ECONOMICS OF DEVELOPMENT

SIXTH EDITION

ECONOMICS OF DEVELOPMENT

SIXTH EDITION

Dwight H. Perkins
Harvard University

Steven Radelet
Center for Global Development

David L. Lindauer
Wellesley College

W. W. Norton & Company
New York • London

W. W. Norton & Company has been independent since its founding in 1923, when William Warder Norton and Mary D. Herter Norton first published lectures delivered at the People's Institute, the adult education division of New York City's Cooper Union. The Nortons soon expanded their program beyond the Institute, publishing books by celebrated academics from America and abroad. By mid-century, the two major pillars of Norton's publishing program–trade books and college texts–were firmly established. In the 1950s, the Norton family transferred control of the company to its employees, and today–with a staff of four hundred and a comparable number of trade, college, and professional titles published each year–W. W. Norton & Company stands as the largest and oldest publishing house owned wholly by its employees.

Editor: Jack Repcheck
Editorial Assistant: Mikael Awake
Project Editor: Carla L. Talmadge
Production Manager: Christopher Granville
Managing Editor, College: Marian Johnson
Book Design: JoAnn Simony
Figures: John McAusland
Composition: Roberta Flechner
Manufacturing: Maple-Vail

Library of Congress Cataloging-in-Publication Data
Perkins, Dwight H. (Dwight Heald), 1934–
     Economics of development / Dwight H. Perkins, Steven Radelet, David L. Lindauer.—6th ed.
        p. cm.
     Rev. ed. of: Economics of development / Dwight H. Perkins . . . [et al.]. 5th ed.
     Includes bibliographical references and index.
     ISBN-13: 978-0-393-92652-1
     ISBN-10: 0-393-92652-4
     1. Developing countries—Economic policy.   2. Economic development.   I. Radelet,
Steven C., 1957–   II. Lindauer, David L., 1952–   III. Economics of development.   IV. Title.
     HC59.7.E314   2006
     338.9—dc22   2006040053

W. W. Norton & Company, Inc., 500 Fifth Avenue, New York, N.Y. 10110
                        www.wwnorton.com

W. W. Norton & Company Ltd., Castle House, 75/76 Wells Street, London W1T 3QT

2 3 4 5 6 7 8 9 0

To Michael Roemer.
Friend, colleague, co-author:
his contributions to the alleviation
of world poverty will endure.

Brief Contents

Contents

PART TWO
Distribution and Human Resources

6 Inequality and Poverty   189

7 Population   237

8 Education   275

9 Health   315

PART THREE
Saving, Investment, and Capital Flows

10 Saving and Resource Mobilization   365

11 Investment, Productivity, and Growth   399

12 Fiscal Policy   429

13 Financial Policy   473

PART FOUR
Production and Trade

Preface

Today's developing nations have faced low incomes and poverty for centuries. But the explicit study of their economic circumstances remains a relatively new field. Many economists cite an article by Paul Rosenstein-Rodan, "Problems of Industrialization of Eastern and South-Eastern Europe," which appeared in the *Economic Journal* in 1943, as the first publication in the field of development economics. Earlier economic writing, going back to Adam Smith and David Ricardo, also was concerned with the subject of economic growth. But what was unique about the article by Rosenstein-Rodan was its focus on the specific problems facing what we today refer to as developing nations.

Forty years passed between the publication of Rosenstein-Rodan's seminal article and the release of the first edition of *Economics of Development* in 1983. Over these four decades the field of development economics emerged. Theories were advanced explaining why some nations grow while others do not; data on economic variables in poor nations were obtained and analyzed; and, perhaps most important, the varied experience of economic growth and development versus economic stagnation and decline informed economists who studied the development process, including the four original authors of this textbook.

More than twenty years have passed since the first edition of *Economics of Development*. Each subsequent edition has incorporated new ideas and new data and provided fresh insights from the experiences of the nations that make up the developing world. This latest edition continues that tradition. While there is much that is new in this sixth edition, the five distinguishing features of this text remain the same:

- It is based primarily on the real-world experiences of developing countries. It explores broad trends and patterns and uses numerous real-country examples and cases to illustrate major points, many of which are drawn from the authors' own experiences.
- It draws heavily on the empirical work of economists who believe that attention to the data not only reveals what the development process entails but permits us to test our beliefs about how that process works.
- It relies on the theoretical tools of neoclassical economics to investigate and analyze these real-world experiences in the belief that these tools contribute substantially to our understanding of economic development.
- It highlights the diversity of development experience and recognizes that the lessons of theory and history can be applied only within certain institutional and national contexts.
- It recognizes the centrality of the political and institutional environment in which economic development takes place.

As in previous editions, the sixth edition of *Economics of Development* is intended to be both accessible and comprehensive. The discussion is *accessible* to those students, whether undergraduates or those pursuing advanced degrees in international relations, public policy, and related fields, who have only an elementary background in economics. At the same time, the text provides a *comprehensive* introduction to all students, including those with significant training in economics, who are taking their first course in development economics.

Major Changes for the Sixth Edition

The sixth edition of *Economics of Development* is the most significant revision of the book in over a decade. The substantial changes reflect the contributions of two new coauthors over the last two editions—Steve Radelet in the fifth edition and David Lindauer in the sixth—working alongside original coauthor Dwight Perkins. The sixth edition features several brand-new chapters and fundamental revisions of several others. The new and revised chapters have more of an empirical orientation than in previous editions, taking full advantage of research on development economics over the past decade. In addition, there are more and better tables, charts, and other exhibits chronicling the lessons and remaining controversies of the development field.

New Chapters

Chapter 2 (Measuring Economic Growth and Development) explores different approaches to defining what is meant by economic development. This new chapter documents both the historical record and the recent experience of economic growth in the different regions of the world. The chapter introduces the Human Development Index and the Millennium Development goals and considers the strengths and weaknesses of these measures along with more traditional indicators of development.

The material on economic growth (Chapter 2 of the previous edition) has been divided into two new chapters (Chapters 3 and 4), providing a much deeper, richer, and easier-to-teach treatment of the topic.

Chapter 3 (Economic Growth: Concepts and Patterns) provides substantial data in easy-to-read tables and charts, concentrating on broad trends across regions and time. Drawing from the main results of the vast literature on growth regressions (without actually showing the regressions!), Chapter 3 identifies the basic determinants of economic growth and examines current debates over the main drivers of growth.

Chapter 4 (Theories of Economic Growth) provides a more rigorous treatment of growth models, including the basic Harrod-Domar and the workhorse Solow growth models. With two chapters, instructors can teach both or (for less-advanced students) skip the more rigorous chapter.

Chapter 11 (Investment, Productivity, and Growth) combines material on investment from several previous chapters into a more coherent and updated chapter. It analyzes key issues about foreign direct investment in the context of debates on globalization and explores new data on the costs to investment and impact on growth of government bureaucracy, corruption, and regulation.

Chapter 14 (Foreign Aid) is an entirely new chapter, offering the most comprehensive and up-to-date treatment of the topic in any undergraduate textbook. It reviews trends in aid, its purposes and rationales (both economic and political), and ongoing debates about aid effectiveness, aid dependency, conditionality, and improving donor practices. It also analyzes the difficulties inherent in strengthening aid programs in the context of a principal-agent framework.

Substantially Revised Chapters

Chapter 1 (Patterns of Development) has an entirely new introduction. The opening vignette from earlier editions of a young Malaysian woman is now complemented by two more vignettes, of an Ethiopian man and a Ukrainian couple. Just as the Malaysian vignette was based on real circumstances, the new vignettes help to chronicle the range of development experiences over the past quarter of a century. These vignettes give a human face to development. The remainder of Chapter 1 has been totally updated with new displays of trends in the structural changes central to the development process.

Chapter 5 (States and Markets) builds on earlier editions and revisits the time-less debate over reliance on markets versus government control. Building on the policy debate over stabilization policies and structural adjustment, the chapter brings in new evidence on the experience with reform in China, Indonesia, Russia, Vietnam, and elsewhere. The chapter concludes with new material on the Washington Consensus, one of the more contentious areas of debate in the development field today.

The entire block of chapters on human welfare and human resources (Chapters 6 to 9) has been completely rewritten. They include new figures, tables, and text boxes and explore the most current topics and debates in these key areas.

Chapter 6 (Inequality and Poverty) provides students with a comprehensive introduction to alternative measures of inequality and poverty. It then provides up-to-date data on trends in these vital outcomes. The chapter discusses current debates on the relationships between growth, poverty, and inequality and on the impact of globalization on poverty and inequality. It adds new material on global inequality and explores why global inequality matters in development.

Chapter 7 (Population) thoroughly updates the discussion on the growth in world population, changes in demographic trends, and the impacts of population and demographic changes on growth and development. It also looks at measures taken by individual countries, including China, to control population growth. New text boxes are included on population momentum, age structure and dependency burdens, and the problem of "missing women."

Chapter 8 (Education) is thoroughly revised. The chapter identifies the revolution in schooling that has taken place over the past three decades, highlighting trends in enrollment patterns, including male/female differences in schooling and learning outcomes. The chapter examines issues surrounding investments in education and their relationship with development. It introduces the latest experimental evidence on improving school outcomes and takes students to the frontier of knowledge about schooling and development.

Chapter 9 (Health) examines the substantial improvements in human health that have transpired in the last forty years and the key factors behind those changes. It considers the interactions between health and economic development and then explores the significant threats posed by disease, including HIV/AIDS, malaria, and tuberculosis. It explores the great successes in improving international health, including eradicating polio in Latin America and the use of oral rehydration therapies to prevent deaths from diarrheal diseases. The chapter considers the growing challenges from weak health systems, weakening antibiotics, and both new and familiar diseases.

Chapter 15 (Foreign Debt and Financial Crises) bridges the 1980s debt crises to current initiatives to forgive the debts of low-income countries, exploring different restructuring options and the reasons that some countries might choose to default on their debts. It also updates the material on the financial crises that plagued Argentina, Brazil, Indonesia, Korea, Russia, Thailand, Turkey, and several other countries.

Chapter 19 (Trade and Development) has been thoroughly rewritten to introduce much more data on trade flows and explore current debates on trade and globalization. It adds significant new material that explores the rise of China and India, the impact of trade protectionism in rich countries on the economies of poor countries, the current round of trade talks under the auspices of the WTO, and debates about sweatshops and concerns about a "race to the bottom" in wages and working conditions.

About the Authors

Of the four original authors of *Economics of Development* only Dwight Perkins remains as an active contributor to this edition. Michael Roemer's death in 1996 took from the development field one of its most thoughtful and productive writers and practitioners. Mike, in many ways, was the single most important contributor to the earlier editions and his legacy endures in this sixth edition. Malcolm Gillis, an expert in issues of public finance and economic development, played the central role in getting this book started in the early 1980s. He later went on to a distinguished career as president of Rice University, from which he recently retired. Donald Snodgrass, who has also retired, at least from the writing of textbooks, was responsible for Part 3, Human Resources, for the first five editions. Both Malcolm Gillis's and Donald Snodgrass's strong contributions are evident in the current edition as well. The new authors are privileged to be part of a text that, thanks to the scholarship of the original authors, helped to define the field of development economics.

Dwight H. Perkins is the H. H. Burbank Professor of Political Economy at Harvard University and former director of the Harvard Institute for International Development. Professor Perkins is a leading scholar on the economies of East and Southeast Asia. The publication of the sixth edition coincides with the end of his full-time teaching career at Harvard. Professor Perkins's legacy is contained not only in the many chapters he has contributed to *Economics of Development* and in his many scholarly books and articles, but also in the thousands of students he has taught over his distinguished academic career (including his two coauthors on the sixth edition!).

Steven Radelet joined *Economics of Development* for its fifth edition. At the time he was a fellow at Harvard's Institute for International Development and taught in both Harvard's economics department and the Kennedy School of Government. He subsequently was deputy assistant secretary of the U.S. Treasury for Africa, the Middle East, and South Asia and is currently a senior fellow at the Center for Global Development and teaches part-time at Stanford University. He is an expert on foreign aid, developing country debt and financial crises, and economic growth and has extensive experience in West Africa and Southeast Asia.

David L. Lindauer is the Stanford Calderwood Professor of Economics at Wellesley College, where he has taught since 1981. He frequently serves as a consultant to the World Bank and was a faculty associate of the Harvard Institute for International Development. Professor Lindauer's area of expertise is in labor economics. He has worked on labor market issues in East and Southeast Asia, Sub-Saharan Africa, and elsewhere. Professor Lindauer, an award-winning teacher of economics, brings his considerable experience teaching undergraduates to the sixth edition.

Acknowledgments

Any textbook that makes it to a sixth edition accumulates many debts to colleagues who read chapters, provided feedback, or contributed in some way to the success and longevity of the work. We owe many thanks to many people. In these acknowledgments, we wish to thank those individuals who contributed to this edition.

David L. Lindauer thanks his research assistants, Adrienne Hathaway and Diane Lee. They did a tremendous job creating the charts and figures in many of the chapters. Both participated in Wellesley College's Research Experience for Undergraduates summer program and were supported by a grant from the National Science Foundation. He also wishes to thank Ann Velenchik and Akila Weerapana (Wellesley College); Anne Dronnier, Deon Filmer, Manny Jimenez, Claudio Montenegro, Harry Patrinos, Lant Pritchett, and Martin Ravallion (World Bank); Paul Glewwe (Minnesota); Susan Greenhalgh (UC Irvine); Dean Jamison (UCLA); Johannes Linn (Brookings); Carrie Hessler-Radelet (John Snow, Inc.); Jennifer Sebstad; and Margaret Stassen. And he wants to thank his family: Margaret, Joanna, Alexa, and Dana. Without their support this project would never have been completed.

Steven Radelet thanks his research assistants Sarah Yerkes, Rikhil Bhavnani, and Bilal Siddiqi. All three, particularly Sarah, spent hours gathering, cleaning, and organizing data to create many of the tables and figures in the text as well as providing useful comments. He also wishes to thank several colleagues for their insights and input: Nancy Birdsall, Michael Clemens, William Cline, Ruth Levine, and Peter Timmer (Center for Global Development); Bruce Bolnick (Nathan Associates); Carol Lancaster and Theodore Moran (Georgetown University); Barbara Bruns (World Bank); and Howard Pack (University of Pennsylvania). Nancy Birdsall, Ed Scott, and Susan Nichols at the Center for Global Development deserve special thanks for their support. He also wants to thank students from Stanford University who provided extensive comments on early drafts of several chapters, including Aisha Ali, Albert Chang, Adam Isen, Aron Kirschner, Julie Lien, Mojan Movassate, David Post, and Julia Speigel. He is eternally grateful for the support and endless patience of his family: Carrie, Meghan, and Sam Radelet.

Dwight H. Perkins is grateful to the hundreds of colleagues and students from around the developing world and at Harvard and other universities in the United States and elsewhere who, over the past five decades, have taught him what he knows about development economics; and to his wife, Julie, who has joined him on many of his trips to developing countries.

All three of us wish to thank everyone at W. W. Norton and Company for their continued support. For the sixth edition we are especially grateful for the guidance and efforts of Jack Repcheck and Mikael Awake, and for earlier assistance from Karl Bakeman. We also want to thank Rick Rawlins, who designed the cover of this edition.

D.H.P. *Cambridge*
S.R. *Washington, D.C.*
D.L.L. *Wellesley*

International Development Resources on the Internet

International Organizations

1. The World Bank (*www.worldbank.org*) hosts specific sites dedicated to country information (*www.worldbank.org/html/extdr/regions.htm*), data on a range of development indicators (*www.worldbank.org/data*), specific development themes (*www.worldbank.org/html/extdr/thematic.htm*), poverty reduction (*www.worldbank.org/poverty*), and governance and anticorruption *(www.worldbank.org/wbi/governance)*.

2. The International Monetary Fund (*www.imf.org*) hosts individual country information (*www.imf.org/external/country/index.htm*) and an index of over 100 economic, commodity, and development organizations (*www.imf.org/np/sec/decdo/contents.htm*).

3. African Development Bank (*www.afdb.org*), Asian Development Bank (*www.adb.org*), and Inter-American Development Bank (*www.iadb.org*).

4. The United Nations development organizations, including the United Nations Development Programme (*www.undp.org*), the Food and Agriculture Organization (*www.fao.org*), the World Health Organization (*www.who.org*), the United Nations Children's Fund (*www.unicef.org*), the Joint United Nations Programme on HIV/AIDS (*www.unaids.org*), and the United Nations Millennium Project with information on the Millennium Development Goals (*www.unmillenniumproject.org*).

Independent Research Organizations

5. The Center for Global Development (*www.cgdev.org*).

6. The Center for International Development at Harvard University (*www.cid.harvard.edu*).

7. The Earth Institute at Columbia University (*www.earthinstitute.columbia.edu*).

8. The Overseas Development Institute (*www.odi.org.uk*).

9. The World Institute for Development Economics Research (*www.wider.unu.edu*).

10. The World Resources Institute (*www.wri.org*).

Information Gateways

11. The Development Gateway (*www.developmentgateway.org*).

12. ELDIS: The Electronic Development and Environment Information System (*www.ids.ac.uk/eldis/eldis.html*).

13. The International Development Research Centre (*www.idrc.ca/library/world*).

14. Netaid.org (*www.netaid.org*).

15. Oneworld.net (*www.oneworld.org*).

Data Sources

In addition to the other sites listed, the following offer useful data:

16. The Center for International Comparisons (Penn World Tables, (*www.pwt.econ.upenn.edu*).

17. The Development Assistance Committee of the Organization for Economic Cooperation and Development (*www.oecd.org/dac*).

18. The Living Standards Measurement Study of Household Surveys (*www.worldbank.org/LSMS*).

19. The Roubini Global Economics Monitor (*www.rgemonitor.com*).

20. The World Factbook (*www.cia.gov/cia/publications/factbook*).

Non-Governmental Organizations and Advocacy Groups

21. Action Aid (*www.actionaid.org*).

22. Debt, AIDS, Trade in Africa (DATA, *www.data.org*).

23. The ONE Campaign (*www.one.org*).

24. OXFAM (*www.oxfam.org*).

Foundations

25. The Bill and Melinda Gates Foundation (*www.gatesfoundation.org*).
26. The Ford Foundation (*www.fordfound.org*).
27. The Open Society Institute (*www.soros.org*).
28. The Rockefeller Foundation (*www.rockfound.org*).
29. The William and Flora Hewlett Foundation (*www.hewlett.org*).

PART ONE

Development and Growth

Patterns of Development

Malaysia

Several decades ago, when she was 17 years old, Rachmina Abdullah did something no girl from her village had ever done before. She left her home in a beautiful but poor part of the state of Kedah in Malaysia, where people grow rice in the valleys and tap rubber trees in the nearby hills, and went to work in an electronics plant in the busy city of Penang, 75 miles away. Rachmina's family was poor even by the modest standards of her village, and her parents welcomed the opportunity for their daughter to earn her own keep and possibly even send money back to help them feed and clothe the family, deal with recurrent emergencies, and raise their five younger children. With these benefits in mind, they set aside their reservations about their unmarried daughter's unheard-of plan to go off by herself to work in the city.

[1]The three narratives that follow are fictional. The vignette on Malaysia is loosely based on Fatimah Daud, "*Minah Karan.*" *The Truth about Malaysian Factory Girls* (Kuala Lumpur: Berita Publishing, 1985), and Kamal Salih and Mei Ling Young, "Changing Conditions of Labour in the Semiconductor Industry in Malaysia," *Labour and Society* 14 (1989), 59–80. The narratives on Ethiopia and Ukraine are based on our discussions with experts who have lived and worked in these nations. The individuals who are named are constructs rather than actual people. Data used in all three vignettes are from *World Development Indicators Online.*

Rachmina got a job assembling integrated circuits in a factory owned by a Japanese company. Every day, she patiently soldered hundreds of tiny wires onto minute silicon chips. It was tedious, repetitive work that had to be performed at high speed and with flawless accuracy. With a long day of hard work with few breaks, Rachmina could earn the equivalent of $2.50.

Since their wages were low, Rachmina and her colleagues welcomed opportunities to work overtime. Often they put in two or three extra hours in a day, for up to seven days a week. They particularly liked working Sundays and holidays, when double wages were paid. With overtime work and occasional bonuses, Rachmina was able to earn about $80 a month. She shared a small house in a squatter area with seven other factory workers. By living simply and inexpensively, most of the young women managed to set aside $5 to $20 a month to send to their families in the villages, and generally enjoyed the unfamiliar freedom of living apart from their families.

Five years later, Rachmina, who had accumulated $400 in savings, decided it was time to return to her village, where she soon married a local man and settled down. She later had two children—fewer than her old friends that had stayed in the village and married earlier. Her savings helped provide for her family and she was able to enroll her children in the local school.

Rachmina's chance to work in an electronics factory came about because, in the 1970s, American and Japanese electronics manufacturers were moving into export processing zones (EPZs) established by the Malaysian government. The national unemployment rate was high, and the government was particularly anxious to find more urban, nonagricultural jobs for the indigenous Malay population.

In the mid-1970s, demand for electronic devices was growing by leaps and bounds, and international firms were looking for overseas locations where they could carry out parts of their operations at lower cost. The first beneficiaries of this migration were the newly industrializing nations of East Asia: Hong Kong, Singapore, South Korea, and Taiwan. Malaysia, with its good infrastructure and English-speaking workforce, also attracted foreign investors. Although the wages were lower than those paid in Japan and the United States, they were much higher than most Malays could earn through farm work, and people lined up for the opportunity to secure these prized jobs. Malaysia, which previously had been known mainly for the export of rubber, tin, and palm oil, became one of the world's largest exporters of electronic components and other labor-intensive manufactured goods. Partly because of these exports, Malaysia became one of the fastest growing economies in the world, and a leading development success story. The income of the average Malay nearly *quadrupled* in real terms between 1970 and 2003, life expectancy rose from 61 to 73 years, infant mortality fell from 46 to 7 children per thousand, and the adult literacy rate jumped from 58 to 90 percent.

Ethiopia

On another continent and at about the same time that Rachmina was on her way to begin working in Penang, Getachew was born in Ethiopia. Getachew's family and many of his relatives lived in a rural area outside of Dese, a drought-affected area in Amhara region and a day's bus ride from the capital city of Addis Ababa. The family lived in a thatched hut and had few possessions. They owned cooking utensils, some blankets and clothing, a radio and a bicycle. Getachew's sisters spent two hours a day fetching water from a small stream outside their village. The village did not have a paved road or electricity. In addition to growing *tef,* a cereal crop similar to millet, the family grew vegetables and relied on its own production for most of its consumption needs. The family was especially proud of their livestock. Getachew's father raised and traded oxen, which earned the family most of their meager cash income.

Getachew was the fifth of eight children, one of whom died at birth and another before her third birthday. Getachew received five years of schooling, but the years were not in succession. In some years, he needed to work with his father and brothers tending the family's crops and livestock. In other years, the family did not have enough money to pay for uniforms and other school fees, and could afford to send only one or two of their children to school. Priority was given to Getachew's older brothers. By the time he was 16, Getachew was able to read and write, although not well.

Getachew and his family have known hard times. His mother died shortly after the birth of her last child. This was due, in part, to her weakened state following the drought and famine in 1984 and compounded by multiple births and lack of emergency postpartum care. Despite worldwide attention to Ethiopia's plight that year, relief came too late to help them. The area has been affected by drought and shortages of food since then but none as severe. Political transition in 1991 brought a lot of uncertainty, even to the countryside. The village school remained closed that year, as the teacher returned to live in the capital. Prices for everything went up at the same time that Getachew's father earned little for his oxen. In 1998, war broke out between Ethiopia and neighboring Eritrea but, fortunately, Getachew was staying with his brother in Addis at the time and able to escape the draft. However, several of his friends were conscripted to serve. One lost a leg during the war and returned home but was no longer much help tending livestock. Another now has AIDS and, without treatment, is sick most of the time and probably does not have long to live.

Getachew's second oldest brother was a truck driver and occasionally provided the family with goods and cash. Getachew went with his brother to Addis Ababa and lived there for a time, finding only occasional casual day labor. Life was hard in the city, in some ways harder than in the countryside. Back home everyone lived similarly. In Addis, more people had money to spend while

Getachew did not. When his father fell ill from tuberculosis, Getachew went back to help out at home. He would like to get married but land has become increasingly scarce in his village and it is unclear when he will be able to support a family of his own.

Getachew's life is much like his father's had been and parallels that of most Ethiopians and many Africans. Per capita incomes in 2003 are about at the same levels as in 1981. In the intervening years, incomes at times have increased and at other times declined, but overall, economic stagnation has characterized the nation. Infant mortality rates have fallen from an estimated 160 per thousand in 1970 to 112 per thousand in 2003, but life expectancy remains at just 42 years. National elections in 2005 are an indication of a movement toward a more democratic government, but Getachew and millions of other Ethiopians are not sure if this will improve their lives.

Ukraine

Unlike Getachew or Rachmina, Viktor and Yulia are relatively well educated. Both were born in L'viv in Western Ukraine, about 300 miles from the capital, Kyiv. They graduated from secondary school in 1980 and went on to study for several more years at the local polytechnic institute, which is where they met. Viktor studied engineering and Yulia architectural drawing. After finishing their studies, they married and Viktor began work at a local glass factory. Yulia was hired by a municipal agency. As was common during the Soviet era, the couple moved into the one-bedroom apartment where Yulia's parents lived. Viktor and Yulia owned a refrigerator and other kitchen appliances, a television, furniture, some musical instruments, many books, and a telephone. They went on vacations, often going to a state-subsidized "sanatorium" in the Carpathian Mountains in Ukraine's southwest. Their daughter, Tetiana, was born in 1986 and Yulia was able to take a paid maternity leave.

Viktor's and Yulia's lifestyle in the 1980s was certainly modest by American or Western European standards. They enjoyed few luxuries but most of their everyday needs were met. Often this required standing on long lines at government stores for staples such as bread, cooking oil, milk, and sugar. They also had their own garden plot where they grew flowers, fruit, and vegetables. Occasionally they purchased goods in the *gray market* (technically illegal but not enforced) that came from Poland. Health care and day care were publicly provided.

Like many other ethnic Ukrainians in L'viv, Viktor, Yulia and her parents longed for national independence. They spoke and maintained their native language even though the official language of the Soviet Union was Russian. Beyond their nationalist leanings, they thought their lives would be better in a less-centralized economy but were unaware of the severe consequences the breakup of the Soviet Union would entail.

Ukraine became independent in December 1991 with 90 percent of voters in support of a referendum on independence. Street celebrations and emotional speeches about freedom marked the event. But independence also had negative consequences. Trade with Russia collapsed and, with it, orders at the glass factory where Viktor was employed. Viktor was paid less and less often. A common refrain heard throughout the former Soviet Union was "they pretend to pay us and we pretend to work." Ukraine relied on energy supplies from Russia, but without foreign exchange to pay for them, Russian fuel exports dwindled and many Ukrainians had to endure cold winters without much heat in their homes or offices. Mismanagement of the domestic economy led to hyperinflation in 1993–94, with prices rising almost 5,000 percent. The hyperinflation destroyed the purchasing power of pensioners, like Yulia's aging parents, and others living on fixed incomes. The health care system fell apart. Medicine, at times, had to be obtained on the black market, and one could never be sure of its efficacy. Life became harsher, with more anxiety, stress, and uncertainty about the future.

Ukrainians had hoped that after independence foreign investment would flow into their country. It did not. Foreigners would look at what was there and find existing technology backward, products of poor quality, and corruption rife. Instead of foreign purchase of factories, company officials often stripped factories of whatever assets they had and kept the proceeds to themselves. Per capita income in 1998 was only 40 percent of its pretransition peak in 1989. By 2003, it had risen to slightly over half its estimated level in 1989. Life expectancy for Ukrainian men fell from 66 years in 1985 to 63 years in 2003.

Viktor was one of many Ukrainian men who had a difficult time with the transition. He could not adjust to changing circumstances and never found a new job. He spent a lot of time at home, doing some carpentry and other odd jobs now and then. His health was poor, the result of smoking too much and, Yulia believes, the environmental hazards of the glass factory. Many of Viktor's friends from the factory have similar health problems; a few have died prematurely. Yulia is holding the family together. She has reinvented herself. She still is employed at the municipal agency, although her wages are seldom paid. Instead, she spends much of her time at work and at night drawing plans for some of the newly rich Ukrainians who are building summer villas and renovating apartments. She prefers not to discuss where the money to pay for these villas, and for her services, is coming from.

Yulia and Viktor still must care for Yulia's parents and are devoted to their daughter. They are anxious for Tetiana to continue with her education and learn English, which they see as key to her future. The entire family was encouraged by the ultimate victory of Viktor Yushchenko in the 2004–05 presidential elections. Yushchenko, a charismatic leader who is both Western oriented and a Ukrainian nationalist, won despite widespread election fraud and an attempt on his life. The new president and families like Yulia and Viktor's have many challenges ahead of them. There are reasons to be hopeful. Trade and investment are growing, and there is increasing integration with the West and a revitalized Russian economy. But ingrained problems of corruption, cronyism, and unresponsive public institutions remain.

Development and Globalization

These three "development vignettes," about Malaysia, Ethiopia, and Ukraine, are meant to capture the range of experience of individual nations over the past two to three decades. Some nations, including Malaysia, have experienced historically unprecedented rates of economic growth, which have dramatically changed the lives of their populations. In other parts of the world, including Ethiopia and much of sub-Saharan Africa, economic change has been minimal and standards of living have remained more or less the same from one generation to the next. A third group of nations experienced a fundamental transition from one economic system to another. In some instances, including Ukraine, this resulted in an abrupt and steep decline in living standards, which only recently has begun to rebound. Understanding the causes and consequences of these different patterns of economic development is the central goal of this textbook.

Economic growth, stagnation, and transition have had a profound impact, respectively, on the lives of Rachmina, Getachew, Viktor and Yulia, and on the more than 5 billion people of the developing countries these individuals are meant to personify. But, as different as the outcomes have been, all have been affected by dramatic changes both within their borders and outside of them.

- Political systems have undergone profound changes, especially since the end of the cold war. Many low-income countries have adopted democratic political systems since the early 1990s. The relationship between these political changes and the process of economic development and poverty reduction remains a matter of considerable debate.
- Substantial demographic shifts have led to a fall in population growth rates in many countries, with a corresponding growth in the share of workers in the population and a decline in the number of dependent children. Looking forward, more low-income countries will soon see large segments of the population reaching retirement age, with important implications for saving, tax revenues, pension systems, and social programs.
- The spread of endemic disease, particularly the HIV/AIDS pandemic, threatens development progress in many countries. In more than half a dozen African countries, more than a quarter of the adult population is HIV-positive, and the pandemic is spreading in China, India, Russia, and other parts of the world. HIV/AIDS, malaria, tuberculosis, and other diseases bring a heavy human toll and substantial economic costs.

- Global trade has grown rapidly in line with sharply falling transportation and communication costs, giving rise to far more sophisticated global production networks. Instead of products being made start-to-finish in one location, firms in one country specialize in one part of the production process, while firms in another country play a different role. There has been a dramatic shift away from producing goods for the local market under government protection toward greater integration with global markets.[2]

- Capital moves much more quickly across borders than it did several decades ago. More sophisticated financial instruments and a greater emphasis on private capital has opened opportunities for low-income countries to access foreign capital for local investment. In some countries, however, rapid financial liberalization led to deep financial crises when local financial institutions were weak and foreign capital was quickly withdrawn.

- Information and ideas spread much faster around the globe than in earlier times. Communications technology has created new opportunities for low-income countries to create jobs that provide services via satellite and through the internet, such as accounting, data entry, or telephone help lines.

Many forces are at work behind these changes. One of the most important is the process of globalization. **Globalization** is a term used by different people to mean many different things and covers more than just economics. Columbia University economist Jagdish Bhagwati defines *economic globalization* as the integration of national economies into the international economy through trade in goods and services (such as tourism), direct foreign investment, short-term capital flows, international movements of people, and flows of technology. Globalization has important noneconomic aspects as well, including cultural, communications, and political integration. It is not a new phenomenon: The early voyages of Ferdinand Magellan, Christopher Columbus, Zheng He, Marco Polo, and others opened an early epoch of globalization, and the late nineteenth and early twentieth centuries saw increased global integration until the process abruptly ended with the onset of World War I. But the current era has included more parts of the world and affected far more people than earlier episodes.

---

[2]Malaysia has most obviously been helped by this process, while at least in the short run, Ukraine has been hurt. Even rural Ethiopians who engage in subsistence agriculture are not insulated from global economic events. The Asian financial crisis of the late 1990s provides an example. The crisis resulted in a sharp decline in the demand for shoes, handbags, and other goods made from leather. This in turn lowered the demand and price for animal hides, a traditional Ethiopian export, and reduced the cash income of rural Ethiopians who might have had no idea why the prices they received for their animal skins had fallen.

These broad global trends and the individual stories of Rachmina, Getachew, Viktor, and Yulia raise many issues central to the process of economic development addressed in this book. Who benefits from foreign investment and integration with global trading networks and who loses? How do governments promote investment, industrialization, and exports? How does the shift from agriculture to manufacturing affect the lives of the majority of people in developing countries who still are rural and poor? How do countries educate their citizens and protect their health, enabling them to become productive workers in more-advanced, globally interconnected industries? This book explores the economics of these and other issues in an attempt to understand why some countries develop rapidly while others seem not to develop at all. Remember that within each nation are people like Rachmina, Getachew, Viktor, and Yulia, whose lives are deeply affected by the progress their nations make along the path toward economic development.

RICH AND POOR COUNTRIES

The countries with which this book is concerned have been labeled with many different terms. The most popular classifications implicitly put all countries on a continuum based on their degree of development. Therefore, we speak of the distinctions between developed and underdeveloped countries, more- and less-developed ones, or to recognize continuing change, **developed** and **developing** countries. The degree of optimism implicit in *developing countries* and the handy acronym **LDCs** for *less-developed countries*, make these the two most widely used terms, although they suffer from the problem that *developed* implies the process is fully complete for wealthier countries.[3] Richer countries frequently are called **industrialized countries,** in recognition of the close association between development and industrialization. Some Asian, Eastern European, and Latin American economies, whose industrial output is growing rapidly, are sometimes called **emerging economies.** The highest-income countries sometimes are referred to as postindustrial countries or service-based economies, since services (finance, research and development, medical services, etc.), not manufacturing, account for the largest and most rapidly growing share of their economies.

---

[3]The initials LDCs also have been used, especially by the United Nations, to designate the "least-developed countries," those with the lowest incomes per capita (among other characteristics).

The rich-poor dichotomy, based simply on income levels, has been refined by the World Bank[4] to yield a four-part classification:

- **Low-income economies,** with average incomes less than $765 per capita in 2003, converted into dollars at the current exchange rate.
- **Lower middle-income economies,** with incomes between $765 and $3,035.
- **Upper middle-income economies,** with incomes between $3,035 and $9,385.
- **High-income economies,** mostly members of the Organization for Economic Cooperation and Development (OECD), with incomes over $9,385 per capita.

Two anomalous groups fit uneasily into this taxonomy. A number of petroleum exporters such as Brunei and Kuwait, whose incomes often fall into the high-income range, have economies that are more traditional than the typical upper-middle income or industrialized country. Many of the economies of Eastern Europe, including Russia and Ukraine, have incomes that qualify them as middle income, although some of them may be better described as **transitional economies,** moving from controlled to market-oriented development.

A term in vogue during the 1980s, especially in international forums, was the **third world.** Perhaps the best way to define it is by elimination. Take away the industrialized (OECD) economies of Western Europe, North America, and the Pacific (the "first" world, although it was rarely called that) and the industrialized, formerly centrally planned economies of Eastern Europe (the "second" world), and the rest of the countries constitute the third world. This terminology is used much less frequently today. The geographic configuration of the third world has led to a parallel distinction of **North** (first and second worlds) versus **South,** which still has some currency. But the south or third world encompasses a wide variety of countries, from wealthy oil exporters to very low-income, poorly endowed countries.

It is important to be aware of these various terms and classifications and recognize their exceptions and inconsistencies, but it is not wise to dwell too long on them. No system can capture all the important dimensions of development and provide a perfectly consistent, manageable framework.

[4]The World Bank, formally the International Bank for Reconstruction and Development (IBRD), borrows funds on private capital markets in developed countries and lends to the developing countries and, through its affiliate, the International Development Association (IDA), receives contributions from the governments of developed countries and lends to the low-income countries at very low interest rates with long repayment periods. The Bank, as it often is referred to, is perhaps the world's most important and influential development agency. Its role is explored in more detail in the discussion of foreign aid in Chapter 14.

GROWTH AND DEVELOPMENT

While the labels used to distinguish one set of countries from another can vary, one must be more careful with the terms used to describe the development process itself. The terms *economic growth* and *economic development* sometimes are used interchangeably, but they are fundamentally different. **Economic growth** refers to a rise in national or per capita income and product. If the production of goods and services in a country rises, by whatever means, and along with it average income increases, the country has achieved "economic growth." **Economic development** implies more, particularly improvements in health, education, and other aspects of human welfare. Countries that increase their income but do not also raise life expectancy, reduce infant mortality, and increase literacy rates are missing out on some important aspects of development. If all of the increased income is concentrated in the hands of a few rich elite or spent on monuments or a military apparatus, there has been very little development in the sense that we mean.

Development is also usually accompanied by significant shifts in the structure of the economy, as more and more people typically shift away from rural agricultural production to urban-based and higher-paying employment, usually in manufacturing or services. Economic growth without structural change is often an indicator of the new income being concentrated in the hands of a few people. Situations of growth without development are the exceptions rather than the rule, but they do happen. For example, the recent discovery and development of vast oil deposits off the coast of Equatorial Guinea has raised the per capita income of this small nation on the west coast of Africa from about $700 in 1990 to over $3,700. By 2003, Equatorial Guinea had a per capita income comparable to Costa Rica's but this is where the similarity between the two nations ends. Despite its sudden high level of per capita income there has been little transformation yet in the low levels of education and health or of the economic activity of most Equatorial Guineans.

Two of the most important structural changes that usually accompany economic development are the rising share of industry, along with the falling share of agriculture, in the national product and the increasing percentage of people who live in cities rather than the countryside. In addition, countries that enter into economic development usually pass through periods of accelerating, then decelerating, population growth, during which the country's age structure changes dramatically. Consumption patterns also evolve as people no longer have to spend all their income on necessities but instead move on to consumer durables and eventually to leisure-time products and services. If growth benefits only a tiny, wealthy minority, whether domestic or foreign, it is not development. We have more to say about alternative ways of defining economic development in Chapter 2.

Modern economic growth, the term used by Nobel laureate Simon Kuznets, refers to the current economic epoch as contrasted with, say, the epoch of merchant capitalism or the epoch of feudalism. The epoch of modern economic growth still is evolving, so all its features are not yet clear; but the key element has been the application of science to problems of economic production, which in turn has led to industrialization, urbanization, and even explosive growth in population. Finally, it always should be kept in mind that, while economic development and modern economic growth involve much more than a rise in per capita income or product, no sustained development can occur without economic growth.

A DEVELOPMENT CONTINUUM

Much can be learned from a perusal of Table 1–1 and Figures 1–1 to 1–4 about the nature of structural change during development and the many differences within the developing world. These data are mostly from the World Bank's *World Development Indicators* and other international agencies.

The first two columns of Table 1–1 show two different measures of each country's income. Comparing incomes is not as straightforward as it may seem, because it requires converting each country's income, initially measured in its local currency (such as Indian rupees), into a common currency, typically into U.S. dollars. However, the fluctuation of exchange rates over time means that dollar incomes, and country rankings, change frequently, even though the underlying situation—people's real welfare—has changed very little. One way to deal with this is to convert the value of each country's output (or income) into a common set of prices. Thus, a haircut in India is priced the same as one in the United States, as is a ton of wheat, a telephone, or a car.

This way of comparing average incomes is called the **purchasing power parity,** or PPP, method. It gives a more accurate comparison of incomes among countries and is discussed at greater length in Chapter 2 and used throughout this book. Column 1 of Table 1–1 shows countries ranked in order of ascending PPP income per capita. The conventional measure of income, converted at the dollar exchange rate, is shown in the second column for comparison.

One way to avoid the problems of comparing incomes is to use physical measures of structural change. One example is a country's per capita consumption of energy. Figure 1–1 shows how closely energy use per capita is correlated with GDP per capita.[5] A predominant structural characteristic of development is

---

[5]The regression lines shown in the graphs have been calculated for countries in our sample only. These countries have been chosen for their general interest rather than because they are a statistically representative sample.

TABLE 1-1. Development Characteristics of Income Groups and Selected Countries

INCOME GROUP AND COUNTRY	GNI PER CAPITA, PPP (US$, 2003)	GNI PER CAPITA, (US$, 2003)	ENERGY USE (KG OF OIL EQUIVALENT PER CAPITA, 2002)	RURAL POPULATION (% OF TOTAL, 2003)	LIFE EXPECTANCY AT BIRTH (YEARS, 2003)	ADULT LITERACY (%) MALES	FEMALES
Income group							
Low income	2,110	440	493	70	58	68	48
Lower-middle income	5,500	1,490	1,227	50	69	88	86
Upper-middle income	9,990	5,440	2,232	25	74	90	90
High income	29,580	28,600	5,395	20	78	N.A.	N.A.
Low income							
Tanzania	620	300	408	65	43	85	69
Ethiopia	710	90	297	83	42	49	34
Nigeria	900	350	718	53	45	74	59
Mali	960	290	N.A.	68	41	27	12
Kenya	1,030	400	489	64	45	90	79
Senegal	1,620	540	319	50	52	49	30
Bangladesh	1,870	400	155	73	62	50	31
Cameroon	1,990	630	417	49	48	77	60
Pakistan	2,040	520	454	66	64	53	29
Ghana	2,190	320	411	63	54	82	66
India	2,880	540	513	72	63	68	45
Lower-middle income							
Bolivia	2,490	900	499	36	64	93	81
Honduras	2,590	970	504	45	66	80	80
Indonesia	3,210	810	737	56	67	92	83
Sri Lanka	3,740	930	430	76	74	95	90
Egypt	3,940	1,390	789	57	69	67	44
Philippines	4,640	1,080	525	39	70	93	93
China	4,980	1,100	960	61	71	95	87
Peru	5,080	2,140	450	26	70	91	80
Colombia	6,410	1,810	625	24	72	92	92
Brazil	7,510	2,720	1,093	17	69	86	87
Upper-middle income							
Malaysia	8,970	3,880	2,129	41	73	92	85
Mexico	8,980	6,230	1,560	25	74	93	89
Argentina	11,410	3,810	1,543	11	75	97	97
Saudi Arabia	13,230	9,240	5,775	13	73	84	69
Hungary	13,840	6,350	2,505	35	73	99	99
High income							
Korea, Rep. of	18,000	12,030	4,272	17	74	99	96
United Kingdom	27,690	28,320	3,824	10	78	99 (total population)	
Germany	27,610	25,270	4,198	12	78	99 (total population)	
Japan	28,450	34,180	4,058	21	82	99	99
United States	37,750	37,870	7,943	22	77	97	97

Sources: *World Development Indicators* database, 0-devdata.worldbank.org.luna.wellesley.edu/dataonline/, accessed May 2005; UNESCO Institute for Statistics, Literacy and Non Formal Education Section, "Estimated Illiteracy Rate and Illiterate Population Aged 15 and Older, by Country, 1970–2015," July 2002 assessment, www.uis.unesco.org/TEMPLATE/html/Exceltables/education/View_Table_Literacy_Country_Age15+.xls., accessed May 2005; CIA, "Germany," "Japan," "United Kingdom," "United States," *The World Factbook* 2005, www.cia.gov/cia/publications/factbook/, accessed June 2005.

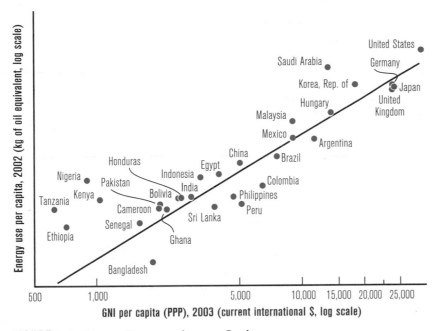

FIGURE 1-1. Energy Consumption per Capita

Source: *World Development Indicators* database, 0-devdata.worldbank.org.luna.wellesley.edu/
dataonline/, accessed May 2005.

the growing share of both income produced and labor employed in industry. Table 1–1 and Figure 1–2 reflect this trend, inversely, in the share of the population living in rural areas. This share declines from an average of 70 percent for low-income countries to only 20 percent for high-income countries.

Table 1-1 shows two other key indicators of development: life expectancy and literacy. Both are correlated with per capita income, as shown in Figures 1–3 and 1–4. Life expectancy, averaging less than 60 years in low-income countries, rises to 78 years on average for high-income countries. Changes in adult literacy, especially among women, are equally dramatic. In some of the poorest countries, less than one third of females 15 years and over is able to read. Upper middle-income countries have increased female literacy rates to 90 percent on average, and in the high-income countries, more than 95 percent of all adults, men and women, are literate.

Each category includes considerable variance and hence some interesting exceptions. China consumes more energy per capita than other countries with similar incomes, while the Philippines, with a similar per capita income level, consumes substantially less (Figure 1–1). The rural population share in Sri Lanka is about double that of Bolivia, even though Bolivia has a much lower per capita income (PPP, Figure 1–2). Chinese and Sri Lankans live nearly as long as Hungarians and Argentines, even though incomes in the latter countries are more than two to three times those in the former countries (Figure 1–3). Kenya, Indonesia, and Peru all report female adult literacy of about 80 percent but have widely varying per capita income levels. Ghana and Pakistan have similar incomes,

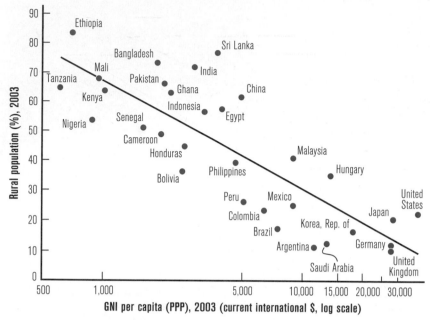

FIGURE 1-2. Rural Population

Source: *World Development Indicators* database, 0-devdata.worldbank.org.luna.wellesley.edu/dataonline/, accessed May 2005.

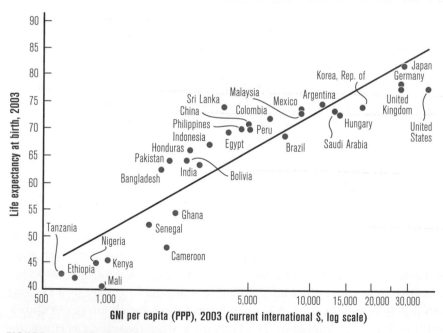

FIGURE 1-3. Life Expectancy

Source: *World Development Indicators* database, 0-devdata.worldbank.org.luna.wellesley.edu/dataonline/, accessed May 2005.

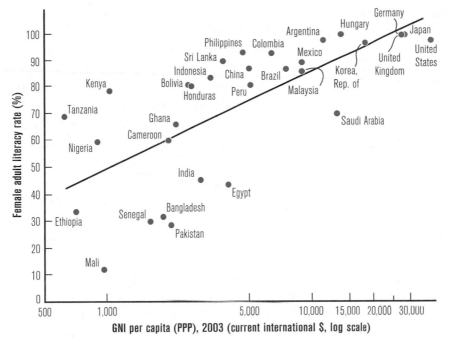

FIGURE 1-4. **Female Adult Literacy**

Sources: *World Development Indicators* database, 0-devdata.worldbank.org.luna.wellesley.edu/
dataonline/, accessed May 2005; UNESCO Institute for Statistics, Literacy and Non Formal
Education Section. "Estimated Illiteracy Rate and Illiterate Population Aged 15 and Older, by
Country, 1970–2015," July 2002 assessment, www.uis.unesco.org/TEMPLATE/html/Exceltables/
education/View_Table_Literacy_Country_Age15+.xls., accessed May 2005; CIA, "Germany,"
"Japan," "United Kingdom," "United States," *The World Factbook 2005*, www.cia.gov/cia/
publications/factbook/, accessed June 2005.

about $2,100 (PPP), but two thirds of Ghanaian women are literate as compared
to less than one third of Pakistani women (Figure 1–4).

A GLANCE AT HISTORY

This diversity in income and literacy is part of a much larger set of variations
among developing countries that often have their origins in different historical
experiences. A key characteristic of modern economic growth is that it did not
begin everywhere in the world at the same time. Instead, it spread slowly across
Europe and North America but, except for Japan, did not occur outside of areas
dominated by European culture until the 1950s and 1960s. In parts of the world,
it has yet to begin.

Even within Europe on the eve of industrialization, there were great differences among societies, and these differences had much to do with why develop-

ment began first in Western Europe and spread only gradually to the East. In England, for example, laborers were free to change jobs and migrate to distant places, and commerce and banking had reached a high level of sophistication in the centuries preceding the Industrial Revolution. But Russia in the mid-nineteenth century was still feudal: Most peasants were tied to their lord's estate for life, and finance, industry, and transport was in a primitive state.

In Asia, Latin America, and Africa, the range of political and cultural experiences is more diverse than that which existed within Europe. Great empires, such as those of China and Japan, experienced over a thousand years of self-governance, and they thought of themselves as a single, unified people, rather than a collection of ethnically distinct tribes or regions. By premodern standards, China and Japan also had high levels of urbanization and commerce, and they shared Confucian values, which emphasize the importance of education. Long years of comparative stability contributed to a population increase that resulted in the great shortage of arable land relative to population, which still exists in the region. Because of the comparative sophistication of premodern commerce in East Asia, European and American merchants never were able to play a significant role in the management of domestic commerce in the region. As Chinese and Japanese merchants gradually acquired an understanding of foreign markets, they were able to compete successfully with representatives of the industrialized world in that sphere as well.

At the other end of this historical spectrum of unified self-government and relative commercial sophistication are several Southeast Asian and most African nations. Indonesia and Nigeria, for example, really were the arbitrary creations of Dutch and British colonialism, respectively, which brought together diverse groups of people who spoke different languages and had no history of working together under a shared government. These diverse groups had little desire to maintain the externally imposed boundaries of the colonial powers. The results in the 1950s in Nigeria and the 1960s in Indonesia were wars fought to keep their new countries together. Similar civil wars threatened to break up the nation in the Democratic Republic of the Congo and Sudan in the 1990s and into the twenty-first century. Even Europe was not immune to this kind of antidevelopment chaos, as the breakup of Yugoslavia into several independent nations in the late 1990s demonstrates.

Experience with commerce in many parts of Southeast Asia and Africa also was quite limited. Throughout the colonial era in Indonesia and many parts of sub-Saharan Africa, foreign trade and large-scale domestic commerce were almost entirely in the hands of Europeans. Local people sometimes controlled small-scale commerce, particularly in the countryside, but large-scale and long-distance commerce usually was in the hands of minorities who had immigrated from other poor but commercially more-advanced countries. Therefore, local commerce in much of Southeast Asia was in the hands of local Chinese; in East

Africa, commerce was managed mainly by immigrants from the Indian subcontinent; while in West Africa, Lebanese often played a central role. Because of inexperience, the local people could not effectively compete with either these immigrant groups or the Europeans; and because they could not compete, they gained little experience with trade or finance. This was one of the many vicious circles so common to the plight of poor countries.

Not all experiences with colonialism were the same. In India, a tiny number of British ruled a vastly populated subcontinent. By necessity, the British had to train large numbers of Indians to handle all but the very top jobs in the bureaucracy and army. At the time of independence in 1947, Indians already were running most of their own affairs because enough trained and experienced personnel were available to do so. But Indonesia had fewer than a thousand university or other post-secondary school graduates at the time of independence, and the Congo had hardly any. Prior to independence even the lower levels of the bureaucracy in Indonesia had been run by the Dutch and those in the Congo by Belgians. In comparison, India and China in the 1940s had hundreds of thousands of university graduates.

Latin America's historical heritage is different from that of either Asia or Africa. Independence in most of the region was achieved in the early nineteenth century, not after World War II, as in Asia and Africa. Although there were local populations in the region when the Europeans first arrived, the indigenous populations were killed, suppressed, or enslaved. So, to meet growing labor requirements, the elites turned to voluntary and forced immigration of Europeans and Africans. Spanish and Portuguese immigrants ruled; Africans were enslaved until late in the nineteenth century. Ignored or pushed aside, some of the original population survived, but in varying numbers: Peru and Bolivia maintained large indigenous populations, whereas in Argentina, native peoples nearly disappeared.

North America above the Rio Grande also was peopled by immigrants who suppressed the local population. In both North and South America, slavery existed in some regions and not in others, but there were important differences between the types of colonial rule. In the North, the indigenous population was more thoroughly suppressed; hence, it was small and isolated and not a factor when economic development began. European immigrants were from the economically most-advanced parts of Europe, where feudal values and structures already had been partially dismantled. But Spanish and Portuguese immigrants came from an area that, by the nineteenth century, was one of the more-backward parts of Europe. The feudal values and structures that still dominated this region accompanied these colonists to the New World. Likewise, there were great differences within Latin America. Argentina, for example, is largely a nation of European immigrants; Mexico, Peru, and Bolivia have large indigenous populations; a large minority of Brazilians and virtually all Haitians are descended from former African slaves.

It is impossible to summarize all the important differences among countries in the developing world, but those with the greatest bearing on the potential for modern economic growth in the region would include differences between

- Countries with a long tradition of emphasis on education and an elite that was highly educated, as contrasted with countries where illiteracy was nearly universal.
- Countries with fairly highly developed institutions and systems of commerce, finance, and transport, mainly run by local people versus countries where these activities were monopolized at the time of independence by European or Asian immigrant minorities.
- Countries peopled by those who shared a common language, culture, and sense of national identity versus countries with a great diversity of language and culture and no common sense of national identity or shared common goals.
- Countries with long traditions and institutions of self-government versus those with no experience with even limited self-government until the 1950s or 1960s.
- Countries with adverse geography (landlocked, isolation from major markets, desert, poor agricultural soils, adverse climate, or endemic disease) versus those with more favorable geography.

Multiple Paths to Development: The Concept of Substitutes

Given the great diversity in developing-country experience, it would be a counsel of despair to suggest that the only way to begin development is to recreate the kinds of political, social, and economic conditions that existed in Western Europe or North America when those regions entered into modern economic growth. England prior to the Industrial Revolution had centuries of experience with merchant capitalism, but does it follow that Ghana or Indonesia also must acquire long experience with merchant capitalism before economic development is feasible? If the answer were yes, these countries would be doomed to another century or more of poverty.

Fortunately, there is no standard list of barriers to be overcome or other prerequisites that must be in place before development is possible. The most successful countries share certain characteristics: a capable government, reasonably well-functioning markets and institutions, and healthy and educated people who can work effectively in and manage the enterprises and other organizations that arise in the course of development. But the details can and do differ substantially. As economic historian Alexander Gerschenkron pointed out, for most presumed prerequisites there usually are substitutes or alternative strategies. The main point of this concept is best illustrated with an example from Gerschenkron's own work.[6]

Capital, like labor, is necessary for development. But Karl Marx and others went a step further and argued that there must be an original or prior accumulation of capital before growth can take place. The basic idea came from looking at the experience of England where, Marx argued, trade, exploitation of colonies, piracy, and other related measures led to the accumulation of great wealth that, in the late eighteenth century, could be converted into investment in industry. Is such an accumulation a prerequisite for development everywhere? In the absence of a prior accumulation of capital, does economic development become impossible?

In Europe, the answer clearly was no. Although countries had to find funds that could be invested in industry, these did not have to come out of the accumulated wealth of the past. Germany, for example, had little in the way of an original accumulation of capital when modern economic growth began there. But Germany did have a banking system that could attract funds, which then were lent to industrialists. How banks attract funds is not our concern here; the point is that investors can draw on these funds, and the generation of those funds does not depend in a significant way on long years of prior saving and accumulation by merchants or other wealthy individuals.

Russia in the nineteenth century had neither an original accumulation of wealth nor a banking system capable of creating large enough levels of credit. Instead, Russia turned to the taxing power of the state. The government levied taxes on people and used this revenue for investment in industry. Russia also imported capital from abroad. Thus, in Russia, the government's use of taxation was a substitute for a well-developed banking system, and elsewhere a modern banking system was a substitute for an original accumulation of capital.

Similar examples of substitutes abound in today's world. Latin American countries, for example, rely heavily on financial institutions to mobilize and allocate savings. Sub-Saharan African countries, in contrast, rely more on fiscal institutions (the government budget). Factories in advanced countries with well-developed commercial networks rely on central distributors to supply them with spare parts. Rural industries in China, where commerce is less developed, make spare parts in their own foundries. A number of countries in the developing world today have substantial numbers of people with training and experience in areas relevant to economic development, while the number of such people in other countries, as already pointed out, is very small. The most common substitute for this lack of relevant experience is to import foreigners or

[6]Alexander Gerschenkron, *Economic Backwardness in Historical Perspective* (Cambridge, MA: Harvard University Press, 1962), Chapter 2.

rely on nonindigenous residents who have the required experience. Foreigners frequently are not very good substitutes for experienced local talent, but where the latter is missing, they can sometimes fill the gap until local talent is trained.

In the chapters that follow, we do not look for three or four universal causes of poverty or for certain prerequisites that must be in place before growth is possible. Instead, we attempt to identify some of the more common barriers to development and recognize that the presence of these barriers or the absence of some "prerequisites" does not condemn a country to stagnation and poverty. There usually are ways around, or substitutes for, any single barrier or prerequisite, but the existence of many of these barriers or the absence of a wide variety of desirable preconditions make economic development more difficult and in some cases impossible.

Diversity in Development Achievements

Despite differences in historical experience, policies, and institutions, a large number of less-developed countries have experienced growth in income since 1965 or 1980 and many have enjoyed substantial growth, as Table 1–2 shows. The most rapidly growing economies, with income per capita expanding by 3 percent a year or more since 1980, mostly have been in Asia: China, India, Indonesia, Korea, Malaysia, and Sri Lanka in the table. But several non-Asian countries are among the fast growers, including Botswana, Chile, Estonia, and Mauritius. In fact, from 1965 to 1995, Botswana, a landlocked country in southern Africa, was the single fastest-growing economy in the world, undermining the stereotype that all African countries have been stuck with little growth and development. At the same time, several Asian countries have grown slowly or not at all, including Myanmar (Burma), North Korea, and Papua New Guinea. There are many examples of countries with income growth over 2 percent a year. At 2 percent annual growth, the average income doubles in 35 years; at 4 percent, it doubles in 18 years. In most of these countries, manufacturing grew more rapidly than the gross domestic product and, thus, moved these economies through the inevitable structural change that reduces the share of income produced and labor employed in agriculture. Many other countries experienced slower (albeit positive) growth and development, with incomes growing 1 or 2 percent per year. In still others, incomes stagnated or declined. Most of the countries in this latter group are in Africa, although income also fell elsewhere, including in many of the transition economies of Eastern Europe and Central Asia.

Perhaps the most remarkable changes in low-income countries in recent decades have been the virtually universal improvement in health conditions and the availability of education. From 1965 to 2003, the infant mortality rate fell dramatically in every country listed in Table 1–3, including from 150 to 63 per thousand births in India and from 160 to 53 in Bolivia. This means that in

TABLE 1-2. Growth of Population and Output of Income Groups and Selected Countries, 1965–2003 (percent per year)

INCOME GROUP (2003) AND COUNTRY	POPULATION, 1965–80	POPULATION, 1980–2003	GDP PER CAPITA, 1965–80	GDP PER CAPITA, 1980–2003	INDUSTRY VALUE ADDED, 1965–80	INDUSTRY VALUE ADDED, 1980–2003
Income group						
Low income	2.5	2.2	1.2	2.1	5.3	4.6
Lower-middle income	2.1	1.4	3.8	2.2	6.9	4.3
Upper-middle income	2.0	1.5	3.3	0.8	5.5	2.3
High income	0.9	0.7	3.0	2.1	2.2	2.3
Low income						
Tanzania	3.0	2.9	N.A.	0.8	N.A.	4.5
Ethiopia	2.6	2.6	N.A.	0.1	N.A.	1.1
Nigeria	2.8	2.8	3.3	0.2	12.3	1.5
Mali	2.1	2.5	2.1	0.6	1.7	5.5
Kenya	3.6	2.8	3.3	0.0	9.2	2.7
Senegal	2.8	2.7	−0.8	0.4	3.7	4.2
Bangladesh	2.5	2.1	−1.4	2.2	0.5	6.4
Cameroon	2.7	2.7	2.6	−1.7	7.1	0.2
Pakistan	3.1	2.5	1.9	2.1	6.4	5.4
Ghana	2.4	2.8	−1.0	1.3	1.4	3.5
India	2.3	1.9	1.2	3.6	4.0	6.1
Lower-middle income						
Bolivia	2.4	2.2	0.8	0.4	4.0	2.2
Honduras	3.1	2.9	1.9	0.1	6.2	3.5
Indonesia	2.4	1.6	5.0	3.7	11.5	6.6
Sri Lanka	1.9	1.2	2.5	3.2	4.6	5.5
Egypt	2.1	2.2	3.3	2.3	6.6	4.4
Philippines	2.8	2.3	2.7	0.3	7.3	2.0
China	2.2	1.2	4.2	8.1	9.6	11.5
Peru	2.8	2.0	1.0	−0.3	4.0	2.0
Colombia	2.5	2.0	3.1	1.3	5.6	2.9
Brazil	2.4	1.6	6.0	0.7	9.6	1.6
Upper-middle income						
Malaysia	2.5	2.6	4.6	3.8	7.9	7.6
Mexico	3.0	1.8	3.0	0.6	6.4	2.8
Argentina	1.6	1.2	1.6	0.7	3.2	1.1
Saudi Arabia	4.5	3.7	8.3	−1.9	11.0	1.9
Hungary	0.4	−0.3	4.6	0.9	N.A.	0.4
High income						
Korea, Rep. of	1.9	1.0	6.3	6.0	13.7	8.0
United Kingdom	0.2	0.2	2.1	2.3	0.9	1.7
Germany	0.2	0.3	2.7	1.9	1.3	0.8
Japan	1.2	0.4	5.1	2.2	6.6	2.0
United States	1.0	1.1	2.1	2.1	1.4	2.6

Note: All growth rates are calculated by fitting a linear regression trend line. The regression takes the form, $\ln X_t = a + bt$, where X is the variable and t is time. The regression estimate of b is the annual average growth rate of X.

Source: *World Development Indicators* database, 0-devdata.worldbank.org.luna.wellesley.edu/ dataonline/, accessed June 2005.

TABLE 1-3. Progress in the Social Well-Being of Income Groups and Selected Countries

COUNTRY	INFANT MORTALITY (PER 1,000 LIVE BIRTHS)			PRIMARY SCHOOL ENROLLMENT (PERCENT)*		
	1965	2003	DECLINE	1965	2001	INCREASE
Low income						
Bangladesh	144	46	98	49	98	49
Cameroon	143	95	48	94	107	13
Ethiopia	149	112	37	49	64	15
Ghana	120	59	61	69	81	12
India	150	63	87	74	99	25
Kenya	112	79	33	54	96	42
Mali	207	122	85	24	57	33
Nigeria	177	98	79	32	96	64
Pakistan	149	74	75	40	68	28
Senegal	126	78	48	40	75	35
Tanzania	138	104	34	32	70	38
Lower-middle income						
Bolivia	160	53	107	73	114	41
Brazil	104	33	71	108	148	40
China	90	30	60	89	116	27
Colombia	86	18	68	84	110	26
Egypt	172	33	139	75	97	22
Honduras	128	32	96	80	106	26
Indonesia	128	31	97	72	111	39
Peru	130	26	104	99	120	21
Philippines	72	27	45	113	112	−1
Sri Lanka	63	13	50	93	112	19
Upper-middle income						
Argentina	58	17	41	101	120	19
Hungary	39	8	31	101	101	0
Malaysia	55	7	48	90	95	5
Mexico	82	23	59	92	110	18
Saudi Arabia	148	22	126	24	67	43
High income						
Germany	25	4	21	N.A.	100	N.A.
Japan	18	3	15	100	101	1
Korea, Rep. of	62	5	57	101	102	1
United Kingdom	20	5	15	92	100	8
United States	25	7	18	104	98	−6

*Gross enrollment ratios where the ratio is of total enrollment, regardless of age, to the population of the age group that officially corresponds to the primary level of education. Ratios greater than 100 imply that children outside of the usual age cohort attending primary school are enrolled.

Source: World Bank, *Development Indicators 2004* online; *World Development Indicators* database, 0-devdata.worldbank.org.luna.wellesley.edu/dataonline/, accessed May 2005.

Bolivia, an additional 107 children out of every 1,000 lived to see their first birth-day! Primary school enrollment became nearly universal in middle-income economies and rose dramatically in most of the low-income countries. With few exceptions, more than three quarters of the eligible children attend primary school in poor countries.

It sometimes is easy to become pessimistic about further progress in developing nations, especially when confronted by gloomy predictions about their future economic growth and the myriad problems afflicting them. As an anti-dote to discouragement, one needs to keep in mind the considerable economic development that already has taken place, the strong growth momentum of sev-eral countries in Asia, and the gratifying improvements in health and education that mark even the poorest countries. Indeed, more than 20 countries compris-ing half the world's population that were low-income in 1960 have more than tripled their real incomes in the last two generations.

The study of economic development, however, is not mainly a review of what has and has not been accomplished in the past. It is a field concerned most of all about the future, particularly the future of the least-advantaged peo-ple in the world. To comprehend the future, one must first try to understand how we got to the point where we are now, but the future will not be just a re-play or a projection of trends of the past. New forces are at work that will shape that future. Some of these forces can be seen clearly today. Others that will shape the economic progress of nations are only dimly perceived, if they are seen at all.

Any list of changes in the environment that will make the future of eco-nomic development different from the past should probably start with the infor-mation revolution. The role of greatly enhanced communication around the world as represented by the Internet has sped up the flow of ideas across oceans and borders to an unprecedented degree and made it possible for many kinds of services to be located far from the location where those services ultimately are used. An American business's accounting office might be in a building in Banga-lore, India, rather than in a backroom of the business's operations in Chicago. Lower transport costs, together with better information, contribute to global production networks and the expansion of global trade and investment. The rapid flow of information also is having an impact on politics, by making it harder for authoritarian regimes to control what their people are allowed to know. Partly for this reason, democratic regimes are becoming more the norm than the exception in developing countries, and there is reason to expect this trend to continue.

Not all the foreseeable trends of the future are positive. The scourge of HIV/AIDS is having a devastating impact on populations, particularly those hardest hit in Africa, where life expectancy actually is declining. Environmental degradation is much more serious today than it was a century ago, when Europe and North America were in the early stages of economic growth. Global warming, as a result, is a problem likely to play an important role in our future, whereas it played no role in the past. The one positive change in the environmental sphere is that people around the world are becoming aware of the danger at a much faster pace than in the past. Also a concern is that advanced technology and the information revolution benefit some groups in society, notably the better educated, while leaving behind other large groups.

Some changes likely to occur in the future are positive, but they still create problems for those that have to deal with them. Notable in this category is the rapid aging of populations in the industrialized countries. An aging process also is underway in many developing countries, which have experienced a sharp fall in both their birth and death rates. The result of this **demographic transition,** discussed at length in Chapter 7, is a longer life expectancy for the average person in these countries, clearly a positive change. But the size of the working-age population relative to the size of the retired older population is shrinking dramatically in more and more countries and that puts a large burden on those still in the workforce. The one group of countries that will not have to worry about this problem is that where the birth rate remains high and life expectancy low. Clearly, it is better to have to deal with the problem of an aging population than not to have the problem at all.

We probably are not even aware of many of the forces that will shape the future economic development of nations. No one at the end of the nineteenth century had heard of nuclear energy, DNA, or integrated circuits. No one in the 1970s had heard of HIV/AIDS. Given the pace of change in the current world of the new millennium, similar and possibly greater discoveries will influence profoundly how economies develop. That said, we cannot rely on future discoveries to solve the problems of economic development and poverty among nations. We must try to understand how the nations of the world got to where they are today so that we can do a better job of raising living standards for all in the future.

APPROACHES TO DEVELOPMENT

This book is not for readers looking for a simple explanation of why some countries are still poor or how poverty can be overcome. Library shelves are full of studies explaining how development will occur if only a country will increase the amount it saves and invests or intensify its efforts to export, among other prescriptions. For two decades in the mid-twentieth century, industrialization through import substitution—the replacement of imports with home-produced goods—was considered by many to be the shortest path to development. In the 1970s, labor-intensive techniques, income redistribution, and provision of basic human needs to the poor gained popularity as keys to development. A large majority of economists now counsel governments to depend substantially on markets to set prices and allocate resources and avoid the high protective barriers that go with import substitution. But there are also many who argue against the impact of relatively free trade and increasing globalization because of the perceived loss of jobs that they believe results. A different theme for some analysts is that development will be possible only with a massive shift of resources, in the form of foreign aid and investment, from the richest countries to the poorest. Others call for debt forgiveness for poor nations that have found it difficult to repay earlier loans.

No single factor is responsible for poverty, and no single policy or strategy can set in motion the complex process of economic development. A wide variety of explanations and solutions to the development problem makes sense if placed in the proper context and makes no sense at all outside that set of circumstances. Mobilization of saving is essential for accelerated growth in most cases but sometimes may come second to a redistribution of income, if extreme poverty threatens political stability or forestalls the mobilization of human resources. Import substitution has carried some countries quite far toward economic development, but export promotion has helped others when import substitution bogged down. Prices badly distorted from their free-market values can stifle initiative and hence growth, but removing those distortions leads to development only when other conditions are met as well. Finally, where leaders backed by interests hostile to development rule countries, those leaders and their constituents must be removed from power before growth can occur. Fortunately, the majority of developing countries have governments that want to promote development.

This book is not neutral toward all issues of development. Where controversy exists we shall point it out. Indeed, the authors of this book differ among themselves over some questions of development policy. But we share a common point of view on certain basic points.

This text extensively uses the theoretical tools of mainstream economics in the belief that these tools contribute substantially to our understanding of development problems and their solution. The text does not rely solely or even primarily on theory, however. For five decades and more, development economists and economic historians have been building up an empirical record against which these theories can be tested, and this book draws heavily on many of these empirical studies. We try to give real-country examples for virtually all the major points made in this book. In part, these examples come from the individual country and cross-country comparative studies of others, but they also are drawn extensively from our own personal experiences working on development issues around the world. The several authors who contributed to this textbook, both the current and past editions, have been fortunate enough to study and work over long periods of time in Bolivia, Chile, China, Fiji, the Gambia, Ghana, Indonesia, Kenya, Korea, Malaysia, Nepal, Peru, Samoa, Sri Lanka, Tanzania, Vietnam, and Zambia. At one time or another, at least one from this group of nations has exemplified virtually all the approaches to development now extant.

While this book draws on classical and neoclassical economic theory, development involves major issues for which these economic theories provide no answers or at best provide only partial answers. Economic theory tends to take **institutions** (the existence of markets, a banking system, international trade, government structures, etc.) as a given. But development is concerned with how one creates and strengthens institutions that facilitate development in the first place. How, for example, does a country acquire a government interested in and capable of promoting economic growth? Can efficiently functioning markets be created in countries that currently lack them, or should the state take over the functions normally left to the market elsewhere? Is a fully developed financial system a precondition for growth, or can a country do without at least some parts of such a system? Is land reform necessary for development, and if so, what kind of land reform? What legal systems are needed to support market-based growth? These institutional issues and many others like them are at the heart of the development process and will reappear in different guises in the following chapters.

ORGANIZATION

This book is divided into four parts. Part 1 examines the main factors, both those suggested by economic theory and those supported by empirical investigations, that contribute to differing rates of economic growth. This discussion involves the deliberate choices by governments, including the debate over how economic development should be guided or managed—what is sometimes referred to as the **Washington consensus** that emphasizes reliance on markets versus the critics of that "consensus."

Part 2 goes beyond issues of economic growth and focuses directly on inequality and poverty. Because economic development first and foremost is a process involving people, who are both the prime movers of development and its beneficiaries, Part 2 deals with how human resources are transformed in the process of economic development and how that transformation contributes to the development process itself. Individual chapters are devoted to population, education, and health.

The other major physical input in the growth process is capital. Part 3 is concerned with how capital is mobilized and allocated for development purposes. From where, for example, do the savings come, and how are they transformed into investment? How does government mobilize the resources to finance development? What kind of financial system is consistent with rapid capital accumulation? Will inflation enhance or hinder the process, and what roles will foreign aid and investment play?

Especially in the early stages of development, countries depend heavily on agriculture and on the export of food, fuel, and raw materials. Part 4 discusses strategies to enhance the productivity of such primary industries as a first, and often a continuing, task in stimulating economic development. Ultimately, however, development depends on industrialization. Part 4 also extends the discussion of industrial development, explores trade policies to promote manufactured exports, considers issues of environmental sustainability, and analyzes the macroeconomic management of a developing economy open to world markets.

SUMMARY

- The last 40 years have seen a wide diversity of development experiences around the world. Some countries, including some very large ones like China, India, and Indonesia, have experienced rapid growth and development. Others, particularly many African countries, have experienced stagnation or even a decline in incomes. Understanding the differences in these experiences and the lessons for the future is the core purpose of this book.
- Many different terms are used to differentiate poor from rich countries, but this text mainly uses the terms *developing* and *low-* and *middle-income economies* to refer to those nations with incomes substantially lower than the richest industrial and postindustrial nations.
- Economic growth refers to an increase in gross domestic product (GDP) and total income, while economic development involves, in addition, improvements in health and education and major structural changes, such as industrialization and urbanization. Some countries have economic growth because of the discovery of great mineral wealth but not development, because they retain many of the structural features of a traditional society.
- Developing countries come from a wide variety of historical experiences, and the differences in historical experience have an important influence on contemporary development. Some were colonies whose borders included a diversity of groups and cultures with no history of working and governing together. Others had experienced centuries of

political and cultural unity. Some developing countries had a long history of educating at least the elites while others, including the elites, were mostly illiterate.

- Fortunately, today's developing countries need not duplicate precisely the development experience of the first developing countries of Western Europe and North America anymore than the less-developed parts of Europe (for example, Russia) had to duplicate the development experience of England. For every so-called prerequisite for development to occur, there are usually one or more substitutes that serve as well.

2

Measuring Economic Growth and Development

A Native American saying recommends, "One should not go hunting a bear unless one knows what a bear looks like." This is sound advice for bear hunters; it also has meaning for our inquiry. Understanding how to achieve economic development requires some agreement on what we want to achieve.

The previous chapter already drew a distinction between economic growth and economic development. Economic growth refers to a rise in real national income per capita, that is, a rise in the inflation-adjusted, per person, value of goods and services produced by an economy. This is a relatively objective measure of economic capacity. It is widely recognized and can be computed with varying degrees of accuracy for most economies. There is far less of a consensus on how to define economic development. Most people would include in their definition increases in the material well-being of individuals as well as improvements in basic health and education. Others might add changes in the structure of production (away from agriculture toward manufacturing and services), improvement in the environment, greater economic equality, or an increase in political freedom. Economic development is a normative concept, one not readily captured by any single measure or index.

Students sometimes find discussion of measurement a bit dry, but give this material a chance. If you really are interested in why some nations are poor and others rich, it is essential to be able to track what has happened to an economy over time and make comparisons between countries. If we want to understand why some nations experienced more rapid growth and development than others, we need measures of economic performance that are relatively accurate and comparable. Poor countries are environments where information is scarce and data of questionable quality at times, so we have to assure ourselves that our indicators, though imperfect, are sufficiently robust to help us understand the outcomes we observe. The study of economic development requires us to combine our insights on how economies work with an appeal to the evidence to check if our insights are consistent with experience. Measurement is central to this process and will be an issue we return to throughout this book.

To get started, this chapter introduces measures of national income and considers the problem of making cross-country comparisons when national incomes are expressed in different currencies. Equipped with a means of making comparisons of national income levels, we examine the record both over time and across countries. These data highlight the enormous differences in economic growth that have characterized different regions of the world over the past 500 hundred years as well as over the more recent past. Much of the rest of this book is devoted to understanding what has caused these differences.

Economic growth may be central to achieving economic development, but there is much more to economic development than growth alone. Not only the level of per capita income but how that income is produced, spent, and distributed determines development outcomes. There is much debate about how to define and measure economic development. We introduce two widely cited indicators of economic development, the Human Development Index and the Millennium Development Goals, and consider their strengths and weaknesses. The information presented in this chapter may not make you a better bear hunter, but it will inform the rest of your study of development economics.

MEASURING ECONOMIC GROWTH

At the core of studies of economic growth are changes in national income. Two basic measures of national income are commonly employed. **Gross national product** (**GNP**) is the sum of the value of finished goods and services produced by a society during a given year. GNP excludes intermediate goods (goods used up in the production of other goods, such as the steel used in an automobile or the chips that go into a computer). GNP counts output produced by citizens of the country, including the value of goods and services produced by citizens who live outside its borders. GNP is one of the most common terms used in national income accounting. The World Bank and other multilateral institutions often refer to this same concept as *gross national income* (GNI). **Gross domestic product** (**GDP**) is similar to GNP, except that it counts all output produced within the borders of a country, including output produced by resident foreigners, but excludes the value of production by citizens living abroad. GNP or GDP divided by total population provides a measure of **per capita income.**

The distinction between GNP and GDP can be illustrated using an example from two Southeast Asian economies, Malaysia and the Philippines. Large numbers of Filipinos work in Malaysia and other Asian nations, where there are abundant opportunities for low-skilled and semiskilled workers. The value of the output produced by these Filipino workers counts as part of the Philippines's GNP (since these workers are Philippine nationals) but not as part of the Philippines's GDP (since the work is performed outside of the country). By contrast, the value of this work counts as part of Malaysia's GDP but not its GNP. In 2002, Malaysia, which employs a large number of foreign workers and has many multinationals that repatriate some of their profits, had a GDP about 7 percent greater than its GNP. In the Philippines, which relies heavily on the remittances of Filipinos working abroad, GDP was about 6 percent less than GNP. In most countries the differences between GNP and GDP are smaller. In part because it is easier to track economic activity within a nation's borders, GDP has become the more widely used measure of national income employed by the International Monetary Fund (IMF), United Nations Development Programme, World Bank, and other multilateral agencies as well as by researchers engaged in analyzing cross-country data and trends. We follow this convention and refer primarily to GDP and GDP per capita as measures of national income from here on. Unless otherwise indicated, when discussing trends over time, we refer to **real GDP** and real GDP per capita, that is, per capita gross domestic product adjusted for domestic price inflation.[1]

The contribution of a sector or component of GDP, such as manufacturing or agriculture, is measured by the value added by that sector. **Value added** refers to the incremental gain to the price of a product at a particular stage of production. Thus, the value added of the cotton textile industry is the value of the textiles when they leave the factory minus the value of raw cotton and other materials used in their production. At the same time, the value added is equal to the payments made to the factors of production in the textile industry: wages paid to labor plus profits, interest, depreciation of capital, and rent for buildings and land. Since the total value added at all stages of production equals total output, GDP is a measure of both total *income* and total *output.*

---

[1]Real GDP is computed by deflating nominal GDP (GDP measured in current prices) by a price index. National statistical offices often calculate a variety of price indices, including the consumer price index (CPI), the GDP deflator, and others. What these indices share in common is an attempt to isolate any general increase (or decrease) in the price level for all goods.

Measuring GDP: What Is Left Out?

The proper way to calculate GDP is to add up the value of all the goods and services produced within a country and then sold on the market.[2] The focus on goods and services sold in the market creates a measurement problem, since many valuable contributions to society are excluded from gross domestic product. When housework and child care are performed by paid servants or day-care employees, for example, they are included in GDP, since these services are "sold in the market." However, when unpaid members of the household perform these same services, they do not enter GDP. The scale of this problem tends to be larger in low-income countries and is evident in a poor nation like Cambodia, where almost 50 percent of the labor force is classified as unpaid family workers, most of whom are engaged on family farms producing food and other goods and services for their own consumption.

In Cambodia and most developing countries, a large number of activities do not enter the market. Much of what is produced by the agricultural sector is consumed by the farm household and never exchanged in the marketplace. Strictly speaking, because of the way GDP is defined, one cannot meaningfully discuss the changing contribution of agricultural production in GDP but only the changing contribution of *marketed* agricultural output in GDP. Because this strict definition of GDP would severely limit the usefulness of comparing countries in which agriculture is the dominant sector, the usual practice is to include estimates of farm output consumed by the producer, valued at the prices of marketed farm produce. Despite these adjustments, not all household production is accounted for. As economies grow, more output is transacted in the marketplace and gets included in GDP. The resulting estimates of GDP, therefore, may overestimate the growth in economic activity, since some of what is now captured is merely a transfer of production from within the household to the market.

GDP is a measure of the goods and services produced by an economy. But what about accounting for the "bads" society produces? If a steel mill pollutes a river or the air, the value of the steel produced is included in GDP but the cost of pollution is not deducted. **Net economic welfare (NEW),** a national income measure that attempts to deduct the costs of pollution, crime, congestion, and other "bads," has been proposed by some economists as a better measure of national income but has not been widely adopted. Although there are obvious flaws in GDP as a measure of national income, including the problems of nonmarketed household production and the failure to account for social "bads," there are also many benefits. Having a widely agreed-on approach to measuring national

---

[2]In calculating GDP, goods and services can be valued by using either the prices at which they are sold in the market (GDP at market prices) or the cost of all factor inputs (capital, labor, and land) used in their production (GDP at factor cost).

income facilitates comparisons of nations' economic activity both over time and relative to other countries. Both types of comparisons are essential to understanding the process of economic development.

Exchange-Rate Conversion Problems

A second methodological problem arises when attempting to convert the GDP of different countries into a single currency. To compare the changing economic structure of several countries as per capita income rises, one must measure the per capita income figures in a common currency. The shortcut to accomplishing this goal is to use the official exchange rate between U.S. dollars and each national currency. For example, to convert India's GDP per capita from rupees into U.S. dollars, the official exchange rate between Indian rupees and U.S. dollars (about 45 rupees per U.S. dollar) is used and yields a 2002 estimate of US$470.

A common reaction to this low figure by anyone who has lived in or visited India (or for that matter any developing nation) is that one U.S. dollar goes much further in India than it does in the United States. A basic woman's haircut in a less-affluent part of Mumbai, for example, might cost 180 rupees (US$4 at the official exchange rate) while a basic haircut in a Boston suburb might run US$40. If one can buy more for one dollar in India than one can in the United States—in this example, ten haircuts in Mumbai for the price of one haircut in Boston—then India's true level of per capita income must be higher than the one given by the conversion using the official exchange rate.

There is considerable merit to this argument. One problem with converting per capita income levels from one currency to another is that exchange rates, particularly those of developing countries, can be distorted. Trade restrictions or direct government intervention in setting the exchange rate make it possible for an official exchange rate to be substantially different from a rate determined by a competitive market for foreign exchange.

But even the widespread existence of competitively determined market exchange rates would not eliminate the problem. The huge price difference in haircuts between Boston and Mumbai is not the result of a managed Indian exchanged rate. Instead, a significant part of national income is made up of what are called **nontraded goods and services;** that is, goods that do not and often cannot enter into international trade. Haircuts are one example. Internal transportation, whether by bus, taxi, or train, cannot be traded, although many transport inputs, such automobiles and rail cars, can be imported. Wholesale and retail trade and elementary school education also are nontraded services. Land, homes, and buildings are other obvious examples of goods that are not exchanged across national borders. Generally speaking, whereas the prices of traded goods tend to be similar across countries (since, in the absence of tariffs and other trade barriers, international trade could exploit any price differences), the prices of nontraded goods can differ widely from one country to the next. This is because the markets for nontraded goods are spatially separated and the underlying supply and demand curves can intersect in different places, yielding different prices.

Exchange rates are determined largely by the flow of traded goods and international capital flows and generally do not reflect the relative prices of nontraded goods. As a result, GDP converted to U.S. dollars by market exchange rates gives misleading comparisons if the ratio of prices of nontraded goods to prices of traded goods is different in the countries being compared. The way around this problem is to pick a set of prices for all goods and service prevailing in one country and to use that set of prices to value the goods and services of all countries being compared. In effect, one is calculating a **purchasing power parity (PPP)** exchange rate. Thus, a cement block or a haircut is assigned the same value no matter if is produced in New Delhi or New York.

The essence of the procedure can be illustrated with the simple numerical exercise, presented in Table 2–1. The two economies in the table are called the United States and India for illustrative purposes, and each economy produces one traded commodity (steel) and one nontraded service (retail sales). Each economy produces a different amount of each good. GDP, expressed in local currencies, is equal to the total value of production of steel plus retail sales. The value of the services of retail sales personnel is estimated in the most commonly used way, which is to assume the value of the service is equal to the wages of the worker providing the service. These wages are likely to differ widely across countries and be determined almost exclusively by the domestic labor supply and labor demand conditions. This is because workers cannot easily migrate from one country to another to take advantage of any differences in wages (partly because of immigration rules and partly because the cost of moving to a new country can be high). From the data in Table 2–1 we determine that GDP in the U.S. totals 30 billion dollars and GDP in India is 312 billion rupees.

One way of comparing the GDP levels of the two economies is to convert them into a single currency, say, the U.S. dollar. In this simple world of two goods and two nations, the exchange rate is determined solely by trade in steel. If steel is freely traded between the two countries, then the exchange rate settles where the price per ton of steel in the two countries is equal, that is, where the U.S. price of $200 per ton equals the Indian price of Rs 9000 per ton, or where US$1 = Rs 45.[3] Using this market-determined exchange rate, Indian GDP of Rs 312 billion equals US$6.9 billion, about 23 percent of the U.S. GDP.

---

[3]At any other exchange rate, there would be profitable opportunities to buy more steel from one of the two countries, causing changes in the market for foreign exchange until the two steel prices are equivalent and the exchange rate settles at US$1 = Rs 45. This is sometimes referred to as *the law of one price,* reflecting how opportunities for arbitrage in traded goods lead to price convergence in these goods.

TABLE 2-1. **Exchange Rate versus Purchasing Power Parity Methods of Converting GDP into a Single Currency**

	UNITED STATES			INDIA		
	QUANTITY	PRICE (US$)	VALUE OF OUTPUT (US$ BILLION)	QUANTITY	PRICE (RUPEES)	VALUE OF OUTPUT (BILLION RUPEES)
Steel (million tons)	100	200 per ton	20	8	9,000 per ton	72
Retail sales personnel (millions)	2	5,000 per person per year	10	4	60,000 per person per year	240
Total GDP (local currency)			30			312

Official exchange rate, based on steel prices = 9000/200 or Rs 45 = US$1.

1. Indian GDP in U.S. dollars calculated by using the official exchange rate:

$$312/45 = US\$6.9 \text{ billion.}$$

2. Indian GDP in U.S. dollars calculated by using U.S. prices for each individual product or service and applying that price to Indian quantities (i.e., using purchasing power parity):

Steel	8 million × $200	= $1.6 billion
Retail sales personnel	4 million × $5,000	= $20 billion
GDP		= $21.6 billion.

3. Ratio of PPP calculation of GDP to official exchange rate calculation: 21.6/6.9 = 3.1.

The problem with this comparison is that while Rs 45 and US$1 purchases the same amount of steel in both countries, they purchase different amounts of the nontraded good. To compare the GDP levels of the two nations taking into account this difference in the purchasing power of the respective currencies, we cannot rely on market exchange rates. An alternative approach is to calculate Indian GDP in U.S. dollars using U.S. prices for each product or service and applying those prices to Indian quantities. This PPP calculation results in Indian steel production valued at US$1.6 billion and retail sales valued at US$20 billion, for an estimated Indian GDP of US$21.6 billion. In this example, the PPP calculation of Indian GDP is more than three times as large as the calculation that relied on market exchange rates. In terms of PPP, India's GDP is over 70 percent of the U.S. GDP.

Table 2–1 presents a hypothetical PPP conversion for two countries using two goods. The task becomes significantly more complicated in a world of tens of thousands of goods, with close to 200 nations. The United Nations' International Comparison Program, which began in 1968, tackled this difficult task by deriving a set of **"international" prices** in a common currency. Detailed price data on a basket of hundreds of specific goods have been collected periodically for an ever-increasing number of nations. "International" prices are then derived by aggregating the price data from the individual countries and are used to determine the value of national output at these standardized international prices. Estimates of national income in terms of PPP are reported in the publications of the IMF, World Bank, and other multilateral agencies. Researchers have made extensive use of these data, which also are contained in the Penn World Tables.

Estimates of GNP per capita using official exchange rates and PPP estimates on a select group of countries are presented in Table 2–2. The results are consistent with the finding that the degree to which the official exchange-rate conversion method understates GNP, generally, is related to the average income of the country. For high-income countries, like Germany, Japan, and the United States, whose per capita GNPs were not far apart in 2002, the exchange-rate conversion is a reasonable approximation of what is obtained when converting German and Japanese GNP into U.S. dollars using the PPP method. For India, however, the ratio between the two measures is 5.6 to 1, and for Ethiopia, the ratio at 7.8 to 1 is even greater. With differences of that magnitude, comparisons of per capita income levels using market exchange-rate conversions can be very misleading. Market exchange rates suggest that per capita incomes in the United States were 75 times those in India in 2002. PPP calculations narrow the multiple to about 14 times—still a huge gap but maybe a more reasonable indicator of relative income levels.

TABLE 2-2. Gross National Product per Capita in 2002 (U.S. dollars)

	MEASURED USING OFFICIAL EXCHANGE RATES	MEASURED AT PURCHASING POWER PARITY	RATIO OF PPP CALCULATION TO OFFICIAL EXCHANGE RATE CALCULATION
Japan	34,010	27,380	0.8
United States	35,400	36,110	1.0
Germany	22,740	26,980	1.2
Jamaica	2,690	3,680	1.4
Poland	4,570	10,450	2.3
Egypt, Arab Republic	1,470	3,810	2.6
Brazil	2,830	7,450	2.6
Syrian Arab Republic	1,130	3,470	3.1
Senegal	470	1,540	3.3
Kazakhstan	1,520	5,630	3.7
Indonesia	710	3,070	4.3
China	960	4,520	4.7
Vietnam	430	2,300	5.3
India	470	2,650	5.6
Ethiopia	100	780	7.8

Source: World Bank, *World Development Indicators Online.*

The International Comparison Program provides a consistent set of PPP estimates of national income, but these are only estimates and critics have pointed out flaws in data collection and methodology. Such problems are pervasive whenever one studies the aggregate performance of an economy as it evolves over time or compares the aggregate performance of two different economies. When comparing the steel ingot output of two countries, it is possible to say precisely how many more tons of steel one of the countries produces when compared with the other. There is no comparable precision when one compares large aggregate measures such as GDP. A certain ambiguity always is present when these figures are used to compare income levels, rates of growth, or development patterns across countries or over time. But, despite these ambiguities, much can be learned from the data at hand.

WHAT DO WE MEAN BY ECONOMIC DEVELOPMENT?

As already indicated in Chapter 1, economic growth is a necessary but not sufficient condition for improving the living standards of large numbers of people in countries with low levels of GDP per capita. It is necessary because, if there is no growth, individuals can become better off only through transfers of income and assets from others. In a poor country, even if a small segment of the population is very rich, the potential for this kind of redistribution is severely limited. When GDP per capita is $2,000 (PPP), roughly the level in Ghana and Vietnam, the most a country can do through static income redistribution is to create shared poverty in which each citizen receives $2,000 a year. Economic growth, by contrast, enables some or even all people to become much better off without anyone necessarily becoming worse off.

Economic growth, however, is not a sufficient condition for improving mass living standards. For at least three reasons, it would be wrong to assume that higher per capita GDP necessarily means higher income for all, or even most, families. First, governments promote economic growth not just to improve the welfare of their citizens but also, and sometimes primarily, to augment the power and glory of the state and its rulers. Much of the wealth of ancient Egypt was invested in the pyramids. Developing nations today may expand their militaries, develop weapons of mass destruction, or construct elaborate capital city complexes in deserts and jungles. When the gains from growth are channeled to such expensive projects, they often provide little benefit to the country's citizens. Second, resources may be heavily invested in further growth, with significant consumption gains deferred to a later date. In extreme cases, such as the Soviet collectivization drive of the 1930s, consumption can decline dramatically over long periods. When the Soviet Union fell in 1991, its consumers were still waiting, with growing impatience, for the era of mass consumption to arrive. Normally, the power to suppress consumption to this extent in the name of economic growth is available only to totalitarian governments. Third, income and consumption may increase, but those who already are relatively well-off may get all or most of the benefits. The rich get richer, the old saw says, and the poor get poorer. (In another version, the poor get children.) This is what poor people often think is happening. Sometimes, they are right.

In addition to problems associated with how income is spent and distributed, any definition of economic development must include more than income levels. Income, after all, is only a means to an end, not an end itself. Amartya Sen, economist, philosopher and Nobel laureate, argues that the goal of development is to expand the *capabilities* of people to live the lives they choose to lead. Income is one factor in determining such capabilities and outcomes, but it is not the only one. An individual, for example, might have enough income to afford an adequate diet necessary for good health. But if that individual suffers from a parasitic disease, one for which he or she is unable to get treatment, that person will not be capable of leading the life he or she would like to lead. In his 1998 Nobel address, Sen argued we need to look beyond income poverty and identified four broad factors that condition how well income can be converted into "the capability to live a minimally acceptable life":

- Personal heterogeneities, including age, proneness to illness, or extent of disabilities.
- Environmental diversities, for example, exposure to specific climates requiring different expenditures for shelter, clothing, or fuel depending on whether it is cold or warm.
- Variations in social climate, the impact of crime, civil unrest, and violence.
- Differences in relative deprivation, being relatively impoverished in a richer society reduces the capability to take part in the life of that community.[4]

According to Sen, economic development requires alleviating the sources of "capability deprivation" that prevent people from having the freedom to live the lives they desire.

---

[4]Amartya Sen, "The Possibility of Social Choice," *American Economic Review* 89 (July 1999). See also Sen's book, *Development as Freedom* (New York: Knopf, 1999).

ECONOMIC GROWTH AROUND THE WORLD: A BRIEF OVERVIEW

We now turn from exploring the concepts of economic growth and development to examining the actual performance of countries around the world. We begin by looking at the findings of economic historian Angus Maddison, who estimated income levels and corresponding rates of economic growth for the world economy as far back as the year 1 A.D. Such an exercise requires a lot of conjecture, especially the further back in time one goes. As Maddison argues, during the first millennium, the rate of growth of output was very low, making population growth the critical factor in determining per capita income levels. Estimates of world population can be made going back 2,000 years.

According to Maddison's most recent calculations, average world income in 1000 was virtually the same as it had been 1,000 years earlier.[5] In other words, growth in per capita income between 1 A.D. and 1000 was effectively zero. The next 820 years (from 1000 to 1820) were barely any better, with world income per capita growing, on average, by just 0.05 percent per year. At this rate of growth, it took more than eight centuries for world per capita income to increase by 50 percent. To place this in some perspective, China today is one of the world's fastest growing economies. With over 1 billion people (about four times the entire world's population in 1000), economic growth in China averaged close to 9 percent over the past decade, raising Chinese per capita incomes by 50 percent, not in 820 years, but in 5.

The estimates by Maddison indicate considerable uniformity in per capita incomes throughout the first millennium. The little bit of economic growth that did take place over the next 800 years was centered in Western Europe and in what Maddison calls the Western "offshoots" (Australia, Canada, New Zealand, and the United States). By 1820, these regions already had a decided advantage over the rest of the world. For example, whereas China and India probably were only slightly behind the Western European countries in 1500, average per capita incomes in Western Europe and in their "offshoots" already were double those of China and India by 1820.[6]

---

[5]The data in this section come from Angus Maddison, *The World Economy: Historical Statistics* (Paris: Development Centre of the Organisation for Economic Co-operation and Development, 2003), HS-8: "The World Economy, 1–2001 AD."

[6]For a fascinating account of why regional incomes diverged in the period prior to 1500, see Jared Diamond, *Guns, Germs and Steel: The Fates of Human Societies* (New York: W. W. Norton and Company, 1997). Diamond goes on to ascribe the subsequent divergence of world incomes in the modern era, fundamentally, to these earlier determinants.

Maddison's research suggests that rapid economic growth as we know it really began around 1820. He estimates that over the subsequent 180 years, the average growth in world income increased to 1.2 percent per year. Note that the difference between annual growth of 0.05 percent and 1.2 percent is huge. With the world economy growing at 0.05 percent per year, it would take nearly 1,400 years for average income to double. With annual growth of 1.2 percent, average income doubles in just 58 years.[7] Therefore, the world has changed from no growth at all during the first millennium, to slow growth for most of the second millennium, to a situation where, in the past two centuries, average real income began to double in less than every three generations.

Maddison's estimates of average income levels for the world's major regions between 1820 and 2001 are shown in Figure 2–1. Several features of this data are notable. First, economic growth rates clearly accelerated around the world during this period, especially after 1880. Second, and perhaps most striking, the richest countries recorded the fastest growth rates and the poorest countries recorded the slowest growth rates, at least until 1950. Per capita income in the Western offshoots grew by about 1.6 percent per year between 1820 and 1950, while in Asia it grew by less than 0.25 percent. As a result, the ratio of the average incomes in the richest regions to those in the poorest regions grew from about 3:1 in 1820 to about 15:1 in 1950.

Between 1950 and 2001, the patterns of economic growth changed, at least in several regions. The gap between the Western offshoots and Western Europe, which had been widening through 1950, narrowed significantly. The poorest region in 1950—Asia—recorded the fastest subsequent growth rate (3.3 percent), thereby beginning to close the income gap with the richer regions of the world. By contrast, Latin America's growth stagnated after 1980, and Eastern Europe's collapsed after the fall of the Berlin Wall in 1989. In Africa, as elsewhere, average growth rates accelerated after 1820 and did so again after 1950, in the period associated with the end of the colonial era. But as in Latin America, economic growth in Africa faded after 1980. As a result, the income gap between the world's richest regions, the Western offshoots, and the poorest, Africa, now

---

[7]The "rule of 70" is useful in thinking about the time necessary for incomes (or anything else) to double for a given growth rate. As a close approximation, 70 divided by the annual rate gives the doubling time. Thus, at a growth rate of 2 percent per year, income will double in about 35 years. More precisely, the equation is $Y_t = Y_0 (1 + g)^t$, where Y is per capita income, g is the growth rate expressed as a decimal, and t is years. For Y to double means, $Y_t = 2Y_0$, hence, $2 = (1 + g)^t$. By taking natural logs of both sides and using a bit of algebra, we find that $t = \ln(2)/\ln(1 + g) = 0.693/\ln(1 + g)$. By multiplying the numerator and denominator of this ratio by 100, we get $t = 69.3/(100 \times \ln(1 + g))$. Since $\ln(1 + g)$ is approximately equal to g if g is small, t is approximately equal to 70/g, where g now equals the growth rate expressed as a percentage. With Madisson's estimated annual world growth rate of 1.2 percent since 1820, we solve to find the doubling time of world incomes during this period to be $t = 58$ years.

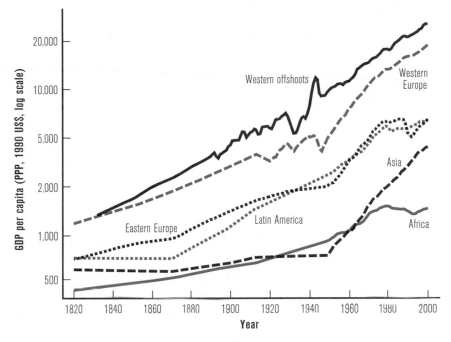

FIGURE 2-1. Levels of GDP per Capita by Region: 1820–2001
Note: Western "offshoots" include Australia, Canada, New Zealand, and the United States.
Source: Maddison www.eco.rug.nl/~Maddison/content.shtml.

stands at 18:1. According to Maddison's work, this is the largest gap in income between rich and poor regions the world has ever known.[8]

Maddison provides an overview of the broad sweep of world economic history, demonstrating how, at the start of the second millennium, income levels in all regions of the world were still roughly similar. By the end of the twentieth century, the opposite was true. The divergence of regional incomes today characterizes the world economy. Table 2–3 takes a closer look at the pattern of growth rates over the past three decades. The selection of decades as the unit of observation is somewhat arbitrary. The 1970s often are associated with two oil price shocks and other significant changes in commodity prices; the 1980s, with the first of a wave of international debt crises; and the 1990s, with the major transition toward market economies, especially in Eastern Europe and the republics of the former Soviet Union. The regional divisions in Table 2–3 differ from those in Maddison and conform to conventions used by the World Bank, a major source of data on economic development. Most of the regional definitions are self-explanatory; however, all high-income economies are combined in one category regardless of geographic location. Therefore, East Asia does not include Japan, Korea, Singapore, Taiwan, and a few small and affluent island

---

[8]Using a somewhat different methodology than that employed by Maddison, similar conclusions are reached by Lant Pritchett, "Divergence, Big Time," *Journal of Economic Perspectives* 11, no. 3 (1997).

TABLE 2-3.   Rate of Growth in Gross Domestic Product per Capita
(percent/year)

	1970–80	1980–90	1990–2002
East Asia and Pacific	4.4	5.7	6.1
Europe and Central Asia	4.4	1.2	−0.6
Latin America and Caribbean	3.1	−0.2	1.3
Middle East and North Africa	2.3	−2.0	1.0
South Asia	1.0	3.2	3.5
Sub-Saharan Africa	0.5	−1.3	0.1
High income	2.6	2.6	1.8

Source: World Bank, *World Development Indicators Online, World Development Indicators 2003, World Development Report 1995.*

economies. Similarly, Europe and Central Asia refers primarily to Eastern Europe and Central Asia since this category does not include any high-income nation within this region, those with a 2002 GNP per capita above $9,075 (US$).

The growth rates in GDP per capita reported in Table 2–3 highlight the differences in economic growth both between regions and over time.[9] The 1970s were the last decade in which *all* regions experienced positive growth. The 1980s often are referred to as "the lost decade" in Latin American, because of the sharp downturn in regional growth, from +3.1 percent in the 1970s to –0.2 percent in the following ten years. Negative growth and falling per capita income also were features of the Middle East and North Africa region and sub-Saharan Africa in the 1980s and Europe and Central Asia in the 1990s. The poor performance of these regions stands in sharp contrast to the accelerating growth rates—and the associated improvements in living standards—in both East and South Asia.[10]

The successful growth performance in Asia and a few countries in other regions, even relative to the high-income economies, illustrates an observation by economic historian Alexander Gerschenkron. When Gerschenkron refers to **"the advantages of backwardness,"** he is not suggesting that it is good to be poor. Instead, he means that being relatively poorer might allow these countries to grow more quickly. For the first nations to experience modern economic growth, in Western Europe and its offshoots, growth rates were constrained by the rate of technological progress. But poor countries could borrow and adapt existing technology and have the potential to grow faster and catch up to the more advanced economies. Over the past three decades, this is what enabled growth

[9]The growth rates in Table 2–3 are based on constant 1995 US$. While large differences in the *level* of GDP per capita are observed depending on whether PPP or market exchange rates are used, this is not the case when comparing *growth rates* of national income.

[10]The regional averages in Table 2–3 are weighted averages, where the weights are the population size of each nation in the region. Such averages are heavily influenced by the experience of the most populous country in the region, especially China in East Asia and India in South Asia, and disguise the wide range in individual country performance. For example, in East Asia, the Philippines annual growth rate from 1970 to 2002 was only 0.5 percent, while Botswana, grew at 5.9 percent per annum, far exceeding not only the sub-Saharan Africa average but the performance of most nations worldwide.

rates in Asia to exceed the growth rates of the high-income region. For development economists, the challenge is to understand why some countries have been able to realize the "advantages of backwardness" while much of the developing world has fallen further behind.

TRENDS IN ECONOMIC DEVELOPMENT

Consistent with the ideas of Amartya Sen, the United Nations Development Programme (UNDP) provides measures of economic development in its annual publication, the *Human Development Report*. The first such report was published in 1990 with "the single goal of putting people back at the center of the development process." Although the terminology is different, human development versus economic development, the idea is the same. The distinction is intended to expand the perception of development as encompassing more than increases in per capita income (Box 2–1).

BOX 2-1 HUMAN DEVELOPMENT DEFINED

Human development is a process of enlarging people's choices. In principle, these choices can be infinite and change over time. But at all levels of development, the three essential ones are for people to lead a long and healthy life, to acquire knowledge, and to have access to resources needed for a decent standard of living. If these essential choices are not available, many other opportunities remain inaccessible.

But human development does not end there. Additional choices, highly valued by many people, range from political, economic and social freedom to opportunities for being creative and productive, and enjoying personal self-respect and guaranteed human rights.

Human development has two sides: the formation of human capabilities—such as improved health, knowledge and skills—and the use people make of their acquired capabilities—for leisure, productive purposes, or being active in cultural, social and political affairs. If the scales of human development do not finely balance the two sides, considerable human frustration may result.

According to this concept of human development, income is clearly only one option that people would like to have, albeit an important one. But it is not the sum total of their lives. Development must, therefore, be more than just the expansion of income and wealth. Its focus must be people.

Source: United Nations Development Programme, *Human Development Report*, 1990 (Oxford: Oxford University Press, 1990), Table 1.1, p. 10. Reprinted by permission of Oxford University Press.

Measuring Human Development

The UNDP attempted to quantify what it saw as the essential determinants of human development: to live a long and healthy life, acquire knowledge, and have access to the resources needed for a decent standard of living. For each of these elements, a specific measure was constructed and aggregated into an index, the **Human Development Index (HDI).** Every year since 1990, the UNDP has calculated the value of the HDI for as many of the world's nations as the data permit and assessed the relative progress of nations in improving human development. Because the HDI combines outcomes with vastly different units of measurement—years for life expectancy, school enrollment rates and percent of literate adults for education, and dollars of income for access to resources— each outcome must be converted into an index number to permit aggregation into a composite measure.

As a proxy for living a long and healthy life, the HDI employs a nation's life expectancy at birth and compares progress on this measure relative to other nations. In a recent HDI, the "goalposts" for assessing life expectancy range from a minimum value of 25 years to a maximum of 85. A country's score essentially is a measure of its own life expectancy compared to these maximum and minimum scores. For example, in 2001, Peru had life expectancy at birth of 69.4 years. Peru's HDI life expectancy index is calculated as $(69.4 - 25)/(85 - 25) = 0.74$; in other words, Peru attained 74 percent of the potential range in life expectancy.

As a proxy for acquiring knowledge, the HDI computes a weighted average of adult literacy and the combined gross enrollment rate of primary, secondary, and tertiary schooling. The adult literacy rate is given a weight of two thirds, while the gross enrollment rate receives a weight of one third. The goalposts here are 0 to 100 percent. With an adult literacy rate of 90 percent and a gross enrollment ratio of 83 percent, Peru's HDI education index is 0.88.

Access to resources is proxied by transforming GDP per capita (PPP US$). The goalposts are $100 to $40,000, where relative standing is determined by taking the logarithms of all dollar values. The transformation into logarithms decreases the significance of income gains the higher is the income. This reflects the *Human Development Report*'s position that there are diminishing returns to income as a means of securing a *decent* standard of living (or, alternatively, that the marginal utility of an extra dollar of income falls as income rises). With a 2001 GDP per capita of $4,570 (PPP), Peru's HDI GDP index equals 0.64, $[\log(\$4,570) - \log(\$100)]/[\log(\$40,000) - \log(\$100)]$. In terms of per capita income performance, Peru has attained 64 percent of the potential range in national income.

The HDI is then computed as the simple average of the three indexes on life expectancy, education, and GDP. This yields an HDI value of 0.752 for Peru, which places it in 82nd place, about halfway, among the 175 nations included in

Human Development Report 2003.[11] Peru's HDI improved from an estimated 0.639 value in 1975, to 0.702 in 1990, to its most recent value of 0.752. These trends suggest progress in Peru's human development over the past 25 years.

What Can We Learn from the Human Development Index?

The basic concept behind human development is one with which many people would agree. But, as we have seen before, when we move from concept to measurement, problems may arise. Many criticisms have been leveled against the HDI since it first was introduced. Some concern limiting the index to only three dimensions of human development. In response, the *Human Development Report* now computes additional indexes focusing on human poverty and gender-related development. Other criticisms concern the choice of goalposts or the equal weight given to life expectancy, education, and income in the composite index. In some instances, there has been a response with adjustments made to how HDI is calculated.[12]

Beyond these criticisms lies the central question of how much of an improvement HDI is over GDP per capita as an index of economic or human development? The *Human Development Report 1990* argued that the two measures show very different outcomes. Figure 2–2 reproduces a diagram that appeared in the 1990 report but uses data and the methodology for calculating HDI from the 2003 report. The upper curve presents the HDI value for all countries ranked from the lowest to highest HDI value. The lower curve shows country rankings according to GDP per capita (PPP). Most countries have a different ranking for GDP per capita than for HDI. Peru has an HDI ranking of 82nd place but a GDP per capita (PPP) ranking that falls to 96th place, suggesting that Peru has made more relative progress in achieving human development than in raising per capita income. The situation in Kuwait is the reverse. It GDP per capita rank, 27th, is much higher than its HDI rank, 46th.

The noticeably different profiles generated by the two curves in Figure 2–2 led the 1990 report to conclude that there is no automatic link between a nation's per capita income and its level of human development. The good news is that human development seems to progress more rapidly than income growth; the troubling news is that economic growth at low income levels seems disconnected from human development.

[11]There are more than 175 recognized nations in the world. The HDI is computed only for members of the United Nations, which eliminates a number of countries (for example, Taiwan). Also excluded are nations for which the necessary data are unavailable. Many of these nations are quite small (Naura and Tonga), while others are so-called failed states where the statistical apparatus has broken down (Afghanistan and Somalia). Despite these omissions, the overwhelming majority of the world's population is covered by the HDI.

[12]*Human Development Report 1993* provides a summary of early critiques of the HDI (pp. 104–14).

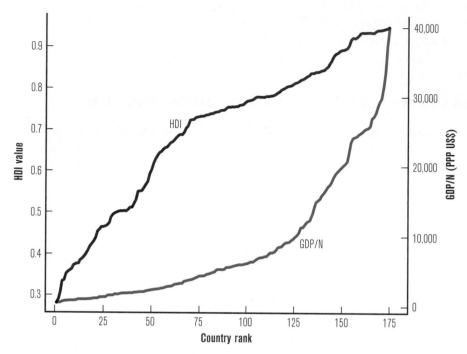

FIGURE 2-2. HDI versus GDP/N Rankings (2001)

Source: *Human Development Report 2003 Online,* hdr.undp.org/reports/global/2003/indicator/
index_indicators.html.

Allen Kelley challenged these conclusions in an article that appeared shortly
after the HDI was introduced.[13] Following Kelley, Figure 2–3 recalculates the relationship shown in Figure 2–2 by mapping per capita income levels using the
same metric for income as contained in the HDI, that is, by using the logarithm
of GDP per capita. The gap between the two measures is reduced substantially
once income is measured in a common manner. This transformation restores
the expected correlation between income levels and human development. We
expect such a result because income remains an important determinant of education and health outcomes.

But there remains more to development than income growth. Figure 2–4
presents another comparison of HDI values and levels of GDP per capita. The
scatter diagram of values for individual countries confirms the trend revealed by
Figure 2–3, rising incomes systematically raise the HDI. But the scatter diagram
also indicates considerable variance around this trend, particularly among low-
and middle-income nations. Swaziland and Ukraine have very similar levels of
per capita GDP (around $4,300 (PPP)) but HIV/AIDS has dramatically lowered
life expectancy to 38 years in Swaziland. Ukraine has not faced a similar health
crisis and life expectancy stands at 69 years. If one compares Algeria and
Panama, both have income levels around $6,000 (PPP), but 92 percent of
Panamian adults are literate while only 68 percent of Algerians are. In terms of

[13]Allen Kelley, "The Human Development Index: 'Handle with Care'," *Population and Development Review* 17, no. 2 (June 1991).

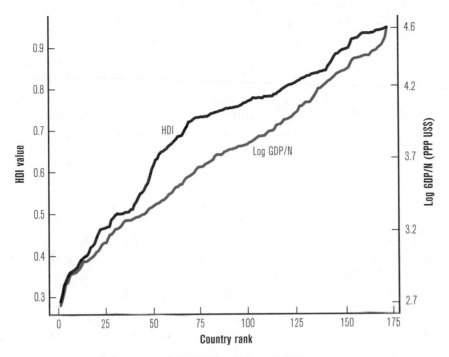

FIGURE 2-3. HDI versus Log GDP/N Rankings (2001)

Source: *Human Development Report 2003 Online,* hdr.undp.org/reports/global/2003/indicator/
index_indicators.html.

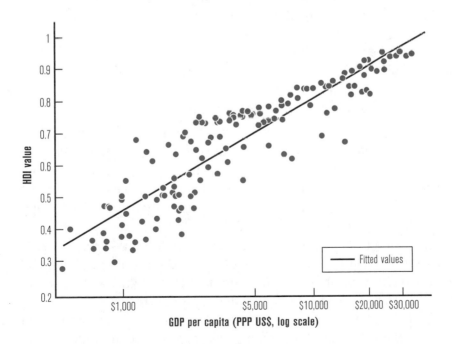

FIGURE 2-4. HDI versus GDP/N by Country

Source: *Human Development Report 2003 Online,* hdr.undp.org/reports/global/2003/indicator/
index_indicators.html.

HDI values, Algeria and Swaziland lay well below the trend line in Figure 2–4, Panama and Ukraine lie well above it.

How much additional insight the HDI offers as a means of measuring economic development remains open to debate. What we can conclude is that alternative measures of economic development confirm the importance of economic growth to the development process while also confirming that improved health and education, as well as other desired outcomes, also depend on factors other than income.

Millennium Development Goals

Defining economic development is inherently difficult. As with any normative concept, people have different opinions as to what should be included in the definition and on what weight to give to different goals. But even without a commonly agreed-on definition, policy makers need specific targets. One such set of targets is contained in the **Millennium Development Goals (MDGs).**

In September 2000, 189 nations adopted the United Nations Millennium Declaration, a broad-reaching document that states a commitment "to making the right to development a reality for everyone and to freeing the entire human race from want."[14] The declaration specifies a set of eight goals consistent with this commitment:

- Goal 1. Eradicate extreme poverty and hunger.
- Goal 2. Achieve universal primary education.
- Goal 3. Promote gender equality and empower women.
- Goal 4. Reduce child mortality.
- Goal 5. Improve maternal health.
- Goal 6. Combat HIV/AIDS, malaria, and other diseases.
- Goal 7. Ensure environmental sustainability.
- Goal 8. Develop a global partnership for development.

To more fully define these goals, a panel of experts developed a comprehensive set of targets and indicators for each of the MDGs. For Goal 4, Reduce child mortality, for example, the target is to reduce by two thirds, between 1990 and 2015, the world's under-five (years of age) mortality rates. Since child mortality rates vary considerably by region, the target is further defined by region. In Latin America in 1990, the under-five mortality rate was 53 deaths per 1,000 children; by 2001, it had fallen to 34; and the MDG for 2015 is a further decline to 17. In sub-Saharan Africa, child mortality is much higher. In 1990, it was 178 annual deaths per 1,000 children; by 2001, it had dropped only slightly to 171; and in 2015, the MDG is to reach a rate of no more than 59 for the region.

The eight MDGs contain 18 targets (Box 2–2), which correspond to 48 indicators. This combination of multiple goals, targets, and indicators is an

[14]United Nations General Assembly, *United Nations Millennium Declaration*, Section III, paragraph 11 (September 18, 2000).

BOX 2-2 TARGETS OF THE MILLENNIUM DEVELOPMENT GOALS

Target 1.   Halve, between 1990 and 2015, the proportion of people whose income is less than one dollar a day.

Target 2.   Halve, between 1990 and 2015, the proportion of people who suffer from hunger.

Target 3.   Ensure that, by 2015, children everywhere, boys and girls alike, will be able to complete a full course of primary schooling.

Target 4.   Eliminate gender disparity in primary and secondary education, preferably by 2005, and to all levels of education no later than 2025.

Target 5.   Reduce by two thirds, between 1990 and 2015, the under-five mortality rate.

Target 6.   Reduce by three quarters, between 1990 and 2015, the maternal mortality ratio.

Target 7.   Have halted by 2015 and begun to reverse the spread of HIV/AIDS.

Target 8.   Have halted by 2015 and begun to reverse the incidence of malaria and other major diseases.

Target 9.   Integrate the principles of sustainable development into country policies and programmes and reverse the loss of environmental resources.

Target 10. Halve by 2015 the proportion of people without sustainable access to safe drinking water.

Target 11. By 2020 to have achieved a significant improvement in the lives of at least 100 million slum dwellers.

Target 12. Develop further an open, rule-based, predictable, non-discriminatory trading and financial system.

Target 13. Address the special needs of the least developed countries.

Target 14. Address the special needs of landlocked countries and small island developing States.

Target 15. Deal comprehensively with the debt problems of developing countries through national and international measures in order to make debt sustainable in the long run.

Target 16. In cooperation with developing countries, develop and implement strategies for decent and productive work for youth.

Target 17. In cooperation with pharmaceutical companies, provide access to affordable essential drugs in developing countries.

Target 18. In cooperation with the private sector, make available the benefits of new technologies, especially information and communications.

Source: United Nations General Assembly, "Road Map towards the Implementation of the United Nations Millennium Declaration," Annex (September 6, 2001).

articulation of what most of the world's governments believe should be achieved in order to make "development a reality for everyone." The millennium declaration even suggests ways in which this development agenda might be financed. Target 13, which focuses on the least-developed or low-income countries, makes recommendations for debt relief and more official development assistance from the rich nations. But none of these recommendations is binding.

Unlike the HDI, which attempted to define human development in a single measure, the MDGs offer an alternative approach. Just as the HDI has been criticized for what it fails to include, the MDGs can be challenged on the basis of including too much, or setting targets that may be either too high or too low based on historical experience.[15] The MDGs also fail to address the fundamental economic problem of trade-offs and priorities. If one cannot fulfill all 18 targets simultaneously, which takes precedence: maternal mortality or access to safe drinking water, reducing hunger or promoting environmental sustainability? This is less of a problem for defining development: Economic development involves all these goals. But it is a practical problem for those charged with realizing this ambitious development agenda.[16]

The MDGs and Economic Growth

The MDGs have been drawn up only recently, but their quantitative targets extend from 1990 to 2015. This permits some midterm assessment of progress to date. Poverty reduction, where poverty is defined as living on less than $1 (U.S., PPP) per day, is on track to meet or exceed the global target by 2015 (although the target will not be met in every country). Access to improved sanitation also is proceeding well. More disappointing are trends in under-five mortality and gender equality in school enrollment, both of which are improving too slowly to meet MDG targets.

Relative success and failure at meeting the MDGs varies not only among specific targets but also by region. Some of the explanation for differential performance is based on disparities in the rate of economic growth within countries and regions. But, as we saw when comparing the HDI with income levels, *some* of the difficulty in achieving specific MDGs also is due to factors beyond economic growth.

Table 2–4 illustrates this conclusion. It shows projected growth in GDP per capita, 2000–15, combined with predictions of how various targets will improve

---

[15]Michael Clemens, Charles Kenny, and Todd Moss, "The Trouble with the MDGs: Confronting Expectations of Aid and Development Success," Working Paper Number 40, Center for Global Development (May 2004).

[16]A strategy for achieving the MDGs is laid out in a report by the UN Millennium Project, *Investing in Development: A Practical Plan to Achieve the UN Millennium Development Goals* (New York: United Nations Development Programme, 2005).

TABLE 2-4. **Economic Growth Alone Is Not Enough to Reach All the Millennium Development Goals**

	ANNUAL AVERAGE GDP PER CAPITA GROWTH 2000–15 (PERCENT PER YEAR)	PEOPLE LIVING ON LESS THAN $1 (US$, PPP) A DAY		PRIMARY SCHOOL COMPLETION RATE		UNDER-FIVE MORTALITY	
		TARGET (PERCENT)	2015 GROWTH ALONE (PERCENT)	TARGET (PERCENT)	2015 GROWTH ALONE (PERCENT)	TARGET (PER 1,000 BIRTHS)	2015 GROWTH ALONE (PER 1,000 BIRTHS)
East Asia	5.4	14	4	100	100	19	26
Europe and Central Asia	3.6	1	1	100	100	15	26
Latin America and the Caribbean	1.8	8	8	100	95	17	30
Middle East and North Africa	1.4	1	1	100	96	25	41
South Asia	3.8	22	15	100	99	43	69
Sub-Saharan Africa	1.2	24	35	100	56	59	151

Source: World Bank, *World Development Report 2004*, Table 1.

as a result of expected economic growth between 2000 and 2015. These outcomes then are compared to region-specific MDGs. Every region but sub-Saharan Africa is projected to meet or exceed Target 1 based on growth alone, halving the proportion of people whose incomes are less than $1 a day. East Asia and Europe and Central Asia are the only regions expected to meet Target 3, universal primary education. Not one region is expected to meet Target 5 based on growth alone, a two-thirds reduction in the child mortality rate.

One reason that sub-Saharan Africa is predicted to do so poorly on all three of these MDGs is because its rate of economic growth is so low. Compared to South Asia, the second poorest region in the world, sub-Saharan Africa is projected to have less than one third the growth rate, accounting for much of the differential performance between these two poor regions. But it is also clear that rapid economic growth is not enough to achieve these MDGs. Even with growth rates well in excess of 3 percent per capita, impressive rates according to the historical data presented earlier, several regions will not fulfill these MDG targets. Better use and distribution of income, specific strategies aimed at some of the targets (such as reducing infant mortality through disease control), combined with economic growth are essential to achieving the United Nations's goal of "freeing the entire human race from want."

IS ECONOMIC GROWTH DESIRABLE?

After discussing the MDGs, which convey the absolute and relative deprivation of so many people around the world, and recognizing the positive correlation between economic growth and human development, it may seem odd to end this chapter by asking, "Is economic growth desirable?" The answer would seem to be an obvious and emphatic, Yes! But there are other perspectives. Some decry the spread of materialism, the Westernization of world cultures, and the destruction of traditional societies that seems to accompany economic growth. Others are troubled by environmental degradation, whether loss of species or global warming, that has accompanied rising per capita incomes. Still others in the high-income world may wonder if we should be so quick to encourage people to follow the path we have taken: seemingly insatiable consumerism, the withering of extended and nuclear families, high levels of stress, and all the other ills associated with modern life.

Survey data on individuals' satisfaction with their lives seem to lend to support to some of these concerns. Richard Easterlin, an economic historian, once observed that, although per capita incomes in the United States had risen dramatically over the preceding half century, people did not seem to be any happier. He based this conclusion on survey data taken over time in which people were asked how happy they were with their lives. Easterlin found similar results for Japan. Figure 2–5 examines this relationship for a cross-section of countries. Drawing on survey data from 42 nations, levels of reported happiness are compared with levels of per capita income. Just as Easterlin found over time in Japan and the United States, looking across countries the figure suggest only a slight tendency for happiness to rise with per capita incomes. In 1996, Norway's GDP per capita (PPP) was 23 times that of Bangladesh, but on a scale of 0–10, Bangladeshis and Norwegians averaged 7.6 and 7.0, respectively, in assessing how happy they were.

Easterlin and others have studied the determinants of happiness and conclude that many factors influence a person's satisfaction with his or her life. A key finding is that we judge ourselves relative to those around us. Someone in Bangladesh does not compare himself to someone in Norway, nor is a Norwegian's happiness a function of Norway's per capita income rank among nations. This may explain the lack of much correlation between happiness and per capita income.

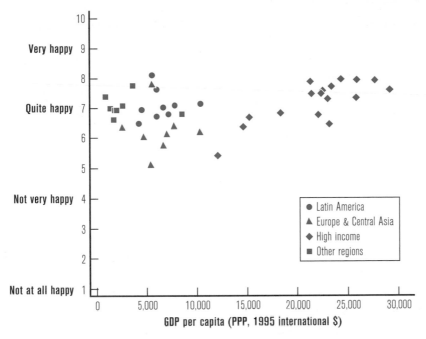

FIGURE 2-5. "How Happy Are You, Taking All Things Together?" Cross-Country Evidence (1995–2002)

Note: Happiness measures the mean happiness of a random group of people, who were asked how happy they are, taking all things together on a scale of 0–10. The data provided were drawn largely from publications on happiness in books and journal articles, as well as from grey reports and other data files.

Source: R. Veenhoven, World Database of Happiness, www2.eur.nl/fsw/research/happiness/index.htm, World Bank, *World Development Indicators Online.*

But the question still remains, if economic growth does not significantly increase happiness, what is the point? Fifty years ago, W. Arthur Lewis, one of the pioneers of the field of development economics who won a Nobel Prize for his contributions, provided an answer. Lewis was writing before there was survey evidence on happiness and at a time when the distinction between the terms economic growth and economic development were not as nuanced as they are today. The concluding chapter of Lewis's 1995 book, *The Theory of Economic Growth,* is entitled, "Is Economic Growth Desirable?" Lewis answers the question as follows:

> The advantage of economic growth is not that wealth increases happiness, but that it increases the range of human choice. It is very hard to correlate wealth and happiness. Happiness results from the way one looks at life, taking it as it comes, dwelling on the pleasant rather than the unpleasant, and living without fear of what the future may bring. Wealth would increase happiness if it increased resources more than it increased wants, but it does not necessarily do this. . . . We

certainly cannot say that an increase in wealth makes people happier. We cannot say, either, that an increase in wealth makes people less happy, and even if we could say this, it would not be a decisive argument against economic growth, since happiness is not the only good thing in life. . . . The case for economic growth is that it gives man greater control over his environment, and thereby increases his freedom.[17]

SUMMARY

- Understanding the process of economic development requires methods of measuring economic performance across countries and over time. GDP per capita is a measure of the aggregate value of national output and, despite a number of limitations, is the most common standard for measuring economic growth.

- For cross-country comparisons, GDP per capita is best measured in terms of purchasing power parity (PPP). PPP estimates are superior to comparisons based solely on market exchange rates. Market exchange rates tend to underestimate the GDP levels of poorer nations. This is because market exchange rates are based on traded goods and capital flows and fail to account for the much lower prices of nontraded goods in poor nations. The PPP estimates obtained from the UN's International Comparison Program correct this problem by expressing every nation's GDP per capita in terms of a common set of "international prices."

- Angus Maddison provides a broad overview of economic growth over the past 2,000 years. For most of this period and in most regions, growth in output was just about sufficient to match growth in population, resulting in more or less stagnant per capita incomes. According to Maddison, modern economic growth began only around 1820, with the escalation of growth rates in Western Europe and its Offshoots. These regions had achieved higher per capita income levels by 1500 but accelerated these differences, especially, over the last 180 years. Rapid growth rates began to characterize other regions, especially in Asia, only in the decades following 1950. As a result of these divergent patterns of economic growth, there is greater disparity in world incomes today than ever before.

[17]W. Arthur Lewis, *The Theory of Economic Growth* (Homewood, IL: Richard D. Irwin, Inc., 1955), 420–21.

- Unlike economic growth, which is a relatively objective measure of economic capacity, economic development is a normative concept. Various scholars and organizations offer specific indicators or goals for achieving development. Prominent among these is the Human Development Index (HDI), a composite measure reflecting the goals of leading a long life, acquiring knowledge, and achieving material well-being. The Millennium Development Goals (MDGs) rely on a multiplicity of goals and targets for advancing human well-being within the next decade.
- Analysis of the HDI and the MDGs reveals the centrality of economic growth to achieving both. HDI ranks are highly correlated with per capita income levels, and differential performance in achieving specific MDGs often is tied to differential growth performance. But economic growth is not a panacea. Achieving economic development also involves questions of distribution and strategies to reach specific development targets.
- Citizens of rich nations can engage in a debate over whether further economic growth will advance their well-being, but this is not a meaningful debate for poor nations. Even if rising per capita incomes are not well correlated with perceptions of happiness, economic growth and development are essential for poor nations as means of increasing choices and advancing human freedoms.

Economic Growth: Concepts and Patterns

Why are some countries rich and others poor? Why do some economies grow quickly with their citizens enjoying rapid increases in their average incomes, while others grow slowly or not at all? How did some East Asian countries advance from poverty to relative prosperity in just 30 years, while many African countries remain mired in deep poverty, with few signs of sustained growth and development? These are some of the most important questions in the study of economics and indeed touch on some of the deepest problems facing human society.

As we saw in the last chapter, rapid economic growth and wide divergences of economic performance across countries actually are fairly recent phenomena in world history. Up until about 500 years ago—a relatively short period of time in human history—most people lived in conditions that we now would consider abject poverty. Housing was poor, food supplies were highly variable and dependent on the weather, nutrition was inadequate, disease was common, health care was rudimentary, and life spans rarely exceeded 40 years. Even as recently as 125 years ago, the vast majority of people living in the world's most modern cities, including New York, London, and Paris, lived in extremely difficult conditions on very meager incomes. At the beginning of the twenty-first century, however, income levels around the world generally are both much higher and far more diverse. A significant minority of the world's population has recorded relatively rapid and sustained income growth during the last several decades and now enjoys much longer and healthier lives, high levels of education, and much-improved standards of living. Other countries have achieved important but more modest gains and now are considered to be middle-income countries. The majority of the world's population, however, continues to live in poverty, in most cases better off than their ancestors but living at levels of income and welfare far below those of the world's richest countries.

Economic growth and economic development are not synonymous, as we discovered in Chapter 2. Yet economic growth is at the heart of the development process, and sustained development and poverty reduction cannot occur in the absence of economic growth. The next two chapters explore in some detail the puzzles of economic growth and divergent levels of income across countries. Our objectives are to better understand the processes by which economies grow and develop and the characteristics that distinguish rapidly growing economies from those with slower growth. This chapter explores the basic empirical data on economic growth, the concepts underlying the leading ideas of what causes growth, and some of the patterns of changing economic structure that typically accompany growth. Chapter 4 expands the analysis by introducing some formal models of economic growth. Later chapters explore some of the other dimensions of development introduced earlier, including the distribution of income, poverty, and improvements in health and education.

DIVERGENT PATTERNS OF ECONOMIC GROWTH SINCE 1960

As we begin to explore differences in growth rates, consider Thailand and Zambia. In 1960, the annual income of the average Thai and the average Zambian were about the same, around $1,100 in Thailand and $1,200 in Zambia in constant 1996 purchasing power parity dollars. Since that time, Thailand achieved very rapid economic growth of around 4.5 percent per person per year, so that the average income in Thailand is now more than $7,000. In 2002, the income of the average Thai was well more than *six times* higher in real terms than that of his or her grandparents 40 years ago. As a result, Thais can consume much more (and much higher-quality) food, housing, clothing, health care, education, and consumer goods. Thais are better off in other ways as well: life expectancy increased from 53 to 69 years, infant mortality dropped from 103 to 24 per thousand (meaning that an additional 79 children per thousand infants lived beyond their first birthday), and the percentage of adults that were literate grew from 80 (in 1970) to 93 percent. In Zambia, by contrast, average income actually fell by 0.6 percent per year to around $900, about 20 percent lower than in 1960. Life expectancy fell from 42 to 37 years, to a large extent because of the dramatic spread of the HIV/AIDS pandemic in the 1990s. Infant mortality rates improved (from 126 to 102 per thousand), as did literacy rates (from 48 to 80 percent), but overall Zambians are arguably worse off than their parents and grandparents.

The different growth records of Thailand and Zambia are mirrored by the experiences of many other developing countries, as shown in Table 3–1. Several

TABLE 3-1.   Economic Growth across Countries, 1960–2003
(1996 constant purchasing power parity prices)

COUNTRY	GDP PER CAPITA (1996 PPP) 1960	GDP PER CAPITA (1996 PPP) 2003	RATIO OF 2003 TO 1960 GDP/CAPITA	AVERAGE ANNUAL GROWTH RATE (%)	INCOME AS A SHARE OF U.S. INCOME 1960	INCOME AS A SHARE OF U.S. INCOME 2003
Negative growth						
Madagascar	1,240	764	0.62	−1.26	0.10	0.02
Nigeria	1,033	992	0.96	−1.05	0.08	0.02
Venezuela	7,841	4,647	0.59	−0.67	0.64	0.13
Zambia	1,207	828	0.69	−0.63	0.10	0.02
Chad	1,212	1,143	0.94	−0.38	0.10	0.03
Senegal	1,818	1,557	0.86	−0.22	0.15	0.04
Slow growth						
Rwanda	938	1,198	1.28	0.13	0.08	0.03
Papua New Guinea	2,177	2,474	1.14	0.38	0.18	0.06
Argentina	7,371	11,436	1.55	0.61	0.60	0.30
El Salvador	3,310	4,517	1.36	0.71	0.27	0.13
Jamaica	2,746	3,877	1.41	0.82	0.22	0.10
Peru	3,228	4,969	1.54	0.89	0.26	0.13
Kenya	796	980	1.23	1.02	0.06	0.03
South Africa	4,962	9,774	1.97	1.07	0.40	0.27
Ghana	866	2,114	2.44	1.17	0.07	0.06
Philippines	2,015	4,082	2.03	1.29	0.16	0.12
Moderate growth						
Lesotho	698	2,419	3.47	2.16	0.06	0.08
Sri Lanka	1,333	3,569	2.68	2.17	0.11	0.10
Turkey	2,688	6,398	2.38	2.22	0.22	0.18
Chile	3,853	9,706	2.52	2.45	0.31	0.26
Egypt	1,478	3,731	2.52	2.60	0.12	0.10
Brazil	2,371	7,360	3.10	2.71	0.19	0.20
Pakistan	633	1,981	3.13	2.74	0.05	0.05
India	847	2,732	3.23	2.74	0.07	0.08
Dominican Republic	1,695	6,445	3.80	2.84	0.14	0.17
Rapid growth						
Indonesia	936	3,175	3.39	3.33	0.08	0.09
Malaysia	2,119	8,986	4.24	3.7	0.17	0.24
Mauritius	3,158	10,662	3.38	3.79	0.26	0.30
China	682	4,726	6.93	4.47	0.06	0.13
Thailand	1,091	7,175	6.58	4.62	0.09	0.20
Botswana	958	8,232	8.59	5.33	0.08	0.22
South Korea	1,495	16,977	11.36	5.97	0.12	0.48
Singapore	2,161	23,127	10.70	6.30	0.18	0.64
Industrialized countries						
Japan	4,545	26,420	5.81	4.11	0.37	0.75
France	7,825	26,146	3.34	2.60	0.64	0.73
United States	12,273	35,484	2.89	2.43	1.00	1.00
Canada	10,384	28,981	2.79	2.35	0.85	0.80
United Kingdom	9,674	25,645	2.65	2.01	0.79	0.73

Source: *Penn World Tables* 6.1; World Bank, *World Development Indicators* CD, 2005.
Note: Growth rates in the fourth column are trend-growth calculated by ordinary least squares regressions, and do not necessarily match endpoint-to-endpoint growth rates. Thus, the ordering of magnitudes in the third and fourth columns sometimes differ.

other countries join Zambia in the unfortunate experience of shrinking incomes, including Madagascar, Venezuela, and Chad. Since incomes were very low to begin with in many of these countries, negative growth has been a major tragedy. A second group of countries attained positive growth but at relatively slow rates. Average incomes in these countries increased but not by as much as in many other countries around the world. In Peru, for example, per capita growth averaged about 1 percent per year since 1960, enough for incomes to increase by 50 percent, but less than what many Peruvians may have hoped for.

A third group of countries has been more successful and has achieved moderate growth, shown in the table as per capita growth between 2 and 3 percent per year. By world historical standards (calculated by Angus Maddison and shown in the last chapter in Figure 2–1), these growth rates are relatively high, and they allowed for solid increases in average income. For example, Egypt recorded growth of 2.6 percent a year, enough for average income to nearly triple in 40 years, a significant achievement. India, home to over 1 billion people, recorded similar growth.

A fourth group of countries has done even better, recording rapid growth of more than 3 percent per capita per year. A few have achieved extraordinary growth exceeding 5 percent, including Singapore, South Korea, and Botswana. These are some of the fastest growth rates ever recorded over a 40-year period in the history of the world, and they have led to enormous changes. In Singapore, income expanded by a mind-boggling factor of *11*, while in Botswana (see Box 3–1), average income is nearly *nine times* what it was 40 years ago. (Unfortunately, Botswana's great success is now threatened by the HIV/AIDS pandemic, as we discuss later in the book.) China, where growth has averaged 4.5 percent per year (with almost all of it coming after 1980, meaning the growth rate since then has been much faster), has undergone perhaps the most remarkable transformation of all: for one-fifth of the world's population, including a huge number of people living in or near poverty, average incomes have increased by a factor of six. China's rapid growth is one of the most important events of the last century, and its continued growth will have profound implications for the next century and beyond.

There are some clear regional differences in growth rates, as the data in Table 3–1 suggest and as we saw in Chapter 2 in Table 2–3. Most of the rapidly growing countries are in East Asia, while most of the slowly growing countries are in Africa. But beware of taking these general statements too far, because there are important exceptions. In East Asia, Myanmar (Burma), Laos, and Papua New Guinea all recorded slow growth, and the Philippines' performance has been modest at best. In Africa, Botswana and Mauritius are among the fastest growing countries in the world, and tiny Lesotho and Swaziland have also achieved steady growth. Indeed, in more than 25 developing countries, real incomes more than doubled since 1960, only about half of which are in Asia.

BOX 3-1 BOTSWANA'S REMARKABLE ECONOMIC DEVELOPMENT[1]

Whereas most of sub-Saharan Africa has achieved little or no economic growth over the past 40 years, Botswana stands out as a clear exception. Indeed, during the 20-year period between 1970 and 1990, Botswana was the fastest growing economy in the world, with growth averaging an astonishing 7.9 percent per year, easily outpacing the more widely noted rapid growth in Singapore (6.3 percent), Korea (6.9 percent), and other countries around the world. Table 3–1 shows that over the slightly longer period from 1960 to 2002, Botswana's growth was the third fastest in the world. Over the 40-year period, average real income increased by a factor of nine in just two generations. A wide array of other development indicators improved dramatically as well. Life expectancy increased from 46 to 61 years in 1987 (before plunging again because of the AIDS pandemic), infant mortality fell from 118 to 74 per thousand, and literacy rates jumped from 46 percent (in 1970) to 79 percent.

Botswana did not seem to have strong prospects when it achieved independence from Great Britain in 1965. At that point, there were only 12 kilometers of paved road in the entire country. Only 22 Batswana had graduated from university and only 100 had graduated from secondary school. The country is landlocked, and more than 80 percent of the land area is in the Kalahari Desert, leaving only a small amount of arable land. Yet, despite the long odds, Botswana prospered. What was behind this remarkable transformation?

Diamonds are part of the story, as Botswana sits atop some of the world's richest diamond deposits, and mining now accounts for about 40 percent of the country's output. But the answer is not that simple: Many other developing countries have rich natural resources; and in many cases, these have created more problems than benefits (see Chapter 17). More broadly, most observers point to Botswana's strong policies and institutions as key determinants of its development success.

Botswana clearly managed its resources much more prudently than other countries. Most of the receipts were invested productively: Botswana has built an impressive infrastructure, with paved roads to much of the country, a reasonably reliable electricity generation and distribution system, a substantial stock of housing, and many schools and clinics. Some of the diamond receipts were saved as reserves to help manage macroeconomic fluctuations. Corruption has been much less of a problem than in other countries. Overall macroeconomic policies were strong, with relatively low inflation for the most part, and supporting fiscal, monetary, and exchange-rate policies. Trade policies were relatively open, with the external tariff set through Botswana's membership in the South African Customs Union. The public sector has remained small, with a civil service based on merit rather than patronage and relatively few state-owned companies. Property rights and other legal protections basically were well respected. Stronger economic management, in turn, may have been partly due to the fact that Botswana is a democracy, and one of the few countries in Africa that has been so since independence.

However, not everything in Botswana is positive. Income inequality is high and has not declined over time. Unemployment remains high, particularly for migrants coming from rural to urban areas. While democratic traditions are strong with fair elections and a vibrant free press, one party has dominated politics since independence. The biggest concern, however, is HIV/AIDS. According to the World Health Organization, Botswana has the second-highest prevalence of HIV in the world with over 35 percent of the adult population HIV-positive. The scourge of HIV/AIDS threatens to turn back much of the progress Botswana has realized in recent decades. With all that Botswana has achieved, its greatest challenge may lie ahead in fighting the disease and ensuring continued growth and development in the future.

[1]This box draws heavily from the accounts given by Daron Acemoglu, Simon Johnson, and James Robinson, "An African success Story," in Dani Rodrik, ed., *In Search of Prosperity: Analytic Narratives on Economic Growth* (Princeton, NJ: Princeton University Press, 2003); and Clark Leith, "Why Botswana Prospered," University of Western Ontario (2000), www.ssc.uwo.ca/economics/faculty/Leith/Botswana.pdf.

Remember, apparently small differences in growth rates can make a huge difference, especially over time. The difference between 1 percent growth and 2 percent growth is huge: It is not a 1 percent difference but a 100 percent difference. With growth of 1 percent per year, average income increases by about 50 percent over 40 years, and incomes double in about 70 years. With 2 percent growth, average income increases by 120 percent over 40 years, and it only takes 35 years for income to double.

FACTOR ACCUMULATION, PRODUCTIVITY GROWTH, AND ECONOMIC GROWTH

Economists have been trying to understand the determinants of economic growth and the characteristics that distinguish fast-growing from slower-growing countries at least since Adam Smith wrote *An Inquiry into the Nature and Causes of the Wealth of Nations,* published in 1776. More than 200 years later, our knowledge about the growth process has expanded but is far from complete. A broad range of factors could plausibly be important to growth, including the amount and type of investment, education and health-care systems, natural resources and geographical endowments, the quality of government institutions, and the choice of public policy. All these play some role, as we see later in the chapter, but some are more central to the process of growth than others.

At the core of most theories of economic growth is a relationship between the basic factors of production—capital and labor—and total economic production. Some countries also are endowed with specific natural resources assets such as petroleum deposits, gold, rubber, land, rich agricultural soil, forests, lakes, and oceans. These assets are often included as parts of a broad definition of the capital stock, but sometimes are treated separately. For simplicity, we focus our analysis on capital and labor. Depending on the products being produced, different combinations of these inputs are required. Growing rice requires significant amounts of labor (at least around planting and harvesting time), but not much machinery other than a plow. Garment production also requires lots of unskilled labor, but needs many sewing machines as well as decent infrastructure to get goods to overseas markets. A steel or chemical factory requires substantial amounts of machinery and other capital, including a reliable source of energy, and (relatively) less labor.

A country's total output—and thus its total income—is determined by how much capital and labor it has available and how productively it uses these assets. In turn, *increasing* the amount of production—that is, economic growth—depends on increasing the amount of capital and labor available and increasing the productivity of those assets. In other words, economic growth depends on two basic processes:

- **Factor accumulation,** defined as increasing the size of the capital stock or the labor force. Producing more goods and services requires more machines, factories, buildings, roads, ports, electricity generators, computers, and tools along with more and better educated workers to put this capital equipment to work.
- **Productivity growth,** defined as increasing the amount of output produced by each machine or worker. Productivity can be increased in two broad ways. The first is to improve the **efficiency** with which current factors are being used. A small furniture maker might initially have each worker make a chair from start to finish. By reorganizing his workers so each specializes in one task (e.g., cutting, assembling, finishing), he might increase total production. The second is through **technological change,** through which new ideas, new machines, or new ways of organizing production can increase growth. Countries that can either invent new technologies or quickly adopt technologies invented elsewhere (a more relevant path for most developing countries) can achieve more rapid economic growth than other countries. Productivity growth often entails shifting resources from producing one good to another. The process of economic growth in low-income countries almost always

corresponds to major structural shifts in the composition of output, generally from agriculture to industry, as we discuss later in the chapter.

One way to explore how factor accumulation and productivity growth affect output and economic growth is by examining a **production function,** which characterizes how inputs (capital and labor) are combined to produce various levels of output. Figure 3–1 shows an example of a common production function. The horizontal axis shows one measure of factor inputs (the amount of capital per worker), while the vertical axis shows the amount of output per worker (in this example, pairs of running shoes). Combining capital and labor into the single "capital per worker" term is a convenient way to simplify the analysis, but it also reflects the dominant role that capital has played in thinking on economic growth over the years. In most models, insufficient capital is seen as the binding constraint on growth. Labor is usually assumed to be in plentiful supply, based on the observation of unemployed or underemployed workers. Thus, in this formulation, increasing the amount of capital available for each worker is seen as key to growth.

Factor accumulation is shown in panel a of Figure 3–1 as a movement to the right along the horizontal axis. As the economy accumulates more capital for each of its workers, output expands, shown by the upward slope of the production function. Note that we draw this particular production function such that it begins to flatten out as capital per worker expands, a characteristic that we explore more fully later. In this case, as the value of capital per worker increases from $10,000 to $15,000, output per worker grows from 2,500 to 2,800 pairs of shoes. The movement from point *a* to point *b* on the production function is the process of economic growth. Of course, growth of this magnitude (12 percent) does not happen instantaneously. It might take two years or so, in which case the annual rate of growth would be a brisk 5.8 percent.

Panel b of Figure 3–1 shows the relationship between productivity change and economic growth. As the factors of production are used more efficiently or as new technology is adopted, the production function shifts upward. With this productivity gain, any amount of capital per worker produces more output than it did before. The production function shifts upward so that $10,000 worth of capital per worker can now produce 3,000 pairs of running shoes, whereas it originally produced 2,500 pairs. This expansion of output of 20 percent might take four years, in which case the annual rate of growth would be 4.7 percent. In this case, the movement along the path from point *a* to point *c* depicts the process of economic growth through productivity gains.

Understanding that factor accumulation and productivity gains are at the heart of the growth process is important but takes us only so far. To gain a deeper understanding of growth, we must understand what drives factor accumulation and productivity growth themselves. We begin with saving and investment.

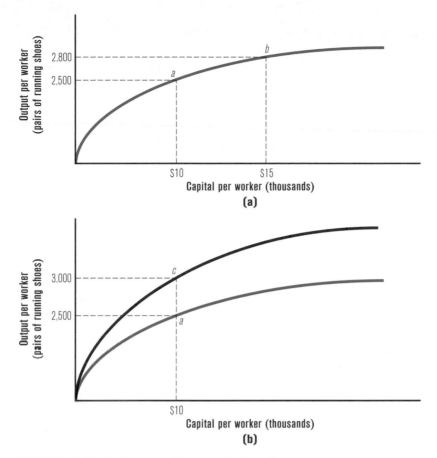

FIGURE 3-1. Basic Sources of Economic Growth
(a) Factor accumulation. As capital per worker expands, output per
worker increases.
(b) Productivity gains. As the factors of production are used more
efficiently or the economy acquires new technology, the same level of
capital per worker can produce more output.

SAVING, INVESTMENT, AND CAPITAL ACCUMULATION

Perhaps the most influential model of economic growth was developed by MIT
economist Robert Solow 1956.[1] At the heart of the **Solow model** (which we explore in depth in Chapter 4) and many other influential growth models is the
process of capital accumulation. As mentioned previously, these models typically give much less attention to the process of expanding the labor force (since
labor is not seen as a binding constraint on growth), which usually is assumed

---

[1]Robert Solow, "A Contribution to the Theory of Economic Growth," *Quarterly Journal of Economics* 70 (February 1956), 65–94; and "Technical Change and the Aggregate Production Function,"
Review of Economics and Statistics 39 (August 1957), 312–20.

to grow in line with the population. The key ideas in these kinds of models are relatively straightforward:

- *New investment increases the capital stock.* Investment in new factories or machines directly increases the capital stock, which facilitates greater production. For the capital stock to grow, the value of new investment must be greater than the amount of depreciation of existing capital. Factories and machines deteriorate over time, and a certain amount of new investment is needed simply to keep pace and maintain the current size of the capital stock. Investment greater than the amount of depreciation directly adds to the capital stock. Investment must be greater than depreciation and the growth of the labor force for there to be an increase in capital per worker.
- *Investment is financed by saving.* We know from standard national accounts identities that investment equals saving.[2] Thus, the models postulate that the key to increasing investment (and the capital stock) is to increase saving.
- *Saving comes from current income.* Households save whatever income they do not consume. Corporations save in the form of retained earnings after distribution of dividends to stockholders. Governments either add to saving to the extent that they receive tax payments in excess of government current (noninvestment) spending (that is, a budget surplus, excluding investment spending) or detract from saving if they spend more than tax receipts (a budget deficit, excluding investment spending). We discuss these concepts in more depth in Chapter 12. Gross domestic saving, which combines all three sources of saving, provides the resources to finance investment.[3]

A key decision facing households, corporations, and governments is how much income to consume and how much to save. Individuals do not care about the level of capital or even the level of output, but they do care about the amount of goods and services they consume. However, there is a clear trade-off: The more that is consumed now, the less is available for saving and therefore for investment, growth, and increased future consumption. On the one hand, people prefer to consume sooner rather than later. Given a choice between better housing now or in five years, everyone would choose now. On the other hand,

---

[2]On the production side of the national accounts (for a closed economy with no trade), everything that is produced (total output, usually designated as Y) must be used for either consumption (C) or investment (I). On the income side, total income (also designated as Y, since the value of total output must equal total income) is either used to purchase consumption goods (C) or saved (S). Putting these two identities together, since Y and C appear in both, saving must be equal to investment.

[3]In an open economy with trade and international capital flows, foreign saving (e.g., borrowing from an overseas bank) can add to the total pool of available saving.

people also recognize that consuming all income now is shortsighted. At a minimum, enough needs to be saved to compensate for depreciation of existing assets: to fix the roof on the house when it leaks, repair the motorbike, or replace a worn-out hoe. Additional saving can provide the basis for even higher income in the future. In essence, deferring current consumption can lead to greater consumption later. For example, a farmer who wants to buy a water buffalo may have to reduce her consumption for several years to save enough to eventually make the purchase. The farmer's reward comes later, when (ideally) the water buffalo increases farm production and income by far more than the amount saved, allowing for even larger consumption in the future.

However, as the last sentence hints, although generating saving and investment is necessary for growth, it is not sufficient. The investments actually have to pay off with higher income in the future, and not all investments do so. The farmer who buys the water buffalo will not earn her reward if the field is too rocky to plow or the land does not have enough nutrients to support the crop. If the government forces down the price of the crop (for example, to try to keep food prices low for urban consumers), the farmer's income will fall and the investment will be much less profitable. If property rights are not secure, the farmer could lose the water buffalo or her land. Changes in world market prices (well out of the farmer's control) could also affect her income. These issues highlight a key point: *Sustaining economic growth requires both generating new investment and ensuring that the investment is productive.* This idea is a recurrent theme in the next two chapters and throughout this book.

SOURCES OF GROWTH ANALYSIS

So far we identified factor accumulation and productivity gains as the two core determinants of growth. But how important are each of these in explaining growth? Robert Solow pioneered early efforts to quantify the contribution of each of the proximate causes of increased output—capital accumulation, labor accumulation, and productivity gains—to economic growth. This approach is more of an accounting framework based on actual data than an economic model. It seeks to answer the following question: What proportions of recorded economic growth can we attribute to growth in the capital stock, growth of the labor force, and changes in overall productivity?[4]

[4]Solow, "Technical Change and the Aggregate Production Function." A year before Solow's paper, Moses Abramovitz found similar estimates of the contribution of productivity gains to U.S. growth between 1870 and 1953 using a less formal methodology. See Moses Abramovitz, "Resource and Output Trends in the United States since 1870," *American Economic Review* 46, no. 2 (May 1956), 5–23.

Solow's procedure usually is referred to as **growth accounting** or **sources of growth analysis.** He starts with a standard production function relating the contribution of labor and capital to aggregate production, then adds a term to capture **total factor productivity (TFP).** TFP is meant to measure the contribution to production of efficiency, technology, and other influences on productivity. This production function is then converted into a form that makes it possible to measure the contribution of changes in each term—expansion of the labor force, additions to the capital stock, and growth in TFP—to overall growth. The resulting equation is

$$g_Y = (W_K \times g_K) + (W_L \times g_L) + a. \qquad [3\text{--}1]$$

In this equation, g_Y stands for the growth of total income or GDP; that is, g_Y is the rate of economic growth (note that it is not per capita growth). Similarly, g_K and g_L are the growth rates of the capital stock (K) and the labor force (L), respectively. W_L and W_K represent the shares in total income of wages and returns on capital, respectively. For example, if 60 percent of all income comes from wages and the remaining 40 percent comes from returns on capital (e.g., interest payments and rent), then $W_L = 0.60$ and $W_K = 0.40$. These two shares must add up to 100 percent, since all income must be allocated to either workers or the owners of capital. The final term, a, is the rate of change in TFP. The equation should make intuitive sense: It shows us how the growth in output depends on the growth in inputs (K and L) and the growth in the productivity of those inputs (a).

The basic procedure is to substitute actual data for all the variables in equation 3–1 except a, which cannot be measured directly, then calculate a as the residual. In this way, the contribution of each of these variables to growth can be measured and identified. A straightforward numerical example illustrates the way in which this equation is used. From the statistical records of a developing country, we find the following values for the variables in the equation:

g_Y = 0.05 (GDP growth rate of 5 percent a year),
g_K = 0.07 (capital stock growth of 7 percent a year),
g_L = 0.02 (labor force growth of 2 percent a year),
W_L = 0.6 (the share of labor in national income is 60 percent),
W_K = 0.4 (the share of capital is 40 percent).

By substituting these figures into equation 3–1, we get

$$0.05 = (0.4 \times 0.07) + (0.6 \times 0.02) + a.$$

Solving for a, we find that $a = 0.01$, meaning that TFP growth is 1 percent per year. These figures tell us the degree to which capital accumulation, labor accumulation, and TFP growth each contribute to the overall rate of growth of 5 percent. TFP growth of 1 percent counts for one fifth (20 percent) of total growth.

The growth in the capital stock accounts for slightly more than half (56 percent) the total growth; that is, $(0.4 \times 0.07)/0.05$. Finally, growth in the labor force accounts for the remaining 24 percent of total growth; that is, $(0.02 \times 0.6)/0.05$. In this particular example, capital accumulation is the main driver of growth, with labor accumulation and TFP growth each contributing similar amounts.

This type of accounting analysis has been used widely in many countries to examine the sources of growth, with particular attention paid to calculating TFP growth. Before examining some of these results, however, it is important to recognize the limits of this kind of study. There are two kinds of problems, at least:

- First, a represents a combination of influences that this analysis cannot entirely disentangle. Should improvements in a be attributed to efficiency gains stemming from improved trade policies, reduced corruption, or streamlined bureaucratic procedures? Or are they due to the introduction of faster computers, new seed varieties for agricultural crops, or other technologies? The limited growth accounting framework cannot definitively answer these questions without adding many more variables for which data do not exist (although that has not stopped analysts from assigning their own favorite explanation to the results).
- Second, a invariably is measured inaccurately, since it is the residual in the equation. All economic data are measured with some inevitable errors, including all the data used in equation 3–1. As a result, in addition to TFP, a captures the net effect of all the errors and omissions in the other data.

What is labeled TFP actually, in practice, is a combination of errors in the data, omission of other factors that should be included in the growth equation, as well as efficiency gains and changes in technology. As a result, there is a danger in trying to read too much into these data when analysts interpret them as strictly efficiency gains or the effects of new technology. In reality, rather than truly being TFP growth, a simply is the part of measured growth that cannot be explained by data on the traditional factors of production. For this reason, economist Moses Abramovitz famously referred to the residual a as a *measure of our ignorance* about the growth process.[5]

Sources of growth analyses have been carried out for many countries. Solow's initial study on the United States attributed a surprisingly large share of growth to the residual and a correspondingly small share to changes in the capital stock: 88 percent to TFP growth and only 12 percent to increases in capital

---

[5]Moses Abramovitz, "Resource and Output Trends in the United States since 1870," *American Economic Review* 46, no. 2 (May 1956), 5–23.

per worker. Subsequent work by Abramovitz, Edward Denison, Dale Jorgenson, and others attempted to measure in a more precise way the contribution of various inputs to the growth process. They divided labor into different skill categories, based on the amounts of formal education workers had received. A worker having a high school education and earning $20,000 a year is treated as the equivalent of two people having only primary school education and earning $10,000 a year each. Similar procedures are used to measure the increase in productivity that occurs when workers shift from low-productivity occupations in rural areas to higher-productivity occupations in urban areas. Other methods are used to measure improvements in the quality of capital and increasing economies of scale.

Many of these more detailed analyses of the U.S. economy found results similar to Solow's initial work: The bulk of the growth process could be attributed to the residual, with relatively small amounts apportioned to various categories of labor, capital, and other inputs. Over the years, many more studies have been completed for the industrialized countries. Increases in the capital stock frequently account for less than half the increase in output, particularly in rapidly growing countries. These results came as a bit of a surprise for most economists, since most basic models put capital formation at the heart of the growth process.

Similar studies have now been carried out for a wide range of developing countries. Data problems and price distortions tend to be more severe for developing countries than for the industrialized countries, making the results even harder to interpret. Few developing countries, for example, have reliable measures for differences in the quality of alternative capital input and labor skill categories. Generally speaking, sources of growth analyses in developing countries attribute a larger role to capital formation than in the industrialized country studies. This is consistent with the idea that developing countries have lower levels of capital per worker than the industrialized countries and can catch up (or converge incomes) through the investment process. Furthermore, much of the capital equipment imported by developing countries (counted as investment) embodies advances in technology. Therefore, the mobilization of capital remains a major concern of policy makers in developing countries.

Economists Barry Bosworth and Susan Collins explored the relative contributions of physical capital, human capital (in the form of education), and TFP to economic growth in a large number of countries around the world since 1960. Some of their results are shown in Table 3–2.[6] As with other studies, they found a fairly consistent pattern that capital accumulation was the main contributor to growth for developing countries, whereas for industrialized countries, the main

---

[6]Susan M. Collins and Barry Bosworth, "The Empirics of Growth: An Update," *Brookings Papers on Economic Activity* 2 (2003), 113–79.

TABLE 3-2. Sources of Growth in East Asia and Other Regions, 1960–2000
(average annual growth rate, %)

	GROWTH OF OUTPUT PER WORKER	CONTRIBUTION BY COMPONENT		
		PHYSICAL CAPITAL PER WORKER	EDUCATION PER WORKER	TOTAL FACTOR PRODUCTIVITY
Brazil				
1970s	4.86	2.02	0.12	2.72
1980s	−1.63	0.16	0.68	−2.47
1990s	0.71	0.07	0.38	0.25
Ecuador				
1970s	5.96	1.05	0.89	4.03
1980s	−1.42	−0.28	0.16	−1.30
1990s	−1.40	−0.46	0.31	−1.24
Egypt				
1970s	4.39	2.33	0.54	1.52
1980s	2.91	1.98	0.89	0.03
1990s	1.46	−0.12	0.64	0.94
Ethiopia				
1970s	0.55	0.22	0.13	0.20
1980s	−1.74	1.11	0.27	−3.12
1990s	1.84	0.81	0.29	0.74
Ghana				
1970s	−2.01	−0.24	0.24	−2.00
1980s	1.14	−1.23	0.15	−0.07
1990s	1.62	0.80	0.16	0.65
India				
1970s	0.70	0.61	0.36	−0.27
1980s	3.91	1.06	0.36	2.48
1990s	3.13	1.35	0.49	1.29
Singapore				
1970s	4.41	3.53	0.11	0.78
1980s	3.79	2.01	0.39	1.38
1990s	5.08	1.96	0.91	2.22
Taiwan				
1970s	5.93	3.69	1.11	1.14
1980s	5.36	2.19	0.24	2.94
1990s	4.84	2.66	0.41	1.77
United States				
1970s	0.83	0.11	0.71	0.01
1980s	1.82	0.55	0.12	1.15
1990s	1.84	0.74	0.11	0.98
Africa				
1970s	1.03	1.28	0.08	−0.32
1980s	−1.06	−0.07	0.42	−1.41
1990s	−0.16	−0.09	0.40	−0.48
East Asia				
1970s	4.27	2.74	0.67	0.86
1980s	4.36	2.45	0.66	1.25
1990s	3.36	2.35	0.50	0.52
Industrial countries				
1970s	1.75	0.95	0.52	0.28
1980s	1.82	0.69	0.24	0.90
1990s	1.52	0.75	0.22	0.54
Latin America				
1970s	2.69	1.25	0.34	1.10
1980s	−1.77	0.04	0.47	−2.28
1990s	0.91	0.16	0.34	0.41
Middle East				
1970s	1.92	2.08	0.45	−0.61
1980s	1.15	0.55	0.53	0.07
1990s	0.84	0.34	0.52	−0.01
South Asia				
1970s	0.68	0.56	0.34	−0.23
1980s	3.67	1.02	0.40	2.25
1990s	2.78	1.19	0.42	1.17

Source: Susan M. Collins and Barry Bosworth, "The Empirics of Growth: An Update," *Brookings Papers on Economic Activity* 2 (2003), 113–79.

contributions were more evenly split between capital accumulation and TFP growth. In East Asia, for example, capital accumulation accounted for about two thirds of total growth, with TFP growth accounting for a smaller share. In comparing TFP growth across countries, the rapidly growing East Asian economies generally (but not always) recorded faster TFP growth than developing countries from other regions of the world. TFP growth in East Asia was generally faster than that of the industrialized countries during the 1970s and 1980s and about the same during the 1990s.

Average TFP growth actually was negative in the 1970s, 1980s, and 1990s in Africa, during the 1980s in Latin America, during the 1970s in South Asia, and during the 1970s and 1990s in the Middle East! What does this mean? Inputs actually became less productive over time. This might be the result of capital and labor lying idle, as often happens during wars, political unrest, or recessions. During Latin America's deep recession, induced by the debt crisis of the 1980s, growth was negative while new investment was essentially zero, implying less productive use of existing capital. Negative TFP growth also might reflect the accumulation of increasingly unproductive assets, like presidential palaces or so-called white elephant projects. For example, Ethiopia built one of the largest tanneries in the world, but it usually operates at a fraction of its capacity, and Nigeria's Ajaokuta steel factory cost nearly $5 billion in construction costs over 25 years and has yet to produce any steel.

In summary, sources of growth analyses suggest that capital accumulation is the main source of growth for developing countries, consistent with the Solow growth model. TFP can play an important part in the growth process in the appropriate policy and structural context. In rapidly growing economies, both factor accumulation and TFP growth appear to play an important role. TFP growth tends to become more important as income rises and is a major contributor to growth in the high-income industrialized countries.

CHARACTERISTICS OF RAPIDLY GROWING COUNTRIES

We identified the key proximate causes of economic growth: factor accumulation (accumulating additional productive assets) and productivity growth. Productivity growth, in turn, comes either from efficiency gains or new technology. Sustaining economic growth requires both generating new investment and ensuring that the new investment is productive. These basic points, however, raise a new set of questions. What are the more fundamental characteristics that explain a country's ability to attract investment and accumulate capital, increase efficiency, and obtain new technologies? More broadly, what are the deep characteristics that distinguish more rapidly growing economies from slowly growing ones?

A large body of research over the last decade tried to answer this question by searching for broad characteristics common to rapidly growing economies. Until relatively recently, it was difficult for researchers to systematically examine these issues due to severe data limitations. Many researchers examined trends in individual countries, but it was difficult to draw general conclusions from these case studies. A few pioneering efforts, such as Irma Adelman and Cynthyia Taft Morris's *Society, Politics, and Economic Development—A Quantitative Approach,*[7] paved the way for today's cross-country empirical growth research. In recent years, this type of research has grown very rapidly, in line with the emergence of many new and large datasets on income in PPP terms, education levels, health characteristics, quality of governance, and a host of related items.[8]

Most of the recent studies are modeled on research conducted by economist Robert Barro in the early 1990s. These studies try to explain the variance in growth rates across countries. With country growth rates as the dependent variable, this approach examines several variables that might affect growth through one of the channels identified earlier (controlling for the initial level of income in each country). These variables include levels of education and health, policy choices, resource endowments, geographic characteristics (latitude, whether the country is landlocked, etc.), political systems, and so on.

This type of research has been controversial, and there is far from a consensus on the exact group of variables that affects growth.[9] For one thing, while this research starts with the Solow model, for many of the variables tested, there is no well-developed theoretical link between the variable and either economic growth or the proximate causes of growth (factor accumulation or productivity growth). The existing theories on economic growth simply are not explicit enough about exactly what variables determine the shape of the production function, the rate of investment, the profitability of investment, efficiency, and the rate of change in technology. As a result, some characteristics may appear

[7]Irma Adelman and Cynthyia Taft Morris, *Society, Politics, and Economic Development—A Quantitative Approach* (Baltimore: Johns Hopkins University Press, 1967).

[8]Some of the most important studies in this body of research include Robert Barro, "Economic Growth in a Cross Section of Countries," *Quarterly Journal of Economics* 106, no. 2 (May 1991), 407–43; Bradford DeLong and Lawrence Summers, "Equipment Investment and Economic Growth," *Quarterly Journal of Economics* 106, no. 2 (May 1991), 445–502; Gregory Mankiw, David Romer, and David Weil, "A Contribution to the Empirics of Economic Growth," *Quarterly Journal of Economics* 107, no. 2 (May 1992), 407–38; and Jeffrey Sachs and Andrew Warner, "Economic Reform and the Process of Global Integration," *Brookings Papers on Economic Activity* 1 (1995). For a review of this literature, see Jonathan Temple, "The New Growth Evidence," *Journal of Economic Literature* 37, no. 1 (March 1999), 112–56.

[9]For critiques of the cross-country approach, see Temple, "The New Growth Evidence," and David Lindauer and Lant Pritchett, "What's the Big Idea? The Third Generation of Policies for Economic Growth," *Economia* 3, no. 1 (Fall 2002).

statistically important in one research study that includes a certain group of variables but unimportant in another study with a different group of variables.[10]

A second issue has to do with interpretation of the statistical results. For example, most economists would agree that high saving rates are associated with rapid economic growth. But which causes which? Higher saving can lead to more rapid growth, as suggested by the Solow model, while faster economic growth might provide more disposable income and a higher saving rate (we discuss this issue more in Chapter 10). In practice, it is a major statistical challenge to precisely estimate the magnitude of these two effects.

Despite these issues, this empirical growth research has helped analysts better understand some of the broad characteristics associated with rapid growth, albeit very imperfectly. The broad thrust of the conclusions from research across countries is consistent with many studies of individual countries. While the debate is far from over about which variables influence long-run growth, how they do so, and the magnitude of the effect, this research has helped provide broad clues about why some economies grow faster than others. The most rapidly growing developing countries tend to share five broad characteristics.[11]

1. Macroeconomic and Political Stability

Stability is good for growth. Economic and political instability undermine investment and growth and are especially hard on the poor, who are least able to protect themselves against volatility. Consider the Democratic Republic of the Congo (formerly Zaire), which suffered through inflation rates averaging an astonishing 2,800 percent per year between 1990 and 2002 and civil and cross-border wars involving troops from at least five other countries. Not surprisingly, its growth and development performance was about the worst in the world: "growth" of –7.2 percent per year (meaning that average incomes fell by 60 percent over 12 years), life expectancy falling from 52 to 45 years, and infant mortality rising from 128 to 139 per thousand.

Relatively low budget deficits over time (with corresponding high rates of government saving), prudent monetary policy (which keeps inflation in check), appropriate exchange rates, suitable financial markets (depending on the stage

---

[10]A seminal study on the robustness of explanatory variables across different specifications is Ross Levine and David Renelt, "A Sensitivity Analysis of Cross-Country Growth Regressions," *American Economic Review* 82, no. 4 (September 1992), 942–63.

[11]Economist Xavier Sala-i-Martin has examined a wide range of studies and identified a list of variables that most consistently and robustly are found to be closely associated with economic growth. See Xavier X. Sala-i-Martin, "I Just Ran Two Million Regressions," *American Economic Review* 87, no. 2 (May 1997), 178–83. The specific list of key areas used here is similar to that suggested by Lawrence Summers and Vinod Thomas in "Recent Lessons of Development," *World Bank Research Observer* 8, no. 2 (July 1993), 241–54.

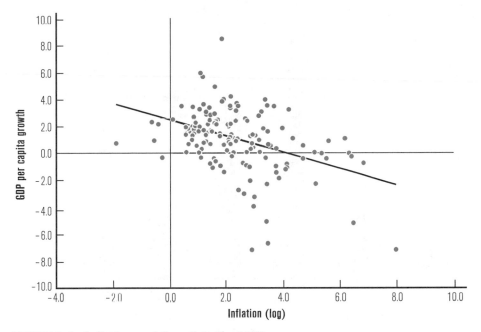

FIGURE 3-2. **Inflation and Growth in the 1990s**
Countries with higher rates of inflation generally have lower rates of economic
growth.
Source: *World Development Indicators 2004.*

of development), and judicious foreign borrowing at sustainable levels are the
key elements to macroeconomic stability. Stability reduces risk for investors,
whether they are multinational conglomerates or coffee farmers considering
planting more trees. High rate of inflation, for example, makes prices and profits
much less predictable, undermining growth (see Figure 3–2). Volatile short-term
capital flows can lead to wide swings in the exchange rate, affecting prices
throughout the economy and undermining investment. In extreme situations,
volatile capital flows can lead to full-blown financial crises, as we explore more
deeply in Chapter 15.

Political stability, not surprisingly, is also good for growth and development.
Civil and cross-border wars, military coups, and other incidences of political instability undermine investment and growth. Once again, the poor are the most
vulnerable and least able to protect themselves from the consequences of political unrest. In the late 1990s, nearly one third of the 42 countries in sub-Saharan
Africa were embroiled in cross-border or civil wars, which took a huge toll on
human lives, infrastructure, institutions, and economic activity and commerce.
Figure 3–3 shows sharp declines in income, averaging 28 percent, following civil
war in seven developing countries. By contrast, most of the relatively successful
developing countries during the last several decades were politically stable for
long periods of time. Although some of the successful countries experienced

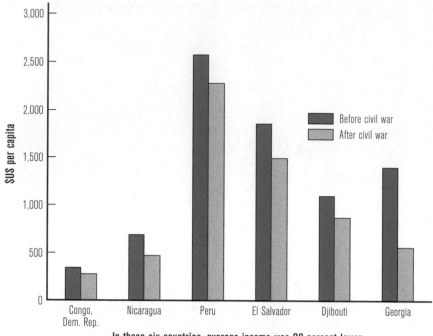

FIGURE 3-3. GDP per Capita before and after a Civil War
In these six countries, average income was 28 percent lower after the civil war than before.

Source: Civil war data from Paul Collier, V. L. Elliot, Håvard Hegre, Anke Hoeffler, Marta Reynal-Querol, and Nicholas Sambanis, *Breaking the Conflict Trap: Civil War and Development Policy* (Washington, DC: World Bank and Oxford University Press, 2003); GDP per capita data from *World Development Indicators 2004*.

periods of instability, for the most part they were short-lived. The economist Paul Collier and others have pointed out the insidious negative cycle of civil war in low-income countries: poverty increases the risk of conflict, and conflict undermines growth and entrenches poverty.[12] Of course, the absence of war is no guarantee of economic growth. Kenya, Jamaica, and Cuba were politically stable for decades but still experienced low growth.

2. Investment in Health and Education

Countries with *longer life expectancy* (and therefore better health) tend to grow faster, after accounting for other factors affecting growth, as shown in Figure

[12]See Paul Collier, "On the Economic Consequences of Civil War," *Oxford Economic Papers* 51 (1999), 168–83; and Paul Collier, V. L. Elliot, Håvard Hegre, Anke Hoeffler, Marta Reynal-Querol, and Nicholas Sambanis, *Breaking the Conflict Trap: Civil War and Development Policy* (Washington, DC: World Bank and Oxford University Press, 2003).

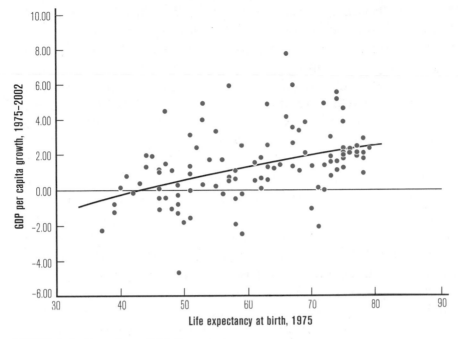

FIGURE 3-4. Growth and Life Expectancy

3–4.[13] A longer life expectancy is indicative of general improvements in the health of a population, which in turn means a healthier and more productive labor force. Thus, one way that life expectancy affects growth is by influencing productivity. In addition, a higher life expectancy also might boost saving and capital accumulation, since businesses may be more likely to invest where workers are healthier and more productive. Moreover, people are more likely to invest in education to deepen their skills if they expect to live longer and reap greater benefits. Accessible basic health-care facilities, clean water and sanitation, disease control programs, and strong reproductive and maternal and child health programs help countries lengthen life expectancy and improve worker productivity.

Malaysia's efforts to reduce malaria and improve health are a good example. When settlers first began to arrive in what is now Kuala Lumpur in the 1850s in search of tin, nearly half died of malaria. A century later, things had improved,

[13]See, for example, World Health Organization, 2001, *Macroeconomics and Health: Investing in Health for Economic Development, Report of the Commission on Macroeconomics and Health* (Geneva: World Health Organization, 2001); David E. Bloom, David Canning, and J. Sevilla, "The Effect of Health on Economic Growth: A Production Function Approach," *World Development* 32 (January 2004), 1–13; and Steven Radelet, Jeffrey Sachs, and Jong-Wha Lee, "The Determinants and Prospects for Economic Growth in Asia," *International Economic Journal* 15, no. 3 (2001), 1–30. For a brief nontechnical summary, see David E. Bloom, David Canning, and Dean Jamison, "Health, Wealth, and Welfare," *Finance and Development* 41, no. 1 (March 2004), 10–15.

but malaria and other diseases were still a problem, and life expectancy in 1960 was just 54 years. Growth during the 1960s was still a respectable 3.4 percent per year. An active government malaria control program began to make significant inroads, and by 1975, the number of malaria cases had been cut by two thirds relative to 1960. Partly as a result, life expectancy increased to 64 years. Improved health (along with several other factors) contributed to a surge in growth, which accelerated to about 5 percent per year between 1976 and 1996. The incidence of malaria has continued to decline, falling to just 11,000 cases in 2001.[14]

Note that the relationship between life expectancy and growth works both ways: Better health helps spur faster growth, while faster growth (and higher income) help improve life expectancy, as we discuss in more detail in Chapter 9. That is, better health is both an *input* to and *outcome* of the growth process. In Chapter 1, we noted the broad association between income levels and life expectancy; and in Chapter 2, we discussed increased life expectancy as an important development goal as part of the Human Development Index. Here, we emphasize the role of good health as an input to the growth process. These two positions are not contradictory—far from it. Rather, they imply a positive reinforcing cycle, in which better health supports faster economic growth, and the higher income from growth facilitates even better health.

Similarly, both *increased levels and improved quality of education* should translate into a more highly skilled workforce and increased productivity. A skilled workforce should be able to work more quickly with fewer errors, use existing machinery more effectively and invent or adapt new technologies more easily. As with better health, a more highly educated workforce may also help attract new investment, thereby contributing to capital accumulation as well. Also, like better health, education has a procyclical relationship with growth, in which better education helps support growth and growth generates the resources to finance stronger educational systems. Education of girls has a particularly strong effect on growth, both the direct impact on their skills and the indirect impact in the next generation on their children's health and education. The impact of education on growth can take a long time, of course, since investments in primary school education today may not show up as improved worker productivity for many years. The quality of service delivery is just as important as quantity. It is not enough to build schools and increase enrollment rates; teachers have to show up, be motivated, and have adequate basic supplies (e.g., textbooks) to do the job.[15]

---

[14]The data on the incidence of malaria come from the Malaysian Ministry of Health, as presented at www.actmalaria.org/downloads/pdf/info/Malaysia.pdf.

[15]These issues are explored more deeply in the World Bank's world development report, *Making Service Work for Poor People* (Washington, DC: World Bank and Oxford University Press, 2004).

As discussed in Chapter 8, most micro-level studies in individual developing countries show very high rates of return to education, especially girl's education. However, in macro-level cross-country studies, the statistical strength of the relationship often is relatively modest. This may be due to difficulties in accurately measuring the quantity and quality of education across a large number of countries in a consistent way. It also suggests that a better-educated workforce is no guarantee of more rapid economic growth. Human capital, just like physical capital, can be squandered in an environment that is not otherwise supportive of economic growth.

3. Effective Governance and Institutions

The role of governance and institutions in economic growth in development began to receive serious attention only beginning in the early 1990s (see Box 3–2). This work was heavily influenced by the research and writing of Nobel Prize-winning economist Douglass C. North of Washington University.[16] Since that time, many studies have found a positive relationship between economic growth and the strength of the rule of law, the extent of corruption, property rights, the quality of government bureaucracies, and other measures of governance and institutional quality.[17]

Stronger governance and institutions help improve the environment for investment by reducing risk and increasing profitability. For example, investors are more likely to make long-term investments where they feel property rights are secure and their factory, machine, or land will not be confiscated. Strong legal systems can help settle commercial disputes in a predictable, rational manner. Low levels of corruption help reduce the costs of investment, reduce risks, and increase productivity, as managers focus their attention on production rather than influencing politicians and government officials. Strong government economic institutions, such as the central bank, ministry of finance, ports authority, and ministry of trade can help establish effective government policies that influence both factor accumulation and productivity.

The most effective governments established institutions that helped facilitate (rather than hinder) strong economic management, effective social programs, and a robust private sector. Governance in the most rapidly growing

---

[16]See, for example, Douglass C. North, *Institutions, Institutional Change and Economic Performance* (New York: Cambridge University Press, 1990).

[17]See, for example, Stephen Knack and Philip Keefer, 1995, "Institutions and Economic Performance: Cross Country Tests Using Alternative Institutional Measures," *Economics and Politics* 7, no. 3, 207–27; Daniel Kaufmann, Aart Kraay, and Pablo Zoido-Lobatón, "Governance Matters," World Bank Policy Research Paper No. 2196 (October 1999); and Daron Acemoglu, Simon Johnson, and James Robinson, "The Colonial Origins of Comparative Development: An Empirical Investigation," *American Economic Review* 91, no. 5 (December 2001), 1369–1401.

BOX 3-2 INSTITUTIONS, GOVERNANCE, AND GROWTH[1]

The role of institutions and governance in supporting and sustaining economic growth began to receive strong attention in the 1990s, following the path breaking work by Nobel Prize-winning economist Douglass C. North.[2] In its broadest definition, institutions include a society's formal rules (e.g., constitutions, laws, and regulations), informal constraints (e.g., conventions, norms, traditions, and self-enforced codes of conduct), and the organizations that operate within these rules and constraints.[3] There are many different kinds of institutions that influence growth and development. Dani Rodrik and Arvind Sumbramanian suggest four broad types of economic institutions, to which we add a fifth for political institutions:

- *Market-creating institutions* protect property rights, ensure that contracts are enforced, minimize corruption, and generally support the rule of law. Without these institutions in place, markets are likely to not exist or to perform poorly; by contrast, strengthening them can help boost investment and entrepreneurship. Examples include an independent judiciary, an effective police force, and enforceable contracts.
- *Market-regulating institutions* deal with market failures such as imperfect information, externalities, and economies of scale. These institutions limit monopoly power and help provide the basis for building and managing public goods, such as roads and fisheries. Examples include regulatory agencies in telecommunications, transportation, water and forestry resources, and financial services.
- *Market-stabilizing institutions* ensure low inflation, minimize macroeconomic volatility, ensure fiscal stability, and avert financial crises. Central banks, exchange rate systems, ministries of finance, and fiscal and budgetary rules are all market-stabilizing institutions.
- *Market-legitimizing institutions* provide social protection and insurance, focus on redistribution, and manage conflict. These institutions help protect individuals and corporations from shocks or disasters or from adverse market outcomes. Examples include pension systems, unemployment insurance schemes, welfare programs, and other social funds.
- *Political institutions* determine how society is governed and the extent of political participation. In many countries, there is a strong focus on the key institutions that support democracy, including a free press, elections, competitive political parties, and participatory politics.

A large body of evidence now shows a robust relationship between stronger institutions, rapid economic growth, and improved development outcomes. The evidence is based partly on major advancements in the ability to better measure governance and institutions, such as the data compiled by Dani Kauffman and Aart Kraay at the World Bank Institute.[4] Strong institutions are central to managing financial systems, building public education and health systems, ensuring efficient trade and commerce, and governing legal systems. Much of neoclassical economic theory on well-functioning markets is based on the assumption that fundamental institutions are in place (such as contract enforcement, perfect information, and the rule of law). But, in many low-income countries, these key institutions are weak or nonexistent.

Understanding the importance of institutions for growth brings us only so far, however. Economic analysis tells us very little about the specific forms of institutions that are best suited for a particular environment (e.g., common law versus civil law). There is significant debate about which institutions are most important for low-income countries, their specific form, and the relative importance of institutions versus other factors. Although some analysts claim that institutions dominate all other factors in the growth process, the bulk of the evidence suggests that other factors play an important role, such as policies, geography, and resource endowments. Indeed, much of the research indicates that institutions themselves are heavily influenced by geography, history, resource endowments, and the extent of integration with the global economy.

Perhaps even more important, theory and research do not tell us much about how institutions change and how a country with weak institutions can best strengthen them. Institutions change only slowly, but fortunately they do change. Deepening our understanding of how institutions affect growth and development, the appropriate form for institutions in different circumstances, and how institutions change over time are major challenges for economists and development specialists in the future.

[1] This text draws heavily on the discussion of institutions found in *Finance and Development* (June 2003), particularly "The Primacy of Institutions (and What This Does and Does Not Mean)" by Dani Rodrik and Arvind Subramanian, and "Institutions Matter, But Not for Everything" by Jeffrey D. Sachs.

[2] Douglass C. North, *Institutions, Institutional Change, and Economic Performance* (New York: Cambridge University Press, 1990).

[3] North distinguishes between the formal rules and informal constraints (which he includes in his definition of institutions) and organizations (which he excludes). He refers to institutions as the *rules of the game* and organizations as *the players.* In common usage, however, many people use the term *institutions* to cover both the rules and the organizations.

[4] Available at www.worldbank.org/wbi/governance/data.html.

countries varied widely from very effective (Singapore and Botswana) to more mixed (Indonesia and Thailand) but generally was better than in slower-growing countries.

Figure 3–5 shows a scatter plot of the relationship between one measure of governance and economic growth. This measure, taken from the World Bank

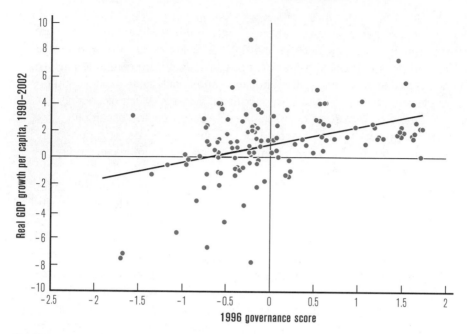

FIGURE 3-5. **Governance and Growth**

Note: Governance scores are the simple average of the voice and accountability, political stability, rule of law, government effectiveness, regulatory quality, and control of corruption components of the governance data set constructed by Daniel Kaufmann, Aart Kraay, and Massimo Mastruzzi, as described in "Governance Matters III: Governance Indicators for 1996–2002."

Institute's Governance Data Set, is based on surveys gauging perceptions about the quality of six dimensions of governance: voice and accountability (a measure of political participation), political stability and absence of violence, government effectiveness, regulatory quality, rule of law, and control of corruption.[18] While there is much variance in the data, there is a clear upward trend in which countries with stronger governance ratings achieved faster economic growth. Chile's governance scores are in the top quartile for the world (a score of 1.03 in the scale used in Figure 3–5, in which zero is the world median), and it achieved growth of over 4 percent per capita between 1990 and 2002. Chile scored particularly well in regulatory quality, rule of law, and control of corruption. By contrast, Ukraine scored in the bottom third with its governance score of –0.5, and its growth rate was –4.8 percent. Of course, other factors contributed to Chile and Ukraine's growth record, but economists increasingly understand the role of good governance and strong institutions in the development process.

[18]The data can be found at www.worldbank.org/wbi/governance/data.html and is described in D. Kaufmann, A. Kraay, and M. Mastruzzi, "Governance Matters III: Governance Indicators for 1996–2002," World Bank Policy Research Working Paper 3106, 2003.

4. Favorable Environment for Private Enterprise

Sustained economic growth requires millions of private individuals to make decisions every day regarding saving, investment, education, and job opportunities. Small-scale farmers, business owners, factory workers, and market stall vendors all strive every day to increase their incomes, and the regulatory and policy environment has a significant effect on their success or failure. For many countries, *agricultural policies* are central to the growth process. Where governments have pushed farmgate prices low to keep food prices cheap or forced farmers to sell their products to government-owned marketing boards, agricultural production (and farmer income) has suffered. The most dramatic example of reducing restrictions of farmers is China's moves to decollectivize agricultural production in the early 1980s and allow farmers to sell their produce on markets. China's agricultural output soared in the decade that followed. Farmers need reasonable access to fertilizers, seeds, and pesticides; and the construction of rural roads has had a dramatic impact on rural incomes in many countries, such as Indonesia. Absolute free markets are not necessarily the solution—some countries have subsidized fertilizer or other inputs to encourage their use, while others have used buffer stocks to counter large swings in prices—but policies that consistently push against markets (rather than helping to strengthen markets) almost always fail in the long run.

The climate for small-scale businesses and manufacturing is also important for long-term growth. While some regulation is crucial for well-functioning markets, most governments in developing countries impose unnecessarily high costs on businesses through licensing, permits, and other restrictions. Hernando de Soto's *The Mystery of Capital* demonstrated the damaging effects of heavy business regulation and weak property rights.[19] When the regulatory burden to start a business is high, fewer entrepreneurs bother to start businesses, and when they do, they tend to operate on a smaller scale and in the informal sector. Moreover, government investments in infrastructure, at the core of capital formation, are central. No matter how favorable the policy environment, business cannot operate if the electricity shuts off every day, the water is brown, and the phones do not work.

One of the most important (and controversial) factors influencing growth is *openness to foreign trade*. Almost all (but not quite all) economists agree on the advantages of open trade as a way to encourage growth. Looking back at the countries in Table 3–1, all the rapid growers were relatively open to international trade in the sense of focusing on labor-intensive exports competing on world

---

[19]Hernando de Soto, *The Mystery of Capital: Why Capitalism Triumphs in the West and Fails Everywhere Else* (New York: Basic Books, 2000). For data on the costs of business regulation, see the World Bank's *Doing Business in 2005: Removing Obstacles to Growth*.

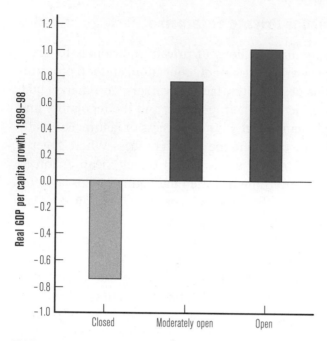

FIGURE 3-6. Openness and Growth

markets (not necessarily open to all imports). More open trade allows firms to specialize, increase efficiency, reduce costs by purchasing from the world's least expensive suppliers, and gain access to the leading-edge technologies. It tends to change the allocation of capital, labor, and other resources from less-productive to more-productive activities. In these ways, trade can both enhance productivity and encourage investment in new profitable opportunities. However, more open trade also increases vulnerability to shocks on world markets (such as volatile prices). Economists debate the magnitude of the gains from trade, the impact on poverty, and the precise policy changes that are most important to encouraging more open trade, as we discuss in Chapter 19.

The evidence supporting a positive relationship between trade and growth is strong. In his analysis of the characteristics most consistently identified in the research as related to growth, Xavier Sala-i-Martin found a strong negative relationship between measures of distortion in the exchange rate (for example, a large difference between the official exchange rates and the "street" rate) and economic growth. Jeffrey Frankel and David Romer also find a strong relationship between trade and growth.[20] The Sachs-Warner study mentioned earlier and others have found that countries that have been consistently "open" to the world trading system have recorded more rapid rates of economic growth. Figure 3–6 shows the average growth rates for countries that were closed, moderately open, and more

[20]Xavier X. Sala-i-Martin, "I Just Ran Two Million Regressions"; Jeffrey Frankel and David Romer, "Does Trade Cause Growth?" *American Economic Review* 89, no. 3 (June 1999), 379–99.

fully open to trade according to the Sachs-Warner classification (see note 23 on page 96). Open countries recorded substantially higher growth rates than countries closed to trade.

However, not all kinds of export products necessarily enhance growth. In particular, while exports of labor-intensive manufactured products (such as clothing, shoes, textiles, and toys) have been strongly associated with poverty reduction and economic growth, natural-resource-based exports have not, at least in recent years. Historically, many countries with rich natural-resource endowments have had strong economic performance, including the United States, Australia, New Zealand, Denmark, and the Netherlands. But, since the 1970s, the relationship between natural resource exports and economic growth generally has been negative. A large number of resource-rich developing countries have fared poorly and recorded very slow growth, including Nigeria, Angola, Bolivia, Colombia, the Congo, Venezuela, Mozambique, Nicaragua, Myanmar, and others. We discuss exports of primary products in more detail in Chapter 17.

5. Favorable Geography

A striking fact is that there are no rich economies located between the Tropic of Cancer and the Tropic of Capricorn other than Singapore and a few small, oil-rich countries. Figure 3–7 shows that the poorest countries in the world are

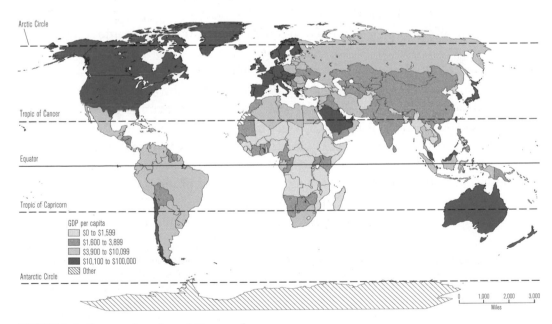

FIGURE 3-7. Income Levels and Geography
Almost all high-income countries are located in temperate zones, while most countries in the tropics are poor.

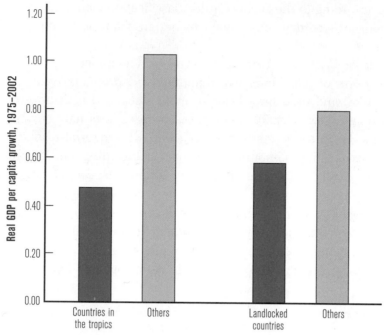

FIGURE 3-8. **Geography and Growth**

almost all in the tropics, while the richest countries tend to be in more temperate zones. Even within the temperate zones, the regions closer to the tropics tend to be less well-off: Northern Europe is richer than southern Europe, the northern part of the United States is wealthier than the southern parts, and southern Brazil is better off than the north. In Latin America and Africa, the wealthiest countries are located in the temperate south: Chile, Argentina, and South Africa.

Several studies have shown a strong relationship between location in the tropics, other geographical characteristics, and growth.[21] Figure 3–8 shows that the average growth rate between 1975 and 2002 for countries located in the tropics was less than 0.5 percent, while for countries outside the tropics the rate was over 1 percent, more than twice as high. Tropical countries have to deal with a greater burden from virulent diseases, erratic climate, and at least in some areas, very poor-quality soil for agriculture. Most of the world's most virulent diseases are centered in the tropics, including malaria and HIV/AIDS. These diseases seriously undermine worker productivity and add to health-care costs.

---

[21]Recent studies that explore the impact of geographical factors on levels of income and growth rates include Robert Hall and Charles Jones, "Why Do Some Countries Produce So Much More Output per Worker Than Others?" *Quarterly Journal of Economics* 114 (February 1999), 83–116; Steven Radelet and Jeffrey Sachs, "Shipping Costs, Manufactured Exports, and Economic Growth," Harvard Institute for International Development, January 1998; and John Gallup and Jeffrey Sachs, "Geography and Economic Development," in Boris Pleskovic and Joseph Stiglitz, eds., *World Bank Annual Conference on Development Economics 1998* (Washington, DC: World Bank, 1998), 127–78.

Similarly, although erratic climate can occur anywhere around the world, floods, droughts, and violent storms tend to be more concentrated in the tropics. Hurricanes and typhoons, of course, are by definition tropical phenomena. Hotter climates make a long, hard day of outdoor work much more difficult, reducing labor productivity (one way Singapore has compensated for being in the tropics is by air conditioning the vast majority of buildings in the country, a step that is much easier for a small city-state like Singapore than for most other countries). And while some tropical regions have very fertile soils (as in the rich lands in Java, one of the main islands of Indonesia), most of the great Sahara desert is in the tropics, as are the arid lands of northern Brazil. These characteristics work to reduce both factor productivity and the incentives for investment and factor accumulation. Location in the tropics does not necessarily preclude growth and development, since some of the burdens at least partially can be alleviated through policies and institutional development, but it clearly creates difficulties and obstacles that make growth and development more difficult.

Another geographical feature that can affect growth is isolation from major markets, such as for landlocked countries and small island nations, such as in the Pacific Ocean. These isolated countries face higher transport costs and fewer economic opportunities than coastal economies and countries located nearer to major markets. Landlocked African countries face overland shipping costs that can be three times higher than their coastal neighbors'. Higher transport costs make imports more expensive, which both reduces income left for consumption and raises production costs. They also make it more expensive to export products to other countries, reducing profits.

Not all landlocked countries have had poor economic performance. Switzerland and Austria are in some ways the exceptions that prove the rule. Although they are landlocked, they are far from being isolated, as they are located in the heart of Europe. Perhaps the clearest exception is Botswana, which has deftly managed its vast diamond mines to generate sustained growth for the last four decades. Figure 3–8 shows that economic growth in landlocked countries has averaged 0.58 percent since 1975 (excluding Botswana, this figure falls to 0.41 percent), while in coastal economies, growth averaged 0.80 percent, about one third higher (and nearly twice as high excluding Botswana). Being landlocked does not mean growth is impossible, but it does limit options and add to production costs. Geographical isolation can be overcome by investments that reduce overland transport costs (e.g., better roads or trucks) or by producing goods that rely more on air rather than sea transport. Landlocked Uganda, for example, grows flowers near its international airport for export to Europe. Advancements in satellite communications open up new possibilities for isolated countries, such as data entry or accounting services provided for firms located in other countries.

Note that some countries face multiple geographical obstacles that significantly limit their development options. Perhaps the most challenging are the landlocked countries in the midst of the Sahara desert, including Mali, Burkina Faso, Niger, Chad, Sudan, and Ethiopia, each of which is among the very poorest countries in the world. These countries have far fewer options and face much more difficult challenges than the average developing country.

These five broad areas are not a complete list of the characteristics that influence factor accumulation, productivity, and economic growth, but they are among the most prominent attributes identified by research and experience. It is important to recognize that this list is not absolute: there is significant variation across countries, and these characteristics are neither a guarantee of success nor a set of rigid requirements for growth. Some countries have done relatively well in many of these areas and still have not experienced rapid economic growth. At the same time, while almost all of the fastest-growing countries score well in most of these areas, some do not. Our understanding of the precise pathways through which each of these factors influence growth is far from complete. However, the evidence does show that these characteristics are among the most important factors supporting factor accumulation, productivity, and growth.

DIMINISHING RETURNS AND THE PRODUCTION FUNCTION

For output and income to continue to grow over time, a country must continue to attract investment and achieve productivity gains. But as the capital stock grows, the magnitude of the impact of new investment on growth may change. In fact, most growth models are based on the assumption that the return on investment declines as the capital stock grows. To show this, we reproduce the production function in Figure 3–1 in Figure 3–9, except now we can think of it as representing the aggregate production function for the economy rather than for one shoe factory. This production function is drawn in a particular way to incorporate the important but common assumption of **diminishing returns to capital,** or more precisely, a **diminishing marginal product of capital.** This property is indicated by the gradual flattening (or declining slope) of the curve as capital per worker grows.

Looking first at production function I (the top curve), at low levels of capital per worker (such as point *a*), new investment leads to relatively large increases in output per worker. But at higher levels of capital per worker (such as point *b*), the same amount of new investment leads to a smaller increment in output. Each addition of a unit of capital per worker (moving to the right along the horizontal axis) yields smaller and smaller increases in output per worker. More generally,

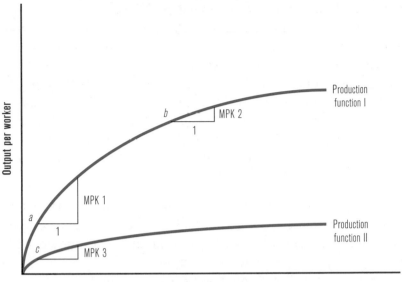

FIGURE 3-9. Diminishing Marginal Product of Capital
Along production function I, an addition of 1 unit of capital per worker at point *a* yields a much larger increase in output per worker than the same investment at point *b*. On production function II, at any level of capital per worker, any new investment will yield a smaller increase in output than at the same level of capital per worker as production function II.

giving workers more and more machinery yields smaller and smaller additions to output. For example, a bread company that purchases its first oven can rapidly increase its output. A second oven further expands production but probably not by quite as much as the first oven. By the time the company buys its tenth oven (without adding any new workers), the increment to bread production is much smaller than it was with the first oven.

Not all production functions feature diminishing returns. Some are based on constant returns, in which additions to capital continually yield the same increase in output. In a diagram such as Figure 3–9, a constant-returns production function appears as a straight line drawn from the origin. Production functions for some products conceivably can incorporate increasing returns, which appear as an upward sloping curve. We briefly examine some of these alternatives in the next chapter. But diminishing returns for new capital investment is the basis for some of the most influential growth models, including the Solow model. The assumption of diminishing returns is focused on factor accumulation, in particular capital accumulation. Increases in output stemming from productivity gains are not necessarily subject to diminishing returns.

The assumption of a diminishing marginal product of capital has many implications, but three are particularly important for developing countries. Consider countries located toward the left on the horizontal axis of Figure 3–9, such as at point *a*. These countries have both relatively small amounts of capital per worker and low levels of output per worker. *The latter means, by definition, that these countries are relatively poor.* By contrast, countries toward the right have both higher levels of capital per worker and more output per worker, the latter implying that they are relatively rich. In general, low-income countries tend to have much less capital per worker than richer countries. Therefore, if all else is equal between the two countries—a crucial qualifier—new investment in a poor country will tend to have a much larger impact on output than the same investment in a rich country. The three key implications are as follows:

1. If all else is equal, poor countries have the *potential* to grow more rapidly than rich countries. In the figure, a country located at point *a* has the potential to grow more rapidly than a country at point *b*, since the same investment will lead to a larger increase in output.
2. As countries become richer (and capital stocks become larger), growth rates tend to slow. In other words, as a country moves along the production function from point *a* to point *b* over a long period of time, its growth rate tends to decline.
3. Since poor countries have the *potential* to grow faster than rich countries, they can catch up and close the gap in relative income. To the extent this happens (which we explore later), income levels between rich and poor countries would converge over time.

These are very powerful implications. It is important to recognize that they rest on the assumptions that all else is equal between the two countries and that growth is derived primarily from capital accumulation rather than productivity gains (which are not necessarily subject to diminishing returns). For all else to be equal, both countries have to be operating along the same production function, have access to the same technology, and have similar saving rates. If they are not, the predictions for rich and poor countries do not necessarily hold. Consider, for example, a poor country operating on the bottom production function in Figure 3–9. This curve is much flatter, so that each new investment leads to less growth than in the top function. A country on this curve might differ from countries operating on the top production function, for instance, because it does not have access to the same technology or faces endemic disease. For this country, even though it has low levels of capital per worker, new investments do not yield such large increases in output. Thus, comparing a poor country at point *c* with a rich country at point *b*, the poor country will not necessarily grow faster and catch up. The phrase *ceteris paribus* (all else being equal), which is much used and often overlooked in economics, is of great importance in the convergence debate.

THE CONVERGENCE DEBATE

If it were true that poorer countries could grow fast while richer countries experience slower growth, poorer countries (at least those in which "all else is equal") could begin to catch up and see their income levels begin to converge with the rich countries. Has this actually happened?

The short answer is that it has for some countries but not for most. Consider the example of Japan. In the 1960s, Japan's income per capita was only about 35 percent of average U.S. income, and it had a much smaller capital stock, giving it the potential for very rapid growth. (We use the United States as the benchmark for convergence since it has among the highest per capita incomes in the world and is usually considered the global technological leader.) Indeed, Japan's growth rate exceeded 9 percent during the 1960s. By the time Japan had reached 70 percent of U.S. income in the late 1970s, its growth rate had slowed to about 4 percent. As its income continued to grow, its growth rate fell further, and growth was very slow after Japan reached about 85 percent of U.S. income in the early 1990s. Japan's experience illustrates the preceding three points very well: (a) When it was relatively poor, it could grow fast; (b) as its income increased, its growth rate declined; and (c) as a result, its income converged significantly toward U.S. income. People who boldly predicted in the 1960s and 1970s that Japan could grow at 7 to 9 percent per year indefinitely—and many people did—ignored the impact of diminishing returns of capital on long-term growth rates.

Japan is not the only country whose income has converged with the world leaders since 1960. Look again at the group of rapidly growing countries shown at the beginning of the chapter at the bottom of Table 3–1. All the countries shown were relatively poor in 1960, and all grew by an average of between 3 to 7 percent per capita or more for 40 years. Rich countries cannot grow that fast over a period of many years (in the absence of a continuous infusion of new technology), but poor countries can, since they start with low levels of capital.

However, being poor and having low levels of capital per worker by no means guarantees rapid growth. As the upper sections of the table show, many low-income countries recorded very low growth. Not only did these countries not catch up, they fell further behind and their incomes diverged further from the world leaders. The point is that low-income countries have the potential for rapid growth—*if* they can attract new investment and *if* that new investment actually pays off with a large increment in output.

Looking beyond the experience of a few individual countries, is there a general tendency for poor countries to grow faster and catch up with the richer countries? Broadly across all countries, the short answer is no. Figure 3–10 shows the initial level of per capita income in 1965 and subsequent rates of growth for 124 countries from around the world. If it were true that poor countries were growing faster than rich countries, the graph would show a clear downward slope from left to right. Poor countries would record a high rate of growth (and appear in the upper left part of the figure) and rich countries would display a slower growth rate (and be in the bottom right). But there is no clear pattern evident in the figure. Some poor countries have grown quickly, but others have recorded very low (even negative) rates of growth. The same is true for middle-income countries. The only part that seems accurate is that almost all the rich countries display relatively slow growth rates, as expected. These results have been documented in many studies using more sophisticated statistical techniques. The empirical fact is clear: There has been no *general* tendency for poor countries to catch up to the world leaders. If anything, the opposite has been true. As we saw in Figure 2–1, for the last two centuries, the gap between the richest and poorest regions of the world has grown, implying a divergence of incomes for these countries.

However, this simple graph does not really do justice to the predictions of convergence, which are based on the critical assumption that all else is equal across countries. This assumption clearly is not true for all countries in the world. Instead, if convergence were to occur, we should expect to find it among countries that share some broad key characteristics, such as a similar underly-

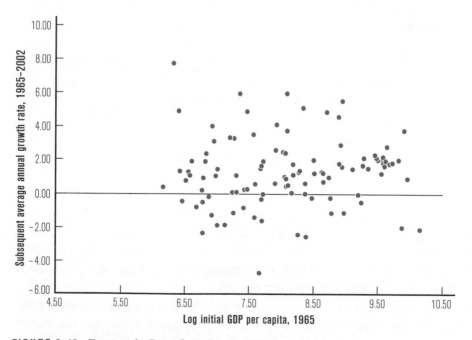

FIGURE 3-10. Economic Growth and Initial GDP per Capita

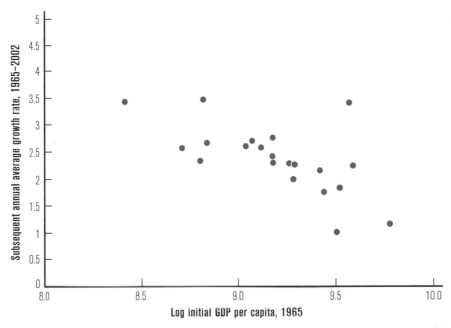

FIGURE 3-11. Conditional Convergence among the OECD Countries

ing production function and similar rates of saving, population growth, depreci-ation, and technology growth. Some of the poor countries in Figure 3–10, for ex-ample, have low saving rates or very little growth in technology compared with other countries and, therefore, have much less potential for rapid growth. To see if the convergence predictions of the Solow model hold under these stricter con-ditions, we have to dig a little deeper.

The trick is to find a group of countries that plausibly share some critical characteristics that might put them on roughly the same (or similar) production functions. William Baumol initially tackled this issue by examining the evidence for convergence among a narrower group of broadly similar countries, the industrialized countries.[22] The plausible assumption is that production processes, technology accumulation, and other factors are roughly similar across this group. Figure 3–11 shows the evidence for convergence between 1965 and 2002 among the 21 countries that were members of the Organization for Economic Coopera-tion and Development in 1965. The pattern is strikingly different from in Figure 3–10. The 8 OECD countries with the lowest average incomes in 1965 (Portugal, Greece, Ireland, Japan, Spain, Italy, Austria, and Finland) recorded economic growth rates of 2.3 percent or better between 1965 and 2002, whereas 10 of the 11 highest income countries all grew at less than 2.3 percent per year (the exception

[22]William J. Baumol, "Productivity Growth, Convergence, and Welfare: What the Long-Run Data Show," *American Economic Review* 76 (December 1986), 1072–85.

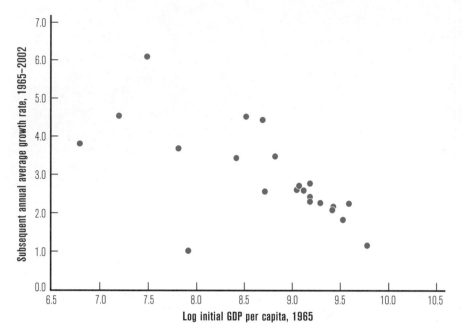

FIGURE 3-12. Conditional Convergence among Open Economies

was Luxembourg, which grew at 3.4 percent per year). The downward slope of the figure shows a clear tendency toward convergence of average incomes across these countries.

Another approach is to pick a group of countries from all income levels that are similar in their policy choices, geographic characteristics, or some other variable. Economists Jeffrey Sachs and Andrew Warner, for example, examined the evidence for convergence among all countries that had been consistently open to world trade since 1965.[23] "Open" economies are similar in that they have similar (global) markets for their products, purchase their inputs on world markets, and can acquire new technology relatively quickly from other open economies through imports of new machinery and their connections to global production networks (we discuss these issues more in Chapter 19). Figure 3–12 shows a strong tendency for convergence of incomes among the group of 25 countries identified as most "open" by Sachs and Warner. Among poorer countries that have been open to world trade, there has been a propensity for rapid economic growth and catching up with richer countries. Prominent examples of

[23]A country was considered to be "open" if it met five criteria: (1) its average tariff rates were less than 40 percent, (2) its nontariff barriers (e.g., quotas) covered less than 40 percent of imports, (3) the premium on the unofficial parallel market exchange rate did not exceeding 20 percent, (4) there were no state monopolies on major exports, and (5) it was not a socialist economy. We discuss these issues more in Chapter 19. See Jeffrey Sachs and Andrew Warner, "Economic Reform and the Process of Global Integration," *Brookings Papers on Economic Activity* 1 (1995), 1–118.

this tendency include Indonesia, Korea, Malaysia, Mauritius, Singapore, Taiwan, and Thailand.

A growing body of more-sophisticated econometric studies that control for a wide range of other variables has reached the same conclusion, including those studies cited earlier that identified some of the key characteristics associated with growth. Once we take into account differences in important government policies, saving (or investment) rates, natural resource abundance, and geographic characteristics (such as being landlocked) that influence the production process, there is a tendency for poorer countries to grow faster than rich countries. Therefore, while there is no evidence for "absolute convergence" of income levels among all countries, there is evidence for "conditional convergence" of incomes once we control (or condition) for differences in key characteristics that might influence growth.

ECONOMIC GROWTH AND STRUCTURAL CHANGE

So far, we examined some of the broad patterns of economic growth, along with some of the proximate and deeper causes of growth. We also saw that the pace of growth is likely to slow as the capital stock grows. But we said little about the particular products that an economy produces and how the composition of output changes during the course of development. Economic growth involves more than increases in per capita output and rises in total factor productivity: As growth proceeds over time, the structure of the economy tends to change in several important ways. Four broad and interrelated changes stand out:

1. The share of total output produced by the agricultural sector declines, while the share of total output from industry and services increases.
2. The portion of the labor force engaged in agriculture declines (although not as rapidly as the decline in agriculture's share of production), while the portion of the workforce in industry and services rises.
3. The population becomes more urbanized as households move from rural areas to cities, and cities grow over time.
4. A larger share of goods and services are sold through markets, since many goods and services that, at an earlier stage of development, are produced by households for their own use instead begin to be produced by enterprises that sell these goods and services through markets.

Further changes tend to occur at later stages of development. For example, within industry there is also structural change. Countries starting down the path of industrialization usually begin with simple labor-intensive processes, such as making shoes and garments, then move to more complex, capital-intensive or technologically based industries, such as petrochemicals, microchips, or auto-mobiles. Here, we briefly examine these shifts in the structure of output as growth takes place. In later chapters (notably Chapters 16 and 18), we look at development within agriculture and industry in more detail.

Every country that experienced sustained economic growth and develop-ment has seen the share of agriculture in GDP fall and the share of industry rise as growth proceeds. Although it is possible to conceive of a situation in which a country moves from poverty to relative wealth while concentrating on agricul-ture, no country has done so. Figure 3–13 shows this shift for four countries: Brazil, Malaysia, Mauritius, and Tunisia. These four countries are quite different in their location, size, and the products they produce, yet each shows the same basic pattern.

There are two principal reasons for the fall in agriculture's share of produc-tion. The first is **Engel's law.** In the nineteenth century, Ernst Engel observed that, as family income rises, the proportion of income spent on food declines. As peo-ple become richer, they may spend more on food, but not in proportion to the rise in income. Once a family is able to meet its basic food requirements, a dou-bling of income does not result in family members consuming twice as much food. Expenditures on food may rise as individuals eat slightly more food or shift to higher-quality or more-expensive foods, but these expenditures tend to rise less than proportionally with income. Instead, people spend more of their budget on clothing, housing, consumer goods, and recreation. Since the main function of the agricultural sector is to produce food, it follows that demand for

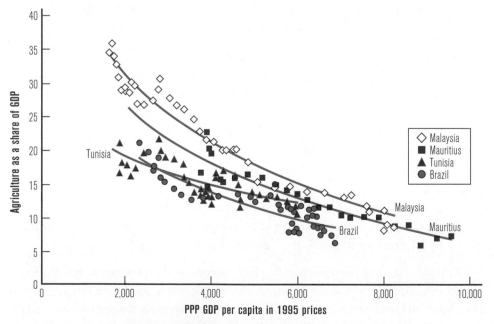

FIGURE 3-13. Income Level and the Share of Agriculture in the Economy
Sources: *World Development Indicators 2004* and *Penn World Tables* 6.1.

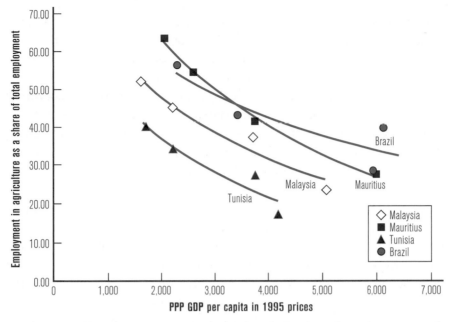

FIGURE 3-14. Employment in Agriculture as a Share of Total Employment and Income

Sources: *World Development Indicators 2004; Penn World Tables* 6.1; and Donald Larson and Yair Mundlak, 1997, "On the Intersectoral Migration of Agricultural Labor," *Economic Development and Cultural Change* 45, no. 2 (1997), 295–319.

agricultural output does not grow as rapidly as demand for industrial products and services; hence, the share of agriculture in national product declines. This relationship holds for *all* countries that experience sustained development.

A second reason reinforces the impact of the first: Productivity gains in agriculture free up workers and allow them to begin to produce nonagricultural goods and services. New seeds, fertilizers, machinery, or use of improved farming methods means that fewer workers are needed to produce the same (or even more) agricultural output. This change frees workers to begin to make clothing, shoes, toys, and other products. Thus, the share of workers in the agricultural sector declines as incomes rise, as shown in Figure 3–14. The United States proceeded perhaps further in this transformation than any other country. In the eighteenth and nineteenth centuries the majority of Americans worked on farms and concentrated most of their efforts (especially at the earliest stages) on producing enough food and other products for their own households. But, today, an individual farmer in the United States can produce enough food to feed, and feed very well, another 70–80 people. As a result only 3 percent of the workforce of the United States is in farming with the other 97 percent able to work in industry and services.

The rising share of industrial production also helps explain why, as incomes rise, an increasing percentage of a country's population lives in cities rather than in the countryside. This trend is illustrated for the same four countries in Figure 3–15. In Brazil, Malaysia, and Tunisia, there has been a clear shift of the population from rural to urban areas. Mauritius does not follow the pattern: The island economy is small enough that, as manufacturing and tourism began to supplant agriculture, workers could easily commute the hour or so to the urban areas by bus and did not have to move. But this is an exception to the general pattern.

Why does the population tend to move to urban areas? There are **economies of scale** in the manufacture of many industrial products, which implies that output per unit of input rises as firm size increases. That is, a large enterprise in industries producing toys or steel produce more output per dollar of input than a smaller enterprise. Large-scale industrial production requires a nearby population center to provide the workforce. Furthermore, it makes sense for many different kinds of industrial enterprises to locate near each other, so that common support facilities, such as electric power stations, transport, and wholesalers, also can operate at an efficient level. The result is that industrialization leads to the growth of cities. At the same time, this change tends to increase the share of manufacturing and some services that are actually counted as part of GDP. In the rural economies of most poor countries, for example, food processing is done in the home and usually not included in GDP calculations. In urbanized countries, food processing often is done in large factories, and the value added produced by these factories is included in the share of the manufacturing sector.

Even though the rising share of manufacturing in GDP and the declining share of agriculture is a pattern common to all countries, it does not follow that

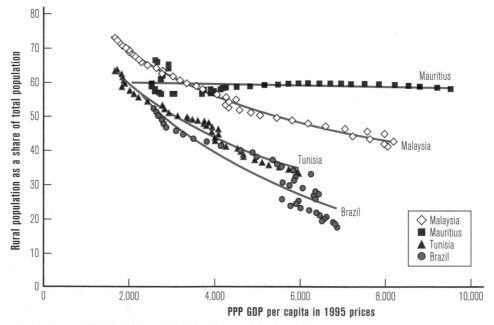

FIGURE 3-15. **Share of Rural Population and Income**
Sources: *World Development Indicators 2004; Penn World Tables* 6.1, and Food and Agriculture Organization, FAOSTAT.

the precise patterns or rates of change are the same in each country. In fact, they can differ substantially, as we saw clearly with the case of urbanization (or lack thereof) in Mauritius. Hollis Chenery and his coauthors were pioneers in analyzing the relationships between growth and structural change. They found that the pattern of change in the shares of agriculture and industry varied depending on the size of the country and its natural resource endowments (e.g., whether it has petroleum or gold deposits), among other factors.[24] Figures 3–13 through 3–15 illustrate that, while each country follows the same general pattern, the precise relationship differs in each country.

Although agriculture tends to diminish in its importance relative to GDP as income rises, it does not follow that policy makers should concentrate on industry and forget about agriculture. Many countries have tried to accelerate the pace of industrial change while ignoring agriculture, and it has almost always been a disaster. China, for instance, learned this the hard way in the 1950s, during its ill-fated Great Leap Forward. The government tried to follow the Soviet example of putting most of its investment into industry, hoping that agriculture would somehow take care of itself. Disastrous harvests followed in 1959 through 1961, with widespread famine. This forced the government to shift direction and put more resources, notably chemical fertilizer, into agriculture, but machinery, steel, and related industries continued to receive the lion's share of investment. Food production grew but only fast enough to hold per capita consumption constant, since population grew at 2 percent a year. In the 1970s, the government greatly increased the share of investment going to agriculture, and in the 1980s, it took the even more radical step of abandoning collectivized agriculture. These steps laid the foundation for a rapid increase in agricultural production and productivity, which in turn helped provide the basis for rapid industrial growth.

Many other countries around the world similarly tried to force the pace of industrialization through price and investment policies while neglecting agriculture, but the results were almost always disappointing. Over time, more governments have come to recognize that increases in agricultural productivity are necessary to free resources for industry, so investments in agriculture are required even as its importance in GDP declines. Investments in rural roads or research into new seed or fertilizer varieties lead to increases in agricultural productivity that free resources for use in industrial production. We explore this important set of topics more fully in Chapter 16.

[24]Hollis B. Chenery and Moises Syrquin, *Patterns of Development, 1950–1970* (London: Oxford University Press, 1975); and Hollis B. Chenery and Lance J. Taylor, "Development Patterns: Among Countries and over Time," *Review of Economics and Statistics* (November 1968), 391–416. Also see Moshe Syrquin, "Patterns of Structural Change," in *Handbook of Development Economics,* vol. 1, Hollis B. Chenery and T. N. Srinivasan, eds. (Amsterdam: North-Holland, 1988); and Dwight Perkins and Moshe Syrquin, "Large Countries: The Influence of Size," in *Handbook of Development Economics,* vol. 2, Hollis B. Chenery and T. N. Srinivasan, eds. (Amsterdam: North-Holland, 1989).

SUMMARY

- Economic growth is not the same as economic development. Development is a much broader concept, but since growth raises average income, it is central to the development process.
- Economic growth depends on two basic processes: factor accumulation and productivity growth. Capital accumulation depends on saving, which requires individuals to defer current consumption to finance investment to increase future output. Productivity growth comes either from improving efficiency or acquiring new technology.
- Sources of growth analyses indicate that capital accumulation tends to contribute substantially to growth in low-income countries, while increases in the size and quality of the labor force and productivity growth also make important contributions. Productivity growth tends to account for a larger share of growth in high-income countries.
- Some of the key country characteristics most closely associated with rapid growth include economic and political stability, investments in health and education, strong governance and institutions, a favorable environment for private enterprise (including agricultural, regulatory, and trade policies), and more-favorable geography. But our understanding of precisely how these and other factors affect the growth process is far from complete.
- Since low-income countries have relatively low amounts of capital per worker, they have the *potential* for rapid economic growth, *if* they can attract new investment and *if* that new investment actually increases output.
- Some poor countries have achieved rapid growth and seen their incomes converge with those of richer countries, but many have not and have seen their incomes fall further behind. There is no evidence of *absolute* convergence across countries, but there is some evidence of *conditional* convergence, in which countries sharing certain characteristics are able to achieve rapid growth and begin to catch up with the richer countries.
- Economic growth over sustained periods is accompanied by important structural shifts, in which the share of agriculture in GDP falls, the share of industry rises, and the population tends to shift from rural to urban areas.

Theories of
Economic Growth

I n opening his Marshall Lecture at Cambridge University in 1985, Nobel Prize-winning economist Robert Lucas focused on a vexing puzzle: the vast differences in incomes between rich and poor countries around the world. "The diversity across countries in measured per-capita income levels," he said with some astonishment, "is literally too great to be believed." After describing the extraordinary growth and transformation in East Asia since 1960 that had begun to close the gap in incomes for some countries, he declared:

> I do not see how one can look at figures like these without seeing them as representing *possibilities*. Is there some action a government of India could take that would lead the Indian economy to grow like Indonesia's or Egypt's? If so, what exactly? If not, what is it about the "nature of India" that makes it so? The consequences for human welfare involved in questions like these are simply staggering: Once one starts to think about them it is hard to think of anything else.[1]

Lucas's challenge contributed to a significant resurgence in debate about and research on the process of economic growth. We began to explore these issues in the last chapter by examining some of the basic processes and patterns that characterize economic growth in low-income countries. We emphasized that growth depends on two processes: the *accumulation of assets* (such as capital, labor, and land), and *making those assets more productive*. Saving and

[1]Robert E. Lucas, "On the Mechanics of Economic Development," *Journal of Monetary Economics* 22, no. 1 (July 1988), 3–42.

investment are central, but investments must be productive for growth to proceed. Our approach was largely empirical, as we examined much of the data on growth and some of the key findings from research on the determinants of growth across countries. We saw that government policy, institutions, political and economic stability, geography, natural resource endowments, and levels of health and education all play some role in influencing economic growth. We emphasized that growth is not the same as development, but it remains absolutely central to the development process.

This chapter develops these ideas more formally by introducing the underlying theory and the most important basic models of economic growth that influence development thinking today. These models provide consistent frameworks for understanding the growth process that augment the empirical approach we took in the last chapter. Here, we identify specific mathematical relationships between the quantity of capital and labor, their productivity, and the resulting aggregate output. Importantly, these models also explore the process of accumulating *additional* capital and labor and *increasing* their productivity, which shifts the model from determining the *level* of output to the *rate of change* of output, which of course is the rate of economic growth. The bulk of the chapter focuses on models in which the factors of production combine to produce a single aggregate product. We then briefly shift to examine some models in which productive inputs can be used in various combinations to produce two different goods: agricultural and industrial products.

As we begin to examine these models, it is useful to consider the words of Robert Solow, the father of modern growth theory, who once wrote: "All theory depends on assumptions that are not quite true. That is what makes it theory. The art of successful theorizing is to make the inevitable simplifying assumptions in such a way that the final results are not very sensitive."[2] The best models are simple, yet still manage to communicate powerful insights into how the real world operates. In this spirit, the models presented here make assumptions that clearly are not true but allow us to simplify the framework and make it easier to grasp key concepts and insights. For example, we begin by assuming that our prototype economy has one type of homogeneous worker and one type of capital good that combine to produce one standard product. No economy in the world has characteristics even closely resembling these assumptions, but making these assumptions allows us to cut through many details and get to the core concepts of the theory of economic growth.

[2]Robert Solow, "A Contribution to the Theory of Economic Growth," *Quarterly Journal of Economics* 70 (February 1956), 65–94.

THE BASIC GROWTH MODEL

The most fundamental models of economic output and economic growth are based on a small number of equations that relate saving, investment, and population growth to the size of the workforce and capital stock and, in turn, to aggregate production of a single good. These models initially focus on the *levels* of investment, labor, productivity, and output. It then becomes straightforward to examine the *changes* in these variables. Our ultimate focus is to explore the key determinants of the *change in output,* that is, on the rate of economic growth. The version of the basic model that we examine here has five equations: (1) an aggregate production function, (2) an equation determining the level of saving, (3) the saving-investment identity, (4) a statement relating new investment to changes in the capital stock, and (5) an expression for the growth rate of the labor force.[3] We examine each of these in turn.

Standard growth models have at their core one or a series of **production functions.** At the individual firm or microeconomic level, these production functions relate the number of employees and machines to the size of the firm's output. For example, the production function for a textile factory would reveal how much more output the factory could produce if it hired (say) 50 additional workers and purchased five more looms. Production functions often are derived from engineering specifications that relate given amounts of physical input to the amount of physical output that can be produced with that input. At the national or economywide level, production functions describe the relationship of the size of a country's total labor force and the value of its capital stock with the level of that country's gross domestic product (its total output). These economywide relationships are called **aggregate production functions.**

Our first equation is an aggregate production function. If Y represents total output (and therefore total income), K is the capital stock, and L is the labor supply; at the most general level, the aggregate production function can be expressed as follows:

$$Y = F(K, L) \qquad\qquad [4\text{--}1]$$

This expression indicates that output is a function (denoted by F) of the capital stock and the labor supply. As the capital stock and labor supply grow, output expands. Economic growth occurs by increasing either the capital stock (through new investment in factories, machinery, equipment, roads, and other infrastructure), the size of the labor force, or both. The exact form of the function F (stating

---

[3]This five-equation presentation is based on teaching notes compiled by World Bank economist Shantayanan Devarajan, to whom we are indebted.

precisely *how much* output expands in response to changes in K and L) is what distinguishes many different models of growth, as we will see later in the chapter. The other four equations of the model describe how these increases in K and L come about.

Equations 4–2 through 4–4 are closely linked and together describe how the capital stock (K) changes over time. These three equations first calculate total saving, then relate saving to new investment, and finally describe how new investment changes the size of the capital stock. To calculate saving, we take the most straightforward approach and assume that saving is a fixed share of income:

$$S = s \times Y \qquad\qquad [4\text{--}2]$$

In this equation, S (upper case) represents the total value of saving, and s (lower case) represents the average saving rate. For example, if the average saving rate is 20 percent and total income is $10 billion, then the value of saving in any year is $2 billion. We assume that the saving rate s is a constant, which for most countries is between 10 and 40 percent (typically averaging between 20 and 25 percent), although for some countries it can be higher or lower. In China and Singapore, saving rates exceed 40 percent, while in Bolivia the saving rate averaged around 10 percent in the 1990s. Actual saving behavior is more complex than this simple model suggests (as we discuss in Chapter 10), but this formulation is sufficient for us to explore the basic relationships between saving, investment, and growth.

The next equation relates total saving (S) to investment (I). In our model, with only one good, there is no international trade (since everyone makes the same product, there is no reason to trade). In a closed economy (one without trade or foreign borrowing), saving must be equal to investment. All output of goods and services produced by the economy must be used for either current consumption or investment, while all income earned by households must be either consumed or saved. Since output is equal to income, it follows that saving must equal investment. This relationship is expressed as follows:

$$S = I \qquad\qquad [4\text{--}3]$$

We are now in a position to show how the capital stock changes over time. Two main forces determine changes in the capital stock: new investment (which adds to the capital stock) and depreciation (which slowly erodes the value of the existing capital stock over time). Using the Greek letter delta (Δ) to represent the *change* in the value of a variable, we express the change in the capital stock as ΔK, which is determined as follows:

$$\Delta K = I - (d \times K) \qquad\qquad [4\text{--}4]$$

In this expression d is the rate of depreciation. The first term (I) indicates that the capital stock *increases* each year by the amount of new investment. The second term $-(d \times K)$ shows that the capital stock *decreases* every year because of the depreciation of existing capital. We assume here that the depreciation rate is a constant, usually in the range of 2 to 10 percent.

To see how this works, let us continue our earlier example, in which total income is $10 billion and saving (and therefore investment) is $2 billion. Say that the value of the existing capital stock is $30 billion and the annual rate of depreciation is 3 percent. In this example, the capital stock increases by $2 billion because of new investment but also decreases by $0.9 billion (3 percent $\times$ $30 billion) because of depreciation. Equation 4–4 puts together these two effects, calculating the change in the capital stock as $\Delta K = I - (d \times K) =$ $2 billion $-$ (0.03 $\times$ $30 billion) = $1.1 billion. Thus, the capital stock increases from $30 billion to $31.1 billion. This new value of the capital stock then is inserted into the production function in equation 4–1, allowing for the calculation of a new level of output, Y.

The fifth and final equation of the model focuses on the supply of labor. To keep things simple, we assume that the labor force grows exactly as fast as the total population. Over long periods of time, this assumption is fairly accurate. If n is equal to the growth rate of both the population and the labor force, then the change in the labor force (ΔL) is represented by

$$\Delta L = n \times L \qquad \text{[4–5]}$$

If the labor force consists of 1 million people and the population (and labor force) is growing by 2 percent, the labor force increases annually by 20,000 (1 million $\times$ 0.02) workers. The labor force now consists of 1.02 million people, a figure that can be inserted into the production function for L to calculate the new level of output.

These five equations represent the complete model.[4] Collectively, they can be used to examine how changes in population, saving, and investment initially affect the capital stock and labor supply and ultimately determine economic output. New saving generates additional investment, which adds to the capital stock and allows for increased output. New workers add further to the economy's capacity to increase production.

One way these five equations can be simplified slightly is to combine equations 4–2, 4–3, and 4–4. The aggregate level of saving (in equation 4–2) determines the level of investment in equation 4–3, which (together with depreciation) determines changes in the capital stock in equation 4–4. Combining these three equations gives

$$\Delta K = sY - d \times K \qquad \text{[4–6]}$$

---

[4]Note that, since the model has five equations and five variables (Y, K, L, I, and S), it always can be solved. In addition, there are three fixed parameters (d, s, and n), the values of which are assumed to be fixed exogenously, or outside the system.

This equation states that the change in the capital stock (ΔK) is equal to saving (sY) minus depreciation (dK). This expression allows us to calculate the change in the capital stock and enter the new value directly into the aggregate production function in equation 4–1.

THE HARROD-DOMAR GROWTH MODEL

As we have stressed, the aggregate production function (shown earlier as equation 4–1) is at the heart of every model of economic growth. This function can take many different forms, depending on what we believe is the true relationship between the factors of production (K and L) and aggregate output. This relationship depends on (among other things) the mix of economic activities (e.g., agriculture, heavy industry, light labor, intensive manufacturing, high-technology processes, services), the level of technology, and other factors. Indeed, much of the theoretical debate in the academic literature on economic growth is about how to best represent the aggregate production process.

The Fixed-Coefficient Production Function

One special type of a simple production function is shown in Figure 4-1. Output in this figure is represented by **isoquants,** which are combinations of the inputs (labor and capital in this case) that produce equal amounts of output. For example, on the first (innermost) isoquant, it takes capital (plant and equipment) of $10 million and 100 workers to produce 100,000 keyboards per year (point *a*). Alternatively, on the second isoquant, $20 million of capital and 200 workers can produce 200,000 keyboards (point *b*). Only two isoquants are shown in this diagram, but a nearly infinite number of isoquants are possible, each for a different level of output.

The L-shape of the isoquants is characteristic of a particular type of production function known as **fixed-coefficient production functions.** These production functions are based on the assumption that capital and labor need to be used in a fixed proportion to each other to produce different levels of output. In Figure 4–1, for the first isoquant, the **capital-labor ratio** is 10 million:100, or 100,000:1. In other words, $100,000 in capital must be matched with one worker to produce the given output. For the second isoquant, the ratio is the same: $20 million:200, or 100,000:1.

Note that, with this kind of production function, if more workers are added *without* investing in more capital, output does *not* rise. Look again at the first isoquant, starting at the elbow (with 100 workers and $10 million in capital). If the firm adds more workers (say, increasing to 200 workers) without adding new

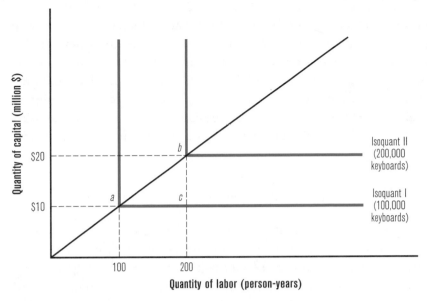

FIGURE 4-1. Production Function with Fixed Coefficients
With constant returns to scale, the isoquants will be L-shaped and the
production function will be the straight line through their minimum-
combination points.

machines, it moves horizontally to the right along the first isoquant to point *c*.
But at this point, or at any other point on this isoquant, the firm still produces
just 100,000 keyboards. In this kind of production function, new workers need
more machines to increase output. Adding new workers without machines
results in idle workers, with no increase in output. Similarly, more machinery
without additional workers results in underused machines. On each isoquant,
the most efficient production point is at the elbow, where the minimum
amounts of capital and labor are used. To use any more of either factor without
increasing the other is a waste.

The production function cuts across the isoquants and connects the most
efficient combinations of labor and capital needed to produce any level of output. In this example, the production function is the ray that connects points *a*
and *b* (along with the points at the elbow of any other isoquants that might be
drawn in for other levels of production).

The production function depicted in Figure 4–1 also is drawn with **constant
returns to scale,** so if capital is doubled to $20 million and labor is doubled to
200 workers, output also exactly doubles to 200,000 keyboards per year.[5] With
this further assumption, two more ratios remain constant at any level of output:

---

[5]More generally, in a constant-returns-to-scale production function, if we multiply both capital
and labor by any number, *w,* output multiplies by the same number. In other words, the production
function has the following property: $wY = F(wK, wL)$.

capital to output and labor to output. If keyboards are valued at $50 each, then 100,000 keyboards are worth $5 million. In this case, in the first isoquant, $10 million in capital is needed to produce $5 million worth of keyboards, so the **capital-output ratio** is $10 million:$5 million, or 2:1. In the second isoquant the ratio is the same ($20 million:$10 million, or 2:1). Similarly, for each isoquant the **labor-output ratio** is also a constant, in this case equal to 1:50,000, meaning that each worker produces $50,000 worth of keyboards, or 1,000 keyboards each.

The Capital-Output Ratio and the Harrod-Domar Framework

The fixed-coefficient, constant-returns-to-scale production function is the centerpiece of a well-known early model of economic growth that was developed independently during the 1940s by economists Roy Harrod of England and Evsey Domar of MIT, primarily to explain the relationship between growth and unemployment in advanced capitalist societies.[6] It ultimately focuses attention on the role of capital accumulation in the growth process. The **Harrod-Domar model** has been used extensively (perhaps even overused) in developing countries to examine the relationship between growth and capital requirements. The model is based on the real-world observation that some labor is unemployed and proceeds on the basis that capital is the binding constraint on production and growth. In the model, the production function has a very precise form, in which output is assumed to be a *linear* function of capital (and only capital). As usual, the model begins by specifying the level of output, which we later modify to explore changes in output, or economic growth. The production function is specified as follows:

$$Y = 1/v \times K \quad \text{or} \quad Y = K/v \qquad [4\text{--}7]$$

where v is a constant. In this equation, the capital stock is multiplied by the fixed number $1/v$ to calculate aggregate production. If $v = 3$ and a firm has $30 million in capital, its annual output would be $10 million. It is difficult to imagine a simpler production function. The constant v turns out to be the capital-output ratio, since by rearranging the terms in equation 4–7, we find

$$v = K/Y \qquad [4\text{--}8]$$

The capital-output ratio is a very important parameter in this model, so it is worth dwelling for a moment on its meaning. This ratio essentially is a measure

[6]Roy F. Harrod, "An Essay in Dynamic Theory," *Economic Journal* (1939), 14–33; Evsey Domar, "Capital Expansion, Rate of Growth, and Employment," *Econometrica* (1946), 137–47; and "Expansion and Employment," *American Economic Review* 37 (1947), 34–55.

of the productivity of capital or investment. In the earlier example in Figure 4–1, it took $10 million in investment in new plant and new equipment to produce $5 million worth of keyboards, implying a capital-output ratio of 2:1 (or just 2). A larger v implies that more capital is needed to produce the same amount of output. So, instead, if v were 4, then $20 million in investment would be needed to produce $5 million worth of keyboards.

The capital-output ratio provides an indication of the capital intensity of the production process. In the basic growth model, this ratio varies across countries for two reasons: either the countries use different technologies to produce the same good or they produce a different mix of goods. Where farmers produce maize using tractors, the capital-output ratio will be much higher than in countries where farmers rely on a large number of workers using hoes and other hand tools. At the same time, in countries that produce a larger share of **capital-intensive products** (i.e., those that require relatively more machinery, such as automobiles, petrochemicals, and steel), v is higher than in countries producing more **labor-intensive products** (such as textiles, basic agriculture, and footwear). In practice, as economists move from the v of the model to actually measuring it in the real world, the observed capital-output ratio can also vary for a third reason: differences in efficiency. A larger measured v can indicate less-efficient production when capital is not being used as productively as possible. A factory with lots of idle machinery and poorly organized production processes has a higher capital-output ratio than a more-efficiently managed factory.

Economists often calculate the **incremental capital-output ratio** (ICOR) to determine the impact on output of additional (or incremental) capital. The incremental capital-output ratio measures the productivity of additional capital, while the (average) capital-output ratio refers to the relationship between a country's total stock of capital and its total national product. In the Harrod-Domar model, since the capital-output ratio is assumed to remain constant, the average capital-output ratio is equal to the incremental capital-output ratio, so the ICOR $= v$.

So far, we have been discussing total output, not growth in output. The production function in equation 4–7 easily can be converted to relate *changes* in output to *changes* in the capital stock:

$$\Delta Y = \Delta K / v \qquad [4\text{–}9]$$

The growth rate of output, g, is simply the increment in output divided by the total amount of output, $\Delta Y/Y$. If we divide both sides of equation 4–9 by Y, then

$$g = \Delta Y / Y = \Delta K / Yv \qquad [4\text{–}10]$$

Finally, from equation 4–6, we know that the change in the capital stock ΔK is equal to saving minus the depreciation of capital ($\Delta K = sY - d \times K$). Substituting the right-hand side of equation 4–6 into the term for ΔK in equation 4–10 and simplifying[7] leads to the basic Harrod-Domar relationship for an economy:

$$g = (s/v) - d \qquad\qquad [4\text{--}11]$$

Underlying this equation is the view that capital created by investment is the main determinant of growth in output and that saving makes investment possible.[8] It rivets attention on two keys to the growth process: saving (s) and the productivity of capital (v). The message from this model is clear: Save more and make productive investments, and your economy will grow.

Economic analysts can use this framework either to predict growth or to calculate the amount of saving required to achieve a target growth rate. The first step is to try to estimate the incremental capital-output ratio (v) and depreciation rate (d). With a given saving rate, predicting the growth rate is straightforward. If the saving (or investment) rate is 24 percent, the incremental capital-output ratio is 3, and the depreciation rate is 5 percent, then the economy can be expected to grow by 3 percent (since $0.24/3 - 0.05 = 0.03$).

How does this model work in practice? Consider Malaysia, which from 1999 to 2001 had an investment rate of about 27 percent and recorded a GDP growth of about 5.0 percent per year. Assuming a depreciation rate of 5 percent, the implied incremental capital-output ratio was approximately $v = 2.7$.[9] Would these figures have helped the Malaysian government predict the 2002 growth rate? In 2002, the investment rate was 24.4 percent, so the Harrod-Domar model would have predicted growth of 4.0 percent ($g = 0.244/2.7 - 0.05$). The actual growth rate in 2002 was 4.1 percent, very close to the model's predictions. However, as we shall see later, the model is not always so accurate.

Strengths and Weaknesses of the Harrod-Domar Framework

The basic strength of the Harrod-Domar model is its simplicity. The data requirements are small, and the equation is easy to use and to estimate. And, as we saw with the example of Malaysia, the model can be accurate from one year to the next. Generally speaking, in the absence of severe economic shocks (such as a drought, a financial crisis, or large changes in export or import prices), the model can do a reasonable job of estimating expected growth rates in most countries over very short periods of time (a few years). Another strength is its focus on the key role of saving. As discussed in Chapter 3, indi-

[7]Substituting equation 4–6 into 4–10 leads to $g = (sY - d \times K)/Y \times 1/v$, which can be simplified to $g = (s - d \times K/Y) \times 1/v$. Since $K/Y = v$, we have $g = (s - dv) \times 1/v$, which leads to $g = s/v - d$.

[8]For an important early contribution to the discussion of the importance of capital accumulation to the growth process, see Joan Robinson, *The Accumulation of Capital* (London: Macmillan, 1956).

[9]Since $g = s/v - d$, then $v = s/(g + d)$. For Malaysia between 1999 and 2001, $v = 0.27(0.05 + 0.05) = 2.7$.

vidual decisions about how much income to save and consume are central to the growth process. People prefer to consume sooner rather than later, but the more that is consumed, the less can be saved to finance investment. The Harrod-Domar model makes it clear that saving is crucial for income to grow over time.

The model, however, has some major weaknesses. One follows directly from the strong focus on saving. Although saving is necessary for growth, the simple form of the model implies that it is also sufficient, which it is not. As pointed out in Chapter 3, the investments financed by saving actually have to pay off with higher income in the future, and not all investments do so. Poor investment decisions, changing government policies, volatile world prices, or simply bad luck can alter the impact of new investment on output and growth. Sustained growth depends both on generating new investment and ensuring that investments are productive over time. In this vein, the allocation of resources across different sectors and firms can be an important determinant of output and growth. Since (for simplicity) the Harrod-Domar assumes only one sector, it leaves out these important allocation issues.

Perhaps the most important limitations in the model stem from the rigid assumptions of fixed capital-to-labor, capital-to-output, and labor-to-output ratios, which imply very little flexibility in the economy over time. In order to keep these ratios constant, capital, labor, and output must all grow at exactly the same rate, which is highly unlikely to happen in real economies. To see why these growth rates must all be the same, consider the growth rate of capital. If the capital stock grew any faster or slower than output at rate g, the capital-output ratio would change. Thus the capital stock must grow at g to keep the capital-output ratio constant over time. With respect to labor, in our original five-equation model, we stipulated (in equation 4–5) that the labor force would grow at exactly the same pace as the population at rate n. Therefore, the only way that the capital stock and the labor force can grow at the same rate is if n happens to be equal to g. This happens only when $n = g = s/v - d$, and there is no particular reason to believe the population will grow at that rate.

In this model, the economy remains in equilibrium with full employment of the labor force and the capital stock *only* under the very special circumstances that labor, capital and output all grow at the rate g. On the one hand, if n is larger than g, the labor force grows faster than the capital stock. In essence, the saving rate is not high enough to support investment in new machinery sufficient to employ all new workers. A growing number of workers do not have jobs and unemployment rises indefinitely. On the other hand, if g (or $s/v - d$) is larger than n, the capital stock grows faster than the workforce. There are not enough workers for all the available machines, and capital becomes idle. The actual growth rate of the economy no longer is g, as the model stipulates, but slows to n, with output constrained by the number of available workers.

So, unless $s/v - d$ (or g) is exactly equal to n, either labor or capital is not fully employed and the economy is not in a stable equilibrium. This characteristic of the Harrod-Domar model has come to be known as the *knife-edge* problem. As long as $g = n$, the economy remains in equilibrium, but as soon as either the capital stock or the labor force grows faster than the other, the economy falls off the edge with continuously growing unemployment of either capital or labor.

The rigid assumptions of fixed capital-output, labor-output, and capital-labor ratios may be reasonably accurate for short periods of time or in very special circumstances but almost always are inaccurate over time as an economy evolves and develops. Each of these varies among countries and, for a single country, over time. Consider the incremental capital-output ratio. The productivity of capital can change in response to policy changes, which in turn affects v. Moreover, the capital intensity of the production process can and usually does change over time. A poor country with a low saving rate and surplus labor (unemployed and underemployed workers) can achieve higher growth rates by utilizing as much labor as possible and thus relatively less capital. For example, a country relying heavily on labor-intensive agricultural production will record a low v. As economies grow and per capita income rises, the labor surplus diminishes and economies shift gradually toward more capital-intensive production. As a result, the ICOR shifts upward. Thus, a higher v may not necessarily imply inefficiency or slower growth. ICORs can also shift through market mechanisms, as prices of labor and capital change in response to changes in supplies. As growth takes place, saving tends to become relatively more abundant and hence the price of capital falls while employment and wages rise. Therefore, all producers increasingly economize on labor and use more capital and the ICOR tends to rise.

Consider again the example of Malaysia. The ICOR changed from approximately 1.6 between 1965 and 1980, to 2.6 between 1980 and 1995, to (as stated previously) 2.7 between 1999 and 2001 as Malaysia gradually moved into more capital-intensive production processes. To continue to use the 1965–80 ICOR in 2002 would have been very misleading and betrayed a significant misunderstanding of the growth process. The structure of the economy had changed substantially during that time period and, with it, the ICOR. Thailand provides a similar example, as described in Box 4–1.

As a result of these rigidities, the Harrod-Domar framework tends to become increasingly inaccurate over longer periods of time as the actual ICOR changes and, with it, the capital-labor ratio. In a world with fixed-coefficient production functions, little room is left for a factory manager to increase output by hiring one more worker without buying a machine to go with the worker or to purchase more machines for the current workforce to use. The fixed-proportion production function does not allow for any **substitution** between capital and labor in the production process. In the real world, of course, at least some substitution

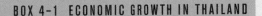

BOX 4-1 ECONOMIC GROWTH IN THAILAND

In the 1960s, Thailand's agrarian economy depended heavily on rice, maize, rubber, and other agricultural products. About three quarters of the Thai population derived its income from agricultural activities. GDP per capita in 1960 (measured in 1996 purchasing power parity terms) was around $1,100, less than one tenth the average income in the United States. Life expectancy was 53 years and the infant mortality rate was 103 per 1,000 births. Few observers expected Thailand to develop rapidly.

However, since the mid-1960s, the Thai economy has grown rapidly (if not always steadily), benefiting from relatively sound economic management and a favorable external environment. The government regularly achieved surpluses on the current account of its budget and used these funds (plus modest inflows of foreign assistance) to finance investments in rural roads, irrigation, power, telecommunications, and other basic infrastructure. At least until the mid-1990s, the government's fiscal, monetary, and exchange rate policies kept the macroeconomy relatively stable with fairly low inflation, despite the turbulent period of world oil price shocks in the 1970s and 1980s. Beginning in the 1970s, the government began to remove trade restrictions and promote the production of labor-intensive manufactured exports. These products found a ready market in the booming Japanese economy of the 1980s and provided a growing number of jobs for Thai workers.

Thailand's ability to make investments and deepen its capital stock depended on its capacity to save. The country's saving rate averaged about 20 percent in the 1960s, already high for developing countries, and increased steadily over time to an average of 35 percent in the 1990s. These high saving rates, combined with relatively prudent economic policies and Japan's economic boom, supported very rapid economic growth and development.

Thailand's development experience has been far from completely smooth, however. In mid-1997, a major financial crisis erupted. Huge short-term offshore borrowing combined with a fixed exchange rate and weak financial institutions led to a collapse of a real estate bubble, rapid capital flight, a substantial depreciation of the Thai baht, and a deep recession (see Chapter 15). In some ways, Thailand had become the victim of its own success, with its rapid growth attracting significant numbers of investors looking to gain quick profits, who rapidly fled once the bubble began to collapse. After two years of negative growth (with GDP falling 10 percent in 1998), the economy began to recover and growth rebounded to 3.5 percent between 1999 and 2003.

Over the longer period between 1960 and 2003, per capita growth averaged 4.6 percent, so that the average income in Thailand is now more than six times higher than it was in 1960. Life expectancy grew to 69 years, infant mortality

fell to 24 per thousand, and adult literacy reached 93 percent. During this period, the structure of the economy changed significantly. By 2003, manufacturing
accounted for well over 30 percent of GNP, up from just 14 percent in 1965,
while the share of agricultural production dropped commensurately. The composition of exports shifted away from rice, maize, and other agricultural commodities toward labor-intensive manufactured products, which now account for more
than 80 percent of all exports. As the Harrod-Domar and Solow models predict,
Thailand's high saving rate and resulting capital accumulation was accompanied
by a dramatic increase in output (and income) per capita. Contrary to the Harrod-
Domar model, however, the ICOR did not remain constant. As the stock of capital
grew and the economy shifted toward more capital-intensive production techniques, the ICOR increased from 2.6 in the 1970s to 4.1 in the 1990s. The rising
ICOR indicated that, as the Thai economy expanded and the level of capital per
worker increased, an ever-larger increment of new capital was required to bring
about a given increase in total output, a characteristic captured by the neoclassical model of economic growth.

between labor and capital is possible in most production processes. As we see in
the next section, adding this feature to the model allows for a much richer exploration of the growth process.

A final weakness of the Harrod-Domar model is the absence of any role for
technological change. Advances in technology generally are thought to play a
critical role in long-term growth and development by contributing to increased
productivity of all factors of production. In Figure 4–1, increased factor productivity and technical change can be represented by an inward shift of each isoquant toward the origin, implying that less labor and capital would be needed to
produce the same amount of output. The simplest way to capture this in the
Harrod-Domar framework is to introduce a smaller ICOR, but of course, this
would contradict the idea of a constant ICOR.

Despite these weaknesses, the Harrod-Domar model is still used to a surprisingly wide extent. Economist William Easterly documented how the World
Bank and other institutions use the model to calculate "financing gaps" between
the amount of available saving and the amount of investment supposedly
needed to achieve a target growth rate.[10] He shows how simplistic and sometimes careless use of the model can lead to weak analysis and faulty conclusions. In essence, analysts enamored by the simplicity of the model tend to
overlook its shortcomings when applying it to the real world.

---

[10]See William Easterly, "Aid for Investment," *The Elusive Quest for Growth* (Cambridge, MA: MIT
Press: 2001), Chapter 2; and William Easterly, "The Ghost of the Financing Gap: Testing the Growth
Model of the International Financial Institutions," *Journal of Development Economics* 60, no. 2
(December 1999), 423–38.

The Harrod-Domar model provides some useful insights but does not take us very far. The fixed-coefficient assumption provides the model with very little flexibility and does not capture the ability of real world firms to change the mix of inputs in the production process. The model can be reasonably accurate from one year to the next (in the absence of shocks), and it rightly focuses attention on the importance of saving. But it is quite inaccurate for most countries over longer periods of time and implies that saving is sufficient for growth, when it is not. Indeed, in the late 1950s, Evsey Domar expressed strong doubts about his own model, pointing out that it originally was designed to explore employment issues in advanced economies rather than growth per se and was too rigid to be useful for explaining long-term growth.[11] Instead, he endorsed the new growth model of Robert Solow, to which we now turn our attention.

THE SOLOW (NEOCLASSICAL) GROWTH MODEL

The Neoclassical Production Function

In 1956, MIT-economist Robert Solow introduced a new model of economic growth that was a big step forward from the Harrod-Domar framework.[12] Solow recognized the problems that arose from the rigid production function in the Harrod-Domar model. Solow's answer was to drop the fixed-coefficients production function and replace it with a **neoclassical production function** that allows for more flexibility and substitution between the factors of production. In the Solow model, the capital-output and capital-labor ratios no longer are fixed but vary, depending on the relative endowments of capital and labor in the economy and the production process. Like the Harrod-Domar model, the Solow model was developed to analyze industrialized economies, but it has been used extensively to explore economic growth in all countries around the world, including developing countries. The Solow model has been enormously influential and remains at the core of most theories of economic growth in developing countries.

The isoquants that underlie the neoclassical production function are shown in Figure 4–2. Note that the isoquants are curved, rather than L-shaped as in the

---

[11]Evsey Domar, *Essays in the Theory of Economic Growth* (Oxford: Oxford University Press, 1957).

[12]The two classic references of Solow's work are "A Contribution to the Theory of Economic Growth" and "Technical Change and the Aggregate Production Function," *Review of Economics and Statistics* 39 (August 1957), 312–20. For an excellent and very thorough undergraduate exposition of the Solow and other models of economic growth, see Charles I. Jones. *Introduction to Economic Growth* (New York: W. W. Norton and Company, 2001). In 1987, Solow was awarded the Nobel Prize in Economics, primarily for his work on growth theory.

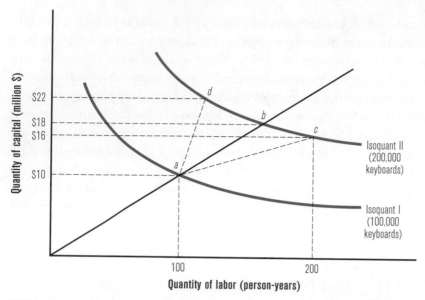

FIGURE 4-2. Neoclassical (variable proportions) Production Function
Instead of requiring fixed factor proportions, as in Figure 4–1, output can
be achieved with varying combinations of labor and capital. This is called
a *neoclassical* production function. The isoquants are curved, rather than
L-shaped.

fixed-coefficient model. In this figure, at point *a*, $10 million of capital and 100
workers combine to produce 100,000 keyboards, which would be valued at $5
million (since, as stated in the earlier section, keyboards are priced at $50 each).
Starting from this point, output could be expanded in any of three ways. If the
firm's managers decided to expand at constant factor proportions and move to
point *b* on isoquant II to produce 200,000 keyboards, the situation would be
identical to the fixed proportions case of Figure 4–1. The capital-output ratio at
both points *a* and *b* would be 2:1, as it was before ($10 million of capital pro-
duces $5 million of keyboards at point *a*, and $20 million of capital produces $10
million of keyboards at point *b*). Note that the Solow model retains from the
Harrod-Domar model the assumption of constant returns to scale, so that a
doubling of labor and capital leads to a doubling of output. But by dropping the
fixed-coefficients assumption, production of 200,000 keyboards could be
achieved by using different combinations of capital and labor. For example, the
firm could use more labor and less capital (a more labor-intensive method),
such as at point *c* on isoquant II. In that case, the capital-output ratio falls to
1.7:1 ($17 million in capital to produce $10 million in keyboards). Alternatively,
the firm could choose a more capital-intensive method, such as at point *d* on
isoquant II, where the capital-output ratio would rise to 2.4:1.

   If the production function facing a country is neoclassical, then the capital-
output ratio becomes a variable influenced by relative prices, policies, and other

factors. Considering production functions like those in Figure 4–2 from the industry level, government policy could induce manufacturers and farmers to employ more labor-intensive technologies (for example, through an increase in the tax rate on capital purchases). At the level of the whole economy, policy changes could encourage labor-intensive technologies as well as investment in the more labor-intensive industries and so reduce the demand for investment and saving on both counts. The kinds of tools that policy makers use to try to reduce the capital-output ratio are discussed in depth in several chapters later in this text.

The Basic Equations of the Solow Model

The Solow model is understood most easily by expressing all the key variables in per-worker terms (e.g., output per worker and capital per worker). To do so, we divide both sides of the production function in equation 4–1 by L, so that it takes the form

$$Y/L = F(K/L, 1) \qquad [4\text{–}12]$$

The equation shows that output per worker is a function of capital per worker.[13] If we use lower case letters to represent quantities in per-worker terms, then y is output per worker (that is, $y = Y/L$) and k is capital per worker ($k = K/L$). This gives us the first equation of the Solow model, in which the production function can be written simply as

$$y = f(k) \qquad [4\text{–}13]$$

Solow's model assumes a production function with the familiar property of **diminishing returns to capital.** With a fixed labor supply, giving workers an initial amount of machinery to work with results in large gains in output. But as these workers are given more and more machinery, the addition to output from each new machine gets smaller and smaller. An aggregate production function with this property is shown graphically in Figure 4–3. The horizontal axis represents capital per worker (k), and the vertical axis shows output per worker (y). The slope of the curve declines as the capital stock increases, reflecting the assumption of the diminishing marginal product of capital. Each movement to the right on the horizontal axis yields a smaller and smaller increase in output per worker.

The first equation of the Solow model tells us that capital per worker is fundamental to the growth process. In turn, the second equation focuses on the determinants of changes in capital per worker. This second equation can be derived

---

[13]We can divide both sides by L because the Solow model (like the Harrod-Domar model) assumes the production function exhibits constant returns to scale and has the property that $wY = F(wK, wL)$. To express the Solow model in per-worker terms, we let $w = 1/L$.

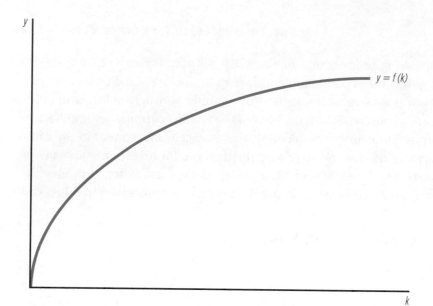

FIGURE 4-3. The Production Function in the Solow Growth Model
The neoclassical production function in the Solow model displays
diminishing returns to capital, so that each additional increment in
capital per worker (k) is associated with smaller increases in output per
worker (y).

from equation 4–6[14] and shows that capital accumulation depends on saving, the
growth rate of the labor force, and depreciation:

$$\Delta k = sy - (n + d)k \qquad\qquad [4\text{–}14]$$

This is a very important equation, so we should understand exactly what it
means. It states that the change in capital per worker (Δk) is determined by
three things:

1. *The Δk is positively related to saving per worker.* Since s is the saving rate
   and y is income (or output) per worker, the term sy is equal to saving per

[14]To derive equation 4–14, we begin by dividing both sides of equation 4–6 by K so that

$$\Delta K/K = sY/K - d$$

We then focus on the capital per worker ratio, $k = K/L$. The growth rate of k is equal to the growth rate of K
minus the growth rate of L:

$$\Delta k/k = \Delta K/K - \Delta L/L$$

With a little rearranging of terms, this equation can be written as $\Delta K/K = \Delta k/k + \Delta L/L$. We earlier assumed
that both the population and the labor force were growing at rate n, so $\Delta L/L = n$. By substitution we obtain

$$\Delta K/K = \Delta k/k + n$$

Note that, in both the first equation of the footnote and this most recent equation, the left-hand side is
equal to $\Delta K/K$. This implies that the right-hand sides of these two equations are equal to each other, as follows:

$$\Delta k/k + n = sY/K - d$$

By subtracting n from both sides and multiplying through by k, we find that

$$\Delta k = sy - nk - dk \quad \text{or} \quad \Delta k = sy - (n + d)k$$

worker. As saving per worker increases, so does investment per worker, and the capital stock per worker (k) grows.

2. *The Δk is negatively related to population growth.* This is shown by the term $-nk$. Each year, because of growth in the population and labor force, there are nL new workers. If there were no new investment, the increase in the labor force would mean that capital *per worker* (k) falls. Equation 4–14 states that capital per worker falls by exactly nk.

3. *Depreciation erodes the capital stock.* Each year, the amount of capital per worker falls by the amount $-dk$ simply because of depreciation.

Therefore, saving (and investment) adds to capital per worker, while labor force growth and depreciation reduce capital per worker. When saving per capita, sy, is larger than the amount of new capital needed to compensate for labor force growth and depreciation, $(n + d)k$, then Δk is a positive number. This implies that capital per worker k increases.

The process through which the economy increases the amount of capital per worker, k, is called **capital deepening.** Economies in which workers have access to more machines, computers, trucks, and other equipment have a deeper capital base than economies with less machinery, and these economies are able to produce more output per worker.

In some economies, however, the amount of saving is just enough to provide the same amount of capital to new workers and compensate for depreciation. An increase in the capital stock that just keeps pace with the expanding labor force and depreciation is called **capital widening** (referring to a "widening" of both the total amount of capital and the size of the workforce). Capital widening occurs when sy is exactly equal to $(n + d)k$, implying no change in k. Using this terminology, equation 4–14 can be restated as saying that *capital deepening (Δk) is equal to saving per worker (sy) minus the amount needed for capital widening* $[(n + d)k]$.

A country with a high saving rate easily can deepen its capital base and rapidly expand the amount of capital per worker, thus providing the basis for growth in output. In Singapore, for example, where the saving rate has averaged more than 40 percent for many years, it is not difficult to provide capital to the growing labor force and make up for depreciation and still have plenty left over to supply existing workers with additional capital. By contrast, Kenya, with a saving rate of about 15 percent (and lower in recent years), has much less saving to spare for capital deepening after providing machines to new workers and making up for depreciation. As a result, capital per worker does not grow as quickly, and neither does output (or income) per worker. Partly because of this large difference in saving rates, output per person in Singapore grew by an average of 6.3 percent per year between 1960 and 2002, while Kenya's growth averaged about 1 percent.

We can summarize the two basic equations of the Solow model as follows. The first ($y = f(k)$) simply states that output per worker (or income per capita) depends on the amount of capital per worker. The second equation, $\Delta k = sy - (n + d)k$, says that changes in capital per worker depends on saving, the population growth rate, and depreciation. Thus, as in the Harrod-Domar model, saving plays a central role in the Solow model. However, the relationship between saving and growth is not linear, because of diminishing returns to capital in the production function. In addition, the Solow model introduces a role for the population growth rate and allows for substitution between capital and labor in the growth process.

Now that we are equipped with the basic model, we can proceed to analyze the effects of changes in the saving rate, population growth, and depreciation on economic output and economic growth. This is accomplished most easily by examining the model in graphical form.

The Solow Diagram

The diagram of the Solow model consists of three curves, shown in Figure 4–4. The first is the production function $y = f(k)$, given by equation 4–13. The second is a saving function, which is derived directly from the production function. The new curve shows saving per capita, sy, calculated by multiplying both sides of equation 4–13 by the saving rate, so that $sy = s \times f(k)$. Since saving is assumed to be a fixed fraction of income (with s between 0 and 1), the saving function has the same shape as the production function but shifts it downward by the factor s. The third curve is the line $(n + d)k$, which is a straight line through the origin with the slope $(n + d)$. This line represents the amount of new capital needed as a result of growth in the labor force and depreciation just to keep capital per worker (k) constant. Note that the second and third curves are diagrammatic representations of the two right-hand terms of equation 4–14.

The second and third curves intersect at point A, where $k = k_0$. (Note that, on the production function above the sy curve, $k = k_0$ corresponds to a point directly above A where $y = y_0$ on the vertical axis.) At point A, sy is exactly equal to $(n + d)k$, so capital per worker does not change and k remains constant. At other points along the horizontal axis, the *vertical difference* between the sy curve and the $(n + d)k$ line determines the *change* in capital per worker. To the left of point A (say, where $k = k_1$ and on the production function $y = y_1$), the amount of saving in the economy per person (sy) is larger than the amount of saving needed to compensate for new workers and depreciation ($(n + d)k$). As a result, the amount of capital per person (k) grows (capital deepening) and the economy shifts to the right along the horizontal axis. The economy continues to shift to the right as long as the sy curve is *above* the $(n + d)k$ curve, until eventually the economy reaches an equilibrium at point A. In terms of the production func-

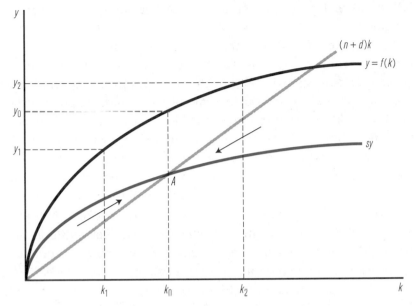

FIGURE 4-4. The Basic Solow Growth Model Diagram
In the basic Solow diagram, Point A is the only place where the amount
of new saving sy is exactly equal to the amount of new capital needed
for growth in the workforce and depreciation $(n + d)$. Point A is the
steady state level of capital per worker and output per worker.

tion, the shift to the right implies an increase in output per worker, y (or income
per capita), from y_1 to y_0. To the right of point A (say, where $k = k_2$ and $y = y_2$), saving per capita is smaller than the amount needed for new workers and deprecia-
tion, so capital per worker falls and the economy shifts to the left along the
horizontal axis. Once again, this shift continues until the economy reaches
point A. The shift to the left corresponds to a decline in output per worker from
y_2 to y_0.

Point A is the only place where the amount of new saving, sy, is exactly equal
to the amount of new capital needed for growth in the workforce and depreciation. Therefore, at this point, the amount of capital per worker, k, remains constant. Saving per worker (on the vertical axis of the saving function) also
remains constant, as does output per worker (or income per capita) on the production function, with $y = y_0$. As a result, point A is called the **steady state** of the
Solow model. Output per capita at the steady state (y_0) is alternatively referred
to as the **steady state, long run,** or **potential level of output per worker.**

It is very important to note, however, that all the values that remain constant are expressed as *per worker.* Although output per worker is constant, *total*
output continues to grow at rate n, the same rate the population and workforce
grow. In other words, *at the steady state GDP (Y) grows at the rate n, but GDP per
capita (y) is constant (average income remains unchanged).* Similarly, although

capital per worker and saving per worker are constant at point A, total capital and total saving grow.

In Chapter 3, we explored three critical implications of the assumption of diminishing marginal product of capital: (1) Poor countries have the *potential* for relatively rapid economic growth, (2) growth rates tend to slow as incomes rise, and (3) as a result of the first two, the incomes of poor countries potentially can begin to converge with those of the rich countries over time. The graphical representation of the Solow model reinforces these points. Consider the situation to the far left of point A where k and y are low (i.e., in a relatively poor country). Under these circumstances, the requirements for capital widening are relatively small, so sy tends to be greater than $(n + d)k$, and both k and y grow. The relatively steep slope of the production function at points where k and y are low implies that, for a given increment in k, the change in y is relatively large, *so output per worker and per capita income grow relatively quickly.* As the economy grows and moves toward point A (and income increases), growth in y slows until it stops at point A. This implies that, for higher-income countries (where y and k are relatively large), the rate of growth in y tends to be smaller. Therefore, when countries move along the same production function and have the same steady state level of y—crucial assumptions—*poorer countries have the potential to grow faster than richer countries and eventually "catch up" to the same level of income per capita at point A.* Chapter 3 explored the empirical evidence on this question and found that there is no evidence of *absolute* convergence of incomes across all countries. However, we saw evidence for *conditional* convergence, in which incomes converge among countries that share in common critical characteristics, such as similar trade policies, suggesting that they operate along similar production functions.

Changes in the Saving Rate and Population Growth Rate in the Solow Model

Both the Solow and Harrod-Domar models put saving (and investment) at the core of the growth process. In the Harrod-Domar model, an increase in the saving rate translates directly (and linearly) into an increase in aggregate output. What is the impact of a higher saving rate in the Solow model?

As shown in Figure 4–5, increasing the saving rate from s to s' shifts the saving function sy up to $s'y$, without shifting either the production function or the capital widening line $(n + d)k$. The increase in the saving rate means that saving per worker (and investment per worker) now is greater than $(n + d)k$, so k gradually increases. The economy shifts to a new long-run equilibrium at point B. In the process, capital per worker increases from k_0 to k_3 and output per worker increases from y_0 to y_3. The aggregate economy initially grows at a rate faster than its steady-state growth rate of n until it reaches point B, where the long-run

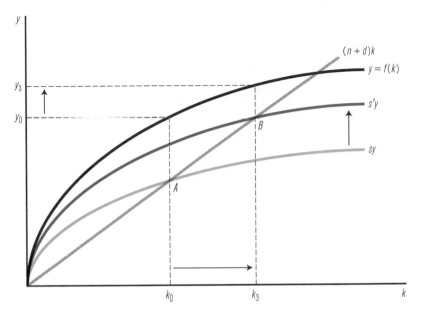

FIGURE 4-5. An Increase in the Saving Rate in the Solow Model
An increase in the saving rate from s to s' results in an upward shift in the
capital deepening curve, so that capital per worker increases from k_0 to k_1.

growth rate reverts to n. Thus, the higher saving rate leads to more investment, a
permanently higher stock of capital per worker, and a permanently higher level
of income (or output) per worker. In other words, the Solow model predicts that
economies that save more have higher standards of living than those that save
less. (The increase in per capita income, however, is smaller than for a similar
increase in s in the Harrod-Domar model, since the Solow model has diminishing returns in production.) Higher saving also leads to a *temporary* increase in
the economic growth rate as the steady state shifts from A to B. However, the increase in the saving rate does *not* result in a permanent increase in the long-run
rate of output growth, which remains at n.

The Solow diagram also can be used to evaluate the impact of a change in
the population (or labor force) growth rate. An increase in the population
growth rate from n to n' rotates the capital widening line to the left from $(n + d)k$
to $(n' + d)k$, as shown in Figure 4–6. The production and saving functions do not
change. Since now there are more workers, savings per worker (sy) becomes
smaller and no longer is large enough to keep capital per worker constant.
Therefore, k begins to decline and the economy moves to a new steady state, C.
Since there are more workers, capital per worker declines from k_0 to k_4 and saving per worker falls from sy_0 to sy_4. Output per worker (or income per capita)
also declines, from y_0 to y_4. Thus, an increase in the population growth rate leads
to lower average income in the Solow model. Note, however, that the new
steady-state growth rate of the entire economy has increased from n to n' at

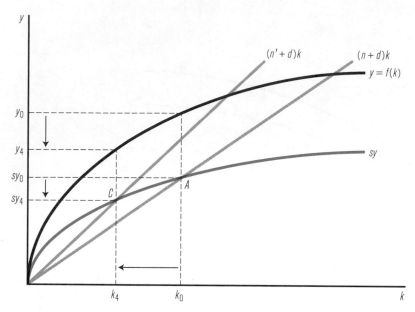

FIGURE 4-6. Changes in the Population Growth Rate in the Solow Model
An increase in the rate of population growth from n to n' causes the
capital widening curve to rotate to the left. Equilibrium capital per worker
drops from k_0 to k_4.

point C. In other words, with a higher population growth rate, Y needs to grow
faster to keep y constant.[15] By contrast, a *reduction* in the population growth rate
rotates the $(n + d)k$ line to the right and leads to a process of capital deepening,
with an increase in both k and in the steady-state level of income per worker, y.
However, the relationship between population growth and economic growth is
not quite so simple, as described in Box 4–2.

The Solow growth model (as described to this point) suggests that growth
rates differ across countries for two main reasons.

1. Two countries with the same current level of income may experience dif-
    ferent growth rates *if one has a higher steady-state level of income than
    the other*. To the extent that two countries with the same current level of
    income have different aggregate production functions, saving rates, pop-
    ulation growth rates, or rates of change in technology (described later),
    their steady-state income levels will differ and so will their growth rates
    during the transition to their respective steady states.

---

[15]A similar exercise can be used to determine the impact of an increase in the depreciation rate,
d. Such an increase results in a reduction in k and y to a lower steady-state income per capita. The
subtle difference between an increase in n and an increase in d is that the latter case does not lead to
a change in the long-run growth rate of Y, which remains equal to n.

BOX 4-2 POPULATION GROWTH AND ECONOMIC GROWTH

The inverse correlation between population growth and economic growth suggested by the Solow model has a lot of intuitive appeal. Countries like Guinea-Bissau, Madagascar, Niger, and Yemen have some of the world's fastest rates of population growth. They are also among some of the poorest nations in the world. But closer inspection of the Solow model reveals other predictions about how population growth may affect economic growth, and a further examination of empirical trends suggests a much more complex relationship.

Figure 4–6 illustrates that, in the Solow model, an increase in the rate of population growth lowers the steady-state level of income, y. However, y refers to output per *worker* while the more common measure of aggregate economic welfare is output per *person, y^**. These two measures of output, of course, are related to one another, as follows:

$$y^* = y \times (N/\text{Pop})$$

where N equals the number of workers and Pop is the total population. Differences in the level of output per capita, therefore, depend on both the amount of output per worker and the ratio of workers to total population. Growth in per capita output, similarly, depends on growth in output per worker and the growth in the worker-to-population ratio.

The Solow model suggests that more rapid population growth reduces capital deepening and, hence, reduces growth in output per worker. But the effect of population growth on the ratio of workers to total population is more complex. It depends on the age structure of the population. Because of rapid population growth, most developing countries have a young age structure, with a larger share of younger people than is the case in developed nations that have growing populations of more elderly people. As a result of previously higher population growth rates, many developing nations today are experiencing an increase in their ratio of workers to total population. This positive effect of a changing age structure on per capita incomes, sometimes referred to as a *demographic gift*, can play a positive and large role in determining economic growth rates.

The impact of population growth on economic growth goes beyond its effects on capital widening and a nation's age structure. In the Solow model, saving and technological change are considered exogenous. But population growth can affect these parameters as well. The net effect of population growth on economic growth is therefore an empirical matter. Simple correlations between economic growth and population growth show no systematic relationship (see Figure 7–5). More sophisticated econometric investigations generally maintain this finding. Population growth influences many aspects of economic growth and development, not only those described by the Solow model.

2. Two countries with the same long-run steady-state level of income may have different growth rates *if they are in different points in the transition to the steady state*. For example, consider two countries that are identical in every way except that one has a higher saving rate than the other and, so, initially has a higher steady-state level of income. At the steady states, the country with the higher saving rate has a higher level of output per worker, but both are growing at the rate *n*. If the country with the lower saving rate suddenly increases its saving to match the other country, its growth rate will be higher than the other country until it catches up at the new steady state. Thus, even though everything is identical in the two countries, their growth rates may differ during the transition to the steady state, which may take many years.

Technological Change in the Solow Model

The Solow model, as described to this point, is a powerful tool for analyzing the interrelationships between saving, investment, population growth, output, and economic growth. However, the unsettling conclusion of the basic model is that, once the economy reaches its long-run potential level of income, economic growth simply matches population growth, with no chance for sustained increases in average income. How can the model explain the historical fact reported in Chapter 2 that many of the world's countries have seen steady growth in average incomes since 1820? Solow's answer was **technological change.**[16] According to this idea, a key reason why France, Germany, the United Kingdom, the United States, and other high-income countries have been able to sustain growth in per capita income over very long periods of time is that technological progress has allowed output per worker to continue to grow. To incorporate an economy's ability to produce more output with the same amount of capital and labor, we slightly modify the original production function and introduce a variable, *T*, to represent technological progress, as follows:

$$Y = F(K, T \times L) \qquad [4\text{--}15]$$

In this specification, technology is introduced in such a way that it directly enhances the input of labor, as shown by the specification in which *L* is multiplied by *T*. This type of technological change is referred to as *labor augmenting.*[17] As technology improves (*T* rises), the efficiency and productivity of labor

---

[16]See Robert Solow, "Technical Change and the Aggregate Production Function." For an early discussion about the relationship between capital accumulation and technological progress, see Joan Robinson, *Essays in the Theory of Economic Growth* (London: Macmillan, 1962).

[17]Two other possibilities are "capital-augmenting" technological change ($Y = F(T \times K, L)$), which enhances capital inputs, and "Hicks-neutral" technological change ($Y = F(T \times K, T \times L)$), which enhances both capital and labor input. For our purposes, the specific way in which technology is introduced does not affect the basic conclusions of the model.

increases, since the same amount of labor can now produce more output. Increases in T can result from improvements in technology in the scientific sense (new inventions and processes) or in terms of **human capital,** such as improvements in the health, education, or skills of the workforce.[18]

The combined term $T \times L$ is sometimes referred to as the amount of **effective units of labor.** The expression $T \times L$ measures both the amount of labor and its efficiency in the production process. An increase in either T or L increases the amount of effective labor and therefore increases aggregate production. For example, an insurance sales office can increase its effective workforce by either adding new workers or giving each worker a faster computer or better cell phone. An increase in T differs from an increase in L, however, since the rise in aggregate income from new technology does not need to be shared with additional workers. Therefore, *technological change allows output (and income) per worker to increase.*

Solow specified technological change as exogenous to the model, that is, determined independent of all the variables and parameters specified in the model. He did not spell out exactly how technological change takes place or how the growth process itself might affect it. Wherever it came from, however, new technology clearly added to the ability of the factors of production to increase output. In this sense, technological change has been called "manna from heaven" in the Solow model.

The usual assumption is that technology improves at a constant rate, which we denote by the Greek letter theta (θ), so that $\Delta T/T = \theta$. If technology grows at 1 percent per year, then each worker becomes 1 percent more productive each year. With the workforce growing at n, growth in the effective supply of labor is equal to $n + \theta$. If the workforce (and population) grows by 2 percent per year and technology grows by 1 percent per year, the effective supply of labor increases by 3 percent per year.

To show technological change in the Solow diagram, we need to modify our notation. Whereas earlier we expressed y and k in terms of output and capital *per worker,* we now need to express these variables in terms of output and capital *per effective worker.* The change is straightforward. Instead of dividing Y and K by L as previously (to obtain y and k), we now divide each by $(T \times L)$. Thus, **output per effective worker** (y_e) is defined as $y_e = Y/(T \times L)$. Similarly, **capital per effective worker** (k_e) is defined as $k_e = K/(T \times L)$.[19]

---

[18]Keep in mind, however, that, while these two broad categories of improvements in technology have similar general effects in this aggregate model, their true effects are somewhat different in the real world. Technological change in the mechanical sense or from the spread of a new idea can be shared widely across the workforce and considered a public good. Improvements in human capital, by contrast, are specific to individual workers and are not necessarily widely shared. However, both have the effect of augmenting the supply of labor and increasing total output.

[19]Note that this is consistent with the earlier notation. If there is no technological change (our earlier assumption), so that $T = 1$ (and remains unchanged), then $y_e = y$ and $k_e = k$.

With these changes, the production function can be written as $y_e = f(k_e)$ and saving per effective worker expressed as sy_e. With effective labor now growing at the rate $n + \theta$, the capital accumulation equation (4–14) changes to

$$\Delta k_e = sy_e - (n + d + \theta)k_e \qquad [4\text{--}16]$$

The new term $(n + d + \theta)k_e$ is larger than the original $(n + d)k$, indicating that more capital is needed to keep capital *per effective worker* constant.

These changes are shown in Figure 4–7, which looks very similar to the basic Solow diagram, with only a slight change in notation. There still is one steady-state point, at which saving per effective worker is just equal to the amount of new capital needed to compensate for changes in the size of the workforce, depreciation, and technological change in order to keep capital per effective worker constant.

One change, however, is very important. At the steady state, output per *effective* worker is constant, rather than output per worker. *Total output now grows at the rate $n + \theta$, so that output per actual worker (or income per person) increases at rate θ.* Therefore, with the introduction of technology, the model now incorporates the possibility of an economy experiencing sustained growth in per capita income at rate θ. This mechanism provides a plausible explanation for why the industrialized countries never seem to reach a steady state with constant output per worker but instead historically have recorded growth in output per worker of between 1 and 2 percent per year.

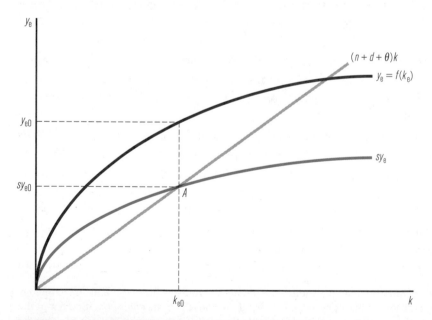

FIGURE 4-7. The Solow Model with Technical Change
In the Solow model with technical change, the equilibrium level of effective capital per worker (k_{e0}) is determined by point A, the intersection of the effective capital widening curve ($n + d + \theta$) and the effective saving curve (sy_e).

Strengths and Weaknesses of the Solow Framework

Although the Solow model is more complex than the Harrod-Domar framework, it is a more powerful tool for understanding the growth process. By replacing the fixed coefficients production function with a neoclassical one, the model provides more reasonable flexibility of factor proportions in the production process. Like the Harrod-Domar framework, it emphasizes the important role of factor accumulation and saving, but its assumption of diminishing marginal product of capital provides more realism and accuracy over time. It departs significantly from the Harrod-Domar framework in distinguishing the current level of income per worker from the long-run steady-state level and focuses attention on the transition path to that steady state. The model provides powerful insights into the relationship between saving, investment, population growth, and technological change on the steady-state level of output per worker. As the empirical evidence on convergence of incomes presented in Chapter 3 suggests, it does a much better job, albeit far from perfect, of describing real world outcomes than the Harrod-Domar model.

However, the focus on the role of factor accumulation and productivity (including technology) as the proximate determinants of the steady state raises a new set of questions that the model does not answer. What are the more fundamental determinants of factor accumulation and productivity that affect the steady state and the rate of economic growth? The empirical evidence in Chapter 3 suggests that the most rapidly growing developing countries share certain common characteristics: economic and political stability, relatively better health and education, stronger governance and institutions, more open trade policies, and more favorable geography. Box 4–3 provides an estimate of the quantitative importance of these factors in East Asia's rapid growth relative to other countries. In the language of the Solow model, these characteristics operate through factor accumulation and productivity to help determine the precise shape of the production function and the steady-state level of output per worker. Changing any of these factors—say, encouraging more open trade— changes the steady-state level of output per worker and therefore the current rate of economic growth as the economy adjusts to the new steady state. Thus, the model helps us focus attention on these more fundamental influences on the steady state and the growth rate, but it does not provide a full understanding of the precise pathways through which these factors influence output and growth.

A particularly important contribution of the model is the simple yet powerful insights it provides into the role of technological change in the growth process. The model illustrates how the acquisition of new technology, either from domestic innovation or importing new technologies from abroad, can provide a powerful fillip to growth. For policy makers, a key question then becomes

BOX 4-3 EXPLAINING DIFFERENCES IN GROWTH RATES

Many recent studies have shown that the initial levels of income, openness to trade, healthy populations, effective governance, favorable geography, and high saving rates all contribute to rapid economic growth. But which are most important? One study sought to explain differences in growth during the period 1965–90 between three groups of countries: 10 East and Southeast Asian countries (in which per capita growth averaged 4.6 percent), 17 sub-Saharan African countries (in which growth averaged 0.6 percent), and 21 Latin American countries (in which growth averaged 0.7 percent).[1]

Policy variables explained much of the difference in growth rates. The East and Southeast Asian countries recorded higher government saving rates, were more open to trade, and had higher-quality government institutions. Together, the differences in these policies accounted for 1.7 percentage points of the 4.0 percentage point difference between the East and Southeast Asian and sub-Saharan African growth rates, and 1.8 percentage points of the difference between East and Southeast Asia and Latin America. Openness to trade stood out as the single most-important policy choice affecting these growth rates.

Initial levels of income also were important, as the Solow model predicts. Since the Latin American countries had higher average income (and therefore greater output per worker) than the East Asian countries in 1965, the Solow model would predict somewhat slower growth in Latin America. Sure enough, this study estimates that Latin America's higher initial income slowed its growth rate by 1.2 percentage points relative to East and Southeast Asia, after controlling for other factors. By contrast, the sub-Saharan African countries had lower average initial income, indicating that (all else being equal) these countries could have grown 1.0 percentage point faster than the East and Southeast Asian countries, rather than the actual outcome of 4.0 percentage points slower. This suggests that the other factors had to account for a full 5.0 percentage point difference in growth rates between East and Southeast Asia and sub-Saharan Africa.

Initial levels of health, as indicated by life expectancy at birth, were a major factor contributing to sub-Saharan Africa's slow growth. Life expectancy at birth averaged 41 years in sub-Saharan Africa in 1965, compared to 55 years in East and Southeast Asia. The study estimates that this reduced sub-Saharan Africa's growth rate by 1.3 percentage points relative to East and Southeast Asia. By contrast, since average life expectancy in Latin America in 1965 was almost the

[1]Steven Radelet, Jeffrey Sachs, and Jong-Wha Lee (2001), "The Determinants and Prospects for Economic Growth in Asia," *International Economic Journal* 15, no. 3 (Autumn), 1–30. These results also are summarized in the Asian Development Bank's study *Emerging Asia: Changes and Challenges* (Manila: Asian Development Bank, 1997), 79–82.

same as in East and Southeast Asia, health explains little of the difference in growth between these regions.

Favorable geography helped East and Southeast Asia grow faster. The combination of fewer landlocked countries, longer average coastline, fewer countries located in the deep tropics, and less dependence on natural resource exports all favored Asia. Taken together, these factors accounted for 1.0 percentage point of East and Southeast Asia's rapid growth compared to sub-Saharan Africa, and 0.6 percentage points relative to Latin America. Differences in initial levels of education and the changing demographic structure of the population accounted for the remaining differences in growth rates across these regions.

Of course, this simple accounting framework does not fully explain the complex relationships that underlie economic growth. Each of the variables in the study captures a range of other factors that affect growth rates. For example, differences in government saving rates probably reflect differences in fiscal policy, inflation rates, political stability, and many other factors. Because of lack of sufficient data, the analysis omits several factors (such as environmental degradation) that may be important. And it certainly does not begin to explain why different policy choices were made in different countries. As a result, studies like these should be seen as a first step to understanding growth, rather than as a precise explanation for the many complex differences across countries.

how to best acquire new technologies. For most low-income countries, while some domestic innovation is possible, for many industries it is probably most cost-effective for entrepreneurs to acquire the bulk of their new technologies from other countries (one of the benefits of "globalization") and adapt them to local circumstances.

As with all models, the Solow model has some important limitations. One, as pointed out, is the lack of direct insight on the fundamental factors influencing the steady state. Another is that, since the model includes just one sector, it does not shed light on the role of the allocation of capital and labor *among* various sectors (e.g., agriculture and industry), which can have an important influence on productivity. All economies produce a mix of different goods and services, each of which uses different combinations of capital and labor (and different kinds of technology) and has different productivities and potentials for growth. In the final section of this chapter, we shift from a one-sector to a two-sector model and explore some of the dynamic interactions between agriculture and industry and how they can affect growth. Finally, the Solow model takes as given the saving rate, growth of the labor supply, the skill level of the workforce, and the rate of technological change. These assumptions help simplify the model, but as a result we learn little about the underlying determinants of these parameters and how they might change during the process of development.

Beyond Solow: New Approaches to Growth

A new generation of models takes off where Solow left off, by moving beyond the assumptions of an exogenously fixed saving rate, growth rate of the labor supply, workforce skill level, and pace of technological change. In reality, the values of these parameters are not just given but are determined partially by government policies, economic structure, and the pace of growth itself. Economists have begun to develop more-sophisticated models in which one or more of these variables is determined within the model (that is, these variables become endogenous to the model).[20]

These models depart from the Solow framework by assuming that the national economy is subject to **increasing returns to scale,** rather than constant returns to scale. A doubling of capital, labor, and other factors of production leads to *more* than a doubling of output. To the extent this occurs, the impact of investment on both physical capital and human capital would be larger than suggested by Solow.

How can a doubling of capital and labor lead to more than a doubling of output? Consider investments in research or education that not only have a positive effect on the firm or the individual making the investment but also have a positive "spillover" effect on others in the economy. This beneficial effect on others, called a **positive externality,** results in a larger impact from the investment on the entire economy. The benefits from Henry Ford's development of the production line system, for example, were certainly large for the Ford Motor Company, but they were even larger for the economy as a whole because knowledge of this new technique soon spilled over to other firms that could benefit from Ford's new approach.

Similarly, investments in research and development (R&D) lead to new knowledge that accrues not only to those that make the investment but to others that eventually gain access to the knowledge. The gain from education is determined not just by how much a scientist's or manager's productivity is raised by investment in his or her own education. If many scientists and managers invest in their own education, there then will be many educated people who will learn from each other, increasing the benefits from education. An isolated scientist working alone is not as productive as one who can interact with dozens of well-educated colleagues. This interaction constitutes the externality. In the

[20]The seminal contributions to the new growth theory are Paul Romer, "Increasing Returns and Long-Run Growth," *Journal of Political Economy* 94 (October 1986), 1002–37; Robert Lucas, "On the Mechanics of Economic Development," *Journal of Monetary Economics* 22 (January 1988), 3–42; and Paul Romer, "Endogenous Technological Change," *Journal of Political Economy* 98 (October 1990), S71–S102.

context of the "sources of growth" analysis introduced in Chapter 3, such externalities suggest that the measured contribution of physical and human capital to growth may be larger than that captured by the Solow framework. Among other implications, this outcome could account for a significant portion of the residual in the Solow accounting framework, meaning that actual TFP growth is smaller than many studies have suggested.

Another important implication is that economies with increasing returns to scale do not necessarily reach a steady-state level of income as in the Solow framework. When the externalities from new investment are large, diminishing returns to capital do not necessarily set in, so growth rates do not slow, and the economy does not necessarily reach a steady state. As a result, an increase in the saving rate can lead to a *permanent* increase in the rate of economic growth. These models, therefore, can explain the observed fact of continued per capita growth in many countries without relying on exogenous technological change. Moreover, they do not necessarily lead to the conclusion that poor countries will grow faster than rich countries, since growth does not necessarily slow as incomes rise, so there is no expectation of convergence of incomes. Initial disparities in income can remain, or even enlarge, if richer countries make investments that encompass larger externalities.

Since growth can perpetuate in these models without relying on an assumption of exogenous technological change, they often are referred to as **endogenous growth models.** They are potentially important for explaining continued growth in industrialized countries that never reach a steady state, especially those engaged in research and development of new ideas on the cutting edge of technology.

For developing countries, the new models reinforce some of the main messages of the Solow and Harrod-Domar models. Like their forerunners, these models show the importance of factor accumulation and increases in productivity in the growth process. In fact, the potential benefits from both of these sources of growth are even greater in endogenous growth models because of potential positive externalities. Thus, the core messages of saving, investing in health and education, using the factors of production as productively and efficiently as possible, and seeking out appropriate new technologies are consistent across all these models.

The applicability of endogenous growth models to developing countries remains a subject of debate, however, since many low-income countries can achieve rapid growth by adapting the technologies developed in countries with more advanced research capacities rather than making the investments in research and development themselves. For many low-income countries, the Solow model's assumptions of exogenous technological change and constant returns to scale in the aggregate production function may be more appropriate.

TWO-SECTOR MODELS

One of the limitations of both the Harrod-Domar and Solow models is that capital and labor combine to produce just one product, when in reality all economies produce multiple goods and services. Although single-good models have the great advantage of simplicity, they do not explore production in different sectors such as agriculture, industry, or services (such as banking or tourism); the allocation of capital, labor, and land across these different activities; and the implications for growth. We saw in Chapter 3 that the decline in the share of agriculture and rise in the share of industry in GDP is at the core of long-term growth and development, suggesting that a more differentiated approach might shed some light on the growth process.

Like the one-good models, two-sector models recognize the prime importance of labor and capital in the growth process. Some versions put particular emphasis on land as a key component of the capital stock for agricultural production to incorporate some of the key features of land (e.g., that it cannot be moved from one location to another and the total stock of arable land cannot easily be expanded). Perhaps more important, two-sector models can explore differences in both the levels and growth rates of productivity in different activities and the implications for relative wages (and returns on capital investment), the allocation of labor and capital across the two sectors, and the potential for migration of labor from rural (agricultural) areas to urban (industrial areas). Two-sector models, therefore, ask slightly different questions than one-sector models and are able to shed light on different aspects of the growth process.

The Labor Surplus Model

Two-sector models have a long tradition in economic thinking. The best-known of the early models appeared in David Ricardo's *The Principles of Political Economy and Taxation,* published in 1817. In his model, Ricardo included two basic assumptions that have played an important role in two-sector models ever since.

1. He assumed that agricultural production was subject to **diminishing returns,** since crops require land and the supply of arable land is limited. To increase production, Ricardo felt, farmers would have to move onto poorer and poorer land, and therefore each new acre of land matched with the same amount of labor would produce less grain.
2. Ricardo formulated a concept that today is called **labor surplus.** Britain, in the early nineteenth century, still had a large agricultural workforce,

perhaps more than was necessary to produce sufficient food for all consumers. Ricardo believed that the industrial sector could draw away "surplus labor" from the farms without reducing total agricultural production or causing a rise in wages in either urban or rural areas.

Labor surplus, to the extent that it exists, is closely related to concepts such as **rural unemployment** and underemployment or disguised unemployment. Very few people in rural areas of developing countries are unemployed in the strict sense. While most rural people have jobs, those jobs are not very productive and do not require full-time effort. In many cases there is not enough work to employ the entire rural workforce full time, especially year-round. Instead members of farm families share the workload and all work part time. Economists call this **underemployment** or **disguised unemployment.**

The two-sector models we examine here focus on employment and are designed to answer several questions. How does surplus labor (or very low-productivity labor) in agriculture affect industry? Can workers move to industry without causing a fall in agricultural production, thus expanding total economic output? How fast must agriculture grow to avoid becoming a drag on industry and overall economic development? And will accelerated population growth help or make matters worse?

The modern version of the two-sector labor-surplus model was first developed by W. Arthur Lewis in 1955.[21] Lewis, like Ricardo before him, pays particular attention to the implications of surplus labor for income distribution. Our concern here, however, is with the relationship between industry and agriculture, and for that, we use a version of the model formulated by John Fei and Gustav Ranis in 1964.[22]

Our starting point is the agricultural sector and the **agricultural production function.** We assume two inputs, labor and land, produce an output, such as grain. The production function of Figure 4–8 is similar to, but differs slightly from, the production function for the Solow model shown in Figure 4–3. Instead of showing output as a function of capital per worker, agricultural output is shown as a function of labor per unit of land. Since any increase in labor must be combined with the existing stock of land (or perhaps new land of decreasing quality), the production function exhibits diminishing returns, just as the Solow model shows diminishing returns to additional capital for a given amount of labor. Put differently, in this model the **marginal product of labor** falls as the amount of labor increases, whereas in the Solow model the marginal product of *capital* falls as the capital stock increases.

[21]W. Arthur Lewis, *The Theory of Economic Growth* (Homewood, IL: Irwin, 1955).
[22]John C. H. Fei and Gustav Ranis, *Development of the Labor Surplus Economy* (Homewood, IL: Irwin, 1964).

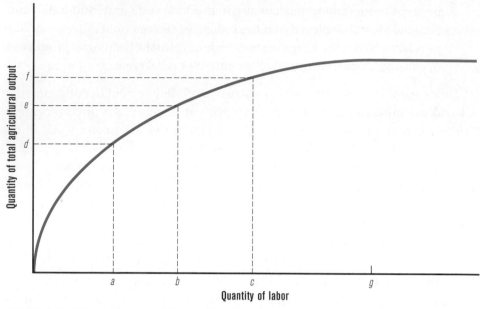

FIGURE 4-8. The Agricultural Production Function
In this figure, a rise in the labor force from *a* to *b* leads to an increase in output of *de*; an equal increase in labor from *b* to *c* leads to a smaller rise in output. At point *g*, further increases in the amount of labor used lead to no rise in output at all. Beyond point *g*, the marginal product of labor is zero or negative, so additional labor causes no increase or reduction in output.

The labor surplus model, however, takes diminishing returns to its extreme: it assumes that at some point, further additions of labor make zero (or even negative) contribution to output. The marginal product of labor (MPL) is allowed to fall to zero. This could happen if all arable land were fully utilized and already so many workers were available that adding new ones would not result in more grain being produced. This situation corresponds to points to the right of point *g* on the horizontal axis in Figure 4–8.

The next step is to show how rural wages are determined. The standard assumption in all labor surplus models beginning with Ricardo is that rural wages do not fall below a minimum level, regardless of how many workers are available. More specifically, the usual assumption is that rural wages do not fall below the **average product** of farm labor. The logic behind this view is that a member of a farm household will not look for work outside the household unless he or she can earn at least as much as he or she would receive by staying at home. At home, total food production would be divided equally among all members of the household, so each person consumes the average product of household production. A slightly different, but comparable concept is that wages are not allowed to fall below a **subsistence level.** In this view, no one would look for work off the farm for wages that were below the amount needed for a minimum level of subsistence. The minimum wage, however determined, sometimes is called an **institutionally fixed wage** to contrast it with wages determined by market forces.

If the MPL falls to zero while wages remain at some minimum level, a wedge emerges between the MPL and the wage rate. This is the key characteristic that distinguishes labor surplus models from standard neoclassical models with perfectly competitive markets (examined in the next subsection) in which the MPL equals the wage rate. Labor surplus models include not just the possibility that the MPL falls to zero, but situations in which the MPL is above zero but less than the rural minimum wage.

These concepts are presented in Figure 4–9, which is derived directly from Figure 4–8, but with several changes. To begin with, the horizontal axis is flipped, so that moving to the right represents a decline in the number of agricultural workers. At the origin, the horizontal axis represents the point where the entire labor force works in agriculture, with no one working in industry. Next, whereas the vertical axis in Figure 4-8 represents the total agricultural product, in Figure 4-9, it is converted to represent the marginal product per unit of labor. Thus, when moving to the right, as the number of agricultural workers declines, the MPL begins to increase (corresponding to Figure 4–8 in which increases in the number of workers leads to diminishing returns to labor).

The minimum or subsistence wage is represented by the dotted line *hi*. Agricultural wages remain at this level until the MPL (represented by the solid curve) rises above this minimum, which occurs at point *i*. Thereafter, agricultural wages rise, following the marginal product curve as more labor is drawn away from the sector. This curve plays a dual role: It shows both the agricultural

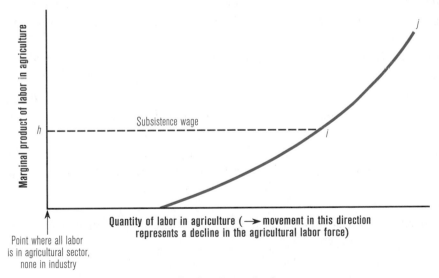

FIGURE 4-9. Modern Product of Labor in Agriculture
As the quantity of agricultural labor decreases, the marginal product increases.

wage and the minimum amount that industry must pay to lure workers off the farm. To hire workers away from the farm, factories have to pay at least as much as the workers are earning on the farm. Therefore, the line *hij* in Figure 4–9 can be thought of as the **supply curve of labor facing the industrial sector.** Actually the usual assumption is that the supply curve of labor in industry is a bit above the line *hij* because factories must pay farmers a bit more than they receive in agriculture to get them to move.

The key feature of this supply curve of labor is that, unlike more common supply curves, it does not rise continuously as one moves from left to right but instead has a substantial horizontal portion. Formally, this means that the supply curve of labor up to point *i* is **perfectly elastic. Elasticity** is a measure of responsiveness, equal to the percentage change in one variable (in this case, the supply of labor) arising from a percentage change in another variable (in this case, wages).[23] The elasticity becomes very large when small changes in wages induce very large changes in the supply of labor. Perfect elasticity occurs when the ratio of these two percentages equals infinity. From the point of view of the industrial sector, this means that this sector can hire as many workers as it wants without having to raise wages, at least until the amount of labor is increased beyond point *i*. To the right of this point, sometime called the *turning point,* industrial wages rise as firms draw more workers from the agricultural sector.

Figure 4–10 shows the supply and demand for labor for the industrial market. The supply curve *kk′* is taken directly from Figure 4–9, and shows the wages that industry has to pay to draw workers from agriculture. The amount $0k$ on the vertical axis in Figure 4–10 is assumed to be slightly higher than the subsistence wage in Figure 4–9, as discussed previously. The supply curve turns up when the withdrawal of labor from agriculture no longer can be accomplished without a decline in the agricultural output (when the MPL rises above 0), because at that point, the relative price of agricultural produce rises and this necessitates a commensurate rise in urban wages. In other words, since after the turning point agricultural production is falling, the price of food rises and industry must pay its workers more to compensate for the higher price of food. The demand curve for labor in industry *m* displays the usual downward-sloping quality and shows the wages that the industrial sector is willing to pay for different quantities of labor. This demand curve is determined by the marginal product of labor in

---

[23]More formally, the elasticity is the ratio of the percentage change in the supply of labor ($\Delta L/L$) to the percentage change in the wage rate ($\Delta W/W$):

$$\text{Elasticity} = \Delta L/L \div \Delta W/W$$

In the case of perfect elasticity, this ratio approaches infinity.

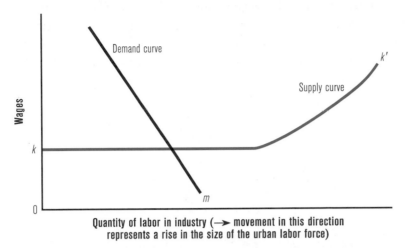

FIGURE 4-10. The Supply and Demand for Industrial Labor
The supply curve kk' is drawn directly from Figure 4–9. Demand m is
derived from the industrial production function.

industry and can be derived from the industrial production function. To simplify our exposition, we do not show the details of this derivation.

The final step is to combine Figures 4–8, 4–9, and 4–10 into a complete version of the model, which is shown in Figure 4–11. Panel A at the bottom of the
figure is the agricultural production function of Figure 4–8 with the horizontal
axis flipped. An increase in the number of agricultural workers is shown as a
movement from right to left from the origin (0 workers in agriculture) to point p,
which is the initial size of the total labor force. Many versions of this model use
total population rather than the labor force, and this switch has little effect if the
labor force is closely correlated with total population. Panel B shows the MPL
curve from Figure 4–9, and Panel C (at the top) shows the supply and demand
curves for labor in the industrial sector from Figure 4–10. In all three panels, a
movement from left to right represents both a decline in the agricultural labor
force and a rise in the industrial labor force; that is, a transfer of labor from agriculture to industry.

If a labor-surplus economy starts with its entire population in agriculture, it
can remove a large part of that population (pg) and move it to industry or other
employment with no reduction in farm output. Industry must pay those workers a wage a bit above subsistence (the difference between the vertical distance
$p''k$ in Panel C and $p'h$ in Panel B) to get the workers to move. As long as there is
some way of moving the food consumed by this labor from the rural to the
urban area, industrialization can proceed without reducing agricultural output,
implying an increase in total GDP.

As industry continues to grow, however, it eventually exhausts the supply of surplus labor. Further removal of labor from agriculture leads to a reduction in farm output. A shift in industrial labor demand to m in Panel C forces industry to pay higher wages to compensate workers for the higher price of food. The rise

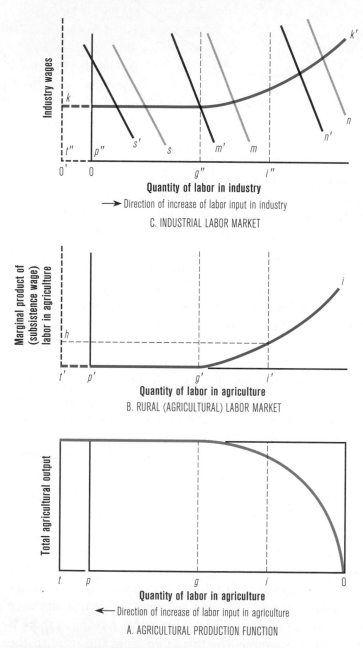

FIGURE 4-11. The Two-Sector Labor-Surplus Model
The limit imposed by the country's population (0 to p in Part A), coupled with the agricultural production function, allows us to analyze the effects of industry wages on the mix between agricultural and industrial labor.

in the price of agricultural output relative to the price of industrial output (which has not changed) sometimes is described as the terms of trade between industry and agriculture turning against industry and in favor of agriculture. The rising price of food as workers move to industry—that is, the shift in the terms of trade—accounts for the rise in the supply curve of labor between g'' and i'' in Panel C.

The Fei-Ranis model can be used to explore the implications of population growth and a rise in agricultural productivity, among other things. To simplify, if one assumes a close relationship between population and the labor force, then an increase in population from p to t increases the length of the horizontal axis in all three panels. Note, however, that additional workers (or a larger population) do not increase agricultural output at all. The elastic portion of both the urban and rural labor supply curves are extended by $p't'$ and $p''t''$, respectively, thus postponing the day when industrialization causes wages to rise.[24]

Most important, if the population rises with no increase in food output, the average amount of food available per capita falls. From the standpoint of everyone but a few employers who want to keep wages low and profits high, population growth is an unqualified disaster. Wages actually may fall in the urban areas, and the welfare of the great mass of farmers certainly falls. It is a model such as this, even if only imperfectly understood, that people often have in mind when they speak of population growth in wholly negative terms.

Britain's economy displayed labor surplus characteristics during Ricardo's time. In the middle of the twentieth century China, India, Indonesia, and some countries in Africa appear to have had surplus labor, but there are few such situations today. The most recent major example of a clear application of the model is China from the 1950s through the 1970s (see Box 4–4), but China's surplus labor was fully absorbed by the 1980s. More common is a situation in which a withdrawal of labor leads to a small but positive decline in agricultural production, which brings us to the neoclassical two-sector model.

The Neoclassical Two-Sector Model

The neoclassical model differs from the labor surplus model in two key ways: (1) The MPL in agriculture is never zero, and (2) there is no institutionally fixed minimum wage, so wages always equal the MPL.

---

[24]In the industrial labor supply and demand part of Figure 4–11, part C, it also is necessary to move the labor demand curves to the left since the 0 point on the horizontal axis has been moved to the left. These new demand curves, s', m', and n', therefore, really are the same as s, m, and n. That is, the quantity of labor demanded at any given price is the same for s' as s, and so on.

BOX 4-4 LABOR SURPLUS IN CHINA

In China, by the 1950s most arable land already was under cultivation and further increases in population and the labor force contributed little to increases in agricultural output. Urban wages rose in the early 1950s but then leveled off and remained unchanged for 20 years, between 1957 and 1977. If allowed to do so, tens of millions of farm laborers would happily have migrated to the cities despite urban wage stagnation. Only legal restrictions on rural-urban migration, backed by more than a little force, held this migration to levels well below what would have been required to absorb the surplus. Population growth that averaged 2 percent a year up until the mid-1970s continued to swell the ranks of those interested in leaving the countryside. In short, during this period China was a labor-surplus country.

China invested in agriculture but only enough to maintain, not to raise, per capita food production. The rural-urban migration that occurred was not fast enough to eliminate the agricultural labor surplus, but it was enough to require farmers to sell more of their production to the cities. Thus, the prices paid to farmers for their produce were gradually raised, while the prices paid by farmers for urban products remained constant or fell; that is, the rural-urban terms of trade shifted slowly but markedly in favor of agriculture.

To get out of this labor-surplus situation, the Chinese government after 1978 had to both accelerate the transfer of workers from agricultural to urban employment and take steps to keep the agricultural pool of surplus labor from constantly replenishing itself. Accelerating the growth of urban employment was accomplished by encouraging production of labor-intensive consumer goods (textiles, electronics, etc.) and service industries (restaurants, taxis, etc.). To feed this increase in urban population, the government increased food imports, shifted more investment funds to agriculture, and allowed a further improvement in rural-urban terms of trade.

To keep the rural pool of surplus labor from replenishing itself, the Chinese government attacked the surplus at its source through a massive (and controversial) effort to bring down the birth rate. By 1980, China's population growth rate had slowed from 2 to 1.2 percent a year, and the rate has stayed below 1.5 percent ever since. Rapid industrial and services growth in and around the cities and in the countryside itself has absorbed roughly 10 million new workers a year. In 1991, the workforce in agriculture reached its peak and declined steadily since then. The agricultural labor force that accounted for 70.5 percent of total employment in 1978 reached a key milestone in 1997, when it fell to 49.9 percent, signifying that for the first time in Chinese history, less than half the people employed in the country were farmers.

A simple neoclassical model is presented in Figure 4–12, showing the same three panels as Figure 4–11. The agricultural production function in Panel A is never flat, and the marginal product of labor curve in Panel B is always rising. Correspondingly, the supply curve of labor to industry in Panel C no longer has a horizontal section. At every point, the removal of workers from agriculture

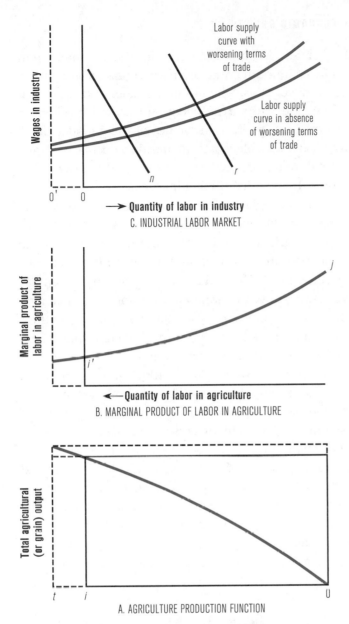

FIGURE 4-12. **Neoclassical Two-Sector Model**

The key difference between Figures 4–11 and 4–12 is the agricultural production function (Figure 4–12A). Limited land resources do lead to slightly diminishing returns in the agricultural sector, but the curve never flattens out; that is, the marginal product of labor never falls to a minimum subsistence or **institutionally fixed** wage in Figure 4–12B. Instead wages always are determined by the marginal product of labor in agriculture. Finally, the supply curve of labor to industry no longer has a horizontal section. Since the removal of labor from agriculture increases the marginal product of labor remaining in agriculture, industry must pay an amount equal to that marginal product plus a premium to get labor to migrate to the cities. The supply cuve of labor to industry rises for another reason as well. As labor is removed from agriculture, farm output falls; and to extract enough food from the agricultural sector to pay its workers, industry must pay higher and higher prices for food. Only if industry is in a position to import food from abroad will it be able to avoid these worsening terms of trade. If imports are not available, rising agricultural prices will lead to a higher value of output and hence higher wages for workers in agriculture. As in the labor-surplus case, industry will have to pay correspondingly higher wages to attract labor.

reduces agricultural production and increases the MPL for those remaining in agriculture. Industry must pay an amount equal to that marginal product (plus a premium) to get workers to move. Thus, whereas in the labor surplus model industrial production can increase without reducing agricultural production (leading to an unambiguous increase in GNP), in the neoclassical model an increase in industrial production can take place only alongside a decrease in agricultural production. The total value of GNP rises only to the extent that industrial production rises more than agricultural output falls.

The implications of population or labor force growth in the neoclassical model are quite different from what they were in the labor surplus model. An increase in population and labor in agriculture raises farm output (see dashed line t in Figure 4–12A), since the agricultural production function continues to rise with more labor and never flattens out. Thus, in a neoclassical model, population growth is not such a wholly negative phenomenon. The increase in labor is much less of a drain on food availability, since that labor is able to produce much or all of its own requirements, and there is no surplus of labor that can be transferred without a consequent reduction in agricultural output.

If industry is to develop successfully, simultaneous efforts must be made to ensure that agriculture grows fast enough to feed workers in both the rural and urban sectors at ever-higher levels of consumption and prevent the terms of trade from turning against industry. A stagnant agricultural sector with little new investment or technological progress causes the wages of urban workers to rise rapidly and thereby cuts into profits and the funds available for industrial development. In other words, investments in improved agricultural technology or rural roads (which reduce the cost of transporting farm inputs and outputs, including food) help the industrial sector by reducing its costs. Whereas in the labor-surplus model policy makers can ignore agriculture until the surplus of labor is exhausted, in the neoclassical model there must be a balance between industry and agriculture.

SUMMARY

- Formal growth models provide a more precise mechanism to explore the contributions to economic growth of both factor accumulation and productivity gains. These models allow us to better understand the implications of changes in saving rates, population growth rates, technological change, and other related factors on output and growth.
- The Harrod-Domar model assumes a fixed-coefficients production function, which helps simplify the model but introduces strict rigidity in the mix of capital and labor needed for any level of output. In this

model, growth is directly related to saving in inverse proportion to the incremental capital-output ratio (ICOR).

- The Harrod-Domar model usefully emphasizes the role of saving, but at the same time overemphasizes its importance by implying that saving (and investment) is sufficient for sustained growth, which it is not. Also, the model does not directly address changes in productivity. In addition, the model's assumption of a fixed ICOR leads to increasing inaccuracy over time as the structure of production evolves and the marginal product of capital changes.

- The Solow model improves on some of the weaknesses in the Harrod-Domar framework and has become the most influential growth model in economics. The model allows for more flexibility in the mix of capital and labor in the production process and introduces the powerful concept of diminishing marginal product of capital. It allows for exploration of the impact on growth of changes in the saving rate, the population growth rate, and technological change. The model helps to provide a deeper understanding of a much wider range of growth experiences than the Harrod-Domar model. Nevertheless, the model does not provide a full explanation for growth. It does not provide insights into the more fundamental causes of factor accumulation and productivity growth and, as a one-sector model, does not address the issue of resource allocation across sectors.

- The Solow model has several powerful implications, including (1) poor countries have the *potential* to grow relatively rapidly; (2) growth rates tend to slow as incomes rise; (3) across countries that share important common characteristics, the incomes of poor countries potentially can converge with those of the rich countries; and (4) acquiring new technology is central to both accelerating and sustaining economic growth.

- Two-sector models provide insights into the interaction between agriculture and industry. The labor surplus model suggests that industry can grow without reducing agricultural output. It also concludes that, where there is surplus labor and limited ability to expand food production, population growth can be a disaster. Most economies, however, do not have a surplus of labor, so industrial expansion occurs alongside a fall in agricultural production, and population growth does not necessarily have a negative impact on economic growth.

5

States and Markets

On March 6, 1957, with great celebration, Ghana became the first sub-Saharan African country to gain its independence. Optimism was in the air: Ghana was the world's largest cocoa producer, it had the highest per capita income in sub-Saharan Africa (except South Africa), and its foreign exchange reserves were equivalent to over three years of imports. Ghana's prospects looked bright, and many observers believed that it had all the ingredients to outperform most other developing countries, including those in Asia.

But it was not to be. President Kwame Nkrumah, who was brilliant in leading Ghana to independence, proved to be much less effective as an economic and political leader. In a push for rapid industrialization, Nkrumah introduced extensive state intervention in the economy, with many controlled prices, restrictions on trade and investment, and state-owned enterprises. Based on its cocoa earnings, Ghana borrowed heavily to establish a wide range of industries designed to substitute for imports and process many of Ghana's raw materials. But cocoa prices collapsed in the mid-1960s, and the state's heavy hand led to widespread corruption, poor investment decisions, distorted prices, and growing instability. In 1966, a group of army officers overthrew Nkrumah in what was only the first of a series of coups and countercoups over the next 17 years. The economy fluctuated wildly, with growth plunging to –6 percent in 1966, then climbing to 7 percent in 1970 as cocoa prices recovered, only to collapse again to –5 percent two years later and to a disastrous –14 percent in 1975. By 1983, the economy had collapsed. Cocoa production was only half as large as it once had been, inflation exceeded 120 percent, "growth" had been worse than –6 percent for three years in a row, and per capita income was about one-third lower than it had been twenty six years before at independence.

In 1983, President Jerry Rawlings (who had taken power himself in a coup two years earlier as Flight Lieutenant Rawlings), with few options at his disposal, turned to the International Monetary Fund (IMF) and World Bank for financial assistance and, in return, accepted their strict conditions for changes in economic policy. Rawlings introduced Ghana's Economic Recovery Program, which in many ways was a prototype for reform programs introduced by many other developing countries under the auspices of the IMF and World Bank in the 1980s and early 1990s. The reforms were widespread: Ghana devalued its currency, freed interest rates from restrictions, and substantially reduced its budget deficit. It removed or modified a range of price controls (including raising the price paid to cocoa farmers), reduced tariffs on many imported products, and otherwise took steps to liberalize the trade regime. It partially or fully privatized dozens of enterprises over several years, including transport, the marketing of cocoa, banking, and other areas. The IMF and World Bank heralded Ghana's progress in reforms and predicted that these changes would lay the foundation for greater macroeconomic stability, sustained economic growth, and a reduction in poverty.

The results were a clear improvement and yet a disappointment to many advocates of reform. The economy stabilized: inflation fell (although it still remained relatively high, above 20 percent), the trade deficit shrank, and foreign exchange reserves grew. Growth became far less volatile and was positive each year after 1983. But the rapid growth that many had hoped for was elusive. Per capita income grew 1.6 percent per year in the ten years from 1985 through 1994—certainly an improvement over the collapse of the 1970s and early 1980s, but hardly the rapid growth seen in many other developing countries. Subsequent growth has been a bit better, averaging 2.2 percent from 1995 through 2003, but still not what reformists and their sponsors in the IMF and World Bank had forecast. Ghana's per capita income in 2003 was about what it had been in 1960, and nearly half the population lived under the international poverty line of $1 a day.

Ghana's experience was in many ways typical of a large number of developing countries. Heavy state intervention and control, combined with volatile world prices and other shocks, led to poor economic performance in the 1970s. There was a widespread view that governments in too many countries had mismanaged their economies, tolerated excessive inflation, and intervened far too heavily in setting prices and taking over productive enterprises. The 1980s saw a significant shift away from government intervention to more market-based reforms through **stabilization** and **structural adjustment programs** supported by financing from the IMF and World Bank. There was widespread agreement on both the general thrust and the specific details of these programs, so much so that the reform agenda became known as the **Washington Consensus,** a term that for many people soon became synonymous with neoclassical and pure free-market economics.[1] However, many countries achieved stabilization but not the rapid growth that had been envisioned.

At about the same time, substantial economic changes were happening in China and Vietnam, followed later by revolutionary political and economic reforms in many other countries following the fall of the Berlin Wall in 1989 and the dissolution of Soviet Union. Prior to these events, these countries rejected market forces in favor of **centrally planned,** or **command economies.** The inefficiency of the command economy led to slow growth or outright stagnation and leaders in these countries concluded that they had to move toward some kind of market system. As the 1990s unfolded, these countries increasingly turned to the World Bank, the IMF, and Western economists for help in thinking through what a movement toward a market economy would involve. Ideas honed in part on the experience with Latin America and on neoclassical economic theory were applied to the very different circumstances of Eastern Europe and the nations of the former Soviet Union. There were major differences over the pace and sequence with which reforms should be carried out, but at least in much of the international community, there was a consensus on what the elements of the reforms should be.

In this chapter, we examine the long-standing debates about the role of markets and the state in development, and the widespread economic reforms introduced around the world in the 1980s and 1990s. We begin with a general discussion about the advantages of markets, the potential for market failures, and government's potential role for helping to correct or minimize those failures. We then explore the reform programs of the 1980s and 1990s, the emergence of the "Washington Consensus" and the retreat from that consensus as reform programs were only partially successful. Most economists conclude that many of these market-oriented reforms are necessary but that they are not sufficient to lay the foundation for sustained growth in many developing countries.

MARKETS AND MARKET FAILURES

Powerful arguments support the view that most (although not necessarily all) economic activities should be governed by markets, rather than by administrative intervention by the state. These arguments are based on the principles of market economies familiar to those who have taken an introductory course in microeconomics.

---

[1]As we discuss later in the chapter, the term was coined by John Williamson, "What Washington Means by Policy Reform," in John Williamson, ed., *Latin American Adjustment: How Much Has Happened?* (Washington, DC: Institute for International Economics, 1990).

First and most important, markets that meet certain conditions can allocate thousands of different products among consumers, reflecting their preferences, and thousands of productive inputs among producers, getting the maximum output from available inputs. These complex allocation tasks, if handled by the state, as in the former Soviet Union, require large government bureaucracies with attendant high costs for decision making and control.

Second, markets frequently are more flexible than governments and better able to adapt to changing conditions and quickly provide incentives for growth, innovation, and structural change that governments either cannot manage or are slow to achieve. A change in the price of an output or input leads to an almost immediate response by profit-oriented producers and consumers. In contrast, when government bureaucracies are in charge of allocation, changes often must wait for a political consensus to evolve before taking action.

Third, markets enhance competition, which motivates producers (farmers, industrial firms, service industries, and individual workers) to operate as efficiently as possible and reduce costs (raise productivity) whenever they can. When market forces do not guide production decisions, the incentive for productivity gains is weaker. Price distortions draw labor, capital, and other factors into less-productive employment. Government regulations establish incentives for rent seeking and bribery; entrepreneurs and managers then spend more time dealing with and influencing government officials and less time making their plants run more efficiently. When governments themselves enter into production through state-owned enterprises, the profit motive of their managers is diluted by political and bureaucratic concerns.

Fourth, reliance on markets provides greater scope for the dispersion of economic power. Decision making in a market system is decentralized down to producers and consumers rather than centralized at upper levels of the government bureaucracy. Decentralization puts decision making closer to the actual producers, who are usually the persons best informed about how their firms should respond to particular situations. The resulting economic pluralism, in turn, is one element tending to encourage democratic government and individual liberties.

Despite these substantial advantages, in some circumstances, markets do not perform well on their own. These circumstances, as pointed out already, were widely believed to apply to most developing economies in the 1950s and 1960s. Economists have identified a number of such **market failures** that can apply to any economy, whether rich or poor, but sometimes are more pervasive in low-income settings:

1. Modern economies often are marked by growing concentration and **monopoly** or **oligopoly power,** where one or a few sellers gain control of a market. In developing countries, **economies of scale** (the decline of unit

costs as output rises) may be so large relative to market size that monopoly is inevitable in some industries, while oligopoly is the rule in many others. In much of mining, manufacturing, utilities, airlines, communications, and wholesale trade, monopoly or oligopoly are common. In large economies, governments can try to limit the exercise of monopoly pricing in some sectors by regulating the size of firms and breaking up the largest ones. In all economies, competing imports, actual or potential, curtail monopoly power in manufacturing industries and in some services by forcing domestic firms to meet competition from abroad. If the government cannot prevent monopoly pricing, it can capture some of the benefits from monopolists by taxing the resulting profits at high rates. What often happens is that corruption and cronyism maintain private monopolies. In some instances, state enterprises become monopoly suppliers and the underlying inefficiencies remain unresolved.

2. **External economies** are the benefits of a project, such as a hydroelectric dam, enjoyed by people not connected with the project, such as the downstream farmer whose production rises because the dam prevents floods. External economies are important benefits in many infrastructure investments, such as dams, roads, railroads, and irrigation schemes. Although in principle the beneficiaries could be charged for all external benefits, in practice they cannot be. It may be difficult and costly to control access to the facilities and difficult even to identify the beneficiaries or the extent to which they benefit. Because private investors cannot easily charge for externalities and such projects take large investments with long repayment periods, private investors are unlikely to undertake them. Governments do so instead.

3. **External diseconomies** are costs not borne by the firm. The pollution of air and water is a widely recognized problem in the industrial world and increasingly so in developing countries. Polluters could bear all the costs of reduced emissions and effluents, but they benefit only as average members of the population of the affected area, so have little incentive to control pollution on their own. The same situation arises with **common resources,** such as forests, fisheries, or open grazing land, that can be used by many people who do not own these resources.

4. Markets may not facilitate the changes in economic structure required for development. The most frequently cited example is the **infant industry,** one brand new to a society, whose productivity increases and costs fall over time because managers and workers are "learning by doing." Although the industry can become profitable over several years, investors may be unwilling to finance the new firms. This can justify a **protective tariff** (a tax on competing imports) or **initial subsidy** (where the government bears some startup costs) to make an infant industry more profitable

in the short run. But the long-run gains in productivity may be realized only if the tariff or subsidy is gradually reduced and the new industry eventually is forced to compete with imports (or other domestic firms). The infant industry argument was a major rationale for the introduction and widespread use of restrictions in the form of tariffs and quotas on the import of industrial products in a wide range of developing countries beginning in most of these countries soon after they achieved independence.

5. **Underdeveloped institutions** exclude large numbers of potential consumers and producers from the market. In developed economies, consumers "vote" with their dollars for the goods the economy should produce. But, in developing economies, remoteness, poverty, and illiteracy prevent many subsistence farmers, rural laborers, and their families from "voting" in goods, services, and financial markets, so these groups have little influence on the types of goods and services supplied. Special efforts are required to bring them into the monetary economy. Even for those in the monetary economy, there is **inadequate information** about markets and products; and so many consumers remain ignorant about the goods and services being offered, workers know little about job opportunities, and producers cannot easily learn about changing market conditions. Similarly, investors, producers, and traders find it difficult to hedge against the **risks** of doing business in changing circumstances, because financial, commodity, and insurance markets are underdeveloped or missing altogether. Weak judicial systems may mean that contracts are not honored or property rights are not enforced, adding to investment uncertainties. The government may have to encourage or establish some of these missing institutions to help markets function better.

6. Economywide markets for labor, credit, and foreign exchange do not always adjust rapidly enough to balance supply and demand as conditions change, and **macroeconomic imbalances** characterize every modern economy. Wages that adjust slowly, low short-run elasticities of supply or demand, and misinformed expectations that can cause shortages and surpluses—all these problems may require government intervention, such as monetary management, fiscal policy, exchange rate adjustments, and incomes policies. We will learn more about such **macroeconomic management** tools throughout this book.

7. To a considerable extent, market economies require intervention not only because of inherent market failures but also because societies impose on them **national goals** that even well-functioning markets cannot satisfy. Establishing policies that favor poorer majorities over entrepreneurially accomplished minorities is one example. If the ethnic Chinese in Malaysia and Indonesia or the ethnic Indians and Pakistanis ("Asians") in Kenya and Tanzania already dominate the production and distribution

system of those countries, then unguided economic growth may further improve their relative position over time. To expand the role of the indigenous majority and allow it to "catch up" requires government intervention. Markets might not be very effective in stimulating rapid growth that automatically generates demands for the output of small farmers and the self-employed, creates jobs to absorb poor workers, and generally helps to relieve poverty. Nevertheless, these market forces are often led by—and hence favor—people and firms that already are successful. Thus, market-oriented growth may concentrate incomes. If the redistribution of income from one group to another becomes a government priority, intervention may be appropriate.

There is no debate between market adherents and those who favor more intervention over the existence of these market failures, but there is considerable debate over their relative importance and the right policy approaches to respond to these failures. Most economists would agree that market failures tend to be more prevalent in low-income countries where infrastructure is inadequate, markets are segmented (e.g., roads do not fully connect buyers and sellers, so markets do not fully clear), institutions are weak, contract enforcement is incomplete, and markets are small. Thus, often a theoretical case may be made for government interventions to overcome market failures, and sometimes carefully designed interventions can help make markets work better or guard against some of the potentially adverse outcomes of markets. Unfortunately, sometimes interventions can make the situation worse, and government failures can outweigh market failures. The particular interventions governments choose are not always ideal, and they often work against the goals they are supposed to achieve. Moreover, sometimes governments misuse these arguments to support interventions that have other underlying purposes, such as exerting political control over minority groups or ensuring easy profits for political cronies. Even when market failures are recognized, there is ample room for debate about what actions, if any, are desirable for governments to take. These debates and differing views about the capability of governments and the desirability of having governments intervene in markets have led to changes over time in the most prevalent views of the role of governments and markets in developing countries.

MARKET PESSIMISTS AND MARKET OPTIMISTS

Perceptions about market failures of various kinds and a lack of faith in the efficacy of markets were major reasons why so many developing countries in the 1950s and 1960s chose to introduce a wide variety of government controls over the economy.[2] The roots of market pessimism go back to the Great Depression of the 1930s and the period following World War II. The Depression destroyed confidence in market capitalism. The antidote to depression offered by John Maynard Keynes—and accepted for decades by most economists and governments—was active intervention to stimulate the economy through fiscal policy. Price controls and quantity rationing helped guide the U.S. economy through World War II. In the 1930s and 1940s, when war and widespread trade barriers made export-oriented development strategies almost impossible, building one's own industrial capacity behind high tariff walls seemed to make sense.

In Asia and Africa, economies had been highly regulated by the colonial powers before and after the war. After independence in 1947, India's new leaders followed the interventionist tendencies of Fabian socialism and the British Raj for a planned and regulated economy. As other countries in Asia and Africa emerged from colonialism over the next two decades, many of them emulated India. The Soviet Union's rapid industrialization under communism also impressed the leaders of these newly emerging countries. The older, independent countries of Latin America, especially Argentina, Brazil, and Mexico, had taken advantage of the war to build their own industries to supply goods once imported from the United States. After the war, Argentine dictator Juan Peron and others built on this base a highly protected manufacturing system that spurred industrial growth for a time.

Economic thought encouraged these tendencies. Underlying the views of many thinkers, ancient and modern, is the view that markets lead to outcomes that are arbitrary, capricious, or worse. Karl Marx's belief in the chaotic nature of markets had a major influence on those who designed the economic systems of the Soviet Union and China. Three strands of twentieth-century development literature reinforced the case for a strong government role. First, Paul Rosenstein-Rodan's 1943 theory of **"balanced growth"** or the **"big push"** argued that, to create markets for industrial output, all industries would have to grow together, each employing workers who would demand the output of other industries. The market alone would never yield such a big push, so government planning, direct investment, and control would be necessary. Even Albert Hirschman's 1958 retort—that **unbalanced growth** and induced shortages provided a more-effective path to industrialization—invited intervention, import protection, and large government investment in infrastructure.

A second and more influential strand ran through the trade literature. Latin American economist Raul Prebisch and European economist Hans Singer argued

[2]Parts of this section are drawn from Michael Roemer and Steven Radelet, "Macroeconomic Reform in Developing Countries," in Dwight Perkins and Michael Roemer, eds., *Reforming Economic Systems in Developing Countries,* Harvard Institute for International Development (Cambridge, MA: Harvard University Press, 1991).

that the terms of trade for primary product producers—the relative prices of their exports compared to their imports—had been declining for decades and were destined to continue to decline, and that world demand for primary products was likely to grow only slowly.[3] This combination would condemn developing countries to slow growth or stagnation in both exports and income. This **export pessimism** was taken as strong support for a strategy of **import substitution,** which required government intervention to protect local manufacturers. Since protection had been the dominant strategy for industrialization in Europe and North America in the nineteenth and early twentieth centuries, import substitution seemed to be a promising course of action.

The third strand suggested that agriculture was not a promising road to development and implicitly encouraged a rapid shift to industry. Perhaps the most influential article of all was W. Arthur Lewis's 1954 theory of the labor-surplus economy, described in Chapter 4. Although Lewis did not advocate intervention, one inference of his theory was the need to transform a developing economy rapidly away from traditional, stagnant agriculture toward dynamic industry. These changes, as the Soviet Union and China appeared to show, could be accomplished by a command economy.

These historic and intellectual tendencies influenced many governments to try a range of interventions in search of economic development, often with the support of Western aid agencies and academics: protective tariffs and other import controls; taxes on primary exports; controls over prices of key commodities, interest rates, and the exchange rate; minimum wage and benefit regulations; government permits and licenses to control key investments; government ownership of key industries, and so on. By the early 1970s, the vast majority of developing countries were mixed economies with a strong dose of controls. Governments, not markets, often occupied the commanding heights of the economy.

The pendulum began to swing away from strong government controls and interventions toward more market-based approaches in the 1970s. The roll call of developing countries undertaking market reforms—Bolivia and Chile, Ghana and Tanzania, India and Indonesia—grew throughout the 1980s and 1990s. In the communist world, China led the way after the death of Mao Zedong in 1976. The end of Soviet domination led the countries of Eastern Europe to seek market solutions that would make them more like Western Europe and allow them to join the European Union.

---

[3]United Nations (by Raul Prebish), *The Economic Development of Latin America and Its Principal Problems* (Lake Success, NY: United Nations, 1950); and Hans W. Singer, "The Distribution of Trade between Investing and Borrowing Countries," *American Economic Review* 40 (1950), 470–85. See also Ragnar Nurske, *Equilibrium Growth and the World Economy* (Cambridge, MA: Harvard University Press, 1961).

By the 1960s, many neoclassical economists began to promote the virtues of market-oriented, outward-looking development. Chicago economist Theodore Schultz won his Nobel Prize partly for work showing that so-called traditional farmers were rational decision makers whose techniques were well adapted to the conditions and constraints they faced. One implication was that market incentives, accompanied by new technologies, would induce farmers to change their methods and raise productivity.[4] By the late 1970s, a series of country studies by trade economists Bela Balassa, Jagdish Bhagwati, and Anne Krueger had established a strong empirical case that outward-looking strategies work better than import substitution.[5] At the core of the argument for market-guided development is the proposition of neoclassical economics that markets create competition and competition stimulates productive investments.

The rapid and sustained growth of the East Asian "newly industrialized countries," beginning in the mid-1960s, also seemed to support a move to more market-based approaches. Hong Kong, Singapore, South Korea, and Taiwan all achieved economic growth rates of 6 to 9 percent a year for many years. Hong Kong and Singapore had economies governed largely by market forces. South Korea and to a lesser degree Taiwan used more mixed approaches, with the government intervening forcefully in some areas, while allowing markets to work in others (Box 5–1). What these four had in common was a strategy of depending heavily on export growth to lead development. This "outward-looking" strategy is explored in Chapter 19. In essence, by inducing private firms to seek markets overseas, these countries took advantage of the large world markets and simultaneously exposed their manufacturing firms to the discipline of competition in international markets. This competitive industrial base permitted the four East Asian countries to sail through the economic crisis of the 1970s and 1980s with relative ease, although many did not fare so well in the crisis of 1997–98.[6]

Perhaps the most important reason for the push toward more market-based approaches was the poor performance of countries that had relied on a stronger and more central role for governments in the market. Protection and import substitution spurred industrial growth at first, but then industrial development sput-

[4]Theodore W. Schultz, *Transforming Traditional Agriculture* (New Haven, CT: Yale University Press, 1964).

[5]Bela Balassa, "Exports and Economic Growth: Further Evidence," *Journal of Development Economics* 5, no. 2 (1978), 181–89; Jagdish Bhagwati, *Foreign Exchange Regimes and Economic Development: Anatomy and Consequences of Exchange Control Regimes* (Cambridge, MA: Ballinger Press, 1978); and Anne O. Krueger, *Foreign Exchange Regimes and Economic Development: Liberalization Attempts and Consequences* (Cambridge, MA: Ballinger Press, 1978).

[6]The World Bank on various occasions attempted to draw lessons for other developing countries from this East Asian experience. See World Bank, *The East Asian Miracle* (New York: Oxford University Press, 1993) and the follow-on volume done after the financial crisis, Joseph E. Stiglitz and Shahid Yusuf, eds., *Rethinking the East Asian Miracle* (Oxford: Oxford University Press, 2001).

South Korea in the 1960s and 1970s pursued an industrial policy that involved heavy intervention by the government to promote exports, in general, and specific industries, in particular. The government provided bank loans to favored industries at below-market rates, gave these industries special access to government-controlled foreign exchange and imports, and helped build the infrastructure they required. The president of the country even met monthly with the heads of the major industries to review and help solve their problems, many of them related to intervention by government in their efforts to expand. The government saw itself as correcting for market failures, even though many of these market failures were the creation of earlier and continuing government controls that were part of its import-substituting policies.

These industrial policies in the 1960s and 1970s appear to have worked reasonably well, although the heavy industry and chemical industry drive of the 1970s remains controversial to this day. President Park Chung Hee, who led this effort, kept politics and corruption out of most of these industrial policy decisions. Because he ran an authoritarian regime supported mainly by a modern army, he felt no need to use industrial policies to pay off his political supporters. By the early 1980s, however, many Korean economists and others felt that this activist government industrial policy was causing too many economic distortions and the country should move toward a more market-oriented system. Moving toward a market system proved to be difficult because of promises made to private companies that had carried out the government's wishes in the past. They felt that they had an implicit guarantee that they would be helped out if, by doing the government's bidding, they got into trouble. In the 1980s, they did get into trouble and the government spent much of its time in that decade providing subsidies and other means of support to these firms.

By the 1990s, Korea had a democratic government led, from 1992 to 1997, by President Kim Young Sam, who had little interest in an activist industrial policy. Like his predecessors, however, he saw how these policies could be used to raise large sums of money to support his political campaigns. Increasingly the criteria for getting government support for a particular firm or industry depended on whether that firm contributed to the political campaigns. Such contributions existed in the 1960s and 1970s as well, but they were not allowed to influence major industrial policy decisions. By contrast, in the 1990s, industrial policy interventions were driven more by politics than by a concern for building efficient, competitive industries. Industrial policy in the earlier period had produced such firms as POSCO, one of the largest and most efficient steel companies in the world, a firm that remained profitable right through the Asian financial crisis of 1997–99. The industrial policy in the 1990s produced such firms as the Hanbo steel company, whose bankruptcy contributed in a significant way to Korea's involvement in the Asian financial crisis.

Finally, in the 1998–2004 period, the Korean government under two new presidents, Kim Dae Jung and then Roh Moo-Hyun, began to make a major effort to get the government out of the business of supporting particular industries and firms. The objective was to create a level playing field for all but to do so without triggering another financial crisis caused by the collapse of the older firms that had relied so much on government support. Moving away from extensive government intervention and relying entirely on market forces, however, is not as simple as simply telling the government to stop intervening. In many cases, the government felt it had to introduce new interventions to undo the damage of previous ones.

tered in country after country.[7] Price interventions generally had unintended consequences: High protective barriers bred inefficient manufacturing; interest rate ceilings suppressed the evolution of financial systems, depressed monetary savings, and encouraged credit rationing and unproductive investment; minimum wages, if they had any impact at all, stifled employment growth and exacerbated inequalities; and ceilings on food prices and taxes on agricultural exports discouraged farmers and retarded productivity growth in agriculture.

Controls by government engendered political and bureaucratic reactions by private entrepreneurs and managers, instead of the innovative and competitive behavior needed for sustained development. Regulations created higher-than-necessary profits, which economists call **rents,** for those able to gain favorable treatment from bureaucrats or to evade the rules. Widespread corruption and other forms of **rent seeking** diverted the energy of entrepreneurs, investors, managers, and traders from productive activities; wasted scarce resources; and reduced economic growth.[8] The almost universal proliferation of public enterprises into everything from hotels to steel mills often extended ineffectual bureaucratic behavior into activities that private enterprises could have handled more effectively and more efficiently.

---

[7]In 1970, influential studies by economists at Williams College and Oxford University chronicled the failures of import substitution and all the interventions that generally accompanied it. See Henry J. Bruton, "The Import Substitution Strategy of Economic Development," *Pakistan Development Review* 10 (1970), 123–46; and Ian Little, Tibor Scitovsky, and Maurice Scott, *Industry and Trade in Some Developing Countries* (London: Oxford University Press, 1970).

[8]Anne O. Krueger, "The Political Economy of the Rent-Seeking Society," *American Economic Review* 64, no. 3 (1974).

The explosive rise of oil prices in the 1970s, then their precipitate fall in the 1980s, and the accompanying accumulations of unserviceable debt exposed the failures of some interventionist development strategies and led to the first developing-country debt crisis. By the early 1980s, many developing countries faced stagnating or negative growth, growing budget and trade deficits, rising inflation, increasing debt burdens, and diminishing foreign exchange reserves. Whereas economic growth for all low-income countries averaged 1.8 percent per year between 1960 and 1971, between 1972 and 1984, growth fell to 0.6 percent per year. In sub-Saharan Africa, average growth fell from 2.6 percent to –0.2 percent. Large macroeconomic imbalances could not be sustained as financing options disappeared. Under these circumstances, many countries had little choice but to adjust their policies and restructure their economies, which led to a major rethinking on the appropriate balance between government interventions and more-open markets.

IMPLEMENTING MARKET REFORMS

As countries began to introduce adjustment and reform programs in response to these problems, big questions remained on the details: how much to adjust and reform, in what way, and with what role for governments and markets? Countries turned to the **International Monetary Fund (IMF)** and **World Bank** for financing, which the two organizations provided if countries implemented specific adjustment and reform measures. These two multilateral organizations, founded in the aftermath of the Great Depression and World War II, became the major sources of financing for low-income and many middle-income countries in the 1980s. The IMF's main purpose is to provide temporary financing to countries facing significant balance-of-payments problems. IMF funds are used to shore up the country's foreign exchange reserves and stabilize the currency, not to finance investment or development projects. By contrast, the World Bank provides direct development finance for roads, schools, agriculture, and a wide variety of other projects and programs. To receive financing from the IMF and World Bank, countries must agree to undertake policy reforms, some of them controversial, typically aimed at reducing the government budget deficit, reducing inflation, opening the economy to more trade, privatizing state-owned companies, and other reforms.

The reform programs implemented under the auspices of the IMF and World Bank had two broad components: stabilization and structural adjustment. **Stabilization** refers to correcting imbalances in foreign payments, government budgets, and the money supply, with the aim of controlling inflation and otherwise reducing macroeconomic instability. **Structural adjustment** is much broader and includes reforms aimed at changing the structure of the economy to be more market based, produce more tradable goods, and increase economic efficiency and flexibility. Structural adjustment programs generally included privatization, liberalization, deregulation, trade reform, and other broad economic reforms. The specific details of stabilization and structural adjustment policies differ across countries. In the sections that follow, we describe some of the main components introduced as parts of these programs.

STABILIZATION OF THE MACROECONOMY

A well-functioning market economy requires macroeconomic stability. Large and chronic budget deficits absorb private savings and foreign funds that are needed for the productive investments so central to economic growth. The need to finance budget deficits often leads to the printing of money and inflation, which increases risks, further undermines investment, and imposes particular hardships for the poor.

Inflation distorts relative prices and the decisions based on them. Groups organized to wield political power, such as unionized labor, large firms, the military, and civil servants, compete intensely to protect their shares of the national income. The result is a distortion of relative prices away from scarcity values to reflect instead the outcome of these political struggles. Relative prices themselves become volatile and so reduce the information they convey to participants in the economy. For example, **real interest rates** (interest rates corrected for inflation) can become negative, which reduces the supply of long-term funds for investment. Exchange rates can become **overvalued:** As the local currency (say, pesos) loses its value through inflation, the central bank offers too few pesos to people selling dollars, which discourages exports and encourages imports. In both instances excess demand arises—for credit when real interest rates are negative; for foreign exchange when currencies are overvalued— leading to nonmarket forms of allocation and a less-productive use of these vital resources.

These distortions and the uncertainty about future rates of inflation cause people either to acquire land, gold, and other assets whose prices rise with inflation or transfer their financial wealth overseas. As a result, investment in productive assets tends to fall. With rapid inflation, entrepreneurs and managers spend more time trying to profit from inflation and devote correspondingly less energy to producing more efficiently. After all, large and sustained productivity gains might reduce costs by 3 to 5 percent a year, not much compared to rates of inflation from tens to hundreds of percent a year. High inflation is particularly bad for the poor and those on fixed incomes, since they are much less able to move financial assets to offshore banks or purchase land and gold as means to protect themselves from rapidly rising prices.

Strong evidence demonstrates that macroeconomic stability is necessary, although far from sufficient, to promote economic growth. Chapter 3 discussed the relationship between macroeconomic and political stability and economic growth, and Figure 3–2 showed the strong negative relationship between inflation and growth in the 1990s. Between 1990 and 2003, countries with inflation rates above 15 percent averaged economic growth per capita of –0.4 percent; those with inflation rates below 15 percent averaged growth of 1.7 percent per year. In the Democratic Republic of the Congo (formerly Zaire), inflation averaged an astonishing 2,800 percent per year. Meanwhile, economic "growth" averaged –7.2 percent per year, meaning that over 13 years average income fell by more than half.

Stabilization programs are designed to stem inflation and correct the other imbalances associated with it, notably deficits in the government budget and the balance of foreign payments. Typical IMF stabilization programs contain some or all of the following remedies:

1. A reduction in the government's budget deficit, through higher taxes and reduced expenditure, since deficits are financed either by money creation or borrowing from private savers, which "crowds out" private investment.
2. Restrictions on central bank credit to the government and commercial banks, to control growth of the money supply.
3. Adjustment of the exchange rate, either through devaluation (shifting to a new fixed exchange rate requiring more local currency per dollar) or through a float (allowing the exchange rate to move based on supply and demand conditions), which raises the price of foreign exchange in domestic currency and helps correct balance-of-payments deficits by stimulating exports and restraining the demand for imports.
4. Removing price controls (or adjusting administered prices) so that markets can reduce the distortions in relative prices. Interest rates, food prices, utility rates, fuel prices, and transport fares often are affected.
5. Introducing targets for restraining wage increases, since wages that increase faster than productivity push up the cost of production and contribute to inflation (Box 5–2).

When deficits in the budget or balance of payments occur, they must be either reduced through economic adjustment or financed. The IMF provides loans to help finance the balance-of-payments gap, which is intended to ease the pain of stabilization by permitting the corrective measures to be less drastic than they otherwise would have to be. However, the disbursement of IMF loans is contingent on successful implementation of the measures designed to stabilize the

BOX 5-2 STABILIZATION THAT WORKED: BOLIVIA, 1985-86

From August 1984 to August 1985, prices in Bolivia rose by 20,000 percent, the most rapid inflation in Latin American history. During September 1985, inflation was stopped cold and prices actually began to fall. How did this happen?

The hyperinflation of 1984–85 was the culmination of events under the regime of President Siles Zuazo, which in 1982 became Bolivia's first elected government in 18 years. Declining foreign aid and commercial bank inflows, combined with rising international interest rates and debt payments, led to a growing payments deficit: Net resource flows into Bolivia declined by 10 percent of GDP over three years to a net outflow of $190 million in 1983. To compensate for this loss of revenue, the government resorted to central bank credit and thus increased the money supply. This, combined with wage increases granted to organized labor, caused accelerating inflation. Rising prices caused a precipitate decline in tax revenues, from 9 percent of the GDP in 1981 to only 1.3 percent in 1985, and led to a rapid depreciation of the exchange rate, both of which fed back into higher inflation. By 1985, the public had lost all confidence in the boliviano and most transactions were denominated in dollars.

In August 1985, the newly elected government of President Victor Paz Estenssoro took power and instituted a radical stabilization program along orthodox lines. The boliviano was devalued and made fully convertible into dollars; a sharp rise in the prices of goods and services sold by government corporations, together with a freeze on public sector wages, immediately cut the budget deficit; a tax reform was proposed and later enacted to increase revenues and avoid future deficits; the Treasury went on a cash-flow basis, spending no more than its incoming cash revenues. The elimination of the deficit reduced the need to obtain central bank credit and so restricted the money supply; this in turn curbed price increases and stabilized the new exchange rate. In contrast to other Latin American stabilizations, no price controls were employed and some existing controls were eliminated. The stabilization was aided by funding from a standby agreement with the IMF and the subsequent resumption of financing from donors, including the World Bank. But the moratorium on debt payments to commercial banks, begun under the Siles government, was maintained.

The abrupt elimination of the government's deficit and its ability to stabilize the exchange rate made its program credible to the public. The Paz government's task was easier because the previous government's policies had been completely discredited and the economy was in a shambles. The government was even able to carry out the kind of unpopular measures that might have toppled other regimes, notably the layoff of 21,000 workers employed by the inefficient government tin mining company, COMIBOL, and the sharp curtailment of government expenditures. After the first few months of dramatic reform, inflation did resume, but at levels of 10 to 15 percent, some of the lowest rates in Latin America at the time.

Sources: Juan Antonio Morales and Jeffrey D. Sachs, "Bolivia's Economic Crisis," in Jeffrey D. Sachs, ed., *Developing Country Debt and the World Economy* (Chicago: University of Chicago Press, 1989); and Jeffrey D. Sachs, "The Bolivian Hyperinflation and Stabilization," *American Economic Review,* 77, no. 2 (May 1987).

economy. This quid pro quo (loans in return for policy reform) is known as **conditionality.**

IMF stabilization measures are often controversial, not least because, in effect, they are painful medicine designed to prevent even more painful outcomes. Most economists recognize that imbalances, particularly budget deficits, have to be corrected and inflation curbed if growth and development are to be sustained. But debates remain over the extent of the adjustment needed, the particular measures involved, and the speed of adjustment. Should stabilization aim to reduce inflation to 5 percent or is 10 percent sufficient? Will expenditure cuts unnecessarily undermine critical social investments in health and education? Stabilization is likely to require some rise in unemployment and a decline in income for some groups, although the imbalances themselves might have caused similar problems. The more abruptly these measures are enforced, the greater will be the dislocation. Yet a gradual implementation may undermine the government's credibility and make it more difficult to complete the stabilization.

When control of inflation has to be combined with a major restructuring of the economy, the dislocation can be particularly severe. This situation, in essence, was the case in much of Central and Eastern Europe, Russia, and Vietnam during the first half of the 1990s. The structural changes there led to both a loss in revenue, as existing sources of tax revenue disappeared, and an increase in government expenditures to bail out the many loss-making state enterprises, losses due in large part to the difficulties these enterprises were having in adjusting to a market system. Formally, these enterprises received loans from the central bank, but since no one expected the loans to be repaid, in reality they were subsidies from the government budget. Closing down the loss-making enterprises would have reduced expenditures and hence inflation pressure, but it also would have thrown large numbers of people out of work. Russia was unable or unwilling to face the political consequences of what the leaders believed would be large-scale unemployment, so inflation continued at 10 to 20 percent per month (which when compounded over the course of a year produces annual inflation rates of 300 to 900 percent). Vietnam, with a much smaller state-enterprise sector, cut back sharply on subsidies to state enterprises and thereby reduced inflation from around 70 percent a year in 1990–91 to well under 20 percent a year in 1992–93 and low rates of inflation have prevailed there ever since.

Even where the restructuring of the economy is less drastic than what was attempted in Russia or Eastern Europe, inflation may be difficult to bring down. Prices for many consumer products, services and some manufactured goods are flexible. But, in some industries, especially those with a few large-scale firms, fixed pricing may prevail. Many governments also like to keep prices fixed for staple food products and gasoline, among other products. In countries with entrenched and politicized labor unions and concentrated industries, prices are more likely to be inflexible. When in addition, the income distribution is very unequal, a government often is unable to win a broad consensus on stabilization measures. These conditions were characteristic of some Latin American countries, where the experience with stabilization programs has been mixed, with many notable failures, such as Brazil and Argentina in the 1980s and Argentina again at the beginning of the twenty-first century, and some successes, notably Bolivia in 1985. In Asia, governments have been better able to use stabilization packages to correct budget and payments imbalances and control inflation.

STRUCTURAL ADJUSTMENT

Once stabilization has been achieved, or even while it is being achieved, the other elements of a well-functioning market system must be put in place through structural adjustment measures. The IMF and the World Bank often make such measures conditions for their continued lending in crisis situations, even though most structural adjustment often takes years or longer to accomplish.

A critical step at the outset is to make as many goods as possible available for purchase on the market rather than through some allocation mechanism of the government bureaucracy. Nonmarket distribution was most prevalent in the economies that patterned themselves after the centrally planned command economies of the Soviet Union, but the problem also exists where restrictions on imports are based on quantitative controls allocated by a government bureaucracy, as in India, especially prior to its reform program of the early 1990s. Similarly, inadequate infrastructure can disrupt markets. If a village is not connected by basic roads, many goods and services are unavailable to people who live there.

An important element in trade reform is to remove government quotas and licenses to allow imports to be allocated by markets rather than by the government. In the agricultural sector, fertilizer and pesticides sometimes are distributed through a state commercial network in amounts determined by the government, rather than by farmers' willingness to purchase and use these inputs. Most of these interventions in mixed economies were justified at their origin by market failures and distributional arguments. Others, restrictions on foreign investment, for example, are justified on political or security grounds. When restriction is piled on restriction, however, the cumulative effect is to remove large parts of the economy from participation in the market.

Adjusting Prices

Shifting prices toward scarcity values, sometimes called *getting prices right*, is critical to ensuring that goods are allocated to their highest-priority uses. What this means in practice is that prices should not be distorted in a major way by restrictions on trade, government price controls, and any other measures that lead prices to depart from their scarcity value in the economy.

Relative prices are the signals that tell firms how to manage their resources to earn the highest rewards. If the relative prices reflect the real scarcities in the economy, firms that maximize profits and consumers who maximize their utility automatically act to make the most out of all resources on behalf of the economy as a whole. Scarce resources, such as capital or energy, should have relatively high prices to conserve their use; abundant resources, such as unskilled labor in poor economies, should receive a market-determined wage rate. Attempts to raise the rate of pay or degree of job security, via minimum wage regulations, mandatory and generous fringe benefits, or onerous restrictions on dismissals, may result in less employment and a failure of firms to use intensively a nation's abundant factors of production.

Despite these advantages of market-determined prices, governments regularly intervene to set prices and shield them from market influences. In principle, these price controls are designed to correct for market failures and thus bring prices in line with real scarcities. In reality, price setting generally is a process based on political and not economic objectives. More often than not, government interventions lead prices further away from real economic scarcities.

A major objective of structural adjustment reforms, therefore, is to reduce or remove these distortions generated by government intervention. In the majority of developing countries, the list of distorted prices is long: high and uneven tariffs, cheap interest rates on loans (that discourage saving and lead to poor loan decisions), high minimum wages that help some workers but hurt others, subsidized fuel or food, limits on prices paid to farmers to control food prices, to name just a few. For every government-determined price, there are winners, who receive more for their output or pay less for their inputs, and losers. Price distortions most-often occur when the beneficiaries of a price change are few and concentrated, while the losers are large in number and dispersed. A tariff raises profits for the well-connected factory owner. But even though millions of people might be paying a higher price, they are scattered unevenly across the country and unlikely to organize to protest the increase. Since the tariff is built into retail prices, consumers may not even be aware that government intervention caused the higher prices. The owners of the company, however, know and are happy to share their increased profits with those who helped them.

Sometimes, correcting a distortion may lead to lower prices, as in removing a tariff, but it can lead to higher consumer prices, as in the removal of food or fuel subsidies. These subsidies are often paid for out of the budget and can be major contributors to budget deficits and inflation, or they can use scarce tax revenues that might be better spent on schools, roads, or health clinics. However, removing these subsidies can create enormous political pressures, since consumers immediately see the costs but not always the benefits. Removal of a food or fuel subsidy frequently triggers rioting that can topple governments.

Structural adjustment reforms designed to correct price distortions, therefore, frequently run into stiff resistance, either because they hurt powerful and well-connected people or because they affect many consumers. In Central and Eastern Europe, Russia, and China, most state enterprises saw themselves as beneficiaries of state price controls because it meant that they received key inputs at artificially low prices. To get around the resistance of large state enterprises, China created a dual price system where steel going to a large enterprise in accordance with the annual plan was charged a low state-set price, while all other steel was sold on the market at much higher market-determined prices. This dual system overcame much of the political resistance to price reform, but it also created opportunities for corruption by those who could use their influence to buy at the low state price and quickly resell at the high market price, corruption that contributed to the discontent that fueled the demonstrations on Tiananmen Square in 1989. Many of the other socialist and former socialist countries, from Russia to Vietnam, therefore, opted for eliminating state-set prices altogether and using one market-determined price for most goods and services. By the latter half of the 1990s, China had largely eliminated the two-price system in favor of a unified market-price system. The gradual elimination of the dual price system resulted in part from deliberate decisions by the Chinese government to reduce the quantity of goods sold at low state-set prices. For the most part, however, the state-set prices disappeared because producers increasingly were unwilling to sell their goods at below market prices, and they found numerous ways to circumvent government instructions requiring them to do so.

Ensuring Competition

In many developing countries, markets often are not fully competitive. Foreign competition is sometimes considered unfair, because foreign firms have years more experience than the country's new domestic firms. The solution often is to prohibit entry into the domestic market by foreign firms. Competition between domestic firms also is seen to waste resources. Why have three firms when one or two can produce all that is required? Fewer firms can achieve economies of scale and produce at lower average cost. Competition is disorderly, so the argument goes, and some firms will fail and put people out of work.

Competition pressures all firms to produce at the lowest possible price; for monopolies no such pressure exists. State-owned monopolies can set prices high enough to cover their high costs and sell goods of inferior quality. Under the circumstances, why bother working hard to lower costs and increase efficieny? Industries built behind a wall of protection from foreign imports may never be able to compete in foreign markets. Managers in these industries put most of their energy into lobbying to maintain that protection, rather than learning how to meet the competition. Centrally managed economies, such as those of the Soviet Union and China before reforms, allowed little real competition among enterprises. In China in the 1970s, even small-scale county-owned enterprises were given a monopoly over the local county market. Command economies were notorious for their profligate waste of resources in terms of both producing goods at high cost and often failing to produce the goods consumers wanted to buy.

Reform programs attempt to introduce competition into markets where it has been limited or absent. Competition among domestic firms can be fostered simply by dismantling import or investment licensing, quotas over output, controls over prices, or other government interventions that give some firms advantages over others. In China, one of the first reform steps was to abolish all regional or local monopolies and thus force enterprises in different regions to compete with each other. If the domestic market is small and one or a few firms dominate the industry, the only viable competition comes from abroad, in the form of competing imports. Therefore, the deregulation of import controls and reduction of tariffs provide the competitive stimulus for improved productivity and higher quality.

Critics of strong market-based approaches do not directly challenge the view that competition promotes productivity growth and deregulation and import liberalization enhance competition. Instead, they argue that import controls can be usefully maintained for a time to allow domestic firms to learn their businesses well enough to compete. Market adherents do not dispute this view on a theoretical level, but they challenge whether governments are capable of making these kinds of infant industry policies function as they should. Too often, in this view, infant industry protection arguments become an excuse to maintain support for inefficient but politically influential industries, as we discuss further in Chapter 19.

Other critics of neoclassical market-based approaches stress that regulations are needed to protect vulnerable groups in the society from the predatory practices of some firms or the unfettered workings of the market. Subsidies for food or low interest rates on rural loans are seen by some as supporting the poor. Income distribution arguments of this sort, however, have often been used to support government regulations that have more to do with enhancing the powers and perquisites of the regulators and much less to do with anything that really helps eradicate poverty.

Privatization

A well-functioning market requires that producers behave in accordance with one critical rule: to **maximize profits** by increasing their sales or cutting their costs. Where households are the main producers, as in farming, where the family farm is the main form of production, profit maximization happens more or less automatically. This is also true for many privately owned companies operating in competitive markets. But some producers maximize company profits not by creating a better product or reducing production costs but by lobbying governments to provide large subsidies or restrict competition. Structural adjustment programs that call for broad privatization of public enterprises typically assume that producers automatically maximize profits if firms are privately owned, but that is not always the case.

Increasing the role of the market often works most easily in agriculture. Theodore Schultz, one of the pioneers of development economics, emphasized that farmers, like owners of small businesses, are profit maximizers. If prices are raised on a particular crop, say coffee in Kenya, farmers plant more land in coffee but less in grain, because by doing so they raise their income. Reform therefore can be effective simply by freeing up prices of agricultural products so that prices reflect society's demand for those products and making inputs such as fertilizer available through the market rather than through state trading companies. Family farmers respond to deregulated prices and supplies because it is profitable for them to do so.

A key reason for the success of the Chinese and Vietnamese reform efforts was that both countries began with reforms in agriculture and small-scale trading. The collective farms and communes were broken up, and the land was turned over to be farmed by individual profit- or income-maximizing households. The crops raised on this land then could be sold on the freed-up rural markets. In both China and Vietnam, farm output increased dramatically after these reforms were introduced and so added credibility to the overall reform effort. Small-scale industrial and commercial enterprises behave much like family farmers. Managers and owners are the same people and increased profits go directly to the managers.

In the case of **state-owned enterprises,** the owner (the government) has goals other than profit maximization. Government-appointed managers often are directed to keep their prices low to help consumers, to employ more people than needed, to invest and locate in less-developed (and less-profitable) regions, to contribute to the political campaigns of the ruling party, and much else. Profits and efficiency may not even be a specified goal.

Creating Market-Supporting Institutions

A well-functioning market requires a range of supporting **institutions.** Markets are built on the idea of enforceable contracts, which in turn depends on a strong legal system. Financial systems require a competent central bank to manage currencies, set monetary policies, and enforce prudent regulations for the banking system. Government bureaucracies need to be relatively competent and able to control corruption. Well-functioning markets require these and other economic institutions, but in many low-income countries these institutions are weak or in the early stages of development.

One critical issue in giving both owners and managers the right incentives for efficient market behavior is how to create property rights or a full sense of ownership for those who have decision-making authority over the enterprise. **Property rights,** to be meaningful, must be *well defined* and *exclusive*. If they are neither, then others will lay claim to the property and no one will know who really has decision-making authority. Property rights must also be *secure* for long and indefinite periods. Otherwise, those who have these rights will take a very short-term view, knowing that they will not be around to reap either the rewards or the punishments for long-run success or failure. An enterprise decision maker who can sell the enterprise will want to maintain its value and not lower its price by running the enterprise into the ground. And property rights must be *enforceable*, usually through a well-established legal system, although there are other enforcement mechanisms. Most developing countries, however, lack well-established legal systems and creating them is one of the biggest challenges they face. Most state enterprises fail to meet these property rights requirements: In most cases, neither the managers nor the supervising ministry officials have well-defined, secure, and transferable rights to the enterprise.

Strong market adherents see privatization of all or most state-owned firms as part of the solution to the profit maximization and property rights problems, along with strengthening requisite institutions. Efforts have been made to privatize state-owned firms in both mixed economies and in the former Soviet-style command economies. In some cases, usually in mixed economies, enterprises are sold off one by one over a long period. In other cases, the effort has been rapid and across the board. The Russian privatization program of the first half of the 1990s is one of the more interesting cases of the latter approach. Vouchers were given to four groups: the general public, local governments, managers of privatizing state enterprises, and workers of those enterprises. These vouchers through an auction system could then be used to purchase a share of ownership in enterprises undergoing privatization, which by 1994 represented more than two thirds of all state-owned firms.[9]

Russia represented a particularly severe case of an absence of property rights and other key supporting institutions prior to privatization. The central government was too weak to protect state assets. Workers, managers, and local governments had little incentive to help the center because there was nothing in it for them. So workers and managers who had temporary control of state assets took the opportunity to sell them for personal profit. Privatization therefore was designed to end the theft of assets by giving those with control over them a stake in their preservation and efficient use. Unfortunately for Russia, obtaining secure property rights and good enterprise management requires more than just privatization of state assets, so the performance of Russian industry did not improve as much as many of the advocates of privatization had hoped. Support for privatization and secure property rights was further undermined when, at a later stage, the government transferred some of the state's most-valuable assets to political friends in private deals rather than through an open competitive process.

Privatization also may not always be necessary to create the required property rights. China's township and village enterprises, for example, were owned by townships or villages. In many cases, the local government officials at this level behaved as profit-maximizing entrepreneurs and the township population as a whole clearly saw the relationship between the effectiveness of the local enterprise and its own personal rewards. Public pension funds and other forms of public mutual funds also may serve as effective owners of state firms, if those funds are clearly profit oriented and have the right to hire and fire enterprise managers by electing their representatives to the enterprise board of directors. Experiments of this sort are underway in places as diverse as Central Europe, China, and Malaysia.

One critical and often underappreciated step is to create an independent, honest, and competent judicial system to solve the economic disputes that inevitably arise. The international financial institutions sometimes have made the strengthening of basic institutions such as the legal system a condition of loans, but creating such institutions as an efficient, honest, competent, and independent judicial system is difficult to accomplish and can take generations to complete and thus probably is not an appropriate component for IMF or World Bank loan conditionality. Modern societies that want to be well governed, however, need independent judiciaries for all kinds of reasons beyond those of settling

---

[9]Maxim Boycko, Andrei Shleifer, and Robert Vishny, *Privatizing Russia* (Cambridge, MA: MIT Press, 1995).

commercial disputes, hence there is a powerful incentive to build strong legal systems even without outside pressure whatever amount of time it may take.[10]

TIMING MARKET-ENHANCING REFORMS

One of the most-controversial issues in introducing market enhancing reforms is not over the specific content of the reforms themselves but over the timing and speed with which they are to be adopted. The specific reforms themselves, after all, are based on the economic theory of markets, a theory developed over more than two centuries and accepted by most economists. There is no comparable theoretical base for deciding when reforms should be introduced and whether reforms should be introduced rapidly or slowly and in all of the economy at once or sector by sector. It is generally the case that the view of the international financial institutions, particularly the IMF, tends to favor faster over slower reform, but some of the IMF's greatest critics have advocated the most rapid version of market-enhancing reforms in certain circumstances, sometimes referred to as **shock therapy.**

What can be said about the timing and speed of market enhancing reforms? There are times in a country's history when economic and political forces provide a brief opportunity for dramatic reforms. Probably the single most-convincing observation on timing, by political scientist Joan Nelson, is that the beginning of a new regime is the time to act.[11] New regimes of any kind have a brief initial period when they can blame problems on the previous government. Early success obviously has political benefits for the regime. But, as time goes on, growing ties between the government and its supporters in the private sector make policy change increasingly dangerous for any regime. In these circumstances, credibility probably is served by rapid, decisive, comprehensive action.

The more complex and multifaceted the reform process becomes, however, the more difficult it is to act in a way that achieves across-the-board changes. The task in Russia, Vietnam, and much of Central and Eastern Europe was to achieve macroeconomic stability, but it also was to create a complete market economy where little or none had existed before. Enterprises, private and public, had to

---

[10]For a more in-depth discussion of the relationship between a well-functioning market with good corporate governance and the development of an independent, competent, and efficient legal system in Asia, see Dwight H. Perkins, "Corporate Governance, Industrial Policy, and the Rule of Law," in Shahid Yusuf, M. Anjum Altaf, and Kaoru Nabeshima, eds., *Global Change and East Asian Policy Initiatives* (Oxford: Oxford University Press, 2004), 293–336.

[11]Joan Nelson, "The Political Economy of Stabilization: Commitment, Capacity and Public Response," *World Development* 12, no. 10 (1984), 983–1006.

learn how to act in a completely different environment. Property rights had to be established where none had existed before, and a supporting legal system had to be designed and made to work.

Polish reformers, among the first to try shock therapy or the big-bang approach to reform, tried to do everything at once. The early reform efforts in Russia associated with Yegor Gaidar, the Russian prime minister in the early 1990s, attempted to do something similar. The approach called for an immediate halt to inflation by stopping the growth in the money supply, freeing up all prices, and privatizing the state-owned sectors of the economy. In terms of economic theory, abstracted from politics, doing everything at once made a degree of sense. If all the elements of a market system are in place, the market will work better than if only some elements are in place.

In practice, shock treatment, at least in its initial form, proved impossible to implement. State enterprises could not adjust to the new situation quickly, so many of them ran deeply into the red. Rather than letting these enterprises go bankrupt, throwing large numbers of people out of work, the central bank kept the enterprises alive by giving them large loans, which no one expected them to pay back to the bank. Increased loans raised the money supply and so kept inflation at high levels. Freeing up prices put goods back on the shelves of stores, but left those with incomes that did not adjust to inflation in a difficult situation. This, in essence, is what happened in Russia in the first half of the 1990s. Some former socialist countries did better, others worse.

Virtually all of Central and Eastern Europe and the republics of the former Soviet Union experienced deep declines in the gross domestic product that lasted for years and full recovery was not achieved in some cases until the beginning of the twenty-first century, if then. The problems of introducing a market system were compounded by the need to downsize the overblown military establishment and establish new trading relationships after the breakup of the communist trading bloc. Recession brought parties to power promising to slow the reform or even reverse it. By the late 1990s and the beginning of the twenty-first century, however, the countries that had gone the furthest in transforming their economic system to one based mainly (although not exclusively) on market forces with secure property rights also were the economies where full recovery and renewed growth were first achieved. Poland, in particular, stood out in this respect.

China and Vietnam in the 1980s through to the beginning of the twenty-first century demonstrated, for some countries at least, that there was a more gradual approach to replacing a command system with a market system. Both began by freeing up prices and reestablishing household-based farming in the agricultural sector. They then freed up inputs and prices to the industrial sector and so created the conditions, in China at least, for a boom in small- and medium-scale industries. These industries in turn put competitive pressure on the large enterprises to become more effective at marketing their products and lowering their costs. While these changes were going on, the Chinese GDP grew at an average of 9 percent a year, and the Vietnamese GDP rose to over 7 percent a year by 1992 through to the first years of the twenty-first century.

China's and Vietnam's experience, however, does not prove that gradualism is the right answer for all countries. The large-scale state enterprise sector, the most difficult to reform, was a much smaller share of the economy in China and Vietnam than in Russia or Poland. China and Vietnam could afford to delay the full marketization of the large-scale state sector while they transformed the other three quarters of the economy; however, as of the new century, problems with loss-making state enterprises loom as one of China's major economic challenges (Box 5–3). In Russia and much of Eastern Europe, the large-scale state sector constituted most of the economy. Delaying reform of that sector meant delaying the entire effort to introduce a market economy.

Most developing economies, however, have at least some elements of a market system in place, and few have economies completely dominated by large-scale state enterprises. In these economies, piecemeal reform of one sector rather than the whole economy often is possible. Import liberalization can occur across the board, or it can begin with a few commodities and then spread to others. Customs procedures can be streamlined even if many tariffs remain high, and quotas can be abolished and replaced with tariffs. There is a danger that political resistance to gradual change will build, because the costs may be more apparent than the benefits, but this could happen with across-the-board liberalization as well. What is feasible in individual countries will depend on the nature of the government and the base of its political support.

Even in market-dominated economies, however, structural adjustment reforms may not always be able to be carried out gradually over time and in a piecemeal fashion. In many Latin American countries, trade liberalization is difficult if one cannot control inflation. And controlling inflation is difficult because the government is committed to supporting large vested interests at a level that cannot be paid for from existing sources of revenue; hence, there is a rise in the money supply and more inflation. Many of these vested interests are the very workers and capitalists who own and work in the import-substituting industries that will be hurt by trade liberalization. Structural impediments to reform of this type are deeply rooted in the social and political systems of the country and may not be changeable without some radical across-the-board restructuring.

For all the complexity involved in meeting these conditions for efficient markets, an increasing number of countries are making the effort to do so. Some of the most successful efforts have been in Asia. Hong Kong and Singapore were relatively free-market economies from the beginning. South Korea used government controls extensively in the 1970s but systematically dismantled many of

BOX 5-3 CHINA JOINS THE WTO TO SPEED THE TRANSITION TO THE MARKET, 1999-2001

In the early 1990s, China had largely completed the process of putting in place a market system in agriculture, domestic commerce, and for its small- and medium-scale township and village industrial enterprises. But the large state-owned enterprises that dominated such sectors as steel, machinery, and automobiles resisted the changes required by a market system. They continued to fight for easy credit from the banking system, and when that was not available, they simply stopped paying their suppliers. The government, they assumed, always would bail them out because the government was afraid of the political consequences of the rising unemployment that would occur if these enterprises stopped production and laid off workers. As long as the state-owned industrial enterprises remained unreformed, it also was difficult to make the banks behave the way they should in a market system.

In 1997 and 1998, however, the government began to push hard to reform the state-owned enterprises and the banks, including pushing hard for redundant workers to be laid off. To further emphasize how serious the government was, then Premier Zhu Rongji, on a trip to the United States in 1999, announced that he was willing to open up the Chinese economy to foreign competition to an unprecedented degree. His immediate purpose was to conclude a trade agreement with the United States that would allow China to become a member of the World Trade Organization (WTO).

The magnitude of the concessions that China said it would agree to, however, made it clear that China's goals had as much to do with its own domestic reforms as it did with its desire for membership in the WTO. Foreign competition for the banks as well as such industries as automobiles was to be the vehicle for forcing these sectors to reform. All manner of protection for these industries and financial institutions was to be abolished or sharply reduced, and foreign ownership was to be allowed in many financial sectors where previously it had not been allowed. The European Union agreed to a similar list of concessions in May 2000, and China was formally accepted for membership in the WTO at the end of 2001, thus ensuring a wave of competitive pressures that would assist China to complete its transition to a market economy.

the controls in the 1980s and 1990s. Even when the Asian financial crisis hit Korea hard after 1997, the government, rather than backing away from market-oriented reforms, redoubled its efforts to dismantle most of the restrictions on the free movement of goods, services, and capital that remained, although they remained wary of international flows of short-term capital, as this was at the core of the crisis, as described in Chapter 15. Taiwan based its remarkable growth on small firms guided by market forces. China was one of the first avowedly socialist economies to introduce market reforms, first into agriculture and, after 1984 with less complete success, into industry. Indonesia moved from a government-regulated industrial and financial system in the 1970s to a more market-oriented economy in the 1980s and 1990s,[12] although the financial crisis of the late 1990s forced some backtracking as the government attempted to deal with the collapse of the Indonesian financial system.

In Latin America, many market reforms have stumbled over failed stabilization programs, including those in Argentina and Brazil during the 1980s and Argentina again at the turn to the twenty-first century. In its almost two decades of stabilization and structural adjustment, Chile took many wrong turns but found a workable formula starting in the mid-1980s. Mexico deregulated its trade and industry in the 1990s while meeting large debt payments, a process reinforced by signing the North American Free Trade Agreement (NAFTA). In Africa, the most notable reforms have been attempted in Ghana, Mozambique, Tanzania, and Uganda, which had fallen into stagnation or even economic anarchy before righting themselves. Kenya, never in such dire straights, flirted with mild reforms that produced marginal results.

THE CREDIBILITY OF REFORMS

Less controversial than the question of timing and speed is the issue of the **credibility** of the reform effort. Success in reforming an economy depends crucially on the credibility of the entire package.[13] If budget deficits remain high or, for any other reason, money creation is not slowed, the public will anticipate continued or higher inflation. If the real exchange rate is allowed to appreciate because inflation outruns nominal devaluation, as happened in Chile and elsewhere, export industries become unattractive to investors.[14] If import liberalization is undertaken tentatively or past attempts are reversed, investors will put their money into the old protected industries. To establish credibility, governments need to manage their reform programs decisively, despite their complexity. They also may need to

[12]David Lindauer and Michael Roemer, *Asia and Africa: Legacies and Opportunities in Development* (San Francisco: ICS Press, 1994).

[13]Nelson, "The Political Economy of Stabilization."

[14]The real exchange rate (RER, discussed in Chapter 17) is the nominal exchange rate times the relative prices of traded goods (whose prices are determined by international markets) and nontradable goods (whose prices are determined by domestic supply and demand conditions). The RER provides a measure of the relative incentives for firms to produce tradable goods (exportables and importables) rather than nontradable goods. Inflation raises the prices of nontradables, weakening the incentives to produce exportables and importables.

"lock in" reforms by making commitments that are difficult to reverse. Many reforms, especially in Africa, started by freeing the exchange rate and foreign exchange flows from all controls; this forces the government to reduce its deficit and contain money supply growth to avoid massive depreciation and capital outflow. One of the more-decisive government efforts to establish the credibility of trade liberalization was the decision of Mexico to negotiate and sign the NAFTA. Opponents desiring to reverse these reductions in trade barriers must first contend with an international treaty.

Credibility also depends on the public's perceptions about stabilization and liberalization. In judging the effects of policies, the public is most likely to compare situations before and after, when the proper comparison is with and without. A stabilized economy may look worse than the observed precrisis economy but could well be an improvement over the situation that might have developed without stabilization, which of course cannot be observed. Leaders and officials in many countries have a deep-seated statist bias toward controls and often maintain an illusion that government controls are effective when they are not. These perceptions by government and the public make it more difficult to plan and implement reforms. Disappointing results with past stabilization and reform efforts make it more difficult to convince the public to support new initiatives.

The influence of international financial institutions on credibility is two edged. The International Monetary Fund and the World Bank provide additional resources that can ease the transition while reforms are being implemented. Foreign financing can enhance the position of reforming elements within a government and be used by government to sell stabilization programs to the public. However, additional resources also make the crisis seem less intense and reforms less necessary. Moreover, an IMF presence can become a focal point for political opposition to economic change. Although governments of countries such as Egypt, Russia, and Zambia have deflected public ire by ceasing at times to negotiate with the IMF, usually the result has been to delay stabilization, not eliminate its necessity.

Public debt plays a similarly dual role. To a point, the need to pay off foreign creditors can be used to steel the public to a degree of austerity. But, at some point, debt becomes a liability, as the public begins to wonder why its standard of living should decline so that foreign bankers' profits can be maintained. To some extent, the balance depends on public perceptions about whether the funds that were borrowed were used effectively or wasted and whether reforms can help improve standards of living while allowing debt commitments to be repaid.

Ultimately these questions about what market-enhancing reforms should be introduced and how and with what speed they should be introduced depend not just on the short-term credibility of the reform effort, but on the long-term impact of that effort. If the reforms lead to increased economic growth that is widely shared, they are likely to be sustained as has been the case in much of

East Asia. If they do not lead to rises in the standard of living of most of the people, as, for example, in Bolivia and other countries in Latin America, political support for reform will erode over time.[15]

THE WASHINGTON CONSENSUS

Moving from these broad discussions of the key components of market-based reforms to detailed steps in specific countries is far from straightforward. Individual characteristics vary widely, and the specific actions taken in one country may be inapplicable or inappropriate in another. Nevertheless as the movement toward reform gained steam in the mid- and late-1980s, the IMF and World Bank tended to require specific steps that were very similar across many countries.

In a seminal essay published in 1990, economist John Williamson of the Institute for International Economics recognized the growing strong agreement among the IMF, the World Bank, the U.S. government, and other key international actors on the steps that were necessary for Latin American countries to reform their economies.[16] Williamson labeled this broadly agreed reform agenda *the Washington Consensus*. Williamson's purpose was to identify "the lowest common denominator" of policy advice prevailing at the time. In so doing, he highlighted how these policies differed from the conventional wisdom that had prevailed 20 years before. The ten components of Williamson's consensus are

1. *Fiscal discipline.* Balanced government budgets are essential to avoid inflation, balance of payments deficits, and capital flight. Government budget deficits of more than 1 or 2 percent of GDP are considered to be excessive and evidence of policy failure.

[15]For a pessimistic view of the impact of market-oriented reforms in the 1980s and 1990s by someone who cannot be considered a critic of those reforms, see William Easterly, "The Lost Decades: Explaining Developing Countries' Stagnation in Spite of Policy Reform 1980–1998," *Journal of Economic Growth* 6, no. 2 (June 2001): 135–57. For a more complete presentation of Easterly's views, see his *The Elusive Quest for Growth: Economists' Adventures and Misadventures in the Tropics* (Cambridge, MA: MIT Press, 2002).

[16]John Williamson (1990) "What Washington Means by Policy Reform," in John Williamson, ed., *Latin American Adjustment.* Years later, John Williamson reflected on the origins of the term *the Washington Consensus.* "The story of the Washington Consensus dates back to 1989 . . . [T]he Institute of International Economics decided to convene a conference at which authors from 10 Latin American nations would present papers detailing what had been happening in their respective countries. To make sure that they all addressed a common set of questions, I wrote a background paper in which I listed 10 policy reforms that I argued almost everyone in Washington thought were needed in Latin America as of that date. I labeled this reform agenda the 'Washington Consensus,' never dreaming that I was coining a term that would become a war cry in ideological debates for more than a decade." See John Williamson, "From Reform Agenda to Damaged Brand Name," *Finance and Development* (September 2003), 10.

2. *Reordering public expenditure priorities.* Expenditures on subsidies of various kinds (gasoline, food, and many other products) and politically sensitive areas, including the military, should be cut back and instead should be concentrated on education, health, key infrastructure, and maintaining essential public administration (but cutting back on bloated bureaucracies).

3. *Tax reform.* To alleviate budget deficits, improve incentives, and achieve equity, reforms call for modest marginal tax rates and a broadening of the tax base.

4. *Liberalization of interest rates.* Market forces should determine interest rates and the allocation of credit. Interest rates need to be positive in real terms; that is, the nominal interest rate should be higher than the rate of inflation.

5. *Competitive exchange rates.* The exchange rate also should be determined by market forces and at a level that maintains a balance-of-payments equilibrium and, in particular, facilitates the expansion of exports.

6. *Trade liberalization.* Elimination of quantitative restrictions (import quotas and import licensing) and a move toward uniform and low tariffs on imported goods. Such measures, in part, would encourage domestic firms to sell to foreign markets rather than focus on protected domestic ones.

7. *Liberalization of foreign direct investment.* Restrictions on foreign direct investment should be removed so as to facilitate the inflow of needed capital, skills, and know-how.

8. *Privatization.* Public enterprises should be privatized, to both relieve pressures on the government budget (from subsidies to loss-making public enterprises) and promote greater efficiency. This reflects the prevailing view that private firms generally are more efficient than those in the public sector.

9. *Deregulation.* The primary vehicle for promoting competition within the domestic economy is to greatly reduce or eliminate government regulation, especially those that limit the entry and exit of firms. However, regulations that ensure safety, environmental protection, and the supervision of the banking sector remain justified.

10. *Secure property rights.* Private property rights matter and steps should be taken to strengthen these rights, including providing them at reasonable cost to the small-scale, informal sector.

Williamson's original essay was written at the end of what is sometimes called a *lost decade* for economic growth and development in Latin America. The paper was meant both as a *description* of the policy reforms recommended to Latin American economies and a *prescription* for reforms needed in the region. This package of reforms, or close variants of it, which advocated prudent macroeconomic policies, greater outward orientation, and increased reliance on free markets, was also applied outside of Latin America. After the fall of the Berlin Wall in 1989, a large group of transition economies emerged, and they were encouraged to pursue similar policies. Sub-Saharan Africa, which had been stuck in its own growth crisis, also was urged to follow this same approach. When financial crises reemerged, first in Mexico in 1994, then in East Asia in 1997, followed soon thereafter by crises in Russia, Brazil, Turkey, and Argentina, elements of the Washington Consensus were applied to these situations, even though the underlying reasons for financial crises (see Chapter 15) often are different from a failure to achieve sustained economic growth.

The 1980s and 1990s witnessed significant shift toward the reform agenda captured by the Washington Consensus. The pendulum swung away from state planning toward the market. Fiscal discipline became more widespread, with budgets moving in the direction of greater balance; hyperinflation that especially had plagued Latin America became less common; exchange rates worldwide became less overvalued, with black market premiums tending to fall if not disappear entirely; financial repression (where nominal interest rates are held below the rate of price inflation, with governments allocating scarce credit to favored firms) was practiced less often; produce market boards were disbanded and other forms of direct price control dismantled; trade barriers were reduced and privatization of state-owned enterprises proceeded on all continents.[17]

But despite all these reforms, which certainly were not universal and were uneven in their application and implementation, the hoped-for economic growth was not realized. Sub-Saharan Africa, despite a decade of reforms, had little to show for it, at least in many countries. The transition experience of economies in Eastern Europe and Central Asia went much worse than anticipated, at least initially. Growth in Latin America was slightly higher in the 1990s than in the 1980s, but much lower than in Asia; and Argentina, Brazil, Mexico, and several other countries were buffeted by major financial crises.

What went wrong? Here, there is no consensus. One argument often made is that the Washington Consensus remains a reasonable strategy; the problem is that it has not always been implemented despite claims that it has. Privatization, for example, did not simply mean the selling of state assets; it implied a

---

[17]In Latin America, "[f]iscal discipline reduced the average budget deficit from 5 percent of GDP to about 2 percent—and lowered public external debt from about 50 percent of GDP to less than 20 percent. Trade liberalization brought average tariffs down from more than 40 percent to nearly 10 percent . . . Banks, power plants, telecommunication systems, and even roads and water and health services were sold off to the private sector. More than 800 public enterprises were privatized between 1988 and 1997." Nancy Birdsall and Augusto de la Torre, *Washington Contentious: Economic Policies for Social Equity in Latin America* (Washington, DC: Carnegie Endowment for International Peace, 2001).

turn toward competitive markets. If instead, formerly state monopolies were sold at discount prices and transformed into private monopolies, as often happened in Russia and elsewhere, then it is little surprise that the benefits of privatization were not realized. Analogously, in Argentina, some would claim that the national government practiced the fiscal discipline mandated by the Washington Consensus. But large and powerful provincial governments did not, instead running large deficits that eventually undermined macroeconomic reforms and led to the economy's collapse. Moreover, while many countries reduced tariff and quotas on imports, exporters still faced high business costs that made them uncompetitive on global markets, undermining the export growth strategy.

It may also be that more time was needed for economies to respond to the policy changes. These reforms called for significant structural changes and economic agents need to become convinced reforms are permanent and respond accordingly. The first decade of the twenty-first century has seen progress in more of the former transition economies, and several sub-Saharan African economies are now showing signs of sustained economic growth. In the eight years from 1998 to 2004, 15 sub-Saharan African countries (not counting oil exporters that benefited from high world oil prices) recorded average per capita growth rates of 2.0 percent or more, a significant improvement over earlier years, although it is too early to know whether this progress will be sustained. It may be too soon to write off the key reforms captured by the Washington Consensus as a development strategy, as the effects are still in process.

But there are also signs of a retreat from the Washington Consensus as a comprehensive package of economic reforms. Some identify the Washington Consensus as a set of necessary but not sufficient conditions for economic growth and development. John Williamson himself revisited his original position, revising some of the recommendations and adding several more. Fiscal discipline, for example, remains essential but is only one element in raising national savings; something has to be done to increase private savings as well. Liberalization of interest rates is subsumed under a broader call for financial liberalization. Williamson also rethought his stance on exchange rate policy, where there was less of a consensus than he had at first thought. Most significant, he added to the list the need for institutional reforms and, at least in the case of Latin America, actions to address the "appalling" inequality of the region, which both constrains the rate of growth and limits the ability of economic growth to reduce poverty.[18]

The importance of adopting institutional reforms to accompany macroeconomic stabilization policies, greater openness, and a turn toward more-

---

[18]John Williamson, "The Washington Consensus Revisited," in Louis Emmerij, ed., *Economic and Social Development into the XXI Century* (Washington, DC: Inter-American Development Bank, 1997).

competitive markets became a focus of attention throughout the 1990s. It was not enough to change economic policies. Nations need adequate supervision of banks, police that protect citizens rather than exploit them, an independent central bank, and a legal system that can be counted on to resolve disputes fairly. Moises Naim, the editor of *Foreign Policy,* put this well in an article, "Washington Consensus or Washington Confusion?":

> An exchange rate that made a country's product cheaper abroad was not enough to sustain an export-led strategy of economic growth if inefficiency and corruption paralyzed the ports, and fiscal reform mattered little if taxes could not be collected. The elimination of restrictions on foreign investment, while indispensable for attracting foreign capital, was far from sufficient to make a country internationally competitive in the race to attract long-term foreign investment. A reliable justice system, a well-educated work force, and an efficient telecommunications infrastructure were some of the additional factors that would give a country an edge in its effort to attract foreign investors. In short, it became apparent that stronger, more effective institutions were urgently needed to complement macroeconomic policy changes.[19]

What Williamson, Naim, and others were saying was that economic reforms alone were not enough. Weak institutions and corruption were crippling reform efforts and good governance was a critical complement of more-market-friendly policies.

Others with a different view doubt the wisdom and underlying premises of the Washington Consensus in the first place (Box 5–4). Harvard economist Dani Rodrik argues that the benefits of greater openness may have been oversold.[20] Certainly, the financial crises of the 1990s exposed the vulnerabilities that more open capital flows (not necessarily trade flows) can engender. Rodrik and others are quick to point out two of the great success cases of the past two decades, China and India. Both can be seen as cautious reformers that moved in the direction of market forces rather than the state as the primary guide of the economy, but neither country can be seen as a charter member of the Washington Consensus. Privatization, deregulation, and openness proceeded slowly in China and India (although China in particular has promoted labor-intensive manufactured exports), and yet both have grown very rapidly over the past 20 years. Earlier success stories, including Korea, Malaysia, and Taiwan, also do not readily fit the mold, although Hong Kong and to a slightly lesser extent Singapore come close. Korea, Malaysia, and Taiwan all pursued some policies that

[19]Moises Naim, "Washington Consensus or Washington Confusion?" *Foreign Policy* (Spring 2000), 93.
　　[20]Dani Rodrik, *Has Globalization Gone Too Far?* (Washington, DC: Institute for International Economics, 1997).

BOX 5-4 THE WASHINGTON CONSENSUS— "A DAMAGED BRAND NAME"

One other group opposes the Washington Consensus. This is a large and somewhat amorphous group that has included antiglobalization activists, politicians, and at times, Joseph Stiglitz, a Nobel laureate in economics. What this group shares in common is their redefinition of the Washington Consensus. Instead of identifying Williamson's term with its original (or even updated) list of policy reforms, this group labels the Washington Consensus as a strategy of pure neoliberalism or market fundamentalism. In this populist interpretation, the Washington Consensus is a pseudonym for minimal governments and the supremacy of market forces.

Closer examination of Williamson's policy recommendations reveals that they are a long way from pure laissez-faire. The Washington Consensus calls for restoring fiscal discipline but does not recommend slashing government spending. It does not argue for cutting taxes or increasing the money supply at a fixed rate. Williamson does not advocate balanced budgets, oppose redistributive government spending, or call for the removal of capital controls. As Williamson writes, "As a statement of the neoliberal creed, the consensus was quite deficient."

But, despite his protestations, Williamson lost control of the meaning of the term he created. It had acquired a life of its own. In 2002, during his campaign for president of Brazil, Luiz Inacio Lula da Silva campaigned by promising to abolish the Washington Consensus and the economic model it represented. But at the same time he reassured voters that he would not let inflation return to Brazil, he favored a more outward orientation for the economy, and the private sector was to play a key role in the nation's future. Lula succeeded in endorsing many of the reforms that were part of the Washington Consensus while condemning the populist interpretation of what this reform agenda was all about.

It is not surprising that, by 2003, Williamson suggested that maybe it was time to drop the phrase *the Washington Consensus* from the vocabulary.

Sources: John Williamson, "What Should the World Bank Think about the Washington Consensus?" *World Bank Research Observer* 15, no. 2 (August 2000) and "From Reform Agenda to Damaged Brand Name," *Finance and Development* (September 2003).

would be considered unorthodox by the standards of the Washington Consensus, including the use of directed credit, public ownership of banks and some industries, and restrictions on capital flows.[21] (Of course, these same policies were used elsewhere without much success.)

[21]Frances Stewart, "John Williamson and the Washington Consensus Revisited," in Louis Emmerij, ed., *Economic and Social Development;* and Nancy Birdsall, Dani Rodrik, and Arvind Subramanian, "How to Help Poor Countries," *Foreign Affairs* (July–August 2005).

Even critics of the Washington Consensus generally agree on the importance of macroeconomic stability, outward orientation, good governance, and market-based incentives. But moving from these general principles to specific policies tailored to the circumstances of individual nations is the hard part. Many, if not most, of the successful economies of the past half century have not pursued the comprehensive structural reforms spelled out in Williamson's original list. There is a need for some policy autonomy and experimentation as nations find what works for them. Initiating and sustaining economic growth and development is a deep challenge. Part of that challenge remains finding the proper balance between the role of the state and of markets.

SUMMARY

- There are strong arguments supporting the view that most economic activities should be governed by markets rather than government controls. But markets can fail for several reasons, and market failures tend to be more prevalent in low-income countries.
- Governments can sometimes take steps to make markets work better, such as by building infrastructure, establishing strong legal systems, and building other key institutions. But poorly designed government interventions can make outcomes worse.
- There is a long-standing debate about the appropriate circumstances for government intervention in developing countries. The prevailing wisdom from the 1950s through the mid-1970s was that a strong role for the state was central to the development process. But disappointing outcomes in many countries, coupled with the success of several countries in East Asia, led to a major shift toward more outward and market-oriented strategies, often as part of reform programs.
- At the core of many reform programs supported by the IMF and the World Bank were stabilization policies aimed at controlling inflation, reducing the budget and balance-of-payments deficits, and otherwise improving macroeconomic stability. Many countries also introduced structural adjustment policies designed to make the economy more market oriented, shift production toward tradable goods, and enhance flexibility and efficiency. Key steps included removing trade barriers to open the economy to international competition, freeing prices or adjusting them to reflect their scarcity values, and privatizing state-owned assets.
- By the early 1990s, there was widespread agreement on the key elements of reform programs, characterized by what came to be known as

the Washington Consensus. The key policies focused on budget reforms, trade, exchange rates, foreign direct investment, privatization, broader deregulation, and property rights.

- However, despite all the reforms, the growth response in many countries has been less than what was hoped for. Some analysts argue that the reforms were not fully implemented, more time is needed for the reforms to have their full impact, or the reform agenda did not sufficiently emphasize strong institutions and good governance. For others, many of the specific measures advocated by the IMF and World Bank were too rigid and did not allow for sufficient flexibility and autonomy. Debates continue about the appropriate balance between markets and states in developing countries.

PART TWO

Distribution and Human Resources

Inequality and Poverty

6

Bangladesh is one of the world's most heavily populated low-income nations. In 2003, average income among Bangladesh's 140 million was $1,770 (US$, PPP). On a daily basis, this amounts to about $5 per person per day, which would permit a meager standard of living at best. But $5 per day refers only to the average, the income level that would prevail if GDP was divided equally among the entire population, which, of course, it is not. What income level is earned by those who fall below the "average"? How much do the poorest Bangladeshis depend on for their survival? Evidence from the World Bank suggests that 36 percent of Bangladeshis, some 50 million people, survive on "$1 a day" or less, the standard international definition for absolute poverty.[1]

At a global level, over 1 billion people, or almost one out of every six people, are estimated to live below the "$1 a day" poverty line; 2.7 billion people, about half the world's population, survive on less than "$2 a day." For most readers of

[1]The World Bank's international poverty line originally referred to $1 a day, in 1985 US$ (PPP). It was later revised to $1.08 a day, in 1993 US$ (PPP). Adjusting for U.S. price inflation, results in a 2000–01 poverty line of about $1.30. We refer to the 1993 $1.08 per day poverty line in quotation marks as "$1 a day." Similarly, the $2 a day poverty line is about $2.60 per day in 2000–01 and is referred to as "$2 a day." The selection of these poverty lines is discussed later in the chapter. Global poverty estimates refer to 2001 and are from Shaohua Chen and Martin Ravallion, "How Have the World's Poorest Fared since the Early 1980s?" *World Bank Research Observer* 19, no. 2 (2004). Estimates for Bangladesh and other countries referred to in this chapter are from *World Development Indicators Online* unless otherwise indicated.

this book, who are enrolled in a college or university, the idea of living on "$1 or $2 a day" is close to inconceivable. But these are the circumstances facing millions of Bangladeshis and billions of people worldwide in their daily lives.

The major explanation for the degree of absolute poverty in Bangladesh and other low income nations is the low level of total production and GDP per capita. But this is not the only factor. Mexico is an upper-middle-income nation with a 2003 GDP per capita income of $9,168 (US$, PPP), five times the level in Bangladesh. If GDP was distributed equally in Mexico, each Mexican would have $25 per day. But income is not equally shared in Mexico, or in Bangladesh, or for that matter in any other country. The richest 20 percent of Mexicans receive over 50 percent of total household income, almost *15 times* as much as the poorest 20 percent. This combination of the level and distribution of income in Mexico results in over 10 million Mexicans (about 10 percent of the population) living below the "$1 a day" poverty line.

Raising people out of poverty requires economic growth. Increases in GDP per capita typically benefit those below the poverty line as well as those who live near to or considerably above it. Without sustained economic growth, the most Bangladesh could achieve is the low level of income that $5 a day permits. But the distribution of national income plays a vital role, too. Inequality affects the amount of poverty generated by a given level of income; inequality may affect growth just as growth may affect levels of inequality; and inequality *itself* is something people care about, independent of its effects on poverty and growth.

If both economic growth and distribution affect poverty levels, what does this suggest about policy? Toward the end of this chapter, we consider potential elements of a pro-poor development strategy. These elements include encouraging more rapid economic growth, improving opportunities for the poor via investments in basic education and health care, and designing social safety nets and other programs for especially vulnerable groups.

MEASURING INEQUALITY

Economists often are interested in the distribution of *income* among *households* within a *nation*. But these are not the only dimensions of inequality we might want to investigate. Instead of income, development economists often look at the distribution of household *consumption,* usually measured by household expenditures, whether in-kind or in money terms. In poor countries income can be hard to measure, especially among subsistence farm households who consume rather than market most of what they produce. Consumption also may be a more-reliable indicator of welfare than income, in part, because consumption tends not to fluctuate as much as income from one period to the next.

One might also be interested in the distribution of *wealth,* which always is more unequal than either the distribution of income or consumption. Distributions of assets, whether of land or education, are useful in understanding the opportunities individuals have to be productive and generate household income. The distribution of income depends on ownership of factors of production (including the value of the labor services that one "owns") and the role each factor plays in the production process. Ownership of land and capital often is highly concentrated, so anything that enhances the relative returns to these factors makes the distribution of income more unequal. Conversely, relatively higher wages for unskilled labor, the most widely distributed factor of production in developing nations, tends to lead to a more equal distribution.

In addition to deciding whether to look at the distribution of income or consumption (or of assets or wealth) *within* one nation, one might want to look at how each is distributed *among* nations. We assess the level of global inequality at the end of the chapter. One can also look within the household at patterns of intrahousehold inequality, which are critical for understanding gender issues and the welfare of children. No matter what dimension of distribution one is interested in, one needs a set of analytical tools for describing and understanding distributional outcomes.

The simplest way of depicting any distribution is to display its **frequency distribution,** which tells us how many (or what percent of) families or individuals receive different amounts of income. The top panel of Figure 6–1 presents the frequency distribution of household consumption per capita for Bangladesh in 2000. This distribution is based on a survey of about 7,000 Bangladeshi families, selected to represent the over 24 million households in Bangladesh. Surveyed households responded to detailed questionnaires about their sources of income and consumption of a wide variety of goods. Researchers used this information to derive an estimate of each household's per capita consumption.

Figure 6–1 tells us the percentage of individuals with different levels of annual consumption starting from the lowest reported level and rising in increments of 650 taka, the Bangladeshi currency, an amount equal to $55 ($US, PPP). Almost 1 million people, less than 1 percent of Bangladesh's population, reported the lowest annual consumption expenditures in the survey, under 3,250 taka per year (<$270, PPP); 8.4 percent (the highest bar in the figure) had per capita consumption of between 5,850 and 6,500 taka (around $500, PPP); and less than half of 1 percent had the top amounts reported in Figure 6–1, over 22,750 taka (almost $1,900, PPP). There are households with higher consumption in Bangladesh. Figure 6–1 reports the distribution for only 95 percent of

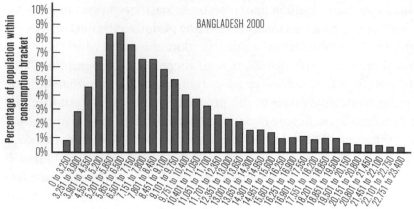

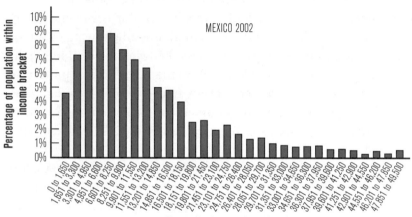

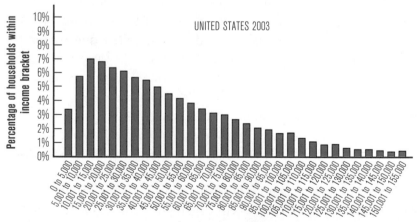

FIGURE 6-1. **The Distribution of Income: Bangladesh, Mexico, and the United States**

Sources: Collaboration with Claudio E. Montenegro, World Bank; *U.S. Current Population Survey*, March supplement, March 2004.

individuals ranked by per capita consumption. Had the top 5 percent been included in the figure, "the tail" of the distribution would continue to extend much farther to the right of the diagram.[2]

Take a look at the shape of the frequency distribution for Bangladesh in Figure 6–1. The distribution is not rectangular, with every level of consumption represented by the same percentage of individuals, nor was it expected to be. The height of the bars, each bar representing a different consumption level, initially rises and then grows progressively shorter. The distribution also is not a normal distribution, the so-called bell curve, with which you may be familiar from courses in statistics. If consumption or income were distributed normally, there would be an equal number of households on either side of the mean and symmetric tails to the distribution suggesting equal numbers at both low and high consumption or incomes. IQs are distributed normally but consumption and income are not. The distribution instead is described as lognormal, meaning that if you took the logarithms of household consumption or incomes and redrew the frequency distribution it would approximate the more familiar bell curve. If distributions were very equal, there would be a small number of very tall bars in the middle of the diagram, indicating that just about everyone had nearly the same level of consumption.

The lognormal distribution captures what you already know about incomes. In virtually all societies there are a relatively small number of rich households (captured in the long, flat tail to the right) and a much larger number of lower-income families who make up "the hump" of the distribution, which is located at the lower end of the income range. This particular shape of the distribution of income is not unique to Bangladesh. Similar distributional outcomes characterize low-, middle-, and high-income economies. The two lower panels of Figure 6–1 illustrate this point. These income distributions are based on micro-level household surveys for Mexico and the United States. Note that all three nations exhibit a similar lognormal distribution, each with its own long, flat tail to the right.

Bangladesh, Mexico, and the United States all have similarly shaped frequency distributions but they are not identical. This means that the degree of inequality in the three nations varies. To get a sense of the differences we need to rearrange the data contained in the frequency distributions; these distributions

[2]Household income and expenditures surveys, like the one for Bangladesh, often fail to capture two groups of households. Both the poorest and richest families are likely to be underrepresented. The poorest families, including those who are homeless and live in places such as railway stations or river gullies, tend not to be adequately enumerated. Similarly, the most affluent, few in number, are unlikely to be part of the statistical sample. There also is a tendency for more affluent households not to respond to such surveys or to underreport their incomes. Even in the best of surveys, the degree of inequality may be underestimated.

TABLE 6-1. Size Distributions of Consumption or Income within Quintiles in Bangladesh, Mexico, and the United States

| | SHARE OF TOTAL CONSUMPTION OR INCOME | | |
QUINTILE	BANGLADESH (2000)	MEXICO (2002)	UNITED STATES (2003)
Bottom 20%	9.0	3.5	3.4
Second 20%	12.5	8.2	8.7
Third 20%	16.0	13.3	14.8
Fourth 20%	21.5	21.2	23.4
Top 20%	41.0	53.7	49.8

Sources: Collaboration with Claudio E. Montenegro, World Bank; *U.S. Current Population Survey*, March supplement, March 2004.

have complex shapes and are difficult to compare whether across nations or within nations over time. Calculating the **size distribution** provides an easier way of identifying the degree of inequality present in the underlying distribution.

Size distributions tell us the share of total consumption or income received by different groups of households ranked according to their consumption or income level. One can rank households or individuals by deciles or even percentiles, but the convention is to report on quintiles, ranking households from the poorest 20 percent, to the next 20 percent, all the way to the richest 20 percent of households. In the case of Bangladesh, each quintile represents almost 30 million people. Summing all individual consumption expenditures in each quintile and dividing by the country's total consumption yields each quintile's share.

Table 6–1 contains World Bank estimates of the size distribution of consumption for Bangladesh and household income for Mexico and the United States. This way of presenting the data makes it clear that, of the three nations, Bangladesh has the relatively most equal distribution since the quintile shares are closer to one another than is the case in either Mexico or the United States. (If the distribution were completely equal, each quintile would receive 20 percent of the total.) In Bangladesh, the top 20 percent receive 41 percent of total household consumption, about 4.5 times the amount received by the poorest 20 percent. In Mexico and the United States, the ratio is much larger, roughly 15:1.[3] Some of

[3]Unlike most low- and middle-income nations, the United States has a comprehensive system of taxation of household incomes and government transfer payments (e.g., social security). The data reported here are for money incomes before taxes and after cash transfer payments. Noncash transfers, such as Medicare, are not accounted for. Once taxes and all government transfer payments are included, the distribution becomes somewhat more equal. The top 20/bottom 20 ratio falls to closer to 10:1.

these differences are due to what precisely is being measured—consumption or income and whether on a per capita or household basis—but much of the difference is due to the underlying distribution within each nation.

The size distribution provides a means for introducing some other techniques commonly used to measure inequality, including some that reduce the entire distribution to a single number. Data from the size distribution can be used to draw a **Lorenz curve** (Figure 6–2), named after Max Lorenz, a statistician who first wrote an article using this technique in 1905. Income recipients are arrayed from lowest to highest income along the horizontal axis. The curve itself shows the share of total income received by any cumulative percentage of recipients. Its shape indicates the degree of inequality in the income distribution. By definition, the curve must touch the 45° line at both the lower-left corner (0 percent of recipients must receive 0 percent of income) and the upper-right corner (100 percent of recipients must receive 100 percent of income). If everyone had the same income, the Lorenz curve would lie along the 45° line (perfect equality). If only one household received income and all other households had none, the curve would trace the bottom and right-hand borders of the diagram (perfect inequality). In all actual cases the Lorenz curve lies somewhere in between. Inequality is greater, the farther the Lorenz curve bends away from the 45° line of perfect equality (the larger the shaded area, *A*). In comparing Lorenz curves, either for the same country at different points of time or for different countries,

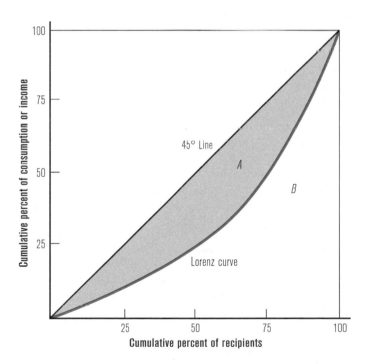

FIGURE 6-2. **Lorenz Curve**

the separate curves often intersect. When this happens it is ambiguous if inequality has increased or decreased over time (or if one country has more inequality than the other.)[4]

Single numbers often are used to describe the distribution of income. One commonly used statistic is the ratio of the income share of the top 20 percent of households to the share received by the bottom 20 or 40 percent. The most frequently used statistic, the **Gini coefficient** (named after Corrado Gini, an Italian statistician), can be derived from the Lorenz curve. This ratio is understood most easily as the value of area A divided by area $A + B$ in Figure 6–2.[5] The larger is the share of the area between the 45° line and the Lorenz curve, the higher is the value of the Gini. The theoretical range of the Gini coefficient is from 0 (perfect equality) to 1 (perfect inequality). In practice, values measured in national income distributions have a much narrower range, ordinarily from about 0.25 to 0.60.

Collapsing all the information contained in the frequency distribution into a single number inevitably results in some loss of information about the underlying distribution. Paraguay and South Africa both report Gini coefficients of 0.578, but the underlying distributions are not identical. Both nations have very high degrees of inequality, but in South Africa the lowest quintile received 3.5 percent of income, in Paraguay only 2.2 percent. From the perspective of the poor in these countries, a more than 1 percentage point difference in income shares is a significant amount. Another criticism of the Gini coefficient is that it is more sensitive to changes in some parts of the distribution than others. This characteristic is evident in a comparison of inequality in China and Zimbabwe. In both nations, the lowest quintile receives about 4.6 percent of income. Despite this similarity, China's Gini at 0.447 is much lower than Zimbabwe's at 0.568. The reason is the gap in amounts received by the richest quintile: 50 percent in China versus 56 percent in Zimbabwe. Despite these shortcomings of the Gini, the desire among researchers to summarize inequality in a single number combined with some other attractive properties of the Gini, including its geometric interpretation using Lorenz curves, has encouraged its widespread use.[6]

---

[4]The reason for this ambiguity should be clear. Draw two Lorenz curves and label the point of intersection X. Below point X, there is relatively more equality along the Lorenz curve closer to the 45° line; but above point X, there is relatively more equality along the other Lorenz curve. Since both Lorenz curves have sections of greater equality, there is no way to decide, overall, if one represents a more equal distribution than the other.

[5]The Gini coefficient can be calculated using a relatively complex formula based on the absolute income differences across all observations in a population, which are then normalized by both the size and mean income of the population.

[6]There are other single number measures of inequality in addition to the Gini coefficient and top 20/bottom 20 or 40 ratios. Discussion of the alternatives and the desirable properties of any measure of inequality can be found in Gary Fields, *Distribution and Development: A New Look at the Developing World* (Cambridge, MA: MIT Press, 2001).

PATTERNS OF INEQUALITY

Simon Kuznets, one of the early Nobel Prize winners in economics and a pioneer of empirical work on the processes of economic growth and development, was one of the first economists to investigate patterns of inequality. In his presidential address to the 1954 meeting of the American Economics Association, Kuznets reported on historical data on income shares for England, Germany, and the United States. He then introduced a few data points for the developing world: Ceylon (now Sri Lanka), India, and Puerto Rico. The data were so limited that Kuznets did not include them in a table or figure; he simply listed them in the text.[7] Some 50 years later, researchers are far less constrained. Data on inequality are available for most nations of the world, although for most countries they are updated only once or twice a decade. The quality and comparability of these data also are sometimes a concern: The World Bank, one of the primary compilers of such information, offers more than the usual caveats about data comparability across countries and over time.

Table 6–2 presents estimates of Gini coefficients of the distribution of household consumption or income for countries by region. (All capital letters indicate that the distribution is based on income not consumption, the former associated with more inequality than the latter since consumption tends to vary less over time than income.) Nations are divided into three categories of income inequality: low (with Ginis <0.40), medium (0.40–0.50), and high (>0.50). What is immediately apparent is the variance in inequality both within and across regions. There is evidence of a tendency toward higher inequality in Latin America and parts of Africa (especially Southern Africa). Low inequality is characteristic of South Asia, the transition economies of Eastern Europe and Central Asia, and among most of the high-income Organization of Economic Cooperation and Development (OECD) economies, with the exception of the United States. Much of East Asia falls in the medium range of income inequality.

What explains these differences? Does it have to do with specific characteristics of different regions or are regions a proxy for something else, perhaps, income level? One idea with a long history is that economic growth itself may be associated with the degree of inequality. The basic intuition is that growth is an inherently unbalanced process. Some individuals capture the benefits of growth early on, and it takes time for others to benefit and for returns to equalize.

---

[7]Simon Kuznets, "Economic Growth and Income Inequality," *American Economic Review* 45, no. 1 (1955).

TABLE 6-2. Gini Coefficients by Country and Region

	LEVEL OF INEQUALITY		
	LOW (GINI <0.400)	MEDIUM (0.400 ≤ GINI < 0.500)	HIGH (GINI ≥ 0.500)
Africa	Ethiopia (0.300) Burundi (0.333) Egypt (0.344) Algeria (0.353) Mauritania (0.390) Morocco (0.395) Mozambique (0.396) Tunisia (0.398)	Ghana (0.408) Senegal (0.413) Kenya (0.425) Cameroon (0.446) Côte d'Ivoire (0.446) The Gambia (0.475) Madagascar (0.475) Burkina Faso (0.482)	Malawi (0.503) Niger (0.505) Nigeria (0.506) Zambia (0.526) Zimbabwe (0.568) South Africa (0.578) Lesotho (0.632)
Asia	Mongolia (0.303) TAIWAN (0.312) Bangladesh (0.318) India (0.325) Pakistan (0.330) Indonesia (0.343) ISRAEL (0.355) Jordan (0.364) Nepal (0.367) Lao, PDR (0.370) Vietnam (0.370)	Cambodia (0.404) SINGAPORE (0.425) Iran, Islamic Rep. (0.430) Thailand (0.432) China (0.447) Philippines (0.461) MALAYSIA (0.492)	Papua New Guinea (0.509)
Europe and Central Asia	CZECH REPUBLIC (0.254) SLOVAK REPUBLIC (0.258) Bosnia and Herzegovina (0.262) Uzbekistan (0.268) Hungary (0.269) SLOVENIA (0.284) Croatia (0.290) Ukraine (0.290) Romania 0(.303) Belarus (0.304) Russian Federation (0.310) BULGARIA (0.319) Lithuania (0.319) Kazakhstan (0.323) Tajikistan (0.326) LATVIA (0.336) Poland (0.341) Kyrgyz Republic (0.348) Albania (0.353) Azerbaijan (0.365) Georgia (0.369) Moldova (0.369) ESTONIA (0.372)	Turkey (0.400) Turkmenistan (0.408)	

TABLE 6-2. Continued

	LEVEL OF INEQUALITY		
	LOW (GINI <0.400)	MEDIUM (0.400 ≤ GINI < 0.500)	HIGH (GINI ≥ 0.500)
Latin America and the Caribbean	Jamaica (0.379)	Nicaragua (0.431) Ecuador (0.437) URUGUAY (0.446) Bolivia (0.447) COSTA RICA (0.465) DOMINICAN REPUBLIC (0.474) VENEZUELA (0.491) PERU (0.498)	ARGENTINA (0.522) EL SALVADOR (0.532) Mexico (0.546) HONDURAS (0.550) PANAMA (0.564) CHILE (0.571) COLOMBIA (0.576) PARAGUAY (0.578) BRAZIL (0.593) GUATEMALA (0.599)
High Income (OECD)	DENMARK (0.247) SWEDEN (0.250) BELGIUM (0.250) NORWAY (0.258) FINLAND (0.269) GERMANY (0.283) AUSTRIA (0.300) NETHERLANDS (0.309) KOREA, REP. (0.316) FRANCE (0.327) CANADA (0.331) GREECE (0.354) IRELAND (0.359) ITALY (0.360) UNITED KINGDOM (0.360) NEW ZEALAND (0.362) PORTUGAL (0.385)	UNITED STATES (0.408)	

Note: Country names written in all capital letters denote that Gini coefficients were calculated using income share data; those written conventionally were calculated using expenditure share data. Ginis are based on data from different years, 1995–2002.

Sources: "Table 2.7: Distribution of Income or Consumption," *2005 World Development Indicators* (Washington, DC: World Bank, March 2005); Data for Taiwan, UNU/WIDER World Income Inequality Database. Luxembourg Income Study (Source 1). Survey of Personal Income Distribution, Taiwan Area (Survey/Source 2), V 2.0a, June 2005, available at www.wider.unu.edu/wiid/wiid.htm, accessed June 2005.

Growth and Inequality

Kuznets was one of the first economists to speculate on the relationship between growth and inequality, suggesting that inequality might first increase as a nation makes the transition from a mostly agricultural economy to an industrial one. The underlying mechanism for this rise in income inequality is the result of differences in the returns to factors of production between agriculture (where they are lower and less dispersed) and industry. When everyone works in agriculture income is distributed relatively equally, but as industrialization and urbanization progress, inequality rises. As more factors make the transition from farm to factory inequality may then start to fall. Kuznets readily acknowledged that the basis for this relationship was "perhaps 5 per cent empirical information and 95 per cent speculation, some of it possibly tainted by wishful thinking."

Other economists offered alternative explanations for an association between growth and inequality. W. Arthur Lewis, also a Nobel Prize winner, developed a theoretical model that predicts rising inequality followed by a "turning point," which eventually leads to a decline in inequality. Employing a two-sector model (like the one introduced in Chapter 4), the modern or industrial sector faces "unlimited supplies" of labor as it is able to draw workers with low or even zero marginal product from agriculture. With wages held down by the elastic supply of workers, industrial growth is accompanied by a rising share of profits. As average incomes rise, labor receives a smaller share of the total, increasing inequality. The turning point is reached when all the "surplus labor" has been absorbed and the supply of labor becomes more inelastic. Wages and labor's share of income then start to rise and inequality falls.[8]

In Lewis's **surplus labor model,** inequality is not just a necessary effect of economic growth; it is a cause of growth. A distribution of income that favors high-income groups contributes to growth because profit earners save to obtain funds for expanding their enterprises. The more income they receive, the more they invest. Their saving and investment increase the economy's productive capacity and thus bring about output growth. Not only does inequality contribute to growth according to Lewis, but attempts to redistribute income "prematurely" run the risk that economic growth will be slowed. These were powerful conclusions. Could they be maintained in light of the empirical evidence on economic growth and inequality?

The ideas of Kuznets, Lewis, and others about growth and inequality held considerable sway among development economists for several decades. During the 1960s, a period of strong growth in many regions, some economists wondered why growth was not yielding more rapid reductions in poverty. One idea

[8]W. Arthur Lewis, "Economic Development with Unlimited Supplies of Labor," *Manchester School* 22 (1954).

was that the relationship that came to be known as Kuznets inverted-U, or more simply, as the **Kuznets curve,** might be at work. Fifteen to 20 years after Kuznets's original paper, researchers were armed with more data on inequality and reexamined the relationship using primarily cross-section analyses of countries, including many developing countries. A key assumption in this approach was that nations at different levels of per capita income could approximate what individual nations might experience over time as they achieved economic growth. Studies using this approach supported the existence of the Kuznets curve.[9] The tendency for inequality to rise and then fall with rising levels of per capita income was maintained as a stylized fact about development until the late 1980s. Subsequent research has overturned this perspective.

Better and more abundant data on income inequality, especially time-series data on individual countries, coupled with more rigorous econometric methods, permitted researchers to identify patterns over time within individual nations. In India, a low-income nation with generally low-income inequality, there is evidence of some decline in inequality from 1950 until the mid-1960s, but since then there is no distinct trend in either direction.[10] India has been and remains a nation with a relatively equal distribution of income. Figure 6–3 illustrates the trend in the Gini coefficient since 1980 for Chile and Taiwan. Chile, one of Latin America's most successful economies, has been a middle-income nation throughout this period; Taiwan has gone from middle- to high-income status. Chile's Gini coefficient fluctuates from year to year but exhibits no particular pattern over time, although there is an upturn in the final year data are available. What is most apparent in Chile's case is the persistence of a relatively high level of inequality. Taiwan exhibits less fluctuation. It traces a slow and modest rise in inequality since 1980. The most notable feature of Taiwanese experience is the persistence of very low levels of inequality.[11] There is no evidence of any inverted U for either India, Chile, or Taiwan.

One should not generalize from a few cases, so it is important to look at the experience of a larger numbers of nations. Researchers who have done so find little evidence of a general tendency for income inequality to first rise and then fall with economic growth. It is as common for Gini coefficients to rise as per

[9]Montek S. Ahluwalia, "Inequality, Poverty and Development," *Journal of Development Economics* 3 (1976).

[10]Michael Bruno, Martin Ravallion, and Lyn Squire, "Equity and Growth in Developing Countries: Old and New Perspectives on the Policy Issues," in Vito Tanzi and Ke-young Chu, eds., *Income Distribution and High-Quality Growth* (Cambridge, MA: MIT Press, 1998).

[11]Taiwan's record of rapid economic growth with low income inequality is somewhat unique. Some transition economies have similarly low or even lower levels of income inequality but none has yet achieved Taiwan's per capita income level. Among rapidly growing economies, China has achieved similar growth rates, although not yet for as many years, but China has done so with significantly higher inequality. The same is true for Malaysia, Thailand, and Singapore. Korea's record on growth and inequality comes closest to Taiwan's.

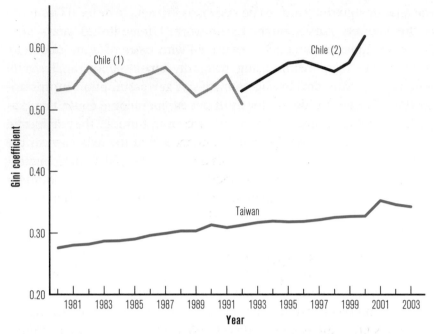

FIGURE 6-3. Trends in Inequality, Gini Coefficients in Chile and Taiwan
Two series are used for Chile because one continuous series is not available
for the entire time period. Series 1 relies primarily on gross income and
Series 2 on disposable income.

Sources: Data for Chile: UNU/WIDER World Income Inequality Database, Chile MIDEPLAN
1994; Deininger and Squire data set, Measuring Income Inequality, available at
www.worldbank.org/research/growth/dddeisqu.htm; World Bank 2004 (Source 1),
Caracterization Socioeconomica Nacional (CASEN) and Encuesta Nacional de Empleo
(Survey/Source 2), V 2.0a, June 2005, available at www.wider.unu.edu/wiid/wiid.htm,
accessed June 2005; data for Taiwan, UNU/WIDER World Income Inequality Database,
Taiwan CSO 2003, Taiwan CSO 2004 (Source 1), The Survey of Family Income and
Expenditure (Survey/ Source 2), V 2.0a, June 2005, available at www.wider.unu.edu/wiid/
wiid.htm, accessed June 2005.

capita income grows as it is for them to fall.[12] The persistence of a given level of
inequality within nations may be the strongest trend. Support for the Kuznets
curve in earlier cross-section analysis was driven by the higher inequality of a
subset of middle-income nations. Better econometric tests reveal that the
inverted U was driven not by economic growth but by the coincidence of Latin
America's high levels of inequality and middle-income ranking. Investigation of
the Kuznets curve offers a cautionary tale for empirical work on developing

---

[12]Klaus Deininger and Lyn Squire, "New Ways of Looking at Old Issues: Inequality and Growth,"
Journal of Development Economics 57 (1998); Martin Ravallion and Shaohua Chen, "What Can New
Survey Data Tell Us about Recent Changes in Distribution and Poverty?" *World Bank Economic
Review* 11, no. 2 (1997).

nations. Patterns observed across nations may not always provide reliable insight into what ultimately are dynamic processes that occur within nations.[13]

Rejection of the Kuznets curve as an overall tendency does not imply that economic growth has no impact on inequality nor that something like the Kuznets curve might occur in some countries. The lack of one general pattern simply confirms the complexity of the process that determines inequality. Research on the Kuznets curve identifies the large role played by country- or region-specific circumstances, which appear far more important in determining distributional outcomes than the level of per capita income. This is an encouraging finding. That all nations do not follow a similar distributional path suggests that there may be greater scope for government policy to influence the distributional outcomes that accompany economic growth.

What Else Might Cause Inequality?

If inequality is not systematically associated with the level of income, what else accounts for the observed differences across countries and regions shown in Table 6–2? There is little doubt that history and politics have played an important role. An obvious example is South Africa, which has one of the world's highest levels of income inequality. For decades, the apartheid government excluded blacks and other nonwhite South Africans from owning prime agricultural land, getting a decent education, and living in major urban areas. The legacy of these policies remains today, reflected in South Africa's highly unequal distribution of income. (South Africa's Gini coefficient in 2000 was 0.58.)

History and politics also played key roles in other parts of the world. At the end of World War II, the United States administered a land reform in South Korea as part of the dissolution of 50 years of Japanese colonial rule. These reforms redistributed land from Japanese to Korean households, providing millions of Korean families with a key asset from which they could earn a living. Low levels of inequality in Eastern Europe and Central Asia are, in part, the product of years of legislated wages and state ownership of the means of production. Citizens of these countries had limited opportunity to accumulate any productive asset other than an education. It is not surprising that, with the turn toward the market, inequality is now rising in many of these countries; in some of them this is happening alongside renewed economic growth.

---

[13]Even the experience of the United States now rejects Kuznets's original hypothesis. Income inequality in the United States fell over the four decades following the great Depression. But, after 1975, during a period of continued growth in the U.S. economy, household incomes became increasingly *unequal*, counter to the predictions of the Kuznets curve. Economists believe technological change, immigration, and increased international trade are some of the factors that explain this post-1975 shift.

Some of the high levels of inequality in Latin America may be traced to patterns of land ownership dating back centuries. Not only was the colonial legacy part of this process, but the demands of specific crops, including the advantages of plantation-style agriculture, were a factor. In East Asia, rice cultivation was better suited to family farming and established a basis for higher income equality in this region. Mineral wealth, whether in diamonds or oil, also tends to produce higher inequality. Factor endowments shaped distributional outcomes in the past and continue to do so today.

Resource endowments and the "persistence of the past" play significant roles in shaping a nation's distribution of income, but policy choices made today also affect these outcomes. Government policy influences the accumulation of assets, including education. Policy decisions affect the diffusion of technology and access to markets, which condition productivity growth and the returns to factors of production. Taxes and government spending, including expenditures on social safety nets, directly influence how income is divided. The level of inequality in any nation is the result of complex interactions among history, politics, resource endowments, market forces, and government policies.

WHY INEQUALITY MATTERS

If economic development requires a reduction in the amount of poverty, then the simplest explanation for why income inequality matters is that the degree of inequality plus the level of income determines the extent of poverty. Even without a discussion of how to define poverty (which we get to shortly), some examples of the relationship between economic growth, income inequality, and poverty should be clear. If an economy grows and inequality remains unchanged, the income of the poor has grown in line with everyone else's. The poorest quintiles have more income, potentially helping to raise some households out of poverty. Similarly, if per capita income remains unchanged and inequality rises, the poorest quintiles have less income and some households probably have fallen into poverty. These propositions merely express the basic mathematics governing the relationship among poverty, growth, and inequality.

But inequality and growth are not determined independent of one another. There may not be one systematic tendency for how inequality changes as nations grow, but inequality often changes with rising per capita incomes. Similarly, inequality may affect the rate of growth an economy achieves. Do nations with more inequality tend to experience slower growth, thus doubly hurting the well-being of the poor? Finally, income inequality also matters in its own right.

Societies have preferences concerning inequality and may (or may not) wish for their governments to intervene to achieve distributional outcomes.

Just as there has been a long debate over the impact of growth on inequality, there is ongoing debate over how inequality affects economic growth. As discussed previously in this chapter, some early theories of economic development concluded that inequality might raise growth rates. By concentrating income in fewer hands, there might be more savings available to finance investments critical for capital accumulation. But this simple view of distribution and growth fails to capture other channels in which income inequality can be a drag on economic growth. Contemporary discussion of the relationship between inequality and growth explores these channels.

When inequality is high, worthwhile investments may not be undertaken. Poor people may have promising investment opportunities. Buying a farm animal or improving irrigation, investing in a piece of a equipment or building a store, or sending a child to school all may yield a good economic return. But the individuals or families may not undertake these investments because they cannot afford them. Credit market imperfections and the inability of the poor to offer lenders collateral lowers the amount of productive investment they engage in and leads to less economic growth. If the economy had a more equal distribution, more of these productive investments could be financed and pursued.

Another channel that links inequality and growth is through the political process. There are numerous "political economy" connections between distribution and growth. Some argue that, when inequality is high, the rich use their wealth to secure outcomes favorable to their interests, influencing everything from government spending (disproportionate amounts spent on public universities, which the children of the rich attend, than on primary schools) to trade policy (using tariffs and other forms of trade protection to maintain domestic monopolies). These policies can lead to inefficient outcomes that lower growth rates. Others argue the opposite political response. When inequality is high, populist movements may arise that focus more on redistribution and less on growth, leading, for example, to higher taxes and less investment. High inequality also tends to be associated with more violence, both personal and political, which in turn can reallocate expenditures to less productive activities (more police and private security services) and discourage greater investment.

Given the multitude of connections between inequality and growth, the net effect is an empirical matter. Studies that attempt to sort out the relationship tend to rely on the cross-country growth regressions introduced in Chapter 3. Early studies found statistical support that high initial inequality, especially of landholdings, was associated with slower subsequent growth. But later studies, using larger data sets and different econometric techniques, either found no such effect or even an opposing one.[14] The inconclusive nature of these results is not surprising, given both the complexity and potential circularity of the relationship. Inequality affects growth and growth affects inequality, complicating statistical identification. It also is unlikely that one systematic pattern describes the relationship between inequality and growth for all countries at all times. This does not imply that, in a specific-country context, inequality and growth are unrelated. High inequality may be a constraint on growth, but relaxing this constraint is always a daunting challenge for policy makers.

MEASURING POVERTY

People sometimes refer to inequality and poverty as if they were the same thing. They are not. Inequality is an important determinant of poverty, but the two concepts are distinct. To see why, consider the following. Assume your lot in life was to fall in the bottom quintile of the income distribution. If you could pick the nation you would live in, would it be one where the bottom 20 percent received 3.4, 3.5, or 9.0 percent of household income? If you answer, the nation where the poorest receive 9.0 percent, you are confusing inequality with poverty. You also probably are forgetting the results presented in Table 6–1. Recall from that table that the share of the poorest quintile in Bangladesh was 9.0 percent, in Mexico 3.5 percent and in the United States only 3.4 percent!

It should be obvious why you would pick being poor in the United States over being poor in Bangladesh or Mexico. To fall in the lowest quintile in the United States does not mean you are likely to be a homeless person. The bottom 20 percent refers to almost 60 million people. Some of these people are homeless but the overwhelming majority is not. Almost all live in a permanent dwelling with electricity, a gas or electric stove, clean water, and indoor plumbing. Most have access to medical care, even if it means an emergency room at a local hospital, and, during childhood, receive a full regimen of vaccinations against many infectious diseases. The likelihood of contracting malaria or dying of a diarrheal disease is remote, although both were common in the United States in its earlier history. For those with children, the probability of an infant dying before its first birthday is low and that child is likely to receive at least 12 years of education. Those in the bottom quintile in the United States are likely to own a television and telephone, perhaps a car, and have some access to a computer, for example, at a public library if not in their own homes.

[14]Two frequently cited papers that reach opposite conclusions relating inequality and growth are Alberto Alesina and Dani Rodrik, "Distributive Politics and Economic Growth," *Quarterly Journal of Economics* 109, no. 2 (1994), and Kristin Forbes, "A Reassessment of the Relationship between Inequality and Growth," *American Economic Review* 90, no. 4 (2000).

The poorest 20 percent are poor relative to most other Americans and may find this demoralizing, but they have a substantially higher material standard of living than the poor in either Bangladesh or Mexico. No one in the bottom quintile in Bangladesh (or for that matter in most any quintile) is likely to receive the health or education benefits or the material goods consumed by America's poorest individuals. The almost 30 million individuals who make up the bottom quintile in Bangladesh are likely to live in the most rudimentary of dwellings, those that can be washed away in a bad storm. Food often is scarce and clean water unavailable. Living with intestinal parasites is a regular occurrence; infectious diseases take a regular toll on young and old; and infant deaths are a common event. School enrollment rates are rising, but the educational attainment of a poor Bangladeshi, especially among females, is a fraction of their American counterparts. Consumer goods consist of a few articles of clothing, some cooking utensils and little else. Most of those in the bottom 20 percent have never placed a phone call or clicked on a mouse. The bottom quintile in the United States receives only 3.4 percent of household income, while the bottom quintile in Bangladesh consumes 9.0 percent of total consumption expenditures in Bangladesh. But America's bottom 20 percent shares a much larger amount of *total* income and, therefore, enjoys a higher standard of living even if its relative share is so much less.

Poverty Lines

Just as a set of analytical tools is needed for describing and understanding distributional outcomes, a similar set of tools is needed to define and measure poverty. We focus mostly on a consumption or income definition of **absolute poverty,** but it is important to recognize that poverty is multidimensional and encompasses deprivations not readily captured by income measures alone. This should be a familiar idea, since it parallels the debate over how to define economic development. Both the Human Development Index and the Millennium Development Goals go well beyond GDP per capita as a measure of well-being and similar approaches are used in defining poverty.

Poverty lines, defined as having a certain amount of taka or pesos or dollars to spend per day, can capture the degree of material deprivation but may not reflect securing basic health and education. A family may have sufficient funds to purchase a minimal basket of food, but if they have no ready access to safe drinking water, food purchases are no guarantee of meeting nutritional needs. In this critical sense, access to safe drinking water joins money income as a determinant of absolute poverty. The availability of public services, including basic health and education, can have an impact on poverty status today and the transmission of poverty across generations, independent of current consumption levels. Another dimension of poverty is vulnerability to adverse shocks.

Expenditures in one period may raise a family above the poverty line, but in a subsequent period, natural disasters, economywide downturns, or even the ill health or death of a family's breadwinner can push the family below the poverty line. Families often move in and out of poverty and reducing vulnerability is intrinsic to improving well-being.

Poverty is multidimensional and it is possible to quantify many of its dimensions. A great deal of attention is paid to quantifying income or consumption poverty. Development economists often use a definition of absolute poverty where a specific monetary value is defined as a dividing line between the poor and nonpoor. Most nations define their own poverty lines, usually basing the amount on the per capita cost of some minimal consumption basket of food and a few other necessities (see Box 6–1). Food dominates these consumption bundles since it may account for two thirds to three quarters of poor people's total expenditures. In many low-income nations, poverty lines are based on a standard of obtaining 2000 or more calories per day. While these caloric requirements seem "scientific," the actual poverty line remains a social construct. The food purchased to achieve these calories depends upon what individuals actually choose to buy. Expenditures even lower than the poverty line might achieve required calories but hardly anyone would actually purchase such a consumption basket.

Often governments specify more than one poverty line. Because of regional price differences, distinct poverty lines may be applied in urban versus rural areas or, as is the case in Bangladesh, for different regions of the country. Once a poverty line (or lines) is established and expressed in a nation's own currency, that level of consumption or income has to be adjusted on an annual basis to account for changes in the price of the underlying bundle of goods. The goal is to maintain a constant poverty line over time where what is being held constant is the ability to purchase the core consumption basket of food and other necessities.[15] This permits policy makers and researchers to chart the progress a country or region is making in lifting people out of absolute poverty.

Most nations have their own poverty lines and these could be used to make international comparisons. One could compare (or combine) the number who are deemed poor in Bangladesh, with daily per person regional poverty lines of between, roughly, 19 to 32 taka (US$1.70 to $2.80, PPP), with the number said to be poor in Mexico, with poverty lines of 30 to 45 pesos (US$4.60 to $6.60, PPP),

---

[15]Poverty lines also can be expressed in relative terms. In the European Union, poverty is sometimes defined as living below 60 percent of median income. With this definition, the poverty line does not represent the ability to purchase a fixed bundle of goods but changes as median incomes change. Using this approach, absolute poverty declines only if incomes become more equally distributed, not if there is a general increase in per capita incomes.

Instead of one official poverty line, Bangladesh has many. Separate poverty lines exist for each of 14 regions to reflect varying costs. Regional lines are further divided into upper and lower levels to capture different intensities of poverty. All poverty lines are based on securing a minimum daily caloric intake of 2,112 calories. The representative bundle of food to obtain these calories was specified in the early 1990s and includes 11 items: rice, wheat, pulses, milk, oil, meat, freshwater fish, potatoes, other vegetables, sugar, and fruit. The cost of this bundle is adjusted using a domestic price index. The lower poverty line in each region represents the level of poverty at which a person does not have the resources to meet both food and nonfood requirements and must sacrifice some minimum daily caloric requirement to afford essential nonfood needs. The upper poverty line represents a level of poverty at which a person is able to meet minimum daily food requirements and afford some nonfood expenditures.

Mexico has three official poverty lines that capture a range of conditions of poverty. Within these lines, there is differentiation between rural and urban populations. The lowest poverty line is estimated by calculating the cost of a representative bundle of food, taking into account the differing nutritional requirements of rural versus urban dwellers in terms of daily calories and grams of protein. Falling below this poverty line indicates that a person cannot meet even these minimal daily nutrition requirements. Falling below the second poverty line means the person does not have the resources to meet both daily nutritional requirements and minimum health and educational expenses. The third line is one where resources are insufficient to pay for all necessary costs of living, including food, education, health, clothing and footwear, housing, and public transportation expenses.

The United States also specifies multiple poverty lines which vary, not by location, but according to household size and age of household members. U.S. poverty lines, like those in Bangladesh and Mexico, start with the cost of a basket of food items. Designed to meet a person's nutritional needs at minimum cost, the bundle of food items used is still based on a 1955 survey of household food consumption. It included servings of milk, cheese, and ice cream; meat, poultry, and fish; eggs; dry beans, peas, and nuts; flour, cereal, and baked goods; citrus fruit and tomatoes; dark-green and deep-yellow vegetables; potatoes; other vegetables and fruits; fats and oils; and sugars and sweets. The cost of the bundle of food was multiplied by 3 to arrive at the poverty threshold because the 1955 survey found that the average family of three or more people spent approximately one third of its disposable income on food. Since adopting these poverty lines in 1965, the dollar value is adjusted annually to account for price inflation. Neither the bundle of food items nor the portion of income a family spends on food has been adjusted in 50 years, despite changes in diets and evidence that even poor Americans spend less than one third of their after tax income on food.

Sources: Fernando Cortés Cáceres et al. "Evolución y características de la pobreza en México en la última década del siglo XX," Secretaría de Desarrollo Social, Mexico, August 2002, available at, June 30, 2005, www.sedesol.gob.mx/publicaciones/libros/evolucion.pdf; Eloise Cofer, Evelyn Grossman, and Faith Clark. "Family Food Plans and Food Costs: For Nutritionists and Other Leaders Who Develop or Use Food Plans," Home Economics Research Report No. 20. (Washington, DC: U.S. Government Printing Office, November 1962), available at, July 5, 2005, aspe.hhs.gov/poverty/familyfoodplan.pdf.

and in the United States, with a daily per person poverty line of around $16.[16] This would offer a measure of poverty as perceived by each nation. But the resulting differences in poverty rates across nations would itself be a function of the poverty line each nation chooses. An alternative and more widely adopted approach is to establish a single global poverty line. By applying one common poverty line, most often the $1 a day or $2 a day measures, it may be possible to obtain a more consistent picture of the degree of absolute poverty across countries and regions, and of how the number of poor are changing over time.

$1 a Day

The global poverty line of $1 a day has its origins in the late 1980s, when the World Bank prepared its 1990 *World Development Report* (WDR). This series of reports, issued annually and considered the World Bank's flagship publication, selects a different theme each year for investigation. The 1990 edition was devoted to examining global poverty. To assess the extent of absolute poverty in the world, the 1990 WDR examined a set of 34 country-specific poverty lines from both developing and developed nations. As expected, these poverty lines generally rose with income level. Focusing only on the low-income nations in this group, the country-specific poverty lines tended to fall within a range of $275 to $370, measured in terms of 1985 PPP dollars per person per year. The upper bound of this range, just over $1 a day, was adopted as a global poverty threshold. Applying the $1 a day poverty line to estimates of the frequency distributions of consumption per capita in low- and middle-income nations, the 1990 WDR concluded that 1.12 billion people, one third the population of the developing world in 1985, lived in absolute poverty.

To chart changes in poverty over time, it is necessary to increase the poverty line in local currencies in response to changes in domestic prices. Ideally, this would be done using a price index based on the goods the poor tend to consume. In practice, a nation's consumer price index is used. To assess what has happened to regional and global poverty since the 1980s, researchers have done more than just adjust the original $1 a day poverty line by domestic price inflation. Because of improving PPP estimates, based on better data and more countries, the World Bank re-estimated its global poverty line in preparation for the

---

[16] The United States defines poverty depending on the size and composition of a household. Households with children or elderly members are assumed to have different food requirements, leading to different poverty lines. Households with more members are assumed to achieve economies of scale in consumption and this, too, affects their poverty lines. Daily per capita requirements in 2004 range from $27 for a household with one nonelderly member to $10.50 for a household of eight with six children. Since the majority of households in the United States have five or fewer members, the $16 amount refers to the average poverty line for households from one to five members. The reported values for Bangladesh and Mexico refer to their "upper" poverty lines discussed in Box 6–1 for the years 2000 and 2002, respectively.

2000–01, *World Development Report, Attacking Poverty.* The new poverty line continues to be based on a subset of country-specific poverty lines and yields a value of $1.08 per person per day, now referenced to 1993 PPP dollars. This is still referred to as the $1 a day poverty line. (Recall from note 1, we refer to the 1993 $1.08 per day poverty line *in quotation marks* as "$1 a day.") For the most recent year available, 2001, 1.09 billion people lived below "$1 a day," almost the same as the 1985 number that was based on the slightly lower poverty line. But, in 2001, this number represented 21.1 percent of the population of the developing world, a significantly lower percentage of the population living in absolute poverty than in 1985.

Before investigating regional trends in poverty, it is worth examining the use of poverty lines in a bit more detail and defining some alternative measures of poverty that can be based on such lines. Figure 6–4 reproduces the frequency distribution of consumption per capita in Bangladesh in 2000, inserting the "$1 a day" poverty line (expressed in taka per year and adjusted for domestic price inflation from 1993 to 2000). Individuals with consumption below the poverty line, some 36 percent of all Bangladeshis, are considered absolutely poor. It should be evident that there is something arbitrary about this distinction between the poor and nonpoor. Is someone with a few taka more of consumption expenditures living that much differently than someone just below the poverty line? This arbitrary character of poverty lines is inevitable. But poverty lines still are useful in providing a sense of the extent of absolute poverty, a means for assessing the success

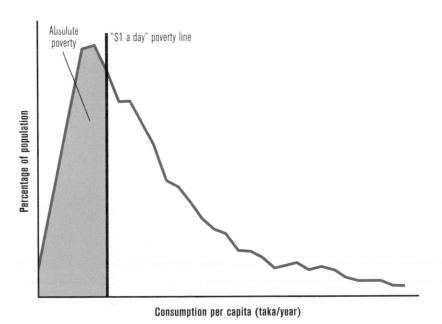

FIGURE 6-4. **Absolute Poverty in Bangladesh**
Source: Collaboration with Claudio E. Montenegro, World Bank.

of policies designed to alleviate poverty, and a mechanism for calling attention to and mobilizing support for reducing human deprivation. Strategies that succeed in reducing the numbers below the poverty line usually spill over and also help the "near poor," those just to the right of the poverty line in the frequency distribution.

Once a poverty line is selected, the extent of absolute poverty can be identified in a number of ways. The simplest is to report the number of people below the poverty line. Equally straightforward is the **headcount index,** the ratio of the number below the poverty line to total population. A third measure, the **poverty gap,** describes the severity of poverty. The severity of poverty refers to both how many people fall below the poverty line and how far they are from that line. Look again at Figure 6–4. Imagine if the frequency distribution below the "$1 a day" poverty line was more rectangular, that is, if the distribution was somewhat higher closer to the origin and somewhat lower closer to the poverty line. This would mean that poverty was more severe. The same number of individuals might fall below the poverty line but the total amount of income they need to get to the poverty line is greater. The poverty gap (PG) captures these differences, and can be calculated as

$$PG = [(PL - MC)/PL] \times HI$$

where PL stands for the poverty line, MC is mean consumption per capita of all individuals below the poverty line, and HI is the headcount index. The bracketed term in the equation indicates in relative terms how far the average poor person is from the poverty line; the headcount index then weights this amount by the percent of poor people in the population. The poverty gap, a measure of how much income is needed to get the poor to the poverty line, rises the further mean consumption of the poor is from the poverty line and the higher the share of the population below the poverty line.

HOW MUCH POVERTY IS THERE?

Figure 6–5 presents one consistent set of estimates, by World Bank economists Shaohua Chen and Martin Ravallion, of the trend in world poverty between 1981 and 2001. Employing the 1993 "$1 a day" poverty line, the good news is that the number of people living in absolute poverty fell by almost 400 million people, from 1.48 to 1.09 billion. Even more dramatic, the share of developing country populations below this standard fell from 40 percent to 21 percent in just two decades. This represents an incredible achievement in reducing human deprivation. The bad news is that 1.09 billion people in poverty still accounts for one out of every five people living in the low- and middle-income nations. A closer look at regional patterns reveals how isolated and uneven the fall in poverty has

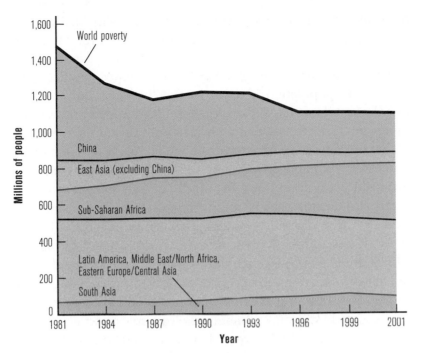

FIGURE 6-5. Number of People Living below "$1 a Day"
Source: Shoahua Chen and Martin Ravallion, "How Have the World's Poorest Fared Since the Early 1980s?" *World Bank Research Observer* 19, no. 2 (2004).

been. Almost the entire decline occurred in East Asia, and within East Asia most of the decline is due to China's success. Half of China's success—lifting over 200 million Chinese above "$1 a day"—occurred in just three years, 1981 to 1984. It took 15 more years to raise another 200 million Chinese above the poverty line. Many observers trace the success achieved between 1981 and 1984 to economic reforms that began in the late 1970s. These reforms decollectivized agriculture and encouraged farm households to produce and market more of their output, pulling them out of poverty.

Poverty reduction was dramatic throughout all of East Asia, with large declines in Indonesia, Malaysia, South Korea, Taiwan, and Thailand. But, in absolute terms, given the size of China's population, China's success dominates the global decline. By comparison, South Asia, dominated by India, saw much less improvement. The decline was only 40 million people, not 420 million, as in East Asia. In sub-Saharan Africa, the trend was the opposite. As the population of this region grew, so did absolute poverty, from 164 million in 1981 to 313 million in 2001.[17] Trends in other regions add little to the aggregate picture for two

[17]Chen and Ravallion, "How Have the World's Poorest Fared . . . ?" point out that the earlier are their estimates, the less confident they are in the results because of the paucity of household surveys form the early 1980s. This is especially the case in Africa. The trend toward increasing absolute poverty in sub-Saharan Africa is not in doubt but the magnitude of this increase may not be precise.

reasons: their population size is relatively small and, as mostly middle-income nations, the share of their populations living at only "$1 a day" was and remains low.

In 1981, the low- and middle-income nations had a combined population of 3.7 billion. By 2001, that population had grown to 5.2 billion. But absolute poverty did not rise by 1.5 billion, it fell! Trends in absolute numbers are one way to mark the progress made against absolute poverty. But it is not the only way. The headcount index presents poverty relative to population size and reinforces both the good and bad news on poverty (Table 6–3). In 1981, China's headcount index was 64 percent; by 2001, it was down to only 17 percent. In South Asia, the incidence of poverty also declined significantly, from just over 50 percent to 31 percent. Sub-Saharan Africa showed a modest increase. With the headcount index remaining in the low to mid 40 percent range, Africa's rapid population growth resulted in its almost doubling the number living below "$1 a day." Latin America also had limited success at decreasing its poverty rate, remaining in the vicinity of 10 percent. The transition experience in Eastern Europe and Central Asia mirrors what we already know from Chapter 2. Economic growth collapsed in the 1990s and as a result absolute poverty, barely known in the 1980s, rose quickly reaching an estimated 6 percent in 1999, but then fell back to under 4 percent in 2001.

For the world as a whole, there has been a significant decline in the proportion who experience the grinding poverty of living below "$1 a day." Forty percent of the developing world or, adding in the developed nations, 33 percent of the entire world population, fell below the "$1 a day" poverty line in 1981. Twenty years later, this ratio stood at 21 percent of the developing world and 18 percent of total world population. Even after excluding China's historic success, the incidence of poverty has fallen significantly in many parts of the world. Can similar progress be made over the next twenty years?

Before trying to answer that question, it is worth considering the severity of poverty as measured by the poverty gap (Table 6–3). In 1981, absolute poverty was severe in the most populous regions of the developing world. In East and South Asia, as well as in sub-Saharan Africa, the poverty gap ranged from 16 to 21 percent. But, by 2001, the poverty gap had fallen to single digits everywhere but in sub-Saharan Africa, where it increased. Over 1 billion people still lived on less than "$1 a day" in 2001, but most of them had gotten a good deal closer to this bare minimum of consumption. China's success at lowering its poverty gap from 23 to 4 percent is a remarkable achievement in human history. It also holds some promise for what is possible and, therefore, what nations in Africa might achieve in the next few decades. Much of Africa began the twenty-first century with a poverty gap similar to China's level 20 years earlier. However, the challenge facing Africa is greater. In 1981, China had a more equal distribution of income than is typical of most African nations. Therefore, African growth rates have to be even

TABLE 6-3. Absolute Poverty by Region, 1981–2001

REGION	NUMBER OF POOR (MILLIONS)			HEADCOUNT INDEX (PERCENT)			POVERTY GAP (PERCENT)		
	1981	1990	2001	1981	1990	2001	1981	1990	2001
East Asia	796	472	271	58	30	15	21	8	3
(China only)	**(634)**	**(375)**	**(212)**	**(64)**	**(33)**	**(17)**	**(23)**	**(9)**	**(4)**
South Asia	475	462	431	52	41	31	16	11	6
Sub-Saharan Africa	164	227	313	42	45	46	17	19	21
Latin America and Caribbean	36	49	50	10	11	10	3	4	3
Middle East and North Africa	9	6	7	5	2	2	1	<1	<1
Eastern Europe and Central Asia	3	2	17	<1	<1	4	<1	<1	<1
Total	**1482**	**1219**	**1089**	**40**	**28**	**21**	**14**	**8**	**6**
(Total excluding China)	(848)	(844)	(877)	(32)	(26)	(23)	(N.A.)	(N.A.)	(N.A.)

Note: Absolute poverty refers to a poverty line of $1.08 a day (PPP, 1993). Total refers to low- and middle-income nations only.
Source: Shoahua Chen and Martin Ravallion, "How Have the World's Poorest Fared Since the Early 1980s?" *World Bank Research Observer* 19, no. 2 (2004).

faster than China's or policies of redistribution greater for absolute poverty to fall as rapidly. It is hard to envision such outcomes. China benefited from a fundamental transformation in its economy, which brought tremendous economic progress. It is hard to identify anything in Africa comparable to China's transition out of socialism and toward the market that has the potential to produce sustained growth rates in output approaching double digits. Reducing absolute poverty in sub-Saharan Africa remains a huge challenge to both African nations and the global community.

Dissenting Opinions on the Extent of Absolute Poverty

With something as complex as estimating the amount of absolute poverty in the world, it should come as no surprise that not everyone agrees with the numbers. Some criticize the amounts as too low, others claim they are too high. One set of criticism concerns the choice of the poverty line; the other, the numbers who fall below "$1 and $2 a day."

The somewhat arbitrary nature of any poverty line already has been identified. Is someone living on just less than "$1 a day" poor while someone consuming just over "$1 a day" not poor? Some commentators also see "$1 a day" as simply too low a threshold for defining absolute poverty at a global level. The "$1 a day" cutoff has been described as "extreme poverty," even "destitution,"

BOX 6-2   WHO IS *NOT* POOR?

Economist Lant Pritchett argues against both "$1 a day" and even "$2 a day" as legitimate measures of *global* poverty. He suggests instead a poverty line no less than $15 a day (2000, PPP), close to the lower bound of the prevailing poverty lines in high income nations. Pritchett argues as follows:

> Because poverty is a social construct each country should be free to set its own definitions of poverty and its own poverty line. . . . But for setting a common, international standard for income poverty—for what constitutes "unacceptable" deprivation in the human condition or "inadequate income in a globalized world—it seems grossly unfair that a person is "poor" if born in one country and yet is "not poor" with a level of real income *ten times* lower if born in another. That is, while India might set a poverty line that is attuned to its capabilities and circumstances and the USA another, for international comparisons choosing the lower line implies that what is "unacceptable" deprivation for a US resident is acceptable for another human being simply because of their residence.

Pritchett goes on to demonstrate that both the "$1 and $2 a day" poverty lines are grossly inconsistent with achieving minimally acceptable levels of such indicators of physical well-being as infant mortality and stunting, the latter referring to the fraction of children whose height for their age is less than two standard deviations less than medical norms.

Pritchett recommends defining "$1 a day" as "destitution," "$2 a day" as "extreme poverty," and "$15 a day" as *global* poverty. He concludes, "This simple shift in definitions allows continuity and comparability with previous measures of poverty while embracing a new bold vision of what the dream of a world free of poverty really means."

Source: Lant Pritchett, "Who Is *Not* Poor? Proposing a Higher International Standard for Poverty," CGD Working Paper No. 33, Center for Global Development (November 2003).

and may be too low to serve as an effective benchmark for poverty alleviation. Others have been critical of what they consider the particularly arbitrary nature of the "$1 a day" poverty line. They argue that the use of one global poverty line bears too little relationship to country-specific poverty lines and therefore defines a poverty line that may have little relevance to the bundle of goods poor people need to purchase to attain their basic needs.[18] This latter argument has special merit for middle-income nations whose poverty lines tend to be above "$1 a day." Still others contend that even "$2 a day" is too low a threshold for a *global* poverty line (Box 6–2).

---

[18]See T. N. Srinivasan and the other contributors to "Dollar a Day: How Much Does It Say?" *in Focus,* International Poverty Centre, United Nations Development Programme (September 2004).

Recognizing some of these criticisms, the World Bank also reports on a "$2 a day" poverty line ($2.15, 1993 PPP), which is more in line with standards adopted by middle-income economies. At "$2 a day," world poverty obviously is higher than at "$1 a day." In 2001, 2.7 billion people, just over half the population of all low- and middle-income economies fell below this poverty line. Regional headcount indices reach as high as 77 percent in South Asia and sub-Saharan Africa. China stands at 47 percent and Latin America at 25 percent. When comparing world regions, at "$2 a day," poverty is most severe in sub-Saharan Africa (it has the highest poverty gap), but there are still three times the number of poor in all of Asia than in sub-Saharan Africa (Figure 6–6). At a global level, progress has been achieved since 1981, when the low- and middle-income "$2 a day" headcount ratio was 67 percent, but the decline has been smaller than for "$1 a day." The apparent "bunching up" of people between "$1 to $2 a day" reveals the vulnerability so many of the world's population faces to economic crises, at both the household and aggregate levels. Falling into extreme poverty is a reality facing hundreds of millions of people.

While no one disputes the widespread nature of absolute poverty nor the severity of the problem in Africa, there is a debate over magnitudes. Economist Xavier Sala-i-Martin and others employ the "$1 and $2 a day" threshold but claim that the estimates of the World Bank of how many people fall below these

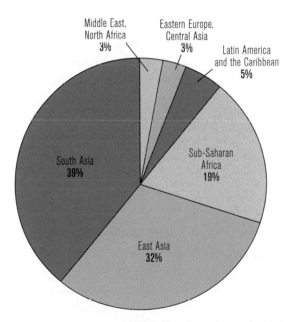

FIGURE 6-6. Regional Distribution of People Living below the "$2 a Day" Poverty Line, 2001

Source: Shoahua Chen and Martin Ravallion, "How Have the World's Poorest Fared since the Early 1980s?" *World Bank Research Observer* 19, no. 2 (2004).

poverty lines are too high.[19] Instead of the World Bank's estimate of over 1 billion poor in 2001, Sala-i-Martin identifies only 3.5 *million* people living below "$1 a day" in 1998, the latest year in his study. The World Bank's global headcount ratio in 2001 is 18 percent, Sala-i-Martin's is 7 percent. These are significant differences that are not easily reconciled. Some of the difference is due to the use of income versus consumption data by Sala-i-Martin. Holding the poverty line constant, poverty estimates must be lower when income is used since, at an aggregate level, income exceeds consumption. Another distinction involves the World Bank's reliance on household surveys versus the alternative of using national income data. Household surveys tend to yield lower levels of consumption, in part, because of the systematic bias due to better-off families having lower response rates to such surveys. But explaining the large gap in estimates based on these different sources remains a puzzle to researchers. What is reassuring is that it is the levels and not the trends in poverty that are so different between the two approaches. Both approaches reveal significant declines in the rate of poverty since 1980 in East and South Asia, and both highlight the worsening situation in Africa. It may be hard to specify the precise number of people that face absolute poverty but there is little doubt that reducing human deprivation remains a formidable challenge.

Who Are the Poor?

If the World Bank's estimates are correct and nearly four out of every five Africans and South Asians live below the "$2 a day" poverty line, it might be easier to identify the nonpoor than the poor. This is a somewhat cynical response to the question "Who are the poor?" Even though the majority of African and South Asian populations live in conditions that qualify as poverty, some live well below the poverty line and are poorer than others. There are defining characteristics of extreme poverty.

Rural poverty rates tend to be higher than urban rates. This may come as a surprise to the casual observer who contrasts the image of rural villages, with their open spaces and often picturesque arrangements of straw huts and basic dwellings, with the urban squalor, densely settled and seeming disorganization in the shantytowns and favelas[20] common to large cities in low- and middle-income nations. What the casual observer fails to see are the lack of opportunities in rural areas. There are fewer ways to earn income, less education and health care, and

---

[19]Xavier Sala-i-Martin, "The World Distribution of Income," NBER Working Paper No. 8933 (May 2002) and Surji Bhalla, *Imagine There's No Country—Poverty, Inequality and Growth in the Era of Globalization* (Washington, DC: Institute for International Economics, 2002).

[20]The origin of the word *favela* is the Morro de Favela hillside in Rio de Janeiro, Brazil, where freed slaves established a community of squatters in the late nineteenth century. Over time the term has been adopted to describe any urban slum, especially in Latin America.

often more vulnerability to the weather and forces of nature. Individuals often choose to leave the countryside for the slums of the city because there are more economic opportunities in urban areas. Within rural areas, poverty often is most common among landless casual laborers or, in sub-Saharan Africa, among pastoralists.

In addition to the rural-urban divide, poverty rates vary by regions within countries. Two examples are the Northeast of Brazil and the Indian state of Utter Pradesh, which have been pockets of deep and persistent poverty for decades. The persistence of regional poverty reflects both the limits of spreading development from one region to another and the constraints individuals may face in escaping poverty by migrating from one region to another. Poverty also has a racial and ethnic face. Scheduled castes in India, certain ethnic minorities in Eastern Europe, and indigenous groups in the Andean region all experience poverty rates in excess of others in their societies.

Are Women Poorer than Men?

Looking at poverty from the perspective of gender requires consideration of intra-household distribution, the sharing of resources within family units. Most studies of gender roles and opportunities in developing and developed nations conclude that women are disadvantaged relative to men along many dimensions.[21] Women have less access to property rights, including ownership of land and often are denied inheritance. Girls have tended to receive less primary and secondary education than boys, although in many countries and regions this is no longer the case. Labor markets tend to discriminate against women, paying them less than men for the same work. Combining the work done at home with that done for income, women tend to work many more hours per week. Domestic violence against women is all too common. Sex-selective abortion favors the birth of boys over girls in many parts of the world.

Given all these disadvantages, the feminization of poverty seems straightforward. But it is not. Measures of individual consumption are based on household data, and it is difficult to disentangle who consumes what within the family. Some goods, including housing, are jointly consumed. Given the lack of data on individual consumption by gender, some studies compare poverty rates between households headed by men and women. The results are inconclusive. Some categories of women-headed households do quite poorly. In many parts of the world, widows without male heirs (India) and elderly women on pensions (Eastern Europe) have particularly high poverty rates. But other women-headed households, including unmarried women working in urban areas or married

---

[21]This discussion draws from World Bank, *Engendering Development* (Washington, DC: Oxford University Press, 2001).

women with husbands working abroad and sending remittances, may experience lower than average poverty rates. Studies of nutrition that assess the degree to which the needs of females versus males are met find some evidence of the relative deprivation of females but the results vary widely across regions and even within countries. Despite the lack of evidence on the feminization of poverty, it is hard to imagine that reducing gender inequality would not also help to reduce the poverty of girls and boys and women and men.

STRATEGIES TO REDUCE POVERTY

The World Bank's 1990 WDR not only provided an estimate of the amount of world poverty, it outlined a strategy for alleviating world poverty. The strategy had two elements: (1) promote market-oriented economic growth and (2) direct basic health and education services to the poor. Market-oriented growth included many of the familiar recommendations of the "Washington Consensus": macroeconomic stability, greater economic openness to trade and investment, increased public investment in infrastructure, improved credit markets, and the like. Combined, these policies would lead to labor-demanding growth, which would benefit the poor since the primary asset the poor rely on is their labor. The second element of the strategy called for investing in people. Directing government health and education services to the poor would increase their productivity and thereby contribute to poverty reduction. A third but less emphasized part of the strategy was to develop social safety nets to assist those unable to take advantage of market opportunities. This group included the sick and the old but also all those who suffered from such systemic shocks as natural disasters or macroeconomic crises.

Economic growth plays a central role in the poverty reduction strategies proposed by the World Bank in both the 1990 WDR and its sequel in 2000–01. But there are dissenting voices. In 1996, the United Nations Development Progamme (UNDP), another multilateral agency devoted to development problems, wrote in its flagship publication, *The Human Development Report,* "Policymakers are often mesmerized by the quantity of growth. They need to be more concerned with its structure and quality." The report goes on to specify problems with economic growth that is "*jobless*—where the overall economy grows but does not expand opportunities for employment"; "*ruthless*—where the fruits of economic growth mostly benefit the rich, leaving millions of people struggling in ever-deepening poverty"; "*voiceless*—where growth in the economy has not been accompanied by an extension of democracy or empowerment"; *rootless*—which causes people's cultural identity to wither"; and *"futureless*—where the present generation squanders resources needed by future generations."[22]

The UNDP report raises many concerns. One of them is to question whether (or at least how often) economic growth is good for the poor, or whether the benefits are more likely to be concentrated on the rich. The basic mathematics of growth, distribution, and poverty suggests that, generally, growth should be good for the poor. Earlier in this chapter, we saw that inequality does not systematically increase with economic growth. This implies that in most cases growth should benefit the poor just as it benefits others in a society. As long as GDP grows faster than population, average incomes within each quintile usually also increase. Numerous studies support this conclusion.

"Growth Is Good for the Poor"

Figure 6–7 reproduces the data from one of these studies.[23] Each observation compares the growth in income of the poor, here defined as the bottom 20 percent of the income distribution, with overall economic growth (growth in GDP per capita). Each observation refers to a growth spell of five or more years in a given country. In many cases, there is more than one observation per country. This occurs when information on the distribution of income is available for multiple years. Growth spells have a median length of six years. These spells occur between the years 1956 to 1999, with most taking place in the 1980s and 1990s. Not all countries are represented in the data set, but there is good coverage by region and for the world population as a whole.[24]

The trend in Figure 6–7 is consistent with the view that growth tends to be good for the poor. The fitted regression line has a *positive* slope of 1.2, indicating that, *on average,* the incomes of the poor grow at about the same rate as GDP per capita. The estimated slope is greater than 1.0, which means that, if GDP per capita grows, say, at 5 percent, the regression predicts that the incomes of the poor will grow by 6 percent. Looking at the variance in outcomes, most observations lie in the quadrant where both the growth in per capita income and the growth in the incomes of the poor are positive. This quadrant can be further

[22]United Nations Development Programme, *Human Development Report,* 1996 (New York: Oxford University Press, 1996), 3–4.

[23]David Dollar and Aart Kraay, "Growth Is Good for the Poor," *Journal of Economic Growth* 7, no. 3 (2002). Earlier studies that reached similar conclusions are Michael Roemer and Mary Kay Gugerty, "Does Economic Growth Reduce Poverty?" CAER Discussion Paper No. 5, Harvard Institute for International Development (1997); and John Gallup, Steve Radelet, and Andrew Warner, "Economic Growth and the Income of the Poor," CAER Discussion Paper No. 36, Harvard Institute for International Development (1999).

[24]Departing from the original study, the OECD economies are excluded from the figure as are a few statistical outliers.

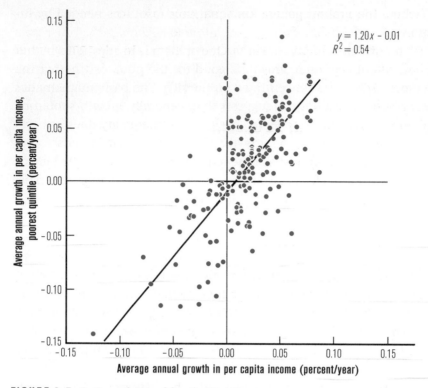

FIGURE 6-7. Is Growth Good for the Poor?

Source: David Dollar and Aart Kraay. "Growth Is Good for the Poor," *Journal of Economic Growth* (September 1, 2002), available at (Dataset), econ.worldbank.org/external/default/main?theSitePK=477872&contentMDK=20355294&menuPK=836389&pagePK=64168182&piPK=64168060, accessed July 2005.

divided in two. More than half the observations lie above the 45° line (not shown), where the incomes of the poor grow faster than average incomes. Growth is still "good for the poor" among the observations that lie below the 45° line but above the *x*-axis. In these cases the incomes of the poor grow at a rate somewhat less than the rest of the economy.

Returning to Figure 6–7, there also are cases of **immiserizing growth,** situations where the poor witness a decline in their average incomes despite growth in the economy. The UNDP's concern over *ruthless* growth appears to have merit in some cases. In about one in five cases of positive economic growth, the income levels of the poor decrease. For Latin America this occurs about one third of the time. Rapid growth, however, minimizes such outcomes. In these data, when growth is over 5 percent, there were only two cases of immiserizing growth.[25] Rapid growth seems especially good for the poor and nonpoor alike. The opposite also is true. The poor are particularly vulnerable during periods of

[25]The two cases are Puerto Rico (1963–69) and Singapore (1978–83).

economic decline. This is shown in the lower left-hand quadrant, where many of the observations lie well below the regression line (a substantial number from Eastern Europe and Central Asia during the late 1980s and early 1990s). While there are important exceptions, the empirical record suggests that economic growth benefits the poor more often than it leaves the poor behind.

Sometimes Growth May Not Be Enough

The centrality of economic growth in achieving economic development is a major theme of this textbook, as is the role of markets in achieving more rapid economic growth. But, in some situations, more than economic growth and market forces may be needed to reduce absolute poverty. First, there are the cases just identified, where the well-being of the bottom quintile falls despite increases in GDP per capita. These are cases where the increase in income inequality that accompanied economic growth was so large as to reverse any potential gains for the poor from rising GDP per capita. Researchers have not yet identified the pattern of growth or the type of government policies that characterize these stark exceptions to "growth is good for the poor."

Second, note that the data in Figure 6–7 are based on a measure of relative rather than absolute poverty. The vertical axis measures changes in the mean income of the bottom 20 percent, not changes in the headcount index or poverty gap based on "$1 or $2 a day" poverty lines. This makes a difference. Imagine an economy where average incomes are low and inequality is high. If the bottom 20 percent only receives 2 to 3 percent of total income, as they do in many countries in Latin American and Southern Africa, even if the incomes of the poorest quintile grow at the same rate as average incomes, the well-being of the poor make little progress. Few of the poor cross the poverty line, because the initial share of income accruing to them is so low. When high levels of inequality further reduce the prospects for more rapid economic growth, the situation of the poor is that much worse.

The cases of immiserizing growth and income inequality high enough that growth produces meager benefits are infrequent. More common is a third situation, where distributional changes reduce the amount of poverty alleviation generated by economic growth. Latin America during the 1990s experienced only modest economic growth, but it also was accompanied by rising income inequality. Even the modest growth that was achieved, assuming no change in inequality, would have reduced the numbers living under "$2 a day" by 90 million people.[26] But, because inequality increased during the 1990s, the number of people living in poverty fell by only 45 million. Poverty in Latin America would have fallen further had there been both faster growth and less inequality.

---

[26]"Is Growth Enough?" *Latin American Economic Policies* 14 (Inter-American Development Bank, 2001).

Last, the data in Figure 6–7 report on rates of growth. But how does growth affect the *absolute amount* of income individuals in different quintiles actually receive? Even when the growth in income of the poor exceeds that of the rich, higher income quintiles usually still receive a much larger increase in absolute income. This is because a small percentage of a large number always represents much more additional income than a larger percentage of a small number. Consider the cases of Bangladesh and Mexico presented at the beginning of this chapter. If economic growth is distributionally neutral (GDP per capita rises but inequality remain the same), then for each increase of 100 taka or 100 pesos going to someone in the bottom 20 percent, someone in the top 20 percent, on average, receives roughly 450 more taka in Bangladesh and 1,500 more pesos in Mexico. In other words, even when growth is good for the poor, the absolute income gap between rich and poor continues to widen. But the poor do gain as the number below the poverty line falls.

Pro-Poor Growth

With increasing attention paid to global poverty, captured by the Millennium Development Goal of cutting in half by 2015 the numbers living below "$1 a day," development experts frequently refer to the need for development strategies that adopt a poverty focus (Box 6–3). Sometimes this is referred to as **pro-poor growth.** This is not a well-defined term. Pro-poor growth sometimes is described as the situation where income growth among the poor is faster than average income growth. The problem with this definition is that it would favor a situation where the incomes of the poor grew, say, at 3 percent while GDP per capita grew at 2 percent, over the case where the incomes of the poor grew at 4 percent while GDP per capita grew at 6 percent. But more rapid poverty reduction would occur in the latter. This is more than a hypothetical distinction, China's experience reflects the second scenario.

While not well-defined, at least the intentions of pro-poor growth are clear. What can governments do to achieve economic growth that rapidly improves the well-being of the poor? Answers lie in better understanding the complex interactions among growth, inequality, and poverty. Pro-poor growth does not represent a choice between being pro-growth versus pro-poor. The strategy calls for combining more rapid growth with increased opportunities for the poor to participate in that growth. Policies that both accelerate growth and address inequality are needed to achieve these goals.

The Washington Consensus and the Poor

Far more-rapid economic growth in most low- and middle-income nations is essential for poverty reduction. Those who question whether growth is good for the poor also may be skeptical about the ability of markets to help poor people.

BOX 6-3 WHY SHOULD DEVELOPMENT STRATEGIES HAVE A POVERTY FOCUS?

In an interview appearing in *Finance and Development,* a journal of the International Monetary Fund, Harvard University economist Dani Rodrik makes a compelling case for reform strategies to adopt a poverty focus.

First, in considering social welfare, most people, and democratically elected governments in particular, would give more weight to the well-being of the poor than to that of the rich. The economy's growth rate is not a sufficient statistic for making welfare evaluations because it ignores not only the level of income but also its distribution. A policy that increases the income of the poor by one rupee can be worthwhile at the margin, even if it costs the rest of society more than a rupee. From this perspective, it may be entirely rational and proper for a government considering two competing growth strategies to choose the one that has a greater potential payoff for the poor, even if its impact on overall growth is less assured.

Second, even if the welfare of the poor does not receive extra weight, interventions aimed at helping the poor may still be the most effective way to raise average incomes. Poverty is naturally associated with market imperfections and incompleteness. The poor remain poor because they cannot borrow against future earnings to invest in education, skills, new crops, and entrepreneurial activities. They are cut off from economic activity because they are deprived of many collective goods (such as property rights, public safety, and infrastructure) and lack information about market opportunities. It is a standard tenet of economic theory that raising real average incomes requires interventions designed to close gaps between private and social costs. There will be a preponderance of such opportunities where there is a preponderance of poverty.

Third, focusing on poverty is also warranted from the perspective of a broader, capabilities-oriented approach to development. An exclusive focus on consumption or income levels constitutes too narrow an approach to development. As Nobel Laureate Amartya Sen has emphasized, the overarching goal of development is to maximize people's ability to lead the kind of life they value. The poor face the greatest hurdles in this area and are therefore the most deserving of urgent policy attention.

Source: Excerpted from, Dani Rodrik "Growth versus Poverty Reduction: A Hollow Debate," *Finance and Development* 37, no. 4 (December 2000).

Competition may be seen as exploiting poor people, by paying them "too little" for their labor or by charging "too much" for the inputs they purchase or the goods they buy. Policies associated with the Washington Consensus often are viewed critically, as protecting the interests of rich countries or rich citizens in poor nations at the expense of the masses of poor people in low- and middle-income countries. But are these criticisms valid? Can market-friendly strategies serve the interests of the poor? Here, we review two main elements of the Washington Consensus—macroeconomic stability and economic openness—and their impact on the poor.

Achieving macroeconomic stability is central to the Washington Consensus. Maintaining fiscal discipline and reducing price inflation are key features of macroeconomic stability. Such stability usually entails reducing budget deficits, achieved by cutting government expenditures. This in turn often brings forth protests that the poor are hurt by reduced government spending on basic services. There can be considerable truth to such concerns, but it is not the whole picture. Government spending frequently fails to reach the poor, as programs, including those on health and education, often are targeted at higher income quintiles.

Maintaining unsustainable budget deficits also leads to price inflation, which tends to hurt the poor much more than the rich. Higher income individuals have ways to avoid the negative consequences of rapid price inflation. They can send their savings abroad or hold their wealth in land or real estate, which often are a hedge against inflation. But the poor lack these options. What minimal savings they have can disappear under persistent price inflation; the costs of even their minimal borrowing escalate; and any type of fixed income, for example, a pension, soon becomes relatively worthless. Price inflation usually leads to the depreciation of the currency, which raises the price of imported goods. While this affects the luxury purchases of the rich it also affects the poor, as prices rise for fuel and other essential commodities. When fuel prices go up, transport costs increase, affecting many items the poor depend on. Price inflation also acts like a brake on investment and economic growth, and slower economic growth is not in the interests of the poor. Overall, macroeconomic stability tends to be good for both economic growth and the poor.

The Washington Consensus calls for trade liberalization and greater economic openness. This entails reducing trade barriers, encouraging foreign direct investment and freeing up exchange rates. Antiglobalization advocates see such measures as hurting the poor, who cannot protect themselves from the vagaries of world capital markets or the onslaught of cheap exports. Once again, there is merit to these positions in some circumstances. The Asian financial crisis of the late 1990s hurt both rich and poor in many economies. Cheap crops, the result (in part) of farm subsidies in the European Union and the United States, hurt farmers in some economies. Cotton growers in West Africa are an often-cited example.

But there is another side to increased economic openness. If nations export goods in which they have a comparative advantage, low-income nations are likely to specialize in goods that rely on unskilled labor. This leads to an increase in the employment of such workers and, over time, to an increase in their wages. Since poverty is likely to be common among the least skilled, trade increases labor demand and reduces poverty. Greater openness, including the exchange of technology and the capital accumulation that results from foreign direct investment, can improve productivity and raise overall economic growth. In addition, trade may also reduce the prices the poor must pay for goods and services, further improving their welfare.

The textbook case for trade is compelling and the success in poverty reduction throughout Asia often identifies trade as an engine of growth, especially exports of labor-intensive manufactured products. But there is more to economic openness than increasing exports, and a full account of the impact of globalization on poverty does not yield one simple conclusion. Trade reform can help some of the poor but hurt others. In Mexico, the NAFTA agreement brought more liberalized trade, which hurt farmers who previously were protected by tariffs on corn at the same time that it helped those who found employment in the growing export sector. Since the same individuals need not have left the farm for the factory, trade reform increased the poverty of some and decreased it for others. (See Chapter 19 for a fuller account of the impact of trade on growth, development, and poverty.[27]) Trade reforms illustrate an important principle: Market forces create new opportunities that benefit some and hurt others. Helping the poor get the most out of new opportunities is a challenge facing all economies.

Improving Opportunities for the Poor

Improving the operation of markets helps the poor only if they can take advantage of these opportunities. This is why expanding basic education and health services are often main elements of strategies to reduce poverty. Education tends to make people more productive. It permits them to process new information and take advantage of new opportunities, whether new seed varieties that increase farm yields; new jobs that require the ability to read and write; or new medicines that increase child survival or improve adult health. Education is not a panacea. In a bad economic environment, even education can yield a low return (see Chapter 8). But, without an education, many of the poor may get trapped in intergenerational cycles of poverty. Similar arguments can be made for the importance of basic health (see Chapter 9). The debilitating effects of a host of diseases, including malaria, HIV/AIDS, and many others, prevent those who are infected from engaging in work and seizing new opportunities. No matter how well markets work, if someone is too sick to take advantage of such opportunities poverty persists.

Investing in human capital is part of an agenda for improving the opportunities of the poor. Other reforms also warrant consideration. Most of the poor

[27]Also see Ann Harrison, ed., *Globalization and Poverty* (Chicago: University of Chicago Press, forthcoming).

live in rural areas and either directly or indirectly depend on agriculture as a source of income. Studies on India find that growth in the rural economy alleviates both rural and urban poverty, while urban growth primarily reduces only urban poverty.[28] Supporting the rural economy is not something governments in low- and middle-income nations always do. More attention needs to be paid to rural infrastructure, including better roads and telecommunications, so that poor farmers can more easily market their crops and obtain information about prices. Tube wells for safe drinking water, improved irrigation, agriculture extension services, research and development on crop varieties, and expanded access to credit are other interventions that can contribute to the improved performance of the rural economy and a decline in rural poverty. (See Chapter 16 for further discussion of agricultural development.)

Spending more on the poor, whether on their education or health care, on the infrastructure on which they depend, or in the rural economy where most of the poor live, means spending less on other groups in society. Reforming the allocation of government expenditures can be both pro-poor and pro-growth. But it is bound to encounter resistance as domestic interest groups act to maintain government expenditures they have come to expect. Even more controversial are proposals to redistribute assets to the poor, most often land.

Explanations for the economic growth and success at poverty alleviation among East Asian countries, including China, Korea, and Taiwan, often point to the role played by earlier policies of land redistribution. These were fairly radical interventions that included the expropriation of land by the state with minimal or no compensation to owners. Land reforms in East Asia occurred during times of extreme political upheaval, whether social revolution in China or the end of foreign occupation in Korea. Despite the ultimate success of these economies and the role redistribution of agricultural land played in their subsequent economic development, land reforms and other types of asset redistribution receive less support today. They often are seen as politically difficult, if not infeasible, by both national governments and multilateral institutions like the International Monetary Fund and World Bank. Land reforms also have gone badly in many countries. Zimbabwe's land reform is but one element of the destructive actions taken by the government of Robert Mugabe that turned Zimbabwe from a net food exporter into a nation dependent on food aid. Zimbabwe's experience is an extreme example; it demonstrates that redistributing assets, alone, offers little promise of alleviating poverty. A much broader set of complementary policies are needed to permit the poor to take advantage of any increase in their assets. But, even when such policies are in place, asset redistribution often is politically too difficult to play much of a role in a pro-poor growth strategy.

[28]Martin Ravallion and Gaurav Datt, "Why Has Economic Growth Been More Pro-Poor in Some States of India than Others?" *Journal of Development Economics* 68 (2002).

Income Transfers and Safety Nets

Every nation has individuals who are beyond the reach of the market. They include those who are too old, too young, or too sick to work and without family networks to care for them. There are also situations in which systemic shocks, whether due to natural catastrophes or economic crises, require government action since the marketplace cannot resolve them.

Situations of chronic poverty tend to call for income transfers. These may take the form of cash grants but, in developing economies, more often involve food pricing or food distribution programs. The challenge facing such programs is to make them cost effective and have them reach the target population and not "leak" to higher-income groups. Food price subsidies aid the poor but also subsidize the purchases of the nonpoor. The net result can be an unsustainable fiscal burden on the budget. Food stamp programs have been used in some countries and can be better targeted to those most in need. But such programs are expensive to administer and may lack broad political support.

Social safety nets are similar to income transfers but, in their design, recognize that household poverty often is transitory rather than chronic. Panel data that trace individuals or households over time find that there are fewer families who are always poor than there are families who are poor some of the time. This outcome is true in low- and middle-income economies as well as in high-income settings. The transitory nature of poverty does not minimize the hardship families endure nor does it imply that those living at just over a nation's poverty line are satisfying their material needs. But it does recommend designing policies that help individuals and households, not in a permanent fashion but when income and consumption shortfalls occur. Public employment schemes are one example.

The Employment Guarantee Scheme (EGS) in the Indian state of Maharashtra and the Trabajar program in Argentina were designed to insure poor people with a source of income and reduce the variability of their incomes. The EGS guarantees employment within a few weeks of the individual's request and provides a job relatively close to a person's home. These jobs involve public works, such as road construction and repair, irrigation systems, and prevention of soil erosion. To solve the targeting problem, wages in public employment schemes must be kept low relative to market alternatives. This maintains the cost effectiveness of the scheme by minimizing the numbers who are not poor from seeking these jobs. By offering the prevailing market wage for unskilled rural labor, EGS encourages self-targeting, the likelihood that those who choose to participate are individuals the program is intended to benefit. To encourage self-targeting Trabajar in Argentina offered a monthly wage set at 75 percent of the average monthly earnings of workers in the bottom 10 percent of households living in and around Buenos Aires. Evaluation of these public employment schemes finds that they were well used and well targeted. ESG provides about 100 million person-days of employment, varying both by season and year. Participation falls during the busy season in agriculture, confirming that poor families use the program to counter the variability in monthly incomes. The overwhelming majority of participants in the ESG and Trabajar programs are from the lowest income deciles. Participants realize significant increases in their incomes, lifting many above poverty.[29]

GLOBAL INEQUALITY AND "THE END OF POVERTY"

Our discussion of inequality and poverty reduction focused on nations. We looked carefully at levels and trends in inequality within nations and pro-poor policies that governments might pursue. Most policy making occurs at a national level, so this focus is warranted. But there is also a global dimension to issues of inequality and poverty. The gap between rich and poor across countries tends to be greater than it is within most nations. Should anything be done to change this outcome? Is reducing world poverty a global goal, and is there a role for actions that go beyond the nation-state? There is considerable debate over the answers to these questions.

A simple way of portraying global inequality is to divide the world into the high- versus low- and middle-income economies. In 2003, the high-income nations accounted for 15 percent of world population and consumed 56 percent of world output. The low- and middle-income nations represented the rest, 85 percent of world population consuming 44 percent of world output. This level of global inequality is comparable to that in Brazil and South Africa, two of the world's most unequal nations. This degree of global inequality is not a recent outcome. In 1980, the results were similar: The high-income nations represented 18 percent of world population and consumed 62 percent of world output.[30] This simple division of the world provides a fairly reliable snapshot of global inequality, but it ignores important differences between countries within each of these groups. In addition, not everyone in a high-income economy is rich nor is everyone in a low-income nation poor. To resolve these problems, three measures often are used in debates over whether the world is becoming a more, or less, equal place.

One approach is to define **international inequality** by comparing average incomes across countries. For some questions, it is appropriate to rely on this

---

[29]World Bank, "Principles of Successful Workfare Programs," *World Development Report 2000/2001: Attacking Poverty* (Washington, DC: World Bank, 2001), Box 8.9.

[30]The share of world output refers to gross national income measured in terms of PPP. If GNI is measured at market exchange rates, the high-income nations' share of GNI was close to 80 percent in both 1980 and 2003.

method. For example, the convergence debate, discussed in Chapter 3, asks whether there is a tendency for the income levels across nations to converge over time. Comparing mean incomes is warranted here. This approach treats each of the world's roughly 200 nations equally, whether Tuvalu, with a population of 11,000, or China with 1.3 billion people. But for a discussion of human welfare, treating each nation the same without regard to its population seems less warranted. An alternative index of international inequality is to weight each nation's mean income by its population. A population-weighted measure of international inequality is better suited for some questions but still leaves a key issue unresolved. By multiplying the average level of income by population no account is taken of the domestic distribution of income, everyone in China (or Tuvalu) is assumed to have the same income as everyone else. To get around this problem, one needs a measure of **global inequality** that compares the income (or consumption) of each individual regardless of where that person lives. Such a measure describes inequality among all individuals not just among all nations. Not surprisingly, the level of inequality and its trend varies according to which of these definitions is employed.

Figure 6–8 compares two estimates of international inequality, one weighted and the other unweighted by population, from 1961 to 2000. The data for these comparisons are readily available, requiring only GDP per capita (PPP) and population by country. Gini coefficients are estimated annually for each of

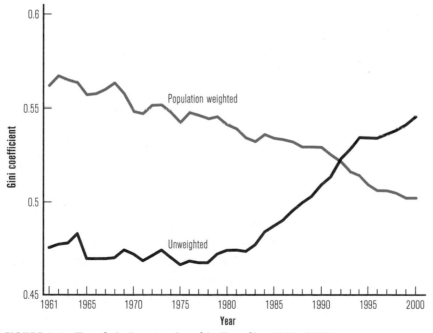

FIGURE 6-8. **Trends in International in Equality, 1961–2000**
Source: Branko Milanovic, *Worlds Apart: Measuring International and Global Inequality*
(Princeton, NJ: Princeton University Press, 2005).

these series. The two trends in international inequality could not be more different. Economist Branko Milanovic refers to these differences as "the mother of all
inequality disputes."[31] The unweighted trend (counting each country the same)
shows little systematic change until the early 1980s, after which there is an
almost continuous rise in inequality. The weighted series (giving larger countries more influence) shows the opposite, a decreasing trend especially since
1980. The difference is easy to explain.

The rise in the unweighted measure of international inequality reflects the regional growth trends we first encountered in Chapter 2. The 1980s were a "lost
decade" for Latin America, with debt crises followed by economic stagnation and
decline. In the 1990s, the transition experience in Eastern Europe and Central Asia
also was accompanied by steep declines in income. These reversals of fortune contrast with positive growth in the high-income economies and parts of Asia. Sub-
Saharan Africa's persistently low incomes increase *the level* of global inequality, but
Africa's growth tragedy plays less of a role in *increasing* international inequality.
This is because low growth has characterized the region since the early 1970s.

The population-weighted measure of international inequality shows an altogether different trend. For four decades, the measure has declined, picking up
speed during the 1990s. Given the construction of this measure, what happened in
heavily populated nations drives the outcome. China's experience explains much
of the observed trend, with economic growth in India contributing but to a lesser
degree. China's post-1978 economic transformation quickly moved the nation
from low- to middle-income status. This closed some of the gap between China
and the high-income nations, especially the heavily populated United States, but
increased the income gap between China and the remaining low-income nations.
On net, the Chinese population's move toward "the middle" of the world distribution of income resulted in a significant decline in the population-weighted Gini
ratio. Continued rapid growth in China, however, could one day lead to a rise in
world inequality if growth in low-income regions fails to accelerate.

But we are not done. Population-weighted international inequality, by
assigning all citizens the same level of per capita income (or consumption),
assumes "perfect income equality" within nations. This is a poor assumption for
measuring inequality among people. To correct this problem requires more than
data on GDP per capita and population size. Household-level data are needed to
assign a more precise estimate of income levels to each person in the world. Some
studies employ techniques to extrapolate such information further back in time.
Others focus on the period since the mid-1980s when household data for a large
percentage of world population became available. There is considerable variance
in the level of global inequality predicted by these various studies and no consen-

---

[31]Branko Milanovic, *Worlds Apart: Measuring International and Global Inequality* (Princeton, NJ:
Princeton University Press, 2005). Much of the subsequent discussion of trends in global inequality
draws from this source.

sus on trends in recent decades. But what all these studies show is that global inequality is significantly higher than population-weighted international inequality.[32] China, India, and the United States contribute significantly to this outcome. All three have had economic growth accompanied by rising Gini coefficients at home.

Global inequality at the beginning of the twenty-first century, as captured by estimates of global Gini coefficients, ranges from about 0.60 to 0.80. This is a large range, which has created considerable controversy and debate over data and methods. But, despite the academic disagreements, what is clear is that global inequality exceeds the level of inequality of almost any nation in the world. It should come as no surprise that the world is a very unequal place, but the *degree* of inequality is striking.

Is your response to the evidence on the degree of global inequality, "Something should be done about this!" If it is, it is important to be clear on the nature of the problems created by global inequality that you wish to resolve. Consider the following: Global inequality would be lower if, all else equal, economic growth in high-income economies was slower. Some may be in favor of slower economic growth in the United States and elsewhere, but their reasons may have little to do with global inequality or the well-being of people in poor nations. You may reject the relentless consumerism of the United States. Americans buy ever-larger houses, fill them with a seemingly endless supply of goods, and drive bigger vehicles on increasingly congested roads. There is much in the lifestyles and consumption habits of high-income economies to criticize. But slower economic growth in rich nations, even if it led to lower global inequality, might have an adverse impact on low- and middle-income nations. If rich nations grew more slowly, their demand for goods from other nations would fall and affect growth rates elsewhere. Global inequality brought about by slower growth in high-income economies could prove a detriment to progress in reducing global poverty. There is no reason to believe that if the United States grew more slowly, Africa or some other poor region would grow more quickly. In all likelihood, the opposite would be true.

There are many ways in which global inequality could be lower today. If instead of slower growth in the rich nations, what if, over the past 20 years, income inequality in China had not risen? Remember that China has had an exceptionally high growth rate for more than two decades and has been able to lift over 400 million of its citizens above the "$1 a day" poverty line. China's economic miracle also contributed to reducing global inequality, but the effect would have been even greater if income inequality within China had not risen. Could China have grown rapidly, dramatically reduced poverty, *and* kept its level of inequality from rising? We really do not know, since we cannot observe the counterfactual. But there is some chance that lower inequality within China might have required slower economic growth.

---

[32]Reviews of alternative studies can be found in Milanovic, ibid., 119–27 and in the *World Development Report 2006: Equity and Development* (Washington, DC: World Bank, 2006), Chapter 9.

Calls for reducing global inequality may be misplaced unless proper consideration is taken of how greater equality might be achieved. Even before considering how to achieve greater global equality, the question remains, Why do so? We have encountered some of these arguments before on a national level and some are also applicable on a global level. First, on the grounds of economic efficiency, the concentration of world incomes may lower productivity growth. Market failures limit poor people from borrowing to finance worthwhile projects and some redistribution of income could increase the return on total global investments. Second, it may be in the self-interest of higher-income households, wherever they may live, to support redistribution. Health risks, for example, cross borders faster than in the past. The rapid transmission of HIV/AIDS across continents is one example. Concern over the global spread of SARS and, more recently, Avian flu are two more. A redistribution of world resources might mitigate the health risks facing both the poor and the rich. Another reason why it may be in the interest of high-income households to favor greater global equality is that, in an information age, people around the world are aware of the gap between rich and poor. This knowledge and frustration over feeling "left out" may play a destabilizing role in international affairs that affect the interests of the rich as well as the poor. Third, a more equitable distribution may be the right thing to strive for on moral grounds. Philosophers have been writing about this subject since Plato. Global inequality, especially given the size of the absolute income gap between those on the top versus those on the bottom, should be seen as an opportunity to address the absolute poverty that has been a central focus of this chapter.

If those in higher income quintiles are averse to high levels of inequality and willing to move toward a world of less poverty and greater equality of incomes and opportunity, what might they do? Columbia University economist Jeffrey Sachs offers both a diagnosis and a blueprint. In his book *The End of Poverty,* he writes

> The greatest tragedy of our time is that about one sixth of humanity is not even on the development ladder. A large number of the extreme poor are caught in a poverty trap, unable on their own to escape from extreme material deprivation. They are trapped by disease, physical isolation, climate stress, environmental degradation, and by extreme poverty itself. Even though life-saving solutions exist to increase their chances for survival—whether in the form of new farming techniques, or essential medicines, or bed nets that can limit the transmission of malaria—these families and their governments simply lack the financial means to make these critical investments. The world's poor know about the development ladder: they are tantalized by images of affluence from halfway around the world. But they are not able to get a first foothold on the ladder, and so cannot even begin the climb out of poverty.[33]

Sachs proposes a global compact to end absolute poverty by 2025. As with any compact there are at least two parties, poor countries and rich ones. Poor

---

[33]Jeffrey Sachs, *The End of Poverty: Economic Possibilities for Our Time* (New York: Penguin Press, 2005), 19–20.

countries are to be held accountable for their efforts to reduce poverty. Corrupt regimes and those that pursue war rather than development cannot be part of this compact. Sachs makes it clear, however, that even among those low- and middle-income nations that sign onto the compact, their actions, alone, may not be enough to end poverty. Conditions in parts of Africa are so dire that lacking the basics (food, clean water, medicines, and health care facilities) many of the poor, in Sachs words, are "too poor to stay alive."

Given the degree of absolute poverty in the world there is a need for rich nations to do more to alleviate poverty. Some of Sachs's suggestions meet with wide support among development economists: the need for rich countries to keep their markets open to exports from poor nations and the need for rich nations to invest in global public goods such as basic science on combating tropical diseases and developing new technologies to improve agricultural yields. Other elements of his global compact are more controversial: the need for better environmental stewardship by the rich nations to minimize the impact of climate change on poor nations; the need for debt forgiveness of the accumulated international debts of poor nations owed to multilateral institutions like the IMF and World Bank; and the need for a significant increase in the foreign aid from rich nations to poor ones. We explore these ideas in later chapters. Despite disagreement about elements of this global compact to end poverty, it is hard to argue against one of its central ideas: Rich nations have a critical role to play in reducing global poverty.

SUMMARY

- The number in poverty in a given country depends on both the level of per capita income or consumption and its distribution. Distributional outcomes are described using size distributions, which report inequality in terms of shares going to each population quintile ranked from poorest to richest; the Lorenz curve, which offers a geometric portrait of inequality; and the Gini coefficient, which provides a single summary statistic.
- Income and consumption inequality exhibits significant regional variation. Latin America and sub-Saharan Africa have relatively high levels of inequality; Eastern Europe and Central Asia, South Asia, and the high-income economies generally have low levels; inequality in East Asia falls in the medium range. These regional patterns seem to have less to do with the *level* of per capita income than with underlying historical and political determinants, as well as factor endowments;
- According to World Bank studies, in 2001 over 1 billion people, representing 21 percent of the developing world's population, lived below the international poverty line of "$1 a day," sometimes referred to as *absolute poverty* or even *destitution*. The number of people living in

absolute poverty declined by almost 400 million between 1981 and 2001. Most of this decline happened in East Asia, especially in China.

- Because world population grew significantly from 1981 to 2001, success at poverty reduction can also be measured in relative terms. Estimates of the headcount index suggest that the incidence of poverty fell significantly in East and South Asia. In sub-Saharan Africa, the level remains at over 40 percent and changed little over time. Most of the world's poor live in East and South Asia, although both the poverty rate (headcount index) and the severity of poverty (poverty gap) is highest in sub-Saharan Africa.

- Poverty tends to be greater in rural than in urban areas. Racial and ethnic minorities often face higher poverty rates. Women are discriminated against throughout the world. In the labor market, they earn lower wages; often they are denied inheritance or the right to own land; and traditionally they have received less education than men. However, because household resources tend to be shared, the result of intra-household distribution decisions, there is less evidence that poverty rates for women are higher than for men.

- Empirical studies confirm that economic growth tends to be "good for the poor." Looking across countries, the incomes of the bottom 20 percent grew at the same rate as GDP per capita. This is an average tendency, and in some cases, somewhat more prevalent in Latin America, the average income of the poorest quintile *fell* despite increases in GDP per capita. This is much less likely to occur when growth rates are rapid and exceed 5 percent.

- *Pro-poor growth* refers to a development strategy that combines more rapid economic growth with increased opportunities for the poor to participate in the economy. Many economists believe that market-friendly policies, including maintaining fiscal discipline, reducing price inflation, and increasing economic openness, serve the interests of the poor. But these interventions alone are not enough; some of the poor will benefit and others will be hurt. Governments must also invest in the education and health of the poor and in the infrastructure on which the poor rely. Social safety nets are needed for those unable to take advantage of the opportunities markets provide.

- Just as we can measure inequality within nations, it is possible to estimate the degree of global inequality. The most comprehensive measure of global inequality compares the income (or consumption) of each individual regardless of where that person lives. Estimates of this measure report Gini coefficients of global inequality of 0.60–0.80, values higher than for almost any single nation. Given both the level of absolute poverty in the world and the degree of global income inequality, it is important to consider the steps rich nations can take to help poor nations.

7 Population

In 1973, marking the completion of his first term as president of the World Bank, Robert McNamara wrote *One Hundred Countries, Two Billion People*, which brings together his basic views on economic development. There is no ambiguity about McNamara's beliefs. He writes, "The greatest single obstacle to the economic and social advancement of the majority of the peoples in the underdeveloped world is rampant population growth."[1]

Before coming to the World Bank, McNamara was a professor at the Harvard Business School, president of the Ford Motor Corporation, and Secretary of Defense in the Kennedy and Johnson administrations. A man of incredible intellectual reach, McNamara understood much about the role of capital accumulation and technological change and their contributions to economic growth. But he maintained the view that rapid population growth was a threat that would have "catastrophic consequences" unless dealt with. "The underdeveloped world needs investment capital for a whole gamut of productive projects, but nothing would be more unwise than to allow these projects to fail because they are finally overwhelmed by a tidal wave of population."[2]

The "Two Billion People" in the title of McNamara's book refer to the early 1960s when the world's population was close to 3 billion, with 2 billion, or about two thirds of the total, living in the developing nations. Since then, the world has added over 3 billion more people reaching 6.5 billion by the end of 2005, over 5 billion of whom reside in low- and middle-income economies.

---

[1]Robert McNamara, *One Hundred Countries, Two Billion People* (New York: Praeger, 1973), p. 31.
[2]Ibid.

Despite this massive increase in numbers of people, the views of James Wolfensohn, World Bank president from 1995 to 2005, could not be more different from those of his predecessor. Wolfensohn's speeches and publications reveal only limited reference to population growth. Most often these references indicate how population growth exacerbates another problem, whether improving access to clean water or making a dent in the numbers suffering from absolute poverty. The discussion of population and reproductive health on the World Bank's website notes, "Today the Bank and its client countries . . . are using new approaches to improving women's health and helping couples to plan their families." There is no sense that population growth is the greatest obstacle or even one of the greatest obstacles to development.

Was McNamara unnecessarily alarmist? Was James Wolfensohn making an irreversible mistake by not focusing on rising population numbers? Is the United Nations similarly wrong in not including reductions in population growth as one of the Millennium Development Goals (introduced in Chapter 2)? We begin to address these questions by reviewing the world's population history and exploring the demographic transition that has characterized today's high-income nations and increasingly the low- and middle-income nations as well. We also consider population projections for the future before turning our attention to the complex relationship between population growth and economic development. This relationship is viewed both at an aggregate level and at the level of individual families making decisions about how many children to have. We conclude by reviewing the options nations face in pursuing policies to limit the size of their populations.

A BRIEF HISTORY OF WORLD POPULATION

Anthropologists debate when our first ancestors appeared. For our purposes, we do not have to go that far back in time. We might begin at the end of the last ice age, about 13,000 years ago, when humans on all continents were still living as Stone Age hunter gathers; or 12,000 years ago with the first signs of agricultural settlements; or 7,000 years ago with the first indications of urbanization. For most of the thousands of years since then, population growth has been close to zero, with annual births roughly offsetting annual deaths. Opportunities for human survival slowly improved and by 1 A.D. the world's population is estimated at about 230 million.[3] To gain some perspective on this number, today Indonesia by itself has a population of 220 million.

---

[3]Angus Maddison, *The World Economy: Historical Statistics* (Paris: Development Centre of the Organisation for Economic Co-operation and Development, 2003), HS-8, "The World Economy, 1–2001 A.D."

Figure 7–1 charts world population from 1 A.D. through the present. This figure makes it abundantly clear that population growth is a recent and unprecedented event in human history. From the beginning of human settlements, it took more than 10,000 years for the world's population to reach 1 billion in 1804. But the next billion were added in less than 125 years and, for the last four decades, each additional billion people got added every 12 to 14 years. No wonder Robert McNamara was so worried!

We have a broad understanding of how world population went from a period of relatively small and stable population numbers to the 6.5 billion (and still growing) that inhabit the planet today. The introduction of settled agriculture revolutionized the earth's capacity to sustain human life. During the years leading up to the Industrial Revolution of the late eighteenth and early nineteenth centuries, the food supply grew and became more reliable. The death rate fell, life expectancy increased, and population growth gradually accelerated. This growth, however, was set back at intervals by famines, plagues, and wars, any of which could wipe out as much as half of the population in a given area. As late as the fourteenth century, the Black Death (bubonic plague) killed one third of the population of Europe. Despite these catastrophic events, by 1800, the world's population had grown to about 1 billion, implying an annual growth rate of only 0.08 percent between 1 A.D. to 1800.

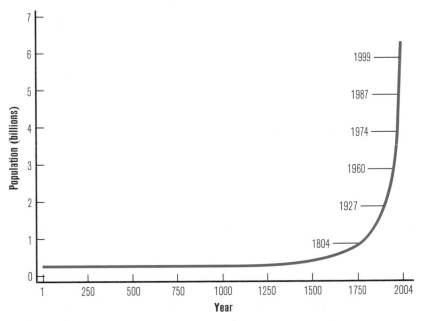

FIGURE 7-1. World Population Growth through History: Years Needed to Add 1 Billion More People

Source: Maddison, www.eco.rug.nl/~Maddison/content.shtml, PRB 2003 Population Data Sheet.

The Industrial Revolution, which marked the start of modern economic growth, further expanded the earth's population-**carrying capacity.** Innovations in agriculture matched innovations in industry, permitting labor to be transferred to industry while the productivity of the remaining agricultural laborers rose fast enough to feed the growing urban population. Transcontinental railroads and fast, reliable ocean shipping further boosted world food output in the late nineteenth century, making it possible to grow more basic foodstuffs in the areas best suited for this activity and get supplies to food-deficit areas quickly in emergencies. Famines, especially in what are now the high-income nations, decreased in frequency and severity. Food prices fell. Meanwhile, modern medicine, sanitation, and pharmaceutical production began to develop. All these factors helped reduce the death rate and accelerate population growth. By 1945, the population of the world was slightly less than 2.5 billion, meaning that global population grew by 0.6 percent per year between 1800 and 1945.

After World War II, there were further dramatic improvements in food supply and disease control. Techniques introduced in the developed countries during the preceding era spread throughout the globe. The result was a veritable revolution in falling death rates and rising life expectancy in both the developed and the developing world. Plummeting death rates in many areas raised population growth rates to levels the world had never known before. Reference to a worldwide **"population explosion,"** unthinkable for most of human history, became commonplace in the 1960s and 1970s as the world's population grew to 3 and then 4 billion. World population passed 5 billion in 1987 and 6 billion in 1999, with almost all the growth in numbers occurring in the developing countries. Between 1945 and 2004, the growth in world population averaged an historically unprecedented rate of 1.6 percent per annum.

The Demographic Transition

The relationship between annual births and deaths determines population growth. Figure 7–2 depicts the basic stages in the **demographic transition** in a now developed nation, Finland. Finland's experience is typical of what most high-income countries have experienced over the past several centuries. The top line in the figure refers to the **crude birth rate,** the number of live births per year per 1,000 people. The lower line refers to the **crude death rate,** the number of deaths per year also per 1,000 people. The difference between these two rates, the excess of births over deaths, is the rate of **natural increase** in the population, which often is expressed as a percentage. For the world as a whole, the natural increase in the population equals the population growth rate; for an individual country, population growth is the difference between the rate of natural increase and net migration.

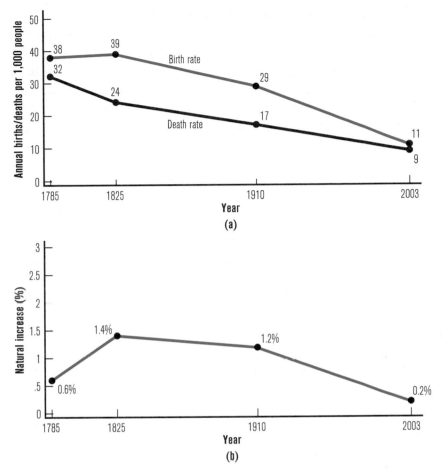

FIGURE 7-2. Demographic Transition for Finland, 1785–2003

Source: The Population Reference Bureau's *Population Handbook*, 4th ed., 1997; *World Population Data Sheet 2003*.

For hundreds of years prior to the eighteenth century, Finland was in the first stage of the classic demographic transition. High birth rates were matched by high death rates and the natural increase in population was close to zero. In some years, births exceeded deaths; in other years, the opposite occurred. By 1785, prior to the start of industrialization and the first year for which data are available, Finland still had high birth and death rates but enough of a gap between the two resulted in a 0.6 percent rate of natural increase. If this rate had been maintained, it would have taken 117 years for Finland's population to double.

By the early 1800s, Finland was in the second stage of the demographic transition, characterized by death rates declining more quickly than birth rates. This was before the advent of modern medicine and public health interventions; so much of this decline can be attributed to improved nutrition as food supplies became more abundant and less variable. With no change in the birth rate and a fall in deaths, the rate of natural increase in the population reached 1.4 percent by 1830. At this rate, the population would double in 50 years. After 1830, death rates continued to fall but not as quickly. At the same time, birth rates started to drop as Finnish families decided to have fewer children. Note that they did so in the absence of modern forms of contraception. Finland was now in the third stage of the demographic transition, with birth rates falling more quickly than death rates. By 1915, Finland's natural increase in population had slowed to 1.2 percent.

By 2003, Finland reached the fourth stage of its demographic transition in which its population growth had fallen close to zero, this time with low birth and death rates. The nation had gone from relatively high birth and death rates producing a low rate of population growth prior to 1785, through a period of more rapid natural increase in the nineteenth and early twentieth centuries, back down to a very low rate of population growth characterized by both low birth and death rates. Today, Finland has a population of 5 million, growing at 0.2 percent per annum. Abstracting from changes due to migration, at this rate Finland's population would require 350 years to double in size. But Finland's population probably will never double again. As has happened elsewhere in Europe, birth rates may fall even further and the crude death rate will rise as the population ages. In coming decades, Finland may even experience negative population growth, just as Germany and Italy already are.

Based on the few observations available, Finland's rate of natural increase never exceeded 1.4 percent. Compare this to the experience of the developing countries where, as a group, the rate of natural increase reached 2.5 percent during the 1960s. Even today, Pakistan's population is growing by 2.7 percent, Honduras's by 2.9 percent, and Madagascar's by 3.0 percent. Why draw so much attention to a one or one and a half percentage point difference in population growth rates? Because doubling time drops from 50 years at a growth rate of 1.4 percent to only 28 years at 2.5 percent to 23 years at 3.0 percent. Seemingly small differences in growth rates provide societies with even less time to achieve a demographic transition before population levels increase by substantial amounts.

Clearly, there are major differences between the historical experience of today's industrialized nations and the contemporary demographic transition of the developing nations. Figure 7–3 portrays the movement of crude birth and death rate for the less developed nations as a group from 1950 to 2000. The bottom panel of the figure charts the corresponding rate of natural increase over the same years. By 1950, the rate of natural increase in the developing nations was 2.1 percent, far larger than the rate ever experienced by today's industrialized countries. The higher rate was the result of somewhat higher birth rates than historically had been the case in today's high-income nations due, in part,

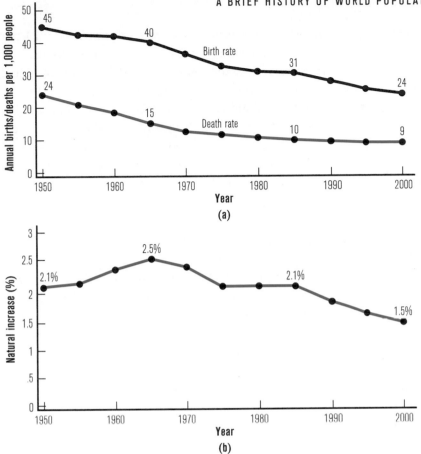

FIGURE 7-3. Demographic Transition for Less-Developed Regions, 1950–2000

Source: Population Division of the Department of Economic and Social Affairs of the United Nations Secretariat, *World Population Prospects: The 2002 Revision* and *World Urbanization Prospects: The 2001 Revision*, available at esa.un.org/unpp.

to earlier age at marriage. Of even greater significance, the decline in death rates in the developing nations began at much lower levels of per capita income and fell much faster than it had historically in the now developed countries. This was due, in part, to the transfer of public health interventions and other medical advances, including vaccines and improvements in water and sanitation services, from the developed to the developing world.

Between 1950 and 1970, death rates in the developing world continued to drop faster than birth rates and the natural increase in populations rose. It peaked at around 2.5 percent in the late 1960s, shortly before Robert McNamara warned of the catastrophic consequences of rapid population growth. With little evidence of falling birth rates, it is not surprising that McNamara was so alarmist about population trends. But a demographic transition already was underway. Between 1950 and 2000, the crude birth rate fell from 45 to 24 per 1,000, and even though death rates also fell, from 24 to 9,[4] the natural increase of the developing nations slowed to 1.5 percent, still high by historical standards but with an unmistakable trend. In all regions of the world and in almost every nation, women started having fewer children and **total fertility rates (TFRs)** fell (Box 7–1). These trends help to explain why the World Bank and other multilateral organizations appear less concerned about population growth today. The world population is still growing and will continue to do so for many more generations, but the *rate of growth* has slowed and a "population explosion" no longer seems an appropriate metaphor.

The Demographic Situation Today

In 2002, the world population approached 6.2 billion. Only 15 percent resided in the high-income countries, 85 percent lived in the low- and middle-income nations (Table 7–1). Almost one out of every three inhabitants of the planet lived in East Asia. China alone accounted for just under 20 percent of world population. South Asia, dominated by India's 1 billion inhabitants, represented another 23 percent of the world's people. Sub-Saharan Africa accounted for a bit more than one-tenth of world population but this share is expected to rise in the future. Rising death rates due to the HIV/AIDS crisis may change these outcomes, but at 2.1 percent, sub-Saharan Africa had the most rapid rate of natural increase in population of any region.

The situation in the high-income countries could not be more different from that in sub-Saharan Africa. With aging populations, crude death rates are likely to rise; and with declining fertility, crude birth rates will fall. Rates of natural increase already have slowed to 0.3 percent. Almost all *population growth* in the high-income countries is attributable to immigration, with openness to immigrants at a higher level in Australia, Canada, New Zealand, and the United States than in Europe or Japan. Total fertility rates in many of the high-income economies already have dropped below replacement levels, where the TFR is less than or equal to 2.1. Women must have at least two children each during their childbearing years for the population to replace itself. Allowing for infant and child mortality, demographers estimate that the replacement level of total fertility is around 2.1. In countries, including Germany, Italy, and Japan, where the TFR is below the replacement level and immigration rates also are low, policy

---

[4]Careful inspection of Figures 7–2 and 7–3 reveals that the death rate in 2003 in Finland, at 9 per 1,000 people, is identical to the death rate in 2000 in the less-developed regions. This does not mean that life expectancy and the overall survival chances in the two places are the same. If one compares age-specific mortality rates, survival probabilities in Finland exceed those of the developing countries for every age group, especially for infants. But, in the aggregate, since Finland has a much older population than the developing world, the crude death rates, coincidentally, average to the same number.

BOX 7-1 TOTAL FERTILITY RATES

Another way to assess population trends is to examine fertility behavior. One of the most common measures of fertility is the total fertility rate. TFR sometimes is thought of as a measure of the average number of children a woman will bear, but this is not entirely correct. TFR is a *synthetic* measure. It sums the age-specific fertility rates of women in a given year, where age-specific fertility rates refer to the average number of births born to women of a specific age (usually, 15–19, 20–24, . . . , 40–44). In other words, TFR is the number of children the average woman would have in her lifetime if age-specific fertility rates remained constant. But these rates change over time, as younger women delay having their children and women have fewer children overall. TFR is a reliable indicator of the number of children women *currently* are having and trends in TFR reveal a great deal about the world's demographic transition.

The figure in this box charts TFRs over the past 40 years for the World Bank's seven geographical regions. In 1962, in Africa, Asia, and Latin America, TFR was 6 children or more. Only the high-income economies and the nations of Europe and Central Asia had reached low TFRs of fewer than 3 children. Over the next four decades and at varying speeds, fertility rates fell in every region. In East and South Asia and in Latin America and the Middle East, TFR fell by half or more. Sub-Saharan Africa's demographic transition took longer to begin but even in this poorest part of the world, TFR, now at 5.1 children per woman, has fallen by more than 1 child since 1982. Most demographers expect the decline in Africa's TFR to follow that of other regions and to continue to fall.

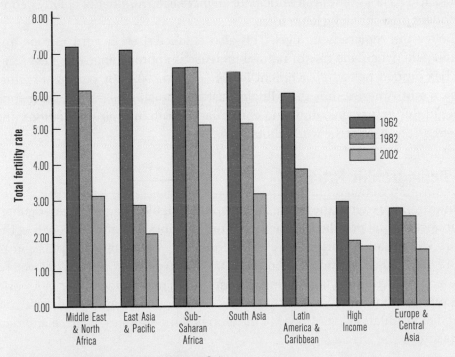

Source: *World Development Indicators Online.*

TABLE 7-1. Levels and Trends in World Population, 2002

	TOTAL POPULATION		POPULATION GROWTH		
	NUMBER (MILLIONS)	PERCENT OF TOTAL	BIRTH RATE (PER 1,000)	DEATH RATE (PER 1,000)	NATURAL INCREASE (PERCENT)
World	6,199	100	21	9	1.2
Income category					
Low income	2,270	37	29	11	1.8
Middle income	2,963	48	17	8	0.9
High income	966	15	12	9	0.3
Region					
East Asia	1,839	30	16	8	0.9
South Asia	1,401	23	26	9	1.7
High income	966	15	12	9	0.3
Sub-Saharan Africa	688	11	39	18	2.1
Latin America	525	8	21	6	1.5
Europe and Central Asia	472	8	13	12	0.1
Middle East and North Africa	306	5	24	6	1.8

Source: World Bank, *World Development Indicators Online.*

makers are concerned about a population implosion rather than a population explosion. These societies can anticipate an increasing number of elderly people dependent on a shrinking labor force.

Below the replacement level, TFR also characterizes Eastern Europe and Central Asia, where the rate of natural increase is approaching zero. East Asia's TFR has dipped below replacement levels (2.05 in 2002). By contrast, neither Africa, Latin America, nor the Middle East has progressed as far along their demographic transitions, implying continued growth in their populations and an increasing share of the world's total.

The Demographic Future

When extrapolated into the future, even modest population growth rates generate projected total populations that seem unthinkable. Continued growth at the world's 2002 rate of natural increase, 1.2 percent, would bring population to over 12 billion by 2050 and 24 billion by 2100. This type of projection, beloved by some popular writers, is frightening to many. It is hard to imagine life in a world with two to four times as many people as there are today. How will this expanded population live? How will the globe's finite supplies of space and natural resources be affected?

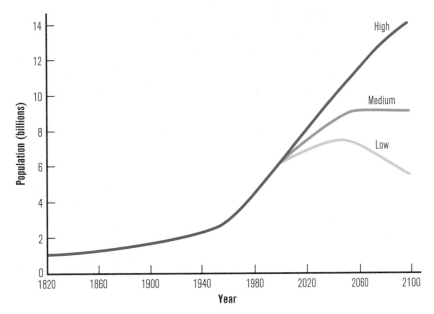

FIGURE 7-4. World Population Historical Trends and Projections
UN population projections for 2000–2100. The scenarios presented here represent different future levels of fertility.

Source: Maddison, available at www.eco.rug.nl/~Maddison/content.shtml; UN Population Division of the Department of Economic and Social Affairs of the United Nations Secretariat, *The World Population in 2300*, draft.

While a significant increase in world population can be expected during your lifetime, it is unlikely to double. Linear extrapolations of current trends are badly misleading because after accelerating for more than two centuries, world population growth has been slowing down for the past four decades. This trend is likely to continue but no one can be certain how quick the transition to lower fertility levels will be or whether there will be any reversals in recent trends.

Every few years the United Nations produces forecasts of future population growth.[5] These projections offer a variety of scenarios based on a similar set of assumptions about declining mortality but using different assumptions about the amount and speed of fertility declines. Figure 7–4 combines estimates of world population from 1820 to 2000 with the UN's low-, medium-, and high-population projections for the twenty-first century. The high scenario assumes the world TFR does not reach replacement levels and predicts an expanding world population until 2100. The medium scenario has the world reaching slightly less than replacement levels by 2050. Under the medium variant, world

[5]In addition to the UN, the International Institute for Applied Systems Analysis in Austria, the U.S. Census Bureau, and the World Bank produce independent population projections. A useful introduction to how such projections are made appears in Brian O'Neill and Deborah Balk, "World Population Futures," *Population Bulletin* (Population Reference Bureau) 56, no. 3 (September 2001).

population rises to almost 9 billion by 2050, at which time, the total population begins to level off. The low scenario assumes a future TFR well below replacement levels. Under these assumptions world population hits a maximum of 7.4 billion in 2050 and begins to decline thereafter. The UN offers the three variants as alternative projections without assigning probabilities to which outcomes are more likely.

What all three scenarios share in common is the projection that world population will continue to grow over the next 50 years, in other words, over the adult lifetime of a university student today. They differ in the size of the projected growth within a range of 1.3 to 4.5 billion. There are three basic reasons for this projected continued increase. The first two explain why the TFR may remain above replacement levels: (1) a desire for large families and (2) a failure to achieve the desired number of children (so-called, unwanted children). The third reason is **population momentum,** a demographic concept requiring some explanation.

Populations that have been growing rapidly, as they have been especially in the developing world, have large numbers of people in, or about to enter, the most fertile age brackets. Even if all the world's couples today were to start having just enough children to replace themselves, the total population would continue to grow for many more decades before eventually leveling off. This is because today's children, who outnumber their parents, will become tomorrow's parents. Stated differently, past fertility decisions echo far into the future (Box 7–2). Population momentum alone could add several billion more people to the world's population in the twenty-first century.[6]

Another way of appreciating the demographic future is to focus on specific countries, especially those projected to be the world's most populous. Table 7–2 lists the ten most-populous nations in 2050 according to the UN's medium-variant projections. The table also lists the population of these countries in 2000. These ten nations are projected to account for 5 billion people in 2050, slightly over half of the projected world population at that time.

China, India, and the United States will continue to be the three most-populated nations, although India will replace China in the top spot. Increases in China's population, which already is well below TFR replacement levels, will be due exclusively to population momentum; in the United States, immigration will be the primary factor for increasing numbers; and in India, both population momentum and fertility above replacement levels will contribute to a projected increase of 514 million *more* inhabitants than the 1 billion who live in India today.

[6]John Bongaarts estimated that half of the projected increase in the world's population during the twenty-first century could be attributed to population momentum alone. John Bongaarts, "Population Policy Options in the Developing World," *Science* 263, no. 5148 (February 11, 1994).

BOX 7-2 POPULATION MOMENTUM

The impact of population momentum on future population levels can be illustrated by the following example of two families. The first generation of each family consists of one man and one woman. Each woman has four children over her reproductive life. This second generation includes four females and four males.

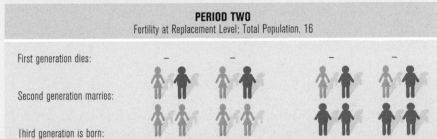

PERIOD ONE
Fertility above Replacement Level; Total Population, 12

First generation:

Second generation:

In period two, the first generation dies and everyone in the second generation marries. Each woman in the four resulting couples has two children, producing a third generation of four males and four females. Even though the second generation reaches replacement levels of fertility, population momentum causes a 33 percent increase in total population, from 12 to 16, between period one and period two.

PERIOD TWO
Fertility at Replacement Level; Total Population, 16

First generation dies:

Second generation marries:

Third generation is born:

The process is repeated in period three. The second generation dies; the third generation marries and produces a fourth generation. If the third generation remains at replacement levels of fertility, the total population stabilizes. The size of the steady-state population in the final period is the result not only of the fertility decisions of the second and third generations, but of those of the first generation as well.

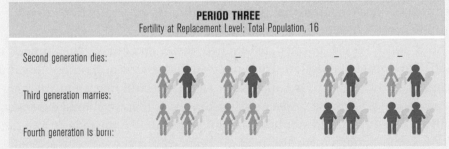

PERIOD THREE
Fertility at Replacement Level; Total Population, 16

Second generation dies:

Third generation marries:

Fourth generation is born:

Population momentum also can work in reverse. If subsequent generations have lower than replacement fertility, the decline in total population could be rapid, reflecting the fertility decisions of both current and previous generations.

TABLE 7-2. Projections: The World's Ten Most-Populous Nations in 2050

COUNTRY	2050 POPULATION (MILLIONS)	RANK	2000 POPULATION (MILLIONS)	RANK	POPULATION INCREASE (MILLIONS)	CHANGE (PERCENT)
India	1,531	1	1,017	2	514	51
China	1,395	2	1,275	1	120	9
United States	409	3	285	3	124	44
Pakistan	349	4	143	7	206	144
Indonesia	294	5	212	4	82	39
Nigeria	258	6	115	10	143	124
Bangladesh	255	7	138	8	117	85
Brazil	233	8	172	5	61	35
Ethiopia	171	9	66	18	105	159
Congo, Democratic Republic	152	10	49	24	103	210
Total (share of world's population)	5,047(0.57)		3,472 (0.57)		1,575 (0.55)	

Note: Projections are based on the UN's medium variant. Population increase as a share of the world's population is the absolute increase in population divided by the change in population.
Source: United Nations, *World Population Prospects, The 2002 Revision,* Tables 2, 9.

Just as striking are the expected population gains elsewhere in South Asia. Pakistan is projected to increase its population by 144 percent and Bangladesh by 84 percent. In sub-Saharan Africa, the Democratic Republic of the Congo, Ethiopia, and Nigeria all are projected to experience even greater percentage increases in their populations. Projections for the Congo and Ethiopia are so large as to catapult these nations into the top-ten category in 2050, replacing Japan and Russia, which were among the top ten in 2000.

It must be remembered that all these estimates of population trends are only projections, which become less and less reliable the further out in time one goes, and much could happen to change these outcomes. The impact of HIV/AIDS on future population size is not well understood and other infectious diseases, some unknown today, may arise. Civil strife and migration will play a role as well. But what these projections make clear is that we should expect significant increases in world population, almost exclusively in today's low- and middle-income nations, over the next 50 years. Given the current difficulties many of these nations currently face, the challenge of achieving economic development for ever-larger numbers of people seems daunting.

THE CAUSES OF POPULATION GROWTH

Discussions of the world's population future often turn acrimonious. Questions of whether and whose populations are to be limited and by what means are sensitive. Before we can confront such issues intelligently, we must consider what is known about both the causes and the effects of rapid population growth. We must concern ourselves with the two-way relationship between the growth of population and economic development, that is, with how population growth affects economic development and how economic development affects population growth. We deal with the latter relationship first.

Thomas Malthus, Population "Pessimist"

The most famous and influential demographic theorist of all time was **Thomas Malthus** (1766–1834). Malthus believed that "the passion between the sexes" would cause population to expand as long and far as food supplies permitted. People generally would not limit procreation below the biological maximum. Should wages somehow rise above the subsistence level, workers would marry younger and have more children, more of whom would survive. But this situation could be only temporary. In time, the rise in population would create an increase in labor supply, which would press against fixed land resources. Eventually, through diminishing returns, food prices would rise and real wages would fall back to the subsistence level. If this process went too far, famines and rising deaths would result. Malthus did not think that the growth of the food supply could stay ahead of population growth in the long run. In a famous example, he argued that food supplies grow according to an arithmetic (additive) progression, while population follows an explosive geometric (multiplicative) progression.

In the grim Malthusian world, population growth is limited primarily by factors working through the death rate, what he called *positive checks*. In this deceptively mild phrase, Malthus included all the disasters that exterminate people in large numbers: epidemics, famines, and wars. These phenomena, he believed, generally constitute the operative limitation on population. Only in later editions of his famous *Essay on the Principle of Population* did he concede the possibility of a second, less drastic, category of limiting factors: "preventive checks" that work through the birthrate. Here, Malthus had in mind primarily measures of "restraint," such as a later age of marriage. Unlike latter-day "Malthusians," he did not advocate birth control, which as a minister he considered immoral. Although he grudgingly admitted that humanity might voluntarily control its own numerical growth, Malthus invested little hope in the possibility.

The gloominess of the Malthusian theory is understandable when one considers that its author lived during the early years of the Industrial Revolution. In all prior history, population had tended to expand in response to economic gains. With unprecedented economic growth underway in the world he knew, what could Malthus expect except an acceleration of natural increase as death rates fell? That indeed was happening during his lifetime.

Malthus did not live to witness the rest of the European demographic transition. The early decline in death rates was followed, with a lag, by a fall in fertility; beginning in the middle of the nineteenth century, wages began to increase dramatically in contrast to Malthus's prediction. Why did all this happen? Wages rose, despite accelerating population growth, because capital accumulation and technical change offset any tendency for the marginal product of labor to decline. Death rates fell through a combination of higher incomes (better nutrition and living conditions) and better preventive and curative health measures. The fall in the birthrate is harder to understand. There are both biological and economic reasons to expect, as Malthus did, that fertility would rise, not fall, as income went up. Healthier, better-fed women have a greater biological capacity to conceive, carry a child full term, and give birth to a healthy infant. Also, people might marry earlier when times are good, and better-off families have the financial capacity to support more children. Why, then, do increases in income seem to lead to declines in fertility? An answer to this question must be sought in post-Malthusian demographic theory.

Why Birth Rates Decline

Two kinds of demographic change affect the crude birth rate. The first is change in the population shares of different age groups. A rise in the share of people of reproductive age (roughly 15 to 45) increases the birth rate, as we saw earlier in the discussion of population momentum. Conversely, if the proportion of older people in the population goes up, as is happening in many industrial countries today, the birth rate drops. The second factor is fertility, the rate at which women have children.

Why, then, do people have as many children as they do? Is it because they are moved by Malthus's "passion between the sexes" and do not know how to prevent the resulting births? Or is it because they are tradition-bound and custom-ridden? Or is it rational in some economic and social settings to have large families? All three positions have some merit. The case for the first one, implicitly, is what those who recommend providing birth control as a response to rapid population growth probably have in mind. A Latin American doctor at an international conference put it bluntly. "People don't really want children," he said. "They want sex and don't know how to avoid the births that result." This viewpoint captures the element of spontaneity inevitably present in the reproductive process. Yet the evidence suggests that all societies consciously control human fertility. Rarely does the number of children that the average woman has over her childbearing years even approach her biological capacity to bear children. One exceptional case is that of the Hutterites, a communal sect that left Russia and settled in Canada and the northern Great Plains in the late 1800s. The group's religious beliefs and lifestyle encouraged maximum fertility. Hutterite women, on average, bore over 10 children, a fertility rate no contemporary low- or middle-income nation comes close to approaching. All societies practice some methods of controlling their numbers whether by aborting pregnancies, disposing of unwanted infants, or inhibiting conception. (Recall our earlier discussion of fertility decline in nineteenth-century Finland.)

As for the second proposition, it has been said that many children are the social norm in traditional societies, that society looks askance at couples who have no or few children, that a man who lacks wealth at least can have children, and that a woman's principal socially recognized function in a traditional society is to bear and rear children. Such norms and attitudes are important, but they probably are not the decisive factors in human fertility. Fertility is determined by a complex combination of forces. Social scientists in recent years have given increasing credence to elements of individual rationality in the process. Simply stated, they believe that most families in traditional societies have many children because it is in their interest to do so.

This brings us to the third explanation. Although some might regard it as a cold, inhumane way of looking at the matter, it is nevertheless true that children impose certain costs on their parents and confer certain benefits. In some low-income settings, especially in rural areas, children may supplement family earnings by working. On family farms and in other household enterprises, there usually is something that even a young child can do to increase production. In many poor societies, large numbers of children work outside the home. In the longer run, children also provide a form of social security, which is important in societies that lack institutional programs to assist the elderly. In some cultures, it is considered especially important to have a son who survives to adulthood; if infant and child mortality is high, this can motivate couples to keep having children until two or three sons have been born, just to be safe. In addition to these economic benefits, which are probably more important in a low-income society than a more-affluent one, children also can yield psychic benefits (and costs!), as all parents know.

The economic costs of children can be divided into explicit and implicit costs. Children entail cash outlays for food, clothing, shelter, and often for education. Implicit costs arise when child care by a member of the family, usually the mother, involves a loss of earning time. Some of the costs felt by parents parallel the costs of population growth experienced at the national level. For example, more children in a family may mean smaller inheritances of agricultural land, an example of a natural resource constraint operating at the family level. Similarly, it may be harder to send all the children in a larger family to school; this reflects the pressures on social investment felt when population growth is rapid.

Viewing childbearing as an economic decision has several important implications:

1. Fertility should be higher when children earn income or contribute to household enterprises than when they do not.
2. Reducing infant deaths should lower fertility, because fewer births are needed to produce a given desired number of surviving children.
3. The introduction of an institutionalized social security system should lower fertility by reducing the need for parents to depend on their children for support in their old age.
4. Fertility should fall when there is an increase in opportunities for women to work in jobs that are relatively incompatible with childbearing, essentially work outside the home.
5. Fertility should be higher when income is higher because the explicit costs are more easily borne.

The first four predictions have received substantial support from empirical studies. The fifth, however, conflicts with observation. Fertility usually is negatively related to income. The negative relationship shows up both in time-series data (that is, fertility usually declines over time as income rises) and in cross-section data (fertility generally is higher in poor countries than in rich ones; also, in most societies, middle- and upper-income families have fewer children than poor families).

Several theorists have wrestled with the seeming anomaly that household demand for children falls as income rises; in other words, children are "inferior goods." Economist Gary Becker of the University of Chicago, a pioneer of **"the new household economics,"** analyzes children as a kind of consumer durable that yields benefits over time.[7] Couples maximize a joint (expected) utility function in which the "goods" they can "buy" are (1) number of living children, (2) "child quality" (a vector of characteristics including education and health), and (3) conventional goods and services. The constraints faced by parents in Becker's model are (1) their time and (2) the cost of purchased goods and services.

Becker explains the fall in fertility as income rises over time by saying that the cost of children tends to rise, especially because the opportunity cost of the parents' time, particularly the mother's, goes up. The familiar income and substitution effects that result from any price change are at work here. As a woman's

---

[7]Gary Becker, *A Treatise on the Family* (Cambridge, MA: Harvard University Press, 1981).

market wage rises, her income also rises, leading to an increase in her demand for any normal good, presumably including the demand for more children. But as a woman's wage rises, the opportunity cost of her time also goes up, so the "price" of raising children rises. As a result, her demand for any activity that is intensive in the use of her time decreases, including child rearing. If the substitution effect is greater than the income effect, couples may decide to have fewer offspring. Becker also argues that given the rising cost of child *quantity*, many parents opt to invest in child *quality* and spend more time and money on a smaller number of children. Wanting "higher-quality" children as income rises also reverts the demand for children back to the demand for a "normal good."

Much of Becker's work on the family was directed at understanding declining fertility levels in the United States and other high-income economies. But the application of "the new household economics" to the circumstances of developing nations also offers keen insights. Replacing Malthus's assumption that people are driven solely by their passions, fertility now is seen as the outcome of a rational process. This does not mean that every child born, in rich and poor nations alike, is the result of a conscious cost-benefit calculation. Economics rarely can explain individual outcomes; its power is in explaining average tendencies. What "the new household economics" suggests is that rich and poor people alike weigh the consequences of their actions, and to understand behavior, we may gain more insights by assuming people act in what they perceive as their own best interests. Having large numbers of children then may be seen not as an irrational act but as the result of the difficult choices poor people face. For poor families, having many children may make economic sense.

"The new household economics" provides insights into the fertility decisions of families in the developing world and, in so doing, raises an apparent contradiction. If individual decisions about fertility are rational and in the perceived best interest of the family, why did Robert McNamara, and many others, identify population growth as "the greatest single obstacle" to economic development? How could rational decisions at the household level result in so dire a societywide outcome?

POPULATION GROWTH AND ECONOMIC DEVELOPMENT

Even if population growth is not "the greatest" obstacle, has population growth been a major impediment to achieving economic development and is it still one today? To a casual observer, who has spent time in Cairo or Calcutta, Manila or Mexico City, or in hundreds of other cities or villages in the developing world, the answer might seem obvious. Looking at the masses of poor people in these places, it would be hard not to conclude that the situation could be measurably improved if only there were fewer people. (A casual observer might draw the same conclusion in New York or Tokyo.)

But more than casual observation is needed to understand the complex relationship between population growth and economic development, especially if one is going to consider policy interventions to reduce population growth. First, we must be clear on the question we are asking. We cannot ask whether people who have been born would have been better off having never been born. This is a question economics cannot possibly answer. Our question can be only whether per capita income, life expectancy, educational attainment, or any other indicator of economic development would be higher if a nation's population had grown more slowly. Given the centrality of economic growth to the development process, much of our attention is on the relationship between population growth and economic growth.

Figure 7–5 is a scatter diagram of the trend growth rate in GDP per capita against the trend growth rate in population from 1990–2002, for 125 low- and middle-income countries for which there are data. There is considerable variance in both growth rates. During these years, the range in annual GDP per capita growth was from +8.8 percent in China to –7.5 percent in Tajikistan. Population growth, the difference between the rate of natural increase and net migration, ranged from +3.7 percent in Jordan, where both the natural increase and immigration were high, to –1.3 percent in Armenia, where both were low.

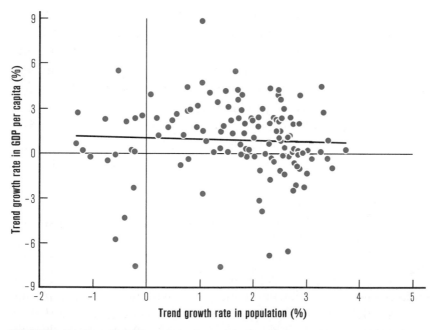

FIGURE 7-5. Growth in Population versus Growth in GDP per Capita, Low- and Middle-Income Economies, 1990–2002

Source: World Bank, *World Development Indicators Online.*

The casual observer who was *sure* that population growth slowed down economic growth might be surprised by Figure 7–5. Instead of an expected downward and statistically significant trend, the scatter diagram reveals no discernible pattern between the two variables. The fitted trend line is flat with a slope that is not significantly different from zero.

The lack of a simple correlation between economic and population growth is neither a new finding nor one dependent on the years chosen. Simon Kuznets, a Nobel Prize winner in economics and a pioneer in the use of data to examine trends in economic growth, reported on the lack of correlation between population growth and per capita output growth for 40 less-developed nations between the early 1950s and 1964.[8] His findings of a lack of correlation between population growth and economic growth had a significant impact on the conclusions of a major United Nations report on population released in 1973. Similar studies have been conducted since Kuznets's work, many of which also report a low correlation between the two growth rates over various time periods.[9]

The findings of Figure 7–5 may be surprising, but they should not be misinterpreted. All they show is a lack of *simple correlation* between contemporaneous growth rates in population and per capita output. This does not mean that population has no effect on economic growth; it simply means that the relationship potentially is much more complex than can be revealed by simple correlation. Numerous criticisms can be leveled against the absence of a trend in the figure. What other factors affect economic growth that need to be controlled for before assessing the marginal impact of population growth; what is the direction of causality between economic growth and population growth; and what are the appropriate lags between changes in population growth and subsequent impacts on growth—is a decade long enough to determine the true relationship?[10]

---

[8]For the 40 less-developed countries in Kuznets's sample, the rank correlation between rates of population growth and growth in per capita GDP was 0.111. From Simon Kuznets, "Population and Economic Growth," *Proceedings of the American Philosophical Society* 3 (June 1967) as reported in, United Nations, *The Determinants and Consequences of Population Trends*, Department of Social Affairs, Population Division, Population Studies No. 17 (New York: United Nations, 1973).

[9]Discussion of these studies can be found in Allen Kelley and Robert Schmidt, "Economic and Demographic Change: A Synthesis of Models, Findings and Perspectives," in Nancy Birdsall, Allen Kelley, and Steven Sinding, eds., *Population Matters: Demographic Change, Economic Growth, and Poverty in the Developing World* (Oxford: Oxford University Press, 2001). The 1980s are one period in which a significant negative relationship between population growth and economic growth is apparent.

[10]Problems with direction of causality are evident when one examines simple correlations between population growth and economic growth over longer periods of time. A trend line fitted to growth rates over 30 years has the expected negative and significant coefficient. Is this because population growth effects take decades to be realized? Or is it because causality runs in the other direction? Higher growth rates over longer periods of time imply sustained increases in income levels, which lead to declining fertility and, hence, slower population growth.

   The lack of correlation in Figure 7–5 opens up rather than closes the discussion of how population growth affects economic growth. At a minimum, it challenges the *naïve view* of how these growth rates are related. The growth rate in GDP per capita equals the growth rate of GDP minus the growth rate in population.[11] The naïve view then holds that, for any given rate of GDP growth, economic growth would be faster the slower the growth in population. This conclusion is true, but its implicit assumption is not. Growth in output is not independent of growth in the population. The simplest reason is that children born today are the labor force of the future, and labor, along with land and capital, is one of the main factors of production for any economy. Stated differently, population growth affects both the level of GDP and how many people must share in that GDP. Once one recognizes these connections, the critical question becomes how population growth affects the core determinants of economic growth: the accumulation of factors of production and the productivity of those factors. Given the number of ways in which population growth can affect these determinants, the absence of a simple correlation between economic growth and population growth is less of a surprise.

Population and Accumulation

A pioneering model of population's effect on material welfare was written in 1958 by demographer Ansley Coale and economist Edgar Hoover.[12] Their work falls squarely into the camp of **population "pessimists"** or antinatalists, those who perceive population growth as harmful to economic development. Coale and Hoover argued that a reduction in birth rate could raise per capita income in three important ways. First, lower fertility levels would slow future labor force growth. The amount of investment then needed to provide a constant amount of capital per worker for a growing number of workers (*capital widening*) would go down and permit more investment to be used to increase capital per worker (*capital deepening*).[13] Second, with lower fertility and fewer children, public funds could be diverted away from education and health expenditures and toward physical capital, which Coale and Hoover assumed would be a more pro-

---

[11]The growth rate of any fraction, A/B, is equal to the growth of the numerator, A, minus the growth of the denominator, B. This is because the growth rate of any variable, X, can be found by taking the derivative of the log of the variable with respect to time: $d(\ln X)/dt = (dX/dt)/X = g(X)$, where g is the rate of growth. If $X = (A/B)$, then $\ln(A/B) = \ln A - \ln B$, and $d[\ln(A/B)]/dt = d(\ln A)/dt - d(\ln B)/dt$, or $g(A/B) = g(A) - g(B)$. In the case of GDP per capita, $g(\text{GDP}/\text{population}) = g(\text{GDP}) - g(\text{population})$.

[12]Ainsley Coale and Edgar Hoover, *Population Growth and Economic Development in Low-Income Countries: A Case Study of India's Prospects* (Princeton, NJ: Princeton University Press, 1958).

[13]The implications of capital widening and capital deepening for economic growth are developed more fully in Chapter 4's discussion of the Solow growth model.

ductive use of government spending. Third, slower population growth would lower the **dependency ratio,** the ratio of the non-working-age population (usually 0–14 and 65 and over) to the working age population (Box 7–3). A lower dependency ratio, in turn, would reduce consumption and increase saving at any given level of income, permitting a higher rate of asset accumulation. Taken together, these three benefits from slower population growth could raise income levels at both the household and aggregate levels.

Coale and Hoover's conclusions, generally, have not been supported by later research.[14] For a given amount of investment, a larger labor force results in less capital per worker, but the quantitative significance of this effect on output appears small. Coale and Hoover's concern about the diversion of resources toward education also has not held up to later research. Demographic factors do not exert much of an independent effect on the share of GDP allocated to education and other social welfare programs. In addition, education and health increasingly are seen, not as consumption expenditures, but as investments in human capital that may have returns equal to or higher than the returns on investments in physical capital.

The third relationship highlighted by Coale and Hoover, among population growth, dependency ratios, and saving, has attracted a great deal of analysis. Some studies find little correlation. This may be because business and government saving are relatively independent of demographic change. Even household saving may be fairly insensitive to changes in population growth if most saving comes from wealthy families. Such households' saving behavior would be affected by neither their own fertility decisions nor those of the poor. On the other hand, there is cross-country evidence that, as the share rises of the population 15 years of age and younger, the aggregate saving rate falls (see Chapter 10).

Recent work on how population growth affects economic growth draws attention to the various demographic factors that determine population growth. It recommends decomposing population growth into its distinct causes. For example, an overall decrease in mortality rates increases population growth but does not change a nation's dependency ratio. A decrease in fertility, however, lowers both population growth and the dependency ratio. If dependency ratios are a determinant of economic growth, population growth then is a poor proxy for this effect. Applying these concepts to East Asia, researchers have argued that the region's demographic transition was both the result of and contributed substantially to the region's rapid economic growth.[15]

---

[14]A good survey is Nancy Birdsall, "Economic Analysis of Rapid Population Growth," *World Bank Research Observer* 4, no. 1 (January 1989).

[15]Discussion of these "new" demographic analyses can be found in David Bloom and Jeffrey Williamson, "Demographic Transitions and Economic Miracles in Emerging Asia," *World Bank Economic Review* 12, no. 3 (1998) and in Nancy Birdsall et al., *Population Matters.*

BOX 7-3 POPULATION GROWTH, AGE STRUCTURE, AND DEPENDENCY RATIOS

In 2003, Nigeria had a population of 134 million people (the world's ninth most-populous nation) as compared to Russia with 145 million (the world's eighth most-populous nation.) Although similar in population size, the two nations are at very different points in their demographic transitions. Nigeria has a total fertility rate of 5.8; Russia's is 1.3. Nigeria's population growth rate, 1990–2002, was +2.7 percent per year; Russia's was −0.28 percent. Only recently has Nigeria reached the stage of the demographic transition where birth rates have started to fall. Russia passed through this phase decades ago.

Differences in crude birth and death rates, in addition to their impact on population growth, have a large impact on a nation's age structure. Population pyramids (see the figure) illustrate these effects. Each bar of the pyramid refers to the number of males and females, respectively, in a given age cohort. Nigeria has the distinctive population pyramid of a nation where population growth is rapid. Each age cohort is larger than the one born before it, the result of both high fertility and population momentum. In contrast, Russia's population pyramid is more rectangular, the result of low population growth. The base of Russia's pyramid is narrowing because fertility has fallen below replacement levels. (Differences among population cohorts also reflect historical events. Russia's 55–59-year-old cohort is especially small because this group was born between 1941 and 1945, during the World War II. Low fertility and high infant mortality during these years explains the shortfall in this age cohort today.)

Nigeria's youth dependency ratio, the number of youths (0–14) divided by the number of people of working age (15–64), obviously is higher than Russia's. The ratio equals 0.87 for Nigeria and only 0.26 for Russia. But Russia has a higher elderly (>64) dependency ratio of 0.18 as compared to Nigeria's 0.06. Differences in age structure have important implications for every aspect of a society, from what it consumes, to how it votes, to the culture it creates. What implications differences in dependency ratios have for overall economic growth and development is considered in the text.

Population and Productivity

In addition to its potential effects on the accumulation process, population growth also can influence the other important determinant of economic growth, the productivity of assets. Concern over these impacts dates back to Thomas Malthus. Malthus saw population growth leading to an inevitable

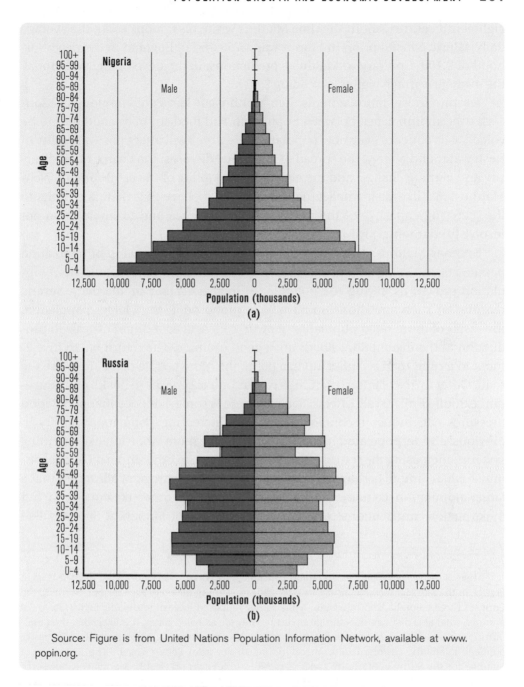

Source: Figure is from United Nations Population Information Network, available at www. popin.org.

decline in agricultural productivity and having devastating consequences for humanity. What Malthus did not envisage is the revolution in agricultural technology that would raise, not lower, the productivity of land. Malthus never would have believed that, in a world of 6.5 billion people, individuals, on average, would eat better than they did in his day, when world population was closer to 1 billion. Economic historian Robert Fogel cites evidence that, in the late eighteenth century, about the time Malthus wrote his famous essay, the average daily caloric consumption in France was 1,753 and in England in the neighborhood of 2,100. Contrary to Malthus's predictions, in the developing world today the average is much higher, exceeding 2,600.[16]

Despite these improvements, neo-Malthusian ideas still are popular. Concern over an imbalance between population and food supplies continues to be voiced as is concern over how population pressures will affect the availability of fresh water and energy, the spread of infectious diseases, the degree of biodiversity and climate change, and the overall sustainability of the environment. Neo-Malthusians, like their intellectual predecessor, believe that there are limits to the "carrying capacity" of the planet and that science and technology cannot resolve fundamental problems of diminishing returns.[17]

Thomas Malthus's thinking placed him squarely in the camp of population pessimists. But some later economists, **population "optimists,"** would view population growth as having the potential to increase factor productivity. Several reasons for such a relationship have been proposed. First, a larger population, the result of more rapid population growth, can yield economies of scale in production and consumption. Roads are a good example. The return on an investment in a rural road is higher, up to a point, the more people there are to use the road. Other forms of infrastructure as well as public services in health and education exhibit similar scale effects. Second, there is some evidence that population pressures can induce technological change. Increasing population density in previously underpopulated regions can encourage more labor-intensive farming systems, increasing the return to land and, perhaps, to other inputs. Third, economist Julian Simon, perhaps the greatest population optimist of all, argues that a larger population contains more entrepreneurs and other creators, who can make major contributions to solving the problems of humanity. Simon called

---

[16]There is a group of countries that today consume fewer than 1,750 calories per day, the level in France in the late eighteenth century. In 1999–2001, this group included Afghanistan, Burundi, the Congo, Eritrea, Somalia, and Tajikistan. While all but Tajikistan has extraordinarily high TFRs of 6.0 or more, what also distinguishes this group is that they are all failed states. It is likely that their malnutrition is caused less by "overpopulation" than by the disruption of agriculture due to massive political instability. Historical data on caloric intake are from Robert Fogel, "The Relevance of Malthus for the Study of Mortality Today: Long-Run Influences on Health, Mortality, Labor Force Participation, and Population Growth" in Kerstin Lindahl-Kiessling and Hans Landberg, eds., *Population, Economic Development, and the Environment* (Oxford: Oxford University Press, 1994), 231–84. Current data are from FAO, *The State of Food Insecurity in the World, 2003* (accessed from www.fao.org).

[17]The neo-Malthusian perspective is presented in Lester Brown, Gary Gardner, and Brian Halweil, *Beyond Malthus: Nineteen Dimensions of the Population Challenge* (New York: W. W. Norton and Company, 1999). The opposing view, that the planet is not overreaching its carrying capacity, is presented in Bjorn Lomborg, *The Skeptical Environmentalist: Measuring the Real State of the World* (Cambridge: Cambridge University Press, 2001).

human ingenuity the "ultimate resource" that can overcome any depletion of other resources.[18]

Just as is true for the population pessimists, empirical support for the positions of the population optimists is spotty. Scale effects exist but often are realized at population densities that already have been achieved; a possible exception is some sparsely settled regions of Africa. Diseconomies of scale also exist and city sizes in parts of the world may be approaching those levels. Finally, there is no simple one-for-one correspondence between population pressures and technological change. Population is only one of many factors that affect the nature and quality of the institutional environment that conditions the introduction of new technologies and methods of production. Green Revolution technologies, which can dramatically increase agricultural output for specific crops such as rice and wheat, have been adopted in some densely populated areas but not in others. This suggests that population pressures alone have not been the deciding factor.

Population and Market Failures

In addition to the population pessimists and the population optimists, who present such conflicting views, there is a third school of thought on population and development, the **population "revisionists."** The revisionists situate themselves between the two extreme camps, arguing that there is no "one size that fits all" on population matters. Because of the varied influences of population growth on economic and social variables, growing populations may or may not be detrimental to economic development depending on time, place, and circumstances.

The revisionists also bring together micro models of fertility behavior with macro assessments of the consequences of population growth. This merging of micro and macro is critical. According to the prevailing microeconomic model of fertility, individuals have control over their fertility decisions and behave rationally. In other words, couples, on average, make decisions on the number of children they want in their own best interest. If this insight is correct, how is it possible that actually tens of millions of rational individual decisions concerning the number of children to have could result in detrimental outcomes for nations or for even for the planet as whole? The revisionist answer is a familiar one to economists: **market failures,** situations in which the costs or benefits of reproductive behavior by individuals (households) are not fully borne by them.

Revisionists agree with some neo-Malthusians that rapid population growth may hasten depletion of natural resources or harm the environment. But unlike

---

[18]The seminal work on population pressures inducing changes in agricultural production is Ester Boserup, *The Conditions of Agricultural Growth* (Chicago: Aldine, 1965.) On human ingenuity, see Julian Simon, *The Ultimate Resource* (Princeton, NJ: Princeton University Press, 1981).

the neo-Malthusians, revisionists argue the fundamental problem is not too many people, but the lack of well-defined property rights. As in the classic "Tragedy of the Commons," population growth can destroy a common resource—for example, common grazing lands or a fishery—because no one family takes into consideration the impact of its use on others. A larger family might help that family gain greater benefits from the common resource (at least in the short run) but, at the same time, help speed its destruction, to the detriment of all.[19] A similar argument can be made about many government services, whether in education, health, sanitation, or transport. Each family may be acting rationally, but if the population grows too quickly, government services may not expand quickly enough. The resulting congestion of government services may produce lower quality of life for all. The root cause of the problem is not population growth but the inability of government to finance the increased demand for publicly provided goods and services. In both these examples, population growth may exacerbate an existing market failure.

Revisionists also call attention to a failure in the market for contraception. If there are poor, incomplete, or imperfect markets either for information on contraception or for the contraceptives themselves, women have more children than they "want" and population growth is higher. One study reports that, in Haiti in 2000, 40 percent of women 15–49 years old preferred to avoid a pregnancy but were not using contraception.[20] To the extent that this was the result of a lack of information about or access to birth control, there is a market failure for contraceptives. In such circumstances, fertility levels do not fully reflect individual preferences and are too high. The ultimate source of the market failure is less apparent. Is it due to lack of information, government restrictions on the sale of birth control devices, or something else? The price of birth control is far less than the price of raising a child. Free markets deliver Coca-Cola worldwide, why not contraceptives?[21]

In addition to drawing attention to market failures, population revisionists focus on the impact of fertility decisions on dimensions of human welfare other than growth in per capita income, such as income distribution. At a household level, high fertility may benefit parents, in terms of earnings from child labor and old age support. But these same advantages for parents may work to the disadvantage of children, if they result in fewer resources available per child for human capital investments. Higher-birth-order children may be at a particular disadvantage. Looking across households, since higher fertility is inversely correlated with household income level, more rapid population growth may increase income inequality and worsen poverty outcomes.

[19]Garret Hardin, "The Tragedy of the Commons," *Science* 162, no. 1 (1968), 243–48.

[20]Population Reference Bureau, www.prb.org, Graphics Bank, Family Planning.

[21]Adapted from William Easterly, *The Elusive Quest for Growth* (Cambridge, MA: MIT Press, 2001), 89–90.

Population revisionists have contributed to the otherwise polarized debate on population between the pessimists and optimists. The revisionists emphasize that rapid population growth is unlikely to be the primary impediment to economic development, focusing instead on how population growth can exacerbate the failings in other markets or particular government policies. Even these negative effects are likely to be mitigated over the long run as households adjust to changing circumstances. Despite their more nuanced approach, the population revisionists seem unable to identify the specific circumstances and country settings where market failures are large and policies to limit births are warranted. Their perspectives, however, help frame the debate over appropriate population policies.

POPULATION POLICY

While economic analysis cannot provide a definitive answer as to where, or even whether, intervention is warranted to slow population growth, most governments in developing nations and most donors favor slower population growth. In pursuit of this objective, governments implement a variety of population policies. Economic reasoning can help evaluate the relative merits of specific policies when the stated goal is to lower population growth rates.

The growth of a population can be reduced either by lowering the birth rate or raising the death rate. In practice, the only acceptable policy solution is reducing the birth rate. No one would advocate increasing the death rate as a way to slow population growth, but nations and donors do not always follow a strictly antimortality approach. The slow donor response to the HIV/AIDS crisis in sub-Saharan Africa is a case in point.

If slowing the rate of population growth is the goal, then reducing the birth rate is the solution. This can be achieved by reducing the share of the population of reproductive age or the fertility rate. Raising the average age of women at childbearing slows down population momentum and, in time, leads to a reduction in the share of the population of reproductive age. Providing women with more education and better employment opportunities can achieve these results. These interventions will also reduce fertility levels. And reduction in fertility, whether by direct or indirect means, is the primary target of population policies.

Two controversies surround population policies aimed at reducing fertility. One is the debate over the significance of family planning efforts versus broad-based socioeconomic development. The other is the debate over the use of relatively authoritarian tactics, including elements of China's 1979 "one-child campaign," to achieve population goals. Before getting to either of these controversies, we can identify some noncontroversial elements of population policy.

Educating girls is one of the least controversial and most effective means of achieving a long-term decline in fertility. As predicted by "the new household economics," women with more education have a higher opportunity cost of time and choose to have fewer children. This result has been born out empirically by numerous studies. (Figure 7–6 provides evidence from four nations.) Because educating girls is valuable in its own right, all schools of thought on population agree to support improvements in girl's education. Any subsequent impact on fertility is as much a consequence as a motivation for such policies. The same can be said for interventions that reduce infant and child mortality. Such interventions, usually involving prenatal care, better birthing practices, and health initiatives directed at the young, can significantly improve survival chances. These interventions need not be motivated by a desire to lower fertility, even though they have this effect.

All policies that promote economic development and lead to more education, better health, higher per capita incomes, and less poverty are associated with declining fertility, even if this is not their primary purpose. At the first United Nations World Population Conference, held in Bucharest in 1974, a popular slogan was, "Take care of the people and the population will take care of itself." Some development specialists go so far as to conclude that economic development is the best contraceptive. But others disagree and argue that more direct interventions to control fertility outcomes are needed.

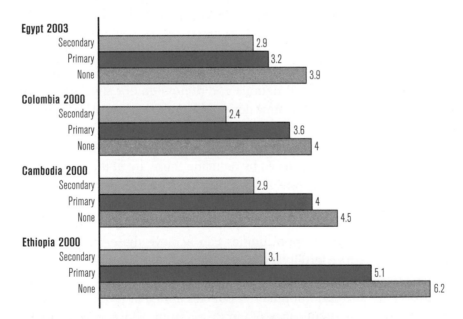

FIGURE 7-6. **Total Fertility Rates by Mother's Education**

Note: Secondary refers to having attended secondary school or higher, except in Colombia where it refers only to having attended secondary school.

Source: ORC Macro, country final reports, Demographic and Health Surveys, available at www.measuredhs.com.

Family Planning

Family planning refers to a range of reproductive health information and services. It includes information on contraception and provision of contraceptives of various types, often highly subsidized or delivered at no cost to the user. Without government family planning services, couples could purchase contraceptives available at market prices or could control their fertility using traditional methods (abstinence, rhythm method, withdrawal). More modern forms of contraception (condoms; hormone therapies including birth control pills, patches, and injections; IUDs, male and female sterilization), however, are more reliable and associated with a greater probability of achieving desired fertility. One of the most important contributions of family planning services, whether provided publicly or through the market, is to help families reach their desired fertility levels. As levels of desired fertility fall, modern forms of contraception provide the means for achieving these goals.

Some population specialists also draw attention to the significant proportion of births in the developing world that is "unwanted." Information on unwanted births is obtained from household survey data in which women report the number of births they have had as well as the number of children they would like to have. Using data from the 1970s and 1980s, demographer John Bongaarts estimated that approximately one out of every four children born in the developing world (excluding China) was unwanted.[22] Estimates for the late 1990s suggest smaller numbers; for a sample of countries representing 60 percent of world population, the total "not wanted" was 11 percent with another 16 percent "wanted later."[23] Reducing the number of unwanted births is another way of reducing population growth. Whether family planning programs are effective at reducing unwanted births is a matter of debate. Using data from the 1970s and 1980s, development economist Lant Pritchett found little correlation between contraceptive prevalence and excess births (the difference between desired and actual fertility.)[24]

Family planning programs also may influence individual preferences about how many children to have. This dimension of family planning efforts involves providing information, counseling, and various forms of "persuasion" concerning the number and spacing of children. Public campaigns to discourage high fertility are employed by many countries. In the 1980s, the slogan of India's National Family Planning Commission launched was *"Hum Do, Hamaray Do,"* which when translated means "Us Two, Our Two," or for two parents, two kids— a model family. The slogan was displayed widely on the sides of buses, bill-

---

[22]John Bongaarts, "Population Policy Options," 771–76.

[23]Population Reference Bureau, *Family Planning Worldwide: 2002 Data Sheet.*

[24]Lant Pritchett, "Desired Fertility and the Impact of Population Policies," *Population and Development Review* 20, no. 1 (March 1994), 1–55.

boards, and in TV advertisements and came with a logo, a silhouette of two parents holding the hands of two children, a boy in shorts and a pigtailed girl in skirts. In Indonesia, the *"Dua cukup"* program recommended "two is enough"; in the Philippines, public ads showed two happy children and advised, "If you love them, plan for them"; and in Zimbabwe, a family planning poster suggested, "A small family brings a better life." These campaigns can affect social norms and the desire to have many children.

Family planning information also can be more personalized. One widely studied program of this type began in the late 1970s in the Matlab region of Bangladesh. It included fortnightly visits to each married woman in half the villages in the region. The visit was from a project employee, who discussed family planning needs and provided contraceptives. As a result of these visits, fertility rates fell dramatically by 1.6 births relative to the half of villages in the region that did not receive such visits. An important lesson of the Matlab experiment is that family planning can be effective at reducing fertility but it can entail substantial costs. Pritchett estimated that the fortnightly field visits, free contraceptives, and administrative expenses per woman amounted to 10 percent of per capita income, sums that could not be sustained at a national level.[25]

Family planning programs need not be as expensive as in the Matlab program to be effective, but the general point remains. If the goal is to reduce fertility levels, is it better to devote scarce resources to expand family planning programs, or might it be more effective to devote these same resources to general improvements in socioeconomic status, which, in turn, could result in an equal or greater decline in fertility? In their evaluations of Indonesia's rapid decline in fertility rates, economists Paul Gertler and John Molyneaux determined that heavy subsidization of contraceptives, representing about half of the family planning program's expenditures, had a marginal impact on reducing fertility. Expansion of the distribution network into rural areas had a more significant effect. But most of the increased use of contraceptives was induced through economic development and the improved education and opportunities facing Indonesian women.[26]

Family planning may not play a large independent role in reducing fertility but this does not suggest that governments should abandon these programs or limit the availability of contraceptives. Modern forms of contraception enable families to better control their fertility. In this sense, family planning and development are complements, not substitutes. Family planning services also help people lead healthier and more satisfying lives. By being better able to time pregnancies, women can better space their children. Children born three to five years apart have higher rates of survival than children born within two years of

---

[25]Ibid., p. 37.

[26]Paul Gertler and John Molyneaux, "How Economic Development and Family Planning Programs Combined to Reduce Indonesian Fertility," *Demography* 31, no. 1 (February 1994), 33–63; and John Molyneaux and Paul Gertler, "The Impact of Targeted Family Planning Programs in Indonesia," *Population and Development Review* 26, supplement (2000), 61–85.

one another. Avoiding unintended pregnancies can also reduce the need for abortions. In many low- and middle-income nations, abortions are illegal and take place under unsafe circumstances, contributing to maternal mortality. Increased use of contraceptives can help reduce the amount of premature death of both women and children in poor nations.

The 1994 Cairo International Conference on Population and Development endorsed the idea that family planning be replaced by a broader program of reproductive health. The World Health Organization defines the goals of this new approach as follows:

> Reproductive health implies that people are able to have a responsible, satisfying, and safe sex life and that they have the capability to reproduce and the freedom to decide if, when, and how often they do so. Implicit in this last condition are the right of men and women to have access to safe, affordable, and acceptable methods of fertility regulation of their choice, and the right of access to appropriate health care services that will enable women to go safely through pregnancy and childbirth and provide couples with the best chance of having a healthy infant.[27]

Authoritarian Approaches

Some countries, concerned over the growth of their populations, have resorted to relatively authoritarian approaches to reduce their birth rates. In India, during the 1970s, the government added male sterilization to its list of promoted family planning methods. It did so because the government felt unable to control population growth by conventional means. Incentives were offered to men who agreed to be sterilized, and quotas were assigned to officials charged with carrying out the pro gram. Problems arose when force allegedly was used against low-status individuals by officials anxious to fill their quotas. The sterilization campaign provoked an adverse political reaction because the methods of population control were regarded as excessively zealous and callous in their disregard of individual rights. Indira Gandhi's surprising defeat in India's 1977 general election was attributed in part to the population policy of her emergency government.

China's experience has been different. Chinese leaders have expressed concern about the size of the nation's population since the census of 1953 revealed a population of almost 600 million. Modest attempts to influence fertility outcomes followed, but not until 1971 was a more aggressive stance adopted. In that year the "planned births" campaign was initiated and established three reproductive norms, *wan, xi, shao* ("later, longer, fewer"): later marriage, longer spacing between births, and fewer children. To implement these norms, birth targets were set for administrative units at all levels throughout China. The responsibility for achieving these targets was placed in the hands of officials heading units ranging from provinces of 2 to 90 million people down to production brigades of 250 to 800. The

[27]Cited in World Bank, *Population and Development* (Washington, DC: World Bank, 1994), p. 81.

national government held information and motivation campaigns to persuade people to have fewer children, but it was left to local officials to fill out many details of the program and finance much of its cost. In China's villages, where much of the population lived, IUD insertions, abortions, and later sterilizations were offered. A wider range of contraceptives was provided in the cities. National spokespeople maintained that participation in the program was voluntary, but local officials with targets to fulfill often applied pressure. At the production brigade level, birth planning became intensely personal, as couples were required to seek approval to have a child in a particular year. (The application might be accepted or they might be asked to wait a year or two.)

The *wan xi shao* campaign began by discouraging couples from having more than two children; by the end of the 1970s, couples were encouraged to have only one. During the 1970s, total fertility rates in China plummeted from around six children per woman to less than three, a rate of fertility decline without precedent in world history. But, despite lowered fertility, population projections continued to cause concern, and in 1979, the **"one-child" campaign** was promulgated. Couples, initially, were required to apply for official approval before conceiving the one child that was allowed. Those who complied could receive income supplements, extra maternity leave, and preferential treatment when applying for public housing. Couples bearing more than one child might be fined or lose access to education or other privileges. Early in the campaign, the government employed harsh methods to enforce its population goals. A system of incentives and penalties, plus other forms of social pressure, moved women to undergo sterilization after two births. China's one-child approach has gone through various phases since its inception, with periods of stricter and looser interpretations. Since the late 1980s, rural couples in most provinces were allowed to have two children if their first was a daughter. Chinese couples still are obliged to strictly limit the number of children they have but elements of the earlier coercion to force such outcomes have waned.[28]

Several lessons can be learned from China's experience. First, the dramatic decline in fertility that took place in China is the result of more than the government's population policies. At the same time that these programs were implemented, economic reforms ushered in a period of rapid economic growth, which decreased desired fertility. Even without the one-child campaign, Chinese fertility levels would have fallen but probably not as far. Second, the sharp fall in births may have longer-term adverse consequences. China will face a rapidly aging population in the decades ahead, which may stress both private and public systems of old-age support. China also faces a growing imbalance between the number of males and females (Box 7–4). This is the result of a traditional

---

[28]For a survey of demographic trends and policies in the People's Republic of China, see Nancy Riley, "China's Population: New Trends and Challenges," Population Reference Bureau *Population Bulletin* 59, no. 2 (June 2004).

BOX 7-4 MISSING GIRLS, MISSING WOMEN

Most parents believe that the chances of having a daughter or a son are 50–50. But this is not true. For most human populations, the expected ratio of boys to girls at birth is closer to 105:100. Scientists are not entirely sure why this is the case, but believe it is related to biological weaknesses in males resulting in higher mortality rates for boy versus girl infants. Since more than biology determines survival, social scientists draw attention to sex ratios, at birth and throughout the life cycle, when they deviate from what is expected in a gender-neutral environment.

The chart in this box compares the sex ratio of children 0–4 years old in various regions. Europe and North America have ratios close to 105:100. The lower ratios in some regions may be due to a tendency for populations of African descent to record male to female ratios at birth closer to 102:100 or the higher rates of male infant and child mortality. The most striking result is the pattern in East Asia, where there were close to 111 boys for every 100 girls. This is neither a recent outcome nor is it biologically driven. The shortage of girls 0–4 is the result of long-standing son preference in the region. In previous periods, the shortage of young females was the result of deliberate female infanticide and neglect. Today, sex-selective abortion is another mechanism causing male children to outnumber female children, one facilitated by the increasing availability of ultrasound and other prenatal screening devices.

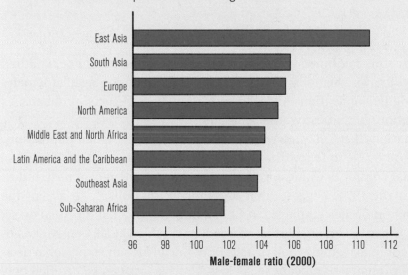

Source: Figure is from United Nations Population Information Network.

Sex-selective abortions, abandonment of female infants, and differential neglect of girls, especially in medical care, are all means of realizing son preference. They are common in many parts of East Asia but none more so than in China. China's 2000 census reported the highest sex ratios at birth in the world, 120 boys for every 100 girls. While son preference has a long history in China, the one-child campaign and the overall move to low fertility rates among Chinese households, have contributed to these outcomes. In 1982, at the beginning of the one-child policy, the sex ratio of first births was 107; second births, 105; and all subsequent births, 110. The change by 2000 was dramatic. The sex ratio of first births in China was still 107; but for second births it rose to 152, and for any subsequent births it was almost 160. Second and higher-order births represented only one third of all births in 2000, but sex selection for these births resulted in the high and grossly imbalanced sex ratio for all Chinese births.

China is not alone in this extreme form of discrimination against females. Amartya Sen examined the issue of differential mortality of males versus females and found that survival chances vary across countries and over the life cycle. In India, the differential shows up less at birth and more during childhood and the late teen years. Sen and other researchers conclude that more than *100 million women are missing* worldwide, 80 million from China and India combined, as a result of sex-selective abortions and the relative neglect of girls and women. Despite the attention Sen and others have drawn to the issue of "missing women," global pressure to change these outcomes has been minimal.

Sources: Nancy E. Riley, "China's Population: New Trends and Challenges," Population Reference Bureau *Population Bulletin* 59, no. 2 (June 2004); Amartya Sen, "More than 100 Million Women Are Missing," *New York Review of Books* (December 20, 1990); Stephan Klasen and Claudia Wink, " 'Missing Women': Revisiting the Debate," *Feminist Economics* 9, nos. 2–3 (November 2003).

preference for sons combined with policies that limited the number of children a couple could have. This most severe form of discrimination against females has human rights implications and may result in a host of social problems for future generations of Chinese women and men.

Finally, nations that today are worried about the growth in their populations are unlikely to be able to follow the Chinese approach. Few states can exercise as much social control as Chinese governments have in the recent past. India's experience in the 1970s suggests that a democracy is unlikely to accept the authoritarian approaches employed in China. But, even if a nation could do so, should they? Amartya Sen argues that, if freedom is valued at all, depriving people of the freedom to regulate their own fertility, one of life's most personal decisions, must represent a significant social loss.[29] Such a loss can be justified only if the social cost of not intervening is high. As this chapter has shown, it is hard to make the case that individuals systematically make poor decisions when it

[29]Amartya Sen, "Population: Delusion and Reality," *The New York Review of Books* 41, no. 15 (September 22, 1994).

comes to childbearing or that the negative externalities of these decisions are large. If this is true, what justification is there for coercion to regulate fertility? Noncoercive approaches, including broad-based socioeconomic improvements, can achieve similar ends and should be pursued instead.

SUMMARY

- The twentieth century will be remembered for populating the planet. In 1900, the world population stood at about 1.5 billion. By 2000, there were over 6 billion people; 5 billion living in developing nations. In no prior century did the world population increase by even 1 billion. The world population growth has slowed since the 1960s, and current projections do not envision that the twenty-first century will see increases as large as those of the last century.

- The driving force behind the population increases of the last 100 years is the demographic transition, especially in the developing world. Improvements in nutrition, medical knowledge, and public health led to a rapid decline in death rates. Birth rates took longer to fall, and in the interim, the rate of natural increase in the populations of low- and middle-income nations soared to unprecedented levels. Today, most regions of the world are experiencing a decline in fertility and are approaching replacement levels. Sub-Saharan Africa is the one exception, where total fertility remains high, but even in this region, some decline is in evidence.

- There is considerable debate over the consequences of population growth on economic development. Evidence from the 1990s and earlier decades suggests the absence of a simple correlation between population growth and economic growth. This is because of the multitude of ways population growth affects the determinants of growth; population growth, for example, may inhibit capital deepening but it also may encourage institutional and technological innovations that increase factor productivity.

- In trying to understand the impact of population growth on economic development it is important to reconcile micro behavior with macro outcomes. If individual couples are making rational choices over the number of children they have, then at a macro level, why might a problem arise? The answer is market failures; for example, if the social costs of raising children exceed the private costs. In practice, it has proven difficult to identify the precise circumstances where this happens and how large are the resulting costs.

- The debate over whether population growth is an obstacle to economic development is reflected in the choice of population policies governments pursue. If household behavior is rational and market failures are small, then development may be the best contraceptive. With better education, especially for girls; better employment opportunities, especially for women; and improved health care, especially for the young; couples desire fewer children. Family planning programs also may influence social norms about family size and can assist individuals in attaining desired fertility levels in a safe and reliable manner.

- Some governments, especially in China, decided that the macro consequences of population growth are so negative that authoritarian steps must be taken to limit fertility. Such approaches have proven effective at reducing fertility levels and rates of population growth. But their development benefits are less obvious. Coercive population policies entail high social costs and loss of individual freedom. It is difficult to justify these actions with such limited evidence that reduced fertility contributes to faster economic growth and development.

8

Education

B elief in the importance of education for economic development is not a new idea. The Chinese philosopher Guan Zhong, writing in the seventh century B.C., advised, "If you plan for a year, plant a seed. If for ten years, plant a tree. If for a hundred years, teach the people. When you sow a seed once, you will reap a single harvest. When you teach the people, you will reap a hundred harvests."

Contemporary scholars voice similar perspectives. Nobel laureate Theodore Schultz, in his 1960 presidential address to the American Economics Association, highlighted the importance of investing in people. Schultz referred to the acquisition of skills and knowledge as investments in **human capital.** Economists consider resources spent on physical capital as an investment that yields a future return, rather than as consumption. Schultz argued that expenditures on people should be viewed in a similar way. He believed that most of the "impressive rise" in the earnings of workers in the industrialized countries was due to the growth in human capital and a limiting factor in the advance of poor countries was insufficient investment in people.[1]

Among the major categories of human capital investments, Schultz included formal education at the elementary, secondary, and higher levels; health services; and on-the-job training. In this chapter, we focus on formal education, specifically on schooling, and its implications for economic growth

[1]Theodore W. Schultz, "Investment in Human Capital," *American Economic Review* 51, 1 (March 1961), 1–17.

and development. In the next chapter, we consider health. On-the-job training includes everything from a parent teaching a child to farm, to an apprentice learning a craft from a master tradesman, to a multinational corporation offering courses to newly hired or experienced workers. All these forms of on-the-job training are important sources of human capital investment, but they ordinarily take place with limited amounts of policy intervention and public spending, especially when compared to education and health care. Schooling also provides *general* human capital, which is a prerequisite to the *specific* human capital more often associated with on-the-job training. For these reasons, we restrict our attention in this chapter to schooling.

Over the past 40 years, there has been tremendous growth in schooling in all regions of the world. In 1960, 68 percent of all adults in the developing world are estimated never to have attended school. By 2000, this percentage had fallen almost by half to 37 percent. At current enrollment rates, this percentage will fall even further in the decades ahead. In many countries expansion in schooling has contributed significantly to the human capital of the labor force and subsequent economic growth and development. But, in other settings, schooling has not yet delivered what Guan Zhong and Theodore Schultz predicted in terms of growth and development. It is not that the Chinese philosopher and the American Nobel laureate were wrong. Instead, education, like so many other prescriptions for economic development, is not a panacea. It is not the sole determinant of economic success. If economic conditions do not encourage productive economic activity, the demand for educated workers will be weak, and even those with schooling may struggle to generate income for themselves and their families.

After considering recent trends in schooling and learning, this chapter examines the evidence on schooling as an investment. Schooling generally displays attractive private and social rates of return, but even when this is the case, spending on schooling often delivers less than it might. Countries often underinvest in schooling overall, misallocate resources across the different levels of schooling, and inefficiently use resources within schools themselves. In some cases, the problem is insufficient or misallocated resources; in others, it is a lack of accountability among teachers, principals, and others responsible for the education of the young. The seventh century Chinese philosopher Guan Zhong may have been right in his overall view of education but he did not spell out the details: How does one induce parents to send and keep their children in school; how does one combat rampant absenteeism among many teachers; and, even more fundamental, how does one increase the amount of learning students achieve by attending school?

TRENDS AND PATTERNS

If you are reading this book for a course in development economics, you are among a privileged group in the world who has the opportunity to attend university. You may not feel part of an especially select group as you make your way through the crowded hallways of your college or university, but you are part of one. Worldwide, gross enrollment rates in any type of tertiary education (schooling beyond high school) amount to about one out of every four members of your age group. In the high-income countries, the rate is close to 60 percent; in the middle-income nations, it falls to 22 percent; and in the low-income countries, it drops to only 10 percent. Even more striking is comparing yourself to the generations that came before you. In Indonesia, out of the *entire* adult age population (ages 25–64) only 2.4 percent received any schooling beyond the secondary level; in Tunisia, only 3.9 percent did; in Brazil, only 7.5 percent. The experience of your age cohort, as compared to the schooling experience of earlier generations, tells us a lot about the stocks and flows of education in the world today. **Stocks** refer to the amount of schooling embodied in a population; **flows,** to the net change in those stocks as the result of school enrollment patterns.

Stocks and Flows

The scarcity of education in the developing nations is evident in the data on the levels of schooling completed among today's adult population (Figure 8–1). In the United States, an advanced economy, only 3 percent of adults did not complete six years of schooling (that is, did not complete primary school). The situation in low- and middle-income nations could not be more different. In Brazil and Indonesia, about one out of every three adults did not attend or complete primary school; in Tunisia, the ratio is almost two out of every three adults. Household data from the two Indian states of Uttar Pradesh and Bihar tell a similar story. In these two states, which have a combined population of 250 million people and are among the poorest states in India and, hence, are among the poorest people in the world, over two thirds of the adult population did not complete primary school; *over 60 percent never even attended school.*

Minimal levels of education characterize today's labor force in many low- and middle-income countries, but the situation is changing. Throughout the world, parents and governments, as well as bilateral donors and international agencies, are advocating that current and future generations receive more schooling. This trend is evident in a comparison of school enrollment rates by

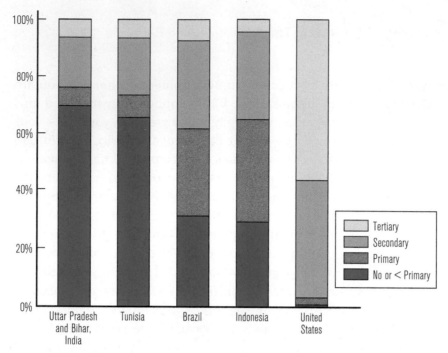

FIGURE 8-1. Educational Attainment of the Adult Population (ages 25–64)

Note: Data for Uttar Pradesh and Bihar, India refer to 1997–98. Data for Tunisia, Brazil, and Indonesia refer to 1999. Data for the United States refer to 2003.

Source: Living Standards Measurement Study, *Survey of Living Conditions, Uttar Pradesh and Bihar;* U.S. Census Bureau, available at www.census.gov/population/socdemo/ education/cps2003/tab01-01.xls; UNESCO.

region over the past three decades (Table 8–1). At the primary school level, **gross enrollment rates** either have been high for decades (East Asia, Europe and Central Asia, Latin America) or have expanded rapidly (Middle East and North Africa, South Asia). In relative terms, sub-Saharan Africa's primary school enrollment rates have grown rapidly but still remain well below the levels reached in all other regions. Taken together, regional trends indicate real progress in increasing the amount of schooling children receive.

Gross enrollment rates refer to the total number of children enrolled in a given school category divided by the number of children of the age group that officially corresponds to that level of schooling. In the case of primary school, the relevant age group usually is 6–11 years old. If older children (or younger ones) enroll in primary school, the gross enrollment ratio can exceed 100, as it does in East Asia and Latin America. Gross enrollment ratios that exceed 100 often are a mixed blessing. The good news is that they indicate lots of children are enrolled in school; the bad news is that they usually are the result of high dropout rates, where children enroll, then leave school, and later return to repeat a grade. If repetition rates are high, as they often are in poor countries,

TABLE 8-1. Changes in Schooling, Gross Enrollment Rates, by Region, 1970–2000

REGION	PRIMARY		SECONDARY		TERTIARY	
	1970	2000	1970	2000	1970	2000
East Asia and Pacific	89.4	111.4	23.8	66.4	1.1	14.4
Europe and Central Asia	99.3[a]	99.5	86.2[a]	85.6	30.9[a]	46.0
Latin America and Caribbean	107.2	124.7	27.6	84.8	6.2	22.6
Middle East and North Africa	70.1	95.6	23.5	70.3	4.4	20.7[b]
South Asia	70.6	94.8	23.0	48.0	4.2	10.0
Sub-Saharan Africa	51.0	81.7	6.3	25.7[b]	0.8	3.6[b]
High income	100.0	101.9	75.0	106.0	26.2	61.1

[a]Due to insufficient data for 1970, the values for Europe and Central Asia refer to 1980.
[b]Values refer to the late 1990s.
Source: World Bank, *World Development Indicators Online.*

gross enrollment rates can be high even though a substantial number of children never attend school.[2]

Alternative measures of school attendance take account of this problem. **Net enrollment rates** refer to enrollments of only those of the relevant age group. **Grade survival rates** estimate how many children actually complete a certain grade level. Estimates of these measures confirm the substantial progress nations have made in expanding primary education but also highlight that universal *completion* of primary school remains a challenge. In 2000, net enrollment ratios in low- and middle-income countries were 85 and 88 percent, respectively; in sub-Saharan Africa they were only 56 percent. Estimates of grade survival rates suggest that one out of five children in the poorest nations did not complete even four years of schooling; in middle-income nations, more than one in ten failed to do so. These failures are most pronounced among the poorest children, those with families in the bottom quintile of the income distribution. In Madagascar, only 4 percent of children from the poorest quintile completed five years of schooling, compared to over 50 percent of children from the richest quintile. Because of these tendencies, the Millennium Development

[2]Paul Glewwe and Michael Kremer offer the following hypothetical example, "In a school system with 6 years of primary education, a 100 percent gross enrollment rate is consistent with 75 percent of children taking 8 years to complete primary school (because each child repeats two grades) and 25 percent of children never attending school." From "Schools, Teachers, and Education Outcomes in Developing Countries," in E. Hanushek and F. Welch, eds., *Handbook on the Economics of Education* (Boston: Elsevier, forthcoming).

Goal of achieving universal primary education for all children by 2015 is unlikely to be met in all but a few regions of the world.

Achieving universal primary education remains an important goal. Another challenge is to expand secondary and tertiary enrollments. Huge enrollment gains in secondary education have been realized in virtually all regions (Table 8–1). Latin America's gains are the greatest, with gross secondary school enrollment expanding from approximately 28 to 85 percent between 1970 and 2000. The poorest regions, sub-Saharan Africa and South Asia, still lag the other regions, but much progress has been made in 30 years. Not surprising, both the absolute level and expansion of tertiary enrollments remain low in all developing regions. Even the current star performers in terms of economic growth, East and South Asia, do not stand out in terms of their expansion of secondary or tertiary enrollments. Faced with limited resources, governments must decide whether to allocate additional resources to achieving universal primary education or to expanding opportunities at either the secondary or tertiary levels. These are controversial issue we return to later in the chapter.

Trends in school enrollment rates across regions, combined with the age structure of today's developing world, tell us how human capital endowments will change in the decades ahead. Subsequent generations will be more numerous and have more schooling than their parents. This trend already is evident. Figure 8–2 provides estimates of the growth in the average years of schooling

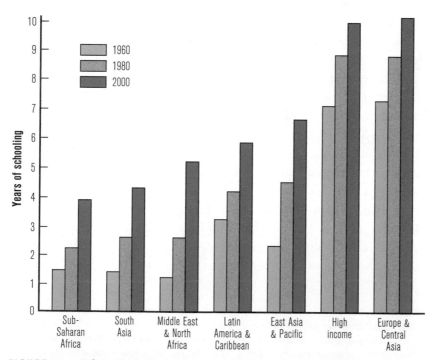

FIGURE 8-2. **Educational Attainment, Adult Population 25 and over**
Source: Robert Barro and Jong-Wha Lee. "International Data on Educational Attainment: Updates and Implications" (Center for International Development, Harvard University, 2000).

completed by adults 25 and over for all regions between 1960 and 2000.[3] As expected, the average years of schooling have increased everywhere. What is striking about these numbers is the extent of this increase. Most of the developing world has seen a doubling, in some cases a tripling, in the mean educational attainment of its potential workforce. East Asia has gone from a predicted mean of 2.3 years to 6.5 years of schooling; South Asia from 1.3 to 4.2 years, and the Middle East and North Africa from only 1.1 years to 5.1 years. The average level of educational attainment may still seem extremely low, especially relative to the high-income economies, but remember these are population means. People in their fifties and sixties with no or little schooling are averaged together with people in their twenties and thirties whose educational attainment exceeds the mean. The trend is unmistakable, younger workers are entering the labor force with more years of schooling and are enriching the human capital of the developing nations. It is fair to say that, during the past 30 years, there has been a global revolution in the provision of schooling.

Boys versus Girls

Progress has been achieved not only in the number of years of schooling received, but also in the distribution of who receives this schooling. There has been considerable progress in spreading the opportunity to attend school to girls as well as boys, although girls' education still lags behinds boys'. Favoring the education of boys over girls is a longstanding and pervasive practice throughout much of the world, but this practice is changing. Estimates of average years of schooling for men and women over the age of 25 reveal a gender gap that has declined significantly over the past four decades. For all developing nations, the mean number of years of schooling for men in 1960 was only 2.4 years and for women even less, 1.2 years. Taking the ratio of the two, women completed only 50 percent the schooling of men. By 1980, this gap had barely narrowed with the gender ratio at 56 percent. Much more progress has been made since 1980. For the developing world as a whole in 2000, adult women were estimated to have completed an average of 4.0 years of schooling as compared to 5.7 years for adult men, meaning a gender ratio of 70 percent.

Regional patterns show considerable variation (Table 8–2) around these trends. All regions have narrowed the gender gap in schooling, with Europe and

---

[3]Calculating average years of schooling for a nation would seem a straightforward task. It is not, in part, because census and survey data in many developing nations are not conducted on a regular basis. Economists estimate educational attainment using a perpetual inventory method, which combines available census and survey data reflecting the stock of human capital with information on enrollment and repetition rates, which reflects the flow of schooling. Economists Robert Barro and Jong-Wha Lee provide the most-often-cited estimates and projections of educational attainment. (See Robert Barro and Jong-Wha Lee, "International Data on Educational Attainment: Updates and Implications," CID Working Paper No. 42 [Center for International Development, Harvard University, April 2000]).

TABLE 8-2. **Estimates of School Attainment for Adults 25 and over by Gender and Region, 1960 and 2000**

REGION	1960			2000		
	WOMEN (YEARS)	MEN (YEARS)	RATIO (%)	WOMEN (YEARS)	MEN (YEARS)	RATIO (%)
East Asia and Pacific	1.5	3.0	50	5.9	7.1	84
Europe and Central Asia	6.7	7.8	86	10.0	9.9	102
Latin America and Caribbean	2.8	3.4	83	5.6	5.9	96
Middle East and North Africa	0.8	1.5	51	4.1	6.1	68
South Asia	0.5	2.0	25	2.9	5.4	53
Sub-Saharan Africa	1.0	1.8	59	3.1	4.5	71
High income	6.7	7.2	93	9.6	10.1	95

Source: Robert Barro and Jong-Wha Lee, "International Data on Educational Attainment: Updates and Implications," Table 5.

Central Asia having achieved gender parity. Latin America has risen to advanced country levels, it now has a gender ratio of about 95 percent. South Asia, by comparison, has a long way to go. Estimates for 1960 show that adult women had received virtually no schooling (0.5 years), only 25 percent of what adult men received. By 2000, outcomes had improved. Women averaged 2.9 years of schooling, now about 50 percent of what men completed. South Asia's gender gap is expected to continue to narrow. Today in South Asia, primary school enrollment rates for girls are 85 percent those of boys and secondary school enrollment rates 74 percent. When these young people move on to replace their parents and grandparents in the labor force, the region's stock of human capital will be larger and its distribution between men and women relatively more equal.

Schooling versus Education

Years of schooling and the gender distribution of that schooling are two ways of charting the accumulation of human capital. But schooling is only a means to an end; the real goal is education, that is, the capabilities individuals acquire from time spent studying and learning. Students can sit through many years of schooling and learn very little. Measuring learning outcomes is notoriously difficult within one nation let alone across them. But there have been attempts to apply basic tests of core competencies in reading and mathematics across nations. The results are sobering, because of both the gap between rich and poor nations and the implications for the quality of schooling available in many low- and middle-income nations.

One source of cross-country information on learning outcomes is the Programme for International Student Assessment (PISA). Initially, PISA administered examinations only among OECD members, that is, mostly high-income economies. But interest in their work led to an expansion of testing to some non-OECD and middle-income settings. PISA's goal is to assess how well 15 year olds, an age when many students are approaching the end of their compulsory schooling years, are prepared "to meet the challenges of today's societies." Anywhere from 4,500 to 10,000 students in each country surveyed have been given PISA tests in reading, mathematics, and science. Average scores on the reading test for a subset of participating nations are presented in Figure 8–3. Korea was the nation with the highest mean score. Korean students performed better than

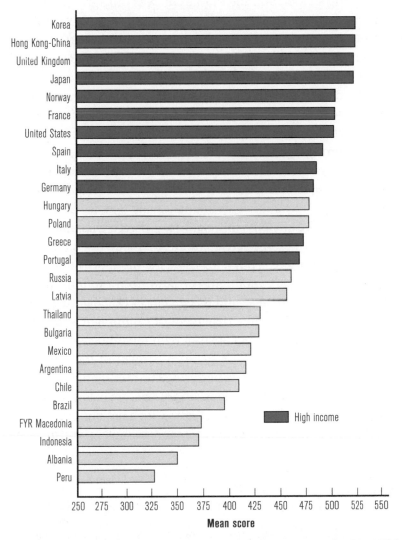

FIGURE 8-3. Learning Outcomes: Reading Achievement of 15 Year Olds, 2003

Source: OECD/UNESCO Institute for Statistics, *Literary Skills for the World of Tomorrow.*

many nations with considerably higher incomes. But Korea is an outlier. Most middle-income nations in the table displayed scores that are lower, in fact, far lower, than even the poorest OECD performers (Greece and Portugal).

The mean score on the reading achievement test was 500 for the OECD nations, with two thirds of all students scoring between 400 and 600. The mean scores of students in Albania, Brazil, Indonesia, Macedonia, and Peru all fell below 400. In Indonesia, PISA reports that over two thirds of all 15 year olds tested have serious difficulties in using reading as a tool to advance and extend their knowledge and skills in other areas. In Peru, three quarters of test takers had such difficulty.[4] Given that these nations have not achieved universal secondary school enrollments, the PISA results actually overestimate the measured abilities of all 15 year olds: Those 15 year olds not in school are unlikely to know as much as those attending school, and the PISA exam was only given to those in school. Results on mathematical skills show an even larger gap in learning among students in OECD countries as compared to those outside of the OECD group. By way of example, the average mathematics score among Brazilian students was on a par with only *the bottom* 2 percent of Danish students.

It is possible that the disparity in results is due to cultural bias, as any test is likely to suffer to some degree from this problem, but the results on relative school performance reported by the PISA study are similar to those from other evaluations. One study from Bangladesh found that 58 percent of a sample of rural children age 11 and older failed to identify seven out of eight letters; a similar percentage had difficulty identifying numbers and geometric shapes. One of the questions from the Third International Mathematics and Science Study asks the following: "Three-fifths of the students in a class are girls. If 5 girls and 5 boys are added, which statement is true? (a) There are more girls than boys; (b) There are the same number of girls as there is boys; (c) There are more boys than girls; (d) You cannot tell whether there are more girls or boys from the information provided." Eighty-two percent of Japanese and 62 percent of U.S. eighth graders provided the correct answer, (a). But only 31 percent of Colombian and South African eighth graders identified the correct answer. With four choices available, random guessing would result in the correct score 25 percent of the time; the school children in Colombia and South Africa performed only marginally better.[5]

That learning outcomes in developing nations, on average, are below the levels prevailing in developed nations is not a surprising finding. Rich nations have many advantages over poorer ones. Children of parents with more schooling tend to have

---

[4]OECD and UNESCO Institute for Statistics, *Literary Skills for the World of Tomorrow: Further Results from PISA 2000* (Paris: OECD, 2003), Figure 2, p. 69.

[5]The Bangladesh results are from Vincent Greaney, Shahidur Khandker, and Mahmudul Alam, *Bangladesh: Assessing Basic Learning Skills* (Dhaka: University Press, 1999) as reported by Glewwe and Kremer, *Handbook on the Economics of Education*. The Trends in International Mathematics and Science Study (TIMSS) results are cited in Lant Pritchett, "Access to Education," in Bjorn Lomborg, *Global Crises, Global Solutions* (London: Cambridge University Press, 2004).

better educational outcomes. The quality of schooling also depends on income levels and demographics. Given the rapid expansion in school enrollments over the past few decades, developing nations had no choice but to focus on expanding quantity, not on improving quality. There simply could not have been, for example, enough experienced teachers and principals to handle the primary and secondary schooling needs resulting from the developing world's rapid population growth. But what is surprising (and disheartening) is the extent of the learning gap between rich and poor nations. School quality undoubtedly plays a role. Anyone with first-hand experience of schools in poor countries, especially in rural areas, is familiar with the problems: too many unqualified teachers, endemic absenteeism among students *and* teachers, too few books and other teaching materials. In such environments, it is not surprising that learning outcomes are so poor.

THE BENEFITS OF EDUCATION

Despite problems of low quality, the demand for education remains high in most countries. Parents want their children to have better lives and often see getting an education as a way to achieve them. In terms of material well-being, what parents perceive is borne out by the data. On average, people with more schooling earn more than people with less schooling. Few economic outcomes are as robust as is the relationship between earnings and schooling. Primary school graduates tend to earn more than those with no schooling; secondary school graduates earn more than their counterparts who only completed primary school; and those with tertiary education tend to earn more than those with less education. Of course, these are average tendencies. A professor with many years of schooling may earn less than a plumber who went to school for many fewer years, but on average, the relationship holds. It holds for both men and women; it holds in fast growing economies and stagnant ones; and it holds across income levels and regions.

Figure 8–4 illustrates the relationship between schooling and earnings for one country, Nicaragua. Using household data from 1998, Figure 8–4 charts **age-earnings profiles** for men and women separately, by level of education attained. Workers at all schooling levels tend to see their earnings rise quickly in their early years, reach a plateau, and sometimes fall off in later years. The more educated is the worker, the higher the age-earnings profile tends to be. In Nicaragua, the earnings premiums for more educated men are unambiguous. As level of schooling rises, each age-earnings profile lies above the one that preceded it. For Nicaraguan women, the trends are not as definitive due, in part, to the relatively small number of observations on working women in this data set. A larger sample would most likely produce the nonoverlapping earnings profiles that characterize Nicaraguan men.

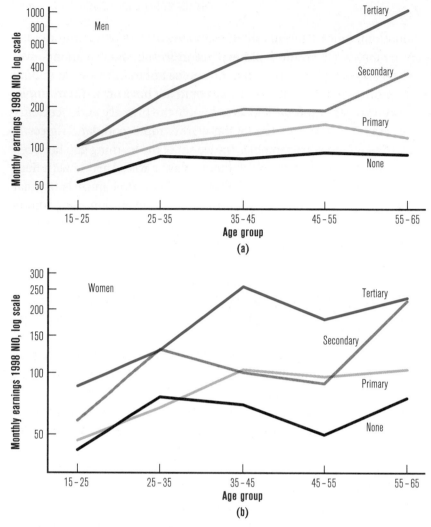

FIGURE 8-4. **Earnings by Age, Education, and Gender, Nicaragua, 1998**
Source: World Bank, Nicaragua Living Standards Measurement Study Survey E.M.N.V. 1998,
available at www.worldbank.org/lsms/country/ni98/ni98docs.html#English.

Comparison of the earnings of Nicaraguan men and women reveals one other relationship. At every education level women tend to earn less than their male counterparts, a worldwide result almost as common as the tendency for earnings to rise with education levels.

Education as an Investment

If Figure 8–4 were reproduced for any country the results would be similar: People with more years of schooling tend to earn more than people with fewer years. The figure also proves useful in thinking about education as an investment. Economists define investment as the flow of resources into the production of new capital. In the case of schooling, resources by both governments and households are spent in the expectation that schooling produces human capital. The expectation is also that these investments will yield a positive return. By attending school, an individual hopes to acquire human capital, which makes that individual more productive and, therefore, better compensated. This relationship holds whether the individual becomes a farmer or trader, laborer or artisan, professional or government official.

There are several benefits to thinking of education as an investment. Schooling competes with many other activities on which governments and households spend their scarce resources. How does a government decide how much to devote to schooling? Should more resources be spent on schools as opposed to health clinics, tube wells for clean water, or rural roads? Even within the education sector, how should a government allocate its spending: Is achieving universal primary education a better use of resources than expanding colleges and universities? Governments must make these decisions and thinking about education as an investment can help. Households make similar decisions. When education is viewed as an investment it becomes easier to understand why some families send their children to work and not to school, while other families do everything in their power to make sure a child receives an education.

Figure 8–5 illustrates the factors that determine the **private return** on schooling. The figure presents two stylized streams of future earnings, one for an individual who only completes primary school and the other for someone

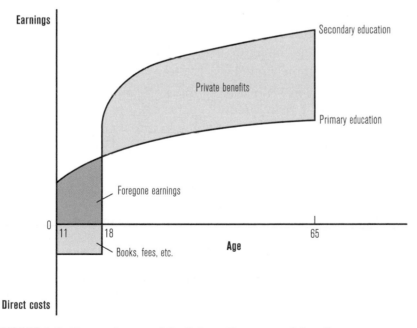

FIGURE 8-5. **Determinants of the Private Returns to Schooling**

who goes on and completes a secondary education. Figure 8–5 considers two groups of individuals, both of whom have completed primary school and are now 11 years old. One group does not continue with its education and begins to work. The earnings profile of this group is the one associated with primary education only. The other group completes secondary education and remains in school until age 18. For ease of exposition, we assume that individuals do not work while in school and, therefore, have zero earnings while in school. Once secondary school is completed, this group follows the higher of the two earnings profiles. The private pecuniary benefits of a secondary education, as we saw in Figure 8–4, are the difference in earnings the individual expects to receive beyond what a primary school graduate might earn.

But costs also are associated with the decision to remain in school. These costs include any foregone earnings, sacrificed because the individual is in school and not working. These costs may seem low for a young person considering attending primary or secondary school. But for the majority of households in the developing nations, the opportunity cost of sending a child to school are real. In peasant households, for example, children work in the fields, take care of animals, or watch siblings, permitting others, including adults, to be engaged in farming or other productive activities. In addition to foregone earnings, households face direct costs in sending a child to school. These costs may include school or uniform fees, payments for books and other materials, transportation costs, or other "unofficial" fees to ensure a child gets the attention of a teacher. Although the sums may seem small, to a poor family they may be overwhelming.

To think of education as an investment, we need a systematic way to compare the costs and benefits of schooling depicted in Figure 8–5. Economists argue that one cannot simply add up the costs and compare them to the benefits because money received in the future is worth less than money that can be spent today. Such positive time preference is the result of both uncertainty about the future and the opportunity cost of resources, namely, the returns an alternative investment might yield. Future benefits need to be **discounted** to compare them to current costs. One way of doing so is to compute the **present value (PV)** of all costs and benefits.[6]

---

[6]The need to discount future benefits can be motivated by the following example. If you are asked to trade $100 today in return for $100 one year from now, you likely will not accept the offer. Beyond any uncertainty you may have about being paid back in 12 months, you could do better by depositing your $100 in a relatively safe alternative, like a bank account. If that account offers you a 5 percent return, your $100 today is worth $105 one year from now, $110.25 in two years, and so forth. This is the familiar process of compounding. Discounting future benefits employs the same logic but working in reverse. The present value of some future benefit is the amount of money that, if available today, by virtue of compounding, would equal that amount. If the opportunity cost of your capital is 5 percent, the present value of $105 received one year from now equals [$105/(1 + 0.05)] = $100; similarly, the present value of $110.25 received in two years also is $100 since [$110.25/(1 + 0.05)²] = $100.

Completing secondary school results in earnings whose PV can be computed as,

$$PV_B = \sum_{t=1}^{n} B_t / (1+i)^t \qquad \text{[8–1]}$$

where PV_B equals the sum of the present value of all future private benefits (the earnings differential received by those with more schooling) over an individual's n years of working; B_t equals the benefits in year t; and i is the interest rate (the household's opportunity cost of capital), which discounts future benefits. A similar calculation can be made for the private costs of schooling (or for any other investment option):

$$PV_C = \sum_{t=1}^{n} C_t / (1+i)^t \qquad \text{[8–2]}$$

where PV_C now refers to the sum of the present value of all anticipated private costs and C_t equals the costs, including foregone earnings while attending school plus any direct costs paid by the household, incurred in each of the t years.

There are several ways one can then determine whether a particular investment is worthwhile. In the analysis of education, a common way is to estimate an internal rate of return for the investment. The **internal rate of return** is a derived interest rate, r, which equates PV_B to PV_C. In other words, the level of r such that

$$\sum_{t=1}^{n} (B_t - C_t) / (1+r)^t = 0 \qquad \text{[8–3]}$$

Even though the dollar value of the private benefits of an education is likely to far exceed the dollar value of the private costs, a value for r can be found because future benefits, occurring many years from now, are much more heavily discounted than costs incurred more immediately. Once the private rate of return to schooling is estimated, it can be compared to the internal rates of return available to other household investments. This helps rank the economic benefits of education as compared to alternative uses of household resources.

Schooling represents not only a private investment, it also is a social one. We, therefore, also can define a **social return** to schooling. Figure 8–6 presents a schematic representation. On the cost side, schooling entails more than the foregone earnings of the individual and the payments of households. Primary school is "free" in most parts of the world, yet someone pays for teachers, the construction of schools, and the like. When evaluating education as an investment from society's perspective, these costs must be taken into consideration. The social return includes all the costs entailed in the provision of schooling. On the benefit side, schooling benefits the individual through higher earnings but schooling may also produce a positive **externality:** benefits that accrue to mem-

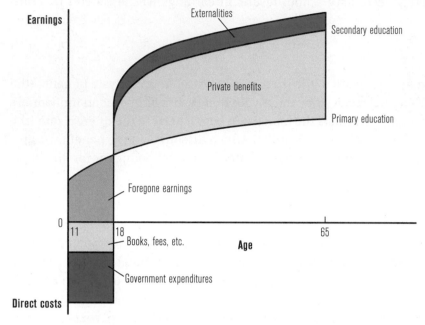

FIGURE 8-6. Determinants of the Social Returns to Schooling
Note: For ease of exposition, the figure is drawn without any positive externalities arising from primary education.

bers of society above and beyond the benefits to the individual who receives the education. Potential positive externalities from school include health spillovers (the children of educated mothers tend to be healthier, which benefits children in other families because it reduces the transmission rate of certain diseases), reductions in crime, and more-informed political participation and decisions. More schooling, especially higher education, may also lead to technological progress that is not fully captured by private returns. In calculating a social internal rate of return to education the equation is the same as in 8–3 but all the benefits of schooling, not just private earnings, and all the costs, private and public, should be included.

Internal Rates of Return to Schooling

For any investment, the lower the costs and the greater the benefits, the higher is the return. With the help of Figure 8–5 we can see what this implies about schooling. Forgone earnings represent a significant cost of schooling, and the older is the student, the higher these forgone earnings will be. This suggests, ceteris paribus, that the private return to schooling will be higher at the primary levels than at the secondary level and higher at the secondary than the tertiary level.

This does not mean that an individual with only a primary education will earn more than someone with a university degree; we know this is not true. But, by comparing discounted marginal costs with discounted marginal benefits, the private return on primary school may be higher than for any other level of education.

At all levels of schooling, private rates of return may be higher in developing than developed nations. This may seem surprising given the much higher wages and salaries workers earn in high income nations. But, remember, rates of return measure something different than the level of earnings. Take the case of graduates of tertiary education. Given the relative scarcity of students with a tertiary education in poorer nations, the pay premium to having such an education may be greater than the relative pay gap between university and high school graduates in richer nations. It is the relative scarcity of labor skills, a combination of the strength of labor demand and the extent of labor supply, that determines the attractiveness of schooling as an investment. In poorer nations, educated workers are relatively scarce, often making schooling (at the primary, secondary, and tertiary levels) an investment with a higher rate of return than in advanced economies, where educated workers are far more abundant.

Estimated Rates of Return

Moving from the conceptual to the empirical, a large number of rate-of-return estimates for schooling are available for both developed and developing nations. To interpret these estimates it is important to be familiar with many of their implicit assumptions. First, there is no way of knowing what anyone's future earnings will be. Economists use the current earnings of individuals at various ages as an estimate of the expected age-earnings profile of someone with a particular level of education. Substituting such cross-sectional findings (comparing wages for different ages at one point in time) for what may happen over time to the wages of individuals as they grow older over time is a common empirical technique in economics; however, especially in a rapidly changing economy, estimates based on cross-sectional findings may not be a good proxy for events that will occur in the future. Second, estimates of the return on education require some measure of individual earnings. In low-income nations and in many middle-income nations as well, the vast majority of workers do not work for wages. They are self-employed, often subsistence farmers or unpaid family workers engaged in petty trading or other informal sector activity. Such workers do not report the kind of earnings data included in standard rate of return on schooling estimations. By relying only on those who receive earnings, most rate of return estimates are based on a fraction of a nation's labor force.

Keeping these caveats in mind, Table 8–3 presents estimates of annual private and social internal rates of return for schooling by income category. The

TABLE 8-3. Returns to Schooling by Level and Country Income Group

INCOME CATEGORY	PRIVATE RATE OF RETURN			"SOCIAL" RATE OF RETURN		
	PRIMARY	SECONDARY	TERTIARY	PRIMARY	SECONDARY	TERTIARY
Low income	25.8	19.9	26.0	21.3	15.7	11.2
Middle income	27.4	18.0	19.3	18.8	12.9	11.3
High income	N.A.	12.2	12.4	N.A.	10.3	9.5

Notes: These estimates of "social" rates of return account for only government expenditures on schooling and do not include estimates of any positive externalities resulting from schooling.

Given the small number of workers in high-income nations with only primary educations, most studies of high-income nations do no provide estimated rates of return to primary education.

Source: G. Psacharopoulus and H. Patrinos, "Returns to Investment in Education: A Further Update," *Education Economics* 12, no. 2 (August 2004).

results are from a meta-analysis by World Bank economists, George Psacharopoulos and Harry Patrinos. In this and earlier studies, the authors compiled the results of internal rate-of-return calculations for over 75 nations. Some of these studies refer to outcomes as far back as the late 1950s, while others refer to the 1990s.[7] The internal rates of return estimated for individual countries are then averaged together and presented as a mean value for each income category and region. These are simple cross-country averages and are not weighted by population size. They are *real* rates of return, since they are based on cross-sectional estimates that measure earnings in the same current dollars.

A number of patterns can be observed in the data. Returns on all levels of schooling and in all income categories are high, almost always in double digits. The attractiveness of such returns can be illustrated by comparing them to estimates of the return on other investment opportunities. For example, U.S. government securities, one of the world's safest investments, have yielded an average real (inflation-adjusted) return of about 1 percent over the last 50 years; an index of the U.S. stock market, a significantly riskier investment, over the same period yields a real return of around 7 percent. Of course, most families do not choose between investing in U.S. stocks or government securities versus sending a child to primary school; a comparison of these rates of return is intended only to put into perspective the relative magnitude of the returns to schooling (Box 8-1).

Table 8-3 also finds, as expected, that the returns to schooling tend to be greater the poorer is the country. This is especially evident when comparing low- and middle-income nations to the high-income economies. (The results

---

[7]George Psacharopoulos and Harry Patrinos, "Returns to Investment in Education: A Further Update," *Education Economics* 12, no. 2 (August 2004). Psacharopoulos has been estimating and reporting on rates of return to education in published work since 1973 (George Psacharopoulos, *Returns to Education: An International Comparison* [San Francisco: Elsevier, Jossey-Bass, 1973]) with the compilation appearing in 1994 widely reproduced in development textbooks, including earlier editions of this book, and in other works on development economics. See George Psacharopoulos, "Returns to Investment in Education: A Global Update," *World Development* 22, no. 9 (September 1994).

BOX 8-1 ESTIMATING RATES OF RETURN FROM WAGE EQUATIONS

Conceptually, the notion of rates of return to schooling is relatively straightforward. Estimating such returns is more complex. In addition to the approach described in the text, one of the most common approaches is to estimate the impact on earnings of schooling, age, and other demographic characteristics. Data on these variables can be obtained from either household or firm surveys and used to estimate a human capital earnings function or wage equation like the following:

$$\ln E_i = \alpha + \beta_1 S_i + \beta_2 EXP_i + \beta_3 EXP_i^2 + \varepsilon_i$$

where E_i refers to the earnings or wages of each individual; S_i, the years of schooling completed; and EXP_i and EXP_i^2, the years of work experience of the individual and its square, often approximated by the individual's age and its square. The reason for including the squared term is to capture the expected nonlinearity in age-earnings profiles, since earnings tend to rise at a decreasing rate over a worker's lifetime. The regression equation also includes an error term, ε_i.

In this specification of the wage equation, the coefficient on schooling (β_1), where $\beta_1 = (\partial E / E)/\partial S$, provides an estimate of the average percent increase in earnings received by workers per additional year of schooling. It is an estimate of how wages in an economy vary by education for the year in which the data are obtained.

The term β_1 is also interpreted as the average annual private rate of return to one additional year of schooling, regardless of the level of schooling already attained. This interpretation requires a number of assumptions, including the same assumption used in the internal-rate-of-return calculation: that earnings differentials by education *in a cross-section* are a good approximation of what will happen to pay differentials *over time* as workers age. Another assumption (one not required by the internal-rate-of-return approach) requires that foregone earnings represent the only private cost of schooling. In some instances these are reasonable assumptions, in others not.

Estimates of β_1 vary widely. Wage equations for the United States have been estimated since the 1970s, yielding private rates of return to one additional year of schooling ranging from 5 to 15 percent. Studies that address particular econometric problems inherent in the basic wage equation suggest the actual range in the United States may be narrower, falling between 7 and 9 percent. In the recent survey article by George Psacharopoulos and Harry Patrinos (cited in the text), the range for low- and middle-income nations is 7 to 12 percent. These results support the view that schooling tends to yield an attractive private economic return relative to many alternative investments in rich and poor nations alike.

are not as strong, nor even always in the expected direction, when comparing low- to middle-income countries.) Looking across levels of schooling, returns are highest for primary schooling. This is because the opportunity cost of attending school in terms of foregone earnings is least when attending primary school and rises thereafter. This suggests that the returns to secondary school should also exceed those of a tertiary education. But, according to the results in Table 8–3, this is not the case in any income category. This may be due to much larger pay differentials between tertiary and secondary school graduates versus between secondary and primary school graduates. Or it may reflect opportunities tertiary school students have to earn some income while studying (so there is less cost from foregone earnings), including receipt of government stipends for attending a school, a common practice in many developing nations, especially during the time period of the studies represented in the table.

Estimated "social" returns in Table 8–3 are lower than private ones at every level of schooling. Theoretically (see Figure 8–6), this need not be the case. If positive externalities are sufficiently large, social returns could exceed the private rate of return even if social costs are greater than private costs. However, no direct means are available for estimating the positive externalities of schooling; the average "social" rates of return to schooling reported in Table 8–3 account for only social costs, not social benefits, hence our use of quotation marks around the word *social*. By incorporating the full cost of schooling but not any positive externalities, "social" returns for a given level of schooling must be less than the corresponding private return. Note also that the relative gap between private and social returns is especially large for tertiary schooling in low- and middle-income nations. This reflects the relatively high per pupil cost and high degree of state subsidy for tertiary education, often including free tuition. Even though these "social" returns are below private returns, these rates are sufficiently high to make schooling an attractive public investment as compared to many alternatives, including investments in physical capital.

The social returns to educating girls appear to be especially high. In the data compiled by George Psacharopoulos and Harry Patrinos there is no clear gender pattern to *private returns* to schooling: Men have a higher return to primary schooling; women, a higher return to secondary schooling; and for tertiary schooling the returns are about the same. The variance in these outcomes by region and country also is large. But there is evidence to believe that the social return to educating girls exceeds that of boys because of the positive health and fertility externalities that are generated. This is because educating women reduces child mortality by more than educating men; educating women reduces fertility and, in so doing, reduces maternal mortality; and educating women reduces the spread of HIV/AIDS by more than educating men. A 1992 study concluded that providing 1,000 girls in India with an extra year of primary school would avert 2 maternal deaths, 43 infant deaths, and 300 births. The cost of providing this education was about 60 percent of the estimated discounted social benefit, suggesting a huge social rate of return on sending girls to school.[8]

Controversies and Puzzles

The estimates of internal rates of return to education presented in Table 8–3 are subject to some controversy. We already have pointed out the limitations of using cross-section results to approximate a time series event, especially in environments where labor market outcomes are changing rapidly. Another concern is the quality of studies included in the Psacharopoulus compilations. One critical review of rate of return estimates for Africa found many of the original rate of return studies were based on guesstimates by consultants of prevailing wages rather than on data from surveys. Other problems included limiting observations only to those workers earning wages, that is, to those employed in the formal sector.[9] Private rates of return to primary education for Africa in Psacharopoulus's sample range from 7.9 in Tanzania in 1991 to 99 percent in Botswana and Liberia in 1983. This large a range in estimates does strain the creditability of the reported findings. Better data and more careful analysis might result in smaller estimates of the average returns to schooling, especially for low-income nations.

Another criticism of studies that form the basis of the results reported in Table 8–3 is the failure to account for all the school costs facing families. In Honduras, for example, the private return to primary school is estimated at 21 percent, if it is assumed that there are no direct costs to the family of attending school and if the child is considered to have foregone earnings only during the last two years of primary school, at ages 11 and 12. If the actual direct costs for uniforms, school supplies, transportation, and other parental contributions are included, the private returns drop to 16 percent; if foregone earnings are added for age 10, the returns drop to below 15 percent.[10] These criticisms challenge the magnitude of some of the reported rates of return to schooling but generally do not reverse the conclusion that schooling has a sufficiently high rate of return to make it a good investment for both the individual and society.

Beyond disagreements about how high the rate of return to schooling is for different levels of schooling and for different countries and regions, several puzzles emerge about the relationship between these returns and both microeconomic and macroeconomic outcomes. One of the microeconomic puzzles concerns schooling and learning. The key issue is why does education have an economic return? The usual answer is that education provides the individual

[8]Lawrence Summers, "Investing in All the People: Educating Women in Developing Countries," EDI Seminar Paper No. 45 (Washington, DC: World Bank, 1994).

[9]Paul Bennell, "Rates of Return to Education: Does the Conventional Pattern Prevail in sub-Saharan Africa?" *World Development* 24, no. 1 (January 1996).

[10]Patrick McEwan, "Private Costs and the Rate of Return to Education," *Applied Economic Letters* 6 (1999).

with cognitive skills, skills learned as distinct from innate ability, which makes him or her more productive in the marketplace. Higher productivity, in turn, is associated with higher compensation, a result that holds if one is discussing farm labor or professionals (Box 8–2). If schools produce cognitive skills, then we expect to observe a positive correlation between years of schooling and earnings and a positive rate of return on attending school. The puzzle involves results reported earlier in the chapter that schooling in many developing countries appears to produce little in the way of learning. If true, why in these settings is there a continued association between schooling and earnings and significant rates of return to education? Sorting out this puzzle requires data that better match learning outcomes and subsequent labor market earnings.

One of the macroeconomic puzzles results from trying to reconcile another set of empirical observations. Earlier in this chapter, we reported on trends in schooling by region. The evidence is clear. There has been rapid growth in schooling throughout the world over the past decades, resulting in some convergence in years of schooling per worker across countries. Given the rates of return to education reported by Psacharopoulos and others, such an expansion of schooling should have produced more rapid aggregate economic growth in many regions and some convergence in incomes. This is expected, since schooling has grown much more rapidly in developing than developed nations and the returns to schooling are higher in low- and middle-income nations than in high-income settings. But this is not what the aggregate data show. Instead, there has been considerable divergence in per capita incomes at the same time that there has been some convergence in schooling.

Schooling, of course, is not the only determinant of aggregate growth, and other factors may be more important in determining growth rates of GDP per capita. But there remains something disconcerting about the micro evidence on (a) the accumulation of schooling and (b) the attractive rates of return to these investments and the subsequent lack of evidence that increased schooling results in significantly higher economic growth rates. Exploration of this puzzle led one researcher to ask, "Where has all the education gone?" and then to speculate that, in environments not conducive to growth, those with more education may engage in rent seeking and other unproductive activities that are privately remunerative but "socially dysfunctional."[11] This may be part of the explanation but a fuller reconciliation of micro and macro evidence on schooling outcomes remains a challenge for future research.

---

[11]Excellent discussion of the macroeconomic puzzles involving schooling and economic growth can be found in Lant Pritchett, "Where Has All the Education Gone?" *World Bank Economic Review* 15, no. 3 (2001) and "Does Learning to Add Up Add Up? The Returns to Schooling in Aggregate Data," *Handbook on the Economics of Education* (Boston: Elsevier, forthcoming). A less-technical review of some of these points can be found in William Easterly, "Educated for What?" in *The Elusive Quest for Growth* (Cambridge, MA: MIT Press, 2001).

BOX 8-2 RETURNS TO SCHOOLING AND INCOME OPPORTUNITIES

In a series of studies, Andrew Foster and Mark Rosenzweig, economists at Brown and Yale Universities, respectively, examine the interaction between returns to schooling and technological change in agriculture. Their core argument is that schooling has a return primarily when new income-generating opportunities arise. In one study of worker productivity, data were assembled on workers engaged primarily in harvesting in Bukidnon, the Philippines. Controlling for a worker's physical ability, proxied by gender and height, there was no impact of the worker's education on the wage received. In this situation, workers performed a routine task and little was gained from additional schooling.

A different outcome was observed in India. In a study of over 4,000 rural households between the years 1968 and 1981, the authors assessed the impact schooling had on farm profitability. The time period studied covered the introduction of the "Green Revolution" to India, when imported high-yield variety (HYV) seeds were introduced that could dramatically increase farm output (usually because it permitted double and even triple cropping during a calendar year). HYV seeds are particularly sensitive to the use of complementary inputs including irrigation and fertilizer, and it was especially important for farmers to be able to learn how to use these seeds, since the required farming techniques were different from traditional methods.

In areas where conditions were suitable for the introduction of the HYV, farmers with primary schooling had higher profits than those without schooling, holding all other inputs constant. Investments in education had a high return to these farmers because of increased returns to learning and new information. In other areas of the country, including the Indian state of Kerala, where farmers had above average years of schooling, conditions were not suitable for the new seeds. These farmers got little return because there were no new opportunities that required education.

Rosenzweig concludes that, "schooling returns are high when the returns to learning are also high." This can be because of a new technology, like the Green Revolution or new opportunities created by changes in market or political regimes. Not only do those with more schooling reap a return in these situations; they also tend to invest more heavily in the schooling of their children. School enrollment rates increased more rapidly in those Indian communities that benefited from the technological change than in those that did not.

Sources: Andrew Foster and Mark Rosenzweig, "Technical Change and Human-Capital Returns and Investments: Evidence from the Green Revolution," *American Economic Review* 86, no. 4 (September 1996); and Mark Rosenzweig, "Why Are There Returns to Schooling?" *American Economic Review* 85, no. 2 (May 1995).

MAKING SCHOOLING MORE PRODUCTIVE

Despite the controversies and puzzles over the rate of return to schooling, no one would conclude that parents or governments in developing nations should invest in less schooling. Schooling has benefits that go well beyond narrow economic returns. It often is considered a merit good, a good that a society determines all members should have access to regardless of ability to pay. There is also evidence that schooling improves health, with educated mothers having healthier children. Schooling further is associated with declining fertility. The challenge facing policy makers and all those concerned with promoting economic development is to understand how to make schooling a better investment: better for students and their families who devote so much of their time to education, and better for governments and donors who finance much of the direct costs.

Rates of return on schooling depend on what happens both in schools and in the labor market after students graduate. Much of this textbook is devoted to the latter, to understanding how to increase the rate of economic growth in an economy and with it an increase in the demand for labor. We will not go over these elements again here. But it is worth noting that low returns to education often have a lot to do with failures to increase the demand for labor. High unemployment among school leavers, including graduates of universities, often reflects failures in promoting economic growth rather than failures in schools. This has been true in transition economies but also is apparent in countries such as Argentina and Egypt, which have not made good use of the human capital they accumulated. High dropout rates, as well as low and even declining school enrollment rates (the latter occurred throughout sub-Saharan Africa during the 1990s), may have as much to do with low returns in the labor market as with a family's resource constraints or problems with the schools themselves. Students and their families may decide that the benefits of schooling do not justify the costs. And in many instances they may be right. The provision of schooling is no guarantee that getting an education will yield a high return. Problems with labor demand highlight that schooling is not a panacea; it is not *the one solution* to problems of poverty and economic backwardness.

But problems on the demand side do not imply that the supply of education is without problems. The remainder of this chapter focuses on the supply of education in an attempt to understand how investments in schooling can be made more productive. In many countries schooling is not doing as much as it can to promote development. Some of the reasons for this are that there is an underinvestment in schooling overall, governments misallocate resources across different levels of schooling, and there are systematic inefficiencies in the use of resources within schools.

Underinvestment

Despite attractive economic returns and other benefits to schooling, many developing countries spend too little on educating their children. Determining the "right amount" that should be spent is no simple matter. First, estimates of rates of return are imprecise at best; second, spending more money on schooling is no guarantee that the money will be well spent and produce better education outcomes. But money does matter and cross-country data reveal considerable variance in public spending on schooling (comparable data on private spending are not available). In Figure 8–7, among low- and lower-middle-income nations, the range in public expenditures as a share of GDP is from about 1 to 11 percent. We cannot be sure that the average spending share within these income groups is "the right amount," especially since we do not know the corresponding amount of private spending. But nations such as Cambodia, Pakistan, and Zambia, where public spending on schooling is under 2 percent of GDP (well below the 3.4 percent median of the low-income group) stand as candidates for increasing the amount their governments spend on education. Similarly, Ecuador, Georgia, and Indonesia devote less than half the lower-middle-income median of 4.9 percent of GDP to schooling and may be seriously underinvesting in education. To the extent that any of these and other countries also have a high dependency burden of young people, they especially need to devote a larger share of GDP to schooling since those expenditures must be spread among a large number of students.

There are many explanations for why nations may underinvest in schooling. One is as a response to fiscal crises. Education and the social sectors in general, as opposed to the military or debt service, often are victims of budget cuts. Economic downturns and negative growth rates have impacts on education spending and can result in an entire cohort of children getting less schooling than would have been the case in a more stable economy. Protecting schooling and the other social sectors is a major challenge facing nations pursuing the structural adjustment programs discussed in Chapter 5.

Misallocation

Misallocation of resources between different levels of schooling refers to government decisions on how much to spend on primary, secondary, and tertiary levels. The estimates of internal rates of return to schooling in Table 8–3 indicate

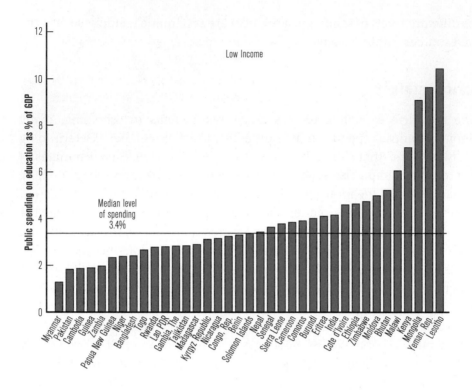

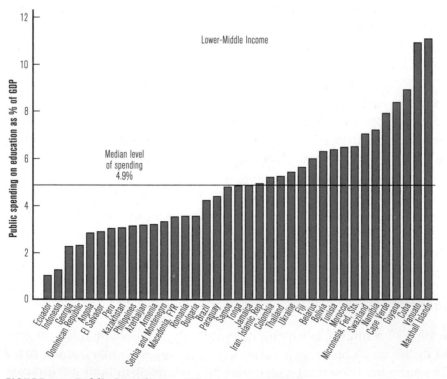

FIGURE 8-7. Public Spending on Education, Early 2000s

Source: *World Development Indicators* database, //0-devdata.worldbank.org.luna.wellesley.edu/
dataonline/, accessed September 2005.

that the "social" returns are highest for primary school followed by secondary then tertiary schooling. Given the construction of these estimates the results are not surprising. The direct costs of tertiary schooling (which includes everything from junior colleges through PhDs) per student, including expenditures on computers, laboratories, libraries, professors, and the like, are much higher than the per student costs of either primary or secondary education. Since the government often pays for all or most of these costs, "social" returns to higher education are going to be significantly less than private returns. This, in turn, suggests that governments should initially allocate more resources to primary schools. Once universal primary education is achieved, more resources should be devoted to secondary schools. According to this logic, tertiary education should have the lowest priority.[12]

Such conclusions encounter much opposition. First, the estimates in Table 8–3 do not take account of any (difficult to measure) positive externalities associated with different levels of education. If a nation has a chronic shortage of trained professionals in agronomy, engineering, finance, medicine, and other fields, developing such skills may yield a large social return. Second, modernization, the goal of many nations, means having the things advanced nations have, including universities and the graduates they produce. To some, the argument that more resources should be devoted to lower rather than higher levels of schooling is reminiscent of the colonial era, when education of native populations was suppressed, leaving many nations with a minuscule number of educated citizens at the time of independence. Third, support for continued government spending on tertiary education comes from those who benefit from such spending. Often it is the children of the elite that disproportionately gain admission to national universities. Such families may have their own resources that could be devoted to higher education, but they are pleased to have the state finance their children's higher education. When this occurs, government spending on tertiary education is both inefficient and an inequitable use of public resources.

Evidence on the potential misallocation of public resources among different levels of schooling is suggested by comparing enrollment rates and expenditure patterns on tertiary education. Among the 19 sub-Saharan African countries for which the relevant data are available, the median gross enrollment rate for tertiary education is 3 percent while the median share of total education expenditures devoted to the tertiary sector is 17 percent. In Latin America, enrollment

[12]The theoretical rule that governments should follow is really more subtle. Governments should allocate resources to equate the marginal rate of return on its investment. Internal rates of return refer to average returns (the average for all graduates of primary, secondary, or tertiary schooling) not the marginal return, which refers to the economic rate of return for the last student educated. When a particular level of schooling gets close to universal enrollment and completion, it is likely that the marginal social return will be below the average return, perhaps, well below it.

rates are eight times bigger—the median is 24 percent—but the expenditure share is the same as in sub-Saharan Africa. In the high-income economies, the median gross enrollment rate is 57 percent but the expenditure share is only 23 percent.

Gaps between enrollment rates and expenditure shares suggest that a closer look needs to be given to how the money is being spent. Much higher expenditures per student enrolled in tertiary institutions in some countries stem from generous allowances given to those enrolled in university, in essence, paying students to obtain an education that is likely to yield them considerably higher earnings in the future. In 2004, most undergraduate students in Senegal received a monthly scholarship in local currency equivalent to about $70 at current exchange rates. Monthly GDP per capita in Senegal is under $50 per month. Students in Senegal and elsewhere often receive generous amounts of money to pursue their studies. Noneducational expenditures in the form of student allowances and scholarships as well as subsidized housing, health care, loans, and so on, accounted for 50 percent of public expenditures on tertiary education among francophone African countries, 20 percent in Latin America, and only 14 percent in OECD countries. Such allowances often are on top of free tuition.[13] With growing numbers of tertiary school students, such expenditures are adding further stress to tight education budgets.

These spending practices also represent an inefficient use of public resources. First and as already noted, given the much lower costs per pupil, the returns to primary education may be higher than those to tertiary education. Second, paying students to attend university can distort incentives, prolonging years spent in school and even influencing what students choose to study. In the 1990s, some Malaysian officials expressed concern that Malaysian students who were fully funded by the government to pursue university education in the United States were majoring in Malaysian studies rather than in technical areas such as engineering and medicine. Students who have to pay for at least some of their education may exercise more care in their field of study, making sure that the education they are helping to pay for will improve their opportunities in the labor market. Third, given the tendency for those of higher socioeconomic status to have the opportunity to attend tertiary education, allowances and free tuition is a regressive use of public money. A review of enrollment in public and private tertiary schools in Latin America found that 75 percent of the students in Colombia were from the top two quintiles of the distribution of income; in Mexico, it was 83 percent, and in Brazil, 92 percent.[14]

---

[13]World Bank, *Constructing Knowledge Societies: New Challenges for Tertiary Education* (Washington, DC: World Bank, 2002), 51–52.

[14]*Constructing Knowledge Societies*, Appendix Table K.1, p. 195.

One approach to the misallocation of resources across schooling levels is to have university students pay for some of their education. This can be justified because higher education is likely to have a good private rate of return, even if the student pays (including taking out loans) for some of his or her education. The use of tuition reduces public contributions and permits some shifting of state spending from tertiary to primary and secondary schooling. The economic logic of charging students, especially those with the ability to pay, for some of the cost of their tertiary schooling may be clear, but instituting such fees may be far from straightforward. In Mexico, the constitution calls for free public education at all levels. Confronted with rising numbers of university students and the rising costs of providing that education, the National Autonomous University of Mexico (UNAM) in 1999 decided to raise student fees from the level last set in 1948. By 1999, these fees, adjusted for price inflation, amounted to only 2 cents ($US) per year. The administration of UNAM proposed new fees of about $150 for those with the economic means to cover these costs. Such fees would have offset less than 10 percent of the government's expenditures on the university. In response to the proposal, many of the school's 270,000 students went on strike and the school remained closed for almost a full year. In the end, the school modified its proposal, making the $150 fee voluntary, and the university's president resigned. Despite the economic logic behind the user fees, on the grounds of both economic efficiency and social equity, the politics surrounding the proposal made it unworkable.

Improving Schools

In addition to spending more on schooling overall and reallocating some expenditures from tertiary to lower levels, the use of resources within schools needs to be improved. Parents complain about schools in almost every community in the world, from suburban Boston to rural India. Some of these complaints are the same, "My child is not getting enough attention" or "My child is not learning enough." But some are quite different, "Why are teachers absent so much of the time?" or "Why are there no books for students to read?" In some instances the solutions to these problems require more financial resources; in others, they require spending available resources better; and in still others, the problems are less about resources than about holding teachers and principals more accountable for their actions.

Inefficient use of resources and lack of accountability within schools are not new issues. But recent research has given new insight into these long-standing concerns. Retrospective studies of policy changes provide one opportunity to assess different strategies. A new area of research employs the use of randomized trials, similar to studies in medicine, where one group receives a "treatment" and outcomes are compared to a "control" group. Insights obtained from both types of research offer suggestions on how to improve the participation and retention of students as well as how to enhance student learning.[15]

Reducing the Costs of Going to School

Earlier we noted that the Millennium Development Goal of achieving universal primary education by 2015 is not likely to be achieved. Data on grade survival rates suggest that 20 percent of children in low-income nations do not complete even four years of schooling. One reason why children may not be in school is because there is no conveniently located school to attend. This certainly can be a problem in remote regions, and many children continue to travel long distances to get to school. However, research findings suggest lack of attendance is much more often a problem of household demand than of school supply.[16]

On the demand side, households may not send their children to school, including to primary school, because poor families cannot afford the fees required for school attendance. These can be user charges to attend school or fees to pay for textbooks or mandatory school uniforms. A school uniform in Kenya costs $6, a nontrivial amount in a nation where one fifth of the population lives below the "$1 a day" poverty line. Starting in the late 1990s, governments in several East African nations (including Kenya, Tanzania, Uganda, and Zambia) eliminated all user charges for primary schools; in some cases, school uniforms were no longer compulsory. Governments subsequently reported substantial increases in enrollment.

It is not surprising that eliminating school fees would lead to an increase in enrollment, but it comes at a cost. Many families previously had paid the fees and sent their children to school. By eliminating fees, the government lost much-needed revenue to pay for teachers and other school needs. Financing schooling now requires new revenues or reallocating funds from some other use. The critical economic question is whether reducing school fees represents an efficient use of resources. Michael Kremer, a development economist at Harvard University and a leading proponent of the use of randomized trials and other experimental approaches, evaluated one program in Kenya where 7 out of 14 poorly performing schools were randomly selected. The "treatment" schools provided free uniforms and textbooks to their students, paid for by a Dutch non-

---

[15]Two earlier reviews of resource use and schooling are World Bank, *Financing Education in Developing Countries* (Washington, DC: World Bank, 1986) and *Priorities and Strategies for Education* (Washington, DC: World Bank, 1995). Two recent and valuable surveys of improving school outcomes in developing nations are Paul Glewwe and Michael Kremer, "Schools, Teachers, and Education Outcomes in Developing Countries," *Handbook on the Economics of Education* (Boston: Elsevier, forthcoming); and Lant Pritchett, "Access to Education." The remainder of this chapter draws heavily from these two works.

[16]Lant Pritchett, "Access to Education."

government organization, and also received improved classrooms. Dropout rates fell considerably, and many students from nearby schools transferred into the treatment group, raising class size by 50 percent. Kremer and his coauthors concluded that the financial benefit of free uniforms was a significant factor in improving school attendance. They also concluded that, since parents accepted larger class sizes in return for these benefits, the government could have reallocated education spending trading off larger classes for lower fees and thereby increasing school completion rates.[17]

Another approach to increasing enrollments and school retention is to design means-tested and targeted programs where families are paid to send their children to school. Several countries have adopted this approach. Bolsa Escola (school grants) in Brazil and the PROGRESA (Programa de Educación Salud y Alimentación) program in Mexico provide modest stipends to millions of poor families as long as their children remain in school. Both have been associated with gains in enrollment and retention (Box 8–3). The Food for Schooling program in Bangladesh provides a free monthly ration of wheat or other grains to eligible families, where eligibility is means tested. To qualify, households must own less than half an acre of land, the household head must be a woman, a day laborer, or work in a very low-wage activity. The family can consume the grain or can sell it and use the cash for other expenses. To maintain eligibility, children must attend 85 percent of classes each month. The program has been successful in increasing primary school enrollment, promoting school attendance, and reducing dropout rates, especially among girls.

The programs in Bangladesh, Brazil, and Mexico all have multiple aims and can be seen as part of a package to alleviate poverty. If such transfers of cash or grain were going to be made on poverty grounds alone, then making them conditional on sending children to school makes the education component highly cost-effective. If they are intended primarily as interventions to expand enrollment and school retention, cost-effectiveness depends, in part, on how carefully the targeting is done. If eligibility is too broad, recipients will include families that already were sending their children to school and the cash or food expenditures will yield no marginal improvements in schooling for these households.

Inefficient Use of Resources

Improving the efficient use of resources within schools also involves making decisions about spending. Should scarce resources be allocated to buildings or teachers, to teachers or school supplies (blackboards, desks, textbooks, etc.), or to any of a number of other alternatives? The problems that schools in poor

[17]Paul Glewwe and Michael Kremer, "Schools, Teachers, and Education Outcomes."

BOX 8-3 MEXICO'S PROGRESA

When Ernesto Zedillo became Mexico's president in 1995, a fifth of the population could not afford the minimum daily nutritional requirements, 10 million Mexicans lacked access to basic health services, more than 1.5 million children were out of school, and student absenteeism and school desertions were three times higher in poor and remote areas than in the rest of the country. His administration decided that a new approach to poverty alleviation was needed. The Education, Health, and Nutrition Programs of Mexico, called PROGRESA, introduced a set of *conditional cash transfers* to poor families—the families would receive cash if their children were enrolled in school and if family members visited health clinics for checkups and nutritional and hygiene information.

The program was intended to remedy several shortcomings of earlier programs. First, it would counter the bias in poor families toward consumption by bolstering investment in human capital. Second, it would recognize the interdependencies among education, health, and nutrition. Third, it would link cash transfers to household behavior, aiming at changing attitudes. Fourth, to reduce political interference, the program's goals, rules, requirements, and evaluation methods would be widely publicized.

Children over the age of 7 were eligible for education transfers. Benefits increased by grade (since the opportunity costs of being in school increase with age) and were higher for girls in middle school, to encourage their enrollment. To retain the benefits, children needed to maintain an 85 percent attendance record and could not repeat a grade more than once. Transfers went to mothers, who were thought to be more responsible for caring for children. In 1999, the average monthly transfer was around $24 per family, nearly 20 percent of mean household consumption before the program.

By the end of 2002, the program had about 21 million beneficiaries, roughly a fifth of the Mexican population. Almost 60 percent of program transfers went to households in the poorest 20 percent of the national income distribution and more than 80 percent went to the poorest 40 percent.

Girls' enrollment in middle school rose from 67 percent to around 75 percent, and boys' from 73 percent to 78 percent. Most of the increase came from increases in the transition from primary to middle school. The program worked primarily by keeping children in school, not by encouraging those who had dropped out to return. The impact on learning is less clear. Teachers report improvements, attributing them to better attendance, student interest, and nutrition. But a study conducted one year after the program started found no difference in test scores.

Source: Adapted from World Bank, "Spotlight on *PROGRESA*," *2004 World Development Report, Making Services Work for Poor People* (Washington, DC: World Bank and Oxford University Press, 2004), 30–31.

nations face can be overwhelming. There usually are shortages of everything. There are too few textbooks and sometimes there are none. Roofs leak and many students are crammed around simple desks if there are desks at all. Teachers often are untrained and children often too sick to learn effectively. Deciding on how to allocate resources in such environments is not easy and research does not always provide clear guidelines.

In the 1980s, some of the debate over resource allocation within schools concerned building schools versus expenditures on recurrent costs to run schools. These recurrent costs included teacher and administrative salaries as well as nonwage expenditures on school supplies and equipment. Donors, who often financed much of the spending on schools, especially in low-income nations, had a preference for constructing new school buildings. The donors could point to the tangible product of their aid, something constituents back home might want to see. Donors also expected a partnership with those governments who received aid and assumed that governments would cover the recurrent costs. The result of these arrangements often was the construction of schools, often at higher standards than needed and sometimes requiring imported building materials, met by an underfunding of recurrent costs. Schools without teachers or classrooms without chalk or writing paper often resulted.

This approach changed by the 1990s. Concern over the quantity and availability of schools diminished and increasing attention was paid to improving the quality of schools. Resources were redirected toward recurrent expenditures, especially nonwage items. But this approach also proved wanting; improvements in learning outcomes remained elusive.

One cost-effective intervention for increasing school attendance (in addition to lowering fees) is not an educational input; it is biannual dosages of albendazole or praziquantel, two medications used to reduce intestinal worms such as hookworms or schistosomes. Such intestinal worms affect a quarter of the world's population and are especially common among children. On the basis of randomized trials, students in some schools in the Busia district of rural Kenya received treatments and others did not. Researchers found that school absenteeism decreased by 25 percent in treatment versus nontreatment schools. Some children who previously were weak or listless were able to attend school because of the treatments; in other cases, deworming improved concentration and may have made attending more worthwhile. Beyond its effect on school attendance, these drugs also improved health outcomes. The intervention is highly cost-effective because the treatment cost is low, about $0.50 per child per year. Deworming increased school attendance by an average of 0.15 years per pupil or $3.50 per an additional full year of school participation. (By comparison, school uniforms cost $6 per child. Because provision of school uniforms increased school attendance at a somewhat lower rate than deworming, the school uniform program was less cost effective at $99 per additional year of school participation.) Even though deworming was associated with improved school attendance, there was no discernible improvement in learning as measured by student test scores.[18]

More traditional school input issues involve reducing class size, increasing the availability of textbooks and other instructional materials, and improving teacher training. Evidence on each of these interventions highlights the difficulty in determining how to improve resource use within schools. Appropriate class size is a matter of debate in school systems throughout the world, in rich and poor nations alike. The basic argument is straightforward. In smaller classes, teachers can provide more attention, even individualized work, for each student. Running a 25-pupil class of 7 year olds (let alone 13 year olds) is daunting enough, what must it be like to teach a class two, three, or more times as large?

Eric Hanushek, a senior fellow at the Hoover Institution and a leading expert on the economics of education in the United States, surveyed almost 100 studies on the determinants of student test scores in developing countries. Of the 30 studies that looked at class size, 8 found a statistically significant positive effect (the fewer students per teacher, the better students performed); 8 found a statistically significant negative effect (the fewer students per teacher, the *worse* students performed); and 14 found no significant effect at all.[19] We need to be careful interpreting these findings. They do not suggest that class size never matters; the results say only that there is no evidence of a robust and significant correlation (let alone causation) between class size and student performance.[20] In some instances, reducing class sizes is warranted; in others, the extra expenditure on teachers and additional classrooms yields no return. Without being able even to identify a simple correlation between reduced class size and stu-

---

[18]Edward Miguel and Michael Kremer, "Worms: Identifying Impacts on Education and Health in the Presence of Treatment Externalities," *Econometrica* 72, no. 1 (2004).

[19]Eric Hanushek, "Interpreting Recent Research on Schooling in Developing Countries," *World Bank Research Observer* 10, no. 2 (1995). In an earlier study, Hanushek reached the same conclusion about the impact of class size on student performance in the United States ("The Economics of Schooling: Production and Efficiency in Public Schools," *Journal of Economic Literature* 24 [1986]).

[20]One of the difficulties of identifying the impact of class size on student learning is the problem of *endogeneity.* Class size may not be determined independent of other determinants of student performance. For example, if school administrators decide to keep class sizes small for students who are disruptive or have difficulty learning, in the hope that teachers can manage such classes better if they have fewer students, then class size will be inversely correlated with student performance but not a cause of low performance. Similarly, if better-educated and higher-income communities effectively lobby for more teachers and smaller classes, class size will be positively correlated with better student performance even though better performance may mostly be due to having students with better-educated parents enrolled in smaller classes. Once again the *independent effect* of class size on performance would be hard to identify.

dent achievement, it is that much harder to move to the question of cost-effectiveness or economic efficiency of allocating scarce resources so that outcomes per dollar are equalized across alternative inputs.

The failure to easily identify strategies to improve student outcomes is not restricted to studies of student-teacher ratios. Studies of textbook use or teacher training yield a similar range of outcomes. According to the survey by Paul Glewwe and Michael Kremer, the introduction of textbooks in Jamaican primary schools improved reading scores, while in the Philippines the impact of textbooks was "unstable," including positive *and negative* effects on the mathematics and reading scores of first graders. A randomized trial in rural Kenya found no evidence that provision of textbooks improved scores for the average student. However, students who were above average before textbooks were provided realized improvements. This may be because textbooks provided by the government were in English, often the second or even third language of many local children, and only the most able students had sufficient English language skills to benefit from the textbooks they received. Studies of teacher training, like those on class size and textbook use, yield similarly ambiguous results.

The conclusion that should be drawn from these results is not that the status quo should be accepted or that nothing can be done. Most schools in developing nations can do better. But one single intervention will not work all the time. Local conditions make a difference. Identifying workable solutions is difficult because of the complexity of the education production function, the way in which schools combine inputs (students, teachers, classrooms, textbooks, etc.) to produce outputs (learning). There is so much heterogeneity in students that it is no wonder it is difficult to discern differences between one school's approach and the next's.[21] Causality is another problem. In a study of reading and mathematic achievement in Ghanaian middle schools, one of the most statistically significant variables in raising student test scores was repairing leaking roofs. Maybe this was because by repairing the leaks school remained open and students attended school more often, which led to greater learning. Or Glewwe and Kremer hypothesize, "[p]erhaps the underlying relationship is that more motivated teachers, principals and parents were more likely to keep the building in good order." If the latter explains the statistical finding, then a nationwide initiative to repair leaky school roofs will not yield the hoped for improvement in children's learning.

[21]"[I]n the PISA examinations in Brazil 55 percent of the total variation in child performance was within schools. Of the remaining 45 percent that was due to differences in averages across schools, 24 percentage points were due to the fact that student background varied across schools. This means that the *maximum* amount of student performance that could be explained by *everything* about the schools is 20 percent of the observed variation in student scores. This poses large problems for the researcher in trying to disentangle the causes of higher student performance, as modest amounts of sorting by parents and students into schools can lead to large bias in estimates of the relationship between school factors such as class size and learning outcomes." Lant Pritchett, "Access to Education," p. 202.

It Is About More than the Money

If there has been a trend in thinking about education and development, it has gone from concern primarily over increasing the quantity of schooling, achieved by building more schools, hiring more teachers, and most recently, reducing the cost of attending, to improving the quality of schools by improving the amounts and mix of inputs within schools themselves. Both these approaches have had some measure of success, with the huge increases in enrollments discussed earlier and success in learning outcomes, at least in some settings, due to different or better use of school inputs. But widespread and persistently low student achievement has resulted in a call not only for more money but for reform of school systems. School reform and more resources need not be substitutes. Both may be required to realize better outcomes, but more money without school reforms will be insufficient to achieve these ends. Calls for school reforms echo those for institutional reforms in other areas of government. Improvements in governance are needed not only to improve the climate for private enterprises and encourage investment in physical capital; they are needed to improve investment in human capital.

The need for improved accountability among teachers is starkly demonstrated by a recent nationwide study of teacher absence in India.[22] Researchers made three unannounced visits to 3,700 Indian primary schools. The presence or absence of teachers assigned to each school was determined by *direct physical verification*, that is, by a member of the research project looking for the teacher in the school building and not by checking logbooks or other records. On average, one in four primary school teachers was absent on the day of a visit. And only 45 percent (less than half) of primary school teachers were actively engaged in teaching their students at the time of the visit. Some percentage of these absences and involvement in nonteaching matters was due to excused absences for health or other reasons or performing required administrative or other duties. But even after correcting for these factors the degree of absence remains high.

The authors of the India study looked at the correlates of teacher absence and did not find that relatively higher pay or more education among teachers reduces absences. Stronger ties to the local community do not seem to play much of a role either. Schools with better infrastructure (e.g., with electricity or staff toilets), more frequent inspections, and closer proximity to roads have lowered absenteeism somewhat but the overwhelming conclusion is that getting more teachers to do their jobs is a significant challenge. The research includes similar investigations in other countries. While India's teacher absence rate is on

---

[22]Michael Kremer et al., "Teacher Absence in India: A Snapshot," *Journal of the European Economic Association* 3, nos. 2–3 (April–May 2005).

the high end (Uganda is higher at 27 percent), rates of 14 percent in Peru, 15 percent in Papua New Guinea, and 19 percent in Indonesia are not encouraging. Discussion of appropriate curriculums, better teaching methods, or more school resources almost seem secondary if so many teachers are not minimally engaged in the daily routines of educating their pupils. In explaining why teacher absence is so high, Michael Kremer and his coauthors note that teachers face little risk of being fired. They found that only one head teacher (school principal) in nearly 3,000 primary schools had ever dismissed a teacher for repeated absences. The absence of "sticks" is one explanation for high absence rates but the problem of accountability runs far deeper.

Teacher absence, or for that matter the absence of health workers or any number of other government workers, is not the only example of the breakdown in accountability that compromises the delivery of public services in low- and middle-income nations.[23] In another often-cited study, researchers "followed the money" allocated by Uganda's national government for local primary schools.[24] Despite the government authorizing 20 percent of public expenditures to education, most of it to primary education, a program to finance nonwage expenditures rarely resulted in money reaching the schools it was intended for. Over the period 1991–95, an average of only 13 percent of such grants actually reached the schools; almost three quarters of the 250 primary schools surveyed in the study received less than 5 percent of what had been authorized. Local officials and politicians captured much of the money along the way.

Unlike the teacher absence problem, which still persists, the study that identified massive leakage of funds in Uganda led to a number of institutional improvements. The central government responded to the initial study and launched an information campaign, where the amounts of centrally disbursed grants were reported in newspapers. Primary schools were also required to post notices of grants actually received. Local parent teacher associations (PTAs), which are very powerful in the Ugandan school system, thus were made aware of grants due their schools and could monitor outcomes. By reducing information asymmetries, it was possible to hold local officials more accountable. The information campaign, coupled with more attention from central government officials (including stiff penalties against offenders), increased the receipt of funds by schools from 20 percent in 1995 to 80 percent in 2001.[25]

---

[23]The problem of improving service delivery by the public sector is the focus of the *2004 World Development Report, Making Services Work for Poor People* (Washington, DC: World Bank and Oxford University Press, 2004). Specific chapters are devoted to basic education, health and nutrition, and drinking water, sanitation, and electricity.

[24]Ritva Reinikka and Jakob Svensson, "Local Capture: Evidence from a Central Government Transfer Program in Uganda," *Quarterly Journal of Economics* 119, no. 2 (May 2004).

[25]Ritva Reinikka and Jakob Svensson, "The Power of Information: Evidence from a Newspaper Campaign to Reduce Capture," Policy Research Paper 3239 (World Bank, March 2004).

The Ugandan example ultimately relied on local or community control as a means of increasing accountability, this time of local officials who received funds from the central government. Expanding local control, often through decentralization of authority over schools, is one of several reform strategies to hold all providers—officials who control funds as well teachers and principals— more accountable. The Educo program (Educación con Participación de la Communidad) in El Salvador provides another example of this approach.

A prolonged civil war in the 1980s left the Salvadorian school system in a woeful state. One third of the country's primary schools were closed, and in many regions, traditional government schools, and their teachers, were viewed with distrust by local people who may have been fighting against the government. During the war some communities had recruited local teachers and established community schools in place of government-run ones. Seizing on this model, the government decided to incorporate community schools into the national system and encourage new ones to open. These *popular* schools enter into one-year renewable agreements with the Ministry of Education. The local schools are run by parent groups, which receive grants from the government, hire teachers on renewable contracts, and determine the salaries and other terms of these contracts. Turnover rates are high; teachers who are frequently absent or perform poorly are dismissed. Parents visit schools more often and are more involved than in traditional schools. The results of these arrangements are encouraging. Educo reached far into the countryside. Rural primary school enrollments grew rapidly with most new students enrolled in the *popular* schools. Student performance in Educo and traditional schools was comparable. This was an impressive outcome, since Educo students tended to come from poorer and less-educated families than students who attended the traditional government schools.[26]

The relative success of Educo does not mean that all school systems should adopt a similar model or that greater parent involvement and control always improves school outcomes. But the Salvadorian case does speak to the ability of nations to experiment with alternative modes of service delivery. Debate over school reforms includes many alternatives to community-based schools. Charter schools share some similarities with community schools. They are financed by the government but have considerable autonomy on how they run themselves, ranging from deciding on curriculums to teacher salaries. Those responsible for the schools (whether principals, teachers, parent groups, or some combination) sign a "charter" with the government with clearly stated performance expectations. If these expectations are not realized the charter is not renewed. Market-based programs are another approach. They attempt to expand school choice by enabling parents to pick between traditional govern-

---

[26]World Bank, *2004 World Development Report*, 131–32.

ment schools and alternatives whether run by nongovernment organizations, religious groups, or the private sector. School vouchers can be used to enable parents to choose where to send their children. By increasing the range of suppliers it is hoped that competitive forces lead to improvements in school operation, teaching, and ultimately, the education children receive.

School reforms are part of a larger agenda of institutional reforms that many nations, whether low, middle or high income, are pursuing to improve schooling, health, and other outcomes. Evidence from such reforms indicates that "one size does not fit all" and continued experimentation and evaluation is needed to identify what works in different settings. School systems need to enroll and retain more students and improve learning outcomes at all levels of education. To do so, schools need clear objectives, adequate financing, and some autonomy on how to operate and achieve stated goals. Schools also must be held accountable to the taxpayers (at home and abroad) who finance school systems and, most important, to the students and their parents who count on schools to provide an education.

SUMMARY

- By historical standards, the last four decades have witnessed a revolutionary change in the number of men and *women* who have attended school and received a basic education. By 2000, two thirds of the developing world's adults had attended school as children. These investments in human capital have profound implications for improving the well-being of much of humanity in the twenty-first century.

- Despite these achievements, much remains to be done. Four out of every five children in the world live in low- and middle-income nations, and far too many of them have never attended school or failed to complete even four years of primary school. And those who have attended school often learned far too little, with their education lagging well behind what comparably aged children have mastered in high-income nations.

- Attending school remains a worthwhile private and social investment. In every nation, on average, if you have more years of schooling, you earn more than those with less schooling. Estimated rates of return, which take account of both the benefits and costs of schooling, indicate that schooling yields attractive returns when compared to other investments.

- Rates of return vary by school level, with the highest "social" returns to primary schooling and the lowest to tertiary levels. Educating girls in many settings also has a high social rate of return, in part, because of the positive health externalities that result from having more-educated mothers.

- Private returns are estimated to be especially high for primary school (where foregone earnings are low) but are also in the double digits for secondary schooling. Private returns to tertiary school often are high in developing nations, because educated workers are relatively scarce and receive a premium in the labor market and because tuition and other costs of attending tertiary schools are paid for by the government (tax-payers), not the individual.

- But schooling is not a panacea. Many nations have expanded enroll-ments and sent their young people through years of schooling and still have not grown. In a bad economic environment, schooling, like other investments, can be wasted. Increasing the demand for all workers, both educated and not educated, raises the private and social return on education and remains a key challenge to achieve economic development.

- Much also needs to be done to make schools more productive. Some developing nations underinvest in education overall; many misallocate resources by spending too much on the tertiary sector at the expense of primary and secondary levels; and most could improve the use of resources within schools themselves. Improvements include every-thing from increasing the health of children to changing the mix of inputs used in schools often with more resources directed at instruc-tional materials and other school supplies.

- Unfortunately, simple prescriptions for how to improve schools and learning outcomes are hard to come by. Decreasing user fees and other costs can increase enrollment and get the children of poor families to enroll and stay in school. But once children are in school, increasing student performance remains a challenge worldwide. Changing the mix of school inputs is important but making teachers, administrators, and government officials accountable for school outcomes may be the most important factor of all.

9

Health

Grab a pencil, here comes a pop quiz. In 2005, Denmark, a high-income nation, had a population of 5.4 million people. With a death rate of 10/1,000, about 54,000 Danes died that year. Here is your first question: What was the median age of those who died? In other words, pick the age where half of those who died were older and half were younger than that age. Now turn to Sierra Leone, one of the poorest nations in the world, which has a population about the same size as Denmark's. But Sierra Leone's death rate in 2005 was much higher, estimated at 24/1,000, resulting in roughly 130,000 deaths. Here is your second question: What was the median age of those who died in Sierra Leone? Write down your predictions; we will provide the answers in a moment.

The difference in the age distribution of deaths between a very poor nation like Sierra Leone and a wealthy developed country like Denmark is that most deaths occur before age five in Sierra Leone, while most deaths occur among the elderly in Denmark. This is graphically illustrated by the age pyramids in Figure 9–1. We examined age pyramids in Chapter 7, contrasting those of rapidly versus slowly growing populations (Box 7–3). The age pyramids of Figure 9–1 look entirely different. They refer to only those who died in a given year. In Sierra Leone, more deaths occur in the first four years of life than in all other age brackets combined; in Denmark, child deaths rarely occur. Here are the answers to the quiz: The median age of death in Denmark is 77; in Sierra Leone, it is under 4. The striking difference in these numbers tells us a lot about life and death in the richest and poorest nations of the world.

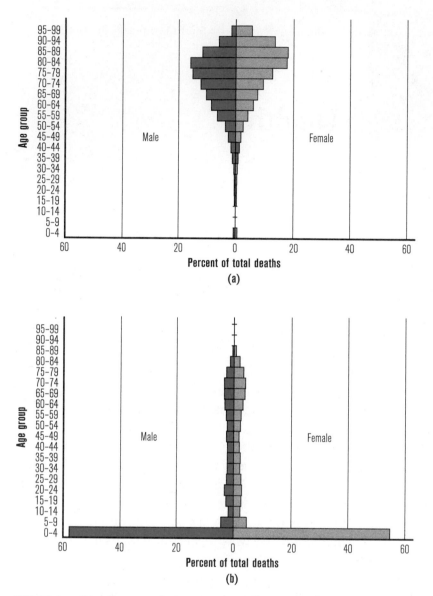

FIGURE 9-1. Distribution of Age at Death in (a) Denmark and (b) Sierra Leone, 2005 (values in graphs are projections)

Source: World Bank, *Health Financing Revisited,* processed (Washington, DC: World Bank, 2005).

One of the best indicators of a county's overall health status is the **under-five mortality rate.** This measure is the probability (expressed as per 1,000 live births) that a child born in a specific year dies before reaching five years of age, if subjected to current age-specific mortality rates. In Sierra Leone, there were 283 deaths to children under-five per 1,000 compared to only 5 in Denmark

TABLE 9-1. Selected Health-Related Measures for Sierra Leone and Denmark
            (early 2000s)

	SIERRA LEONE	DENMARK
Mortality statistics		
Life expectancy at birth (years)		
Both sexes	38	77
Males	37	75
Females	39	80
Mortality rates (per 1,000)		
Neonatal (first 28 days)	56	4
Under five	283	5
Adult (15–60 years) men	597	121
Adult (15–60 years) women	517	73
Healthy life expectancy at birth (HALE, years)		
Males	27	69
Females	30	71
Morbidity statistics		
Children under five stunted for age (%)	34	–
Children under five underweight for age (%)	27	–
Environmental risk factors		
Access to improved water sources, urban	75	100
Access to improved water sources, rural	46	100
Access to improved sanitation, urban	53	–
Access to improved sanitation, rural	30	–
Health services coverage		
Immunization coverage among one year olds (%)		
Measles	73	96
Diptheria, tetanus, pertussis, three doses	70	96
Births attended by skilled health personnel (%)	42	–
Health system statistics		
Number of physicians per 10,000	0.7	29
Number of nurses and midwives per 10,000	3.8	74
Number of health workers per 10,000	4.5	103
Hospital beds per 10,000	–	41
Per capita total expenditures on health (US$, PPP)	27	2,583

Source: *World Health Report 2005,* statistical annexes (Geneva: World Health Organization, 2005), available at www.who.int.

(Table 9–1). About 20 percent of all under-five mortality occurs in the first month of life in Sierra Leone. Early childhood is an especially risky period for Sierra Leone's children.

There are many explanations for the massive disparity in the chances that a child born in Sierra Leone versus one born in Denmark will survive and for the lower health status of the rest of the population these numbers suggest. At birth, less than half of all mothers in Sierra Leone is tended to by a skilled health worker; in Denmark, such services are available to all mothers. In Sierra Leone, malnutrition is common, especially among children. One out of every three children under-five is stunted and 27 percent are underweight. **Stunting** refers to the percentage of children under-five years that have a height-for-age ratio less than two standard deviations below the **World Health Organization (WHO)** global reference median. Being **underweight** refers to the percentage of children under-five years that have a weight-for-age ratio less than two standard deviations below the WHO global reference median. Both such outcomes are rare in Denmark.

The majority of rural inhabitants in Sierra Leone have no access to clean water or improved sanitation and many in the urban areas lack those services as well. Everyone in Denmark has access to safe drinking water and modern sanitation. Almost all one year olds (96 percent) are immunized in Denmark for measles and receive three doses of DTP (diphtheria, tetanus, and pertussis or whooping cough; DTP3) vaccine. Seventy-three percent of one year olds in Sierra Leone are immunized for measles and 70 percent for DTP3; 30 percent are not immunized and at risk of infection. A person who gets sick in Denmark has many more resources to turn to for medical care. Denmark has more than 20 times the number of health workers per 10,000 persons than Sierra Leone (103 versus 4.5). There are 29 trained physicians per 10,000 people in Denmark; in Sierra Leone, there is less than 1. Denmark also spends almost 100 times as much per person per year on health care ($2,583 versus $27; US$, PPP). Poor access to health services from childhood through adulthood increases adult mortality. In Sierra Leone, adult men are five times more likely to die than in Denmark; adult women are seven times more likely.

The data for Denmark and Sierra Leone reflect the experience of their geographical regions, Europe and Africa. Africa has the highest rate of under-five mortality with 171 deaths per 1,000 compared to 23 per 1,000 for Europe, the region with the lowest rate[1] (Table 9–2). The Eastern Mediterranean region, which includes twenty-one nations in North Africa and the Middle East, has the next highest regional under-five mortality rate at 92; and South-East Asia, encompassing 11 nations including Bangladesh, India, and Indonesia, is the third highest at 78. Poor health outcomes are correlated with low incomes, which in turn are associated with low levels of education and environmental risk factors such as lack of access to safe drinking water and the absence of improved sanitation, especially in rural areas. Absence of medical personnel

---

[1]WHO is the primary UN agency responsible for global health issues. WHO data rely on a regional breakdown that is different from the one used by the World Bank and frequently referred to throughout this textbook.

and low levels of health spending are other characteristics of high mortality among both children and adults. As we shall see, low incomes explain much, but certainly not all, of the disparity in health outcomes across countries and regions.

TABLE 9-2. **Selected Health-Related Measures for WHO Regions (early 2000s)**

	AFRICAN REGION	AMERICAS	SOUTHEAST ASIA
Mortality statistics			
Life expectancy at birth (years), males	46	71	61
Life expectancy at birth (years), females	48	77	64
Mortality rates (per 1,000)			
Neonatal (first 28 days)	43	12	38
Under five	171	25	78
Adult (15–60 years) men	522	179	275
Adult (15–60 years) women	466	102	212
Healthy life expectancy at birth (HALE, years), males	40	62	54
Healthy life expectancy at birth (HALE, years), females	42	67	55
Morbidity statistics			
Number of adults and children living with HIV (millions)	25.3	3.2	6.4
Adult (15–49) rate of people living with HIV (%)	7.1	0.7	0.7
Children under five stunted for age (%)	37	10	36
Children under five underweight for age (%)	26	5	37
Environmental risk factors			
Access to improved water sources, urban	84	97	94
Access to improved water sources, rural	45	80	79
Access to improved sanitation, urban	58	91	65
Access to improved sanitation, rural	28	64	28
Health services coverage			
Immunization coverage among one year olds (%)			
Measles	63	93	71
Diptheria, tetanus, pertussis, three doses	61	91	73
Births attended by skilled health personnel (%)	43	87	45
Health system statistics			
Number of physicians per 10,000	1.8	21.8	5
Number of nurses and midwives per 10,000	8.8	40.8	7.4
Number of health workers per 10,000	10.6	62.6	12.4
Hospital beds per 10,000	–	26	17
Per capita total expenditures on health (US$, PPP)	101	2,221	101

TABLE 9-2. (Continued)

	EUROPEAN REGION	EASTERN MEDITERRANEAN	WESTERN PACIFIC REGION
Mortality statistics			
Life expectancy at birth (years), males	68	61	70
Life expectancy at birth (years), females	77	64	74
Mortality rates (per 1,000)			
Neonatal (first 28 days)	11	40	19
Under five	23	92	36
Adult (15–60 years) men	234	257	164
Adult (15–60 years) women	100	187	100
Healthy life expectancy at birth (HALE, years), males	62	53	63
Healthy life expectancy at birth (HALE, years), females	68	54	66
Morbidity statistics			
Number of adults and children living with HIV (millions)	2.0	0.7	1.7
Adult (15–49) rate of people living with HIV (%)	0.4	0.3	0.2
Children under five stunted for age (%)	–	20	11
Children under five underweight for age (%)	–	18	8
Environmental risk factors			
Access to improved water sources, urban	99	92	93
Access to improved water sources, rural	83	75	69
Access to improved sanitation, urban	94	86	75
Access to improved sanitation, rural	67	39	34
Health services coverage			
Immunization coverage among one year olds (%)			
Measles	90	75	85
Diptheria, tetanus, pertussis, three doses	91	77	89
Births attended by skilled health personnel (%)	94	48	92
Health system statistics			
Number of physicians per 10,000	33.1	10.1	15.8
Number of nurses and midwives per 10,000	72	13.7	19.7
Number of health workers per 10,000	105.1	23.8	35.5
Hospital beds per 10,000	67	16	34
Per capita total expenditures on health (US$, PPP)	1,331	187	443

Source: *World Health Report 2005,* statistical annexes (Geneva: World Health Organization, 2005), available at www.who.int.

WHAT IS HEALTH?

The WHO defines *health* as a state of complete mental, physical, and social well-being and not merely the absence of disease.[2] However, such a complex construct would be difficult to measure and likely vary between cultures and over time. The measures most often used to express health are those that describe the absence of health: mortality and morbidity statistics. **Mortality** measures deaths in a population; **morbidity** measures rates of disease and illness.

Since death is an unambiguous event indicating a complete failure of health, mortality statistics offer a summary of a population's health status and reveal much about a population's standard of living and health care. Most countries record and publish death rates with various levels of coverage and accuracy. In a very poor country, such as Sierra Leone, less than 25 percent of deaths were covered by the country's own vital registration system. In such cases, mortality rates are estimated from sample surveys or other existing data.

Perhaps the most common summary statistic that is used to provide a snapshot of a country's health status is **life expectancy,** which is derived from data on mortality. Because death rates are affected by factors such as age, sex, and race, life expectancy is often calculated for specific demographic subgroups. The life expectancy for a male born in 2003 in Sierra Leone was 37 years and 39 years for a female. A Danish baby boy born in 2003 had a life expectancy of 75 and a girl had a life expectancy of 80. To put these numbers in some historical perspective, life expectancy in Sierra Leone today is about what it was in the United States in 1850.[3]

One might think that in a country where life expectancy is 38 (or 77) years that most people die by that age. That is clearly not the case, as Figure 9–1 demonstrates. Many people have shorter lives while others live well past the average life expectancy. Confusion arises because life expectancy is an average with variance around the mean and it is a "synthetic" statistic. It is based on the probability of surviving from one year to the next assuming that today's age-specific death rates remain unchanged into the future. But this is unlikely. Rising incomes and advances in medicine suggest that age-specific death rates are likely to fall in coming decades, expanding lifetimes beyond the predictions of current life expectancy estimates. However, new diseases, like HIV/AIDS, can cause the opposite, leading to shorter lifetimes and declining life expectancy.

---

[2]Preamble to the Constitution of the World Health Organization as adopted by the International Health Conference, New York, June 19–22, 1946. The definition has not been amended since 1948.

[3]Life expectancy at birth in Massachusetts in 1850 was 38 years for males and 40 years for females.

Box 9–1 describes in detail how life expectancy is computed using data from 1995 for Malaysia. Even though life expectancy in Malaysia was 69 years, people in the 70–75 age group had a life expectancy of 10 more years, a sort of "bonus" for surviving. In countries with high infant mortality, like Sierra Leone, life expectancy for children who survive the early years can be higher than at birth. For example, life expectancy at birth for Sierra Leone was 34 years in 2001. For the 5–9 age group, life expectancy was 44 additional years for a total of 49 years for a 5 year old, a full 15 years more than a newborn.[4] A 5-year-old child in Sierra Leone today will probably live even longer than 49 years. Now that years of civil war finally have ended in Sierra Leone, it is hoped that economic growth and development can begin. If this happens, age-specific death rates should start to fall and Sierra Leone's children should tend to live beyond current estimates of life expectancy.

Cause-specific death rates provide information on why people die and can be a useful policy tool. Morbidity statistics provide information on how people live, whether they live in full health or experience disabilities that may limit their participation in work or family life. Researchers have developed several innovative approaches to measuring health status that address the limitations of morbidity and mortality statistics by combining the information from both into a single unit. The WHO uses a single measure of death and disability that recognizes that years lived with a disability are not the same as healthy years. **Health-adjusted life expectancy (HALE)** reduces life expectancy by years spent with disabilities where disabilities are weighted according to their level of severity and duration. The balance remaining is the expected number of years of healthy life.[5]

Using the HALE measure, healthy life expectancy in Sierra Leone for males is cut by 10 years from 37 to 27 and for females it is reduced from 39 to 30. This is the lowest healthy life expectancy of all 192 WHO member countries. In Denmark, disabilities reduce healthy life expectancy from 75 to 69 for males. Females in Denmark suffer fewer disabilities and live 71 "healthy" years compared to an average life expectancy of 75. Years lost to disability are substantially higher in poorer countries because some limitations strike children and young adults, such as injury, blindness, paralysis, and the debilitating effects of several tropical diseases such as malaria. People in the healthiest regions (Europe) lose about 9 percent of their lives to disability, versus 15 percent in the least healthy region (Africa) (Table 9–2). The impact of disability on healthy life expectancy in Latin America and South Asia is also about 15 percent.

---

[4]World Health Organization, WHO Statistical Information System (WHOSIS), WHO Statistics, Burden of Disease Statistics, Life Tables for 191 Countries.

[5]*World Health Report 2002: Reducing Risks, Promoting Healthy Life* (Geneva: World Health Organization, 2002), statistical annex.

BOX 9-1 LIFE EXPECTANCY

Life expectancy is an estimate of the *average* number of additional years a person could expect to live if the age-specific death rates for a given year prevail for the rest of the person's life. Life expectancy is a hypothetical measure, because it is based on current death rates and actual death rates change (they usually fall) over the course of an individual's lifetime.

Life tables are used to calculate life expectancy; with life expectancy at birth the most commonly cited life expectancy measure. The table in this box contains selected portions of a life table for men in Malaysia in 1995. Age-specific death rates are applied to a hypothetical population of 100,000 people born in the same year. Column 1 shows the proportion of each age group dying in each age interval. These data are based on the observed mortality experience of the Malaysian population.

Column 2 shows the number of people alive at the beginning of each age interval, starting with 100,000 at birth. Each age group contains the population that survived from the immediately preceding group. Column 3 shows the number who would die within each age interval (Column 1 × Column 2 = Column 3). Column 4 shows the total number of person-years that would be lived within each age interval, including estimates of those who remain alive for only part of the interval. Column 5 shows the total number of years of life to be shared by the population in the age interval in all subsequent intervals. This measure takes into account the frequency of deaths that will occur in this *and subsequent intervals.* As age increases and the population shrinks, the total person-years that the survivors have to live necessarily diminish.

Abridged Life Table for Males in Malaysia, 1995

	1	2	3	4	5	6
AGE	PROPORTION DYING IN THE AGE INTERVAL	NUMBER LIVING AT THE BEGINNING OF THE AGE INTERVAL	NUMBER DYING DURING THE AGE INTERVAL	PERSONS-YEARS LIVED		YEARS OF LIFE REMAINING (LIFE EXPECTANCY)
				IN THE AGE INTERVAL	IN THIS AND SUBSEQUENT INTERVALS	
<1	0.01190	100,000	1,190	98,901	6,938,406	69.38
1–5	0.00341	98,810	337	394,437	6,839,505	69.22
5–10	0.00237	98,473	233	491,782	6,445,067	65.15
10–15	0.00270	98,240	265	490,536	5,953,285	60.60
–	–	–	–	–	–	–
65–70	0.16050	70,833	11,368	325,743	928,004	13.10
70–75	0.25762	59,464	15,319	259,024	602,260	10.13
75–80	0.34357	44,145	15,167	182,808	343,237	7.78
80+	1.00000	28,978	28,978	160,428	160,428	5.54

Source: Department of Statistics, Malaysia, 1997.

Life expectancy is shown in Column 6. The total person-years lived in a given interval plus subsequent intervals, when divided by the number of persons living at the beginning of that interval, equals life expectancy – the average number of years remaining for a person at a given age interval (Column 5 ÷ Column 2 = Column 6). For example, dividing the number of person-years associated with Malaysian men who survive to age 70 (602,260) by the number of these men (59,464) shows they have an additional life expectancy of 10.1 years. With age, life expectancy actually rises, a kind of "bonus" for surviving. The 59,464 Malaysian men who survive to age 70 can expect to live more than 10 additional years, well past their life expectancy at birth of 69 years.

Source: Adapted from, Arthur Haupt and Thomas T. Kane, *Population Handbook,* 5th ed. (Washington, DC: Population Reference Bureau, 2004), 29–30.

Transitions in Global Health

The past two centuries have seen a remarkable improvement in health and life expectancy. Until 1800, life expectancy at birth averaged around 30 years, but it could be lower. In France between 1740 and 1790, life expectancy of males fluctuated between 24 and 28 years. In England between the 1500s and the 1870s, life expectancy ranged from 28 to 42 with an average of only 35 years.[6] Many people died in infancy or early childhood while a few lived on to old age. Life expectancy steadily increased since the late nineteenth century, making dramatic gains in the twentieth century. From 1960 to 2003, life expectancy around the world increased from 50 to 67 years (Table 9–3). Among the low- and middle-income countries, the increase is especially dramatic. Life expectancy was only 44 years in 1960; in 2003, it was 65 years, almost a 50 percent increase. By comparison, the increase in the high-income countries over this time period was nine years, from 69 to 78. This smaller increase is because the high-income countries had achieved significant gains in life expectancy earlier in their history.

All regions of the world experienced gains in life expectancy since 1960, whether or not they also experienced economic growth. In East Asia, where economic growth has been rapid (and China dominates the regional average), life expectancy has risen from only 39 years in 1960 to 70 years in 2003. In 2003, per capita income in East Asia was only 16 percent that of high-income countries, but its life expectancy was already 90 percent the level achieved by high-income nations. Despite its slow growth between 1960 and 1990, South Asia added almost five years of increased life expectancy per decade. Latin America, even with its "lost decades," by 2003, had achieved the world's second-highest regional life expectancy, at 71 years.

But not all the news is this positive. Sub-Saharan Africa experienced an increase in life expectancy between 1960 and the early 1990s, but many African nations recorded declines since then due to HIV/AIDS, as young adults and children die prematurely. Tragically, life expectancy in parts of Southern Africa has been reduced by 20 years.[7] Life expectancy declined in some other countries as well. In Russia, life expectancy fell sharply in the 1990s. Between 1990 and 1994, life expectancy for Russian men fell from 64 years to 58 years and for Russian women from 74 to 71 years.[8] Increases in cardiovascular disease (heart disease and stroke) and injuries accounted for two thirds of the decline in life expectancy. Causes for this decline include high rates of tobacco and alcohol consumption, poor nutrition, depression, and a deteriorating health system. The underlying causes of these determinants of increased morbidity and mor-

[6]James C. Rile, *Rising Life Expectancy: A Global History* (Cambridge: Cambridge University Press, 2001).

[7]*World Health Report 2003* (Geneva: World Health Organization, 2003).

[8]Francis Notzon et al., "Causes of Declining Life Expectancy in Russia," *JAMA* 279, no. 10 (1998), 793–800.

TABLE 9-3. Increased Life Expectancy, 1960–2003

REGION	LIFE EXPECTANCY, YEARS			CHANGE IN YEARS PER DECADE	
	1960	1990	2003	1960–90	1990–2003
Low and middle income	44	63	65	6.3	1.5
East Asia and Pacific	39	67	70	9.3	2.3
Europe and Central Asia	N.A.	69	68	N.A.	−0.8
Latin America and Caribbean	56	68	71	4.0	2.3
Middle East and North Africa	47	64	68	5.7	3.1
South Asia	44	58	63	4.7	3.8
Sub-Saharan Africa	40	50	46	3.3	−3.1
High income	69	76	78	2.3	1.5
World	50	65	67	5.0	1.5

Sources: David Bloom, David Canning, and Dean T. Jamison, "Health, Wealth, and Welfare," *Health and Development: A Compilation of Articles from Finance and Development.* (Washington, DC: International Monetary Fund, December 2004) and *World Development Indicators Online.*

tality have been traced to both the cumulative effects of often poor living standards under communist rule of the Soviet Union and to the upheaval and stresses associated with Russia's transition.

The examples from Africa and Russia demonstrate that declines in health and life expectancy can take place rapidly. But these outcomes remain exceptions to the general trend of improving health and increasing life expectancy. The gaps in health outcomes between the richest and poorest regions of the world have become markedly smaller since 1960. The difference in life expectancy between low- and middle-income as compared to high-income nations was 25 years in 1960 but fell to only 13 years by 1990. Despite a lack of income convergence across nations (see Chapter 3), there is strong evidence of a convergence in life expectancy.[9]

The Epidemiologic Transition

Dramatic improvements in life expectancy and reductions in infant and child mortality during the past century resulted in equally dramatic demographic and socioeconomic changes. These changes led to the lower fertility rates and slower

[9]In the second half of the twentieth century, world life expectancy (computed as life expectancy by country weighted by each country's population) rose by about 18 years, while the weighted standard deviation *fell* from 13 to 7 years. See Charles Kenny, "Why Are We Worried about Income? Nearly Everything That Matters Is Converging," *World Development* 33, no. 1 (January 2005). See also Gary S. Becker, Tomas J. Philipson, and Rodrigo R. Soares, "The Quantity and Quality of Life and the Evolution of World Inequality," *American Economic Review* 95, no. 1 (2005), 277–91.

rates of population growth discussed in Chapter 7. Worldwide, youth dependency declined while elderly dependency rose. In 1970, 40 percent of the populations of all low- and middle-income nations were children 14 years and under. In 2004, the percentage had fallen to 30 percent. The elderly, those 65 and older, were only 4 percent of the population of developing nations in 1970 and today are still only 6 percent as compared to 14 percent in the high-income countries. But, in coming decades, demographic change will accelerate as the consequences of the developing world's transition from high to low population growth rates combine with falling child mortality and rising life expectancy.

As societies age and health improves, the pattern of diseases and causes of death also shift in a generally predictable pattern. This shift in disease pattern is referred to as the **epidemiologic transition.** One early characterization of the epidemiologic transition identified three main stages, the age of pestilence and famine, the age of receding pandemics, and the age of degenerative and human-made diseases.[10] The age of pestilence and famine, which covered most of human history, was a time of frequent epidemics and famines. Chronic malnutrition existed, as did severe maternal and child health problems. Health outcomes were affected by environmental problems such as unsafe water, inadequate sanitation, and poor housing. During the age of receding pandemics, death rates fell as infectious disease and famines declined. As people lived longer, they began to experience heart disease and cancer in greater numbers. In the age of degenerative and human-made diseases, mortality rates are low and chronic degenerative diseases, such as heart disease, diabetes, and hypertension, and human-made diseases, the result of smoking, excessive use of alcohol, and environmental pollution, take the place of infectious diseases as the primary causes of death. Changes have been made to this initial theory, but it remains a useful framework.

Some researchers add other stages of epidemiologic transitions, such as emerging and re-emerging infectious disease.[11] Old infectious diseases may cause increased morbidity and mortality due to resistance to antimicrobial therapies, as is the case for drug resistant tuberculosis, and new pathogens continue to emerge. HIV/AIDS is the best known of these new infections, although other new infectious diseases have emerged over the past 30 years, including the Ebola virus, SARS (severe acute respiratory syndrome), and recent strains of avian flu.[12]

---

[10]A. R. Omran, "The Epidemiologic Transition: A Theory of the Epidemiology of Population Change," *Millbank Memorial Fund Quarterly* 49, no. 4 (1971), 509–37.

[11]Ronald Barrett, Christopher W. Kuzawa, Thomas McDade, and George J. Armelagos, "Emerging and Re-emerging Infectious Diseases: The Third Epidemiologic Transition," *Annual Review of Anthropology* 27 (1998), 247–71.

[12]The U.S. Centers of Disease Control and Prevention (CDC) maintain a list of emerging and re-emerging infectious diseases. In 2005, the list included over 50 diseases (www.cdc.gov). See also David Satcher, "Emerging Infections: Getting Ahead of the Curve," *Emerging Infectious Diseases* 1, no. 1 (January–March 1995), 1–6.

TABLE 9-4. Mortality by Cause, 1998 (total mortality, %)

CAUSE OF DEATH	WORLD	HIGH INCOME	LOW AND MIDDLE INCOME	SUB-SAHARAN AFRICA	INDIA	LATIN AMERICA	CHINA
I. Communicable diseases, maternal and perinatal conditions, and nutritional deficiencies	30	6	35	66	42	23	11
II. Noncommunicable conditions	59	88	54	22	48	62	77
III. Injuries	11	6	11	12	10	15	12

Source: *World Health Report 1999: Making a Difference* (Geneva: World Health Organization 1999), annex table 2.

The twentieth century has seen a major shift in causes of death and disability from infectious diseases to noncommunicable disease. However, not all countries made this transition fully. Many of the poorest countries and poor subpopulations in middle-income countries still suffer from high rates of infectious diseases, maternal and perinatal conditions, and nutritional deficiencies that ceased to be problems in high-income nations. Table 9–4 demonstrates the extent of these disparities. Globally, 59 percent of mortality is due to noncommunicable conditions such as cardiovascular disease and cancer, 30 percent of mortality is due to communicable conditions, and 11 percent is due to injuries. High-income countries have greatly reduced mortality from communicable disease to only 6 percent, with 88 percent due to noncommunicable conditions. In stark contrast, 66 percent of mortality in sub-Saharan Africa remains due to communicable diseases and only 22 percent to noncommunicable conditions. The situation in India (characteristic of all of South Asia) and Latin America lies in between sub-Saharan Africa and the high-income countries. The differences in causes of death are also seen in Table 9–5. In high-income European countries, such as Denmark, all but one of the ten leading causes of death is from noncommunicable disease. In sub-Saharan Africa, the top six leading causes of mortality are infectious conditions.

China, a country that experienced rapid economic growth, also experienced a substantial epidemiologic transition. Despite still being a lower-middle-income nation, the distribution of the causes of death in China is rapidly approaching those of the high-income nations (Table 9–4). A recent study found that heart diseases, cancers, and strokes are the leading causes of death, accounting for approximately two thirds of total deaths among adults 40 years

TABLE 9-5. Leading Causes of Mortality, 1998

RANK	CAUSE	% OF TOTAL
World		
1	Ischaemic heart disease (II)	13.7
2	Cerebrovascular disease (II)	9.5
3	Acute lower respiratory infections (I)	6.4
4	HIV/AIDS (I)	4.2
5	Chronic obstructive pulmonary disease (II)	4.2
6	Diarrheal diseases (I)	4.1
7	Perinatal conditions (I)	4.0
8	Tuberculosis (I)	2.8
9	Cancer of the trachea/bronchus/lung (II)	2.3
10	Road traffic accidents (III)	2.2
	Total for ten causes	50.4
Sub-Saharan Africa		
1	HIV/AIDS (I)	19.0
2	Malaria (I)	10.0
3	Acute lower respiratory infections (I)	8.2
4	Diarrhoeal diseases (I)	7.6
5	Perinatal condiitons (I)	5.5
6	Measles (I)	5.2
7	Cerebrovascular disease (II)	4.7
8	War (III)	3.2
9	Ischemic heart disease (II)	2.9
10	Homicide and violence (III)	2.8
	Total for ten causes	69.1
Europe, high income		
1	Ischaemic heart disease (II)	23.8
2	Cerebrovascular disease (II)	11.3
3	Other cardiac diseases (II)	9.1
4	Cancer of the trachea/bronchus/lung (II)	5.2
5	Other cancers (II)	4.6
6	Acute lower respiratory infections (I)	3.9
7	Chronic obstructive pulmonary disease (II)	3.5
8	Cancer of the colon/rectum (II)	3.0
9	Other digestive diseases (II)	2.1
10	Cancer of the breast (II)	2.0
	Total for ten causes	68.5

Note: (I) Communicable diseases; (II) noncommunicable conditions; (III) injuries.
Source: World Health Organization, *The World Health Report 1999: Making a Difference.* (Geneva: World Health Organization, 1999), annex table 4 (all member states). Africa and Europe are calculated from annex table 2.

and older. As recently as the early 1960s, famines in China accounted for tens of millions of deaths. China no longer faces the threat of famine but must instead contend with the more "modern" health risks of smoking, obesity, HIV and other emerging diseases, and the various causes of cancers, heart disease, and other noncommunicable conditions.

THE DETERMINANTS OF IMPROVED HEALTH

Improved health and increases in life expectancy are due to several factors. Major advances in agriculture and food distribution in Europe led to the disappearance of famine and starvation, a concern up to the nineteenth century in some parts of the region. Famines were common and devastating in East and South Asia throughout much of the twentieth century. With few exceptions, North Korea being one, famine no longer appears as a threat in most of Asia. The same cannot be said for sub-Saharan Africa, where famines still occur regularly. Even without famine, malnutrition continues to plague billions of people in Africa and elsewhere and contributes to lower life expectancy. Malnutrition makes individuals more susceptible to infections and less able to fight them off.

Rising incomes generally allow for better nutrition and housing and improved survival rates. Throughout the twentieth century, life expectancy has been strongly associated with per capita income. Life expectancy rises rapidly with income, especially at low levels of income. Increased income allows people, particularly the poor, to buy more food, better housing, and more health care. However, since 1900, on an almost decade by decade basis, life expectancy has shifted upward, so that more health is realized for a given income. This upward shift indicates that health depends on more than income.[13]

Public health measures such as clean water, sanitation, and food regulation contributed to the decline in child mortality in the late nineteenth century and continue to do so today. In the late nineteenth century, Robert Koch showed that the bacterium *M. tuberculosis* causes tuberculosis and people began to understand about germs. Many other pioneers of science and medicine, such as Louis Pasteur and Joseph Lister, made equally important discoveries. Simple precautions such as preparing food and disposing of waste hygienically, eliminating flies and rodents, and quarantining the sick had far-reaching benefits. The discovery that cholera and typhoid were transmitted through impure water dates to the 1850s, but access to safe drinking water is still far from universal. Medical technology became important to controlling infectious diseases in the 1930s, when antibacterial drugs and new vaccines were introduced. All these developments, coupled with the rise of public health institutions that provide for improved sanitation, distribute vaccines, control disease vectors such as mosquitoes, and offer surveillance of disease outbreaks, protect societies against the major infectious causes of death.

---

[13]"Health in Developing Countries: Successes and Challenges," in *World Development Report 1993: Investing in Health* (Oxford: World Bank, published by Oxford University Press, 1993), Chapter 1, 17–36.

The critical role of science and institutions as determinants of health, independent of income, is reflected in the historical record. In 1900, life expectancy in the United States was 47 years and per capita income $4,600 (US$, 2000). Compare this to the situation in low- and middle-income countries in 2003. Life expectancy is substantially higher at 65 years, even though per capita income, at $3,700 (US$, 2000, PPP) was 20 percent lower. The explanation is straightforward. Penicillin and other antibiotics were unknown in 1900. Urban living conditions were overcrowded and few vaccines were available. Infectious diseases took their toll on the United States population just as they do in many low-income nations today.

Finally, education plays an important role in improving health. This was not always the case. Child mortality differed little by education or income in the United States in the last decade of the nineteenth century, but these factors made a big difference in the early twentieth century. The implication is that affluence and education did not matter much until the underlying scientific knowledge was present. Better-educated individuals acquire and use new information more quickly. This helps to explain the large differences in child mortality by mother's education observed in developing countries.[14]

HEALTH, INCOME, AND GROWTH

As we indicated before, in both rich and poor countries, there is a strong positive relationship between better health and economic growth, income levels, and poverty. In Chapter 3 (Figure 3–4), we saw that countries with higher life expectancy have faster economic growth. Figure 9–2 takes a different perspective, showing the relationship between under-five mortality and the *level* of income. Mortality rates are highest in the poorest countries, and they drop off sharply in conjunction with higher incomes. In countries with per capita income below $2,000 (US$, PPP), on average, 140 out of every 1,000 children do not live to their fifth birthday. Incredibly, one out of seven children in these countries does not live to see his or her fifth birthday. For incomes between $4,000 and $6,000, the child mortality rate is much lower, falling to just 39 per 1,000. For countries with incomes above $10,000, only 12 out of 1,000 die early in life.

Since key measures of health are strongly related to both income levels and growth rates, it should be no surprise that they are also strongly related to poverty. Figure 9–3 makes the link with poverty, showing that countries with higher life expectancies have much lower rates of poverty. In countries with life

---

[14]"Health in Developing Countries."

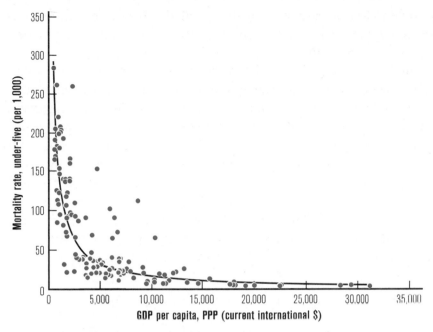

FIGURE 9-2. Child Mortality and Income (2003)

Based on data for 2003 from 137 countries of all income levels around the world.

Source: *World Development Indicators 2005.*

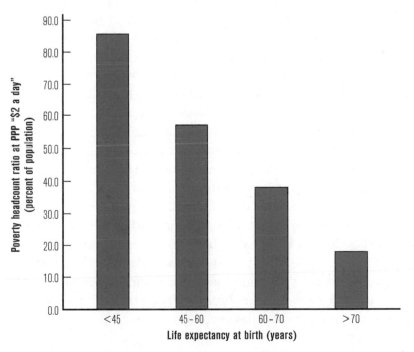

FIGURE 9-3. Poverty and Life Expectancy (1998–2003 average)

Source: *World Development Indicators 2005.*

expectancy below 45 years, 86 percent of the population lives below the $2 a day poverty line; in countries with life expectancy greater than 70 years, only 18 percent live below the poverty line.

The strength of these relationships is not in doubt. The question is this: What is causing what? Higher income and reductions in poverty could lead to better health. But the causality could run the opposite direction, improved health could lead to faster economic growth, higher incomes, and less poverty. In fact, both channels probably are at work. Better health and higher incomes work together in a mutually reinforcing and virtuous cycle, in which improvements in health support faster economic growth leading to higher incomes and higher incomes facilitate even better health. Unfortunately, the cycle can also work in reverse, as declines in income can weaken health (as in Russia and other transition economies), and the onset of new diseases, such as HIV/AIDS, can lead to a fall in income.

Higher Income Improves Health

As incomes increase, individuals, households, and societies at large are able to increase spending on a range of goods and services that directly or indirectly improve health. Individuals and households can buy more and better food, so there is a strong causal link from higher income to improved nutrition to better health.[15] Research shows that, as incomes rise, child height (an indicator of nutrition) tends to increase in many low-income countries. With higher incomes, poor households can more easily afford clean water and basic sanitation facilities, either as an outhouse or through indoor plumbing, which can help control disease. Also, as incomes rise, poor households can afford better shelter, which in turn should keep them healthier. They are also more likely to be able and willing to seek medical care when it is needed, either because they can afford the transportation costs to the clinic or pay for medicines or other out-of-pocket expenses. For individuals living on subsistence incomes, paying for even the most basic medicines and health care can sometimes be a struggle. Oral rehydration therapy (ORT), a simple mixture of water, salts, and sugar is an effective treatment for common, and often fatal, diarrheal diseases in children. At 33 cents per treatment it is also extremely inexpensive, especially when viewed relative to its life-saving benefits. Insecticide treated bed nets have proven effective at reducing exposure to mosquitoes that transmit malaria. At $3 per net, they also are inexpensive. But in some of the poorest parts of the world, where these interventions are most needed, even these minimal costs can be too high for a poor family. As incomes rise, such expenditures become more routine.

---

[15]For a good survey on these issues, see John Strauss and Duncan Thomas, "Health, Nutrition and Economic Development," *Journal of Economic Literature* 36 (June 1998).

For society as a whole, as incomes rise, there is greater ability to build public health clinics and hospitals, train more doctors and nurses, and pay for public health services such as immunization campaigns or insect spraying programs. Poor countries cannot afford to build the same kinds of public and private health systems that richer countries can, and they may not be able to afford to pay their doctors and nurses the kinds of salaries needed to keep them home, rather than taking positions in richer countries. Interruptions in the supply of electricity can reduce the efficacy of medications; for example, many vaccines need to be kept refrigerated prior to inoculation, and when the electricity grid fails, the stock of vaccines is damaged. It is not uncommon in developing countries to find hospitals and clinics without medicines or clean water. Often, because operating budgets are so small and patients cannot afford to pay much, the patient's family must supply basic food and care to a family member in the hospital. As a society's income rises, it is much better able to pay for a reasonable health care system. In sub-Saharan Africa, where incomes average $1,850 (US$, PPP), spending 2 percent of national income on public health translates to $37 per person per year. In Latin America, where incomes average a much higher $7,660 (US$, PPP), the same 2 percent allocation to public health provides $153 per person per year, which can buy far more hospital beds and medicine.

Economists Lant Pritchett of the World Bank and Lawrence Summers of Harvard University provide one estimate of the potential impact of rising incomes on health. They find that the long-run income elasticity of under-five mortality is between –0.2 and –0.4, meaning that each 10 percent increase in income is associated with a 2–4 percent decline in child mortality rates. According to this result, if income growth in low- and middle-income nations during the 1980s had been 1 percent higher, as many as half a million child deaths would have been averted in 1990 alone.[16]

The *level* of per capita income, of course, is not the only determinant of health outcomes. The *distribution* of income matters, too. To the extent that a household's command over resources influences morbidity and mortality, for any given level of per capita income, the more equal is the distribution, the better the expected aggregate health outcome. But health is responsive to more than the level and distribution of income. The creation and dissemination of medical knowledge and public health practices was central to the historical rise in life expectancy in the now-developed nations (Box 9–2). The diffusion of this knowledge to poor nations today remains a key determinant of health outcomes in developing countries. It is also a determinant somewhat independent of the per capita income levels of the poorer nations. This is another example of economic historian Alexander Gerschenkron's hypothesis about "the advantages of

---

[16]Lant Pritchett and Lawrence H. Summers, "Wealthier Is Healthier," *Journal of Human Resources* 31, no. 4 (1996), 841–68.

BOX 9-2 "HOW BENEFICENT IS THE MARKET? A LOOK AT THE MODERN HISTORY OF MORTALITY"

Richard Easterlin, a distinguished economic historian and demographer, investigated the reasons behind the decline in mortality rates that began in Europe in the nineteenth century. While rising levels of income improved nutrition and generally contributed to increased resistance to disease, economic growth in this period also increased exposure to disease as industrialization gave rise to urbanization and the concentration of people in closer quarters.

In explaining the great improvement in life expectancy that occurred in parts of Europe in the nineteenth century, Easterlin identifies the centrality of scientific discoveries and the role of public health initiatives. Easterlin also reflects on the role of markets versus the state in achieving these outcomes:

> Only with the growth, first, of epidemiological and, then, bacterial knowledge did effective techniques emerge for controlling infectious disease. These techniques focused primarily on the prevention of the spread of disease—first via controlling the mode of transmission, and subsequently via immunization. It is these methods of prevention that have been chiefly responsible for the great improvement in life expectancy. In the last half century the advance of knowledge has added methods of curing disease to the arsenal available to fight infectious disease, particularly with the development of antibiotics, but the great bulk of the reduction in infectious disease has been accomplished largely by preventive methods.
>
> The control of infectious disease involves serious issues of market failure—information failures, externalities, public goods, principal-agent problems, and so forth. The market cannot be counted on for such things as the provision of pure water and milk, the proper disposal of sewage, control of pests such as mosquitoes and rats, the supply of uncontaminated food and other manufactured products, immunization of children and adults against major infectious diseases, and the dissemination of new knowledge regarding personal hygiene, infant and child care, food handling and preparation, care of the sick, and the like. There is also a serious market failure problem with regard to the distribution of anti-microbials because of externalities associated with the development of disease-resistant bacteria.
>
> The title of this article posed the question, how beneficent is the market? The ubiquity of market failure in the control of major infectious disease supplies the answer: if improvement of life expectancy is one's concern, the market cannot do the job . . . [T]he assumption that the market, in solving the problem of economic growth, will solve that of human development is belied by the lessons of experience. Rather than a story of the success of free market institutions, the history of mortality is testimony to the critical need for collective action.

Source: Richard A. Easterlin, "How Beneficent Is the Market? A Look at the Modern History of Mortality," *European Review of Economic History* 3 (December 1999), 286–88.

backwardness." Poor countries can learn from the scientific knowledge, most of it generated in the developed nations, about disease transmission and interventions to promote health and extend people's lives.

Better Health Increases Growth and Incomes

There is increasingly strong evidence of the causality also running in the opposite direction, in which improved health leads to faster economic growth, higher incomes, and reduced poverty. Several studies have shown that higher life expectancy in an early period (say, 1960) leads to faster subsequent economic growth (say, from 1960–2000). The relationship is usually found to have diminishing returns, meaning that an extra year of life expectancy at birth has a big effect on growth when life expectancy is 45 years but a smaller effect when life expectancy reaches 70 years. A typical estimate suggests that, after controlling for other factors that influence growth, each 10 percent improvement in life expectancy at birth translates into an increase of 0.3–0.4 percentage points per year in economic growth. The difference between life expectancy of 70 years in a high-income country and 45 years in a low-income country translates into faster growth of about 1.5 percentage points per year.[17]

Even if higher life expectancy did not translate into more-rapid growth or higher annual income, it would translate to higher *lifetime* earnings. Consider the differences in well-being between an average resident of Botswana and the United States. In Botswana, average income in 1997 was about $6,320 in PPP terms, whereas in the United States it was about $30,000. At first glance, it would appear that income in the United States was five times higher per person. But an average 22-year-old in Botswana with 12 years of education (and annual income much higher than the average) has a lifetime expected income of about $385,000, whereas a similarly educated 22-year-old American, because of a longer expected life span, has a lifetime expected income of around $3,600,000. In terms of (undiscounted) lifetime incomes rather than annual incomes, the income gap is closer to ten times with all of the attendant implications for greater consumption, savings and investment.[18]

Better health increases life expectancy. It also affects both fundamental causes of economic growth: productivity gains and increased investment.

---

[17]World Health Organization, *Macroeconomics and Health: Investing in Health for Economic Development*, Report of the Commission on Macroeconomics and Health (Geneva: World Health Organization, 2001). To allow for diminishing returns, most models estimate the relationship between the natural logarithm of life expectancy at birth on growth, with the typical coefficient of a round 3.5. The calculation is $3.5 \times [\ln(70) - \ln(45)]$, which equals around 1.5 percent per year.

[18]From World Health Organization, *Macroeconomics and Health*, p. 25.

Health and Productivity

Healthier people tend to be more economically productive, since they are more energetic and mentally more alert. A healthier worker is able to harvest more crops, build more furniture, assemble more computers, or make more service calls than a worker that is ill or lethargic. A study of sugarcane workers in Tanzania showed that workers with schistosomiasis, a disease caused by a parasitic worm that causes fever, aches, and fatigue, were able to cut much less cane and therefore earn much less in wages (since they were paid by the amount they cut) than workers in the same estate that did not have the disease.[19] Healthier workers not only are more productive while they work, they lose fewer workdays because of illness. The types of work available to many low-income, low-skilled workers typically rely more on strength and endurance than higher-skilled desk jobs, putting a premium on physical health. Moreover, aside from their own health, if a worker's family is healthier, the worker loses fewer workdays in caring for family members that are ill. A dramatic example of the latter point involves HIV/AIDS. Firms in southern Africa, where HIV prevalence rates are the highest in the world, lose workdays due not only to the illnesses of employees but also in time lost to attending the high number of funerals of coworkers and family members.

A family member's health can also have an impact on children's education, which in turn has implications for future income. Families that cope with long-term illnesses, such as HIV/AIDS or tuberculosis of an adult, may rely on children to work the fields, find other ways to bring in income or care for the sick family member, thus preventing the child from attending school and investing in his or her own human capital. The poor health of a child can reduce cognitive ability in students and undermines schooling through absenteeism and shorter attention spans. As noted in the previous chapter, experimental evidence from Kenya finds that students in schools that received a simple treatment for hookworms had significantly higher attendance rates than children in schools without treatment programs. Moreover, when child mortality declines, parents tend to have fewer children, allowing them to invest more in each child's health and education, as discussed in Chapter 7.

Childhood health can affect labor productivity years later when children grow older and join the workforce. The early effects of health on physical strength and cognitive ability can have lasting impacts. Nobel laureate Robert Fogel found a strong relationship between nutrition, body size, and labor productivity.[20] Research on Brazil, inspired by Fogel's earlier work, identifies a rela-

---

[19]A. Fenwick and B.M. Figenschou, "The Effect of *Schistosoma mansoni* on the Productivity of Cane Workers in a Sugar Estate in Tanzania," *Bulletin of the World Health Organization* 47, no. 5 (September 1972), 567–72.

[20]See, for example, Robert Fogel, "New Findings on Secular Nutrition and Mortality: Some Implications for Population Theory," in M. R. Rosensweig and O. Stark, eds., *Handbook of Population and Family Economics*, vol. 1a (Amsterdam: Elsevier Science, 1997), 433–81.

tionship between a worker's height and wages. Taller workers, who, after controlling for other factors, are likely to have had better nutrition during childhood, earn much higher wages, reflecting higher levels of productivity. The relationship in Brazil is strong: A 1 percent increase in height is associated with a nearly 8 percent increase in wages. When workers are healthier and more productive, firms are willing to pay them higher wages.

Health and Investment

Beyond its impact on labor productivity, improved health can influence the other key channel for achieving economic growth, increased saving and investment.

As people expect to live longer, they have greater incentives to make long-term investments in their farm or other business and their human capital. By contrast, people with poor health have to divert more of their income into medical expenses, reducing their capacity to save. Poor people facing catastrophic illness sometimes must sell some of their assets, such as livestock or farm tools, thus depleting their capital stock, to pay for medicines or simply to feed their family if they no longer can work. Health can also affect public saving and investment. Governments fighting endemic diseases must allocate more of their spending to these purposes, reducing the amount available for building roads or other capital investment.

In South Africa, the high prevalence of HIV/AIDS is viewed as both a public health challenge and as a macroeconomic problem that reduces economic growth. The disease reduced the size of the workforce and its productivity, at the same time as it has decreased the ability of households, firms, and the government to invest in the future. Households face lost labor income and increased expenditures on health; firms confront increased expenditures on health benefits and insurance, higher absenteeism and job turnover, and greater training costs due to premature deaths; and government finds that health expenditures crowd out other high-priority expenditures. Some studies suggest that HIV/AIDS may currently cost South Africa a full percentage point of annual economic growth.[21]

Reduction or elimination of diseases can help substantially increase the amount of usable productive assets, including land. The classic example of disease impeding a critical investment is the construction of the Panama Canal in the late nineteenth century (Box 9–3). Contemporary examples include large tracts of land rendered uninhabitable by endemic disease. The dramatic reduction of river blindness in West Africa allowed increased farming in the fertile lands near riverbanks that previously were breeding grounds for the disease (see

[21]Jeffrey D. Lewis, "Assessing the Demographic and Economic Impact of HIV/AIDS," in Kyle Kauffman and David Lindauer, eds., *AIDS and South Africa: The Social Expression of a Pandemic* (Hampshire, U.K.: Palgrave Macmillan, 2004).

Box 14–3 for a discussion of the fight against river blindness in the context of foreign aid programs). Schistosomiasis makes it unsafe for people to enter lakes and streams in sections of Africa, and trypanosomiasis (sleeping sickness) restricts the range of the livestock industry. The reduction of malaria allowed farmers to work new lands in Malaysia, Sri Lanka, and the Terrai area of northern India. Singapore's economic prosperity was made possible partly because rampant malaria was brought under control on the island. Similarly, disease can undermine foreign investment, as investors shun environments where HIV/AIDS, malaria, tuberculosis, and other diseases are more prevalent.

THREE CRITICAL DISEASES

Dramatic changes have taken place in global health. The reduction of infectious disease allowed the survival of many individuals to old age. Reductions in fertility rates contribute to a change in population structure so that the elderly represent a larger portion of the population, imposing new demands on health care systems. The process of industrialization, urbanization, and modernization create its own set of health problems. Pollution damages the environment and affects health. Increased tobacco use adds to the burden of diseases such as lung cancer and heart disease. Alcohol abuse, injuries, and stress create their own set of health problems. A shift in diet from vegetables and cereals to highly processed foodstuffs coupled with a decline in activity levels leads to rising obesity in both rich and poor nations, and contributes to chronic illnesses.

While the burden of noncommunicable disease grows, the unfinished agenda of infectious diseases remains. There is a great disparity between what has been achieved in health care between the developed and developing nations and even between groups within nations. The rest of this chapter focuses on a handful of diseases that are preventable, treatable, or curable yet pose significant problems in developing countries. This is followed by examples of how countries and the international community have addressed some of these and other diseases. A disease-based approach offers a snapshot of some of the health issues facing developing countries and some of the ways these challenges have been met.

Three of the developing world's most prominent and deadly infectious diseases are HIV/AIDS, malaria, and tuberculosis (Box 9–4). They are the first, second, and eleventh leading causes of death in Africa. These three diseases have spread steadily in recent decades and together kill nearly 6 million people every year. Relative to high-income countries, the burden of these diseases (in terms of deaths per capita) is 30 times greater in developing countries, resulting in

BOX 9-3 MALARIA, YELLOW FEVER, AND THE PANAMA CANAL

On February 1, 1881, capitalized by over 100,000 mostly small investors, the French Compagnie Universelle du Canal Interocéanique began work on a canal that would cross the Isthmus of Panama and unite the Atlantic and Pacific Oceans. Ferdinand de Lesseps, builder of the Suez Canal, led the project. In the first months, the digging progressed slowly but steadily. Then, the rains began, and the crew soon discovered what they were up against: mile upon mile of impassable jungle, day upon day of torrential rain, insects, snakes, swamps, heat, and endemic disease—smallpox, malaria, and yellow fever.

In 1881, the company recorded about 60 deaths from disease. In 1882, the number doubled, and the following year, 420 died. The most common killers were malaria and yellow fever. Because the company often fired sick men to reduce medical costs, the numbers probably reflect low estimates. By the time the company halted the project and went out of business in December 1888, about $300 million had been spent, and 20,000 men had died.

In 1904, the American president, Theodore Roosevelt, instigated a treaty with Panama that gave the United States the right to build the canal and created a 10-mile wide Canal Zone of what amounted to sovereign American territory surrounding the waterway. The United States army dispatched surgeon Colonel William Gorgas to Panama to tackle malaria and yellow fever. Gorgas was fresh from Havana where he had helped eradicate yellow fever, following discoveries by his colleague Major Walter Reed and others that the disease was carried by a mosquito. The fight against yellow fever also substantially reduced malaria, building on discoveries by British bacteriologist Ronald Ross that the parasite that causes malaria was transmitted by the anopheles mosquito.

The efforts to control the two diseases were successful. Yellow fever was totally eradicated. Deaths due to malaria in employees dropped from 11.6 per 1,000 in November 1906 to 1.2 per 1,000 in December 1909. But the impact spread well beyond the Canal workers. Deaths from malaria in the Panamanian population fell from 16.2 per 1,000 in July 1906 to 2.6 per 1,000 in December 1909. The canal was completed in 1914, once of the greatest construction miracles of the early of the twentieth century. The project powerfully demonstrated that malaria and yellow fever could be controlled over a wide geographical area, paving the way for investment and increased economic activity.

Sources: Adapted from the Public Broadcasting Service's film series *The American Experience: The Story of Theodore Roosevelt,* "TR's Legacy—The Panama Canal," www.pbs.org/wgbh/amex/tr/panama.html; and Centers for Disease Control and Prevention, *Malaria: The Panama Canal,* www.cdc.gov/malaria/history/panama_canal.htm.

tremendous economic loss and social disintegration. One of the many tragedies of each of these diseases is that they are preventable and, with adequate resources and institutions, can be treated effectively.

HIV/AIDS[22]

Although HIV/AIDS has affected humans since at least the 1930s, it was virtually unknown until it was first recognized in 1981. Since then, the pandemic[23] has spread inexorably around the globe, exacting a terrible toll on the health and welfare of the world's poorest communities. More than 40 million people were living with HIV/AIDS in 2005, about 1 of every 160 people in the world, and about 3 million people died that year of AIDS-related causes. HIV/AIDS is the leading cause of death among adults aged 15–59 worldwide and has killed an estimated 20 million people.

Sub-Saharan Africa bears the largest burden, with two thirds the world's infection, even though it is home to only one tenth the world's population. Across sub-Saharan Africa nearly 1 in 13 adults carries the virus, but huge variations exist across the region. Some West African countries, such as Senegal, have maintained adult prevalence rates of less than 1 percent for more than a decade. In these low-prevalence countries, the disease is confined primarily within groups that practice high-risk behavior, such as sex workers and their clients. In southern Africa, HIV/AIDS has taken hold within the general population. In Swaziland, prevalence rates among pregnant women are a mind-boggling 43 percent. In six countries in southern Africa, more than one fifth of all adults are HIV positive: Botswana, Lesotho, Namibia, South Africa, Swaziland, and Zimbabwe. Nearly 1 million people died of HIV/AIDS-related causes in 2004 in southern Africa, one third the global total.

The sliver of good news is that prevalence rates are beginning to fall in three African countries (Kenya, Uganda, and Zimbabwe), representing an important achievement in turning the tide on the pandemic. However, even these trends convey a mixed message. Some claim that declines in prevalence rates in Uganda can be attributed at least partially to behavioral changes linked to the government's ABC program, promoting Abstinence, Being faithful to one partner, and using Condoms. But recent studies demonstrated that, in some regions of the country, falling prevalence rates are less the result of behavioral change

[22]This section draws on information from UNAIDS, *2005 Report on the Global AIDS Epidemic* (Geneva: UNAIDS, 2005); the Global Fund, *2004 Disease Report* (Geneva: The Global Fund to Fight AIDS, Tuberculosis, and Malaria, 2004), and information from the websites of the WHO and the U.S. Centers for Disease Control.

[23]HIV/AIDS is usually referred to as a pandemic rather than an epidemic. Both terms often refer to the spread of an infectious disease. *Epidemics* refer to an illness that shows up in a larger number of cases than is normally expected. *Pandemics* refer to an even higher number of cases spread over a larger geographic area.

BOX 9-4 HIV/AIDS, MALARIA, AND TUBERCULOSIS: SOME BASICS

HIV stands for human immunodeficiency virus. Once infected with HIV, a person will always carry the virus. The disease primarily is a sexually transmitted disease, but it can also be transmitted through needles or contaminated blood. Over time, HIV infects and kills white blood cells called CD4 lymphocytes (or T cells), leaving the body unable to fight off infections and cancers. **AIDS** stands for acquired immune deficiency syndrome and is caused by HIV. A person with AIDS has an immune system so weakened by HIV that he or she usually becomes sick from one of several opportunistic infections or cancers, such as pneumonia, KS (Kaposi sarcoma), diarrhea, or tuberculosis. AIDS usually takes several years to develop from the time a person acquires HIV, usually between 2 to 10 years. AIDS can be treated but not cured. With successful antiretroviral (ARV) therapy, which requires medication for life, the body can remain healthy and fight off most viruses and bacteria; and people living with HIV can resume a relatively normal life.

Malaria is a serious and sometimes fatal disease caused by a plasmodium parasite transmitted by the female *anopheles* mosquito. The mosquito transmits malaria by taking blood from an infected individual and passing it to another. Malaria can also be transmitted by blood transfusion and contaminated needles and syringes. Patients with malaria typically are very sick with high fevers, shaking chills, and flu-like illness. Four species of plasmodium infect humans, but the most dangerous is *P. Falciparum,* which causes the most severe disease and deaths and is most prevalent in sub-Saharan Africa and some parts of Southeast Asia. Although malaria can be a fatal disease, illness and death from malaria are largely preventable.

Tuberculosis (TB) is a bacterium that infects the lungs and is spread through the air when someone with active TB coughs, sneezes, talks, or otherwise releases tiny microscopic droplets of *M. tuberculosis,* which then enter the respiratory system of another person. Because proximity and poor ventilation speed transmission, TB is a particular problem in densely populated or enclosed settings, such as urban slums or prisons. Each person with active TB infects an average of 10 to 15 people each year. Only about 10 percent of people infected with the bacterium develop active TB and the accompanying symptoms: fever, weight loss, chronic cough, chest pain, bloody sputum, loss of appetite, and night sweats. A third of those with active TB die within a few weeks or months if they are not treated. The remainder struggle with recurrent infections or the disease goes into remission, where it re-emerges from time to time to cause pain, fever, and possibly death. The HIV epidemic fueled the resurgence of TB. HIV weakens the immune system, and people who are infected with HIV are particularly vulnerable to TB. Antibiotics to treat and cure TB patients have been available for over 50 years. Successful treatment requires strict patient compliance. Antibiotics must be taken regularly for six months or more. Failure to do so has contributed to the spread of multidrug-resistant TB, which is much harder to cure.

Sources: "HIV InSite," University of California at San Francisco; WHO; Centers for Disease Control and Prevention; and the Global Fund to Fight AIDS, Tuberculosis, and Malaria.

than of high mortality. Because of AIDS-related deaths, there are simply fewer HIV positive adults in 2003 than there were a decade earlier.[24]

The pandemic is less severe in other regions but still a major threat that continues to spread. Adult prevalence rates exceed 2 percent in the Caribbean, where AIDS is the leading cause of death among young adults. In Asia, Thailand has implemented a successful campaign to limit the spread of the disease, but in other countries, the number of infected people is growing rapidly. According to some estimates, by 2010, India will have the largest number of infected people in the world. Unsafe blood transfusion practices in China account for about one quarter of HIV cases; injecting-drug users over 40 percent; and heterosexual transmission, especially involving sex workers, another 20 percent. Increases among injection-drug users in Russia, Ukraine, and other countries in Eastern Europe and Central Asia contributed to a growing problem in that region.

Women are increasingly vulnerable to HIV, and globally, girls and women account for almost half of those living with HIV. In Africa, the picture is especially grim for young women, where three quarters of those living with HIV/AIDS between the ages of 15 and 24 are female. Socioeconomic factors contribute significantly to women's vulnerability to HIV infection. Most are infected by partners who practice high-risk behavior. Compounding this problem is that as many as nine out of ten HIV-positive people in sub-Saharan Africa do not know that they are infected. Social disempowerment and lack of access to HIV education or services further contribute to the soaring pandemic among women. In 24 sub-Saharan countries, two thirds or more of young women aged 15–24 years lack comprehensive knowledge of HIV transmission.[25] Children are also increasingly vulnerable, with over 2 million children infected and over half a million deaths every year. The vast majority of infected children acquire HIV through transmission from their mother during pregnancy, labor and delivery, or breastfeeding. Antiretroviral drugs, such as nevirapine, significantly reduce mother to child transmission, but still are not widely available in sub-Saharan Africa.

The HIV/AIDS pandemic has had a crippling effect on many countries that were making significant progress in health. Whereas most countries in sub-Saharan Africa had achieved steady increases in life expectancy in the 1960s, 1970s, and early 1980s, in several countries, this progress stopped in the late 1980s and has since reversed. Figure 9–4 shows changes in life expectancy for six

---

[24]In the Rakai region in Uganda, researchers attribute approximately 5 percentage points of the 6.2 percent decline in HIV prevalence between 1994 and 2003 to increased mortality. UNAIDS, *AIDS Epidemic Update* (December 2005), p. 26.

[25]UNAIDS and World Health Organization, "HIV Infection Rates Decreasing in Several Countries but Global Number of People Living with HIV Continues to Rise," press release (November 21, 2005), available at www.unaids.org.

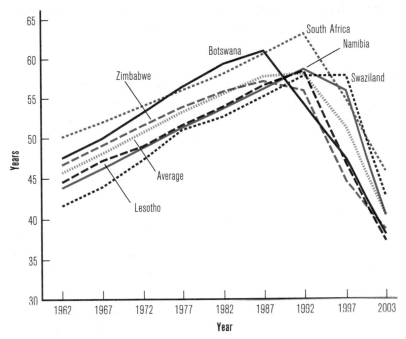

FIGURE 9-4. Life Expectancy at Birth in Selected Most-HIV-Affected Countries

Source: World Bank, *World Development Indicators 2005*.

of the most severely infected countries. Tragically, life expectancy has dropped from an average of 58 years in 1992 to just 40 years in 2003.

The effects on communities and families are devastating as parents, children, and community leaders become sick and die. Unlike most other diseases, HIV/AIDS attacks primarily young adults and the economically active segment of the population. Other diseases tend to incapacitate the very young, the old, or those already weakened by other conditions. HIV/AIDS is different. In Africa, HIV disproportionately destroys the lives of society's most productive members. Households face catastrophe as income earners fall ill and eventually succumb to the disease. The long duration of AIDS illness makes it particularly costly. In addition to these losses, others in the family must stop work to care for those that are ill. Small farms and gardens go untended and children may be taken out of school to tend to sick family members or to go to work to earn extra income. Families become further impoverished as they face increasing medical costs and have less income to pay for food, clothing, or other expenses. In some cases, funeral costs may be higher than health care costs and add to a family's burden. Studies in Tanzania and Thailand estimate that the cost of medical care and funerals can be greater than the household's annual income triggering borrowing, asset sales or other coping strategies that can have long-term financial welfare implications.[26] Many of the effects of HIV/AIDS are intergenerational: There are now 14 million AIDS orphans worldwide, where one or both parents have died from the disease.

Combating the epidemic requires strong national and international commitment. Until scientists develop other interventions, such as a cure or preventive vaccine, the key to halting the spread of the disease is strong prevention programs coupled with adequate care and treatment. In richer countries, where people can afford treatment, the development of ARVs has made AIDS a chronic disease that can be managed, rather than a fatal disease, allowing those infected to resume a relatively normal lifestyle. Death rates for HIV/AIDS in Europe and North America fell by 80 percent in the four years after the introduction of anti-retroviral therapy. Prophylactic treatment with ARVs in combination with other interventions has almost entirely eliminated HIV infection in infants in industrialized countries.[27] But for most people in the poorest countries, ARVs remain out of reach. Only about one in ten Africans that need treatment has access to these drugs. Beginning in 2003, access to ARVs in developing countries began to improve, and in a few countries, treatment coverage is now widespread. In Argentina, Brazil, Chile, and Cuba, more than 80 percent of those that need ARVs are now receiving them, but these are exceptions rather than the norm.

Delivering antiretroviral therapy on a global level requires not only good science and health policy but also political and economic initiatives. The most cost-effective way to provide the massive quantities of drugs required at hugely discounted prices is to encourage the manufacture of generic versions of these antiretroviral agents. Issues of trade-related intellectual property rights and patents must be considered here. One challenge is to encourage such manufacture while providing incentives for major pharmaceutical companies to develop newer medicines, as patients develop resistance to the current stock.[28]

The international community was slow to respond to the growing crisis during the 1990s, but that has begun to change. In 1996, only about US$300 million was available to fight the disease globally. By 2003, an estimated US$4.7 billion was available, a figure that includes not just donor funds but the steadily

[26]Steven Russell, "The Economic Burden of Illness for Households: A Review of Cost of Illness and Coping Strategy Studies Focusing on Malaria, Tuberculosis and HIV/AIDS." Disease Control Priorities Project (DCPP) Working Paper 15, August 2003, available at www.fic.nih.gov/dcpp/. Funeral costs have become a significant expense to both households and firms. They have become so common that firms are beginning to limit the number of days that employees can take for funeral leave each month. This is an issue, in part, because family members often are buried in their traditional villages, requiring days of travel for mourners.

[27]World Health Organization, *World Health Report 2004: Changing History* (Geneva: World Health Organization, 2004).

[28]Diane V. Havlir and Scott M. Hammer, "Patents versus Patients? Antiretroviral Therapy in India," *New England Journal of Medicine* 353, no. 8 (August 25, 2005), 749–51.

increasing funding that comes from country governments and "out-of-pocket" spending by directly affected individuals and families. Yet this amount is less than half what UNAIDS has estimated was required in 2005 and only a quarter of what will be required by 2007. Finding the needed funds will be a huge challenge, and even when they are found, they will have significant opportunity costs as funding is diverted from other key challenges to fight HIV/AIDS.

Malaria[29]

Malaria is estimated to claim the lives of 2,000 children every day and is a major contributor to illness in the developing world. WHO estimates that approximately 40 percent of the world's population is at risk of malaria in over 107 countries, primarily poor countries located in the tropics. Malaria contributes to over 1.25 million deaths and 500 million cases of severe illness each year. Africa, again, bears the heaviest burden, with about 60 percent of the cases of clinical malaria and 80 percent of the world's malaria deaths. Almost one fifth of the deaths in children under five in Africa are from malaria. Malaria also continues to be a problem in Southeast Asia, India, South America and some parts of Oceania.

Most diseases in developing countries have a disproportionate impact on the poor, but this is especially the case with malaria. Poor families are more likely to live in slum areas or in the countryside where malaria is common, less likely to be able to afford simple prevention steps (like purchasing insecticide-treated bed nets), and less likely to receive treatment once fever strikes. About 58 percent of malaria deaths occur in the poorest 20 percent of the world's population, a higher percentage than for any other disease of major public health importance. Figure 9–5 shows that, in ten districts in Zambia, 75 percent of children from the poorest quintile had malaria, whereas only one third of children from the richest quintile were infected.

Many countries have begun to make progress in reducing malaria. Prevention strategies include the use of insecticide-treated bed nets for those at highest risk of malaria, intermittent preventive drug treatment of pregnant women, and spraying with insecticides and other forms of vector control. For those who become sick with malaria, the disease can be controlled with early treatment. As of yet, there is no vaccine against the disease, although research is underway to find one. Unfortunately, since this is a disease of the poor, commercial opportunities are limited for selling a vaccine and recouping expensive research and

[29]This section draws in information from UNICEF and WHO, *2005 World Malaria Report*; the Global Fund, *2004 Disease Report*; and Tina Rosenberg, "What the World Needs Now Is DDT," *New York Times* (April 11, 2004).

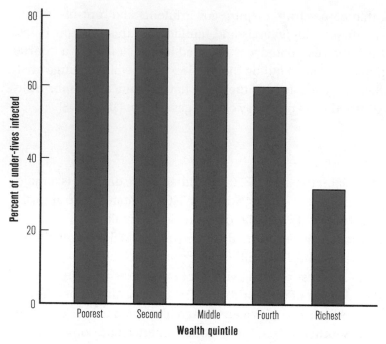

FIGURE 9-5. **Parasite Prevalence Is Higher in Poor Children**
The prevalence of malaria infection was higher in under-fives from
poorer families in ten districts surveyed in Zambia.
Source: WHO, *Africa Malaria Report 2003,* Fig. 1.6.

development costs, and research on this vaccine has been underfunded. Box
9–5 describes one innovative idea aimed at overcoming this market failure.

Malaria can have substantial economic costs on top of its public health
impact. Research by economists John Gallup and Jeffrey Sachs concluded that
the presence of a high malaria burden reduces economic growth by 1.3 percent
per year.[30] Although that figure probably incorporates the impact of other diseases that occur in tandem with malaria (such as HIV/AIDS), there is little doubt
that malaria creates a heavy burden in countries with high prevalence rates.
Malaria programs can be very cost effective. One study, based on data from sub-
Saharan Africa, estimated that the net benefits of a complete package of malaria
interventions were about 18 times higher than the costs.[31]

But even cost-effective programs can prove controversial. The insecticide of
choice for combating malaria is DDT (dichloro-diphenyl-trichloroethane) but
donors rarely pay for its use. The irony is that DDT was once used extensively

[30]John Gallup and Jeffrey Sachs, "The Economic Burden of Malaria," *American Journal of Tropical
Medicine and Hygiene Special Supplement* (June 2001).
  [31]Global Fund, *2001 Disease Report,* p. 37.

BOX 9-5 MAKING MARKETS FOR VACCINES

Vaccines save 3 million lives a year, prevent long-term disability and illness in millions more, and are one of the most cost-effective ways of enhancing health and reducing poverty in developing countries. Yet, there are no vaccines for some of today's biggest killers, such as malaria, HIV, and tuberculosis; and new vaccines developed for hepatitis B, pneumococus, rotavirus, and cervical cancer, which kill millions of people are year, are not affordable in developing countries. If vaccines are so cost effective and save so many lives, why are vaccines not being developed and used for these killer diseases?

In some cases, the science is highly uncertain, such as for HIV. But in other cases, private firms that conduct much of the research and development (R&D) for vaccines have no financial incentive to do so for diseases that affect mainly poor countries. The costs of developing these vaccines are high and incomes in many poor countries too low to afford them. Once vaccines are developed, governments often use their buying power to try to push down the price, further reducing the incentives for firms to invest in R&D and productive capacity. Private markets fail to develop vaccines because a price that is low enough for developing countries to afford is too low to create incentives for private companies to invest in developing new vaccines or production facilities for existing vaccines.

Many of the most widely used vaccines are aimed at diseases that affect children in both rich and poor countries, such as diphtheria, tetanus, pertussis, and polio. Since these vaccines are used around the world, the market is large enough to cover a pharmaceutical company's costs for both R&D and production. In some cases, vaccines could be sold at a higher price in richer countries, to recover R&D costs, and a lower price in poorer countries. But some of the highest-priority diseases for developing countries lack the high priority for rich countries. AIDS, diarrheal diseases, malaria, and other diseases, which are some of the biggest killers in developing countries, are not nearly as high on the list for rich countries, so the total potential market for vaccines for these diseases is much more limited. The pharmaceutical industry tends to respond to where the financial pay-off is the greatest, serving the health needs of the richer countries while neglecting diseases concentrated in low-income countries.

The costs of development and the risks of failure for vaccines are high. Vaccine development can take 7 to 20 years for basic research, clinical testing, regulatory approval, production, and distribution; and even the most promising vaccine candidates can fail at any stage. Estimates of the total costs of developing a new vaccine vary but range from several hundred million dollars to $1.5 billion. It is not realistic to hope that private companies will spend the money necessary to develop urgently needed vaccines then just give them away or sell them at a low price to poor countries.

One new idea to overcome this market failure is for donors to provide an advance market commitment (AMC) to provide private firms the financial returns they need to develop new vaccines while keeping the cost low for consumers in low-income countries. Sponsors and donors, such as governments, international agencies, or foundations, make binding commitments to pay for a desired vaccine if and when it is developed. Developing countries would decide whether to buy a vaccine at a low and affordable price, and sponsors would commit to provide the balance up to a guaranteed price, thus providing market returns for the vaccine developer that are comparable to other products. Once a specified number of vaccines was purchased at the guaranteed price (enough to cover R&D costs), the supplier would be committed to selling further treatments at a lower, affordable price without the sponsor's top-up. This step would ensure that developing countries could afford to continue purchasing the vaccine once payments under the commitment had been made.

A commitment creating a market comparable to the sales revenue of an average new medicine would cost about $3 billion. As an example, sponsors could make a legally binding commitment to purchase 200 million treatments of a malaria vaccine for $15 each. Poorer nations would decide to buy the vaccine at a low price (say, $1 per treatment) and the sponsors would provide the additional $14. After the first 200 million treatments, the company would be committed to sell additional treatments at $1, enough to cover ongoing production costs. These purchases, along with sales to the military, travelers, and some middle-income countries that can afford a higher price, would create the $3 billion market.

This approach complements rather than substitutes for other approaches for developing vaccines, such as support for public research facilities and universities. R&D in public health often involves government-funded research into the "public good" of knowledge about diseases, which can then be appropriated by the private sector for commercial development. AMC provides clear incentives for private firms to invest in the development of critical vaccines. It also respects intellectual property rights for vaccines and removes pressures on firms to sell new products at a loss. For donors, there would be no cost unless a vaccine is actually developed, minimizing their risks. AMC would use public funds to make markets work more effectively to solve some of the developing countries' most pressing health problems.

Source: The idea for the AMC was developed by a working group hosted by the Center for Global Development and is based on an earlier idea by Harvard University economist Michael Kremer. See Owen Barder, Michael Kremer, and Ruth Levine, *Making Markets for Vaccines: Ideas to Action* (Washington, DC: Center for Global Development, 2005). Much of the text in this box is drawn from this report. Also see Michael Kremer and Rachel Glennerster, *Strong Medicine: Creating Incentives for Pharmaceutical Research on Neglected Diseases* (Princeton, NJ: Princeton University Press, 2004).

and successfully in the United States, Southern Europe, and many developing countries as a means of malaria control and eradication. But overuse of DDT in the United States, especially to control agricultural pests, was linked to environmental damage affecting wildlife. Author and social activist Rachel Carson brought attention to the problem in her seminal book, *Silent Spring,* published in 1962. (The title refers to the impact of DDT on bird populations.) DDT use eventually was banned in the United States and other countries, but remains a highly effective and inexpensive (its patent expired long ago) means of eradicating the mosquito that transmits malaria. When sprayed on the interior walls of dwellings (the preferred mode for preventing the spread of malaria), DDT has minimal environmental consequences and has not been found harmful to humans. But given its pariah status in the West and the fear of maintaining a "double standard" (selling an insecticide to poor countries that is banned in rich ones), DDT has not played a significant role in saving lives in Africa and other malaria-endemic regions for many years.

The level of international attention to and spending on malaria control in poor regions has been dismal. In the early 2000s, spending was less than US$100 million per year, while the actual needs were more than an order of magnitude greater. Estimates by the WHO find that effective malaria prevention will require US$2.5 billion as of 2007 and US$4 billion per year as of 2015.[32]

Tuberculosis

Until 20 years ago, tuberculosis (TB) was uncommon in the industrialized world and many assumed that the disease had been largely conquered. But, in recent years, TB reemerged as a virulent killer. More than 2 billion people, one third of the world's population, are infected with the TB bacterium. Most people who are infected carry the bacterium in their body without symptoms, but each year 8 million people develop "active" TB and exhibit fever and other symptoms. TB causes or contributes to 2 million deaths each year, with 90 percent of the deaths occurring in developing countries. About half of those that die also are infected with HIV, which weakens the immune system and makes people more vulnerable to developing active TB.

As with other diseases, the poor are particularly vulnerable to TB. Studies in India have shown that the prevalence of TB is two to four times higher among groups with low income and no schooling. The poor are more likely to live in overcrowded conditions where the airborne bacterium can spread easily. Poor nutrition and inadequate sanitation also add to the risk. And as with other diseases, once the poor are infected, they are less likely to be diagnosed and

[32]Jefferey Sachs and Pia Malaney, "The Economical and Social Burden of Malaria," *Nature* 415, no. 7 (February 2002), 680–85.

treated. The economic costs of TB can be significant, stemming from lost work for the patient and caregivers, extra nutritional needs, treatment costs, transportation to and from clinics, and withdrawal of children from schools. In the developing world, an adult with TB can lose an average of three to four months of work.[33] Every year in India alone, more than 300,000 children leave school because of their *parent's* TB. By some estimates, TB depletes the incomes of the world's poorest communities by up to $12 billion every year, and lost productivity can cost an economy on the order of 4–7 percent of GDP.[34]

The internationally recommended strategy to control TB is DOTS, or directly observed treatment, short course, which combines a regular TB drug dosage with clinical observation visits. Full treatment takes many months, but unfortunately some patients stop taking their medicines during that period because they start to feel better or the drug supply is unreliable. This may lead to the emergence of drug-resistant TB. A particularly dangerous form of drug-resistant TB is multidrug-resistant TB (MDR-TB). Rates of MDR-TB are high in some countries, including Russia, and threaten TB-control efforts. From a public health perspective, poorly supervised or incomplete treatment of TB is worse than no treatment at all. When people fail to complete the treatment regime, they may remain infectious and develop a resistance to treatment. People they infect have the same drug-resistant strain. While drug-resistant TB generally is treatable, it requires extensive chemotherapy (up to two years of treatment) that is often prohibitively expensive (often more than 100 times more expensive than treatment of drug-susceptible TB) and more toxic to patients. Direct observation of treatment helps TB patients to adhere to treatment. According to WHO, the DOTS strategy produces cure rates of up to 95 percent, even in the poorest countries. A six-month supply of drugs for treatment under the DOTS strategy costs as little as $10 per patient. The World Bank has identified the DOTS strategy as one of the most cost effective of all health interventions.[35]

For DOTS to be effective, there must be access to TB sputum microscopy for TB detection; standardized short-course treatment of six–eight months, including direct observation of treatment; an uninterrupted supply of high-quality drugs; a reporting system to monitor patient outcome and program performance; and a political commitment to sustained TB control. Since its inception, more than 17 million TB patients have been treated under DOTS and 182 countries have adopted the DOTS strategy. However, a quarter of the world's population still has no access to DOTS services.

---

[33]World Health Organization, *Treatment of Tuberculosis: Guidelines for National Programmes,* 3rd ed. (Geneva: World Health Organization, 2003).

[34]Global Fund, *2004 Disease Report,* p. 26.

[35]World Health Organization, Tuberculosis: Fact Sheet No. 104 (Geneva: World Health Organization, 2005).

WHAT WORKS? SOME SUCCESSES IN GLOBAL HEALTH

Despite many challenges to health in the developing world, there are also many successes. The examples that follow recount specific actions by the health sector that saved millions of lives and improved millions more. These cases are excerpted from *Millions Saved: Proven Successes in Global Health*, by Ruth Levine and the What Works Working Group.[36] (The What Works Working Group is a group of 15 development specialists convened by the Center for Global Development.) *Millions Saved* describes 17 successful public health interventions in the developing world, all of which were substantial in nature. They comprise programs that were implemented on a national, regional, or global scale; addressed problems of substantial public health significance; demonstrated a clear and measurable impact on a population's health; lasted at least five consecutive years; and were cost effective.

The cases presented in *Millions Saved* demonstrate what the health sector can do, even in the poorest countries. Innovative interventions that involve the community can reach the most remote regions. These cases also demonstrate that governments in poor countries can get the job done including being the chief sources of funds for the interventions. In almost all the cases, the public sector, so often maligned for its corruption and inefficiency, was responsible for delivering care to the affected populations. The interventions included technological developments as well as basic changes in behavior that had a great impact on health. In the control of guinea worm in Africa, for example, families learned to filter their water conscientiously; and in the fight against deaths from dehydration due to diarrheal disease in Bangladesh, mothers learned how to mix a simple salt and sugar solution and taught the technique to their daughters. Interventions can also benefit from international coalitions or partnerships. Such cooperative ventures can break through bureaucracies, provide funding, bring technical capabilities, and generate the political will to sustain an effort in the face of competing priorities. It is also possible to determine whether improvements in health outcomes are due to specific interventions; in most cases, because special efforts were made to collect data that look at outcomes. Finally, these cases illustrate that success comes in all shapes: disease-specific programs, initiatives that improve access and quality, traditional public health interventions, and legal and regulatory reforms all can work, individually or in combination.

[36]Ruth Levine and the What Works Working Group with Molly Kinder, *Millions Saved: Proven Successes in Global Health* (Washington, DC: Center for Global Development, 2004). We summarize 5 of the 17 cases presented. Interested students should consult *Millions Saved* for more complete coverage of these five cases and to learn about the other cases not included here.

Preventing HIV/AIDS in Thailand

Well-documented stories of large-scale success in HIV prevention are few, although many small programs have been shown to be effective. But in Thailand, a large-scale program was successful in changing behaviors associated with increased risk of HIV among sex workers and those who use their services. Thai authorities initially recognized the severity of the situation in 1988, when the first wave of HIV infections spread among injecting-drug users. Between 1989 and 1990, they found that brothel-based sex workers infected with HIV tripled from 3.1 percent to 9.3 percent, and a year later it reached 15 percent. Over the same period, the proportion of male conscripts who were HIV positive when tested on entry to the army rose from 0.5 percent to 3 percent, a sixfold increase in only two years.

While prostitution is illegal in Thailand, and there was fear that the government's intervention could imply that it tolerated or even condoned it, officials agreed that the higher priority was preventing HIV from spreading further. To do this the government launched the "100 percent condom program," in which all sex workers in brothels were required to use condoms with clients. There was one straightforward rule: no condom, no sex. By creating a "monopoly environment," clients, most of whom preferred unprotected sex, could not go elsewhere to find it. Health officials provided free boxes of condoms and local police held meetings with brothel owners and sex workers. Men seeking treatment for sexually transmitted diseases were asked to name the brothel they had used, and health officials would then visit the establishment to provide more information. In principle, the police could shut down any brothel that failed to adopt the policy. Such sanctions were used a few times early on but authorities generally preferred to work with the brothels rather than alienate them.

The campaign was successful: Nationwide condom use in brothels increased from 14 percent in 1989 to more than 90 percent in 1992. The number of new cases of sexually transmitted infections fell from 200,000 in 1989 to 15,000 in 2001; the rate of new HIV infections fell fivefold between 1991 and 1993–95. The program may have prevented 200,000 HIV infections during the 1990s.

Thailand's remarkable success in slowing its HIV/AIDS epidemic to date will continue to require vigorous support. While the program was successful among sex workers, the program did little to encourage men and women, especially among teens and young adults, to use condoms in casual but noncommercial sex. This suggests that a substantial risk remains that HIV will spread through unprotected sex in Thailand. In addition, HIV continues to spread among injecting-drug users, where the rate is now as high as 50 percent. The cost of treating AIDS with antiretroviral drugs, as well as the cost of treating opportunistic infections, is a major challenge facing the Thai government and its citizens. The expense of the governments ARV program, in part, is responsible for a two thirds decline between 1997 and 2004 in the budget for HIV prevention.

Controlling Tuberculosis in China

Tuberculosis is the leading cause of death from infectious disease among adults in China. In 1990, 360,000 people in China died from the disease. In 1991, China revitalized its TB program and launched the ten year Infectious and Endemic Disease Control Project to curb its TB epidemic in 13 of its 31 mainland provinces. The program adopted the DOTS strategy. Trained health workers watched patients at local TB dispensaries every other day for six months as they swallowed their antibiotic treatment. Information on each treatment was sent to the county TB dispensary, and treatment outcomes were sent quarterly to the National Tuberculosis Project Office.

China achieved a 95 percent cure rate for new cases within two years of adopting DOTS, and a cure rate of 90 percent for those who had previously undergone unsuccessful treatment. The number of people with TB declined by over 37 percent between 1990 and 2000, and an estimated 30,000 TB deaths were prevented each year. The program cost $130 million in total. The World Bank and WHO estimate that successful treatment was achieved at less than $100 per person. One life year was saved for an estimated $15 to $20.

Despite China's success in curing TB, the program achieved lower-than-hoped-for rates of case detection. China is not alone in this shortcoming and had an experience similar to other high-burden countries. One of the main contributing factors to the low case detection rate was inadequate referral of suspected TB cases from hospitals to the TB dispensaries. Because hospitals can charge for TB diagnosis and treatment, they have little economic incentive to direct patients to the dispensaries. As a result, despite regulations requiring referrals to dispensaries, most TB patients are diagnosed in hospitals where treatment is often abandoned prematurely.

TB remains a deadly threat in China. More than 400 million people are infected and 10 percent of these will develop active TB. The government of China faces the challenge of maintaining high cure rates in the provinces covered by the project while scaling up the DOTS program to the remaining half of the population. Expertise is being marshaled to identify new ways for hospitals to work with TB dispensaries to increase case detection rates. With international financial commitment and technical cooperation, China hopes to achieve its goal and significantly reduce the health burden due to TB.

Eradicating Smallpox

Smallpox, which had affected 10–15 million people globally in 1966 and resulted in 1.5 to 2 million deaths, has been completely eradicated. The last recorded case of smallpox occurred in Somalia in 1977. Its eradication has been heralded as one of the greatest achievements of public health in world history. In addition to the direct impact on smallpox, the campaign brought important benefits to other health issues, such as improvements in routine immunization. During the smallpox eradication campaign it was discovered that more than one vaccine could be given at a time, an idea now taken for granted. In 1970, an Expanded Program on Immunization was proposed that sought to add several vaccines to routine smallpox inoculation. By 1990, 80 percent of the children throughout the developing world were receiving vaccines against six childhood killers, compared to only 5 percent when the program started.

The cost of smallpox eradication can be compared to its benefits, captured by the costs of the disease that have been averted. In developing countries, the costs averted include expenditures for caring for patients as well as to lost economic productivity due to illness. In 1976, it was estimated that the cost of caring for someone with smallpox in India was about $3 per patient, which translated to an annual cost of $12 million due to the widespread nature of the disease. Although $3 per patient may seem small, bear in mind that, in many developing countries, public health spending in total is typically only $7–8 per person. In addition to the costs of care, by one estimate, India lost about $700 million each year due to diminished economic performance. Assuming 1.5 million deaths due to smallpox worldwide in 1967, smallpox cost developing countries at least $1 billion each year at the start of the eradication campaign.

In the industrialized countries, eradication allowed governments to save the cost of vaccination programs that had been in place to prevent the reintroduction of the disease. In the United States, the bill for 5.6 million primary vaccinations and 8.6 million revaccinations in 1968 alone was $92.8 million, about $6.50 a vaccination. With other indirect costs of the vaccination program, expenditures in all developed countries were around $350 million per year. Therefore, combining developing and industrialized countries, the estimated global costs, both direct and indirect, of smallpox in the late 1960s was more than $1.35 billion per year. This figure represents the benefits of eradication.

The ultimate expenditures of the intensified eradication program were around $23 million per year over 1967 to 1979, including $98 million from international contributions and $200 million from the endemic countries. Thus, the benefits of eradication far outweighed the costs. It has since been calculated that the largest donor, the United States, saves the total of all its contributions every 26 days, making smallpox prevention through vaccination one of the most cost-beneficial health interventions of our time.

Eliminating Polio in Latin America

The world's largest public health campaign, the Global Polio Eradication Initiative, follows in the footsteps of smallpox eradication. The initiative is within reach of its goal. In 1988, 125 countries were endemic for polio with an estimated 350,000 cases. By 2006, the number of cases had dropped to below 1,400 and only six countries and territories remained polio endemic: Afghanistan, Egypt, India, Niger, Nigeria, and the Palestinian Territories. However, poliovirus continues to spread to previously polio-free regions. Ten previously polio-free countries were reinfected in late 2004 and 2005. Worldwide success is due to the coordinated efforts of regional and international polio eradication campaigns that have immunized hundreds of millions of children. The regional polio campaign in the Americas eliminated polio in just six years.

Polio, short for poliomyelitis, is caused by the intestinal poliovirus. Its most feared effect, paralysis, develops in less than 1 percent of all victims, when the virus affects the central nervous system. The most serious form of the disease causes paralysis that leaves a person unable to swallow or breath. Respiratory support is needed to keep patients alive and mortality runs as high as 40 percent.

In the 1930s and 1940, following a series of polio outbreaks, the American public called for a vaccine. The mobilization effort was led by the disease's most famous victim, U.S. President Franklin D. Roosevelt. In 1938, President Roosevelt created the National Foundation for Infantile Paralysis, later renamed the March of Dimes, to raise funds "a dime at a time" to support the quest for a vaccine. In 1952, the campaign paid off with Dr. Jonas Salk's discovery of an inactivated polio vaccine, IPV. Between 1955 and 1961, more than 300 million doses were administered in the United States resulting in a 90 percent drop in the incidence of polio. In 1961, a second scientific breakthrough resulted in a new form of the vaccine. Dr. Albert Sabin's oral polio vaccine, OPV, had several advantages over the previous vaccine. The vaccine prevented paralysis, as did the IPV, but OPV went further by helping to halt person-to-person transmission. At approximately $0.05 per dose, OPV is cheaper than its predecessor, and since it is an oral vaccine that requires no needles, it is easier to administer on a wide scale by volunteers.

Successful vaccination programs in Latin America eventually led the Pan American Health Organization in 1985 to launch a program to eradicate polio from the Americas. The immunization strategy of the campaign centered around three primary components: achieving and maintaining high immunization coverage, prompt identification of new cases, and aggressive control of outbreaks. In countries where polio was endemic, national vaccine days (NVDs) were held twice a year, one to two months apart, reaching nearly all children younger than five. The NVDs were designed to vaccinate as many children as possible. While aggressive vaccination strategies helped slow polio's transmission in most of the region, the disease still lingered.

Operation Mop Up was launched in 1989 to aggressively tackle the virus in its final bastions. The initiative targeted the communities where polio cases had been reported, where coverage was low, or where overcrowding, poor sanitation, weak health care infrastructure or heavy migration pervaded. In these communities, house-to-house vaccination campaigns were held to finally wipe out the disease. The last reported case was in Peru in 1991. Polio was declared eradicated from the Americas a few years later when no further cases emerged.

Administration of an oral polio vaccine proved both inexpensive and cost effective. The cost of immunizing a child with three doses of the polio vaccine (along with diphtheria, tetanus, and pertussis vaccine) is just $21. Even without taking into consideration such benefits as increased productivity, strengthened capacity to fight other diseases, and reduced pain and suffering, the polio eradication campaign was economically justified based on the savings of medical costs for treatment and rehabilitation alone. The first five years of the polio campaign cost $120 million: $74 from national sources and $46 million from international donors. Taking into consideration the saving from treatment, donor contributions paid for themselves in 15 years. Today, war and politics, not money, are the primary barriers to the total eradication of this disease.

Preventing Deaths from Diarrheal Disease

Diarrheal disease is one of the leading causes of death among children, causing nearly 20 percent of all child deaths. Worldwide, dehydration from diarrhea kills between 1.4 and 2.5 million babies each year, mostly in developing countries where children suffer an average of three episodes a year. Nearly 20 out of 1,000 children die of diarrheal disease before the age of two. This is a great public health failure because such deaths easily can be prevented at very low cost. Nevertheless, there has been some progress. Many countries, including Egypt, as documented later, have succeeded in disseminating knowledge about a life-saving treatment that resulted in dramatic declines in mortality associated with diarrhea and a large improvement in infant and child survival.

Diarrhea is an intestinal disorder characterized by abnormally frequent and watery stools. It is caused by a number of agents, including bacteria, protozoa, and viruses. Unclean water, dirty hands during eating, and spoiled food are the primary sources of transmission. The most-effective modes of prevention include improved water supply and sanitation, improved hygiene, and immunization against measles (which can cause diarrhea). Dehydration is the most serious effect of diarrhea. When fluid loss reaches 10 percent of body weight, dehydration becomes fatal. In cases that are not fatal, dehydration can leave a child susceptible to future infections.

Avoiding death from dehydration requires the swift restoration of lost fluids and electrolytes. Until the development of oral rehydration therapy in the 1960s, the only effective treatment was through intravenous (IV) infusions in a hospital or clinic. IV therapy is not a treatment of choice in the developing world because of its high cost, the hardship of traveling to clinics, and shortage of both trained personnel and supplies. Many people turn to drugs, including antibiotics, which can stop diarrhea. However, the majority of these drugs have no proven health benefit and some can cause dangerous side effects.

Oral rehydration therapy has been called the most-important medical discovery of the twentieth century. Developed in the 1960s in Bangladesh and India, it consists of a simple solution of water, salt, and sugar that is as effective in halting dehydration as intravenous therapy. It is immensely cheaper, at just a few cents per dose, safer and easier to administer, and more practical for mass treatment. The effectiveness of ORT therapy was proven during cholera outbreaks in refugee camps on the border of India and Bangladesh in the 1970s. In 1971, the war for independence in what is now Bangladesh created 10 million refugees. The unsanitary conditions in overcrowded refugee camps resulted in outbreaks of cholera with fatality rates approaching 30 percent. Resources were not available for mass treatment with IV fluids. Oral treatment was proposed as an alternative. The results were extraordinary. Cholera fatalities in the camp using ORT dropped to less than 4 percent, compared to 20–30 percent in camps treated with intravenous therapy.

Egypt was one of the early pioneers of national-level administration of oral rehydration therapy. In 1977, diarrhea caused at least half the infant deaths in Egypt, a country that experienced a relatively high infant mortality rate of 100 per 1,000 live births. Therefore, 1 in 20 children died of diarrhea before his or her first birthday. That year packets of oral rehydration salts were introduced at public clinics and for sale at pharmacies, but few mothers were aware of the treatment and even fewer used it. In 1982, only 10–20 percent of diarrhea cases used the packets of oral rehydration salts. Physicians also did not recommend them.

In 1980, the government launched the Strengthening of Rural Health Delivery Project to test how mothers and physicians could be persuaded to use ORT. Initially, in 29 rural villages, nurses taught mothers in their homes how to use ORT and physicians were educated about the therapy. ORT use rose dramatically, and as a result, child mortality was 38 percent lower than in control villages and diarrhea-associated mortality during the peak season was 45 percent lower. Based on the success of these community trials, in 1981 Egypt began a massive program to promote ORT use among the country's 41 million residents. Financial and technical support came from the U.S. Agency for International Development (USAID) and the public health organization John Snow, Inc. The program involved the entire Ministry of Health, other branches of government, WHO, and UNICEF. The program worked through the existing health infrastructure in order to strengthen the capacity of the health services to deliver care.[37]

[37]M. el-Rafie et al., "The Effect of Diarrheal Disease Control on Infant and Childhood Mortality in Egypt: Report from the National Control of Diarrheal Diseases Project," *The Lancet* 335, no. 8690 (March 17, 1990).

The program used several innovative approaches to increase the use of ORT. Packets were redesigned in smaller quantities and the project logo became the most recognized product label in Egypt. Production and distribution channels were developed. Health workers, nurses, and physicians were trained. A mass media campaign was launched in 1984 that took advantage of the 90 percent of households that had televisions. The campaign was very successful. By 1986, nearly 99 percent of mothers were aware of ORT. Infant mortality dropped by 36 percent and child (under-five) mortality by 43 percent between 1982 and 1987. Mortality due to diarrhea dropped 82 percent among infants and 62 percent among children during this same period. The program achieved success with an extremely cost-effective intervention. The average cost per child treated with ORT was less than $6, and the cost per death averted was between $100 and $200.

ORT continues to be the most cost-effective means of treating dehydration and its use has been adapted to the unique challenges found in different countries. In Bangladesh, where 90 percent of the population of over 100 million lives in rural areas with poor transportation in a country ten times the size of Egypt, distribution of ORT packets was not feasible. In 1980, a program to promote ORT in rural Bangladesh began by training workers to go door to door and teach mothers about dehydration and ORT. Mothers were also taught how to make a homemade solution by mixing a three-finger pinch of salt, a fistful of sugar, and a liter of water. (Today, packaged oral rehydration salts are available in most of the country.) Between 1980 and 1990, 13 million mothers were taught to make oral rehydration mixtures. An evaluation of more than 7,000 households found that between 25 and 52 percent of cases of severe diarrhea used the mixture. Today, the usage rate of ORT in Bangladesh is 80 percent and part of Bangladeshi culture. An increase in the use of ORT across the globe has helped slash diarrhea mortality rates in children by at least half. ORT saves the lives of an estimated 1 million children each year.

Lessons Learned

There is no simple prescription for success that comes out of comparing the cases presented in *Millions Saved*. Nor can one easily place blame for the dismal failures that let HIV/AIDS ravage Southern Africa or prolonged malaria's devastating toll on so many. Poverty is one of the explanations for the failures but it is insufficient. Even poor nations have had success in combating diseases. The health sector is one with pervasive market failures: There are all the common problems of negative externalities, principal-agent problems, information failures, and public goods. An inability to resolve these issues reflects equally pervasive government failures at the local, national, and international levels.

Successful health initiatives are characterized by strong leadership. The former World Bank president, Robert McNamara, was personally committed to controlling river blindness in West Africa; the Thai government had charismatic leaders with the vision to launch a program to prevent the spread of HIV/AIDS; and Egyptian officials stood firmly behind plans to expand ORT from community trials to a national program. In contrast, South African president Nelson Mandela and Thabo Mbeki generally ignored HIV/AIDS as an issue until the disease had already turned into a pandemic and national tragedy. Malaria, after having been resolved in the developed nations, has been neglected elsewhere.

In addition to strong leadership and program champions, one needs a combination of a technological solution and an affordable delivery system. Affordability can require concessions made by patent holders, as is happening with generic ARVs mass produced by pharmaceutical companies in Brazil and India. Public-private partnerships also have worked, where drugs are provided at cost and distribution is handled by government authorities. Donors, whether public or private, can play important roles. The Global Fund to Fight AIDS, Tuberculosis, and Malaria; USAID; the World Bank; and others have provided critical finance as has the private Bill and Melinda Gates Foundation. Local commitment is equally essential. Delivering improved health requires the actions of millions of individuals, whether those trained as doctors, nurses, or engineers or relatively unskilled workers and volunteers who watch patients take their medications as part of DOTS programs or help administer oral vaccines in remote villages.

HEALTH CHALLENGES

The challenge for the twenty-first century is to continue the battle against communicable disease while developing strategies to combat emerging epidemics of noncommunicable conditions. The developing world continues to face the illnesses of poverty. Over 10 million children and half a million mothers die each year, even though most of these deaths can be avoided through cost-effective vaccine programs, rehydration therapy for diarrheal diseases, improved nutrition status, and better birthing practices. Many people believe that infectious diseases in low- and middle-income countries should be a high priority, because the technical means exist to control them and they disproportionately affect the young. The Millennium Development Goals (MDGs) placed maternal and child health as a high priority and an integral part of poverty reduction. Over the past decade, the MDGs have moved maternal and child health from a primarily technical concern to one that is increasingly seen as a "moral and political imperative."[38]

[38]*World Health Report 2005: Make Every Mother and Child Count* (Geneva: World Health Organization, 2005), p. 3.

The battle against infectious disease will be ongoing this century. New diseases will emerge and, in a more globalized world, move quickly across borders. Drug resistance will make disease eradication all that much harder, as the discovery of new drugs races against the ability of microbes to adapt and mutate into even-more-virulent strains. But infectious diseases are not the only challenge the low- and middle-income nations face. The *2002 World Health Report: Reducing Risks, Promoting Healthy Life* highlights other factors that have adverse effects on health. The report identifies ten major global risk factors in terms of the burden of disease. Listed in order of their expected health risks, they include underweight children; unsafe sex; high blood pressure; tobacco consumption; alcohol consumption; unsafe water, sanitation, and hygiene; iron deficiency; indoor smoke from solid fuels; high cholesterol; and obesity and physical inactivity. These ten risk factors already account for more than one third of deaths worldwide.

Underweight children are strongly related to poverty as are unsafe water, inadequate sanitation, and indoor air pollution. Unsafe sex is the main factor in the spread of HIV/AIDS, with a major impact in the poor countries of Africa and Asia. Some of these risk factors, such as high blood pressure and high cholesterol, tobacco and excessive alcohol consumption, obesity and physical inactivity, are more commonly associated with wealthy societies. However, with epidemiologic transitions, poor and middle-income countries increasingly face these risks as well. For improvements in health and life expectancy to continue, it will be necessary to address this *double burden* of disease in the decades ahead.

SUMMARY

- Life expectancy is among the most common measures for assessing health outcomes. In 2003, the high-income nations had life expectancy at birth of 78 years; in Latin America, 71 years; in South Asia, 63 years; and in sub-Saharan Africa, only 46 years. Most of the differences can be explained by the much higher rates of mortality during the first five years of life in poorer regions.
- Since the 1960s, the gap in life expectancy between nations, unlike the gap in per capita incomes, has fallen rapidly. Many low- and middle-income nations have made substantial and historically unprecedented progress in increasing life expectancy. This stands as one of the great successes of human development in the past half century. There are some exceptions, including many nations in sub-Saharan Africa,

Russia, and elsewhere in the former Soviet Union, where life expectancy has declined since 1990.

- In many developing nations, where life expectancy has risen and fertility fallen, the age structure of the population has changed and so has the pattern of disease. This has resulted in an epidemiologic transition. Heart disease, a noncommunicable disease, is now the leading cause of death worldwide. Diseases common in high-income nations, including heart disease and cancers, are becoming more prevalent in low- and middle-income nations. But infectious diseases, which take a relatively small toll in high-income nations, remain a major threat to children and adults in developing countries.

- Improving health requires economic growth and rising levels of per capita income. But significant improvements in health can occur even at low incomes. Preventative measures long practiced in developed countries are vital. They include access to clean water and proper sanitation, control of insects and other disease vectors, and widespread vaccination programs. In addition to these public health measures, education, especially of females, is correlated with better health outcomes.

- Health and income are elements of a virtuous circle, where increases in income lead to better health and better health leads to higher income. Better health helps children remain at school and makes workers more productive in their fields and at their jobs. Better health increases the opportunity nations and individuals face to save and invest in their futures. Higher incomes, in turn, permit governments and families to devote more resources, whether for water, sanitation, vaccines, drugs, or health workers, to improving health.

- Infectious disease continues to plague poor nations. HIV/AIDS, malaria, and tuberculosis are three of the best known. Together they kill 6 million people a year, accounting for about 10 percent of all deaths worldwide. Other infectious diseases kill millions more, especially children, and debilitate those who are sick but do not die. Many of these infectious diseases, including HIV/AIDS, malaria, and tuberculosis, are preventable and, with adequate resources and institutions, can be treated effectively. That this is not happening is both an economic failure and a human tragedy.

- The spread of HIV/AIDS, the failure to attack malaria, and the reemergence of TB, including new drug-resistant strains, provide evidence of what has gone wrong in addressing world health. But there are also abundant examples of health successes, ranging from the eradication of smallpox, to the near eradication of polio, to the diffusion of oral rehydration therapies as a means of saving children from diarrheal diseases.

- The challenge of the twenty-first century will be for low- and middle-income countries to win the battle against both old and new infectious diseases, while addressing the increasing prevalence of chronic non-communicable diseases long associated with higher incomes.

PART THREE

Saving, Investment, and Capital Flows

10

Saving and Resource Mobilization

An old saw claims that "It takes money to make money." Although not always absolutely true, this idea is at the heart of the relationships between saving, investment, and economic growth: Creating new income often requires putting aside some current income to buy machines, materials, or supplies. Purchasing farm tools, acquiring additional sewing machines, buying a new goat, expanding a factory, or building a new rural feeder road are all forms of investment that require financing that comes from saving. It is not true, as some people claim, that one already has to be rich to make new investments. But it is true that the resources needed to make new investments come from income: Someone has to be willing to sacrifice greater consumption from current income to provide the resources necessary for investment for future gain. The saving can come from a variety of sources, including the individual that makes the investment, a private loan or gift from family or friends, a bank loan drawing on its customer's savings, an equity investment from a foreign company, a small loan from a microfinance agency, a nation's tax revenue for public investments, or a grant from a foreign aid agency that uses its own country's saving.

The view that capital formation is the single most-important determinant of growth and development, called **capital fundamentalism,** was at the heart of development strategies in many countries in the 1950s and 1960s. At that time, the development problem was widely seen as one of simply securing investment resources sufficient to generate some chosen target rate of national income growth. Theories of economic growth reflected this idea. The Harrod-

Domar model gives near absolute prominence to capital accumulation. The Solow model features much more-realistic diminishing returns to capital and allows for technical change but still retains a central role for capital formation. As we have seen throughout this book, accumulation of physical capital no longer is viewed as a simple panacea for poor countries. Capital accumulation remains necessary for growth and development, but it is not sufficient. We now recognize the important roles played by investments in health and education, as well as the importance of institutional development, good governance, international trade, and macroeconomic stability, which encourage *productive* investments and an efficient use of a nation's savings. Establishing an environment for productive investment not only helps a country gets more "bang for the buck" from its saving but also helps encourage more overall saving. Only when societies are able to maintain saving and investment at a sizable proportion of GDP and ensure reasonably productive investment can they sustain even mildly robust growth rates over long periods of time.

Many of the most successful developing countries over the last several decades have saving rates of 30 percent or more. China, for example, saves over 40 percent of its income, providing a substantial base for new investment. How is it that some countries are able to achieve such high rates of saving, while others struggle to save much less? Once countries save, what determines how and where the funds are invested?

The next six chapters explore in some depth different forms of saving, the factors that influence saving and investment, capital flows across international borders, and the financial institutions that undergird saving and investment in developing countries. In this chapter, we focus on the key role of saving, its main sources, and its major determinants. Chapter 11 explores investment, emphasizing the importance of the productivity of investment as well as its size and distinguishing between public and private investment and between domestic and foreign investment. Chapter 12 investigates fiscal policy and the tools used by governments to collect revenues to finance public expenditures and generate public sector saving, which can be used to finance public investment. Chapter 13 focuses on financial markets and monetary policy, providing an overview of the key issues in strengthening private financial markets that help generate saving and channel it to productive investment. Chapter 14 is the first of two chapters exploring foreign sources of saving. It looks closely at foreign aid, which is an important (and sometimes controversial) source of financing for both investment and consumption in many of the poorest countries in the world. Chapter 15 concludes the section by examining foreign debt and other foreign financial flows, which can help propel economic growth but also can precipitate financial crises, like those that swept through many emerging market countries in the late 1990s and early 2000s.

This chapter begins by exploring the closely intertwined trends in saving and investment around the world in recent decades. We then focus more narrowly on saving, examining different types of saving from households, corporations, governments, and foreign entities. The chapter concludes by analyzing the key determinants of saving, and why individuals choose to save rather than consume.

SAVING AND INVESTMENT AROUND THE WORLD

Saving and investment rates vary widely around the world, even among countries at similar levels of development. Azerbaijan and Armenia both have per capita incomes of around $2,800 (PPP), but Azerbaijan saved 21 percent of its income between 1999 and 2003, while Armenia's saving rate was –1 percent, meaning it consumed more than it produced. Despite the differences across countries, several broad global trends are evident. First, investment rates generally have increased over the last several decades, often financed through foreign saving rather than domestic saving. Second, domestic saving rates have tended to decline slightly in many, but not all, countries. Third, saving rates tend to be lower for low-income countries and higher for middle-income and high-income countries, but there is wide variation, particularly among low-income countries. Fourth, there is a strong relationship between saving rates and economic growth, although the direction of causality is unclear.

Table 10–1 shows basic data on investment, domestic saving, and foreign saving for a group of 25 countries, representing a wide range in per capita income, natural resource endowments, and other key characteristics. It also shows the averages for groups of countries classified by the World Bank as low income, lower-middle income, upper-middle income, and high income. The average investment ratios for 60 low-income countries for which complete data are available increased substantially between the period 1965–69 and 1999–2003 from 15 to 21 percent. This change represents a substantial increase of about 40 percent in the share of GDP devoted to investment in the world's poorest countries during the last four decades. Although the investment rate rose for most low-income countries, it did not do so in all cases. In Kenya, investment fell from 19 percent to 14 percent of GDP between the two periods, and in Pakistan it fell slightly from 17 to 16 percent of GDP.

Investment ratios also rose for lower-middle-income countries, growing from 22 to 27 percent of GDP. China had the highest investment rate in this group of countries (and one of the highest in the world) at 39 percent of GDP. In contrast to the first two country groups, the average investment ratio for the upper-middle-income countries basically remained unchanged at 19 percent of GDP. For the high-income countries, investment ratios actually fell slightly, on average, from 23 to 21 percent. The United Kingdom, the United States, and many other industrialized countries saw their investment ratios decline. Japan's investment ratio

TABLE 10-1. **Gross Domestic Investment and Saving, 1965–2003**

COUNTRY OR CATEGORY	GROSS DOMESTIC INVESTMENT (% OF GDP)		GROSS DOMESTIC SAVING (% OF GDP)	
	1965–69*	1999–2003	1965–69*	1999–2003
Bangladesh	12	23	8	17
Cameroon	13	18	11	19
Ghana	13	23	9	7
India	16	23	14	22
Indonesia	9	15	5	24
Kenya	19	14	19	8
Mali	17	22	8	12
Nigeria	14	23	8	25
Pakistan	17	16	10	14
Senegal	8	19	5	10
60 low-income countries	15	21	13	20
Brazil	20	20	20	21
China	22	39	29	42
Colombia	20	14	19	14
Egypt, Arab Republic	15	18	12	12
Honduras	18	31	16	15
Peru	31	20	29	18
Philippines	21	20	19	19
49 lower-middle-income countries*	22	27	23	27
Argentina	22	15	23	20
Hungary	29	28	29	25
Malaysia	18	24	22	44
Mexico	20	22	18	20
29 upper-middle-income countries	19	19	24	23
Japan	35	25	36	27
Korea, Republic	24	29	13	31
United Kingdom	20	17	20	15
United States	20	19	20	16
36 high-income countries	23	21	25	21

*Gross domestic saving figures in China are for 1970 and 1998–2002.

Note: Country group data are simple (unweighted) averages for all countries with available data, including 60 low-income countries (with 2002 general national income, or GNI, per capita of $735 or less), 49 lower-middle-income countries (with GNI per capita between $735 and $2,935), 29 upper-middle-income countries (with GNI per capita between $2,936 and $9,075), and 36 high-income countries (with GNI per capita of $9,076 or more).

For the lower-middle income countries, the dates for the first period are 1970 through 1974.

Sources: *World Development Indicators 2005* and Penn World Tables 6.1.

TABLE 10-1. (Continued)

COUNTRY OR CATEGORY	FOREIGN SAVING (RESOURCE GAP) (% OF GDP)		AVERAGE ANNUAL GDP GROWTH PER CAPTIA (%)
	1965–69*	1999–2003	1965–2003
Bangladesh	3	5	1.0
Cameroon	1	−1	0.8
Ghana	4	16	−0.1
India	2	1	2.7
Indonesia	4	−8	4.0
Kenya	−1	6	1.2
Mali	9	10	0.8
Nigeria	5	−2	0.3
Pakistan	7	1	2.3
Senegal	3	9	0.0
60 low-income countries	2	2	1.6
Brazil	0	0	2.4
China	−7	−3	6.6
Colombia	1	0	1.8
Egypt, Arab Republic	3	6	2.7
Honduras	1	16	0.7
Peru	2	1	0.3
Philippines	1	1	1.2
49 lower-middle-income countries*	−1	−1	2.8
Argentina	−1	−5	0.5
Hungary	0	3	2.7
Malaysia	−5	−21	3.9
Mexico	2	2	1.7
29 upper-middle-income countries	−5	−4	1.6
Japan	−1	−2	3.4
Korea, Republic	11	−1	6.1
United Kingdom	0	2	2.1
United States	0	3	2.1
36 high-income countries	−2	0	2.5

fell precipitously, especially in the 1990s, as its economy became mired in a deep and prolonged recession, but it still remained relatively high at 25 percent.

How was this rise in investment in emerging economies financed? Table 10–1 shows two broad components of total saving: domestic saving and foreign saving. **Domestic saving** comes from individuals, households, the government, and corporations. **Foreign saving** consists of saving by foreign countries that is used to finance local investment. Borrowing from foreign banks, investment from multinational corporations and foreign aid are all examples of foreign saving. The amount of foreign saving sometimes is referred to as the **resource gap** (defined as investment minus domestic saving), with some analysts and policy makers speaking of the need to fill this gap with *foreign saving*. The language of a "gap" that needs to be "filled" comes from the image of a domestic entrepreneur or government agency with a good investment project searching for financing and finding it abroad. Sometimes, this characterization is accurate, such as if a private company is looking for financing for a factory expansion or the government is seeking foreign aid for a road project. But, sometimes, the language is misleading. For example, a foreign company might decide that it wants to build its next factory in this country, in which case the investment and the foreign saving come together in a package, and there is no "gap" that needs to be "filled." In other cases foreign financiers arrive with their funding in search of good investment opportunities, such as in the local stock market.

Domestic saving ratios followed a pattern broadly similar to investment, although there was much more variation across countries. Overall, domestic saving rates rose for the majority of developing countries. But these averages mask some major differences in the saving performances across different countries. For many counties, such as Bangladesh, Cameroon, China, India, Indonesia, and Malaysia, domestic saving rates rose significantly between the two periods. For others, such as Ghana, Kenya, Columbia, and Peru, domestic saving rates fell. Among countries in this table, domestic saving rates in 1998–2002 ranged from 7 percent in Ghana to an astonishing 42 percent in China.[1]

As with domestic saving, foreign saving varies widely across countries. On average, low-income countries have positive foreign saving, meaning they are investing more than they are saving domestically and drawing saving from the rest of the world. Many of the upper-middle-income and upper-income countries have small or even negative "resource gaps." A negative resource gap (or negative foreign saving) implies the country is a net lender to the rest of the world (that is, it saves more than it invests at home), and the saving is used to finance investments abroad. One reason for this pattern is that low-income countries receive more foreign aid than middle-income countries, which is a form of foreign saving.

---

[1]For an overview of saving trends, see Norman Loayza, Humberto Lopez, Klaus Schmidt-Hebbel, and Luis Serven, "Saving in the World: Stylized Facts," World Bank, November 1998, available at www.worldbank.org/research/projects/savings/savinwld.htm.

Low- and middle-income countries also tend to be net recipients of foreign direct investment and other private financial flows, which is another form of foreign saving. Rich countries tend to invest some of their savings in low- and middle-income countries in hopes of earning a higher rate of return than they can at home, as predicted by the Solow model. But there are exceptions to these patterns. Low-income China saves more than it invests, and sends some of the surplus to the United States to partly finance the latter's resource gap.

Saving rates generally tend to be higher in countries with higher income but not always, as shown in Figure 10–1. Middle-income countries typically have higher saving rates than low-income counties, but there is much less difference in saving rates between middle-income and high-income countries. Low-income countries tend to have both the lowest average saving rate and the widest variation in saving rates. Countries with average incomes below $5,000 (PPP) have saving rates ranging from –20 percent to 40 percent or more. There is much less variation in saving rates for middle- and high-income countries. In particular, there are far fewer countries with low or negative saving rates. All of the countries in the figure with average income higher than about $7,000 (about the income of Tunisia) have saving rates of at least 10 percent.

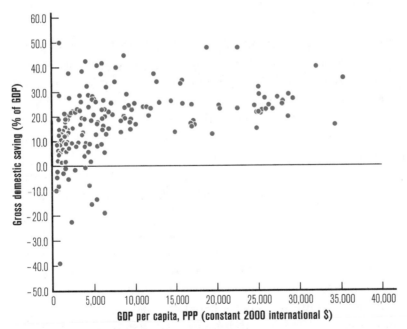

FIGURE 10-1. **Income and Saving, 1999–2003**
Saving rates tend to be lower, on average, for the poorest countries and higher for middle income and upper income countries. Some of the richest countries, however, have lower savings rates than some middle-income countries. There is substantial variation in saving rates across countries, especially among low-income countries.
Source: *World Development Indicators 2005.*

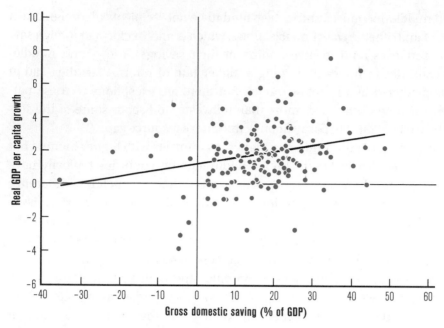

FIGURE 10-2. **Saving and Growth, 1994–2003**
Higher saving rates tend to be associated with faster economic growth, but the
direction of causality is unclear.

The standard view is that poor countries tend to save less than middle- and
high-income countries simply because they have less money available for saving after subsistence needs are met. But the relationship between income and
saving is far from absolute. China (42 percent), Malaysia (44 percent), and Korea
(31 percent) all had higher saving rates than the United Kingdom (15 percent)
and the United States (16 percent). The relatively low saving rates in some of the
richest countries may be partly due to the large numbers of retirees living in
these countries, which tends to dampen saving rates, since people in retirement
are drawing down their accumulated savings rather than generating new saving.
Some economists have hypothesized an "inverted U" relationship between
income and saving, in which saving is low or even negative in low-income countries, higher for middle-income countries, and then lower again for the richest
countries.[2] But there is no simple, single relationship between saving and
income across all countries.

Countries with higher domestic saving generally also have faster growth
rates, as shown in Figure 10–2. The idea that higher saving and investment supports faster economic growth is at the core of almost all growth models,

---

[2]See P. Masson, T. Bayoumi, and H. Samiei, "International Evidence on the Determinants of Pri-
vate Saving," *World Bank Economic Review* 12, no. 3 (December 1998), 483–501; and Masao Ogaki,
Jonathan Ostry, and Carmen Reinhart, "Saving Behavior in Low- and Middle-Income Developing
Countries: A Comparison," Working Paper WP/95/3, International Monetary Fund 1995.

although the emphasis on capital accumulation varies across these models. From an empirical standpoint, the strong relationship between saving, investment, and economic growth has been well established through sources of growth analysis and studies of total factor productivity growth, as described in Chapter 3. In industrial societies, the expansion of physical capital inputs typically accounts for about half the growth in aggregate income. The rapid growth of East Asia's "miracle economies" went hand in glove with high levels of saving and investment in both physical and human capital. However, the direction of causality between saving and growth is not clear. It seems to work at least partially in both directions, in which higher saving contributes to more rapid growth, and higher growth stimulates increased saving and investment. Moreover, simple sources of growth studies take us only so far. While pointing to the importance of capital accumulation, they tell us very little about why some societies have been more successful in generating high rates of saving and investment and why some economies have invested their resources more productively than others.

A SAVING TAXONOMY

All investment ultimately must be financed by saving by either domestic entities (e.g., firms, the government, households) or by foreigners. A private firm, for example, finances its investment either through contributions by equity holders (which ultimately come from these individuals' personal savings) or bank loans (which are other individuals' savings). Governments finance public investments through tax contributions, which at one level can be thought of as a form of forced saving. To the extent that an economy is open to trade and international financial transactions, it can finance some of its investment by drawing on saving from other countries. For example, a company in Venezuela might decide to borrow from a bank located in New York, in which case it is drawing on another country's saving, which we refer to as *foreign saving*.

In turn, domestic saving may be broken down into two components: private domestic saving (S_p) and government (or public sector) saving (S_g).[3] Private

---

[3]A further distinction can be made between domestic saving and national saving, which is roughly equivalent to the difference between gross domestic product (GDP) and gross national product (GNP). Domestic saving measures all saving that takes place within the borders of a country, whether by citizens or foreigners resident in the country (including foreign corporations). It does not include saving by citizens living abroad or the foreign operations of domestic firms operating abroad. National saving includes savings of all citizens of a country regardless of where they live. It does not include the saving of foreign residents or firms inside a country's borders. The distinction is important in some countries, such as the Philippines, where the remittances of citizens working overseas constitutes an important part of national saving. In this chapter, we use the two terms interchangeably.

domestic saving arises from two sources: corporate saving and household saving. **Corporate saving** is defined as the retained earnings of corporate enterprises (corporate income after taxes minus dividends paid to shareholders). **Household saving** is the part of household income not consumed. Household saving can come from wage income that is not spent on consumer goods, but it also includes saving from unincorporated enterprises (single proprietorships, partnerships, and other noncorporate forms of business enterprise). In most developing countries, unincorporated business enterprise (farms, market stalls, and other small businesses) is by far the dominant form of business organization. Household saving can be held in many forms, but poor households (especially in more remote rural areas) are unlikely to use formal saving institutions (like banks) and instead may use their saving to directly purchase investment goods such as jewelry or livestock. These purchases might lead to a positive rate of return later if they can be sold for more than they were purchased, but they also provide a way to save in a nonliquid form that is less tempting to spend quickly but can be accessed in emergencies.

Private saving typically accounts for three quarters or more of total saving in most developing countries and between 10 and 20 percent of income, as shown in Table 10–2. In a few countries, the private saving ratio is even higher. Between 1999 and 2003 private saving accounted for more than 20 percent of GDP in China, India, Malaysia, and South Korea, with China leading the way with an extraordinary rate of 47 percent. In a handful of countries, private saving is less than 10 percent of income, including Burundi, the Dominican Republic, Morocco, Senegal, and Sri Lanka.

Until fairly recently, economists, aid donors, and many policy makers in developing countries tended to view private domestic saving as of secondary importance relative to government saving and foreign aid as a source of investment finance. Partly, this was due to the belief that government and foreign saving could be influenced more easily by policy than private saving. However, in recent years, much more attention has been given to issues of mobilizing private saving and channeling it into productive investment.

Government saving consists primarily of budgetary saving that arises from any excess of government revenues over government consumption. Government consumption is defined as all *current* expenditure plus outlays for military hardware and includes expenditures for food subsidies, civil servant and police salaries, fuel, stationery, arms, maintenance of roads and bridges, and interest on the national debt. It does not include expenditures for building roads, bridges, schools, and other physical infrastructure, which are classified as investment (or capital) spending. Government saving, in turn, is used to finance public investment. Therefore, a country could have positive public saving even when the overall government budget is in deficit, when consumption plus investment spending is larger than total revenue. For example, if government

TABLE 10-2. Gross Domestic, Government, and Private Saving, 1975–2003
(percent of GDP)

COUNTRY	GROSS DOMESTIC SAVING		GOVERNMENT SAVING		PRIVATE SAVING	
	1975–79	1999–2003	1975–79	1999–2003	1975–79	1999–2003
Chile	17.4	24.1	15.8	9.6	1.6	14.6
China	32.2	42.2	N.A.	−5.0	N.A.	47.2
Columbia	20.6	14.3	3.1	−3.4	17.5	17.7
Dominican Republic	18.2	16.0	9.8	9.5	8.4	6.5
India	18.7	22.0	1.3	−0.9	17.4	23.0
Indonesia	28.5	22.7	8.7	11.8	19.8	11.0
Kuwait	59.0	24.7	27.4	9.5	31.6	15.2
Malaysia	29.8	44.3	6.4	10.4	23.4	33.9
Mexico	22.5	19.9	2.4	2.5	20.1	17.4
Morocco	12.2	19.1	4.2	9.8	8.0	9.3
Pakistan	7.4	14.5	3.1	3.3	4.4	11.2
Peru	18.0	18.3	2.2	5.5	15.8	12.7
Philippines	26.7	18.8	4.1	2.6	22.7	16.2
Senegal	5.8	9.5	3.1	4.0	2.7	5.5
South Africa	31.0	18.7	7.0	8.8	24.0	10.0
South Korea	26.4	32.8	5.8	9.3	20.6	23.5
Sri Lanka	13.8	16.6	11.1	7.6	2.8	9.0
United States	19.7	15.8	1.2	4.0	18.4	11.8

Note: N.A. means data are not available.
Sources: *World Development Indicators 2005*. Government saving data for China are calculated using revenue data from *China's Growth and Integration into the World Economy*, Occasional Paper 32 (Washington, DC: International Monetary Fund, 2004).

consumption expenditure equals 20 percent of GDP, public investment spending is 5 percent of GDP, and revenues are 22 percent of GDP, government saving is 2 percent of GDP even though the total budget deficit is 3 percent of GDP. In a very few countries, saving by government-owned enterprises (such as a state-owned oil company) also contributes to public-sector saving. More often, however, government-owned enterprises operate at a loss and detract from public saving by requiring government subsidies to remain in operation.

Foreign saving comes in two basic forms. **Official foreign saving,** some of which is referred to as *foreign aid* or *official development assistance,* consists of grants and loans from other governments or international government organizations such as the World Bank, the regional development banks (including the African, Asian, or Inter-American Development Banks), or the United Nations Development Program. We discuss foreign aid in detail in Chapter 14. **Private foreign saving** is made up of debt finance (or **external commercial borrowing**) and equity finance. Foreign equity finance usually is classified as either **direct foreign investment** (when foreigners take a direct ownership share in a domestic firm) or

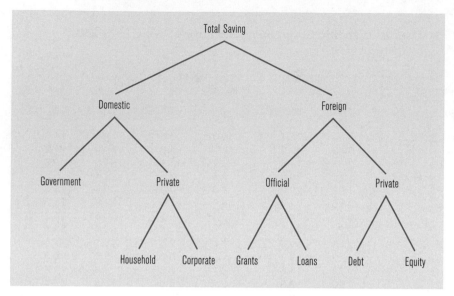

FIGURE 10-3. **Interrelationship of Key Components of Saving**

portfolio investment (when foreigners purchase equities through the domestic stock market).

The importance of different types of saving differs greatly among developing countries, depending on country characteristics such as the level of per capita income, natural resource endowments, and the composition of GDP (i.e., between agriculture and industry), and government policies. We summarize the various key components of saving and their interrelationships in Figure 10–3.

HOUSEHOLD SAVING AND CONSUMPTION

Individuals and households save for two main reasons. First, they want to generate higher future income by saving and investing some of their current income. Second, they want to save some current income to protect themselves from the risk of unexpected falls in income in the future, whether from a drought that undermines next year's food crop; the loss of productive assets from fire, flood, theft, or disease (e.g., that kills livestock); or other loss of income. This "precautionary" motive can be particularly important for poor people living on subsistence levels, where a sudden loss of income could be catastrophic, or where insurance markets are not well developed and individuals, families, and businesses must self-insure against the risks of a sudden loss of income or assets.

Given these motivations, a key decision is how much to save and how much to consume. The more a person saves, the more he or she can invest to increase future income and the more he or she can safeguard against future shocks. But saving comes at a cost: The only way to save is to reduce current consumption. Households will sacrifice current consumption to save only if they believe either that the ensuing investment will increase their income and consumption in the future or they will need to draw on that saving to finance basic consumption in the event of a severe income shock. A wide variety of factors might influence saving: the current level of income, anticipated future levels of income, the number of dependents that must be supported, the opportunities for productive investment, and the quality of the financial institutions through which some saving might be channeled.

Theories of household saving behavior initially were developed as part of the postwar Keynesian revolution in economics to explain saving patterns in industrial countries. Although the relevance of these theories to developing countries has been debated,[4] they nevertheless form the foundation of our basic understanding of saving and consumption behavior. We first examine household saving and then turn to corporate saving.

All theories of household saving behavior seek to explain three observed patterns: (1) within a particular country at a given time, higher-income households tend to save larger fractions of their income than lower-income households; (2) within a particular country over time, household saving ratios tend to be roughly constant, more so in industrial than developing countries; and (3) across countries, household saving ratios vary with no clear relationship to income. To help reconcile these "stylized facts," we consider four alternative explanations of household saving behavior: the Keynesian absolute-income model, the relative-income hypothesis, the Friedman permanent-income model, and the life-cycle hypothesis.

The Keynesian Absolute-Income Hypothesis

Economists once widely believed in the general applicability of a simple relationship between aggregate income, saving, and consumption. Household saving, and consumption were viewed as directly dependent on current **disposable income,** the amount of income available after payment of taxes.[5] The famed

---

[4]See especially Angus Deaton, "Saving in Developing Countries: Theory and Review," *Proceedings of the World Bank Annual Conference on Development Economics* (Washington, DC: World Bank, 1989).

[5]Tax payments vary widely from 10 to 40 percent of income, leaving disposable income of between 60 and 90 percent of GDP. By definition, all disposable income must be either consumed or saved, so consumption plus saving equals disposable income. More formally, from the standard national accounts identities, $Y = C + S + T$, where Y is total income, C is consumption, S is saving, and T is tax payments. Disposable income (Y_d) is defined as $Y_d = Y - T$. Thus, $Y_d = C + S$, meaning that all disposable income is either consumed or saved.

British economist John Maynard Keynes first propounded what came to be known as the **Keynesian absolute-income hypothesis** in the 1930s. The idea is straightforward: as aggregate disposable income rises, the national propensity to save increases, while the propensity to consume declines. To see Keynes's idea, it is easiest to start by examining the connection between aggregate *consumption* and disposable income, which he proposed to be as follows:

$$C = \bar{C} + (1 - s)Y_d \qquad\qquad [10\text{--}1]$$

where C = private consumption, Y_d = current disposable income, and s = the marginal propensity to save from disposable income $(0 < s < 1)$.[6] Since s is the marginal propensity to save, $1 - s$ is the marginal propensity to consume. Thus, if $s = 0.15$, then for each peso of additional disposable income, 15 percent is saved and 85 percent is consumed. $\bar{C}$ is a constant indicating a minimum level of consumption. Individuals will never allow consumption to fall below this level, regardless of how low income falls. The term $\bar{C}$ is sometimes called **autonomous consumption,** since it is independent of income. Even if disposable income falls to zero, aggregate consumption will not fall to zero but will be maintained at $\bar{C}$. In this case, consumption would be greater than income, which means that saving would be negative. That is, the country would have to borrow or receive grants to maintain the minimum level of aggregate consumption.

Alternatively, since consumption is equal to disposable income minus saving, equation 10–1 can be converted into an equivalent saving function as follows:[7]

$$S = -\bar{C} + sY_d \qquad\qquad [10\text{--}2]$$

where S = the value of private saving. The equation says that, for each additional peso of disposable income, a fixed share (s) will be saved. In this formulation, the constant $-\bar{C}$ is less than zero, which is just the flip side of the constant $\bar{C}$ in the consumption function. The negative sign means that saving could be negative in an amount up to the value of autonomous consumption. Thus as income falls and approaches zero, consumption never falls below $\bar{C}$ and saving becomes negative and approaches $-\bar{C}$. Negative saving rates are unusual but not unheard of, especially in low-income countries in the midst of civil conflict. Sierra Leone endured a brutal civil war during the 1990s, during which its income plummeted. But consumption did not fall quite as far, so the country recorded a saving rate of about –4 percent.

The consumption function is shown in Figure 10–4, which plots disposable income along the horizontal axis and consumption and saving on the vertical

---

[6]Note that, in this formulation, s is the share of household saving in *disposable* income, not *total* income.

[7]Since consumption plus saving equals disposable income, $C = Y_d - S$. Substituting this identity into equation 10–1 for the C term yields $Y_d - S = \bar{C} + (1 - s)Y_d$. Rearranging terms yields equation 10–2.

axis. The 45-degree line shows all points at which consumption would exactly equal disposable income. The vertical distance between the 45-degree line and the line representing the consumption function shows the amount of saving. The consumption function intercepts the vertical axis at point $\bar{C}$, depicting that this is the minimum level of consumption when disposable income is zero. For all points to the left of point A, the consumption line is above the 45-degree line, indicating that consumption exceeds income and saving is negative. To the right of point A income exceeds consumption and saving is positive.

It is important to stress the difference between the *marginal* saving rate and the *average* saving rate. Focusing on the saving function, whereas the marginal saving rate s is a constant, saving as a fraction of income will rise as income grows. For example, if disposable income Y_d is 1,000 pesos, $\bar{C}$ is 100 pesos, and s is 0.25, then total saving is 150 pesos. The average saving rate is 15 percent (150/1,000), while the marginal saving rate is 25 percent. If disposable income doubles to 2,000 pesos, the marginal propensity to save tells us that 25 percent of that additional income (250 pesos) is saved. Total saving now is 400 pesos, so that the average saving rate now is 20 percent. Correspondingly, consumption as a share of total income falls from 85 to 80 percent as disposable income rises from 1,000 pesos to 2,000 pesos.

Although the Keynesian formulation has some appeal because of its simplicity, the historical record in both developed and developing countries provides it with only very weak empirical support. At best, the Keynesian

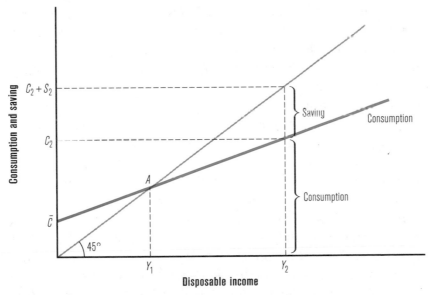

FIGURE 10-4. **The Keynesian Absolute Income Hypothesis**
For each additional peso of disposable income, a fixed share is consumed and a fixed share is saved. To the left of point A, consumption exceeds disposable income and saving is negative; to the right of point A, saving is positive.

hypothesis may depict saving behavior over the very short term, but it breaks down as a long-run proposition. Although average saving rates tend to rise as income grows, they do not do so with a fixed marginal propensity to save as assumed by this model.

The Relative-Income Hypothesis

An alternative view of the income-consumption relationship, the **relative-income hypothesis,** focuses on the longer term. It tries to take into account the idea that as income increases, saving rises less and consumption rises more than the Keynsian model suggests. In its simplest form, this hypothesis is based on the idea that consumption and saving depend not only on current income but also on *previous* levels of both income and consumption. One form of the relative-income hypothesis, called the **Duesenberry hypothesis** after economist James Duesenberry, can be expressed as follows:

$$C_1 = (\bar{C} + bC_h) + (1 - s)Y_{d1} \qquad [10\text{--}3]$$

where C_1 is consumption in period 1, C_h is the previous high level of consumption, and Y_{d1} is disposable income in period 1. The constant b is the share of the previous high level of consumption that is maintained regardless of the current level of income, with $0 < b < 1$.

The difference between equations 10–1 and 10–3 is the addition of bC_h to the constant term, which implies that consumption in the current period is partly dependent on the previous high level of consumption. The basic idea is that short-run consumption in an economy tends to ratchet upward over time as income grows. Each time individuals reach a new high level of consumption, they adjust upward their autonomous level of consumption for all subsequent periods. But, in the short run, they are reluctant to reduce consumption levels and slow to raise them in response to temporary changes in disposable income. In essence, when income changes, consumers are expected initially to adjust their saving up or down with little change in consumption, then adjust consumption more slowly over time.

The relationship between the Keynesian absolute-income hypothesis and the Duesenberry relative-income hypothesis is depicted in Figure 10–5. Each of the parallel short-run consumption functions is similar to the consumption function shown in Figure 10–4. But, as disposable income grows and individuals achieve a new high level of consumption (C_h in equation 10–3), their consumption function shifts up to a new level. In geometric terms, the addition of the bC_h term shifts the consumption function upward with the y-intercept term $(\bar{C} + bC_h)$ increasing as the previous high level of consumption (C_h) increases.

The Duesenberry hypothesis was formulated as an explanation for consumption and saving behavior for the United States. Later researchers argued

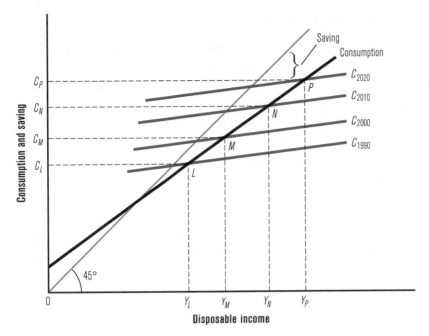

FIGURE 10-5. **Consumption and Saving in the Short and Long Term with Rising Income over Time**
The 45° line shows all points at which consumption plus saving is equal to income. Four short-run consumption functions are shown for each of the years 1990, 2000, 2010, and 2020, representing what people would have spent at various levels of income in those years. The flatness of these curves reflects consumers' reluctance to change consumption habits in the short run. The points L through P trace out a long-term consumption path.

that it also might be applicable to developing countries. Some have suggested that a *demonstration effect* operates to cause consumption in developing countries to ratchet upward as incomes grow. In this view, internationally mobile upper-income groups in the developing countries are thought to emulate high-consumption patterns of the wealthiest income groups in developed countries; successively lower-income groups tend to emulate the patterns of higher-income groups, so that consumption in the society as a whole tends to be a high and stable function of income.[8]

---

[8]Early studies of saving behavior among high-income elites in developing countries include Nicholas Kaldor, "Problemas Económicos de Chile," *El Trimestre Economico* 26, no. 102 (April–June 1959), 193, 211–12; Robert H. Frank, "The Demand for Unobservable and Other Non-Positional Goods," *American Economic Review* 75 (March 1985), 101–16; and Philip Musgrove, "Income Distribution and Aggregate Consumption Function," *Journal of Political Economy* 2, no. 88 (June 1980), 504–25.

The Permanent-Income Hypothesis

One of the most influential approaches to explaining consumption and saving behavior is the **permanent-income hypothesis,** first formulated by Nobel Prize laureate Milton Friedman at the University of Chicago in the 1950s. In the Friedman view, income consists of two components: permanent income and transitory income. The basic idea is that individuals expect to live for many years, and they make consumption decisions over a time horizon that includes their entire life span. The permanent-income component should not be confused with expected lifetime earnings. Rather it should be viewed as the mean income at any time that the household regards as permanent, which in turn depends on both its time horizon and foresight. **Permanent income** usually includes the yield from accumulated wealth, including both physical and human capital assets (education and so on). **Transitory income** includes unexpected, nonrecurring income such as that arising from changes in asset values, changes in relative prices, an unexpected bonus from work, lottery winnings, and other unpredictable windfalls. Friedman believed that individuals could predict the magnitude of permanent income over their lifetimes with a reasonable degree of accuracy. He argued they gear their consumption to what they perceive to be their normal, or permanent, income, which tends to be stable over time.

In the most-restrictive variant of the permanent-income hypothesis, consumption tends to be a constant proportion (approaching 100 percent) of permanent income. Hence, any saving that occurs will come primarily from transitory income. Econometric research has called into question the strong assumption that households consume 100 percent of permanent income. Nevertheless, some studies show a fairly high propensity to consume out of permanent income.

The permanent-income hypothesis may be expressed as

$$S = -\bar{C} + s_p Y_p + s_t Y_t \qquad [10\text{--}4]$$

where Y_p is permanent disposable income, Y_t is transitory disposable income, and s_p and s_t are the marginal propensities to save from permanent and transitory income, respectively. As noted, in the most extreme version, $s_p = 0$ and $s_t = 1$, so all saving arises from the transitory component of income, and this entire component is saved. Modified versions of the permanent-income hypothesis hold only that the rate of saving out of permanent income is constant over a person's lifetime and that, although the propensity to save out of transitory income is high, not all transitory income is saved. Equation 10–4 can represent this version with $0 < s_p < s_t < 1$.

Several studies have sought to test the applicability of the permanent-income hypothesis to developing countries in Asia and Latin America. The results are far from conclusive, but overall they lend some support to the modified versions of the hypothesis: People tend to save a higher proportion of transitory relative to permanent income. A particularly interesting study by Angus Deaton, based on the framework of permanent-income models, stresses the importance of precautionary motives in household saving behavior, particularly among poor rural families in developing countries. Deaton argues that, for these groups, saving is not so much a matter of accumulation as it is a method of smoothing consumption in the face of volatile income. Poor families living at subsistence levels save in years of relative abundance (perhaps in the form of buying additional small livestock, purchasing simple jewelry, or adding to seed stocks) and draw on that saving in times of scarcity, such as during a drought. Essentially, Deaton says that poor rural households dissave as often as they save and behave as if their primary motive for saving is to protect their living standards against disasters.[9]

Another offshoot of the permanent income hypothesis is the idea that changes in a country's international terms of trade (the relative price of exports to imports) might influence saving rates, known as the Harberger-Laursen-Meltzer effect. In this view, an increase in the terms of trade increases income, which in turn should increase saving. However, the effect on saving depends on the extent to which the change in the terms of trade is perceived to be temporary or permanent. Specifically, a permanent change in the terms of trade (and therefore a change in permanent income) would have a relatively small effect on saving, while a temporary change (corresponding to a change in transitory income) would have a larger effect on saving.[10]

The Life-Cycle Hypothesis

The **life-cycle model** of saving is similar to the permanent-income model, in that it postulates that saving and consumption depend on expectations about future income in addition to actual current income. However, the life-cycle model, associated most closely with Nobel Prize-winning economist Franco Modigliani, is more specific about how saving and consumption would be

[9]Deaton, "Saving in Developing Countries," 61–81.

[10]The original idea is formulated in two articles: Arnold C. Harberger, "Currency Depreciation, Income, and the Balance of Trade," *Journal of Political Economy* 58 (1950), 47–60; and Svend Laursen and Lloyd A. Metzler, "Flexible Exchange Rates and the Theory of Employment," *Review of Economics and Statistics* 32 (November 1950), 281–99. Subsequent explorations of the empirical evidence include Maurice Obstfeld, "Aggregate Spending and the Terms of Trade: Is There a Laursen-Metzler Effect?" *Quarterly Journal of Economics* 97, no. 1 (1982), 251–70; J. D. Ostry and Carmen Reinhart, "Private Saving and Terms of Trade Shocks," *IMF Staff Papers* 39 (September 1992), 495–517; and Masson et al., "International Evidence on the Determinants of Private Saving."

expected to vary systematically during a person's lifetime.[11] In this model, young adults tend to have lower saving rates because they have lower incomes (and expect higher incomes in the future) and are raising children. Indeed, many people would be expected actually to dissave (go into debt) during this stage of life. Saving rates tend to rise and peak toward the middle and end of a person's working years, when incomes are higher and there are fewer consumption-related expenses for children. During this stage of life, people accumulate the bulk of their saving to be used during retirement. Once workers retire, their income falls and they again dissave by drawing down on their previous saving. Thus, saving rates tend to be low or even negative during the younger years, high during middle age, and negative again after retirement.

The life-cycle hypothesis suggests that the demographic structure of a society may have a strong effect on overall saving rates. As discussed in Chapter 7, all societies tend to pass through a demographic transition with three basic stages: (1) high birth and death rates, with low population growth; (2) falling death rates, with continued high birth rates and consequently high population growth rates; and (3) falling birth rates with continued low death rates and lower population growth. As countries pass through these stages, the share of the population too young to work, of working age, or retired tends to change dramatically; and saving rates may change with them. A society in stage 2 of the demographic transition is likely to have a relatively large number of surviving children because of falling death rates and continued high birth rates. Children, of course, earn very little or no income, so their consumption effectively is negative saving. At this stage of the demographic transition, each worker in the society has more young dependents to care for, so saving rates are expected to be relatively low. Later on, as a country enters stage 3 of the transition, the number of children tends to fall and the large number of children from the previous generation enters the workforce. As a result, society as a whole tends to have a far larger share of workers and fewer dependents. Since each worker has fewer children to care for, saving rates are expected to rise. Later still, these workers retire and saving rates tend to decline. This hypothesis is consistent with an income-saving relationship in which saving rates are high for middle-income countries and lower for high-income countries. Higher income countries tend to have longer life expectancies and more people living in retirement, which would suggest lower average saving rates for these countries.

---

[11]See Franco Modigliani and Richard Brumberg, "Utility Analysis and the Consumption Function: An Interpretation of Cross-Section Data," in K. Kurihara, ed., *Post Keynesian Economics* (New Brunswick, NJ: Rutgers University Press, 1954); and Alberto Aldo and Franco Modigliani, "The Life-Cycle Hypothesis of Saving: Aggregate Implications and Tests," *American Economic Review* (March 1963). For a classic early work on the subject, see Ansley J. Coale and Edgar M. Hoover, *Population Growth and Economic Development in Low-Income Countries* (Princeton, NJ: Princeton University Press, 1958).

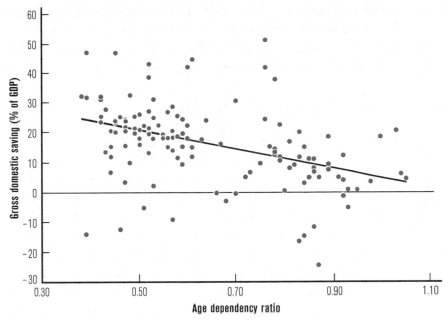

FIGURE 10-6. **Gross Domestic Saving and the Age Dependency Ratio, 2003**
As the age dependency ratio increases, because there are either more children or more retired adults per worker, the saving rate tends to decline. However, there is significant variation within this relationship.

Figure 10–6 shows the relationship between saving rates and the "dependency ratio," which compares the size of the dependent population (children and retirees, the population aged 0 to 15 years and those over 60) to the working-age population. The figure shows the tendency for saving rates to be lower in countries with larger number of dependents relative to the workforce. Note that there is significant variation around the line, meaning that the relationship does not necessarily hold in all countries. Although some studies have found little connection between dependency ratios and saving rates, most others have detected a strong relationship.[12] The relationship seems to be more robust with respect to the young-age dependency ratio (the ratio of the population between 0 and 15

[12]Studies that find no relationship between demographic structure and saving include Angus Deaton, *Understanding Consumption* (Oxford: Clarendon Press, 1992); and M. Gersovitz, "Savings and Development," in Hollis Chenery and T. N. Srinivasan, eds., *Handbook of Development Economics*, vol. 1 (Amsterdam: North-Holland, 1988). Studies that reach the opposite conclusion include Sebastian Edwards, "Why Are Saving Rates So Different across Countries? An International Comparative Analysis," NBER Working Paper 5097 (Cambridge, MA: National Bureau of Economic Research, 1996); Masson et al., "International Evidence on the Determinants of Private Saving"; Norman Loayza, Klaus Schmidt-Hebbel, and Luis Serven, "What Drives Private Saving across the World?" *Review of Economics and Statistics* 82, no. 2 (May 2000), 165–81; and Steven Radelet, Jeffrey Sachs, and Jong-Wha Lee, "Economic Growth in Asia" (Cambridge, MA: Harvard Institute for International Development, May 1997).

years of age to the working-age population). The evidence is weaker with respect to the old-age dependency ratio, which compares the size of the population aged over 60 to the working-age population, suggesting that this cohort may not reduce its saving as much as the life-cycle theory suggests.

Growth and Saving: Which Causes Which?

Each of these models views the level of income (whether current, relative, or permanent) as the principal determinant of saving. They differ in their perspectives on both the magnitude of the effect and the channel through which income operates, but all agree that higher levels of income should be associated in some way with higher amounts of saving, as we saw in Figure 10–1. In their basic form, they do not explicitly incorporate the impact of economic growth, but they imply that faster growth should be associated with higher rates of saving. In the relative income hypothesis, for example, as incomes increase, initially saving increases and later consumption adjusts. As incomes grow faster, saving would be expected to increase faster. Similarly, Franco Modigliani argued that one implication of his life-cycle hypothesis is that growth would lead to higher saving rates, but in a very different way.[13] Economic growth would accrue income to workers, rather than dependents, meaning that the worker's share of total income would increase. Even if neither group changed their saving rate, since workers have a higher saving rate than dependents, their growing share of income would lead to an increase in the average saving rate.

Note the implied direction of causality: From this perspective, faster economic growth and higher income lead to higher rates of saving. This is the opposite direction of the causality incorporated into most growth models, where higher saving leads to greater capital accumulation and faster growth. But recall the precise predication of the Solow model, discussed in Chapter 4: A higher saving rate leads to faster growth only during the transition period to a higher steady-state level of output per worker, not to a permanently higher rate of growth. In any case, both ideas predict a positive relationship between saving and growth, but they have different views of which one is pushing which. Earlier, in Figure 10–2, we saw that faster economic growth is associated with higher saving, but the figure does not tell us the direction of causality.

Several studies have suggested that the dominant effect runs from faster growth to higher saving.[14] Economist Dani Rodrik has pointed out that, in many of the fast-growing East Asian countries, sharp increases in saving occurred *after*

---

[13]Franco Modigliani, "The Life-Cycle Hypothesis of Saving, the Demand for Wealth, and the Supply of Capital," *Social Research* 33 (Summer 1966), 160–217.

[14]See, for example, Christopher Carroll and David Weil, "Saving and Growth: A Reinterpretation," NBER Discussion Paper No. 4470 (Cambridge, MA: National Bureau of Economic Research, September 1993); and Dani Rodrik, "Saving Transitions," *World Bank Economic Review* 14, no. 3 (September 2000), 481–507.

growth accelerated. However, there is no broad consensus on the causality issue. It may well be that the relationship works both ways: Higher rates of saving can support faster growth (at least during a transition period to a new steady-state level of income, as in the Solow growth model), while faster growth can lead to higher saving. At the same time, both saving and growth simultaneously are influenced by a range of other factors, including government policies, trade orientation, demographic structure, macroeconomic and political stability, and other factors.

Other Determinants of Private Saving

Each of these models provides some insight into saving behavior in both industrialized and developing countries, but they take us only so far. One weakness of these models is that, while each views income as the principal determinant of saving behavior, in reality income by no means is the only determinant, particularly in developing countries. Analysts have suggested a range of other possible influences on private saving, including demographic structure, as discussed previously. A different possibility is the location (rural versus urban) of a country's population. There appears to be some tendency around the world for rural households to save higher fractions of their income than urban households with comparable income levels. This behavior is consistent with the permanent-income hypothesis and Deaton's views on precautionary saving, because farmer's incomes are more variable than those of urban wage earners.

Others have stressed the structure and quality of financial markets, as discussed in Chapter 13. Two issues are relevant: interest rates and the strength of financial institutions. On the first, although many analysts have suggested that low interest rates discourage saving and high interest rates have the opposite effect, there is little empirical support for this proposition. On the second, more recent studies have focused attention on the institutional basis (or lack thereof) for saving in developing countries. Formal saving and credit markets often are segmented and closed to much of the population in developing countries. The absence of mortgage markets means that people must accumulate a large share of saving in advance of a housing purchase. Similarly, "missing" markets for pensions, insurance, and consumer credit may be associated with higher rates of saving. In this view, precautionary motives may play a large role in mobilizing saving, as households save out of current income to protect themselves from adverse shocks in the future. Thus, more-sophisticated financial markets may be associated with *lower* rates of saving.[15] This rationale provides another reason why rural households might save more than urban households: Since rural

---

[15]For more discussion of these issues, see T. N. Srinivasan, "Saving in the Development Process," in James H. Gapinski, ed., *The Economics of Saving* (Norwell, MA: Kluwer Academic Publishers, 1993).

households are less connected to formal financial markets, they cannot tap into "pooled" saving systems (such as banks, pension systems, or insurance companies) and must save more to cover their own needs.

In the end, despite many plausible theories about the determinants of private saving, the empirical evidence is fairly weak. Private saving data from developing countries are notoriously poor, since they often are measured as the residual from the national accounts and therefore include large errors and omissions. Even with good data, saving studies are bedeviled by identification, causality, and bias problems. Therefore, many questions remain about the determinants of household saving in developing countries.

CORPORATE SAVING

We have seen that there is no shortage of hypotheses purporting to explain the determinants of household saving. However, there are far fewer theories explaining corporate saving, even in the industrialized countries. In the industrialized countries, the share of corporate saving in total income typically is less than 5 percent, and the share of corporate saving in total net private saving typically is less than 25 percent. For example, in the early 1990s, corporate saving was about 2 percent of disposable income in Japan and the United States, 3 percent in Belgium and France, and about 1 percent in Canada. Only in Denmark, the Netherlands, and Spain did the figure exceed 5 percent. Such data are available for only a few developing countries and not always very reliable. World Bank data suggest that in the early 1990s corporate saving accounted for 7 percent of disposable income in Colombia, 2 percent in Korea, and around 0 percent in the Philippines.

Corporate saving is relatively small in most developing countries primarily because the corporate sector generally is small. For a variety of reasons, there are fewer pressures and incentives in developing countries for doing business in the corporate form (as opposed to operating as an unincorporated business). The principal reasons for organizing as a corporation in the private sector are to limit the liability of enterprise owners to amounts invested in a business and to facilitate enterprise finance through the issue of equity shares (stocks). Although these advantages are substantial in higher-income countries with well-developed commercial codes, civil court systems, and capital markets, they are smaller in most developing countries, where the collection of commercial claims (for example, company debts) through the courts is relatively difficult and where capital markets are poorly developed, when they exist at all.

As usual, however, there are important exceptions to these generalizations. In some developing countries, corporations are both numerous and quite large.

Fortune magazine's annual list of the 500 largest corporations outside the United States includes several dozen from developing countries.[16] Examples include conglomerates such as Samsung Electronics in South Korea, Shanghai Automotive in China, the diversified firm Reliance Industries in India, petroleum companies such as Mexico's PEMEX and Venezuela's PDVSA, and financial conglomerates such as Taiwan's Cathay Life and Brazil's Banco Bradesco. But, except in a few countries such as Korea and Brazil, even in middle-income countries, such corporations are not numerous, ordinarily do not account for a large share of private-sector business activity, and do not provide a high proportion of domestic saving.

In all but a few of the highest-income developing countries, the great bulk of private sector farming and commercial and manufacturing activity is conducted by unincorporated, typically family-owned enterprises. Some of these businesses fall into the category of medium-scale establishments (from 20 to 99 workers). The great majority are small-scale operations with fewer than 20 employees. The noncorporate sector, including most small family farms, manages to generate more than half of all domestic saving in most developing countries, and this sector is the only consistent source of surplus in the sense that its saving exceeds its investment. For those closely held, largely family-owned and -managed firms, enterprise profits become an important part not only of corporate saving but also of gross household income. The available evidence indicates, and economic theory suggests, that household saving accounts for the overwhelming share of private saving in developing countries and the chief source of household saving probably is household income from unincorporated enterprises.

GOVERNMENT SAVING

Unlike private saving, there are no well-developed theories for government saving and consumption behavior. Government saving arises when tax revenues exceed public consumption expenditures (that is, government spending excluding public investment expenditures).[17] Government saving in most countries tends to be smaller than private saving (although not always), typically averaging between 3 and 10 percent of GDP in most developing countries, as shown earlier in Table 10–2. In some countries, where governments run large budget deficits, government saving can be negative. But in a few countries, government

---

[16]*Fortune* magazine, "The Fortune Global 500," annual.

[17]In some countries saving by government-owned enterprises contributes to government saving, but it generally plays a minor role, so our discussion of government saving is confined to budgetary saving.

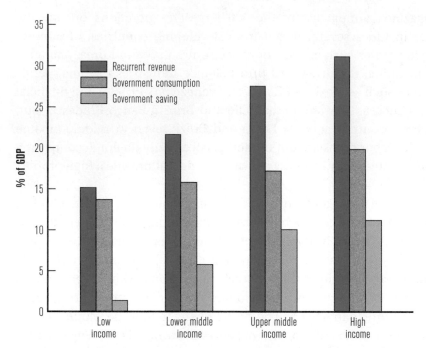

FIGURE 10-7. Government Revenue, Consumption, and Saving, 1990–2002
Tax revenues as a share of income tend to be much smaller in low-income
countries than high-income countries. Government consumption also grows
with income but not nearly as much. Therefore, government saving generally
is much smaller in low-income countries than high-income countries.

saving actually exceeds private saving, such as in the Dominican Republic. Government saving also tends to be much smaller in low-income countries than in middle- or upper-income countries, as shown in Figure 10–7. As discussed later, one reason for this outcome is that poorer countries generally do not generate as much tax revenue as richer countries.

Even though government saving usually is smaller than private saving, historically it has been given strong emphasis in development policy. This is partly because private saving often is seen as inherently constrained by such factors as low per capita income and high private consumption propensities among wealthy families with the greatest capacity for saving. But it is also because government saving can be controlled more directly by policy makers, and the public sector investment financed by that saving (roads, bridges, ports) plays an important role in supporting economic growth.

Government saving can be changed by either increasing revenues or reducing consumption expenditures. Historically, most effort has focused on increasing tax revenues, either by strengthening tax structures and collection systems or by altering tax rates. In this line of thinking, tax ratios in many developing countries are too low, and policy changes aimed at increasing tax revenues help increase domestic saving (and ultimately the rate of economic growth). But there are several steps in between, and the extent to which this occurs depends on three key questions:

1. To what extent can governments increase the tax ratio, if they want to do so?
2. Will an increase in the tax ratio lead to an increase government saving?
3. Will an increase in government saving increase total domestic saving?

On the first question, it is not easy to judge the appropriate level of taxation in developing countries. If taxes are too low, governments cannot provide essential services, such as basic education, public health, a well-functioning judicial system, basic security, and public infrastructure. Tax rates that are too high (or fall too heavily on some groups) can undermine private entrepreneurs and reduce the incentives for new investment and economic growth. These issues are discussed in more depth in Chapter 12. As a general matter, developing countries generally do not (and cannot be expected to) have tax ratios as high as is common in wealthier countries (except for developing countries with significant natural-resource endowments, which are easier to tax). Moreover, it is not easy to increase tax collection in developing countries, if for no other reason than their much lower per capita income allows a much smaller margin for taxation after subsistence needs are met. Figure 10-7 shows that, whereas typical tax ratios for low-income countries average around 15 percent, the ratio of government revenue to GDP in the industrialized countries averages around 30 percent and can be much higher.

Turning to the second question, a higher tax ratio does not necessarily lead to a higher government saving rate. It depends on what the government does with the revenue. To the extent that it spends the revenue on consumption (i.e., higher salaries or increased supplies), government saving does not increase; to the extent it uses the revenue to reduce a budget deficit or for investment, government saving increases. More specifically, the impact of increased tax revenue on the government saving rate depends on the government's propensity to save (as opposed to consume) out of an additional peso of tax revenue. In many countries, the government's marginal propensity to save out of taxes has been sufficiently small that higher taxes often have had relatively little effect on government saving and in some cases none at all.

It is worth emphasizing that increasing government consumption (rather than saving) may or may not be bad policy. Some consumption expenditures may be a waste, such as fancy cars, luxurious government offices, or a rapid buildup of military purchases. But other consumption expenditures may be vitally important, such as purchasing vaccines; making salary adjustments to keep and attract qualified civil servants; maintaining roads, schools, health facilities, and communication networks; and strengthening the judicial system or financial institutions.

Government consumption tends to rise less sharply with income than does revenue, as shown in Figure 10–7. There is much less difference in government consumption ratios between low-income countries (14 percent) and high-income countries (19 percent) than there is in tax ratios. This difference leads to a substantial divergence in average government saving rates. The poorest countries tend to have very low (and sometimes negative) government saving rates, averaging around 2 percent of GDP. Government saving rates tend to rise with income as tax ratios increase, averaging 11 percent of GDP for the richest countries.

On the third question, perhaps counterintuitively, an increase in government saving does not automatically increase domestic saving. How can this be, since government saving plus private saving equals domestic saving? It depends on how private saving responds to the increase in government saving. If the government raises taxes, government saving might increase, but private individuals might respond by lowering their saving to pay the higher taxes, thereby dampening the impact on aggregate domestic saving. Thus the effect on saving of raising taxes depends on both the government's and the private sector's propensity to save out of the marginal dollar of income. As a general statement, increased tax revenue increases the domestic saving rate only if the government's propensity to save is greater than the private sector's propensity to save.

Debates about the private sector's reaction to increased government saving date back at least as far as the early part of the nineteenth century to the writings of the great British economist David Ricardo. Ricardo postulated—and largely rejected—the idea that, under certain circumstances, a change in taxes will have absolutely no effect on total domestic saving. Ricardo's theory has come to be known as **Ricardian equivalence:** Any increase in public saving is offset by an equivalent decline in private saving, with total domestic saving remaining unchanged. The basic idea is that, when private actors receive a tax cut and see that government spending does not change, they anticipate a commensurate tax increase in the future and prepare for it by increasing their current saving. Thus, if the government reduces taxes, government saving may fall, but households and firms increase private saving in anticipation of a future tax increase. The fall in government saving is offset exactly by a rise in private saving, and the tax cut has no impact on total saving. Similarly, a tax increase may lead to higher government saving, but private saving is expected to decline by the same amount with no change in total saving. Ricardo's original idea was rejuvenated and formalized by economist Robert Barro in 1979.[18]

Ultimately, of course, this is an empirical issue that comes down to measuring the extent to which private agents alter their saving behavior in response to changes in government tax and expenditure policies. The abundance of evi-

---

[18]Robert Barro, "Are Government Bonds Net Wealth?" *Journal of Political Economy* (November–December 1979).

dence suggests partial, but only partial, truth to Ricardo's hypothesis. Many studies have shown that an increase in government saving tends to be associated with a decline in private saving, but by less than the strict one-to-one relationship postulated by Ricardo. Most studies have found an offset of between 0.40 and 0.65, meaning that a 1 percentage point of GDP increase in the government saving rate is associated with a 0.40–0.65 percentage point decline in the private saving rate. This would imply a net increase in the total domestic saving rate of between 0.35 and 0.60 percentage points.[19]

The salutatory impact of higher government saving may go beyond the effect on domestic saving. Since higher government saving is derived largely from smaller budget deficits, it reduces the government's borrowing requirements. Government deficits typically are financed through domestic money creation (i.e., borrowing from the central bank, which prints money to fund the deficit) or by borrowing in either local or overseas markets. As a result, larger budget deficits can lead to higher rates of inflation (from money creation), larger government debts, or both. Lower budget deficits (or higher public saving) tend to have the opposite outcomes: lower inflation and indebtedness. Thus, higher public saving is likely to enhance general macroeconomic stability.

FOREIGN SAVING

Historically, many countries have augmented domestic saving with foreign saving to help finance investment and growth. The United States relied heavily on foreign saving, particularly during the antebellum period from 1835 to 1860 and again in the late nineteenth century to finance, among other things, the expansion of the railway system. Likewise, Russia used foreign saving to help propel its development in the three decades before World War I and the Communist revolution. However, not all countries have followed this pattern: Japan became a wealthy nation even though it actively discouraged inflows of foreign saving and investment throughout its history. Therefore, foreign saving can help development but is not necessarily essential for it.

Whereas, in decades past, some developing countries actively tried to shut out private capital flows, today almost all developing countries actively try to encourage them. But controversy surrounds foreign aid, foreign investment, short-term private capital flows, and the debt that has accrued from foreign borrowing. The

---

[19]See, for example, Sebastian Edwards, "Why Are Saving Rates So Different across Countries? An International Comparative Analysis," NBER Working Paper No. 507 (Cambridge, MA: National Bureau of Economic Research, April 1995); Masson et al., "International Evidence on the Determinants of Private Saving"; Loayza et al., "What Drives Private Saving Across the World?"; and Radelet et al., "Economic Growth in Asia."

remainder of this chapter provides a brief overview of some basic concepts and data on foreign saving. Chapter 14 explores foreign aid in detail, and Chapter 15 examines issues related to private capital flows, foreign debt, and financial crises related to short-term foreign capital flows.

The relationships between investment, domestic saving, foreign saving, and the trade balance can best be seen from standard national accounts identities, which tell us that total investment (I) must equal total saving (S), which in turn consists of domestic saving (S_d) and foreign saving (S_f). To see this, recall from the income side of the national accounts that

$$Y = C + I + G + X - M \qquad [10\text{--}5]$$

where G is government consumption, X is exports of goods and services, and M is imports of goods and services. On the expenditure side, all income must be consumed, saved, or given to the government as taxes:

$$Y = C + S_p + T \qquad [10\text{--}6]$$

Note that the saving term in this identity refers to private saving. Since both equations equal Y, the right-hand sides must be equal:

$$C + I + G + X - M = C + S_p + T \qquad [10\text{--}7]$$

Subtracting C from both sides and rearranging the terms yields

$$I = (T - G) + S_p + (M - X) \qquad [10\text{--}8]$$

The first term on the right-hand side ($T - G$) is government saving, and the second term (S_p) is private saving. The third term ($M - X$) is both the current account deficit of the balance of payments and foreign saving. When a country's imports (M) exceed its exports (X), the difference must be financed by inflows of capital from abroad (foreign aid, bank loans, equity flows, etc.), which is foreign saving. The right-hand side of the equation is the sum of domestic and foreign saving, yielding

$$I = S_d + S_f \qquad [10\text{--}9]$$

or the more traditional

$$I - S_d = M - X \qquad [10\text{--}10]$$

Thus, as the difference between investment and domestic saving grows (or shrinks), the trade deficit grows (or shrinks) commensurately. The two balances must move together in tandem. One can think of this in many ways. As investment increases (without an increase in domestic saving), imports tend to increase and exports decrease to provide the materials needed for the investment project. A firm building a new factory requires steel, cement, lumber, and machinery, which can come from either new imports or purchasing the goods domestically, leaving less for export. Alternatively, an export boom without a commensurate increase in imports generates profits that can contribute to domestic saving, closing the gap between investment and domestic saving.

Foreign saving includes both a public sector component (called *official foreign saving*) and a private component. Most **official foreign saving** is foreign aid provided on **concessional terms** as either *grants* (outright gifts) or *"soft" loans*, meaning that they bear lower interest rates and longer repayment periods than would be available in private international capital markets. Industrialized country governments and international agencies also provide some financing as loans on commercial terms *("hard" loans)*, particularly to middle-income countries. Aid can be further divided into *bilateral aid*, given directly by one government to another, and *multilateral aid*, in which the funds flow from donor governments to international agencies like the United Nations, the World Bank, and the regional development banks, which in turn grant or lend the funds to recipient developing countries. Finally, aid can be in the form of *technical assistance*, the provision of skilled individuals to augment national expertise; *financial assistance*, the provision of money for projects and programs; or commodity assistance, the transfer of specific goods, such as food or gasoline.

Private foreign saving consists of four elements. *Foreign direct investment* is made by nonresidents, typically but not always by multinational corporations, in enterprises located in host countries. "Direct" investment implies that funds go directly to an enterprise (as opposed to indirectly through a stock market) with the foreigner gaining full or partial control of the enterprise. *Portfolio investment* is the purchase by foreigners of host country bonds or stocks, without managerial control. Portfolio investment was a very important form of financing in the nineteenth and early twentieth centuries, but fell into disuse after World War II. It revived again in the 1990s, however, as rich-country investors showed interest in emerging stock and bond markets, especially in Asia and increasingly in Latin America. *Commercial bank lending* to developing country governments and enterprises supplanted portfolio investment in importance for a time but waned beginning in the 1980s when debt crises afflicted many developing countries. It expanded quickly in the early 1990s, then dropped sharply toward the end of the decade, as several developing countries experienced major financial crises. Finally, exporting firms from the industrialized countries, their commercial banks, and official banks (such as the U.S. Export-Import Bank) offer *export credits* (or credit guarantees) to firms in developing countries that import from the industrialized countries. These credits help the exporters promote sales by permitting delayed payment, often at commercial interest rates.

Capital flows to developing countries changed dramatically in several important ways between 1990 and 2003, as shown in Table 10–3. First, private capital flows grew extremely rapidly until 1996, growing from $55 billion to $281 billion. All the major categories of private finance expanded rapidly: long-term loans, short-term loans, portfolio equity, and foreign direct investment. But this trend changed abruptly in 1997 following the financial crises that struck Thailand,

TABLE 10-3. Capital Flows to Developing Countries, 1990–2003
(billion US$)

	1990	1996	2000	2003
Inflows	107.0	307.1	206.2	272.1
Official development finance	51.8	25.8	28.1	23.7
Grants (excluding technical assistance)	25.4	23.0	23.2	38.0
Official loans (net)	26.4	2.8	4.9	−14.3
Private finance	55.2	281.3	178.1	248.4
Long-term debt flows (net)	16.6	82.5	7.4	22.9
Short-term debt flows (net)	13.2	37.4	−7.9	49.0
Portfolio investment	3.4	32.9	12.4	24.8
Foreign direct investment	22.1	128.6	166.2	151.8
Outflows	53.5	200.5	226.6	346.9
Accumulation of reserves	32.4	90.4	46.8	291.9
FDI from developing countries	5.0	10.0	16.5	24.0
Other items/errors and ommissions	16.1	100.1	163.3	31.0
Total	53.5	106.6	−20.4	−74.8
Memo item: Aggregate current account balance of developing countries				
Excluding grants	−53.5	−106.6	20.4	74.8
Including grants	−28.1	−83.6	43.6	112.8

Source: World Bank, *Global Development Finance* 2005 and IMF, *International Financial Statistics,* annual yearbook.

Indonesia, Korea, Russia, and several other countries. Private capital flows fell sharply for several years, and then grew again between 2000 and 2003.

Second, and in sharp contrast to private flows, official development flows fell during the 1990s. In particular, net official lending dropped significantly and turned negative, meaning that developing countries were repaying old loans more than they were receiving new loans from donor governments. Whereas official development finance and private finance were about the same size in 1990, private flows were ten times larger in 2003. While these two patterns hold for developing countries as a whole, the patterns differ between low-income and middle-income countries. In particular, as shown in Table 10–4, the large increase in private capital flows was concentrated in middle-income countries. Private capital flows to low-income countries were small in 1990, and while they were larger in 2003, the increase accounted for a relatively small share of the increase in total private capital flows. Official flows to low-income countries were only slightly larger in 2003 than they were in 1990; in middle-income countries, they were substantially smaller.

Third, whereas capital inflows to developing countries in aggregate grew rapidly, capital outflows grew even more rapidly. The aggregate current account deficit of developing countries (shown at the bottom of Table 10–3) moved from a deficit position to a surplus position in 2000. In other words, aggregate exports of all goods and services exceeded imports of goods and services, so developing countries as a whole were exporting capital to the richer countries. Correspondingly, total net capital flows (or net foreign saving, summing together all inflows and outflows) shifted from positive to negative. The main channel through which this occurred was a small number of developing countries running large balance of payments surpluses and accumulating foreign exchange reserves, including China, Korea, Taiwan, and a few other countries. Typically they (along with other central banks in developing countries) hold their foreign exchange reserves in one of two ways: (1) as deposits in banks in the United States, Europe, or Japan, which is a form of saving available to finance new loans in those countries; or (2) by purchasing government securities, such as U.S. Treasury bills. China's central bank (the People's Bank of China) became one of the largest purchasers of U.S. Treasury bills. In effect, the balance of payments surpluses generated by these countries are providing the saving necessary to finance the U.S. budget deficit. Historically and under normal circumstances, capital tends to flow from rich countries (which tend to have larger capital stocks) to low-income countries (where capital is scarce), but since 2000 that pattern has been reversed. However, this pattern is heavily concentrated in a small number of developing countries that are exporting a large amount of capital by accumulating reserves. The majority of low-income countries continue to be net importers of capital from rich countries.

TABLE 10-4. **Capital Inflows to Developing Countries by Income Category, 1990–2003 (billion US$)**

	1990	2003
All developing countries		
Official flows (net)	51.8	23.7
Grants (excluding technical assistance) and concessional loans	39.8	42.2
Nonconcessional loans	11.9	−18.5
Private flows	55.2	248.4
Total	107.0	272.1
Middle-income countries		
Official flows (net)	27.6	−4.2
Grants and concessional loans	17.9	10.7
Nonconcessional loans	9.7	−14.9
Private flows	47.3	227.4
Total	74.9	223.3
Low-income countries		
Official flows (net)	24.2	27.9
Grants and concessional loans	21.9	31.5
Nonconcessional loans	2.3	−3.6
Private flows	7.9	21.0
Total	32.1	48.8

Source: World Bank, *Global Development Finance*, 2005.

SUMMARY

- Domestic saving rates rose for many developing countries in recent decades but not all. The increase was particularly notable for several countries in East Asia. Investment rates (as a share of GDP) rose at a similar rate. Saving rates tend to be lower for low-income countries and higher for middle-income and high-income countries, but there is wide variation, particularly among low-income countries.

- Income levels are a central determinant of saving rates, but theories and empirical evidence differ on the precise connection. Generally, higher income levels are associated with higher rates of saving. Some theories stress the absolute level of income, while others stress relative income, the composition of income between permanent and transitory components, or changes in income over the course of a lifetime.

- There is a clear positive relationship between saving and economic growth, although the direction of causality is unclear. Higher saving can lead to faster growth by financing productive investment; at the same time, faster growth provides more income, which in turn can facilitate greater saving.

- Government saving makes an important contribution to total saving in many developing countries, although it is usually much smaller than private saving. An increase in government saving generally increases total domestic saving but typically by less than one for one, as it can be partially offset by a decline in private saving. Government saving tends to rise with average income, driven mainly by increased government revenue collections.

- Foreign saving is relatively small compared to domestic saving, but is often more controversial. The composition of foreign capital flows has changed markedly since the early 1990s. The amount of official finance flowing to low-income countries dropped sharply. By contrast, private finance grew even more quickly, at least until severe financial crises affected several countries in the late 1990s. The increase in private capital flows has been concentrated in middle-income countries, with much less flowing to low-income countries. In a change from the normal pattern, in recent years, some developing countries, including China, have been providing financing to rich countries.

11 Investment, Productivity, and Growth

Nazma, a seamstress in Calcutta, has had a run of good luck. Business has been brisk, and she can hardly keep up with the steady stream of new customers that want her to make new clothes. Now Nazma faces a key decision: Should she buy another sewing machine and hire another seamstress? The initial cost would be high, and it would be a struggle at first to pay for the machine and the additional wages. But, if business remains strong and the electricity keeps working, in a few months she could pay off the sewing machine and earn a little extra income. The extra money surely would be helpful in paying school fees for her young children. Still, it would be a risky step, and there would be no guarantee of success.

Every day, people in developing countries face similar decisions. Should a farmer buy a new ox or plough and try to acquire rights to farm some new land? Should the senior manager of a small toy-making operation take the big step and start her own business? Should the government build new rural feeder roads to help stimulate agricultural production, or would it make more sense to build some new schools? Should a multinational cell phone maker build a new factory in Thailand, South Africa, or Costa Rica? These decisions have an enormous impact on individual welfare, economic growth, poverty reduction, and development.

What influences these decisions? How can developing countries encourage more investment and help ensure that investments are productive? Investors are interested in investments that are as profitable as possible, which in turn means they want to keep their costs low and be able to sell their products easily and for a good price. They are also interested in minimizing their risks, meaning they want to be confident they can control their costs, keep production lines operating on schedule, and be able to sell their products in reasonably stable markets. Profitability is a useful first indicator of the value of an investment, and most projects that are privately profitable help stimulate growth and development. But this is not always the case, especially if profits can be made only through subsidies or price distortions that incur costs on others. The challenge for policy makers is to create an environment where scarce resources are allocated efficiently and invested where they will be beneficial for growth and development.

In many low-income countries, there appear to be abundant opportunities for increased investment that could have significant economic and social benefits, but these investments do not happen. Roads are absent or of poor quality, electricity and telecommunications facilities are in short supply and unreliable, and there seems to be many workers with few factories to employ them. Sometimes, this is because investment funds are not always available, but it is also because the investments that do take place are not always particularly productive. But this in itself is a puzzle: The Solow growth model suggests that, in low-income countries where capital is scarce, new investment has the *potential* to be highly productive, but that is not always the case. The questions about the quantity and productivity of investment become more complicated when foreigners make the investments. Although foreign capital appears to be a ready source of additional investment funds, foreign investment does not always have a good reputation, and in some cases, even where it is productive, it is not always welcomed.

This chapter explores the key issues surrounding investment and development. It describes different types of investment and stresses the importance of both the quantity and quality of investment. The chapter reviews cost-benefit analysis, one of the basic techniques for evaluating investment decisions and examines a range of factors that influence business costs, profitability, and productivity, including red tape, corruption, market restrictions, institutional quality, and trade policies. It then explores some of the issues surrounding foreign direct investment (FDI)—historically the most controversial form of investment—and the policies implemented by some developing countries to either encourage or regulate FDI.

TYPES OF INVESTMENT

Investment spending comes in many forms. The first important distinction is between public and private investment. In many countries, **public investment** by the government is one of the most important components of annual budgets and long-range development strategies. The basic economic rationale for public investment is to finance projects for which the benefits accruing to a private investor are too small to make the venture profitable but the benefits to society more broadly can be quite large. For example, while all firms and households benefit from roads that connect cities, villages, farms, factories, markets, and ports, it typically will not be financially profitable for any single firm to build roads for its own benefit. The cost of building the road simply is too high. Moreover, once the road is built, others can use it without having borne the cost of the initial investment, so every individual and firm has the incentive to wait for someone else to build it. This benefit to those that do not bear the cost is a positive **externality** of the investment. One possible solution to this dilemma is toll roads that charge a fee to users, but these generally are unworkable except for certain highways and bridges. The more common solution is that each firm and household indirectly pays a relatively small share of the cost of the road through tax payments, and the government builds the road for public use.

Governments in developing countries play the central role in building infrastructure, including roads, ports, power, water, and telecommunications facilities. Roads are important not only to connect urban commercial facilities but to connect remote villages to markets so they can buy goods more cheaply and sell their products at better prices to a larger market. In this way, building rural roads can be an important ingredient in the alleviation of rural poverty. Deep-sea ports help facilitate fast and inexpensive international shipments of both imports and exports. Reliable power supplies help avoid costly production shutdowns and reduce production costs. Appropriate telecommunication facilities have become ever more important for telephone, fax, and Internet connections; and they open new opportunities for developing country firms to provide services (such as "backroom accounting") to global markets. In addition, the public sector plays the major role in building schools, hospitals, clinics, and other related facilities in most countries, developed and developing.

Of course, this does not mean that all public sector infrastructure investments are a good idea—governments have been known to build fancy super-highways connecting the capital city to the president's village or large showcase dam projects that never pay for themselves. As discussed later in the chapter, the acid tests for public investment decisions are whether the net present value (NPV) of the investment is greater than 0 and greater than the NPV of other possible public investments. Each investment project should generate more economic resources than it costs to undertake and generate a greater return than all of the other available investment options. Unfortunately, many investment projects in developing countries fail to meet these two basic tests.

While public investment lays much of the foundation to create an environment conducive to growth, **private investment** is much larger and provides the dynamism for the vast majority of new jobs, new technologies, and growth in economic output. Private investors buy better tools and machines for their family farms, invest in bicycles to deliver water in urban areas, build a small shop to sell groceries on a street corner, or expand their factories to increase production. In the late 1990s, the private sector accounted for two thirds of investment in East and South Asia and sub-Saharan Africa, three quarters of investment in Europe and Central Asia, and fully 84 percent of investment in Latin America.[1] In some countries, the share is much lower, such as in China, Haiti, and Mozambique, where the private sector accounts for about half of investment. But in most developing countries, the private sector is the main channel for investment.

EFFECTIVE USE OF CAPITAL

Not surprisingly, investment has a strong relationship with economic growth, as shown in Figure 11–1. This relationship is very similar to the one between saving and growth shown in the last chapter. Like the saving-growth relationship, although the positive relationship is clear, the direction of causality is not obvious. In many countries, it operates both ways in a reinforcing cycle: An increase in investment, especially if it is highly productive, leads to more rapid economic growth. But faster growth also can lead to more investment, as new investors recognize the potential profits that can be realized in a rapidly growing economy.

Governments in developing countries face the dual challenges of creating an environment that will encourage both *high levels* of private investment and *more-productive* investment. The two are closely related. The more productive is investment in terms of rates of return to investors, the easier it is to encourage a greater volume of investment. At the same time, however, as the Solow model points out, as the volume of investment increases, its marginal productivity tends to fall, unless policy changes or new technologies are introduced that further enhance productivity.

If basic macroeconomic prices (exchange rates, interest rates, wage rates) are approximately equal to scarcity values for factors of production, scarce capital is likely to be deployed where it can be applied effectively. In many developing countries, however, distortions in prices (e.g., through subsidies on certain types of fuel or high tariffs on imported capital goods) negatively affect both the volume and allocation of investment, lowering the productivity of investment and ultimately the rates of economic growth.

To see the importance of the productivity of investment, consider a hypothetical example of two small low-income countries that initially are identical in many important respects. Each had per capita income of PPP $1,600 in 2005, a

---

[1]World Bank, *World Development Report 1999/2000* (Washington, DC: World Bank, 1999), Appendix Table 16.

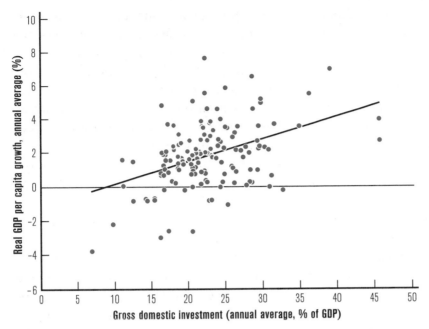

FIGURE 11-1. Investment and Growth, 1994–2003
In a sample of 147 countries from around the world of all income levels, the average annual rate of investment has a positive relationship with the average annual growth rate. As with saving and growth, the direction of causality is not clear and may operate both ways.
Source: World Bank, *World Development Indicators*.

population of 6.25 million, and therefore a total GDP of $10 billion. Each has an investment ratio of 18 percent and similar patterns of exports, imports, agriculture, and industry. From 2000 to 2005, both followed similar development strategies and recorded marginal products of capital (MPKs) of 0.30 (meaning that each dollar of investment yielded 0.30 dollars of additional output each year). As a result, each experienced a real GDP growth rate of about 5.4 percent (the investment ratio, 18 percent, times the MPK, 0.30, ignoring depreciation) over the five-year period.

In 2005, new governments in both countries decided to change their development policies. Country A's government began to provide subsidies for large-scale, capital-intensive investments in chemical factories, paper mills, and steel mills. However, although investors supported the subsidies, since the necessary raw materials were fairly expensive and managers and workers did not have the appropriate skill background (which is why businesses had avoided these activities before the subsidies), the MPK fell from 0.30 to 0.25.

Country B, on the other hand, decided to emphasize labor-intensive investments in agriculture and industry, including textiles, food processing, coastal fisheries, and shoe manufacturing. The government built feeder roads to support these activities, eliminated some outdated regulations that unnecessarily slowed production, and reduced tariffs on inputs to lower production costs. The MPK rose from 0.30 to 0.33.

To see the impact of the difference in productivity, first assume that the quantity of investment remains unchanged. In Country A with an MPK of 0.25, investment of 18 percent of GDP increases output by 4.5 percent (ignoring depreciation), but in Country B with an MPK of 0.33, the same investment leads to growth of 6 percent. Country A would have to save and invest 24 percent of GDP to achieve an annual growth of 6 percent. That is, saving would have to be one-third higher to compensate for the difference between a MPK of 0.33 and an MPK of 0.25.

Next, consider the implications over time under two investment scenarios: a "low" case, in which investment expands by 5 percent per year (not to be confused with an increase of 5 percentage points in the investment-GDP ratio) and the "high" case in which investment grows by 10 percent per year as shown in Table 11–1. The table shows that the efficiency with which capital is used can be as important for growth than raising the volume of investment. Compare the outcomes when investment in Country A expands by 10 percent per year (the "high case") while in Country B it grows by just 5 percent per year (the "low case"). Because of the higher productivity, GDP in Country B is higher than in Country A in each year, *even when the growth rate of investment in Country A is twice as large as in Country B*. In this scenario, after five years, investment in

TABLE 11-1. **GDP and Investment with Different Investment Productivities (million US$)**

	INVESTMENT GROWTH RATE (%)	2005	2006	2007	2008	2009	2010	AVERAGE ANNUAL GROWTH (%)	2010 INVESTMENT/ GDP
Available investment funds									
I. Low case	5.0	1800	1890	1985	2084	2188	2297	5.0	
II. High case	10.0	1800	1980	2178	2396	2635	2899	10.0	
GDP in Country A (MPK of 0.25)									
I. Low case	5.0	10,000	10,450	10,923	11,419	11,940	12,487	4.5	18.4
II. High case	10.0	10,000	10,450	10,945	11,490	12,088	12,747	5.0	22.7
GDP in Country B (MPK of 0.33)									
I. Low case	5.0	10,000	10,594	11,218	11,873	12,560	13,282	5.8	17.3
II. High case	10.0	10,000	10,594	11,247	11,966	12,757	13,626	6.4	16.9

Note: To simplify the presentation, we assume that investment in any year affects output in the following year. Therefore, the calculation for GDP in Country A in 2006 for the low case is as follows: Investment in 2005 of $1,800 million times an MPK of 0.25 leads to increased output of $450 million, so GDP in 2006 is $10,450. All other figures are calculated in a similar fashion.

Country A reaches 22.7 percent of GDP, whereas it falls slightly to 17.3 percent of GDP in Country B.[2] Even with this large difference in investment rates, Country B achieves faster growth because of its higher MPK. As a result, citizens in Country B must make a much smaller sacrifice than the citizens of Country A in terms of forgoing current consumption for saving to increase their income and welfare.

The difference is even larger if investment were to grow at 10 percent per annum in each country. In this case, aggregate income in Country B is 7 percent higher than in Country A by 2010, even though they began at the same level. Although a 7 percent difference in total income after five years may not seem large, it is quite significant. At this rate, after 50 years, total income in Country B would be *double* that of Country A.

COST-BENEFIT ANALYSIS

This simple example illustrates the importance of investment quality in spurring growth from an economywide perspective. But individual investors do not base their decisions on the economywide MPK, they base it on the potential costs and benefits of specific projects. If the costs are too high, the expected payoffs too low, or the risks too great, they will not make the investment. One of the most powerful tools that investors use to evaluate potential investments is **cost-benefit analysis,** or **project appraisal.**

Present Value

The investor's calculation normally involves four steps. First, the firm will forecast the **net cash flow** of an investment, measuring the difference between the cash revenues from the sale of the product and the cash outlays on investment, material inputs, salaries and wages, purchased services, and other items.

Second, investors have to adjust their valuation of costs and benefits depending on whether they happen soon or far into the future. Investors recognize that cash received in the future is less valuable than cash received immediately, because in the interim they could earn interest (or profits) on these funds by investing them in bonds or savings accounts (or in additional, revenue-earning production facilities). Any firm or individual asked to choose between $1,000 today or $1,000 next year would take the money now and place it in a savings account earning, say, 2 percent a year. Then, after one year, the interest payment would boost the savings account balance to $1,020. Equivalently, the

[2]The investment ratio in Country B falls slightly because investment is growing at 5 percent and GDP is growing at 5.8 percent.

prospect of $1,000 a year from now should be evaluated as equivalent today to only $1,000/1.02 = $980. This process of reducing the value of future flows is called **discounting.** Since the interest rate provides a first approximation of the rate at which future cash flows must be discounted, it is usually called the **discount rate.** Discounting takes place over several years, so the discount rate must be compounded over time. In the second year another 2 percent would be earned on the balance of $1,020, and increase it to $1,040.40. The payment of $1,000 two years from now then would be discounted to yield a **present value** of only $1,000/1.040 = $961. A general expression for the present value, P, is

$$P = F/(1 + i)^t \qquad [11\text{--}1]$$

where F = the value in the future, i = the discount rate, and t = time, usually represented by the number of years. As the interest rate or the number of years increases, the present value of the future cash flow decreases. Note that because project appraisals are most conveniently done at **constant prices,** netting out inflation, the discount rate is a **real rate of interest,** net of inflation.

Investment projects usually have negative cash flows in the early years, when there are large expenditures, then generate positive cash flows in later years, as the new facilities begin to earn revenues. Such a **time profile** of net cash flow is depicted in Figure 11–2; it is the most common of several possible profiles. To summarize the value of this net cash flow in a single number, each year's net cash flow is divided by the respective discount factor and the resulting present values are added to give the **net present value** (NPV):

$$NPV = \Sigma(B_t - C_t)/(1 + i)^t \qquad [11\text{--}2]$$

where B_t and C_t are the benefits (revenue) and costs in each year t and i is the discount rate. For a firm, the correct discount rate is the average cost at which additional funds may be obtained from all sources (that is, the firm's cost of capital).

If the net present value of a project happens to equal 0, the project will yield a net cash flow just large enough to cover all the projects costs. In that case, when NPV = 0, the discount rate has a special name, the **internal rate of return (IRR),** a term we introduced in the Chapter 8 discussion of education as an investment. If the net present value is positive, then the project can cover all its financial costs with some profit left over for the firm. If negative, the project cannot cover its financial costs and should not be undertaken. The higher is the net present value, the better the project. If the cash flow of Figure 11–2 is discounted at a rate of 8 percent, the net present value is a positive $1,358 (Table 11–2). This calculation indicates that the investment will earn enough to repay the total costs ($2,500 over years 0 and 1) with a (discounted) surplus of $1,358.

Third, investors must consider the risks to both the costs and the benefits of their investments. Simple NPV analysis such as that in Table 11–2 can be misleading because it generates a single summary number for the answer, giving a false sense of precision. In reality, investors cannot be sure in advance of all the

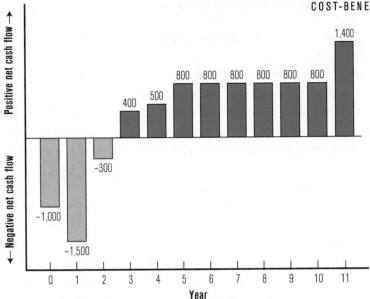

FIGURE 11-2. Time Profile for Investment: Net Cash Flow
The cash flow of a project can be represented by a bar diagram. Cash
outflows are shown by bars below the horizontal axis, inflows by bars
above the axis. Year 0 and 1 show investment in construction and
equipment, hence negative cash flows; year 2 is the startup period;
years 3 and 4 show gradually increasing output and cash inflows;
years 5 through 10 show steady output and cash inflows; and the
project is assumed to end in year 11, when the salvage value of
equipment swells the cash inflow.

TABLE 11-2. Net Present Value

YEAR	CASH FLOW FROM FIGURE 11-2 (DOLLARS)	DISCOUNT FACTOR AT 8%	PRESENT VALUE (DOLLARS)
0	−1,000	1	−1,000
1	−1,500	0.926	−1,389
2	−300	0.857	−257
3	400	0.794	318
4	500	0.735	368
5	800	0.681	544
6	800	0.63	504
7	800	0.583	467
8	800	0.54	432
9	800	0.5	400
10	800	0.463	371
11	1,400	0.429	600
Net Present Value			1,358

Notes: The discount factor is calculated as $1/(1 + i)^t$ from equation 11–2. The present value in each year is
calculated as the cash flow times the discount factor. The net present value is the sum of the present value in
each year.

costs or the cash flows their investment might generate. Fuel prices might sky-rocket, or electricity supplies might be cut off, forcing the investor to either buy a new generator or curtail production. The prices for their products might be either much higher or lower than the original projections. Political instability might increase costs and disrupt the firm's ability to purchase supplies or sell its products. Therefore, prudent investors calculate a range of NPVs for their investment based on best case and worse case scenarios, testing the sensitivity of the outcome to changes in specific costs or benefits. An investor may decide not to make an investment even if it generates a positive NPV under baseline calculations if the risks around actually achieving that outcome are too great.

Fourth, investors must compare across projects. Just because a project generates a positive NPV does not mean it is the best possible use of investment funds, especially if the firm has a set of alternative projects to consider and a budget that can accommodate several but not all of them. Under these circumstances, investors should select the set of projects that will yield the highest total net present value for the entire investment budget.

Opportunity Costs

Every investment uses goods and services that could otherwise be used for other purposes. In evaluating the investment from an economywide perspective, these goods and services should be valued in terms of the net benefits they would have provided if used in some alternative project. These benefits from alternative uses are known as **opportunity costs.** For example, an investment in a dam requires saving that otherwise could be invested in a rural road or in elementary schools. Cotton used in a textile factory otherwise could have been exported and sold abroad. The labor used to build a road might have otherwise been used to sink water wells or grow millet. For a private firm, the cost is the market value that it pays for wages, goods, and services. For society at large, the cost is the value of the resources in terms of their next best use. Public sector investments, in particular, should be evaluated using opportunity costs rather than market costs where the two differ.

The opportunity cost to society might differ from the market wage rate if, for example, the government pays wages higher than the market clearing value. If ten farm workers take jobs building a new highway, their opportunity cost is the value of the lost agricultural output due to their leaving the farm, net of the non-labor recurrent costs of producing that output. This reduction in net output is the value of the **marginal revenue product** and, in this situation, is equal to the opportunity cost of labor.[3] Similarly, if the highway project means that savings

---

[3]The value of the marginal product of a factor of production can be calculated as the price of a commodity multiplied by the additional physical output that results when one unit of the factor is added to the production process with all other factors held constant.

will be drawn away from other projects that on average would have earned a return of 5 percent, then the opportunity cost of capital is 5 percent; and this should be used as the discount rate in evaluating the project, even if the government borrows money at 2 percent.

In some countries, the market price of foreign exchange might differ from the opportunity cost, especially in countries where governments manipulate or control the exchange rate. Cotton used in a textile mill otherwise might have been exported; if so, its opportunity cost would be the foreign currency it would have earned as an export. If the cloth produced by the mill would have been imported in the absence of the project, its opportunity cost (a benefit in this case) would be the foreign exchange that otherwise would have been spent on cloth imports.

Shadow Prices

The opportunity costs of goods and services for the economy as a whole are called **shadow prices** or **economic opportunity costs.** The first approximation of a shadow price (for land, labor, capital, and foreign exchange) is the price paid by private participants in the market. Interference in the market distorts market prices from their economic opportunity cost: taxes and subsidies of all kinds, monopoly power, minimum wages, interest rate controls, tariffs and import quotas, price controls, and so forth. When a firm undertakes investment analysis, it conducts a **commercial project appraisal** based on market prices and focusing on profitability. When governments consider public investments, they want to measure the full economic impact of the investment on the country. To do so, they must use shadow prices where market prices do not fully reflect true scarcity values. This kind of evaluation is called **economic project appraisal.** To estimate shadow prices, market prices must be adjusted to reflect full opportunity costs.

Estimating shadow prices is not easy and requires intimate knowledge of the workings of an economy, both its macroeconomic relationships and the microeconomic behavior of its factor markets. But such adjustment can be important. In many countries, the shadow foreign exchange rate is higher than the official rate in terms of local currency per dollar. In most cases, this reflects the impact of import duties and quotas or intervention by central banks in establishing or modifying the exchange rate. As a consequence, any export project that earns more foreign exchange than it uses or any import-substituting project that saves more than it uses gets a boost from the shadow exchange rate. Although the salaries and wages of skilled employees usually require no adjustment from market to shadow prices, frequently the opportunity cost of unskilled workers is lower than the wage in formal urban labor markets. Therefore, any project using unskilled labor, especially if it is located in a rural area, gets a boost because the shadow wage reduces costs without changing benefits.

TABLE 11-3. **Effects of Shadow Pricing on Cost-Benefit Analysis**

PROJECT	INVESTMENT (FIRST YEAR)	NET ANNUAL CASH FLOW (NEXT 5 YEARS)	NET PRESENT VALUE (10%)
1. Take two projects with identical cash flows. Project A earns more net foreign exchange and uses more labor than project B:			
A. Textile mill, of which	−1,000	+300	+137
Net foreign exchanged earned	−500	+400	
Wages paid	−350	−100	
B. Telecommunications system, of which	−1,000	+300	+137
Net foreign exchange earned	−800	0	
Wages paid	−100	−50	
2. The shadow wage is 75% of market wage, so all wage costs are reduced by 25%. This results in the following net cash flows:			
A. Textile mill	−913	+325	+319
B. Telecommunications system	−975	+313	+212
3. The shadow exchange rate is 20% above official rate, so the net foreign exchange flow is raised by 20%. This results in the following net cash flows:			
A. Textile mill	−1,100	+380	+340
B. Telecommunication system	−1,160	+300	−23

Discount rates might also be adjusted from market interest rates to shadow discount rates if a government treats capital as a very scarce factor of production or if it has a strong preference for projects that realize their benefits relatively quickly. This approach would tend to discourage any public investment project with high initial investment costs, long gestation periods, and low net cash flows. A higher social discount rate would favor projects that generate their net benefits early, because these can be reinvested in other productive projects for continued growth and projects that use relatively abundant factors of production, especially labor, instead of scarce ones, like capital.

An illustration of the power of shadow pricing is contained in Table 11–3, which depicts two projects with identical cash flows. One project (the textile mill) earns more foreign exchange but uses more labor. Because the shadow wage rate is below the market rate, the economic net present value (NPV) of both projects is raised, but the more labor-intensive textile project benefits more (shown in part 2 of the table). When the shadow exchange rate is applied, the NPV of the textile mill is raised considerably, and that of the telecommunications system becomes negative (part 3).

Welfare Weights

Under some circumstances, governments want to incorporate broader social goals into the evaluation of public sector projects, such as the impact on income distribution, poverty alleviation, or environmental degradation. To do so, governments can use welfare weights to further adjust shadow prices in a project analysis. This process might place a higher value on net additional income to certain target groups, such as the very poor. Then, projects generating more income for these groups have higher NPVs than otherwise and tend to be selected more frequently. Similarly, it might adjust benefits to capture environmental goals or further reduce the shadow wage rate if it was particularly interested in creating new jobs. When welfare weights are introduced or shadow prices are further adjusted to reflect social goals, the process is called **social project appraisal**.

The method potentially is powerful but has its dangers as well. Welfare weights are arbitrary, subject to policy makers' or politicians' judgment. This, in itself, is not bad, but these weights can so overwhelm economically based shadow prices that project selection comes down to a choice based almost entirely on arbitrary weights. This gives a false sense of precision, and sometimes can be misused.

ENCOURAGING PRODUCTIVE PRIVATE INVESTMENT

Public sector investments make an important contribution to growth in terms of building infrastructure, ensuring reliable utilities, building schools and health clinics, and in other areas. But private sector investment is much larger than public sector investment in most countries and is the primary driver for job creation, increased productivity, and long-term growth and development. As we have seen, investors make investments if the financial benefits (appropriately discounted) exceed the costs, taking into account various risks. To encourage economically productive and profitable investment, then, policy makers need to focus on steps that can reduce production costs and help create reasonably stable markets. What key factors affect investment decisions?

Investors clearly place a high priority on **macroeconomic and political stability.** High rates of inflation, volatile exchange rates, or recurring financial crises raise production costs and create substantial risks for investors, thus deterring investment even in projects that might be profitable. Investment also tends to be much lower in countries with greater political instability from military coups, civil conflict, or frequent demonstrations or strikes.

For many investors, **infrastructure** is a critical issue. If electricity and water are too expensive or too unreliable, investment will suffer. Roads that are of poor quality (causing frequent truck breakdowns) or too congested (causing long delays) unnecessarily increase costs. If port facilities are too small, poorly located, or too congested, investors are deterred. Countries with poor infrastructure often cannot attract investment, unless they have lower costs in other areas, such as wage rates. In effect, unreliable or high-cost infrastructure reduces productivity and limits the wages that investors might be willing to pay to run a business.

Trade policy and economic openness can have a major impact on investment, but while many investors value greater openness, some investors want specific trade restrictions that can help them be more profitable. Greater openness can encourage investors, since high tariffs or quotas on imported inputs raise costs and sometimes force firms to use lower-quality substitutes. Greater openness also tends to encourage more diffusion of technology and ideas from abroad, which can help make investments more productive. For firms producing exports, openness also allows for larger markets, since firms can more easily sell either to the domestic market or abroad. But other investors are attracted by high tariff barriers that protect the goods and services they produce. It is easy to attract investment in steel: All a government need do is impose very high tariffs on steel imports. High tariffs would assure local steelmakers of a secure market and allow them to raise prices without worrying about competition, but this kind of investment raises steel prices for everyone else and probably is not in the best interests of the country, as we discuss later.

One of the most important factors influencing both the size and productivity of investment is the quality of **institutions and governance.** Stronger institutions and better governance can help both reduce risks and lower costs, which should both encourage greater investment and make investment more productive. Where property rights are secure and contracts are enforced by the court system, investors are much more likely to make larger, long-term investments. If investors think that court systems or government regulatory bodies are unpredictable, they may go elsewhere or not invest at all. Widespread corruption can add to costs or make investors feel that their competitors may be able to "buy" rules or regulations that give them an unfair advantage. Higher crime rates can make investors feel less secure, add to their risks, and increase their costs because of the burden of extra security measures. By contrast, where institutions work better, greater investment is more likely. Effective policy makers in key economic institutions (such as the central bank and the ministry of finance), the court system, parliament, and the head of state's office can give investors greater confidence that the government will implement sound and consistent economic policies.

Evidence suggests a positive relationship between perceptions of the quality of institutions and governance and investment (Figure 11–3). This measure, taken from the World Bank Institute's Governance Research Indicators dataset, is based on surveys gauging perceptions about the quality of six dimensions of governance: voice and accountability (a measure of political participation), political stability and absence of violence, government effectiveness, regulatory

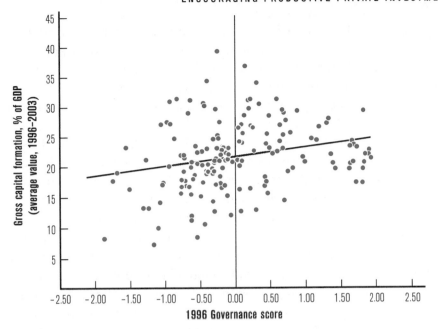

FIGURE 11-3. **Governance and Investment**
Governance scores in 1996 are positively associated with average
investment in subsequent years. The data are for 164 countries of all
income levels. Governance scores are the simple average of the voice and
accountability, political stability, rule of law, government effectiveness,
regulatory quality, and control of corruption components of the governance
dataset constructed by World Bank researchers Daniel Kaufmann, Aart
Kraay, and Massimo Mastruzzi, as described in "Governance Matters IV:
Governance Indicators for 1996–2004."

quality, rule of law, and control of corruption.[4] While there is some variation
around the trend line, countries with higher governance scores generally attract
larger amounts of investment.

Investors are also interested in the basic **costs of doing business,** including
starting a business, hiring and firing workers, obtaining business licenses, getting credit, registering property, and enforcing contracts.[5] Path-breaking work in
this area was done by Peruvian economist Hernando de Soto in his 1989 book
The Other Path.[6] De Soto and his team established a small textile factory on the

[4]The data can be found at www.worldbank.org/wbi/governance/data.html and are described in
D. Kaufmann A. Kraay, and M. Mastruzzi, "Governance Matters III: Governance Indicators for
1996–2002," World Bank Policy Research Working Paper 3106 (Washington, DC: World Bank, 2003).

[5]For in-depth analysis and comparison of business costs across countries, see *Doing Business in
2005: Removing Obstacles to Growth* (Washington, DC: World Bank, 2005), and *World Development
Report 2005: A Better Investment Climate for Everyone* (Washington, DC: World Bank, 2004).

[6]Hernando de Soto, *The Other Path: The Invisible Revolution in the Third World* (New York:
Harper & Row, 1989).

outskirts of Lima and documented all the obstacles and bureaucratic procedures necessary to get the operation legally started. It took 289 days and cost $1,231, about 20 percent more than the average Peruvian's annual income. Facing these kinds of startup costs, many investors are forced to give up their investment plans, especially small-scale investors that are less able to overcome these initial costs.

Peru's experience was not an exception. The World Bank found that businesses in poor countries face much larger regulatory burdens than those in rich countries: three times the administrative costs, nearly twice as many bureaucratic procedures, and fewer than half the property rights protections. According to the World Bank, in 2004, it took 153 days to start a business in Mozambique, but just 3 days in Canada. It took 21 procedures to register commercial property in Nigeria, but just 3 in Finland.[7] These burdens increase costs, reduce profitability, keep wages down, and generally reduce investment. They seem to have an especially large impact on the poor, since they impose particularly high costs on small family businesses. They also vary widely across countries, as shown in Table 11–4. In Bolivia, starting a business costs the equivalent of 174 percent of average income, whereas in Vietnam (with the same per capita income) it costs 29 percent. The cost differences can have a major impact on investment decisions.

Sometimes, these high costs arise from too much government involvement, but sometimes, they are the consequence of too little, as when court systems are overburdened and cannot decide cases, police departments are understaffed and have too little equipment to provide adequate security, or property cannot be adequately registered or titled. In a more recent book, *The Mystery of Capital*, de Soto argues that the poor in developing countries have substantial assets that they are unable to use to leverage investment because of weak institutions and inadequate rules and procedures.[8] For example, land holdings often cannot be properly registered and titled, so the poor cannot use land to secure bank loans. In the United States and other industrialized countries, the ability to show clear title to land and pledge it as an asset in return for a loan lies at the foundation of long-term credit markets. The weaknesses or absence of titling systems in many developing countries is an important reason for the lack of long-term credit markets, which in turn restricts opportunities for investment and economic growth.

---

[7]World Bank, *Doing Business in 2005*, p. 3.
[8]Hernando de Soto, *The Mystery of Capital: Why Capitalism Triumphs in the West and Fails Everywhere Else* (New York: Basic Books, 2000).

TABLE 11-4. Costs of Starting a Business, 2004 (% of GDP)

	COSTS OF STARTING A BUSINESS, 2004 (% OF GDP)
Congo	603
Cambodia	480
Bolivia	174
Nicaragua	170
Malawi	141
Uganda	131
Bangladesh	91
Nepal	74
Egypt	63
Kenya	53
India	50
Pakistan	36
Greece	35
Vietnam	29
Zambia	23
Korea, Rep.	18
Jamaica	15
Kyrgyz Republic	12
Botswana	11
Chile	10
South Africa	9
Mongolia	8
Armenia	7
Russian Federation	7
Singapore	1
Sweden	1
United States	1

Source: World Bank, *Doing Business in 2005.*

FOREIGN DIRECT INVESTMENT

The vast majority of investment in developing countries is undertaken by local citizens, either through small individual projects, larger investments by local firms, or by the government. But in some countries, an increasingly larger share of investment is made by foreign individuals or firms. Since 1990, **foreign direct investment (FDI)** has been the largest of all international capital flows to middle-income developing countries, larger than either cross-border bank lending or foreign aid (in low-income countries, FDI is smaller). FDI is defined as a long-term investment in which a nonresident entity exerts significant management control (usually at least 10 percent of voting stock) over an enterprise in the host country. A second type of cross-border investment is **portfolio equity,** in which an investor takes a smaller stake in an enterprise, either through a direct purchase or through a stock exchange. Portfolio equity flows to developing countries grew very rapidly in the early 1990s, but then fell sharply following the financial crises of 1997 and 1998. Even at their peak, however, portfolio flows were still less than one fifth the size of FDI and about half the size of long-term international commercial bank loans.

In the 1960s and 1970s, many developing countries were suspicious of FDI and often took steps to actively discourage it. At the time, because of the recent colonial history in many countries and the sometimes offensive behavior of certain foreign investors in taking advantage of weak political and legal systems to gain monopoly rights and make huge profits, this suspicion often was well founded. Starting in the mid-1980s, however, these attitudes began to change, and developing countries increasingly sought to attract FDI as a means of financing investment, creating jobs, and importing technology and ideas. As shown in the last chapter in Table 10–3, FDI to developing countries grew rapidly from $22 billion in 1990 to $166 billion in 2000 before tapering slightly to $152 billion in 2003 (more than half of all foreign capital flows). The sharp increase was due partly to worldwide advances in technology in communications and transportation (and the accompanying reduction in costs) and was closely related to the rapid expansion in world trade during the period. It was also is the result of much greater enthusiasm on the part of developing countries in trying to attract FDI.

FDI continues to generate extensive controversy on a range of issues, including repatriation of profits, loss of control over domestic natural resources to foreign-owned entities, the extent of the transfer of technology, the impact on tax revenues, and the content of incentive packages. For some, foreign ownership of domestic companies should always be discouraged, even if it brings economic benefits. For others, FDI is a critical avenue to integrate the domestic economy with global markets that brings with it new technology and skills. As we shall see, the evidence on the relationship between FDI and development suggests that is hard to make broad generalizations and the impact depends critically on the purpose and type of the investment, as well as policies and institutions in the recipient country. FDI in firms producing manufactured products sold on competitive global markets is more likely to be positively related to economic growth and other development outcomes, whereas FDI in firms producing primary products or manufactures or services for protected domestic markets tends to have more mixed outcomes.

FDI Patterns and Products

The majority of direct foreign investment in developing countries is undertaken by **multinational corporations (MNCs),** sometimes also called *transnational*

TABLE 11-5. The Size of Selected Multinational Corporations, 2004
(billion US$)

RANK IN 2004*	COMPANY (COUNTRY)	SALES	ASSETS	EMPLOYEES (000S)
1	Wal-Mart Stores (U.S.)	263.0	104.9	1,500.0
10	General Motors (U.S.)	195.3	448.5	326.0
25	Honda Motor (Japan)	72.3	80.1	131.6
50	Cardinal Health (U.S.)	56.8	18.5	50.0
100	BASF (Germany)	37.8	42.4	87.2
500	Toronto-Dominion Bank (Canada)	10.8	207.5	41.9
Largest developing-country MNCs				
46	State Grid (China)	58.3	127.1	750.3
52	China National Petroleum (China)	56.4	97.7	1024.4
54	Sinopec (China)	55.1	67.6	854.7
55	Samsung Electronics (South Korea)	54.4	57.1	94.2
66	Pemex (Mexico)	49.2	74.1	138.2
76	PDVSA (Venezuela)	46.0	58.0	27.4

*Ranked according to sales.
Sources: "Global 500: World's Largest Corporations," *Fortune* (July 26, 2004); and World Bank, *World Development Report.*

corporations (TNCs). A multinational corporation is a firm that controls assets of enterprises located in countries other than its home country in which foreign operations are central to its profitability. Multinational enterprises are quite diverse, coming in all sizes, from all regions of the world, and engaged in a wide variety of activities. The majority of MNCs are from industrialized countries, but a growing number are based in developing countries (Table 11–5). Eight developing countries had companies in *Fortune* magazine's list of the world's largest 500 firms in 2004, including Korea (nine entries), China (six), and Brazil (four). Most MNCs are private corporations, but not all: *Fortune*'s top 500 includes a number of giant, state-owned companies producing petroleum and steel, such as China National Petroleum and Mexico's PEMEX. But multinationals are not always large; small companies, especially in East and Southeast Asia, have been investing overseas for many years, particularly producing labor-intensive manufactured products such as textiles, shoes, toys, and electronics.

Not surprisingly, the vast majority of FDI comes from rich country investors. Globally, most multinational investment also is directed toward other wealthy countries, but the share aimed at developing countries has been rising. In the late 1980s, less than one fourth of global FDI flows were directed toward developing countries; in the early 1990s, the share reached 42 percent before declining to

35 percent by 2003.[9] However, FDI is highly concentrated in a few developing countries. In 2003, two thirds of all FDI in developing countries went to just ten countries. One country, China (including Hong Kong), received an incredible 34 percent of the total. By contrast, the 49 countries that the United Nations classifies as low income received less than 4 percent and sub-Saharan Africa received just 5 percent of the total.[10]

FDI is aimed at a very wide range of activities that are sometimes difficult to classify, but three broad categories stand out:

1. Natural resource-based activities, such as petroleum, minerals, and agricultural production. Firms engaged in these activities tend to be quite large and the investments very capital intensive. These investments usually are negotiated directly with the host government, and the government is often a partner in the investment.

2. Manufacturing and services aimed at the domestic market in the host country, including consumer goods (e.g., processed food or apparel), capital-intensive products such as steel or chemicals, and a range of services, including transportation, communication, finance, electricity, business services, and retail trade. In many cases, these activities are protected at least partially against competition from imports through tariffs or other restrictions.

3. Labor-intensive manufacturing aimed for export on world markets, including apparel, electronics, food processing, footwear, textiles, and toys. Firms in these activities tend to be efficient and competitive, but they also can move quickly from one country to another in response to changes in production costs or macroeconomic or political instability.

Benefits and Drawbacks of Foreign Direct Investment

Viewed most narrowly, FDI is a **source of capital** that adds to total investment. FDI is relatively small compared to domestic investment, but its share has grown in the last two decades: It accounted for just over 10 percent of all investment in developing countries in 2003 compared to about 2 percent in 1990.[11] But its importance varies widely, even among the largest developing country recipients, as shown in Table 11–6. In some countries, FDI can be equivalent to well over 10 percent of GDP in some years, especially in countries with oil or other natural resources such as Azerbaijan, Equatorial Guinea, and Angola. In other countries, FDI is less than 1 percent. China receives more FDI than any other

---

[9]United Nations Conference on Trade and Development, *World Investment Report 2004*, p. 3.
[10]World Investment Report, Annex Table B-1.
[11]World Investment Report, p. 4.

TABLE 11-6. Foreign Direct Investment in Developing Countries, 1980–2003
(ranked by 2003 dollar amount)

	1980	1990	2003	SHARE OF GDP (%) 2003
China	57	3,487	53,505	3.8%
Mexico	2,090	2,549	10,783	1.7%
Brazil	1,911	989	10,144	2.1%
Russian Federation			7,958	1.8%
India	79	237	4,269	0.7%
Poland	10	89	4,123	2.0%
Azerbaijan			3,285	46.0%
Chile	213	661	2,982	4.1%
Venezuela	55	451	2,520	3.0%
Hungary	1	311	2,506	3.0%
Malaysia	934	2,332	2,473	2.4%
Morocco	89	165	2,279	5.2%
Kazakhstan			2,088	7.0%
Thailand	190	2,444	1,949	1.4%
Romania			1,844	3.2%
Colombia	157	500	1,746	2.2%
Turkey	18	684	1,562	0.6%
Vietnam		180	1,450	3.7%
Equatorial Guinea		11	1,431	49.1%
Ukraine			1,424	2.9%
Bulgaria			1,419	7.1%
Angola	37	−335	1,415	10.7%
Peru	27	41	1,377	2.3%
Serbia and Montenegro			1,360	6.6%
Sudan			1,349	7.6%
Nigeria	−739	588	1,200	2.1%
Argentina	678	1,836	1,020	0.8%

Source: World Bank, *Global Development Finance, 2005;* and World Bank, *World Development Report 2005.*

developing country, amounting to over $50 billion in 2003, or nearly 4 percent of its GDP.

Foreign capital in general tends to be more volatile than domestic capital, but FDI is usually more stable than other forms of private foreign capital. One key reason is that FDI is often attracted by either resource endowments or long-term fundamental economic strengths, factors that generally do not change as quickly as interest rates and exchange rates, which are stronger determinants of short-term bank loans and portfolio capital. Moreover, since FDI is characterized by significant management control in large, fixed-production facilities such as factories and mines, investors are less likely (and less able) to flee during economic downturns. During the 1997–98 Asian financial crises, FDI fell somewhat but much less than bank loans and portfolio capital, which dropped sharply.

Along with providing new capital, recipient countries hope that FDI will add to the demand for labor and **generate employment.** Not surprisingly, since FDI is a relatively small source of investment in most developing countries, its contribution to employment also tends to be small, accounting for less than 5 percent of total employment in most developing countries. However, the impact on employment varies greatly depending on the activity. FDI focused on resource-based capital-intensive industries, such as mining or petroleum, creates relatively few jobs, while investments in labor-intensive manufacturing create more jobs. The impact of FDI on wages and working conditions is controversial, with some people charging that MNCs pay low wages and impose harsh working conditions. While conditions vary and this may be true in some instances, on the whole, evidence suggests that MNCs pay higher average wages and have better average working conditions than domestic firms.[12]

Another benefit of at least some kinds of FDI, especially FDI in manufactured exports, is that it can help increase **specialization** in production. When firms in developing countries are part of a global production process, they can focus on the particular activity where they have a comparative advantage and produce most efficiently. Although domestically financed investment can also engage in very specialized production, FDI has the advantage of stronger links to other parts of a global chain. Firms in the automobile business need not make the entire car (and if they did, they might not be able to compete on world markets). Instead, they can specialize in assembly, production of basic components (such as door parts or wiring), manufacturing of more sophisticated parts (e.g., engines or transmissions), design, or other aspects of the production process. In today's production environment, it is difficult to classify an automobile as American, German, Japanese, or Korean, since various parts are made all over the world. Moreover, the particular activity that makes sense in an economy can change over time as resource endowments, skills, and economic policies change. When Intel made its first investments in the electronics industry in Malaysia in the early 1970s, it focused on low-skill activities such as simple assembly. Over the years, as the Malaysian workforce gained new skills and more Malaysians became experienced managers, activity shifted toward production of basic parts (e.g., keyboards), then to more-advanced components (such as microprocessors), and later to testing and research. More recently, electronics production in the Philippines has followed a similar progression.

FDI can also bring with it **access to world markets.** Developing countries capable of producing at competitive costs often find it difficult to penetrate foreign markets. Many multinationals, particularly in natural resources, chemicals, and other heavy industries, are vertically integrated, oligopolistic firms, for

[12]Edward Graham, *Fighting the Wrong Enemy: Antiglobal Activists and Multinational Enterprises* (Washington, DC: Institute for International Economics, 2000), Chapter 4.

which many transactions take place within the firm. Multinationals develop preferential access to customers by fashioning and adhering to long-term contracts in standardized products, such as petroleum, or by acquiring a reputation for delivering a specialized product of satisfactory quality on a reliable schedule, as in electronics and engineering. On their own, firms from developing country often require years to overcome such marketing advantages, and an affiliation with an MNC can help accelerate the process.

Among the most important potential benefits from foreign investment is the **transfer of technology, skills, and ideas.** Because much of the world's research and development activity takes place within North America, Europe, and East Asia, firms from these areas are a potentially rich source of innovative products, machinery, manufacturing processes, marketing methods, quality control, and managerial approaches. MNCs potentially can bring these new ideas and technologies with them, helping reduce costs and increase productivity in the host country. FDI is most valuable when these kinds of benefits spread beyond the local affiliate of the MNC itself and help other local firms and enterprises, generating positive externalities called **spillovers.** For example, local firms competing against the MNC may observe and adopt the technology brought from abroad to try to improve their own productivity. A domestic furniture maker might learn about new machinery, a special technique to finish wood products, or a different way to organize production that could lower its costs and increase its competitiveness. Competition from the MNC can push rival firms to reduce their costs through more-efficient use of all inputs and by introducing new technologies and techniques, generating an indirect benefit to all firms that buy from the MNC and its competitors.

While this kind of "horizontal" spillover to competitors can be important, MNCs clearly have the incentive to limit technology transfer to their rivals. They have stronger incentives to encourage "vertical" spillovers to firms operating up and down the supply chain that either sell to or buy from the MNC. MNCs want their local suppliers to produce at the lowest possible cost, so it is in their interest to work with suppliers to increase the suppliers' productivity by introducing new methods to improve quality and reliability and reduce costs. These changes provide indirect benefits to other firms that buy from these suppliers.[13]

One important way these kinds of spillovers can occur is through the **training of workers and managers.** Most developing countries do not have many well-trained managers with experience in organizing and operating large industrial

[13]See Howard Pack and Kamal Saggi, "Vertical Technology Transfer via International Outsourcing," *Journal of Development Economics* 65, no. 2 (2001), 389–415; and Garrick Blalock and Paul Gertler, "Foreign Direct Investment and Externalities: The Case for Public Intervention," in Theodore Moran, Edward Graham, and Magnus Blomstrom, eds., *Does Foreign Direct Investment Promote Development?* (Washington, DC: Institute for International Economics and Center for Global Development, 2004).

projects, such as those undertaken by multinational firms. MNCs have the incentive to train local managers and workers (both their own employees and their supplier's) and, in some circumstances, will send employees abroad to the parent company for training in production methods or management techniques. It is not uncommon for local managers to spend six months or more working in the parent company, then return to senior positions in the local affiliate. The immediate impact is to help increase productivity and profitability of the MNC. However, over time, these managers and workers may move to other firms or even start their own companies, bringing this new knowledge with them. When textile companies began to move from Korea and Taiwan to Indonesia in the 1980s, initially most senior managers were expatriates. Over time, more Indonesians were trained to fill these positions, and eventually some started their own companies that competed against the MNCs. When Mauritius first began to produce textiles and footwear in the early 1980s, virtually 100 percent of the export firms were foreign owned, but within 15 years, foreign firms controlled just 50 percent of total equity capital.[14]

However, just as FDI can create positive spillovers, it can create negative ones. MNCs might create air or water pollution or cause other environmental damage, generating a negative externality for the host country. (Of course, local investors also sometimes cause environmental damage, in some cases even worse damage.) While some MNCs have been guilty of causing extreme environmental damage, others bring with them cleaner and more efficient production techniques that help reduce environmental damage, as discussed in Chapter 20.

FDI in protected or inefficient activities can lead to net economic losses rather than gains by misallocating capital, labor, and other resources. For example, if a government encourages an MNC to invest in a petrochemicals company that can be profitable only with government subsidies or regulations that limit competition (like high import tariffs on competing products), the costs to the country are likely to be higher than the benefits. Firms operating under protection tend to use more outdated technologies and are less likely to be able to compete eventually on world markets. The firm might boast large profits and appear to be thriving, but the costs to taxpayers and to downstream customers forced to pay higher prices might be even larger.

Perhaps the biggest concern about FDI is the loss of local control over business. MNCs can drive out local businesses, and even where this might be economically efficient it can be politically very unpopular. A large efficient MNC can drive out small local business that operate at higher costs, particularly in countries with high trade barriers and other regulations where local firms may be relatively weak. Also, MNCs are more likely to repatriate their profits abroad, although some reinvest locally (and many local businesses also send their profits abroad). Concerns are most acute for the largest MNCs, whose size and control over resources often match and sometimes outstrip that of the recipient

---

[14]See Blalock and Gertler, "Foreign Direct Investment and Externalities."

country governments. Investment by a multinational corporation raises the specter of interference by, and dependence on, foreign economic powers beyond the control of the host country. In some cases valid social preferences over the control and distribution of income might outweigh economic efficiency arguments.

FDI and Growth

Ultimately, broad general statements about whether FDI is beneficial or harmful are difficult to make and can be misleading. Since FDI is so varied, much depends on the specific activity, the actions taken by the MNC and the government, and the reaction by local suppliers, competitors, and customers. Debate continues as to the existence and magnitude of spillovers, both positive and negative. As a result, research examining the relationships between FDI and growth has reached mixed conclusions. Some research has found a positive relationship, particularly where the workforce in the recipient country has achieved a minimum level of education, whereas other studies have found no relationship or even a negative one.[15]

Clearer patterns begin to emerge when researchers take into account the purpose and context of the FDI. Foreign investment that produces for the domestic market and relies heavily on subsidies or protection from competition is much less likely to be beneficial and may even generate economic losses for the host country. FDI in natural-resource-based industries depends heavily on the impact of the industries themselves. As described in Chapter 17, while primary product exports have at times helped spur development in some countries (such as diamonds in Botswana and petroleum in Malaysia and Indonesia), in other countries, natural resource abundance has been as much as curse as a blessing, such as petroleum in Nigeria or Venezuela, copper in Zambia, and diamonds in the Democratic Republic of the Congo and Sierra Leone.

FDI aimed at firms producing manufactured exports and operating in competitive global markets most often is found to have a positive relationship with growth and development. This type of activity tends to be economically efficient and conducive to importation of new technologies, training new workers and managers, and positive spillovers to suppliers and even competitors. Georgetown University economist Theodore Moran finds significant differences in

[15]The research on FDI, spillovers, and growth is extensive. For an example of a study finding a positive relationship in the presence of a minimum level of education in the recipient country, see E. Borensztein, J DeGregorio, and Jong-Wha Lee, "How Does Foreign Investment Affect Growth?" *Journal of International Economics* 45, no. 1 (1998), 115–72. For an influential study finding negative spillovers in Venezuela, see Brian Aitken and Ann E. Harrison, "Do Domestic Firms Benefit from Direct Foreign Investment? Evidence from Venezuela," *American Economic Review* 89, no. 3 (June 1999), 605–18. For a recent survey, see Robert Lipsey and Fredrick Sjöholm, "The Impact of Inward FDI on Host Countries: Why Such Different Answers?" in Moran et al., *Does Foreign Direct Investment Promote Development?*

operating characteristics between subsidiaries that are integrated into the international sourcing networks of their parent multinationals and those that serve protected domestic markets. Where parent firms use local affiliates as a part of a strategy to remain competitive in international markets, they maintain those affiliates at the cutting edge of technology, management, and quality control. But Moran finds that FDI in protected industries can hinder an economy, as these firms typically use older technologies and operate under restrictions that raise costs, hinder exports, and reduce productivity gains.[16]

Policies toward Foreign Direct Investment

Developing countries interested in attracting FDI and assuring maximum benefit generally use some combination of three broad strategies:

1. Improve the general environment for all kinds of investment (foreign or domestic) by strengthening infrastructure, reducing red tape, and improving the quality of labor.
2. Introduce specific policies and incentives to attract FDI, such as export processing zones, worker training, import protection, or tax holidays.
3. Impose requirements on MNCs (such as limits on equity holdings or repatriation of profits) in an attempt to capture more benefits locally.

IMPROVE THE GENERAL INVESTMENT ENVIRONMENT

The least-controversial approach, and one that can bring benefits beyond those associated with FDI, is to take steps to improve the general environment for investment and business operations. As we have already seen, businesses in poor countries face much larger regulatory burdens and higher costs than those in rich countries. To try to improve the general investment environment, governments can improve road and ports infrastructure, invest in utilities to make them more reliable and less expensive, reduce trade tariffs, strengthen the judicial process and the rule of law, and reduce unnecessary regulations and "red tape" that add to the cost of doing business. These steps should help attract new investment, both domestic and foreign, and help make existing investments more productive and profitable.

INTRODUCE POLICIES AND INCENTIVES AIMED SPECIFICALLY AT ATTRACTING FDI

The question of whether governments should take specific measures to encourage FDI even more than domestic investment turns on views on the existence and size of spillovers: If FDI brings with it positive spillovers that generate benefits to firms other than the MNC, then policies and incentives aimed specifically at attracting FDI may be appropriate. Where there are few if any positive

[16]Theodore Moran, "How Does FDI Affect Host Country Development? Using Industry Case Studies to Make Reliable Generalizations," in Moran et al., *Does Foreign Direct Investment Promote Development?*

spillovers and possibly negative ones, the argument for government action and special treatment is much weaker.

Three kinds of specific policies are common. First, host governments can provide effective and timely **information** to potential investors that markets might not provide on their own. Investors might not come to a particular country if they simply do not know much about it. Many governments in developing countries have established investment promotion agencies to "market" their countries and provide information on business costs, port facilities, natural resources, levels of education, climate, and other factors that might make their country attractive to investors. In some countries, this kind of promotion can help, but in others, it seems to make little difference.

Second, governments can undertake specific expenditures aimed at making their country more attractive for FDI. Many governments have established industrial parks or **export-processing zones (EPZs)** to increase investment and manufactured exports. The basic idea is that building infrastructure and improving the investment climate for an entire economy are likely to take a long time, so as an interim measure, the government could establish an enclave located near port facilities in which infrastructure is of high quality, utilities are reliable and of relatively low cost, and there are fewer regulations and less red tape. Typically, countries welcome both domestic and foreign investment in EPZs, but FDI tends to account for a greater share of the investment. Most of the countries that have been highly successful in producing manufactured exports have established EPZs or similar facilities, including EPZs in Malaysia, Korea, Mauritius, the Dominican Republic, and Indonesia; special economic zones in China; and maquiladoras in Mexico and similar stand-alone facilities in Tunisia and other countries. But EPZs and related facilities are not always successful and have failed when they have been poorly located, badly managed, or in other ways added to rather than reduced producer's costs.

Third and more controversial, governments can provide specific incentives to MNCs to increase their profitability, including protection from import competition, subsidies, or tax breaks. Governments provide **protection** by introducing tariffs and quotas to reduce imports of competing goods or provide outright monopoly control over local markets. These steps are most relevant for FDI aimed at producing for the domestic market, rather than for exporters. Because import protection and monopoly control create higher domestic prices and profits, in effect local consumers pay higher prices as a transfer to the multinationals' foreign stockholders. Since evidence suggests that FDI aimed for protected domestic markets brings with it the least benefits (and sometimes net economic losses), it is often difficult to justify this kind of intervention.

Perhaps the most controversial of all steps taken to encourage FDI is **income tax incentives.** While these incentives can take a wide variety of forms, the most common is *income tax holidays,* which exempt firms from paying taxes on corporate income, usually for three to six years. Most countries otherwise would tax profits at rates anywhere from 20 percent to as high as 50 percent. For tax holidays to help the multinationals, they must be creditable against income taxes due to their home country governments. Otherwise, if home countries tax firms on worldwide income, as all industrial countries except France do, then the MNC would pay less tax to the developing country but more to its home country. In effect, taxes foregone by the developing country would simply be transferred to tax revenues of the multinational's home country. Most industrial countries now permit their firms to take credit for tax holidays granted abroad through tax treaties negotiated between host- and home-country governments.

There is substantial debate about the circumstances, if any, under which tax holidays are justified. Most studies conclude that, for many kinds of FDI, income tax holidays have only marginal effects on multinational investment decisions and reward the multinationals for doing what they would have done in any case. This is especially true for firms attracted by natural resources or those intending to produce in protected domestic markets of the host countries. Under these circumstances, MNCs are attracted by specific characteristics of the host country, such as the presence of gold or petroleum deposits or a large domestic consumer market. These MNCs may have few other serious location options, so tax treatment may not be a critical factor in their investment decision. Moreover, tax holidays cannot turn an unprofitable investment into a profitable one: Taxes become relevant only once a firm is earning profits.

Evidence suggests that export-oriented, labor-intensive, "footloose" industries may be more sensitive to tax holidays and other incentives, since they have a much wider set of location options. Firms producing electronics products, shoes, textiles, clothing, games, and toys can choose among dozens of countries that offer the basics of political and economic stability, relatively low transport costs, and a pool of unskilled and semiskilled workers. Under these circumstances, tax holidays may be an important factor for the MNC in choosing its location. Since research suggests that these kinds of investments are more likely to provide positive spillovers to the host country, limited tax holidays may be justified. These steps always are controversial, however, as local firms and other MNCs quickly demand similar tax treatment, and it may be difficult for governments to resist this pressure.

REQUIREMENTS AND RESTRICTIONS ON FDI

Many governments impose restrictions and requirements on MNCs in an attempt to capture as much as possible of the expected benefits from foreign direct investment, including performance requirements, local ownership requirements, labor requirements, and restrictions on profit repatriation. It is possible that these policies can increase the benefits to the host country; however, under most circumstances, they discourage FDI.

Many host countries have made it mandatory for foreign investors to sell a specified share of equity, usually at least 51 percent, to local partners to form **joint ventures.** Through local ownership requirements, host governments hope to ensure the transfer of technology and managerial skills, limit the repatriation of profits, and maintain local control. However, parent multinationals often are more reluctant to allow diffusion of technology to joint ventures than to wholly owned subsidiaries. Moreover, many local joint-venture partnerships are pro forma arrangements involving local elites close to the centers of political power with little knowledge or expertise in business that simply receive occasional payment from the MNC as a figurehead partner. This is not always the case, however. In some cases, skilled local partners eventually can take greater control and possibly buy out the MNC.

Many countries impose **domestic content requirements** on MNCs, requiring them to purchase a certain share of their inputs locally (as opposed to through imports), often with the share increasing over time. The idea is to encourage local suppliers and ensure stronger links between the MNC and local firms. Ideally, MNCs would choose to purchase locally in any case, but when they are forced to do so it usually indicates that the local suppliers are not producing at low enough price and high enough quality to compete with imports. Thus, these requirements add directly to the costs of the MNC and can discourage investment. Similar **production requirements** can be aimed at labor or technology transfer. Policies that make foreign firms utilize local personnel are aimed not only at job creation but also at increasing absorptive capacity for the transfer of technology from multinationals. Developing countries have tried to promote technology transfer by imposing standards requiring multinational firms to import only the most-advanced capital equipment rather than used machinery. Other common restrictions include ceilings on repatriation of profits to the parent corporation and stiff taxes on profit remittances. As with domestic content requirements, if not carefully designed, these restrictions can deter investment and may do little in the long run to help transfer benefits to local entities.

Overall, the accumulated evidence indicates that some types of FDI bring large benefits and others bring small or even negative benefits. This suggests that the best general policy is to get the basics right to make the investment climate more attractive for both domestic and foreign investment: reliable transportation, power, and communications facilities; freedom from unnecessary or onerous government regulations; capable institutions; adherence to the rule of law; macroeconomic and political stability; and labor markets in which wages are matched by productivity. In addition to this general approach, special public investments or incentives should be used carefully and reserved for FDI in which the potential for positive spillovers is greatest, usually labor-intensive manufactured and service exports, where clear performance targets can be established and profits depend on efficient operation.

SUMMARY

- Both public investment and private investment are central to economic growth and development. Public investment generally focuses on roads, ports, telecommunications facilities, schools, and health facilities. Private investment tends to be much larger than public investment and provides the dynamism for the vast majority of new jobs, new technologies, and growth in economic output.

- The quantity and productivity of investment are closely related. Countries that establish an environment in which investment is highly productive are likely to attract larger volumes of investment; at the same time, as investment volumes increase, productivity tends to decline. Increasing the productivity of investment can have as large or larger impact on growth than increasing the volume of investment.

- Cost-benefit analysis provides a rigorous technique for evaluating both public and private investments and calculating the net present value over time of each investment. This technique can be used for commercial evaluation (to calculate private-sector financial benefits), economic evaluation (to measure the economic costs and benefits to society as a whole), or social evaluation (incorporating the impact of investments on important social goals).

- The key factors that influence investment include macroeconomic and political stability, infrastructure, economic openness, institutional quality and governance, regulatory quality, and the basic costs of doing business. These features influence both the quality of investment and its ultimate productivity.

- Foreign direct investment can generate important benefits, but not all FDI is alike. FDI focused on firms producing exports on competitive global markets appears to be most beneficial, creating jobs and bringing new technologies and ideas from abroad, among other "spillovers." FDI for natural resources or for firms operating in protected domestic markets generally has had more mixed benefits and sometimes has been costly to recipient countries.

- Policies specifically aimed at attracting FDI, such as tax holidays, are more controversial than those aimed at improving the general investment environment. These approaches may be effective for some kinds of investors (especially "footloose" investors that can easily change locations) but costly to recipient countries in other situations.

12

Fiscal Policy

The next two chapters focus on two sets of government policy instruments that operate across all sectors of an economy: fiscal policy and financial policy. Both sets of instruments can play critical roles, for good and ill, in the mobilization of domestic saving. Moreover, both types of policies have far-reaching effects on income distribution, employment, efficiency, and economic stability. In this chapter, we focus on **fiscal policy,** which encompasses all measures pertaining to the level and structure of government expenditures and revenues. **Financial policy,** the subject of Chapter 13, includes monetary policy and a wide variety of policy measures affecting the growth and allocation of financial assets in an economy.

As the terms are used in this book, **government revenues** consist of all tax and nontax revenues flowing to the government treasury, including surpluses of public enterprises owned by governments and domestic borrowing by the treasury. **Government expenditures** are all outlays from the government budget, including those for current expenditures, such as civil service salaries, maintenance, military costs, interest payments, and subsidies to cover losses by public enterprise. The other major category on the expenditure side is capital expenditures, sometimes also referred to as *development expenditures,* such as outlays for construction of irrigation canals, roads, and schools and for the purchase of nonmilitary equipment owned by government.

Fiscal policy operates through both the tax and expenditure sides of the government budget. The locus of decision making on fiscal policy in developing countries typically is split between two agencies: the Ministry of Finance (the

Treasury Department) and the Ministry (or Board) of Planning. In most countries, the Ministry of Finance is assigned primary responsibility for the design and implementation of tax policy and decisions concerning current government consumption expenditures. The Ministry of Planning sometimes holds sway on decisions concerning government capital expenditures. Some economists and policy makers reserve the term *fiscal policy* for that which is done by the Ministry of Finance and the term *development policy* for that which is under the ultimate control of the Ministry of Planning. But the distinction between public capital and consumption spending essentially is an arbitrary one, in both theory and practice.

THE GOVERNMENT BUDGET: GENERAL CONSIDERATIONS

Much of economic policy operates through the expenditure and tax sides of the government budget. To be sure, many government activities have an importance out of proportion to their relative significance in the overall government budget. This is particularly true for the conduct of financial policy; government regulation of competition, trade, and investment; and operations of public enterprises. In this chapter, the term *public sector* refers only to that part of government operations reflected in the expenditure side of the budget.

All societies, from those organized under laissez-faire principles to those organized under socialism, require a public sector, simply because, even under the best conditions, the market mechanism cannot perform all economic functions desired by households. Because of *public goods* and other types of *market failures* discussed in Chapter 5 and elsewhere, the market alone cannot satisfy all consumer wants, even when societies have a strong preference for decentralized decision making. For private goods, such as rice, saris, or TV sets, the signals provided by unfettered competitive market mechanisms guide producers to satisfy consumer demand efficiently. For pure public goods, the market fails entirely. There are few examples of pure public goods; national defense and lighthouses generally are cited as illustrations. The term *public good* refers to a good or service that exhibits two traits: nonrival consumption and nonexcludability.

In *nonrival consumption,* one person's use of a good does not reduce the benefits available to others. That being the case, no one has any incentive to offer to pay for the good: If it is available to one, it is available to all. *Nonexcludability* means that it is either impossible or prohibitively expensive to exclude anyone from the benefits once the good is available. In either case, the private market cannot provide the good: Market failure is total. For most public goods, the characteristics of nonrival consumption and nonexcludability are present but less pronounced and the market can function only in an inefficient way. Examples include vaccination against contagious diseases, primary education, police protection, and mosquito abatement. Therefore, it is evident that the appropriate role of the public sector, to a significant degree, is a technical issue. Extension of the public sector beyond that required to provide public goods and correct for other market failures is an ideological issue, to be settled through a political process. Most countries, industrial and developing, have extended the size of the public sector well beyond that required for technical reasons, to include income redistribution, provision of pension schemes, and ownership and operation of airlines, shipping, utilities, manufacturing enterprises, and banks. Government investment, particularly in developing countries, also tends to account for a large share, often as much as half, of all capital formation.

GOVERNMENT EXPENDITURES

In the late 1800s, German political theorist Adolph Wagner propounded his famous *law of expanding state activity*. The thrust of Wagner's law was that the relative size of the public sector in the economy has an inherent tendency to grow as per capita income increases. Although few fiscal economists accept Wagner's law without several qualifications, poor countries do have smaller public sectors than rich ones, when size of the public sector is measured as the ratio of government expenditure to GDP.

Two classes of expenditure account for most of the difference between high-income and developing countries' outlays as a share of GDP. Military expenditures in the industrial countries used to be at 5 percent, or about double the share of national product in the developing countries, but military expenditures in high-income countries have come down sharply as a share of GDP since the end of the Cold War and levels of military spending are now quite similar across income levels (see Figure 12–1). Expenditures on health are between 0 and 3 percent in the low- and lower-middle-income countries listed in Table 12–1, but between 2 and 7 percent of GDP in the upper-middle-income and high-income countries in the same table. But social protection accounts for most of the difference: In Germany, this accounts for as much as 18 percent of GDP while in Zimbabwe, social protection accounts for only 6 percent of GDP.

Hundreds of books and articles have been written on the reasons for differences in government expenditure across countries and through time. The results of the studies often conflict. Although associated with income growth, these differences do not seem to be related in any systematic way to population growth, but may be strongly influenced by other demographic factors, such as urbanization.

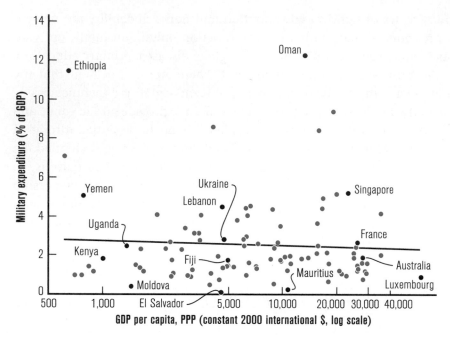

FIGURE 12-1. Military Expenditure as a Share of GDP (country data range from 1995 to 2003)

Source: *World Development Indicators* database, 0-devdata.worldbank.org.luna.
wellesley.edu/dataonline/, accessed July 2005.

TABLE 12-1. Central Government Expenditure as a Share of GDP

	YEAR	TOTAL OUTLAY	GENERAL PUBLIC SERVICES	DEFENSE	HEALTH	EDUCATION	SOCIAL PROTECTION	ECONOMIC AFFAIRS
				PERCENT OF GDP				
Low income								
India	2003	16	10	2	0	0	N.A.	3
Madagascar	2002	14	6	0	1	3	0	2
Zimbabwe	1997	34	8	2	3	8	6	2
Lower-middle income								
Bolivia	2003	31	6	2	3	7	5	5
Thailand	2003	17	2	1	2	4	2	4
Tunisia	2003	32	5	2	2	6	7	5
Upper-middle income								
Brazil	1998	27	8	1	2	2	13	1
Czech Republic	2003	41	5	2	7	4	13	6
Mauritius	2003	24	6	0	2	4	5	3
High income								
Korea, Rep.	2001	20	5	3	0	4	3	4
Germany	2003	33	4	1	6	0	18	2
United States	2003	21	3	4	5	1	7	1

Note: The percentages accruing to the components of total outlay do not sum to the percentage of GDP that total outlay accounts for because a few categories of expenditures are not included in the table.
Source: International Monetary Fund, *Government Financial Statistics Yearbook 2004*, 12–16, 27–31.

Current and Recurrent Expenditures

The current expenditure side of the budget includes expenditures that must be made annually as long as the government is involved in any particular activity. These expenditures also often are referred to as *recurrent expenditures,* because they recur year after year, in contrast with capital expenditures, which come to an end when a bridge or highway is completed and turned over to the operating authorities. Table 12–2 breaks down central government expenditure into five categories: (1) compensation of employees; (2) the use of goods and services, including equipment and materials for use by public sector employees, maintenance, and all spending on military equipment; (3) interest payments on the government debt; (4) subsidies, grants, and other social benefits to individuals, international organizations, foreign governments, and producers; and (5) other expenses. The table shows a wide variance in the proportions of total expenditure devoted to each category. Some of this is related to the stage of development: Richer countries have larger social welfare programs that cause subsidies, grants, and other social benefits to be a much higher share of expenditures than in most lower-income countries. Huge differences in interest payments on public debt reflect differing policy choices and alternative ways to manage—or mismanage—economies. And, in some cases, accounting practices may be responsible for differences in the way expenditures are reported.

TABLE 12-2. Composition of Government Expenses, by Type

| | | | PERCENT OF TOTAL EXPENSES | | | | |
	YEAR	EXPENSES (% OF GDP)	COMPENSATION OF EMPLOYEES	USE OF GOODS AND SERVICES	INTEREST	SUBSIDIES GRANTS, AND SOCIAL BENEFITS	OTHER EXPENSES
Low income							
India	2003	16	9	13	27	29	1
Madagascar	2002	9	49	18	13	10	10
Zimbabwe	1997	32	38	13	21	28	0
Lower-middle income							
Bolivia	2003	29	24	17	9	45	4
Thailand	2003	15	36	26	7	25	6
Russian Federation	2003	23	18	19	7	55	1
Upper-middle income							
Brazil	1998	26	13	10	15	63	0
Czech Republic	2003	40	9	7	2	59	24
Mauritius	2003	20	38	13	14	33	3
High income							
Korea, Rep.	2001	19	11	12	6	56	15
Germany	2003	33	5	4	6	81	3
United States	2003	21	13	15	9	62	1

Source: International Monetary Fund, *Government Financial Statistics Yearbook 2004,* 12–17, 22–26.

A pervasive belief is that recurrent expenditures in some sense are less important and should have a lower priority than public investment or capital expenditures. Recurrent costs of public investment programs by convention are labeled *government consumption,* implying that increases for such purposes do not increase productive capacity. But governments often focus so much on capital expenditures that they make inadequate provision for the recurrent operational and maintenance costs of previous investments. In many parts of the developing world, public sector capital is underutilized and allowed to decay because of inadequate provision for the recurrent expenditure requirements of the project.

As indicated already, the division between recurrent and capital expenditures also can be somewhat arbitrary. Recurrent outlays on education and health, for example, are investments in human capital that can have major long-term benefits to economic development as discussed in Chapters 8 and 9.

Wages and Salaries

Wages and salaries constitute a large fraction of recurrent outlays of governments, especially in the low- and lower-middle-income countries: In Table 12–2, four of the six countries in this category devote approximately a quarter or more of their total expenses to wages and salaries.

The stereotypical image of public sector bureaucracies in developing countries is one of bloated payrolls and inefficient, corrupt, even indolent behavior. The evidence for this view essentially is anecdotal. Reliable international comparisons of civil service performance are almost nonexistent. It is easy to accumulate anecdotes involving bureaucratic snafus, stupidities, corruption, and shortsightedness in both developing and developed societies. No firm judgment can be made on the extent of overstaffing of public agencies or overremuneration of officials or bureaucratic extravagance in developing countries relative to industrial countries: Civil service payrolls in Massachusetts and New Jersey may be as bloated as in many developing countries. And, despite examples of gross venality and blatant use of political patronage in public sector hiring in segments of the civil service systems of some developing countries (and many U.S. cities), there also are examples of first-rate professionalism and codes of conduct that may rival those found in industrial countries, as in the Singapore and Hong Kong civil service systems.

In some countries, the salary bill for civil servants could be compressed sufficiently to augment government savings. But, in others, like Bolivia, Peru, and Kenya, civil service salaries remain so low relative to those available in the private sector that it has been difficult to attract and hold the type of qualified public-sector managers, secretaries, and technicians essential for efficient government operation.

About the only safe generalization that can be made about civil service systems in developing countries is that they appear no more, or less, responsive to the socioeconomic changes that accompany development than any other group in society. In the 1950s, it was almost impossible to discuss Latin American development without hearing repeated mention of the "antidevelopmental" effects of the famous *mordida* (bite) then commonly demanded by civil servants for doing what they should—or should not—be doing. It was commonly believed then that such behavior was the result of both low civil service salaries and unalterable cultural habits. Low civil service salaries contribute to the problem, but culture probably has relatively little explanatory power. When low salaries are combined with high customs duties, government licensing of all kinds of economic activity, and other such discretionary authority in the hands of government officials, the temptation on the part of many of those officials to ask for side payments can become irresistible. One powerful motive behind the decision of many countries to move toward greater reliance on unfettered market forces is that this eliminated many of the opportunities for inappropriate side payments. That made it easier for the government to focus on the more limited number of cases of inappropriate official behavior that remained. Singapore and Hong Kong are good examples of how government actions of this sort have reduced rent seeking to levels well below those found in much of the rest of the world, including in the richest nations.

Purchases of Goods and Services

Governments need supplies, such as paper, computers, and fuel, to perform their functions; they also purchase services, such as construction, transportation, and janitorial work, from private firms. If a road maintenance crew consists of employees of the Ministry of Works, their salaries come under the heading *compensation of employees* and their supplies are categorized as *use of goods and services* in Table 12–2. But, if the ministry hires a private contractor instead, all the expenditure falls under *use of goods and services*. Two important items in this category are *maintenance and repair* and some nonwage *military spending*.

If there is waste in government procurement in some areas, there are other areas where, for lack of funds, governments have been too miserly in appropriating funds. As already suggested, this is particularly true with regard to **maintenance costs** for the upkeep of the public-sector capital stock and many vital operating expenses. The phenomenon is aptly characterized by Peter Heller:

> In Colombia, new tarmac roads have suffered rapid and premature deterioration for lack of maintenance. Throughout West Africa, many new schools have opened without qualified teachers, educational materials, or equipment. Agricultural

projects are often starved for extension workers, fertilizer, or seeds. In the Sahel, pastoral wells constructed for livestock projects have fallen into disrepair. In Bolivia, doctors are often stranded at rural health centers for lack of gasoline for their vehicles.[1]

Underfinancing of recurrent costs is pervasive across countries, including the United States, where items such as bridge maintenance have been long postponed in many states. In developing countries, however, this pattern is exacerbated by the policies of aid donors, who strongly support capital projects but, as a matter of policy, have been reluctant to support the recurrent costs of these projects. As a result, painfully accumulated public-sector capital stock tends to deteriorate rapidly until eventually it is beyond maintenance and requires new construction. Few countries are in a position to expand public savings by further compressing this category of recurrent expenditures.

The share of **military spending** in government expenditure as a fraction of GDP shows no trend as incomes rise (Figure 12–1). On average the low- and middle-income countries spend about the same share of their national incomes (between 2 and 3 percent) on the military as high-income countries. High-income countries a decade and more ago typically spent a higher percentage than that on the military, but the end of the Cold War contributed to cutbacks in the military budgets of these countries. Burundi, Ethiopia, Israel, Jordan, Kuwait, and Oman all spent more than 7 percent of their GDPs on military expenditures. Some other high spenders are Greece, Iran, Lebanon, Pakistan, Singapore, Turkey, the United States, and Yemen, all at over 4 percent of GDP.

Military spending is directed toward noneconomic goals, such as defense against external threats and internal instability. What is known about the impact of military spending on economic growth? Clearly, all countries could expand public savings significantly by reducing military spending. Beyond that, the topic is controversial. Nevertheless, research suggests that high military spending has many more negative effects on growth than positive ones, including the large contributions made by military spending to debt in some countries, the diversion of scarce resources from more-productive civilian uses, and the effects of highly import-intensive military outlays on balance-of-payments deficits.[2]

Interest Payments

Interest on government debt is a major cost for many developing countries, accounting for more than a fifth of total expenses in India and Zimbabwe (Table 12–2). Chapter 15 discusses the debt crises caused by overborrowing by devel-

---

[1]Peter Heller, "Underfinancing of Recurrent Development Costs," *Finance and Development* 16, no. 1 (March 1979), 38–41.

[2]Anita Bhatia, *Military Expenditure and Economic Growth* (Washington, DC: World Bank, 1987).

oping countries, especially in Latin America and Africa. The Asian financial crisis that began in 1997 also involved excessive borrowing, but unlike the earlier Latin American and African cases, most of the Asian borrowing was by the private sector and the banking system. In the Asian case, therefore, the borrowing did not show up on the expenditure ledgers of the government. In situations where the government is or has been a major borrower, interest on government debt reflects past decisions about deficit finance and external borrowing. Interest outlays are difficult to reduce in the short term, even if budgets are balanced and borrowing ceases. Debt payments can be radically reduced if a government defaults on its debt obligations, like Bolivia and Peru in the 1980s. Indonesia in the late 1990s did not formally default on its government debt, but it did restructure that debt in agreement with the Paris Club, thus reducing its interest payments. Debt payments can also be radically reduced if the lenders agree to a debt moratorium or debt forgiveness. From the debt crisis of the 1980s through the beginning of the twenty-first century, many people from politicians to rock stars have advocated debt forgiveness for the poorest countries and some official debt relief programs are now in place. The issue of debt will be discussed further in Chapter 15.

Subsidies

A variety of subsidies and other transfers account for substantial shares of expenditures in developing and industrial countries. In Table 12–2, the shares range from 10 percent in Madagascar to more than 50 percent in the Russian Federation, Brazil, the Czech Republic, the Republic of Korea, Germany, and the United States. This category includes subsidies to consumers, social welfare payments, and subsidies to loss-making state-owned enterprises, as well transfers to international organizations and foreign governments.

Consumer subsidies are particularly common for basic foods. Countries such as Colombia, Egypt, India, Indonesia, and Sri Lanka have provided large subsidies on purchases of staple foods such as rice or wheat flour. A typical mechanism is to distribute price-controlled foods through state-owned entities, then absorb losses in food distribution through budgetary transfers to these enterprises (see Chapter 16). When the world price of oil rose during the 1970s, most oil-producing countries (and a few oil importers) generously subsidized the domestic use of refined products; a few, such as Venezuela, still do. Budgetary subsidies also have been common for rural electrification (Malaysia and the Philippines), contraceptive devices (Indonesia), fertilizer (Indonesia and Sri Lanka), bank interest payments on savings deposits (Indonesia), and urban bus services (Colombia, Indonesia, and others).

As incomes rise, countries typically undertake social welfare programs that transfer funds to citizens for medical care and retirement. The high share of subsidies and other transfers for the industrial countries in Table 12–2 reflects programs such as Medicare, Medicaid, and Social Security in the United States. The transition economies took on heavy obligations of this sort under their communist regimes (note the Czech Republic's 59 percent share in Table 12–2) and now find these obligations especially burdensome. Developing countries, especially middle-income economies, also are moving toward medical and pension plans that may swell their outlays on transfers in the future. Some of these will fund themselves through contributions from those who will benefit, as is true for some of the programs in the rich countries. But experience suggests that contributions will fall short of benefits and governments will bear part of the burden.

In virtually all developing countries employing budgetary subsidies, the stated purpose has been income redistribution. For foods, especially grains, the argument appears plausible, even if the ultimate effect is not always what was intended. Heavy subsidies on fertilizer use in Indonesia had a high payoff in greater rice production and rural income. The role of many other subsidies in securing goals of income redistribution is less clear, however, as we shall see. Whatever the ultimate impact of budget subsidies on income distribution, clearly, in many countries, substantial sums are involved and efforts to remove or reduce them meet with strong resistance virtually everywhere. Riots have occurred following the reduction of food subsidies in Sri Lanka, Egypt, Turkey, Zambia, and other countries; and social disturbances followed the reduction of gasoline subsidies in Indonesia, Colombia, and Thailand, when these were coupled with increases in urban bus fares. It is clear why governments often view proposals to reduce subsidies with even more reservation than proposals for tax increases. Yet, by the late 1980s through to the first decade of the twenty-first century, the need to stabilize economies by reducing budget deficits had become so acute that many countries were forced to shrink their subsidies.

State-Owned Enterprises

A significant portion of governmental outlays for subsidies and other transfers has been devoted to covering large deficits in state-owned enterprises (SOEs). Five decades ago, SOEs were not numerous in developing countries and, with notable exceptions such as Turkey and Mexico, typically were confined to a few sectors of their economies. Commonly, SOEs were limited to the so-called natural monopolies (decreasing-cost public utilities); monopoly production of sumptuary products such as liquor, beer, and tobacco; and so-called basic necessities such as salt and matches.[3]

---

[3]For a good discussion of some of the reasons for the development of large public enterprise sectors in developing nations, see R. P. Short, "The Rule of Public Enterprises: An International Statistical Comparison," IMF department memo 83/34, 1983, International Monetary Fund, Washington, DC.

With independence after World War II, there was a rapid expansion in the number and relative importance of state enterprises in developing economies. This was particularly so in Africa, where more than half the SOEs were established between 1967 and 1980; in Tanzania alone, the number of state enterprises increased tenfold from 1965 through 1985.[4] By 1980, SOEs were common, and often dominant, in manufacturing, construction, banking services, natural resource industries, and agriculture. Although SOEs typically were small-scale undertakings in most developing countries prior to 1950, many now are among the largest firms in their countries, and some are among the largest enterprises in their fields anywhere the world.

Deficits in the state enterprises averaged 4 percent of the GDP across all developing countries in the mid-1970s. The problem worsened in the early 1980s, particularly in such countries as Brazil, Costa Rica, the Dominican Republic, Ecuador, Egypt, the Philippines, Turkey, and Venezuela, where SOE deficits reached between 3 and 12 percent of the GDP. In all these countries, the rest of the public sector would have generated a fiscal surplus, excluding the net transfers to the state enterprises.[5] By the late 1980s and through the first decade of the twenty-first century, the drain of SOE subsidies on government budgets has led to efforts by many developing countries to eliminate these subsidies by privatizing their SOEs. International aid agencies frequently have made SOE privatization a condition for further assistance. Privatization, however, has been a slow process, because it has been actively resisted by SOE managers and workers, not to mention politicians that use SOE employment as a patronage machine for their supporters. In countries where a large part of the private sector is controlled by minorities, as is the case with the Chinese minority in Southeast Asia or the South Asian minority in East Africa, the majority population often fears that privatization is simply a way of turning even more of modern business over to the minority.

Intergovernment Transfers

Transfers from central to subnational governments conventionally are treated as recurrent expenditures, even though subnational governments (provinces, departments, counties, municipalities) may use the proceeds for capital formation, such as construction of schools and hospitals. However, some countries, such as Indonesia, classify some transfers as capital spending and others as consumption, so international comparisons are difficult. In a few cases, subnational governments with small transfers have access to rich sources of revenue. This is true for Bolivia, where oil-producing provinces receive large oil royalties,

---

[4] *World Development Report 1988* (New York: Oxford University Press for the World Bank, 1988).
[5] *World Development Report 1988*, p. 171.

and for Malaysia, where the state governments of Sabah and Sarawak earned substantial tax revenues from the export of tropical timber. In most unitary states, such as Chile, government affairs at virtually all levels are run from the capital, and subnational units of governments have few responsibilities to go with their limited sources of local revenue.

Elsewhere, including many federal countries, transfer of funds from the central government to subnational units is essential because the center has monopolized the most productive sources of tax revenue. In most cases, national governments impose income taxes because subnational governments lack the resources and skill required to administer such a complex tax and could not do so effectively anyway because the income tax base easily can migrate within a country. Similarly, the major source of tax revenue for some developing countries, import duties, must remain a central government resource, since most countries have only a few serviceable ports.

We have just seen that there are few easy ways to reduce government recurrent expenditure to achieve higher public savings. The scope for doing so often is greatest in the areas of military spending and subsidies to cover deficits of state-owned enterprises. Together, these two categories of recurrent spending can account for 7–10 percent of GDP.

TAX POLICY AND PUBLIC SAVING

For much of the postwar period, extending well into the 1970s, the most widely prescribed measures to boost public saving were policies to raise tax collections, especially increased tax rates and new taxes. This tendency was reinforced by policies of aid donors and the advice of foreign experts, who encouraged countries to generate high tax ratios, by making full use of their taxable capacity. **Taxable capacity** was determined in terms of an index composed of per capita income, mineral and oil exports, and the share of foreign trade in the GDP. High values for these variables suggested higher taxable capacity, either because of a higher margin of income over subsistence (high per capita income) or because of the accessibility of the tax base in oil- and mineral-exporting economies and highly open economies. Exports and imports easily are taxed, because they pass through bottlenecks (ports), where they are tracked more easily than items in domestic trade.

By the mid-1980s and through the first decade of the twenty-first century, however, a wide consensus shared by development specialists and government officials was that high tax ratios were not necessarily a virtue nor low tax ratios a vice in mobilizing domestic savings. Tax ratios reflect both opportunity and ideology. Sub-Saharan African countries in particular tend to tax themselves more heavily relative to their taxable capacities than countries in Asia.[6] Ideology may be a factor, but a high tax ratio may reflect that opportunities for mobilizing other types of savings, especially private savings, are limited because of poorly developed and organized financial systems. Latin American countries tend to dominate any list of countries with low tax effort. This may merely reflect the relatively greater ease with which private savings can be mobilized through the financial system in Latin America. Since 1945, extended periods of robust growth of organized financial markets have occurred in many Latin American countries, particularly in Mexico, Brazil, Argentina, and Chile and later in Colombia and Venezuela.

Tax measures can be used to expand public saving or shrink a destabilizing government deficit, except where taxes are so high that they result in lower domestic savings overall. Even when the government's marginal propensity to consume is significantly less than 1, there is no guarantee that the higher public saving made possible by higher tax revenues will result in an appreciable expansion of *overall* national saving. As shown later in this chapter, some part of any higher taxes will come out of private saving.

A number of tax measures are available for increasing public saving or reducing destabilizing deficits, including (1) periodic increases in rates imposed under existing taxes; (2) enactment of new taxes to tap previously unutilized sources of revenue; (3) improvements in tax administration that allow greater collection under existing taxes at present tax rates by reducing tax avoidance and evasion; and (4) major reform of the entire tax structure, involving elements of options 1, 2, and 3. For many countries, options 1 and 2 offer only slight hope for increased collections. Options 3 and 4 perhaps are the more difficult to implement but, if feasible, are much more likely to achieve the desired results.

As incomes rise, so does the share of gross national income (GNI) collected in tax revenues, from 16 percent on average for low-income countries to 27 percent for high-income countries. Table 12–3 shows that the composition of tax revenue may also differ markedly between developing and developed countries; while 45 percent of Madagascar's tax revenue in 2002 came from taxes on international trade, only 6 percent of the Republic of Korea's tax revenue came from taxes on international trade in 2001. Import and export duties, in particular, decline as incomes rise. Domestic income taxes tend to rise with increasing incomes. Some of the reasons for these variations are explored in the next sections.

---

[6]For the late 1970s, the average tax ratio for sub-Saharan African countries was 18 percent; that for Asia was but 15 percent. By 1985, tax revenues as a percent of GDP were about 23 percent in Africa, 16 percent in East Asia, and only 12 percent in South Asia. See Vito Tanzi, "Quantitative Aspects of Tax Systems in Developing Countries," in David Newberry and Nicholas Stern, eds., *The Theory of Taxation for Developing Countries* (London: Oxford University Press, 1987); and World Bank, *World Development Report 1988*, p. 82.

TABLE 12-3. Composition of Tax Systems by Type of Tax

	YEAR	TOTAL TAXES (% OF GDP)	COMPOSITION OF TAXES (% OF TOTAL TAXES)			
			DOMESTIC INCOME TAXES	TAXES ON GOODS AND SERVICES	TAXES ON INTERNATIONAL TRADE	OTHER TAXES
Low income						
India	2003	9	38	42	20	0
Madagascar	2002	8	23	30	45	2
Zimbabwe	1997	25	48	26	23	2
Lower-middle income						
Bolivia	2003	13	11	68	6	15
Thailand	2003	15	36	51	12	1
Russian Federation	2003	13	9	65	26	0
Upper-middle income						
Brazil	1998	12	50	43	6	0
Czech Republic	2003	17	42	54	2	2
Mauritius	2003	17	16	54	25	5
High income						
Korea, Republic	2001	15	37	46	6	11
Germany	2003	23	50	46	0	3
United States	2003	19	59	24	1	16

Note: Domestic income taxes are the sum of taxes on income, profits, and capital gains and taxes on payroll and the workforce. Other taxes are the sum of the taxes named such by in the *Government Financial Statistics Yearbook 2004* and taxes on property. All data represent central government tax revenues except for the United States and Germany; because of their federal systems, general government tax revenue data were used.
Source: International Monetary Fund, *Government Financial Statistics Yearbook 2004*, 17–21.

Taxes on International Trade

Although reliance on the taxes of foreign trade has diminished in recent years, particularly in middle-income countries, tax revenue structures in developing countries historically have depended heavily on import duties. Many low-income countries remain markedly dependent on import duties. This is particularly so for countries like the Gambia, Uganda, Rwanda, Sudan, Togo, and Yemen, where at least half the total government revenue comes from taxes on imports. Dependence on import duties is much less marked in middle-income countries, which have developed alternative sources of tax revenue.

For most countries, attempts to raise revenues through higher duties are infeasible and undesirable on economic grounds. Higher import duties intensify the incentive for smuggling or evading tariffs. Various studies have shown that, for countries with already high duty rates, the incentive to smuggle increases disproportionately with further increases. Therefore, a 10 percent rise in duty rates can result in an increase in smuggling activity by more than 10 per-

BOX 12-1   TAX RATES AND SMUGGLING: COLOMBIA

In Colombia, before 1969, when the import duty rate on cigarettes was over 100 percent, it was virtually impossible to purchase duty-paid cigarettes. At such high rates, import duty collections on cigarettes were nil and the market was flooded with smuggled foreign brands. In 1969, the duty rate was reduced to 30 percent. Cigarette smuggling on the poorly policed Caribbean coast of that country continued, but duty-paid packages began to appear in the mountainous interior, and duty collections on this product soared. Smuggling profits possible under a 30 percent duty were no longer high enough to compensate smugglers for the risks of arrest. Similar phenomena have been observed in Indonesia, Bolivia, and elsewhere.

cent, as illustrated by the case study of Colombia (Box 12–1). And, in mountainous countries, such as Afghanistan and Bolivia, or archipelago countries, such as Indonesia and the Philippines, borders are especially porous to smuggled imports.

Reliance on import duties for additional revenues may be infeasible for another reason. Except in open economies such as Hong Kong, Singapore, and Malaysia, the typical structure of import duties in developing countries, as explained in greater detail in Chapter 19, is heavily cascaded: The highest rates of duty in virtually all countries are imposed on consumer durable goods, particularly luxury goods (appliances, cameras, and so on); lower rates are applied on such intermediate goods as cement and leather; and the lowest duty rates are put on capital goods and imported items viewed as basic necessities (food, grains, fish, kerosene). When countries have sought additional revenues from tariffs, consumer goods already subject to high tariffs have been taxed even higher. Higher rates on necessities were considered inadvisable for equity reasons, and higher rates on capital goods and intermediate goods were deemed unacceptable for fear this would retard industrialization programs. But the enactment of higher duties on consumer goods, particularly luxury consumer goods, generally did not produce higher revenue. The reason is simple: The price elasticity of demand is not 0 for any consumer good, and for many already subject to very high duties, price elasticity is relatively high, in some cases –2.0 or more. For an import already subject to a 150 percent duty, such as stereos, and with a demand price elasticity of –2.0, a 10 percent increase in duty rates actually would decrease tax revenue on this item by about 2 percent.[7]

[7]This result comes from applying the formula where R = total duty collections on stereos, t = rate of duty, and E = price elasticity of demand.

Export taxes are constitutionally prohibited in the United States and extremely rare in other industrial countries. But export taxes are not uncommon in developing countries, particularly in tropical Africa and Southeast Asia. Taxes ordinarily are imposed on exports of raw materials such as timber (Ivory Coast and Liberia), tin (Malaysia), jute (Pakistan), and diamonds (Botswana) and on foodstuffs such as coffee (Colombia), peanuts (the Gambia and Senegal), cocoa (Ghana), and tea (Sri Lanka).

Twenty developing countries relied on export taxes for more than 10 percent of total tax revenue in the 1980s, but in only seven countries, primarily low-income African countries, do export taxes account for more than 20 percent of revenue. Export taxes often are imposed in the belief that they are paid by foreign consumers. That is, the taxes themselves are thought to be exported to consumers abroad, along with the materials. But the conditions necessary for exporting taxes on exports to foreign consumers rarely are present.

Export taxes also are employed to promote nonrevenue goals, including increased processing of raw materials within natural-resource-exporting developing countries. This is done by imposing high rates of export tax on unprocessed exports (cocoa beans or logs) and lower or no rates of tax on processed items fabricated from raw materials (chocolate and plywood). In principle, this use of export taxes should increase the local value added on natural resource exports and thereby generate greater employment and capital income for the local economy. Unfortunately, in many cases, the result has been that a government gives up more in export tax revenues than its country gains in additional local value added, particularly when processed raw materials are exported tax free. One study documents several instances in Southeast Asia and Africa where the additional value added gained in heavily protected local processing of logs into plywood typically was less than half the amount of export tax revenue that would have been collected had timber been exported in the form of logs.[8]

Personal and Corporate Income Taxes

Harried ministers of finance, perceiving slack in personal and corporate income taxes, often resort to rate increases in these taxes, with no change in the tax base. The results usually are disappointing, particularly for the personal income tax. Even in middle-income countries, only a very small proportion of the population is covered by the personal income tax: only 2 percent in the 1970s in Ghana, Peru, and almost all other developing countries, although higher in Kenya and Turkey. In contrast, well over half the adult population in the United

---

[8]Robert Repetto and Malcolm Gillis, eds., *Public Policies and the Misuse of Forest Resources* (New York: Cambridge University Press, 1988), "Conclusions," Chapter 10.

States filed income tax returns in the 1990s. Therefore, few developing countries can rely heavily on the personal income tax for revenues. Whereas the personal income tax accounts for well over half of all federal tax in the United States (not including Social Security and Medicare payments), rarely does the personal income tax account for close to that much of total central government revenues in developing countries.

In Colombia, for instance, the personal income tax is as well developed as in any developing country. Yet, even though this tax typically is responsible for as much as 15–18 percent of national government revenues, a large share of it is paid by a small number of people: In the early 1970s, the top 4 percent of households paid two thirds of the total tax.[9] In general, personal income taxes are paid largely by urban elites. Not only are these groups usually the most vocal politically, but over the years, they have developed such a variety of devices for tax evasion and avoidance that rate increases stand little chance of raising additional revenues.

Rate increases for corporate taxes usually are not productive, either. In only 16 of 82 developing countries did the corporation income tax account for more than 20 percent of total taxes in the 1980s. In 1996, corporate taxes and personal income taxes taken together accounted for more than 30 percent of all revenue in only a third of a sample of 60 developing countries. And, in most of these countries, corporate tax collections usually originated with foreign natural-resource firms. Except for several middle-income countries, such as Argentina, Korea, Taiwan, and Mexico, the corporate form of doing business covers but a small portion of the private sector. To be sure, most state-owned firms are corporations, but few such firms outside the natural-resources sector earn sizable taxable profits. Even fewer pay substantial income taxes.

Sales and Excise Taxes

A much more-promising source of additional government revenue is indirect taxes on domestic transactions, such as sales and excise taxes. **Sales taxes,** including **value-added taxes,** are broad-based consumption taxes imposed on all products except those specifically exempted, such as food, farm inputs, and medicine. **Excise taxes** also are taxes on consumption, but these levies are imposed only on specifically enumerated items, typically tobacco, alcoholic beverages, gambling, and motor fuel. On average, developing countries depend on domestic commodity taxes for a substantial share nearly a third of total revenues (Table 12–3).

Virtually every developing country imposes some form of sales tax. In most, the tax is not applied to retail sales because of the burdensome administrative

[9]Malcolm Gillis and Charles E. McLure, Jr., "Taxation and Income Distribution: The Colombian Tax Reform of 1974," *Journal of Development Economics* 5, no. 3 (September 1978), 237.

requirements of collecting taxes from thousands of small retailers. In the past, as in Chile before 1970 and in some Indian states, the tax was imposed as a gross turnover tax collected at all levels of production and distribution, with harmful implications for efficiency, income distribution, and virtually every objective of tax policy. In developing countries, administrative problems are more tractable when the sales tax is confined to the manufacturing level: A much smaller number of firms is involved and the output of manufacturers is far more homogeneous than sales of retailers or wholesalers. For these reasons many low-income countries have utilized either the single-stage or the value-added form of manufacturers' tax, usually exempting very small producers. This kind of sales tax, however, involves more economic distortions than either a wholesale or a retail tax, and for that reason as well as for revenue motives, more and more middle-income countries have turned to taxes at the retail level.[10]

Increasingly, these taxes have taken the form of one or another variant of the value-added tax (VAT), widely seen as the most effective method of taxing consumption yet developed. Nearly 60 countries, including all members of the European Community, have adapted the VAT since it was first adopted in its comprehensive retail form in Brazil in 1967.[11] Over 40 developing countries had adopted the tax by 1994, either to replace older, outdated forms of sales taxes or to allow them to reduce reliance on harder-to-collect income and property taxes. Table 12–4 provides a chronology of adoption for the VAT in 44 selected developing countries, as well as the share of the VAT in GDP and overall tax revenues.

Virtually all developing and industrial countries using the VAT have chosen to extend the tax through the retail level. A VAT extended through the retail level has a tax base virtually identical to a single stage of retail sales tax and, when imposed at the same rate as the latter tax, generates almost identical revenues. Both are indirect taxes on consumption.[12]

Excise taxes might appear to represent an ideal source of additional tax revenue. These typically are imposed on sumptuary items having relatively inelastic demand. When the price elasticity of demand for such products is very low (as for tobacco products) or relatively low (as for alcoholic beverages), an increase in excise tax rates will induce little reduction in consumption of the taxed good. If price elasticity is as low as –0.2, not uncommon for cigarettes, then an additional 10 percent excise tax on this product would yield an 8 percent increase in tax revenues. Moreover, it is a hallowed theorem in optimal tax theory that taxes levied on

---

[10]For a full discussion of the distortions involved in different forms of sales tax, see John Due and Raymond Mikesell, *Sales Taxation: State and Local Structure and Administration* (Baltimore: Johns Hopkins Press, 1983).

[11]Carl Shoup, "Choosing among Types of VAT," in Malcolm Gillis, Carl Shoup, and Gerry Sicat, eds., *Value-Added Taxation in Developing Countries* (Washington, DC: World Bank, 1990).

[12]As used in virtually all developing and in all industrial countries, the VAT properly is seen as an indirect tax on consumption: The base of the tax includes only consumption goods and services. A VAT can be structured so that the tax base is all income, but this tax is more difficult to administer and has been used in few countries (Argentina, Turkey). See Shoup, "Choosing among Types of VAT."

TABLE 12-4. Value-Added Taxation

COUNTRY	YEAR VAT INTRODUCED	VAT REVENUES AS % OF GDP	VAT REVENUES AS % OF TOTAL TAX REVENUE	BASIC VAT RATE (%)	OTHER VAT RATES (%)
Low income					
Malawi	1989	6	31	20	
Kenya	1990	8	31	18	
Lower-middle income					
Pakistan	1990	2	10	15	
Nicaragua	1975	2	13	10	
El Salvador	1992	4	37	10	
Bolivia	1973	5	32	14.92	
The Philippines	1988	2	10	10	
Romania	1993	7	19	18	
Sri Lanka	1995	6	30	25	
Indonesia	1985	4	22	10	
Peru	1976	3	32	18	
Morocco	1986	6	21	19	
Paraguay	1993	3	24	10	
Ecuador	1970	3	17	10	
Upper-middle income					
Bulgaria	1994	3	7	18	
Tunisia	1988	3	10	17	6, 29
Turkey	1985	5	24	15	1, 8, 23
Brazil	1967	1	4	11	9
Panama	1977	2	6	5	10
Hungary	1988	8	14	25	10
Thailand	1992	3	19	7	
Uruguay	1968	7	22	22	12
Mexico	1980	3	19	10	
Greece	1987	14	39	18	4, 8
Chile	1975	9	37	18	
Venezuela	1993	1	3	10	
Korea, Republic	1977	4	23	10	2, 3, 5
High income					
Portugal	1986	7	17	16	5, 30
Ireland	1972	8	19	21	12.5
Spain	1986	4	14	15	3, 6
New Zealand	1986	6	18	12.5	
Israel	1976	12	31	17	6.5
Finland	1994	9	27	22	9, 12
United Kingdom	1973	7	19	17.5	
The Netherlands	1969	7	14	17.5	6
Sweden	1969	9	21	25	12, 21
Italy	1973	5	13	19	4, 9, 12
Norway	1970	9	18	22	
Belgium	1971	7	16	20.5	1, 6, 12
Austria	1973	6	16	20	10, 32
Denmark	1967	10	25	25	
France	1968	8	19	18.6	2.1, 5.5
Japan	1989	1	8	3	4.5
Germany	1968	4	14	15	7

Source: World Bank, *World Development Report 1994* (Washington, DC: The World Bank, 1994), Table 11; IMF, *Government Finance Statistics Yearbook 1994*, 42–43; and Glenn P. Jenkins, "Economic Reform and Institutional Innovation," unpublished paper, April 11, 1995.

items with inelastic demand and supply involve the smallest losses in economic efficiency, or what is the same thing, the least excess burden. **Excess burden** is defined as a loss in private welfare above the amount of government revenue collected from a tax.[13] Further, many agree, with much justification, that consumption of both tobacco and alcohol should be discouraged on health grounds.

All three considerations would seem to argue for heavy reliance on excise taxes in developing countries. However, unfortunately, in addition to low price elasticity, items such as tobacco and alcoholic beverages have low income elasticity and so tend to be more important in the budgets of low-income than high-income households. It follows that excise taxes on sumptuary items are decidedly regressive: Poor people pay a higher proportion of their income in excise taxes than rich people, a serious matter when the sumptuary items constitute a substantial portion of spending by poor people, as in most developing countries. In Indonesia, for example, the poorest 20 percent of Javanese households spent about 5 percent of total income on heavily taxed cigarettes in 1976, as opposed to 3.5 percent of income for persons with income more than five times as high.

New Sources of Tax Revenues

If higher rates on existing taxes are unlikely to raise revenues much, a second option for increasing public savings is to tap entirely new sources of tax revenues. In many developing countries, whether by accident, design, or simply inertia, many sources of tax revenue may have been overlooked entirely. Many countries have not collected taxes on motor vehicle registrations; some have not utilized urban property taxes as a significant source of revenue; many have not applied corporation income taxes to the income of state-owned enterprises. Kenya, for example, does not seriously tax farm land, and a few countries, such as Indonesia until 1984, do not collect personal income taxes on the salaries of civil servants.

The service sector furnishes other examples. Telephone service exists in all but the very poorest countries and is widespread in many but often untaxed. Some service establishments, such as restaurants and cabarets, are commonly taxed, but services of beauty shops, parking lots, tire-recap businesses, photo-finishing firms, modern laundries, and foreign-travel agencies are among the more common items excluded from the tax base. Not only is taxation of this category of spending attractive from a revenue standpoint, in developing countries, such services typically face relatively income-elastic demand. Because families with higher incomes purchase proportionately more of these items, they would tend to bear the greater burden of taxation, consistent with the equity objectives of fiscal policy. However, these services constitute a small fraction of consumption, even for upper-income groups, so their revenue potential is limited.

[13]For a further discussion of optimal taxation and excess burden, see Figure 12–2, later in this chapter, and also Joseph Stiglitz, *Economics of the Public Sector* (New York: W. W. Norton and Company, 1988).

Changes in Tax Administration

A far more-significant option for increasing tax revenues is to implement changes in tax administration that permit more taxes to be collected from existing tax sources, even at unchanged tax rates. The potential for increased revenues from such action is very large and seldom realized in virtually all developing countries. Shortages of well-trained tax administrators, excessively complex tax laws, light penalties for tax evasion, corruption, and outdated techniques of tax administration combine to make tax evasion one of the most intractable problems of economic policy in developing countries.

The case studies, which suggest the magnitude of the problem in India and Bolivia (Box 12–2), are typical of many, perhaps most, other developing countries.

BOX 12–2 TAX ADMINISTRATION IN INDIA AND BOLIVIA IN THE 1980s

India during the 1980s provides one of the more-egregious examples of poor tax administration. During the fiscal year 1981, for example, it was found that taxes were avoided on at least 40 and possibly 60 percent of potentially taxable income. Almost 70 percent of the taxpayers covered by a survey openly admitted bribing tax officials, and three quarters of the tax auditors admitted accepting bribes to reduce tax payments. The cost of a bribe was commonly known to be about 20 percent of the taxes avoided.

In Bolivia during the same period, the tax system was chaotic. More than 400 separate taxes were levied by the national, regional, and city governments. Taxpayer records were out of date, and tax collections were recorded more than a year after they had been paid. Of 120,000 registered taxpayers, one third paid no taxes at all, while 20,000 taxpayers who did pay were not on the register. The administration had all but ceased its data processing. Administration had gotten so bad that the government was helpless to collect taxes during the hyperinflation of the mid-1980s. Tax collections fell to only 1 percent of the GDP. Faced with this chaos, the Bolivian government reformed its tax administration, simplifying it drastically. This, together with price stabilization, enabled the government to collect revenues equivalent to over 7 percent of the GDP by 1990, a low ratio by world standards but a vast improvement for Bolivia.

Sources: Omkar Goswami, Amal Sanyal, and Ira N. Gang, "Taxes, Corruption and Bribes: A Model of Indian Public Finance," in Michael Roemer and Christine Jones, eds., *Markets in Developing Countries: Parallel, Fragmented and Black* (San Francisco: ICS Press, 1991), 201–13; Carlos A. Silvani and Alberto H. J. Radano, "Tax Administration Reform in Bolivia and Uruguay," in Richard M. Bird and Milka Casanegra de Jantscher, eds., *Improving Tax Administration in Developing Countries* (Washington, DC: International Monetary Fund, 1992), 19–59.

These examples suggest that efforts to collect a greater share of the taxes due under the current law can increase revenues substantially. But the kinds of administrative reforms required are difficult to implement and especially difficult to sustain. Even Bolivia's successful reform raised its tax ratio to only 7 percent of GDP. Korea, a country noted for its efficient and determined administration, failed in the 1960s to reach its goal of increasing collections by 40 percent through more effective enforcement, although it was able to reduce underreporting of nonagricultural personal income from 75 percent to slightly under 50 percent. Although administrative reform can help and be important at any stage of development, better tax administration tends to improve with economic development. In a lower-middle-income country like Jamaica, more than a third of the potential tax base escapes taxation, compared to less than 15 percent in the United States or Canada.[14]

Fundamental Tax Reform

The final policy option available for increasing tax revenues is the most difficult to implement but the most effective when it can be done. Fundamental tax reform requires junking old tax systems and replacing them with completely new tax laws and regulations. Implementing tax reform engenders enormous technical and informational, not to mention political, difficulties in all countries. In general, governments resist genuine efforts to reform the tax structure until a fiscal crisis, in the form of massive budgetary deficits, threatens. Even during a fiscal crisis, it is difficult to mobilize a political consensus to allow unpopular tax measures to pass. Tax policies that protect favored groups and distort the allocation of resources did not just happen; more likely, they were enacted at the behest of someone, ordinarily the privileged and the powerful.

Probably, more has been said, to less effect, about tax reform than almost any topic in economic policy. This is no less true for the United States than for the 50-odd developing countries where major tax reform efforts have been mounted since 1950. That the process is painful and slow is evident from the experience of several countries: In the United States, the time lag between the birth of tax innovations (tax credit for child-care expenses, inflation proofing of the tax system) and their implementation usually is at least 15 years. If anything, the lag may be slightly shorter in developing countries.

In spite of the difficulties involved, some countries were able to carry through fundamental reforms in tax structure and administration before 1980. The classic example is Japan in the 1880s, when that society began its transformation to a modern industrial power. Korea implemented a major tax reform

---

[14]James Alm, Roy Bahl, and Matthew Murray, "Tax Base Erosion in Developing Countries," *Economic Development and Cultural Change* 39, no. 4 (July 1991), 849–72.

program in the early 1960s, as did Colombia (Box 12–3) and Chile in the 1970s. But, also during the 1970s, major tax reform efforts went for naught in many more countries: Bolivia, Ghana, Liberia, and Peru, among others.

Since 1980, however, the pace of tax reform has quickened notably, in both developing and industrial countries, with many similarities in the various

BOX 12-3 LESSONS FROM COMPREHENSIVE TAX REFORM: COLOMBIA

In 1974, Colombia implemented one of the most ambitious tax reform programs undertaken. The Colombian experience illustrates both the potential payoffs and the difficulties involved in any serious tax reform effort.

In the last quarter of 1974, the new government of Alfonso Lopez Michelsen, in the midst of a national crisis, enacted a tax reform of very large magnitude. The reform, nearly a decade in the making, was engineered by an extraordinary group of officials as well versed in fiscal economics as any treasury department in the world. The reform package was comprehensive: It involved nearly all tax sources. It was geared to all four fiscal policy objectives: growth, equity, stability, and efficiency. The instruments employed were well suited to the objectives sought. The reform contained measures to increase progressivity that still are absent in tax systems of the United States and Canada. Numerous anomalies in the tax system that encouraged waste and inefficiency in the private sectors were introduced and allowed to stand for a short time before they were struck down by the Colombian Supreme Court.

The reform's most striking initial achievements were its effects on tax-revenue growth and income distribution. In the first year following the reform, tax revenues grew by 45 percent, more than twice the growth rate in revenues in the years prior to the reform. The early impact on income distribution was just as striking: In its first year, the reform shifted as much as 1.5 percent of GDP away from the top 20 percent of the income earners, a rare feat.

Many of the achievements of the reform effort proved short-lived, however. The reform initially caught most powerful economic interests with their defenses down. But by 1976, groups injured by the reform were able to have many key measures watered down or repealed, and taxpayers began to develop defense mechanisms against the new law and exploit loopholes uncovered by the best legal minds in the country. Also, the reform effort paid far too little attention to the practical problems of implementation and the strengthening of tax collection procedures. Nevertheless, many of the innovations introduced in 1974 survived relatively intact through 1980, and many revenue-hungry and equity-oriented tax officials in other Latin American countries viewed much of the 1974 reform package as a model worth detailed study.

reform programs. Throughout much of the postwar period, tax systems commonly were fine-tuned to achieve a wide variety of nonrevenue objectives. In particular, governments in developed and developing nations alike commonly sought substantial income redistribution through the use of steeply progressive tax rates. Also, complex and largely impossible to administer systems of tax incentives were widely used in attempts to redirect resources to high-priority economic sectors and promote foreign investment, regional development, and even stock exchanges.

While fine-tuning tax systems someday may yield the desired results, this requires, at a minimum, strong machinery for tax administration and traditions of taxpayer compliance. Within developing countries, at least, there has been growing recognition that these conditions seldom prevail. Consequently, governments increasingly have turned away from reliance on steeply progressive tax rates and complicated, costly tax incentive programs.

The 1980s through the beginning of the twenty-first century saw a worldwide movement toward an entirely different type of tax system, with a shift toward vastly simplified taxes imposed at much flatter rates and with much broader bases[15] and increasingly greater reliance on consumption rather than income taxation. Tax reform programs in Bolivia, Chile, Colombia, India, Indonesia, Jamaica, and Malawi exemplify most of these trends.[16]

Two aspects of this worldwide movement in tax reform are especially salient. First, the top marginal income tax rates of 60–70 percent were not uncommon from 1945 to 1979. But, since 1984, country after country has slashed the top marginal rate, often substantially. Table 12–5 shows how some developing countries have reduced the top marginal rate of income tax, many of them quite dramatically. During the same period, many industrial nations ranging from Australia and Austria through the United Kingdom and the United States also cut the top rate sharply.

In many of these cases, sharp cutbacks in the highest tax rates were accompanied by reforms involving a very substantial broadening of the income tax base, through the reduction of special tax incentives, abolition of tax shelters, and the like. This pattern was especially notable in Bolivia, Colombia, Indonesia, Jamaica, and Sri Lanka, so that, even with a rate reduction, higher-income groups often ended up paying a higher proportion of total taxes than before.

Reasons for the worldwide shift toward lower tax rates on broader income tax bases are not difficult to find. First, income taxes imposed at high marginal rates have proven difficult or impossible to administrate, even in wealthy coun-

---

[15]Joseph A. Pechman, ed., *World Tax Reform: A Progress Report* (Washington, DC: Brookings Institute, 1988), "Introduction," p. 13.

[16]A number of these cases are discussed in Malcolm Gillis, ed., *Tax Reform in Developing Countries* (Durham, NC: Duke University Press, 1989).

TABLE 12-5. Countries Reducing Highest Rates of Income Tax, 1984–2002

COUNTRY	1984	2002
Low income		
Tanzania	75	30
Uganda (1985)	70	30
India	62	30
Kenya	65	30
Nigeria	70	25
Senegal (1985)	65	50
Ghana	65	30
Zimbabwe (1985)	61	46
Lower-middle income		
Papua New Guinea	50	47
Pakistan (1985)	60	35
Bolivia	40	13
The Philippines (1985)	60	32
Sri Lanka	55	35
Indonesia	45	35
Peru (1985)	50	27
Guatemala	42	31
Jamaica	58	25
Upper-middle income		
Botswana	75	25
Brazil (1985)	60	28
Costa Rica (1985)	50	25
Colombia	49	35
Thailand (1985)	65	37
Argentina (1985)	45	35
Mexico (1985)	55	40
Malaysia	55	28
Chile (1985)	56	43
Trinidad and Tobago	70	35
High income		
Singapore	45	26

Sources: George J. Yost, III, ed., *1994 International Tax Summaries, Coopers & Lybrand International Tax Network* (New York: Wiley, 1994); Glenn P. Jenkins, "Tax Reform: Lessons Learned," in Dwight H. Perkins and Michael Roemer, eds., *Reforming Economic Systems in Developing Countries* (Cambridge, MA: Harvard Institute for International Development, 1991); and *World Development Report 1998/99* (Washington, DC: World Bank, 1999), 222–23.

tries such as the United States. With high marginal tax rates, the incentives to evade taxes (through concealment of income) or avoid taxes (by hiring expensive legal talent to devise tax shelters) are very high. Second, the growing mobility of capital across international boundaries has meant that the risk of capital flight from a particular country increases when that country's top rates of income tax exceed those prevailing in industrial nations, where tax rates have been falling.[17] Third, the operation of the income tax systems of such developed nations at the United States and Japan has placed downward pressure on the tax rates everywhere. This is because of the *foreign income tax credit*, wherein a country like the United States allows foreign income taxes to be credited (subtracted) from U.S. taxes due on income repatriated from abroad. This credit could be used, however, only up to the amount of tax payable at U.S. rates, which was reduced from 50 to 28 percent in 1986. Finally, high marginal rates of income tax did not prove to be particularly efficacious in correcting severe inequalities in income distribution in either rich or poor countries.

The second striking feature of recent tax reforms worldwide has been the steadily growing number of countries adopting the value-added tax. Several reasons account for the popularity of the VAT: The two most important are its reputation as a "money machine" and its administrative advantages, relative to other forms of sales taxes and income taxes.[18]

The record of the VAT in generating large amounts of revenue quickly and in a comparatively painless fashion has given it a reputation as a money machine. Although this reputation stems largely from the experience in European countries, the record in developing countries does lend some support to the alleged revenue advantages of the VAT. In Indonesia, the 4 percent share of the value-added tax in GDP in 1987 was nearly three times the share garnered in 1983 by the taxes it replaced. And, for 14 of the 27 low- and middle-income countries in Table 12–4, the share of the VAT in GDP was higher than 3 percent in about half these cases and the VAT usually constituted at least 20 percent of total tax revenue. Still, in six of the countries listed in Table 12–4, the VAT revenues were 2 percent or less of GDP. Notwithstanding the marked revenue success of the VAT in nations such as Brazil, Chile, and Indonesia, its reputation as a money machine appears to have been at least slightly overstated.

Twenty years ago, it was common to hear the claim that the VAT was largely self-administering. This is not so, but the tax-credit type of VAT has three principal advantages over single-stage retail and nonretail sales taxes in limiting the scope for evasion. First, the VAT is self-policing to some extent because under-payment of the tax by a seller (except, of course, a retail firm) reduces the tax credit available to the buying firm. Even so, firms that also are subject to income taxes have incentives to suppress information on purchases and sales to avoid both the value-added and income taxes. Also, this possible advantage of the VAT is diminished when evasion at the final (retail) stage of distribution is endemic. Second, cross-checking of invoices enables the tax administration to match

[17]For a cogent discussion of the implications for taxation of growing international mobility of financial and physical capital, see Dwight R. Lee and Richard B. McKenzie, "The International Political Economy of Declining Tax Rates," *National Tax Journal* 42, no. 2 (March 1989), 79–87.

[18]For a full statement of these reasons, see Alan A. Tait, *Value-Added Tax* (Washington, DC: International Monetary Fund, 1988), Chapter 1.

invoices received by purchasers against those retained by sellers. The cross-check feature is a valuable aid in audit activities but no substitute for a true, systematic audit. Third, that a large share of the VAT is collected prior to the retail level is an advantage particularly because, in most developing countries, an abundance of small-scale retail firms do not keep adequate records. In sum, the administrative advantages of the VAT are very real, if sometimes exaggerated by enthusiastic proponents.[19]

TAXES AND PRIVATE INVESTMENT

Fiscal policy influences capital formation in the private sector by affecting both the capacity and the incentive to save and by affecting incentives to invest in private projects. Taxes impinge more directly, but not necessarily more importantly, on both sets of incentives than government expenditures and is our prime focus here.

Taxes and Private Saving

An increase in taxes on households will come partly out of consumption and partly out of saving, but the effects of taxes in reducing consumption and saving, respectively, is a matter of some dispute. Some cross-country studies of saving behavior suggest that increases in taxes in developing countries merely reduce private-sector consumption with little or no effect on saving. Other studies conclude that there is a high degree of substitutability between private savings and taxes. The truth probably lies slightly closer to the latter observation.

Different taxes have different types of impact on the **capacity to save.** Although heavy sales taxes on highly price-elastic items of luxury consumption curtail the rates of growth in the consumption of such items, heavy taxes on corporate income may come in large part at the expense of business savings that might have been plowed back into company investment. Where upper-income groups have a high propensity to consume, as often has been argued to hold for the elite in many Latin American countries, increased taxes on them may have little impact on private savings. But where the same groups display strong saving propensities, as many argue is true for some ethnic minorities in Africa and Southeast Asia, higher taxes have a relatively greater impact on saving. Further, heavier taxes on foreign natural-resource firms ordinarily have minimal negative

---

[19]For a succinct summary of some of these issues, see John F. Due, "Some Unresolved Issues in Design and Implementation of Value-Added Taxes," *National Tax Journal* 42, no. 4 (December 1990), 383–98.

impact on the availability of private domestic savings unless such firms have local joint-venture partners and cut their dividends to them in response to reduced profitability.

There is less uncertainty concerning the effect of different forms of taxes on **incentives to save,** but even here, offsetting considerations are present. Taxes on consumption probably impinge less severely on private savings than taxes on income in most developing societies. Perhaps the only exception to this statement arises when households save primarily for the later purchase of items subject to heavy consumption taxes. Some observers have argued that this motivation for saving is common in many low-income countries, where the nature of extended-family relationships makes household saving difficult. In some societies, households with incomes above subsistence share resources with poorer households within the family group to help them meet subsistence needs. This pattern is characteristic of many African countries and many parts of rural Asia. Under such circumstances household saving is devoted largely to the purchase of prized durable goods, such as transistor radios, bicycles, and sewing machines. In high- and middle-income countries, these typically are viewed as consumer goods that are strong candidates for taxation. But, in some poorer countries, heavy taxation of such items may well reduce incentives to save. It is even questionable whether products such as bicycles, sewing machines, and even small outboard motors should be viewed as consumer goods in many low-income societies. Purchasing a bicycle or a small outboard may allow a rural family to market garden produce and fish more easily, whereas sewing machines ordinarily are bought to generate extra income for the household.

On balance, consumption-based taxes probably are more favorable for growth in private saving than income-based taxes. Virtually all developing countries tax consumption through such indirect means as sales and excise taxes. These levies, although not inherently regressive, often are perceived to be. This perception has led many tax reformers to argue for direct taxes on consumption. Under a direct consumption tax, taxpayers annually would report total consumption as well as income. Consumption below the level thought minimally necessary for an adequate living standard would be exempt, and any consumption above that level would be taxed at rates that rise progressively with total consumption. If such a levy could be administered, it would stimulate savings, since a household could reduce its tax liability by not spending. Direct consumption taxes have been seriously proposed for the United States, Great Britain, Sweden, and Australia. Among developing countries, they have been proposed for India, Guyana, and Sri Lanka and actually enacted in India in the 1950s. The Indian experiment was short-lived, however, as the tax involved required information beyond the capacities of the tax administration at the time; it proved impossible to administer. But, at the beginning of the twenty-first century, the administrative problems, both real and imaginary, of direct consumption taxes are not so great as to preclude their consideration in many developing and industrial countries.

Taxes can affect incentives to save in other ways. To the extent that national savings rates are responsive to the after-tax rate of return on savings (a question examined in the next chapter), heavy taxes on income from capital (dividends and interest) reduce the volume of private savings available for investment. Likewise, to the extent that people save mainly to finance retirement, social security taxes also can reduce private and aggregate national saving if the social security system is financed on a pay-as-you-go basis (that is, from current revenues), as in the United States, Colombia, the Philippines, and India. Under a social security system financed in this manner, it is argued that individuals covered by the system reduce their saving in anticipation of receiving future social security benefits. But there is no corresponding increase in public saving because the social security taxes paid by those covered now are not set aside and invested but rather are used to pay benefits to those already retired.

This is an important point, because many proposals have been made—and some enacted—for social security systems in Asia and Latin America intended to help increase the national saving rate. The argument that social security systems can foster domestic saving is correct only under two circumstances, both relatively uncommon in developing countries. First, social security systems that operate as true retirement funds clearly can help mobilize capital resources, provided the funds are invested in projects with an adequate social marginal rate of return. Under such *provident funds,* the taxes collected from those covered are invested by the government in assets that earn returns; payments are made to retirees out of these returns rather than from taxes collected by those still working, as under the pay-as-you-go system. Under this approach, used in Chile and Singapore and for some workers in Malaysia and a few other countries, any decline in the private savings of those paying social security taxes largely is offset by a concomitant rise in public savings. But the use of provident funds is not widespread.

Even the pay-as-you-go system can increase national saving rates in its early years of operation if benefits are denied to those who retired before the system was implemented and if social security tax rates are set high enough to cover benefit payments for the first decade or so. In the early years, the number of workers covered is large relative to the number of retirees, so that the disbursement of benefits is small compared to the inflow of revenues. Therefore, a government seeking new temporary sources of public saving could enact a pay-as-you-go system for social security that would serve this purpose for a few years. Sooner or later, however, such a system would tend to reduce overall domestic saving, although not necessarily by as much as the social security taxes paid by covered workers.

Taxes and Capital Mobility

If a country's tax system operates to reduce private savings, it will tend to curtail private domestic investment. Beyond that effect, taxes can affect both the amount and allocation of private domestic investment undertaken out of any given volume of private capital available for investment.

In spite of exchange controls and similar restrictions, capital tends to be fairly mobile across international boundaries. If opportunities for earning returns abroad promise higher after-tax returns than those available in a particular developing country, domestic capital tends to flow to these opportunities. Of course, a critical factor determining after-tax returns in a given country is the nature of taxes on capital there. Suppose, for example, that capital owners in the Philippines, on the average, can secure before-tax returns equal to 15 percent of their investments and capital income in that country is subject to a 50 percent tax. After-tax returns are then 7.5 percent. The same funds invested in well-developed capital markets in Hong Kong, where capital is less scarce, might obtain only a 12 percent return before taxes, but are taxed at only, say, 15 percent. The after-tax return in Hong Kong is therefore 10.2 percent. The difference of 2.7 percent in after-tax returns may be large enough to induce movement of Philippines savings to Hong Kong. In general, countries that attempt to impose substantially heavier taxes on capital income often experience outflows of domestic savings to countries employing lower tax rates on capital. This movement is quite distinct from the type of *capital flight* from developing to developed countries often observed in countries experiencing severe domestic political turmoil or exchange-rate uncertainties.

No shortage of low-tax foreign opportunities faces domestic savers in developing countries. *Tax havens* such as Panama and the Bahamas have been attractive to Latin American investors since the 1960s. Likewise, the Hong Kong and Singapore financial markets draw substantial inflows of savings from other Asian countries. Increasingly, enterprises from countries such as India, with relatively high taxes on capital income, have become major investors in other developing countries where after-tax returns are higher than at home.

Most countries have recognized that capital is fairly mobile across national boundaries and sought to keep taxes on capital income from reaching levels much above those prevailing worldwide. This is evident from an inspection of corporate income tax rates in most developing countries. In Latin America, corporate tax rates typically are found in a band of from 25 to 40 percent, compared to 34 percent in the United States in 1990. In Southeast Asia, corporate tax rates, other than those of Hong Kong, cluster in a narrow range of 30–40 percent; the rate in Hong Kong is less than 20 percent.

Countries have sought to impede the outward mobility of capital through such devices as controls on movement of foreign exchange and imposition of domestic taxes on worldwide income of residents. Flourishing business in tax-haven countries, coupled with very large investment holdings by citizens of developing countries in the United States, Switzerland, Hong Kong, and Singapore, are ample testament to the limited effectiveness of such controls.

Partly to stem capital outflow and direct private investment into high-priority areas, such as basic industry, exports, or backward regions, many developing country governments selectively offer substantial tax incentives to domestic investors. The two main types of incentives are income tax holidays, in which approved investments are exempted from income tax obligations for specified periods ranging from three to ten years, and tax credits for investment, in which a government allows an investor to subtract some portion of initial investment (usually 20–25 percent) from his or her income tax liabilities. On rare occasions, these types of incentives for domestic investment have produced the desired results, but these devices suffer from a number of administrative and efficiency limitations. Because of these limitations, in 1984, Indonesia abolished all tax incentives and replaced them with the most effective tax incentive ever offered: lower tax rates for all firms.

INCOME DISTRIBUTION

As indicated in Chapter 6, a basic thrust of economic policy in many developing countries has been the mitigation of extreme income inequality. For decades, developed and developing countries alike have sought to use the fiscal system, particularly taxation, to redress income inequalities generated by the operation of the private market. Social philosophers from John Stuart Mill and eminent nineteenth-century Chilean historian Francisco Encina to John Rawls in the 1970s have sought to establish a philosophical basis for income redistribution, primarily through progressive taxes. Karl Marx also favored steeply progressive taxes in bourgeois societies but for reasons other than income redistribution. Rather, in Marx's view, heavy taxes on capitalists were essential for speeding the decline of the capitalist state and its replacement by a socialist order.

No scientific basis is used to determine the optimal degree of income redistribution in any society. And across developing countries different views prevail as to the ideal distribution of income. But, in virtually all countries, the notion of *fiscal equity* permeates discussions of budgetary operations. In the overwhelming majority of countries, fiscal equity typically is defined in terms of the impact of tax and expenditure policy on the distribution of economic well-being. Progressive taxes, those that bear more heavily on better-off citizens than on poor ones, and expenditures whose benefits are concentrated on the least advantaged are viewed as more equitable than regressive taxes and expenditures.

Taxation and Equity

On the tax side of the budget, the materialistic conception of equity requires that most taxes be based on the **ability to pay.** The ability to pay can be measured by income, consumption, wealth, or some combination of all three. Clearly, individuals with higher incomes over their life spans have a greater ability to pay taxes, quite apart from the moral question of whether they should do so. Indeed, the redistribution impact of taxation almost always is expressed in terms of its effects on income. However, philosophers since the time of Hobbes have argued that consumption furnishes a better index of ability to pay than income; in this view, tax obligations are best geared to what people take out of society (consume) rather than what they put into society (as measured by income).

In practice, developing countries have relied heavily on these two measures of ability in fashioning tax systems. Personal and corporate income taxes employ income as the indicator; sales taxes and customs duties are indirect assessments of taxes on consumption. But the ability to pay is not the exclusive guide to the assessment of taxes in all countries. Religious and cultural values often provide other bases for establishing tax liability. Nevertheless, most societies largely define equity in taxation as requiring taxation on the basis of ability to pay, and this is commonly interpreted to mean progressivity. At a minimum, equity usually is assumed to require the avoidance of regressive taxes whenever possible. A number of tax instruments have been employed to secure greater progressivity in principle, if not in practice; all suffer from limitations to one degree or another.

Personal Income Taxes

The most widely used device for securing greater progressivity has been steeply progressive rates under the personal income tax. In some countries in some periods, nominal or legal marginal income tax rates have reached very high levels, even for relatively low incomes. Thus, for example, tax rates applicable to any income in excess of $1,000 in Indonesia in 1967 reached 75 percent, largely because tax rates were not indexed to rapid inflation; in Algeria in the 1960s, all income in excess of $10,000 was subject to marginal tax rates of nearly 100 percent; Tanzania imposed top marginal rates of 95 percent as late as 1981.

Although, in most developing countries, marginal income tax rates are considerably lower than the preceding examples and, as is apparent from Table 12–5, have been falling, some countries still attempt to impose rates in excess of 50 percent.[20] Countries such as Brazil, Colombia, Costa Rica, Singapore, and Sri

---

[20]Ten of the 16 countries imposing income tax rates in excess of 50 percent in 1989 were in Africa, two were in Latin America, and the remainder were in Asia.

Lanka generally hold maximum marginal rates to 40 percent or slightly less, and the maximum income tax rate in Indonesia has been 35 percent since that country implemented tax reform in 1984.

If the tax administration machinery functioned well and capital were immobile among countries, the pattern of actual tax payments of high-income taxpayers would resemble the legal, or theoretical, patterns just described. In fact, in most countries, **effective taxes** (the taxes actually collected as a percent of income) fall well short of theoretical liabilities. Faced with high income tax rates, taxpayers everywhere tend to react in three ways: (1) They evade taxes by concealing income, particularly capital income not subject to withholding arrangements; (2) they avoid taxes by altering economic behavior to reduce tax liability, whether by supplying fewer labor services, shipping capital to tax havens abroad, or hiring lawyers to find loopholes in the tax law; and (3) they bribe tax assessors to accept false returns.

For all these reasons, the achievement of substantial income redistribution through progressive income taxes has proven difficult in all countries, including the United States and the three Scandinavian nations where tax rates were long among the world's most progressive. Tax avoidance is the favored avenue for reducing tax liability in the United States, where use of the other methods can result in imprisonment. But, where tax enforcement is relatively weak, particularly where criminal penalties for evasion are absent and tax officials deeply underpaid, tax evasion and bribery are utilized more commonly. The scope for substantial redistribution through the income tax therefore is even more limited in developing countries than in the United States or Sweden.

Notwithstanding these problems, a significant share of the income of the wealthiest members of society is caught in the income tax net in many developing countries. Revenues from personal income tax collections in countries such as Colombia, South Korea, and Chile have been as high as 15 percent of total taxes and in a few others have run between 5 and 10 percent of the total. In virtually all developing countries, the entirety of such taxes is collected from the top 20 percent of the income distribution. This means, of course, that the very presence of an income tax, even one imposed at proportional rather than progressive rates, tends to reduce income inequality. Income taxes, together with taxes on luxury consumption, constitute about the only feasible means of approaching income redistribution goals through the tax side of the budget.

Taxes on Luxury Consumption

In view of the difficulties of securing a significant redistribution through income taxes, many countries have sought to employ heavy indirect taxes on luxury consumption as a means of enhancing the progressivity of the tax system. Efforts to achieve this goal usually center on internal indirect taxes, such as sales taxes, and on customs duties on imports, but not excises on tobacco and alcohol.

Several developing countries have found that, provided tax rates are kept to enforceable levels, high rates of internal indirect taxes on luxury goods and services, coupled with lower taxes on less income-elastic items, can contribute to greater progressivity in the tax system. For revenue purposes, countries typically impose basic rates of sales taxes on nonluxuries at between 4 and 8 percent of manufacturers' values. This is equivalent to retail taxes of between 2 and 4 percent because taxes imposed at this level exclude wholesale and retail margins. Food, except that consumed in restaurants, almost always is exempted from any sales tax intended to promote redistributive goals. In developing countries, the exemption of food by itself renders most sales taxes at least faintly progressive, given the high proportion (up to 40 percent in many middle-income countries) of income of poor households spent on food. Sales taxes involving a limited number of luxury rates of between 20 and 30 percent at the manufacturers' level have been found to be workable in countries such as Colombia, Chile, Taiwan, and Korea.

The redistributive potential of sales tax rates differentiated in this way, however, is limited by the same administrative and compliance constraints standing in the way of the heavier use of income taxation in developing countries. While sales taxes are not as difficult to administer as income taxes, they do not collect themselves. A manufacturer's sales tax system employing three or even four rates may be administratively feasible in most countries, even when the highest rate approaches 40 percent. Rates much higher than that or reliance on a profusion of rates in an attempt to fine-tune the tax lead to substantial incentives and opportunities for tax evasion. Jamaica had over 15 rates prior to 1986, and Chile had over 20 from 1960 to 1970. In recognition of these problems, Indonesia adopted a flat-rate manufacturers' tax in 1985: The tax applies at a rate of 10 percent on *all* manufactured items and imports. The tax nevertheless is slightly progressive, since it does not apply to items that do not go through a manufacturing process, including most foodstuffs consumed by low-income families.

Although the use of internal indirect taxes, such as sales taxes, can contribute to income redistribution goals without causing serious misallocation of resources, the same cannot be said for the use of customs duties. Sales taxes are imposed on all taxable goods without regard to national origin, including goods produced domestically as well as abroad. Tariffs apply only to imported goods. Virtually all countries, developed and developing, utilize customs duties to protect existing domestic industry. Developing countries in particular employ customs duties as the principal means of encouraging domestic industry to produce goods that formerly were imported. This strategy, called **import substitution,** is examined at length in Chapter 19.

Deliberate policies to encourage import substitution through the use of high protective tariffs, under certain conditions, might lead to results sought by policy makers. But accidental import substitution arises when tariffs are used for purposes other than protection, and this is unlikely to have positive results. Many countries, as already pointed out, use high tariffs to achieve heavier taxation of luxury consumption. Often heavy tariffs are imposed on imported luxury items for which there is no intention of encouraging domestic production. Therefore, many Latin American and some Asian countries have levied customs tariffs of 100–150 percent of value on such appliances as electric knives, hair dryers, sporting goods, videocassette recorders, and mechanical toys. For most countries, these items are clearly highly income elastic and apt candidates for luxury taxation.

But efforts to tax luxuries through high customs duties lead to unintended, and almost irresistible, incentives for domestic production or assembly of such products. In virtually all countries save the very poorest, alert domestic and foreign entrepreneurs have been quick to seize on such opportunities. By the time local assembly operations are established, they usually can make a politically convincing case that the duties should be retained to enable local production to continue, even when the value added domestically is as low as 10 percent of the value of the product. Such operations, if subject to any local sales taxes, usually succeed in being taxed at the basic tax rate, usually 5 to 10 percent. By relying on tariffs for luxury taxation, the government ultimately forgoes the revenues it previously collected from duties on luxury goods, as well as severely undermining the very aims of luxury taxation.

If, instead, higher luxury rates on imports are imposed under a sales tax collected on both imports and any domestic production that may develop, unintended import substitution can be avoided. The use of import tariffs for luxury taxation—indeed, for any purpose other than providing protection to domestic industry—is one illustration of the general problem of using one economic policy instrument (tariffs) to achieve more than one purpose (protection, luxury taxation, and revenue). Reliance on import duties for revenue is subject to the same pitfalls just discussed. If it is desired to increase government revenue from imports, a 10 percent sales tax applied both to imports and any future domestic production yields at least as much revenue as a 10 percent import duty, without leading to accidental protection.

Corporate Income and Property Taxes: The Incidence Problem

Income taxes on domestic corporations and property taxes often are mentioned as possible methods for securing income redistribution through the budget. Corporate income ultimately is received, through dividends and capital gains, almost exclusively by the upper 5–10 percent of the income distribution. Also, ownership of wealth, which in many lower-income countries largely takes the form of land, tends to be even more concentrated than income. But, to a greater extent in developing than in developed countries, efforts to secure significant fiscal redistribution through heavier taxes on domestic corporations and property are limited both by administrative and economic realities.

Administrative problems bedevil efforts to collect income taxes from domestic firms to at least as great an extent as for income taxes on individuals. Hence, in many countries, such as Pakistan, where corporate taxes on local firms have been important, as much as two thirds to three fourths of nonoil corporate taxes flow from state-owned firms, not from private firms owned by high-income individuals. Taxes on land should be subject to less-severe administrative problems, since it is an asset that cannot be hidden easily. However, land valuation for tax purposes has proven difficult even in Canada and the United States. It is more difficult in developing countries. Other than Colombia, few developing countries have been able to assess property at anything approaching its true value.

Economic realities hinder efforts to achieve greater progressivity in the tax system through heavier use of corporate and land taxes, because of the tendency for taxation to unintentionally burden groups other than those directly taxed. This is the **incidence** problem. The incidence of a tax is its ultimate impact, not who actually pays the tax to the government, but whose income finally is affected by the tax when all economic agents have adjusted in response to the tax. The point of incidence is not always the point of initial impact. Taxes on domestic corporations may reduce the income of capitalists, who in turn might shift their investment patterns to reduce taxation. The income of the workers they employ and the prices charged to consumers may be affected as well. In the end, taxes on land and improvement may not much reduce the incomes of landholders but may be reflected in higher prices charged to consumers. Ultimately, all taxes are paid by people, not by things such as corporations and property parcels.

The implications of incidence issues may be illuminated by a simple application of incidence analysis to the corporation income tax. Consider a profit-maximizing company that has no significant monopoly power in the domestic market. If taxes on the company's income are increased in 2004, then after-tax returns to its shareholders in 2004 are reduced by the full amount of the tax. In the short term, the incidence of the tax clearly is on shareholders. Since shareholders everywhere are concentrated in higher-income groups, the tax is progressive in the short run. If capital were immobile, unable to leave the corporate sector, the long-term incidence of the tax also would rest on shareholders and the tax would be progressive in the long run as well.

But, in the long run, capital can move out of the corporate sector. To the extent that capital is mobile domestically but not internationally, the corporate tax also is progressive in the long run. Returns on capital remaining in the corporate sector is reduced by the tax. Untaxed capital owners employed outside the corporate sector also suffer a reduction in returns, because movement of capital from the taxed corporate sector drives down the rate of return in the nontaxed sector. Because the corporate tax reduces returns to capital throughout the economy, all capital owners suffer, including owners of housing assets, and in a closed economy, the long-run incidence again is progressive.

However, few if any developing economies are completely closed; indeed, we saw in previous chapters that capital in recent years has become much more mobile internationally. To the extent that capital can move across national borders and higher returns are available in other countries, domestic capital migrates to escape higher corporate taxes. But, as capital leaves an economy, both new and replacement investment and, ultimately, output are curtailed and the marginal productivity of workers falls. Prices of items produced with domestic capital, therefore, rise. In this way, an increase in corporate taxes may be borne by domestic consumers, who pay higher prices for the reduced supply of corporate-sector goods. Similarly, domestic workers, whose income is reduced when production is curtailed, may bear a part of the burden of the corporate tax.

Hence, the corporate tax may be regressive (worsen the income distribution) in the long run. The degree of regressivity depends on whether consumption by low-income groups is more or less capital intensive and on the relative position in the income distribution of workers losing their jobs or suffering declining real wages. In the end, capital owners may suffer no significant decline in income. Although, under other plausible conditions, an increase in the corporation income tax may not result in greater relative burdens on capitalists, this scenario is sufficient to illustrate that often the intentions of a redistributive tax policy may be thwarted by all the workings of the economy. Therefore, policy makers cannot be sure that all taxes imposed on wealthy capital owners ultimately are paid by them.

Limited Effects of Redistribution Policy

The foregoing discussion suggests that, whereas some tax instruments may achieve income redistribution in developing countries, the opportunities for doing so are limited in most countries, a conclusion supported by a large number of empirical studies. With few exceptions, these studies show that the failure to administer personal income taxes effectively—the failure to utilize the limited opportunities for heavier taxes on luxury consumption, overreliance on revenue-productive but regressive excise taxes, and inclusion of food in sales taxes, all these combined—reduces significantly the redistribution impact of tax systems. By and large, tax systems in developing countries tend to produce a burden roughly proportional across income groups, with some tendency for progressivity at the very top of the income scale. As a result, the very wealthy pay a somewhat greater proportion of their income in taxes than the poor, but the poor still pay substantial taxes: at least 10 percent of their income in many cases studied (Argentina, urban Brazil, Colombia, Jamaica, and six others).[21] This is the predominant pattern even in countries, such as Colombia, Jamaica, Tanzania, and Chile before 1970, that placed strong policy emphasis on the use of tax tools to reduce income inequality. Of course, in the absence of such efforts, the after-tax distribution of income may have been even more unequal. This suggests that, although difficult to implement and often disappointing in results, tax reforms intended to reduce income inequality are not futile exercises and they may prevent taxes from making the poor worse off.

Expenditures and Equity

The limits of tax policy suggest that, if the budget is to serve redistribution purposes, the primary emphasis must be on expenditure policy. Indeed, where redistribution through expenditures has been a high priority of governments, the results generally have been encouraging. The effects of government expenditure on income distribution are even more difficult to measure than those of taxes. But both the qualitative and quantitative evidence available strongly indicate that, in developing countries, budget expenditures may transfer very substantial resources to lower-income households, in some cases as much as 50 percent of their income. And the pattern of benefits tends to be progressive: A much higher fraction of income goes to the poor households than to those in the upper reaches of the income distribution.

One study found that, in Malaysia in the late 1960s, the combined effect of taxes and recurrent government consumption expenditures was to transfer 5 percent of GNI from the two highest income classes to the two lowest income groups, with more than three quarters of the transfer going to the poor. This figure understates the actual extent of the redistribution impact of expenditures since it does not include the effects of public investment, which was perhaps the most important tool of fiscal redistribution in Malaysia from 1968 to the beginning of the twenty-first century.[22] Another study found that, in Indonesia in 1980, the tax system was only slightly progressive. But the expenditure side of the budget, with its emphasis on food subsidies and primary education, markedly helped the poor: Benefits from government expenditure were slightly more than 50 percent of the income of the poorest income group.[23] Similarly, an exhaustive study of the net incidence of the Chilean budget for 1969 shows that, although the tax system had virtually no effect on income distribution, govern-

---

[21]These Latin American studies have been summarized in Richard M. Bird and Luc Henry DeWulf, "Taxation and Income Distribution in Latin America: A Critical View of Empirical Studies," *International Monetary Fund Staff Papers* 20 (November 1975), 639–62. Results of studies on Indonesia and Jamaica may be found in Gillis, *Tax Reform*, Chapters 4 and 5.

[22]Donald R. Snodgrass, "The Fiscal System of Malaysia as an Income Redistributor in West Malaysia," *Public Finance* 29, no. 1 (January 1972), 56–76.

[23]Malcolm Gillis, "Micro and Macroeconomics of Tax Reform: Indonesia," *Journal of Development Economics* 19, no. 2 (1986), 42–46.

BOX 12–4 IRRIGATION AND EQUITY

Many economists have long believed that government investment in irrigation in developing countries was bound to result in significant benefits for poor rural households, primarily by the effects of increased irrigation on agricultural productivity. However, this view was widely questioned by many analysts in the 1970s. They claimed that irrigation tends to be adopted faster and more completely by large farmers at the expense of small farmers and landless laborers, because the large farmers then are better able to buy out the small ones and the technology associated with irrigation is laborsaving.

Studies sponsored by the International Food Policy Research Institute (IFPRI) tend to confirm the older view: Government investment in irrigation has not benefited the larger farmers more than small farmers and landless laborers. Rather, these studies find that the latter groups have made major increases in their incomes as a result of irrigation. This research focused on ten project sites in Indonesia, Thailand, and the Philippines. It found no tendency to merge farms after the introduction of irrigation and, particularly in Indonesia, the gains to landowners accrued primarily to small farmers. Further, gains to landless labor were substantial, however these are measured, because irrigated areas use more workers per acre than nonirrigated farms.

Source: *IFPRI Report* 8, no. 1 (January 1986).

ment expenditures favored the poor. The lowest-income groups received only about 7.5 percent of national income but about 15–18 percent of the benefits from government expenditures.[24]

Obviously, not all government expenditures are effective in reducing income inequality. Some, like interest payments on government debt, have the opposite effect because interest income is concentrated in upper income groups. But it is not difficult to identify those categories of budget outlays that tend to have the most marked effects on the income of the poor. Public expenditures on primary, but not university, education tend strongly to reduce income inequality (Chapter 8). Government spending for public health programs, particularly water supplies, sanitation, nutritional programs, and rural health clinics, also can have a clearly progressive impact (Chapter 9). Although many poor people live in huge cities such as Jakarta, São Paulo, Mexico City, Lagos, and Calcutta, in most developing countries, most of the poorest people live in rural areas and wealthy people tend to live in urban areas. Hence, programs that reallocate government spending to rural areas (irrigation programs, secondary roads, erosion control) may tend to reduce income inequality overall, particularly in the case of irrigation (Box 12–4).

[24]Alejandro Foxley, Eduardo Aninat, and J. P. Arellano, *Redistributive Efforts of Government Programs* (Elmsford, NY: Pergamon Press, 1980), Chapter 6.

Subsidies for consumption of basic foodstuffs also can result in substantial redistribution, provided food subsidy programs are not accompanied by oppressive price controls on the production of food by poor farmers. Subsidies to subnational governments often are used to finance the provision of basic human needs, such as water, sewerage, education, and health services, all of which have benefits concentrated in lower-income classes. Housing subsidies favor the poor less frequently, since many programs for housing subsidies (Indonesia, Ghana, Pakistan) in reality are confined largely to government employees, a group that in most countries is relatively well off.

Not all subsidy programs contribute to income redistribution, even when redistribution is the announced goal. The most striking example has been that of subsidies for the consumption of petroleum products, particularly kerosene, in Bolivia, Colombia, Indonesia, Pakistan, and several other oil-producing countries. In all four cases mentioned, a principal justification offered for such subsidies was to assist low-income groups. In Bolivia through 1980 and in Colombia through 1974, this argument was extended to cover gasoline consumption, even though in both countries automobile ownership was confined largely to the upper 5 percent of the income distribution and, in both, urban bus transport already was heavily subsidized. In Indonesia, gasoline was subsidized only lightly, but budget subsidies held the prices of kerosene and diesel fuel at less than half the cost of production and distribution. Although it seems plausible that kerosene subsidies strongly favor the poor, this is not the case. The poorest 40 percent of families consume only 20 percent of the kerosene sold. Therefore, for every $1 of subsidy to the poor, relatively high-income families received $4 of benefit. And, since kerosene can be substituted for diesel fuel, the subsidy program included it as well to prevent diesel users from switching. The result was that subsidies to kerosene and diesel fuel averaged about 5 percent of total tax revenues in Indonesia from 1979 to 1981, a figure exceeding total capital expenditures for education during that period.

Fiscal policy to redistribute income must be viewed in perspective. It is not the only and not always the most effective instrument for redistribution. Other chapters draw attention to the pivotal importance for income distribution of land tenure, the terms of trade between rural and urban areas, the growth of employment, the relative prices of labor and capital, the openness and market orientation of the economy, and other factors. Taxation and government expenditures can affect most of those factors to some extent, but other, more-direct policy instruments may have greater impact on income distribution. Each of these instruments, some of which force radical changes in the economy, has its economic and political dangers. But a government determined on a more-equitable income distribution probably needs to employ all these measures, including progressive taxation and expenditure policies, to some degree.

ECONOMIC EFFICIENCY AND THE BUDGET

Sources of Inefficiency

On the expenditure side of the budget, the tool we call *social cost-benefit analysis* can be deployed to enhance efficiency (reduce waste) in government spending. On the tax side, promotion of economic efficiency is more problematic.

All taxes, save lump-sum levies (poll taxes), lead to inefficiencies to one degree or another. Lump-sum taxes are not realistic options for raising government revenues given their high degree of regressivity. The objective, therefore, is to minimize tax-induced inefficiencies consistent with other goals of tax policy. In most developing societies, this objective largely reduces to the necessity to identify examples of waste engendered by taxes and purge them from the system. If a particular feature of a tax system involves large efficiency losses, called *excess burden* in fiscal economics, and at the same time contributes little or nothing to such other policy goals as income redistribution, then that feature is an obvious candidate for abolition. A full discussion of those elements of tax systems that qualify for such treatment is properly the subject of an extended public finance monograph. We can do little more here than indicate some of the principal examples.

A major source of inefficiency in taxation is excessive costs of tax administration. In some countries and for some taxes, these costs have been so high that they call into question the desirability of using certain taxes for any purposes. This is true for certain kinds of narrow-based stamp taxes widely used in Latin America to collect government revenue on the documentation of transfer of assets, rental agreements, checks, and ordinary business transactions. Many stamp taxes cost more to administer than they collect in revenue.

In some countries, even broad-based taxes have had inordinately high costs of collection. For example, sales taxes in Chile and Ecuador in the 1960s cost $1 in administration for every $4 collected, as opposed to about $1 per $100 for most state sales taxes in the United States. And, because taxes on capital gains are so difficult to administer everywhere, including North America, the cost of collecting this component of income taxes often exceeds the revenue in developing countries.

Many developing countries, from Ghana to Colombia to Indonesia, have offered substantial tax incentives to encourage investment in particular activities and regions. Many of these, particularly income tax holidays for approved firms, have proven very difficult to administer and few have led to the desired result.[25] Given persistently pressing revenue requirements in most countries, granting liberal tax incentives may have no effect other than requiring higher rates of tax on

[25]See, for example, Arnold C. Harberger, "Principles of Taxation Applied to Developing Countries: What Have We Learned?" in Michael Boskin and Charles E. McLure, Jr., eds., *World Tax Reform: Case Studies of Developed and Developing Countries* (San Francisco: ICS Press, 1990).

taxpayers who do not qualify for incentives. It is a dictum of fiscal theory that economic waste (inefficiency) arising from taxation increases by the square of the tax rate employed, not proportionately. Therefore, it is not difficult to see that unsuccessful tax incentive programs involve inefficiencies for the economy as a whole that are not compensated for by any significant benefits. Largely for this reason, Indonesia abolished all forms of tax incentives in a sweeping tax reform in 1984.

Finally, some features of major tax sources involve needless waste. From the earlier discussion of the use of import duties for luxury tax purposes, it is clear that this often is a major source of inefficiency. The use of progressive tax rates in a corporation income tax (as in Colombia until 1974, Venezuela, Mexico, Brazil, Ghana, and a score of other countries) is another example. Progressive rates of corporate tax, where they cannot be enforced, do little to contribute to income redistribution; and where they can be enforced, they lead to several kinds of waste. Two of the most important are fragmentation of business firms and inefficiency in business operations. The incentive for fragmentation is evident: Rather than be subject to high marginal rates of taxes, firms tend to split into smaller units and lose any cost advantages of size. Where high progressive rates are employed for company income, the tax takes a high proportion (say, 70 percent) of each additional dollar of earnings, so the incentive to control costs within the firm is reduced. For example, for a firm facing a marginal tax rate of 70 percent, an additional outlay of $1,000 for materials involves a net cost to the firm of only $300, because at the same time taxes are reduced by $700.

Neutrality and Efficiency: Lessons from Experience

Experience around the world, both in developed and developing countries, seems to indicate that, in societies where efficiency in taxation matters, this objective is best pursued by reliance on taxes that are as neutral as possible. A **neutral tax** is one that does not lead to a material change in the structure of private incentives that would prevail in the absence of the tax. A neutral tax system, then, is one that relies, to the extent possible, on uniform rates: a tax on all income at a flat rate or a sales tax with the same rate applied to all food and services. A neutral tax system cannot be an efficient tax system.

An **efficient tax system** involves a minimum amount of excess burden for raising a required amount of revenue, where the *excess burden* of a tax is the loss in total welfare, over and above the amount of tax revenues collected by the government. Figure 12–2 demonstrates how the excess burden of, say, a commodity tax is the greater the more elastic is the demand or the supply of the taxed item. Case 1 depicts the inelastic case, good A, while Case 2 shows the elastic case, good B. Constant marginal costs (MC) are assumed in both cases and at the same level for both goods to portray more starkly the contrasting results achieved in those cases. Before the tax is imposed on either good, the equilibrium price and quantity are P_a and Q_a for good A and P_b and Q_b for good B. Now, we impose a tax rate (t) on both goods. The new equilibrium (posttax) magnitudes are P_{at} and Q_{at}

for good A and P_{bt} and Q_{bt} for good B. For good A, the total amount of government revenue is the rectangle $P_aP_{at}cd$. The total loss in consumer surplus arising from the tax is the trapezoid $P_aP_{at}ce$. The excess of the loss in consumer surplus over the amount of government revenue is the conventional measure of efficiency loss from a tax, or excess burden. For good A, the excess burden is the small triangle cde. By similar reasoning, the excess burden in the case of good B is the larger triangle fgh. We see that taxes of equivalent rates involve more excess burden when imposed on goods with elastic demand.

We can see that efficient taxation requires neither uniformity nor neutrality but many different tax rates on different goods, with tax rates lower for goods with elastic demand and higher for goods with inelastic demand. This is known as the **Ramsey rule,** or the **inverse elasticity rule.** The problem is that a tax system under this rule would be decidedly regressive: The highest taxes would be required on foodstuffs, drinking water, and sumptuary items. Taxes would be lower on items such as clothing, services, and foreign travel, which tend to be both price and income elastic.

The principle of neutrality in taxation is not nearly as intellectually satisfying a guide to tax policy as efficient taxation. Nevertheless, neutral taxation is to be preferred as one of the underlying principles of taxation, along with equity, until such time as analysts are able to identify optimal departures from neutrality—and uniformity in tax rates—in real-world settings. More intellectually satisfying tax policies also must wait until such time as administrative capacities are equal to the task of operating necessarily complicated structures of efficient or optimal taxes.

There is a paradox here. Neutral, uniform-rate taxes are less suited for efficiency goals than perfectly administered efficient taxes. Yet neutral tax systems are more likely to enhance efficiency in the economy than efficient or optimal

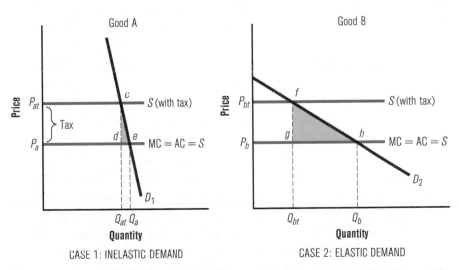

FIGURE 12-2. Taxation and Efficiency: Excess Burden of Commodity Taxes with Constant Marginal (MC) and Average Costs (AC), under Competition
The shaded area in each case represents the excess burden of equal tax rates imposed on different goods. The greater is the elasticity, the greater the excess burden.

systems, since neutral systems with uniform rates can be administered most easily and are much less vulnerable to evasion. This is not to say that neutrality has ever been or should be the overriding goal of tax policy. Governments often undertake very deliberate departures from neutral tax treatment of certain sectors or groups of society to achieve other policy goals. But, in real-world settings, these departures involve costs, not only in terms of tax administration but often in both equity and efficiency terms as well. It is important that these costs be made as transparent as possible, so that policy makers may weigh them against expected gains from nonneutrality, including efficiency gains. Under the present technology, major departures from neutrality in taxation are not likely to yield benefits commensurate with the costs. Neutrality in taxation may be the most advisable guide to efficiency in taxation for some time to come.

SUMMARY

- The expenditure side of the government budget is made up of capital or development items together with a wide variety of current use expenditures that are called *recurrent costs*. Developing country governments and donor aid programs frequently waste capital by neglecting the recurrent costs needed to maintain that capital.
- Developing countries rely mainly on indirect taxes (sales or value-added taxes and customs duties) rather than income and capital gains taxes, because the latter are extremely difficult and expensive to administer in developing countries and thus produce less revenue.
- Tax reform in developing countries generally involves simplifying the tax system (one or a small number of different tax rates) and introducing taxes such as the value-added tax that have some self-enforcement properties. Greater complexity in the tax code leads to greater difficulty and greater corruption in administering the code. Simplified tax codes also reduce the distortions in the economy introduced by taxes.
- Taxation on the basis of an individual's ability to pay (higher-income people pay a larger share of their income in taxes), is a fundamental principle of equity. A good tax system is thus progressive rather than regressive, but progressive tax systems are extremely difficult to administer, particularly in developing countries, except in limited areas such as the exemption of food from sales taxes. When one looks at the actual incidence of taxes on high- and low-income earners, taxes that are designed to be progressive often turn out to be the opposite, and tax reform needs to take this into account.

13

Financial Policy

A country's **financial system** consists of a variety of interconnected financial institutions, both formal and informal. Except in a handful of countries (including Liberia, Panama, Hong Kong, and several Francophone African countries), a central bank lies at the core of the organized financial system and is responsible for the control of the money supply and the general supervision of organized financial activity. Virtually everywhere, and particularly in developing countries, the commercial banking system is the most visible and vital component of the formal financial system, as acceptor of deposits and grantor of shorter-term credit. Other elements of the formal financial system include savings banks, insurance companies, and in a growing number of middle-income countries, pension funds and investment banks specializing in long-term credit, as well as emerging stock exchanges. Coexisting with these modern financial institutions are the informal and largely unregulated systems of finance, including pawnshops, local moneylenders, trade credit, and other informal arrangements involving the borrowing and lending of money, such as intrafamily transfers and cooperative credit. In very low-income countries, or even in some middle-income countries, the informal financial sector may rival the formal system in size.

Financial policy embraces all measures intended to affect the growth, utilization, efficiency, and diversification of the financial system. In North America and Western Europe, the term *financial policy* ordinarily is used as a synonym for *monetary policy,* the use of monetary instruments to reduce instability caused by fluctuations in either internal or external markets. In the United

States, these instruments include open-market operations, changes in legal reserve requirements of commercial banks, and shifts in central-bank (Federal Reserve) lending (rediscount) rates to commercial banks; these terms are explained later in the chapter. In developing countries, the term *financial policy* typically has a much broader meaning. Monetary policy is part of financial policy but so are measures intended to encourage the growth of savings in the form of financial assets, develop money and capital markets, and allocate credit among different economic sectors. Also of central importance, as the Asian financial crisis of 1997–98 reminded us, are regulatory and supervisory systems that oversee capital markets.

THE FUNCTIONS OF A FINANCIAL SYSTEM

The financial system provides four basic services essential for the smooth functioning of an economy. First, it provides a medium of exchange and a store of value, called *money*, which also serves as a unit of account to measure the value of the transactions. Second, it provides channels for mobilizing savings from numerous sources and channeling them to investors, a process called *financial intermediation*. Third, it provides a means of transferring and distributing risk across the economy. Fourth, it provides a set of policy instruments for the stabilization of economic activity.

Money and the Money Supply

An economy without money as a **medium of exchange** is primitive. Trade between individuals must take the form of high-cost, inefficient barter transactions. In a barter economy, goods have prices, but they are expressed in the relative prices of physical commodities: so many kilos of rice for so many liters of kerosene, so many meters of rope for so many pairs of sandals, and so on. Trading under such circumstances involves onerous information costs.

Few societies have ever relied heavily on barter because of the high costs implicit in this means of exchange. At some point, prices of goods and services begin to be expressed in terms of one or more universally accepted and durable commodities, like gold and silver, or even beads and cowrie shells. The rise of commodity money diminishes the transaction and storage costs of trade but still involves problems of making exchanges across space and time. Gold and silver prices fluctuate, and the commodities therefore are not fully reliable as **units of account.** As specialization within an economy increases, financial instruments backed by commodities appear. In the last century, with the rise of central banking all over the world, currency evolved into *fiat* money, debt issued by central banks that is legal tender. It is backed not by commodities of equivalent value but only by the full faith and credit of the central bank.

As markets widen and specialization proceeds apace, a need arises for still another financial instrument, **transferable deposits.** In the normal course of development, *checking* or *demand deposits* (deposits that may be transferred to any economic agent at the demand of the depositor) appear first and ordinarily bear little or no interest. Rising levels of economic activity, however, create increasing needs for transaction balances; individuals always will maintain some balances in demand deposits to meet these needs but tend to economize on the levels of such deposits if no interest is paid on them. With further monetization still another financial instrument begins to grow in importance, *time deposits,* which also are legally transferable on demand but sometimes only after stated periods. Time deposits involve contractual interest payments; higher interest rates induce people to hold greater amounts of deposits in this form.

While checking (demand) and time deposits are **liabilities** (or debts) of commercial banks, they are **financial assets** for the persons who hold them. Both demand and time deposits are known as *liquid financial assets.* Unlike *nonfinancial assets* that also can be held by households and businesses (inventories, gold, and land), demand and time deposits can be quickly and conveniently converted into their currency equivalents. *Currency,* by definition, is the most liquid of all assets. The concept of liquid financial assets is an important one in any discussion of financial policy in developing countries. For most developing countries, the movement of savers in and out of liquid financial assets may be the prime factor behind the success or failure of a financial policy. We will see that long-term shifts from tangible, or nonfinancial, physical assets to financial assets, particularly liquid assets, bodes well not only for economic growth but also for economic stability.

A country's **money supply** may be defined as the sum of all liquid assets in the financial system. While not all economists agree about what constitutes a liquid financial asset, most vastly prefer this money supply concept to those commonly employed in early postwar monetary analysis. Formerly, the money supply was conventionally defined as the sum of only two liquid financial assets: currency in circulation outside banks (*C*) plus demand deposits (*D*), which together are known as M1 *(narrow money).* However, it later became clear that, because depositors tend to view time and savings deposits (*T*) as almost as liquid as demand deposits, the former also should be included in any workable concept of money supply, called M2 *(broad money).* Finally, for high-income countries, specialized deposit-taking financial institutions have arisen and offer an array of options to savers other than those available in commercial and savings banks. The liabilities of these specialized institutions (*O*) are included in M3 *(total liquid liabilities),* the broadest measure of money. Thus,

$$M1 = C + D \qquad [13\text{--}1]$$

$$M2 = M1 + T \qquad [13\text{--}2]$$

$$M3 = M2 + O \qquad [13\text{--}3]$$

For most low-income countries and many middle-income countries, liquid financial assets constitute by far the greatest share of outstanding financial assets. But, as income growth continues and the financial system matures, less-liquid financial assets assume progressively greater importance. These include primary securities such as stocks, bonds (issued both by government and firms), and other financial claims on tangible (physical) assets that are convertible into currency equivalents with only some risk of loss to the asset holder and are hence less liquid than demand or time deposits.

The evolution of financial activity follows no set pattern across countries. Differing economic conditions and policies may result in widely divergent patterns of financial growth. Nevertheless, as per capita income rises, money increases as a ratio to GDP. Table 13–1 shows these patterns for broad money, M2. For all income classes shown in the table, the ratio of M2 to the GDP rose substantially from 1970

TABLE 13-1. **Broad Money (M2) as a Percentage of GDP, 1970 and 2002**

	PERCENT OF GDP			PERCENT OF GDP	
	1970	2002		1970	2002
Low-income countries	19	48	Upper-middle-income countries	18	40
Ethiopia	–	48	Colombia	18	27
Tanzania	–	20	Argentina	21	26
India	21	59	Mexico	15	21
Bangladesh	–	37	Malaysia	30	101
Kenya	27	38	Korea, Republic	29	83
Nigeria	9	28			
Ghana	18	26	High-income countries	60	83*
Honduras	19	50	Saudi Arabia	14	50
			Japan	68	131
Low- and middle-income countries	22	68	United States	62	69
Pakistan	41	49			
Bolivia	15	42			
Cameroon	14	19			
The Philippines	23	56			
Sri Lanka	22	37			
Indonesia	8	54			
Peru	18	32			
Egypt	34	81			

*2001 data.

Source: World Bank, *World Development Indicators 2004*, online at worldbank.publications.org/subscriptions/WDI.

to 1997. This reflects both economic growth and changing policies. Looking across countries, however, the pattern is not so clear-cut. On average, the advanced, high-income economies had much higher monetization ratios than the middle- and low-income countries. But no clear differences are found in the averages for lower-, lower-middle-, and upper-middle-income country groups. The variance among countries, even with similar income, is notable, as is the range among developing countries. The ratio of M2 varies from lows of 14–15 percent for low-income Nigeria and middle-income Peru and Argentina to highs of over 70 percent for Ethiopia, one of the poorest countries in the world, and middle-income Egypt and Malaysia. Even among industrial countries, Japan's ratio is two thirds higher than those of Germany and the United States.

Liquid assets are not the only source of financial growth, however. As financial markets widen with the spread of the money economy, they also tend to deepen as a greater variety of financial assets begin to appear. With rising incomes, a growing proportion of financial growth tends to come in the form of nonliquid financial assets, such as primary securities, suitable as a basis for the type of longer-term finance that commercial banking systems cannot easily provide. The **financial ratio** (the ratio of net financial assets to GDP) tends to rise steadily from less than 20 percent of GDP in very poor countries, such as Haiti or Chad, to between 60 and 80 percent in higher-income countries, such as Brazil, South Korea, and Venezuela. Malaysia by 1985 had reached the extraordinarily high level for a developing country of 200 percent. In very high-income countries, including Canada and the United States, total financial assets are also nearly twice as large as GDP, and three times GDP in Japan.[1] Here again, there is no evidence of immutable laws of financial development. Many very high-income industrial countries, including France and Holland, have financial ratios a third that of Japan. And many higher-income developing countries, particularly those with long inflationary histories (Uruguay, Brazil, Argentina), display a lower ratio of financial assets to GDP than poorer countries such as India and Thailand (89 and 65 percent, respectively).

Financial Intermediation

As financial structures become increasingly rich and diversified in terms of financial assets, institutions, and markets, the function of money as a medium of exchange, store of value, and unit of account tends to be taken for granted, except in situations of runaway inflation. As financial development proceeds, the ability of the financial system to perform its second major function, financial intermediation, grows as well. The process of financial intermediation involves gathering savings from multitudinous savers and channeling them to a much smaller but still sizable number of investors. With a few exceptions,

---

[1]World Bank, *World Development Report 1989*, p. 39.

households are the only net savers in developing countries. At early stages of economic development, a preponderant share of intermediation activities tends to be concentrated in commercial banks. As development proceeds, new forms of financial intermediaries begin to appear and gradually assume a growing share of the intermediation function. These include investment banks, insurance companies, pension funds, and securities markets.

Financial intermediation activities are best measured through use of **flow-of-funds accounts,** which display the uses of finance by different economic sectors together with the sources of savings by sectors. Unfortunately, reliable flow-of-funds tables are available for only a few countries at present, and cross-country generalization about intermediation based on such tables is not yet possible. In the absence of flow-of-funds accounts, we employ the liquid asset–GDP ratio as an approximate measure of financial intermediation.

Financial intermediation is best seen as one of several alternative technologies for mobilizing and allocating savings. The fiscal system discussed in Chapter 12 furnishes another alternative, and we see in the next chapter that reliance on foreign savings constitutes still another. Further, we will observe in this chapter that inflation also has been employed as a means of mobilizing resources for the public sector. Indeed, a decision to rely more heavily on financial intermediation as a means of investment finance is tantamount to a decision to rely less heavily on the government budget, foreign aid and foreign investment, and inflation to achieve the same purpose.

Transformation and Distribution of Risk

Another major service provided by a well-functioning financial system is the transformation and distribution of risk. All economic activities involve risk taking, but some undertakings involve more risk than others. Individual savers and investors tend to be risk averse; the marginal loss of a dollar appears more important to them than the marginal gain of a dollar. But the degree of risk aversion differs among individuals. When risk cannot be diversified, or pooled, across a large number of individuals, savers and investors demand greater returns, or premiums, for bearing risk; and activities involving high risk tend not to be undertaken. But high-risk activities may well offer the greatest returns to the economy as a whole. A well-functioning financial system furnishes a means for diversifying, or pooling, risk among a large number of savers and investors. The system may offer assets with differing degrees of risk. Financial institutions that specialize in assessing and managing risks can assign them to individuals having different attitudes toward and perceptions of risk. Indeed, a perfectly functioning financial system can reduce all risk premiums to zero, except for those *systematic risks* that never can be diversified away from the domestic economy, such as those arising from national disasters and recessions in the world economy.

Stabilization

Finally, the financial system provides instruments for the stabilization of economic activity in addition to those available under fiscal policy and direct controls. All economies experience cyclical changes in production, employment, and prices. Governments often attempt to compensate for these fluctuations through policies affecting the money supply. Because unemployment in developing countries rarely is of the type that can be cured by monetary expansion, the use of financial policy for stabilization purposes generally focuses on efforts to control inflation. As the economic crisis that began in Asia in 1997 demonstrated, however, the financial system itself can become a major source of instability in the country. From the beginning of the twenty-first century, as a result, financial policy also has focused on more than simply whether the supply of money is growing too rapidly or too slowly. Policy makers have had to devote much attention to ensuring the integrity and stability of banks and other nonbank financial institutions to avoid a severe recession brought on by financial panic. In the discussion that follows, we focus first on the use of the financial system to control inflation and then return to the issue of how the financial system should be designed and managed to avoid panic and recession.

INFLATION AND SAVINGS MOBILIZATION

By the 1980s to the present, **price inflation,** defined as a sustained increase in the overall price level, generally was regarded as a malady, which in its milder forms was annoying but tolerable and in its moderate form corrosive but not fatal. Runaway inflation, also known as *hyperinflation,* however, always has been recognized as severely destructive of economic processes, with few offsetting benefits. Whereas a number of influential thinkers in the 1950s and 1960s advocated some degree of moderate inflation (for example, inflation rates between 8 and 12 percent) as a tool for promoting growth, few adherents of this view remain, for reasons discussed later. Many others did not actively advocate inflation but tended to have a higher threshold of tolerance for a steadily rising general price level than now is common. They believed that development inevitably involved trade-offs between inflation and unemployment and that the wise course was to resolve the trade-off in favor of less unemployment and more inflation. Today, few economists still believe in a fixed, long-term relation between inflation and unemployment, and a growing body of evidence, some of it presented in Chapter 5, demonstrates that restraining inflation may enhance, rather than retard, prospects for long-run growth.

Inflation Episodes

Inflationary experiences vary widely among developing countries and generalizations are difficult to make. Nevertheless, postwar economic history offers some interesting national and regional contrasts in both susceptibility to and tolerance for different levels of inflation. The period prior to the early 1970s was one of relative price stability in developing countries. In the southern cone of Latin America, however, particularly in Argentina, Brazil, and Chile, **chronic inflation** (prices rising 25–50 percent per year for three years or more) was an enduring fact of economic life for much of the past four decades. The experience of these countries indicates that a long period of double-digit inflation does not necessarily lead to national economic calamity in all societies. In all, 35 countries experienced chronic inflation from 1950 to 1997, as shown in Table 13–2.

However, a tolerable rate of inflation in one country may constitute economic trauma in another. This may be seen more readily by considering the often progressive inflationary disease, acute inflation. **Acute inflation,** defined here as inflation in excess of 50 percent for three or more consecutive years, was experienced by 33 countries over the postwar period, in some cases more than once per country. For Brazil, the progression from chronic to acute inflation did not result in any noticeable slowing of that country's relatively robust economic growth, whatever it may have meant for income distribution. In Ghana, on the other hand, a decade of acute inflation coincided with a decade of decline in GDP per capita. Although it may be tempting to attribute economic retrogression in Ghana to acute inflation, it is more likely that the same policies that led to sustained inflation, not the inflation itself, were responsible for declines in living standards there.[2]

Although acute inflation has proven toxic to economic development in some settings and only bothersome in others, **runaway (hyper)inflation** almost always has had a devastating effect. Inflation rates in excess of 200 percent per year represent an inflationary process that is clearly out of control; 22 countries have undergone this traumatic experience since 1950. One recent major bout of runaway inflationary experience occurred in three Latin American countries: Bolivia and Argentina in 1985, Argentina again in 1988–90, and Peru in 1988–91. In Bolivia, the annual rate of inflation over a period of several months in 1985 accelerated to a rate of nearly 4,000 percent. In Argentina, the monthly rate of price increases was 30.5 percent in June 1985 alone; on an annual basis, that would have been an inflation rate of 2,340 percent. In both Bolivia and

---

[2]For a diagnosis of the causes of the Ghanian economic decline after 1962, see Michael Roemer, "Ghana, 1950 to 1980: Missed Opportunities," and Yaw Ansu, "Comments," both in Arnold C. Haberger, ed., *World Economic Growth* (San Francisco: ICS Press, 1984), 201–30.

TABLE 13-2. Inflation Outliers: Episodes of Chronic, Acute, and Runaway Inflation among Developing Countries, 1948–2002 (average annual rates)

	CHRONIC INFLATION (25–50%, 3 YEARS)		ACUTE INFLATION (50–100%, 3 YEARS)		RUNAWAY INFLATION (200+%, 1 YEAR)	
	YEARS	RATE	YEARS	RATE	YEARS	RATE
Angola					1993–96	858
					1997–2000	170
Argentina	1950–74	27	1977–82	147	1976	443
			1986–87	111	1983–85	529
					1988–91	1,400
Armenia					1990–97	700
Azerbaijian					1990–96*	590
Belarus			1997–2002	87	1990–96*	715
Bolivia	1979–81	33	1952–59	117	1983–86	1,132
Brazil	1957–78	36	1979–84	108	1985	227
					1986	145
					1987–93	831
Chile	1952–71	29			1973–76	308
	1978–80	36				
	1983–85	26				
Colombia	1979–82	26				
	1988–92	28				
Dominican Republic			1988–92	51		
Ecuador	1997–2001	49				
Georgia					1990–96*	2,279
Ghana	1986–90	32	1976–83	73		
			1995–97	75		
Indonesia					1965–68	306
Kazakhstan					1990–96*	605
Kyrgyz Republic					1990–96*	256
Latvia					1990–96*	111
Lithuania					1990–96*	179
Malawi	1998–2001	33				
Mexico			1982–88	70		
			1992	116		
Nicaragua	1979–84	33			1985–91	2,130
Paraguay			1951–53	81		
Peru	1975–77	32	1950–55	102	1988–91	1,694
			1978–87	85		
Romania			1991–93	132		
			1997–92	56		
Russia	1996–99	42	1993–95	376		
Sierra Leone			1983–92	81		
South Korea			1950–55	95		
Tajikistan					1990–96*	394
Turkmenistan					1990–96*	1,074
Tanzania	1980–89	27				
Turkey	1981–87	38	1978–80	69		
			1988–2002	70		
Uganda	1990–92	37	1981–89	101		
Ukraine					1993–95	1,167
Uruguay	1948–65	26	1965–68	83		
	1981–83	34	1972–80	68		
			1984–92	76		
Venezuela	1987–92	40				
	1993–98	43				
Zaire/Congo	1981–82	36	1976–80	68	1991–92	2,987
			1983–90	68	1992–95	3,206
					1996–2002	218
Zambia	1985–87	44	1988–92	113		
			1993–96	71		

*For a number of the former Soviet republics, the GDP price deflator data are given for the entire period 1990–96, not broken down by year. See World Bank, *World Development Indicators 1998,* 230–32.

Source: IMF, *International Financial Statistics Yearbook 1994,* 2003.

Argentina for much of 1985, workers had little choice but to spend their pay-checks within minutes of receipt, for fear that prices would double or triple over the next week. In Peru, hyperinflation in 1989 gave birth to publications devoted only to the tracking of inflation (see Box 13–1). In the 1990s, hyperinflation was experienced by virtually all the new republics formed after the breakup of the Soviet Union. In the first part of the 1990s, inflation reached a rate of nearly 400 percent a year in Russia over a period of several years and over 1,000 percent a year in Georgia and Turkmenistan. In the latter two countries, civil war put heavy demands on government expenditures while reducing the ability of those governments to collect taxes, leading them to finance their activities by printing money. In Africa in the 1990s, civil war in Angola and the Congo also led to infla-tion rates of over 1,000 percent per year.

The 35 countries in Table 13–2 brought on inflation in three different ways. In one group (including Argentina, Chile, Ghana, Indonesia, Peru, Russia, and Ukraine), large budget deficits relative to GDP were financed by borrowing from the central bank. In a second group (Paraguay in the early 1950s and Brazil and Uruguay before 1974), inflation was caused by a massive expansion of credit to the private sector. And in Nicaragua, Sierra Leone, Uganda, Angola, the Congo, and several of the nations created out of the former Soviet Union, political strife or civil war exacerbated the fiscal and monetary causes of inflation. Whatever the initial impetus to inflation, as we shall see, once it begins to accelerate, the public begins to expect inflation to continue, and this leads to even-higher, more-sustained price increases.

For developing countries as a group, Table 13–3 shows that, on average, inflation was only 13 percent a year until the oil crisis began in 1973 but jumped to 21 percent a year during the period of rising oil prices until 1981. Inflation

TABLE 13-3. **Inflation by Regional Groupings, 1964–2001**
(percent per annum)

	1963-73	1973-81	1981-86	1986-92	1992-95	1995-98	1998-2001
World	26.3	13.8	14.1	21.1	19.2	6.8	4.2
Industrial countries	24.6	10.3	24.9	4.0	2.5	1.9	1.8
Developing countries	12.9	20.7	32.0	55.0	47.9	12.6	7.1
Africa	24.9	17.3	29.0	25.4	40.2	12.1	8.2
Asia	13.5	28.8	26.8	9.0	11.6	6.9	2.4
Middle East	24.2	16.6	18.8	14.0	15.0	9.5	5.5
Latin America and							
Caribbean	18.4	43.7	98.0	232.8	216.5	15.5	8.4

Source: IMF, *International Financial Statistics Yearbook 1994, 1998, 2003*, 76–80, 108–9.

BOX 13-1   HYPERINFLATION IN PERU, 1988-90

The economic and social havoc wrought by hyperinflation is difficult to comprehend for those who have not lived through the experience. The Peruvian hyperinflation, which began in 1988 and continued until 1991, provides some rueful examples.

The inflationary process was triggered by large budgetary deficits and sustained by subsequent ongoing deficits, virtual economic collapse, and steadily rising inflationary expectations. Peru already had experienced two serious bouts with acute inflation since 1950 (see Table 13–2), but the pace of inflation in 1989 was the highest in the nation's history: 28 percent per month, or about 2,000 percent per year. Moreover, inflation accelerated in the first six weeks of 1990, as prices rose by 6 percent per week, or about 1 percent per day. From January 1989 to December 1990, the value of the Peruvian currency (the intis) on the free market fell from 1,200 intis per dollar to 436,000 intis per dollar.

This hyperinflation may turn out to be one of the best documented in history: In 1988, Richard Webb, an internationally respected Peruvian economist, began to publish a magazine devoted essentially to helping producers and consumers cope with the chaos associated with runaway inflation. The magazine, called *Cuanto?* (*How Much?*) appeared monthly. It not only provided details on price developments for a large number of commodities and services but managed to extract what little humor there is in a situation where the price of a movie ticket rises while people are waiting in line to buy it or a taxi driver must carry his fare money in a burlap bag because the domestic currency collected in fares each evening is too bulky to fit in his trousers.

But precious little is funny about hyperinflation. In Peru, it was a story of government employees going without pay for weeks at a time, of indices of poverty nearly doubling from 1987 to 1989, further impoverishing the poorest 40 percent of the population. It was a story of precipitous decline in gross domestic product and the rise of pervasive black markets in everything from dollars to gasoline to cement. It was a time when, on each payday, laborers rushed to the market to buy their weekly food supplies before they were marked up overnight. It was a tale of wide variations in price rises, where prices for such items as pencils and chicken increased by more than 25 times from February 1989 to February 1990, but prices of light bulbs and telephone services increased "only" tenfold.

Imagine life in Lima, the capital city, in the first few weeks of 1990, for a middle-income family trying to survive. For the first 40 days of the year, increases in the price of dying outpaced the price of living: The cost of funerals rose 79 percent, while house rent rose by 56 percent and the price of restaurant meals and haircuts increased by 44 percent.

By mid-1990, the economic paralysis of Peru was virtually complete. Peru's hyperinflation ended in 1992 (although inflation remained acute at 75 percent) as government reduced its budget deficit to 1 percent of GDP.

then accelerated to more than 30 percent a year even as oil prices began falling and exceeded 50 percent a year after oil prices collapsed in 1986. In the 1990s, these high rates of inflation continued through the first half of the decade and then slowed markedly after 1995. The principal exceptions were the states of the former Soviet Union, where triple-digit inflation in many cases continued into the twenty-first century. The industrial countries, in contrast, had much lower inflation throughout and the highest price increases coincided with the rise in oil prices.

These averages conceal more than they reveal, however. Asian countries, with moderate inflation before the oil crisis, were adept at stabilizing their economies and reducing inflation to single digits during and after the rise in energy prices. African countries went in the opposite direction: They accepted the "imported" inflation from higher oil prices (and their own commodity price boom) during the 1970s then, in the 1980s, chose to finance their deficits, using foreign aid and domestic borrowing, rather than reduce them. Latin America stands out as the region of highest inflation prior to the 1990s and prior to the breakup of the Soviet Union into independent republics. Not only did many Latin American countries borrow extensively during the 1970s to cover external deficits, they also refused to reduce their fiscal deficits when those loans had to be repaid, at higher interest rates, during the early 1980s. Inflationary deficit financing intensified throughout the 1980s in many countries. By the 1990s, however, particularly after 1995, there was a strong trend in both Africa and Latin America toward reduced deficits and lower inflation, as it became clear that economic growth was unlikely until inflation had been quenched. In Latin America in the 1990s and through the turn to the new century, only Brazil continued to experience triple digit inflation, while major economies such as Argentina, Mexico, Chile, and Bolivia saw the rate of price increase fall below 20 percent a year.

Forced Mobilization of Savings

Chapter 12 identified a number of problems involved in the use of conventional taxes, such as income and sales taxes, for mobilizing public-sector savings. Another form of taxation is inflation. Governments from the time of the Roman Empire have recognized inflation as an alternative means of securing resources for the state. All that is required is that the stock of money be expanded at a sufficiently rapid rate to result in increases in the general price level and people be willing to hold some money balances even as the values of these holdings decline. Inflation then acts as a tax on money holdings. At 15 percent inflation, the annual tax on currency is 13 percent, and at 40 percent inflation the tax is 29 percent.[3] These are higher annual tax rates than any country has ever managed to impose successfully on any physical asset, such as housing, automobiles, or equipment. Under extremely high rates of inflation, as in the German hyperinflation of 1922–23 or the Peruvian inflation of 1988–90, households attempt to reduce holdings of money balances to virtually nothing. However, except during runaway inflation, because money is so convenient as a means of exchange and unit of account, people always hold some money balances, even if they must pay fairly heavy inflation taxes for the convenience.

Difficulties in collecting conventional taxes, the apparent ease of collecting inflation taxes, the convenience properties of money balances, and the view that inflation taxes are progressive (richer people hold higher money balances) have led some policy makers and economists to view inflation as a desirable means of development finance. During the 1950s and 1960s, the influential United Nations Economic Commission for Latin America saw moderate inflation as a means of "greasing the wheels" of development, forcing savings from holders of money balances and transferring such savings to governments strapped for investment resources. Accordingly, much effort was expended in the search for what was viewed as an "optimal" rate of inflation for developing societies: The rate that maximizes tax collections, including both conventional taxes and inflation rates.

Implementation of such a forced-saving strategy tends to curtail private investment, since some of the inflation tax comes out of money balances that would have been used for investment in the private sector. However, proponents of tax maximization through inflation assumed that the government's marginal propensity to invest out of inflation taxes exceeded that of the private sector and the government would invest in real assets as productive as the private investment it displaced. Therefore, it was thought, forced-savings strategies would never reduce total investment.

Two implicit assumptions lay behind the argument that the forced-savings strategy would improve economic welfare in developing countries. Collections of conventional taxes were believed to be highly responsive to inflationary

---

[3]Say, the nominal value of money balances at the beginning of a year is M_n, equal to the real value, M_r. Now, if price inflation proceeds at a rate p per year, then after one year the real value of money balances would be

$$M_r' = M_r / (1 + p)$$

The tax on these balances is $T = M_r - M_r'$ and the tax rate is

$$t = \frac{M_r - M_t'}{M_r} = 1 - \frac{1}{1+p} = \frac{p}{1+p}$$

If $p = 40$ percent, $t = p/(1 + p) = 29$ percent.

growth; that is, the revenue elasticity of the conventional tax system with respect to nominal income growth is greater than 1.[4] And efficiency losses from inflation taxes were thought to be less than efficiency losses from the use of conventional taxes to increase government revenues. Indeed, it can be shown that, under circumstances where (1) a government's marginal propensity to invest out of inflation taxes is unity or greater, (2) the revenue elasticity of the tax system also is unity or greater, and (3) the marginal efficiency costs of inflation taxes are less than those for explicit taxes, the growth-maximizing rate of inflation may be as high as 30 percent. However, these assumptions are so far divorced from economic realities in developing countries as to undermine severely, if not demolish, the case for forced savings through inflation.

First, little evidence has found that governments anywhere have a marginal propensity to invest out of inflation taxes that is near unity. For tax maximization through inflation to simulate growth, a government's marginal propensity to invest would have to rise with inflation. Research by George von Furstenberg of the IMF and others find no support at all for even the weakest form of this hypothesis. Second, the net result of even moderate inflation on a government's total revenues (conventional taxes plus inflation taxes) actually may be to decrease the government's ability to expand total investment. This may occur easily if the revenue elasticity of the tax structure is less than unity, as is the case in many, but not all, developing countries. In such cases, the growth in collections from conventional taxes lags well behind nominal GNP growth. Particularly in the early stages of an inflationary process, part of the higher inflation tax collections are offset by a decline in the real value of conventional tax collections. Third, available evidence suggests that, once inflation exceeds 2 percent per annum, the incremental efficiency losses from inflation taxes tend strongly to outweigh those from conventional taxes.[5] And it is well to note that, since 1973, typical inflation rates in developing countries have been far above 2 percent (Table 13–3).

At best, then, government mobilization of resources through inflation is a knife-edge strategy. Inflation rates must be kept high enough to yield substantial

---

[4]The revenue elasticity (E_R) measures the responsiveness of the tax system to growth in GDP. It is defined as the percent of change in tax collections divided by the percent of change in GDP, where Y = GDP, or

$$E_R = \frac{\Delta T / T}{\Delta Y / Y}$$

If $E_R > 1$, then the tax system is revenue elastic and taxes rise proportionally more than national income. For example, if $E_R = 1.2$, then, for every 10 percent increase in GDP, tax collections rise by 12 percent. If $E_R < 1$, the tax system is revenue inelastic; if $E_R = 0.8$, then, with a 10 percent increase in GDP, tax collections rise by 8 percent.

[5]George M. von Furstenberg, "Inflation, Taxes and Welfare in LDCs," *Public Finance* 35, no. 2 (1980), 700–1.

inflation taxes but not so high as to cause holders of liquid assets to undertake wholesale shifts into real assets to escape the tax. Inflation rates must be kept low enough that collections from conventional taxes do not lag far behind growth in nominal income and efficiency losses from inflation do not greatly exceed efficiency losses from higher conventional tax revenues. Paradoxically, then, the inflation tax device can work best where it is needed the least, in those countries having tax systems most responsive to growth in the overall GDP and involving low efficiency costs. Countries with revenue-elastic tax systems do not need to resort to inflation in an attempt to finance expanded government investment. In this sense, tax reform can be seen as a substitute for inflationary finance but not the other way around.

Inflation as a Stimulus to Investment

The forced-savings doctrine was not the only argument employed in favor of purposeful inflation. For more than 50 years, some economists argued that, even in industrial countries, rising prices can act as a stimulus to private business enterprise, as inflation was thought to be helpful in drawing labor and capital out of declining sectors of the economy and into dynamic ones. If true for industrial societies, then, it was reasoned, the argument might apply with special force in developing countries, where rigidities, bottlenecks, and barriers to mobility were such that resources were particularly likely to be trapped in low-productivity uses. Inflation, it was argued, would help to speed the reallocation of labor and capital out of traditional or subsistence sectors into the modern sectors with the greatest development potential. Therefore, moderate inflation was seen not only as inevitable but desirable: A progressive government would actively seek some target rate of inflation, perhaps as high as 10 percent, to spur development.

Experience with development since 1950 strongly suggests that some inflation indeed is inevitable in developing societies seeking rapid growth in per capita income: Factors of production are relatively immobile in the short run, and imbalances and bottlenecks in supply develop in spite of the most careful planning. However, the deliberate use of sustained inflation to spur development is likely to achieve the desired results only under a limited set of circumstances.

First, if inflation is the result of deliberate policy or can otherwise be anticipated, then in a sustained inflationary process, the approaching rise in prices causes individuals and firms to adjust their expectations of inflation. To the extent that the inflation is anticipated, the supposed beneficial effects never occur; people already have taken them into account in their decision making.[6]

---

[6]This observation dates at least as far back as the early 1930s, to Swedish economist Knut Wicksell. It contains the germ of the idea behind the rational-expectations school of thought of the 1970s and 1980s.

For industrial societies, it would be difficult, at least for an economist, to accept the idea that behavior does not ultimately adjust to expectations of inflation. In developing countries, where all markets, including the market for information, tend to be more imperfect than in developed countries, it might be argued that firms and individuals are less efficient in collecting and using information, including that pertinent to the formation of price expectations. Thus, inflation may not be fully foreseen throughout the economy; consequently, rising prices may result in some stimulus to development in the short term. But it should be recognized that, over the longer run, a successful policy of deliberate inflation depends on people not understanding the policy.

Second, the argument that deliberate inflation enhances private-sector performance overlooks the effects of inflation on risk taking. Inflation increases the risk of all investment decisions. Suppose that businesses can anticipate inflation with a margin of error of plus or minus 20 percent of the actual rate. (If the margin of error is wider, the effects about to be described are more pronounced.) If inflation has been running at 5 percent per year, there may be a general expectation that it will settle within the range of 4–6 percent in the near future. But, if inflation has been running at substantially higher rates, say, 30 percent, then expectations of future inflation rationally may be in the much broader range of 24–36 percent. The entrepreneur, therefore, faces far higher levels of uncertainty in planning investments and production. The more uncertain the future and future returns are, the more likely is the entrepreneur to reduce his or her risks. Investments with long lives (long gestation periods) tend to be more risky than those with short lives. Thus, inflation tends to reduce private-sector investment in projects with a long-term horizon; the inhibiting effects rise with the rate of inflation. Unfortunately, these often are precisely the types of investments most likely to involve high payoffs in terms of income growth for society as a whole.

Finally, inflation may severely curtail private-sector investment by constricting the flow of funds to the organized financial system if nominal interest rates are not allowed to rise as rapidly as the expected rate of inflation. As we see in the next sections, such situations are typical under strategies of shallow financial development.

In any case, many of the arguments developed in favor of deliberate inflation may have been little more than efforts to rationalize the failure of many governments (particularly in Latin America) to bring inflation under control. In most cases, inflation in developed and developing countries has been more a consequence of policy miscalculation or economic dislocation (oil-price shocks, civil wars, agricultural disasters, and so on) than a consciously chosen instrument of economic growth. Some reflective observers of inflationary dynamics, such as Albert Hirschman, have maintained that inflation usually is not the outcome of a systematic set of choices designed to promote growth and other policy objectives. Rather, inflation usually represents the consequences of government temporizing, postponing difficult decisions that might shatter a fragile consensus in governments with sharply divided constituencies.[7] Measures to increase collection from conventional taxes or reduce government spending on programs enacted at the behest of powerful vested interests are examples of such difficult decisions. Avoiding such stabilizing changes is tantamount to choosing inflation, in the hope that, at some point in the future, a more enduring coalition of constituencies can be assembled to directly confront difficult issues. Seen this way, inflation results not by design but by default.

Inflation and Interest Rates

The concept of real interest rates is central to the understanding of the implications of financial policy for growth and development. Interest rates may be viewed as the price of financial assets. The **nominal interest rate** on loans is the stated rate agreed between lender and borrower at the time of contracting a loan. The nominal rate of interest on deposits is the rate offered savers at the time the deposit is made. The nominal rate is an obligation to pay (on loans) or a right to receive (on deposits) interest at a fixed rate regardless of the rate of inflation. Currency, which is a debt of the central bank but a financial asset for currency holders, bears a *nominal* interest rate of 0. In some countries, such as Indonesia, Turkey, and South Korea, interest is paid on demand deposits, but typically this asset also receives a nominal return of 0. Time deposits (including savings accounts) always bear positive nominal interest rates, ranging from as high as 30 percent in Indonesia in 1974 (for deposits committed for a two-year term) to as low as 4 percent in Ghana in the early 1970s. When an enterprise borrows from a commercial bank, the interest rate it agrees to pay usually is quoted in nominal terms; that is, independent of any changes in the general level of prices. Because costs are incurred in intermediating between savers and investors, the nominal lending rates must exceed nominal deposit rates or financial intermediaries operate at a loss. However, in some countries, governments, as a part of broader antiinflationary programs, deliberately have set lending rates below deposit rates and subsidized banks to cover their losses, as in Korea (1960s) and Indonesia (1968–80).

Nominal interest rates (those quoted by banks on loans and deposits) often are subject to maximum ceilings imposed by governments. For example, usury laws and conventions throughout much of the history of the United States limit nominal interest rates that can be charged on loans both to private citizens and the government. Similar laws have operated in developing countries. Also, several

---

[7]Albert O. Hirschman, *Journeys toward Progress: Studies of Economic Policy-Making in Latin America* (New York: Twentieth Century Fund, 1963), 208–9.8. Maxwell J. Fry, *Money, Interest and Banking in Economic Development*, 2d ed. (Baltimore: Johns Hopkins Press, 1995),162–69.

organized religions support limitations on nominal rates to limit usury; this adds moral force to conventions limiting interest rates.

Nominal interest rates are significant for financial development because the nominal rate governs the real interest rate. The **real interest rate** is the nominal interest rate adjusted for inflation, or more precisely, the inflation rate expected by the public. Consider two depositors in different countries in otherwise identical circumstances, except that in one country the inflation rate is expected to be 5 percent and in the other at 10 percent. If both receive nominal interest rates of 6 percent, then the real rate of interest in the first case is a positive 1 percent and in the second case is a negative 4 percent. The prospective value of the deposit rises in the first and falls in the second.

Borrowers as well as depositors respond ultimately to real, not nominal, rates of interest. At sustained high rates of inflation, say, 30 percent per year, borrowers are quite willing, indeed eager, to pay nominal interest rates of 30 percent per year, for loans that are costless: They can be repaid in money with purchasing power well below that at the time of borrowing. Where legal ceilings do not apply on nominal interest rates, they tend to adjust as expected inflation rises and falls. However, in many countries, at least until recent financial market reforms, governments placed ceilings on nominal interest rates. Inflation often exceeded these ceilings, and this resulted in negative real rates.

The relationship between real and nominal interest rates can be illustrated with a one-year deposit of $1 that pays a nominal rate of interest, i. At the end of the year, the deposit is nominally worth $1 + i$. If inflation is p per year, then the *real* value of the deposit at the end of the year is only $(1 + i)/(1 + p)$. Then, the real rate of interest, r, is this value minus the original deposit of $1, or

$$r = (1 + i)/(1 + p) - 1 \qquad [13\text{--}4]$$

Note that, in this formula, we must express rates in fractions, not percentages: 6 percent becomes 0.06.

For example, in Ecuador in 1992, the deposit rate was 34 percent and inflation was 45 percent. The real rate of interest on deposits was

$$r = (1 + 0.34)/(1 + 0.45) - 1 = -0.076 = -7.6 \text{ percent}$$

This means that a depositor, at the end of a year, would have lost 7.6 percent of the value of his or her funds, equivalent to a tax of 7.6 percent on those assets.

When inflation and interest rates are low, say, below 10 percent, the real rate of interest can be approximated by a simple formula:

$$r = i - p \qquad [13\text{--}5]$$

In Malaysia, where the deposit rate was 7 percent in 1992 and inflation was nearly 5 percent, the real rate of interest was $7 - 5 = 2$ percent a year.

In cases where conventional income taxes are collected on interest income, the tax (at rate t) also must be deducted from the nominal rate to arrive at the real deposit rate net of taxes:

$$r_n = \frac{1+i(1-t)}{1+p} - 1 = \frac{i(1-t)-p}{1+p} \qquad [13\text{--}6]$$

Therefore, with only a 20 percent income tax on interest, equation 13–6 shows that the real rate of deposit interest in Ecuador would have been –12 percent. Most countries impose taxes on interest income.

This discussion of inflation and real interest rates brings us to the point where we may evaluate the role of financial policy in a systematic fashion. We shall see that the real interest rate is critical in determining the extent to which the financial system is able to *mobilize and allocate* savings for development finance. It is important to note that this is not the same thing as saying that higher real interest rates induce households to save higher proportions of their income than at lower real interest rates. This implies that the interest elasticity of savings is greater than 0. But, if savings and consumption decisions are responsive to the real rate of interest, the effects of financial policy on income growth are magnified.

INTEREST RATES AND SAVING DECISIONS

In evaluating the impact of financial policy on economic growth, it is important to distinguish between the implications of real interest rates for consumption-saving decisions, on the one hand, and for decisions about the uses of savings, including the channels through which savings flow, on the other. Debate over the first question revolves around estimates of the interest elasticity of savings (ε_{sr}); debate over the second is couched in terms of the elasticity of demand for liquid assets with respect to the real interest rate (ε_{lr}).

Where both elasticities are 0, financial policy can play only a minimal role in the development process. Where both elasticities are high and positive, the scope for growth-oriented financial policy can be substantial. Where ε_{sr} is small or 0 but ε_{lr} is positive and large, financial policy still may have a significant impact on savings mobilization through the financial system. Virtually all economists can agree that the real interest rate has a significant impact on the demand for liquid assets; that is, with higher real rates, a higher proportion of savings are channeled through the financial system. But the evidence is mixed on the extent to which higher real interest rates may stimulate savings and, thus, increase the ratio of national savings to gross national product.

Econometric tests on national savings rates by financial economist Maxwell Fry note that, in Asia, where real interest rates generally have been positive over the past two decades, the ratio of gross national saving to GNP rises about 0.1 percentage point for each 1 percentage point rise in the real deposit rate. This response, although statistically significant, is too small to justify a rise in interest rates as the main approach to raising national savings. But Fry cites other studies that find higher elasticities of savings to real interest rates in much of the developing world except Latin America, where the elasticity is close to 0. There appears to be a consensus that saving rates are determined more by income and economic and demographic structure than interest rates. In Asia, it appears that savings rates are also affected by the availability of banking services, as measured by the number of bank branches per 1,000 people.

Whereas the role of the real interest rate in consumption-saving decisions is a matter of some dispute, the role of real interest rates in influencing the demand for liquid assets rarely is questioned, whether in developed or developing countries. Indeed, there is evidence that the real interest rate paid on deposits plays an even greater role in liquid-asset demand in developing than industrial countries. Furthermore, experience with marked adjustments in real interest rates in Korea (1965), Indonesia (1968–69, 1974, and 1983), Taiwan (1962), and a host of Latin American countries strongly indicates the significance of real interest rates for growth in money holdings and demand and time deposits (M2).

Liquid assets, or financial assets in general, represent one form in which savings out of past or current income can be held. The demand for liquid assets in economies where nominal interest rates are not allowed to adjust fully to expected rates of inflation, as has been true for many developing countries, typically is represented as a function of income, the real interest rate, and the real rate of return available on nonfinancial assets:

$$L/P = d + d_1 Y + d_2 g + d_3 r \qquad\qquad [13\text{--}7]$$

where L = liquid asset holdings, P = price level, Y = real income (that is, money income deflated by the price level), g = real return on nonfinancial assets, r = the real interest rate on deposits, and d = a constant; d_1 and d_3 are expected to be positive and d_2 negative.

The values for the parameters in equation 13–7 are readily understandable. As real income (Y) grows, the public wants to hold more purchasing power in the form of cash and demand and time deposits, the principal forms of financial assets available in developing countries. In particular, d_1 is positive because, at higher levels of real income, higher real levels of liquid balances are needed to carry out transactions and meet contingencies. Clearly, liquid-asset balances furnish a convenience service to asset holders. In industrial societies with highly developed financial systems and securities markets, it might be reasonable to expect something like a proportional relationship between the growth in income and the growth in demand for liquid assets. However, in developing countries, the demand for liquid assets, given relative price stability, may rise at a faster rate than income because of the paucity of other financial assets in which to hold savings. That is, in developing countries, the income elasticity of demand for liquid assets may be expected to exceed unity. Indeed, even for middle-income countries such as Malaysia, the demand for liquid assets grew twice as fast as real income from 1970 to the eve of the financial crisis in 1997–98. For many Latin American countries the long-run income elasticity of money demand also often is above unity. In such circumstances the rate of increase in the supply of liquid assets (M2) can exceed the rate of income growth by a substantial margin and price stability still can be maintained.

The sign for d_2, the coefficient of the return on nonfinancial assets, is negative, since liquid assets are not the only repository for domestic savings. A range of assets, including nonfinancial assets and, in higher-income countries, nonliquid financial assets such as securities, are available to savers. Higher returns on these nonliquid assets relative to liquid assets induce a shift of savings out of the latter.

The coefficient d_3 of the real deposit rate has a positive sign, for at higher levels of real interest rates, the public is willing to hold larger liquid balances. Where r is negative, holders of all liquid assets pay hidden inflation taxes on their balances. Because higher rates of the inflation tax are imposed on non-interest-bearing assets (cash and demand deposits) than on interest-bearing time deposits, savers are less willing to hold liquid assets.

Numerous studies have been made of the demand for liquid assets in a variety of developing countries over the past several decades. In these studies, estimates of the elasticity of demand for liquid assets with respect to real interest rates vary according to differing economic conditions across countries. However, in country after country, real interest rates have been a powerful factor affecting liquid asset demand. In Asia, where controls over interest rates have been most widely liberalized for the longest time, sharp increases in the real interest rate on time deposits (from negative to positive levels) have resulted in dramatic growth in the share of liquid assets in GDP. On the other hand, many Latin American and African countries have allowed real interest rates to remain negative over long periods. Consequently, growth in the demand for liquid assets was minimal in these countries. In most, the share of liquid assets in the GDP either declined or remained constant until after financial reforms were implemented in the 1980s or 1990s.

TABLE 13-4. Real Lending Interest Rates, 1980 and 2004

	1980	2002
Low-income countries		
Ethiopia	−	17
Tanzania	−	12
India	4	9
Bangladesh	−5	12
Kenya	−2	9
Nigeria	−4	12
Ghana	−21	−
Honduras	0.3	16
Lower-middle-income countries		
Bolivia	2	17
Cameroon	−1	17
The Philippines	0	4
Sri Lanka	−1	4
Indonesia	−	11
Peru	−	14
Egypt	−4	9
Upper-middle-income countries		
Brazil	−	50
Hungary	−	0
Colombia	−	10
Argentina	−	16
Mexico	−	3
Malaysia	1	3
Korea	−5	5
High-income countries		
United Kingdom	−3	1
Japan	3	4
Germany	7	8
United States	6	3

Source: World Bank, *World Development Indicators 2004*, at WDI online.

Table 13–4 presents the real interest rates on deposits and bank loans for a number of developing countries. In 1980, there was a preponderance of negative real rates on both deposits and loans. But, by 1992, after financial market reforms and stabilization programs in many countries, most countries had positive real rates. Comparison with Table 13–1 shows many cases in which a marked rise in real interest rates or the maintenance of positive real rates over the period was accompanied by a jump in the ratio of broad money to GDP: India, Honduras, Bolivia, the Philippines, Sri Lanka, Indonesia, Egypt, Mexico, and Korea.

FINANCIAL DEVELOPMENT

Shallow Finance and Deep Finance

Policies for **financial deepening** seek to promote growth in the real size of the financial system, the growth of financial assets at a pace faster than income growth. In all but the highest-income developing countries, private-sector financial savings predominantly take the form of currency and deposits in commercial banks, savings and loan associations, postal savings accounts, and in some countries, mortgage banks. For most developing countries, growth in the real size of the financial system is reflected primarily in growth in the share of liquid assets in GDP. In contrast, under **shallow finance,** the ratio of liquid assets to GDP grows slowly or not at all over time and typically falls: The real size of the financial system shrinks. Countries able to mobilize large volumes of government or foreign savings can sustain high growth rates even under shallow finance policies, although even these countries may find financial deepening attractive for reasons of employment and income distribution. But, for countries where mobilization of government savings is difficult and foreign savings scarce or unwanted, deep finance may be essential for sustained income growth. This is because growth in the share of liquid assets in GDP provides an approximate indication of the banking system's ability to increase its lending for investment purposes. We will see that the hallmark of a deep financial strategy is avoidance of negative real interest rates; shallow finance, on the other hand, typically involves sharply negative real interest rates.

Growth in the real size of the financial system enhances its capacity for intermediation, gathering savings from diverse private sources and channeling these savings into productive investment. The need for financial intermediation arises because savings endowments do not necessarily correspond to investment opportunities. Those individuals with the greatest capacity to save usually are not those with the entrepreneurial talents required for mounting new investment projects. Except in very simple, rudimentary economies, mechanisms are required to channel savings efficiently from savers to entrepreneurs. In rudimentary economies, production in farming, industry, and other activities is small scale and involves traditional technologies. Producers ordinarily can finance most of their modest investment requirements from their own current savings or those of their families (self-finance). Small-scale enterprises employing traditional technologies have an important role to play in development (see Chapter 18). Yet, at some stage, improvement in productivity (and, therefore, living standards) in any economy requires adoption of newer technologies. These typically involve lumpy investments that ordinarily are well beyond the financial capacity of all but the wealthiest families. Where enterprise finance is restricted to current family savings, only very wealthy groups can adopt such innovations. Thus, a heavy reliance on self-finance tends to be associated with both low productivity and, usually, persistent income inequality.

A restriction to self-financing also guarantees that many productive opportunities involving high private and social payoffs will never be seized, because the resources of even the small number of very wealthy are not unlimited. Innovative, smaller-scale investors are not the only groups that fare poorly where financial intermediation is poorly developed; savers are penalized as well. Let us first examine the case where even the most basic financial intermediaries, commercial banks, are absent. Under these circumstances, the domestic options open to savers are limited to forms of savings, such as acquisition of gold and jewelry, purchase of land and consumer durable goods, or other relatively sterile forms of investment in physical assets. Alternatively, wealthier savers may ship their savings abroad. The common feature of all such investments is that the resources devoted to them are inaccessible to those domestic entrepreneurs who would adopt new technology, begin new firms, or expand production in existing enterprises. Savings in the form of physical assets like gold may be plentiful, as in France or India, but this type of savings effectively is locked away from investors. At a minimum, such investments may be trapped in declining sectors of the economy, unable to flow to sectors with the brightest investment prospects.

However, even where financial intermediation is poorly developed, individuals have the option of holding some of their savings in the form of currency. Additions to cash hoards are superior to investment in unproductive physical assets from an economywide point of view, since at least this serves to curtail the demand for physical assets, reduce upward pressures on their prices, and thus moderate domestic inflation. Nevertheless, savings held in this form still are relatively inaccessible to investors.

There now are virtually no societies where financial systems are as rudimentary as those just sketched. All developing countries have financial institutions, however embryonic, to serve as intermediaries between savers and investors, even where these intermediaries are limited to commercial banks that accept checking (demand) and time (savings) deposits from savers, to relend to prospective investors for a short term. Intermediation flourishes under deep finance, but under strategies of shallow finance intermediation is constricted and the financial system can contribute little to further the goals of economic growth. Later, we see that shallow finance may have unintended effects on employment and income distribution as well.

Shallow Financial Strategy

Shallow financial policies have a number of earmarks: high legal reserve requirements on commercial banks, pervasive nonprice rationing of credit, and most of all, sharply negative real interest rates. Countries rarely, if ever, have consciously and deliberately adopted strategies of shallow finance. Rather, the repression of the financial system flows logically from certain policies intended to encourage, not hinder, investment.

In developed and developing countries alike, policy makers often have viewed low nominal rates of interest as essential for the expansion of investment and controlled interest rate levels tightly. Indeed, so long as the supply of investment funds is unlimited, low interest rates foster all types of investment activities, as even projects with low returns appear more attractive to investors. In accordance with that observation and in the belief that low interest rates are particularly essential to assist small enterprises and small farmers, governments often have placed low ceilings on nominal interest rates charged on all types of loans. These low ceilings are quite apart from special credit programs involving subsidized credit for special classes of borrowers. Because financial institutions ultimately must cover costs (or else be subsidized by governments), low legal ceilings on nominal loan rates mean low nominal interest rates on deposits as well.

As long as inflation is held in check, low ceilings on nominal loan and deposit interest rates may not retard growth, even when these ceilings are set below the opportunity cost of capital. Indeed, the United States over the period 1800–1979 managed rather respectable rates of income growth even in the presence of a set of archaic usury laws and other interest rate controls that (particularly before 1970) often involved artificially low, administered ceilings on interest rates. Even so, throughout most of the period before 1979, real interest rates in the United States remained positive; periods in which real interest rates were sharply negative were intermittent and confined to wartime (1812, 1861, 1917–18, and 1940–46).[8]

Usury laws and other forms of interest rate ceilings have been common in developing countries as well. For all the reasons just given plus one more, financial officials in many developing countries, observing gross imperfections in financial markets, have concluded that the market should not be permitted to determine interest rates. Monopoly (or oligopoly) power in financial markets, particularly in commercial banking, in fact provides ample scope for the banks and other lenders to exercise market power in setting interest rates on loans at levels higher than the opportunity cost of capital.

[8]Steven C. Leuthold, "Interest Rates, Inflation and Deflation," *Financial Analysis Journal* (January–February 1981), 28–51.

There are ample observations of gross imperfections in financial systems in developing countries. Barriers to entry into banking and finance often allow a few large banks and other financial institutions to possess an inordinate degree of control over financial markets and thus exercise monopoly power in setting interest rates. Often these barriers are a direct result of government policies. Governments have prohibited new entrants into the field, adopted such stringent financial requirements for entry that only the very wealthy could amass the needed capital, or reserved permission for entry to political favorites who were attracted to banking and finance largely by the monopoly returns available when entry was restricted.

In this way, one set of government policies, entry restrictions, helps give rise to the need for extensive controls on prices charged by financial institutions. Typically, these controls take the form of interest rate ceilings imposed to limit the scope of monopoly power in the financial system. Controls by themselves do not necessarily lead to shallow finance. Rather, a combination of rigid ceilings on nominal interest rates and inflation impedes financial development and ultimately retards income growth.

Few economists believe that steeply positive real interest rates are essential for healthy growth in the real size of the financial system. In fact, the Chilean experience with very high real interest rates from 1981 to 1983 strongly suggests the opposite. Indeed, there is no widely accepted answer to the question, What level of real interest rates is required for steady development of the financial system? Clearly, the required real rate differs across countries in different circumstances. In some, financial growth may continue even at 0 or mildly negative real interest rates; for others, moderately high positive real rates of between 3 and 5 percent may be essential.

Apart from a few Latin American countries and Indonesia, most developing countries were able to keep rates of inflation at or below 5–6 percent prior to 1973. Inasmuch as nominal deposit rates typically were between 3 and 5 percent, real interest rates tended to be slightly positive or only mildly negative. When inflation accelerated in many developing countries after 1973, because few countries made more than marginal adjustments in nominal deposit rates, real interest rates turned significantly negative in many nations, as Table 13–4 shows for 1980. Negative interest rates endured in a few African and Latin American countries in the period 1983–89.

When real interest rates turn significantly negative, the maintenance of low nominal rates for promoting investment and income growth becomes counterproductive. Inflation taxes on liquid financial assets bring real growth in the financial system to a halt. Sharply negative real rates lead to a shrinkage in the system, as the demand for liquid assets contracts. This tendency is evident from a comparison of Tables 13–1 and 13–4, which shows the tendency for negative real interest rates to be associated with decreases in the degree of monetization in countries such as Argentina, Ghana, Nigeria, and Peru.

Contraction in the financial system results in a reduction in the real supply of credit and thus constricts investment in productive assets. Under such circumstances, nonprice rationing of investible resources must occur and can take many forms. In most developing countries, only those borrowers with either the highest-quality collateral or the "soundest" social and political connections or those willing to make the largest side payments (bribes) to bank officers are successful in securing finance from the organized financial system. These criteria do not yield allocations of credit to the most-productive investment opportunities.

Negative real interest rates make marginal, low-yielding, traditional types of investment appear attractive to investors. Banks and financial institutions find such projects attractive as well, since they may be the safest and the simplest to finance and involve the most creditworthy borrowers. Satisfying the financial requirements of such investors constricts the pool of resources available to firms with riskier projects offering greater possibilities for high yields. Additionally, in the presence of substantial inflation, interest rate ceilings discourage risk taking by the financial institutions themselves, since under such circumstances they cannot charge higher interest rates (risk premia) on promising but risky projects. Also, negative real interest rates are inimical to employment growth, as they make projects with relatively high capital-output ratios appear more attractive than if real interest rates were positive. This implicit subsidy to capital-intensive methods of production reduces the jobs created for each dollar of investment, even as the ability of the financial system to finance investment is shrinking.

Negative real rates of interest tend to lower the marginal efficiency of investment in all the ways described. In terms of the Harrod-Domar model described in Chapter 4, shallow financial strategies cause higher capital-output ratios. Consequently, growth in national income and, therefore, growth in savings tend to be lower than when real rates are positive. Therefore, shallow finance retards income and employment growth even if the interest elasticity of savings is 0. And if savings decisions are responsive to real interest rates, then shallow finance have even more serious implications for income growth, as the ratio of private savings to the GDP also contracts.

Deep Financial Strategy

Deep finance as a strategy has several objectives: (1) mobilizing a larger volume of savings from the domestic economy, that is, increasing the ratio of national savings to the GDP (where the interest elasticity of savings is thought to be positive and significant); (2) enhancing the accessibility of savings for all types of domestic investors; (3) securing a more-efficient allocation of investment throughout the economy; and (4) permitting the financial process to mobilize and allocate savings to reduce reliance on the fiscal process, foreign aid, and inflation.

A permanent move toward policies involving positive real interest rates or, at a minimum, avoidance of sharply negative real rates is the essence of deep finance. In turn, this requires either financial liberalization that allows higher nominal rates on deposits and loans, curbing the rate of inflation, or some combination of both.

Given the difficulties involved in securing quick results in reducing inflation to levels consistent with positive real rates of interest, the first step involved in a shift from shallow to deep financial strategies ordinarily is to raise the ceilings on nominal rates for both deposits and loans. In some cases, this has required nominal interest rates as high as 30 percent on time deposits (Korea in 1966, Indonesia in 1968 and 1974).[9] In extreme cases of acute inflation, the initial step has involved raising ceilings on nominal deposit rates to as much as 50 percent in Argentina and Uruguay in 1976 and to nearly 200 percent in Chile in 1974 (where real interest rates nevertheless remained negative until 1976). As the real rate moves toward positive levels, savers strongly tend to increase their holdings of liquid assets; this allows a real expansion in the supply of credit to investors. Marked increases in flow of savings to financial institutions have been observed when nominal rates were increased substantially, as in Uruguay in 1976, Indonesia in 1968–69 and 1983, and Taiwan and South Korea in 1965. Notable responses also have occurred in countries where mildly negative real rates were moved closer to positive levels through increases in nominal rates: These include India and Sri Lanka after 1977 and Turkey after 1980.

Available evidence suggests that countries that attempt to maintain modestly positive real interest rates over long periods tend to be among those with the highest rates of financial growth, as we already noted in comparing Tables 13–1 and 13–4. Nevertheless, one can have too much of a good thing. One factor contributing to sharply negative real GDP growth rates in Chile in 1982 and 1983 was the emergence of very high real interest rates in 1981 and 1982. The nominal interest rate on loans increased sharply, while at the same time there was a very large and unexpected drop in inflation: The real interest rate soared above 30 percent.[10]

---

[9]Ceilings rarely need be increased to the point where they match the *current* rate of inflation. For example, in Indonesia in 1974, the nominal ceiling on two-year time deposits was raised to only 30 percent, even though inflation over the previous 12 months was 42 percent. The increase in nominal rates, coupled with a battery of other measures, convinced depositors that real rates soon would be positive. All that is required is that the inflation expected by savers be reduced to levels closer to the nominal deposit rate.

[10]The Chilean real GDP declined by 13.2 percent in 1982 and by 2.3 percent in 1983. For a comprehensive discussion of the Chilean economic debacle of 1982–83, see Sebastian Edwards, "Stabilization with Liberalization: An Evaluation of Chile's Experiment with Free-Market Policies 1973–83," *Economic Development and Cultural Change* 27 (September 1985), 224–53.

Where finance is deep, inflation tends to be moderate; therefore, savers are not subject to persistently high inflation taxes on liquid-asset holdings. That being the case, they are less inclined to shift their savings into much more lightly taxed domestic assets such as gold, land, or durable goods and foreign assets such as currencies or land and securities. Rather, financial resources that otherwise may have been utilized for these purposes flow to the financial system, where they are more accessible to prospective investors. Nonprice rationing of credit, inevitable under shallow finance, diminishes as well. As a result, the capacity of the financial system to identify and support socially profitable investment opportunities expands: Higher-risk, higher-yielding investment projects stand a far better chance of securing finance under deep than shallow finance. Growth prospects are enhanced accordingly.

The preceding discussion represents but a sketch of policies designed to promote financial deepening. The focus has been on the real interest rate on deposits and loans when, in fact, a variety of other policies may be involved. These include central bank payment of interest on commercial bank reserves and avoidance of high legal reserve requirements to commercial banks. That positive real interest rates tend to lead to growth in the real size of banking systems now rarely is questioned. Such a development substantially enlarges the real flow of short-term credit, the stock in trade of commercial banks. However, investment finance problems do not end with the provision of a growing real flow of short-term credit. As economies move to higher levels of per capita income, the pattern of investment shifts toward longer horizons. Longer-term investment requires longer-term finance. Commercial banks everywhere are ill-suited for providing substantial amounts of long-term finance, given that their deposits primarily are of a short-term nature.

Therefore, as financial and economic development proceeds, the need for institutions specializing in longer-term finance rises accordingly: Insurance companies, investment banks, and ultimately equity markets (stock exchanges) become important elements in financial intermediation. Nevertheless, the type of well-functioning commercial bank system that tends to develop under deep finance almost always is a necessary condition for the successful emergence and long-term vitality of institutions specializing in longer-term investment finance. Where entry into financial activities is only lightly restricted, longer-term financial institutions may appear spontaneously.

Earlier we observed that entry into the financial field rarely is easy, and other factors also often lead to gross imperfections in financial markets. Under such circumstances, many developing-country governments have found intervention essential to develop financial institutions specializing in longer-term finance. Intervention may take the form of establishment of government-owned development banks and other specialized institutions to act as distributors of government funds intended as a source of longer-term finance, as in Indonesia and Pakistan. In Mexico and Colombia, governments provided strong incentives for private-sector establishment of long-term financial institutions. Other governments sought to create conditions favorable for the emergence of primary securities (stocks and bonds) markets, the source par excellence for long-term finance. In cases where these measures have been undertaken in the context of financial markets with strong commercial banking systems (Hong Kong, Singapore, Brazil, and Mexico), efforts to encourage long-term finance have met with some success. In cases where commercial banking has been poorly developed as a consequence of shallow finance (Ghana, Uruguay before 1976) or the government has sought to "force feed" embryonic securities markets through tax incentives and other subsidies (Indonesia before 1988, Kenya, Turkey), the promotional policies have been less effective.

Panic, Moral Hazard, and Financial Collapse

Prior to the late 1990s, policy makers and students of financial systems development were concerned largely with how to gradually achieve financial deepening over the long term through the kinds of measures discussed in the previous sections of this chapter. In 1994, however, Mexico was hit by very rapid withdrawals of foreign capital and a cessation of international lines of credit, leading to what became known as the *peso crisis*. The Mexican economy contracted sharply, and the crisis spread to Argentina, Venezuela, and several other economies. In the middle of 1997, financial panic struck again, hitting first in Thailand and then in three other Asian countries and eventually spreading as far as Russia and Brazil. These events reminded policy makers and analysts alike of the risk of outright collapse of the financial system. Nations that had appeared to have developed deeper and stronger financial systems suddenly found themselves with large numbers of bankrupt commercial banks and nonbank financial institutions that were in even worse condition. On these countries' stock markets, share values of listed companies fell to a small fraction of what they had been only a few months earlier.

Financial panics have occurred throughout the history of banking. Economists have long recognized that financial markets tend to be prone to instability and panic. Events similar to the Asian financial crisis have been recurring in slightly different forms since the development of banks and the emergence of international capital flows several centuries ago. Prominent examples include the Dutch tulip mania of 1636, the bank panics in the United States in the late nineteenth century, and the global financial collapse and Depression that began in 1929. Economist Charles Kindleberger chronicled the long history of these phenomena in his classic work *Manias, Panics, and Crashes: A History of Financial Crises.*[11]

---

[11]New York: John Wiley and Sons, 3rd ed., 1996.

Banks, as pointed out previously, must be prepared to pay their depositors immediately on demand, but banks lend for longer periods. This situation does not create a problem as long as only a few depositors ask for their money at any given time. But, sometimes, rumors spread that the bank may be in trouble and in danger of defaulting on its obligations to its depositors. It may not matter whether the rumor is true or not as long as a large number of depositors believe it might be true. Depositors rush to the bank to get their money, and the bank lacks enough cash on hand or readily available from nearby sources to satisfy so many customers. As a result, the bank must sell off its assets (long-term loans, for example) to other banks and financial institutions, often at a large discount. Even a previously healthy bank under such circumstances can go bankrupt. Panics of this sort were common through the nineteenth century and the early part of the twentieth century.

Financial crises occur less frequently in industrialized economies today because these countries have put into place mechanisms and institutions specifically designed to reduce the frequency and severity of financial crises. The United States' experiences with severe banking crises in 1873, 1893, and 1907 helped bring about the establishment of the Federal Reserve System beginning in 1913. The Federal Reserve, like other central banks around the world, stands ready to act as a "lender of last resort" and provide financing to commercial banks that face a sudden creditor run. With this mechanism in place, there is no need for a bank to hurriedly sell off its assets at discounted prices.[12] Industrialized countries also provide deposit insurance, ultimately backed by the government, to assure bank depositors that they will get their money back, even in the event that their bank runs out of funds. The Federal Deposit Insurance Corporation insures deposits in U.S. banks up to $100,000. Depositors, therefore, no longer have to rush to the bank and remove their money every time they fear the bank might be in trouble. In addition, most industrialized countries have well-defined and transparent systems for managing bankruptcies and other debt workouts. These mechanisms provide a way to both stop a creditor panic (the court has the authority to declare a standstill on debt payments) and sort out creditor claims on a bankrupt corporation. These institutions have reduced (but not completely eliminated) financial crises in the industrialized countries.[13]

As Southeast Asia in 1997 demonstrated, however, some situations still could lead to financial panic and a run on the banks and other financial institutions. A critical feature of the Southeast and East Asian situation was that the banks of Thailand, Indonesia, Malaysia, and South Korea had borrowed heavily

---

[12]The United States used this mechanism effectively in October 1987 to mitigate the impact of a severe stock market crash.

[13]The most prominent recent example of a financial crisis in the United States is the savings and loan crisis of the early 1990s.

outside their countries and thus acquired debts that had to be repaid in foreign exchange, such as U.S. dollars or yen. The next chapter deals with the circumstances that led the banks to borrow abroad. Here, we simply note that these Asian banks acquired large liabilities that were not protected by deposit insurance. The ability of the banks to repay also depended on their ability to buy foreign exchange from the central bank, preferably at the same exchange rate at which they had borrowed the money. But, in the case of the Southeast and East Asian countries, the central banks ran out of foreign exchange and had to allow the exchange rate to devalue. Where, in early 1997, 25 Thai baht could buy 1 U.S. dollar, by the end of the year it took 50 baht to buy a dollar. A bank that had borrowed $100 million, expecting to use 2.5 billion baht to repay the loan (plus interest) now had to find 5 billion baht to do so. In effect, the size of the bank's debt, in terms of baht, had doubled almost overnight.

As foreign lenders began to realize what was happening, they panicked, much like depositors in the days before deposit insurance would have panicked. Even lenders who previously felt there was nothing to worry about rushed to get their money out, because the first people in line were the ones most likely to get their money. As with a fire in a crowded theater, those first out the door are the most likely to survive. The panic that began in Thailand soon spread to Malaysia and Indonesia and then even to the considerably more advanced economy of South Korea. When the panic finally subsided, many of the banks and nonbank financial institutions in these countries were insolvent. In the case of Indonesia in 1998, despite nearly a decade of banking reform, virtually all the banks were insolvent.

If foreign borrowing by the banks created conditions that could lead to panic, why did so many banks and nonbank financial institutions take the risk of borrowing so much in foreign exchange? Why, in turn, did the foreign lenders lend? Some of the behavior of both the borrowers and lenders can be attributed to ignorance. Neither fully realized the dangers entailed in their actions. Among foreign lenders, for example, there was a widespread belief that Asia was the place to make high rates of return on their investments, a belief often based on little more than that everyone else in their business thought this was the case. It is not uncommon for investors to behave more like a herd of animals than careful calculators of risks and rewards. This kind of behavior, therefore, often is referred to as **herd** behavior.

But there was another important reason why borrowers and investors alike were willing to take these risks. They believed the risks were not that great because they counted on being helped out if they got into trouble. The investors counted on their own governments (in Japan, Europe, and the United States) together with the International Monetary Fund to protect them from default by the Asian banks. The Asian banks and nonbank financial institutions, in turn, counted on their own governments to bail them out if they got into trouble. The political and personal ties between the bankers and the government were very close in all four of the hard-hit Asian countries, and in the past, the government frequently had stepped in to help out when one bank or another got into trouble. The willingness of governments to step in when these borrowers and lenders got into trouble created a situation that economists refer to as *moral hazard.* **Moral hazard** refers to the situation where an effort to protect people or institutions from risky behavior actually tends to encourage people and institutions to increase their willingness to practice risky behavior. Governments, by protecting lenders and borrowers in the past, thus contributed to the risky behavior that led to the Asian financial crisis of 1997–98.

The development of a sound financial system, therefore, requires more than a government that ensures that real interest rates are positive, important as that is. Financial institutions, if they are to survive a crisis like the one that occurred in 1997–98, must learn that they have to be able to stand on their own feet in such a crisis. They must carefully calculate the risks of their actions and avoid practices that would require them to turn to the government in a crisis. The Asian banking systems that came closest to meeting this standard, those of Singapore and Hong Kong, weathered the 1997–98 crisis without getting into serious trouble.

There is also an important role for government in ensuring that the banks maintain sound lending practices. Rather than simply bailing out the banks when they get into trouble, government regulators need to regularly inspect the banks to ensure that they are classifying their loans properly, what is called **prudential regulation.** Banks in trouble are prone to classifying **nonperforming loans,** loans that are not being repaid on time or repaid at all, as if they were performing and being repaid on time. The method for doing this is to make new loans to these borrowers so that they can pay off their old loans. If the original loan is not being repaid on time, the new loan will not be repaid either, but to the outside observer who does not have access to the nature of the loan, that loan appears to be in the process of repayment. A bank that is loaded down with nonperforming loans and in fact may be bankrupt (its liabilities are greater than its assets) may appear healthy for some time with such procedures, but the ultimate collapse will be that much more devastating. Good prudential regulation by government inspectors can force the bank to change these practices or go out of business much earlier than otherwise would be the case. In Asia in the 1990s, however, prudential regulation in many of the countries was weak, and this contributed to the general weakness of the financial system. These weak financial systems, in turn, made the financial crisis of 1997–98 more severe than otherwise would have been the case. We return to the lessons of the Asian financial in the next chapter.

Informal Credit Markets

The discussion of financial development has dealt with modern credit institutions, the formal market. But, in many developing countries, **informal credit markets** coexist with modern financial institutions. These markets arise in many forms. In rural India, village moneylenders make loans to local farmers who have no access to commercial banks. In Ghana and other West African countries, market women give credit to farmers by paying for crops in advance of harvest, and they assist their customers by selling finished goods on credit. In South Korea, established lenders actually make loans on the street outside modern banks; this justifies their designation as the *curb market*. In much of rural Africa, wealthy family members make loans to less fortunate kin; and all over the developing world, there are cooperative arrangements to raise funds and share credit among members. Even in modern economies, pawnbrokers and others give credit outside the formal credit system.

Informal credit generally is financed by the savings of relatively wealthy individuals, such as local landowners, traders, family members who have moved into lucrative jobs or businesses, and the pooled efforts of cooperative societies. But informal lenders also may have access to the formal banking system and borrow there, to relend to customers with no access to banks. How can they do this if the banks cannot? First, because they know their borrowers so well and may have familial, social, or other ties to them, informal lenders face lower risks than distant, large banks that might loan to the same borrowers. Loan recovery rates are higher (usually much higher than found in large banks in developing countries) because those who borrow in informal markets know that the availability of loans in the future is dependent on repaying current loans. Second, they also face lower administrative costs in making loans. Of course, moneylenders charge very high interest rates; and this is a third reason they coexist with banks, which are often prevented by law from charging rates high enough to cover the risks and costs of loans in small amounts to very small firms and low-income borrowers.

As modern credit institutions evolve, especially under deep financial policies, they draw customers and resources from the informal market. First, some of the largest and most creditworthy borrowers from informal lenders eventually qualify as borrowers in the formal market. Second, some moneylenders themselves may establish credit institutions within the informal system. Third, banks begin to attract savings from a wider group of households, some of which previously had directed their savings into informal channels. On all counts, the informal market is likely to shrink in size and coverage, although it rarely totally disappears even in high-income countries. The process may leave behind several kinds of borrowers, such as small farmers, traders, artisans, and manufacturers, who still depend on the shrinking informal market

BOX 13-2   SMALL-SCALE SAVINGS AND CREDIT INSTITUTIONS: BANGLADESH AND INDONESIA

In a number of countries, most notably in Bangladesh and Indonesia, formal credit institutions have attempted to bridge the gap between small-scale borrowers in the informal sector and the formal financial system.

In Bangladesh, the Grameen Bank, founded by Muhammad Yunus over three decades ago, provides credit to people in about a third of the country's 68,000 villages. The average loan is under $100 and the maximum is $200. Of the borrowers, 65 percent are landless women and all loan recipients are poor. Loans are made to individual women, but only through local groups that provide social pressure for repayment. The loans are not heavily subsidized and the recovery rate exceeds 97 percent. The Grameen Bank is more than a financial institution, however. Its loans require recipients to accept certain "social disciplines," such as cleanliness and family planning, and the bank provides such services as advice on home construction and access to education for some borrowers.[1]

In Indonesia, a government bank, the Bank Rakyat Indonesia (BRI) provides full banking services, both loans and savings deposit facilities, to farmers, traders, and other small-scale borrowers, through their branches in over 3,000 villages. BRI charged market rates of interest, around 30 percent a year, on its loans and paid attractive rates, about 12 percent, on deposits. These rates changed during the financial crisis of 1997–98, largely because of the high inflation in that period, but the basic rate-setting principles remained the same. In the absence of inflation, rates of 30 percent on loans may seem high, but they were considerably below the rates charged by informal money lenders. At these rates, the BRI was able to attract sufficient savings deposits to more than finance its loan program. Roughly 97 percent of the loans are repaid on time. In addition, the program is a major generator of profits for the BRI, something that cannot be said about many of its credit programs for large-scale producers and borrowers.[2]

[1]World Bank, *World Development Report 1989,* p. 117; and A. Wahid, *The Grameen Bank: Poverty Relief* (Boulder, CO: Westview Press, 1993).

[2]Richard H. Patten and Jay Rosengard, *Progress with Profits: The Development of Rural Baking in Indonesia* (San Francisco: ICS Press, 1991); and Marguerite Robinson, "Rural Financial Intermediation: Lessons from Indonesia," development discussion paper No. 434, Harvard Institute for International Development, October 1992.

for their credit (see Box 13–2). Competitive, efficient, and varied financial institutions—the kind encouraged by deep financial policies—have incentives to integrate borrowers into the modern market and thus reduce the adverse impacts of financial development on those who once depended on informal credit markets.

MONETARY POLICY AND PRICE STABILITY

We saw from Table 13–3 that inflation largely was conquered in Asia during the 1970s, but accelerated in Latin America and Africa during and especially after the oil-price boom of the 1970s. In the 1990s, however, attempts to control inflation were more serious and widespread with the notable exception of the republics formed out of the collapse of the Soviet Union. Even in these former Soviet republics, inflation at the beginning of the twenty-first century was down to single digits except for Belarus. Monetary policy is the principal instrument used to achieve price stability.

Monetary Policy and Exchange-Rate Regimes

Appropriate use of monetary policy in controlling inflation depends critically on the type of exchange-rate regime used by a country. Exchange-rate regimes form a continuum with fixed (pegged) exchange rates at one end and floating (flexible) exchange rates at the other. Under a **fixed-exchange-rate** system, a country attempts to maintain the value of its currency in a fixed relation to another currency, say, the U.S. dollar: The value of the local currency is **pegged** to the dollar. This is done through intervention by the country's monetary authorities in the market for foreign exchange and requires the maintenance of substantial **international reserves** (reserves of foreign currencies), usually equivalent to the value of four or more months' worth of imports.

For example, consider the case of Thailand, where from 1987 to early 1997 the Thai currency, the baht, was fixed at an exchange rate close to 25 baht to US$1. Because the exchange rate, if left to its own devices, would change from day to day to reflect changes in both the demand for and supply of exports and imports and capital flows, to defend the peg, the government must be prepared to use the country's international reserves to buy or sell dollars at an exchange rate of 25 to 1 to keep the exchange rate from moving. If, for example, a poor domestic harvest caused the nation to increase its food imports, the baht-dollar exchange rate would tend to rise (the baht would depreciate, as its dollar value falls) in the absence of any net sales of dollars from Thailand's international reserves. To sustain a fixed exchange rate, of course, the country must have sufficient foreign exchange reserves to keep on buying baht at that fixed rate. In 1997, as already pointed out, because of large capital outflows, Thailand actually ran out of foreign exchange and had to abandon its support of the pegged rate.

Under freely **floating rates,** the authorities simply allow the value of local currency vis-à-vis foreign ones to be determined by market forces. Between the two ends of this continuum (see Figure 13–1) lie a number of intermediate

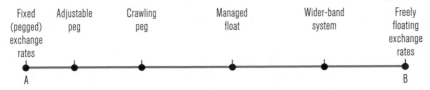

FIGURE 13-1. **Continuum of Prototypes of Exchange-Rate Regimes**
As one moves from point *A* on the left to point *B* on the right, both the
frequency of intervention by domestic monetary authorities and the required
level of international reserves tend to be lower. Under a pure fixed-exchange-
rate regime (point *A*) authorities intervene so that the value of the currency
vis-à-vis another, say, the U.S. dollar, is maintained at a constant rate. Under a
freely floating-exchange-rate regime, authorities do not intervene in the
market for foreign exchange, and there is minimal need for international
reserves; indeed, there can be no balance-of-payments deficit.

options.[14] Closest to the floating-exchange-rate option is the *wider band* system,
where the exchange rate of a country is allowed to float or fluctuate within a pre-
defined band of values, say, between 23 and 27 baht to US$1. But, when condi-
tions threaten to push the value of the currency beyond the band, the
authorities intervene by buying or selling local currency as appropriate to stay
within the band. Further along the continuum away from floating rates is the
managed float, where the authorities are committed to defend no particular
exchange rate, but they nevertheless intervene continuously at their discretion.
A country with steadily shrinking international reserves, for example, might
allow the value of its currency to depreciate against the value of other currencies; that is, allow the exchange rate to rise against other currencies.

   Two other systems are closely related hybrids of fixed and floating rules. The
crawling peg, used over a long period by Brazil, Colombia, and Indonesia,
involves pegging the local currency against some other currency but changing
this in gradual, periodic steps to adjust for any differential between the country's inflation rate and the world inflation rate. Closest to a fixed-exchange-rate
system is the *adjustable peg,* involving a commitment by the monetary authorities to defend the local exchange rate at a fixed parity (peg), while reserving the
right to change that rate when circumstances require.

   Two very rigid forms of pegged exchange rates that a small number of countries have adopted are currency boards and "dollarization." With a *currency
board,* the government issues domestic currency only when it is fully backed by
available foreign exchange reserves at the given exchange rate. Currency in

[14]For a full discussion of these and other types of exchange-rate regimes, see John Williamson,
The Open Economy and the World Economy (New York: Basic Books, 1983), 238–41; or Anne O.
Krueger, *Exchange Rate Determination* (New York: Cambridge University Press, 1983), 123–36.

circulation increases when additional foreign exchange becomes available (say, through increased export receipts) and decreases when foreign exchange becomes scarcer (say, through an increase in imports or capital outflows). This system assures that the country will not run out of foreign exchange. However, the main instrument of adjustment becomes domestic interest rates, which increase when foreign exchange (and domestic currency) becomes scarcer, and decline when foreign exchange becomes more available. Hong Kong, Bulgaria, Argentina, Brunei, Djibouti, Estonia, and Lithuania all have or have had currency boards. With *dollarization*, one country adopts another country's currency, as Panama did many years ago when it adopted the U.S. dollar as its currency. Most economists believe that currency boards and dollarization are appropriate in only a very limited number of developing countries that are small, very open to trade, and not vulnerable to large commodity price swings. In Hong Kong, the currency board system works reasonably well although high interest rates and hence slower growth were required to prevent large currency outflows during and immediately after the Asian financial crisis. In Argentina at the beginning of the twenty-first century, the inability of the central government to rein in excessive local government spending caused pressures on reserves that ultimately made it impossible to maintain the peg to the dollar that was essential to the continuance of the currency board.

The currencies of all the major industrial countries have floated vis-à-vis one another since the early 1970s, with occasional intervention by national monetary authorities to prevent very sharp swings in rates. Most developing countries have adhered to either the adjustable-peg or the crawling-peg system, although an increasing number, particularly in Africa, have been adopting floating-rate systems as part of stabilization programs. Since, in practice, both pegged systems operate for particular periods like fixed-rate regimes, for our analysis, we focus most of our attention on monetary policy issues arising under fixed exchange rates in small, open economies.

Sources of Inflation

In open developing economies with fixed exchange rates, the rate of monetary expansion no longer is under the complete control of domestic monetary authorities. Rather, countries with fixed exchange rates may be viewed as sharing essentially the same money supply, because the money of each can be converted into that of the others at a fixed parity.[15] Under such circumstances, the stock of money (M), by definition, is the sum of two components: the amount of

---

[15]This section draws substantially on syntheses of monetary and international economics by Arnold C. Harberger. See his "A Primer on Inflation," and "The Inflation Syndrome," papers presented in the Political Economy Lecture Series, Harvard University, March 19, 1981.

domestic credit of the banking system that is outstanding (DC) and the stock of international reserves of that country (IR), measured in terms of domestic currency. The money supply, therefore, has a domestic component and an international component, so we have

$$M = DC + IR \qquad\qquad [13\text{--}8]$$

Changes in the domestic money stock can occur either through expansion of domestic credit or by monetary movements that lead to changes in international reserves. That is,

$$\Delta M = \Delta DC = \Delta IR \qquad\qquad [13\text{--}9]$$

Under fixed exchange rates, a central bank of any small country can control DC, the domestic component, but has only very limited control over IR, the international component. Under such circumstances, developing countries that attempt to keep the rate of domestic inflation below the world inflation rate (through restrictive policies on domestic credit) are unable to realize this goal. If, fueled by monetary expansion abroad (growth in the world money supply), world inflation initially is running in excess of domestic inflation, the prices of internationally traded goods rise relative to those of domestic, nontraded goods.[16] Imports fall, exports rise, and the balance of payments moves toward surplus and causes a rise in international reserves. Therefore, the foreign components of the money stock rise. This is tantamount to an "importation of money" and eventually undoes the effort to prevent importation of world inflation. Again, a small country on fixed exchange rates can do little to maintain its inflation rate below that of the rest of the world. For very open countries with few restrictions on the movement of goods and capital into and out of the country, the adjustment to world inflation can be very rapid (less than a year). For less-open countries with substantial restrictions on international trade and payments, the process takes longer, but the outcome is inevitable under fixed exchange rates.

The fact that financial policy for stabilization in countries with fixed exchange rates is heavily constrained by international developments sometimes is taken to mean that changes in the domestic component of the money stock have no impact on prices in economies adhering to fixed exchange rates. On the contrary, excessive expansion in money and credit surely will result in domestically generated inflation that, depending on the rate of expansion, for a time, can be well in excess of world inflation rates. However, such a situation cannot continue for long, as excess money creation spills over into the balance of payments via increased imports and leads to a drain on international reserves and, ultimately,

---

[16]This is but one of several mechanisms that led to changes in international reserves sufficient to thwart efforts by developing countries to insulate themselves from world inflation.

an inability to maintain the fixed exchange rate. As reserves dwindle, the country no longer can defend its exchange rate and devaluation becomes inevitable.[17] Inflation, therefore, can be transmitted to small, open economies through the working of the world economy or generated by domestic developments.

A growing number of developing countries have begun to employ floating exchange rates (point *B* on the continuum in Figure 13–1). A floating exchange-rate regime allows countries to insulate themselves from world inflation. Under such a system, the rise in world prices attendant on world inflation would initially favor exports from the country and discourage imports. As a consequence, the current account of the country's balance of payments improves, international reserves rise, and the exchange rate soon appreciates (fewer baht are required to buy dollars, for instance). The appreciation in the country's exchange rate cancels out external price increases and prevents the importation of world inflation.

Under any exchange-rate regime, domestically generated inflation may result from excessive increases in domestic credit from the banking system to either the public or private sector. Budget deficits of the central government, for example, must be financed by borrowing, but the embryonic nature of money and capital markets in most developing countries generally means that governments facing deficits ordinarily must resort to borrowing from the central bank. Borrowing from the central bank is equivalent to direct money creation via the printing press. The result is a direct addition to the reserve base of the monetary system, an increase in so-called high-powered money. It is important, however, to recognize that not all budgetary deficits are inflationary. We have seen that a growing economy is characterized by a growing demand for liquid assets, including money. Moderate budgetary deficits year after year, financed by the central bank, can help satisfy this requirement without leading to inflation. In general, the money stock may expand at least as fast as the growth in real income, with little or no inflationary consequences.

Earlier we saw that liquid assets normally are between 40 and 50 percent of GDP in developing countries (with wide variations), equivalent to roughly four to six months of income. Therefore, the public generally is willing to hold this much in money balances. A deficit of 2 percent of GDP financed by money creation adds only marginally to the money supply and easily may be accepted by the public. But a deficit of 8 percent of GDP increases the stock of money by an amount equal to one more month of income, an amount the public may be unwilling to hold (unless nominal interest rates on deposits are greatly increased). The excess spills over into higher prices.

---

[17]Import controls frequently are used to stem the drain of reserves and avoid devaluation for a time. But import controls engender another set of distortions and inefficiencies, explored in Chapter 19, that eventually require more drastic measures, including devaluation.

Use of bank credit to finance government deficits has not been the only source of inflationary monetary expansion in developing countries. Sometimes excessive growth of credit to the private sector has played a more-significant role in domestically generated inflationary processes. Nevertheless, as a general rule, inflation rates that are much in excess of world inflation usually have been traceable to budgetary deficits.

It is evident, then, that, for countries attempting to maintain fixed exchange rates, efforts to avoid price increases in excess of world inflation must be a matter primarily of fiscal policy, not monetary policy. If budget deficits are not held to levels consistent with world inflation, even very deft deployment of monetary policy instruments are unable to prevent rapid inflation, devaluation, or both. There still is a role for monetary policy in developing countries, but that role must be largely passive. Resourceful use of monetary policy can help by not making things worse and moderating strong inflationary pressures until the budget can be brought under control, provided the latter is done fairly quickly.

We have seen that monetary factors are causes of inflation in both fixed- and floating-exchange-rate countries. In the case of fixed exchange rates, both world monetary expansion and domestic monetary expansion generate inflation; in flexible-exchange-rate countries, inflation arises from domestic monetary sources. But, thus far, no mention has been made of so-called nonmonetary causes of inflation. It seems plausible that internal and external shocks, such as those arising from widespread crop failure in the domestic economy or a drastic increase in prices of imported energy, could have important effects on inflation in countries suffering such shocks. This is true, but the mechanism whereby nonmonetary factors may initiate or worsen inflation needs to be clearly portrayed.

Nonmonetary disturbances indeed may precipitate policy reactions that lead to domestic monetary expansion large enough to accommodate higher relative prices of food or oil and large enough to cause inflation. In the absence of accommodating monetary expansion in the face of such shocks, inflation can be contained, but at some cost. In practice, failure to allow the money supply to expand to accommodate higher relative prices of important goods leads to increases in unemployment that most governments find unacceptable. Therefore, as a matter of course, governments in such cases usually attempt to allow monetary expansion sufficient to avoid unwanted consequences for employment. But it is important to remember that, however advisable monetary accommodation may be on social and employment grounds, expansion in the money stock is required to fuel inflation, whatever external or internal factors may precipitate the expansion. This truth, known for centuries, often is incorrectly interpreted to mean that nonmonetary factors cannot "cause" inflation. They can, but only through an expansion of the national or international stock of money or both.

Controlling Inflation through Monetary Policy

The array of available instruments for anti-inflationary monetary policy in developed countries include (1) open-market operations, in which the central bank can directly contract bank reserves by sales of government securities;[18] (2) increases in legal reserve requirements of banks, so that a given volume of reserves support a lower stock of money (and reduce the credit expansion multiplier as well); (3) increases in rediscount rates, so that commercial bank borrowing from the central bank becomes less attractive; and (4) moral suasion, where the exhortations of monetary authorities are expected to lead to restraint in bank lending policies.

For virtually all developing countries, the first instrument (open market operations) is not available for inflation control. Securities markets typically are absent or not sufficiently well developed to allow the exercise of this powerful and flexible instrument, although some countries, including the Philippines and Brazil, utilized the tool to a limited degree. The other three monetary policy instruments are employed, with varying degrees of success, in developing countries. In addition, developing countries often resort to two other tools employed only infrequently in developed countries: (5) credit ceilings imposed by the central bank on the banking system and (6) adjustments in allowable nominal rates of interest on deposits and loans. Governments attempting to control inflation usually resort to all or many of these instruments, often together but sometimes separately, occasionally experiencing temporary success, as in Argentina in 1985, and occasionally enjoying transitory success, as in Indonesia in 1967 and 1968 and in Bolivia in 1985–86.

Reserve Requirements

All central banks require commercial banks to immobilize a portion of their deposits in the form of legal services that may not be lent to prospective customers. For example, legal reserve requirements for Indonesian and Malaysian banks in the late 1970s were expressed as 30 percent of deposits in domestic currency in the former and 20 percent of all deposits in the latter. Thus, in

---

[18]Open-market operations are used as an instrument of monetary policy in countries with well-developed financial markets. When the Federal Reserve System in the United States or a central bank in Europe wants to curtail the growth of the money supply, it sells government securities (bonds, bills) on the open market. When a buyer pays for the securities, the effect is to reduce directly the reserves of the banking system, since the funds are transferred from commercial bank deposits or household cash holdings to the account of the Federal Reserve. When the Federal Reserve wants to expand the money supply, it buys securities on the open market and thus directly adds to bank reserves.

Malaysia, for example, banks were required to add 20 units of currency to reserves for every 100 units of deposits. These figures are not too far out of line with legal reserve requirements in many industrial nations, where reserve ratios of 15 percent for demand deposits and 5 percent for time deposits are common.

Increases in reserve requirements can be used to help moderate inflation. An upward adjustment in reserve requirements works in two ways: It reduces the stock of money that can be supported by a given amount of reserves, and it reduces the money multiplier. The first effect induces banks to contract credit outstanding; the second reduces the growth in the money stock possible from any future increment to reserves.[19] Changes in legal reserve requirements usually are employed only as a last-ditch measure, although China raised reserve requirements in 2004 when price increases were still modest but rising. Even small changes in the required ratio of reserves to deposits can have a very disruptive impact on commercial bank operations unless banks are given sufficient time to adjust.

Credit Ceilings

In some countries, such as Indonesia from 1947 to 1983 or China in 1994 through 1996 and at various other times in Malaysia, Sri Lanka, and Chile, credit ceilings have been used as supplementary instruments of inflation control. Indeed, the International Monetary Fund often requires countries seeking balance-of-payments support to adopt credit ceilings as a prerequisite for IMF assistance. General ceilings of domestic credit expansion represent a useful method of controlling growth in the domestic components of the money supply. Credit ceilings, however, do not allow full control of money-supply growth in developing countries operating under fixed-exchange-rate regimes, since the monetary authorities have no control over foreign components of the money supply. Nevertheless, general credit ceilings sometimes can be usefully deployed in combating inflation in countries not experiencing major imbalances in external payments. Unfortunately, ceilings work the least well where they are needed the most, since countries attempting to deal with chronic inflation usually are those experiencing the most destabilizing changes in their international reserve positions. Finally, general credit ceilings are unlikely to have much effect on inflation unless the government simultaneously takes steps

---

[19]In its simplest form the money multiplier (m) can be expressed as

$$m = (c + 1)/(c + k)$$

where c = the ratio of currency outside banks to deposits and k = the ratio of reserves to deposits. If k is raised, then m falls.

to reduce the budgetary deficits that, except in major oil-exporting countries, typically are the root causes of chronic, acute, and especially runaway inflation.

Countries often supplement general credit ceilings with specific ceilings on lending to particular sectors of the economy. Indonesia attempted to fine-tune credit controls in this way from 1974 to 1983, with poor results. The system of ceilings was so detailed and cumbersome that domestic banks were unable to come close to exhausting the ceilings. Excess reserves arose. The banks had little choice but to place their excess reserves in deposits overseas, primarily in banks in Singapore. As a result, many domestic firms in Jakarta were forced to seek credit from Singapore banks, which held well over a billion dollars of deposits from Jakarta banks that might have been lent to domestic firms at a lower rate in the absence of credit ceilings. China, in the first part of the twenty-first century, placed ceilings on credit to real estate developers in what was believed to be an overheated real estate market but with only limited impact on investments in this area.

Interest-Rate Regulation and Moral Suasion

In most industrial countries, the central bank can influence interest rates by varying the *rediscount rate* charged on central bank loans to commercial banks that require additional liquidity. Because the rediscount rate is central to commercial banks' operations, it is important in determining the market rate of interest on both deposits and loans. As more developing countries adopt financial reforms that free interest rates from central bank control, they are better able to use the rediscount rate as a tool for influencing market interest rates.

In developing countries that controlled rates on loans and deposits, the controlled rates have been instruments of anti-inflationary packages. Since 1973, the use of such interest rate adjustments have been common in Latin America, and increases in deposit rates and loan rates were major elements in the stabilization programs of South Korea and Taiwan in the mid-1960s and Indonesia in both 1968 and 1974. The objective in each case was twofold, to stimulate the demand for liquid assets and to discourage the loan demand for marginal investment projects by private-sector borrowers. The extent to which such measures can be successful depends on the interest elasticity of the demand for liquid assets and the interest elasticity of the demand for loans. In most of the cases just cited, particularly in the three Asian countries, both sets of elasticities evidently were sufficiently high, as the stabilization packages succeeded to a large degree.

Moral suasion by the monetary authorities, sometimes called *open-mouth operations* or *jawbone control*, is practiced no less extensively in developing than in developed countries. Warnings and exhortations to commercial banks to restrict lending or to encourage them to focus lending on particular activities have been quite common in Ghana. They also were used at various times in Malaysia, Singapore, Brazil, and elsewhere, sometimes prior to the imposition of credit ceilings and often to reinforce pressure on banks to adhere to ceilings. In both developed and developing countries, however, moral suasion has proven credible only when accompanied by forceful use of more tangible instruments of monetary control.

SUMMARY

- The money supply is made up of the liquid assets of an economy but the degree of liquidity of particular assets varies, leading to different, more-precise definitions of the money supply.
- The rate of inflation varies greatly among developing economies. Inflation, in effect, is a tax on those who hold money balances, and a moderate rate of inflation can sometimes increase government savings and investment, but the higher is the rate of inflation, the more people shift away from liquid assets, thus undermining any attempt to raise savings and investment in this way.
- The nominal rate of interest is the agreed-on rate between lenders and borrowers, but the real rate of interest, the nominal rate adjusted for inflation, most influences whether individuals are willing to hold liquid assets or not.
- Positive real interest rates are necessary for financial deepening, defined as the rising ratio of liquid assets to GDP. Negative real interest rates have the opposite affect. Financial deepening generally supports growth, although growth sometimes still occurs in its absence.
- Financial panics have been present throughout the last several centuries, but countries have learned how to eliminate some of the reasons for financial panic. As the experience in the late 1990s of several countries around the world demonstrated, however, there are reasons why panics can still occur.
- Exchange rate management ranges from fixed exchange rates, where the local currency is pegged to the dollar or some other currency, to floating rates that move with market forces. In small countries with fixed-rate systems, worldwide inflation is transferred rapidly to the country with the fixed exchange rate. With floating rates, inflation arises mainly from domestic, not international, sources.

- A variety of mechanisms for controlling inflation are at the disposal of the central bank, all of which must, in one way or another, reduce the growth rate of the money supply. Mechanisms such as open-market operations are generally more efficient than mechanisms such as credit ceilings, but most developing countries are not in a position to conduct open-market sales and purchases of government bonds. Credit ceilings and increased bank reserve requirements are less efficient but are effective in lowering the growth of the money supply and inflation.

14

Foreign Aid

Rich countries must recognize that even with action on trade or agricultural subsidies, there is still a fundamental need to boost resources for developing countries. We estimate that it will take on the order of an additional $40 to $60 billion a year to reach the Millennium Development Goals—roughly a doubling of current aid flows—to roughly 0.5 percent of GNP, still well below the 0.7 target agreed to by global leaders years ago. . . . Does anybody really believe that the goal of halving absolute poverty by 2015 is not worth this investment? (World Bank President James Wolfensohn, 2002)[1]

I have long opposed foreign aid programs that have lined the pockets of corrupt dictators, while funding the salaries of a growing, bloated bureaucracy. (U.S. Senator Jesse Helms, January 11, 2001)[2]

T hese two viewpoints succinctly reveal the diversity of opinions and the contours of the debates about foreign aid. Foreign aid has always been controversial. As early as 1947 Congressman (later Senator) Everett Dirksen of Illinois labeled the **Marshall Plan,** a post–World War II aid program for European reconstruction now seen as one of the most highly regarded aid programs of all time, as "Operation Rat-Hole." Prominent economists such as Peter Bauer and Nobel laureate Milton Friedman have strongly criticized aid. Bauer

[1]James Wolfensohn, "A Partnership for Development and Peace," in World Bank (Washington, DC: World Bank, 2002), *A Case for Aid,* p. 11.

[2]Jesse Helms, "Towards a Compassionate Conservative Foreign Policy." Remarks delivered at the American Enterprise Institute, January 11, 2001. www.aei.org/news/newsID.17927/news_detail.asp.

believed that aid only enriches elites in recipient countries and famously quipped "aid is a process by which the poor in rich countries subsidize the rich in poor countries."[3] Friedman argued, beginning in the 1950s, that aid only strengthened and enlarged central governments, and as a result, aid did more harm than good. Critics, from both left and right, see aid as a political tool that distorts incentives, invites corruption, and entrenches corrupt dictators and elite business interests. Many believe that aid has little effect on growth and often has done more harm than good for the world's poor. They cite the widespread poverty in Africa and South Asia despite four decades of aid and point to countries that have received significant amounts of aid and have had disastrous growth records, including the Democratic Republic of the Congo (formerly Zaire), Haiti, Papua New Guinea, and Zambia. Critics call for aid programs to be dramatically reformed, substantially curtailed, or eliminated altogether.

By contrast, supporters see foreign aid as an important ingredient in fighting poverty and accelerating economic growth in developing countries, especially in the very poorest countries, where people may not be able to generate the resources needed to finance investment or health and education programs. Equally prominent economists, such as Columbia University's Jeffrey Sachs and Nobel laureate Joseph Stiglitz, argue that, although aid has not always worked well, it has been critical for poverty reduction and growth in many countries and helped prevent even worse performance in many other countries. Advocates argue that many of the weaknesses of aid have more to do with the donors than with the recipients, and since substantial amounts of aid are given for political purposes, it should not be surprising that it has not always been effective in fostering development. They point to a range of successful aid recipients such as Botswana, Korea, Indonesia, and Taiwan, and (more recently) Uganda and Mozambique, along with broader aid-financed initiatives such as the Green Revolution, the campaign against river blindness, and the introduction of oral rehydration therapy. They note that in the 40 years since aid became widespread in the 1960s, poverty indicators have fallen in many countries, and health and education indicators have risen faster than during any other 40-year period in human history.

Since its modern origins in the aftermath of World War II, foreign aid has become the dominant form of international capital flow from richest to the poorest countries, as well as a way to provide technical expertise and donate commodities such as rice, wheat, and fuel. While it plays a much less significant role in middle-income countries, it remains as much a source of debate and

---

[3]Bauer, Peter, *Dissent on Development* (Cambridge, MA: Harvard University Press, 1972). For a more recent critique of aid, see William Easterly, *The Elusive Quest for Growth: Economists Adventures and Misadventures in the Tropics* (Cambridge, MA: MIT Press, 2001).

controversy there as in other countries. Foreign aid to low- and middle-income countries totaled $79 billion in 2004, and including aid to richer countries and the former states of the Soviet Union, the total topped $84 billion. More than 37 governments around the world provided aid in 2004 and 150 countries received at least some aid inflows. For some countries, the amounts were trivial, amounting to half of a percent of GDP or less. In others aid flows were substantial, totaling 20 percent of GDP or more.

This chapter explores the motivations for and impacts of foreign aid. The empirical evidence on aid effectiveness is decidedly mixed, with some research showing little or no relationship between aid and development and others showing a positive impact. On balance, the evidence suggests that aid has supported growth and development in some countries and contributed to more broad-based improvements in certain areas, such as health and agricultural technology. But, in other countries, it had little effect and did not spur growth; in some countries, it probably held back the process of development, particularly when donors have given it to political allies with corrupt or ineffective governments that showed only faint interest in economic development.

This mixed record has led to sharp debates. Where, when, and how should aid be provided? Which countries are most likely to use aid effectively? Who should have the major responsibility for designing and implementing aid programs? What kinds of conditions should donors impose on recipients? And how can donors ensure that aid is not wasted and gets to the people who need it most and can use it most effectively?

DONORS AND RECIPIENTS

What Is Foreign Aid?

Foreign aid consists of financial flows, technical assistance, and commodities given by the residents of one country to the residents of another country, either as grants or as subsidized loans. Aid can be given or received by governments, charities, foundations, businesses, or individuals. Not all transfers from wealthy countries to poor countries are considered to be foreign aid (or the equivalent term, **foreign assistance**). It depends on who gives it, what it is given for, and the terms on which it is provided. A commercial loan from Citibank to build an electricity generator is not aid nor is a grant from the British government to purchase military equipment. However, a grant from the British government to build an electricity generator counts as foreign aid.

The official source for definitions, data and information on foreign aid is the Development Assistance Committee (DAC) of the Organization for Economic

Cooperation and Development (OECD), an international organization with membership consisting of the governments of 30 industrialized countries, including almost all the major donors. According to the DAC, to be counted as foreign aid the assistance must meet two criteria:

1. It must be designed to promote economic development and welfare as its main objective (thus excluding aid for military or other nondevelopment purposes).
2. It must be provided as either a grant or a subsidized loan.

The grants and subsidized loans that make up foreign aid are often referred to as **concessional assistance,** whereas loans that carry market or near-market terms (and therefore are not foreign aid) are categorized as **nonconcessional assistance.**[4] Distinguishing between subsidized and nonsubsidized loans requires a precise definition. According to the DAC, a loan counts as aid if it has a "grant element" of 25 percent or more, meaning that the present value of the loan (taking into account its interest rate and maturity structure) must be at least 25 percent below the present value of a comparable loan at market interest rates (usually assumed by the DAC, rather arbitrarily, to be 10 percent with no grace period). Thus, the grant element is zero for a loan carrying a 10 percent interest rate, 100 percent for an outright grant, and something in-between for other loans.

Using this definition, the DAC groups aid flows into three broad categories. **Official development assistance (ODA)** is the largest, consisting of aid provided by donor governments (hence the term *official*) to low- and middle-income countries. **Official assistance (OA)** is aid provided by governments to richer countries with per capita incomes higher than approximately $9,000[5] (including the Bahamas, Cyprus, Israel, and Singapore) and countries that were formerly part of the Soviet Union or its satellites (including Hungary, Poland, Romania, and Russia). **Private voluntary assistance** includes grants from nongovernment organizations, religious groups, charities, foundations, and private companies.

WHO GIVES AID?

Although economic assistance from one country to another has occurred for centuries, today's foreign aid programs trace their origins to the 1940s and the establishment of the United Nations, the World Bank, the International Mone-

---

[4]Nonconcessional loans from donor agencies are counted as part of official development *finance* but not as official development *assistance.*

[5]More precisely, assistance to countries with per capita incomes (for three consecutive years) above the World Bank's "high-income" threshold is normally counted as OA, but the DAC makes some exceptions.

BOX 14-1 THE MARSHALL PLAN

When World War II ended in 1945, world leaders hoped that Europe would not require much outside assistance, and that the key economies (especially Britain and France) could quickly rebuild themselves. But, by 1947, there had been little progress, and there was growing concern that discontent in Europe could encourage the spread of communism or fascism. U.S. Secretary of State George Marshall proposed a new approach to reconstruction at a commencement address at Harvard University on June 5, 1947, in which the United States would provide substantial amounts of funding, but only if the European nations, for the first time, could work together to draw up rational plans for reconstruction.

Despite some objections by isolationist members of the U.S. Congress, President Truman signed legislation funding the program, officially called the European Recovery Program, in April 1948. By June 1952 (when the program officially ended), the United States had provided $13.3 billion in assistance (equivalent to over $100 billion in today's dollars) to 16 countries in Europe. Almost 90 percent of the funds were provided as grants. The largest recipients in dollar terms were the United Kingdom, France, Italy, Germany, and the Netherlands. For most of the major recipients, funding exceeded 1 percent of GDP. From the perspective of the United States, these were large commitments representing 1.5 percent of U.S. GDP. The Marshall Plan was almost ten times larger than current U.S. official development assistance, which in 2004 was 0.16 percent of U.S. GDP.

The Marshall Plan is generally regarded as having been a huge success in helping stimulate rapid growth and recovery in Europe (although some analysts believe that recovery was already underway and would have occurred without the funding). While the Marshall Plan is often held up as a model (Marshall won the Nobel Prize for Peace, in 1953), it differed in many ways from today's aid programs. Most important, it was aimed at countries that already had relatively high incomes, highly skilled workforces, and established financial and legal institutions, characteristics absent from most low-income countries. The Marshall Plan was designed to help relatively advanced countries rebuild infrastructure and rebound to their earlier levels of productive capacity, whereas today's aid programs are aimed at the much more difficult task of initiating growth and development in countries where it (by and large) has yet to occur. Nevertheless, the Marshall Plan and its perceived success provided the foundation for today's aid programs.

tary Fund, and the Marshall Plan (Box 14–1). Historically, most aid has been given as **bilateral assistance** directly from one country to another. Some of the major bilateral aid agencies today include the United States Agency for International Development (USAID), the United Kingdom's Department for International Development (DfID), the Japanese International Cooperation Agency

(JICA), the Saudi Fund for International Development, and the International Development Agencies of Canada (CIDA) and Sweden (SIDA). Some governments have multiple bilateral aid agencies. The U.S. government has 18 departments and agencies that provide bilateral aid, including USAID; the Peace Corps; the Departments of Agriculture, Defense, Health and Human Services, State, and Treasury; the Millennium Challenge Corporation (established in 2004); and several others. While most bilateral aid is provided to recipient country governments, some is disbursed to churches, research organizations, universities, private schools and clinics, and local nonprofit agencies. Even private companies sometimes receive foreign assistance, such as U.S. assistance through "enterprise funds" that make investments in firms (such as in Poland in the early 1990s) or aid to micro-finance agencies, like the Grameen Bank in Bangladesh, that provide loans to small-scale entrepreneurs.

In terms of total dollars, the United States has consistently been the world's largest donor, except for a few years in the mid-1990s, when Japan provided the largest amount of aid. In 2004, the United States provided $19 billion in aid to low-income countries (ODA), with Japan, France, the United Kingdom, and Germany the next-largest donor countries (Figure 14–1). (Including OA, the United States provided a total of $20.5 billion.) However, when aid is measured as a

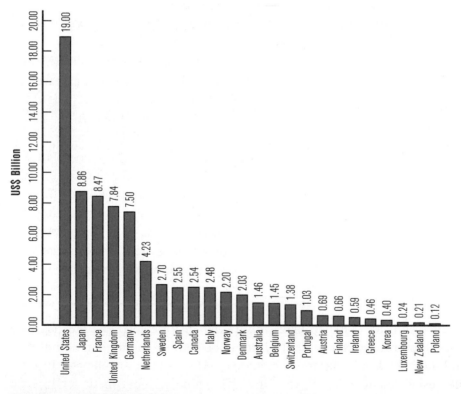

FIGURE 14–1. **Net Official Development Assistance in 2004**

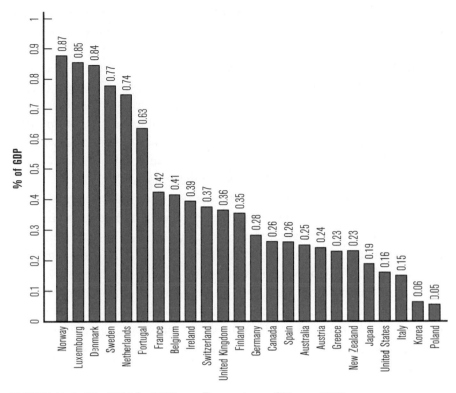

FIGURE 14-2. **Net ODA in 2004 as a Percentage of Donor GDP**

share of the donor's income, a different pattern emerges (Figure 14–2). The most generous donors from this perspective are Norway, Luxembourg, Denmark, Sweden, and the Netherlands, each of which provided between 0.74 and 0.87 percent of GDP in ODA in 2004.[6] The United States is one of the smallest donors by this measure, with ODA in 2004 equivalent to about 0.16 percent of U.S. income. This figure is about half its 1970 level of 0.32 percent and less than one-third the average during the 1960s, when ODA averaged 0.51 percent of U.S. income. Foreign aid makes up about three quarters of 1 percent of the U.S. federal budget. This is much smaller than the public believes: Surveys show that Americans believe that the United States spends upwards of 15–20 percent of its budget on foreign aid.[7] Although U.S. ODA levels as a share of income are small compared with other countries, the United States and other rich countries affect

[6] In 2002 and 2003, the largest donor in the world measured as a share of its income was Saudi Arabia, which provided more than 1 percent of its GDP in both years. Saudi Arabia had been a much smaller donor until it increased assistance to Afghanistan and several other countries in the aftermath of the September 11 terrorist attacks on the United States, and it is uncertain whether this trend will continue over a longer period of time.

[7] See, for example, Program on International Policy Attitudes, "Americans on Foreign Aid and World Hunger: A Study of U.S. Public Attitudes," 2001, www.pipa.org/OnlineReports/BFW/questionnaire.html.

poor countries in many more ways than just foreign aid: Policies on trade, technology, migration, security, and others areas are also important, as described in Box 14–2.

In nominal terms, global ODA increased steadily from the 1960s until it reached a peak of $60 billion in 1991, just after the end of the Cold War (Figure 14–3). Aid flows then declined sharply, falling to just under $48 billion in 1997, before rebounding again to reach $69 billion in 2004 (all these figures would be slightly higher if they included OA). In real terms, total ODA in 2004 was less than the levels of the late 1980s and early 1990s. Measured as a share of donor income, ODA fell sharply during the 1990s and rebounded only slightly.

The values in Figures 14–1 and 14–2 include both the amounts that donors give directly as bilateral aid and the amounts they provide indirectly as **multilateral aid,** which pools together resources from many donors. The major multilateral institutions include the World Bank; the International Monetary Fund; the African, Asian, and Inter-American Development Banks; the United Nations; and the European Commission. The basic rationale for multilateral institutions is that they can provide larger amounts of aid with (presumably) lower bureaucratic costs (since donors do not have to duplicate efforts in each country) and fewer political ties (since funding decisions cannot be driven as easily by the political concerns of a single donor).

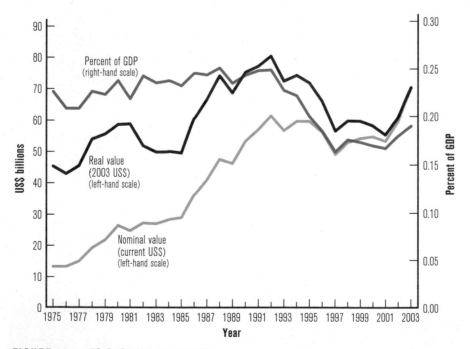

FIGURE 14–3. Global ODA 1975–2003

In nominal terms, global ODA grew until the early 1990s, then fell and rebounded again. In real terms, ODA was at about the same level between 1997 and 2002 as it had been in the late 1970s. ODA as a share of donor income fell sharply in the early 1990s and rebounded only slightly.

BOX 14-2 THE "COMMITMENT TO DEVELOPMENT" INDEX

Rich countries affect poor countries in many ways, including through their policies on foreign aid, trade, migration, military spending, and the environment. Sometimes, these policies help poor countries; sometimes, they hurt. Open-trade policies can help provide markets for poor countries, but tariffs and quotas imposed by rich countries can keep poor countries out and slow their growth and development. To capture these broader channels beyond aid, the Center for Global Development and *Foreign Policy* magazine produce an annual "Commitment to Development Index" that ranks 21 of the world's richest countries on the quality of their policies that affect poor countries in seven areas:

1. Foreign aid, both in terms of its quantity (the amount of both government aid and private charitable contributions) and its quality, in terms of how it is given, to whom, and how much is required to be spent in the donor country.
2. Trade policies, capturing tariffs, quotas, and subsidies for domestic farmers that impede trade or otherwise disadvantage poor countries trying to compete in rich-country markets.
3. Foreign investment policies, including tax rates; programs that provide political risk insurance for investors against coups or other political instability; and other related policies.
4. Migration, capturing the extent to which policies ease or hinder migration (particularly of unskilled rather than skilled workers) from poor to rich countries.
5. Environmental policies, including greenhouse gas emissions, fishing subsidies, or other actions that lead to environmental degradation in poor countries.
6. Security, including financial contributions to peacekeeping operations, naval operations that secure international shipping lanes, and penalties for certain arms exports.
7. Technology, including policies that support research and development and protection of intellectual property rights that enable creation and dissemination of innovations that help poor countries (like vaccines).

In 2005, Denmark came out on top, thanks to its large foreign aid program (relative to its size), its contributions to international peacekeeping, and falling greenhouse gas emissions. The United States ranked twelfth, scoring relatively well on trade and investment policies but poorly on aid programs, because of their small size relative to U.S. income and their poor quality. Japan ranked at the bottom, with weak scores on aid, trade, migration, and security. As with any composite ranking, the Commitment to Development Index is far from perfect, and different assumptions could change the rankings. Its intent, however, is not to be definitive in the rankings but to generate debate and discussion on the many different ways that rich countries affect poor countries, and on how the most important policies can be improved.

Source: David Roodman, *The Commitment to Development Index: 2005 Edition* (Washington, DC: Center for Global Development, 2005). Available at www.cgdev.org/doc/cdi/technicaldescrip05.pdf.

The largest multilateral agency is the **World Bank,** which began as the International Bank for Reconstruction and Development (IBRD) after its founding at a conference held in Bretton Woods, New Hampshire, in July 1944. The word *reconstruction* in the IBRD's title describes its first task, which was to help finance the reconstruction of Europe after World War II. The World Bank group today consists of five affiliated institutions operating in over 100 countries: the IBRD, the International Development Association (IDA), the International Finance Corporation (IFC), the Multilateral Investment Guarantee Agency (MIGA), and the International Centre for Settlement of Investment Disputes (ICSID). Most of the funding provided by the World Bank is *not* foreign aid. The IBRD lends to middle-income countries at market rates. It obtains its funds by borrowing on world capital markets then relends them to member countries at slightly higher rates. Since the IBRD has an excellent credit rating, it is able to borrow and relend to developing countries at much cheaper rates than the recipients could obtain on their own in private markets. The IFC lends on commercial terms and takes minority equity positions in private companies. The MIGA provides guarantees to private foreign investors against loss caused by noncommercial (political) risks, and the ICSID helps settle investment disputes between foreign investors and host countries.

The only part of the World Bank that actually provides foreign aid is the IDA. Donor governments contribute funds to the IDA, which uses it to provide highly concessional loans and grants to low-income countries. Funds from the IDA are used for a wide variety of development purposes, including building roads and ports, funding agricultural research and extension, purchasing medicines and schoolbooks, and training government officials. Its standard loan terms include a "service charge" of less than 1 percent per year and a repayment period of between 20 and 40 years, including a 10-year "grace" period during which no repayment is required. IDA provides 15–20 percent of its financing as grants, a share that has risen in recent years. To be eligible for IDA funds, countries must have (2004) per capita income of less than $965 (although the World Bank makes a few exceptions) and not have access to borrowing on private international capital markets. About 80 countries are eligible to borrow from the IDA. The largest borrowers in 2004 were India, Bangladesh, the Democratic Republic of the Congo, Uganda, Ethiopia, and Vietnam. The IDA disbursed about $6.9 billion in 2003; after repayments from borrowers, it provided *net* ODA of $5.2 billion.

The World Bank is owned and controlled by its 184 member governments, with each member having a voting share determined by the size of its shareholding, which in turn is roughly commensurate with its portion of global GDP. The voting shares differ somewhat across the five bank agencies, with the U.S. the largest shareholder in both the IBRD (17 percent) and the IDA (14 percent). The next-largest shareholders are Japan, Germany, the United Kingdom, and France.

The **International Monetary Fund (IMF)** was also founded at the 1944 Bretton Woods conference.[8] The IMF's original mission was to reestablish an international system of stable national currencies as part of an effort to rejuvenate world trade after World War II. All the IMF's early programs were in today's industrialized countries, with frequent lending operations with the United States, the United Kingdom, France, Germany, and other countries until the early 1970s. The IMF played a very limited role in developing countries until the late 1970s and early 1980s, when many low-income countries began to face severe balance-of-payments problems and debt crises.

Today all of the fund's operations are in low- or middle-income countries. It had programs in 54 countries in 2004. Its main purpose is to provide temporary financing to countries facing significant balance of payments problems stemming from a sharp fall in export prices, a rise in import prices (for example, from an increase in world oil prices), a financial crisis that leads to significant international capital flight, or other shocks. IMF funds are used to shore up the country's

---

[8]The third organization that was meant to be launched at Bretton Woods was the International Trade Organization (ITO). However, the U.S. Congress failed to pass the legislation necessary to ensure U.S. participation, and the ITO never came into existence. Instead, the international community established the General Agreement on Tariffs and Trade, which was the forerunner of today's World Trade Organization.

foreign exchange reserves and stabilize the currency, *not* to finance investment projects or consumption. The IMF is concerned primarily with helping countries achieve and maintain macroeconomic stability rather than directly supporting economic growth and development (although, of course, a stable environment is important for long-run growth). To receive IMF financing, countries must agree (sometimes controversially) to undertake policy reforms typically aimed at reducing the government budget deficit, tightening monetary policy, increasing the flexibility of the exchange rate, and quickly reducing the current account deficit to restore macroeconomic stability.

The vast majority of the IMF's financing is *not* foreign aid. For its emergency loans (called *stand-by credits*) it typically lends money for a one- to three-year period and charges market interest rates. Only about 10 percent of the IMF's outstanding loans are categorized as ODA, all of it provided to low-income countries through its Poverty Reduction and Growth facility. Its gross ODA disbursements in 2003 were $1.1 billion, but after repayment, net ODA disbursements were just $9 million (although due to unevenness in repayment, net disbursements in 2002 were $567 million). Although IMF programs are designed to be short term, in many instances they are renewed for many years. The IMF had continuous or nearly continuous programs throughout the 1980s and 1990s in Bolivia, Ghana, Malawi, the Philippines, Uganda, and several other countries.

Africa, Asia, and Latin America each has its own **regional development bank:** the African Development Bank, the Asian Development Bank, and the Inter-American Development Bank.[9] Like the World Bank, each of the major regional banks provides financing on both concessional and nonconcessional terms, depending on the income level of the borrower. Regional member countries and the major aid donors contribute to the capital of these banks, which also borrow on private capital markets to finance "hard" (nonconcessional) loans and receive contributions from aid donors for their "soft" (concessional) loan and grant operations. Other multilateral donors include the European Union (EU), the Organization of Petroleum Exporting Countries (OPEC) Fund, and the Islamic Development Bank.

The United Nations' foreign assistance programs amounted to about $3.5 billion in 2003, all of it provided as grants. Much of this assistance comes as technical cooperation (consultants, advisers, and other expertise), primarily from the United Nations Development Program (UNDP), the UN Population Fund (UNFPA), and the World Health Organization (WHO). Other UN agencies provide grants for development projects and humanitarian assistance, including the World Food Program (WFP), the UN Children's Fund (UNICEF, winner of the 1965 Nobel Prize for Peace), and the UN High Commission on Refugees (UNHCR).

---

[9]A fourth, the European Bank for Reconstruction and Development, finances investment in Eastern Europe and Central Asia, but almost none of its finance is concessional.

Private Foreign Aid

Not all foreign aid is provided by governments. Private foundations such as the Aga Khan Foundation and the Bill and Melinda Gates Foundation provide significant amounts of assistance to low-income countries, as do charitable groups such as Catholic Relief Services, the Nobel Peace Prize–winning Médecins Sans Frontières (Doctors without Borders), and the Red Cross and Red Crescent Societies. Some of these efforts are focused on specific issues. Rotary International provided significant financing aimed at eradicating polio, with substantial success. Religiously based "mission" schools and hospitals operate in low-income countries around the world, in many cases providing vital services to the poor. Some agencies operate as public-private partnerships, such as the Global Fund to Fight AIDS, Tuberculosis, and Malaria, a foundation based in Switzerland that receives funding from both governments and private sources. In addition, some multinational companies provide charitable donations in the countries in which they operate. According to estimates from the DAC, total aid from private sources reached $10.2 billion in 2003, of which $6.3 billion originated in the United States. These figures almost certainly understate the true amount of private foreign aid, since private charities do not have to report their donations, and the DAC has no way to accurately track these numbers. But, even if accurately counted, the amounts would not be large. In the case of the United States, these amounts are equivalent to about 6 cents per American per day.

Who Receives Foreign Aid?

One hundred fifty countries and territories around the world received aid in 2003. Table 14–1 shows the largest ten recipients, each of which received more than $1 billion. Total dollar amounts are important, but they do not tell the entire story. On a per capita basis, the aid flows to some of these countries are fairly small. Bangladesh received $1.4 billion in aid in 2002, which sounds like a big number, but Bangladesh is a very large country with 138 million people. ODA inflows were equivalent to just 2 percent of its GDP, or about $10 per Bangladeshi, the cost of a few kilograms of rice. But for some of the big recipients with smaller populations, the amounts involved are quite large. Jordan received $1.2 billion in 2004, which for its 5.3 million people worked out to be about $233 dollars per person. For other (mostly smaller) countries, a little bit of aid goes a long way. Tiny Sao Tome and Principe received just $38 million in aid, but this translated into 75 percent of GDP and about $240 per person.

The difference in the apparent magnitudes of aid as a share of GDP (which in some cases appear relatively large) and aid per capita (which seems much smaller) often reflects the very low GDP in recipient countries. Uganda's per capita income is $240 in nominal dollar terms, so aid receipts of 11 percent of

TABLE 14-1.   Major Official Aid Recipients in 2003

RANK	COUNTRY	TOTAL AID (MILLIONS OF CURRENT US$)
1	Iraq	2,265
2	Vietnam	1,769
3	Indonesia	1,743
4	Tanzania	1,669
5	Ethiopia	1,504
6	Bangladesh	1,393
7	China	1,325
8	Serbia and Montenegro	1,317
9	Russian Federation	1,255
10	Jordan	1,234
		AID % OF GNI
1	Sao Tome and Principe	75
2	Guinea-Bissau	64
3	Timor-Leste	48
4	Micronesia, Fed. Sts.	44
5	Marshall Islands	41
6	Burundi	39
7	Sierra Leone	39
8	Eritrea	34
9	Malawi	30
10	Liberia	28
		AID PER CAPITA (CURRENT US$)
1	French Polynesia	2,134
2	New Caledonia	2,022
3	Marshall Islands	1,076
4	Micronesia, Fed. Sts.	923
5	Cape Verde	306
6	West Bank and Gaza	289
7	Tonga	270
8	Sao Tome and Principe	239
9	Jordan	233
10	Kiribati	191

Source: World Bank, *World Development Indicators 2005.*

GDP (which seems large) translate to only about $26 per person. Ethiopia, Haiti, and Egypt received aid equivalent to 22, 5, and 1 percent of GDP, respectively, but in each case the aid amounted to about $19 per person, so it would not be accurate to say that Ethiopia receives much more aid than Egypt. A high aid-to-GDP ratio can indicate a large amount of aid, but it can also result from low GDP.

On a regional basis, sub-Saharan African countries received aid flows averaging 6 percent of GDP in 2002, or $34 per person (Table 14–2). Two other regions, Europe and Central Asia and North Africa and the Middle East, received

TABLE 14-2. **Official Aid Receipts by Region, 2003**

	MILLIONS OF US$	PERCENT OF GDP	DOLLARS PER PERSON
Sub-Saharan Africa	24,144	6.0	34
South Asia	6,169	0.8	4
East Asia and Pacific	7,140	0.4	4
Europe and Central Asia	10,465	0.8	22
Middle East and North Africa	7,628	1.0	24
Latin America and Caribbean	6,153	0.4	12
Low income	32,135	3.0	14
Lower-middle income	21,775	0.5	8
Upper-middle income	3,778	0.2	11
High income	1,273	0.0	1

Source: World Bank, *World Development Indicators 2005.*

more than $20 per person, although aid receipts were a much smaller share of their incomes. For low-income countries around the world, donors provided aid averaging about $14 per recipient. Donors provide almost the same amount per person to upper-middle incomes, although this translates to a much lower share of their income.

Generally speaking, aid is an important type of capital flow for low-income countries but not most middle-income countries. Aid flows averaged 3 percent of GDP in low-income countries in 2003 but just 0.2 percent of GDP in upper-middle-income countries. As discussed in Chapter 10, in the 1990s private capital flows grew sharply in middle-income countries, more than compensating for a fall in aid. In low-income countries, private capital rose much more slowly and remained significantly smaller than aid.

The Motivations for Aid

What determines to whom donors provide aid and how much they give? Donors have a variety of motivations in providing aid, only some of which are directly related to economic development.

FOREIGN POLICY OBJECTIVES AND POLITICAL ALLIANCES

There is little question that foreign policy and political relationships are the key determinants of aid flows. During the Cold War, both the United States and the Soviet Union used aid to vie for the support of developing countries around the world. The United States provided significant amounts of aid to countries fighting communist insurgencies with little regard as to whether the aid was used for development, including Vietnam in the 1960s; Indonesia, the Philippines, and Zaire in the 1970s and 1980s; and several countries in Central America in the

1980s. The Soviet Union countered with aid to North Korea, Cuba, and countries across Eastern Europe. Both sides vied for support in newly independent countries across Africa and used aid to gain support for crucial votes in the United Nations or other world bodies. The United States and the Soviet Union are not the only countries to have used aid in this kind of competitive way: Taiwan and China have used aid (among other policy tools) to try to gain support and recognition for their governments from countries around the world.

Many donors provide significant aid to their former colonies as a means of retaining some political influence. Being a former colony substantially increases the probability of receiving aid flows. Between 1970 and 1994, 99.6 percent of Portugal's aid went to former colonies, whereas 78 percent of aid from the United Kingdom and between 50 and 60 percent of aid from Australia, Belgium, and France went to their former colonies.[10]

For the United States, the most important geopolitical concern outside of the Cold War has been the Middle East. Since 1980, the two largest recipients of U.S. foreign aid (including both OA and ODA) have been Israel and Egypt, as the United States provided financial support to back the Camp David peace agreement signed by those two countries in November 1979. More recently, the largest U.S. aid recipients are countries important in the war on terrorism, such as Afghanistan, Pakistan, and Jordan. Beginning in 2002, Iraq became the largest recipient of U.S. aid (and the largest aid recipient in the world), and its reconstruction is likely to become the largest single foreign aid program ever recorded.

INCOME LEVELS AND POVERTY

Income and poverty are important considerations in aid allocation, at least for some donors, although not as much as is sometimes assumed.[11] For many people in rich countries, the main rationale for aid is to help those in most need in the poorest countries. Income levels and poverty influence both the amount of aid donors provide and the extent of its concessionality. Donors generally provide their most concessional aid to the poorest countries and give fewer grants and subsidized loans for higher-income countries. Some aid programs are designed explicitly with this objective in mind. The World Bank's IDA program has an income ceiling (as do the concessional windows of the regional development banks). Once countries reach that ceiling ($965 per capita in 2004), in most cases, they "graduate" from IDA to nonconcessional IBRD loans. Other programs have less formal graduation rules but still tend to provide less aid as incomes grow.

As incomes of the poorest countries rise, the composition of their capital inflows tends to change, with aid flows declining and private capital inflows

---

[10]Alberto Alesina and David Dollar, "Who Gives Foreign Aid to Whom and Why?" *Journal of Economic Growth* (March 2000), 33–63.

[11]Alesina and Dollar, "Who Gives Foreign Aid?" found that income levels were the primary motivation for aid from Denmark, Finland, Norway, and Sweden.

increasing. There are exceptions, both ways. India receives relatively small amounts of aid (per capita or as a share of GDP) relative to other countries with similar incomes; and Israel, French Polynesia, and Poland receive quite large amounts of aid, even though they have relatively high per capita incomes. Botswana received aid flows equivalent to 15 percent of GDP in the early 1970s, when its income averaged less than $800 per capita, but with its average income now over $4,000, aid flows have declined to less than 1 percent of GDP.

The transition from high to low aid receipts generally takes many years. Consider a country like Mozambique, with a 2004 per capita income of $250. Its income would have to nearly quadruple before it reaches $965 and "graduates" from IDA and (typically) begins to shift from ODA to nonconcessional finance. If its income grows at a very brisk 5 percent per capita per year, it will take 27 years for Mozambique to reach $965 per capita. At a more modest but still rapid growth rate of 3 percent per capita per year, the transition will take 46 years. One recent study calculated that, for the most successful countries, the "half-life" of aid is about 12 years, meaning that aid falls to about 50 percent of its peak level after 12 years and about 25 percent of its peak after 24 years.[12] So, for many of the poorest countries, a rapid transition to private capital flows is unlikely.

COUNTRY SIZE

Donors provide much more aid (either as a share of GDP or per person) to smaller countries than to large countries. If donors were concerned strictly with allocating aid to where the largest numbers of poor people live, much more aid would go to China, India, Indonesia, Bangladesh, and Pakistan. However, the very size of some of these countries sometimes daunts donors. They prefer to provide aid to smaller countries, where it can make a more noticeable difference. Aid of $50 million can make a huge difference in the Gambia, but would not be noticed in India. For political reasons, donors generally want to influence as many countries as possible, which tends to lead to a disproportionate amount of aid going to small countries. A vote in the UN General Assembly counts the same if it is from a small country or a large one, so donors try to influence as many small countries as possible.

COMMERCIAL TIES

Bilateral aid is often designed at least partially to help support the economic interests of certain firms or sectors in the donor country. Multilateral aid is less prone to these pressures, although by no means immune. Many analysts have concluded that commercial ties are an important determinant of Japan's aid.

[12]Michael Clemens and Steven Radelet, "The Millennium Challenge Account: How Much Is Too Much, How Long Is Long Enough?" Working Paper No. 23 (February 2003), Center for Global Development, Washington, DC.

Food donations help support the farmers that produce the crops in the United States and European Union. Many donors "tie" portions of their aid to purchases within the donor country. Automobiles, airline tickets, and consulting services financed by U.S. foreign aid, in most cases, must be purchased from U.S. firms. Tying aid has a long history: Much of the machinery and equipment for the Marshall Plan was purchased from U.S. companies, and all of it had to be shipped across the Atlantic on U.S. merchant vessels. Tying aid probably helps strengthen political support for aid programs within donor countries, but it adds to the costs of aid programs and makes them less effective. One study found that tying aid added 15–20 percent to its cost, meaning that recipients received less of a benefit from the aid notionally allocated to their country.

DEMOCRACY

Historically, donors have provided foreign assistance with little regard to whether recipient country governments were authoritarian or democratic. This was particularly the case during the Cold War, but since the breakup of the Soviet Union, donors have tended to increase their aid to countries that become democracies. More aid has been aimed at strengthening fragile democracies, supporting the transition of nondemocracies to democracies, or building democratic institutions, including financing for parliaments, election monitoring systems, and groups supporting civil rights and free speech. Alberto Alesina and David Dollar, in a study covering the years 1970 through 1994, found that the typical country received a 50 percent increase in aid after switching to become a democracy.

AID, GROWTH, AND DEVELOPMENT

Many people think of foreign aid primarily as either building infrastructure (such as roads or dams) or providing emergency relief to refugees, but it purposes often are more diverse. Most foreign aid is designed to meet one or more of four broad economic and development objectives:

1. To stimulate economic growth through building infrastructure, supporting productive sectors such as agriculture, or bringing new ideas and technologies.
2. To promote other development objectives, such as strengthening education, health, environmental, or political systems.
3. To support subsistence consumption of food and other commodities, especially in emergency situations following natural disasters or humanitarian crises.
4. To help stabilize an economy following economic shocks.

The extent to which aid has been successful in helping achieve these objectives is a matter of continued debate and controversy.

Despite these broader objectives for aid, economic growth has always been the main yardstick used to judge aid's effectiveness, with more aid expected to lead to faster growth. But, at a very broad level, there is no apparent simple relationship between aid and growth, as shown in Figure 14–4. Some countries that received large amounts of aid recorded rapid growth, while others recorded slow or even negative growth. At the same time, some countries that received very little aid did very well, while others did not.

What does the absence of a simple relationship mean? For some analysts, it is evidence of a failure of aid to achieve its basic objectives. But, for others, this simple correlation is misleading, since other factors affect both aid and growth. Some countries that received large amounts of aid may face endemic disease or poor geography or may be emerging from long-standing civil conflict, in which case aid might have a positive impact on growth even if the overall growth performance remains weak. Or the causality could run in the opposite direction: Donors give more aid to countries with slow growth rates and much less to rapid growers like China. These analysts suggest that, once these other factors are taken into consideration, a positive relationship emerges. Still others conclude that aid works well under certain circumstances but fails in others. Aid might help spur growth in countries with reasonably good economic policies but fail

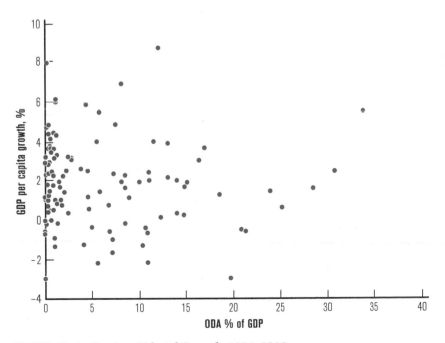

FIGURE 14-4. **Foreign Aid and Growth, 1994–2003**

to do so where corruption is rife and the economy is badly mismanaged. In this view, while the overall trend line is important, the variance around the trend and the reasons for that variance are also critical in understanding the true underlying relationships.

Debate on these issues has been ongoing for many years, and continues today. There is general agreement on some broad issues. Even aid pessimists (at least most of them) agree that aid has been successful in some countries (such as in Botswana or Indonesia or more recently in Mozambique and Tanzania), that aid has helped improve health by supplying essential medicines, and that aid is an important vehicle in providing emergency relief following natural disasters. Similarly, aid optimists concede that much aid has been wasted or stolen, such as by the Marcos regime in the Philippines and the Duvalier regime in Haiti, and that, even under the best circumstances, aid can have adverse incentives on economic activity. Debate continues on the overall general trends, the conditions under which aid works or does not work, and on what steps can be taken to make aid more effective. Empirical evidence is mixed, with different studies reaching different conclusions depending on the time frame, countries involved, and assumptions underlying the research. We summarize these by looking at three views on aid and growth.

View 1. Although Not Always Successful, on Average, Aid Has a Positive Impact on Economic Growth and Development

The clearest economic rationale for aid is to promote growth by financing new investment, especially investment in public goods. Aid used to build roads, ports, electricity generators, schools, and other infrastructure augments the process of capital accumulation, which (if the investments are productive) should accelerate the rate of growth. This motivation for aid has been invoked since the Marshall Plan. Indeed, early analyses of foreign aid, such as Walter Rostow's popular 1960 book *The Stages of Economic Growth,* saw aid wholly in terms of financing investment and adding to the capital stock.[13] This idea is fully consistent with the Harrod-Domar model that views capital formation as the main driver of growth, as well as with the Solow model, which sees capital accumulation as important for growth, albeit with diminishing returns and with a strong role for new technology. In the context of these models, aid adds to the

---

[13]W. W. Rostow, *The Stages of Economic Growth: A Non-Communist Manifesto* (Cambridge, UK: Cambridge University Press, 1960).

total amount of saving, which increases investment and the capital stock, which in turn accelerates the rate of economic growth.[14]

In this view, poor countries are unable to generate sufficient amounts of saving on their own to finance the investment necessary to initiate growth, or if they do they can finance only very slow growth. As discussed in Chapter 10, saving rates tend to be low in the very poorest countries, and even where they are moderately high, the actual amount of saving is low. A country with per capita income of $200 and a saving rate of 10 percent generates saving of $20 per person per year, which cannot purchase much in terms of capital goods. In the strongest version of this view, the poorest countries may be stuck in a **poverty trap,** in which their income is too low to generate the saving necessary to initiate the process of sustained growth.[15] Total saving may be too small to compensate for depreciation, let alone add to the capital stock. In a more moderate version, the poorest countries may be able to save enough to begin to grow, but only at very slow rates. Thus, aid flows provide a way to augment domestic saving and accelerate the growth process.

Aid can also support growth by building knowledge and transferring new ideas, technology, and best practices from one country to another. Some aid helps support research in low-income countries that can accelerate the pace of growth. One of the best examples is aid-funded research in the 1960s and 1970s on new varieties of seeds, fertilizers, and pesticides that helped transform agriculture in Asia through what became known as the *Green Revolution*. Similarly, a significant portion of aid finances advisors and technical assistance that ultimately is aimed at strengthening institutions and increasing productivity. This kind of aid, when it is effective, can be thought of as shifting the production function upward, thereby helping increase the rate of growth.[16]

Several studies, although far from all, found a positive relationship between aid and growth, on average, after controlling for the impact of other factors on growth. In particular, beginning in the mid-1990s researchers began to investigate whether aid might spur growth, albeit with diminishing returns; that is, small amounts of aid might have a relatively large impact on growth, but each additional dollar of aid might have less effect. This may seem like an obvious point, since it is the standard assumption about capital accumulation in most growth models (e.g., the Solow model), but surprisingly, earlier research tested

---

[14]As discussed in Chapter 4, in the Harrod-Domar model the effect is a permanent increase in the growth rate; in the Solow model it is a transitory increase in the growth rate until the economy achieves a new steady level of output.

[15]See Jeffrey Sachs et al., "Ending Africa's Poverty Trap," *Brookings Papers on Economic Activity* 1 (2004), 117–240.

[16]In the Solow model, the increase in the rate of growth lasts only during the transition to a new steady-state level of income.

only a linear relationship. Many (but not all) of the studies that allow for diminishing returns and control for other variables find a positive relationship, on average, between total aid and growth.[17] In terms of Figure 14–4, these studies find that other variables, such as geography, political conflict, policies, and institutions explain much of the variance in growth rates among aid recipients. They conclude that, after controlling for these variables and allowing for diminishing returns, a positive relationship between aid and growth emerges, albeit with important variance around the trend line. This view is captured by the top panel of Figure 14–5. But as we shall see, other research reached quite different conclusions, so the debate about the relationship between aid and growth remains open.

In addition, for defenders of View 1, aid can have a positive impact on other important development objectives that may affect growth only indirectly or affect it only after a long period of time, such as health, education, or the environment. Similarly, it can provide emergency assistance or humanitarian relief or be used to help achieve macroeconomic stability. We briefly review each of these in turn.

PROMOTING HEALTH, EDUCATION, AND THE ENVIRONMENT

Nearly half of all aid flows are aimed at improving health, education, the environment, and other objectives. Aid that finances immunizations, medical supplies, medicines, bed nets (to prevent the spread of malaria), clean water, and school supplies is meant to help provide essential goods and services to people too poor to afford them. In economic terms, most of these kinds of expenditures count as additions to consumption rather than investment (although some aid for education and health, such as building schools and clinics, count as investment).

Economic growth is often a secondary, long-term objective of this kind of aid. Healthier, better-educated workers should be more productive, shifting the production function and expanding output and income. A similar argument can be made for at least some aid aimed at protecting the environment. Improving forest or fisheries management, cleaning water supplies, or reducing air pollution can improve welfare and increase productivity over time. The impact on growth, however, can take a long time to materialize. Programs to immunize

---

[17]Cross-country econometric studies that allow for diminishing returns typically do so by including both aid and aid squared as determinants of growth. This specification yields a parabola in which aid has a positive effect on growth with diminishing returns, but in theory, with enough aid, the marginal impact could be negative. However, in these studies, the data points are concentrated on the upward portion of the curve, so they do not conclude that large amounts of aid have a negative impact. See, for example, Carl-Johan Dalgaard, Henrik Hansen, and Finn Tarp (2004), "On the Empirics of Foreign Aid and Growth," *Economic Journal* 114, no. 496 (2004), 191–216; Robert Lensink and Howard White, "Are There Negative Returns to Aid?" *Journal of Development Studies* 37, no. 6 (2001), 42–65; and Henrik Hansen, and Finn Tarp, "Aid and Growth Regressions," *Journal of Development Economics* 64 (2001), 547–70.

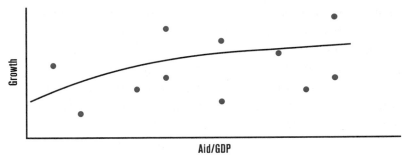

View 1 Aid has a positive impact on growth with diminishing returns, after controlling for the impact of other variables.

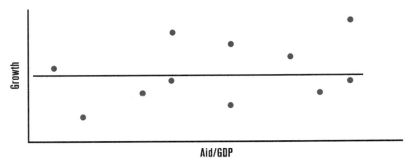

View 2 Aid has little or no impact on growth and may have a negative impact.

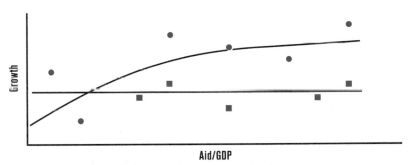

View 3 Aid has a positive impact on growth in some circumstances (the circles) but no impact in others (the squares).

FIGURE 14-5. Three Views on Aid and Growth

children or improve the quality of primary schools do not affect labor productivity until these children join the workforce, which is many years after the aid was received.

Research on the relationship between aid and other development outcomes tends to concentrate on evaluating specific projects and interventions rather than broad cross-country trends. As with growth, in many cases, aid appears to have had a strong impact on health and education, along with many interventions that failed. Perhaps the best documented are aid-financed interventions in health. A group of experts convened by the Center for Global Development documented 17 cases of large health interventions in developing countries that have been very successful in improving health outcomes and saving lives, several of which are discussed in Chapter 9 (see Box 14–3).[18] A massive global effort spearheaded by the World Health Organization succeeded in completely eradicating smallpox from the world in 1977, perhaps the greatest public health achievement ever. A worldwide effort to fight polio, supported by both government aid agencies and private donors such as Rotary International, succeeded in nearly eliminating the disease. The introduction of oral rehyrdration therapy has saved millions of lives after being developed first in East Pakistan (now Bangladesh) in the 1970s. In Egypt, a donor-funded oral rehydration program helped reduce infant diarrheal deaths by an astonishing 82 percent between 1982 and 1987.

There have also been several successful education initiatives.[19] A girls' primary school education initiative in Balochistanm, Pakistan, led to a tripling of the number of schools, a more than doubling of girls' enrolment, and an increase in the girls' primary school completion rate from 7 to 30 percent between 1990 and 1998. In Ethiopia, a systemwide set of education reforms implemented in the 1990s with the support of USAID, the World Bank, and UNICEF led to the construction of many new schools, increasing the number of teachers and improving their training, and expanding the availability of textbooks. Between 1991 and 2001, the overall primary school enrolment ratio increased from 20 to 57 percent, and the girls' enrolment ratio jumped from 12 to 47 percent. In Indonesia, donors partially supported the construction of over 61,000 primary schools in the mid-1970s, which MIT economist Esther Duflo showed led to significant increases in educational attainment and increased wages for school graduates.[20]

These individual success stories only tell part of the story. There also have been many failures, where donors provided funding for health and education reforms that did not happen, for technical assistance that did not help, or for interventions that led to little change in health or education. But beyond case studies, little systematic evidence has been gathered on the circumstances under which aid-financed interventions in health and education have been successful and where they have not.

PROVIDING EMERGENCY ASSISTANCE AND HUMANITARIAN RELIEF

About one tenth of all foreign aid provides emergency relief following natural disasters or humanitarian crises. Relief programs following earthquakes, floods,

---

[18]Ruth Levine with Molly Kinder, *Millions Saved: Proven Success in Global Health* (Washington, DC: Center for Global Development, 2004).

[19]For a summary of successful education interventions, see Maria Beatriz Orlando, "Success Stories in Policy Interventions towards High Quality Universal Primary Education" (Washington, DC: Center for Global Development, 2004).

[20]Esther Duflo, "Schooling and Labor Market Consequences of School Construction in Indonesia: Evidence from and Unusual Policy Experiment" *American Economic Review* (September 2001).

BOX 14-3   CONTROLLING RIVER BLINDNESS IN SUB-SAHARAN AFRICA[1]

Onchocerciasis, or "river blindness," is a pernicious, parasitic disease that afflicts approximately 18 million people worldwide, with well over 99 percent of its victims in sub-Saharan Africa. Spread through the bite of an infected blackfly living near fast-moving waters, river blindness causes symptoms such as disabling itching, rashes, muscle pain, skin lesions, and in its most severe cases, blindness.

In 1974, governments and donors in 11 West African countries jointly launched the Onchocerciasis Control Program.[2] At the time, 2.5 million of the area's 30 million inhabitants were infected with the disease, and approximately 100,000 were blind. The primary intervention was weekly aerial spraying of larvicide during rainy seasons along the region's waterways to control the disease-spreading blackflies. The aerial spraying, augmented by hand spraying of breeding grounds, persisted even through civil and regional conflicts and coups. In 1987, the program began distributing the drug ivermectin, which treats the disease's symptoms with a single annual dose.

The program was implemented through unusual cooperation between several governments and a wide range of donors. It was launched under the leadership of the World Health Organization, the World Bank, the Food and Agricutlure Organization, and the United Nations Development Programme. Twenty-two donor countries contributed $560 million to support the 28-year project, with much of the financing provided through long-term commitments. The pharmaceutical company, Merck, Inc., donated ivermectin to the program beginning in 1987, pledging to provide it to anyone that needed it as long as they needed it, making the donation program one of the largest public-private partnerships ever created. Governments and NGOs in the recipient countries were critical to implementing the program efffectively.

The program achieved impressive success between 1974 and its conclusion in 2002. Transmission was halted completely in all 11 West African countries involved. Six hundred thousand cases of blindness were prevented, and 18 million children born in the program area are now free from the risk of the disease. In addition to the striking health benefits, the economic impact has been impressive. An estimated 25 million hectares of arable land, enough to feed 17 million people, are now safe for resettlement. In Burkina Faso, 15 percent of the country's land that had been deserted because of onchocerciasis has been completely reclaimed, and its new residents now enjoy a thriving agricultural economy.

The program was extremely cost effective, with a yearly cost of less than $1 per protected person. The World Bank calculated that the annual return on investment (attributable mainly to increased agricultural output) to be 20 percent, and it is estimated that $3.7 billion will be generated from improved labor and agricultural productivity.

[1]Ruth Levine with Molly Kinder, *Millions Saved: Proven Success in Global Health* (Washington, DC: Center for Global Development, 2004), Chapter 6.
[2]Benin, Burkina Faso, Cote d'Ivoire, Ghana, Guinea, Guinea-Bissau, Mali, Niger, Senegal, and Togo.

or other disasters typically provide food, clothing, basic medicines and drugs, and other items to help meet subsistence needs. Similarly, humanitarian aid assists people living in refugee camps and those displaced by war or other conflict. From an economic point of view, most of this aid is meant to support basic consumption rather than growth per se, although some of it is used to rebuild ruined infrastructure and help output from collapsing further than it otherwise might following disasters.

SUPPORTING ECONOMIC AND POLITICAL STABILITY

Some aid is provided to help countries facing macroeconomic instability. A fall in export prices, a rise in import prices, or an economic shock, such as a drought, flood, or earthquake, can lead to a sharp depreciation of the exchange rate, which in turn can ripple through the economy and increase the prices of traded goods and services. Aid inflows add to the supply of foreign exchange and can help moderate the pressure on the exchange rate. The IMF plays the leading role in this area, with other donors such as the World Bank providing supporting funds. Aid flows that are a response to a macroeconomic crisis or a natural disaster, as described in the previous paragraph, are inversely correlated with economic growth. Growth falls because of the crisis, and aid increases as a result. These situations account for some of the "below-the-line" cases in Figure 14–4, where aid is associated with negative GDP growth. But, since aid is responding to the low growth, these cases should not be seen as examples of a failure of aid to promote growth and development.

View 2. Aid Has Little or No Effect on Growth and Actually May Undermine Growth

How could aid have no impact or a negative impact on growth, as suggested by the middle panel of Figure 14–5? One simple way is if most of it simply was wasted. If donors build large bureaucracies or spend the money on expensive technical experts from their home country that write reports no one reads, aid will not help growth. Aid that winds up in the personal off-shore bank accounts of government officials or finances a fleet of expensive cars for members of parliament creates little stimulus to growth. If aid builds a road but provides no funds for maintenance, there may be an initial burst of output, but this could be followed by a decline back to previous levels as the road deteriorates. Since donors typically like to finance capital costs of new projects but not maintenance, this is a common problem.

More insidious, if aid breeds corruption, government officials and their cronies spend their time plotting about how to siphon aid money to their own bank accounts rather than increasing output. Aid funds used to pay private contractors for construction projects or delivery of services can create opportunities for kickbacks and other illegal activities, just like any other public funds. One of the strongest critiques of aid and how it might undermine development is that it can prop up malevolent dictators and support political regimes that further impoverish rather than help the poor. U.S. aid to the Marcos regime in the Philippines during the 1970s and 1980s, for example, may have helped support an anticommunist ally but probably also lengthened the time in which his corrupt regime remained in power. The same argument can be made about aid in the 1970s and 1980s to the Central African Republic, Haiti, or Zaire.

But even if aid is not simply wasted or misused, it could have a smaller than expected impact on growth because of diminishing returns to investment as the recipient begins to reach its **absorptive capacity.** Government bureaucracies with relatively few skilled workers might have difficulty overseeing and managing larger and larger aid flows. Purchases of commodities and supplies might strain available warehouses or delivery systems. Large donations of medicines might sit unused because they cannot be delivered on time to clinics. In the long run, an increase in aid flows may help expand absorptive capacity, as it can be used to train and hire more workers, expand warehouse facilities, or build infrastructure to ease bottlenecks, but in the meantime, the impact of aid may be diminished by these constraints.

Perhaps the most important way in which aid could slow growth is by undermining incentives for private sector activity. Large aid flows can spur inflation and cause a real appreciation of the exchange rate, which reduces the profitability of production of all tradable goods. Aid flows can enlarge the size of the government and related services supporting aid projects, drawing workers and investment away from other productive activities such as agro-processing, garments, or footwear exports, which have been important engines for growth in many countries. These "Dutch disease" effects are usually associated with revenues from natural resource export booms (Chapter 17), but can result from aid flows as well. Some analysts believe that large aid flows to Ghana in the late 1980s and early 1990s undermined export incentives.[21] Similarly, food aid can sometimes undermine local food production, as discussed in Box 14-4.

AID, SAVING, AND TAX REVENUE

Aid could also have a smaller-than-expected effect on growth if it has an adverse impact on saving and investment. Early analysts assumed that, since aid is a form of foreign saving, each dollar of aid would add one full dollar to investment. But this is unlikely to happen, for at least two reasons. First, as mentioned previously, not all aid is provided as investment goods or even aimed at increasing investment and growth. Second, even where aid is aimed directly at invest-

---

[21]See Stephen Younger, "Aid and the Dutch Disease: Macroeconomic Management When Everybody Loves You," *World Development* 20, no. 11 (November 1992), 1587–97.

BOX 14-4 FOOD AID AND FOOD PRODUCTION

For many people, it seems obvious that donating food is a good way for rich countries to help poor countries. Although sometimes that is true, under certain circumstances, donations of food can hurt local farmers by undermining the incentives for them to produce food. If all food is produced locally (i.e., there are no imports), then an increase in food from aid donations can shift out the supply curve for food and drive down food prices, benefiting consumers but hurting farmers, as shown in panel (a) of Figure 14–6. In an economy with no commercial imports, food aid shifts the supply curve for food from S_1 to S_2, causing the price to fall from P_0 to P_1. Producers react by reducing output from Q_0 to Q_1, while consumers increase consumption from Q_0 to Q_2, with food aid of $Q_2 - Q_1$ filling the gap. Consumers are clearly better off (important if there is a true food shortage) while producers are worse off.

In an economy that produces some food but imports on the margin, the outcome is different, as shown in panel (b) of Figure 14–6. With a world price of P_W, initial production takes place at Q_3 with consumption at Q_4 and imports of $Q_4 - Q_3$. In this situation, food aid displaces imports, with imports falling to $Q_4 - Q_5$ and food aid making up the difference $Q_5 - Q_3$. Domestic prices, food production, and consumption do not change, with food aid, in effect, saving the economy the cost of the displaced imported food.

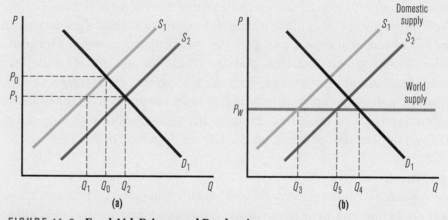

FIGURE 14-6. **Food Aid, Prices, and Production**
(a) Food aid and production in the absence of imports: Food aid lowers prices, benefitting consumers, but displacing local production. (b) Food aid and production with imports: Food aid adds to total supply without affecting prices or displacing production.

ment, the impact could be partially offset by a reduction in either private saving (through a decline in the rate of return on private investment) or government saving (through a fall in tax revenues). If a country that currently invests $100 million per year receives $10 million in new aid for investment (e.g., building roads), it is highly unlikely that total investment will reach $110 million. It is far more likely that, with $10 million in new investment, some of the original $100 million will be shifted into consumption.

The impact of aid on saving is illustrated in Figure 14–7. Before the recipient country obtains aid, it can produce consumption goods and capital goods along the production possibilities frontier P. To simplify, the diagram ignores international trade and other capital inflows, so that consumption initially also must take place somewhere along the production frontier. Community tastes are defined by a set of indifference curves, of which two are shown (labeled I and II). The country's welfare is maximized if it produces and consumes at point A, where the indifference curve I is tangent to the frontier P, with consumption at C_1 and investment (and saving) at I_1. Now donor countries contribute an amount AB of aid with the intention that it be used to raise investment to I_2. However, the aid moves *the consumption frontier* outward from P to P'. Now, the country maximizes its welfare at point D, the tangency between P' and indifference curve I_2, where it consumes C_3 and invests I_3. Of the aid amount AB, AE (equal to $I_3 - I_1$) is invested and BE (equal to $I_2 - I_3$) is consumed. Even if all the

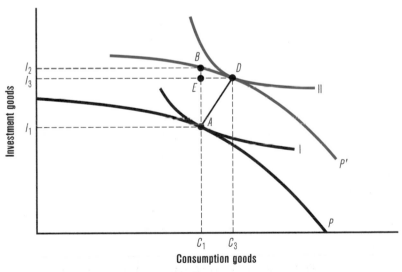

FIGURE 14-7. Impact of Aid on Investment and Consumption
Foreign aid totaling AB turns into actual new investment of only AE, because the country maximizes welfare on the new frontier, P', at point D, not B. P' is not really a "production" frontier but a "supply" frontier.
Source: Adapted from Paul Mosley, "Aid, Savings and Growth Revisited," *Oxford Bulletin of Economics and Statistics* 42 (May 1980), 79–91.

new aid money is invested as intended, some of what the country had invested before is shifted to consumption, so in effect, the aid finances an increase in both investment and consumption, with the precise impact depending on production possibilities, community tastes, and other variables left out of the figure, such as trade. Aid may finance mostly investment if $I_3 - I_1$ is a large percentage of total aid (AB), or it may mostly finance consumption if $I_3 - I_1$ is a small percentage of AB.

Why would the country react in this way and not invest all the aid it receives? Saving always requires a sacrifice of current consumption, based on the anticipation that investment will lead to increased output and greater consumption in the future. When the country receives a new inflow of aid, investment increases and the country is less willing to sacrifice that last dollar of today's consumption to finance the last dollar of investment. Thus, domestic saving falls somewhat, although with the addition of foreign saving from aid total saving (and investment) rises.

When substitutions of these kinds are possible and aid effectively finances activities for which it was not originally intended, aid is said to be **fungible.** This kind of substitution could be good or bad, depending how the money is spent. If donor funds to build a school allow members of the community to save less and purchase more food, clothing, and medicine for their families, few donors would take issue. But, if instead the freed-up funds are used to buy several Mercedes Benzes for the mayor and his staff, donors are likely to be unhappy and economic development is not served.

Aid given as a cash transfer to the budget or as program aid rather than for a specific project deliberately gives the recipient the kinds of choices demonstrated in Figure 14–7. But even if all aid is used for very specific investment projects and the donor audits projects to confirm where the money has been spent, substitution is possible. Project aid might be used, for example, for investment projects that the government would have made without aid. In that case, the government's resources are freed up for other purposes. If the government is intending to build an electricity generator with its own funds, then a donor decides to provide the funding, the government's money is freed up for any purpose the government wishes. Even if aid finances projects that the government was not planning to implement, the government might simply cut back on other projects because it wants to raise the share of consumption for economic or political reasons.

The tendency for aid flows to "stick" as increased government expenditures, rather than result in tax relief or offsetting expenditure reductions in other areas, is sometimes called the *flypaper effect.* Several studies find that $1 in aid translates to less than $1 in government spending, typically in the range of 33–67 cents on the dollar. But some studies for specific countries find a strong flypaper effect, with $1 of aid translating into close to $1 of new spending. One study on Indonesia found that $1 in aid led to $1.50 in government expenditures, suggesting that aid "crowded in" government spending, perhaps by relieving constraints that were limiting government spending.[22]

Aid flows can similarly influence government revenues. A government that receives aid flows is likely to be less willing to raise marginal tax revenue from the general public, especially since taxes are not politically popular. A government without aid inflows might be willing to raise taxes to finance a new hospital, but if a donor finances the hospital, the government has much less incentive to raise the revenue. However, aid could help increase revenues if donors require governments to provide matching funds for a particular activity; if aid helped governments introduce institutional changes to strengthen the tax authority, or in the case of loans, governments knew they would need revenues in the future to repay the loans. The empirical evidence on this effect is mixed: In some countries, aid inflows corresponded with increased revenues, while in other cases, revenues declined.[23] Where revenues declined, the reduction may benefit ordinary citizens, who can save and consume more for their own purposes, which could help accelerate economic growth. Or it may be directed to individuals or businesses with special connections to the government.

Private saving might also be affected by aid inflows. A host of subtle influences from aid on relative prices may contribute to substitution that reduces private saving and "crowds out" private sector investment. Aid inflows could reduce interest rates, which in turn could reduce private saving. If investment is subject to diminishing returns, more capital in general could mean lower returns on investments and hence a greater tendency to consume rather than save in the recipient countries.

It is difficult, if not impossible, for donors to stop this substitution, although they may be able to limit it to some extent. Research suggests that aid funds are fungible, at least partially, meaning that recipients, to some extent, can substitute aid funds from their intended purpose to something else. However, the evidence suggests that aid is not perfectly fungible: Much of it goes to its intended purpose, and recipients cannot or do not transform all aid flows into other purposes.

---

[22]See World Bank, *Assessing Aid: What Works, What Doesn't, and Why* (New York: Oxford University Press, 1998); and Tarhan Feyzioglu, Vinaya Swaroop, and Min Zhu, "A Panel Data Analysis of the Fungibility of Foreign Aid," *World Bank Economic Review* 12, no. 1 (1998). For the study on Indonesia, see Howard Pack and Janet Rothenberg Pack, "Is Foreign Aid Fungible? The Case of Indonesia," *Economic Journal* 100 (March 1990).

[23]For a recent survey, see Mark McGillvary and Oliver Morrisey, "A Review of the Evidence on the Fiscal Effects of Aid," Research Paper no. 01/13 Center for Research in Economic Development and International Trade, Nottingham, UK, 2001. For a classic model on these effects, see Peter Heller, "A Model of Public Fiscal Behavior in Developing Countries: Aid, Investment, and Taxation," *American Economic Review* 65 (1975), 429–45.

AID DEPENDENCY

Some analysts argue that aid loses some of its effectiveness when aid flows are relatively large for long periods of time, because prices, institutions, and expectations adjust to that level and, to some extent, recipients become dependent on aid. This situation can raise several challenges. First, the larger the amount of aid, the greater is the risk of a sudden reduction in aid. Aid flows tend to be more erratic than domestic revenues, and the degree of volatility increases with greater dependence on aid.[24] If donors suddenly reduce aid, whether because they face budget cutbacks, in response to a corruption scandal, a change in government, or for some other reason, the macroeconomic consequences can be difficult to manage. Second, large aid flows give donors substantial leverage over the recipient, so that recipients become more willing to introduce whatever conditions the donors require, good or bad, to ensure that the aid continues to be disbursed. Aid flows thus can weaken public accountability and impede the development of civil society, if the recipient government becomes more responsive to the donors than to its own citizens.

As recipients become more dependent on aid, the process of gradually reducing aid over time as development proceeds becomes more difficult. If aid finances public expenditure, a reduction of aid must be matched with either an increase in revenue or a reduction in expenditure, neither of which is particularly easy or politically popular (although raising revenue is made easier by the process of economic growth). The incentives are strong for recipients to continue to request aid for as long as possible and resist these adjustments. Egypt has been one of the world's largest aid recipients since 1980, and some observers believe that these inflows have taken the pressure off of the government to reduce wasteful expenditures and introduce other needed reforms.

Aid programs may actually weaken the institutions that society needs to enhance the process of development and reduce the need for aid. Budget institutions might be weakened by aid, especially if most aid is disbursed as projects with the money not flowing through the budget. Aid agencies need qualified accounts, economists, and financial specialists to design, monitor, and evaluate their projects. By increasing the demand for these skills, aid agencies bid up their wages, making them more expensive for everyone else, including the government (not to mention domestic firms). Aid agencies sometimes recruit the most able and promising local staff, leaving government agencies and the rest of the economy with less-qualified (and usually lower-paid) staff. In Mozambique, following the end of its civil war in the early 1990s, donors came flooding into the country and recruited many of the most-capable government workers, paying upwards of five times the

---

[24]Aleš Bluír and Javier Hamann, "How Volatile and Unpredictable Are Aid Flows, and What Are the Policy Implications?" IMF Working Paper No. 01/167, International Monetary Fund, Washington, DC, 2001.

government salary and sometimes more than private sector salaries. But the departure of some of its most talented staff deprived the government of needed skills, and weakened government effectiveness as a result.[25]

This process is not limited to the budget office: It can affect the central bank, the ministry of health (which might lose physicians or epidemiologists), the ministry of education, and other agencies. Aid agencies might be able partially to countervail these tendencies by supplying technical assistance to train government workers (although some then take other jobs) or otherwise strengthen institutional system. Over time, there may be some benefit, as the increased wages entice more school graduates to become accountants and financial experts. In any case, aid agencies are often unaware of or do not take into account these possible deleterious impacts.

To some extent, the dependency can work both ways, as aid agencies become accustomed to operating large-scale programs. Donor agencies, in effect, are asked to work themselves out of their jobs by making aid less necessary and less important over time. But, like any agency, most aid agencies like to be bigger and have more aid flows to disburse. Individuals working on specific projects often like to see them continued over time; and the larger the programs, the more influence they may have over government policy choices. Promotions and other rewards often are geared to the size of the aid program they manage. Thus, the incentives facing the donors sometimes encourage dependency between donor and recipient.

Proponents of View 2 point to a body of research that finds little relationship between aid and growth. Keith Griffen and John Enos (1970) were among the first to report empirical research questioning the effectiveness of aid, finding negative simple correlations between aid and growth in 27 countries. Since then, other studies concluded that there is no relationship or even a negative relationship between aid and growth,[26] in contrast to the studies cited earlier that support View 1.

---

[25]Peter Fallon and Luiz Pereira da Silva, "Recognizing Labor Market Constraints: Government-Donor Competition for Manpower in Mozambique," in D. Lindauer and B. Nunberg, eds., *Rehabilitating Government* (Washington, DC: World Bank, 1994).

[26]See, for example, K. B. Griffin and J. L. Enos, "Foreign Assistance: Objectives and Consequences," *Economic Development and Cultural Change* 18, no. 2 (July 1970), 313–27; Paul Mosley, "Aid, Savings, and Growth Revisited," *Oxford Bulletin of Economics and Statistics* 42, no. 2 (1980), 79–96; Peter Boone, "The Impact of Foreign Aid on Savings and Growth," working paper no. 677, Centre for Economic Performance, London School of Economics, London, 1994; William Easterly, Ross Levine, and David Roodman, "New Data, New Doubts: A Comment on Burnside and Dollar's 'Aid, Politics, and Growth'," *American Economic Review* 94, no. 3 (June 2004); David Roodman, "The Anarchy of Numbers: Aid, Development, and Cross-Country Empirics," working paper no. 32, Center for Global Development, Washington, DC, July 2003. For a review, see Michael Clemens, Steven Radelet, and Rikhil Bhavnani, "Counting Chickens When They Hatch: The Short-Term Impact of Aid on Growth," working paper no. 44, Center for Global Development, November 2004.

View 3. Aid Has a Conditional Relationship with Growth, Stimulating Growth Only under Certain Circumstances, Such as in Countries with Good Policies or Institutions

This perspective begins by accepting the idea that aid has had mixed results: Even where research has found a generally positive relationship, no one claims that aid worked across all countries all the time. It recognizes that aid seems to have stimulated growth in some countries under certain circumstances but not in others and focuses on trying to decipher the key characteristics that might explain these differences. This view is represented by the bottom panel of Figure 14–5. Three "conditional" explanations have emerged, suggesting that the relationship between aid and growth might depend on the characteristics of the recipient country, the type of aid being provided, or the way in which donors provide it.

CHARACTERISTICS OF THE RECIPIENT COUNTRY

The most influential of the conditional perspectives is that the impact of aid depends on the quality of institutions and policies in the recipient country. According to this view, in countries with poor macroeconomic and trade policies, high levels of corruption, and low accountability of government officials, aid is likely to have little or no impact. By contrast, in countries with reasonably good policies and institutions, aid programs can help accelerate growth. World Bank researchers Jonathan Isham, Daniel Kaufmann, and Lant Pritchett initiated this line of research by finding that rates of return on aid-financed investments were higher in countries with strong civil liberties and other measures of governance. Craig Burnside and David Dollar took the next step by finding a significant positive relationship between aid and growth in countries with good policies and institutions and no relationship otherwise.[27] Other researchers explored the possibility that the impact of aid may differ depending on the type of government, quality of human capital, location in the tropics (presumably a proxy for health), the magnitude and frequency of export shocks, and other factors.

Although subsequent analysis cast doubt on some of these results, the idea has had an enormous influence on donor policies, probably because the conclusions of a differential effect are consistent with the experience of many development professionals. These findings have led to a shift among donors to be more "selective" in allocating foreign aid, to provide more of it to countries with relatively stronger institutions and policies, as we discuss later in the chapter.

[27]Jonathan Isham, Daniel Kaufmann, and Lant Pritchett, "Governance and Returns on Investment: An Empirical Investigation," Policy Research working paper no. 1550, World Bank, 1995; Craig Burnside and David Dollar, "Aid, Policies, and Growth," *American Economic Review* 90, no. 4 (September 2000), 847–68; Paul Collier and David Dollar, "Aid Allocation and Poverty Reduction," *European Economic Review* 45, no. 1 (2002), 1–26; World Bank, *Assessing Aid: What Works, What Doesn't, and Why* (New York: Oxford University Press, 1998).

TYPE OF AID

Different kinds of aid might affect growth in different ways. One recent study disaggregated aid flows into those most likely and least likely to affect growth within a few years, if at all.[28] It separated aid into three categories:

1. Emergency and humanitarian aid, likely to be negatively associated with growth, since it increases sharply at the same time growth falls because of an economic shock.
2. Aid that might affect growth only after a long period of time, if at all, and so a growth impact may be difficult to detect, such as aid for health, education, the environment, and to support democracy.
3. Aid directly aimed at affecting growth (building roads, ports, and electricity generators, or supporting agriculture).

It found a very strong relationship between the third type of aid and growth, but the relationship with the other types was less detectable. The study found some support for the proposition that the third subcategory of aid had an even stronger impact in countries with stronger institutions.

DONOR PRACTICES

Many analysts argue that differences in donor practices are likely to influence aid effectiveness. Multilateral aid might be more effective in stimulating growth than bilateral aid, since less of it is determined by political factors (although some argue just the opposite, that multilateral agencies tend to be too large and unfocused). Aid "tied" to purchases of good and services in the donor countries or used to finance conferences and international meetings might be less effective than other aid. Large aid bureaucracies add to costs and slow down disbursements, making aid less effective. Donors that coordinate with other funders and recipient governments may be more effective than those that operate completely on their own. Donors with more effective monitoring and evaluation systems might be better able to channel aid to its most productive uses, enhancing overall effectives. An influential view that emerged in the late 1990s is that aid might be more effective where there has been a "participatory approach" among government and community groups in recipient countries in setting priorities and designing aid-supported programs, a topic we return to later in the chapter. Substantial debate centers about these issues and there is little doubt that donor practices are critical, but to date there has been very little systematic research connecting specific donor practices to aid effectiveness.

Research at this more disaggregated and nuanced level, investigating various "conditional" relationships between aid and growth, has just begun. This line of enquiry is promising, but it has yet to reach firm conclusions. In summarizing the

[28]Clemens, Radelet, and Bhavnani, "Counting Chickens When They Hatch."

aid and growth research, it seems that aid has been successful in some countries but not others, with the overall trend a subject of debate. This research is only beginning to scratch more deeply beneath the surface and reveal conclusively what types of aid are most effective, which are ineffective, and the precise conditions under which aid has the largest impact on growth. Just as with the evidence on the causes of economic growth more generally discussed in Chapter 3, there is still much that we do not know about the relationship between aid and growth.

DONOR RELATIONSHIPS WITH RECIPIENT COUNTRIES

The criticisms about foreign aid and the evidence that it appears to have been effective in some countries but not in others led to debates about how aid programs can be improved to more-effectively support growth and development. But the challenge is not easy. Aid programs face some inherent difficulties in trying to achieve a wide range of objectives (which may differ between donor and recipient), provide financial oversight, and ensure results. In this section, we first explore some of the challenges in more depth, then turn to some specific changes that have been suggested and in some cases implemented by donors and recipients in an attempt to make aid more effective.

The Principal-Agent Problem

A key issue facing aid agencies is that there is only an indirect and distant relationship between the people actually providing the financing (taxpayers in donor countries) and the intended ultimate beneficiaries of aid projects (poor people living in low-income countries). Many institutions, organizations, and transactions are in-between; and the decisions made along the way may not be in accord with the wishes or best interests of either the taxpayers or the beneficiaries. All public-sector agencies and many private companies are faced with the **principal-agent problem,** but the international dimension makes it an even greater challenge for aid. Economist Bertin Martens analyzed the principal agency problem for aid agencies, and our account closely follows his.[29]

"Principals" in a private company (the owners), club (the members), or public administration (taxpayers) cannot make all decisions and carry out all tasks themselves, so they must delegate these responsibilities to "agents" to work on their behalf: managers, employees, elected officials, and civil servants. But agents have their own goals and motivations, which may not be the same as the principals'. Agents also have more information than the principals and can use

---

[29]Berten Martens, "Introduction" in Berten Martens, ed., *The Institutional Economics of Foreign Aid* (Cambridge: Cambridge University Press, 2004).

that information in ways that run counter to the principals' interests. Therefore, principals are faced with the problem of writing contracts and establishing rules that more closely align agents' interests with their own. These issues are particularly important for public-sector agencies, since they tend to have multiple objectives (not just profit) and their many principals may not agree on which objective holds the higher priority. These problems make it very difficult to match incentives, such as salary, bonuses, and promotions, with performance indicators.

Most aid programs have a long, complex chain of principal-agent relationships, starting with the taxpayers that delegate authority to elected officials, who in turn become principals that delegate authority to a new set of agents, the heads of aid agencies. These relationships continue to aid agency employees, contractors, and consultants. In the recipient country, similar relationships lie between the ultimate recipients, their government, and those that actually implement programs. In most public agencies, there is considerable slippage throughout these relationships, but the problem is compounded in aid agencies by the physical separation of the original taxpayers and ultimate beneficiaries. In domestic public programs (such as trash collection or local schools), the taxpayers and ultimate beneficiaries are the same people, so they may have clearer information about success or failure and can reward or penalize their agents accordingly by re-electing them or voting them out of office. But this feedback loop is broken for aid agencies, as Martens points out:

> A unique and striking characteristic of foreign aid is that the people for whose benefit aid agencies work are not the same as those from whom the revenues are obtained; they actually live in different countries and different political constituencies. This [separation] blocks the normal performance feedback process: beneficiaries may be able to observe performance but cannot modulate payments (rewards to agents) as a function of performance. Although donors are typically interested in ensuring that their funds are well spent, it is extremely difficult for them to do so, since there is frequently no obvious mechanism for transmitting the beneficiaries' point of view to the sponsors.[30]

The principal-agent problem affects nearly all aspects of aid delivery, including program design, implementation, compensation, incentives, evaluation, and allocation of funding. The problem can never be fully avoided: Private companies face similar issues between owners, managers, and employees, as do private aid foundations and charities. The challenge is to design institutions and incentives to try to mitigate these problems as much as possible to clarify goals, objectives, incentives, and rewards. A key challenge for donors is how best to apply conditions to their loans to encourage recipients to act more in accord with the donors' (and possibly the ultimate beneficiaries') interests and wishes.

---

[30]Martens, "Introduction," p. 14.

Conditionality

Donors often require that recipient countries adopt specific policies, or packages of policies, as prerequisites for funding; and this **conditionality** is one of the most controversial aspects of aid. Broad policy conditions are most often associated with financing from the IMF and World Bank, but all donors use them to some extent. Many bilateral donors take their lead from these two multilateral organizations and do not provide the full amount of their aid until the recipient country has met IMF and World Bank conditions. As discussed in Chapter 5, the IMF typically requires that countries adopt a more flexible exchange rate, smaller budget deficits, slower growth of the money supply, a build-up of foreign exchange reserves, privatization of certain state-owned enterprises, a reduction in import restrictions, and the implementation of broad anticorruption measures. Sometimes, the required reforms may be only distantly related to the main purpose of the funding the IMF provides. World Bank conditions sometimes reinforce these broad policy reforms and may add some sector-specific requirements, such as liberalizing fertilizer markets before providing an agriculture loan.

In many cases, the specific policy conditions required by the IMF and World Bank are justifiable and often supported by at least some people within the recipient governments. But, other times, IMF and World Bank conditions go too far and their conditions are harder to justify, especially when the rationale for specific reforms are less clear-cut and seen by critics as based more on ideology than hard facts and sensible economics. For example, while privatization of state-owned marketing boards, retail outlets, or trading establishments is generally not controversial, privatization of public utilities is much more open to debate. Many countries may need to impose fiscal discipline as required by the IMF, but the fund is often accused of imposing much stricter discipline than is really necessary to achieve stability, at a cost of dampening aggregate consumption and expenditures on important social programs. Sometimes, the donors simply impose too many conditions, seemingly wanting the recipient country to fix everything at once without showing any sense of priority or feasibility. Turkey's "Letter of Intent" with the IMF in April 2003 included a table listing 131 very specific policy actions (with dozens more subcategories of actions) that the government promised to undertake as part of its program.[31] The IMF admitted that, at times, it has gone too far, as with its program in Indonesia following the financial crisis of 1997.

While donors are often criticized for imposing too many conditions, they are almost as often criticized for not imposing *enough* conditions. Some advo-

---

[31]See "Turkey: Letter of Intent," Annex B, April 3, 2003, www.imf.org/external/np/loi/2003/tur/01/index.htm.

cates that criticize the IMF for imposing too much fiscal austerity also insist that it require governments to spend a minimum amount on health and education. The World Bank is often asked to add conditions to force governments to take specific actions, for example, on projects that have potential environmental consequences. This can lead to difficult dilemmas. Sometimes governments ask the World Bank to be one of many cofunders for a project, hoping that World Bank participation will provide credibility and security. In return, the World Bank typically wishes to require environmental safeguards or anticorruption measures. But, since the World Bank is only one lender, its leverage may be limited. If the World Bank requires too many conditions, the government can just go ahead without them (and without the environmental safeguards), but if they ask for too few, they may find themselves funding a project with inadequate conditions.

The rationale for these conditions is straightforward: Donors believe these broad-based conditions are important for growth and development, and without them, providing aid is futile. It is easiest to see this rationale in extreme cases: If government policies have led to high rates of inflation, an overvalued exchange rate, massive inefficiencies and waste of public spending, and extensive corruption, then providing aid, whatever the specific purpose, without requiring fundamental change provides no benefits and perhaps perpetuates the damage. Some even argue that the primary purpose of aid is not the money but for aid to act as a lever for the policy reforms. The conditionality debate is a microcosm of the principal-agent problem: A donor requests a recipient to take specific actions in return for receiving aid, but the recipient may have different objectives and controls sufficient information to make compliance difficult.

Cornell economist Ravi Kanbur points out two further problems with conditionality. First, it is not always clear what conditions are the most appropriate to ensure sustained growth and development. Mahbub ul Haq, an influential development advisor long associated with the UNDP, once commented that sub-Saharan Africa, "often receives more bad policy advice per capita from foreign consultants than any other continent in the world."[32] Development doctrine has swung from a state-led approach in the 1950s and 1960s, to basic human needs in the 1970s, to a macroeconomic approach focused on open markets in the 1980s and 1990s, to a greater focus on institutions beginning in the mid-1990s. As a result, the list of conditions is constantly evolving.

Second, conditionality does not seem to work. Most analysts agree that governments implement reforms only when it is in their interests to do so, and donor conditions have little, if any, impact on that decision. Many donors continue to disburse aid even when recipients fail to meet conditions, sometimes repeatedly so. Over time, recipients learn that aid flows do not necessarily

---

[32]Mahbub ul Haq, "Does Africa Have a Future?" *Earth Times New Service* (January 1998).

depend on meeting stated conditions, a process that gradually undermines the aid institutions and the conditions they attach. Donors are faced with their own internal incentives to continue to disburse aid to support the contractors and recipients that depend on it. They also face a "Samaritan's dilemma," that withdrawing aid would create short-term pain for the very people it is aimed to help.[33]

In the end, there are no clear-cut rules for conditionality. Striking the right balance between responsible oversight and accountability, on the one hand, and ensuring against high bureaucratic obstacles and the imposition of unnecessary controls or unwarranted policy changes, on the other, requires flexibility, judgment, and the ability to balance multiple objectives.

Improving Aid Effectiveness

Since the late 1990s, as global aid flows began to slowly rebound, there has been increased discussion and debate about how aid programs could be strengthened and become more effective in supporting growth and development. These debates recognized some of the weaknesses in aid programs and resulted in some specific ideas for change. In recent years, donor agencies began to put some of these ideas in practice, and some donor practices changed noticeably as a result.

COUNTRY SELECTIVITY

One influential idea is that donors should be more selective about to which countries they provide aid, based on the view that aid works best in countries with good policies and institutions. In the strongest version of this view, aid should be provided *only* to countries that meet these criteria and not otherwise, with more going to countries with the highest levels of poverty. A more moderate view is that *more* aid should be allocated to countries with stronger policies and institutions but continue to provide targeted aid to some countries with relatively poor institutions, especially in postconflict situations. This proposal takes a turn on the conditionality debate: Instead of providing aid to encourage reforms, provide it to countries that already decided to implement key reforms. Economists Paul Collier and David Dollar suggested a "poverty-efficient" allocation of aid in which funding would be provided to the poorest countries with relatively stronger policies and institutions, in order to maximize the impact of aid on global poverty reduction.[34]

---

[33]Ravi Kanbur, "The Economics of International Aid," in Serge Christophe-Kolm and Jean Mercier Ythier, eds., *Handbook of the Economics of Giving, Altruism, and Reciprocity: Applications* (Amsterdam: North Holland, 2006). Also see Jakob Svensson, "Why Conditional Aid Does Not Work and What Can Be Done About It," *Journal of Development Economics* 70, no. 2 (2003), 381–402; and William Easterly, *The Elusive Quest for Growth.*

[34]Collier and Dollar, "Aid Allocation and Poverty Reduction."

Donors began to move in this direction in the past few years. The World Bank uses its Country Policy and Institutional Assessment index to partly determine the allocation of its concessional IDA funds. Several European donors moved toward providing broad budget support or financing for sectorwide approaches (SWAps), but only for a relatively small number of countries considered to be the most responsible. The United States' new Millennium Challenge Corporation provides aid to only a small number of recipient countries, based largely (although not completely) on their performance on 16 indicators of policies and governance.[35]

Since so much aid is allocated for political, security, and other foreign policy reasons, there are limits to how far donors are likely to go in reallocating their aid based on strict economic development criteria. This is especially true for the major bilateral donors but is true for multilateral donors as well. It is perfectly justifiable for countries to use aid as one tool to help achieve legitimate foreign policy goals, such as Middle East peace. One frequent suggestion is for donors to more clearly separate funding primarily aimed at foreign policy goals from funding aimed at development. This would allow programs to be designed, implemented, and evaluated in different ways so donor country governments, their taxpayers, and recipients could better understand and appraise aid effectiveness.

RECIPIENT PARTICIPATION

A second influential idea is that aid has been weakened by donor domination in setting priorities, designing programs and projects, choosing implementers (often consulting firms from the donor country), and monitoring and evaluating results. The idea is that bureaucrats and activists from donor countries design too many programs, leading to a poor choice of priorities, flawed design, or weak commitment among recipients for programs they do not feel are their own. Advocates have pushed for a more "participatory approach" in which various groups in recipient countries (government, NGOs, charities, the private sector) play a more active role. The idea is to eliminate some of the problems in the long chain of principal-agent relationships and more tightly integrate the ultimate beneficiaries in key aspects of the aid-delivery process. This might have two benefits. First, projects might be better designed, with a more accurate view of the highest priorities and the most appropriate implementation methods to meet local needs. Second, increasing recipient participation in the design and implementation process may provide them with more "ownership" of the activity and a higher stake in ensuring its success. One of the first movements in this direction was the introduction of "Poverty Reduction Strategy Papers" as the

---

[35]For an early analysis of the Millennium Challenge Account, see Steven Radelet, *Challenging Foreign Aid: A Policymakers Guide to the Millennium Challenge Account* (Washington, DC: Center for Global Development, 2003). For ongoing analyses, see the CGD website at www.cgdev.org.

basis for World Bank and IMF debt relief and other financing. Similarly, both the Global Fund to Fight AIDS, Tuberculosis, and Malaria and the Millennium Challenge Corporation rely on a significant degree of local participation in designing and implementing the programs they finance.

These programs are relatively new, so while the participatory approach holds out promise, there is no evidence yet on the extent to which (or the circumstances under which) it improves aid effectiveness. There is a clear and inescapable tension between country ownership, on the one hand, and donor priorities and conditionality, on the other. Donors are more likely to facilitate a participatory approach in countries in which governments show a strong commitment to sound development policies and less so in countries with corrupt and dictatorial governments.

HARMONIZATION AND COORDINATION

Managing aid flows from many different donors can be a constant challenge for recipient countries, since different donors tend to implement their own initiatives and insist on using their own unique processes for initiating, implementing, and monitoring projects. Recipients can be overwhelmed by donor requirements to provide multiple project audits, environmental assessments, procurement reports, financial statements, and project updates. According to the World Bank, developing countries typically work with 30 or more aid agencies across a wide variety of sectors, with each sending an average of five missions a year to oversee their projects. Governments can find themselves hosting three or more aid missions a week.[36] Many recipient countries have only a limited number of skilled and highly trained technocrats; and all the donors want to meet with these top people, leaving them with much less time to deal with other pressing concerns. The government of Tanzania, which hosts several hundred aid missions each year, has introduced a "quiet time" from April to August of each year during which it asks donors to minimize meetings and missions so that the government has time to adequately prepare its annual budget.

These concerns have led to numerous suggestions and pledges for donors to more closely coordinate their activities; harmonize their accounting, monitoring, and evaluation systems; or "pool" their funds.[37] Some progress has been made in the form of donors providing more aid as budget support in certain countries, acting together through joint missions, and agreeing to use similar monitoring and evaluation procedures. At the same time, some newer donor initiatives appear to want to use their own new methodologies, which could compound this problem going forward.

---

[36]"Cutting the Red Tape," World Bank Development News Media (February 21, 2003).

[37]Ravi Kanbur and Todd Sandler, "The Future of Development Assistance: Common Pools and International Public Goods," Policy Essay No. 5, Overseas Development Council, Washington, DC, 1999.

RESULTS-BASED MANAGEMENT

The emphasis on demonstrating the effectiveness of aid has led to calls for improved monitoring and evaluation and results-based management. In this view, aid programs should aim to achieve very specific quantitative targets, and decisions about renewing or reallocating aid going forward should be based on those results. There are three basic objectives. First, results-based management can help donors allocate funds toward programs that are working. Second, ongoing reviews can detect problems at an early stage and help modify and strengthen existing programs. Third, donors and recipients can better learn what approaches have worked and what have not. Stronger monitoring and evaluation helps strengthen the principal-agent relationship so that aid agencies have clearer incentives and taxpayers have better information about the impact of aid on its intended beneficiaries.

SUMMARY

- Most aid is given by bilateral donors, but a significant portion is channeled through multilateral agencies. Global aid flows peaked in 1991, then declined in real and nominal terms until 1997, before rebounding again. The United States today provides the largest dollar amount of aid but is among the smallest in terms of aid as a share of its income.
- For some countries, aid flows are large and significant, while in others they are small. Sub-Saharan Africa received aid flows equivalent to about 6 percent of its income in 2004, or about $34 per person. Eastern Europe, Central Asia, North Africa, and the Middle East received more than $20 per person, although aid was a much smaller share of income in these countries. Aid receipts per capita have fallen since 1990 in every region of the world except Eastern Europe and Central Asia.
- For most donors, the primary motivation for providing aid is to support foreign policy objectives and political alliances. Income and poverty tend to be secondary objectives. Country size, commercial and historical ties, and the extent of democracy also play a role.
- There are three broad viewpoints on the relationship among aid, growth, and development. First, some analysts believe that aid supports growth and development by adding to investment and the capital stock, helping in the transfer of technology, supporting key health and education programs, and enhancing economic stability. Second, others believe that aid has no impact on growth and might undermine growth by distorting incentives for private production, encouraging corruption, enlarging the government, or creating aid dependency. Third,

some argue that aid works under certain conditions but not others, depending on the policy and institutional environment in the recipient country, the purpose of the aid, or the donor's practices and procedures. The empirical evidence on these relationships is mixed, with different studies reaching different conclusions.

- Aid can influence both saving rates and tax revenues through a host of subtle impacts on prices, preferences, and incentives. Aid flows add to total saving and investment but less than one for one. The fungibility of aid can cause private and government saving to decline as aid increases. The impact on government revenues varies across countries, with some experiencing a decline and others an increase corresponding to higher aid flows.

- Aid agencies face a classic principal-agent problem, compounded by the fact that the original funders (taxpayers in donor countries) have only indirect and distant connections to the intended ultimate beneficiaries (poor people in low income countries). A particular challenge for donors is how to place appropriate conditions on their aid. Donors often are criticized for putting too many, too few, or the wrong kinds of conditions on aid; and conditionality in general appears to have been largely ineffective.

- In recent years, donors began to try to make aid more effective by becoming more "selective" in choosing recipients, encouraging more participation by recipients in program design and implementation, coordinating more closely with each other, and managing programs based on results. It is too early to judge the effectiveness of these changes, but they are likely to affect aid programs for some time to come.

15

Foreign Debt and Financial Crises

I n the two decades following World War II, Mexico, like most developing countries, had few transactions with international capital markets. The country borrowed relatively little from international banks, and foreign investors only occasionally took a stake in Mexican firms. And, while it borrowed some funds from official lenders (governments and international organizations such as the World Bank), Mexico's total borrowing remained small. At the time, international capital markets were relatively undeveloped compared to today, and they were only just beginning to recover from the disruptions of the two World Wars and the Great Depression. But things began to change in the late 1960s and early 1970s. Capital market instruments became more sophisticated, and the costs of international transactions fell. Bankers and other investors started to look for opportunities outside their traditional Western markets. Official lending increased as well. Mexico, along with many other countries, was eager to expand investment and accelerate growth, and began to look abroad for financing. In the decades since then, Mexico's foreign borrowing has had tremendous impact, both positive and negative, on its economic growth, macroeconomic stability, job creation, and even political dynamics.

Most of Mexico's foreign financing in the early years was in the form of borrowing, especially from private creditors, as opposed to foreign direct investment. Mexico was suspicious of foreign investors and wanted to maintain ownership control of its enterprises, so borrowing was more palatable than foreign direct investment. Foreign commercial banks were more than willing to lend money to the Mexican government, state-owned companies (such as PEMEX, the state oil company), and other businesses. In 1970, Mexico's foreign borrowing from private creditors was relatively small, amounting to $350 million, or about 1 percent of GDP. But by 1980, it was borrowing nearly $15 billion a year from private creditors, about 8 percent of GDP. More than half the debt was "short term," meaning that it had to be repaid (and usually reborrowed) within one year.

At first, the borrowing seemed to help: Mexico's GDP per capita rose 4.2 percent per year between 1972 and 1981, compared with 2.6 percent during the previous seven years. But it turned out that Mexico had borrowed too much too quickly: In August 1982, it shocked the world by declaring that it could not service its debts. The country plunged into a deep economic crisis that led to a sharp reduction in investment, negative growth rates, deep strains on government finance, and considerable economic hardship for millions of Mexicans. Mexico's crisis quickly cascaded to many other developing countries that had borrowed heavily abroad, and the consequences of these crises are still playing out today in some countries. Foreign lending to Mexico plummeted following the crisis before recovering in the early 1990s, only to plunge again when Mexico faced another payments crisis in 1994 and 1995. Since the mid-1990s, Mexico's net foreign borrowing has been negative in most years, meaning that it has been repaying international lenders more than it has been borrowing.

Globally, debt flows to developing countries have followed a pattern similar to Mexico's, swinging back and forth from large inflows to large outflows and then back again. Borrowing from private commercial banks became the dominant form of international capital flows to developing countries, especially middle-income countries, in the 1970s and 1980s, surpassing official borrowing in almost every year. But debt flows fell sharply in the 1980s following the debt crises (Table 15–1). In the early 1990s, private debt flows grew sharply again, quadrupling in size in just six years from $30 billion in 1990 to $120 billion in

TABLE 15-1. Debt Flows to Developing Countries, 1980–2003 (billion US$)

	1980	1990	1996	2000	2003
Private debt finance	70.9	29.8	119.9	−0.4	71.8
Commercial Banks	28.7	3.2	30.7	−5.8	2.5
Bonds	1.1	1.1	49.5	17.5	26.6
Other	11.5	12.3	2.3	−4.3	−6.3
Short-term debt flows (net)	29.5	13.2	37.4	−7.9	49.0
Official debt finance	20.5	26.4	2.8	4.9	−14.3
Bilateral	13.1	11.0	−10.4	−6.9	−16.0
Multilateral	7.4	15.4	13.1	11.8	1.8
Total	91.4	56.2	122.7	4.5	57.6

Sources: World Bank, *Global Development Finance 2005;* and IMF, *International Financial Statistics,* annual yearbook.

1996. But then a series of financial crises struck several emerging markets around the world, starting with Mexico in 1995; then hitting Thailand, Indonesia, and Korea in 1997; Russia and Brazil in 1998; and Turkey and Argentina in 2001. Debt flows collapsed, and by 2001, the $120 billion inflow of five years earlier had completely disappeared. But, once the crises abated, borrowing increased again, and private debt flows rebounded to $72 billion just two years later in 2003. Official borrowing was much smaller and less volatile than private borrowing, but it fell steadily during the 1990s, and by 2003, developing countries as a whole were repaying more to official creditors than they were borrowing. For many of the poorest developing countries, grants, rather than loans, were the dominant source of foreign financing.

Even among the largest borrowers, foreign borrowing has always been small compared to domestic capital flows, in most years accounting for perhaps one fourth or less of available investable funds and only occasionally amounting to more than 3–4 percent of GDP. From the perspective of economic growth models that emphasize the role of capital formation in the growth process (such as the Harrod-Domar and Solow models), private debt flows are only modestly important. But foreign debt plays a more complex role than the basic numbers indicate. The economic impact of debt flows is magnified by their effect on macroeconomic stability, the exchange rate, interest rates, government budgets, and domestic financial institutions and the potential to trigger widespread financial crises.

This chapter explores the advantages, disadvantages, and risks associated with foreign borrowing. It describes various forms of debt, the patterns of debt flows to developing countries over the last several decades, and the basic conditions under which debt is sustainable. It examines in some detail the developing-country debt crises of the 1980s, the ongoing debt problems faced by some low-income countries, and the emerging-market financial crises of the 1990s, then explores the main lessons that have emerged from these crises for debt management in the future. We also probe some of the tough questions that arise when countries default or no longer can pay their debt service: How much should be forgiven? How should the burden of bad loans be shared between creditors and borrowers? And what conditions, if any, should be placed on countries seeking debt forgiveness?

ADVANTAGES AND DISADVANTAGES OF FOREIGN BORROWING

Foreign debt gained a bad reputation following the crises of the 1980s and the late 1990s, in many ways deservedly so. However, prudent borrowing has been an important part of the development strategy of many countries. The United

States borrowed heavily in the middle and late nineteenth century to finance its westward expansion (especially the railroads). Most countries in Western Europe relied on foreign borrowing at one time or another.

From a national perspective, borrowing permits a country to invest more than it can save and import more than it can export. If the additional funds finance productive investment, they should yield sufficient returns to pay the interest and principal on the initial foreign inflows. As we saw in Chapters 3 and 4, since capital is relatively scarce in low-income countries, these countries have the *potential* to realize higher rates of return on investment and more rapid economic growth than richer countries, providing the foundation for lending from rich to low-income countries. Under these circumstances, foreign borrowing can help support growth and development at the same time as it yields attractive returns to the lender.

For countries interested in augmenting domestic saving with foreign capital, borrowing brings several advantages and disadvantages relative to foreign direct investment and other forms of capital. When a domestic firm borrows abroad, there are no controversies over foreign ownership, profit repatriation, tax holidays, and the like that arise with foreign direct investment (FDI). In addition, foreign borrowing can be undertaken much more quickly and easily than FDI. Repayments are limited to the terms of the loan, so if an investment is highly profitable, the home country can keep the profits rather than repatriate them abroad. To simplify only slightly, as long as the rate of return on investment projects exceeds the interest rate on the debt, foreign borrowing can be a very sensible strategy to augment domestic savings, add to investment, and accelerate growth. In addition, borrowing can play a critical stabilization role for countries buffeted by balance of payments shocks. When a country's export prices suddenly collapse or its import prices rise, some temporary borrowing can help bridge the financing gap until prices rebound or the economy can adjust to the change, thus helping ease the costs of adjustment.

However, there are downsides as well. Debts must be paid, even when a project goes bad. Too much borrowing of the wrong kind or for the wrong purposes can leave developing countries vulnerable to sudden capital withdrawals and financial crises. Short-term debt, in particular, can very quickly switch from rapid inflow to rapid outflow, which can cause sudden plunges in exchange rates and skyrocketing interest rates and wreak havoc on banks, private companies, and government budgets.

Borrowing too much to finance consumption or poorly conceived investments also can lead to trouble. Borrowing is much easier politically than raising taxes to pay for spending, especially if governments do not think they will still be in office when it is time to repay. If governments borrow to finance monuments, lavish office buildings, or fleets of expensive cars, there will be no future income stream to repay the debts. But even where governments borrow to finance investments that initially seem sound, sudden drops in export prices, rising interest rates or oil prices, or an unforeseen world recession can turn a worthwhile project into a financial loss. Governments strapped with large debt service payments sometimes face painful choices between repaying foreign lenders as promised, or maintaining spending on health, education, or other important domestic programs.

DEBT SUSTAINABILITY

How much aggregate debt can a country take on before it begins to get into trouble? There is no simple answer. A country's debts are sustainable if they can be serviced without resort to exceptional financing (e.g., a special bailout by friendly donors) and without a major future adjustment in the country's income and expenditure. But every country's situation is different. A country's ability to repay depends on a wide array of factors: the size of its debt, its trade and budget deficits, the interest rate on its debt, the mix of loans and grants it receives, its vulnerability to shocks (e.g., natural disasters such as droughts or hurricanes or a fall in export prices), and the rate of growth of GDP, exports, and government tax revenues.

At a simple level, a country's debt sustainability depends on (1) how much it owes and (2) its capacity to make the required payments. But neither of these is quite as straightforward as they first seem. There are two ways to think about how much the country owes: the total stock of debt and the amount of payments due in a particular year. The usual measure of the total debt stock is the sum of the face value of all debts outstanding, but this can be misleading if a significant portion of debt is subsidized. For example, the World Bank's International Development Association (IDA), the part of the World Bank that provides finance for low-income countries, provides loans with an interest rate of just 0.75 percent and 40 years to repay. Obviously a $100 million dollar loan extended on these terms creates a much smaller burden than a $100 million loan that must be repaid in five years with a market-determined interest rate of 7 percent. Under these circumstances it makes much more sense to calculate the net present value (NPV) of the debt. A loan extended on normal market terms would have an NPV equal to 100 percent of its face value, a grant would have NPV equal to 0, and subsidized loans would have an NPV in between, depending on the interest rate and the maturity structure (that is, the schedule to repay the loan's principal).

Debt service is the amount due for principal and interest payments in a given year. Policy makers need to know how much is due each year, but looking at just one year can be misleading, since it leaves out how much is due the next year or the year after, when a big payment might be due. Thus, an accurate projection of how much debt service is due when is an important component of assessing debt sustainability.

What about the second part of sustainability, a country's *capacity* to pay? Three measures of capacity are most common: GDP, exports, and government tax revenue. GDP is the broadest measure of the economic resources available to repay the debt. The larger a country's productive capacity and corresponding income, the greater its ability to repay debt. But if a country is repaying foreign debt, the real constraint may not be total income, but the ability to earn the dollars (or other foreign exchange) needed to repay the loans denominated in foreign currency. When Thailand, Indonesia, and Korea could not fully service their debts in late 1997, the problem was not a lack of sufficient income, but a lack of available foreign exchange. Under these circumstances, exports earned each year or the stock of foreign exchange reserves held by the central bank may be more suitable indicators of debt servicing capacity. Exports and reserves focus attention on the **external transfer problem,** the challenge of generating sufficient foreign exchange to transfer to external (foreign) creditors. But foreign exchange is not always the binding constraint either. If the government is the major debtor, an important indicator of repayment capacity is its ability to generate tax revenue that can be used to repay the debt. The importance of tax revenues points to the **internal transfer problem,** the government's challenge of raising enough revenue from households and firms to enable the government it to repay the nation's debts.

DEBT INDICATORS

Analysts typically turn these broad measures into ratios with the numerator containing either debt or debt service and the denominator showing a measure of the capacity to repay. The most common debt sustainability indicators include

- *Debt/GDP*, perhaps the broadest measure of debt sustainability, compares total debt to the economy's total capacity to generate resources to repay. A closely related measure uses the net present value: *NPV debt/GDP*. Where most debt is on market terms (e.g., commercial bank loans), the difference between these two measures is small; to the extent debts are contracted on concessional (subsidized) terms, the two differ. Although each country is different, history suggests that debt distress tends to be more likely in countries where the NPV debt/GDP ratio exceeds 30–50 percent.[1]

---

[1]International Monetary Fund, "Debt Sustainability in Low-Income Countries: Proposal for an Operational Framework and Policy Implications," February 3, 2004.

- *Debt/exports* (and NPV debt/exports) compares the total debt to the capacity to generate foreign exchange. A wide range of debt/export ratios might be compatible with sustainability, reflecting the tendency for exports to vary more widely than GDP. Analysts tend to place threshold levels for individuals countries anywhere between 100 and 300 percent, most frequently around 200 percent.
- *Debt/revenue* (or NPV debt/revenue) is most relevant when the government is the largest debtor and there are concerns about its ability to generate tax revenue to repay the loans. Analysts cite ratios of anywhere between 140 and 260 percent as thresholds for individual countries.
- *Debt service/exports* has the great advantage of focusing attention on the amount owed in a single year relative to the export earnings available to make the payments, but it tells less about the overall burden of debt over time. Concern about debt distress tends to grow when this ratio exceeds 20–25 percent.
- *Debt service/revenue* focuses on the government's ability to generate tax revenues to make payments due in a single year. The higher is this ratio, the more tax revenue that must be devoted to making debt payments and the less available for other government expenditures on health, education, infrastructure, or other purposes. History suggests that debt distress tends to appear once this ratio exceeds 10–15 percent.
- *Short-term foreign debt/foreign exchange reserves* focuses on the amount of debt due to be repaid within the next year compared to the available amount of foreign exchange reserves. Analysts suggest that a country is vulnerable to a rapid withdrawal of capital and a financial crisis when this ratio approaches 1:1.

These ratios reflect two broadly different ways that countries can face debt difficulties: insolvency and illiquidity. An **insolvent** borrower lacks the net worth to repay outstanding debts out of future earnings. An **illiquid** borrower lacks the ready cash to repay current debt-servicing obligations, even though it has the net worth to repay the debts in the long term. An illiquid debtor may need cash to make immediate payments, but still has the capacity to repay the debt over time, while an insolvent debtor does not have the income or assets to repay. The debt/GDP ratio in effect is a measure of overall solvency, indicating the value of debt relative to aggregate economic resources (in theory, ideally we would like a measure of overall wealth—the value of all assets—not just annual income, but this is extremely difficult to measure for a country). The debt service/exports, debt service/revenue, and short-term debt/reserves indicators are measures of liquidity, indicating whether a country has the capacity to make the payments due this year.

These ratios appear at first to be simplistic and mechanical, but each captures and depends on important broader features of both the debt and the economy. To see this, we examine two of the ratios in more depth: debt/exports and debt/GDP.

To explore the debt/export ratio, recall that foreign saving (F) equals the difference between imports and exports of goods and nonfactor services ($M - X$), or roughly the current account of the balance of payments. For simplicity, assume all foreign saving is in the form of borrowing. Therefore, the increase in debt in any year is

$$\Delta D = iD + M - X \qquad [15\text{--}1]$$

where ΔD represents the change in the debt stock and i is the average interest rate. For simplicity, assume that X and M grow at the same exponential rate, g_X. In that case, the stock of debt also grows exponentially at the same rate; and in the long run, the ratio of debt to exports settles at

$$D/X = a/(g_X - i) \qquad [15\text{--}2]$$

where a is the ratio of the current account deficit to exports, $(M - X)/X$, and is a constant, assuming that imports and exports grow at the same rate.[2]

Equation 15–2 tells us that the long-run ratio of debt to exports depends on the size of the current account deficit, the growth rate of exports, and the interest rate. If exports are growing faster than the average rate of interest ($g_X > i$), a country can continue to import more than it exports, meaning that a can remain positive. This should make intuitive sense: Borrowing to cover the gap between imports and exports is sustainable so long as exports are growing more than enough to cover interest payments.

Consider a numerical example. If the current account deficit as a share of exports were 8 percent ($a = 8$), the average interest rate were 5 percent, and exports were growing 9 percent a year, then the ratio of debt to exports would settle at 2 (or 200 percent). If exports grew faster than 9 percent, the debt-export ratio would fall. If, on the other hand, export growth fell to 5.5 percent, the debt/export ratio would explode to 1,600 percent. If it fell below the interest rate (either because export growth fell or world interest rates rose), the numerator a also would have to turn negative; that is, the current account deficit would turn to a surplus. The country could no longer run a deficit and borrow to make up the difference; instead it would have to run a surplus of exports over imports and use the balance to repay debts. This is precisely what has happened to many low-income, high-debt countries, with enormous adverse consequences in some cases.

---

[2]Equation 15–1 is solved to yield 15–2 by letting $\Delta D = g_X D$ and substituting into equation 15–1. Then 15–1 becomes $g_X D = iD + M - X$, from which 15–2 can be readily derived (hint: start by dividing each side by X). The result is given by Albert Fishlow, "External Borrowing and Debt Management," in Rudiger Dornbusch and F. Leslie C. H. Helmers, eds., *The Open Economy: Tools for Policymakers in Developing Countries* (New York: Oxford University Press, 1988), 220–21.

Turning to the debt/GDP ratio, instead of examining imports and exports, a similar calculation can be made from the investment-saving perspective. Since we know from Chapter 10 that the current account balance $M - X$ is equal to the investment-saving balance $I - S_d$, equation 15–1 can be converted to the following:

$$\Delta D = iD + I - S_d = iD + vY - sY = iD + (v - s)Y \qquad [15\text{–}3]$$

In this equation, $Y =$ GDP and v and s are the investment and saving shares of GDP, respectively. As with the trade balance perspective, assume that debt and GDP grow at the same exponential rate, g_Y. Then the long-run equilibrium ratio of debt to GDP is

$$D/Y = (v - s)/(g_Y - i) \qquad [15\text{–}4]$$

In this case, if investment exceeds saving by 1 percentage point, the growth rate of GDP (expressed in current dollars) is 7 percent a year, and i averages 5 percent, the debt-GDP ratio settles at 0.5 (or 50 percent). But, if GDP slips to a long-run rate of 5.5 percent, the ratio balloons to 200 percent.

Thus, a country with poor overall economic performance, reflected in low export or GDP growth rates, is far more likely to get into trouble than a country with better performance. Policy makers must take these factors into account in determining how much a country can borrow and on what terms. Strong debt management, however, goes beyond these basics and includes allowing for the risk of a sudden fall in export receipts, higher interest rates, or other adverse shocks. And, as we shall see, the terms on which the debt is obtained (especially the maturity structure) can have a profound impact on vulnerability to a crisis.

FROM DISTRESS TO DEFAULT

Many developing countries have seen their debt ratios climb to uncomfortable levels at one time or another during the last two decades. Sometimes, even countries with good economic management can get into debt difficulties when they face drops in export prices or unexpected increases in import prices, say, from an increase in world oil prices. As debt-service payment burdens grow and it becomes more difficult to service the debts, countries face several important questions and trade-offs. To what extent should they continue to raise taxes and cut spending in order to service debts? At what point do they try to renegotiate the terms of these loans, or in more extreme circumstances, consider outright default?

Most countries rightly see debt agreements as legal contracts in which they have an obligation to fully repay. Most want to avoid default, since it can have significant negative consequences, just as filing for bankruptcy can have adverse consequences for a company. A country defaulting on its debts is likely to have much more difficulty borrowing in the future, at least for some period of time, until their prospects brighten. When creditors begin to lend again, they are likely to charge higher interest rates to compensate for the higher risks. Moreover, the process of renegotiation and restructuring can be time consuming and costly and is something most finance officials would rather avoid. And most countries do not want the stigma and bad publicity that a default might generate.

At the same time, in extreme situations policy makers may see the costs of continuing to service their debts as outweighing the cost of default. Political leaders are willing to ask their citizens to undertake only so much austerity to repay foreign creditors. Moreover, sometimes, it might be fully appropriate for creditors to bear some of the cost of bad loans, especially if they pushed hard to provide funds for questionable projects. To the extent that creditors were partially responsible, they should absorb some of the costs through smaller repayments or even forgiveness of some of the remaining loan. Defaults are not uncommon for either private companies or public entities and certainly are not limited to developing countries (Box 15–1). Defaults occurred frequently in many Latin American and European countries during the nineteenth century and the 1930s. Several U.S. states defaulted on their debts in the nineteenth century.

In addition, it is possible that continued repayment might undermine a country's ability to make future payment to such an extent that both the debtor *and* the creditor would be better off with some debt forgiveness. This situation is known as a **debt overhang:** The debt creates such a drag on growth that it undermines the ability of the country to make repayments.[3] Inflows of foreign financing should have a positive impact on growth, but debt service has a negative impact. As debt service grows, the negative impact becomes larger, and with debt service large enough, the overall impact on growth could be negative.

To see how this could happen, consider the following scenario. A government starts to raise taxes to repay the debt, and private companies and individuals begin to anticipate even higher taxes in the future, so they reduce investment. The growing debt service burden makes lenders more reluctant to provide new finance, as they begin to fear the possibility of default. As debt burdens grow very large, the government begins to face perverse incentives against undertaking stringent adjustment measures. Economic reforms may help the country avoid default, but local citizens bear the cost of adjustment while creditors gain the benefits. Worse policies might lead to poorer economic performance but could lead to a larger debt write-off. Thus, the debt burden becomes a disincentive for the very economic reforms that might be most needed. Empirical evidence on

---

[3]Paul Krugman, 1988, "Financing versus Forgiving a Debt Overhang," *Journal of Development Economics* 29 (November), 253–68; Jeffrey Sachs, "The Debt Overhang of Developing Countries," in R. Findlay, G. Calvo, P. Kouri, and J. Braga de Macedo, eds., *Debt, Stabilization and Development: Essays in Honor of Carlos Diáz Alejandro* (Oxford: Basil Blackwell, 1989).

BOX 15-1 A SHORT HISTORY OF SOVEREIGN LENDING DEFAULT

In 1979, then-Citicorp chairman Walter Wriston famously pronounced that "countries don't go bankrupt." While it may technically be true that a country cannot go bankrupt, the assertion that they cannot default runs counter to the historical record. Default by governments is a practice as old as the concept of credit. Throughout history, there are many examples of countries that have refused to pay their bills or unilaterally written off debts incurred by previous governments.

The first such recorded default occurred in the fourth century B.C. when ten of thirteen Greek city-states with debts to the Delos Temple walked away from their contractual obligations. Not long after, the island of Chios announced publicly that payments on its unsustainable debt would cease until economic conditions improved. Default in ancient times often took the form of currency depreciation, rather than a declaration of bankruptcy. For example, over the course of the three Punic Wars (241–146 B.C.), Rome reduced the metallic content of its monetary unit from twelve ounces to one-half ounce, in a series of de facto government defaults.

The practice of governmental default continued through the Middle Ages and into modern times. An eighteenth-century French minister of finance contended that "each government should default at least once every century, in order to restore equilibrium"! In the nineteenth century, as the practice of lending abroad became more common, government default increased and most European nations at least partially defaulted on their debt commitments. Some defaulted multiple times, with Spain and its seven recorded defaults leading the way. The record in developing nations was similar: every Latin American nation without exception defaulted during the nineteenth century.

While the U.S. government avoided outright default, many individual states defaulted during this period. Some defaulted on civil war debts, while others did so on bonds issued to failed enterprises, usually railroad or bank endeavors. Arkansas and Florida each defaulted three times during the nineteenth century. And at the conclusion of the Spanish American War in 1898, the U.S. government repudiated the debts that had been incurred by Cuba while under Spanish rule.

Germany's reparation obligations following World War I led to protracted debt difficulties that nurtured German grievances in the early 1930s. In the wave of defaults that accompanied the Great Depression of the 1930s, the international capital market collapsed, thereby leading to further widespread default. International capital flows fell sharply during the Depression and World War II, so sovereign defaults were rare in the late 1940s and the 1950s. But the international capital markets gradually revived in the 1960s and 1970s, and the debt crises of the 1980s saw a return to the sovereign defaults that had been common in the nineteenth century.

Adapted from Nancy Birdsall and John Williamson (with Brian Deese), *Delivering on Debt Relief: From IMF Gold to New Aid Architecture,* Center for Global Development and Institute for International Economics, April 2002.

the existence of a debt overhang is mixed, but the idea has been influential in thinking about the rationale for debt restructuring and write-offs in developing countries.

Finally, while debt agreements are legal contracts, under some circumstances, governments may see the agreements as illegitimate, making default an easier option to contemplate. Debts taken on by a military dictator who took power through a coup and stole the money may not be seen as legitimate obligations by a succeeding democratically elected government. We discuss these **odious debts** later in the chapter.

The 1980s Debt Crisis

The questions about default and debt restructuring are much more than hypothetical possibilities: They became very real issues for many developing countries during the last several decades. During the 1970s a large number of developing countries, especially in Latin America, borrowed extensively and accumulated large amounts of debt, so large that, by 1983, long-term debt owed by developing countries to commercial banks had grown from $19 to $307 billion dollars, 16 times larger than it had been in 1970 (Table 15–2). Total debt stocks grew by a factor of 10 between 1970 and 1983, then doubled again in the ten years that followed. But the rapid growth of debt in the 1970s and early 1980s led to trouble for some countries that had accumulated too much debt too fast. In the first half of 1982, eight countries had to reschedule their debt payments (that is, negotiate new terms to stretch out repayment). In August 1982, Mexico stunned global markets by declaring that it could not make its debt payments,

TABLE 15-2. **Long-Term Debt, All Developing Countries, 1970–2003 (billion US$)**

	1970	1983	1993	2003
Stocks				
All sources	61	618	1,316	1,960
Official creditors	33	218	697	805
Private creditors	28	400	619	1,155
Of which, commerical banks	19	307	304	580
Net Flows				
All sources	6.8	50.3	72.6	4.3
Official creditors	3.3	24.3	24.0	−14.3
Private creditors	3.5	26.0	48.6	20.3
Of which, commerical banks	2.4	17.9	4.7	2.5

Source: World Bank, *Global Development Finance 2005*.

signaling the beginning of a much broader series of debt crises affecting dozens of countries. From 1983 to 1987, more than $300 billion of debt repayments had to be rescheduled. Now, almost 30 years later, the effects of these crises are still reverberating in some countries, and the lessons learned are crucial for future economic management in developing countries.

Causes of the Crisis

The crisis resulted from several things going wrong at once: adverse international economic shocks outside of the control of the debtor countries, poor domestic economic management, and bad lending decisions by international banks.[4]

INTERNATIONAL ECONOMIC SHOCKS

In 1973, the Organization of Petroleum Exporting Countries (OPEC) announced that it would restrict oil production, sparking a very sharp increase in world oil prices. Import values and trade deficits immediately increased for oil importers around the world (including developing countries), slowed global economic growth (hampering export markets for many developing countries), and created volatility in a wide range of other commodity markets. In 1979, OPEC again cut back its production, leading to even larger increases in oil prices.

At the same time, the United States' economy was facing a combination of slow growth and accelerating prices. With the economy under pressure, in August 1971, President Richard Nixon released the dollar from the gold standard that had determined its value since the end of World War II. This move led to a sharp depreciation of the dollar and an increase in currency volatility and uncertainty around the world. Large budget deficits emanating from spending on the Vietnam war and the sharp hike in world oil prices added to the pressure. By the end of the 1970s, U.S. inflation reached double digits and interest rates rose very sharply, reaching 16 percent in 1981. The increase in interest rates substantially increased the interest burden for developing country debtors, whose original loans were written with variable interest rates. For a group of 15 countries in Central and South America, the rise in interest rates between 1978 and 1981 added over $13 billion to the costs of servicing their debts in 1981 alone.

[4]A huge literature examines the 1980s debt crisis. We cite some of the key works here. Jeffrey D. Sachs, ed., *Developing Country Debt and Economic Performance* (Cambridge, MA: National Bureau of Economic Research, 1989–1990): Vol. 1, *The International Financial System;* Vol. 2, *Country Studies: Argentina, Bolivia, Brazil, Mexico;* Vol. 3 (with Susan Collins), *Country Studies: Indonesia, Korea, the Philippines, Turkey;* summary volume, *Developing Country Debt and the World Economy.* William Cline, *International Debt: Systematic Risk and Policy Response* (Washington, DC: Institute for International Economics, 1984); *International Debt Reexamined* (Washington, DC: Institute for International Economics, 1995). Ishrat Husain and Ishac Diwan, eds., *Dealing with the Debt Crisis* (Washington, DC: World Bank, 1989), and Joseph Kraft, *The Mexican Rescue* (New York: Group of Thirty, 1984).

DOMESTIC ECONOMIC POLICIES

Even in the face of these shocks, not all debtors suffered equally. South Korea and Indonesia were among the world's largest debtors, yet sound economic policies enabled them to service their debt while continuing to grow throughout the 1980s. In particular, these countries responded by reducing their budget deficits, restraining the expansion of domestic demand, and encouraging export production. But in many other countries, reactions by policy makers exacerbated the crisis.

In the face of rising imports and trade deficits, escalating prices, and growing budget deficits, it was much easier for governments to convince themselves that the oil crisis would be short-lived rather than try to limit demand. Many believed they could borrow to cover the deficits (from either their central banks or from foreign banks) and even increase spending, rather than restrain demand and close the deficits. But this strategy, while perhaps politically expedient in the short run, could not be sustained and typically led to even higher rates of inflation and larger debts.

At the same time, some governments tried to compensate for rising import prices by maintaining an overvalued exchange rate, which restrains price increases for imports and exportable goods. This step is popular with consumers because it makes imports cheaper, but it discourages export growth and encourages capital flight. More generally, countries that had been actively promoting manufactured exports, mainly in East Asia, were in a better position to further spur exports and close their deficits than countries that followed a less open trade strategy, such as in Latin America. Ultimately, countries with overvalued exchange rates and less-active export promotion strategies faced larger current account deficits and, therefore, larger borrowing needs. Instead of improving, their debt crises just got worse.

IMPRUDENT BANK LENDING

The foreign banks also bear some responsibility for making poor lending decisions. Banks were more than happy to keep lending to governments, even after the economic situation began to deteriorate and normal lending strategies suggested more prudence. Banks believed that, since the debts were **sovereign** (that is, either contracted or guaranteed by governments), they did not have to worry as much about the normal risks of default. And once the banks were heavily involved, further lending seemed a sensible way to keep debtor countries liquid enough to continue servicing earlier loans. Banks were encouraged by their own governments and the international agencies, all of which hoped that more lending would help countries grow out of the crisis, especially once the world economy recovered from its instability.

Impact on the Borrowers

Once it became clear that many debtors would be unable to meet their obligations, the commercial banks stopped making new loans. From 1980 to 1982, private creditors provided more than $50 billion a year in new lending to developing countries; in 1987, the net resource flow was essentially zero.

The impact on the most indebted countries was severe. In effect, countries very quickly had to turn from net borrowers into net repayers of loans. We know that net capital inflows always must equal the current account deficit, which in turn is equal to the balance of investment over domestic saving:

$$\text{Net capital inflows} = M - X = I - S_d \qquad [15\text{--}5]$$

Prior to the crisis, foreign borrowing (and other capital inflows) allowed the countries to finance imports in excess of exports and investment in excess of saving. But when countries began to default on the loans, banks demanded immediate repayment and reduced new lending. In the absence of other new capital inflows, countries had to reverse the signs and run a surplus of exports over imports and of saving over investment. Economic growth fell abruptly. Many governments found it difficult to raise taxes and reduce spending (to increase domestic saving), so they resorted to inflationary financing, which further destabilized the economy.

These kinds of dramatic changes were clearly evident in Mexico before and after the 1982 crisis, as shown in Table 15–3. In the five years up to and including 1981, imports exceeded exports in Mexico by the equivalent of about 2 percent of GDP and investment exceeded domestic saving by the same amount. There

TABLE 15-3. **Mexico before and after the 1982 Debt Crisis**

	BEFORE THE CRISIS, 1977–81	AFTER THE CRISIS, 1982–86
Exports of goods and services (% of GDP)	9.6	16.9
Imports of goods and services (% of GDP)	11.5	10.6
Resource balance (% of GDP)	−2.0	6.3
Gross domestic investment (% of GDP)	24.7	20.4
Gross domestic savings (% of GDP)	22.7	26.7
Saving-investment gap (% of GDP)	−2.0	6.3
Gross domestic investment (real, average annual growth)	13.0	−12.2
GDP (real, average annual growth %)	7.6	−0.6
GDP per capita (real, average annual growth %)	5.0	−2.9
Inflation, consumer prices (average annual %)	23.7	73.2

Source: World Bank, *World Development Indicators.*

was strong growth in investment, GDP, and GDP per capita. But the crisis changed everything. Between 1982 and 1986, imports fell and exports expanded sharply, providing the trade surplus necessary to pay foreign creditors. The **resource balance** (the excess of exports over imports, and the opposite of net capital inflows) shifted by a huge 8.3 percent of GDP (from –2 percent to +6.3 percent). Investment fell by over 4 percent of GDP, and domestic saving rose by a similar amount. GDP per capita fell, the budget deficit grew, and inflation skyrocketed to 73 percent per year.

These kinds of adjustments were not limited to Mexico. Between 1978 and 1981, a group of 15 heavily indebted countries imported about $9 billion more than they exported. But from 1983 to 1988, they were forced into a reverse transfer of almost $34 billion a year to service their debt. From 1970 to 1981, these countries had enjoyed per capita income growth of 2.7 percent a year, invested 25 percent of their GDP, and tolerated inflation of 39 percent a year on average. During the debt crisis, however, from 1982 to 1988, GDP growth per capita was –0.7 percent a year, investment fell to 18 percent of GDP, and annual inflation grew to 149 percent.[5]

Escape from the Crisis, for Some Countries

For the international commercial banks and many of the countries that had borrowed from them, especially the middle-income countries, the debt crisis of the 1980s essentially was over by the mid-1990s. For other countries (mainly low-income countries in sub-Saharan Africa, South Asia, and Central America) that had borrowed predominantly from other governments and the international financial institutions, the debt crisis lingered unresolved into the new century.

Debt ratios improved substantially for Latin American countries from the 1980s to the 1990s and were much lower in 2003 compared to their previous high levels (Table 15–4). Latin American debtors worked out of insolvency through debt relief agreements that involved a combination of several forms of debt restructuring and reorganization:

- *Refinancing*, involving making new loans to repay the old. In a refinancing, the amount of debt owed does not change, but the terms for repayments are eased, usually through longer repayment periods and perhaps lower interest rates.
- *Rescheduling*, closely related to refinancing, in which the original loans stay on the books, but the schedule of payments is altered to allow longer repayment periods and possibly lower interest rates.

[5]Rudiger Dornbusch, "Background Paper," in Twentieth Century Fund Task Force on International Debt, *The Road to Economic Recovery* (New York: Priority Publications, 1989), p. 31.

TABLE 15-4. **Debt Ratios, Developing Countries, 1980–2003 (percent)**

	MAXIMUM	
	1980–97	2003
All developing countries		
Long-term debt to GNP	43	30
Long-term debt to exports	203	90
Total debt service to exports	33	16
Latin American countries		
Long-term debt to GNP	60	38
Long-term debt to exports	343	149
Total debt service to exports	48	29
Selected countries: Total debt service to exports		2002
Argentina	83	13
Bolivia	63	26
Brazil	82	61
Chile	71	32
Mexico	51	23

Source: *Global Development Finance 2004.*

- *Reduction,* in which the amount actually owed is reduced (i.e., for-given), either partly (a write-down) or completely (a write-off).
- *Buybacks,* whereby the debtor buys the loan from the creditor, usually for a percentage of the face value of the debt. Creditors might prefer getting an assured payment today for part of the debt rather than taking the risk of less payment later.
- *Debt-equity swaps,* in which creditors are given equity in a company (such as a state-owned telecommunications company) in return for eliminating the debt outstanding.

Strategies to resolve the 1980s debt crisis evolved slowly in two broad stages. In 1985, nearly three years after Mexico first defaulted, U.S. Secretary of the Treasury James Baker announced what came to be known as the **Baker Plan.** This two-pronged strategy involved providing new finance to the debtor countries in return for them undertaking significant economic reforms aimed at stabilizing their economies and reducing their current account deficits. The plan did not reduce the amount of debt; it was based on the assumption that, with enough new financing and economic adjustment, the debtor countries could begin to grow and would fully repay the banks.

Financing was provided in part by the creditor banks refinancing and restructuring existing debts and partly through new funds provided by the IMF, World Bank, and official aid agencies. The new financing provided some breathing room for the debtors, as it reduced the amount of immediate adjustment necessary in the current account deficit. But adjustment was still necessary. The policy adjustment programs involved a range of steps aimed at reducing deficits in the government budget and the balance of payments, containing inflation, stimulating savings, and generating more resources for investment and debt service. These **stabilization and structural adjustment programs,** which were designed and overseen by the IMF and World Bank, typically involved devaluing the currency (or allowing it to depreciate through a float) to reduce imports and stimulate exports, cutting government expenditures, raising taxes, reducing growth in the money supply, and closing loss-making state companies.

These programs, already discussed in Chapter 5, were controversial, and the austerity measures created huge burdens on the ordinary citizens of debtor countries in the form of reduced income, higher taxes and fees, reduced services from government, and other adjustments. Critics argued that, while some of these steps were necessary, the programs were not always well designed and required more austerity than was necessary while creating little burden for the creditors. Although it was hoped that this combination of new money and policy reforms eventually would allow countries to resume growth and fully repay the banks, in the end, the Baker Plan proved insufficient to resolve the debt crisis.

The key breakthrough came in 1989, when new U.S. Secretary of the Treasury Nicholas Brady unveiled a different strategy, this time incorporating the idea that the value of the debt would be written down and the commercial banks would share in some of the losses. The **Brady Plan** recognized that debtor countries needed a permanent reduction of their debt burdens to get back on sound economic footing. The strategy called for banks and debtor governments to renegotiate debts on a case-by-case basis from a "menu" of options including reducing the face value of the debt, reducing the interest rate, providing new loans, and other forms of restructuring. The debtor countries issued new bonds to the banks, called **Brady bonds,** to replace the old debt. The amount of debt relief encompassed in these deals varied from country to country. Mexico's commercial bank debt was reduced by about 35 percent, whereas Costa Rica's was reduced by about 65 percent. By May 1994, Brady deals were in place covering about $190 billion in debt for 18 countries, including Poland, Ecuador, Venezuela, the Philippines, Brazil, Peru, the Ivory Coast, and other countries. Over $60 billion in debt had been forgiven. As with the Baker Plan, the new scheme included stabilization and structural adjustment programs under the auspices of the IMF and World Bank, new lending from these organizations, and bilateral debt relief.

The key to the program was the recognition by the international community and the creditor banks that by continuing to insist on full repayment, they were undermining the strength of these economies and ultimately receiving less repayment than they would under a negotiated settlement. By the early 1990s, growth had resumed and prices had stabilized. Net capital inflows, after falling to $10 billion per year between 1983 and 1989, rose to $60 billion in 1992. Debt reduction alone could not have solved the crisis, but debt reduction combined with new financing, strong adjustment efforts by the countries themselves and, importantly, the revival of the world economy in the early 1990s, helped bring an end to the crisis, at least for some countries. A similar approach would be adopted for other heavily indebted nations almost a decade later.

THE DEBT CRISIS IN LOW-INCOME COUNTRIES

Although the debt crisis effectively ended in the early 1990s for most middle-income countries that had borrowed heavily from commercial banks, it continued for many low-income countries, especially many countries in Africa. Most of the debts of these countries are owed to either official multilateral organizations, such as the IMF and World Bank, or to donor governments, rather than to commercial banks. Thus, although the terms of the debts were more generous (and usually subsidized), the Brady Plan was not a solution for these countries, since it was designed for commercial banks, ultimately providing the creditor with new bonds that it could sell on private bond markets. Different approaches were needed for these countries.

Low-income countries borrowed in the 1970s and 1980s for many of the same reasons as other developing countries. They were hit by the same set of strong international economic shocks: high oil import prices, low commodity prices, the end of the gold standard, and weak market demand in the industrialized countries. These challenges were even more difficult to meet in the poorest countries, which had a limited number of well-trained financial and economic experts, many of which had gained their independence only recently and had new and untested government institutions. The impact of these shocks was exacerbated in many countries by a prolonged period of economic mismanagement. Governments kept budget deficits high, erected significant barriers to trade, distorted market prices, and failed to provide basic infrastructure and health and education services.

Even where economic policies later improved, however, growth remained elusive, partly because many of these countries also face very difficult geographical challenges, such as being landlocked, located in the tropics (where disease is much more virulent), or located in or near the Sahara Desert. Several currently are ravaged by the HIV/AIDS pandemic, which further undermines their capacity for sustained economic growth and repayment of debt.

As with the debt crisis in Latin America, creditors sometimes added to the crisis by making loans for bad projects (many designed by the very same donors that provided the loans), although in this case the major creditors were government and multilateral agencies rather than commercial banks. In some cases industrialized country governments provided loans for poor investments and grandiose consumption projects in an attempt to win countries over to one side or the other of the Cold War. Some Western loans supported corrupt governments that had little intention or capability of repaying the loans to finance presidential palaces, showcase steel mills, and other wasteful expenditures.

During the 1980s and early 1990s, the international community's strategy for the low-income countries had two components, similar to the original Baker plan: provide new finance in return for significant economic reforms in the hopes that the debtor countries could grow out of their difficulties. Beginning in 1988, the financing was augmented by partial write-downs from government creditors. Multilateral creditors, including the IMF, World Bank, or other multilateral organizations (such as the African and Asian Development Banks) offered no write-downs until 1996.

Debt Reduction in Low-Income Countries

Individual creditor governments provide debt rescheduling and debt reduction through an informal group called the **Paris Club.** The governments of the United States, the United Kingdom, Japan, Germany, France, and 14 other creditor countries coordinate to offer common terms for debt restructuring to each debtor. The first meeting was in 1956, when Argentina met with a group of its creditors in Paris. Since that time, the Paris Club has negotiated over 400 agreements with at least 80 different countries. Until 1988, all Paris Club agreements involved debt rescheduling rather than reduction. Since then, agreements typically provide debt rescheduling for middle-income countries and partial debt reduction coupled with rescheduling for low-income countries. The first debt reduction deals in 1988 provided 33 percent reduction for certain qualifying debts; by 1999, the Paris Club was providing 90 percent reduction for at least some debts owed by certain countries. Many creditor governments have gone further and provided 100 percent debt relief in some circumstances.

The arguments for providing debt relief to the poorest countries were similar but not identical to those made for the middle-income countries. The first argument was a variant of debt overhang: The debts were so large that they were impeding growth and development, partially by undermining private sector incentives, but also by impeding the government's ability to make critical investments in health, education, and infrastructure.

The second argument was that the creditor governments and institutions should not have been providing so much of their financing as loans to the world's poorest countries in the first place, since history suggested that accelerating growth sufficiently to repay the loans would be a major challenge. The world's poorest countries have had the most difficulty in initiating and sustaining growth, for reasons that we discussed: adverse geography, disease burdens, weak institutions, frequent climate and trade shocks, and poor policies. Providing loans to these countries rather than outright grants was based on the presumption that growth could be turned around relatively easily, providing these countries with the basis to repay their loans. But for many of the world's poorest countries, growth rates remained low, debts piled up, and many countries were able to service their loans only by receiving new loans.

The third argument is that creditors knowingly lent money to dictatorships to garner their political support, even when the dictators wasted and stole the money. Once the dictators left, the citizens of the country were left with the responsibility of repaying these debts. The Democratic Republic of the Congo, formerly Zaire, piled up large debts under the ruthless dictatorship of Mobutu Sese Seko, as Western donors happily lent him more money, even when it was obvious that most of the money was wasted or stolen. Many argue that *odious debts* (obligations accumulated by an illegitimate government in the name of a country) should be forgiven, with the costs born by the creditor (Box 15–2). The United States, which often has resisted attempts by some countries to claim odious debts, pushed hard in 2004 for other countries to forgive debts owed by Iraq. Although the United States was careful to avoid the term odious debt because of the legal precedent, it nonetheless argued that Iraq's debts were amassed by an illegitimate dictator and were a large impediment to future growth. In November 2004, the Paris Club agreed to cancel over \$29 billion of Iraq's debts and reschedule and additional \$7 billion, by far the largest debt forgiveness operation ever undertaken for a single country.

The Heavily Indebted Poor-Country Initiative

By the middle of the 1990s, it was becoming increasingly clear that some of the poorest and most heavily indebted countries would not be able to repay their debts. Most of these countries almost never actually defaulted on their debt payments: Instead, as the debt payments grew, the creditors lent them new money so they could repay the old, a strategy known as **defensive lending** (since the loans defend the creditor against the possibility of the debtor defaulting). But this strategy could not be sustained indefinitely, and debt levels continued to grow while growth rates remained stubbornly low.

In 1996, the international community recognized that deeper debt reduction would be necessarily. The World Bank and IMF, in conjunction with other multilateral agencies and creditor governments, launched the rather awkwardly named *heavily indebted poor-country* (HIPC) initiative.[6] The HIPCs include 38

[6]For a thorough analysis of the HIPC program and related debt issues, see Nancy Birdsall and John Williamson (with Brian Deese), *Delivering on Debt Relief: From IMF Gold to New Aid Architecture* (Washington, DC: Center for Global Development and Institute for International Economics, April 2002).

BOX 15-2 ODIOUS DEBT

Under the law in many countries, *individuals* do not have to repay if others fraudulently borrow in their name and *corporations* are not liable for contracts that their chief executive officers enter into without proper authority. The legal doctrine of odious debt makes an analogous argument that sovereign debt that is incurred without the consent of the people and that does not benefit the people should not be transferable to a successor government, especially if creditors are aware of these facts in advance. But many developing countries carry debt incurred by rulers who borrowed without the people's consent and who used the funds either to repress the people or for personal gain.

The doctrine of odious debt originated in 1898 after the Spanish American War. During peace negotiations, the United States argued that neither it nor Cuba should be responsible for debt the colonial rulers had incurred without the consent of the Cuban people and had not used for their benefit. Although Spain never accepted the validity of this argument, the United States implicitly prevailed, and Spain took responsibility for the Cuban debt under the Paris peace treaty.

Though legal scholars elaborated the details of the doctrine of odious debt, it has gained little momentum within the international legal community—still, many countries could qualify. For example, through the 1980s, South Africa's apartheid regime borrowed from private banks, devoting a large percentage of its budget to financing the military and police and repressing the black majority. The South African people now bear the debts of their repressors. Despite appeals—from the archbishop of Cape Town and South Africa's Truth and Reconciliation Commission—to have the apartheid-era debt written off, the postapartheid government has accepted responsibility for it, perhaps out of fear that defaulting would make the country seem not to be playing by the rules of capitalism and would hurt its chances of attracting foreign investment. South Africa is not poor enough to qualify for debt relief under the HIPC Initiative.

Among other dramatic instances of odious debt, Anastasio Somoza was reported to have looted $100–500 million from Nicaragua by the time he was overthrown in 1979; Ferdinand Marcos amassed a personal fortune of $10 billion in the Philippines; Mobutu Sese Seko expropriated a reported $4 billion from the Democratic Republic of the Congo (then Zaire); and Jean-Claude Duvalier reportedly absconded with $900 million from Haiti. Some of the money that built these fortunes was drawn from amounts that these dictators borrowed in the name of their people. Recently, the United States successfully argued that debts accumulated by Saddam Hussein in Iraq were illegitimate and should be forgiven, although, to avoid setting a legal precedent for other countries to follow, the United States did not use the "odious debt" terminology. The international community forgave over $29 billion in Iraqi debt in 2004.

Economists Michael Kremer and Seema Jayachandran have argued for the creation of an independent institution to assess whether regimes are legitimate and declare sovereign debt incurred by illegitimate regimes odious and thus not the obligation of successor governments.

Adapted from Michael Kremer and Seema Jayachandran, "Odious Debts," *Finance and Development* 39-2 (June 2002).

countries with per capita incomes below $900 (converted using official exchange rates rather than PPP) and with NPV debt/export ratios exceeding 150 percent.[7] Most had much higher debts. From 1982 to 1992, the NPV debt/export ratio deteriorated from an average of 266 percent to 620 percent for the HIPCs. The new initiative had two key features, deeper debt relief from bilateral government creditors (initially up to 80 percent of qualifying debts, then in 1999 up to 90 percent), and for the first time ever, partial write-downs of debts owed to the multilateral agencies.

The first version of the HIPC initiative turned out to be too cumbersome and time consuming to be effective. In the first three years, only five countries received debt relief, and the amounts involved were relatively small. In 1999 a new, "enhanced" HIPC initiative was introduced to provide more relief and provide it more quickly.

To be eligible for debt reduction, a country must first establish a track record of good economic policies, as determined by the IMF and World Bank, usually including a stable macroeconomic environment, lower trade restrictions, policies to support private-sector growth, and strengthening of the financial and legal systems. Countries must develop **Poverty Reduction Strategy Papers,** detailing their plans for growth, development, and poverty reduction. Once countries establish this track record, they reach the **decision point,** where creditors provide interim relief; that is, they forgive debt payments as they fall due, but do not yet forgive the stock of debt. Countries that maintain strong economic policies for an additional year or more and carry out specific reforms determined at the decision point reach the **completion point,** at which time they receive irrevocable debt reduction.

Under the program as it was conducted until 2005, countries that reach the completion point received debt reduction sufficient to reduce their NPV debt/export ratio to 150 percent, a level the IMF and World Bank deem to be the threshold for sustainable debt for low-income countries. Two features of this approach are noteworthy. First, a single threshold level is used for all countries. Basic economics would suggest that each country can sustain a different level of debt, but politically and institutionally, it was simpler for these organizations to treat all countries the same. Second, note that whereas the Paris Club forgives a percentage of debt, HIPC forgives the excess over the threshold. Thus, a country with a NPV debt/export ratio of 200 percent would receive 25 percent debt forgiveness, while a country with a 300 percent ratio would receive a 50 percent write-off.

[7]In certain circumstances, where countries have very open economies and the NPV/export ratio may not be appropriate (because large exports drive down the ratio), countries qualify if the NPV debt/revenue ratio is above 250 percent. For more information on HIPC, see the World Bank website at www.worldbank.org/hipc/.

In 2005, the shareholders of the IMF, World Bank, and African Development Bank decided to go a step further and offer 100 percent forgiveness of all obligations owed to the three organizations for countries that reached the completion point. This step represented a major change and is the first time any of the organizations provided 100 percent forgiveness.

As of mid-2005, 18 HIPC countries had reached completion point, 9 were at the decision point, and 11 others (several mired in civil conflict) were technically eligible but had made little progress. The 27 countries that reached their decision or completion points had received debt relief amounting to $54 billion. The average debt service/export ratio fell from an average of about 16 percent in 1998 to 7 percent in 2004, while debt service/revenues fell from 24 percent to 12 percent. In many countries, the benefits from the program were already evident. For example, Ghana used its savings to construct 509 new classroom blocks around the country, provide microcredit to about 43,000 farmers, and fund 560 sanitation and 141 water projects. Both Uganda (Box 15–3) and Tanzania used some of their saving to eliminate primary school fees, leading to sharp increases in school enrolment.

The HIPC initiative demonstrates that, even after policy makers decided that some debt forgiveness is warranted, they face several key questions. These issues are more difficult in forgiving debts owed to government and multilateral institutions, since market-based mechanisms are less relevant. Which countries should be eligible, and which should not (that is, what are the right cutoffs for "poor" and "heavily indebted")? How much debt should be forgiven and over what time frame? Should the debtors be expected to undertake policy conditions in return for debt relief, and if so, what conditions (and determined by whom)? How should the cost burden be shared? There are no obvious right or wrong answers to these questions, since they involve economic, financial, political, and institutional considerations, so these issues continue to be major challenges for policy makers in the years ahead.

EMERGING MARKET FINANCIAL CRISES

International capital flows played a central role in a series of financial crises that struck several developing countries starting in the mid-1990s, including Argentina, Brazil, Ecuador, Indonesia, Korea, Mexico, Russia, Thailand, Turkey, Uruguay, and Venezuela. These crises had some similarities with the 1980s and HIPC debt crises, but some critical differences as well. In most cases they struck very suddenly and ferociously, with enormous economic and financial consequences in a matter of weeks and months. Moreover, several of the worst-hit countries previously had strong economic performance and been favorites of

BOX 15-3 DEBT RELIEF IN UGANDA

When Uganda gained its independence from Britain in 1962, there was wide-spread optimism that its vibrant agricultural base and diverse, talented people could provide the basis for sustained economic development. However, political instability in the late 1960s and a 1971 coup led by Idi Amin ushered in a long period of political terror and economic destruction. By the time Yoweri Musevini assumed power in 1986, Uganda was one of the poorest countries in the world. Food production had fallen by a third in fifteen years; average income had declined by over 40 percent; and life expectancy was just forty-eight years.

The new government embarked on a broad-based economic rebuilding program that focused on rehabilitating infrastructure, restoring macroeconomic balance, lowering barriers to trade, and investing in the social sectors. In the fifteen years that followed, the economy staged a remarkable recovery. Average income increased by nearly 60 percent, and the share of the population living below the poverty line fell from 56 to 44 percent. By the mid-1990s, however, Uganda had accumulated a substantial debt burden. By 1993, total external debt was more than twelve times the value of annual exports, one of the highest such ratios in the world (total debt equal to twice the value of exports is generally considered a heavy burden). Two thirds of the debt was owed to multilateral agencies, so the traditional methods for debt relief (for private sector or bilateral debt) had limited potential.

In April 1998, Uganda was the first country to become eligible for debt reduction under the HIPC initiative. In the first formulation of the program, Uganda received about $650 million in debt relief, reducing its $3.2 billion debt stock by about 20 percent. Two years later, Uganda became the first country to qualify for the enhanced HIPC program, which offered deeper debt relief. This second phase reduced Uganda's debts by about $1.3 billion, bringing the total debt reduction to approximately $2 billion. These steps reduced Uganda's debt service payments by about $80 million per year, or about two thirds of debt service payments due. In 2005, Uganda became eligible for 100 percent forgiveness of debts owed to the IMF, World Bank, and African Development Banks. Uganda's early success with the program was encouraging: It sharply increased the net primary school enrollment rate from 62 to 86 percent between 1992 and 2003, raised investments in farm-to-market roads by 75 percent, and brought the share of the urban population with access to safe water from 54 percent in 2000 to 65 percent in 2003 (however, the country also increased its military spending in response to regional conflicts). GDP per capita grew about 3.6 percent between 1995 and 2004, increasing average income by over 40 percent.

This information is drawn primarily from the World Bank websites on the HIPC program and the country page for Uganda (www.worldbank.org).

the international capital markets. These crises led to dramatic falls in GDP and investment, major disruptions of trade and banking relationships, widespread unemployment, and increases in poverty. They also led to widespread rethinking of both the role of foreign capital flows (especially short-term flows) and the proper timing and sequencing of financial liberalization in the development process.

At the heart of these crises were huge, sudden reversals of international private capital flows. Economies that had been receiving relatively large amounts of private capital suddenly were faced with withdrawals of lines of credit, demands to repay debts, an exodus of portfolio capital, and offshore flight by domestic investors. Table 15–5 shows both the rapid buildup in lending and the depth and speed of the subsequent reversal in capital flows for five Asian crisis economies: Indonesia, Malaysia, the Philippines, South Korea, and Thailand. Net private capital flows to these five countries more than doubled *in just two years,* from $40 billion in 1994 to $103 billion in 1996. Net commercial bank lending alone nearly tripled from $24 billion to $65 billion. But, in the last six months of 1997, the private capital inflow of $103 billion suddenly turned into an outflow of $1 billion. This net reversal of capital flows of $104 billion was equivalent to about 10 percent of the combined precrisis GDPs of these five countries. Mexico suffered a similar fate during its 1994 crisis. The reversal in capital flows amounted to $40 billion over two years, equivalent to about 9 percent of GDP. Other crisis countries followed a similar pattern. With withdrawals of those magnitudes, it is little wonder these countries were plunged into crisis.

As must be the case, the reversals in capital flow immediately led to dramatic changes in trade balances, saving-investment gaps, and overall economic activity. In the five Asian crisis countries, current account balances changed from deficits averaging 5 percent of GDP in 1996 to surpluses averaging 5 percent of GDP in 1998. Economic output fell sharply in each of the crisis countries in either the year of the crisis or the year after (depending mainly on how early

TABLE 15-5. **Five Asian Economies: Private External Financing before and after the Crises (billion US$)**

	1994	1995	1996	1997	1998
Net private flows	40.5	77.4	103.2	−1.1	−28.3
Equity investment	12.2	15.5	19.7	3.6	8.5
Private creditors	28.2	61.8	83.5	−4.7	−36.8
Commercial banks	24.0	49.5	65.3	−25.6	−35.0
Nonbank private creditors	4.2	12.4	18.2	21.0	−1.7

Note: The economies of South Korea, Indonesia, Malaysia, Thailand, and the Philippines.
Source: Institute of International Finance, Inc. "Capital Flows to Emerging Market Economies," January, 1999.

TABLE 15-6. GDP Growth before and after the Crisis

COUNTRY	YEAR OF CRISIS	REAL ANNUAL GDP GROWTH (PERCENT)			
		YEAR PRECEDING CRISIS	YEAR OF CRISIS	YEAR AFTER CRISIS	TWO YEARS AFTER CRISIS
Argentina	1995	5.8	−2.8	5.5	8.1
Argentina	2001	−0.8	−4.4	−10.9	7.0
Brazil	1998	3.3	0.1	0.8	4.4
Indonesia	1997	7.6	4.7	−13.1	0.8
Korea	1997	6.8	5.0	−6.7	10.9
Malaysia	1997	10.0	7.3	−7.4	6.1
Mexico	1995	4.4	−6.2	5.2	6.8
The Philippines	1997	5.8	5.2	−0.6	3.4
Thailand	1997	5.9	−1.4	−10.5	4.4
Turkey	1994	8.0	−5.5	7.2	7.0
Turkey	2001	7.4	−7.5	7.8	4.8
Venezuela	1994	0.3	−2.3	4.0	−0.2

Source: World Bank, *World Development Indicators 2004.*

or late in the year the crisis struck), as shown in Table 15–6. The plunges in GDP growth in Argentina, Indonesia, and Thailand were particularly large. The poor were especially hard hit. For example, urban day laborers trying to eke out a subsistence living by loading trucks or working on construction sites suddenly were thrown out of work. Poverty rates in Indonesia doubled by official estimates from 12 percent to around 22 percent, with some unofficial estimates suggesting even higher levels.

Almost as striking as the collapse in growth was the speed of the rebound, at least in some countries. Argentina, Korea, Malaysia, Mexico, and Turkey all recorded GDP growth of 5 percent or more two years after their respective crises. As we shall see, the relatively rapid recovery is at least partly a reflection of the central role played by creditor panic in many of these crises.

How did the crises happen? The affected countries had several characteristics in common. First, they tended to be middle-income and upper-middle-income countries that had been growing quickly. Second, all had received large flows of private international capital, much of it with short-term maturity structures. Third, they recently had liberalized their financial systems and had recorded a very rapid—perhaps too rapid—expansion of bank lending and other financial services. Fourth, most of the crisis countries had exchange rates heavily controlled by their central banks, often strictly fixed (or pegged) to the U.S. dollar. Fifth, some countries, but not all, had large government budget deficits financed by a combination of borrowing from local and overseas banks and bondholders. These similarities suggest that government policies contributed to the crises, especially banking, financial, and exchange rate policies. However, the quick recovery in several countries, the fact that crises struck so many countries in such a short period of time, and the consistent pattern of rapid buildup and then withdrawal of private foreign capital all suggest that flaws in the operations of international capital markets played an important role as well.

Domestic Economic Weaknesses

Each of the crisis countries had liberalized its financial systems in the late 1980s and early 1990s and had done it in ways that inadvertently left the financial systems fragile and overextended. Entry requirements were eased for banks and other financial institutions, allowing new private banks to open. Governments removed regulations that controlled interest rates and forced banks to allocate credit to particular firms and investment projects, so banks had more flexibility in their lending and interest rate decisions. At the same time, banks were given much greater freedom to raise funds through offshore borrowing, indeed in some countries government policies actively encouraged banks to borrow from foreign banks and relend to domestic companies. In Thailand, total foreign liabilities of banks and financial institutions rose from 5 percent of GDP in 1990 to 28 percent of GDP in 1995, mostly reflecting Thai banks borrowing from foreign commercial banks. The combination of theses changes led to very rapid increases in domestic lending by banks, which grew by the equivalent of more than 50 percent of GDP in just seven years in South Korea, Malaysia, and Thailand.

Of course, financial liberalization can bring about many benefits to developing countries, including the mobilization of additional resources, reduced intermediation costs, and improved allocation of credit. The problem was not financial liberalization per se but how it was done, especially how rapidly it was done. The speed and magnitude of the expansion of financial activities outstripped the government's ability to establish strong legal and supervisory institutions to safeguard the system. Central banks did not have supervisors with the skills and authority necessary to determine which banks were vulnerable and take steps to penalize or close poorly performing institutions. Bank regulations were weak, poorly enforced, or both. In some cases, supervisors were pressured (or bribed) to overlook violations by banks with politically influential owners. As a result, some banks were undercapitalized, nonperforming loans were at high levels, and many prudential regulations were broken with no penalty. Over time, loans tended to go to weaker investment projects and the quality of banks' loan portfolios deteriorated. This left the banks (and the financial systems more broadly) in a vulnerable situation. In Thailand, for example, extensive lending was directed at real estate, construction, and property. When property prices began to fall in late 1996, banks exposed to these markets began to weaken considerably, making these banks' foreign creditors increasingly nervous.

Exchange rate policies added to the problems. Each of the crisis countries had either fixed or heavily managed exchange rate systems; none had fully flexible currencies. Although fixed exchange rates help keep import prices stable and provide a price anchor in a highly inflationary environment, they can create three kinds of problems.

First, they tend to encourage short-term capital inflows, which are especially vulnerable to rapid withdrawals. With fixed exchange rates, investors believe there is little chance they will lose money from a rapid change in the exchange rate. A foreign investor is more likely to buy a one-month bond denominated in Mexican pesos if the investor believes there is little risk that the exchange rate will change during the month. In countries with flexible exchange rates, foreign investors must take into account the risk that a relatively small exchange rate movement quickly could wipe out any gain they realize from higher interest rates.

Second, fixed exchange rates tend to become overvalued, which makes imports cheap and undercuts the profitability of exports. Partly because of their exchange rate policies, the crisis economies generally experienced growing imports, a slowdown in export growth, and a widening of the trade deficit in the years preceding the crisis.

Third, and more subtly, once capital withdrawals begin in the early stages of a crisis, fixed exchange rates tend to help accelerate the withdrawals. Once investors recognize that withdrawals are underway, they begin to speculate against the local currency, betting that the government will have to remove the fixed exchange rate.[8] This speculation adds to the loss of reserves and the pressure on the exchange rate. When the central bank finally runs out of reserves, it has little choice but to allow the currency to float, which usually leads to a very large depreciation. The Thai baht jumped from 25 baht to the dollar in July 1997 to 54 baht to the dollar in January 1998, and the Korean won moved from about 900 won to over 1,900 won to the dollar in just a few months before appreciating back in early 1998. It is easy to see why someone holding assets denominated in either baht or won and expecting a devaluation would have wanted to get money out of these countries as quickly as possible.

---

[8]Such speculation takes place along the lines of the following, very simplified example. A foreign investor believes that the Philippine peso will have to be devalued. The investor takes out a short-term loan of 25 million pesos from a bank in the Philippines. The investor then converts the money into dollars using the current exchange rate of 25 pesos to the dollar, yielding $1 million. If the investor is right and the exchange rate moves, fewer dollars will be required to repay the loan. For example, if the exchange rate moves to 50 pesos to the dollar, the investor need convert only $500,000 dollars to get the 25 million pesos needed to repay the loan, allowing the investor to pocket a tidy profit of the remaining $500,000. This strategy is called *shorting the peso*.

Short-Term Capital Flows

While policy weaknesses undoubtedly created vulnerabilities in these economies, to fully explain the speed and ferocity of the crises we must turn to the operations of the international capital markets and the actions of the foreign creditors.

A key reason that so much capital was able to leave these countries so quickly was that so much of it had very short-term maturity structures. A large portion of the loans to the firms, banks, and governments in the crisis countries was scheduled to be repaid in just a few months or even weeks. These **short-term loans** (with full repayment due in one year or less) were attractive to both borrowers and lenders. For the borrowers, short-term loans generally carry lower interest rates; for the lender, short-term loans carry lower risk (and require less provisioning by the supervisory authorities[9]), since the lender is not exposed over long periods of time. As long as these economies continued to grow, creditors were happy to roll over the loans when they fell due (that is, make a new loan for the same amount to repay the old loan), allowing borrowers to continue their operations. So as long as things are going well, short-term loans *appear* to pose few problems. However, as soon as there is any trouble—or more precisely, as soon as creditors think there *may* be trouble—creditors quickly withdraw their lines of credit and demand immediate repayment of loans. This is precisely what happened in East Asia: When Thailand's economy began to noticeably weaken in late 1996 and early 1997, creditors began to close off their lines of credit and demand repayment, setting off a chain of events that led to financial panic and severe economic crisis.

Economies become vulnerable to a sudden withdrawal of international capital when the short-term foreign exchange *liabilities* of the economy grow in excess of short-term foreign exchange *assets.* In that situation, economies can become *illiquid:* Roughly speaking, there may not be enough dollars (or whatever relevant foreign currency) on hand to pay all the international debts falling due. Table 15–7 shows the size of one significant type of foreign liability for the crisis countries: short-term debts owed to foreign commercial banks by the government, state-owned companies, commercial banks, and private corporations in each economy. The table also shows data for the main liquid foreign exchange asset of an economy: the foreign exchange reserves held by the central bank. The last column shows the key point: In each of the crisis economies, short-term foreign debts exceeded or nearly exceeded the available foreign exchange reserves. In this situation, economies are *vulnerable* to a severe crisis,

---

[9]Central banks require commercial banks to set aside (or provision) a percentage of all new loans to ensure that the bank has some capital on hand in case loans fail. The amount of provisioning varies by the perceived risk of the loan and generally is smaller for short-term loans. In part because banks do not have to provision as much for these loans, short-term loans carry lower interest rates than long-term loans.

TABLE 15-7. **Short-Term Foreign Debt and Reserves
(million US$)**

COUNTRY	PERIOD	SHORT-TERM DEBT	RESERVES	SHORT-TERM DEBT/RESERVES
Crisis countries				
Argentina	June 1995	21,509	10,844	1.98
Argentina	June 2001	40,916	21,077	1.94
Argentina	Sept. 2001	37,792	20,555	1.84
Argentina	Dec. 2001	32,320	14,553	2.22
Brazil	Dec. 1998	41,038	42,580	0.96
Indonesia	June 1997	34,661	20,336	1.70
Korea	June 1997	70,612	34,070	2.07
Malaysia	June 1997	16,268	26,588	0.61
Mexico	Dec. 1994	33,149	6,278	5.28
Philippines	June 1997	8,293	9,781	0.85
Russia	June 1998	34,650	11,161	3.10
Thailand	June 1997	45,567	31,361	1.45
Turkey	June 1994	8,821	4,279	2.06
Turkey	June 2000	26,825	24,742	1.08
Turkey	Sept. 2000	27,845	24,255	1.15
Turkey	Dec. 2000	28,360	22,488	1.26
Venezuela	June 1994	4,382	5,422	0.81
Noncrisis countries				
Chile	June 1997	7,615	17,017	0.45
Colombia	June 1997	6,698	9,940	0.67
Egypt	June 1997	4,166	18,779	0.22
India	June 1997	7,745	25,702	0.30
Jordan	June 1997	582	1,624	0.36
Peru	June 1997	5,368	10,665	0.50
Sri Lanka	June 1997	414	1,770	0.23
Taiwan	June 1997	21,966	90,025	0.24

Sources: Bank for International Settlements, *The Maturity, Sectoral, and Nationality Distribution of International Bank Lending* (Basle, Switzerland: various issues); International Monetary Fund, *International Financial Statistics* (Washington, DC: various issues); Joint BIS-IMF-OECD-WB Statistics on External Debt (30 November 2004).

because if all short-term loans are called in for repayment, not enough foreign exchange is available to repay every debt.

Bear in mind that the short-term bank loans shown in Table 15–7 are just one kind of short-term foreign exchange liability. Other kinds of foreign capital also can be withdrawn quickly, including portfolio equity (i.e., stock purchases), foreign-exchange bank deposits, hedging instruments, and long-term loans with clauses that allow accelerated repayment, but data on these forms of capital are not available. Moreover, the withdrawals generally are not limited to foreigners: local citizens also begin to try to convert their assets out of domestic currency and into dollars (or yen), putting further pressure on the exchange rate. Note that longer-term loans and FDI generally cannot be reversed as quickly as short-term loans and therefore are less prone to rapid withdrawals.

Creditor Panic

These financial crises were at least partially the result of what are known as **rational panics** by the creditors. Under certain circumstances, investors may have the incentive to quickly withdraw their money from an otherwise reasonably healthy economy, if they believe that other investors are about to do the same thing. The classic example from within one economy is a bank run, in which bank depositors suddenly withdraw their funds and deplete the capital of the bank. The particular conditions under which a rational panic can occur are described in Box 15–4.

In an international context, two conditions provide the foundation for such a panic. The first is a high level of short-term foreign liabilities relative to foreign assets. In this situation, each creditor begins to recognize that, if all creditors demanded repayment, not enough foreign exchange would be available to pay everyone. The second is that some event makes creditors believe that other creditors may begin to demand repayment. The event could be a military coup, a natural disaster, a sharp fall in export prices, a fall in property prices that weakens the domestic banking system, or an event in a neighboring country that makes creditors nervous about an entire region. Once creditors believe that others might pull out, the only rational action for each creditor is to immediately demand repayment ahead of everyone else, to avoid being the last in line and left unpaid if foreign exchange reserves are depleted. This is why the very rapid withdrawals are called *rational* panics. The irony, of course, is that the simultaneous

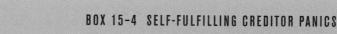

BOX 15-4 SELF-FULFILLING CREDITOR PANICS

Self-fulfilling creditor panics are best understood by beginning with the critical distinction between illiquidity and insolvency. An *insolvent* borrower lacks the net worth to repay outstanding debts out of future earnings. An *illiquid* borrower lacks the ready cash to repay current debt servicing obligations, even though it has the net worth to repay the debts in the long term. A *liquidity crisis* occurs if a solvent but illiquid borrower is unable to borrow fresh funds from the capital markets in order to remain current on debt-servicing obligations. Because the borrower is solvent, capital markets could in principle provide new loans to repay existing debts with the expectation that both the old loans and the new loans will be fully serviced. The unwillingness or inability of the capital market to provide fresh loans to the illiquid borrower is the nub of the matter.

Why might markets fail this way? The primary reason is a problem of collective action. Suppose each individual creditor is too small to provide all of the loans needed by an illiquid debtor. A liquidity crisis results when creditors as a group would be willing to make a new loan, but no individual creditor is willing to make a loan *if the other creditors do not lend as well*. One possible market equilibrium is that no individual creditor is willing to make a loan to an illiquid borrower precisely because each creditor (rationally) expects that no other creditor is ready to make such a loan.

Consider a simple illustration. Suppose that a borrower owes debt D to a large number of existing creditors. The debt requires debt service of θD in period one, and debt service of $(1 + r)(1 - \theta)D$ in period two, where r is the rate of interest charged on the unpaid balance of the loan. The debtor owns an investment project that will pay off Q_2 in the second period. Note that for the project to be profitable, $Q_2/(1 + r)$ must be greater than the present value of total debt service payments in both periods $\theta D + [(1 + r)(1 - \theta)D]/(1 + r)$, which must be equal to D.) The debtor lacks the cash flow to repay θD, since the investment project only pays off in the second period. Moreover, if the debtor defaults, the loan repayment schedule is accelerated (i.e., creditors demand immediate repayment). The investment project is then scrapped, with a salvage value of $Q_1 < D$. In that case, the partial repayment of the outstanding loan from the salvage value is shared among the existing creditors on a *pro rata* basis.

Typically, this solvent but illiquid borrower would borrow a fresh loan L in the first period, use it to repay θD, and then service $(1 - \theta)D + L$ in the second period. Thus, with $L = \theta D$, the total repayment due in the second period is $(1 + r)\,\theta D + (1 + r)(1 - \theta)D = (1 + r)D$, which by assumption is less than Q_2. In this case, then, the project remains profitable.

Suppose, however, that each individual creditor can lend at most λ, where $\lambda \ll D$ (that is, λ is much smaller than D). This lending limit might result from prudential standards imposed on individual bank lenders, which limit their exposure to particular debtors. If only one lender is prepared to lend in the first period, the borrower will be forced into default, since it will not be able to service its debts in the first period. The new creditor lending λ in the first period would then suffer an immediate loss on its loans (indeed, it might receive nothing if repayments are prioritized such that all of the preceding creditors have priority on repayment). Obviously, a first period loan will require at least n_1 new lenders, where $n_1 = \theta D/\lambda$.

There are clearly multiple rational equilibria in this situation. In the normal case, n_1 lenders routinely step forward, the existing debts are serviced, and the future debts are also serviced. The investment project is carried to fruition. In the case of a financial crisis, each individual creditor decides not to lend on the grounds that no other creditor is making loans. The debtor is pushed into default. The debt repayments are accelerated and the investment project is scrapped with sharp economic losses, since the salvage value Q_1 is less than $Q_2/(1 + r)$. Each individual creditor, of course, feels vindicated in its decision not to lend; after all, the debtor immediately goes into default.

From Steven Radelet and Jeffrey D. Sachs, "The East Asian Financial Crisis: Diagnosis, Remedies, Prospects," *Brookings Papers on Economic Activity*, no. 1 (1998), 1–89.

demand for repayment by all the creditors ultimately depletes reserves and brings on the very crisis that all would rather avoid. In this sense, these crises are often referred to as *self-fulfilling:* The fact that more creditors believe that a crisis is possible in itself makes a crisis more likely to actually happen.

In Asia, once Thailand's economy began to slow in late 1996 and early 1997 and banks came under increasing pressure from falling property prices, foreign creditors that had lent to Thai banks began to get nervous and withdraw their loans. Other creditors came to believe that Thailand might run out of foreign exchange reserves, devalue the baht, or both, and began to withdraw their credits. These events ultimately depleted foreign exchange reserves and forced the large depreciation of the baht that began in July 1997. The weaknesses in Thailand made creditors more nervous about its neighbors, specifically Korea, Malaysia, Indonesia, and the Philippines. A similar chain of events (with differences in the specific details and triggering events) occurred in most of the other crisis countries.

Once a panic begins, it tends to perpetuate itself for a period of time, for several reasons. First, as foreign creditors demand repayment and the exchange rate begins to depreciate, local citizens try to convert their financial assets from local to foreign currency, putting additional pressure on reserves and the exchange rate. This was a particularly large problem in Argentina, Brazil, Indonesia, and Russia. Second, the deprecations wreak havoc on the balance sheets of banks and corporations that had borrowed in foreign currency. For example, as the Indonesian rupiah jumped from about 2,500 rupiah to the dollar in mid-1997 to over 10,000 rupiah to the dollar in early 1998, Indonesian corporations with dollar debts had to come up with *four times* more rupiah to make their payments. The crippling effect of the exchange rate movement was obvious to the creditors, so the more the exchange rate fell, the faster the foreign creditors tried to withdraw any remaining loans, putting even more pressure on the exchange rate. Third, as exchange rates fall in one country, creditors begin to believe something similar will happen in neighboring countries, so they start to withdraw their funds from other emerging markets. There was no hint of trouble in Malaysia, Indonesia, and the Philippines until the Thai baht collapsed in July 1997. Within weeks "contagion" had struck, and creditors were withdrawing their money from almost every country in the region.

These emerging market financial crises were not new phenomena. Similar events have been recurring in slightly different forms since the development of banks and the emergence of international capital flows several centuries ago. Economists have long recognized that financial markets (both domestic and international) tend to be prone to instability and panic. Early in the twentieth century, industrialized country governments put into place mechanisms and institutions specifically designed to reduce the frequency and severity of financial crises, including lender-of-last-resort facilities at the central bank, deposit insurance, and bankruptcy procedures, making crises much less common within these countries.

However, these key institutions generally do not exist in international financial markets, leaving these markets vulnerable to panics. When central banks face a run on their foreign exchange reserves (akin to a commercial bank facing a depositor run), no international lender of last resort stands ready to supply it with the foreign exchange it needs to remain liquid (the IMF only partially fulfills this role, as discussed later). Similarly, no international insurance mechanism akin to deposit insurance assures creditors that they will be paid if a borrower defaults. And there is no international bankruptcy court that can call for a mandatory standstill on debt service payments and oversee the distribution of assets when a country cannot meet its short-term foreign currency obligations. On each count, there is extensive debate as to whether these institutions *should* exist and, if so, how they might realistically be designed to operate effectively in an international context, where there is no single legal authority. For example, an international agency that insures creditors could lead to excessive lending to weak companies, since the creditor always could rely on an insurance settlement if the company goes bankrupt. In any event, in the absence of these institutions, international financial markets continue to be prone to rapid oscillations and financial panics.

Stopping Panics

Once a financial panic from international capital withdrawals is underway, it is very hard to stop. There are four basic options:

1. Governments can try to convince foreign creditors and citizens to stop withdrawing funds and even supply new funding. They can reduce the demand for foreign exchange by tightening fiscal and monetary policies and, perhaps, restricting imports. They can also implement policy reforms aimed at correcting perceived weaknesses in the economy. For example, if creditors are worried about the banking sector, reforms to strengthen banks might convince creditors to begin lending again.

2. Governments can try to increase the supply of foreign exchange by borrowing from official sources (such as the International Monetary Fund and World Bank), much like a commercial bank borrows from its central bank in the event of a bank run. New funds can help assure creditors that enough foreign exchange is on hand to pay everyone, if need be, and allow the economy to operate normally.

3. Governments can try to stop the creditor rush for repayment by restructuring foreign debts so they will be repaid over longer periods of time. This option may include a formal debt rescheduling, a limited "standstill" period during which loan repayments are postponed, or in some cases outright default.

4. The government can do nothing (intentionally or unintentionally) and let the panic run its course until all creditors have fled, foreign exchange reserves are exhausted, debts are in default, and the economy is in deep recession. At some point, even in these dire circumstances, some investors will begin to return to take advantage of low asset prices, the foreign exchange market will begin to stabilize (at a greatly depreciated exchange rate), and the economy slowly will begin to recover.

The appropriate combination of policy actions and financing depends on the root causes of the crisis and the perceptions of international creditors, but there is little doubt that both policy adjustments and financing are necessary to avoid complete collapse. The problem, of course, is that correctly diagnosing a panic and prescribing the right response is very difficult when markets are changing rapidly by the hour, little accurate information is available, and the perceptions and reactions of creditors are impossible to measure. It therefore is not surprising that both the affected countries and the international community often make mistakes when dealing with incipient crises, like the ones faced by the emerging market economies.

In most of the affected economies, once the crisis was underway, the government turned to the International Monetary Fund for advice and financial assistance. The IMF was established in 1945 in the aftermath of the Great Depression and World War II to help support stability in the international monetary system, including promoting the balanced expansion of world trade, the stability of exchange rates, and orderly corrections of balance-of-payments problems.[10] It aims to prevent crises or moderate their impact by encouraging countries to adopt what it sees as sound economic and financial polices and by providing temporary financing when necessary to address balance-of-payments problems. The IMF was undoubtedly in a difficult situation in working on these crises. The policies and programs it promoted during the crises were hotly debated, with analysts divided on whether the programs initially helped ease the crisis or unintentionally added to the panic, at least in its early stages, by shaking the confidence of investors and further weakening the economy.[11]

---

[10]See the description of the purposes of the IMF at www.imf.org/external/pubs/ft/exrp/what.htm.

[11]For debates on these issues, see Steven Radelet and Jeffrey D. Sachs, "The East Asian Financial Crisis: Diagnosis, Remedies, Prospects," *Brookings Papers on Economic Activity*, no. 1 (1998), 1–90; Jason Furman and Joseph Stiglitz, "Economic Crises: Evidence and Insights from East Asia," *Brookings Papers on Economic Activity*, no. 2 (1998), 1–136; Martin Feldstein, "Refocussing the IMF," *Foreign Affairs* 77, no. 4 (March–April 1998), 20–33; Stanley Fischer, "In Defense of the IMF," *Foreign Affairs* 77, no. 4 (July–August 1998); Timothy Lane and others, "IMF-Supported Programs in Indonesia, Korea, and Thailand: A Preliminary Assessment," IMF occasional paper no. 178 (1999); World Bank, *East Asia: The Road to Recovery* (Washington, DC: World Bank, 1998); Martin Feldstein, ed., *Economic and Financial Crises in Emerging Market Economies* (Chicago: University of Chicago Press, 2003); Nouriel Roubini and Brad Setser, *Bailouts or Bail-Ins? Responding to Financial Crises in Emerging Economies* (Washington, DC: Institute for International Economics, 2004).

The IMF's initial set of policy prescriptions, consistent with option 1, centered on tightening both fiscal and monetary policies (to reduce aggregate demand and the demand for foreign exchange) and closing weak financial institutions. Each requires a delicate balance. In countries where the fiscal deficits were large and part of the problem (since they required significant financing) such as Argentina and Turkey, some fiscal tightening was necessary. However, in other countries, particularly those in Asia, where the fiscal balance was either a small deficit or even a surplus, tightening fiscal policy was more debatable, and some analysts believe this step may have added to the economic contraction. Tightening monetary policy and raising interest rates is even more complex. On the one hand, high interest rates might attract some foreign currency and slow capital withdrawals. On the other hand, foreign creditors might believe that high interest rates would further weaken banks and corporations, leading them to accelerate their demands for repayment. The empirical evidence on this issue is far from conclusive. Perhaps the most controversial issue was reform of financial institutions. There is no doubt that banking systems were weak and overextended and needed significant reform. However, the very abrupt closure of some of these institutions may have added to the panic in the short run, leading to an acceleration of bank runs as depositors feared their bank would be the next closed.

Actions by governments in several of the crisis economies exacerbated rather than eased the crisis. Thailand's reluctance to float its currency earlier and take steps to address the problems facing banks that were heavily exposed to property markets made the crisis more severe than it otherwise would have been. The Indonesian central bank made huge loans to try to prop up weak banks, ultimately fueling capital flight and further weakening the currency.

Turning to the second option, these programs were supported by substantial financing from the IMF and, in some cases, bilateral funding from the governments of Japan, the United States, and European countries. This financing was designed to augment the foreign exchange reserves of the crisis economies, convince creditors that sufficient funds would be available to repay everyone, and ease pressure on the exchange rate. In several cases, the amount of financing pledged by the international community was extremely large (Table 15–8). International financial commitments to Mexico, Brazil, South Korea, and Turkey all exceeded $30 billion.

The amounts actually disbursed were often smaller, either because the simple announcement of the amounts available helped ease creditor concerns, the crisis began to pass before the full amounts were necessary, or sometimes because the recipient countries did not fulfill specified conditions so funds were withheld. In Mexico, South Korea, Brazil, and Turkey, the funds clearly were sufficiently large to help ease the panic; in other cases, it is less clear the amounts were sufficient. However, some analysts believe that large financing packages

TABLE 15-6. **International Financing for Selected Crisis Countries**

COUNTRY	IMF COMMITMENTS		BILATERAL COMMITMENTS		TOTAL COMMITMENTS		ACTUAL DISBURSEMENTS	
	BILLION $	%GDP	BILLION $	%GDP	BILLION $	%GDP	BILLION $	%GDP
Mexico (1995)	18.9	4.6	20	5.0	38.9	9.6	27.6	6.8
Thailand (1997)	4.0	2.2	10.0	5.5	14.0	7.7	11.2	6.2
Indonesia (1997)	11.3	5.0	15.0	6.6	26.3	11.6	10.8	4.7
Korea (1997)	20.9	4.0	20.0	3.8	40.0	7.7	19.4	3.7
Russia (1998)	15.1	3.5	0	0.0	15.1	3.5	5.1	1.2
Brazil (1998–99)	18.4	2.3	14.5	1.8	32.9	4.1	17.5	2.2
Turkey (1999–2002)	33.8	17.0	0	0.0	33.8	17.0	23.1	11.6
Argentina (2000–01)	22.1	7.8	1.0	0.4	23.1	8.1	13.7	4.8
Uruguay (2002)	2.7	14.5	1.5	8.0	2.7	14.5	2.2	11.8
Brazil (2001–02)	35.1	6.9	0	0.0	35.1	6.9	30.1	5.9

Source: Nouriel Roubini and Brad Setser, *Bailouts or Bail-Ins? Responding to Financial Crises in Emerging Economies* (Washington, DC: Institute for International Economics, 2004).

are harmful in the long run: Some suggest that the bailout of Mexico in 1995 made private creditors more relaxed about lending aggressively to other emerging markets and so may have contributed to the buildup in capital flows that led to other crises in 1997 and 1998. This kind of situation is known as **moral hazard,** the risk that an agreement or contract will alter the behavior of interested parties in perverse ways.[12] In this case, the agreement to bail out Mexico might have led investors to believe they could take greater risks in other emerging markets, as they would get bailed out in the event of another crisis. However, many analysts dispute whether Mexico's bail out had this effect.

Option 3 is to restructure the debts to either stretch out the maturity dates so the debts can be paid later or to write off part or all of the debt. In the most extreme cases, such as Argentina, Ecuador, and Russia, governments adopted a unilateral **standstill**—that is, they halted all debt payments—or simply defaulted. In effect, these steps effectively forced the creditors to provide financing involuntarily, what economists Nouriel Roubini and Brad Setser refer to as "bailing in" the creditors.[13] The option for default is even more complicated when the creditors are not just foreign banks but local banks or citizens that hold government bonds. When governments have borrowed from local banks, defaulting on those debts further weakens the domestic banking system and can lead to a freeze on deposits, obviously a politically unpopular step.[14]

[12]The classic example of moral hazard is insurance markets, where coverage against a loss might increase risk-taking behavior by the insured.

[13]Roubini and Setser, *Bailouts or Bail-Ins?*

[14]Defaulting on debts owed to foreign bank similarly can weaken those banks, but they tend to be a much smaller share of the foreign banks' balance sheets, so the impact is more limited.

Steps less dramatic than outright default are possible and less disruptive. Brazil and Turkey persuaded at least some of the foreign banks to roll over existing lines of credit, but these were not mandatory and many banks did not do so. More-formal restructurings are also an option. Turkey exchanged about $8 billion of short-term local currency debt, held mostly by domestic banks and residents, into longer-term dollar and lira debt. Argentina extended the maturity of about $15 billion in government debt and capitalized interest on another $15 billion in long-term debt. These deals were expensive in terms of the interest rates charged, but they provided immediate financing and avoided the disruptions of default.

Perhaps the most-interesting and -important debt restructuring was in South Korea. In late December 1997, under pressure from the U.S. government and the IMF, the major creditors to South Korea's banks agreed to reschedule about $22 billion in debt payments that were scheduled to fall due in the first quarter of 1998. This step was taken very early in the crisis, and its preventative effect in stopping the panic was immediate: The Korean won began to appreciate and the Korean stock market rebounded the day after the rescheduling was announced. Within weeks, the most intense part of the Korean crisis effectively was over, and the Korean economy rebounded very quickly.

Debt restructurings have several advantages. First, they at least partially share the burden of adjustment between the creditors and debtors, rather than forcing the debtor to make all the adjustments. This is not only fairer, it may have a preventative aspect: with standstills or restructuring realistic possibilities, creditors should be less likely to engage in excessive lending. Second, when debts are restructured less new finance is required from the international community (and its taxpayers). Third, since pressure to immediately repay debts is at heart of the creditor panic, restructuring can have an immediate salutatory effect, as was the case in Korea. Debt restructurings and standstills are the centerpiece of bankruptcy proceedings in most industrialized economies, but engineering them in cross-border situations is much more difficult. Several analysts have suggested different ways to establish an international bankruptcy regime, but putting these ideas into action has proven difficult.

Panics eventually end, even when little or no action is taken to stop them, simply because foreign exchange eventually is depleted, so creditors stop demanding repayment and debt falls into default. But the resulting economic contraction can be very deep, and the financial system can be left in a shambles. In Indonesia, for example, where the financial crisis quickly cascaded into a political crisis that led to widespread rioting and destruction of property and ultimately the resignation of President Suharto in May 1998. GDP contracted by about 15 percent in 1998 before the economy finally began to stabilize in 1999, and it took many years for the economy to recover.

Lessons from the Crises

First, these crises are cautionary tales about rapid financial liberalization and the difficulties involved in building strong institutions in emerging markets. The crisis economies liberalized their financial systems very quickly without fully establishing and strengthening the institutions necessary to oversee and regulate financial transactions. Building well-functioning financial systems remains a major challenge in the development process. These crises suggest that governments should proceed carefully in liberalizing domestic financial transactions and ensuring parallel development of the requisite regulatory institutions.

Second, the crises reveal the vulnerabilities of relying on a fixed exchange rate, at least for countries with large private capital inflows. The conditions under which fixed or floating exchange rates are preferable for long-run growth and development is an open question that economists have debated for two centuries, and the debate is far from resolved. Fixed rates reduce volatility in thin foreign exchange markets and can provide some certainty to skittish investors. But the crises indicate that fixed rates create vulnerability to a panic and ultimately lead to huge economic adjustments when the exchange rate no longer can be defended. Increasingly, many economists suggest that the choice for developing countries is between a very rigidly fixed rate defended with abundant foreign exchange reserves or a freely floating exchange rate. Most economists now tend to believe that the rigid fixed rate options, including a currency board or outright dollarization,[15] are appropriate in only a very limited number of developing countries and flexible exchange rates generally are the preferred choice. However, the debate on this issue is far from over and likely to continue in the years to come.

Third, in terms of foreign capital inflows, there are clear differences between FDI and other long-term capital and short-term capital. Long-term capital flows are much less prone to panic and more strongly associated with long-term investment and growth. Since short-term flows create vulnerability to a panic, governments should be much more careful about, and at times possibly even discourage, short-term flows, especially while they are in the process of strengthening weak financial institutions. Some analysts support restrictions on short-term capital inflows as a temporary step to protect nascent financial systems, so long as the restrictions are limited to short-term capital (there is little support among economists for restrictions on long-term capital or outflows of any kind). Chile has been at the forefront of countries trying to encourage long-

---

[15]Recall from Chapter 13 that, with a currency board, the government issues domestic currency only when it is fully backed by available foreign exchanges reserves at the given (fixed) rate, thereby keeping the ratio of foreign currency to domestic currency constant. With dollarization, a country adopts the dollar (or another widely traded currency) as its legal currency, thereby giving up an independent monetary policy.

term capital flows and discourage short-term flows. During the 1990s, Chile required that foreign investors deposit a share of their investment funds in a non-interest-bearing account for one year, a step that made short-term investment much less profitable. Such restrictions reduced short-term capital flows to Chile without reducing aggregate capital flows.[16]

Fourth, vulnerability to crises can be reduced not only by reducing short-term capital inflows but also by building up foreign exchange reserves. China and Taiwan employed just this kind of "self-insurance" and were able to avoid serious difficulties while crises swirled around them in 1997 and 1998, even though China, in particular, displays some of the same financial sector weaknesses evident in the crisis countries. Although China had over $30 billion in short-term foreign debt in 1997, its foreign exchange reserves were almost $150 billion. After the crises, China continued to build up its reserves, which reached an astonishing $700 billion in 2005. Taiwan, with about $20 billion in short-term debt in 1997, had over $90 billion in reserves, so also was safe from this kind of crisis (it subsequently built its reserves to over $240 billion). Korea, whose reserves had dwindled to about $3 billion when its crisis erupted (compared to $70 billion in short-term debts), subsequently built up its reserves to over $200 billion, effectively ensuring that it will not soon face a similar international payments crisis and have to look to the IMF for emergency financing.

Fifth, the operations of international financial markets and the immediate reactions by the official international community probably added to the severity of the crisis. As a result, there has been widespread discussion about possible reforms to the international financial "architecture." These debates have proceeded on several fronts, including reforming the operations of the IMF itself, strengthening international banking standards, and establishing new international mechanisms for debt standstills and rollovers, but few fundamental changes have been made.[17] As they have been for two centuries, financial crises are likely to continue to be recurring yet difficult-to-predict phenomena affecting emerging markets around the world.

---

[16]For discussions of short-term capital flows, see Richard Cooper, "Should Capital Controls Be Banished?" *Brookings Papers on Economic Activity* 1 (1999), 89–141; Jaime Cardoso and Bernard Laurens, "The Effectiveness of Capital Controls on Inflows: Lessons from the Experience of Chile," IMF Monetary and Exchange Affairs Department, 1998; Sebastian Edwards, "Capital Flows, Real Exchange Rates, and Capital Controls: Some Latin American Experiences," Department of Economics, UCLA, 1998; and Felipe Larraín B., ed., *Capital Flows, Capital Controls, and Currency Crises: Latin America in the 1990s* (Ann Arbor: University of Michigan Press, 2000).

[17]See Roubini and Setser, *Bailouts or Bail-Ins?*; Feldstein, *Economic and Financial Crises in Emerging Market Economies*; Barry Eichengreen, *Toward a New International Financial Architecture: A Practical Post-Asia Agenda* (Washington, DC: Institute for International Economics, February 1999); and Morris Goldstein, *Safeguarding Prosperity in a Global Financial System, Report of an Independent Task Force for the Council on Foreign Relations* (Washington, DC: Institute for International Economics, September 1999).

SUMMARY

- Debt flows to developing countries have oscillated widely since the 1970s. They grew rapidly until the 1980s, then fell in the aftermath of the 1980s debt crises. They accelerated again in the early 1990s, only to drop sharply following the financial crises of the late 1990 then rebound again after 2001. Middle-income countries tend to borrow from both private lenders and official creditors (such as the World Bank), whereas low-income countries borrow mainly from official sources (including IDA loans from the World Bank).

- Debt can play an important role in financing investment and stabilizing an economy buffeted by shocks, but too much borrowing, especially of the wrong kind and for the wrong purposes, can create debt problems. In particular, borrowing for consumption or weak investment projects, borrowing too much when GDP growth or export growth rates remain low, or borrowing too much on short-term debt can leave countries vulnerable to crisis.

- The debt crises of the 1980s caused major economic dislocations in many countries around the world, especially in Latin America. For countries that had borrowed heavily from private commercial banks, the debt crises by and large were resolved through Brady bonds restructurings in the late 1980s and early 1990s. However, for lower-income countries that had borrowed from official sources, debt burdens continued to grow through the 1990s. The heavily indebted poor-country initiative has begun to reduce the debt burdens for some, but not all, the countries.

- The financial crises of the late 1990s struck emerging markets that had borrowed substantial funds with short maturities and had relatively low levels of foreign exchange reserves, fixed exchange rates, and weak financial systems. The rapid withdrawal of funds caused exchange rates to plummet and interest rates to soar and caused significant damage to domestic banks, private companies, government financial accounts, and overall economic well-being.

- International capital flows are more vulnerable to these kinds of crises than domestic capital, since the institutions that can help reduce risks domestically do not operate well across borders, including lender-of-last-resort facilities, deposit insurance, and bankruptcy procedures. Countries have taken steps to minimize their risks by reducing (or restricting) short-term capital flows, building up reserves, introducing more flexible exchange rates, and strengthening financial systems.

PART FOUR

Production and Trade

16

Agriculture

Understanding the nature of agriculture is fundamental to understanding development. The labor-surplus and neoclassical models presented in Chapter 4 dealt primarily with the nature of the relationship between the industrial and agricultural sectors. The problem of income distribution or extremes of poverty within developing nations discussed in Chapter 6 is substantially a question of how to do something about the rural poor. Nutrition, discussed in Chapter 9, is a question of food production and distribution. And the contribution of exports to development, as treated in Chapters 17 and 19 for many countries, is a question of creating agricultural exports.

Much of this book has been about **rural development,** all those activities that affect the well-being of rural populations, including the provision of basic needs, such as food, and the development of human capital in the countryside through education and nutrition programs. This chapter concentrates on problems that have a direct bearing on raising agricultural production and farmers' income. Indirect measures treated elsewhere in this book, even those as crucial as rural education, are dealt with only in passing.

In a sense, agriculture simply is one industry among many, but it is an industry with a difference. To begin with, the agricultural sector in a country at an early developmental stage employs far more people than all other industries and sectors put together, 60–70 percent or more of the total workforce are in agriculture in many of the poorer developing countries, including India and, until the 1990s, China. In contrast, agriculture in developed economies typically employs less than 10 percent of the workforce (4 percent of men and only 1 percent of women in the United States). Second, agricultural activities have existed for thousands of years, ever since humankind gave up hunting and gathering as its main source of food. Because of this long history, the rural economy often is described as **tradition bound.** Generating electric power or manufacturing automobiles can be done only by means based on modern science and engineering, but crops often are grown using techniques developed hundreds or even thousands of years before the advent of modern science. And the rural societies in which traditional techniques are used often develop customs and attitudes that reinforce older ways of doing things and make change difficult.

A third characteristic of agriculture that separates it from other sectors is the crucial importance of land as a factor of production. Other sectors use and require land, but in no other sector does land play such a central role. The availability of cultivable land, whether relatively plentiful in relation to population, as in the Americas, or scarce, as in much of Asia, fundamentally shapes the kind of farming techniques that can be used. Closely related to the central role of land is the influence of weather. No other sector is as subject to the vagaries of the weather as agriculture. Land, like the weather, differs from place to place so that techniques suitable in one place are often of little use elsewhere. The manufacture of steel must adjust to differences in the quality of iron ore from place to place and similar problems occur in other industries, but the basic techniques in much of manufacturing are similar, at least within and often between countries. In agriculture, differences in soil quality, climate, and the availability of water lead to the production of different crops and different ways of raising a particular crop, not only within countries, but even within provinces or counties of a single country.

Finally, agriculture is the only sector that produces food. Humankind can survive without steel or coal or electric power but not without food. For most manufactured products, in fact, there are substitutes, but there is no substitute for food. Food must be either produced within a country or imported.

AGRICULTURE'S ROLE IN ECONOMIC DEVELOPMENT

Agriculture's role in economic development is central because most of the people in poor countries make their living from the land. If leaders are seriously concerned with the welfare of their people, the only ways they can readily improve the welfare for the majority is by helping to raise, first, the farmers' productivity in growing food and cash crops and, second, the prices they receive for those crops. Not all increases in farm output benefit the majority of rural people, of course. The creation of mechanized, large-scale farms in place of small, peasant farms actually may make the majority of the population worse off.

Although it is a necessary condition, raising agricultural output is not by itself sufficient to achieve an increase in rural welfare. We return to this problem later.

Most developing countries must rely on their own agricultural sectors to produce the food consumed by their people, although there are exceptions. Countries with large natural-resource-based exports, such as Malaysia or Saudi Arabia, have the foreign exchange necessary to import much of their food. But most developing countries cannot rely so heavily on foreign exchange earnings to feed their populations.

Farmers in developing countries must produce enough to feed themselves as well as the urban population. Hence, as the proportion of the urban population rises, the productivity of farmers also must rise. If productivity does not rise (and in the absence of food imports), the models in Chapter 4 make it clear that the terms of trade will turn sharply against the industrial sector, cut into profits, and eventually bring growth to a halt.

The agricultural sector's size is the characteristic that gives agriculture such an important role in the provision of factor inputs, notably labor, to industry and the other modern sectors. With 70 percent or more of the population in agriculture, the rural sector is virtually the only source of increased labor power for the urban sector. Importation of labor is possible, and usually the urban sector itself experiences population growth, but neither of these sources is likely to be sufficient for the long-term needs of economic growth. If restrictions are placed on the movement of labor out of agriculture, economic development will be severely crippled. Serfs in Russia through the mid-nineteenth century, for example, were tied to their lord's land by law and hence not free to move to the cities and into industry. Therefore, Russian industry did not begin to grow rapidly until after the serfs were freed. Today such feudal restrictions are increasingly rare, but heavy indebtedness by a farmer to a landlord-moneylender sometimes has the same effect as tying an individual to the land and thus making the individual unavailable to modern industry.

The agricultural sector also can be a major source of capital for modern economic growth. Some writers have even suggested that agriculture is the main or even the sole source of capital in the early stages of development, but this overstates agriculture's role. Capital comes from invested savings and savings from income. However, even in the poorest countries the share of agricultural income in the national product typically is less than half the gross domestic product. Over half the GNP therefore is provided by nonagricultural sectors (industry and services), and these sectors often are important contributors to saving and hence to investment. Furthermore, whereas imports of labor seldom provide a large portion of the domestic labor force, imports of capital, whether in the form of aid or private investment, sometimes do contribute a substantial share of domestic capital formation without drawing on the agricultural sector at all. South Korea is a case in point, where capital formation in the early years of rapid growth was provided mainly by foreign aid and in later years was increasingly paid for from the profits of the industrial sector.

If one treats foreign exchange as a separate factor of production, agriculture has an important role to play in the supply of this factor as well. As indicated in Chapter 17, developing countries' comparative advantage during the early stages of development usually lies with natural resources or agricultural products. In only a few cases is the export of manufactures or services the principal source of foreign exchange for a country in these early stages of modern economic growth. Therefore, unless a country is rich in natural resources, such as petroleum or copper, the agricultural sector plays a key role in providing foreign exchange with which to import capital equipment and intermediate goods that cannot be produced at home.

Finally, the farming population of a developing country, in some cases at least, is an important market for the output of the modern urban sector. The qualification *in some cases* must be added because farm populations in some poor countries purchase very little from modern industry. This is particularly likely where the distribution of income is extremely unequal, with most of the country's income, land, and other wealth in the hands of a small urban and rural upper class. In that situation, the rural population may simply pay taxes and rents to wealthy urban residents and subsist on whatever is left over. Even cheap cloth from urban factories may be beyond the means of a very poor rural population. If income is less unequally distributed, however, the rural sector can be an important source of demand for industrial products. If a large rural market exists, industries can continue to grow after they have saturated urban demand for their product without turning to foreign markets until they are better able to compete.[1]

SELF-SUFFICIENCY AND DWINDLING WORLD FOOD SUPPLIES

One important aspect of agriculture's role in development typically gets a great deal of attention from economic planners, the degree to which a country wishes to achieve food self-sufficiency. **Food self-sufficiency** can take on several different meanings. At one extreme is the view that any dependence on foreign trade is dangerous to a country's economic health, and dependence on food imports

[1]A number of good studies treat the role of agriculture in development, including C. Peter Timmer, *Agriculture and the State* (Ithaca, NY: Cornell University Press, 1991); Thomas P. Tomich, Peter Kilby, and Bruce F. Johnston, *Transforming Agrarian Economies: Opportunities Seized, Opportunities Missed* (Ithaca, NY: Cornell University Press, 1995); and Lloyd Reynolds, *Agriculture in Development Theory* (New Haven, CT: Yale University Press, 1976).

simply is one part of this broader danger. More common is the view that food is a basic or strategic good, not unlike military weapons. If a country is dependent on others for food, hence for its very survival, the suppliers of that food are in a position to bring the dependent country to its knees whenever it suits the supplier countries' purposes. Others argue that population growth is rapidly eating into the world's food surpluses, and countries relying on food imports soon will find themselves paying very high prices to get what they need from the world's dwindling surplus.

The national defense argument for food self-sufficiency may be valid under certain circumstances. Since a discussion of these circumstances would divert us into an analysis of complex international security issues, suffice it to say that the national defense argument frequently is used to justify policies that have little relationship to a country's real security.

The issue of a dwindling world food surplus cannot be dealt with so easily. History does not support the view that world supplies of exportable food are steadily diminishing. Data on world grain exports are presented in Table 16–1. What these and other data indicate is that, although the world grain export surplus and the corresponding size of the deficit in importing countries fluctuates, the overall surplus is growing, not declining. In 1972, for example, bad weather struck a wide part of the globe, including the Soviet Union, China, India, and Indonesia. The resulting surge in demand for grain imports drove prices up sharply in 1973, but prices fell again when production in these deficit areas recovered. The 1972–73 "crisis" was not significantly different in magnitude from other weather-induced fluctuations of the past. After 1973, grain exports rose substantially and prices fell.

TABLE 16-1. **World Cereal Exports (million metric tonnes)**

YEAR	EXPORTS
1962	85
1966	114
1970	113
1974	149
1978	191
1980	216
1985	224
1988	232
1992	250
1996	234
2002	280

Source: Food and Agricultural Organization, FAO, *Trade Yearbook 1972, 1976, 1978, 1987, 1989, 1993,* and *1996* (Rome: 1973, 1977, 1979, 1988, 1990, 1994, 1997) or the FAO website www.fao.org.

Those who speak of an impending world food crisis are implicitly or explicitly forecasting the future. Continued population growth is rapidly pushing people out onto the world's diminishing supply of arable land. In places like Africa's Sahel, agriculture already may have developed beyond the capacity of the land to sustain it. The real issue, however, is not whether the world is running out of surplus land—it is—but whether yields on existing arable land can be raised fast enough to meet the needs of an increasing population with rising per capita incomes. The problem is not one of biology. Research in the plant sciences has shown that yield per acre could be higher than even that of such advanced agricultural systems as Japan's. And most of the world produces food at levels per acre nowhere near those of Japan. Although there is some biological limit to the capacity of the earth to produce food, the planet is not close to that limit today.

The real danger of a long-term food crisis arises from a different source. From a scientific point of view, the countries that could expand food output dramatically may not do so because of internal social and economic barriers to technical progress in agriculture. At the same time, for economic reasons, the world's few food-surplus countries may not be able to continue to expand those surpluses. Therefore, it is possible that the world could face growing food deficits in importing countries that are not matched by rising surpluses in exporting countries. Under such circumstances, food prices rise sharply, and therefore only countries with large foreign exchange earnings could afford to continue to import sufficient food. Some of the poorest countries, including those where food imports make the difference between an adequate diet and severe malnutrition, may not have the foreign exchange earnings needed to maintain required imports. We must emphasize, however, that while the potential for a disaster of this kind is present, it is not today a reality; many economists believe it will never become a reality.[2] A possible future world food crisis is a weak basis for a country's economic planners to place a high priority on the development of agriculture.

FOOD SUPPLY AND FAMINE

Closely related to the desire for food self-sufficiency is the view that a general nationwide shortage of food is the main cause of devastating **famines** that can lead to millions of deaths within a short period in developing countries. This view sees

---

[2]Maldistribution within a country, however, can and does cause severe localized famines, sometimes accompanied by large-scale loss of life. See Jean Drèze and Amartya Sen, *Hunger and Public Action* (London: Oxford University Press [Clarendon], 1989).

prevention of famine as primarily an exercise in raising a nation's food production to ensure there are adequate supplies to meet everyone's minimum needs.

But famine is far more a problem of distribution than of food production. Famines often start as a result of some natural phenomenon such as a drought that destroys an entire year's crop in one or more regions of a country. Human-made disasters such as civil wars, however, can have much the same effect. The central issue is not what caused the crop failure but why no one stepped in to assist those who had lost the means to survive. Even in historical times, governments often saw it as their responsibility to maintain stores of grain against just such contingencies. Why have there been such severe famines as recently as the first decade of the twenty-first century in countries such as Zimbabwe and Ethiopia, when the power of governments to intervene is far greater than it was in the nineteenth century and the means for transporting the grain to the affected areas is readily available? Furthermore, where the government of the famine-affected country is not itself able to mobilize sufficient resources, the international community has stood ready to help out with low-cost or even free supplies of food where necessary. International agencies and nongovernment organizations also sometimes have supplied the means to deliver the food to where it is needed.

Market forces alone often are not adequate to the task of relieving a famine. Large numbers of people in the affected areas have lost most or all their income and are in no position to pay for food. If the famine is in a remote area, as often is the case, transport costs can be high, making it unprofitable for private traders to ship grain to the region, even if people there have some income. Nor are these poor farmers in a position to borrow money to tide them over until they do finally receive a good harvest a year or more down the road.

Governments and nongovernment organizations, therefore, must play a central role in situations such as this, but why then do governments sometimes fail to do so? In the words of Jean Drèze and Amartya Sen, the reason often is "negligence or smugness or callousness on the part of the non-responding authorities."[3] In the Chinese famine of 1959–61, during which roughly 30 million people lost their lives, government officials feared the wrath of Mao Zedong if they criticized his radical agricultural policies by pointing out that they had led to a sharp decline in food output, so they kept quiet. Even the statistical authorities were afraid to report what actually was going on and instead published false figures indicating that the harvest in 1959 had been good when the opposite was the case. Famine in Ethiopia in the 1970s and 1980s also resulted from a government unwilling to admit to itself or the international community that it was unable to deal with the severe drought that had affected parts of the country. When the situation got so bad that the international community was called in to

[3]Drèze and Sen, *Hunger and Public Action*, p. 263.

help out, the government of that time often tried to withhold food from regions of the country that were in rebellion against the government. In an analogous fashion, food became a weapon in the clan warfare that often wracked Somalia through the 1990s.

As Drèze and Sen have pointed out, famines rarely happen where a nation is democratic or governed by some other form of pluralistic politics. They also rarely happen where there are open channels of communication and criticism such as a free press. An open democratic society does not let its government ignore the plight of starving citizens. As the Chinese and Ethiopian cases of several decades ago illustrate, famines are most likely to occur when a government controls all the means of communication and uses them to keep itself in unchallenged control.

Once the attention of the government, nongovernment organizations, and the international community focuses on the problem, many mechanisms can be used to end the starvation. Free shipments of food to central distribution points in the affected region are common. Food-for-work programs sometimes can be even more effective, since the food not only allows the individuals receiving it to survive, but the work they do in exchange can build needed infrastructure such as roads or irrigation systems. The basic point, as stated at the outset of this discussion, is that the distribution problem must be dealt with first. Increasing agricultural production, whether to a self-sufficient level or not, also is desirable, but raising production contributes to a long-term solution. It is not an effective way of dealing with the immediate problem caused by a harvest failure and the resulting famine.

LAND TENURE AND REFORM

Before we focus on agricultural production, we need to explore the problem of land and the way it is owned and organized. Conditions of land tenure set the context within which all efforts to raise agricultural output must operate. Put differently, the property right that matters most in the agricultural sector is the right over the use of land. If that right is well defined as well as exclusive, secure, enforceable, and transferable, then farmers with those rights have an incentive to invest and work the land efficiently.

Patterns of Land Tenure

Land tenure and **land-tenure relations** refer to the way people own land and how they rent it to others to use if they choose not to cultivate it themselves. In Europe during the Middle Ages, for example, a local lord owned a piece of land

and allowed the local peasants to cultivate it. In exchange for cultivating that land, the peasant family had to deliver a part of the harvest to the lord, and members of the peasant family had to perform labor services in the lord's castle. In most cases, the peasant could not freely leave the land to seek work in the city or with another lord. Peasants did flee, but the lord had the right to force them to return if they could be caught. Serfdom, as this system sometimes is called, was only a modest step up from slavery. Serflike land-tenure relations prevail today in only a few remote and backward areas of the globe. The patterns that do exist, however, are diverse, as the following incomplete list makes clear.

- **Large-scale modern farming or ranching** usually refers to a large crop- or cattle-raising acreage that uses some hired labor but where many of the activities are highly mechanized. Many such farms are found in the United States, whereas much of Latin American agriculture is characterized by large modern farms that exist alongside small peasant plots.
- **Plantation agriculture** is a system in which a piece of land is used to raise a cash crop, such as tea or rubber, usually for export. Cultivation is by hired labor who are paid wages, and the plantation is run either by the owner or, more frequently, by a professional manager.
- **Latifundios** is a term used in Latin America and Europe to refer to large estates or ranches on which the hired labor still have a servile (master-servant) relationship to the owner.
- **Family farms or independent peasant proprietors** own plots of land (usually small) and operate them mainly or solely with their own family's labor. This type of tenure is dominant in Asia and Africa and is important in Latin America as well.
- **Tenancy** usually refers to a situation where an individual family farms a piece of land owned by a landlord to whom the farmer pays rent. Much of Asian agriculture is made up of either individual peasant proprietors or tenants.
- **Sharecropping** is a form of tenancy in which the farmer shares the crops with the landlord.
- **Absentee landlords,** who are particularly important in Asia and Latin America, tend to live in cities or other places far away from the land they own. Landlords who live near their land have little to do with it except to collect rents. Some resident landlords provide seeds and certain kinds of capital to tenants.
- **Communal farming** is practiced in parts of Africa, where inhabitants of villages still may own some of their land jointly. Individuals and families may farm plots on communal land, to which they gain access by custom or by allocation from the community's leaders. Europe in an

earlier period also had such common lands, which were used, among other purposes, as pasture for the village cows.

- **Collectivized agriculture** refers to the kinds of agricultural systems found for the most part in the states of the former Soviet Union including Russia, China prior to 1981, and Vietnam prior to 1989. Land, except for small family plots, is owned by a cooperative whose members typically are all or part of the residents of a single village. Management is by a committee elected by the villagers or appointed by government authorities, and members of the cooperative share in the output on the basis of the amount of labor they contribute to it.

There are numerous variations within and among these categories, but this list gives some idea of the great range of land-tenure systems that exist in the developing world. The kind of land-tenure system existing in any given country or region has an important bearing on economic development for several reasons. To begin with, prevailing land-tenure arrangements have a major influence on the welfare of the farm family. A family farming only one or two acres of land that must turn over half its main crop to the landlord has little left over to feed itself or invest in improvements. Such a heavy rent burden may seem harsh, but half or more of the farmers in some major countries, such as China and South Korea before land reform and parts of Latin America and India today, labor under comparable conditions or worse.

A second important impact of the land-tenure system is on the prevailing degree of political stability. Families that own the land they cultivate tend to feel they have a stake in the existing political order, even if they are quite poor. Because they possess land, they have something to lose from turmoil. Landless farm laborers and tenants who can be pushed off the land at the will of a landlord have no such stake in the existing order. The history of many countries with large landless rural populations often are dotted with periodic peasant rebellions. One such rebellion played a major role in bringing the Communists to power in China. Much of the history of modern Mexico has also been shaped by the revolt of the landless.

Tenure and Incentive

Land-tenure systems also have a major impact on agricultural productivity. An individual proprietor who has well-defined, exclusive, and secure rights to land knows that increased effort or skill that leads to a rise in output also improves income. This result does not necessarily follow if the land is owned by someone else and property rights for the farmer are not well defined and secure. Under sharecropping, for example, the landlord gets a percentage share, typically a half of any increase in output. If a tenant's rent contract is only a year or two in length, a rise in output may cause the landlord to threaten eviction of the tenant so that all or much of the increase in production can be captured through a rise in the rent. In some countries, landlords had to draw up land-rental contracts of many years or even a lifetime's duration, precisely because tenants otherwise would have no incentive to invest in improvements or even to maintain existing irrigation and drainage systems.

Farms with large numbers of hired laborers have an even more difficult incentive problem, compounded by a management problem. Farm laborers are paid wages and typically do not benefit at all in any rise in production. One way around this difficulty is to pay on a **piece-rate basis;** that is, to pay workers on the basis of the number of bushels of cotton or tea leaves they pick. But, although this system works at harvest time, it is virtually impossible to pay on a piecework basis for the cultivation of crops. A laborer can be paid by the acre for planting wheat, but it will be many months before it will be possible to tell whether the planting job was done well or carelessly. In a factory, elaborate procedures can be set up by management to check on the pace and quality of work performed. But work in a factory is much easier to reduce to a routine that can be measured and supervised than work on a farm. A thousand different tasks must be performed on a typical farm; and supervision, even in the hands of a skilled manager, is seldom a good substitute for a farmer motivated by the knowledge that extra effort will lead directly to a rise in income.

Incentives under communal farming suffer in a different way. Property rights in this case are not exclusive because the land is owned in common. Each individual family has an incentive to use the land to the maximum extent possible, but no one has much of an incentive to maintain or improve the land because the benefits of individual improvement efforts accrue to everyone who uses the land, not mainly to the individual. Economists call this the **public goods** or **free-rider** problem. Everyone agrees that a fire department is necessary if a town is to avoid conflagration, but few people would voluntarily pay what the fire department is worth. Instead each would pay little or nothing in the hope that neighbors would pay enough to maintain the department, but of course, the neighbors would not pay enough either. The usual solution to this problem is to turn payment over to the town government and allow that government to assess taxes on everyone in town on an equitable basis. Similar solutions are found in communal agriculture. Certain dates can be set aside when everyone in the village is expected to show up and work on a particular land improvement, such as repair of a fence with a neighboring village. But the incentive to work hard in a common effort relies heavily on community social pressure plus the inner goodwill of each individual. If farmers were saints, goodwill would do the job, but for better or worse, farmers are like the rest of us.

Collectivized agriculture has some of the incentive and management problems of both plantation and communal agriculture, but with important differences. Because rights to the land are held in common, the free-rider problem is present, but its impact is modified by paying everyone "work points" on the basis of the amount of work actually done. At the end of the year, the total number of work points earned by collective members is added up and divided into the value of the collective's output to determine the value of each work point. The individual, therefore, has a dual incentive to work hard. More work means more work points, and indirectly it leads to higher collective output and hence a higher total income for that individual.

The incentive issue posed by collective agriculture is whether the work-point system is an adequate substitute for the motivation provided on a family farm, where increased output benefits a farmer's own family and only that family. The main problem with the collective system is that an individual sometimes can earn work points by claiming to have worked hard, when in fact that person was sleeping or leaning on a hoe. The solution to the leaning-on-a-hoe problem is to have the leadership of the collective check up on how hard members are working, but that can introduce the supervision or management problem found in plantation labor; namely, it is extremely difficult to supervise many agricultural activities. In general, both the incentive and managerial problems worsen as the collective unit gets larger. In a unit of 20 or 30 families, the size of the Chinese production teams in the 1970s, families could supervise each other and penalize laggards. But in a unit of several thousand families, the size of the Chinese commune in the late 1950s, family members had little incentive to pressure laggards to work harder because no single individual's work, however poorly done, had much impact on the value of a neighbor's work points. If everyone in the collective thinks this way, of course, the output of the collective will fall. By 1981, the Chinese leadership had decided that even the 20- to 30-family collective unit created incentive and managerial problems, and the leaders introduced reforms that returned Chinese agriculture to a system of family farming.

From an incentive and management point of view, therefore, the family-owned farm would seem to be the ideal system. The analysis so far, however, has left out one very important consideration, economies of scale. In agriculture, economies of scale may exist because certain kinds of machinery can be used efficiently only on large farms. On small farms, tractors or combines may be badly underutilized. Such considerations help explain why many Latin Americans feel that large-scale farming is the most appropriate way to increase agricultural production and exports. Economies of scale may also exist because large collective units are better at mobilizing labor for rural construction activities than individual family farms. We return to the question of scale economies later. Here, all we can conclude is that the question of the ideal type of rural land-tenure system has not been completely resolved.

Land Reform

The reform of land-tenure systems can assume many different forms.[4] Here are some typical measures found in many reforms, starting with the least radical:

- *Reform of rent contracts* ensures the tenure of a tenant farmer. Many tenants farm at the will of the landlord and can be removed easily at the end of a season. Laws requiring long-term contracts that restrict the landlord's right to remove a tenant can markedly improve the tenant's willingness to maintain and invest in the land and also introduce a degree of stability into the family's life. In effect, these kinds of reforms strengthen the property rights of tenants at the expense of those of the landlord but do not necessarily involve a transfer of income from owner to tenant.

- *Rent reduction* typically involves a ceiling on the percentage share of the crop that a landlord can demand as rent. If the percentage share is substantially below what prevailed in the past, the impact both on tenant welfare and the tenant family's surplus available for investment can be substantial.

- *Land to the tiller* (the former tenant) *with compensation* to the landlord for loss of land is a measure that can take many different forms. A government can pass a law setting a ceiling on the number of acres an individual can own and so force individuals to sell all land over that limit. Or the reform law can state that only those who actually till the land can own it, and all other land must be sold. A key issue in this kind of reform is whether the former landlord receives full or only partial compensation for the land that must be sold.

- *Land to the tiller without compensation* involves the most radical transformation of rural relations, except for the further step of collectivization. All land not cultivated by its owner is confiscated, and the former landlord receives nothing in return. Frequently, in such reform, the landlord may lose life as well as land.

The Politics of Land Reform

The main motive for undertaking land reform usually is political, not economic.[5] Two types of politics lead to reform. A society with a large tenant and

---

[4]There are numerous studies of land reform. One of the best-known practitioners was Wolf Ladejinsky. See Louis J. Walinsky, ed., *Agrarian Reform as Unfinished Business: The Selected Papers of Wolf Ladejinsky* (London: Oxford University Press, 1977).

[5]Elias Tuma, *Twenty-Six Centuries of Agrarian Reform: A Comparative Analysis* (Berkeley: University of California Press, 1965).

landless laborer population that is controlled by other classes may find itself faced with increasing rural unrest. In the first type of land reform, to keep this unrest from blowing up into a revolution, bills are passed to reduce the burden on the peasantry and give them a stake in continued stability. In the second type, land reform takes place after a revolution supported by the rural poor has occurred. The main purpose of reform in this case is to consolidate support for the revolution among the rural poor and eliminate the economic base of one of the classes, the landlords, most opposed to the revolution.

The motive behind the Mexican land reforms of the twentieth century, for example, was largely of the first type. Prior to the Mexican Revolution of 1911, land in Mexico had become increasingly concentrated in large haciendas ranging in size from 1,000 to over 400,000 acres. Although the revolution of 1911 was supported by those who had lost their land and other rural poor, those who took power after the revolution largely were from upper-income groups or the small middle class. This new leadership, however, had to deal with the continuing rural unrest that often was ably led by men such as Emiliano Zapata. To meet the challenge of Zapata and people like him, the Mexican government periodically redistributed some arable land, most recently under the government of President Luis Echeverria in the 1970s. Mexican land-tenure relations, however, continue to be characterized by large estates existing alongside small peasant holdings. Reform eliminated some of the more extreme forms of pressure for more radical change, but Mexican agriculture still includes a large, poor, and not very productive rural peasant class.

The Chinese land reform of the 1940s and early 1950s under the leadership of the Communist Party was a reform par excellence of the second type. The communist revolution had been built primarily on the rural poor, and the landlord class was one of the main pillars of support of the existing Kuomintang government. Prior to the reform some 40 percent of the arable land had been farmed by tenants, who typically paid half their main crop to the landlord as rent. The landlord, whether a resident in the village or an absentee, contributed little or nothing other than the land. After the reform, and prior to the collectivization of agriculture in 1955–56, land was owned by the tiller and the landlord received no compensation whatsoever. In fact, many landlords were tried publicly in the villages and either executed or sent off to perform hard labor under harsh conditions.[6]

A more recent example of "land reform" without compensation occurred in Zimbabwe at the turn of the twenty-first century where President Mugabe encouraged landless individuals to simply seize the land of the large farms owned by white farmers. With the government unwilling to enforce their prop-

---

[6]Among the many descriptions of Chinese land reforms is William Hinton's *Fanshen* (New York: Vintage Books, 1966).

erty rights, the white farmers had little choice other than to flee their farms or risk their lives defending them. Whether those who received the land will have secure property rights and farm the land efficiently remains to be seen but initial results contributed directly to famine in Zimbabwe.

The Japanese land reform that followed World War II was different in important respects from the Chinese experience. Land reform in Japan was carried out by the U.S. occupation forces. The occupation government believed that the landlord class had been an important supporter of the forces in Japanese society that brought about World War II. Small peasant proprietors, in contrast, were seen as a solid basis on which to build a future democratic and stable Japan. Since the Americans had won the war, Japanese landlords were not in a position to offer resistance to reform, and a thoroughgoing reform was carried out. Compensation of landlords was provided for in legislation, but inflation soon had the effect of sharply reducing the real value of the amounts offered. As a result Japanese land reform also amounted to confiscation of landlord land with little compensation.[7]

A second feature of land reform efforts is that land reform legislation is extremely difficult to enforce in the absence of a deep commitment from the government. Most developing countries have some kind of land reform legislation on the books, but relatively few have experienced real reform. In some cases, no serious effort is made to enforce the legislation. In other cases, the legislation is enforced but has little effect because of legal loopholes. India provides examples of both kinds of problems. In the Indian state of Bihar, the government awarded substantial tracts of land to the harijan (former untouchable) caste. But Bihar is a state where much of the real power rests in the hands of so-called higher castes, which include many landlords, and these higher castes have forcibly prevented the harijans from taking over the land the government awarded to them. Elsewhere in India, a law limiting the amount of land that can be owned by a single person has been enforced but has had limited real effect. An individual with more land than allowed by law registers the extra land in the name of trusted relatives or associates. For truly enormous landholdings, subterfuges of this kind may be impossible, but most landlords in India possess only several tens or a few hundred acres of land.

Land Reform and Productivity

The impact of land reform on agricultural productivity depends on what kind of system is being reformed as well as the content of the reform measures. Land reform has the greatest positive impact on productivity where the previous system was one of small peasant farms, with high rates of insecure tenancy (for

[7]There are many studies of Japanese land reform, including R. P. Dore, *Land Reform in Japan* (London: Oxford University Press, 1959).

example, one-year contracts) and absentee landlords. Under such conditions reform has little impact on cultivation practices since farms are small both before and after reform. Elimination of landlords also has little effect on productivity because they have nothing to do with farming. On the other hand, turning tenants into owners provides them with well-defined and secure property rights and hence with a greater incentive to invest in improvements. The Chinese, Japanese, and South Korean land reforms of the 1940s and 1950s essentially were of this kind.

At the other extreme are reforms that break up large, highly efficient modern estates or farms and substitute small, inefficient producers. In many parts of the developing world, such as Mexico, Kenya, and Malaysia, large, highly mechanized estates using the most advanced techniques have grown up over time. The incentive problems inherent in the use of hired farm labor at least partially are overcome by the use of skilled professional estate managers. Often these estates are major suppliers of agricultural produce for export and hence a crucial source of the developing country's foreign exchange. If land reform breaks up these estates and turns them over to small peasant proprietors who know little about modern techniques and lack the capital to pay for them, the impact on agricultural productivity can be catastrophic. But there also are examples, as in the Kenyan highlands, where the breakup of large estates into small peasant holdings actually increased productivity, mainly because the small holdings were farmed much more intensively than the large estates. In between these two extremes are a myriad of variations with different impacts on productivity, both positive and negative.

Land Reform and Income Distribution

Land reform has a major impact on the distribution of income in rural areas only if land is taken from landlords without compensation or at least without anything close to full compensation. If former tenants are required to pay landlords the full market value of the land received, the society's distribution of wealth is the same as before. The tenant receives land together with a debt exactly equal to the value of the land, hence no change in net wealth of the former tenants. The former landlord surrenders land but acquires an asset of equal value in the form of a loan to the former tenant. Reform with full compensation may be desirable on productivity grounds because of the advantages of strengthening property rights through owner rather than tenant cultivation, but initially at least, the new owner is just as poor and the new landlord just as rich as before. On the other hand, if the landlord is compensated with bonds paid for out of general tax revenues, the former tenant's income share may rise, provided the taxes to pay for this do not fall primarily on the tenant. The best-known successful land reforms commonly have involved little or no compensation for confiscated assets of landlords. Such was the case in Russia after 1917 and China after 1949, as well as in the Japanese and South Korean reforms after World War II. This discussion of land-tenure relations and their reform sets the scene for the discussion of agricultural production and how it can be raised. Much of the analysis that follows deals with subjects like agricultural research or the uses of chemical fertilizer. But always keep in mind that, behind the use of better techniques and more inputs, the land-tenure system must provide farmers with well-defined, secure, and enforceable property rights and, hence, the incentive to introduce those techniques and inputs, then use them efficiently.

TECHNOLOGY OF AGRICULTURAL PRODUCTION

The popular view of traditional agricultural systems is that they are made up of peasants who have been farming the same way for centuries. The implication is that traditional farmers are bound by custom and incapable of making changes that raise the productivity and efficiency of their efforts. Custom, in turn, is reinforced by values and beliefs often closely tied to religion. Change thus becomes doubly difficult, because to make a change may involve a rejection of deeply held religious beliefs. In this case, only a revolution that completely overturns the traditional society and all it stands for holds out real hope for agricultural development.

Traditional Agriculture

Tradition-bound societies of this type exist in the world, but the description does not fit the great majority of the world's peasant farmers. A great accumulation of evidence suggests that these farmers are efficient. They already have made sensible—sometimes complex and subtle—adaptations to their environment, and they are willing to make further changes to increase their welfare if it is clear that an improvement will result with no unacceptable risk of crop failure and hence starvation.[8]

When traditional agriculture is described as *efficient,* the word is used in the same way as it has been used throughout this book. Given existing technology, traditional farmers get the most output they can from available inputs or they get a given level of output with the smallest possible use of inputs. Foreign advisors, regardless of their background, often have to relearn this fact, sometimes at considerable cost. With a little reflection it is hardly surprising that traditional

[8]A classic statement of this point has been made by Theodore W. Schultz, *Transforming Traditional Agriculture* (New Haven, CT: Yale University Press, 1964).

agriculture tends to be efficient within the limits of traditional techniques. The central characteristic of traditional technology is that it changes very slowly. Farmers therefore are not in a position to respond constantly to changing agricultural methods; instead, they can experiment over long periods of time with alternative techniques until just the right method for the given technology is found. Long periods of time in this context may refer to decades or even centuries. If a slightly deeper method of plowing or a closer planting of seeds will raise yields per acre, for example, one or two more venturesome farmers eventually are going to give such methods a try. At least, they will do so if they have plows capable of deeper cultivation. If the techniques work, their neighbors will observe and eventually follow suit. Given several decades or a century, all farmers in the region will be using similar methods.

This example brings out a closely related characteristic of traditional agriculture. In addition to being efficient, traditional agricultural techniques are not stagnant; they have evolved slowly over time. That peasant farmers in a traditional setting are willing to change if the benefits from a change are clearly perceived has been demonstrated over and over again. Some of the best evidence in support of this willingness to change is that provided by responses to changes in prices. Time and again, as the price of cotton or tobacco or jute has risen relative to other farm prices, farmers, even in some of the poorest countries in the world, have rushed to increase the acreage of these crops. And the reverse has occurred when prices have fallen.

Change in traditional agriculture involved much more than responses to fluctuations in relative prices. Long before the advent of modern science and its application to farming, fundamental advances in all aspects of agricultural technology took place.

Slash-and-Burn Cultivation

One of the most fundamental changes, of course, was the conversion of society from groups of hunters and gatherers of wild plants to groups of settled farmers, who cleared and plowed the land. Initially, settled farming often involved slash-and-burn methods of cultivation. In slash-and-burn agriculture, trees are slashed and fire is used to clear the land. The burnt tree stumps are left in the ground, and cultivation seldom involves much more than poking holes in the ground with a digging stick and dropping seeds into the holes. The original nutrients in the soil plus the nutrients from the burnt ashes make respectable yields possible for a year or two, after which most of the nutrients are used up, weed problems increase, and yields fall off drastically. Farmers then move on to slash and burn a new area, perhaps returning to the first area 20 or 30 years later when the land has regained a sufficient level of plant nutrients. Slash-and-burn agriculture, therefore, often is referred to as a form of **shifting cultivation** or **forest-**

fallow cultivation. This system requires a large amount of land to support a small number of people. Today, the system exists mainly in remote, lightly populated areas, such as in the mountains of Laos and parts of Africa and the Amazon.

The Shortening of Fallow

The evolution from slash-and-burn agriculture to permanent cultivation, in which a crop is grown on a piece of land once every year, can be thought of as a process of gradually shortening the period that land is left fallow. The term *fallow* refers to the time that land is left idle to allow the soil to again accumulate the nutrients essential to successful cultivation. In Europe, the shortening of fallow gradually took place during and after the Middle Ages, and annual cropping did not become common until the latter part of the eighteenth century. In China, the evolution to annual cropping occurred at least a thousand years earlier. In both Europe and China, the driving force behind this evolution was increased population pressure on the land.[9]

The elimination of fallow did not occur automatically or easily. Farmers had to discover ways to restore nutrients in the soil by rotating crops and adding fertilizers such as compost and manure. Ploughs had to be developed to cultivate the land each year yet prevent it from being taken over by grasses. Each of these changes was at least as fundamental as many that have occurred in agriculture in the twentieth century. The difference is that these earlier changes took place over centuries rather than years.

Farming within a Fixed Technology

Once fallow was eliminated, increases in agricultural production could be obtained either by increasing yields on annually cropped land or expanding onto previously uncultivated land. Where population pressure was particularly severe, several centuries ago, grain yields reached levels per hectare higher than those found in many parts of the world even today. In China, for example, two crops a year of rice or of rice and wheat were common before the sixteenth century. By the mid-nineteenth century in both China and Japan, average rice-paddy yields over large areas had passed 2.5 to 3 tons per hectare, whereas in India and Thailand as late as the 1960s average rice yields were under 1.5 tons per hectare. Traditional agriculture was capable of achieving high levels of productivity per unit of land.

What separates traditional from modern agricultural development, therefore, is not the existence of technological progress or the sophistication of the

---

[9]Ester Boserup, *The Conditions of Agricultural Growth: The Economies of Agrarian Change and Population Pressure* (Chicago: Aldine, 1965); and Dwight H. Perkins, *Agricultural Development in China, 1368–1968* (Chicago: Aldine, 1969).

techniques used. Traditional agriculture experienced substantial technological progress, and the techniques used in highly populated areas at least were as sophisticated as many so-called modern techniques found today. The difference between traditional and modern agriculture is in the pace and source of change. In traditional agriculture, change is slow; whereas in modern agriculture, it is rapid. In modern agriculture, scientific research produces most of the new techniques used. In traditional agriculture, new techniques sometimes were the result of the tinkering of individual farmers and at other times new inputs, such as improved seeds, were accidents of nature that led to a variety that produced higher yields or required a shorter growing season.

The principal problem of traditional agriculture, therefore, was that farmers worked most of their lives within a technology that changed very slowly. They could spend their energies raising the efficiency with which they used that technology, but the gains from higher levels of efficient use of a stagnant technique were limited. The improvements in technique that did occur happened over too long an interval of time to have anything but a marginal impact on rural standards of living.

Modernizing Agricultural Technology

Traditional agriculture can be modernized in two ways. The first is technological: Specific inputs and techniques can be combined to produce higher agricultural production. Technological modernization deals with such issues as the role of chemical fertilizer and the relationship of fertilizer's impact to the availability of improved plant varieties and adequate supplies of water. These technological issues are the subject of this and the next section. The second approach to modernization concerns the mobilization of agricultural inputs and techniques in developing countries. How, for example, does a country mobilize labor for rural public works or create institutes that develop new techniques suitable to local conditions? These issues of mobilization and organization are the subject of the following part of this chapter.

There is no universally best technology for agriculture. All agricultural techniques must be adjusted to local soil and climatic conditions and local factor endowments. Even in industry, technology must be adapted to local conditions, but an automobile assembly plant in Ghana will look much like one of similar size in Indonesia. In agriculture, local conditions are fundamental, not secondary. Students from a developing country can be sent to advanced countries to learn how to develop improved plant varieties suitable to their country, but only occasionally will the plant varieties in the advanced country be directly transferable.

Still, generalizations can be made about the characteristics of modern agricultural technology. The technological development that occurs differs markedly depending on whether a country has a large area of arable land and a small declining rural population or a large rural population on a very limited amount of

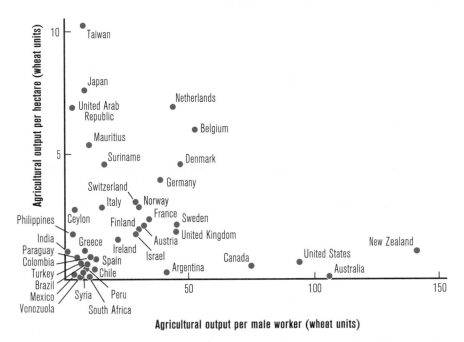

FIGURE 16-1. International Comparison per Male Worker and per Hectare of Agricultural Land

The dot for the United States indicates that U.S. grain output per farm worker was nearly 100 tons of wheat or its equivalent but U.S. yields per hectare were only about 1 ton. Mauritius, in contrast, had over 5 tons of output per hectare but little more than 10 tons per worker. Output data in the diagram are 1957–62 averages; and labor and land data are for the year closest to 1960.

Source: Yujiro Hayami and Vernon W. Ruttan, *Agricultural Development: An International Perspective* (Baltimore: Johns Hopkins Press, 1971), p. 71.

arable land. The problem in the former is to get the most output possible out of its limited rural labor force. The latter country also must raise labor productivity, but the key to success depends primarily on achieving rapid increases in the productivity of the land.[10] The fundamental difference between these two strategies can be illustrated with a simple diagram, Figure 16–1. As the figure makes clear, the United States and Japan have pursued fundamentally different agricultural strategies, and most other countries fall somewhere in between. In the United States, labor productivity is extremely high but yields per hectare are well below those of many countries, including more than a few of the less developed. In contrast, Japanese labor productivity in agriculture is only a fraction of that in the United States, but land productivity is several times that of the United States.

The difference between the two strategies involves basically different technologies. These different technologies often are called the *mechanical package*

[10]The point is that innovation is induced by perceived needs. See Hans P. Binswanger and Vernon W. Ruttan, *Induced Innovation: Technology, Institutions and Development* (Baltimore: Johns Hopkins Press, 1978).

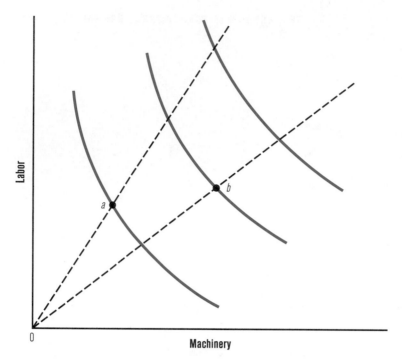

FIGURE 16-2. The Mechanical Package Production Function
The isoquants in this production function represent increases in
agricultural output as one moves out from the point of origin (0).
Movement from point *a* to point *b* represents a shift to the use of
more machinery, which also involves a rise in agricultural output
because machinery is a good substitute for labor.

(of technologies) and the *biological package.* In the **mechanical package,** tractors, combines, and other forms of machinery are used primarily as substitutes
for labor that has left the farm for the cities. In the **biological package,** yields are
raised through the use of improved plant varieties such as hybrid corn or the
new varieties of rice developed at the International Rice Research Institute in
the Philippines. Because of the dramatic effect on yields of some of these new
varieties, the phenomenon often is referred to as the **Green Revolution.** But
these new varieties raise yields only if combined with adequate and timely
water supplies and increased amounts of chemical fertilizer. The basic production functions that describe these two packages therefore are fundamentally different. The isoquants of a production function representing the mechanical
package indicate a high degree of substitutability (Figure 16–2), whereas the isoquants for the biological package are drawn in a way to indicate a high degree of
complementarity (Figure 16–3). The L-shaped isoquants in Figure 16–3 indicate
complementarity because only a limited number of fertilizer and water combinations produce increases in grain output. Continual increases of only one
input, such as fertilizer, runs into diminishing returns and then, where the curve
flattens out, no returns. Even the biological package has some substitutability
but less than in the case of the mechanical package.

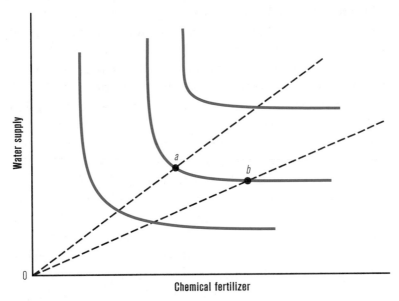

FIGURE 16-3. The Biological Package Production Function
The isoquants in this production function also represent increases in
agricultural output as one moves out from the point of origin (0), but
these isoquants, unlike those in Figure 16–2, indicate little
substitutability between inputs. An increase in fertilizer from point *a*
to point *b*, for example, does not lead to a rise in agricultural output,
because the required increase in water supply to make the fertilizer
effective has not occurred.

The Mechanical Package

To someone familiar with the cornfields of Iowa or the wheat fields of Nebraska
and the Dakotas, mechanization means the use of large John Deere tractors and
combines, metal silos with mechanical loading devices, and numerous other
pieces of expensive equipment. Using such equipment, a single farmer with one
assistant can farm hundreds of acres of land. But mechanization also can occur
profitably on farms of only a few acres. As labor becomes more abundant and
land less so, the mechanical package becomes less important in relation to the
biological package, but mechanization still has a role to play even in poor, labor-
intensive agricultural systems.

Mechanization of agriculture in labor-abundant developing countries primarily is a substitute for labor, just as in the labor-short U.S. Midwest. Even in countries such as China or India, there are periods when the demand for labor exceeds
its supply. When two rice crops are grown each year, for example, the first crop
must be harvested, fields prepared, and the second crop transplanted, all within a
matter of a few weeks. Transporting the harvest to market also takes an enormous
amount of labor if goods must be brought in on carts hauled by men or animals or
as head loads carried by women, as is still the case in much of the developing

world. One driver with a truck can do in a day what might otherwise take dozens of men and women several days to do. Nor can humans or animals working a hand pump or a water wheel move much water to the fields, however hard they work. A small diesel pump can move more water to higher levels than a large number of oxen turning wheels, and oxen cost more to feed than the pump costs to fuel.

Even when labor is extremely inexpensive, therefore, it can be economical to substitute machines for labor in some operations. Over the years manufacturers in Japan and elsewhere have developed whole lines of miniaturized machinery such as hand tractors and rice transplanters to meet this need, and these machines are in widespread use in the developing world. Not all mechanization in the developing world has been economic, however. Frequently tractors and other forms of farm machinery are allowed to enter a country duty free (when other imports have high tariffs) or are subsidized in other ways. Large farmers thus sometimes find it privately profitable to buy tractors and get rid of hired labor when, in the absence of subsidies, they (and the country) would be better off economically using laborers.

A major point of this discussion is that no one agricultural technology is most efficient in all countries. The technology that produces a given level of output at the lowest possible cost in a country with a low per capita income is likely to be very different from the technology that produces the same product at the lowest cost in a country with a high per capita income. The reason is straightforward. Labor in a country with a low per capita income typically is paid much lower wages than in the richer country. Capital conversely often is less expensive in countries with a higher per capita income.

How this works can be illustrated by adding **isocost** lines to Figure 16–2, which is done in Figure 16–4. The isocost lines (*ac* and *bd*) illustrate the various combinations of labor and machinery that can be purchased for a given sum of money, say $1,000, at prices prevailing for machinery and labor in that country. The line *bd* represents the relative costs of these inputs in a high per capita income country, where labor is expensive and capital relatively cheap. The line *ac* represents the situation in a poorer country, where labor is inexpensive and capital is relatively costly. The objective for the efficient farmer is to produce the most output possible at a given cost (or minimize the cost required to produce a given output). For the country with a low per capita income, that most efficient point is at *f*, where its isocost line is tangent to the isoquant *efgh* of the production function. For the country with the higher per capita income and the relatively expensive labor, in contrast, tangency is achieved at point *g* on that same isoquant. At point *g*, the richer country uses substantially more capital and less labor to produce the same level of output as the poorer country producing at point *f*.

In some cases, however, the capital-intensive technology is superior regardless of the relative prices of capital and labor. An example would be the use of tube wells with power pumps to replace wells dug by hand with water obtained with a bucket and rope. The latter uses much more labor but saves little or no capital. This situation is illustrated in Figure 16–5. The isocost lines of both the

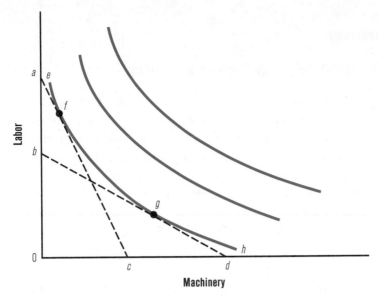

FIGURE 16-4. Choices of Technology with Differing Costs of Capital and Labor
The technology choices here are similar to those in Figure 16–2. Added are the isocost line for the high per capita income country (*bd*) and the low per capita income country (*ac*).

high and low per capita income countries, *ac* and *bd*, are tangent to the production isoquant at almost the same point (*e* is close to *f*). This situation, where efficient substitutability is limited, also commonly is found with respect to some elements in the biological package, to which we now turn.

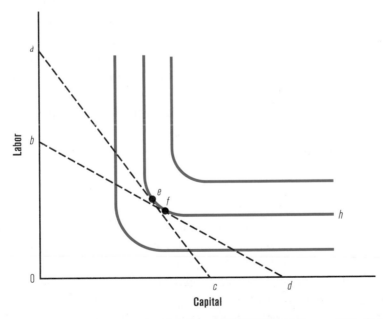

FIGURE 16-5. Choices of Technology with Differing Costs of Capital and Labor and Limited Substitutability between Capital and Labor
This figure is similar to Figure 16–4, except for the use of production function isoquants that indicate limited substitutability between capital and labor.

The Biological Package and the Green Revolution

The main impact of the biological package is to raise yields. Nothing is new about using improved plant varieties in combination with fertilizers and pesticides to raise yields of rice or corn. The use of modern scientific laboratories to develop the new varieties dates back half a century and more. Only since the 1960s, however, have the methods so successful in the industrialized countries been applied throughout the developing countries. The founding of the International Maize and Wheat Improvement Center (CIMMYT[11]) in Mexico and the International Rice Research Institute (IRRI), in the Philippines, marked the beginning of a truly international effort to develop high-yielding varieties of grain suitable to the tropical conditions found in so much of the developing world. National efforts preceded these international centers, and other international centers devoted to the problem of arid and semiarid developing areas and other crops followed. The result has been a steady stream of new, high-yielding varieties of wheat, rice, and other crops that found increasing acceptance in Asia and Latin America and to a lesser degree in Africa.

A rapid increase in the use of chemical fertilizers in the developing world had accompanied the increased use of high-yielding and other improved varieties (see Table 16–2). Prior to World War II, modern chemical fertilizers were virtually unknown in the less-developed countries. By the 1970s, they were in widespread use from Brazil to India. Unlike machinery, chemical fertilizers can be purchased in almost any quantity and even very small amounts help yields. Thus, chemical fertilizers are within the reach of even quite poor peasants. The principal limitations on the greater use of chemical fertilizer have not been the conservatism of the peasants or their poverty, but the availability of supplies and the price at which these supplies have been sold. We return to the price question later in this chapter.

A key component of the biological package is water. Improved plant varieties using more chemical fertilizer lead to dramatically higher yields only when there is an adequate and timely water supply. In much of the U.S. Midwest, rainfall provides all the water required and at the right time. In many parts of the developing world, rainfall often is inadequate or comes at the wrong time. In much of India, the difference between a good crop and a harvest failure still depends primarily on when the monsoon rains arrive and in what amount. As a result, efforts to raise yields in the developing world often have focused on measures to extend irrigation systems so that crops are less dependent on the vagaries of the weather.

Extending the irrigated acreage often has been seen as primarily a financial and engineering problem. If a country had enough money in the 1950s and 1960s (from aid or its own resources), it hired a group of engineers to build a

[11]The acronym refers to the name in Spanish: Centro Internacional de Mejoramiento de Maiz y Trijo.

TABLE 16-2.   Consumption of Chemical Fertilizer in Developing Countries
(1,000 metric tonnes of nutrient)

YEAR	LATIN AMERICA	FAR EAST*	NEAR EAST	AFRICA
1948–49 to 1952–53				
(annual average)	116.5	617.2	93.8	32.5
1961–62 to 1965–66				
(annual average)	609.7	1,839.3	379.3	192.2
1969–70	1,171.7	3,546.3	693.9	395.5
1979–80	6,720	9,473	2,831	1,142
1984	7,293	14,442	4,242	1,482
1988	8,807	19,237	5,019	1,694
1992–93	7,908	24,407	4,632	3,780
2002	13,230	70,210	5,947	4,278

*Far East excludes Asian centrally planned economies in earlier years.
Sources: Food and Agricultural Organization, *Production Yearbook 1970* (Rome: FAO, 1971); *Fertilizer Yearbook 1984* (Rome: FAO, 1985), p. 121; *Fertilizer Yearbook 1989*, 88–89; *Fertilizer Yearbook 1993*, 119–20; and the FAO website, www.fao.org.

dam to create a reservoir and canals to take water to the fields. As one dam project after another was completed, however, it became increasingly apparent that the irrigation potential of these systems was badly underutilized. Engineers could build the dams and the main canals, but they could not always get the farmer to build and maintain the feeder canals to the fields. Who should do the work and who would reap the benefits of these canals became entangled in the conflicting interests and local politics of rural society. Irrigation extension was as much a social as an engineering and ecological question.

More than anything else, the increased use of inputs from this biological package made possible the steady, if unspectacular, expansion of agricultural output that kept the food supply even with, or a bit ahead of, the rise in population (see Table 16–3). In the future, further development of improved varieties

TABLE 16-3.   Food Production per Capita in Developing Countries
(indices 1999–2001 = 100)

YEAR	WORLD	SOUTH AMERICA	ASIA	AFRICA
1975	83.4	70.8	60.6	103.3
1985	90.0	79.7	72.1	91.2
1997	96.8	94.6	93.7	97.6
1999–2001	100.0	100.0	100.0	100.0
2003	101.4	107.5	104.2	98.2

Source: FAO website, www.fao.org.

and expansion of irrigation systems, together with increased chemical fertilizer production, will remain the major contributors to higher yields. The main function of the mechanical package, in contrast, remains freeing labor from the burden of producing food so that it can do other, ideally more productive, tasks. Whether those tasks in fact are more productive depends on what is happening in the rest of the economy.

MOBILIZATION OF AGRICULTURAL INPUTS

Although the technology of increasing agricultural output is well understood, the ways in which the relevant inputs can be mobilized are both complex and much less well understood. Some of the problems already have been touched on, both in the discussion of difficulties in expanding irrigation and in the earlier presentation of the relationship between land tenure systems, individual incentives, and management difficulties. Here, we discuss some of these issues further in the context of the agricultural production function. In brief, the question is, In what alternative ways can a rural society supply itself with the necessary amounts of labor, capital, and improved techniques?

Rural Public Works Projects

Mobilizing labor to raise crops is primarily a question of individual and family incentives. The main determinants of such incentives are the nature of property rights over the use of land and the prices paid and received for agricultural inputs and outputs (treated later in this chapter). Mobilization of labor to create rural capital (roads, irrigation systems, and other parts of the rural infrastructure) is the topic of this section.

The creation of a rural infrastructure through the mobilization of rural labor has long been the dream of economic planners in the developing world. The idea is a simple one. In the off-season, labor in the rural sectors of developing countries is unemployed or underemployed. Therefore, the opportunity cost of using that labor on rural public works projects is zero or near zero (although food consumption may go up for people doing heavy construction work).

To use this labor in factories, factories first must be built, and that requires the use of scarce capital equipment. Furthermore, this equipment lies idle when the rural workers return to the fields to plant and harvest their crops. No such problems exist, however, when off-season, unemployed labor is used to build roads or irrigation canals. There is no need to buy bulldozers and other heavy equipment. If there is enough labor, shovels and baskets to carry dirt can accomplish much the same purpose, and farmers already have shovels and baskets or easily can make them. In the ideal situation, therefore, unemployed workers can be put to work, first making crude construction tools, after which they can begin to create roads and canals. The result is a major expansion in the rural capital stock at little or no cost to society other than the reduced leisure time of rural workers.

Effective implementation of rural public works programs using seasonally unemployed labor, however, has proven extremely difficult. The community development programs of India and elsewhere are widely perceived as failures. Time and again, international aid agencies have started pilot public works projects, only to see the project die quietly when aid money ran out. Of all the problems connected with the mobilization of unemployed rural labor, the most basic has been the lack of connection between those who did the work and those who reaped most of the benefits.

When an irrigation canal or a road is built, the main benefits that result take the form of higher yields on land near the canal or easier access to the market for crops grown on land near the road. Land or people living distant from the canal or road receive fewer benefits or none at all. If the people who own the nearby land are also those who did the work constructing a road or canal, then there is a direct relation between effort and reward. Unfortunately, more often than not, the people who do the work reap few of the rewards. The extreme case is when the land serviced by the new canal or road is owned by absentee landlords. Absentee landlords are never mobilized for rural public works projects. Rather, landless laborers and tenants do all the work, and the landlords benefit in the form of increased rent. Workers on such projects must be paid wages, and these wages tend to be higher than is justified by their productivity. Rural construction with crude tools, after all, is very low-productivity work. If the wages paid exceed the benefits of the project, it is hardly surprising that these projects come to an end when government or aid agency subsidies run out.

Clearly the problem of mobilizing unemployed labor to build rural infrastructure is more difficult than economists and others first thought (see Box 16–1). The complexity of successfully sharing the benefits is such that rural public works, though possible, are not the universal solution to the problem of rural development that some once thought them to be.

Rural Banking and Micro Credit

Farmers like all other producers need capital and most farmers cannot acquire all the capital they need from their personal savings. The poorest farmers may not have any savings at all. Farmers thus often need credit to take full advantage of their production opportunities. But, in traditional agriculture, a farmer usually has only two sources of credit: members of the family and the local moneylender. Since the real interest rates charged by moneylenders typically range to over 100

BOX 16-1 LABOR MOBILIZATION IN CHINESE COMMUNES

Even when land is owned by those who cultivate it, there is a problem of matching effort and reward. A typical project may require the labor of an entire village or several villages, whereas the benefits go primarily to farmers in only one part of the village. The Chinese solution to this problem was to collectivize agriculture by forming people's communes.[1] An entire village owned its land in common. People who participated in public works projects received work points based on the amount of effort expended, just as if they spent their time cultivating crops. When the project was completed, the land in a part of the village would be more productive, but the higher productivity benefited the entire village. The gap between work and reward, in effect, had been closed.

The Chinese commune made possible the more or less voluntary mobilization of large amounts of underemployed rural labor. Hills were leveled to create new fields, new reservoirs dotted the countryside, and roads reached deep into the countryside where only footpaths had existed before. But the Chinese ran into the work-reward problem in a different form. As the rural works projects became larger and larger, it became necessary to mobilize labor from two dozen villages, even though the benefits of the project went largely to only one or two of those villages.

The initial solution to this problem was to pool the land of all two dozen into a single commune. Then, increased productivity on the land around a single village would be shared by all 24 villages, and workers in those villages once again had an incentive to participate in the project. This larger commune, made up of two dozen villages, however, immediately ran into all the incentive and managerial problems common to large collective units. The result was that, despite all the construction activity or even because of it, Chinese agricultural output fell; and small collective units called *production teams* replaced the large communes as the basic agricultural management unit, although the latter continued to exist and perform some functions until China decided to return to household-based agriculture in the early 1980s.

---

[1]When China first collectivized agriculture (1955–57), the Chinese called their rural collectives *producers' cooperatives,* but to simplify the discussion we refer to collectives in all periods as *communes.*

percent a year, a farmer goes to a moneylender only when desperate. Peasants do not borrow from moneylenders to buy more fertilizer or a new pump. Only rarely will such investments be productive enough to make it possible to pay off loans with exceedingly high interest charges. They borrow instead to pay medical bills or provide a dowry to make it possible for a daughter to marry.

There are numerous reasons why urban commercial banks do not move in and take over from the moneylenders. Because of their location, urban banks lack the knowledge and skills necessary to operate efficiently in rural areas. On the other hand, local moneylenders know the reliability of the people to whom they are lending and the quality of land put up as collateral. Individuals without land, of course, have difficulty getting money even from local moneylenders. Women in particular may have difficulty when they farm land registered in the name of an absent husband, a frequent occurrence in Africa, South Asia, and elsewhere.

There are several potential substitutes for the absence of most large urban commercial banks in rural credit markets. One solution is known worldwide as the Grameen Bank model, named after the bank set up in rural Bangladesh to provide credit for the poorest of the poor, particularly landless rural women. The second model, based on the experience of the Indonesian bank, Bank Rakyat Indonesia (or BRI as it is usually referred to, see Box 13–2) revamps the practices of a standard urban commercial bank to make them more appropriate for rural areas. A third, frequently not very successful approach is to create rural credit cooperatives.

The Grameen Bank model is different from conventional banks in that it targets the poorest of the poor, particularly rural women. No collateral is required for a loan, as is customary with standard banking practices, because most of these women have little collateral. The borrower instead is required to join a group, usually a group of women from the same village who provide support to each other to ensure that each one can repay whatever money they have borrowed. The bank personnel as well work with these poor women to help them overcome difficulties that might interfere with their ability to repay the loan. The great strength of the Grameen system is that it reaches many of the poorest members of the community. The main weakness of the system is that Grameen has regularly required subsidies from international aid agencies and others to make up for the fact that the bank is not profitable on its own. Not all rural credit systems have such regular access to these kinds of funds, but Grameen has been successful in obtaining the necessary support over several decades.

In Grameen, as with most other successful micro-credit systems, those who repay their loans are eligible for further credit and access to further credit is probably the single greatest incentive to repay the loan. If the borrowers know that credit is likely to be cut off, they have little incentive to repay their outstanding loans, and banks in such circumstance have little recourse. Many credit systems set up by international aid agencies, in contrast, issue credit only so long as the international aid agency keeps on supplying funds. Since few such agencies supply funds on a regular basis over long periods, the money eventually runs out and borrowers, knowing this is going to happen, have little incentive to pay back their loans, thus accelerating the pace at which these kinds of subsidized operations go out of business.

Another key issue in rural banking is the question of at what level to set interest rates. Many well-meaning people think that the obvious answer is to charge the lowest rate possible, since these are poor people who cannot afford to pay more. But any interest rate that is well below the high moneylender rates in the local credit market are of some benefit to the loan recipients, however poor. Excessively low rates have two particularly debilitating drawbacks. On the one hand, lending rates that do not cover the cost of the loan require the supplier of micro credit to find a steady source of subsidies or go out of business. On the other hand, low interest rates attract politically powerful high-income borrowers who use their influence to divert the subsidized funds to their own uses. Grameen deals with this latter problem by not lending to such people, but rural credit institutions often are in no position to resist such pressures.

Arguably the most creative response by a large urban commercial bank to the special requirements of rural credit is that introduced by the Indonesian state-owned Bank Rakyat Indonesia. The BRI revamped the incentive systems for its rural lending and savings mobilization personnel. They also charged interest rates on loans that were high enough to cover costs and allow for some profit (and also high enough to discourage the politically powerful seeking low-cost funds) but were still only a fraction of the rates charged by rural money-lenders. The introduction of this new lending program (and an accompanying savings program) led to a many-fold rise in rural lending and an even larger increase in rural savings deposits—all happening at the same time that government subsidies to the BRI rural credit program were eliminated. While the "poorest of the poor" were not the major beneficiaries of this program, millions of farmers and small rural businesses that previously had no access to credit were able to obtain loans. Even the Asian financial crisis beginning in 1997 did not fundamentally undermine either the continued expansion or the profitability of this rural credit and savings program.

Credit cooperatives set up by the small farmers are another potential solution to the lack of sufficient credit in rural areas. The idea is that each farmer is capable of saving a small sum, and if these sums are pooled, one or two farmers can borrow a substantial sum to buy a new thresher or pump. The next year it will be another farmer's turn, and so on. In the meantime, those who put their money in the cooperative draw interest and thus are encouraged to save more. But this approach has flaws. Farmers' savings tend to be small, hence the cooperatives tend to be financially weak. More seriously, farmers in developing countries have little experience relevant to the effective operation and management of the cooperatives. In addition, economic, social, and political conflicts within the village may make it impossible to decide something as simple as who will get the next loan.

Because of these and other problems, the establishment of rural credit institutions usually requires significant injections of both money and personnel from outside the village, usually from the government. The entry of the government, however, does not necessarily or even usually solve the underlying difficulties. Governments, in an attempt to use cooperatives to strengthen their political support, charge interest rates that require large continuing subsidies and lead to the diversion of this credit to high-income borrowers as already outlined. Corrupt officials appointed to the cooperatives also sometimes siphon off the funds directly into their own pockets. These problems involved in setting up effective rural credit cooperatives can be overcome with well-trained banking personnel and a strong government administration capable of drawing up sensible procedures and enforcing them properly, but large numbers of well-trained banking personnel and strong government administrations are not common in developing countries.

Real solutions for overcoming the lack of sufficient rural credit, therefore, usually require either a model that makes it possible for regular commercial banks to operate profitably in rural areas with millions of small lenders and savers (the BRI model) or banking to be combined with a political and social movement that can sustain support for lending to the poorest of the poor over decades (the Grameen model) or some combination of the two models.

Extension Services

If one key to rapid progress in rural areas depends on the introduction of new inputs and new techniques, it follows that some of the most important rural institutions are those responsible for speeding the transfer of these new techniques to the farmers. **Extension services,** as these institutions usually are called, provide the key link between the research laboratories or experimental farms and the rural population that ultimately must adopt what the laboratories develop.

The key to the effectiveness of the extension worker is contact and trust. Rural education helps increase the channels of contact, because if farmers can read, contact can be made through the written as well as the spoken word. Trust is necessary, because if there is contact, the farmer may not believe what is read or heard. Trust, of course, depends not only on the extension worker's honesty or personality but, fundamentally, on the competence of the extension worker and the research system. Giving a farmer bad advice that leads to crop failure is likely to close the channels of communication for some time. Making contact and establishing trust is further complicated because extension workers usually are men whereas those doing the farming, particularly in parts of Africa, are women.

These remarks make common sense, but they get at the heart of the failure of extension services in many developing countries. Frequently, training for the extension service is seen not as a way of learning how to help farmers but as a way of entering the government bureaucracy and escaping from the rural areas. Some extension workers are government clerks living in town and just as averse to getting their hands dirty as their colleagues in the tax collection bureau or the post office. Even when they do visit the farmers they are supposed to be helping, they know so little about how farmers really operate that they are incapable of pointing out genuinely useful new methods. Too often, the extension worker visits the village, tells the farmers what is good for them, and departs; the farmers are left to guess as best they can whether the gain from using the new idea is worth the risk of failure.

At the other end of the spectrum are extension workers who are well trained and live in the villages and work closely with the farmers when new techniques are being introduced. A closely related variation on this approach is practiced by CIMMYT, which carries out major parts of its basic research on farmers' fields rather than in separate experimental stations, thus eliminating the physical gap between the experiments and the ultimate farmer beneficiaries.

There is much that we do not yet know about the spread of advanced technology in agriculture, but an effective extension service is only a part of the picture. To a large degree, farmers learn from their neighbors. However, if one local farmer owns 30 acres and farms it with a large tractor and the neighboring farmers have only 5 acres and no tractors, the farmers with 5 acres may feel they have little to learn from the experience of their neighbor. More evidence is required, but technology appears to travel more rapidly when neighboring farms in a country or region are much alike. Extremes of inequality thus may impede technological progress as well as being undesirable on equity grounds. As this discussion of mobilizing rural labor and capital and accelerating the rate of technical advance makes clear, agricultural development in the developing countries is not solely a scientific or engineering problem. It also depends on the quality of government administration at both the central and local levels.

The Development of Rural Markets

One common theme in the preceding chapters has been the importance of avoiding major distortions in the structure of prices. Nowhere is an appropriate price structure more important than in the agricultural sector. But, in agriculture as in other sectors, there first must be a market before prices can have widespread effects. And in the rural areas of developing countries, the existence of an effectively operating market cannot be taken for granted.

Virtually no areas of the world today still have subsistence farming in its purest form. All farmers specialize to some degree and trade their surplus output on some kind of market. Economic development usually is accompanied by the increasing size and sophistication of this rural marketing network, and in turn, that improved network has an important impact on productivity in agriculture. The key to an increasing role for the market is specialization, and specialization depends on economies of scale, low-cost transport, and acceptable risk.

Economies of scale are at the heart of specialization. If everyone could produce everything he or she needed at the lowest possible cost, there would be no need to turn over certain tasks to others. In fact, economies of scale are pervasive. In the most advanced agricultural sectors, such as the U.S. Midwest, farmers grow only one or two crops and rely on the market for all their other needs. In developing countries, the single greatest barrier to taking advantage of these economies of scale is transportation costs. The absence of good roads or trucks to run on them can mean that it can cost as much to move a bulky commodity 50 miles as to produce it in the first place. In the United States, wheat is turned into flour in large mills, and farmers buy bread in the local supermarket like everyone else. In developing countries, only wheat destined for urban consumption is processed in large mills. In rural areas, wheat is processed at home or in village mills, because to take the wheat to a large, distant mill would be prohibitively expensive. In large parts of southern Sudan, to take an extreme but not uncommon example, there are no all-weather roads at all, and large regions are completely cut off from the outside world during the rainy season. Regions such as this cannot readily specialize in crops for sale in the cities or for export abroad.

In large parts of the developing world, therefore, improvements in the transportation system, and hence in marketing, can have a major impact on agricultural productivity. Construction of an all-weather road system in South Korea in the 1970s, for example, made it possible for millions of Korean farmers to increase dramatically their emphasis on vegetables and cash crops destined for urban and export markets. Even the simple device of building paved bicycle paths connecting to the main road made it possible for Hong Kong farmers to expand their vegetable acreage several decades ago. In the absence of refrigerated transportation, many vegetables spoil quickly, and hence it does not pay to raise them if too much time elapses between the harvest and their sale on the market. Furthermore, enormous amounts of labor are required if the vegetables must be carried every day on human backs across muddy fields. The ability to move the vegetables along a paved path on the back of a bicycle can make the difference between growing vegetables or concentrating on rice, which has to be moved to market only once or twice a year.

Even when the transportation system is adequate, farmers in developing countries may limit their dependence on the market because of the risk it entails. While cash crops can fail due to bad weather or pests, the principal risk from market dependence is that the price of the crop being raised will fall sharply by the time the farmer is ready to sell. For large farmers in advanced economies, a fall in price of their main crop leads to a reduction in their income. If the fall is large enough, that farmer may be forced to borrow from a local bank to tide him or her over until prices rise again. Or the farmer merely may have to draw from the family's savings account. In developing countries, a fall in the price of a cash crop, particularly if food prices are rising simultaneously, may lead to a drop in a farm family's income to a level below that necessary to survive. Credit may tide the family over, but interest rates are so high that, once in debt, the farmer may never be able to pay off creditors and loses the land put up as collateral. Most farmers in developing countries avoid becoming dependent on a single cash crop and instead devote part of their land to meeting their family's food requirements. Their average income over the long run might be higher if they planted all their land in cotton or tobacco, but they might not live to see the long run if one or two years of depressed prices wipe them out.

Governments can take measures to reduce both transportation costs (by building roads) and risks (by guaranteeing prices and other similar measures) and thereby develop more efficient markets. But governments also can, and often do, take measures that inhibit the development of rural marketing. Governments around the world seldom have a real understanding of the role of rural traders, of the numerous middle traders who make a marketing system work. Middle traders are seen as exploiters who get between the producer and consumer; they drive down the price paid to the producer and drive up that charged to the consumer to reap huge monopoly profits. In response to political pressures from farmers, governments often have taken over the rural marketing system to improve its operation and eliminate the monopoly profits.[12] The temptation for governments to take this step is particularly strong where the middle traders are of a different race from the majority of the population, as is the case in much of Southeast Asia, where Chinese play a major role in marketing, and in East Africa, where descendants of nineteenth- and early-twentieth-century South Asian immigrants now control the wholesale and retail trade.

Although occasionally government involvement improves rural marketing, more often such involvement is based on a wrong diagnosis of the problem. The price at which a farm product is sold in the cities is markedly higher than the price paid to the farmer, but the difference has little to do with monopoly profits. The real cause is the high cost of transportation and a generally rudimentary system of distribution and marketing. It is not that rural traders get paid so much, it is just that it takes so many of them to get the goods to market. When the government takes over, this basic situation does not change. For a high-cost, private rural trading network the government often substitutes an even higher-cost bureaucratic control of the movement of goods.

AGRICULTURAL PRICE POLICY

This discussion of agricultural development has stressed the central role of institutional change such as land reform and the creation of effective rural credit, marketing, and extension systems. It also has emphasized the impor-

---

[12]The problems created by too much government interference in agricultural marketing in Africa are discussed in Elliot Berg et al., *Accelerated Development in Sub-Saharan Africa* (Washington, DC: World Bank, 1981).

tance of government investment in infrastructure, notably in agricultural research. But the creation of new rural institutions can take a long time. Needed changes in the land tenure system, in particular, can be blocked by powerful interests for decades and longer. Nor can an agricultural research system be created in a few years' time. New plant varieties suitable to local conditions may take a decade to develop. If the plant scientists needed to carry out the research have not yet been trained, the process can take longer.

The Multiple Role of Prices

In one area, however, government intervention has an immediate and often profound positive or negative impact. Most governments in both industrialized and developing countries intervene in agricultural markets to set prices for both the rural producer and the urban consumer. How they intervene can have a profound effect both on agricultural production and consumption. Specifically, the prices at which grain and other agricultural produce are bought and sold play three, and sometimes four, vital roles:

1. The prices paid to farmers and the relation of those prices to the prices farmers pay for key inputs, such as fertilizer, have a major impact on what and how much those farmers can produce.
2. The prices paid to farmers, together with the quantity of produce sold, are the primary determinants of farmers' cash income.
3. The prices at which agricultural products are sold in the cities are major determinants of the cost of living of urban residents in developing countries.
4. The prices of agricultural products, particularly in many African countries, often are controlled by government marketing boards, which manipulate them to earn profits for the government, a slightly disguised form of taxation.[13]

Prices have a profound impact on agricultural production because most farmers, even in very poor countries, are interested in raising their income. While some hold that peasants grow particular crops or use particular inputs because that is the way their grandfathers did it, as pointed out earlier in this chapter, study after study has shown that, when prices change, peasant farmers respond much like any profit-maximizing businessperson operating in a world fraught with uncertainty. If the price of cotton rises relative to, say, corn, farmers will grow more cotton even in very traditional societies.

---

[13]For a full discussion of the multiple role of prices, see C. Peter Timmer, Walter P. Falcon, and Scott R. Pearson, *Food Policy Analysis* (Baltimore: Johns Hopkins Press, 1983); and Isabelle Tsakok, *Agricultural Price Policy: A Practitioner's Guide to Partial-Equilibrium Analysis* (Ithaca, NY: Cornell University Press, 1990).

The most important price relationship from the standpoint of agricultural production is that between farm output and purchased inputs, notably chemical fertilizer. From the farmer's point of view it makes sense to use more chemical fertilizer so long as it increases the value of farm output by more than its cost. (This simply is a manifestation of the profit-maximizing rule that the use of a factor of production should be increased as long as the factor's marginal revenue product exceeds its marginal cost.) The simplest and most-effective ways of increasing rice yields are to raise the price of rice or to lower the price of chemical fertilizer or both. As studies of rice production in Asia have shown, a clear relationship lies between the rice yield per acre in a country and the rice-fertilizer price ratio. Other elements also are at work, but the role of prices is a primary influence. This basic point is illustrated with the diagrams in Figure 16–6.

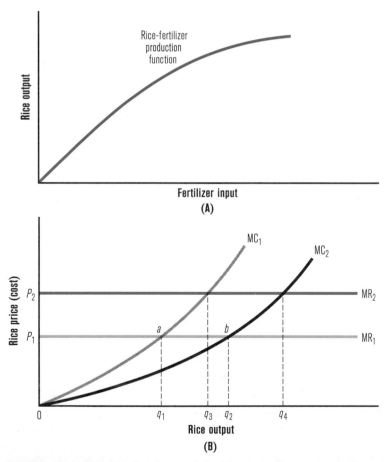

FIGURE 16-6. **Rice Production and the Rice-Fertilizer Price Ratio**

Part A is a simple one-input–one-output production function. The production function is drawn to reflect diminishing returns. If we know the prices of both fertilizer and rice, we easily can derive the marginal cost and marginal revenue curves facing the individual farmer, as is done in Part B.

If the price of fertilizer is lowered, the marginal cost curve falls from MC_1 to MC_2 and rice production rises from q_1 to q_2 as farmers maximize their profits at point b instead of point a by increasing the use of fertilizer. Similarly, a rise in the price from P_1 to P_2 while holding fertilizer prices constant increases rice output from q_1 to q_3.

The Impact of Subsidies

One of the most persistent problems facing planners and politicians in the developing world is the conflict between urban consumers and rural producers over appropriate agricultural prices. Since food purchases account for at least half the budget of urban consumers in most developing countries, a substantial increase in the price of food cuts sharply into the income of all but the richest urban people. Even governments indifferent to the welfare of their poorer urban residents cannot ignore the political impact of major increases in food prices. From Japan in the 1920s to Zambia in the 1990s, food price rises have triggered massive rioting that has threatened the very existence of particular regimes. (This phenomenon is closely akin to, and often part of, the politically dangerous transition from controlled to liberalized economies discussed in Chapter 5.) Because political leaders themselves live in urban areas and urban residents are in a better position than rural villagers to threaten governments, many states attempt to hold down food prices even during periods of general inflationary pressure. The result is depressed prices for farmers that reduce both farm income and farm output.

Especially (but not exclusively) in some developed countries, the political power of the farmers is such that governments raise farm purchase prices to gain rural support. Democracies that still have large or politically powerful rural populations are particularly likely to respond to these pressures. The United States, Japan, and the European Union from the 1960s right through to the twenty-first century and South Korea from the late 1960s and early 1970s are examples. The result is that prices are favorable to higher yields, but the income and production benefits of the higher prices may not be equitably distributed. In some countries, richer farmers who market a high percentage of their output gain most from high prices. Small subsistence farmers market little and hence gain little. In other countries, however, all farmers market a high percentage of their crop and all gain from higher prices. But prices for farmers set above world prices also require the country subsidizing farmers in this way to restrict imports from other lower-cost producers. The surplus production often generated by these high prices is also often exported at below world market prices to the rest of the world, thus depressing prices for agriculture in the countries that receive these subsidized imports. The success of the first trade liberalization effort of the twenty-first century, the Doha Round, depends critically on eliminating many if not all of these subsidies to farmers in the high-income countries of North America, Europe, and Japan. As developing country representatives regularly point out, why should they be expected to liberalize their import trade when the richest countries in the world are restricting trade in the very products where the developing countries have a comparative advantage.

Where both urban and rural residents have considerable political influence, governments sometimes have tried to maintain both low urban food prices and high farm purchase prices. Japan since World War II and South Korea and Mexico in the 1970s pursued this dual goal. Since the government must pick up the deficit resulting from selling food at prices below what it cost to purchase, only governments with large resources or those willing to forgo other high-priority goals can afford this policy. Thus, there is no single right answer to how high prices to farmers should be. Ultimately, the decision turns on political as well as economic judgment.

One common way to subsidize grain marketing is for the government to absorb the often substantial costs of moving grain from the farm to the urban retail market. Who benefits from this process depends on how the subsidy is handled. Several of the possibilities are illustrated in Figure 16–7, in which marketing costs are represented by the vertical distance between the farmer's grain supply curve and the retail supply curve facing urban residents. These costs are assumed to be a constant amount per unit of grain marketed. In a free market without subsidy, the retail price of grain on the urban retail market would be p_1 and the price received by farmers would be p_2. As this diagram indicates, if the subsidy goes to farmers, the result can be either a rise in grain storage or exports. If the subsidy goes to urban consumers, on the other hand, the excess demand leads to a rise in imports.

It is not just foreign trade in grain that is affected by these subsidies. The cost of marketing must be borne by someone, and in these cases, it most likely will be an expenditure item in the government's budget. Or the grain marketing authority may borrow from the central bank to cover its costs but without the ability of ever paying back the loan. The macroeconomic effects of these subsidies can be substantial, particularly in countries where a large portion of marketed agricultural produce is subsidized.

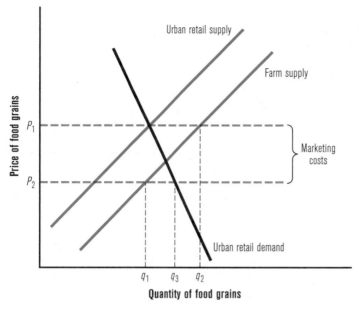

FIGURE 16-7. Effect of a Marketing Subsidy on Supply and Demand for Food Grains

If farmers receive the marketing cost subsidy P_1P_2, then the farmers' price rises to P_1 and farm output rises from q_1 to q_2. Since the food-grain supply now exceeds demand, the excess must be either stored or exported. On the other hand, if urban consumers are given the entire P_1P_2 subsidy, then the price paid by these consumers falls to P_2 and their demand rises from q_1 to q_3. The excess in demand then must be supplied from imports or the government must ration the allocation of food grains to urban consumers.

Source: This diagram is a modified version of that in Timmer, Falcon, and Pearson, *Food Policy Analysis,* p. 198.

Overvalued Exchange Rates

Because the high cost of large subsidies to government marketing boards becomes increasingly obvious to policy makers over time, steps usually are taken to eventually bring these costs under control, even though the political cost can be high. Another way of subsidizing urban consumers or rural producers, however, has a less obvious effect on the government budget but a profound effect on the economy, the use of an *overvalued exchange rate* (see Chapter 19). The impact of an overvalued exchange rate on the grain market is illustrated in Figure 16–8. If, at an equilibrium exchange rate, the world price of grain is P_2, then domestic demand, represented by the curve *DD*, is $0q_4$, and the domestic

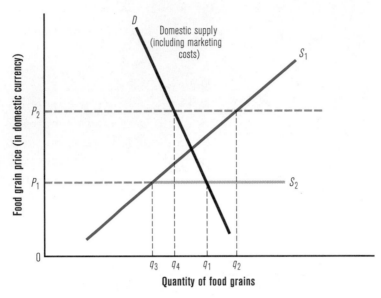

FIGURE 16-8. The Grain Market with an Overvalued Exchange Rate

If the world price of grain is P_2, then domestic demand (D) is q_4, domestic supply is q_2, and the result is excess stocks for storage or export. With an overvalued exchange rate, represented by P_1, however, domestic demand (q_1) exceeds domestic supply (q_3) and requires imports or rationing.

supply of grain exceeds demand by the amount q_4q_2. This excess could be either stored or exported. But, if this nation's currency becomes overvalued, the world price of grain expressed in terms of domestic currency falls from P_2 to P_1. The domestic food-grain supply, in this case, falls to q_3, and the excess of demand at this price, q_3q_1, is made up with imports or by restricting urban demand through rationing. Therefore, although this method of subsidizing urban consumers does not show up as an expenditure item in the government budget or a loss for the grain marketing board, it has a large negative impact on domestic agricultural production. Domestic agricultural production falls from q_2 to q_3.[14]

An undervalued exchange rate, of course, has a positive impact on farm output, but poor urban and rural purchasers of food grain may be forced by high prices to reduce substantially their intake of food; and this may lead to malnutrition and worse. In developing countries, the poor spend a high proportion, over 50 percent, of their budget on food. A price increase for food thus represents a sharp drop in income for these people. They can try to maintain food

[14]For a study of how trade and macroeconomic policies affect agriculture, see Romeo Bautista and Alberto Valdés, *The Bias against Agriculture: Trade and Macroeconomic Policies in Developing Countries* (San Francisco: ICS Press, 1993).

consumption by cutting back on other items in their budget, but these usually are necessities as well.

Agricultural price policies, therefore, have a profound effect on both agricultural production and the standard of living, and even the basic health, of the poorer segments of a country's people. Since agricultural prices and the exchange rate usually are set by the government in developing countries, it technically is a simple matter to change these prices to reflect the objectives of the government. Price changes involve few of the institution-building or implementation problems connected with developing an effective extension system or mobilizing labor for public works projects. Price changes, however, involve readily apparent costs to those on the receiving end of higher prices. If these people are in a position of influence, the political barriers to effective price policy can be formidable.

SUMMARY

- Agriculture contributes to development not only by providing food and raw materials to the population, but as productivity rises in agriculture, the sector also contributes to the supply of labor to the nonagricultural sectors and through higher rural incomes to the demand for nonagricultural as well as agricultural products.
- Famine is more a problem with the distribution of food than with its production. Democracy and a free press can go a long way toward eliminating the dangers of famine arising from government mismanagement of the distribution of food.
- Property rights in the form of the land tenure system is the key institution affecting the incentives of farmers to invest or not to invest in their land. Land reform largely is carried out for political purposes, but how it is done can have a profound impact on both the distribution of rural incomes and on farmer productivity.
- The two key kinds of agricultural inputs are what are often called the *mechanical package* in contrast to the *biological package*. The former involves mainly the substitution of machinery for labor to raise labor productivity, while the latter involves mainly the greater use of chemicals and improved plant varieties to improve the productivity of land.
- Mobilizing agricultural inputs in ways that best increase farmer productivity and incomes involves many institutions: research centers developing new plant varieties, extension systems getting the new discoveries

out to the farmers, and credit systems that provide farmers with the capital they need to implement some of the improved methods.

- Governments regularly attempt to influence the prices paid and received by farmers, and how they do this has a profound impact on agricultural production, farmer incomes, and the political stability of the nation.

17

Primary Exports

I nternational trade is one of the most powerful forces affecting the process of economic development. Trade influences a country's rate of economic growth, income distribution, use of natural resources, and economic and political relationships with the rest of the world. International trade provides firms access to new markets, opens up new opportunities for labor, and gives consumers a much wider and richer array of choices in the goods they buy. Trade allows low-income countries to import the latest machinery and technology without having to develop it on their own and facilitates a much greater flow of information and knowledge between countries. It also creates several challenges for developing countries, including increased competition from foreign firms, instability in world market prices for import and export products, and structural changes inherent in the shift from primary to manufactured products. This chapter begins by describing some general characteristics of exports from developing countries then explains the concept of comparative advantage and its powerful implications for international trade. The bulk of the chapter focuses on countries whose **comparative advantage** lies in primary commodities: food, agricultural raw materials, timber, metal ores, petroleum, and natural gas. Chapter 19 describes development strategies that attempt to change comparative advantage from primary products to manufactures.

EXPORT CHARACTERISTICS OF DEVELOPING COUNTRIES

Developing countries export a wide variety of products, including oil and other petroleum products; minerals such as gold, tin, and copper; food and agricultural cash crops; and manufactured products such as textiles, clothing, footwear, electronics, and toys. The diversity of trade patterns among developing countries is shown in Table 17–1. Not surprisingly, countries tend to export products based on their own particular endowments of the basic factors of production (land, other natural resources, labor, and capital). Natural resources dictate the exports of the oil-rich countries of the Persian Gulf, Southeast Asia, and Latin America; copper exporters such as Zambia, Zaire, Chile, and Peru; and timber exporters like Malaysia and Ghana. Variations in climate (which may be considered a factor of production) helps explain exports of foods such as coffee, cocoa, bananas, and vegetable oils and raw materials such as rubber and cotton. Countries with abundant labor tend to produce export crops that can be produced efficiently with labor-intensive methods, such as coffee, tea, rice, and tobacco, as well as labor-intensive manufactures such as textiles, clothing, and electronic components. At the same time, developing countries tend to import products that rely on factors of production relatively scarce in their countries, especially highly skilled labor. Therefore, almost all developing countries import machinery and other capital equipment, as well as more technologically advanced intermediate products such as chemicals, refined petroleum products, and metals.

Many developing countries are highly dependent on one or just a few primary commodities for the bulk of their export earnings. The extreme cases of export concentration include many of the major petroleum exporters, Ghana in cocoa, the Ivory Coast in cocoa and coffee, Colombia in coffee and cocaine (not a part of the official data), Chile and Zambia in copper, and Jamaica in bauxite and alumina. A few countries have a more diversified export base. In three of the cases shown (Bolivia, Malaysia, and Peru), no one product dominates and at least four commodities each account for 5 percent or more of total export earnings. Not surprisingly, very large countries tend to have a greater variety of natural resources and show a much more diversified export pattern.

Large countries also tend to export less of their total production than smaller countries, since there is a bigger domestic market in which to sell their goods. For example, India, Brazil, Bangladesh, and Pakistan export a low share of gross domestic product, ranging from 7 to 21 percent in 1996. Economists Moises Syrquin and Hollis Chenery verified this general relationship between country size and exports in their statistical analysis of cross-country patterns of

TABLE 17-1. **Export Characteristics of Selected Developing Countries, 1996**

COUNTRY NAME	POPULATION (MILLIONS)	GNP PER CAPITA (CUR. INT'L $S)	EXPORT SHARE OF GDP (%)	MAJOR PRIMARY EXPORTS	SHARE OF PRIMARY GOODS IN MERCHANDISE EXPORTS (%)
India	945	1,580	12	None	26[a]
Indonesia	197	3,310	26	Petroleum	49
Brazil	161	6,340	7	Coffee, iron ore	46
Nigeria	115	870	48	Petroleum	99
Pakistan	125	1,600	17	Cotton, rice	16
Bangladesh	122	1,010	14	Jute goods, raw jute	16[c]
Mexico	93	7,660	32	Petroleum	22
The Philippines	72	3,550	42	Coconut products	16
Thailand	60	6,700	39	Rice, rubber, tapioca	27[a]
Egypt	59	2,860	21	Petroleum, cotton	68
Ethiopia	58	500	13	Coffee, hides	99
Korea, Republic	46	13,080	32	None	8
Colombia	37	6,720	17	Coffee, fuel oil	66
Tanzania	30	610	22	Coffee, cotton	N.A.
Kenya	27	1,130	33	Petroleum, tea, coffee	72
Peru	24	4,410	12	Copper, zinc, petroleum, lead	84
Venezuela	22	8,130	37	Petroleum	88
Malaysia	21	7,410	92	Rubber, palm oil, wood, petroleum	24
Sri Lanka	18	2,290	35	Tea, rubber, coconut	27[b]
Ghana	18	1,790	27	Cocoa, wood	N.A.
Saudi Arabia	19	9,700	43	Petroleum	94
Chile	14	11,700	27	Copper	85
Ivory Coast	14	1,580	45	Coffee, cocoa	N.A.
Guatemala	11	3,820	18	Coffee, sugar	69
Bolivia	8	2,860	20	Tin, gas, zinc, silver	84
Senegal	9	1,650	31	Petroleum products, fish, ground nuts & oil, phosphates	50[a]
Jamaica	3	3,450	55	Alumina, bauxite, sugar	31
Zambia	9	860	38	Copper	95[b]

[a] 1995 data.
[b] 1994 data.
[c] 1993 data.
Source: World Bank, *World Development Indicators 1998*, CD-ROM.

development.[1] They found that, for an average small country with a population of less than 25 million and income per capita of $700 (in 1980 prices), exports of goods and services tend to average about 25 percent of GDP, compared with only 15 percent for a typical large country with the same income. They further found that, as income per capita rose from the neighborhood of $300 to $4,000, the average export share of gross domestic product tended to rise from about 15 to 21 percent. Of course, as with any statistical pattern, there are exceptions to these stylized patterns. Countries of any size that are well endowed with petroleum and other natural resources usually export much more: from 37 percent of GDP for Venezuela; around 30 percent for Chile, Indonesia, and Zambia; to 48 percent for Nigeria. Smaller countries lacking rich resource endowments show a wide range of export ratios, from 13 percent for Ethiopia, around 20 percent for Colombia and Tanzania, to around 40 percent for Thailand and Ivory Coast. Malaysia, rich in natural resources but also successful in the transition to manufactured exports, exports an astounding 92 percent of its GDP.[2]

COMPARATIVE ADVANTAGE

For more than 200 years, trade theorists have tried to explain why nations engage in international trade, what goods and services they trade, and how firms and consumers gain or lose from trade. The workhorse models rely primarily on the **theory of comparative advantage,** which describes trade patterns under assumptions of *static conditions* that hold the factors of production in fixed supply. Comparative advantage has rich implications about the gains from trade. Among the most powerful results are the following:

1. Any country can increase its welfare by trading, because the world market provides an opportunity to buy some goods at relatively low prices.
2. The smaller the country, the greater is this potential gain from trade.
3. A country gains most by exporting commodities that it produces using its abundant factors of production most intensively, while importing goods whose production requires relatively more of scarcer factors of production.

---

[1]Moises Syrquin and Hollis Chenery, "Patterns of Development, 1950–1983," Discussion paper no. 41, World Bank, Washington, DC, 1989, p. 20. Figures are for merchandise exports, excluding the export of services such as tourism and construction.

[2]It is worth noting that official export data often are understated in developing countries. Because the data cover only goods exported through official channels, they omit goods exported through parallel markets in countries like Ethiopia, where civil war prevailed until the early 1990s; Tanzania, where inflation and a controlled exchange rate made export unprofitable through the 1980s; and Colombia and Bolivia, where illegal drugs are important exports.

TABLE 17-2. **Production Costs and Comparative Advantage**

	MEXICO	UNITED STATES
Labor-days to produce		
Vegetables (1 ton)	5	4
Computers (1)	30	20
Relative price (tons of vegetables per computer)	6	5

The first implication is a subtle one that requires elaboration but is one of the most powerful ideas in all of economics. To reiterate, *any* country can engage in and benefit from international trade, including the world's highest-cost and lowest-cost producers of any good. To see why, consider the following highly simplified example. Assume that two countries, which can be called Mexico and the United States, both produce only two products, vegetables and computers, and use only one factor of production, labor, in the production process. The labor required to produce each product differs in the two countries, as shown in Table 17–2.

Note that, in this example, it takes fewer labor days to produce either product in the United States. Nevertheless, the United States is better off if it buys vegetables from Mexico and sells computers in return, even though it can produce vegetables at home with less labor. In the United States, a computer sells for the equivalent of 5 tons of vegetables, since each takes 20 labor-days to produce.[3] In Mexico, however, one computer sells for 6 tons of vegetables, since each takes 30 labor-days to produce. Therefore, the United States is better off selling its computers in Mexico and receiving more vegetables in return for home consumption. So, if labor is shifted away from farming and into computer production, U.S. firms can produce enough computers to satisfy domestic demand and export to Mexico, and U.S. consumers can eat more vegetables. But here is the most surprising result: Mexico also is made better off through the trade. Without trade, Mexico would have to produce 6 tons of vegetables to buy one computer in the home market. By selling to the United States, however, Mexico needs to give up only 5 tons of vegetables to get one computer. Thus, Mexico is better off by switching its labor into producing more vegetables and selling them to the United States.

The important point of this example, and the core of comparative advantage, is that both countries can gain from trade whenever the **relative prices** of commodities in each country differ in the absence of trade. Once the two coun-

[3]If each ton of vegetables requires 4 labor-days to produce, then it takes 5 tons of vegetables to absorb the same labor as one computer, which uses 20 labor-days. This formula for calculating relative prices works in this oversimplified example because labor is the only input into production.

tries begin to trade, the relative prices of commodities begin to shift until they are the same in the two countries. In the example, the relative price of 1 ton of vegetables in terms of computers settles somewhere between five and six (the relative prices prevailing before trade in the United States and Mexico, respectively). The final trade price, which can be called the **world price,** is closer to the initial price in the market of the country whose economy is larger. In our example, the final price in both countries settles closer to 5 tons of vegetables per computer. One implication is that small countries benefit more from trade because the relative price of commodities shifts more, and therefore the gains from trade are greater. To see this, consider an extreme case in which the U.S. economy is so large and trade with Mexico so small that U.S. prices do not shift at all. In this case, the United States does not gain from trade (nor does it lose), while Mexico gains to the full extent of the price difference.

The theory of comparative advantage is posed here in the very simple form developed by David Ricardo during the nineteenth century: two countries, two goods, and only one factor of production (labor). Some of the complexities of the real world can be incorporated into the theory, however. A trading world of many countries can be handled by taking the home country, say, Kenya, and treating the rest of the world as its trading partner. Some of the complexities of many goods are addressed in Chapter 19. Swedish economists Eli Heckscher and Bertil Ohlin expanded the theory during the first half of the twentieth century to deal with two factors of production, such as labor and capital. Under certain conditions the Heckscher-Ohlin theory can be extended to include more factors of production. The Heckscher-Ohlin model leads to an extremely important result: A country exports products that use its abundant factors of production more intensively and imports products that require relatively more of its scarce factors.

The implications of this more general approach to comparative advantage are encapsulated in Figure 17–1. The economy of the **home country** is divided into **exportable goods,** such as vegetables, that are produced using relatively land- and labor-intensive methods, and **importable goods,** such as computers, produced using relatively capital-intensive methods. As shown in the diagram, the home country is relatively well endowed with land and labor, so the production frontier is skewed to the right, depicting the country's greater capacity to produce vegetables than computers. The country's collective utility in consuming these goods is represented by the community indifference curves.

Without trade, the home country achieves its greatest utility by producing and consuming at point *A*, the tangency of the indifference curve *I* and the production frontier. The slope at *A* determines the domestic relative price of vegetables in terms of computers. Assume that the rest of the world is better endowed with capital than labor and land relative to the endowments of the home country

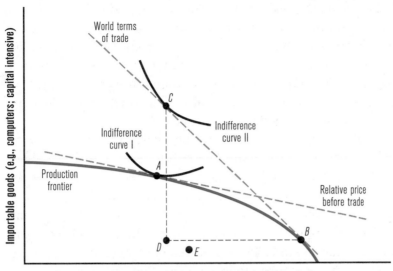

FIGURE 17-1. **Gains from Trade**
Before trade, a country both produces and consumes at a point like *A*.
With trade, a country produces at a point like *B* and can increase its
consumption of both goods and move to a higher indifference curve at *C*.

and world consumers have tastes broadly similar to those of the home country.
Then, in world markets, the relatively higher production of computers compared
to the demand for computers drives its price lower than in the home country;
and the relatively lower production of vegetables compared to the demand for
vegetables drives their price higher than in the home country. Since only relative
prices matter, these two statements mean the same thing: In world markets, the
price of vegetables in terms of computers is higher than in the home country.

This difference in relative prices between the home country and the rest of
the world presents an opportunity for the home country to improve its welfare
through trade. *With trade,* the country, taking advantage of its factor endowment, can produce more vegetables and fewer computers and sell vegetables on
the world market at the higher relative price, the world terms of trade in Figure
17–1. In producing more vegetables, the home country moves along the production frontier from *A* to *B*, where the terms-of-trade line is tangent to the production frontier. With vegetables to export, the country then can import computers
and consume more of *both* goods. The consumption point *C* is determined by
the tangency of the terms of trade line with indifference curve *II*. The country
now exports *BD* of vegetables and imports *DC* of computers, given by the trade
triangle *BCD*. As indifference curve *II* is above and to the right (northeast) of
curve *I*, the country is better off with trade than without it.

The general result is this: Any country, whatever its size and stage of development, can benefit from trade. This is true for large countries like China and India, small countries such as Ghana and Belgium, high-income countries like the United States and Japan, and low-income countries such as Mozambique and Haiti. As long as relative prices at home differ from those on world markets (or would differ in the absence of international trade), countries can increase their aggregate welfare by engaging in international trade.

However, although every country can gain from trade in the aggregate, *not all individuals or groups within each country necessarily gain.* In the vegetables-computers example, vegetable producers gain from trade because they sell more vegetables at a higher price. The consumers of computers also gain, because they can consume more at a lower price. But, once trade begins, computer manufacturers face competition from imports and hence sell fewer computers at a lower price than before, while consumers of vegetables must pay higher prices. Comparative advantage theory tells us that the aggregate gains outweigh the losses for the country as a whole, but that may be cold comfort to producers of computers and consumers of vegetables. The losers from trade may share in the gains if suppliers of capital and labor to the computer industry find it easy to shift into the production of vegetables or if mechanisms exist to transfer income from the gainers to the losers. In most countries, neither condition holds to a sufficient degree, especially in the short to medium term. Therein lies the seed of political opposition to policies that promote freer trade, even though all countries gain from it.

However suggestive the theory of comparative advantage may be for developing countries, it is only the beginning of an explanation of development through international trade. The theory fails to explain growth and structural change because it excludes changes over time in the amount of capital, land, and labor available to producers, as well as improvements in the quality or productivity of those factors. The theory provides no mechanism to explain how economies evolve over time and change the composition of their output, consumption, and trade. It also does not capture the two-way relationship between trade and development. In one direction, as we have seen, increased trade can lead to improved welfare and higher incomes. In the other direction, advances in development go hand in hand with more highly skilled labor and higher-quality capital and machinery, opening up new opportunities for increased trade. To better understand how trade and development affect each other, it is necessary to adopt an eclectic approach, using trade theory where it is useful but reverting frequently to other kinds of analysis. The unifying theme is trade strategies: How different approaches to trade, favoring different types of exports and imports, lead to different kinds of economic development. The first such strategy, **primary-export-led growth** is examined in the balance of this chapter.

PRIMARY EXPORTS AS AN ENGINE OF GROWTH

Before the 1950s, primary produce exports were seen as central to the development process and as the basic engine for economic growth. For most developing countries, following comparative advantage meant exporting food and raw materials, importing machinery and capital goods, and permitting structural change and income growth to take place as a consequence. The United States, Canada, Australia, New Zealand, Denmark, and other countries had achieved higher levels of income at least partly based on their natural resource endowments; and Argentina had gone quite far in that direction. More recently, many developing countries have tried alternative trade strategies, including import substitution and export of labor-intensive manufactures, both discussed in Chapter 18. Nevertheless, primary product exports have remained central to development strategies in a wide range of developing countries, including Botswana, Colombia, Mexico, Ghana, Nigeria, Indonesia, Malaysia, and the Philippines. Primary-export-led growth brings three broad types of benefits to developing countries: improved utilization of existing factors of production, expanded factor endowments, and linkage effects.

Improved Factor Utilization

To begin with, primary-export-led growth can propel an economy both to use more of the available factors of production and use those factors more efficiently. For example, an isolated country, shut off from world markets, might have substantial amounts of land either being used inefficiently or not at all. We saw in the example in Figure 17–1 how a reallocation of the factors of production in a land-abundant, capital-short country could lead to higher income. In this example, all factors of production are fully employed at the outset, as indicated by production taking place at point A along the production frontier. Even with full employment, however, by reallocating resources to produce and export more land-intensive goods (such as vegetables, rice, or cocoa) and import more manufactures (computers, cloth, or chemicals), the country is able to consume more of both kinds of commodities and increase its welfare. The country moves along its production frontier, from A to B in Figure 17–1. Land, the abundant factor of production, is utilized more intensively with trade in the sense that its productivity (the yield per hectare) rises as labor shifts from manufacturing to agriculture.

If land and labor are not fully employed before trade begins, a country can reap even larger gains from trade. This case is represented in Figure 17–1 by points D and E, both of which lie within the production frontier. Trade helps stimulate the economy by bringing this idle land, labor, and capital into the production process, so that the country can produce more of the exportable good and possibly more of the importable good as well. This is represented in Figure 17–1 by the economy moving from point *D* or *E* to point *B* on the production possibility frontier.

This static model of the gains from trade can be applied to the development of several countries (at least with a little imagination and some judicious simplification). In the nineteenth century, the United States and Canada had abundant land in relation to their endowments of labor and capital. Much of this land was idle, so both countries produced at points within their production frontiers. British demand for cotton and wheat enabled North America to bring this land into production and move toward the production frontier by growing cotton and wheat for export, while importing the manufactured goods it could not produce as efficiently as Britain. Much of the great western migration in both the United States and Canada was essentially a process of bringing large tracts of land and other natural resources into the production process. New Zealand and to some extent Australia followed a similar pattern.

Burmese economist Hla Myint has observed that, when parts of Africa and Asia came under European colonization, the consequent expansion of their international trade enabled those areas to utilize their land or labor more intensively to produce tropical foodstuffs such as rice, cocoa, and oil palm for export. Myint applied Adam Smith's term **vent for surplus** to these cases (as well as the cases of surplus land in the Americas and Australia).[4] The concept applies to a situation in which a country has the capacity to produce more than it can sell on the domestic market. Trade enables the country to employ either land or labor more fully and sell the goods produced with its "surplus" land and labor to the rest of the world.

However, when underutilized land or labor was vented as a result of colonization, as was typical during the nineteenth century, the gains from trade often were purchased at a high cost to the indigenous population. Land that may have been idle or utilized at low productivity frequently was taken by force from its occupiers, whether these were Native Americans, the Kikuyu and other peoples of East Africa, or Javanese farmers. Colonizers also used taxation and coercion to keep plantations and mines supplied with low-cost labor in many parts of Africa and Asia. And, especially in British India, the movement along a production frontier toward greater production for export often resulted in cheaper imports that competed directly with traditional handicraft industries, displacing artisans and workers. While the colonial powers could have distributed the gains from trade in ways that benefited indigenous populations enough to compensate them for the losses they bore, often this was not the case.

---

[4]Hla Myint, "The 'Classical Theory' of International Trade and the Underdeveloped Countries," *Economic Journal* 68 (1959), 317–37.

Expanded Factor Endowments

In addition to helping an economy use its *current* factor endowments more intensively and more efficiently, the expansion of primary product exports can lead to the accumulation of additional factors of production, especially capital and labor. More specifically, primary-export-led growth can help spur increases in foreign investment, domestic savings, labor, and skilled personnel to complement the fixed factors of production, land and natural resources. In the context of Figure 17–1, the country would be able to produce more of both exportable and importable goods as its entire production frontier shifted out.

Once the profitable opportunities in tropical agriculture or natural resources become apparent, foreign investment is likely to be attracted to the country, first to exploit the country's comparative advantage and, perhaps eventually, to invest in other sectors. The influx of foreign investors has been a familiar story in all mineral-exporting industries and in many tropical-product industries based on plantation agriculture. Well-known examples include Standard Oil in Venezuela, British Petroleum in Iran, Anaconda in Chile, Alcoa in Jamaica, Lever Brothers and Firestone in West Africa, and United Fruit in Central America. Foreign capital frequently brought migrant labor to the mines and plantations, as occurred in Southern and West Africa, Malaysia, Sri Lanka, and many other places. Both foreign investment and migrant labor, of course, were prominent features in the development in the "new lands" of the Americas and Australia in the nineteenth century. The emergence of new lines of export production also is likely to open up many new profitable outlets for investment that foreign capital will not completely satisfy, whether in the export sector itself or in related industries. These opportunities represent an outward shift in the demand for domestic savings and should induce some supply response and further increase investment in the economy. At least some of the earnings from primary product exports usually are retained as savings (often by the government) that can finance new investment opportunities.

Linkage Effects

Another potential benefit from primary product exports is the possibility of stimulating production in other, related sectors. Indeed, the very notion of export-led growth implies that exports would lead to more broad-based economic growth. Several types of linkages to the rest of the economy are possible, including to upstream or downstream industries, increased production of consumer goods, enhanced infrastructure, more widely available skilled labor, and increased government revenues. Albert O. Hirschman coined the phrase **backward linkage** for the situation in which the growth of one industry (such as textiles) stimulates domestic production of an upstream input (such as cotton or dyestuffs).[5] Backward linkages, which will be discussed again in Chapter 18, are particularly effective when the using industry becomes so large that supplying industries can achieve economies of scale of their own, lower their production costs, and become more competitive in domestic or even export markets. The wheat industry worked this way in North America in the nineteenth century; it created sufficient demand for transportation equipment (especially railway rolling stock) and farm machinery that these industries became established in the United States. In Peru, the rapid expansion of the fishmeal industry during the 1950s and 1960s led directly to the production of fishing boats and processing equipment. In fact, Peru's boat-building industry became efficient enough to export fishing craft to neighboring countries. Growth in the processing-equipment industry gave Peru a start on one kind of capital-goods production that can supply a wide range of food-processing industries.[6]

As these examples suggest, one of the most common backward linkages for primary product exports is between food processing for export (rice, vegetable oils, tea) and a processing-equipment industry. Three conditions contribute to these kinds of linkages. First, production initially should take place in small units that use simple technology to give the fledgling equipment industry a chance to master production techniques and learn its trade by repetitive production. Second, the export industry should grow steadily over time and thus promise a continuing market for its suppliers. Third, the export sector should be large enough to enable equipment manufacturers eventually to achieve scale economies. These conditions were met in fishmeal and can be met in several agricultural fields. But they generally are not satisfied in mining, which typically requires complex equipment for large-scale investments that must be implemented in the shortest time possible, conditions under which domestic infant industries are unlikely to thrive.

Expanded production of primary products also can stimulate **forward linkages** by making lower-cost primary goods available as inputs into other industries. In many developing countries, agricultural products are used as inputs to the food processing industry. Senegal and the Gambia process raw groundnuts (peanuts) into shelled nuts and oil. In Indonesia, forest products are used in furniture production, and Malaysia exports processed rubber and palm oil stemming from its plantation agriculture. Forward linkages can develop for mining and mineral products (i.e., petroleum refining, plastics, or steel) as well, but the more complex production techniques and demand for highly specialized capital and labor make it difficult for most developing countries to compete in these

---

[5]Albert O. Hirschman, *The Strategy of Economic Development* (New Haven, CT: Yale University Press, 1958), Chapter 6.

[6]Michael Roemer, *Fishing for Growth: Export-Led Development in Peru, 1950–1967* (Cambridge, MA: Harvard University Press, 1970).

activities. For example, Venezuela is using its iron ore, natural gas, and hydro-electric power to produce steel, partly for export and partly for domestic use. If, and only if, the domestic steel is cheaper than imported steel, it may stimulate further forward linkages to steel-using industries like construction, transport equipment, processing equipment, and oil derricks.

Consumption linkages develop indirectly as the higher income earned from primary product exports leads to increased demand for a wide range of consumption goods. This type of linkage is most likely to operate if, as a result of expanded exports, a large segment of the labor force is paid wages above previous levels and increased demand centers on mass-produced consumer goods like processed foods, clothing, footwear, furniture, radios, televisions, packaging materials, and so forth. The North American wheat industry, with its extensive endowment of land, high labor productivity, and egalitarian income distribution based on family farms, successfully stimulated local consumer goods industries. Unfortunately, these conditions are not always present in developing countries. Neither plantation agriculture in Africa, with its large labor force but low wages, nor mining industries, which pay high wages but employ relatively few workers, are able to generate adequate demand to stimulate local consumer goods industries.

Infrastructure linkages arise when the provision of overhead capital (roads, railroads, power, water, telecommunications) for the export industry lowers costs and opens new production opportunities for other industries. The classic example is the railroad in the nineteenth-century United States. Built to connect the East Coast with the grain-producing states of the Midwest, it lowered the cost of transporting both input and output for the manufacturing industry in the wheat-exporting region.[7] Harbors and rail and road networks built to facilitate the export of copper in southern Africa, cocoa and timber in Ghana, tea in India, and beef in Argentina have had similar effects on domestic manufacturing industries. Power projects made economically feasible by export industries, such as the Akosombo Dam in Ghana and the Guri Dam in Venezuela, provide cheap power that may encourage the domestic manufacturing industry.

Primary export sectors also may stimulate **human capital linkages** through the development of local entrepreneurs and skilled laborers. The growth of the Peruvian fishmeal industry, with its many small plants, encouraged scores of new entrepreneurs and trained many skilled workers to operate and maintain equipment. These resources then became available for subsequent development. Rubber, palm oil, and tin production for export encouraged entrepreneurs in

[7]Albert Fishlow, *American Railroads and the Transformation of the Antebellum Economy* (Cambridge, MA: Harvard University Press, 1965); and Robert W. Fogel, "Railroads as an Analogy of the Space Effort: Some Economic Aspects," in Bruce Mazlish, ed., *Space Program: An Exploration in Historical Analogy* (Cambridge, MA: MIT Press, 1965).

Malaysia, and small-scale farming for export has proven an outlet for entrepreneurial talent in several African countries.

The best case for petroleum, mining, and some traditional agricultural crops is the **fiscal linkage.** Governments can capture large shares of the economic rents (higher-than-necessary profits) from these exports as taxes or dividends and use the revenue to finance development in other sectors. Governments can choose to spend the revenues on health or education programs or new investment projects, or they can choose to reduce taxes and increase after-tax income. Although a government obviously is better off with than without such revenues, the effectiveness of these revenues in stimulating self-sustaining development in the rest of the economy depends critically on the kinds of programs and interventions the government undertakes.[8]

RECENT EMPIRICAL EVIDENCE ON PRIMARY-EXPORT-LED GROWTH

Since the 1950s, some economists and the leaders of many developing countries have argued that, despite the possible benefits, primary exports other than petroleum cannot effectively lead the way to economic development. The most common arguments have been that the markets for primary products grow too slowly to fuel growth, the prices received for these commodities have been declining, earnings are too unstable, and linkages do not work. We examine each of these arguments in the next section. Here, we examine the direct empirical question, What has been the relationship between primary exports and economic growth in recent decades? A few resource-rich developing countries have performed relatively well, including Botswana, Malaysia, Indonesia, Tunisia, and Mauritius. However, many others have grown very slowly or not at all, such as Nigeria, Zambia, Argentina, Burma, Egypt, Venezuela, and Colombia. At the same time, many of the fastest growing Asian economies are resource poor, including Japan, Korea, Taiwan, Hong Kong, and Singapore. Alan Gelb explored

[8]The impact of export industries on economic development through various forms of linkages is the focus of a body of literature called **staple theory,** which tries to explain differing impact by differing characteristics of production technologies. For examples of the genre, see Robert E. Baldwin, *Economic Development and Export Growth: A Study of Northern Rhodesia, 1920–1960* (Los Angeles: University of California Press, 1966); Douglass C. North, "Location Theory and Regional Economic Growth," *Journal of Political Economy* 63 (1955), 243–85; Roemer, *Fishing for Growth;* and Melville H. Watkins, "A Staple Theory of Economic Growth," *Canadian Journal of Economics and Political Science* 29 (1963), 141–58. Perhaps the ultimate expression of production characteristics and linkages as determinants of development patterns is the essay by Albert O. Hirschman, "A Generalized Linkage Approach to Development, with Special Reference to Staples," in Manning Nash, ed., *Essays on Economic Development and Cultural Change* (Chicago: University of Chicago Press, 1977), 67–98.

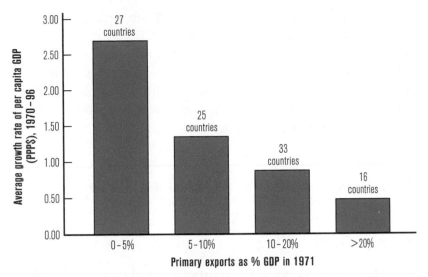

FIGURE 17-2. **Natural Resource Abundance and Economic Growth**
Countries with small amounts of primary product exports have grown
more quickly than resource-abundant countries.
Source: Updated from Steven Radelet, Jeffrey Sachs, and Jong-Wha Lee, "Economic
Growth in Asia," Harvard Institute for International Development, Cambridge, MA, May
1997. Data are from World Bank, *World Development Indicators* (electronic version) and
Penn World Tables, mark 5.6 (website version).

this seeming paradox in the specific case of petroleum exports in *Oil Windfalls:
Blessing or Curse?*[9]

Harvard economists Jeffrey Sachs and Andrew Warner went a step further,
with a systematic econometric exploration of the relationship between primary
product exports and economic growth in a sample of 95 countries from around
the world between 1971 and 1989.[10] Somewhat surprisingly, they found strong
evidence showing that, on average, countries with substantial primary product
exports have grown much more *slowly* than resource-poor countries since the
early 1970s. More specifically, they found that, on average, an increase of 10 percentage points in the ratio of primary exports to GDP was associated with a 0.7
percentage point slower annual rate of growth of per capita income. Figure 17–2
shows the basic negative relationship over a slightly longer time period (1970–96)
for 101 countries. For the 27 countries in which primary exports (in 1971) were
5 percent of GDP or less, annual per capita growth averaged 2.7 percent. By

---

[9]Alan Gelb, *Oil Windfalls: Blessing or Curse?* (New York: Oxford University Press for the World
Bank, 1988). The disappointing performance of several petroleum-exporting countries also is
explored by R. M. Auty in *Resource-Based Industrialization: Sowing the Oil in Eight Developing
Countries* (New York: Oxford University Press, 1990).

[10]Jeffrey Sachs and Andrew Warner, "Natural Resource Abundance and Economic Growth," Discussion paper 517a, Harvard Institute for International Development, Cambridge, MA, October
1995.

contrast, annual per capita growth averaged less than 0.5 percent in the 16 countries with primary exports equal to 20 percent or more of GDP.

How can resource abundance be associated with slower rates of economic growth? After all, primary product exports should raise aggregate wealth and allow a country to increase both its imports and its investment and possibly create some of the linkages described earlier. The next section examines several possible explanations for this apparent puzzle.

BARRIERS TO PRIMARY-EXPORT-LED GROWTH

Sluggish Demand Growth

In a world of balanced economic growth, exporters of primary products could expect their exports to expand at the same pace as the national income of the countries that import primary products and also expect their own income to grow at that rate. The world is not balanced in this way, however, and economists skeptical of primary export potential have cited structural shifts in the industrial world that seem to condemn third world primary exports to slower growth than industrial world income.[11]

One well-known structural shift, captured by **Engel's law,** is that the demand for staple foods and beverages grows more slowly than income. Therefore, as the income of food importers continues to grow, the proportion of their income they spend on food gradually falls. For high-income countries, the income elasticity of demand for food probably is below one half, implying that the demand for food (including food imported from developing countries) tends to lag far behind income growth.

Technological change in manufacturing also works against the consumption of raw materials, in two ways. First, new technologies and improved machinery help firms reduce wastage so that less raw material is needed in the production process. Modern looms waste less cotton yarn, sawmills turn wood shavings into boards, and so forth. Second, new technologies allow for the substitution of synthetics for raw materials. For example, synthetic rubber has replaced natural rubber, fiber optics has substantially reduced the use of copper in wire, and plastic pipes have replaced iron and copper pipe. Metal cans contain less tin, textile production uses more synthetic fibers, and automobiles use fiberglass instead of steel.

---

[11]An early and articulate proponent of this view was Ragnar Nurske, *Equilibrium Growth in the World Economy* (Cambridge, MA: Harvard University Press, 1961), Chapters 10 and 11.

Aggregate data on primary product production and trade confirm this gloomy picture. From 1963 to 1986, while world industrial production grew by 3.9 percent a year, the consumption of natural raw materials grew by only 1.5 percent a year.[12] The share of nonfuel raw materials and food imports in total industrial-country imports has fallen substantially, from 40 percent in 1965 to about 15 percent in 1996. With imports in the industrial world growing at 11 percent a year in value terms, imports of nonfuel raw materials and foodstuffs have grown by only 7.8 percent a year over more than 30 years, too slow to fuel economic development in primary exporting countries.[13]

Despite the broad trend, there are likely to be encouraging prospects for some primary commodities and some primary product exporting countries (see Box 17–1). After all, new technologies can *increase* the demand for raw materials. The invention of the railroad substantially increased the demand for iron and steel, and the development of the electric light bulb and other electric appliances led to a boom in the demand for copper. The demand for petroleum, rubber, aluminum, newsprint, plywood, and vegetable oils also received a substantial boost from technological innovation or from high-income elasticities of demand in the early part of the century. Several commodities experienced substantial export growth rates in the latter half of the twentieth century: Exports of sorghum, wheat, fish, soybeans, vegetable oils, oilseed cake and meal, fertilizers, timber, alumina and aluminum, and nickel, for example, all grew by at least 5 percent a year for at least 20 years after 1960, valued at constant prices.[14] The rapid growth of the Chinese economy led China to rapidly expand imports of petroleum at the beginning of the twenty-first century and together with disruptions in supply contributed to the run-up in oil prices at that time.

Nevertheless, with slower growth in the industrial countries, the impact of Engel's law, and materials-saving innovations, it seems unlikely that the high-income countries will import enough tropical foods and raw materials to fuel an era of rapid development for primary product exporters over the next few decades. Some commodities such as petroleum will face brisk demand growth from time to time and some countries will benefit substantially from producing such exports, but many others will benefit far less.

---

[12]World Bank, *Global Economic Prospects and the Developing Countries* (Washington, DC: World Bank, 1994), 39–40.

[13]*World Development Report 1990*, Tables 14 and 15; and *World Development Report 1994*, Tables 13 and 14.

[14]World Bank, *Commodity Trade and Price Trends*, 1987–88 ed. (Washington, DC: World Bank, 1988); and World Bank, *Price Prospects for Primary Commodities, 1990–2005* (Washington, DC: World Bank, 1993).

BOX 17-1   PRIMARY-EXPORT-LED GROWTH IN MALAYSIA

When Malaysia achieved independence in 1957, it was close to the archetypical single-crop economy: Rubber accounted for well over half its export earnings and about a quarter of Malaysia's gross domestic product. The second largest export, tin, earned between 10 and 20 percent of total export revenues. Neither commodity faced a bright future: Demand for rubber was constrained by the availability of cheap synthetic substitutes and the tin market was plagued by production exceeding likely demand. It would have been natural for the new country's planners to fall prey to the dominant export pessimism of the day and build a development strategy around import substitution.

But Malaysia enjoys a rich resource base with a relatively small population, and its development strategy was based on its comparative advantage. The country invested in research to reduce the costs of growing rubber that maintained its competitiveness with synthetic rubber. Measured relative to import prices, rubber export revenues fell by only 4 percent from 1960 to 1987. At the same time, Malaysia invested in planting oil palm and this new export grew in volume by 15 percent a year from 1960 to 1987. Petroleum exports grew by a steady 8 percent a year, and exports of logs and timber expanded by a total of 82 percent from 1960 to 1987. During this period, Malaysia also invested in manufacturing for export. Although primary products earned over 90 percent of export revenues in 1965, by 1998, manufactures had grown sufficiently to account for 79 percent of export revenues. Thanks to investments in both primary and manufactured exports, Malaysia's total export earnings, deflated by import prices (that is, its income terms of trade; see the next section) grew by 7 percent a year for three decades.

As a consequence of its investments in primary and manufactured exports, Malaysia has sustained rapid economic growth, over 6 percent a year from 1965 through to the first years of the twenty-first century, despite being hit by the 1997–98 financial crisis. Its per capita income of $9,000 (in 2004) in purchasing power parity terms puts Malaysia on a par with Mexico and Greece, even though, in the mid-1960s, its average income was close to that of Zambia and El Salvador. Malaysia's diversified export base, efficient production, and high income provide the resources for continued rapid development.

Source: Data are from the *World Development Report 1990;* World Bank, *World Development Indicators 2000;* and IMF, *International Financial Statistics Yearbook 1990.*

Declining Terms of Trade

An influential school of thought, led by Argentine economist Raul Prebisch and Hans Singer of the University of Sussex, argues that, over the long run, prices for commodity exports on world markets fall relative to prices of manufactured goods.[15] Since most developing countries export primary products and import manufactured goods, such a shift in relative prices means that, over time, developing countries have to export more primary products to import the same amount of manufactured products. One implication of a fall in relative prices, combined with weak growth in demand for primary products in high-income countries, is that countries relying solely on primary product exports are likely to lag behind in the development process. This prominent view came to be known as **export pessimism** and was the root of arguments in favor of import substitution strategies, discussed in Chapter 19.

Empirical tests of the Prebisch-Singer hypothesis have had mixed results. The most commonly used measure of relative prices of traded goods is the commodity or **net barter terms of trade,** T_n. The term T_n is a ratio of two indexes: the average price of a country's exports (P_e) and the average price of its imports (P_m). The commodity terms of trade rise if export prices rise relative to import prices. In his 1950 monograph, Prebisch used data on the terms of trade for Great Britain from the 1870s to the 1930s that seemed to support his contention. Prebisch's data were imperfect, however, and inadvertently biased in favor of his hypothesis. In subsequent years, other economists tried to replicate Prebisch's results using different data sets and various periods of time, with conflicting results.[16] Georgetown University economist John Cuddington and associates used improved data to measure the terms of trade for 24 primary commodities, excluding oil, for the period from 1900 to 1988.[17] Figure 17–3 shows the results. The net barter terms of trade for primary commodities fluctuated widely during the period. Except for a precipitous drop in the early 1920s and again after the mid-1970s, no statistically significant downward trend could be found in the net barter terms of trade.[18] If oil and other fuel prices are included in the index, and there is no reason why they should not be, they would reinforce this conclusion.

[15]United Nations (Raul Prebsich), *The Economic Development of Latin America and Its Principal Problems* (Lake Success, NY: United Nations, 1950); Hans W. Singer, "The Distribution of Trade between Investing and Borrowing Countries," *American Economic Review* 40 (May 1950), 473–85.

[16]For a summary of these results, see Bela Balassa, "Outward Orientation," in Hollis Chenery and T. N. Srinivasan, *Handbook of Development Economics*, vol. 2 (Amsterdam: Elsevier, 1989), 1653–59.

[17]The numerator of T_n, P_e, is a geometric average of the price indexes for 24 nonfuel commodities; the denominator P_m is an index of unit values for manufactured goods. See John T. Cuddington and Carlos M. Urzua, "Trends and Cycles in the Net Barter Terms of Trade: A New Approach," *Economic Journal* 99 (June 1989), 426–42.

[18]This is the conclusion reached by Cuddington and Urzua.

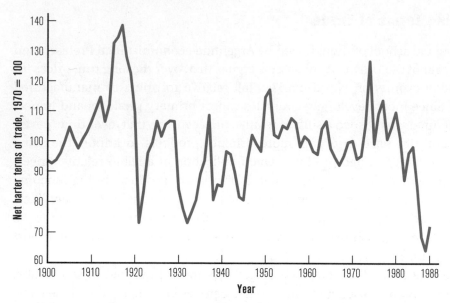

FIGURE 17-3. Net Barter Terms of Trade, Primary Commodities, 1900–88
A geometric index for 24 commodities, excluding fuels, shows no trend over 88
years, despite wide fluctuations and a sharp drop in 1921.
Source: John Cuddington and Hong Wei, "An Empirical Analysis of the Prebisch-Singer
Hypothesis: Aggregation, Model Selection and Implications," in Sir Hans Singer, Neelambar
Hatti, and Rameshwar Tandon, eds., *Export-Led versus Balanced Growth in the 1990s,* New World
Series, vol. 13 (Delhi: B. R. Publishing Corp., 1998).

Some econometricians disagree, however, and, using similar data but different
techniques, find significant declines in the net barter terms of trade of at least
0.7 percent per annum.[19]

Although the Prebisch-Singer hypothesis is properly addressed by looking at
commodity data, the overall terms of trade for a country (including all export
products) is what really matters in its development. Figure 17–4 shows two different measures of the net barter terms of trade since 1950. When oil exporters
are included, the terms of trade of developing countries rose dramatically after
1972 and remained high, despite the fall of oil prices during the 1980s and early
1990s. But the terms of trade for non-oil-exporting developing countries
declined over the period by over 30 percent. Conclusions about the Prebisch-
Singer hypothesis depend critically on the commodities included and the time
period under investigation. Although the very long-term trend is not clear, the
evidence indicates a steady, gradual decline in the terms of trade for nonoil
commodity exporters since 1950.

[19]These studies are summarized by David Sapsford and V. N. Balasubramanyam. "The Long-Run
Behavior of the Relative Price of Primary Commodities: Statistical Evidence and Policy Implications," *World Development* 22, no. 11 (November 1994), 1737–45.

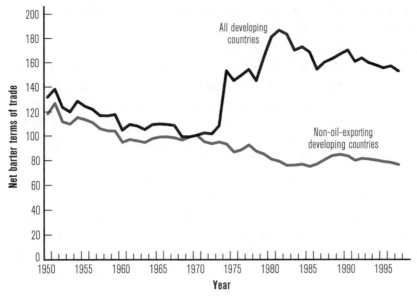

FIGURE 17-4. Net Barter Terms of Trade, 1950–97
Excluding oil, the net barter terms of trade for developing countries has
declined steadily since 1950.

Source: IMF, *International Financial Statistics, 1999.*

However, the net barter terms of trade tell us little about income or welfare,
which ought to be the basis for judging changes in world trade conditions. A better measure of the income effect of price changes would be the **income terms of
trade,** T_i, which measures the purchasing power of exports by comparing an
index of export *revenues* to an index of import *prices*. This is equivalent to the net
barter terms of trade multiplied by the volume of exports (Q_e), or $T_i = P_e Q_e / P_m =
T_n Q_e$. The basic idea is that, if export revenues (not just prices) rise faster than
import prices, the exporting country has the capacity to import more goods and
is better off. The income terms of trade can behave very differently from the net
barter terms of trade if changes in export prices also affect export volumes. If, for
example, Brazil increases its coffee exports and causes the world price to fall,
total coffee revenue could increase. This would happen if prices fell less than in
proportion to the increase in volume (implying that the absolute value of the
demand elasticity for Brazilian coffee is greater than 1).[20] In this case, the net
barter terms of trade fall, but the income terms of trade rise. Assuming the
resources shifted into coffee production could not have produced goods or services of equal value in other sectors, Brazil would be unambiguously better off

[20]The price elasticity of demand for the exports of any one country is $e_i = e_w / s_i$, where e_w is the
worldwide price elasticity of demand for the commodity and s_i is the market share of the country.
Even if e_w is quite low, say, –0.3, if the country's market share is below 30 percent, which would be
quite large, the price elasticity facing that country would be more negative than –1.

than before. For nonoil developing countries as a group, the income terms of trade *rose* about 6 percent a year from 1950 to 1997.

Export prices also might fall because of higher productivity in the primary exporting country. An increase in Brazil's coffee production due to higher productivity may cause world coffee prices to fall. But if the price decline is less than the percentage rise in the productivity (Z_e) in coffee production, the factors engaged in raising coffee beans would be better off than before. The **single factoral terms of trade,** T_S, measures factor income relative to factor inputs and import prices, or $T_S = (P_e/P_m)Z_e = T_n Z_e$. Note that a rise in either the income or single factoral terms of trade implies an improvement in income or welfare relative to that country's previous situation. But if, as often is the case, either index rises less than export volume, this also implies that exporting countries are sharing part of the potential gains with importing countries, as Prebisch and Singer suggest. Although this measure is intuitively appealing, it rarely is used, since data on productivity are not readily available for most developing countries.

Fluctuating Export Earnings

Not only do the net barter terms of trade show a secular decline, they also fluctuate considerably, as is evident from Figures 17–3 and 17–4. If not well managed (see Box 17–2), instability in export earnings can be transmitted to the domestic economy and make domestic demand unstable and investment more risky. Fluctuating domestic demand, coupled with uncertain access to imported materials, would discourage investors and reduce economic growth. Export instability may also confuse the signals conveyed by relative prices (since relative prices regularly fluctuate), so that investors are unsure about the most productive long-term investments. This **signaling effect** raises the capital-output ratio and reduces the growth rate for any given level of investment.

One theory of consumption, the **permanent-income hypothesis** (see Chapter 10), suggests the opposite result, however. Income earners count on some level of relatively certain annual income and try to maintain consumption patterns based largely on that *permanent,* or long-run, income. The more income fluctuates around this permanent level, the more is saved to maintain the permanent level of consumption through good times and bad.[21] If fluctuating export earnings transmit income instability to households, they save more, so the country is able to finance more investment and grow faster. Which effect is likely to dominate?

Economist David Dawe tested these propositions using a measure of export instability that compares deviations in export earnings around a five-year trend

---

[21]Odin Knudsen and Andrew Parnes, *Trade Instability and Economic Development* (Lexington, MA: Heath Lexington Books, 1975), 81–128.

BOX 17-2 GHANA: A CASE OF ARRESTED DEVELOPMENT

At independence in 1957, Ghana probably was the richest country in sub-Saharan Africa, with a per capita income close to $500 (in 1983 prices). By 1983, its per capita income had fallen to $340, below that of Kenya, Sudan, and Pakistan. Many things went wrong for Ghana in that quarter century, but the failure of export policy was crucial.[1] Like Malaysia, Ghana was a one-export country in the late 1950s: Cocoa earned almost 60 percent of export revenues and represented almost a fifth of GDP. In contrast to Malaysia, Ghana under its charismatic leader, Kwame Nkrumah, turned sharply away from its export base to invest in import-substituting industries. In this, it failed. Had exports in agriculture, forestry, and mining been maintained, Ghana might have earned sufficient revenue to make a gradual transition to import substitution. But so abrupt was the disinvestment in primary exports that cocoa exports halved in volume from the early 1960s to the middle 1980s, and other exports did not make up that deficit.

Ghana's failure to utilize its generous export base is made more vivid by the performance of its next-door neighbor, the Ivory Coast. With virtually the same resource base, the Ivory Coast invested enough to maintain its coffee exports and then diversified into cocoa (just as Ghana was disinvesting), wood, and other primary products. Over two decades, export volume more than doubled, and per capita GDP grew to nearly twice that of Ghana, despite substantial immigration from less-prosperous neighboring countries.

Source: *World Development Report 1990;* and World Bank, *World Tables 1989–1990.*
[1]On Ghana's development policies, see Michael Roemer, "Ghana 1950–1980: Missed Opportunities," in Arnold Harberger, ed., *World Economic Growth* (San Francisco: ICS Press, 1984), 201–26.

to gross domestic product. Among a sample of 85 countries over 15 years (1970–85), Dawe found that export instability corresponds with an increase in the ratio of investment to GDP, consistent with the permanent income hypothesis. However, countries with greater instability have lower GDP growth rates.[22] The reason, he suggests, may be that the signaling effect is especially strong and so reduces the productivity of all investment, even as the permanent income effect increases the quantity of investment.

This finding poses a dilemma for development strategy. If its comparative advantage lies in primary exports with fluctuating prices in world markets, will a country's growth be enhanced by following comparative advantage more than it

[22]David C. Dawe, "Essays on Price Stabilization and the Macroeconomy in Low Income Countries," Ph.D. dissertation, Harvard University, May 1993, 50–107.

is hurt by accepting export fluctuations? Case histories of experience in both Asia and Africa suggest that countries following their comparative advantages, even if they lie in primary exports, grow faster than countries that turn away from this path.[23] The key seems to be how these countries manage their export earnings. For example, the effects of export price instability can be mitigated by counter-cyclical fiscal and monetary policies. Moreover, the successful primary exporters diversified their export base, both within primary products and by shifting gradually to manufactured exports, to reduce the instability of total export earnings. They did this by first investing in primary exports, like Malaysia, rather than by turning away from them, like Ghana (see the preceding case studies).

Ineffective Linkages

Another possible explanation for the relatively slow economic growth in primary exporters is that the previously discussed *linkages* with the rest of the economy may have failed to work. For example, the petroleum industry and, with a few exceptions, the mining industry, generally remain *enclaves,* remote from other centers of production and ill adapted to link with the rest of the economy. Neither backward linkages to suppliers of production materials and equipment nor consumption linkages are likely to work. In some instances, railroads and ports built for the mines aid other industries by lowering costs and stimulating investment, but examples of remote or specialized overhead capital also can be found. Liberia's rail and harbor link with its iron mines is poorly placed to stimulate agriculture or other industry, and the pipelines and tanker ports of the petroleum industry have no use outside that sector. Some agricultural export sectors, particularly plantations in colonial Africa, also had few effective linkages, because they used few inputs and paid low wages. However, small-farm, labor-intensive agriculture typically has effective linkages through transport and marketing services and consumer demand by farm families.

Some countries have tried explicitly to encourage forward linkages through taxes or outright bans on the export of primary products. Indonesia, for example, banned the export of logs and heavily taxed the export of sawn wood to encourage the plywood and furniture industries. Since export prices are determined in world markets, export taxes and bans reduce the price of the primary commodity in the domestic market. This helps downstream industries, which get the benefit of lower raw material prices. Farmers, loggers, and miners are taxed to provide greater incentives for processors and manufacturing firms. This is one form of *protection,* similar in its effects to protection against imports, the subject of Chapter 19.

[23]See David L. Lindauer and Michael Roemer, eds., *Asia and Africa: Legacies and Opportunities* (San Francisco: ICS Press, 1994), especially Chapters 1 and 4.

These strategies to encourage downstream processing of primary products may succeed in expanding the industrial base and increasing the economic benefits derived from a natural resource. However, resource processing is no panacea for development. Most of the mineral-processing industries share with mining the characteristics of large scale, capital intensity, sophisticated technology, and high wages, so they tend to be extensions of the export enclave and generate little employment and realize few linkages to the rest of the economy. Nor is there much diversification of risk in moving from crude to refined petroleum exports or from bauxite to aluminum.

Rent Seeking and Corruption

Another possible explanation for the poor performance of primary exporters is that resource abundance leads to increased corruption and rent seeking, as defined in Chapter 5. Large and relatively easy-to-earn profits can be made by the lucky few that gain control over natural resources as, for example, occurred with Russian petroleum in the middle of the 1990s and into the first decade of the twenty-first century. Under these circumstances, entrepreneurial energies are likely to focus on obtaining a larger piece of the existing economic pie, rather than on efforts to enlarge the pie through productivity gains. Economists Philip Lane and Aaron Tornell developed a formal economic model exploring the relationship between resource riches and rent seeking. They show how a commodity boom can lead to a "feeding frenzy," in which intense competition for the resource rents ultimately leads to inefficiency and waste of the potential windfall. In a country with powerful interest groups and weak government institutions, a commodity boom can worsen the distribution of income and reduce the rate of economic growth.[24] Some developing countries have managed to minimize this problem, but corruption often is a significant problem in resource-rich countries.

The Dutch Disease

Booming primary exports may fail to stimulate development for another, more pervasive reason, which has been labeled the **Dutch disease.** This syndrome derives its name from the experience of the Netherlands after 1960, when major reserves of natural gas were discovered. The ensuing export boom and the balance-of-payments surplus promised new prosperity. Instead, however, during the 1970s, the Dutch economy suffered from rising inflation, declining export of manufactures, lower rates of income growth, and rising unemployment. The oil boom of the 1970s and early 1980s produced similar paradoxes in a number of

---

[24]Philip Lane and Aaron Tornell, "Power, Growth, and the Voracity Effect," *Journal of Economic Growth* 1, no. 2 (June 1996), 213–41.

countries, including Saudi Arabia, Nigeria, and Mexico. Economists began to realize that Dutch disease might be a very general phenomenon, applicable to all countries that "enjoy" export booms of primary commodities (see Box 17–3).[25] Because, as we shall see, the influx of foreign exchange itself causes the Dutch disease, the syndrome also can result from large inflows of foreign capital in any form. The import of gold and silver from the Americas, for example, may have helped to retard Spain's growth in the sixteenth century. A surge of foreign investment into the United States probably helped make U.S. industries less competitive in the 1980s. Large foreign aid flows to developing countries can undermine exporting firms' international competitiveness. How can this happen?

One key to this paradox is to understand (1) how export booms affect a country's **real exchange rate** and (2) how the real exchange rate, in turn, affects other industries. The *official* or *nominal exchange rate* simply is the price at which anyone holding foreign exchange, such as dollars, can convert it into local currency, say, pesos in Mexico, naira in Nigeria, or rupiah in Indonesia. Most commonly, the nominal exchange rate is quoted in local currency per unit of foreign currency, say, pesos per dollar. When the exchange rate rises (that is, there are more pesos or naira or rupiah per dollar), the domestic currency is said to *depreciate*, because it takes fewer dollars to buy the same amount of pesos, naira, or rupiah than before.[26] When the exchange rate falls, the domestic currency *appreciates*, because pesos are worth more in dollars than before.

The real exchange rate starts with the nominal exchange rate then incorporates the prices of **tradable goods** and **nontradable goods** to analyze how changing prices and exchange rates affect the incentives for production and consumption. Economists call any good that is or could be imported or exported a **tradable.** Prices for tradable goods generally are determined on world markets and, in most cases, are not affected by domestic conditions in developing countries. **Nontradables** are goods produced domestically and not imported or exported. Prices for nontradables are determined by supply and demand conditions in the domestic market. Examples of nontradables include transportation, construction, electricity and other utilities, household and other personal services, and manufactures or farm products that are heavily protected and not subject to competition from imports.[27]

---

[25]The Dutch disease has been analyzed from a theoretical standpoint by W. Max Corden and S. Peter Neary, "Booming Sector and Deindustrialization in a Small Open Economy," *Economic Journal* 92 (December 1982), 825–48. The application of this theory to developing countries is explored by Michael Roemer, "Dutch Disease in Developing Countries: Swallowing Bitter Medicine," in Matts Lundahl, ed., *The Primary Sector in Economic Development* (London: Croom-Helms, 1985), 234–52.

[26]The language on exchange rate changes sometimes is confusing. When the nominal exchange rate rises, it takes more domestic currency (naira) to buy foreign currency (dollars). Equivalently, this means that it takes fewer dollars to buy naira. In this latter sense, the naira is said to *depreciate*, or lose value, when the exchange rate rises.

[27]The definitions of *tradables* and *nontradables* are made more precise in Chapter 19.

BOX 17-3   NIGERIA: A BAD CASE OF THE DUTCH DISEASE

In 1973–74, the oil embargo imposed by Arab countries, followed by the activation of OPEC as an effective cartel, quadrupled the price of petroleum on world markets. In 1979–80, the price doubled again, so that by the end of 1980 the terms of trade for oil exports, relative to the price of imports, was nearly seven times the level in 1972. In Nigeria, higher export prices generated an "oil windfall" that added 23 percent to the nonmining gross domestic product in the middle 1970s and again in the early 1980s.

Nigeria's political history has been marked by intense competition among ethnic groups, culminating in the Biafran war of the late 1960s, and one of the major battlegrounds of this strife has been the incidence of taxation and government expenditure. Under this kind of pressure, the Nigerian government spent all its oil windfall. Public investment rose from 4 to 30 percent of the nonmining GDP and the average pay for civil servants was doubled in 1975. Much of the new-found revenue was squandered on wasteful projects. The second oil windfall only whetted fiscal appetites even more: From 1981 to 1984, the budget deficit averaged 12 percent of the nonmining GDP.

Fiscal excesses exacerbated the tendency of export windfalls to create inflation. Prices rose while the central bank kept the nominal exchange rate fixed, so that, by 1984, the real exchange rate had appreciated to nearly three times its level in 1970–72. Over the decade ending in 1984, Nigeria's nonoil exports fell almost 90 percent in nominal terms, a classic if extreme symptom of Dutch disease.

Agriculture suffered worst. Because rural constituencies were politically weak, little of the oil windfall was invested in agriculture, while vast amounts were spent, and wasted, on infrastructure and industry. From 1973 to 1984, the quantity of agricultural exports fell by more than two thirds, while both agriculture output per capita and total caloric consumption per capita declined. From 1972 to 1981, growth in the nonmining GDP was a respectable 5.3 percent, but this was only 60 percent of the growth rate during the five years before the oil price boom. It can be argued that Nigeria might have been better off without its oil boom.

Source: This account is based on Henry Bienen, "Nigeria: From Windfall Gains to Welfare Losses?" in Gelb, *Oil Windfalls,* 227–60.

The real exchange rate most commonly is defined as

$$RER = (E_O \times P_T)/P_N \qquad\qquad [17\text{--}1]$$

where RER = an index of the real exchange rate, E_O = an index of the official (nominal) exchange rate, P_T = an index of the prices of tradable goods expressed in foreign currency (e.g., U.S. dollars), and P_N = an index of the domestic price of nontradables. Note that the RER is an index of prices, like the terms of trade, not a price itself. Also note that, since P_T is expressed in foreign currency, by multiplying by E_O, the numerator ($E_O \times P_T$) becomes a domestic currency index of tradables prices. Therefore, the RER can be thought of as the ratio of the price of tradable goods to the price of nontradable goods, all expressed in domestic currency. An increase in the RER—because of either an increase in the exchange rate, a rise in the dollar prices of tradable goods on world markets, or a fall in nontradables prices—suggests that the relative price of tradables in domestic markets has risen. Such a shift should encourage more production of tradable goods and discourage consumption of tradable goods. Following the language of nominal exchange rates, a rise in the RER is referred to as a *real depreciation* of the peso or naira, and a decline in the RER is called a *real appreciation*. Official devaluations, which raise the peso price of dollars, cause the real rate to depreciate, at least initially. The same is true for an increase in world tradable prices. An increase in nontradables prices has the opposite effect, causing the RER to appreciate.[28]

The Dutch disease is a wolf in sheep's clothing because it typically starts with what looks like a good thing: A boom in a country's raw material exports. But the boom in exports can cause a sharp appreciation of the RER, in two ways. First, the influx of foreign exchange from higher export earnings creates a surplus of foreign currency. Unless the central bank tries to maintain the official exchange rate at its former level, this shift in supply causes the currency to appreciate in value. Second, higher income from booming primary exports also spurs faster domestic inflation. It does this because the additional income creates greater demand for all goods and services in the economy. To the extent that this demand spills over into more imports, there is an outflow of foreign exchange but no inflation, because the price of imports is not much affected by demand in a single country. But prices for nontradable goods and services are likely to increase. Due to a limited supply of nontradables, especially in the first months or years of the boom, the greater demand results in higher prices for nontradables (that is, in domestic inflation). From equation 17–1 we know that a rise in nontradable prices causes the RER to decline, or appreciate.

To understand how the real exchange rate becomes the key to the Dutch disease paradox, begin with the impact of the real exchange rate on export industries *other than the booming primary export industry*. Table 17–3 demonstrates that, with a fixed nominal exchange rate, domestic inflation in excess of world inflation (that is, an increase in nontradable prices in excess of tradable prices) causes exporters' profits to decline. This occurs because the wages and the prices of domestic inputs rise faster than the prices of exported output.

---

[28]For a comprehensive discussion of the real exchange rate, see Sebastian Edwards, *Real Exchange Rates, Devaluation and Adjustment: Exchange Rate Policy in Developing Countries* (Cambridge, MA: MIT Press, 1991).

TABLE 17-3. **Effects of Inflation and Devaluation on Exporters' Profits**

Today: Exchange rate = 12 pesos per dollar; real exchange rate = 100

1. Exporter sells goods worth	$100,000
2. For which exporter receives local currency of	P1,200,000
3. If exporter's costs (all domestic nontradables) are	P900,000
4. Then exporter's profits are	P300,000

Three years later, after the primary export boom, because of domestic inflation, nontradables prices have risen 33 percent more than world tradables prices; the real exchange rate has appreciated to 75

1. Exporter sells goods worth	$100,000
2. For which exporter receives local currency of	P1,200,000
3. If exporter's costs (all domestic nontradables) are	P1,200,000
4. Then exporter's profits are	P0

Three years later, but with currency devalued by 33 percent to 16 pesos per dollar; the real exchange rate is restored to 100

1. Exporter sells goods worth	$100,000
2. For which exporter receives local currency of	P1,600,000
3. If exporter's costs (all domestic) are	P1,200,000
4. Then exporter's profits are	P400,000
5. Which, deflated by 33 percent to year-1 prices, again are (in real terms)	P300,000

That, of course, is the same thing as a real rate appreciation, since RER falls in equation 17–1. Note that the same reduction in profitability follows from an appreciation of the nominal exchange rate, that is, from lowering the peso price of a dollar, which is likely to happen with a commodity export boom. If profits for noncommodity exporters fall, they are likely to produce less for export and so reduce the income and employment in export industries. Exporters' profitability could be restored by a nominal devaluation that the offsets the domestic inflation, as shown in the last section of Table 17–3. (For another example, see Box 17–4.)

Now the paradox can be explained. Booming primary exports, by stimulating more rapid domestic inflation and thus causing the real exchange rate to appreciate, render *other* exports less competitive and hence less profitable. Therefore, the "disease" is the deleterious effect of a commodity boom on other export sectors. Producers of tradables, both exporters and import competitors, face rising costs in their purchases of nontradable goods and services, including the wages of their workers. But they cannot charge higher prices because they compete with foreign producers, either as exporters or as import competitors. These farmers and manufacturers face a profit squeeze that causes some of them to reduce production and employment. The boom in primary exports and nontradables is partly offset by a depression in other tradable industries.

If it is relatively easy to move capital and labor between the booming commodity sector and other activities and the booming sector can employ all the factors of production released from other, less-profitable activities, then the

BOX 17-4 INDONESIA: FINDING A CURE

Indonesia was both the poorest and the largest country in the world to receive substantial oil windfalls. At first, the oil boom affected Indonesia much as it did Nigeria. The 1973–74 boom added 16 percent to the nonmining GDP and the 1979–80 price surge raised the windfall to 23 percent. Of the first windfall, the government itself spent more than 60 percent. From 1974 to 1978, the real exchange rate appreciated an average 33 percent over its preboom level, a bit more than in Nigeria at that time.

Yet, the outcome was very different in Indonesia. Throughout the boom period, the government was required to balance its budget each year, and because all controls had been removed from foreign exchange transfers, stringent management of the money supply was necessary to protect foreign exchange reserves. These self-imposed restraints limited the impact of the windfalls on inflation.

The Indonesian government adopted two policies that took advantage of oil windfalls for national development goals. First, investment in agriculture had a high priority, especially the goal of achieving self-sufficiency in rice production. The government financed irrigation systems, encouraged the adoption of new rice varieties, subsidized fertilizer and pesticide sales, provided credit to farmers, invested in rural health and education facilities, and built roads and other infrastructure in rural areas. By the mid-1980s, Indonesia was self-sufficient in rice; and by 1982–83, its total food output per capita was a third above its 1970 level, a performance far above average for all developing and industrial countries over the period.

The second policy was to devalue the exchange rate enough to avoid real appreciation. Major devaluations were imposed in 1978, 1983, and 1986, after which the rate was managed flexibly to maintain its real value. At the end of the oil boom period in 1984, the Indonesian real exchange rate had *de*preciated 8 percent from its 1970–72 average. Consequently, over the period from 1971 to 1984, the quantity of nonoil exports grew by over 7 percent a year; and from 1972 to 1981, the nonmining GDP expanded by over 8 percent a year.

Thus, shrewd policy played a major role in effecting an early cure for incipient Dutch disease. The government placed great stress on integrating the multitude of ethnic groups of this diverse country and so avoided the conflicts over fiscal resources that paralyzed Nigeria. Moreover, the country had an important advantage over other oil exporters: Its large labor force, nearly two thirds of it working in rural areas in 1970, dampened any tendencies for surges in wages and thus in domestic prices throughout the oil boom.

Source: This account is based on Bruce Glassburner, "Indonesia: Windfalls in a Poor Rural Economy," in Gelb, *Oil Windfalls*, 197–226.

commodity boom poses no major problem. As prices for the primary export product rise, labor and capital can move into the booming sector, and the economy is better off as a result. If the boom ends, the factors of production can move back to their previous activity. But this usually is not the case. If the booming sector is highly capital intensive (such as petroleum), few new jobs are created, so unemployment may go up (although the indirect employment effects of the boom in construction and other activities can mitigate this effect). More insidiously, when the boom ends (and booms always end), it is likely to be very difficult to move the factors of production back to their previous employment. After all, manufacturing activities cannot just restart overnight. Moreover, at the end of the boom, wages are likely to fall, so workers are unlikely to be happy to move back to lower-paying jobs. In addition, the boom can lead to social or migratory shifts that are hard to unwind. Nigeria's oil boom (described in Box 17–3) stimulated rural workers to migrate to urban areas to look for new, high-paying construction and civil service jobs. When the oil boom ended, few urban workers wanted to return to rural areas. Many other oil exporters suffered similar fates when petroleum prices fell in the mid-1980s.

Because mineral and other primary sectors typically pay high taxes, commodity booms can lead to a swelling of government revenue. This *fiscal linkage* can be used to stimulate development, especially if the additional revenue is invested in public services, such as infrastructure, education, and health, or to promote efficient investment in tradable sectors, notably agriculture and manufacturing, that have been rendered less competitive by the primary export boom. Although some governments used their fiscal resources effectively during the 1970s oil boom, the record then and after has generally been dismal, with significant resources wasted on frivolous projects. Precisely when fiscal resources are generously available, finance ministers have the most difficult time resisting political and social pressures for higher expenditures. Once again, the big difficulties arise when the boom ends, and government must quickly reduce spending and reverse the commitments made during the good times. As discussed in Chapter 15, some countries borrowed heavily from abroad during the commodity booms of the 1970s on the assumption that export prices would remain high and were left with large foreign debts and a significantly reduced capacity to pay when the boom ended.

The depredations of Dutch disease and other problems with primary product exports often are fatal to development aspirations, as the case study of Nigeria illustrates. But this is not necessarily so. Some countries have turned their resource windfalls into sustained development, such as Indonesia, Botswana, Tunisia, Malaysia, and Chile.[29] The negative relationship between primary prod-

---

[29]World Bank economist Alan Gelb has documents six cases of the Dutch disease in *Oil Windfalls*.

uct exports and economic growth is a tendency, not an absolute straightjacket. Determined governments can take several steps to avoid some of the most difficult problems associated with abundant natural resources.

The best prevention for Dutch disease effects is to avoid or reverse the initial real appreciation of the currency. In most cases, this requires a devaluation of the currency, accompanied by strong restraints on government spending and money creation by the central bank, both aimed at curbing inflation. The government needs to resist demands for expansion and save its new-found revenues until there is time to plan sensible, well-targeted projects with high returns. More generally, the more-successful governments channeled new investments into health, education, and infrastructure development that improves overall well-being, enhances productivity, and opens up economic opportunities outside the primary sector. Such an investment policy accomplishes two things. First, it harnesses export windfalls to finance sound, long-term development. Second, by delaying the new expenditures, the government acts *countercyclically* and so helps stabilize the economy by spending less during the most inflationary period of the export boom and more after the boom has faded.[30] These *stabilization measures* are explored with a rigorous economic model in Chapter 21.

For reasons already discussed in Chapter 5, policies of restraint, essential to stabilization, are seldom popular and often vigorously opposed by political pressure groups. Although the judicious use of commodity revenues is easy to prescribe and essential for an economy's health, the advice often is not taken in sufficient doses to effect a cure.

SUMMARY

- Comparative advantage allows two countries to gain from trade with each other, even where the factor inputs in production are lower for all products in one country than the other.
- Trade, by making it possible to utilize previously unused or underutilized resources, such as land, by creating a *vent for the surplus* of this unused resource, contributed to the early growth of many developing countries as well as such current high-income countries as the United States and Canada.

---

[30]If, however, the permanent-income hypothesis is valid, the households will save much of the windfall and the burden on government is less. David Bevan, Paul Collier, and Jan Gunning, *Controlled Open Economies: A Neoclassical Approach to Structuralism* (London: Oxford University Press [Clarendon], 1990), argue that this was the case in Kenya during the commodity boom of the late 1970s.

- Expanded development of primary exports provided various kinds of linkages that promoted development in other sectors of the economy: backward and forward linkages, but also consumption, infrastructure, human capital, and fiscal linkages.
- The main weakness of reliance on primary exports is that these exports typically grow more slowly than exports of manufactures.
- The export pessimism expressed by economists such as Prebisch and Singer, who argued that the terms of trade steadily would turn against primary products, however, has not been borne out by the data.
- Heavy reliance on the export of primary products does often lead to the phenomenon known as the *Dutch disease*, where a country rich in natural resources actually suffers slower growth as a result of that rich endowment. There are cures for this disease, however, if countries take the necessary steps to prevent waste and corruption in the use of primary export revenues and keep their exchange rate from becoming overvalued.

18

Industry

T he concept of development and the process of industrialization often have been treated as synonymous, ever since the Industrial Revolution enabled Britain to raise its industrial production by 400 percent over the first half of the nineteenth century.[1] From then until the present, the dominant criterion for development has been the rise in per capita income brought about largely by industrialization.

INDUSTRY AS A LEADING SECTOR

From the Chapter 3 discussion of cross-country patterns, we know that higher shares of the gross domestic product generated by industry are closely associated with rising income per capita. Figure 18–1 shows this pattern for manufacturing value added in 1992 for 17 large countries (with populations over 25 million) and 20 small ones. In making such cross-country comparisons, economists conventionally segregate large from small countries. Nations with larger markets are able to develop a wider range of industries sooner in their development, because they can take advantage of *scale economies* within the domestic market.[2] Hence, we expect large countries to industrialize faster than small ones.

[1] E. J. Hobsbawm, *The Pelican Economic History of Britain,* vol. 3, *Industry and Empire* (Baltimore: Johns Hopkins Press, 1969).

[2] The concept of *scale economies* is explained later in this chapter.

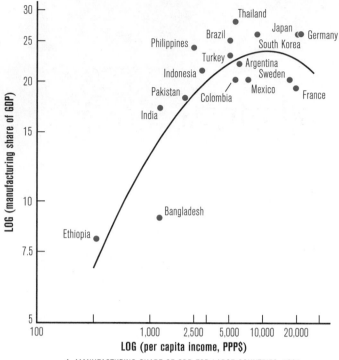

A. MANUFACTURING SHARE OF GDP FOR LARGE COUNTRIES, 1992

FIGURE 18-1. **Manufacturing Share of the GDP, Large and Small Countries, 1992**
Large countries (with populations over 25 million), on average, are more industrialized than small ones at the same incomes. In both cases, there is a tendency for manufacturing value added to rise as a share of GDP as average income rises, up to a level of about $10,000.

Source: *World Development Report 1994* (Washington, DC: The World Bank, 1994), 166–67, 220–21.

Both tendencies are evident in Figure 18–1. At any level of income per person, the average for large countries, determined by the regression line, is higher than for small countries. Yet, for both sets of countries, a strong correlation is found between industrialization and average income. On average, for large countries, as income quintuples from $1,000 to $5,000 per person (in purchasing power parity), manufacturing value added rises from 13 to 22 percent of GDP. In an average small country undergoing the same change in income, the manufacturing share rises more sharply, from about 7 percent to about 17 percent of GNP. A country with per capita income growing at 3 percent a year would take 54 years to make this transition.

The manufacturing share does not grow indefinitely. Somewhere between $10,000 and $20,000 per capita, the ratio of manufacturing value added to GDP begins to decline, as advanced economies move out of manufacturing into

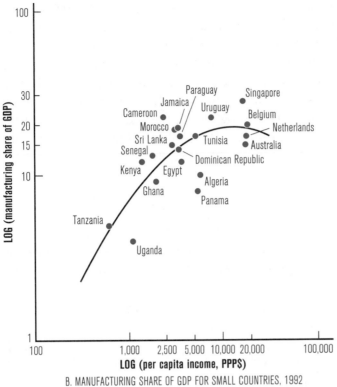

B. MANUFACTURING SHARE OF GDP FOR SMALL COUNTRIES, 1992

FIGURE 18-1.   (**Continued**)

modern service industries. This is indicated in Figure 18–1 by the regression line, which peaks after $10,000 and begins to decline.[3]

But wide variations are evident. Among large countries with similar incomes, Bangladesh has a manufacturing share of only 8 percent, whereas India's is 21 percent; Columbia and Mexico have shares of 20 percent, whereas Thailand's is 28 percent. Among small countries, Uganda's share is only 4 percent in contrast to Kenya at 12 percent, and Panama at 8 percent contrasts with Uruguay at 22 percent. The differences may be due to differing endowments: Columbia's productive agriculture and Mexico's oil deposits give those countries the opportunity to grow with less investment in industry than poorly endowed countries such as South Korea. They may be due to strategy: Thailand and India adopted policies, though very different ones, to speed industrialization. Or differences may be due to location and historical circumstance: Uganda is land-locked and suffered a prolonged civil war while Kenya is centrally placed to serve a regional market and enjoyed relative stability.

[3]The regression equations were of the form log MS $= a + b \log y + c(\log y)^2$, where MS is the manu-facturing share and y is PPP income per capita. The coefficient c is negative and significant in both cases and so gives a curved shape to the regression line.

Cross-country patterns imply that the value added in manufacturing ought to grow more rapidly than GDP in the typical developing country. This prediction is partially borne out by World Bank data. For the low- and middle-income countries as a whole, over the period from 1980 to 1998, manufacturing grew by 3.9 percent a year, compared to 3.4 percent a year for GDP. But this average pattern is not observed in most of the individual countries. Of 42 developing countries for which data are available from 1965 through 1990, for example, manufacturing grew at least 1 percent a year faster than GDP in only 19 of them; in most of the others, the differences in growth rates were less than 1 percent a year.[4]

Linkages

If manufacturing generally and early developing branches of manufacturing in particular are to lead economic development, they ought to have more **backward linkages** than other sectors, in the sense introduced in Chapter 17. There have been several attempts to measure linkages. Those used by Pan Yotopoulos and Jeffrey Nugent seem as easy to understand and useful for our purposes as any.[5] Not surprisingly, linkage formulas depend on input-output tables, which are constructed to display linkages within an economy. A **direct backward linkage** for any industry, j, is measured as

$$L_{bj} = \sum a_{ij} \qquad [18\text{--}1]$$

where L_{bj} = the index of backward linkage and a_{ij} = the Leontief (input-output) coefficient defined in Chapter 3. Thus a measure of backward linkage for any industry is simply the sum of its domestic input coefficients. If, for example, the textile industry adds value equal to 30 percent of its output and imports inputs equivalent to another 15 percent of output, its backward linkage index L_b is 55 percent, the share of domestically purchased inputs $(100 - 30 - 15 = 55)$.

This index captures only the direct links. But, if textile production stimulates cotton growing, might not cotton in turn stimulate fertilizer production? It is easy to incorporate these indirect effects by summing the direct and indirect coefficients of the Leontief inverse, designated r_{ij}, to get

$$L_{tj} = \sum r_{ij} \qquad [18\text{--}2]$$

where L_{tj} = an index of direct plus indirect or **total backward linkages** from the jth industry.

[4]World Bank, *World Development Report 1992* (Washington, DC: World Bank, 1992), 220–21.

[5]Pan A. Yotopoulos and Jeffrey B. Nugent, "A Balanced-Growth Version of the Linkage Hypothesis: A Test," *Quarterly Journal of Economics* 87 (May 1973), 157–71; reprinted in their text, *Economics of Development: Empirical Investigations* (New York: Harper and Row, 1976), 299–306.

There is an analogous simple measure of **direct forward linkages:**

$$L_{fi} = \sum X_{ij}/Z_i \qquad\qquad [18\text{--}3]$$

where L_{fi} = the forward linkage index for the ith industry, X_{ij} = the output of the ith industry purchased by each jth user industry (the row of the input-output table), and Z_i = the production of good i for both intermediate and final use.

Yotopoulos and Nugent use input-output tables for five developing countries (Chile, Greece, Mexico, Spain, and South Korea) to measure the linkage indexes for 18 industries. The results are shown in Table 18–1. For leather, the next-to-last column tells us, for example, that for each additional dollar of leather goods produced, production of all inputs must rise by $2.39. A high index indicates that expansion of the industry will stimulate production in other sectors of the economy. Manufacturing industries dominate the upper ranks of Table 18–1 on the basis of both direct and total backward linkages. The early-developing sectors (leather, clothing, textiles, and food and beverages) represent four of the first five branches ranked by total backward linkages. Primary indus-

TABLE 18-1. **Sectoral Linkage Indexes and Rankings in Five Less-Developed Countries**

	DIRECT FORWARD LINKAGE INDEX		DIRECT BACKWARD LINKAGE INDEX		TOTAL BACKWARD LINKAGE INDEX	
	(L_j)	RANK	(L_b)	RANK	(L_t)	RANK
Leather	0.645	4	0.683	2	2.39	1
Basic metals	0.980	1	0.632	5	2.36	2
Clothing	0.025	18	0.621	6	2.32	3
Textiles	0.590	8	0.621	7	2.24	4
Food and beverage manufactures	0.272	16	0.718	1	2.22	5
Paper	0.788	3	0.648	3	2.17	6
Chemicals and petroleum refining	0.599	7	0.637	4	2.13	7
Metal products and machinery	0.430	13	0.558	9	2.12	8
Wood, furniture	0.582	9	0.620	8	2.07	9
Construction	0.093	17	0.543	10	2.04	10
Printing	0.508	10	0.509	12	1.98	11
Other manufacturers	0.362	15	0.505	13	1.94	12
Rubber	0.453	12	0.481	14	1.93	13
Minerals (nonmetallic)	0.870	2	0.517	11	1.83	14
Agriculture	0.502	11	0.368	15	1.59	15
Utilities	0.614	6	0.296	16	1.49	16
Mining	0.638	5	0.288	17	1.47	17
Service	0.378	14	0.255	18	1.41	18

Note: The countries are Chile, Greece, South Korea, Mexico, and Spain.

Source: Yotopoulos and Nugent, "A Balanced-Growth Version of the Linkage Hypothesis," Table 2, p. 163.

tries, utilities, and services are low on both lists. Hence, an unbalanced-growth strategy, to stimulate investment in other sectors, should begin with the early-developing industries then move to chemicals and metal products. Advocates of import-substitution strategies find sustenance in these findings.

What do these indices really mean? Should a country base its development strategy on them, even if rapid growth is the principal goal? These particular measurement formulas have been attacked for several reasons, many of them sound. But alternative and more-complicated formulations give similar rankings anyway. The real issue is whether a mechanical summing up of input-output coefficients for one country really tells us anything about the dynamic processes of growth in another country. The textile industry, which ranks high in Table 18-1 according to its total backward linkage coefficient, may well require input of cotton and synthetic fibers. But whether this additional demand leads to new investment in farming and chemicals depends on many conditions, none of them reflected in the index. Can cotton be grown in the country at all and, if so, at what cost? It might remain cheaper and to the country's advantage to import cotton and use the land to grow more profitable crops. If cotton already is being grown and exported, can output expand to accommodate the textile plant or would it simply divert exports? Reduced exports, of course, cancel the backward linkage effect.

The potential linkage back to synthetic fibers raises additional issues. Petrochemical industries are subject to substantial economies of scale, and it would take a considerable expansion of the textile industry to justify the very large investment in petrochemicals. If protection is used to keep out imports of synthetic fibers, the textile industry itself suffers higher costs and perhaps loses its impetus to expand. However, some infant supplier industries may have the potential to reduce costs over time, learning by doing, if they are given a chance.

The requirements for effective forward linkages from manufacturing are even more stringent. To continue the example, textiles have a large forward linkage index, primarily to the clothing industry. But does domestic cloth stimulate the clothing industry? It can if textiles can be produced at costs below the world price of imported cloth. Otherwise, the user industry is better off importing its input. If clothing manufacturers are forced, through tariffs or import controls, to use more-expensive domestic cloth, this would discourage, rather than stimulate, the forward linkage.

The static linkage indexes can help direct attention to potential linkages, but detailed studies are required to consider all the relevant conditions and pinpoint the ways in which investment in one industry leads to investment in others. These studies may well show that some manufacturing sectors can lead growth in certain countries. But some of the references cited in Chapter 17 demonstrated that certain primary sectors also generate effective linkages, and no overwhelming case favors manufacturing on this ground.

Urbanization

Since the Industrial Revolution, urbanization and industrialization have moved in tandem. England started the nineteenth century with 30 percent of its people living in cities and ended the century with an urban population share over 70 percent.[6] The trend toward urbanization with industrial development is evident today in cross-country comparisons, depicted in Figure 18–2. As average incomes grow from about $750 per capita (in PPP) to $7,500, both the manufacturing workforce and the urban population grow as shares of the total workforce and population. Beyond $7,500, however, the urban share continues to rise even though manufacturing no longer employs an increasing share of the workers.

What causes rapid urbanization as industrialization proceeds? Several **external economies** (see Chapter 5) benefit manufacturing firms in urban settings. Large populations reduce the firms' costs of recruiting labor of all kinds, but especially skilled workers and technicians. Moreover, in cities, workers usually find their own housing, so firms need not provide it, as they might in rural areas or small towns. **Infrastructure,** including industrial sites, electricity, water, sewage, roads, railroads, and in many cases ports, is provided by the government

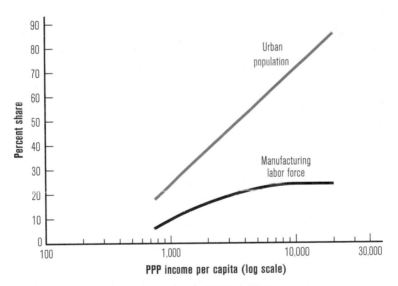

FIGURE 18-2. **Industrialization and Urbanization**
Cross-country regressions indicate that, as GNP per capita rises up to about $7,500, the manufacturing workforce grows from an average 6 percent of the labor force to 24 percent, while the urban share of the population grows from 18 to 66 percent. But urban growth continues, even though manufacturing's share of the workforce levels off.

[6]Hobsbawm, *Industry and Empire,* Figure 13.

in the cities at costs that reflect substantial scale economies. Health and education facilities also are more highly developed in the cities.

Each firm also benefits from the **economies of agglomeration** that result from the presence of many other firms, because a wide range of necessary inputs and services becomes available. Manufacturers can reduce transportation costs and shipping delays if they locate near their suppliers. They benefit from the proximity of repair and other industrial services. Financial markets cluster in cities, where domestic and international communication facilities are available and cheap. Manufacturers need access to banks and other financial institutions. They also need the city's communications to stay in touch with distant suppliers and markets, especially export markets. When the city in question is a national capital, manufacturers may locate there to gain ready access to government officials who control investment licenses and incentives, import allocations, and a myriad of other policy and administrative devices that affect the profitability of the firm. Finally, the strong preferences of capitalists, managers, and technicians for the amenities of large cities can be a significant reason for locating there.

Once a city is established, its large market creates reinforcing attractions. Distribution costs are minimized when the firm locates near its largest market. If the costs of shipping output weigh heavily in firms' costs, and especially if they are more important than the costs of transporting input, firms are pulled toward cities. This attraction is particularly strong in developing countries, where intercity and rural-urban transportation networks are sparse or costly. In developed countries, where transportation networks are dense and efficient, manufacturing tends to be more footloose and seeks out advantages like cheap labor with less regard for transportation costs.

But urbanization has its costs, as the residents of every large city in the world observe daily: overcrowding, unsanitary conditions, displacement of rural migrants, crime. These too have been features of industrialization for two centuries. During the first half of the nineteenth century, London and the other growing cities of Britain were dismal places:

> Smoke hung over them and filth impregnated them . . . the elementary public services: water supply, sanitation, street-cleaning, open spaces, and so on, could not keep pace with the mass migration of men into the cities, thus producing, especially after 1830, epidemics of cholera, typhoid and an appalling constant toll of the two great groups of nineteenth-century urban killers—air pollution and water pollution, or respiratory and intestinal disease. . . . New city populations . . . pressed into overcrowded and bleak slums, whose very sight froze the heart of the observer.[7]

---

[7]Hobsbawm, *Industry and Empire,* p. 86.

Migrants to the large cities of the third world probably need not put up with conditions as bad as those of early nineteenth-century London, but cities like Calcutta, Lagos, and São Paulo contain large slums with many of the same kinds of problems. Industrializing cities become magnets for rural workers seeking jobs at higher wages, a pervasive third world phenomenon. Despite the risks of unemployment and congested living conditions, urban life still is attractive to many rural dwellers, relative to the opportunities available at home. The costs of congestion are external diseconomies: Each new migrant benefits on average but, in so doing, reduces the well-being of all others, even if only slightly. The social costs are high, however, because this marginal reduction in well-being must be added up for all residents of the city.

No government feels comfortable with crowded cities, and many have attempted to stem the flow of migration. Over the long run, this can be done best by encouraging rural development as actively as industrialization, using the wide range of land tenure, investment, price incentive, and other policies described in Chapter 16. A complementary approach is to encourage the dispersal of new industries to smaller cities through the provision of infrastructure, incentives, and controls over location. Spreading investment reduces congestion and also may reduce the cost of migration. Migrants have shorter average distances to travel, so more of them can search for jobs with no commitment to permanent residence in cities remote from their homes. The decentralization of industry has complementary benefits for agriculture; it distributes urban markets and manufactured supplies more widely among the farming population.

Industrial dispersion has costs, however. Infrastructure costs may be greater in small towns, which have not provided as much of the basic facilities as large cities. To this must be added the higher costs of transportation and other infrastructure required to connect dispersed industrial locations. Even with this wider network of transportation and communications in place, private firms and society incur higher costs of hauling freight (both material input and final output) if they do not locate in the most-efficient place. These firms further incur higher costs in communicating with suppliers, customers, and financial institutions, not to mention government officials, and waiting with idle facilities while parts and repair specialists from distant places arrive to fix broken equipment. Whether the benefits of dispersal justify the costs depends on the circumstances. Costs are lower if the population already is dispersed, if several urban centers and connecting infrastructure already exist, and if the new sites have obvious advantages, such as nearby raw materials or abundant water.

INVESTMENT CHOICES IN INDUSTRY

Chapter 4 introduced the proposition that, because factors of production can be substituted for one another in many production processes, economies were able to conserve capital and get more growth out of a given amount of saving. Chapter 4 also used the same analytical device, the neoclassical production function, to demonstrate that policies to make labor less expensive and capital more expensive could move producers toward investments that employ more labor and less capital for a given level of output. Is there enough variance in production techniques to make such policies effective in conserving capital and creating more employment for a given amount of production? For industry, the answer is yes.

Choice of Technique

Table 18–2 illustrates the choice of technology for a single industry, textile weaving. Three alternative technologies are included: an older, semiautomatic loom (T1); a more modern, fully automatic, high-speed loom (T3); and an intermediate technology (T2). More alternatives could have been shown, including hand-loom weaving, which is still used in some Asian countries. As expected, the three technologies show increasing capital intensity, in the sense that the ratio of capital to output rises, and decreasing labor intensity. In addition to capital and labor costs, this table adds consideration of other operating costs, including rental space, power, and differential wastage of the main input, yarn. In many cases, modern equipment conserves both energy and material inputs and lowers production costs.

Analysis of the choice of technology is conveniently done using project analysis as described in Chapter 11. Revenues and costs, including the cost of investment, can be discounted over the life of each technology, and the technology with the highest net present value chosen as the most economic. In Table 18–2, for simplicity, we assume that all techniques produce cloth of equal quality and value, so revenue is not brought into consideration. Instead, the present value of costs is minimized.

The second part of the table presents indicative factor costs for a rich country and a poor one: Workers in the rich country are paid ten times the wage of workers in the poor one, whereas the real interest rate in the poor country is twice that of the rich one. Under those conditions, investors in the rich country minimize costs by choosing the most modern looms, largely because these require so much less labor. Investors in the poor country select the intermediate technology. However, should the annual wage in the poor country be $1,000 a year instead of $1,500, which is a realistic possibility, the oldest and most labor-

TABLE 18-2. Choice of Technology in Textile Weaving

INPUTS (PER MILLION YARDS OF SHIRTING)	ALTERNATIVE TECHNOLOGY[a]		
	T1	T2	T3
1. Equipment cost ($1,000)	80.0	200.0	400.0
2. Labor (person-years)	22.0	11.0	5.0
3. Other costs ($1,000/year)[b]	11.4	9.3	6.7

FACTOR COSTS	RICH COUNTRY	POOR COUNTRY
1. Real interest rate (% per annum)	5.0	10.0
2. Present-value factor (20 years)[c]	12.46	8.51
3. Wages ($1,000/year)	15.0	1.5

PRESENT VALUE OF COSTS ($1,000)[d]	ALTERNATIVE TECHNOLOGY[a]		
	T1	T2	T3
Rich country			
1. Capital charges	80	200	400
2. Wages	4112	2056	935
3. Other costs	142	116	83
4. Total	4334	2372	1418
Poor country			
1. Capital charges	80	200	400
2. Wages	280	140	64
3. Other costs	97	79	57
4. Total	457	419	521

[a]Technologies are T1, semiautomatic loom; T2, intermediate technology; and T3, fully automatic, high-speed loom.
[b]Includes cost of space, power, and wastage of yarn, all of which vary depending on the technology; excludes the common cost of yarn in the finished product.
[c]Present value of $1 per year for 20 years at the interest rate shown in 1.
[d]Wages and other costs are discounted at appropriate interest rate over 20 years using present value factor of factor costs.
Source: Adapted from data in Howard Pack, "The Choice of Technique and Employment in the Textile Industry," in A. S. Bhalla, ed., *Technology and Employment in Industry* (Geneva: International Labour Office, 1975), 153–74.

intensive technology minimizes costs. Figure 18–3 represents these technological choices as a production isoquant similar in a form realistic for alternative technologies in single industries.

The range of technologies represented in Figure 18–3 is realistic for the weaving industry in a developing country. The scope for technological choice in this industry can be indicated by the range of capital-labor ratios from the most- to the least-capital-intensive technology. The capital-labor ratio of technology T3 is 22 times that of technology T1. The study from which these figures are taken gives a similar range for cotton spinning, whereas cement-block making in Kenya alone exhibits a ratio of 11:1.[8]

[8]Howard Pack, "The Choice of Technique and Employment in the Textile Industry," p. 169; and Frances Stewart, "Manufacture of Cement Blocks in Kenya," p. 221, in A. S. Bhalla, ed., *Technology and Employment in Industry* (Geneva: International Labour Organization, 1985).

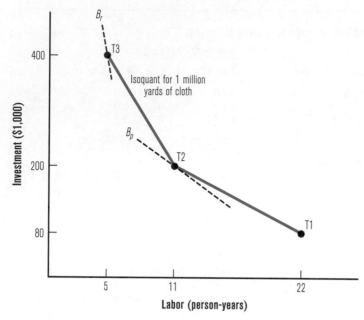

FIGURE 18-3. Technological Choice in the Weaving Industry
Three alternative weaving technologies, T1, T2, and T3, are taken
from Table 18–2. Each represents a different ratio of capital to
labor. Because the industry, or even a single firm, can use any
combination of technologies, production could take place at all
combinations of labor and capital along T1T2 and T2T3. Thus, an
isoquant can be traced from T1 to T2 to T3. The slopes of the
budget lines B_r and B_p represent the ratio of wages to capital
charges for the rich and poor countries, respectively. They
indicate costs are minimized for the rich country by using the
most capital-intensive technology, T3, whereas the poor country
should use intermediate technology, T2. Were wages in the poor
country only slightly lower relative to capital costs, the most
labor-intensive technology, T1, might well be optimal.

Even if the scope is narrowed to a choice between the appropriate technology (T2 for the poor country in Figure 18–3) and the most-capital-intensive alternative (T3), a wide range of technologies is available in several industries. For
shoe manufacturing, the most capital-intensive technology has a capital-labor
ratio 2.8 times that of the appropriate technology; for cotton weaving, the ratio is
4.3 times; for cotton spinning, 7.3 times; for brick making, 13.8 times; for maize
milling, 3.3 times; for sugar processing, 7.8 times; for beer brewing, 1.5 times; for
leather processing, 2.3 times; and for fertilizer manufacturing, 1.1 times.[9]
The cumulative impact of the choice of more-labor-intensive technologies
can be considerable. In one indicative experiment, Howard Pack, an American

[9]Howard Pack, "Aggregate Implications of Factor Substitution in Industry Processes," *Journal of
Development Economics* 11, no. 1 (August 1982), 7.

economist who specializes in the choice of technology, assumes that each of the nine industries listed in the previous paragraph receives $100 million of investment. If all this were spent on the most capital-intensive technology, it would generate employment of 58,000 and a value added of $364 million a year. But, if invested in the appropriate technology instead, the same investment would create over four times the employment (239,000) and 71 percent more value added ($624 million).[10]

Despite the advantages to be gained in both output and employment from using appropriate, more-labor-intensive methods in developing countries, we observe many industrial plants using processes that are too capital intensive. Several possible explanations for this were given in the discussion of the employment problem elsewhere in this text. Market prices of productive factors, for example, typically do not reflect true factor scarcities (opportunity costs or shadow prices) and so distort technology choice. More-labor-intensive methods usually are embodied in older models of equipment, frequently available only as used machinery, which may be difficult to learn about, obtain, and maintain; newer equipment may manufacture products of higher quality and value; or managers may not be skilled in handling large labor forces. These factors often are exaggerated. In any case, most of them can be incorporated in present value calculations that reveal least-cost technologies.

These factors probably do not explain the wide range of technologies, many of them apparently inappropriate, that can be observed in a single country or in similar countries. There may be two further explanations for this. First, different firms can face different factor prices. Foreign firms usually have access to cheaper capital than domestic companies can obtain, so their optimal choice of technology is more capital intensive. (However, this may be countered by the multinational firm's greater knowledge of and easier access to machinery using older techniques, some of which may be in use in older plants of the same company.) Among domestic companies, small firms, with limited access to formal capital markets, may have to pay more for their capital than large firms. Similarly, small firms may escape both unionization and minimum-wage laws and so are able to employ workers at lower costs. In Indonesia, economist Hal Hill observed four textile-weaving technologies in operation, with a capital-output ratio for the most modern looms over 200 times that for traditional handlooms. Two of these technologies represented least-cost choices for their firms. Surprisingly, these were the two most capital intensive. But when shadow prices were used, only the more labor-intensive of the two techniques remained appropriate.[11]

Second, investors may purchase inappropriate equipment because they and their managers have a strong bias toward the most modern machinery and

[10]Pack, "Aggregate Implications of Factor Substitution," p. 10.

[11]Hal Hill, "Choice of Technique in the Indonesian Weaving Industry," *Economic Development and Cultural Change* 31, no. 2 (January 1983), 337–54.

the highest possible quality of output, with less emphasis on profitability and other economic considerations. Harvard management expert Louis Wells called this the behavior of "engineering man."[12] If the characteristics of management constrain the choice of technology, the selection may be technique T3 in Figure 18–3, even though the budget line indicates the choice of technique T2. Such noneconomic behavior is more likely to prevail in highly protected, monopolistic situations, where a decision to produce at less than minimum cost does not threaten the firm's existence. State-owned enterprises are particularly prone to inefficiencies of this type.

Economies of Scale

In decisions about alternative technologies, **economies of scale** may be a crucial consideration. Economists at least since Adam Smith have observed that, for many kinds of production, larger facilities may be able to produce at lower unit costs than small ones. For example, steel produced in a mill designed for 2 million tons a year might cost 15 percent less than steel produced in a mill designed for only 1 million tons. As the scale of output rises, the potential average cost falls. (However, if the larger mill produces only 1 million tons, its average cost is likely to be higher than the small mill, because the small one was designed for lower output and the large one was not.) Readers familiar with the theory of the firm will recognize the concept of **long-run average cost,** the potential unit cost of output when plant size is variable. If the long-run cost curve declines over a range of output relevant to the plant in question, as depicted in Figure 18–4, there are economies of scale.

Scale economies arise for a number of reasons.

1. Some costs, such as research and design efforts or startup costs, may be fixed over a wide range of output.
2. The amount and cost of materials used in capital equipment rises with output but not always in proportion. For example, the capacity of a boiler is related to its volume, which for a sphere varies as the cube of its radius, whereas the material used to build it is related to its area, proportional to the square of the radius.
3. The amount of inventory and other working capital does not rise proportionally to output.
4. Greater scale permits greater specialization of both workers and equipment (a point emphasized by Adam Smith), which in turn permits higher productivity.

[12]Louis T. Wells, Jr., "Economic Man and Engineering Man: Choice of Technique in a Low-Wage Country," in C. P. Timmer et al., eds., *The Choice of Technology in Developing Countries* (Cambridge, MA: Center for International Affairs, Harvard University, 1975), 69–94.

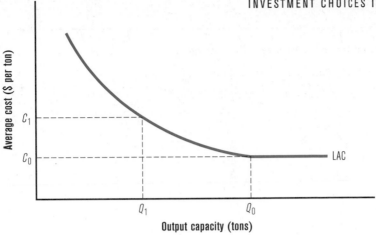

FIGURE 18-4. **Economies of Scale**
The long-run average cost curve, *LAC*, shows the average cost for
plants designed to produce at any capacity. Average cost falls as
capacity rises up to Q_0, sometimes called the *minimum efficient scale.*
Q_1 is half Q_0. The percentage by which C_1 exceeds C_0 is a measure of
the economies to be gained by building plants to a larger scale.

5. Larger production runs reduce the number of times equipment must be
   set up or readjusted for each run. For example, a plant that produces two
   or more products with one machine, such as metal cans of different sizes,
   could be run more efficiently once it has enough volume to produce each
   on a separate machine and reduce setup costs.
6. Larger producers may be able to obtain quantity discounts when they
   procure input.

All these economies apply to individual plants. At the level of the firm, further
economies may arise in management, transportation, marketing, and finance
as more plants are added.

These cost savings can be quite important in manufacturing certain products. Table 18–3 presents data on scale economies for several industries in
Europe in the early 1980s. The **minimum efficient scale** (MES) is defined as a
plant large enough so that no further economies can be gained by building a
larger facility, Q_0 in Figure 18–4. The first column of the table gives the percent
by which the average cost would be greater if a plant were built to a smaller
capacity; the second column shows that capacity (either one third, one half, or
two thirds the MES). In practice, if the largest plant in existence does not
exhaust the potential scale economies, investigators often take that output as
the MES until a larger plant is built.

Some of the cost increases in column 1 are significant: from 11 to 26 percent
for electric motors, steel, synthetic rubber, petrochemicals, Kraft paper, cement,
glass bottles, and flour. However, this is not very meaningful unless we know how

TABLE 18-3. **Economies of Scale in Manufacturing**

PRODUCT	PERCENT INCREASE IN AVERAGE COST	PLANT CAPACITY = THIS % OF MES	MES AS % OF U.K. MARKET
Refrigerators	7	33	85
Electric motors	15	50	60
Steel	11	33	27
Synthetic rubber	15	50	24
Petrochemicals	19	33	23
Tires	5	50	17
Oil refineries	4	33	14
Beer	5	33	12
Kraft paper	13	50	11
Cement	26	33	10
Glass bottles	11	33	5
Dairy products	2	67	1
Flour	21	67	1

Note: Estimates come from studies of European industries conducted from the late 1960s through the early 1980s. *Minimum efficient scale* (MES) is defined as the output beyond which average costs cease to decline (Q_0 in Figure 18–4) or beyond which no larger plants have been built.
Source: Cliff Pratten, "A Survey of the Economies of Scale," in Commission of the European Communities, *Research on the "Cost of Non-Europe,"* vol. 2, *Studies on the Economics of Integration* (Luxembourg: Commission of the European Communities, 1988).

large the MES is relative to the national market. The last column shows how the MES compares to the market in the United Kingdom. For all products except glass, dairy products, and flour, these efficient plants would fill from 10 to 85 percent of British demand for those products. For refrigerators and electric motors, the minimum-efficient-size plant could supply well over half the demand.

The market in the United Kingdom is comparable to that in the largest developing countries, if gross domestic product is measured in terms of purchasing power parity. Over a billion people in China, with PPP average income only an eighth of Britain's, have a GDP 2.5 times that in the United Kingdom; India's GDP is about the same as Britain's; Brazil, Mexico, and Indonesia have economies 60 to 80 percent that of the United Kingdom. But, in Nigeria (the largest economy in Africa), the Philippines, and Pakistan, GDP is only a fifth that of Britain. Moreover, in developing countries, it is likely that the effective demand for modern manufactures is considerably smaller than indicated by the comparison of GDPs, because in Britain a much larger share of the population has reached middle-class standards of income. Where markets are much smaller than the minimum efficient scale, unit costs may be much higher than those indicated in the table. Such an industry would remain viable only if protected from imports and given a monopoly.

The characteristics of these large-scale industries shed light on the industrialization process. Those with largest cost savings and the largest potential market shares are all, with the exception of beer, either producer goods (electric motors, steel, synthetic rubber, for example) or consumer durables (refrigerators and others not shown, such as automobiles). Thus, the nondurable consumer goods industries, such as processed foods, textiles, clothing, and footwear, develop early at least in part because economies of scale are no barrier, except in the smallest economies. The barriers to backward integration also are suggested by scale economies in producer goods.

Despite the scale economies, it may be efficient to build small plants in developing countries. A steel plant, for example, should be built when it can produce at a cost below the price of imported steel. This may happen long before the market grows to accommodate a steel mill of minimum efficient scale. Economic size is only one factor that bears on efficiency. All the others mentioned earlier in this text (productivity, opportunity costs of capital and labor, availability of raw materials and complementary inputs, managerial skills, and market organization) also affect the outcome and may outweigh the effects of scale economies. Techniques such as project appraisal (Chapter 11) can be employed to analyze the impact of these elements on profitability.

Moreover, the domestic market is not the only possibility. The "virtuous circle," through which export markets make it possible to attain scale economies, which in turn increase export competitiveness, was one of the forces behind Britain's Industrial Revolution. Indeed, if a domestic industry in a small developing country were efficient enough to compete with foreign plants at any given output, then scale economies would not matter: The home industry could export enough to achieve any scale desired. Developing countries like South Korea and Brazil achieved scale economies, even in industries like steel and automobiles, with the help of export markets. Economic integration among developing countries may help other countries to do the same.

Small-Scale Industry

Although economies of scale require large plants in some branches of production, in many other industries small- and medium-scale firms can compete effectively with large ones (see Table 18–4). This is especially true in developing countries, where many widely used manufactured items, including most food and tobacco products, textiles, clothing, footwear, furniture and other wood products, cement blocks, bricks, tiles, and various simple metal products, commonly are made by smaller firms.

It often has been argued that developing country governments should promote small-scale industry as either a complement or an alternative to large-scale modern manufacturing. India, probably the postindependence leader in planning for large-scale industrialization, also pursued small-industry development with vigor, a legacy of Ghandi's famous advocacy of small units using traditional technologies. China's use of small-scale rural industry in support of local self-reliance is equally well known (see Box 18–1). E. F. Schumacher, author

BOX 18-1 TOWNSHIP AND VILLAGE ENTERPRISES IN CHINA

The Chinese did what appears to be difficult in market economies: They established modern small- and medium-sized factories in the Chinese countryside. In the first phase of successful development, the emphasis was on the supply of farm inputs, equipment, and consumer goods to communes and other rural customers. Several conditions made possible this early development. China's rural transportation and marketing system was poorly developed, so that rural communities were isolated from urban centers of production. Centralized planning and control of industrial goods intensified this isolation, because communes wanting fertilizer or trucks had to apply to authorities located in urban centers, a process that entailed long delays and often was unsuccessful. It was in the communes' interests for their regions to become self-reliant in agricultural inputs to avoid these delays, and it was also in the planners' interests if local materials, capital, and labor could be used, so that other industrial priorities were not sacrificed. Local industry had the additional advantages of bringing modern technology directly to the countryside and helping narrow the economic and social gaps between farm and city.

This knowledge of technology and how to organize a factory proved to be valuable to China's industrial development effort after market-oriented reforms were introduced in the early 1980s. With the abolition of central planning and the communes, part of the original rationale for these rural industries disappeared, but now these enterprises could buy whatever inputs they wanted and could afford on the open market. Renamed *township and village enterprises,* the factories began pro-

of *Small Is Beautiful,*[13] founded a movement of small-industry enthusiasts. Over the years, very few development plans have failed to pay homage to the goal of small-industry development.

Advocates of small-industry promotion promise a wide range of benefits, including accelerated employment creation, income generation for the poor, dispersal of economic activity to small towns and rural areas, and mobilization of latent entrepreneurial talent. They also argue that support for small enterprise and the **informal sector** creates a wider base of political support for capitalism and free-market policies.[14]

Shortly, we assess the potential of small industry to realize these hopes, but first we need to consider what *small industry* really means. There are several different ways to classify manufacturing plants by scale, none perfect. Classifying by the number of workers employed has the advantage that data are widely

[13]E. F. Schumacher, *Small Is Beautiful* (London: Sphere Books, 1974).
[14]See Hernando deSoto, *The Other Path* (New York: Harper and Row, 1989), and P. N. Dhar and H. F. Lydall, *The Role of Small Enterprises in Indian Economic Development* (Bombay: Asia Publishing House, 1961).

ducing a wider and wider range of products, not only for the countryside but for the urban areas and export as well. Because these enterprises were "owned" locally and relatively small, they were outside the sphere of control of the central ministries in Beijing and could respond freely to market opportunities. Also, because they were small and, unlike the large state enterprises, lacked access to subsidized bank credit, it was acceptable politically to let loss-making township and village enterprises fail. Local governments had no resources to subsidize their losses, so these industries had to work extra hard to make sure they stayed profitable.

Not all areas of the country benefited equally from the development of township and village enterprises, however. The most dynamic development of this sector was in the coastal provinces of China and areas within easy reach of cities. Mountainous regions and other areas remote from good infrastructure and urban markets had fewer township and village enterprises. Therefore, agglomeration effects, as indicated elsewhere in this chapter, mattered as much, if not more, for the smaller-scale township and village enterprises as they did for the large urban manufacturing establishments. The result of these developments was that employment in township and village enterprises rose from 28.3 million workers in 1978 to 69.8 million in 1985 and 130.5 million in 1997. As a percentage of the total industrial output in China, the share of township and village enterprises rose from 22 percent in 1978 to 32 percent in 1985 and 38 percent in 1997. The share of the large state-owned enterprises, in contrast, fell from 78 percent in 1978 to 65 percent in 1985 and 26 percent in 1997 (the share of foreign joint ventures and outright private firms accounted for the remainder). Particularly during the latter half of the 1980s but throughout the 1990s as well, China's industrial and GDP growth rates would have been significantly lower had it not been for the dynamic growth of the township and village enterprise sector.

available. Units with 1–4 workers (usually a proprietor and family members) can be classified as **cottage shops,** whereas larger plants can be divided into small enterprises (sometimes 5–19 workers), medium enterprises (20–99), and large enterprises (100 or more), respectively. Such distinctions are arbitrary. In a large country or a small industrial one, a plant employing 200 workers would be considered small. Moreover, when plants are classified by other criteria, such as capital invested or technology used, they may shift into different categories.

Cottage shops and small enterprises employ one half to three quarters of all manufacturing-sector workers in many low-income countries. Their share in manufacturing value added is likely to be much lower, however, usually about one fourth the total. This marked discrepancy between the employment share and the value-added share shows that the value added per worker is much lower on average in small plants than in large ones. In part, this reflects the greater labor intensity of small plants.

Since low-income countries typically have abundant labor but little capital, most economists would expect labor-intensive technologies to be efficient in these settings. By this line of reasoning, that small firms usually are more labor intensive sometimes is taken to mean that they are more efficient than large firms. As part of the informal sector, small firms may be exempted from, or escape the enforcement of, taxes, minimum-wage laws, employment codes, and other regulations that raise the costs of larger firms. They also may lack access to subsidized loans, foreign exchange at overvalued (cheap) rates, and controlled imports, which artificially lower the costs of larger firms. It has been theorized that this freedom from many sources of factor-price distortion may induce small firms to use resources more efficiently than large firms. Alternatively, however, they might simply use all resources less efficiently. Attempts to measure the relative efficiency of different-size plants in industries where large and small firms coexist generally have been unable to reach solid conclusions.[15] Such comparisons face many difficulties in any case, not least that product quality may differ greatly between large and small firms. Although cottage shops make cheap plastic sandals, for example, large plants may produce shoes of higher quality.

As a country develops, the average size of its industrial plants tends to rise, as implied by Table 18–4. This rise is associated with the expansion of markets, which permits a few firms in some industries to expand and realize economies of scale and thereby beat out their smaller competitors. A related factor is declining transportation and communication costs, which facilitate the integration of national markets and permit goods to be manufactured in least-cost locations then shipped to their final markets. Thus, the "natural monopoly" conferred on smaller local firms by high transportation costs and poor communication begins to break down. Industrialization also tends to narrow productivity and wage differentials among units of different sizes, a condition for the efficient allocation of resources.

The presence of many small firms in most poor countries and the many people who depend on them for a living does not necessarily mean that government should promote or subsidize small-scale industry. Most of the cottage shops and small enterprises in low-income countries probably have little capacity for enterprise growth. They typically provide a living for the proprietor and a few family members at a standard above that of peasant farmers but below that provided by efficient modern firms. Like small family farms, most of these "livelihood enterprises" survive as long as no better economic opportunities present themselves, then gradually disappear as the modern sector of the economy develops and workers move on to higher-productivity employment. Only a few small- and medium-scale enterprises have the potential to modernize themselves, upgrade their technologies, and compete successfully with larger firms. To do so, they usually must define some niche of excellence. The small firms that survive in industrial countries tend to be just as capital-intensive and high tech as larger firms in the same economy and to differ from them only in degree of specialization.

---

[15]Ian M. D. Little, Dipak Mazumdar, and John M. Page, Jr., *Small Manufacturing Enterprises* (New York: Oxford University Press for the World Bank, 1988). They also claim to detect a tendency for medium-size firms to be most efficient.

TABLE 18-4. **Share of Small Establishments in Total Manufacturing Employment, 1980s (percent)**

GDP PER CAPITA	DISTRIBUTION OF EMPLOYMENT BY NUMBER OF WORKERS			
	1–4	5–19	20–99	100+
$100–500	64	7	4	25
$500–1,000	41	12	10	37
$1,000–2,000	11	13	14	61
$2,000–5,000	8	11	17	64
Over $5,000	4	6	20	70

Source: Donald R. Snodgrass and Tyler S. Biggs, *Industrialization and the Small Firm: Patterns and Policies* (San Francisco: ICS Press, 1996).

Can the promotion of small-scale industry deliver the benefits promised by its advocates? Let us examine the evidence on each of the claims noted earlier.

Small plants generally are more labor intensive than large ones, although there are many labor-intensive large firms as well. Labor intensity contributes to equity in countries where income is distributed very unequally and people often have difficulty finding remunerative employment. The amount a worker earns is more important than merely having a job, however; and the level of pay ultimately is linked to productivity. In small industries in the poorest countries, labor productivity is low and most jobs in small firms provide little more than a chance to share in the general poverty. Government policy should aim not just at raising employment but at helping firms of all scales to develop new markets, adopt new technologies, and raise labor productivity. This is more likely to occur in medium-scale firms than in very small ones.

The claim that small-scale industry promotes regional decentralization also needs considerable qualification. Although many small firms are located in rural areas and small towns, these tend to be traditional "livelihood enterprises" that are likely to lose out in the process of industrialization. Keeping them alive through subsidization might increase equity, but at a high cost to efficiency and long-term growth. Modern small firms, in contrast, cluster in large cities, perhaps even more densely than large firms. Large firms are more self-sufficient and rely on economies of scale to lower production costs. Small firms, however, depend more on economies of agglomeration generated by proximity to firms engaged in similar or complementary activities. Most small producers need access to intermediate material inputs and so prefer to be close to ports and other transport facilities. They are less likely than large firms to train their own workers, so they benefit from being near urban growth centers where skilled workers are located.

Small-scale industry indeed serves as a breeding ground for potential entrepreneurs. Most societies have actual or potential entrepreneurs in farming, retail trading, transportation, and other small-scale activities. Small-scale industry represents a feasible step for these entrepreneurs, who would be blocked from entering manufacturing if large amounts of credit and the ability to manage large-scale enterprises were essential. Small enterprises sometimes can be developed in imitation of earlier entrants and so require less-innovative entrepreneurs. Some small firms have the potential to grow to medium or even large enterprises. It is important, however, not to yield to romanticism. Statistically, very few small firms even survive over long periods of time, let alone grow to be medium or large enterprises. The rate of business failure is high among small firms in all countries.

Government can assist by providing a legal system, supporting financial and other institutions, and pursuing market-based policies that permit successful enterprises to flourish and require unsuccessful ones to meet market pressures or give way to more efficient alternatives. Most governments can begin by eliminating the many facets of policy that discriminate against small firms. Controlled imports and subsidized credit seldom reach small firms, whereas licensing requirements, health regulations, zoning restrictions, and other measures often are used actively to discourage small enterprises, especially those operating in the informal sector. In the kind of market-based, outward-looking regime described in Chapter 19, small firms should thrive if they have the economic advantages claimed for them by the advocates of small-scale industrialization.

Even in a deregulated, market-oriented economy, however, many feel that small industry needs special help from government to overcome some of its initial handicaps. A fairly standard package of services is used to provide this assistance.[16] It includes credit, usually provided through a small-industry development bank or similar institution; technical advice, organized along the lines of an agricultural extension service; training programs for managers and skilled workers; help in setting up procurement and marketing channels; and industrial estates that provide sites with infrastructure and a focal point for the assistance package. The idea behind this kind of package is to help inexperienced entrepreneurs over their early hurdles, introduce them to regular marketing channels, and eventually make them self-reliant.

However, the package is expensive and often ineffective. It requires government agencies to contact numerous individual entrepreneurs and offer assistance tailored to their specific needs and thus draws heavily on the government's limited managerial and technical resources. Firms served by these programs often find the advice they receive unhelpful and the places in industrial estates they are offered poorly located or too expensive. Many have failed to repay their loans, and this has sometimes resulted in the bankruptcy of the specialized lending institution. At best, the expense and complexity of small-industry assistance programs limits their outreach to a small fraction of target firms. Nor is it clear that government agencies have the skills and nimbleness required to help small entrepreneurs deal with market situations. Therefore, this approach is no substitute for general economic policies that permit small operators to do what they do best.

[16]See Eugene Staley and Richard Morse, *Modern Small Industry for Developing Countries* (New York: McGraw-Hill, 1965).

Industry and Development Goals

Industrialization is not a panacea for underdevelopment. But two of its strengths are essential for any development program. As suggested by the Lewis-Fei-Ranis two-sector model (Chapter 4), greater productivity in industry is a key to increased per capita income. And manufacturing provides a much larger menu of possibilities for efficient import substitution and increasing exports than is possible with primary industries alone.

Industrialization and rural development must proceed in tandem. Industry can supply agriculture with inputs, especially fertilizer and simple farm equipment, that raise farm productivity. If manufacturing is efficient, these inputs may be supplied more cheaply than imports. The relationship is reciprocal, because agriculture supplies raw materials for manufacturing, such as cotton and other fibers, rubber, or tobacco. Agriculture and industry also provide reciprocal consumer goods markets. If agricultural incomes grow in an egalitarian fashion, which may require land reform and broad-based rural development, then manufacturing enjoys a wide and growing market for its consumer goods, one that may enable it to achieve scale economies in both production and marketing. Similarly, the growth of urban incomes, stimulated by industrial expansion, should provide a continuing stimulus to agricultural output and productivity through increasing demand for food. The key to growing food demand is expanding employment and improved urban income distribution.

Industry by itself cannot generate sufficient jobs to absorb the growing number of workers or to equalize income distribution, especially in the poorest countries. Liberalized economies, with reduced controls and market prices closer to scarcity values, can help arrest the tendency toward capital intensity and inappropriate, modern technologies in manufacturing and thus raise job creation in industry. A renewed emphasis on small industry also may help. Moreover, to the extent that intermediate or innovative technologies are needed to save capital and create more jobs relative to output, an innovative, efficient capital goods industry is an essential part of a development strategy. But, in the final analysis, much of the burden for employment creation and income equalization lies outside industry, in agriculture and the services.

Industry has been seen as a key to another goal of many developing countries, reduced dependence. If a country wants the ability to do without imports of essential commodities, it must develop both an integrated industrial structure and a productive agriculture. If it wishes to exclude foreign political and cultural influence, it must learn to operate its manufacturing plants without foreign help. Much of the discussion about reduced dependence really is about increasing autarky or self-sufficiency; this implies that a country must produce everything it needs. But an alternative goal suggests the capability of producing a wide variety of goods efficiently enough to trade them on world markets and obtaining some goods overseas when it is advantageous to do so. This leads to the outward-looking strategy discussed in the next chapter.

Behind these considerations lurks a hidden development goal, industrialization for its own sake. Despite advice from many quarters to temper their protective and other industrial policies and instead to promote greater efficiency, employment, and equity, many governments continue to establish the most modern, capital-intensive industries available. This cannot be attributed entirely to misguided policy. The desire to have modern industry may be as great for a country as the desire for a radio or car can be for an individual. To the extent that modern manufacturing is a goal in itself, the best that development economists can do is point out how much could be accomplished with alternative policies and measure the costs of industrialization in terms of other goals that remain to be achieved.

SUMMARY

- The share of industry in GDP rises with an increase in per capita income in countries with relatively low levels of income but eventually levels off as income per capita rises above $10,000.
- Individual industries create backward and forward linkages that raise the demand for and stimulate the development of other industries.
- Industrialization is accompanied by urbanization, because many efficiencies and external economies are obtained by one industry locating near others, but many diseconomies in the form of worsened air and water quality also are connected with urbanization, particularly in the early stages of development.
- The most-efficient choices of technology can be analyzed using project appraisal techniques, and poorer countries with large amounts of labor and relatively little capital usually, but not always, benefit from the use of more labor-intensive technology.
- Economies of scale exist in many industries, but the markets in the larger developing countries, particularly those in the middle-income category, are typically large enough to support industries with large scale economies. Developing countries with smaller markets always have the option of achieving economies of scale by exporting the product of these industries.
- Some observers see small-scale industrial firms as the ideal way to pursue industrialization in low-income countries, and small firms provide greater employment and contribute in other ways as well in many circumstances, but small is not always beautiful even in the poorest countries, because such firms have disadvantages as well as advantages.

19

Trade and Development

I n November 2005, the fourth Summit of the Americas was held in Mar del
Plata, Argentina. Thirty-four presidents from the Western Hemisphere
assembled to discuss a Free Trade Area of the Americas, an idea proposed in
1994 by U.S. President Bill Clinton and supported by his successor, George W.
Bush. Mexican President Vicente Fox also backed the proposal, as did other
Latin American leaders. But there were voices of dissent. Populist presidents
from Argentina and Brazil had their doubts. Most critical was Hugo Chavez, the
leftist president of Venezuela, who rallied a crowd of an estimated 25,000 pro-
testers in a stadium near the closed-door meetings proclaiming, "Each one of us
brought a shovel, a gravedigger's shovel, because here in Mar del Plata is the
tomb of the Free Trade Area of the Americas."

Rioting broke out after the rally, something that has happened repeatedly
during official meetings about international trade. The meetings of the World
Trade Organization (WTO) in Seattle in 1999 were disrupted by street protestors
who felt free trade hurt workers in both developing and industrialized nations. In
Cancun, Mexico, in 2003, there also were protests, both among official participants in the trade talks and by demonstrators outside. One of those demonstrators was Lee Kyang Hae, who headed South Korea's Federation of Farmers and
Fishermen. Lee stabbed himself, and later died, in protest against the WTO and
the more open-trade policies it advocated. Lee specifically opposed further trade
liberalization of agriculture, which he believed would ruin the livelihood of many
Korean farmers. As these events demonstrate, globalization and free trade generate some of the world's most heated controversies over economic policy.

But, despite these controversies and concerns, trade among nations has been growing rapidly, and most developing countries are actively trying to expand their trade. Global trade has more than doubled in the last three decades, with trade in developing countries tripling. Developing countries import many more goods and services than they once did, ranging from appliances to pharmaceutical products to sophisticated machinery. They also export much more, including agricultural products, automobile parts, clothing, computers, shoes, toys, oil, minerals, and other raw materials.

Trade provides low- and middle-income nations with significant opportunities to improve welfare and accelerate growth and development. With more open trade, families and businesses have more choices in quality, price, and array of products than if they buy only from domestic firms. Producers have much larger markets to which they can sell. If successful, exporting firms can generate rapid job growth for large numbers of low-skilled workers, which can have a strong impact on poverty reduction. Trade also creates the possibility for the transfer of new technologies from rich to poor countries, which can raise productivity and incomes.

But the news is not all good. Although more open trade creates many winners, it creates losers. Firms and farmers that produce at high prices for the domestic market can be forced out of business, with job losses and other disruptions. Exporters operating on world markets often face the risk of rapidly falling prices or other vagaries of the world market that are out of their control. Poor weather in Nicaragua may undercut its coffee crop, sending up world prices and benefiting coffee farmers in Uganda, but a bumper crop in Vietnam can lead to a drop in prices that can leave the Ugandan farmer with much lower income.

The evidence suggests that, on balance, more open trade is beneficial for developing countries, and leads to more rapid growth and poverty reduction, particularly when exports are focused on labor-intensive products such as agriculture and basic manufacturing. But there is plenty of controversy. Some economists argue that the contribution of trade, while positive, is smaller than many people suggest and other factors are much more important in the development process. There is much debate about the key policies necessary to stimulate trade and the balance between traditional market-oriented policies and government interventions to help spur exports. Some believe that more open trade only creates "sweatshops" and leads to a "race to the bottom" in wages, labor standards, and environmental outcomes. And some argue that multilateral trade negotiations are biased against poor countries, allowing rich countries to continue to protect their own agricultural and textile producers while forcing developing countries to open their economies.

In this chapter, we examine these debates, first by considering recent trends and patterns in trade flows across countries. We then explore the pros and cons of two major trade strategies, import substitution and outward orientation, and review the empirical evidence on trade volumes, trade policies, and economic growth. Finally, we explore several key issues, including the rise of China and India, the sweatshop argument, protection in the industrialized countries, and multilateral trade negotiations.

TRADE TRENDS AND PATTERNS

World trade expanded dramatically during the last several decades, far outpacing global growth in overall output. Figure 19–1 shows changes in exports as a share of GDP for the world as a whole as well as for middle- and low-income countries (the patterns for imports, not shown, are quite similar). Globally, exports nearly doubled from 13 percent of world output in 1970 to 24 percent in 2003. Trade grew particularly quickly in developing countries: In both low- and middle-income countries, exports as a share of GDP almost tripled. The remarkable increase in trade in recent decades is among the clearest indicators of the current era of globalization. There is more to globalization than trade, as it includes more rapid and larger financial flows, greater migration of people, and faster information flows through the Internet and satellite phone connections, among other things. But there is little doubt that trade is one of the most important aspects of

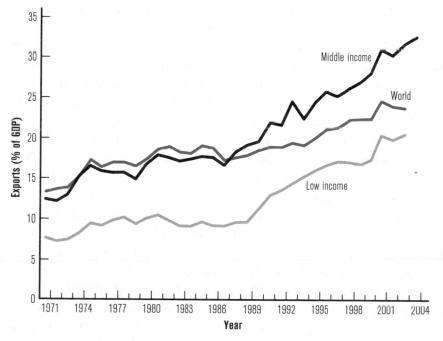

FIGURE 19-1. Exports as a Share of GDP, 1970–2003
Source: World Bank, *World Development Indicators 2005.*

TABLE 19-1. **Regional Participation in International Trade and Capital Flows**
(percent)

REGION	SHARE OF WORLD GDP		SHARE OF WORLD EXPORTS		SHARE OF EXPORTS IN GDP		AVERAGE ANNUAL GROWTH OF EXPORTS	
	1970	2002	1970	2002	1970	2002	1970–86	1986–2002
World	100	100	100	100	13.3	23.9	5.4	6.3
East Asia and Pacific	1.5	5.5	–	9.1	7.1	38.5	–	10.8
Latin America and Caribbean	6.1	6.1	5.0	5.4	9.9	23.4	4.8	7.2
Middle East and North Africa	–	2.1	–	2.5	37.3	33.4	–	0.7
South Asia	1.3	2.0	0.7	1.4	5.1	16.5	5.3	10.7
Sub-Saharan Africa	1.3	1.1	3.6	1.4	22.3	22.4	2.2	3.6
High income	83.7	80.1	72.6	74.5	13.7	33.4	5.7	6.2

Source: World Bank, *World Development Indicators 2005* (Washington, DC: World Bank, 2005).

globalization. For developing countries as a whole, imports plus exports are now equivalent to over 60 percent of total output, indicating that large portions of these economies are influenced by global markets.

There are stark regional differences in these trends. East and Southeast Asia have seen the most rapid *increase* in trade and global integration, with exports growing from 7 percent of GDP in 1970 to 38 percent in 2002 (Table 19–1). This huge change was driven mainly by very rapid growth in manufactured exports, especially in China, which as a large economy dominates the regional average. There were also significant increases in exports in Latin America and South Asia. But, in the Middle East, North Africa, and throughout much of sub-Saharan Africa, there has been much less change. These regions are major exporters of oil and other petroleum products, copper, gold, other raw materials and minerals, and agricultural goods such as cocoa and coffee; but not manufactured goods. In 1970, exports were a much larger share of GDP in the Middle East and North Africa (37 percent) and sub-Saharan Africa (22 percent) than in other major regions, but by 2002, their export-GDP ratio had changed little. Sub-Saharan Africa, in particular, remains dependent on trade, with exports accounting for over one fifth of the region's GDP. But, despite this dependence, sub-Saharan Africa in many ways remains marginalized from world trade. Its exports constituted 3.6 percent of the world total in 1970, but just 1.4 percent in 2002.

As economies grow and the share of trade increases, the products imported and exported tend to change as well. On the import side, as incomes grow, countries typically import more-sophisticated consumer goods and intermediate products as inputs to manufacturing. On the export side, as workers gain new skills and increase productivity, the composition of exports shifts away from primary products (agriculture, minerals, and raw materials) to manufactured products. Table 19–2 shows how the composition of exports has changed for 17 developing countries. In 1970, Mauritius's primary export was sugarcane, with manufactured goods accounting for only 2 percent of exported goods. But, by 2003, three quarters of the value of all exports were from manufactures, as Mauritius became a major producer of textiles and clothing. An almost identical pattern emerged in Sri Lanka, and there were large shifts in several other countries. But, where economic and export growth lagged, such as in Argentina, Honduras, and Senegal, manufactured exports remain a relatively small share of the total.

For those developing nations that have been able to expand their trade, most of the increase has come from trading with industrialized countries rather than with other developing countries. The industrialized countries manufacture the majority of capital goods and many intermediate goods, so they tend to be the origin for most products imported by developing countries. At the same time, they offer the largest markets for developing countries to sell the full range of their export products, whether agricultural products, raw materials, manufactured goods, or services (including everything from call centers to tourism). For most developing countries, this pattern continues today, but it has changed dra-

TABLE 19-2. Shifts in the Composition of Exports, 1970–2003

	SHARES OF TOTAL EXPORTS (%)				GDP GROWTH PER CAPITA (% PER ANNUYM)
	1970		2003		
COUNTRY	PRIMARY	MANUFACTURES	PRIMARY	MANUFACTURES	
Algeria	93	7	48	52	1.0
Argentina	86	14	87	13	0.2
Honduras	92	8	98	2	0.6
India	48	52	23	77	2.8
Indonesia	99	1	19	82	4.1
Korea	23	77	7	93	5.8
Malaysia	93	7	23	77	4.0
Mauritius	98	2	25	75	4.3
Mexico	68	32	73	27	1.5
Pakistan	43	57	10	90	2.0
Peru	99	1	48	52	0.1
Senegal	81	19	78	22	0.1
Singapore	72	28	15	85	5.0
Sri Lanka	99	1	26	74	3.0
Thailand	95	5	15	85	4.5
Tunisia	81	19	19	81	3.0
Venezuela	99	1	66	34	−1.4

Source: World Bank, *World Development Indicators 2004* (Washington, DC: World Bank, 2005).

TABLE 19-3. Intraregional Trade, 1980–2003

REGION	INTRAREGIONAL TRADE (BILLION US$)		TOTAL TRADE BY REGION (BILLION US$)		INTRAREGIONAL TRADE/TOTAL TRADE (PERCENT)	
	1980	2003	1980	2003	1980	2003
Asia	39.9	659.0	168.0	1,382.6	23.7	47.7
Africa*	3.4	9.7	72.3	140.8	4.7	7.1
Middle East	9.1	21.7	110.1	229.5	8.3	9.4
Latin America	22.9	60.8	111.8	339.5	20.5	17.9

*Figures for Africa do not include South Africa because data for South Africa was not available in 1980.
Source: IMF, *Direction of Trade Statistics*, October 2005.

matically in Asia in recent years (Table 19–3). Nearly half of Asia's exports today are sent to other countries in Asia, up from a quarter in 1980. Raw materials and intermediate products produced in one Asian country now are more likely to be exported to a neighboring country for finishing and final export. Moreover, as incomes in Asia have risen dramatically, these countries have become the final destination for many raw material and consumer products. A large portion of Indonesia's natural gas exports go to Korea and other countries in the region. China's dramatic rise is particularly significant: Its imports have grown almost as fast as its exports, and it is now one of the biggest markets in the world. A significant share of China's manufactured export products are assembled using components imported from other countries in the regions. Food products from the Philippines might now be sold in China rather than shipped to the United States.

The extent to which a country trades with the rest of the world depends importantly on the size of its economy (Figure 19-2). Small economies, measured in this instance by total GDP not by GDP per capita, tend to import more than larger ones, as they cannot efficiently produce the full range of consumer goods, intermediate products, and capital equipment demanded by consumers and businesses. Just as a small town cannot offer the same range of stores and services for shoppers as a large town, small economies cannot efficiently produce everything that consumers and businesses would like to buy, so they tend to import more products to satisfy those demands. On the export side, as firms in small economies increase production, they are more likely to be constrained by the limited size of the market and unable to take advantage of economies of scale if they sell only locally. By exporting to global markets, they can sell larger amounts of more-specialized products. Producers in larger economies can sell a much larger share of their output locally without being constrained by market size. In tiny Guyana, imports and exports together are nearly 200 percent of

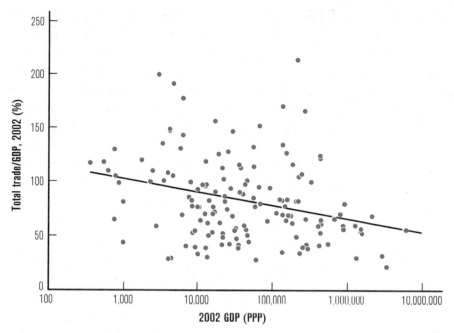

FIGURE 19-2. **Economic Size and Trade**
Smaller economies tend to trade more, and larger economies trade less. The
figure shows total GDP and trade as a share of GDP for 146 countries of all
income levels in 2002.

GDP, and in Mauritius they reach nearly 120 percent of GDP. But in much larger
Brazil and India, the ratios are 29 and 31 percent, respectively.

Trade patterns are also influenced by a country's geographical characteristics, including its access to shipping routes, especially whether or not it is landlocked, and its location relative to major markets. For the last several hundred
years, the cheapest and most important form of transporting goods between
countries was by sea, and to this day, countries with easier access to sea-based
shipping tend to have larger exports and imports than landlocked countries.
Adam Smith recognized the advantages of access to the sea for trade and commerce more than 230 years ago in *The Wealth of Nations:* "As by means of water-
carriage a more extensive market is opened to every sort of industry than what
land-carriage alone can afford it, so it is upon the sea-coast, and along the banks
of navigable rivers, that industry of every kind naturally begins to sub-divide
and improve itself, and it is frequently not till a long time after that those
improvements extend themselves to the inland part of the country."[1]

As Smith predicts, most landlocked countries trade less and have slower economic growth. Landlocked countries face much higher transport costs, as they

---

[1]Adam Smith, *An Inquiry into the Nature and Causes of The Wealth of Nations,* Book 1, Chapter 3,
paragraph 3 (New York: The Modern Library, 1976).

must not only pay for sea-based shipping but overland costs to and from the nearest seaport. These costs can skyrocket when relationships between neighboring countries deteriorate. For example, periodic conflict between Ethiopia and Eritrea has forced some firms in Ethiopia to seek other more distant ports, for example, in Djibouti or Kenya. Landlocked Nepal is almost totally dependent on shipment through India. Sixteen African countries are landlocked, and shipping costs for these countries can be two or three times higher than for their coastal neighbors.[2] As a result, everything that is imported is much more expensive. Similarly, exporters must pay more for shipping, raising the costs of export products and making firms less competitive on world markets.

Some landlocked high-income countries have done well, such as Austria and Switzerland, but they are located in the midst of major markets, are connected with good road networks, and have had good relations with neighboring states, so shipping costs are not a major barrier. Moreover, landlocked countries that ship raw materials for which the margins between production costs and world prices are large are in a better position to export, despite higher shipping costs. Landlocked Botswana has been very successful, as its diamonds bring in plenty of revenue to overcome the higher shipping costs. Uganda's coffee, the nation's primary export, does not enjoy the same advantage. In addition to landlocked countries, small countries isolated from major markets, such as the small island countries of the Pacific Ocean, face similar issues with high shipping costs. As air shipment costs decline these disadvantages are reduced, but the vast majority of trade still takes place by sea.

In addition to geography, government strategies for trade and choices about trade policy determine trade outcomes. Broadly speaking, governments in developing countries have employed two different trade strategies, import substitution and outward-looking development. **Import substitution** is the production of goods and services that replace (or substitute for) imports. Since new firms in developing countries often are unable (initially) to compete on world markets, import substitution protects domestic firms from international competition by erecting trade barriers that make imported products more expensive or more difficult to purchase, with the aim that over time firms will become more efficient and competitive. **Outward orientation** shifts the focus to producing for export for global markets. This strategy is designed to make producers internationally competitive through market forces and strengthening key institutions. The core idea behind import substitution is that newly developing industries cannot survive at first without some protection from imports, giving them the chance to learn and grow. In contrast, the core idea behind an outward-looking trade strategy is for firms to compete internationally to gain access to new technologies,

[2]United Nations Conference on Trade and Development (UNCTAD), *Review of Maritime Transport 1995* (Geneva: United Nations Publications, 1995).

increase efficiency, and enlarge the scope of their potential market. We consider each strategy in turn, exploring the impact of the strategy not only on trade outcomes but on economic growth and development.

IMPORT SUBSTITUTION

Import substitution (IS) has been used as a strategy for industrialization by almost every country in the world at one time or another. Canada, England, France, Germany, Japan, Russia, and the United States all protected their manufacturers against competition from imports following the Industrial Revolution, sometimes for extended periods. In developing countries, IS was adopted throughout Latin America when its primary export markets were severely disrupted by the Great Depression and subsequently by the scarcity of commercial shipping during World War II. Having built up domestic manufacturing capacity during this period, Argentina, Brazil, Colombia, Mexico, and other countries systematically erected barriers to keep out competing imports after the war. In Asia and Africa, most countries adopted IS following World War II, as the newly independent countries wanted to develop their own industrial capacity and reduce their imports from the colonial powers. By the 1960s, IS was the dominant strategy of economic development.

The basic idea of IS is straightforward. For sustained economic development, countries need to shift from primary production to manufacturers to prevent prolonged specialization in low-value-added activities. But, proponents of the strategy argue, firms are unlikely to be able to compete in manufactures immediately and require government assistance to get started. Ideally, the first step is to identify products with large domestic markets, as indicated by substantial imports, and relatively simple production technologies that can be mastered quickly, rather than products requiring advanced machinery and highly skilled labor. Then governments introduce either tariffs or quotas on imports to forcibly increase the price of competing imports. **Tariffs** are taxes imposed on imports at the border; **quotas** are quantitative limits on specified categories of imports. These **protective barriers** raise the price of imports and allow domestic manufacturers to charge higher prices, compensating them for higher production costs and making their operations profitable. But this strategy comes at a cost to consumers, who must pay the higher prices, with commensurate welfare losses as a result.

This stylized approach (focus on relatively simple products with large domestic markets) implies that consumer goods, such as processed foods, beverages, textiles, clothing, and footwear, should be the first targets. By contrast, capital goods should not be heavily protected, since they require more-sophisticated skills and raising their costs hurts all downstream industries and investors that buy capital goods. Nevertheless, many developing countries have used IS to protect steel, machinery, and other capital goods, usually with little success.

Most economists are critical of the IS strategy, but there are valid arguments in favor of this approach, the most compelling of which is the concept of an **infant industry.** Entrepreneurs opening new production facilities in a developing country must compete against firms from industrialized countries that have long experience and mastered both production technologies and marketing. The managers and workers of the new, or "infant," industry must learn to use these technologies efficiently to compete. This process of **learning by doing** can take several years. Advocates of IS argue that, without some form of assistance, these investments are unlikely to take place and developing countries will be unable to learn the skills needed to eventually compete with imports on equal footing. For this strategy to work, however, an infant industry must be capable of eventually competing without protection against imports. This suggests that tariffs should be *temporary* and decline toward zero over time, as productivity increases and production costs fall. For this strategy to be economically worthwhile, the eventual benefits to society of establishing the new industry must exceed the costs to the economy of protection.

To more-fully understand the IS strategy, we first explore the impact of tariffs, quotas and subsidies on imports, production, and consumption. We then briefly examine the relationship between exchange rate policy and trade.

Protective Tariffs

The most direct effect of a protective tariff is to raise the domestic price of the good, say, digital videodisc (DVD) players, above the world price. For the importing country, the world price of imported DVD players is the cost at the port of entry, usually called the *c.i.f. price* (including cost, insurance, and freight) or *border price*. The percentage increase in the domestic price as a result of the tariff is called the **nominal rate of protection.** As shown in Figure 19–3, at the world price P_w (equal to the border price), consumers demand Q_1 DVD players and local producers produce Q_2; the balance, $M_1 = Q_1 - Q_2$, is imported. If an ad valorem (that is, a percentage) tariff t_0 is imposed on imports and the world supply is perfectly elastic, then the domestic price rises to P_d. This reduces the quantity demanded to Q_3 and increases domestic production to Q_4. Imports are reduced to $M_2 = Q_3 - Q_4$.

The increase in domestic output from Q_2 to Q_4 has two effects. First, it increases the *producers' surplus* by an amount given by trapezoid a, which captures the extent to which producers receive a price (P_d) that exceeds their marginal cost of production, represented by the domestic supply schedule. Second, the increase in production entails a *resource cost*, given by triangle b, because it

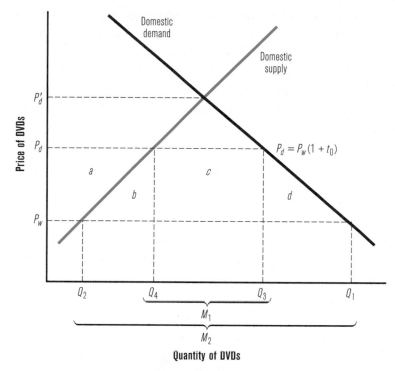

FIGURE 19-3. **Nominal Tariff Protection**

uses labor, machinery, and raw materials that could be used more efficiently to produce something else. The resource cost can be best understood by thinking about the opportunity cost of domestic production. Without the tariff, the nation can import an amount of DVD players equal to Q_2 to Q_4 by paying the world price for them. To produce them at home costs more, by an amount equal to the area of triangle b. Since it costs more to produce at home than to import, the society is using its resources inefficiently.

Consumers pay for protection both by the higher price P_d they pay on all purchases and by reducing consumption from Q_1 to Q_3. Part of what they pay is transferred to the government as tariff revenue that can be used by society for other purposes. This amount is a transfer within society rather than a loss. Revenue is equal to the quantity of imports, M_2, multiplied by the tariff rate times the world price, represented by rectangle $c = (t_0 P_w) \times M_2$. The total cost to consumers is represented by the loss of *consumer surplus,* equal to area $a + b + c + d$. The large loss to consumers is only partially compensated by the gains to either producers (trapezoid a) or the general public (though the tax revenues represented by rectangle c). Area $b + d$, two triangles representing welfare losses not compensated by gains to anyone, called the *deadweight loss,* represents the efficiency loss to the economy. We already identified area b as a loss resulting from the inefficiency of producing the good at home rather than importing it; area d

is the inefficiency resulting from higher prices that reduce the choices available to consumers, sometimes referred to as the *consumption cost* of the tariff. Both these deadweight losses increase as the tariff rate rises. The protective effects of tariffs are really more complex than suggested by the basic diagram of Figure 19–3, since the diagram focuses only on output markets. Much depends on the relationship between tariffs on both the final good and any imported inputs needed to produce that good (Box 19–1).

BOX 19-1 EFFECTIVE RATES OF PROTECTION

How much do tariffs affect producer's incentives to shift production? The tariff rate on competing imports gives us a clue but does not tell the whole story. The tariff rate determines the nominal rate of protection, which focuses on the effect of tariffs on *output* prices. But producers also care about the effect of tariffs on *input* prices and, ultimately, on the margin between revenues and input costs. Whereas a tariff on competing imports helps raise profits, tariffs on intermediate goods reduces them.

The **effective rate of protection (ERP)** measures the protection afforded by the entire structure of tariffs on inputs and outputs.[1] It focuses attention on the impact of trade policies on *value added,* the difference between the selling price of the good and the unit cost of intermediate goods.[2] Value added can be measured in domestic prices as the difference between the domestic price of the product (P_d) and the domestic cost of material inputs per unit of output (C_d), while the value added at world prices is the difference between the world price of the product (P_w) and the costs of inputs valued at world prices (C_w). The ERP is the ratio between the two:

$$\text{ERP} = \frac{\text{value added (domestic prices)}}{\text{value added (world prices)}} - 1 = \frac{P_d - C_d}{P_w - C_w} - 1 \qquad [19\text{--}1]$$

The key difference between domestic prices and world prices is tariffs (and other trade barriers such as quotas that can have similar effects on prices). The tariff on competing imports (t_0) raises the domestic price of the product above the world price, $P_d = P_w[1 + t_0])$, while the average tariff on inputs (t_i) raises the costs of producing it $(C_d = C_w[1 + t_i])$. Thus, domestic prices and costs can be expressed in terms of world prices and tariffs:

$$\text{ERP} = \frac{P_w(1+t_0) - C_w(1+t_i)}{P_w - C_w} - 1 \quad \text{or} \quad \text{ERP} = \frac{P_w t_0 - C_w t_i}{P_w - C_w} \qquad [19\text{--}2]$$

[1]The concept of the effective rate of protection is due to Max Corden, "The Structure of a Tariff System and the Effective Protection Rate," *Journal of Political Economy* 74 (June 1966), 221–37.

[2]Within this margin, the manufacturer must pay all the factors of production: wages, rents, interest on borrowed capital, and profit. Together these payments are equal to the value added.

Since the denominator is the value added calculated at world prices, the ERP measures the impact of all tariffs on the value added, rather than on prices. The measurement of ERP easily can be extended to include quotas, subsides, or other policies that influence output and input prices and thus the value added. To see the powerful insights from the ERP concept, suppose a producer manufactures a DVD player that sells for $100 and costs $60 to produce on world markets, so that value added is $40. Consider the impact on value added of three stylistic cases of tariff policy:

1. *The tariff on output is exactly the same as the tariff on inputs.* Say both t_0 and t_i equal 10 percent. You might think the impact would be neutral, but it is not. The sales price rises to $110 and domestic costs increase to $66, so value added increases by 10 percent to $44. A uniform tariff, 10 percent in this case, provides effective protection on value added of 10 percent, exactly equal to the nominal rate of protection.

2. *The tariff on output is higher than the tariff on inputs.* If $t_0 = 10$ percent but $t_i = 0$, the domestic price rises to $110 and the valued added rises from $40 to $50. Thus, the ERP = 25 percent, much higher than the nominal rate of protection of 10 percent. More generally, if t_0 is greater than t_i, the ERP exceeds the nominal rate of protection. Note the key point here: What seems like a small tariff can have a huge impact on the margin between costs and prices and thus a big impact on producers' incentives to reallocate resources away from sectors with no protection to those with protection. Tariff structures in many countries tend to follow this pattern, escalating from relatively low rates on inputs to higher rates on finished products. Under these circumstances, ERPs of 100 percent are not uncommon.

3. *The tariff on output is lower than the tariff on inputs.* If there is no tariff on competing imports but a 10 percent tariff on inputs ($t_i = 10$ percent), domestic costs rise to $66 but output prices remain at $100. Thus value added falls to $34 and the ERP is a *negative* 15 percent. Although a tariff structure that undermines investment incentives seems unlikely, it is actually fairly common, particularly for agriculture and export products. Governments like to keep food prices low to keep urban consumers happy and so are reluctant to impose duties on food imports. Therefore, protective tariffs on fertilizer, seeds, or irrigation equipment undermine the profitability of agriculture and switch investment out of agriculture. As for exports, governments cannot use tariffs to raise output prices, since exporters sell on world markets. A tariff on inputs raises exporters' costs and reduces incentives to invest in export industries. This pattern of protection is a critical problem undermining the international competitiveness of exporting firms in many developing countries.

Import Quotas

Industries also can be protected through **quantitative restrictions** on imports, usually in the form of *quotas* or *import licensing*. With quotas, the government determines in advance exactly the quantity of imports it wants to allow, whereas with tariffs, the quantity of imports depends on the reactions of producers and consumers, as captured by the elasticities of supply and demand. A quota that limits imports to the same quantity as a tariff has many of the same effects. In terms of Figure 19-3, a quota limiting imports to M_2 forces the domestic price up to P_d, increases domestic production to Q_4, and decreases consumption to Q_3, just as with the tariff. The loss in consumer surplus, deadweight loss, and gain in producer surplus are the same.

But, in two critical respects, import quotas have different effects than tariffs. First, the government does not necessarily collect revenue. To enforce the quota it must issue licenses to a limited number of importers, giving them the right to purchase up to M_2 of imports. If the government simply gives away the licenses with no fee (which many governments do, using the licenses as patronage for politically well-connected importers), license holders earn a windfall profit equal to the area of rectangle c. This is because the importer can purchase the goods at price P_w on the world market and sell them at P_d domestically. This windfall, often called a **quota rent,** can be substantial, so importers expend a great deal of effort to obtain them, including possibly offering large bribes, in effect sharing the quota rent with the right government official. (Under a tariff, importers can also bribe customs officials to avoid paying all of the required tariffs.) Alternatively, and preferably, the government could sell the import licenses at auction. Potential importers would be willing to pay up to an amount c for these licenses, since that is the size of the potential windfall they could earn. A well-functioning auction could yield the government the same revenues as a tariff, although the distribution of quotas often is seen as more costly to administer than tariffs.

Second, market dynamics that shift the supply and demand curves or the world price have very different impacts with tariffs and quotas. Consider a fall in the world price, P_w. With a tariff, both P_w and P_d fall, giving consumers the benefit of the lower price. Consumption increases, domestic production declines, and imports rise to fill the gap. Under a quota, however, imports could not rise. Domestic production and consumption remain unchanged, and the domestic price remains at P_d. The lower world price simply increases the quota rent, with the benefit going directly to import license holders. Put more generally, under most (but not all) circumstances, since tariffs allow changes in imports on the margin, domestic producers and consumers react on the margin to market changes as they would in an open economy; with quotas, they react on the margin as they would in a closed economy. Because of these consequences of quotas, economists prefer tariffs, and trade reforms and international trade agreements often start with the conversion of quotas to equivalent tariffs, which bears the inelegant name **tariffication.**

Production Subsidies

Direct subsidies are an alternative to tariffs or quotas as a means of protecting domestic manufacturers. The United States, the European Union, and Japan all use large subsidies to support agricultural production and protect it from global competitors, often at the expense of potential competitors from developing countries. The impact of subsidies is similar to tariffs in some ways: A 20 percent protective tariff on imports and a 20 percent subsidy on output have identical effects on profits. But the effects on consumers and the government budget can be quite different.

A subsidy of s_0 percent, equal to the earlier tariff of t_0, effectively moves the supply curve from S to S', as shown in Figure 19–4. Production shifts out from Q_2 to Q_4, but prices do not change, so consumers still purchase Q_1 at the original price P_w. Thus, a big advantage of using subsidies is that there is no loss of consumer surplus. The total cost of the subsidy is $a + b$, but in this case, the funds come from the government budget rather than being imposed only on consumers of the particular good. Producers are equally happy with a subsidy or an equivalent tariff. As with the tariff, they gain producer surplus a, with a resource

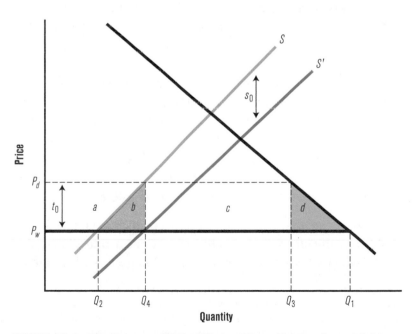

FIGURE 19-4. **The Impact of Subsidies on Firms Competing with Imports**

loss of b. Thus, the deadweight loss is only triangle b, which is smaller than the amount $b + d$ with a tariff.

Economists generally prefer subsidies over tariffs (and tariffs over quotas) because consumers are able to purchase more of the good while society pays no more for production than under an equivalent tariff. The cost is borne by taxpayers as a whole, not just the consumers of the product. Subsidies usually appear as an expenditure item in the government's budget, so there is an annual accounting for the costs of protection. The government, therefore, is more restrained and correspondingly more likely to keep protection moderate and short lived (although industrial-country farm subsidies have continued for many years). Unfortunately, government officials tend to prefer quotas or tariffs over subsidies, precisely because the costs do not appear on the budget and are less obvious to society as a whole.

Exchange-Rate Management

Tariffs, quotas, and subsidies are only some of the tools policy makers can use to influence trade. One of the most powerful instruments they can use is the exchange rate, which often affects more transactions than any other single price in an economy and directly affects the domestic prices of everything traded. Tariffs, quotas, and subsidies are used to support very specific products and sectors by changing the relative price between those products and all other products. The exchange rate, by contrast, has a uniform effect on the prices of all tradable goods[3] but alters the price between tradables (exportables and importables) and nontradables (such as local transportation, power and water supplies, most construction, personal and household services, and government services).

Figure 19–5 illustrates the market for foreign exchange, where exporters supply and importers demand foreign currencies. The vertical axis is the exchange rate measured in the local currency; for example, pesos per dollar. With a floating exchange rate system, a rate of e_e is an equilibrium rate and just clears the market so that the value of imports equals the value of exports with no trade deficit or surplus. But when governments intervene to fix their exchange rate (as described in Chapter 13), two other outcomes are possible.

1. An *overvalued exchange rate*. Historically, many governments have intervened to hold the official exchange rate below e_e at a rate like e_o. An imported cell phone that costs \$200 would cost 2,000 pesos with a market

---

[3]As discussed in Chapter 17, tradable goods include exports, imports, and all goods and services that could be exported or imported, with prices determined on world markets. Nontradable goods are produced locally and not subject to competing imports, with prices determined by local supply and demand conditions.

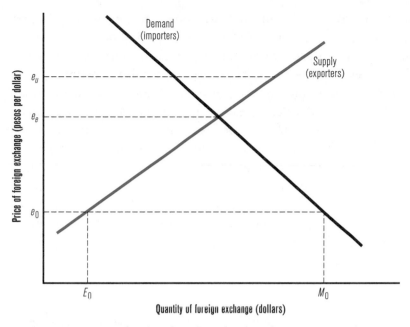

FIGURE 19-5. **Overvalued and Undervalued Exchange Rates**

exchange rate of 10 pesos to the dollar, but at an overvalued rate of 8 pesos per dollar, the phone now costs just 1,600 pesos. At the same time, anything exported and sold in dollars earns fewer pesos. The result is an increase in imports and a fall in exports, with a trade deficit of $M_o - E_o$. Some governments like overvalued exchange rates because they keep imports cheap, and urban consumers (often the political power base including the military) like cheap imports. An overvalued exchange rate can lead to growing trade deficits and cause a variety of problems in terms of accumulating debt and slower growth. But it also runs counter to the IS strategy, as it makes imports even cheaper, undermining the competitiveness of domestic firms. As a result, governments often impose even larger tariffs than they might under a floating exchange rate to provide protection to favored industries and to try to reduce the growing trade deficit. In the 1970s and 1980s, the combination of overvalued exchange rates and pervasive tariffs and quotas was quite common. Today, it is less common, although it is still the policy mix in some countries, such as Egypt.

2. An *undervalued exchange rate.* Some governments follow the opposite strategy and intervene to hold the exchange rate above e_e at a rate like e_u. This approach makes all imports more expensive and, at the same time, makes exports more profitable by increasing their price in domestic currency. Thus, it helps stimulate exports and provides protection to firms competing with imports by raising the price of competitive products. Because imports are more expensive, an undervalued exchange rate

tends to dampen overall consumption, thus increasing saving. The resulting surplus on the balance of payments also allows countries to build up their foreign exchange reserves. While this strategy has some advantages, it also has its costs. It is not popular with consumers, as it acts like a tax on imported consumption goods and reduces consumer welfare, at least in the short run. Reserve accumulation can be helpful to a point, but reserves, by definition, are resources that a society puts aside and does not use for current consumption or investment. Undervalued rates, although not as common as overvalued rates, were used by pro-export regimes such as that in Taiwan during the 1980s. The most important example in the early twenty-first century is China, which quite controversially, has used an undervalued exchange rate to help stimulate exports and restrain imports (Box 19–2).

BOX 19-2 EXCHANGE-RATE POLICY IN CHINA

Is China's exchange rate policy unfair? China has been roundly criticized by some for maintaining an undervalued exchange rate that makes its exports more profitable; others argue that the currency is not seriously misaligned. China keeps its currency, the *renminbi* (RMB), fixed against the U.S. dollar at a rate of RMB 8.1 to the dollar. This new rate follows a 2 percent adjustment in July 2005, when the rate was revalued from RMB 8.28 to the dollar, a rate that had prevailed for a decade.

Several pieces of evidence suggest that the RMB is undervalued; that is, kept at above the market clearing rate, as with exchange rate e_u in Figure 19–5. China's current account surplus (exports minus imports of both goods and services) has grown to more than 3 percent of GDP, as predicted by Figure 19–5. Normally, a current account surplus is matched by an outflow of foreign capital, as countries invest the proceeds abroad. But China attracts net capital *inflows* of an additional 4 percent of GDP, so its overall balance of payments surplus is a very large 7 percent of GDP. This allows China to accumulate foreign exchange reserves, which increased by a breathtaking $500 billion in three years, reaching $769 billion in September 2005, equivalent to over 13 months of imports.

Some suggest that the current account surplus is not all that large by world standards and many of the capital flows are volatile short-run flows, rather than long-term, more-permanent flows that determine the true long-run equilibrium exchange rate. And China's exchange rate is not the only policy that affects these balances. The government maintains an array of restrictions on capital flows, which tend to discourage outflows of capital. In the absence of these controls, the surpluses would not be so large. Even taking these arguments into account, many economists still conclude that the RMB is undervalued, perhaps by 10–20 percent.[1]

An undervalued RMB makes Chinese exports more profitable, and indeed exports doubled between 2001 and 2004, much of it through importing components from other countries in the region and assembling finished products for export. This export growth is a key reason for China's overall economic growth and its impressive reduction in poverty, as many unskilled workers have found jobs in the special economic zones (SEZs, much like EPZs discussed in Box 19–3). The RMB policy helps support China's high saving rate, since imports are more expensive than they otherwise would be, dampening consumption. Moreover, the buildup in reserves also allows China to maintain macroeconomic stability, as it is unlikely to face the kind of capital account crisis many of its neighbors faced in the late 1990s, as described in Chapter 15. China's buildup in reserves is partly a defensive move in response to these crises.

But the policy has its costs, especially the longer it is in place. Restraining consumption reduces the welfare of ordinary Chinese in the short run and may not be all that beneficial on the margin when saving rates approach 40 percent and reserves cover more than one year of imports. Moreover, the fixed rate encourages speculative capital inflows, as investors begin to bet that, at some point, the RMB will be revalued. Investors bringing in $1 dollar today get 8 renminbi in exchange, and if they think that at some point they will only need 7 renminbi to buy it back, they will invest more of their dollars in China. These inflows have contributed to a rapid expansion of credit, as the stock of bank loans outstanding doubled in just two years. The flurry of bank lending increases the possibility of significant numbers of bad loans, which ultimately weaken the banking system. Finally, the fixed exchange rate brings threats of protectionism from trading partners: The U.S. Senate proposed putting a 27 percent tariff on all Chinese imports unless China revalues the RMB by a similar amount. China's exchange rate policy has become a convenient scapegoat for the U.S. trade deficit, even though China's exchange rate contributes relatively little to the deficit compared to other factors more in the control of the United States, particularly its budget deficit and low personal saving rate.

China's exchange rate policy may also have an unintended affect on U.S. interest rates. With its buildup in foreign exchange reserves, China has become of the largest purchasers of U.S. Treasury bills, helping to finance the growing U.S. budget deficit. A revaluation would result in less reserve accumulation and therefore fewer Treasury bill purchases by China, which could contribute to upward pressure on U.S. interest rates.

China's exchange rate policy has contributed to its rapid economic growth and poverty reduction in recent years, and its large reserve holdings help stabilize the economy and reduce the chances of a major capital account crisis. But, over the longer run, there will be little extra benefit for China to continue to accumulate reserves at the expense of consumption. At some point, the government is likely to alter its policy, first by revaluing the RMB to a new level, and eventually by moving to a more flexible exchange rate system.

[1]See Morris Goldstein, "Adjusting China's Exchange Rate Policies" Institute for International Economics, Washington, DC, May 2004.

Outcomes of Import Substitution

Import substitution has the potential to be an effective strategy for certain sectors over a limited period of time. Almost all countries have tried it at one stage or another, and many have achieved some success. But, all too often, the basic conditions for success are not met. In many countries, IS has been used to protect too many activities and remained in place for too long. Developing countries are littered with infants that never grew up and were never able to compete internationally, such as the petrochemical industry of Colombia, the automobile industry of Malaysia, and the textile industry of Kenya. These kinds of firms require protection indefinitely, at continuous cost to the rest of society. Sometimes IS fails because of an initially poor choice to protect the wrong kinds of activities (like steel); often it stems from the reluctance of governments to remove the protection given to politically well-connected industrialists.

Countries introducing import substitution typically record a quick growth spurt during the initial, or *easy, phase of import substitution,* as consumer goods industries expand to meet domestic demand. Once the domestic market is saturated, however, growth typically bogs down. Most developing countries have relatively small internal markets, either because per capita incomes are low or populations are relatively small. As a result, there typically is relatively little competition, and firms cannot take advantage of economies of scale and often produce at less than their minimum efficient size. And, by reducing their commercial links with the rest of the world, import-substituting countries limit their exposure to new technology and ideas. IS has had some limited success in bigger economies with large internal markets, at least for a short period of time, but it generally has been less successful in middle-sized or small economies.

Ironically, many countries that try IS run into balance-of-payments problems from growing trade deficits. Even though the strategy is designed to replace imports with domestic production, not all imports can be replaced (especially capital goods). Since the strategy effectively discourages exports, foreign exchange earnings lag, especially since IS often is accompanied by an overvalued exchange rate. Therefore, many countries following this strategy have had to borrow heavily and found it difficult to meet their debt service requirements.

Underlying the protective regime also is a set of incentives that reward political lobbying, corruption, and bribery more than economic efficiency and competitiveness. When higher domestic costs, reduced import prices, or better-quality foreign goods erode the competitive position of domestic firms, their natural reaction is to turn to the government for enhanced protection. This option blunts the competitive instincts of entrepreneurs, who normally would have to cut costs, improve quality, and thus raise productivity. In this environment, the most successful managers are those who have the political skills or connections with which to bargain effectively, or simply bribe, officials who administer import quotas and determine tariff rates or have close ties with the political and bureaucratic elite.

OUTWARD ORIENTATION AND EXPORT PROMOTION

Since the late 1980s, many countries have shifted the balance of their trade policies away from IS and toward more-outward-oriented trade policies, in which firms compete on global markets. This strategy has many names, including *outward orientation, openness, export orientation,* and *export promotion.*[4] The idea is to introduce policies that encourage firms to produce products that are competitive on world markets, especially labor-intensive manufactured exports and agricultural products, but also competitive substitutes for imports. The key difference with IS is that this strategy uses global competition rather than protection as the main force to encourage investment, productivity gains, learning, and new technology to support growth.[5]

In the typical pattern, in the early stages, firms manufacture and export relatively simple labor-intensive products, such as textiles, clothing, shoes, toys, electronic equipment, and furniture. Some countries also export agricultural products and labor-intensive agro-processing goods, such as cut vegetables, fruit juices, or cut flowers, and increasingly certain services including data entry, basic accounting, or call centers. Then, over time, as workers learn new skills and gain access to improved technology, firms begin to shift to more-sophisticated products (which pay higher wages to match greater productivity and skills) as the country's comparative advantage gradually shifts to manufacturing more-advanced electronics devices, higher-end clothing, and consumer durables.

The shift toward more-outward-oriented policies among developing countries began in the 1960s with the four East Asian Tigers: Hong Kong, Korea, Singapore, and Taiwan. They demonstrated that developing countries could compete on world markets by carving out niche markets in producing labor-intensive manufactured products. Their rapid growth in trade was accompanied

---

[4]Joining a free trade area, as Mexico did with Canada and the United States under NAFTA (North America Free Trade Agreement) can also be seen as a move toward greater outward orientation. However, some free-trade areas or other types of economic integration can be more like import substitution if the combined economies are small and members build tariff walls around themselves, reducing trade with nonmembers.

[5]Four prominent economists who strongly influenced thinking about the shift from inward versus outward strategies are Gustav Ranis, "Industrial Sector Labor Absorption," *Economic Development and Cultural Change* 21 (1973), 387–408; Anne O. Krueger, *Foreign Trade Regimes and Economic Development: Liberalization Attempts and Consequences* (Cambridge, MA: Ballinger, 1978); Jagdish N. Bhagwati, *Foreign Trade Regimes and Economic Development: Anatomy and Consequences of Exchange Control Regimes* (Cambridge, MA: Ballinger, 1978); and Bela Balassa, "The Process of Industrial Development and Alternative Development Strategies," *Essays in International Finance* 141 (1980). For an overview of the shift in thinking about trade policy and development between the 1960s and 1990s, see Anne O. Krueger's presidential address to the American Economics Association "Trade Policy and Economic Development: How We Learn," *American Economic Review* 1, no. 87 (March 1997), 1–22.

by accelerating economic growth, reductions in poverty, and other advancements. Following their example, most of the very rapidly growing developing countries in recent decades have introduced some form of this strategy, including Chile, China, Indonesia, Malaysia, Mauritius, Poland, Thailand, Tunisia, and Vietnam, among others. India's growth rate accelerated in the 1990s as it shifted to a more-outward-oriented strategy.

But not all countries that have shifted to more outward orientation achieved the success they had hoped for. Bolivia, for example, introduced many steps to open its economy, and while growth has recovered from the negative rates that prevailed in the early 1980s, it averaged only about 1.2 percent since the late 1980s. Moreover, the outward-oriented strategy brought with it some controversy. Consistent with Bolivia's experience, some analysts believe that, while there are gains from greater openness and trade, the benefits are not as large as some proponents suggest. Some argue that outward orientation per se is not the key to success, but other factors, such as improved institutions or better governance, support both rapid growth and exports. Others argue that this strategy induces only a "race to the bottom" for low-wage labor and therefore hurts rather than helps development. In the sections that follow, we explore these arguments as well as the available empirical evidence.

Policies Supporting Outward Orientation

The specific policies supporting more outward orientation differ across countries, but all share the common starting point of reducing barriers to imports and constraints on exports. There has been a clear global trend to reduce average tariffs since the early 1980s, as shown in Figure 19–6. Average tariffs in South Asia fell from a very high 65 percent to a (still high) 30 percent, while tariffs, in other regions fell as well. But the core liberalization strategy goes beyond just reducing tariffs and includes removing quotas, reducing other barriers to trade, and shifting domestic prices closer to world prices. In many countries, governments have augmented this agenda by establishing export platform institutions such as export processing zones (EPZs), which aim to create competitive environments for at least some firms. In addition, in some countries, governments have taken additional steps explicitly to tilt incentives even further in favor of exports, either through undervalued exchange rates, export subsidies, or special credit facilities.

The basic steps toward full-fledged liberalization aimed at encouraging exports include the following:

- Remove quotas and tariffs and other forms of protection, especially on capital and intermediate goods.
- Allow the currency to float with a market-determined exchange rate, and ensure macroeconomic stability through prudent monetary and fiscal policies.

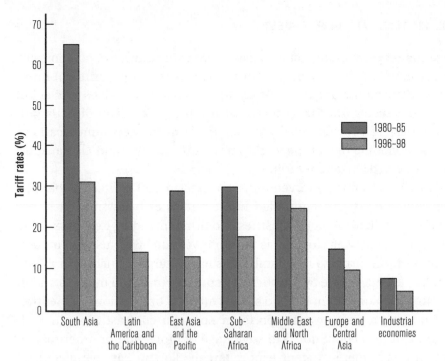

FIGURE 19-6. Average Unweighted Tariff Rates by Region
(Figures for Europe and Central Asia and Industrial Economies reflect
1986–90 data.)

Source: Andrew Berg and Anne Kreuger, "Trade, Growth and Poverty: A Selective Survey,"
Working Paper WP/03/30, International Monetary Fund, Washington, DC, 2003, from World
Bank and World Trade Organization data.

- Reduce unnecessary regulatory burdens, bureaucratic costs, and red
  tape that add to business costs.
- Keep factor markets flexible, especially for labor and credit, with market determined wages and interest rates.

In a full liberalization strategy, these steps are augmented with general
approaches to strengthen infrastructure (especially roads, ports, electricity supplies, and telecommunications to connect firms with the rest of the world and
reduce production costs); invest in education and public health (to ensure a
well-educated, healthy, and productive workforce); and improve governance, so
that property rights are respected. These basic policies will not surprise any student of neoclassical economics. Indeed, outward orientation is often seen as
synonymous with broader market-based and liberalized economic policies. The
neoclassical approach does not prescribe a bias toward exports, but rather a
regime that is neutral in its treatment of exports, import substitutes, and nontraded goods. In this view, the strategy is not aimed at exports per se, but export
growth is likely to follow because the distortions that inhibited exports and
favored other activities are removed.

While this approach has theoretical appeal, few countries actually have followed a pure neoclassical strategy, and some of the successful countries were far

from it in some respects. Hong Kong, at least prior to its return to China in 1997, was the closest, where the economy was very open with few government interventions and distortions. Singapore also followed a fairly liberalized model but nevertheless diverged from the neoclassical norm in that many of its largest export industries are government-owned service firms in telecommunications, port services (including one of the world's best-run airports), and air transport (the world-renowned Singapore Airlines).

Korea was much more interventionist. It erected stiff protective barriers against certain imports and controlled interest rates at below-market levels, directing cheap credit to favored industries and firms, including exporters. What made the approach outward looking is that interventions were used to induce, and sometimes force, firms to meet ambitious export targets. Success or failure was dictated to a large degree by the ability to compete on world markets, rather than domestically.[6] Korea went beyond simple outward orientation and neutrality and introduced a bias toward exports. In Korea, in contrast to an inward-looking regime, a firm could not take advantage of protection or other market distortions unless it met stringent export targets. Korean car manufacturers became competitive on global markets and began to export while selling locally. Some of the tools of protection were used to help fledgling exporters who were learning by doing: adopting new technologies, learning how to master them, reducing costs of production, finding and entering markets overseas, and eventually competing on equal terms with foreign firms.

The strong bias and intervention to support exporters was not the rule for all the Asian exporters. Indonesia, Malaysia, Taiwan, and Thailand used a mixed approach, with less of a bias toward exporters. Although heavily protectionist and interventionist in some areas, most of the industries they supported never became internationally competitive, such as Malaysia's Proton automobiles and Indonesia's IPTN aircraft.[7] Nevertheless, each introduced policies that insulated export industries from the distortions of the home market and permitted firms to buy inputs and sell output at close to world market prices, as the neoclassical strategy dictates, so that a wide range of exporting firms became competitive on international markets.[8]

---

[6]See Marcus Noland and Howard Pack, *Industrial Policy in an Era of Globalization: Lessons From Asia* (Washington, DC: Institute for International Economics, March 2003).

[7]IPTN stands for Industri Pesawat Terbang Nusantara, or the "Archipelago's Aircraft Industry," owned by the Indonesian government.

[8]The revisionist school on Korea, questioning the neoclassical approach, was led by Alice Amsden, *Asia's New Giant: South Korea and Late Industrialization* (New York: Oxford University Press, 1989). Taiwan's interventionist strategy is documented by Robert Wade, *Governing the Market: Economic Theory and the Role of Government in East Asian Industrialization* (Princeton, NJ: Princeton University Press, 1990). The World Bank attempted to reconcile neoclassical and revisionist thinking in its much-discussed book, *The East Asian Miracle: Economic Growth and Public Policy* (Washington, DC: World Bank, 1993).

China, along with Korea and Taiwan in earlier years, used exchange rate policy to favor exporters, as described earlier in Figure 19–5. China pegs its exchange rate above the market-clearing rate, making imports more expensive and exports more profitable. This policy has contributed to China's rapid export growth, its large trade surplus, and the resulting accumulation of foreign exchange reserves. It acts as an indirect subsidy for Chinese exporters. Like all subsidies, it comes at a cost, in this case of making imports more expensive and thus reducing consumption and consumer welfare for the average Chinese. (China's exchange rate policy was discussed in Box 19–2.)

BOX 19-3 EXPORT PROCESSING ZONES AND OTHER EXPORT PLATFORMS

Export processing zones (EPZs), bonded warehouses, duty exemptions systems, and science and technology parks all are examples of institutions and programs designed to establish export platforms, where distortions are reduced and firms can operate more closely to world prices. EPZs are enclaves located physically or administratively outside a country's customs' barrier, typically as fenced-in areas near a port, that provide exporters access to duty-free imports, reduced business regulations, expedited customs clearance, and reasonable infrastructure. Bonded warehouses essentially are single-factory EPZs that can be located anywhere, yet still have many of the other advantages of EPZs.[1] Duty exemption systems allow qualifying firms to import their inputs duty free. Science and technology parks are like EPZs, but with infrastructure specially suited for electronics, pharmaceuticals, biomedical products, or other products related to science and technology.

The basic idea is straightforward. Potential exporters face a variety of challenges, including high tariffs or quotas on their inputs, poor infrastructure, and red tape. The neoclassical solution is to remove all import tariffs and quotas, improve infrastructure, and reduce red tape, as described in the text. The problem is that, for a variety of institutional and political reasons, no country realistically can implement all these steps quickly. Most governments lack the large number of trained personnel to take on so many issues at once, and political forces are likely to fight certain steps, like reducing tariffs. It can take many years for a country to build the infrastructure and introduce all the policy changes needed for firms throughout the economy to become competitive. The export platform approach is to allow one part of the economy to be competitive, while steps are taken over time to introduce economywide changes. Providing an enclave allows some firms, mainly pro-

[1]These factories are called *bonded warehouses* because firms usually post a bond as a guarantee against any duties that might be applicable to imports diverted to the domestic market, and if they sell output locally instead of export it, they are liable to pay the import duties.

ducing labor-intensive manufacturers, to become competitive on world markets before all the required steps are in place for the economy as a whole.

Most of the successful exporting countries established at least one, and in most cases more than one, of these programs. Malaysia relied mainly on EPZs that provided reliable infrastructure and allowed exporters (mainly in electronics) to import and export without being taxed; the government also established bonded warehouses and a duty exemption system for other exporters. Most Korean and Taiwanese exporters used a well-functioning duty exemption and rebate system to obtain inputs at world prices; in addition, a substantial number of firms were set up as bonded warehouses or located in EPZs. Hong Kong and Singapore essentially are citywide EPZs. Indonesia established an agency in the Ministry of Finance that granted exemptions from import licensing restrictions and drawbacks (rebates) for duties paid on imported inputs. The vast majority of Tunisia's manufactured exporters operate as bonded warehouses, whereas Mauritian exporters are located mainly in export processing zones. China's special enterprise zones, located up and down the coast, are the source of most of its manufactured exports. In the early 1990s, the Philippines established EPZs at the former Subic Bay naval base and Clark air force base, where the departing U.S. military forces left behind an extensive high-quality physical infrastructure, which provided the basis for rapid growth in electronics exports and service exports, such as the regional hub for many overnight delivery services at Clark air base.

In the Dominican Republic, exports from EPZs increased by a factor of 5 during the 1990s, and by the end of the decade they accounted for over 80 percent of all exports. Firms export textiles, footwear, electronics, jewelry, and other products, mostly to the United States. EPZ employment reached nearly 200,000 people by the end of the 1990s, about 17 percent of the workforce. About 60 percent of employees are women, a pattern that is typical of many EPZs.[2]

Export platforms have not always been successful. When they are located far from ports in an attempt to spur development in isolated areas, production costs usually are too high for firms to compete. If firms in export platforms still face high regulatory costs or must wait long periods of time for goods to clear customs, they will not be successful on global markets. And export platforms cannot overcome poor macroeconomic management that leads to high inflation or overvalued exchange rates. Egypt's EPZs have not spurred faster export growth, as they still face high production costs. Kenya's bonded warehouses began to expand in the 1980s, but when macroeconomic policies deteriorated and the currency became overvalued in the 1990s, 60 of 70 bonded warehouses closed. But, where export platforms are established as enclaves in which producers face world prices for both inputs and outputs, they have been more successful, and they can be found in the strategy of most rapidly growing manufactured exporters.

[2]Staci Warden, "A Profile of Free Trade Zones in the Dominican Republic," Harvard Institute for International Development, Cambridge, MA, 1999.

Another approach taken in almost all of the countries that have achieved rapid export growth was to establish specialized export platform institutions that enabled exporters to import and sell at close to world market prices, even in the presence of more widespread distortions. The platforms took a variety of forms, including export processing zones (EPZs), bonded warehouses, duty exemption programs, industrial parks, and science and technology parks (Box 19–3). In all cases, exporters pay zero tariffs on imported inputs, receive expedited clearance through customs, and in some cases benefit from specialized infrastructure and reduced bureaucratic and regulatory burdens. These institutions are designed to create a kind of enclave for fledgling export industries, where they could be insulated from the controls and price distortions of the protected domestic market and be better able to compete on world markets.[9] However, while export platforms have been a common feature that contributed to the success of many of the fast-growing countries, they have not always worked well. In many countries, EPZs were poorly located in remote parts of the country, added extra regulations, or in other ways increased producer's costs rather than reduced them. Kenya's EPZs, despite some advantages, could not overcome an overvalued exchange rate and other high regulatory costs that were inimical to growth. These institutions are no silver bullet, but they provide an example of how innovative institutions shaped to a country's specific needs can help support market-based growth.

The Benefits of Outward Orientation

What is it about outward orientation and exports of manufactured products that supports economic growth? The first to answer this question was Adam Smith, who, in *The Wealth of Nations,* articulated the view that more-open trade would lead to a more-efficient allocation of resources through greater competition, which in turn would lead to higher income. In Smith's view, export markets permit factories to produce more of any single item and so to specialize to a greater extent than if they produced only for the home market. Specialization permits each firm to learn more about manufacturing its products efficiently and allows production in greater volumes, which reduces the setup costs of switching from one product to another.

Smith's ideas were later developed more fully into the idea of comparative advantage, as described in Chapter 17: A country gains most by exporting goods and services that use its abundant factors of production most intensively, while

---

[9]See David L. Lindauer and Michael Roemer, eds., *Asia and Africa: Legacies and Opportunities in Development* (San Francisco, ICS Press, 1994), especially Chapters 1 and 11. Also see Steven Radelet, "Manufactured Exports, Export Platforms and Economic Growth," CAER discussion paper no. 42, Harvard Institute for International Development, Cambridge, MA, September 1999.

importing products that require more of scarcer factors of production. For many developing countries, this implies exporting products that use relatively low-skilled and abundant labor, primarily manufacturing and agriculture, and importing more-capital-intensive products that require fewer and more highly skilled workers. The long-term objective is gradually to shift from simple manufacturing and labor-intensive agriculture into more-sophisticated products that generate higher wages, profits, and income. Labor-abundant, capital-scarce developing economies initially should be internationally competitive in labor-intensive products, such as agricultural output, agro-processing, apparel, furniture, shoes, textiles, and toys. Over time, as workers gain more skills and master more-sophisticated technologies, a country's comparative advantage can change, and it can gradually shift to export more-skill-intensive products that bring with it higher income, such as electronics, integrated circuits, refrigerators and other heavy consumer durables, steel, or financial and information services.

The idea that countries would move up the technology ladder by following the countries just ahead of them was coined the *flying geese* model of development by Japanese economist Kaname Akamatsu in the 1930s. The Asian countries to some extent have followed this model. Hong Kong, Korea, and Taiwan took over leadership in textiles and apparel in the late 1960s and early 1970s from Japan as Japan moved into electronics, transport, and other capital goods. A decade or so later, as labor skills improved and wages rose, Korea and Taiwan moved into electronics components, while the textile and apparel industries moved to China, Indonesia, Mauritius, Thailand, and Vietnam. More recently, Malaysia, the Philippines, and Thailand shifted into electronics production.

There are two main channels through which more-open trade can lead to more rapid growth and higher incomes, greater investment and higher productivity. In terms of greater investment, it is possible that protectionist policies through IS might encourage investment by offering firms the opportunity to sell on domestic markets without competition from imports. But the investment tends to grow only until production matches local demand. By contrast, more-open trade policies could encourage investment for a more sustained period, since firms that export to global markets can continue to expand, and new firms producing similar goods can also export. In addition, tariffs on capital goods imports make them more expensive, meaning that, with trade barriers, each dollar of investment buys less capital. Fewer barriers to trade in capital goods make them less expensive, so that more-open trade promotes greater investment. Several research studies found that more-open trade is associated with greater investment.[10]

---

[10]See, for example, Jeffrey Frankel and David Romer, "Does Trade Cause Growth?" *American Economic Review* 89, no. 3 (June 1999), 379–99; Romain Wacziarg, "Measuring the Dynamic Gains from Trade," *World Bank Economic Review* 15, no. 3 (2001), 393–429; and Ross Levine and David Renelt, "A Sensitivity Analysis of Cross Country Growth Regressions," *American Economic Review* 82, no. 4 (September 1992), 942–63.

More-open trade could lead to higher productivity through either increasing efficiency or greater access to new technologies. As Adam Smith suggested, trade increases competition in the domestic market. No firm can gain a monopoly, and competition from abroad stimulates firms to reduce costs and increase their efficiency. Import liberalization also reduces costs for exporters, since they can choose between domestic and imported inputs based on which are cheaper and of higher quality. More-open trade can also help firms take advantage of economies of scale in their production by producing for larger world markets. University of Pennsylvania economist Howard Pack points out that, when export markets exist, labor, capital, and even land can be moved rapidly from low- to high-productivity uses without encountering diminishing returns as quickly as with production for the home market.[11]

Perhaps the most important advantage of manufactured exports is that it provides a channel through which a developing country can gain new technologies and new ideas. The enhanced ability to import capital goods, together with greater exposure to world markets, provides exporters the opportunity to observe the best practices and latest technologies used by leading global firms and adopt the technology most appropriate for their own use. These links provide a powerful means through which firms can learn about new technology, and there is no realistic chance of this occurring if a country is cut off from world markets. UCLA economist Sebastian Edwards examined the relationship between trade policy and total factor productivity growth, using nine different indicators of trade openness, and found a consistently strong positive relationship, regardless of which measure of trade openness he used.[12] The link to increased technology is the main rationale used by those that favor an explicit bias in favor of exports, rather than neutral incentives: By enhancing technology, export growth may bring with it positive externalities that benefit the rest of the economy.

Nevertheless, moving up the production ladder to more-skill-intensive products is a difficult challenge and far from automatic. To some extent, market forces push this process along, as changes in the relative scarcities of the factors of production (land, labor, natural resources, and capital) lead to changes in comparative advantage. But some exporters have had trouble shifting from garment and textiles to electronics and other products, including the Dominican Republic, Indonesia, Mauritius, and Tunisia. More-sophisticated production processes demand better facilities, more-reliable infrastructure, and more-highly-trained workers and managers. And firms from middle-income countries

---

[11]Howard Pack, "Industrialization and Trade," in H. Chenery and T. N. Srinivasan, eds., *Handbook of Development Economics,* vol. 2 (Amsterdam: Elsevier, 1989), 333–80.

[12]Sebastian Edwards, "Openness, Productivity, and Growth: What Do We Really Know?" *Economic Journal* 108 (March 1998), 383–98.

with moderate skill and wage levels, like Mexico, face the challenge of finding a niche between exporters with abundant low-skilled labor (such as China and India) and those with more-skilled labor such as the United States.

TRADE AND GROWTH: THE EMPIRICAL EVIDENCE

The theoretical advantages of more-open trade are not absolute. As described earlier, under certain circumstances, an infant industry strategy also encourages greater investment and productivity gains. Moreover, while theory suggests advantages to open trade, it says little about which types of policies might be most helpful for a country wanting to move in this direction. Therefore, the question of the relationship between trade strategies and economic growth is ultimately an empirical one. What does the evidence suggest about the relationship between openness, growth, and income?

The first type of evidence is anecdotal, looking at various countries' experiences. Most of the fastest-growing economies during the last several decades have been the most resolute in pursuing an outward-oriented strategy. Chile, China, Hong Kong, Indonesia, Korea, Malaysia, Mauritius, Taiwan, Thailand, and Singapore are among the fastest-growing economies and among those most focused on stimulating export growth. China and India were among the most-closed countries to trade in the 1960s and 1970s. As China began to become more outward-oriented in the 1980s and India in the 1990s, both saw their growth rates accelerate sharply. Many factors—economic, political, institutional, geographic, demographic, and cultural—undoubtedly contributed to this strong performance. For example, the Asian countries invested heavily in human and physical capital, which are central to rapid development. But the focus on labor-intensive exports clearly played an important role in making educated labor and capital more productive than they would have been within protected, inward-looking economic regimes. Exports have been referred to as the "engine of growth" in these economies. At the same time, many countries that pursued policy regimes biased against exports tended to grow more slowly, including many nations in Latin America and Africa. The former Soviet Union also can be added to this list; in many ways, the Soviet system was predicated on an import substitution strategy within the Soviet block.

Figure 19–7 shows the strong positive relationship between manufactured exports and growth. This positive relationship does not hold for all exports: We saw in Chapter 17 that there is a negative relationship between primary product exports and growth, which may result from "Dutch-disease" effects, less potential for sustained productivity gains, and the potential for corruption. The positive relationship between manufactured exports and growth is more tightly tied

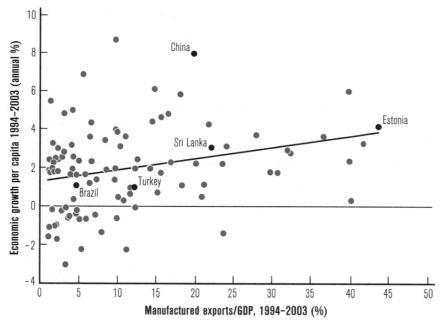

FIGURE 19-7. **Manufactured Exports and Economic Growth, 1994–2003**

to the theoretical rationales given previously: greater scope for competition, specialization, technology transfer, and productivity gains. While some argue for an export-led growth strategy, a more-precise (albeit more-cumbersome) description would be a labor-intensive export led growth strategy.

A large body of more-sophisticated research that controls for the effects of other social, geographic, and economic factors clearly supports the relationship between outward orientation and economic growth. Debates continue about the magnitude of the results, the statistical techniques employed, and the definitions of *openness* used, but the preponderance of research concluded that economies integrated into the world economy perform better than those closed or isolated. Some studies focus on the relationship between trade flows and income or growth, others focus on attributes of trade policy, but both strands of the literature reach the same broad conclusion.

Trade Volumes, Trade Policy, and Growth

In examining the relationship between trade volume and growth, economists Jeffrey Frankel from Harvard University and David Romer from the University of California at Berkeley tackled the difficult issue of the direction of causality. A strong positive relationship between trade and rapid economic growth does not prove that the former is the *cause* of the latter. It is entirely plausible that the causation runs the other way: Rapid income and productivity growth, by increasing productive capacity and reducing costs, can make a country more competitive in world markets and lead to faster growth of manufactured exports. Also possible is that both export growth and economic growth are simultaneously caused by something else, such as improved macroeconomic policies, more-stable political systems, reduced corruption, or increased savings. Frankel and Romer partially addressed the causality issue by tracing the portion of trade due to geographical characteristics (such as a country's size, its location, and whether or not it is landlocked), which tend to be weakly correlated or uncorrelated with other possible determinants of growth. They show that this geographical component of trade has a large but only moderately statistically significant positive effect on income.[13] While the study shows a strong connection from trade to growth and the link to geography demonstrates the importance of favorable location near major markets, it does not tell us much about trade policy. Ultimately, causality is hard to untangle because, to a large extent, export growth and economic growth probably support each other in a virtuous circle: Exporting countries have greater access to new machinery and technology that support growth, while faster economic growth provides the means to finance investments in infrastructure and education that support exports.

To isolate the impact of trade from institutions and other effects, World Bank economists David Dollar and Aart Kraay examined the relationship between *changes* in trade shares and growth, while controlling for several other factors. They found that raising the trade share from 20 to 40 percent of GDP over a decade raised the growth rate by between 0.5 and 1.0 percent per year. A recent survey of several major studies found that, as a mid-range estimate, each 1 percent increase in the (export + import) ÷ GDP ratio (e.g., from 40 to 40.4 percent) was associated with an increase in output per capita of about 0.5 percent over a 10–20 year time horizon.[14]

Measuring the links between specific *trade policies* and growth is more complex, since a range of policies affect trade. Looking at any one policy in isolation from others can provide ambiguous results, as no single policy can fully reflect a country's range of trade policies.[15] Consider import tariffs: China, Korea, Malaysia,

[13]Frankel and Romer, "Does Trade Cause Growth?"

[14]The survey is by William Cline, *Trade Policy and Global Poverty* (Washington, DC: Center for Global Development, 2004), and the research on changes in trade shares is from David Dollar and Aart Kraay "Trade, Growth, and Poverty," Policy Research Department Working Paper No. 2615, World Bank, Washington, DC, 2001. For other studies showing a strong relationship between trade and growth, see Edwards, "Openness, Productivity, and Growth"; Charles Jones and Robert Hall, "Why Do Some Countries Produce So Much More Output per Worker than Others?" *Quarterly Journal of Economics* 114 (February 1999), 83–116; Warcziarg, "Measuring the Dynamic Gains from Trade"; World Bank, *The East Asian Miracle*.

[15]Lant Pritchett, "Measuring Outward Orientation in LDCs: Can It Be Done?" *Journal of Development Economics* 49, no. 2 (1996), 307–35.

and other countries kept tariffs high on many products, while some other countries that reduced average tariff rates were not rewarded with rapid export growth. But the most successful countries did more than just lower average tariffs. The exact policy combination differed, although they all had the common element of zero tariffs on imported inputs and capital goods for exporters, and they took other steps to reduce costs for exporters and to integrate firms with the global economy. But the fact that the policy mix differed makes it harder to measure for research purposes and harder to prescribe the precise steps that other countries might want to take. Moreover, not all countries that began to liberalize their trade policies were rewarded with faster export growth, particularly in Latin America.

Studies that examined combinations of trade policies found a strong relationship between openness and growth. Economists Jeffrey Sachs and Andrew Warner examined the economic growth performance of 79 countries around the world during the period 1970–89 and found that countries with more-open policies and less-biased exchange rates grew about 2 percentage points faster than closed economies.[16] Subsequent research extended their findings throughout the 1990s, albeit usually with a slightly smaller effect. Despite some criticism of their measure of openness, several other studies, using different measures of trade policies, also found a strong relationship with growth.[17]

Skeptics on the strength of the relationship between more-open trade and growth, such as Harvard University economist Dani Rodrik, point to potential weaknesses in the methodologies and data used in some of these studies, and they caution that care should be taken not to draw overly strong conclusions. They point out that studies on the relationship between trade volumes and growth do not directly address the issue of trade policies and studies that examine policies leave open some questions on precisely how to measure policies appropriately, the exact channels through which trade policies affect growth, and the relationships between trade policies and other policies that support growth. Rodrik and others suggest that some of the impact attributed to changes in trade barriers more appropriately should be attributed to stronger institutions, better governance, and improved macroeconomic policies that typically

[16]In their policy index, a country was considered to be "open" if it met five criteria: (1) Its average tariff rate was less than 40 percent, (2) its nontariff barriers (e.g., quotas) covered less than 40 percent of imports, (3) the premium on the unofficial parallel market exchange rate did not exceed 20 percent, (4) there were no state monopolies on major exports, and (5) it was not a socialist economy. See Jeffrey Sachs and Andrew Warner, "Economic Reform and the Process of Global Integration," *Brookings Papers on Economic Activity* 1 (1995), 1–118.

[17]See, for example, Edwards, "Openness, Productivity, and Growth"; Warcziarg, "Measuring the Dynamic Gains from Trade; David Dollar, "Outward-Oriented Developing Countries Really Do Grow More Rapidly: Evidence from 95 LDCs, 1976–85," *Economic Development and Cultural Change* 40, no. 3 (1992), 523–44.

accompany trade reform, rather than trade policies per se.[18] This suggests, not that increased trade will not confer benefits, but that the steps necessary to stimulate economic growth and increased trade go beyond simply reducing tariffs and quotas and include strong macroeconomic management (including sensible exchange rate policy), steps to strengthen key economic and governance institutions, and policies that more broadly improve the environment for investment and productivity growth. The institutional innovations needed to spark growth may be different from those prescribed by a pure neoclassical model, and innovations that work in one country may not be easily replicable in others. In this view, greater integration may follow an initial burst of growth based on these other policy measures, rather than be the root cause. But even these skeptics do not suggest that openness to trade is an ill-advised strategy or that broad trade barriers are conducive to long-run growth.

While outward orientation tends to be associated with faster growth and gains for an economy as a whole, it is important to bear in mind that not every individual benefits from more openness. Some sectors expand as a result of greater openness, but others contract. Owners of firms that previously had been protected from import competition and the workers in those firms lose, at least unless they are able to find work in the expanding sectors. Some farmers may lose out to import competition, while others gain from the expansion of export markets. For example, because of NAFTA, the free-trade agreement between Mexico and the United States, small Mexican farms that grow corn have been severely hurt by imports of much-lower-priced U.S. corn. But other Mexican farmers have done well, as have exporters of manufactures. Mexico's export earnings from horticulture have tripled under NAFTA and export sales to the United States of fresh fruit and vegetables have risen substantially.

The political economy of trade reform is such that often the losers, though fewer in number, are often very vocal in protesting against trade liberalization. It is hard to blame them, as the costs are visible and immediate: People in protected sectors lose their jobs. The gains, while usually larger, are much harder to see initially, as the growth in new investment and employment opportunities takes place only over time, so the winners from more-open trade are more dispersed and less visible at the time of the reforms.

---

[18]See, for example, Dani Rodrik, Arvind Subramanian, and Francesco Trebbi, "Institutions Rule: The Primacy of Institutions over Geography and Integration in Economic Development," *Journal of Economic Growth* 9, no. 2 (2004), 131–65; Francisco Rodriguez and Dani Rodrik, "Trade Policy and Economic Growth: A Skeptic's Guide to Cross-National Evidence," Working Paper No. 7081, National Bureau of Economic Research, Cambridge, MA, April 1999; Dani Rodrik, "Trading in Illusions," *Foreign Policy* (March–April 2001); and Ann Harrison and Gordon Hanson, "Who Gains from Trade Reform? Some Remaining Puzzles," *Journal of Development Economics* 59 (1999), 125–54.

Trade and Poverty Reduction

Less research has been directed at the relationship between trade and poverty reduction, but most of the evidence indicates that greater openness and faster growth in labor-intensive exports is associated with poverty reduction.[19] As discussed in Chapter 6, generally there is a strong relationship between economic growth and poverty reduction. As average incomes rise, income distribution changes relatively little: The income of the very poor also tends to rise, sometimes faster than the average, sometimes slower, but the tendency is for the income of the poor to increase with economic growth. Some of the countries with the fastest growth in labor-intensive exports have seen the most rapid drops in poverty. In China, the percentage of the people living with income under $1 per day dropped from 28 percent to 16 percent between 1987 and 2001; in Indonesia, it fell from 28 percent to 8 percent; and in Thailand, it dropped from 18 to just 2 percent. Two recent studies conclude that a global move toward free trade would lift more than 300 million people out of poverty over the next 10–20 years through its impact on income growth.[20]

One way in which trade liberalization affects poverty is through its impact on consumer prices. As import barriers are removed, prices for many goods purchased by poor families fall, increasing their real income. But the most direct channel through which more outward orientation could reduce poverty is through an increase in the demand for labor. Trade in labor-intensive products, including both agriculture and manufactured products, has the potential to create substantial employment opportunities for low-skilled workers, precisely those living below or near the poverty line. This is what has happened in many of the more outward-oriented economies: New job opportunities help increase the income of the poor and reduce the number of people in poverty. But openness can also lead to job losses in some sectors, such as when protected domestic firms or agricultural products cannot compete effectively with imports, and unskilled workers in those sectors lose their jobs. As we stressed, while more-open trade is likely to benefit an economy as a whole, it does not necessarily benefit every individual. The overall impact depends to a large extent on the mobility of labor: For openness to reduce poverty, unskilled workers need to be

[19]See Ann Harrison, ed., *Globalization and Poverty* (Chicago: University of Chicago Press, forthcoming); Alan Winters, Neil McCulloch, and Andrew McKay, "Trade Liberalization and Poverty: The Evidence So Far," *Journal of Economic Literature* 42 (March 2004), 72–115; Andrew Berg and Anne Krueger, "Trade, Growth, and Poverty: A Selective Survey," Working Paper WP/03/30, International Monetary Fund, Washington, DC, 2003; David Dollar and Aart Kraay, "Trade, Growth, and Poverty," Policy Research Department Working Paper No. 2615, World Bank, Washington, DC, 2001; William Cline, *Trade Policy and Global Poverty*.

[20]Cline, *Trade Policy and Global Poverty*, Chapter 5; and World Bank, "Market Access and the World's Poor," in *Global Economic Prospects and the Developing Countries 2002: Making Trade Work for the World's Poor* (Washington, DC: World Bank, 2002).

able to move from protected sectors (which are contracting) to tradables sectors (which are expanding). Country studies in Colombia and India suggest that trade reforms were associated with an increase in poverty only where inflexible labor laws prevented easy movement of workers from one activity to another.[21]

KEY ISSUES ON THE GLOBAL TRADE AGENDA

Increased Global Competition and the Rise of China and India

The benefits for an individual developing country from greater outward orientation may be smaller in the future than those achieved by the original Asian Tigers. When Hong Kong, Korea, Singapore, and Taiwan began to compete on global markets, there was little competition from other developing countries, so their firms were able to expand and multiply quickly. Today, many more developing countries have adopted this strategy, including giants China and India, generating concerns about tougher competition and falling prices for export products. As new highly efficient producers enter a market, prices often fall in the short run, as new entrants create overcapacity and drive out high-cost producers. Prices for semiconductors fell in the mid-1990s as world productive capacity grew rapidly; coffee prices dropped when Vietnam started producing, hurting some traditional coffee exporters, including Honduras and Uganda; and China's expansion into garment exports put pressure on firms as far away as tiny Lesotho in southern Africa. There is no question that some firms might lose out in the process as others gain.

The long-term evidence, however, suggests that world trade can expand very quickly and accommodate many new firms. Between 1950 and 2003, world exports grew more than three times more quickly than world output, and exports of manufactured products grew most quickly of all. The United States was a huge force in world markets, accounting for 25 percent of world output after World War II, much larger than China today, and there was concern that U.S. firms would dominate all trade. But while the reduction of trade barriers by the United States and its European allies put pressure on some firms as world prices dropped, the changes created many new opportunities for other firms. Similarly, in today's world, as more countries trade, and transport and telecommunication costs continue to drop, the opportunity for firms to specialize increases. Global production networks allow firms from many different countries to contribute to the production of one finished good, with each firm specializing in the particular phase of the production process in which it has

---

[21]See the case studies in Harrison, *Globalization and Poverty.*

comparative advantage. Many exports from China are assembled and finished products built with components, kits, and other materials imported from other countries. A computer from China might include a screen made in Malaysia, a circuit board from Singapore, and a keyboard made in the Philippines. In addition, firms in one country often are better able to serve niche markets for specialized consumer goods that arise in other countries. High-quality fruit from Chile and Ecuador is sent by air overnight and sold in the United States, while roses from Kenya and Uganda are harvested one day and sold the next on the streets of Rotterdam.

As developing countries open to world markets, they also become consumers for other country's exports, not just competitors. Trade is a two-way process. China and India are rapidly increasing their imports as well as their exports, and they are becoming two of the largest markets in the world for other countries. China is now Indonesia's fourth largest export market (after the United States, European Union, and Japan), importing oil and gas, timber, fish, and even some electronics products. The expansion of India and China creates challenges and disruptions as well as opportunities that require adjustment, hurting some firms and helping others, but their expansion does not undermine the basic rationale for the outward-oriented strategy.

Does Outward Orientation Create Sweatshops?

Some critics argue that outward orientation leads to a global sweatshop economy, in which corporations pit workers around the world against each other in a "race to the bottom" to see who will accept the lowest wages, benefits, and environmental standards (we discuss the relationship between trade and environmental standards in Chapter 20). It is understandable how someone looking at the factories that produce shoes and textiles in low-income countries could reach this conclusion. By rich world standards, the wages are very low, often only a few dollars a day or less. Workers labor for long hours in repetitive tasks, often with only limited breaks. In many cases, the conditions are deplorable. This is also true for firms producing for local markets, for agricultural workers, and others.

Low wages are a reflection of the extent of poverty in low-income countries. Wages are set, not by what firms pay in other countries, but by the productivity of local workers (which establishes the demand for labor) and the wages paid to workers' next-best opportunity (which determines the supply of labor.) As we have seen, billions of the world's population live on less than $2 a day. Many toil in backbreaking work in agriculture to try to feed their families, and others work in market stalls, as servants, dock laborers, or in other difficult positions. Many have no job and little or no income at all. A 25-year-old woman machine operator in a textile firm in Nairobi earns about one tenth of what her counterpart earns in Copenhagen or Taipei.[22] This huge gap in pay is not because the Kenyan worker is exploited by her employer or because the Danish or Taiwanese workers are ten times more skilled. It is because pay differences across countries reflect differences in the average level of *economywide* productivity. Workers in Kenya have less physical and human capital to work with and, on average, output per worker is low. Therefore, the market-determined wage is going to be substantially lower than in high-productivity Denmark or Taiwan.

For many people, the opportunity to work in a steady factory job for a few dollars a day is a big improvement over other options and can represent an important first step in rising above subsistence living and out of poverty. Without such options, poverty could be worse, rather than better. Efforts to substantially and immediately raise wages to industrialized-country standards could backfire. Firms forced to pay well above the marginal product of labor hire fewer workers, substitute machines for workers, or simply decide to relocate their operations, making workers even worse off. No one advocates that factory jobs with relatively low wages (by global standards) should be seen as the end goal. Rather, it should be seen as the first step on what ideally will be a dynamic path on which job skills, wages, and standards of living can grow steadily over time. The United States, Japan, and the nations in the European Union all went through a phase of very low wages and difficult working conditions during their transition from agrarian economies to industrialized nations. This is not meant to glorify this phase. It suggests only that there are no shortcuts to achieve economic development. Wages rise as the average productivity of the economy rises, the result of productive investments in both capital and people. Success stories in recent years are those nations that grew rapidly and were able to get through the very low-wage and difficult-working-conditions phase quickly.

The image of a "race to the bottom" suggests that wages steadily *fall* in countries that compete to attract foreign firms that export to world markets. Sometimes wages fall at first for some workers, as uncompetitive protected firms close down, where wages effectively were subsidized by consumers that paid a higher price for protected products. But the typical pattern in countries that shift to outward orientation is not a steady fall in wages but a rise in wages over time as workers gain new skills and factories become more productive. Evidence suggests that, in countries that attracted foreign direct investment, multinational corporations tend to pay higher average wages and have better average working conditions than domestic firms engaged in the same activities. Nike subcontractors in Indonesia pay nearly three times the average annual minimum wage, and workers in foreign-owned apparel and footwear factories in Vietnam rank in the top 20 percent of the population by household expenditure. In Mexico, export-oriented firms pay upward of 50 percent higher wages than

---

[22]Union Bank of Switzerland, "Prices and Earnings," UBS AG, Zurich, 2003.

similar nonexporting firms. Pay for workers in EPZs generally is higher than for similar activities outside of zones.[23]

The concern about the "race to the bottom" goes beyond wages and includes working conditions and labor standards. It generated a broader debate about differing standards and institutions in rich and poor countries and the imposition of standards across borders (see Box 19–4). Advocates of stronger labor standards argue that they are necessary to guard against corporations imposing poor working conditions, such as long hours, short breaks, gender discrimination, poor ventilation, and other problems. Opponents argue that the imposition of stricter standards raises producer costs and discourages investment, thereby hurting workers by costing them their jobs. Despite the sometimes polemic debate, there is ample middle ground. Some standards are widely shared. The International Labour Organization (ILO) refers to these as **core standards:** abolishing forced labor; ending discrimination based on gender, race, ethnicity and religion; eliminating child labor where it is harmful to the child; and permitting freedom of association of workers and the right to collective bargaining. For other improvements in conditions, which often are referred to as **cash standards,** the costs to producers are often small, including providing reasonable work breaks and improving safety conditions (such as unlocking doors, supplying fire extinguishers, and improving ventilation). In other words, some working conditions can be improved without adding significantly to costs and discouraging investment.

There is no question that working conditions are worse in low-income countries than in richer countries and this is the case not just for firms engaged in trade, but for those selling in protected domestic markets and for agriculture. The goal is to improve those conditions over time. Does outward orientation and greater trade make these conditions worse or better? The evidence is not complete, but overall it suggests that working conditions generally improve as economic growth proceeds in outward-oriented countries.[24] This outcome is not always the case. There are situations where investors threaten to go elsewhere if workers are allowed to unionize or individual workers advocating for better conditions lose their jobs, as is the case with nonexporting firms. But in countries

[23]For summaries, see Drusilla Brown, Alan Deardorff, and Robert Stern, "The Effects of Multinational Production on Wages and Working Conditions in Developing Countries," Working Paper No. 9669, National Bureau of Economic Research, Cambridge, MA, April 2003; Theodore H. Moran, *Beyond Sweatshops: Foreign Direct Investment and Globalization in Developing Countries* (Washington, DC: Brookings Institution Press, 2002), p. 7; and Edward Graham, *Fighting the Wrong Enemy: Antiglobal Activists and Multinational Enterprises* (Washington: Institute for International Economics, 2000), Chapter 4.

[24]See Kimberley Ann Elliot and Richard B. Freeman, *Can Labor Standards Improve under Globalization?* (Washington, DC: Institute for International Economics, 2003); Brown et al., "The Effects of Multinational Production; Richard Freeman, "Trade Wars: The Exaggerated Impact of Trade in Economic Debate," Research Paper Series No. 2003/42, University of Nottingham, 2003.

**BOX 19-4 PRINCIPLES FOR WORLD TRADE:
ONE ECONOMIST'S VIEW**

Harvard economist Dani Rodrik, who often warns that some of the evidence on trade and growth might be overstated, offers the following guidelines:

- *Trade is a means to an end, not an end in itself.* Advocates of globalization lecture the rest of the world incessantly about the adjustments countries have to undertake in their policies and institutions to expand their international trade. This way of thinking confuses means with ends. Trade serves at best as an instrument for achieving the goals that societies seek: prosperity, stability, freedom, and quality of life. Reversing our priorities would have a simple but powerful implication. Instead of asking what kind of multilateral trading system maximizes foreign trade and investment opportunities, we would ask what kind of multilateral system best enables nations around the world to pursue their own values and developmental objectives.

- *Countries have the right to protect their own social arrangements and institutions.* Opponents of globalization argue that trade sets off a "race to the bottom," with nations converging toward the lowest levels of environmental, labor, and consumer protections. Advocates counter that there is little evidence that trade leads to the erosion of national standards. One way to cut through this morass is to accept that countries can uphold national standards in these areas, by withholding market access if necessary, when trade demonstrably undermines domestic practices enjoying broad popular support. The WTO already has a "safeguard" system in place to protect firms from import surges. An extension of this principle to protect environmental, labor, or consumer safety standards at home, with appropriate procedural restraints against abuse, might make the world trading system more resilient and less resistant to ad hoc protectionism.

- *But they do not have the right to impose their institutional preferences on others.* Using trade restrictions to uphold our values has to be sharply distinguished from using them to impose these values on other countries. Trade rules should not force Americans to consume shrimp caught in ways that most Americans find unacceptable, but neither should they allow the United States to use trade sanctions to alter the way that foreign nations go about their fishing business. Citizens of rich countries who are genuinely concerned about the state of the environment or workers in the developing world can be more effective through channels other than trade, via diplomacy or foreign aid, for example.

> • *Nondemocratic countries cannot count on the same trade privileges as democratic ones.* National standards (such as on labor and the environment) that deviate from those in trade partners and thereby provide trade advantages are legitimate only to the extent that they are grounded in free choices made by citizens. A democratic country such as India can argue, legitimately, that its practices are consistent with the wishes of its population. But nondemocratic countries do not pass the same prima facie test. The assertion that labor rights and the environment are trampled for the benefit of the few cannot be as easily dismissed in those countries. Consequently, exports of nondemocratic countries deserve greater international scrutiny, particularly when they entail costly dislocations in other countries.
>
> Source: Dani Rodrik, "Five Simple Principles for World Trade," *The American Prospect* (January 17, 2000).

that expanded trade over a sustained period of time, such as Korea, Indonesia, Malaysia, and Mauritius, working conditions improved and are much better than they were in the late 1980s or early 1990s.[25]

In countries where there is little investment and growth, worker conditions tend to stagnate. Moreover, export-oriented firms tend to include a large share of foreign investors, and most studies show that worker conditions tend to be better in foreign-owned factories compared to similar domestically owned factories. This hardly suggests that advocacy efforts are misplaced. Better conditions in foreign-owned firms are partly in response to advocacy: Multinational firms respond to adverse publicity about poor worker conditions and attempt to bring about improvements. But it is hard to find systematic evidence of a decline in worker standards and a "race to the bottom" as countries become more open and expand trade.

Expanding Market Access

Implementing a more-open trade strategy is successful only if there are markets in which developing country exporters can sell their products, and the most important markets are those in the European Union, Japan, and the United States. Generally speaking, these countries have low trade barriers, with relatively low average tariff and quota rates by world standards. But historically, their

---

[25]The evolution of wages and working conditions in Korea is discussed in David L. Lindauer et al., *The Strains of Economic Growth: Labor Unrest and Social Dissatisfaction in Korea* (Cambridge, MA: Harvard Institute of International Development, 1997).

largest trade barriers and greatest protection are precisely on the products in which low-income countries have a comparative advantage: textiles, apparel, and agriculture. While, on the one hand, the world's richest countries advocate free markets and recommend that poor countries shift toward greater outward orientation; on the other hand, they erect trade barriers that impede that process. Going forward, a key question is whether industrialized countries react to greater competition on world markets from China, India, and many other developing countries by imposing greater protectionism or by allowing market access to more products produced in developing countries.

In most years, the United States collects more tariffs on goods from poor countries than rich countries, despite importing much higher-valued goods from rich countries. Consider U.S. imports from France and Bangladesh in 2001. Both countries paid $330 million in tariffs to the United States, but for France, this amount was charged on $31 billion in imports, while for Bangladesh it was charged on $2.5 billion of imports. The implied average tariff on French products was 1 percent, while on products from Bangladesh it was 13 percent. As one example, the United States charges a 32 percent tariff on acrylic sweaters from Bangladesh. Needless to say, protectionism in the United States for making sweaters can hardly be justified by infant industry arguments. Trade barriers in the European Union are even higher, on average, than those in the United States and Japan.

The United States and other industrialized countries also charge higher tariffs on processed goods, such as chocolate and shirts, than on the raw materials needed to make them, such as cocoa and cotton. The United States does not charge a tariff on cocoa beans, but it charges more than 25 cents a pound for certain kinds of chocolate, making it harder for firms in developing countries to compete in those markets. Such mercantilist practices were denounced by Adam Smith over 200 years ago but they remain features of developed nation trade policies.

TEXTILES AND APPAREL

The industrialized countries historically have restricted imports of textiles and apparel through both tariffs and quotas. With respect to quotas, textile and clothing imports were restricted for many decades, until 1995, through an agreement among the industrialized countries called the Multi-Fiber Agreement (MFA). The MFA was replaced in 1995 by the Agreement on Textiles and Clothing (ATC), which was phased out in 2005. Under these arrangements, each industrialized country allowed only up to a certain amount of imports of textiles and clothing from each developing country. Some exporters, like China, Indonesia, and Thailand, easily filled their quota and were not allowed to export more. This helped some other developing countries, as investors began to look at countries like Bangladesh, Lesotho, Mauritius, and Sri Lanka to locate production facilities and export to the industrialized countries. But, because of the quotas, the rich countries imported far less overall than they would have with open markets, which drove up domestic prices and protected domestic textile and apparel makers (and their workers) at the expense of firms and workers in developing countries.

As part of the Uruguay round of international trade negotiations (discussed later), these arrangements governing trade in textiles and apparel were gradually phased out and eliminated in 2005. This was a boon to the most-efficient firms in developing countries that had fully used their quotas, such as China, but created pressures on firms in Bangladesh and other countries that, to some extent, benefited from the quotas. Although the full impact of the phaseout is not yet clear, many firms in developing countries will benefit, while some will lose out.[26] The net impact on developing countries will be positive, but the gains may be concentrated in some countries.

Tariffs on textile and apparel imports remain in place. Although they have been reduced over the years, the average tariff on textiles and apparel in the United States, Europe, and Japan is around 10 percent, which is about two to three times higher than the average tariff on other products. Many of the tariff rates on specific products are even higher. As we saw earlier in the chapter, even modest tariff rates can have a substantial effect on the effective rate of protection, so these tariffs leave firms in developing countries at a significant disadvantage.

AGRICULTURE

The United States, Canada, the European Union, and Japan provide substantial protection to their agricultural producers. The protection comes both through tariff barriers and direct subsidies to producers. As shown in Table 19–4, the magnitude of the protection is quite large, ranging from a tariff equivalent of about 20 percent in the United States to over 80 percent in Japan. A wide range of products is protected, including cotton, dairy products, maize, peanuts, soybeans, sugar, rice, and wheat, among others. Sugar is among the most distorted markets in the world, with the industrialized countries both subsidizing domestic producers and imposing quotas to significantly restrict imports. In recent years, U.S. consumers have paid as much as three times the world price of sugar because of U.S. sugar quotas, which subsequently affects the price of everything from candy to processed foods to soft drinks produced in the United States.

---

[26]Cambodia is another country that benefited from the quota system. But it adopted a unique position, in part, because of pressure from the U.S. government. Cambodian garment exporters agreed to follow strict guidelines on worker rights, hoping that the United States and other developed-nation consumers would be willing to pay more for garments certified to have been produced in factories complying with a number of nonwage labor standards. With the end of the system of managed trade in garments, it remains to be seen whether consumers in industrialized countries will pay more for Cambodian products or simply shop for the lowest-priced goods available.

TABLE 19-4. **Overall Protection in Agriculture (percent tariff equivalent)**

TYPE OF PROTECTION	UNITED STATES	CANADA	EUROPEAN UNION	JAPAN
Tariffs	8.8	30.4	32.6	76.4
Subsidies	10.2	16.8	10.4	3.2
Total	19.9	52.3	46.4	82.1

Source: William Cline, *Trade Policy and Global Poverty* (Washington, DC: Center for Global Development, 2004).

These subsidies provide farmers in industrialized countries with a significant advantage over potential competitors, and weaken the incentives for increased production in developing countries. The subsidies also encourage increased production in the industrialized countries, which adds to the world supply, thereby putting downward pressure on world prices. The World Bank estimates that subsidies depress world rice prices by 33–50 percent, and for sugar and dairy products, by 20–40 percent.[27] As a result, farmers in developing countries receive lower prices, meaning they both produce less and earn less for the amount they produce, reducing their total income.

The politics around agricultural subsidies are very sensitive. Large agricultural corporations in the industrialized countries lobby hard to maintain the subsidies and generally are successful, even though the subsidies are costly to taxpayers. Agriculture subsidies in the European Union and the United States total over $67 billion and about $20 billion per year, respectively, with most of the payments going to large commercial farmers. In one often-cited calculation, the average Japanese cow gets $7 a day from various government subsidies and other forms of protection, while a cow in Europe receives $2.20 a day. This at a time when over 1 billion people in the developing world lives on less than $1 a day. The combined impact of industrial country tariffs, quotas, and subsidies on textiles, apparel, agriculture, and other products is significant. By one estimate, the elimination of industrialized country barriers would add $100 million annually to GDP of poor countries, more than total foreign aid. Two studies find that the elimination of these barriers would lift 300 million or more people out of poverty.[28] It is unlikely that the industrialized countries will reduce these barriers on their own, but they may be more willing to do so in the context of multilateral trade negotiations.

[27]World Bank, *Global Economic Prospects and the Developing Countries 2002.*
[28]World Bank, *Global Economic Prospects and the Developing Countries 2002*; and Cline, *Trade Policy and Global Poverty.*

Multilateral Trade Negotiations and the WTO

With the outbreak of World War I, a long epoch of globalization came to an end as the industrialized countries began to erect high trade barriers, a trend reinforced by the onset of the Great Depression. With the end of World War II, this pattern began to change. Industrialized-country leaders began to reduce tariffs, and they looked for ways to accelerate and consolidate the process. The result was a shift toward **multilateral trade negotiations,** involving many nations simultaneously negotiating reductions in tariffs. The idea was that, with a large international effort in which participants would pledge to reduce their tariffs if other countries did the same, each individual country would be better able to overcome narrow interest groups at home that opposed trade liberalization. These discussions led to a proposal in 1948 to establish an **International Trade Organization (ITO)** as a sister organization to the IMF and World Bank. Although the ITO was never established, multilateral trade negotiations expanded and flourished in the ensuing decades through a less-formal institution known as the **General Agreement on Tariffs and Trade (GATT).**[29] Between 1947 and 1994, eight rounds of multilateral trade negotiations took place through the GATT, covering mostly tariffs but later including quotas, antidumping measures, and other issues.

The Uruguay round of trade negotiations (so named because its initial meeting took place in Punta del Este, Uruguay, in September 1986) was completed in 1994. It was by far the largest trade negotiation ever held, with 123 countries taking part, including for the first time a large number of developing countries. These negotiations led to several key changes:

- The global average tariff on manufactured goods was reduced by about one third.
- Agricultural protection, which the industrialized countries had always excluded from the negotiations, was incorporated for the first time.
- Participants agreed to phase out the Multi-Fiber Agreement and the Agreement on Textiles and Clothing, which restricted textile and clothing imports in the industrial countries, with complete elimination by January 1, 2005.
- Industrial countries, especially the United States, won stricter adherence to *trade-related intellectual property rights*, or TRIPs, that prevent the use of patented material and the production of generic "copycat" products without permission. They also won agreement on new rules on investment and trade in services.

[29]Although the ITO charter was approved at a UN conference in Havana in 1948, the U.S. Congress refused to ratify the agreement, even though the United States had been one of the driving forces behind the ITO idea. In 1950, the U.S. government announced that it no longer would seek congressional ratification of the UN charter, effectively killing the ITO. See the WTO website (www.wto.org) for details.

- The GATT was superseded by a new organization, the **World Trade Organization (WTO),** established on January 1, 1995. In some sense, the establishment of the WTO finally brought into existence (in a different form) the ill-fated ITO. The WTO serves as a central institution for global trade negotiations aimed at establishing a system of rules for fair, open, and undistorted competition, and as a forum for settling disputes among members.

Many developing countries had high hopes at the outset of the Uruguay round, as it was the first in which a large number of low- and middle-income countries were allowed to participate, and it was the first in which industrialized countries, with great reluctance, agreed to include agricultural subsides. Discussions led to what later was called the *grand bargain* between rich countries and low-income countries. The industrialized countries promised (1) significant reduction in tariffs, (2) the end of the Multi-Fiber Agreement, and (3) reductions in agricultural subsidies, with a commitment to even larger reductions in the next round. For their part, developing countries promised (1) larger reductions in their own tariffs; (2) agreement on new rules on investment, services, and TRIPs; and (3) support for the new WTO. This approach represented a significant shift from the traditional GATT approach on reciprocity: Instead of each country agreeing to open its markets on certain goods if the others did the same, the Uruguay round featured an implicit deal in which the richer countries agreed to certain steps in some areas in return for the developing countries agreeing to steps in other areas, many of which went way beyond traditional border barriers.[30]

Despite the increased access in some industrialized country markets, many developing countries eventually were deeply disappointed in the round. There were three broad concerns. First, the industrialized countries' pledge to reduce subsidies for agriculture generally did not materialize. Second, the new agreements on investment, services and TRIPs were much more complicated than simply reducing tariffs or quotas, and as a result, the developing countries had to build domestic institutional and legal expertise that required significant time and money. These changes were a large burden on many low-income countries with a scarcity of high-skilled legal and administrative expertise. The industrialized countries promised to provide technical assistance to help with the transition but often did not fully follow through. Third, the TRIPs agreement resulted in developing countries paying higher prices for medicines and pharmaceutical products covered by patents. For many goods and services, protecting property rights and rewarding those that invest in research and development makes sense, but paying high market prices and preventing the sale of cheaper generic

---

[30]See Sylvia Ostry, "Why Has Globalization Become a Bad Word?" the Alcoa-Intalco Works Distinguished Lecture, Western Washington University, October 25, 2001.

brands became a particularly contentious issue around medicines, particularly those used for treating HIV/AIDS. Only ten years later was there the beginnings of serious discussion about how to make these drugs more affordable for low-income countries, as discussed in Chapter 9.

For many, the Uruguay round came to be considered a "bum deal" rather than a "grand bargain,"[31] and the unhappiness led to raucous demonstrations against the WTO in Seattle in 1999 and at other subsequent WTO meetings. A new round of trade negotiations under the WTO, called the Doha round, is currently underway, with many of the same issues under negotiation. The results of the round will help determine whether or not developing countries perceive that world trading arrangements are fair and will go a long way in determining whether the trend toward greater trade openness continues or the world begins to shift back to more inward-looking approaches.

SUMMARY

- World trade has grown rapidly in recent decades. Total exports as a share of GDP from developing countries have tripled since 1970. Trade tends to be particularly large for small countries and those with access to seaports and near major markets. As economies grow, the composition of trade tends to change, with exports shifting from primary products to simple labor-intensive products to more-sophisticated goods and services.
- Almost all countries have used import substitution at various times. In theory, IS can allow domestic firms to learn production techniques, improve efficiency, and eventually compete on world markets. However, despite some exceptions, more often than not, this strategy leads to slower growth, low efficiency, and weak technology.
- Many developing countries began to shift to more outward-orientated trade strategies in the 1980s. Outward orientation allows firms to become more specialized, sell to larger global markets, and import leading technologies. Most countries that follow this strategy begin with labor-intensive manufacturing and agriculture, with the goal of moving to more-sophisticated products over time. Concerns that this strategy leads to a "race to the bottom" in wages and labor standards generally are not supported by the evidence.
- Evidence suggests a strong positive relationship between trade, trade policy, and growth. Countries with larger amounts of trade or more-

[31]Ostry, "Why Has Globalization Become a Bad Word?"

open trade policies tend to record faster growth and poverty reduction. Some critics, however, find the results less than fully persuasive and suggest that other factors, such as strong institutions and an overall climate that supports investments, are more important in explaining rapid growth.

- Protectionist policies in the industrialized countries impede exports from developing countries, especially in textiles, apparel, and agriculture. It remains to be seen whether the industrialized countries will maintain these barriers and erect new ones as competition from developing countries increases or whether multilateral negotiations can lead to reductions in these barriers and increased opportunities for developing countries.

20

Sustainable Development

W hat is the relationship between economic development, natural resource management, and environmental quality? Is there an inherent trade-off in which economic growth can proceed only at the cost of continued environmental degradation? Or are environmental quality and growth sometimes complementary? A country's environment—its air, water, diversity of biological species, and natural surroundings—are valuable natural resources. These resources can be critical inputs to economic activity, job creation, and growth. Prudent management of fisheries can help provide a sustainable source of food for fishers and their families or support larger-scale commercial fishing. Game parks, beaches, or mountain trails can be the basis for a dynamic tourism sector. At the same time, to some extent, all economic activity uses the environment as a dump for waste products, and environmental damage can have substantial detrimental effects on health and welfare. Contaminated water and the resulting diarrhcal disease kill about 2 million children and causes about 900 million episodes of illness every year. Dust and soot in city air cause between 300,000 to 700,000 premature deaths every year.[1] In addition, soil erosion, water and air pollution, and deforestation can cause substantial economic losses to a wide variety of economic activities. Further, natural resources and wildlife have certain intrinsic value above their relationship to economic activity and human welfare.

[1]*World Development Report 1992: Development and the Environment* (Washington, DC: World Bank, 1992).

Economic development and environmental management often are assumed to be at odds with each other. Many people suppose that rapid growth only comes with environmental degradation, and an improved environment can come only at the cost of reduced growth and development. In some situations, this is true: Rapid economic growth today may create pollution that reduces welfare and incurs cleanup costs in the future. Similarly, if rapid growth today is possible only through depleting a resource (such as clear-cutting forests to support the timber industry), growth may not be sustainable and may come at a very high cost. Moreover, efforts to reduce pollution or better manage the environment can be costly, and hard choices need to be made weighing the costs and benefits. But in other cases there is no such trade-off. In many situations, development and environmental goals are complementary, and reducing environmental degradation can help lower production costs and directly improve economic output and welfare. Reduced air and water pollution, for example, should help support tourism, fisheries development, and agricultural production.

These issues take on greater meaning when going beyond national borders to consider the entire planet. Are we depleting the world's fisheries and cutting down its rainforests so fast that neither can regenerate and large numbers of species are becoming extinct? Will the world run out of minerals, especially fuels, before we can develop technologies for renewable sources of energy? Are we heating earth's atmosphere so much with emissions of carbon dioxide from burning fossil fuels that economic development will change the world's climate, with dramatic and unpredictable effects on human welfare? And will these uses of our natural resource base have cumulative effects that are irreversible if we do not act soon enough?

We cannot attempt to thoroughly answer all of these questions in this chapter. Instead, we attempt to provide some frameworks that can be used to analyze these questions and pinpoint key issues. At the national level, it is not difficult to design policies that promote sustainable development, although governments often find it difficult to implement them. For the earth as a whole, the answers are more speculative and few existing mechanisms enforce solutions to environmental problems.

MARKET FAILURES

Environmental degradation is often the result of market failures, in which market prices deviate from scarcity values and individuals and companies make decisions that maximize their own profits but cause losses for others and society as a whole. A central theme of this chapter is that, within a single country, correcting those market failures and establishing properly working, efficient markets can be among the most powerful and effective mechanisms to promote efficient resource use, reduce environmental degradation, and generate sustainable development. At first blush, that proposition may seem counterintuitive. The point, however, is that environmental degradation often occurs because market participants do not take into account the full costs of their actions on the environment. For example, prices of goods produced in a factory may not include the costs to society of the air pollution generated by that factory. Government policies and interventions aimed at incorporating these costs into market decisions help improve environmental outcomes, make markets work better, and bring broader benefits to society.

Prominent among the market failures affecting resources are **externalities**— *costs* borne by the population at large but not by individual producers and *benefits* that accrue to society but cannot be captured by producers. The most important externalities are those caused by the depletion or degradation of natural resources, including the environment. If resources are depleted at rates faster than they can be replenished or substituted by human-made capital, development will be **unsustainable,** either nationally or globally. If markets fail in this fundamental way, how can they promote sustainable development? To resolve this apparent conflict, we first need to analyze in greater depth the reason that markets fail to allocate natural resources efficiently.

The Commons

During the eighteenth century, as the Industrial Revolution began in England, cows still grazed on the commons of many villages in England and its American colonies. The essence of a village commons was **open access,** free of charge, to any member of the village. The first villagers to take advantage of open access had ample grazing for their livestock; their only cost was the time it would take to herd their animals to the commons, allow them to graze, and herd them home. But the amount of land was fixed and soil fertility and climate limited the quantity of grass. As more villagers used the commons, the grass became sparse, so the animals took longer to feed or, in the case of open rangeland, herders were forced to travel farther to find forage, so that everyone's costs rose. The rising average cost to each herder eventually discouraged grazing on the commons. But the new entrants did not have to pay compensation for the rising costs imposed on each of the previous entrants and more grazing took place than was in the interests of the village as a whole. Eventually, since no one incorporated the full cost of their grazing into their decisions, overgrazing destroyed the commons as a useful source of feed for everyone.

The dilemma of the commons is a widespread phenomenon, applicable to any limited resource to which access is unlimited. Grazing on open range, whether in the U.S. West or the African savannah, has the same outcome. Open access to timberlands or access at fees well below the social cost results in over-logging and the destruction of native forests in Brazil, Ghana, Thailand, and many other tropical countries. Open access to fishing grounds in the North Atlantic, in Peru's Pacific waters, and in some inland lakes in Africa already has depleted fish stocks beyond their ability to regenerate. Free use of water from a stream benefits upland farmers, who have first access to the water, at the expense of downstream farmers, who get less water. Even traffic congestion in cities like Bangkok, Mexico City, or New York fits the description of a common property: City streets, to which access is free, are the common resource; each new vehicle causes worse traffic jams, forcing all previous entrants into longer, most costly commutes.

The earth's environment is composed of several common resources: air and the atmosphere, fresh water and the oceans, the earth's soils and minerals, and the diverse plant and animal species that live in this biosphere. Access to the environment typically is free. When manufacturers and farmers vent their waste into the air or water or create toxic dumps in the ground, they create health problems for the affected population, reduce the value of land in the affected area, destroy recreational potential, and generally reduce the welfare of people who value a clean environment. When lumber companies cut down a rain forest, they destroy the habitat of plant and animal species that are of value to others, including local populations that may harvest them or citizens or tourists who simply like to see them. They also may alter local climates, change patterns of water availability to surrounding farmers, and cause soil erosion. When we include the environment as a common resource, then much private activity generates external costs and market failure becomes a very general phenomenon.

Externalities: A Closer Look

External costs and benefits are at the core of the common resource problem. A new producer creates higher costs for all previous entrants or all producers impose external costs on the general population. In either case, in the absence of regulation, taxes, or property rights for environmental quality, external costs are not borne by the producers who cause them and the prices of their products do not reflect the social costs of production. Thus, more of these resource-depleting or -polluting goods and services are produced and consumed than would be the case if prices reflected external costs. Hence, societies pollute more than their people would choose if markets reflected all social costs.

Figure 20–1 shows this process. In a market with competitive producers, the supply curve S represents private marginal costs. Market equilibrium occurs at price P_1 with output Q_1. But, if this is a polluting industry, the external costs make the social marginal cost, SMC, higher. If these costs were reflected in the

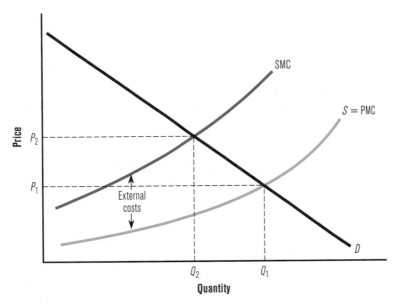

FIGURE 20-1. External Diseconomies
Polluters impose costs on others. If these external costs were reflected
in the firms' costs, the social marginal cost curve, SMC, would prevail,
the market price would be P_2, and output would be Q_2. But, because
the firms do not bear these costs, their private marginal cost curve,
PMC, is lower, so more, Q_1, of the polluting product is produced and
consumed.

market, the price would jump to P_2 and demand, and therefore output, would
be reduced to Q_2. As less of the offending product is grown or manufactured,
there would be less environmental degradation.

Sustainable Harvests

Most common property resources are **renewable resources:** They can regenerate themselves, to some extent if not fully, given time. The village common or
open rangeland reproduces grass each year. Fish breed new stocks, wild animals
replenish their herds, and forests reseed themselves. Air and water cleanse
themselves at least partially of pollutants through biological, chemical, or
mechanical transfers. It is possible to use renewable resources sustainably if
annual harvests do not exceed the annual growth of the stock. The difference
between the rate of harvest and the rate of growth is called the **rate of depletion.**
The faster resources can be replenished, the more they can be used, and the
faster the rate of economic growth that can be sustained indefinitely using the
resource.

For renewable resources, three questions arise: What is the maximum sustainable harvest? What is the economically optimal harvest? And what is the

danger of overexploiting the resource to the point of irretrievable loss or extinction? To begin to answer these questions, we explore a simple model of a fishery. Fish stocks are typically renewable within a relatively short period, so what we conclude about sustainable use of fisheries must apply with greater force to forests or the environment, which take longer to regenerate.

Before fishing begins, the stock of fish (in a lake or an ocean fishery) is large and cannot grow rapidly because its supply of food is limited. When fishing begins, the number of fish declines slightly and food becomes relatively more abundant. The fish can replenish their numbers more rapidly, and the sustainable catch rises. But, as the fishing effort increases, this process reaches a peak, after which the annual growth of the stock declines and so does the sustainable catch. If the fishing effort continues to grow, the fish stock may be so small or so scattered that reproduction cannot replace the catch at any level; this leads to extinction. The fishery model is an alternative way to describe the common resource problem. With the village common, we assumed that more entrants raise the cost for all. With the fishery, even if the costs of operating a boat are constant, the catch per boat declines, as does the fishers' revenues.

Fishing's total costs and revenue are shown in Figure 20–2, which gives total revenue for the fishery on the y axis and the total effort by all those fishing on the x axis. Assuming a constant price for fish, the total revenue curve, TR, first rises with effort, then peaks and begins to fall. At some point, overfishing depletes the stock so much that the fish cannot reproduce at the rate of extraction and become extinct. The total cost of fishing, TC, is assumed to rise linearly: Each boat puts to sea at the same cost, so total cost is simply the unit cost times the number of boats. Note that costs include the minimal profit necessary to keep those fishing in business.[2]

If fishing is done by small, independent operators who have open access, the level of effort increases as long as new entrants earn some net revenue over costs and necessary profit. Fishers earn net revenues up to E_1, the point where TC intersects TR. The last boat to enter the fishery just balances costs and revenues. Note that, because these are total revenue and cost curves, once the marginal boat is in the fishery, no net revenues are left for any of the fishing units. The external costs of exploiting the common fishery have caused this result.

Conceptually, a society wishing to maximize its economic welfare utilizes resources to the point where net present value is maximized for any activity. In the fishery case, that rule is equivalent to maximizing the net revenue to all fishers, which is the difference between total revenue and total cost.[3] We know from

---

[2]For a more complete discussion of the fisheries model, see Tom Tietenberg, *Environmental and Natural Resource Economics,* 5th ed. (New York: Addison-Wesley, 2000).

[3]Here we implicitly assume that the discount rate is 0, so that net benefits tomorrow have the same weight as those today. We relax that assumption in the next section.

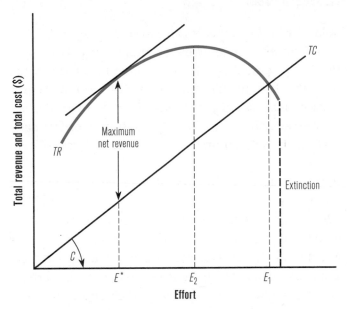

FIGURE 20-2. Fishery Economics
As the level of fishing efforts increases, sustainable total
revenue (*TR*) at first rises, then peaks at E_2, and begins to
fall, until the fish cannot reproduce fast enough to replace
the catch and extinction occurs. The total cost of effort is
TC, assuming each boat puts to sea at the same unit cost.
With open access, effort reaches E_1. The optimal outcome
would maximize the net revenue from the fisheries—the
difference between *TR* and *TC*—at E^*, where marginal
revenue (the slope of *TR*) equals marginal cost (the slope
of *TC*).

microeconomic principles that the maximum net revenue is achieved by equat-
ing the marginal cost and the marginal revenue. In Figure 20–2, the marginal
cost is the slope of the total cost line. The marginal revenue is the increase in the
catch for a unit increase in effort, valued at a constant price, which is the slope
of the TR curve at any point. The slope of TR is the same as the slope of TC at
level of effort E^*. This level of effort, maximizing net revenue, is achieved by a
fishing company that has exclusive rights to the fishery or a government that
regulated access by individual fishers.

Another term for *net revenue* in this case is **resource rent.** A *rent* is a return
to producers in excess of the return necessary to keep them in production.
Because the total cost curve in Figure 20–2 includes necessary profit, any revenue in excess of TC is a rent. Therefore, the rule to optimize the exploitation of
a natural resource (maximize net revenue) is equivalent to prescribing the maximization of resource rents. This is the rule a private owner of the fishery would
follow, just as the private owner of agricultural land would seek to maximize the
rental payments from tenant farmers.

Note that the optimal level of effort E^* is much lower than E_1, the effort expended by fishers with open access. The economically optimal effort also is less than that needed to achieve the biologically determined maximum catch E_2. So long as there is some cost to fishing effort, the economically optimal effort occurs where the TR curve has positive slope, to the left of E_2. It is not in society's interest to extract the maximum sustainable yield from the fishery or from any renewable resource; a society gains maximum welfare by extracting less than the maximum yield.

Can profit-maximizing fishers cause extinction? This could happen in an open-access fishery if the unit cost were so low that the TC line intersected the TR curve along the dashed line, where the stock had become too small to replace the annual catch. It also could happen at a lower level of effort, such as E_1, if environmental conditions caused a reduction in fishes' reproduction rates for a time, so that what had been a sustainable catch became unsustainable. Once overfishing has become apparent, fishers might adjust by reducing their effort. However, consider a lake fisher in Africa: Once he has a boat and net, his cost of fishing is only the opportunity cost of his time, which is probably quite low, while the benefits of withdrawal accrue not to him but to other fishers. Hence, there is little incentive to withdraw from the industry. The exhaustion of fisheries in the North Atlantic, in the Humboldt Current off the coast of Peru, and in some lakes in Africa shows that overfishing is not just a theoretical possibility.

Similar models can be used to describe the exploitation of other renewable resources. The application to game hunting is clear. Where hunting is effectively controlled, as is deer hunting in the United States or the hunting of large cats in many African countries, stocks can be maintained. Where hunting is less effectively controlled, extinction becomes a real possibility, because the cost of hunting is so low. For poachers of elephant and rhinoceros in Africa, costs are low, the value of tusks or horns is very high, and poachers place little value on sustaining stocks into the future. In addition to the clear harm to the animal populations themselves, the economic costs can be significant. The African tourist industry benefits from big game and tries to conserve it, but the poachers do not share in the benefits from this lucrative industry. The reduction in earnings from tourism slows economic growth.

Natural forests regenerate over much longer periods than fish or mammals, and second-growth forest is likely to be different from native stands. Tropical rain-forest species can take 70 years or so to grow to harvestable maturity, and the economic rotation of northern species such as Douglas fir are about the same length. Moreover, if harvesting greatly alters the habitat, regeneration can take longer or become impossible. In parts of Indonesia, inappropriate logging techniques allow the generation of a grass, called *alang-alang,* that has no economic value and prevents both reforestation and farming. In this case, forest land actually is laid to waste.

Environmental amenities, such as clean air and water, have similar properties. Waste can be dumped in them and water can be consumed without permanent impairment, so long as these uses do not exceed the capacity of air and water to cleanse themselves or rainfall to replace groundwater. But, at least until environmental regulation became common over the past two decades, air and water were common properties with virtually free access. The extreme air pollution of cities such as Los Angeles, Mexico City, Bangkok, and Jakarta testify to the overuse of this common resource. Industrial pollution of many waterways in North America, the "killing" of the Aral Sea in Uzbekistan by excessive irrigation that reduced its supply of river water (see Box 20–1), and the dumping of household waste in Asian rivers are examples of burdening water resources beyond their medium-term abilities to cleanse themselves. Private and public wells have seriously depleted aquifers in many places, sometimes to the point of permitting the incursion of seawater, which renders them permanently useless.

BOX 20-1 THE ARAL SEA—THE COST OF IGNORING AN ENVIRONMENTAL ASSET

The Aral Sea watershed now spans the national borders of six countries. Over the past 40 years the excessive water diversion for irrigation along the Amu Darya and Syr Darya Rivers, the two main tributaries of the Aral Sea, caused the volume of the sea to fall by 85 percent, and the sea level by 18 meters, exposing more than 40,000 square kilometers of saline seabed and heavily salinating the remaining water. Today the Aral is divided into a smaller, less saline sea in the north and a larger, saline sea in the south.

LOSS OF FISHERIES
Although Soviet planners realized that greater irrigation would lower the sea's water level, it was thought that the increment in agricultural output of the whole basin would yield significantly higher benefits than any damage caused. Not recognized, however, was that the excessive water withdrawal would make the remaining sea water so much saltier that it would become unfit for higher forms of aquatic life. The once fairly substantial fishing industry has now almost completely disappeared.

A DROP IN AGRICULTURAL OUTPUT
At the same time the combination of excessive irrigation and poor management of the irrigated land has led to waterlogging and increased the salinity of the soil in the entire basin. Almost one third of the irrigated land is now degraded. Effective management in these areas, with an emphasis on environmental assets, could have helped avert the current problems and the environmental degradation surrounding the sea.

It is no longer possible to maintain irrigation and cotton production at levels experienced during the Soviet period. The land degradation, combined with the reduced availability of appropriate agricultural inputs for production after the breakup of the Soviet Union, greatly reduced cotton production, both total yields and productivity per hectare. The original conversion of 7.9 million hectares of desert allowed a rise in Soviet cotton production from 2.2 million tons in 1940 to 9.1 million tons (at its peak) in 1980. Cotton production in Uzbekistan, which accounted for 70 percent of the total production (4 million tons) in 1960, peaked at 5.5 million tons in 1980. By 2000, it was down to 1960 levels, which may be more optimal and sustainable, when large-scale irrigation was beginning.

AN INCREASE IN HEALTH COSTS

The exposed seabed and polluted downstream waters also had high human and health costs. Winds carrying salt from the seabed contaminate lands adjacent to the sea, and increased chemical and pesticide use upstream pollutes drinking water. The people hardest hit live in Karakalpakstan, at the end of the Amu Darya Delta. Reliable data on health costs are hard to obtain. But, by some estimates, maternal deaths in Karakalpakstan in 1994 were 120 per 100,000 live births (twice the national average) and infant mortality was 60 per 1,000 live births (three times the national average). In the past 10–15 years kidney and liver diseases, especially cancers, have increased 30- to 40-fold, arthritic diseases 60-fold, and chronic bronchitis 30-fold.

FULL RESTORATION IS TOO COSTLY, BUT AVOIDANCE OF
FURTHER DECLINE IS NEEDED

It may be too late to fully reverse the damage, but it is possible to stabilize agricultural production in the basin and mitigate negative downstream effects. Restoring the sea to its former level in the next 50 years would mean suspending all irrigation and other water uses in the basin—impossible today, when even water reductions of 3–5 percent meet with strong local opposition from people highly dependent on irrigation. Although the rates of return on the incremental irrigation have not been very high, ranging from 13 percent in the best case scenario (high cotton prices and low irrigation costs) to minus 10 percent in the worst case (low cotton prices and high irrigation costs), better returns can be achieved and agricultural production in the region can be put on a more sustainable path. Estimates put potential efficiency gains through operational improvements, greater participation, and collective action in the use of irrigation water at 20–30 percent, at relatively low financial cost and without constraining production. With these improvements, the decline in sea level could be arrested and some aquatic life could be reintroduced.

Source: World Bank, *World Development Report 2003: Sustainable Development in a Dynamic World*.

The Value of Time

So far, we skirted the issue of time by discussing sustainable harvests as if all years were of equal value. That assumption is unrealistic and especially difficult to sustain in talking about exhaustible resources. We know from the discussion of discounting in Chapter 11 that benefits and costs realized in the future have less present value than those that are realized immediately. If the discount rate (the real interest rate) is r percent per year, then in any future year n, the present value placed on resource flows is $1/(1 + r)^n$.

The more productive is capital and the scarcer are savings that finance investment, the higher is the discount rate and the lower is the value placed on future benefits and costs. In developing countries, we expect real discount rates of 10 percent a year or so; at that rate, a benefit of $100 accruing 15 years from now is worth only $24 today ($100/1.10^{15} = $24). This indicates that people are not so willing to wait long for benefits from their investments. Generally speaking, as a country increases its average income, the lower is the likely return on new investments (because the capital stock has become larger), the more can be saved (because incomes are higher), and the more willing is the population to wait for future benefits; hence, the appropriate discount rate usually is lower. If a country's discount rate were 5 percent a year, the value of $100 of benefits received in 15 years would be $48.

To see how discounting affects the allocation of scarce resources over time, consider an oversimplified but instructive hypothetical example. Let us say that Zambia's copper deposits are expected to last two decades and the government is trying to decide how much copper to extract and export in each of the first and second decades. Zambia's output is large enough to affect the world price. For each decade, the higher the rate of extraction and the more Zambia exports, the lower it will drive the price of copper on world markets. If extraction costs are constant, then in each decade, the net revenue from copper exports (world price less mining cost) declines as more ore is extracted. How much should be mined in each decade?

The answer depends on the **marginal net benefit (MNB),** or the additional revenue net of additional costs from producing one more unit (mining one more ton of copper ore) in each period. The rule for maximizing net benefits over time is to equate the present value of the marginal net benefit for each period; that is, $MNB_1 = MNB_2/(1 + r)$. (In this example, r is the discount rate between decades, not years.) The discount factor $(1 + r)$ on the right-hand side of the equation indicates that Zambia places a lower value on benefits received in the second decade than in the first, since it generally can expect to earn higher income in the future if it can save and invest more today. If the marginal net benefit is higher in period 1 than the discounted benefit in period 2, it pays the country to mine more copper in period 1 and less in period 2, until the present value of the net benefits are equal at the margin. Note that the maximizing condition can be satisfied only if MNB_1 is less than the undiscounted value of MNB_2. Because the price and, therefore, MNB decline as output rises, net benefits are maximized over both decades if Zambia mines and exports more copper in the first decade than in the second.[4]

This highly simplified example has important implications for resource management. First, even though the current generation (which is doing the mining in the first decade) is concerned about the welfare of the next generation, it will consume some of the nonrenewable resource. Second, the current generation should consume more of the resource than the next generation so long as time has value and the discount rate is positive. This will be the case whenever profitable investments are to be made and savings are there to finance them, so that the next generation will have higher income than the current one. Third, the higher the discount rate and the higher the expected level of future income, the more should be exploited by the current generation.

This two-period example easily can be extended to the more realistic case of annual discounting over many years or generations, for both renewable and nonrenewable resources. Discounting applies with particular force to the harvesting and regeneration of natural forests. Assume that a private firm owns a large area of forest with secure rights long into the future and, for simplicity, ignore the nontimber products of the forest. The timber company has three choices. It can fell all the marketable timber now for immediate profit and then invest the proceeds in another business. It can wait for some future time to do the same thing. Or it can harvest the timber continuously over time. These three options are depicted in Figure 20–3.

Felling all trees now brings in the revenue, net of costs, shown in rectangle A. Because this is done in the present, no discounting is necessary. Waiting until some future time to harvest the entire forest yields the revenue in rectangle B. Because world timber prices have been rising at about 2 percent a year in real terms and the trees may produce more volume in the future, the company can expect to earn higher current revenues by waiting, as indicated by the dashed rectangle. But, to compare future revenues B with current revenues A, future revenues must be discounted; this yields the clear rectangle at B. The decision to harvest continuously is shown by option C, the solid line rising continuously over time as prices rise and trees grow; its discounted value is the area under the solid line.

If the discount rate exceeds the rate of price increase plus the rate of timber growth, the value of option A exceeds the discounted value of either B or C. Immediate harvest is likely to be the optimal choice for mature forests, with little or no potential timber growth. But if the forest is not mature, so that potential

---

[4]If Zambia's exports of copper were too small to affect world market prices, this result still would hold if the marginal cost of mining increased with the quantity mined in each period, as well it might.

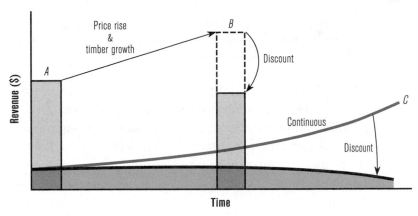

FIGURE 20-3. Discounted Value of Forest Harvest Options
Option *A* is to cut all trees now. Option *B* is to wait for benefits from tree growth and rising real prices, but discounting reduces the present value of future net revenues. Option *C* is a continuous harvest, made more attractive by rapid tree growth and price rises but less so by a high discount rate.

growth is substantial and if the discount rate is not very high, discounted net revenues from a future harvest at *B* or a continuous harvest, option *C*, may exceed those at *A*.

Any of these options can result in a sustainable harvest. Whether trees are logged all at once or continuously, the natural forest can regenerate itself if nearby forests can provide seeds and if the logged land is protected from encroachment by illegal loggers, fuelwood gatherers, herders, or farmers. For some forests, clear-cutting large tracts, as under options *A* and *B*, are compatible with sustainable harvesting. For others, selective and continuous logging is more sustainable. The period for complete regeneration can be long, however. In the Indonesian rain forest, it takes up to 70 years for trees to mature, although it may not be economically efficient to wait for full maturity.

Environmental protection has a similar time dimension. A firm choosing to clean up a degraded environment or stop all pollution faces some immediate costs, or the loss of current output, in favor of greater environmental benefits in the future. The most-serious deterrents to a firm taking such steps are that the benefits of clean air and water and more attractive scenery are external to the firm and most environmental benefits cannot be valued or marketed easily. But, leaving this issue aside, high discount rates, implying a low regard for the future compared to the present, also work against environmental protection or cleanup.

Higher discount rates is one reason that poorer countries may place less emphasis on environmental amenities than richer countries. High discount rates can help explain why Brazil and Malaysia cut down their tropical rain forests at unsustainable rates and why authorities in Mexico City and Bangkok appear less concerned about air pollution than authorities in Los Angeles.

POLICY SOLUTIONS

The market failures that lead to overexploitation of natural resources stem from external costs that are not borne by producers. Even in a well-functioning market economy, externalities require government intervention to make markets work better and to reach efficient market outcomes. Governments can bestow property rights on private users, regulate access to common resources, impose taxes that reflect external costs, and issue tradable access rights. We discuss each of these options in turn.

Property Rights

Common properties generate external costs because no one owns or controls the right to exploit them. For some resources, a simple solution would be to confer ownership, which economists call **property rights,** on a single individual or company. As long as the owner is a profit maximizer and sells output in a competitive market, the socially optimal outcome is achieved without further government intervention.[5] Nor does the owner have to be the producer to achieve optimal resource use. The owner who rents the resource to some of the same producers who previously had common property access maximizes profit by charging rents that limit access and production to the optimal level.

Property rights, to be effective, must be exclusive and well defined, leaving no doubt to the owners and possible competing claimants about what has been conferred and to whom. Rights need to be secure, so that the risk of loss through legal challenge or expropriation is reduced and enforceable through the judicial system. Ownership must be valid over a long-enough horizon that the owners have a stake in the long-term, sustainable exploitation of the resource. Longevity converts the resource into an asset for the producer, who can reap the benefits from investments in improving and sustaining its productivity. And the rights must be transferable, so the owner can realize the benefits of the resource asset by selling the property at any time.[6]

For some resources, such as forests, rangeland, or mineral deposits, the

---

[5]If the owner is a monopolist in the product market, output is below, and the price above, the social optimum. With the possible exception of a few minerals such as diamonds, markets for the products of common resources are fairly competitive (i.e., firms face elastic demand), especially when close substitutes are considered.

[6]Theodore Panayotou, *Green Markets: The Economics of Sustainable Development* (San Francisco: ICS Press, 1993), 35–37.

application of property rights is straightforward. The resource is a tangible property and exclusive ownership is enforceable. The government can privatize the asset by granting or selling rights to private producers. If the right is granted, then the producer gains all the resource rents. If it is sold for a fixed fee, government shares part of the rent. Alternatively, if the property right is auctioned, potential owners bid up the price to the point where they still can earn a reasonable profit on their investment of capital and labor but have forgone most or all the resource rents, which then are captured by the government. Such auction systems now commonly are employed in a few developing and transitional economies, including Malaysia and Romania. Short-run revenue maximization does not necessarily translate into long-run maximization of resource rents, however, if the structure of concession agreements does not promote use of logging methods that ensure regeneration. Concessions to exploit the tropical rain forest are common in Indonesia and Malaysia, although the terms are badly flawed and do not result in optimal regeneration. Most timberland in the United States is privately owned and harvested and replanted on a sustainable basis, although the result often is plantations of uniform species rather than regenerated natural forest.

Property rights can be held by communities. If local populations have traditional access to the forest, for example, and can enforce this right, it is in their interest to achieve optimal output because they benefit from the resulting rents. The struggle over property rights in Brazil's Amazon is in part a conflict between local communities that traditionally have exploited the rain forest sustainably (though perhaps not optimally) and modern companies whose incentives are to overexploit this resource. In Kenya, county councils have been given property rights to some of the game parks that attract international tourists in large numbers; the entry fees charged give local governments an incentive to preserve these assets against poaching and grazing by cattle. Sometimes, cooperation must extend across borders, as with the Nile Basin Initiative, in which ten governments work cooperatively together to manage the common resource of the Nile River basin (see Box 20–2).

For some common property resources, however, it is difficult (and in some cases impossible) to convey property rights as these usually are understood. Both law and ease of access make it impractical to own an ocean and difficult (although not impossible) to own a lake fishery. Nor can a company own the air and water that accommodate its waste, because the polluter cannot easily exclude other users and therefore cannot charge for access to clean air and water. Governments sometimes can create partial property rights in these circumstances by legislating, granting, and enforcing quotas, access permits, licenses to operate, and other legal instruments that give some agents the right to fish, harvest, pollute, or otherwise use a common resource.

BOX 20-2 THE NILE BASIN INITIATIVE

An extraordinary example of cooperation in the management of international river basins is evolving in the Nile River Basin. The Nile, at almost 7,000 kilometers, is the world's longest river. The basin covers 3 million square kilometers and is shared by ten countries: Burundi, the Democratic Republic of the Congo, Egypt, Eritrea, Ethiopia, Kenya, Rwanda, Sudan, Tanzania, and Uganda. Tensions, some ancient, arise because nearby populations rely to a greater or lesser extent on the waters of the Nile for their basic needs and economic growth. For some, the waters of the Nile are perceived as central to their survival.

The countries of the basin are characterized by extreme poverty, widespread conflict, and increasing water scarcity in the face of growing water demands. This instability compounds the challenges of economic growth in the region, as does a growing scarcity of water relative to the basin's burgeoning population. About 150 million people live in the basin today, with growing water demand per capita. More than 300 million people are projected to be living in the basin in 25 years. The pressures on scarce water resources will be very great.

The countries of the Nile have made a conscious decision to use the river as a force to unify and integrate rather than divide and fragment the region, committing themselves to cooperation. Together they launched the Nile Basin Initiative, led by a Council of Ministers of Water Affairs of the Nile Basin, with the support of a Technical Advisory Committee, and a Secretariat in Entebbe, Uganda. The

Government Regulation

As an alternative to conveying private property rights, governments themselves can act as the owners of common resources and directly regulate their use. Governments can limit the quantity of a hunter's kill, a fisher's catch, a logger's haul, a rancher's herd, or a polluter's emissions. And they can regulate the kinds of equipment that can or must be used: Some kinds of fishing nets, boats, or navigation equipment have been banned; hunters may be restricted in their choice of weapons; polluters are required to install equipment that scrubs gas emissions and treats wastewater.

Quantity regulations raise two issues. First, how do the regulators know the optimal levels of access and output? If property rights can be conveyed, efficient outcomes are approached through market forces and no government judgments are needed. But if regulation replaces the market, regulators need to estimate the characteristics of both producers' costs and users' demand for the products of a common resource. To get a sense of these information require-

initiative is a regional partnership within which the countries of the Nile Basin united in common pursuit of the sustainable development and management of the Nile waters. Its Strategic Action Program is guided by a shared vision "to achieve sustainable socioeconomic development through the equitable utilization of, and benefit from, the common Nile Basin water resources." The program includes basinwide projects to lay the foundation for joint action, and two sub-basin programs of cooperative investments that will promote poverty alleviation, growth, and better environmental management. The initiative enjoys the strong support of many donor partners through an International Consortium for Cooperation on the Nile, chaired by the World Bank.

The Nile waters embody both potential for conflict and potential for mutual gain. Unilateral water development strategies in the basin could lead to serious degradation of the river system and greatly increase tensions among riparians. But cooperative development and management of the Nile waters in sustainable ways could increase total river flows and economic benefits, generating opportunities for "win-win" gains that can be shared among the riparians. The Initiative provides an institutional framework to promote this cooperation, built on strong riparian ownership and shared purpose and supported by the international community. Cooperative water resources management might also serve as a catalyst for greater regional integration beyond the river, with benefits far exceeding those from the river itself.

Source: World Bank, *World Development Report 2003: Sustainable Development in a Dynamic World.*

ments, consider the regulation of air pollution.[7] The external costs of pollution are manifest in the reduced welfare of others: poor health, unsightly environment, lower property values, fewer and more expensive recreational possibilities, and possibly reduced productivity and income. If these costs could be measured, they would be depicted by a curve such as MEC in Figure 20–4, which shows the marginal external cost of pollution (measured along the horizontal axis). Those that believe that the costs of pollution are higher than normally recognized or who put a high premium on reducing pollution argue, in effect, that the MEC curve should be shifted up. Wherever it is located, any reduction in pollution (a movement to the left on the horizontal axis) means a reduction in the cost to society from pollution or, equivalently, an increase in the marginal external benefit of abatement.

[7]This approach to the economies of pollution abatement is based on the treatment by David W. Pearce and R. Kerry Turner, *Economics of Natural Resources and the Environment* (Baltimore: Johns Hopkins Press, 1990), Chapters 4–7.

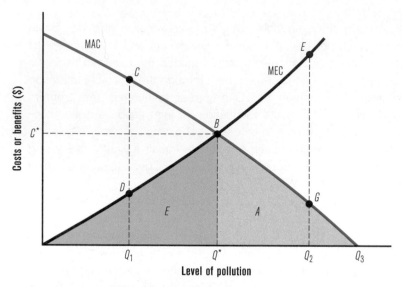

FIGURE 20-4. Optimal Level of Pollution
The marginal external cost of pollutants, borne by the population, is given by MEC; the marginal cost of abatement, borne by the firm, is MAC. The total cost to society (the area E plus A) is minimized and pollution is optimal at Q^*, where MEC = MAC.

However, there is a cost to abating pollution. The polluting firm, say, a petrochemical plant, can reduce its effluents either by changing its production process, installing abatement equipment such as gas scrubbers and water treatment plants, or reducing output. Schedule MAC traces these marginal abatement costs. At any point along MAC, the cost shown is that of the lowest-cost method of abatement. Moving from right (high pollution) to left (lower pollution), MAC rises because it becomes increasingly costly to clean up air or water the stricter are the standards or the lower the level of contamination. It is important to recognize that these costs of abatement, although borne by the petrochemical firm, also are costs to society because they involve either less consumption of petrochemicals or savings spent on abatement that otherwise might have been spent on investment in other goods or services people want. These abatement costs thus have equal weight to the benefits gained by reducing pollution.

Society's (and government's) aim should be to minimize the combined costs of pollution and its abatement. This is achieved at Q^* in Figure 20–4, where MEC = MAC. At this point $Q_3 - Q^*$ of pollution has been abated (assuming for convenience that Q_3 is the maximum amount of pollution), and Q^* of pollution remains. Because these are marginal cost curves, the total external cost of pollution is the area E under MEC from 0 to Q^*. And the total cost or abatement is given by the shaded area A under the MAC curve between Q^* and Q_3. With less pollution, such as Q_1, the marginal abatement cost exceeds the marginal external cost of pollu-

TABLE 20-1. Costs of Environmental Degradation in Asia

| COUNTRY | FORM OF DAMAGE | YEAR | ANNUAL COST | |
			$ MILLION	% GNP
China	Soil erosion, deforestation, water shortage, wetland destruction	1990	13,900–26,000	3.8–7.3
	Health and productivity losses from cities' urban pollution	1990	6,300–9,300	1.7–2.5
	General environmental degradation and pollution	1989	31,000	8.5
Indonesia	Health effects of particulates and lead in Jakarta	1989	2,164	2
Pakistan	Health effects of air and water pollution and productivity losses from deforestation and erosion	Early 1990s	1,700	3.3
Philippines	Health and productivity losses from water and air pollution in Manila vicinity	Early 1990s	335–410	0.8–1.0
Thailand	Health effects of particulates and lead	1989	1,602	

Source: Asian Development Bank, *Emerging Asia: Changes and Challenges.*

tion and the total cost of additional abatement, the area of the trapezoid Q_1Q^*BC, exceeds the net gain from reduced pollution, Q_1Q^*BD. If more pollution is permitted, such as Q_2, the additional external cost, Q^*Q_2EB, exceeds the reduced cost of abatement, Q^*Q_2GB.

Therefore, society is better off with some pollution than with none, because abating the last unit of pollution is expensive relative to its benefits. Similarly, society gains from some exploitation of natural resources, even nonrenewable ones. But how do the regulators, who wish to achieve this optimal level of pollution know what it is? To find Q^*, they have to know all the external costs of pollution, as a function of the levels of contaminants in the air, water, and soil. The costs in some cases are substantial. Soil erosion reduces economic output by an estimated 0.5–1.5 percent per year in Costa Rica, Malawi, Mali, and Mexico.[8] Various studies have estimated that the economic costs of environmental degradation in countries in Asia range from 1 to 9 percent of GDP (Table 20–1). Particulates and lead emissions in Jakarta, Indonesia, cause damage estimated to be up to 2 percent of GDP. In Pakistan, damage from air and water pollution combined with productivity losses from deforestation and soil erosion amount to more than 3 percent of GDP. And the costs of environmental degradation and pollution in China may be the equivalent of a staggering 8.5 percent of GDP.[9]

[8]*World Development Report 1992: Development and the Environment,* p. 56.
[9]These findings are summarized in the Asian Development Bank study, *Emerging Asia: Changes and Challenges* (Manila: ADB, 1997), p. 223.

In addition to these estimates of direct economic costs, finding Q^* requires having a method for estimating the values people place on environmental amenities such as clean air, water, and soil. Survey and other methods are being developed to measure such valuations, but these still are experimental and beyond the scope of governments in many developing countries.[10] Finally, the regulators need to know the costs of abatement. Yet firms subject to regulation have an incentive to overstate these costs in the hope of being allowed to emit more pollutants and avoid abatement costs.

In the absence of such knowledge, regulators must set arbitrary standards based on studies estimating the impact of pollutants on human health, animal survival, forest dieback (from acid rain) and regeneration, and presumed climate changes. Because of the large uncertainty in such estimates and the conflicting objectives of environmental policy, these standards become political issues, subject to contention by interest groups speaking for the environment, the public, industry, and developers. These policy struggles, the establishment of compliance staffs in both the government and polluting firms, and the ensuing lawsuits all add significant costs to the imposition of environmental standards and so reduce the gains to society. In countries with widespread corruption and weak legal institutions, polluting industrialists are likely to use their financial and political muscle to either weaken environmental regulations or simply ignore them.

The second question raised by regulation is its efficiency compared to other methods. Governments have imposed many different methods for restricting access to common resources. They have specified hours or days of access to fisheries; completely barred access to some forests or fisheries; set quotas for individual hunters, loggers, and fishers; limited the specific levels of pollution for each plant in a region; prohibited particularly efficient equipment such as gill nets or even, in Alaska for a time, motorized boats;[11] mandated the use of abatement equipment; and shut off electricity to conserve water in hydroelectric sites. These methods may get the economy closer to the optimal rate of use but are unlikely to achieve it exactly. Even if they did, the outcome would not be optimal for society because the controls themselves impose costs on producers and consumers.

In Figure 20–4, regulators might achieve output Q^* by requiring certain equipment for each plant or setting output quotas for each producer. But, while the MAC curve assumes that each polluter makes the most-efficient choice of technique for abating pollution, regulators are unlikely to know the costs of each option and have little incentive to find the most-efficient way to reduce

---

[10]Paul R. Portney, "The Contingent Valuation Debate: Why Economists Should Care," *Journal of Economic Perspectives* 8, no. 4 (Fall 1994), 3–17.

[11]Tietenberg, *Environmental and Natural Resource Economics*, 4th ed., p. 271.

emissions. So their required method of achieving Q^* is likely to raise the MAC schedule above its minimum and unnecessarily raise the costs borne by society. In controlling the fisheries depicted in Figure 20–2, regulators might achieve optimal catch E^* by enforcing certain practices or prohibiting certain equipment, and so raise the cost of fishing to each entrant. But the higher costs dissipate the rents available from the optimum level of effort, and these rents no longer are available to society for other uses.[12]

Taxation

A third option is that, in principle, the government also could achieve optimal rates of resource use by imposing taxes that reduce the incentive for producers to use common properties or manufacture polluting products.[13] A tax might be imposed on output that represents the external costs of production, so that the private marginal cost schedule shifts up to equal the social marginal cost schedule.[14] This might take the form of a tax on each ton of steel or petrochemicals at a rate representing the external cost of pollution or a tax on gasoline to cover the costs of both pollution and traffic congestion. A tax, equal to the maximum resource rent, could be levied on the level of effort or quantity harvested by fishers or foresters, so that their private costs would induce them collectively to take the optimal harvest.[15]

If the tax is on output or level of effort, the incentive is to reduce production of the good with external costs. If the tax can be levied on the externality itself, there is an additional incentive to invest in reducing external costs. For example, a tax on the quantity of pollutants would give petrochemical plants an incentive to abate pollution, because the tax then is reduced. Malaysia had success with emissions fees on its palm oil industry (see the Box 20–3). China introduced emissions fees on industrial and urban wastewater, air pollution, and solid waste. Several of the transitional economies in Central and Eastern Europe (including Poland, Estonia, Latvia, Russia, Romania, and Bulgaria) experimented with a range of pollution charges, based largely on modifying systems that were in place before the breakup of the Soviet Union in 1989.[16] In general, however, attempts to tax pollutants have had limited success (and even less success in high-income countries

[12]Tietenberg, *Environmental and Natural Resource Economics*, 4th ed., p. 270.

[13]See Gunnar Eskeland and Shantayanan Devarajan, *Taxing Bads by Taxing Goods: Pollution Control with Presumptive Charges* (Washington, DC: World Bank, 1996).

[14]In Figure 20–1, the tax would shift the PMC schedule up to coincide with the SMC schedule.

[15]In Figure 20–2, a tax equal to the maximum resource rent would move the cost schedule up to TC' and induce fishers to expend the optimum effort E^*.

[16]See Robert Bohm, Chazhong Ge, Milton Rusell, Jinnan Wang, and Jintian Yang, "Environmental Taxes: China's Bold New Initiative," *Environment* 40, no. 7 (September 1998); and Randall Bluffstone and Bruce A. Larson, eds., *Controlling Pollution in Transition Economies* (Cheltenham, UK: Edward Elgar, 1997).

BOX 20-3   REDUCING WATER POLLUTION FROM
PALM OIL MILLS IN MALAYSIA

Between 1970 and 1989, Malaysia's output of palm oil, a major export, grew 12-fold. Unfortunately, the processing of palm oil in rural mills generates 2.5 tons of wastewater for every ton of crude palm oil produced. By the late 1970s, effluents from the mills had severely polluted over 40 rivers in Malaysia, mainly by depleting their oxygen. Pollution killed freshwater fish, endangered mangroves on the coast that are essential for traditional marine fisheries, contaminated the major source of drinking water for many rural Malays, and emitted a stench that made several villages uninhabitable.

Water pollution became so serious that, in 1974, the government passed the Environmental Quality Act and in 1975 established the Department of the Environment (DOE). In 1977, the DOE announced standards for the quality of effluents from palm oil mills that were to become increasingly stringent over time. To provide the reluctant mills with incentives to comply, the DOE established a two-part licensing fee with a constant charge per unit of effluent plus an excess fee that varied with the oxygen-depleting potential of the discharge. Therefore the mills could choose their least-cost option: Either pay the costs of reducing and treating their effluent or pay the higher fees for discharging waste that exceeded the environmental quality standard.

The industry responded by developing and installing improved treatment technologies; by developing commercial products, such as fertilizer and animal feed, from their waste products; and by recovering methane that could be used to generate electricity. Over time, the economic incentives became less important as inflation eroded their value, and direct controls became more important. Nevertheless, the market-oriented regime set in motion a sharp reversal of polluting practices. By 1989, even though palm oil production had reached an all-time high, three out of four mills complied with the stringent sixth-generation standards and the oxygen-depleting potential of emitted waste was only 1 percent its mid-1970s level.

Source: Jeffrey R. Vincent, "Reducing Effluent while Raising Affluence," Harvard Institute for International Development, March 1993.

than in developing and transitional economies). Monitoring is difficult (and expensive), charge rates generally are set too low, and tax avoidance can be relatively easy. An alternative might be to tax the polluting product but to reduce or eliminate the tax if pollution abatement equipment is in operation.

Taxes that internalize external costs have two important advantages over regulation. First, they allow the producer to choose the method of reducing access to a common resource, so that rents are not dissipated in wasteful expenditures forced by regulators. The cost savings with this flexibility can be substantial. Studies in the United States comparing the costs of water pollution abatement indicate that "command and control" approaches with strict regulation can cost up to three times more than the alternative least-cost method of achieving the same goal. For air pollution, command and control approaches have been found to cost from 2 to 22 times more than the least-cost alternative.[17] An optimal tax, however, requires the same information as optimal regulation: in the case of pollution, knowledge of the relation between pollution and output, the cost of abatement, and the external costs to the population. However, given a consensus that pollution is too great or a common resource is being overexploited, the government can move in the right direction by imposing an initial tax, observing outcomes, and adjusting the tax rate if necessary.

Second, taxes can generate substantial revenues for the government. By some estimates, carbon taxes (mainly on gasoline) can contribute an estimated 2–8 percent to government revenues in many countries. In Indonesia, estimates in the mid-1990s suggested that increasing stumpage fees on logging concessions could have added an estimated 6–8 percent to government revenues, pollution charges for the greater Jakarta area could have generated 1–2 percent, and congestion charges on urban roads could have added another 2–3 percent to government revenues.[18] These kinds of revenues can be used to fund environmental programs or in other ways to compensate citizens for the harm caused by pollution and other environmental degradation.

Marketable Permits

A fourth intervention is to create a property right where none exists by issuing **marketable permits,** granting the holders the right to harvest a common resource up to a given limit or giving producers a license to pollute the environment up to specified amounts. Although environmentalists sometimes scoff at the notion of a "right" to pollute or exploit resources, this idea recognizes that zero pollution is usually not optimal because of the costs involved in achieving that goal. These permits may be the most-efficient way to reduce pollution and resource overuse, and this approach has been a major innovation of the past decade. The U.S. sulfur dioxide reduction scheme relies on tradable rights, and both Iceland and New Zealand revived fishing stocks by assigning fishing rights at a sustainable level and allowing fishers to trade their quotas freely.

---

[17]These estimates are summarized in Tietenberg, *Environmental and Natural Resource Economics,* 5th ed., 372 and 453.

[18]The figures are from Theodore Panayotou, *Instruments of Change: Motivating and Financing Sustainable Development* (London: Earthscan, 1998).

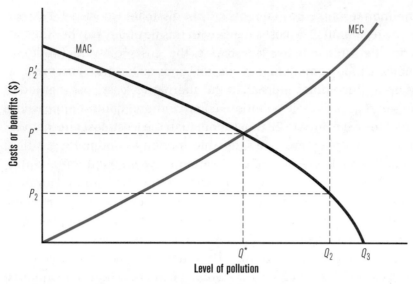

FIGURE 20-5. Marketable Permits to Pollute
The MAC schedule shows the demand for pollution rights. If rights are
issued to pollute up to Q_2, these are worth P_2 to polluters, but the public
places a value of P_2' on reducing pollution. This could be the basis for a
bargain to reduce pollution to the optimal level Q^*.

Figure 20–5 shows how a pollution permit works.[19] The MAC and MEC
curves are copied from Figure 20–4. Say that the government knows the optimal
level of pollution and auctions off emissions permits totaling Q^*. Any firm polluting without a permit, if detected, would be fined or shut down. (Thus, permits have the same enforcement requirements as regulations or taxes.) If MAC
represents the cost of pollution abatement for all firms in the market, they
would bid up the price of permits to P^*. The MAC schedule (moving from right
to left) shows that firms can reduce pollution from Q_3 to Q^* at costs less than P^*.
Additional reductions in pollution would cost more than P^*. Therefore, the MAC
schedule is the demand curve for permits. Either the government can issue a
given number and observe the auction price paid for them or it can set a price
and issue whatever number of permits is demanded by polluters.

What if the government overshoots and either issues Q_2 permits or offers
permits at a price P_2? There would be more pollution than the public would like,
as indicated by the MEC schedule; with Q_2 permits, the public's marginal cost
due to pollution is P_2'. If there is an effective market for permits, those that suffer
from pollution could offer to buy permits from producers. At first, they should be
willing to offer a price of P_2', the marginal benefit to them of less pollution. This

---

[19]This figure is adapted from Pearce and Turner, *Economics of Natural Resources,* 110–13; and
Tietenberg, *Environmental and Natural Resource Economics,* 4th ed., 319–20.

would be more than enough to induce a polluter to sell a permit and reduce emissions at a cost of only P_2. Such bargains would continue, until the public's benefits, given by MEC, just equaled the polluters costs, MAC, which would occur at the optimum level of pollution Q^*, where permits would sell for P^*.

Economist Robert Coase theorized that this is precisely what could happen, even in the absence of government-issued permits.[20] But the requirements of the Coase theorem are stringent and probably not often met in practice. Some countries, such as Indonesia, have had some success with informal regulation to reduce pollution, based largely on making polluters more aware of the pollution they are generating and providing positive publicity to those that reduce their emissions.[21] But to actually move to the optimum level of pollution Q^*, the suffering public would have to incur the costs of organizing to make their bargaining power effective and would have to mobilize funds to match the benefits they would gain from reduced pollution. But, as many of those benefits have no market price (such as improved health, better recreational facilities, or more attractive scenery), it would be difficult to convert them into cash that could compensate polluters. And, in poor societies or among the poor in any country, it seems highly unlikely that the demand for an improved environment could be made effective in a permits market.

It is possible that environmental groups could overcome these obstacles and behave as Coase predicted. They could purchase and then withdraw tradable emission permits from the market. Conservation groups have purchased fishing rights in New Zealand and other countries to reduce the size of the overall catch. And the programs of the Nature Conservancy and other groups to purchase rainforest land in tropical countries, while using a different mechanism, has the same effect of expressing consumer interests in an improved environment through the market.[22]

Even if the market between polluters and suffers is not fully effective, the market among polluters can be highly effective in minimizing the costs of meeting any government-imposed standard for emissions or other limitations to resource use. Assume that the government issues an arbitrary quantity, Q_p, of permits to pollute that would reduce emissions below their current level and

[20]Ronald Coase, "The Problem of Social Cost," *Journal of Law and Economics* 3 (October 1960), 1–44.

[21]Sheoli Pargal and David Wheeler, "Informal Regulation of Industrial Pollution in Developing Countries: Evidence from Indonesia," *Journal of Political Economy* 104, no. 6 (December 1996), 1314–27; Shakeb Afsah and Jeffrey Vincent, "Putting Pressure on Polluters: Indonesia's PROPER Program," available at www.worldbank,org/nipr/work-paper/vincent/index.htm (February 1997).

[22]In one version of this transaction, an environmental group buys some of the host country's debt from disappointed bondholders on the international market, usually at a heavy discount, then agrees not to seek repayment of the loans from the host government. In return, the host country sets aside a negotiated area of rain forest to be preserved as a national park. These are called *debt-for-nature swaps*.

divides these among existing firms by any method, for example, in proportion to their output. Firm 1, with old technology, finds it very costly to reduce its emissions to the new standard represented by the permits. Firm 2, built recently, is capable of reducing its emissions below the level of its permits at low cost. These differences provide the basis for a bargain between the two firms that would benefit society: Firm 2 does more of the abatement (since it can do so at a lower cost), and Firm 1 pays them to do it. Firm 2 sells some of its permits to pollute to Firm 1 at a price above its marginal abatement cost but below the MAC of Firm 1. Both firms are better off: Firm 2 earned revenue in excess of its costs of abatement while Firm 1 paid less than it would have to reduce its pollution. The public also is better off because the reduced emission standard has been met, but at a lower cost than would have been incurred had the initial allocation of permits been enforced.

This powerful result is quite general. It suggests that, whenever a limitation is to be imposed on a private activity, the creation of a marketable property right that firms can buy from and sell to each other can achieve an efficient outcome with minimal government intervention. For that reason, economists recommend that traditional property rights to natural resources, such as forest concessions or licenses to fish and hunt, should be marketable. The use of marketable permits is in its infancy. Considerable experience has been gained in the United States with pollution permits issued to public utilities. The sulfur allowance program in the United States allows utility companies to buy and sell from each other the rights to emit sulfur oxides and penalizes companies that emit more than authorized by their holdings of allowances.[23] In developing and transitional economies, where policy dependence on market forces is a more-recent phenomenon, marketable permits hardly have been tried (although some pilot programs have been introduced in Kazakhstan and Poland[24]) but hold promise for the future if the problems of enforcement can be overcome.

POLICY FAILURES

Although some government intervention is necessary to correct for the market failures associated with natural resources, it is equally true that, all over the world, government policies frequently contribute to wasteful use of resources and the degradation of the environment. Too much intervention or intervention

---

[23] For a brief description of this program, see Tietenberg, *Environmental and Natural Resource Economics*, 5th ed., 396–98.

[24] Jeffrey Vincent and Scott Farrow, "A Survey of Pollution Charge Systems and Key Issues in Policy Design," in Randall Bluffstone and Bruce A. Larson, eds., *Controlling Pollution in Transition Economies* (Cheltenham, UK: Edward Elgar, 1997).

BOX 20-4 SUBSIDIZED DEFORESTATION OF THE AMAZON

The government of Brazil, wishing to promote development in the Amazon, subsidized ranchers to cut down the vast rain forest. Each year throughout the 1970s, 3,000 to 4,000 square miles of the Amazon were deforested, and almost a quarter of the Amazonian state of Rondonia was converted from rain forest to pasture from 1970 to 1985. Not only does pastureland replace the rain forest, but rain forest occupations provided more jobs than the ranching that replaced them. Despite this, the government provided new ranchers with 15-year tax holidays, investment tax credits, exemptions from export taxes and import duties, and loans with interest substantially below market rates. Although a typical subsidized investment was estimated to yield a loss to the economy equivalent to 55 percent of the initial investment, a private rancher was able to earn a return, due to subsidies, equivalent to 250 percent on the amount invested.

Source: Panayotou, *Green Markets*, 14–15.

of the wrong kind can be just as costly as too little intervention. We have seen that, when production has external costs, one approach is to internalize those costs by raising production costs through taxing output or granting marketable property rights. But, instead, governments commonly subsidize or otherwise reduce the costs the production of commodities that degrade natural resources and often compromise property rights in ways that encourage rapacious exploitation. Examples are not hard to find.

Forestry policy has been especially destructive in many tropical countries. For many years Brazil subsidized ranching and other activities that encroached on the Amazon rain forest (see Box 20–4). In the 1990s, Indonesia granted logging concessions for only 20 years with no clearly defined conditions for renewal, which encouraged wasteful logging practices because regeneration times are 70 years. It charged no fees for the concessions, discouraged transfers of the concessions, imposed inadequate taxes and fees that did not encourage conservation, and was ineffective in policing conservation regulations. Thailand's policies were so wanton that its rain forest has all but disappeared, and the Philippines is on the same path.

Trade policy has been equally destructive. Ghana, Indonesia, and Malaysia, for example, placed bans on log exports as a means of promoting wood-processing industries. Export bans drive down the domestic price of tropical hardwood and so make it very profitable for sawmills and plywood mills to purchase logs and export semifinished products. But these industries are usually

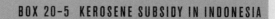

BOX 20-5 KEROSENE SUBSIDY IN INDONESIA

From 1972 to 1984, the government of Indonesia heavily subsidized the consumption of kerosene and other fuels. The kerosene subsidy was justified as an aid to poor rural dwellers, who were thought to use it for cooking, and as a disincentive to harvest fuelwood. The cutting of fuelwood was denuding mountain slopes and causing soil erosion on Java, Indonesia's most densely populated island. But research subsequently discovered that rural families used kerosene predominantly for lighting, not for cooking, so that only about 50,000 acres of forest land was protected each year by the subsidy at a cost of almost $200,000 a year per acre. Replanting programs, in contrast, cost only $1,000 per acre. Moreover, most kerosene turned out to be consumed by the wealthy, not the poor. And the low price of kerosene made it necessary to subsidize diesel fuel as well, because the two fuels could be partially substituted in truck engines, and this caused greater environmental damage. Recognizing the costs of this policy, the government sharply reduced its subsidy on kerosene and other fuels in the mid-1990s. However, large subsidies reemerged following the 1997 Asian financial crisis.

Source: Malcolm Gillis, "Indonesia: Public Policies, Resource Management and the Tropical Forest," in Repetto and Gillis, *Public Policy and the Misuse of Forest Resources.*

inefficient and consume resource rents through higher production costs. Because timber companies cannot export tropical hardwoods, such as ebony and mahogany, as logs, these valuable species are used along with low-value timber to make inexpensive products, such as plywood sent to Japan to make forms for pouring cement. The role of self-imposed log export bans in destroying rain forests should be a warning to northern countries that want to preserve tropical forests by imposing their own import bans on these logs.[25]

Energy pricing is another common policy failure. In oil-rich countries like Nigeria and Venezuela, energy has been kept cheap in an attempt to stimulate industrialization and diversification, and Indonesia subsidized kerosene ostensibly to help the rural poor (see Box 20–5). This policy has multiple adverse effects. It encourages wasteful domestic consumption and reduces the country's petroleum and gas reserves and its export-earning potential. It encourages the use of cars and minibuses and so adds to congestion. Cheap energy promotes

[25]On forest policies, see Robert Repetto and Malcolm Gillis, eds., *Public Policies and the Misuse of Forest Resources* (Cambridge: Cambridge University Press, 1988); and Jeffrey Vincent, "The Tropical Timber Trade and Sustainable Development," *Science* 256 (1992), 1651–55.

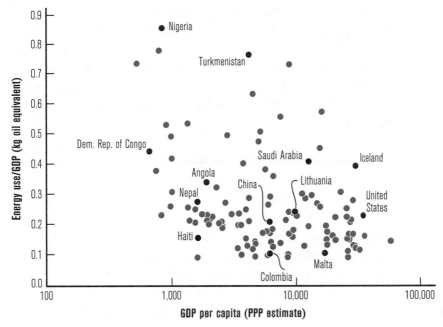

FIGURE 20-6. Energy Use and Income
Energy use varies widely across countries, even among those with similar levels
of income. Some countries have especially high energy use, in some cases,
because of distorted prices and subsidized energy.
Source: World Bank, *World Development Indicators.*

industry ill-suited to the country's endowments. Firms and consumers have little incentive to adopt energy-saving technology. Because burning oil is an
important source of air pollution, all these overuses contribute to environmental degradation. Similarly, some oil importers, such as Egypt, Argentina, China,
and India, subsidized petroleum products by as much as 50 percent of the world
price and so encouraged imports they cannot afford, industries that cannot
compete in world markets, and environmental degradation that market pricing
would have discouraged.[26]

Figure 20–6 shows commercial energy use per unit of GDP for almost 90
countries. The variance, even among poor countries, is notable. Among the high
energy users, mistaken energy policies are not entirely to blame but probably
contributed in countries like Zambia, India, Argentina, South Africa, and
Venezuela, where market prices have been distorted. Even today, Venezuela
prices gasoline at less than 25 U.S. cents a gallon. The consequences of price
distortions are particularly notable in former communist countries (e.g., China,
Poland, Bulgaria, Hungary, and Romania), where markets played very little role

[26]Bjorn Larsen and Anwar Shah, "World Fossil Fuel Subsidies and Global Carbon Emissions,"
Working Paper WPS 1002, World Bank, Washington, DC, October 1992, especially Chart 1.

in resource allocation until the 1990s. Among industrial countries, Norway, Canada, and Finland stand out as particularly high users of energy, a result of their cold climate. The United States uses more total energy than any other country and is among the highest in terms of energy consumption per person. However, energy consumption in the United States is not especially high relative to the total value of production, partly because energy is priced at or above world market levels.

Infrastructure investment is a third area of widespread policy failure. In forestry and energy pricing, governments typically underprice the resource and fail to force private operators to account for external costs. In infrastructure investment, governments often create new external costs and fail to account for them in project planning. Environmental groups have focused much of their ire on investments in power dams, irrigation and flood control systems, roads, and power plants that damage their environments. Dams that flood their upstream areas displace local populations, who sometimes do not fare as well in new locations, and destroy natural habitat. Egypt's huge Aswan Dam controls the floodwaters of the Nile. But prior to the dam, those floodwaters had beneficial effects, replenishing soil and leaching out unwanted salts, so the dam may have reduced agricultural productivity over the long run. This does not mean that dams are necessarily bad ideas but rather the full costs are not always recognized up front and incorporated into prices. Irrigation schemes in Africa at times have encouraged diseases such as schistosomiasis and river blindness (but in other cases have been enormously beneficial in supporting food production). Roads into the rain forest in Brazil and elsewhere not only destroy habitat along the right of way but encourage overexploitation of the forest and surroundings.

A complete project analysis, as discussed in Chapter 11, to some extent, can incorporate the external costs of large projects. The commercial value of land, forests, and inland fisheries can be calculated and added to the costs of projects. More controversially, the cost of illness from some kinds of environmental change can be estimated. Recreational benefit and costs also might be quantified. To the extent possible, the inclusion of these costs and the use of cost-benefit analysis in public investment decisions would help avoid environmentally damaging projects or change designs and reduce external costs. However, many environmental costs cannot be quantified so readily, although applications of nonmarket valuation techniques have expanded readily in the past decade, including in developing countries.[27] Probably more critical, too many governments do not take project appraisal at all seriously. The World Bank, under considerable pressure from environmental groups, now undertakes impact analyses of the investments it

---

[27]For a summary of valuation studies in developing countries, see Stavios Georgiou, Dale Whittington, David Pearce, and Dominic Moran, *Economic Values and the Environment in the Developing World* (Cheltenham, UK: Edward Elgar, 1997).

finances. Several other donors have followed the bank's lead, and this practice is likely to spread.

Perhaps the first step toward an incentive regime that promotes sustainable resource use is to reduce or eliminate subsidies and protective tariffs that encourage production of products that unnecessarily destroy resources. Where this is done, marketable natural resources and sources of pollution bear prices closer to their true scarcity costs. Because external costs and benefits are not reflected in market prices, this is not the only necessary step. Marketable property rights and permits, taxes, or even regulation also is necessary to internalize the externalities and complete the incentive regime. But it is important to recognize that there is no necessary conflict between economic reform and sustainable development.

MEASURING SUSTAINABILITY

Most societies and their governments aim to increase income as rapidly as possible over long periods. How do they ensure that economic growth does not depend unsustainably on the consumption of natural resources? This chapter so far has answered this question in terms of the markets for individual resources, such as fisheries, forests, mineral deposits, and the environment. If a government wished to track the country's success in sustaining its growth, what concepts could it use and how would these be measured?

Natural Capital

The discussion of economic growth in Chapters 3 and 4 emphasized that rising income depends on increases in the capital stock and the productivity with which labor and capital produce goods and services. In standard growth models and other economic analyses, the capital stock is defined as **human-made capital:** machines, buildings, and infrastructure **(made capital),** as well as the education and experience of the labor force **(human capital).** But natural resources can also be considered as a form of capital. Like machines, its value can depreciate over time as it is consumed during production processes. The productivity of made capital and labor decline as natural resources are depleted, unless more resources are discovered, greater amounts are invested in made capital, or technological change increases productivity. This suggests that natural resources also ought to be included as part of capital in economic growth models and measures of national output.

To incorporate natural resources in our thinking about economic growth, economists have developed the concept of natural capital, analogous to that of made capital. **Natural capital** is the value of a country's existing stock of natural resources, including fisheries, forests, mineral deposits, water, and the environment. Natural capital produces goods and services, just like labor and made capital. It usually is depleted during the process of production, just as made capital is depreciated. And through natural growth of renewable resources and investment in discovery of new reserves, natural capital can increase, just as investment increases the stock of made capital.

How can natural capital be measured? Made capital is measured as the cost of investment: If a factory cost $30 million to build and equip, that is the value of the capital stock recorded in the national accounts. In any year, the *gross capital stock* of a country is the sum of the value (after adjusting for inflation) of all such investments over the previous many years. Because the capital stock wears out in the course of production, the stock is reduced each year to account for depreciation. Thus, each year the initial capital stock is increased by the value of investment and decreased by depreciation to calculate the *net capital stock*. If the economy is to grow sustainably, the net capital stock also must continue to grow.

Obviously there is no analogous way of valuing natural capital. But an alternative and economically preferable way of valuing made capital can be applied to natural capital. Capital of any kind produces goods and services into the future. A measure of the net benefits from producing these goods and services is the difference between their market price and the cost of the other inputs, materials and labor, used to produce them. The capital then can be valued as the sum of these future benefits, discounted by the appropriate interest rate. That is, the capital is valued as the *net present value* of the future stream of value added by the capital.

This approach can be used to value natural capital. If a forest is harvested, the logs have a market value determined by their price less the costs of harvesting; that is, their resource rent.[28] The cost of harvesting includes materials, wages, and the minimum necessary return to made capital; that is, the opportunity cost of made capital engaged in logging. The market price of timber varies depending on the quality and volume of the timber, something that can be roughly estimated from the characteristics of forest and logging practices. The value of the forest can be calculated as the discounted present value of the future resource rents, using the prevailing interest rate (see equation 11–2). The annual depletion of the forest simply is the change in this present value.

The application of this approach to fisheries, water supplies, mineral deposits, and soil fertility is straightforward. But the valuation of clean air and water and other environmental amenities is not so simple. The physiological impact of particular pollutants on human well-being is complex, indirect, and not completely understood. Many forms of the impact have no market values.

---

[28]Strictly speaking, the resource rent should be measured using the *marginal* cost of extraction.

And environmentalists suspect that pollution has cumulative, nonlinear effects that are not easily estimated, such as climate change due to the venting of carbon dioxide into the atmosphere (the *greenhouse effect*). Until scientists and economists understand more about the costs of environmental degradation, the valuation of natural capital is likely to be confined to marketable resources like fish, timber, minerals, and water supplies.

Sustainability

If an economy consumes natural capital to produce current income, the economy's capacity to generate income will decline in the future unless the natural capital is replaced. For the moment, consider a constant population. A test for a sustainable economy is its capacity to maintain consumption at a constant level indefinitely. To achieve this, the depletion of natural capital must be replaced by made capital, technological change must be generated to increase the productivity of all capital and labor, or both must be done. This suggests an alternative, if partial, criterion for sustainability: the maintenance of the total stock of capital— natural, made, and human. The depletion of natural capital must be compensated for by net investment in other capital.

Therefore, sustainability can involve the depletion of natural resources and the eventual decline of farming, fishing, forestry, mining, petroleum, and other sectors dependent on natural resources. As these industries decline, others grow, including manufacturing, utilities, construction, finance, transportation, telecommunications, trade, health, education, and other services. When an economy develops from a natural resource base, the net benefits or rents from the primary sectors provide much of the finance for secondary and tertiary industries. And some of the finance may go into research and development of new technologies that will increase productivity.

One other kind of transformation should be noted. In countries almost entirely dependent on natural resources for income, such as oil exporters Kuwait and Brunei, there is little scope for transforming resource rents into other productive capital within the economy. Instead, these countries invest their resource rents in bonds and stocks in the international capital markets or even in the industries of other countries. Brunei, for example, has invested in cattle ranching in Australia and hotels in the United States. As the oil runs out, these countries begin increasingly to live off their investments.

The transformation to made capital does not justify the wanton use of resources. The point is a narrower one, that to some extent growth can be sustained by increasing the made capital stock while the natural capital stock diminishes. Resources should not be wasted simply because made capital can be increased. Instead, they should be used efficiently, in ways described earlier in this chapter. The substitution of made capital for natural capital may not be productive or even possible forever. Natural resources also are used in manufac-turing and services, as raw materials, fuel, and waste sinks. Unless technology continues to reduce this dependence on raw materials, it is possible that a country, or even the planet, may run out of needed resources. Further, if the population is growing and a society wants its income per capita to grow as well, then it becomes necessary to invest more than resource rents to continuously increase the total capital stock. Within these limits, however, some societies may choose to accelerate resource depletion in favor of investment in other indus-tries, and they can do it sustainably if resource rents are invested productively.

Resources and National Income

The concept of sustainability as the transformation of natural into made capital can be reflected in the national accounts, particularly in relation to saving rates. In principle, consumption can be sustained over time only if the value of total assets (in other words, total wealth) does not decline. In turn, maintaining wealth requires saving sufficiently to offset depreciation of existing assets. In standard national accounting, this idea is captured by measuring **net saving** (NS), defined as gross saving (*S*) minus the depreciation of made capital (D_m):

$$NS = S - D_m \qquad\qquad [20\text{--}1]$$

But focusing on depreciation of only made capital is too limited, and in princi-ple the concept should be expanded to include depreciation of natural capital (D_n), including the depletion of energy stocks, dwindling mineral assets, and damage from air pollution. This gives rise to the measurement of **adjusted net saving** (ANS):

$$ANS = S - D_m - D_n \qquad\qquad [20\text{--}2]$$

This corrected definition of net saving suggests that, if enough is saved each year to cover the depreciation of both made and natural capital, the economy can sustain its wealth and its level of consumption. In principle, this idea could be extended to include other assets as well, including human capital, knowl-edge, and social assets. However, measurement difficulties and lack of data make this extension difficult in practice, so we restrict our discussion here to made and natural capital.

   Estimates of adjusted net saving for several regions and countries are given in Table 20–2, showing the costs of depletion of some categories of natural capi-tal.[29] Note the high estimated rates of resource depletion for the Middle East and North Africa, reflecting depletion of oil reserves. Saving rates in the region are

---

[29]This procedure is based on a similar table in the World Bank's *World Development Report 2003: Sustainable Development in a Dynamic World.*

TABLE 20-2. **Estimating Adjusted Net Saving, 2002**
           (percentage of GDP)

INCOME AND REGION	GROSS DOMESTIC SAVING	CONSUMPTION OF FIXED CAPITAL	ENERGY DEPLETION	MINERAL DEPLETION	CARBON DIOXIDE DAMAGE	ADJUSTED NET SAVING
By income						
Low income	21.5	8.4	5.9	0.4	1.3	5.5
Middle income	27.7	10.1	7.7	0.3	1.4	8.2
Low and middle income	26.6	9.8	7.4	0.3	1.4	7.7
High income	17.4	13.1	0.7	0.0	0.3	3.3
By region						
East Asia and Pacific	38.8	9.2	3.4	0.3	1.8	24.1
Europe and Central Asia	22.7	10.5	9.7	0.1	2.1	0.3
Latin America and the Caribbean	19.3	10.3	5.2	0.6	0.5	2.7
Middle East and North Africa	23.4	10.0	26.3	0.1	1.3	−14.3
South Asia	23.1	9.0	2.2	0.3	1.5	10.1
Sub-Saharan Africa	15.9	10.2	8.1	0.5	1.1	−4.0
By country						
Costa Rica	15.1	5.9	0.0	0.0	0.2	9.0
Indonesia	18.2	5.4	8.6	1.2	0.9	2.1
Brazil	19.7	10.8	2.9	1.1	0.5	4.4
The Philippines	24.5	7.9	0.0	0.1	0.7	15.8
Nigeria	13.1	8.3	38.7	0.0	0.5	−34.4
Mexico	18.3	10.5	4.9	0.1	0.5	2.3
Malawi	0.8	7.0	0.0	0.0	0.3	−6.5

Note: Adjusted net saving is equal to net domestic saving (calculated as the difference between gross domestic saving and consumption of fixed capital), minus energy depletion, mineral depletion, and carbon dioxide damage. Other types of depletion (e.g., forest depletion) could be included where data exist.
Source: World Bank, *World Development Indicators 2004*

not large enough to compensate for the consumption of both fixed and natural capital, implying a reduction in net wealth and unsustainable consumption. These data suggest similar problems in both sub-Saharan Africa and to some extent in Eastern Europe and Central Asia, as well as in some individual countries, such as Nigeria, a large oil producer.

Measurement of natural capital depletion still is experimental, and these estimates should be considered highly approximate and illustrative. Even the standard depreciation of made capital is estimated only approximately, if at all, for most developing countries, and the data on depletion of natural capital is even less precise. Partly for that reason, ANS has not been used much in official estimates, and it has hardly affected policy discussions. Yet even rough allowances for natural depletion would be an improvement on current estimates of national product and should lead to better policy. The United Nations and the World Bank are encouraging countries to begin keeping resource and environmental accounts as satellites to their standard national income accounts.[30] As more experience is gained, resource and environmental accounting may become an integral part of the standard national income accounts of many countries.

GLOBAL SUSTAINABILITY

Is economic development sustainable? For any one country, if appropriate economic and resource policies are in place, the answer should be yes, because any single, well-managed country can draw on resources, saving, and technology from other countries. The answer becomes less certain when the whole planet is considered. Scientists are developing complex models to predict whether our economies will exhaust the earth's minerals, soils, forests, and fisheries or cause irreversible damage to the environment, including changes in climate. But the existing models often give uncertain, sometimes unstable or conflicting, results. What are the biases for gloom and for hope?

Malthusian Views

In the early nineteenth century, the famous English demographer Thomas Malthus predicted that growing populations would exhaust the earth's capacity to produce food, until rising death rates and falling birth rates would harshly keep populations in check, as was discussed in Chapter 7. Malthusian ideas remain influential in the early twenty-first century, although the focus has shifted from land and agriculture to all natural resources and the global environment.

The heart of the Malthusian view is the notion that the demand for natural resources is based on the *exponential* growth of both population and income, while the supply of resources either is absolutely limited or can increase only *linearly*. No matter how slow the growth rate, any exponentially expanding demand eventually will overwhelm any fixed or linearly increasing supply, as shown in Figure 20–7. Historically, human societies have been able to avoid the Malthusian trap in three ways. First, science and technology moved fast enough to increase the productivity of land and other natural resources. Second, when resources became scarce, such as wood in England in the seventeenth century

---

[30]See the collection by Ernst Lutz, ed., *Toward Improved Accounting for the Environment* (Washington, DC: World Bank, 1993).

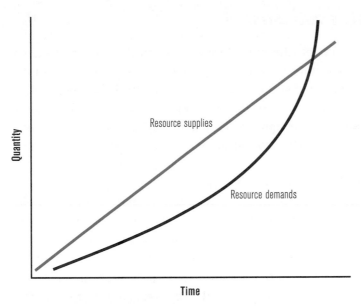

FIGURE 20-7. Global Resource Balance
The Malthusian view is that resource supplies rise at a linear
rate, at best, while demand rises exponentially. If so, demand
eventually must exceed supply.

or coal in the nineteenth, substitutes (coal and later petroleum) were found.
Third, people chose to reduce family size and thus population growth.

The question is whether these processes can continue indefinitely to avoid
Malthusian scarcity. Although the world population growth is slowing, it remains
high enough to expect a doubling of the world's population by the middle of this
century. As development proceeds, especially in populous Asia and in Latin
America, a rising share of this expanding population will aspire to the consumption standards of the northern middle class, which suggests more intensive consumption of resources and pollution of the environment. As nonrenewable fuels
run out and the environment becomes saturated with waste, alternative sources
of materials or new technologies may be substantially more costly than current
ones, which would slow growth. And, if the impact of resource depletion and pollution accelerate and become irreversible, it may be beyond the capability of
humans to develop new technologies fast enough to compensate.[31]

Neoclassical Views

History and economics suggest a more optimistic view. Human societies, in fact,
have been able to evade the Malthusian trap. The hopeful interpretation of this
experience comes from neoclassical economics, which argues that the growing

[31]These views are discussed by Edward B. Barbier, *Economics, Natural-Resource Scarcity and
Development* (London: Earthscan, 1989).

resource scarcity itself has been the main inducement to changes in behavior and technology that helped avoid Malthusian predictions. As one country or the entire earth begins to use more resources such as wood, petroleum, fresh water, or clean air, either the market price of these resources rises or, in the case of unpriced amenities, the cost of using them increases. Higher costs, which often are anticipated, become a signal for several changes that ameliorate the growing resource scarcity.

Rising costs of fuels and raw materials make it profitable to search for new deposits and exploit less-accessible deposits with higher extraction costs. The sharp increase in oil prices resulting from the fuel crisis of the 1970s induced new exploration, which led to new finds of oil and natural gas deposits: Proven global oil reserves rose from 406 billion barrels to 1,189 billion barrels between 1978 and 2004, despite consumption of significant quantities of oil in the interim. Higher costs also mean greater rewards from research into new technologies that increase the productivity of waning resources or make it cheaper to use alternative materials. Even if the costs of using alternatives cannot be reduced, substitutes may become economical as the prices of exhaustible resources go up. Solar energy technically is feasible today but too expensive. If fuel deposits become more expensive to tap, solar energy would be relatively more attractive, even at current costs, and more research would be undertaken to reduce these costs.

Increased scarcity also forces users to conserve. World oil consumption fell in the early 1980s as a result of the sharp prices increases of the late 1970s before rising again as oil became cheap in the 1990s. Rising prices also lead to increased efficiency. The amount of energy required to produce a dollar of world GNP declined by about a quarter between 1970 and 2003. Much of the decline was due to improved technology, such as improvements in automobile engines that reduced fuel consumption with no reduction in output or change in consumers' behavior. In the United States, the stock of cars in 1973 averaged 13 miles per gallon of gasoline; by the mid-1980s average mileage had almost doubled. Of course, the opposite reaction occurs as fuel prices drop. In the 1990s, when world oil prices fell, Americans began to shift back to larger cars and sport-utility vehicles (SUVs) that consume much more gasoline than smaller sedans. As world oil prices rose again to $60 per barrel in 2005, sales of SUVs began to drop off in favor of smaller cars.

A similar process occurs with environmental pollution. Even though many environmental amenities are not marketed, pollution entails costs felt by producers and consumers. Some of these work through the market, for example, as land values fall in polluted areas. Others may have to be artificially introduced by government policies that impose external costs on producers or consumers, as discussed earlier in the chapter. As these costs are felt, the demand rises for new technology or behavioral changes that reduce pollution. Gas scrubbers

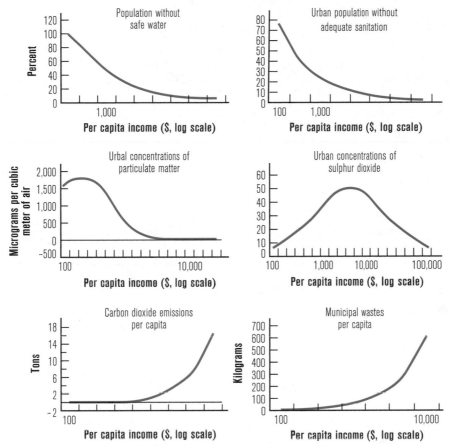

FIGURE 20-8. Income Levels and Various Environmental Indicators
Source: Shafik and Bandyopadhyay, background paper, World Bank, *World Development Report 1992,* Figure 4.

seemed to be a costly imposition on industry at first, but they have become economic and less costly as societies become willing to pay for cleaner air.

The relationship between income levels and environmental indicators tends to follow three broad patterns. Figure 20–8 shows these three broad patterns, as does Figure 20–9, using actual data. Some environmental problems tend to diminish as incomes grow, such as lack of access to safe water and adequate sanitation. Other problems tend to worsen continually as economic output and incomes rise, including municipal wastes and carbon dioxide emissions. In still other cases, environmental problems tend to worsen as incomes grow at low levels of income, then reach a turning point, after which the problem tends to diminish with economic growth. Both air and water pollution tend to follow this pattern. This last pattern is sometimes referred to as an environmental *Kuznets's curve,* since its inverted U shape is reminiscent of the

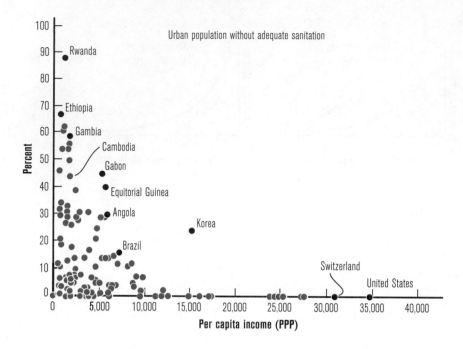

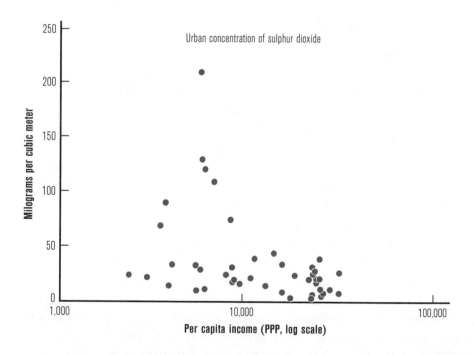

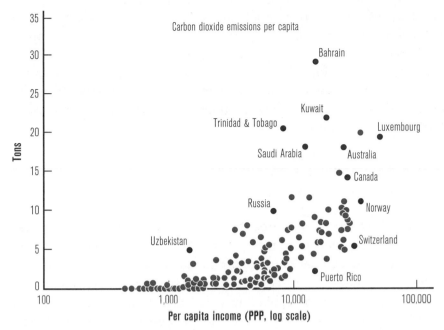

FIGURE 20-9. Income Levels and Environmental Indicators
There is no single relationship between environmental indicators and
income. Some indicators improve with income, and others worsen. Some,
such as concentration of sulphur dioxide, tend to initially worsen and then
later improve as income rises.
Source: World Bank, *World Development Indicators 2004.*

pattern between income levels and income distribution hypothesized by Simon
Kuznets (discussed in Chapter 6).[32]

None of these patterns guarantees that the resource barriers, cumulative
effects, and irreversibilities emphasized by Malthusian views can be overcome.
Perhaps the economic, behavioral, and technological mechanisms of the past
will be swamped by global resource exhaustion. Much will depend on both government policy designs and individual choices. But predictions of exhaustion
that ignore proven adaptive mechanisms are just as likely to be wrong as predictions of sustainable growth that ignore possible irreversibilities. And the cost of
acting on wrong predictions, in either direction, can be large.

From an economic perspective, the soundest strategy for global sustainability would be to move quickly toward more-effective markets, including property
rights, marketable permits, and taxes, so that real resource scarcities are

[32]For further discussion of the relationship between environmental indicators and income, see
World Development Report 1992: Development and the Environment; Gene Grossman and Alan B.
Krueger, "Economic Growth and the Environment," *Quarterly Journal of Economics* (May, 1995),
353–77; and Kenneth Arrow et al., "Economic Growth, Carrying Capacity, and the Environment," *Science* (April 28, 1995), 520–21.

reflected in the prices people pay for all commodities and services. An end to subsidies on fuels, fertilizers, pesticides, water, timber, land clearing, and other destructive uses of resources would be a major step toward sustainability. Most countries are far from this ideal market environment and can reduce resource wastage without jeopardizing economic growth.[33] At the same time, the world needs to invest in better scientific observations and models to see how close humankind really is to exhausting the earth.

Environmental Standards, International Competitiveness, and Trade

The relationship between international trade and environmental quality has been a topic of growing concern in recent years. At the heart of the issue is the convergence of increased globalization of production processes and differences in environmental standards across countries. Some business leaders and policy makers fear that environmental regulations may substantially raise production costs and adversely affect the ability of firms to compete in international markets. Environmental advocates are concerned that the globalization of production will induce firms to move to locations with lax environmental standards to avoid tougher standards at home (the "pollution haven" hypothesis).

These concerns have manifested themselves in several ways. The World Trade Organization (WTO) increasingly is called on to arbitrate disputes that arise from differences in environmental standards across countries. For example, the WTO has been involved in disputes between the United States and India, Pakistan, and Malaysia over exports of shrimp caught by fishing gear that may be environmentally harmful. It also has arbitrated cases affecting pollution, such as high-sulfur oil exported from Venezuela to the United States. Concerns about the environmental impact of trade led to the negotiation of elaborate side agreements as part of the North American Free Trade Agreement between Canada, Mexico, and the United States. Countries with stricter environmental standards have threatened (and sometimes imposed) special duties on imports from countries with weaker standards. Policy makers in many developing countries fear that wealthier countries will use such duties and other regulations as a disguised way to protect industries in high-income countries from competition from abroad. While some people advocate global environmental standards, difficult issues arise about who would set those standards and how they would be enforced.[34]

---

[33]These ideas are developed in Panayotou, *Green Markets*.

[34]For a succinct and accessible review of the relationships between competitiveness and environmental regulation, see Theodore Panayotou and Jeffrey Vincent, "Environmental Regulation and Competitiveness," in the *World Competitiveness Report 1997* (Geneva: World Economic Forum, 1997), 64–73. For a more thorough review, see Adam Jafee et al., "Environmental Regulation and the Competitiveness of US Manufacturing: What Does the Evidence Tell Us?" *Journal of Economic Literature* 33, no. 1 (March 1995), 132–63.

Many of these concerns are based on the notion of a trade-off between environmental standards, on the one hand, and firm productivity and international competitiveness, on the other hand. In this view, strict environmental standards raise production costs by more than the benefits received by the firm, and these additional costs are large enough to harm a firm's competitiveness, perhaps enough to push firms to relocate in other countries.[35] However, as we have seen, this trade-off does not always apply. Stricter environmental standards reduce the costs of some industries. For example, fisheries gain from reduced water pollution, agriculture from improved soil quality, and tourism from lower pollution and improved overall environmental management. And improved worker health should be reflected in higher labor productivity across all industries. In addition to these kinds of benefits, Harvard Business School professor Michael Porter suggested that environmental regulations may improve a firm's productivity by encouraging efficient use of inputs, improved overall management, and technological innovation.[36]

Research into these topics is made difficult by the statistical need to create meaningful measures of environmental regulations and environmental quality that are consistent over time and across countries.[37] Studies in the United States found relatively modest productivity losses from environmental regulations, with small losses in some industries and larger losses in others (such as paper and pulp). Economists Dale Jorgenson and Peter Wilcoxen estimated that pollution controls in the United States reduced GNP by 0.2 percent per year between 1974 and 1985. In a follow-up study, they estimated that, following the enactment of amendments to the Clean Air Act in 1990 that allowed for more flexible, market-based instruments, the loss in annual GNP fell to 0.004 percent per year. These studies, however, did not try to estimate the economic benefit from these controls.[38] Also some suggestive, but not conclusive, evidence supports Porter's hypothesis that environmental standards induce technological innovation and reduce production costs.

[35]See Rudiger Pethig, "Pollution, Welfare, and Environmental Policy in the Theory of Comparative Advantage," *Journal of Environmental Economic Management* 1975, no. 2, 160–69; Horst Seibert, "Environmental Quality and the Gains from Trade," *Kyklos* 3, no. 4 (1975), 657–73; and Martin McGuire, "Regulation, Factor Rewards, and International Trade," *Journal of Public Economics* 17, no. 3 (April 1982), 335–54.

[36]Michael Porter, "America's Green Strategy," *Scientific American* (April 1991), 168; and Michael Porter and Claas van der Linde, "Toward a New Conception of the Environment-Competitiveness Relationship," *Journal of Economic Perspectives* 9, no. 4 (Fall 1995).

[37]This research is summarized in Panayotou and Vincent, "Environmental Regulation and Competitiveness."

[38]Dale Jorgenson and Peter Wilcoxen, "Environmental Regulation and US Economic Growth," *RAND Journal of Economics* 21, no. 2 (Summer 1990), 314–40; and Dale Jorgenson and Peter Wilcoxen, "Impact of Environmental Legislation on US Economic Growth, Investment, and Capital Costs," in Donna Brodsky, ed., *US Environmental Policy and Economic Growth: How Do We Fare?* (Washington, DC: American Council for Capital Formation, 1992).

The "pollution haven" hypothesis, while a seemingly logical concept, does not gain much support from the available evidence. Environmental standards do not appear to have a strong impact on a firm's decision on where to invest and are dwarfed by concerns about macroeconomic and political stability, geographical location, labor costs, and other issues. This is consistent with the finding that the costs of environmental regulation are relatively modest in most industries. These costs would have to be much larger to induce firms to close factories in one country and open new operations in a different country.[39]

Similarly, environmental standards appear to have relatively little impact on trade patterns, again consistent with the idea that, in most industries, these standards have a modest impact on production costs. For example, economists Gene Grossman and Alan Krueger found that higher pollution abatement costs in the United States had no effect on U.S. imports from Mexico, contrary to the fears that some had expressed that these costs would lead to a surge of imports from less-regulated Mexican firms.[40] Moreover, more open trade actually may help reduce pollution in many developing countries. A country completely closed off from trade would have to produce everything for itself, including capital- and pollution-intensive products, such as steel. There is a long history in many developing countries of partially closing off the economy from world trade to protect nascent domestic industries, as discussed in Chapter 19. This strategy can lead to growth of inefficient, high-cost firms that face little competition and have no incentive to reduce costs or use the most appropriate technologies that might reduce pollution. Some of the most heavily polluting industries in developing and transitional economies are "smokestack industries" insulated from trade and competition. One study found that the toxic intensity of manufacturing increased more rapidly in inward-oriented developing countries with policies designed to inhibit trade, while more outward-oriented developing countries recorded either slowly increasing or decreasing levels of toxic intensity in manufacturing.[41]

In sum, the available evidence suggests that the fear that environmental regulations will substantially increase production costs and inhibit the interna-

[39]See David Wheeler and Ashoka Mody, "International Investment Location: The Case of US Firms," *Journal of International Economics* 33, nos. 1–2 (August 1992), 57–72; Robert Repetto, "Jobs, Competitiveness, and Environmental Regulation: What Are the Real Issues?" World Resources Institute, Washington, DC, March 1995; and Panayotou and Vincent, "Environmental Regulation and Competitiveness."

[40]Gene Grossman and Alan Krueger, "Environmental Impacts of a North American Free Trade Agreement," in Peter Garber, ed., *The US-Mexico Free Trade Agreement* (Cambridge, MA: MIT Press, 1993), 13–56.

[41]Hemamala Hettige, Robert Lucas, and David Wheeler, "The Toxic Intensity of Industrial Production: Global Patterns, Trends, and Trade Policy," *American Economic Review* 82, no. 2 (May 1992).

tional competitiveness of firms *in developing countries* appears to be overstated. At the same time, increased trade does not seem to be creating a "race to the bottom," with firms locating where they can pollute more, but rather may create incentives for developing countries to focus production on less pollution-intensive goods and services.

Poverty and the Environment

Rising levels of consumption, especially of an expanding global middle class, are often seen as a major threat to the earth's capacity to sustain living standards. A growing middle class, however, can have two kinds of effects. On the one hand, a growing middle class wants to consume more resources, but on the other hand, it also tends to eventually want, and exert political pressure to get, a cleaner and more-sustainable environment. Whether these opposing tendencies are balanced enough to promote sustainability remains to be seen.

What about the poor? The relationship between poverty and the environment is complex. Asian, African, and Latin American farmers and migrants use slash-and-burn techniques to clear land for farming; African herders graze their livestock on deteriorating common land; poor, rural households throughout the developing world encroach on the forest to obtain wood for charcoal, their most common fuel; local fishers in Africa deplete inland fisheries; and the rivers of densely populated Asia are used simultaneously as common sewers and sources of water. The poor have little margin for subsistence. Struggling to survive today, they heavily discount the future and tend to choose consumption over conservation. In countries where the majority of people are poor enough to exert such pressure on the environment, it is both infeasible and unfair to regulate and tax the access of the poor to common resources. For at least some aspects of environmental degradation, development itself can then be part of the solution: As incomes rise, the poor move away from the margin of subsistence and open opportunities for more sustainable resource use.[42]

Despite considerable truth to this view of poverty and resource use, it is not the whole story. The poor also are victims of resource degradation and have a stake in efficient resource use. Land in central Kenya is exquisitely planted to derive the maximum output from small plots, farmers of arid land in Sudan have developed techniques to make the most of the occasional rainfall, and complex irrigation systems are effectively managed by small farmers in Indonesia. Photographs from the semiarid Machakos District of Kenya show evidence

---

[42]See, for example, World Commission and Development (the Brundtland Commission), *Our Common Future* (New York: Oxford University Press, 1987), 3, 28; and *World Development Report 1992*, 23, 30.

of better soil conservation and more trees today than in the 1920s.[43] Small, poor farmers in the Philippines have organized to prevent the destructive logging of the nearby rain forest. The murder of Chico Menendez, who organized local rubber tappers to protect the Amazon from commercial exploitation, made headlines everywhere. Greenbelt and other grassroots organizations have sprung up in Africa and Asia to protect the environment.[44]

Although extreme poverty undoubtedly makes resource conservation more difficult, the principles of resource policy seem as applicable to poor producers and consumers as to rich ones. Where poor farmers, foresters, or fishers are invested with secure property rights, they act in their own interest to use resources sustainably. Where poor nomads, migrants, and the landless have no property to protect, they are more likely to degrade the environment.

Rich Nations and Poor Nations

Today many people in industrial countries, joined by others in developing countries, are pressing for global action for sustainable resource use. But many developing country governments, with more untapped resources, higher discount rates, and greater pressure for rapid economic growth, resist. Industrial countries would like to preserve tropical rain forests for their many environmental amenities and productive uses. The tropical countries see timber as an important export of growing value and forest land as an opportunity for agricultural expansion. Many people are concerned about global warming, produced mainly by burning fossil fuels. But some in southern countries wonder why they, at lower incomes, have to slow development to help compensate for a problem caused, until now, mainly by industrial growth in the North. China wants to use its abundant coal to fuel rapid income growth for a fifth of the world's population, a vanguard of which is already moving into middle-class consumption patterns. Environmentalists in Europe and North America shudder at the idea of so much production and consumption growth fueled by the most-polluting source of energy in the world.

Therefore, many in the North, joined by others in the South, place a high value on resource and environmental sustainability, while many countries in the South are more concerned about rapid economic growth. These are the conditions for a bargain. Industrial countries should be willing to help finance programs to preserve resources and the environment and permit developing

[43]Mary Tiffen and Michael Mortimore, "Malthus Controverted: The Role of Capital and Technology in Growth and Environment Recovery in Kenya," *World Development* 22, no. 7 (July 1994), 997–1010.

[44]Robin Broad, "The Poor and the Environment: Friends or Foes?" *World Development* 22, no. 6 (June 1994), 811–22.

countries to invest in growth. Debt-for-nature swaps, in which environmental groups from rich countries have paid off poor countries' debts in return for the protection of natural habitats, have been one popular example of such bargains. National and multilateral aid agencies condition their assistance on the kinds of market reforms that promote more-efficient resource use, but they could do this in a more focused way. They also are taking more explicit care about the environmental impact of large projects. Industrial countries might finance the use of new technology that uses resources more efficiently and reduces industrial effluents.[45]

The sustainability of global development therefore may require a transfer of financial and made capital from the industrial to the developing countries in return for the preservation of natural capital in the South, which also will benefit the North. The measure of the North's sincerity in promoting efficient global resource use will be its willingness to make these transfers. But increased efficiency and greater sustainability in resource and environmental management will be beneficial to the developing countries themselves and should be undertaken whether or not a bargain can be struck.

SUMMARY

- In some situations there is a trade-off between economic growth and environmental quality, with expansion of some economic activities coming at the cost of depleted resources or increased pollution. But, in other situations, the two are complements, with prudent resource management a critical component of sustained growth.
- Environmental degradation is often the result of market failures. Firms sometimes overproduce because they do not face the full costs to society of their production decisions. Steps to improve the functioning of markets can help reduce or even reverse the extent of degradation.
- Governments have a variety of policy options that can improve market functions so that both producers and consumers take into account the full costs of resource depletion, pollution, and degradation in their decisions. These include improving property rights, introducing specific regulations, taxation, and sales of marketable permits.
- While well-designed and well-implemented government intervention can help markets function better, bad government policies can have a

---

[45]Theodore Panayotou, "Financing Mechanisms for Agenda 21," Harvard Institute for International Development, 1994.

huge detrimental impact on the environment. Policies that subsidize the overuse of scarce resources or activities that create pollution (e.g., subsidized fuel) can exacerbate resource and environmental management issues.

- For a country's consumption to be sustainable over time, saving has to be large enough to compensate for depreciation of assets, both made and natural. For this condition to hold, adjusted net saving must be positive. Data weaknesses make it difficult to measure adjusted net saving in practice.

- World population growth is slowing, but it continues to put increased pressure on nonrenewable resources, especially in the context of rising living standards. These trends give rise to concerns about the possibility of irreversible resource depletion or exhaustion. However, increased scarcity leads to rising prices of these resources, which tends to reduce consumption and spur new technologies, which can offset, at least to some degree, the impact of higher population and rising living standards.

21

Managing an Open Economy

Economic development takes place in the long term. Most of the processes discussed in the previous chapters, whether improving human welfare, increasing saving, or shifting toward manufactured exports, take years and even decades to bear significant results. If policy makers in developing countries gaze only at the far horizon, however, they are unlikely ever to reach it. Much happens in the short term, within a few months or a couple of years, to throw an economy off balance and make pursuing long-term strategies difficult and sometimes impossible. Policy makers need to emulate the ship's captain, who, always steering toward the port of destination, nevertheless must deal decisively with any storms at sea.

Among the most dangerous and likely of these storms are changes in world prices that throw the balance of payments into deficit, excessive spending that fuels inflation, and droughts or other natural disasters that disrupt production. Unless a government counteracts these economic shocks, they create greater uncertainty and higher risk for private producers and investors, who take evasive action that reduces future investment, worsens the crisis, and causes development efforts to founder.

During the 1970s and 1980s, many economies became unbalanced because of unstable world market conditions: Sharp rises in oil prices during the 1970s were followed by equally precipitate declines in the mid-1980s. A cycle began with rising world inflation during the 1970s, followed by corrective policies, especially in the United States, that included monetary restraint and rising interest rates and led to a world recession in the early 1980s. Wide swings in the major exchange rates characterized both decades.

Some governments, especially those in East and Southeast Asia, managed their economies shrewdly enough to overcome and even benefit from these changing conditions. But a larger number of developing countries were unable to cope. Several governments, particularly in Latin America and Africa, made the situation worse. These governments allowed their exchange rates to become overvalued; this contributed to growing deficits in the balance of payments. These deficits were financed by borrowing abroad, so countries accumulated debt that could not be serviced. These governments also ran budget deficits that had to be financed through the banking system, which expanded the money supply and fed inflation. Many governments then intervened in markets to counter the effects of profligate macroeconomic management.

In Chapter 5 and again in Chapters 13 and 15, we discussed the consequences of such **macroeconomic instability.** Countries with overvalued exchange rates and rapid inflation were unable to grow rapidly, in contrast to those, especially in East and Southeast Asia, with well-managed economics. *Stabilization programs,* many funded by the IMF, are intended to correct these macroeconomic imbalances.

In this chapter, we develop a mechanism for analyzing the macroeconomic policies that a developing country should pursue to stabilize its economy and create a climate for faster economic growth. The model developed here incorporates the two main policy approaches for correcting macroeconomic imbalances: *Reductions in expenditure,* such as lower government budget deficits and slower creation of money, and *adjustments in relative prices,* particularly exchange-rate devaluation.

EQUILIBRIUM IN A SMALL, OPEN ECONOMY[1]

Developing economies have two features central to understanding how macroeconomic imbalances occur and can be corrected. First, they are **open economies,** in that trade and capital flow across their borders in sufficient quantities to influence the domestic economy, particularly prices and the money supply. Most economies are open in this sense, especially since economic reforms in China beginning in the late 1970s and in Eastern Europe and

---

[1]In developing this and the next two sections, we acknowledge an intellectual debt to Shantayanan Devarajan and Dani Rodrik, who wrote an excellent set of notes for their class on macroeconomics for developing countries at Harvard's John F. Kennedy School of Government in the late 1980s and to Richard E. Caves, Jeffrey A. Frankel, and Ronald W. Jones, who develop the open economy model in Chapter 19 of *World Trade and Payments: An Introduction* (Glenview, IL: Scott, Foresman, Little, Brown, 1990).

the states of the former Soviet Union beginning in the early 1990s. Today only a few economies, such as Cuba, North Korea, and Burma, are so heavily protected and regulated (and subject to foreign embargos) that they might not qualify as open to trade and finance.

Second, these are **small economies,** meaning that neither their supply of exports nor their demand for imports has a noticeable impact on the world prices of these commodities and services. Economists call these countries *price takers* in world markets. A number of developing countries can exert some influence over the price of one or two primary exports in world markets: Brazil in coffee, Saudi Arabia in oil, Zambia in copper, South Africa in diamonds, for example. But they almost never affect the price of goods they import, and for macroeconomic purposes, it usually is adequate to model even these countries as price takers.[2]

These two qualities, smallness and openness, are the basis for the **Australian model** of a developing economy.[3] Chapters 17 and 19 used simple general equilibrium models to describe comparative advantage (Figure 17–1) and economic growth through import substitution (Figures 19–4 and 19–5). In those models, the two goods were importables and exportables. The Australian model lumps importables and exportables together as *tradables* and distinguishes these from all other goods and services, called *nontradables.* We used this specification in Chapter 17's discussion of Dutch disease.

Tradable goods and services are those whose prices within the country are determined by supply and demand on world markets. Under the small-economy assumption, these world market prices cannot be influenced by anything that happens within the country and so are *exogenous* to the model (determined outside the model). The domestic price of a tradable good is given by $P_t = eP_t^*$, where e is the nominal exchange rate in local currency per dollar (pesos per dollar for Mexico or rupees per dollar for Pakistan) and P_t^* is the world price of the tradable in dollars. Even if the supply of and demand for tradables change within an economy, the local price will not change because domestic supply and demand have a negligible influence on the world price. Adjustment of the exchange rate changes the domestic price, however. Because this model simplifies all tradables into one composite good, the price of tradables P_t is best thought of as an index, a weighted average of the prices of all tradables, much like a consumer price index.

---

[2]Among developing countries, China and India are large enough that they could become exceptions to the small country rule, given continued growth in China and both greater growth and openness in India.

[3]So called because it was developed by Australian economists, including W. E. G. Salter, "Internal Balance and External Balance: The Role of Price and Expenditure Effects," *Economic Record* (1959), 226–38; Trevor W. Swan, "Economic Control in a Dependent Economy," *Economic Record* 36 (March 1960), 51–66; and W. Max Corden, *Inflation, Exchange Rates and the World Economy* (Chicago: University of Chicago Press, 1977). Australia also is a small, open economy.

   Tradables include exportables, such as coffee in Kenya and Colombia, rice in Thailand, beef in Argentina, cattle in West Africa, palm oil in Malaysia and Indonesia, copper in Peru and Zambia, oil in the Middle East, and textiles and electronics in East Asia, and importables, such as rice in West Africa, oil in Brazil or Korea, and intermediate chemicals and machinery in many developing countries.

   Nontradables are goods and services, such as transportation, construction, retail trade, and household services, that are not easily or conventionally bought or sold outside the country, usually because the costs of transporting them from one country to another are prohibitive or local custom inhibits trade. Prices of nontradables, designated P_n, therefore, are determined by market forces within the economy; any shift in supply or demand changes the price of nontradables. Nontradable prices thus are *endogenous* to the model (determined within the model). The term P_n, like P_t, is a composite or weighted average price incorporating all prices of nontradable goods and services.

Internal and External Balance

Figure 21–1 depicts equilibrium under the Australian model. The vertical axis represents nontradables (N); the horizontal axis takes both the exportables and the importables of previous diagrams (Figures 17–1, 19–3, and 19–4) and treats

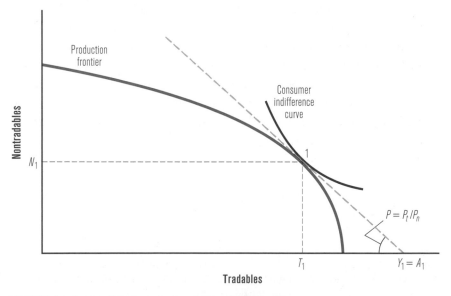

FIGURE 21-1. Equilibrium in the Australian Model
With equilibrium at point 1, the tangency of the production frontier and a community indifference curve, the country produces and consumes T_1 of tradables and N_1 of nontradables. The relative price, P, is a measure of the real exchange rate (see text). National income measured in tradable prices is Y_1.

them together as tradables (T). The production frontier shows the menu of possible outputs of the two kinds of goods, N and T. The community indifference curves show consumer preferences between consumption of tradables and nontradables.

Equilibrium is at point 1, the tangency of a consumer indifference curve and the production possibilities frontier. At this point, the production of tradables, determined by the production frontier at point 1, is T_1, equal to the demand for tradables, determined by the indifference curve at 1; and similarly, for nontradables, supply equals demand at N_1. This is a defining characteristic of equilibrium in the Australian model: At point 1, the markets for both goods are in balance. Put another way, there is **external balance,** because the supply of tradables equals demand, and **internal balance,** because the supply of nontradables equals demand.

The tangency of the indifference curve and production frontier also determines the relative price of tradables in terms of nontradables, $P = P_t/P_n$. The slope of the relative price line gives this price in Figure 21–1. The relative price, P, is an alternative measure of the **real exchange rate,** one of the important innovations of the Australian model.[4] This formulation separates out prices that are under the influence of monetary and fiscal policy and domestic market forces, P_n, from prices that can be changed only by adjustments of the nominal exchange rate, $P_t = eP_t^*$. Note that the slope of the price line that is tangent to the production possibility curve and the consumer indifference curve is the only real exchange rate consistent with equilibrium in the model.

If P rises (the price line becomes steeper in the diagram), tradables become more expensive relative to nontradables. Producers then attempt to switch along the production frontier away from N goods, toward T goods. Consumers attempt to switch in the opposite direction, up along the indifference curve to consume fewer T goods and more N goods. Therefore, a rise in P should increase the surplus of T-good production over consumption.

If the production of T goods exceeds consumption of T goods, there is an external surplus, which is identical to a surplus in the balance of trade. To see this, start with the definition of the trade balance as

$$B_t = E - M \qquad\qquad [21-1]$$

---

[4]Chapters 17 and 19 defined the real exchange-rate index as RER $= R_o P_w/P_d$. The term R_o is an index of the nominal exchange rate, whereas in this chapter we use e, the nominal exchange rate itself. The term P_w is an index of world prices, often the U.S. consumer or wholesale price index and is similar or identical to P^* as measured in practice. But, P_d is a domestic consumer or wholesale price index that includes both tradable and nontradable prices, while P_n is an index of nontradable prices only. Thus, the Australian formulation of the real exchange rate is a more-precise definition than those given in the earlier chapters.

where E and M are exports and imports. Because exports are the surplus of supply over demand for exportable goods, while imports are the opposite, a surplus of demand over supply, we can write the balance of trade as

$B_t =$ value of E-goods supply − value of E-goods demand − (value of
   M-goods demand − value of M-goods supply),

$=$ value of E-goods supply + value of M-goods supply − (value of
   E-goods demand + value of M-goods demand),

$=$ value of tradables supply − value of tradables demand;

or if we let the supply of tradables be X_t and demand be D_t,

$$B_t = P_t X_t - P_t D_t = P_t(X_t - D_t) \qquad [21\text{--}2]$$

In Figure 21–1, with the economy in equilibrium, consumption of tradables is equal to production, so the balance of trade is 0.

The value of income (GDP) also can be found in Figure 21–1. It is the sum of the value of output of N goods (N_1) and T goods (T_1). This value is given by Y_1, the intersection of price line P from point 1 to the T axis.[5] In national income accounting, we distinguish two concepts. Gross domestic *product,* a measure of the value of output, is given by

$$Y = C + I + E - M \qquad [21\text{--}3]$$

where C and I are consumption and investment by both the government and the private sector. Gross domestic *expenditure,* often called **absorption,** is

$$A = C + I = Y + M - E \qquad [21\text{--}4]$$

When, as in Figure 21–1, the economy is in equilibrium, $E = M$ and income equals absorption. Indeed, this is a condition of equilibrium.

This exploration of the Australian model yields three results. First, macroeconomic equilibrium is defined as a balance between supply and demand in two markets: nontradable goods (internal balance) and tradable goods (external balance). Second, to achieve equilibrium in both markets, two conditions must be satisfied: Expenditure (absorption) must equal income, and the relative price of tradables (the real exchange rate) must be at a level that equates demand and supply in both markets (the slope of P in Figure 21–1). Third, this also suggests two remedies for an economy that is out of balance: A government can achieve equilibrium (stabilize the economy) by adjusting absorption, the nominal exchange rate, or both. Generally, both instruments must be used to achieve internal and external balance.

---

[5]Along the T axis, Y_1 is measured in prices of the T good, so $P_t Y_1 = P_t T_1 + P_n N_1$ or $Y_1 = T_1 + (P_n/P_t)N_1$. But $P_n/P_t = \Delta T/\Delta N$, with $\Delta N = N_1$ and $\Delta T = Y_1 - T_1$, the distance along the T axis from T_1 to Y_1. Thus, the value of both goods in T prices is $T_1 + Y_1 - T_1 = Y_1$.

The Phase Diagram

Using the perspective of trade theory, we tie the small, open economy model of macroeconomic management to the tools of analysis already used in this text. But the principles of stabilization can be explored from a more-useful perspective, the **phase diagram.** To develop this approach, consider the markets for tradables and nontradables from the perspective of conventional supply and demand diagrams, as in Figure 21–2.

In these diagrams, we use the real exchange rate, which is the relative price of T goods in terms of N goods (P_t/P_n), as the price in both markets. For tradable goods, that gives a conventional supply and demand diagram: As the price rises, supply increases and demand decreases. But in the nontradables market, a rise in P means a fall in the relative price of N goods, so supply decreases and demand increases. Note that, in both markets, any increase in expenditure, or absorption, A, causes an outward shift of the demand curve: At any price, consumers buy more of both goods.

To use these diagrams as a basis for macroeconomic analysis, we need to change the interpretation of the supply curve for tradables. Until now, we have assumed that all tradables are produced within the home country. But foreign investment and foreign aid can add to the supply of tradables by financing additional imports. Therefore, the supply curve should not be X_t, but $X_t + F$, where F

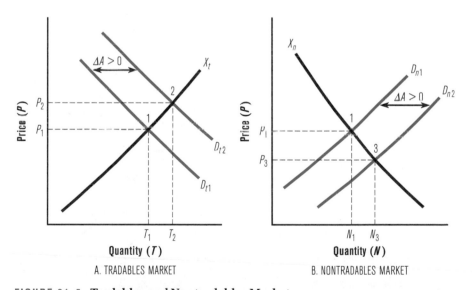

FIGURE 21-2. Tradables and Nontradables Markets
Supply is denoted by X and demand by D. The price, P, in both diagrams is P_t/P_n. In part A, the demand and supply curves for tradables X_t and D_t have the conventional slopes. But, in part B, the slopes are reversed: X_n falls as P rises (because the relative price of N is falling) and D_n rises as P rises. In both markets, demand increases when absorption (expenditure) increases, shown by an outward shift of D_t and D_n.

is the inflow of long-term foreign capital in the form of aid, commercial loans, and investment.

Figure 21–2 constitutes a simple model of the small, open economy that is based on two variables: The real exchange rate P on the vertical axis and absorption A, which determines the position of the demand curves. These, of course, are the conventional variables of microeconomics, price and income. But, in this model, they also are the two main macroeconomic policy tools of government: The exchange rate and the level of expenditure. Because these two variables are central to macroeconomic management, it would be helpful to develop a diagram that uses them explicitly on the axes.

Figure 21–3 does this. It puts the real exchange rate, $P = eP_t^*/P_n$, on the vertical axis and real absorption, A, on the horizontal axis. The diagram also contains two curves, each representing equilibrium in one of the markets. Along the EB, or *external balance*, curve, the T-goods market is in balance ($X_t = D_t$). Along the IB, or *internal balance*, curve, the N-goods market is in balance ($X_n = D_n$).

The slopes of the two curves, EB and IB, can be derived from Figure 21–2. In the tradables market, when absorption is A_1, equilibrium is at P_1, where T_1 is produced and consumed. This equilibrium point 1 also is shown in part A of Figure 21–3. If absorption increases to A_2 in Figure 21–2, the demand curve moves outward and shifts equilibrium to point 2. Note that, with higher absorption, A_2, the real exchange rate, P_2, must be higher to restore equilibrium in the T-goods market. Increased absorption raises the demand for T goods. To meet

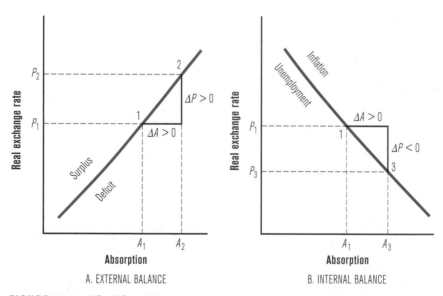

FIGURE 21-3. The Phase Diagram
The axes are the main policy variables, the real exchange rate, P, and real absorption, A. The curves show equilibrium in the T-goods market (external balance, EB) and N-goods market (internal balance, IB).

this demand, it is necessary to raise output, which can be achieved only through a higher relative price of T goods, P_2. This higher price also helps regain balance by reducing the demand for T goods along the new demand curve. Point 2 is transferred to Figure 19–3 at (P_2, A_2).

In the nontradables market, when absorption is A_1, equilibrium is at P_1, where N_1 is produced and consumed. This equilibrium point 1 also is shown in part B of Figure 21–3. If absorption increases to A_2 in Figure 21–2, the demand curve moves outward and shifts equilibrium to point 3. In the N-goods market, higher absorption, A_2, requires a lower, or appreciated, real exchange rate to restore equilibrium. Increased absorption raises demand for N goods, met by raising output, which can be achieved only through a lower relative price of T goods, P_3. This lower real exchange rate, or higher price of N goods, also helps regain balance by reducing the demand for N goods along the new demand curve. Point 3 is transferred to Figure 21–3 at (P_3, A_2).

Figure 21–3 also shows the **zones of imbalance.** In the T-goods market, part A, for any given level of absorption, say, A_1, any real exchange rate greater than P_1 causes external surplus: The production of tradables exceeds the demand for tradables because the relative price, P, is at a more-depreciated level than required for equilibrium. Any real exchange rate below (more appreciated than) P_1 causes an external deficit and the demand exceeds the supply of tradables. Therefore, the zone of surplus is northwest of EB and the zone of deficit is southeast.

In the N-goods market, part B, inflation is to the right of the IB curve, where the demand for N goods exceeds the supply. In that region, for any given real exchange rate, such as P_1, absorption is too high, say, A_3. To the left is the zone of unemployment, where there is an excess supply of N goods. In that region, for any given real exchange rate, say, P_3, absorption is too low, say, A_1.

The meaning of inflation and unemployment is precise in our model but not in the real world. It is best to think of inflation as being an increase in prices faster than is customary in the country in question. That rate would be quite low in Germany, Japan, or China, probably less than 5 percent a year, but quite high in Brazil or Argentina. Unemployment implies not only jobless workers but also idle capital and other factors of production. In other words, there is unemployment when an economy is inside the production frontier in Figure 21–1. A country may have high levels of labor unemployment but be unable to increase output because it is fully utilizing its capital or land.

Equilibrium and Disequilibrium

The two balance curves are put together in Figure 21–4. All along the external balance curve, the demand for T goods equals the supply produced at home plus any net foreign capital inflow. All along the internal balance curve the

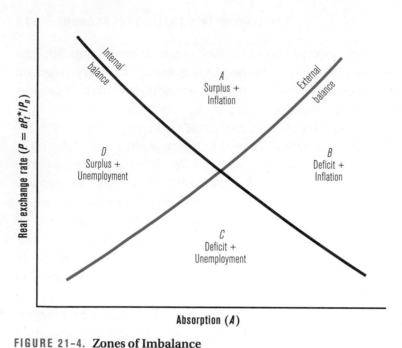

Absorption (*A*)

FIGURE 21-4. Zones of Imbalance
The economy is in equilibrium only at point 1, the intersection of the
EB and IB curves. Zones of imbalance are labeled. For example, in
zone *A* to the north, supply of *T* goods exceeds demand, so there is a
surplus, and demand for *N* goods exceeds supply, so there is inflation.

demand for *N* goods equals the supply of *N* goods. The only point where there is
both internal and external balance (equilibrium in both the *T*- and *N*-goods
markets) is the intersection of the two curves. This is sometimes called the *bliss
point*. It is the same as the tangency of the indifference curve to the production
frontier in Figure 21–1 at point 1. The objective of macroeconomic policy is to
adjust the exchange rate and absorption to keep an economy stable, in both
external and internal balance.

Economies spend considerable time in one of the four zones of imbalance
shown in Figure 21–4. Zone *A* to the north is a region of external surplus and
inflation, where the exchange rate is *undervalued*. In zone *B* to the east of equilibrium, the economy faces inflation and a foreign deficit, due principally to
excessive expenditure (absorption is greater than income). To the south is zone
C, where the exchange rate is *overvalued* (too appreciated) and there is both
unemployment and an external deficit. And west of the bliss point the economy
is in zone *D*, where, because of insufficient absorption, there is unemployment
of all resources but a foreign surplus.

Once in disequilibrium, economies have built-in tendencies to escape back
into balance. Figure 21–5 describes them separately for external balance (part A)
and internal balance (part B). Start with an external surplus, point 1 in part A. The
excess supply of tradables generates two self-correcting tendencies. First, the net
inflow of foreign exchange adds to international reserves. If the central bank takes

no countermeasures, the money supply increases and interest rates fall and induce both consumers and investors to spend more. The increase in absorption moves the economy rightward, back toward external balance. Second, the inflow of foreign exchange creates more demand for the local currency and, if the exchange rate is free to float, forces an appreciation. This is a move downward in the diagram, also toward the EB line. The net result of these two tendencies is the resultant, shown as a solid line in the diagram, heading toward external balance. If, instead, the economy starts in external deficit at point 2, the tendencies are the opposite but the result is the same, a tendency to regain external balance.

The tendency to regain internal balance is shown in part B. When there is inflation (point 3), it affects both the real exchange rate and real absorption. If the nominal exchange rate remains fixed (or is not allowed to depreciate as fast as inflation), the rise in P_n causes a real appreciation. At the same time, the rise in prices can cause a fall in the real value of absorption, assuming that the central bank doe not take steps to increase the money supply to compensate for inflation. Under these assumptions, the economy would move from inflation at point 3 back toward internal balance. Unemployment (point 4) would be self-correcting also, if prices are able to fall as easily as they rise, but this seldom is the case.

Despite these self-correcting tendencies, in practice, they often fail to work smoothly or quickly enough because of *structural rigidities* in the economy. For

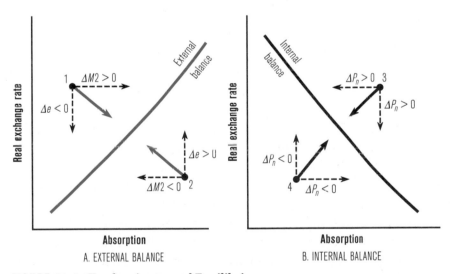

FIGURE 21-5. Tendencies toward Equilibrium
If the economy faces an external surplus (point 1 in part A), reserves and the money supply tend to rise while the exchange rate tends to appreciate; this drives the economy toward external balance. Conversely for a deficit: If the economy faces inflation (point 3 in part B), the rise in prices leads to real appreciation of the exchange rate and a reduction in the real value of absorption; this moves conditions toward internal balance. Conversely for unemployment at point 4, but only if prices can fall flexibly.

instance, exchange-rate changes may take time to affect actual imports and exports, perhaps as long as two years to have a full impact. In economies like Ghana and Zambia, dominated by one or two export products such as cocoa and copper, with long gestation periods for new investment, supply elasticities for tradables may be especially low and foreign deficits can persist for a time despite real devaluations.

Nontradables prices probably rise very quickly when demand exceeds supply, as in part B of Figure 21–5. But in many developing economies, inflation, once started, may resist corrective policies, and prices do not fall so easily when there is unemployment: Unions strike wage bargains that try to maintain real wages by continually raising nominal wages; banks use their market power to keep interest rates high; producers are dependent on imports, whose prices are responsive only to exchange rate adjustments; and large firms with monopoly or oligopoly power keep prices up to cover costs that resist downward pressures. Such rigidities have been cited frequently to explain chronic trade deficits and inflation in Latin America, especially in Argentina and Brazil.

However, arguments about structural rigidities can be overstated. There is some flexibility in production for most export industries, even in the short term. And many producer prices are quite flexible, including those of most farm products, those in the large informal sector, and even those of some modern manufacturing firms. Nevertheless, the automatic tendencies toward external and internal balance depicted in Figure 21–5 are likely to be too slow and politically painful to satisfy most governments.

Not all the barriers to adjustment are structural. Sometimes, policies work against adjustment. When foreign reserves fall, for example, the money supply also falls automatically unless the central bank's policy is to *sterilize* these shifts by expanding domestic credit to compensate for the fall in reserves and keep the money supply from falling. Sterilization prevents the move from points 1 or 2 of Figure 21–5 toward external balance. And nominal exchange rates respond to changing market conditions, as shown in panel A, only if the exchange rate is allowed to float or the government makes frequent adjustments in the nominal exchange rate to match changing economic conditions.

However, the opposite policy, a fixed nominal exchange rate, is needed if inflation in nontradables prices is to cause a real exchange-rate appreciation, as depicted at point 3 of Figure 21–5. This fixed nominal rate is called an exchange rate *anchor,* because the fixed rate alone can halt the upward drift of prices, as the economy moves due south from point 3 in part B. Chile used such an anchor to slow inflation during the late 1970s (see Box 21–1). If government devalues the rate to keep up with inflation, Brazil's practice for many years, then real appreciation is thwarted and there is no anchor. Similarly, real absorption falls with inflation only if the government fixes its expenditure and its deficit in nominal terms and allows inflation to erode the real value of the expenditure and if

BOX 21-1 PIONEERING STABILIZATION: CHILE, 1973-84

In the last year of the Salvatore Allende regime in Chile, when the public sector deficit soared to 30 percent of GDP and was financed mostly by printing money, inflation exceeded 500 percent a year. In 1973, General Augusto Pinochet overthrew Allende and established an autocratic regime. An early goal of his government was to stabilize the economy. It proved to be a difficult task of many years, with important lessons for later stabilizations in Latin America.

Faced by rapid inflation and unsustainable external deficits, the government imposed a fiscal and monetary shock on the economy. The budget deficit was cut to 10.6 percent of GDP in 1974 and again to 2.7 percent in 1975. Monetary policy was tight: From the second quarter of 1975 through the middle of 1976, it has since been estimated, households and firms were willing to hold more money than was in circulation. But inflation persisted; consumer prices nearly doubled in 1977.

Despite draconian measures, prices continued to rise for two reasons. First, the peso was aggressively devalued to improve the foreign balance, the more so because of the 40 percent fall in copper prices in 1975. In 1977, the peso was worth about one-80th its 1973 value against the dollar. Second, wages in the formal sector were determined by rules that permitted adjustments based on the previous year's rate of inflation, a rule that helped to perpetuate the higher rates of earlier years. It also was argued by some that the monetary policy was not stringent enough.

In 1978, the government switched gears and began using the exchange rate as its main anti-inflation weapon. At first a crawling peg was adopted with pre-announced rates, the *tablita,* that did not fully adjust to domestic inflation. In 1979, the rate was fixed at 39 pesos to the dollar for three years. The appreciating real exchange rate, or *anchor,* helped control inflation, which was down to 10 percent by 1982. But it also discouraged export growth and contributed to a growing current-account deficit. At the same time, Chile liberalized its controls over foreign capital flows and attracted large inflows of loans: Net long-term capital rose from negligible amounts before 1978 to average over $2 billion a year in the next five years, equivalent to 8 percent of GDP in 1980. This inflow not only financed the growing current deficit but contributed to the real appreciation of the exchange rate.

Not until after 1984 did Chile finally achieve a semblance of both internal and external balance. It did so through a large real devaluation, approaching 50 percent, supported by tighter fiscal and monetary policies. After a decade and a half of falling income per capita, Chilean incomes grew by 5.8 percent a year from 1985 to 1991.

Source: Based on the account by Vittorio Corbo and Andrés Solimano, "Chile's Experience with Stabilization Revisited," in Michael Bruno et al., *Lessons of Economic Stabilization and Its Aftermath* (Cambridge, MA: MIT Press, 1991).

the central bank restrains the money supply to grow more slowly than inflation. More typically, the fiscal authorities adjust the expenditure, while the monetary authorities adjust both the money supply and the nominal exchange rate, to fully compensate for inflation. In that case, rising prices have no impact on the real exchange rate or real absorption and an inflationary economy remains at point 3 in Figure 21–5.

Stabilization Policies

Whether the barriers to rapid automatic adjustment are inherent in the economic structure or created by policy contradictions, in most cases, governments need to take an active role to stabilize their economies. They have three basic instruments for doing so: exchange-rate management, fiscal policy, and monetary policy.

Alternative **exchange-rate regimes** were introduced in Chapter 13. Governments can vary the exchange rate by having the central bank offer to buy and sell foreign currency at a predetermined or *fixed* official exchange rate (*e* in our nomenclature) that nevertheless can be changed from time to time or by allowing the rate to *float* in the currency market, although the central bank sometimes may intervene to influence the price. An intermediate case is the *crawling peg,* under which the central bank determines the rate but changes it frequently, as often as daily, to ensure that the official rate stays in line with domestic and world inflation; this results in a constant or slowly adjusting real exchange rate (*P*).

Governments have two policies that can influence the level of absorption. **Fiscal policy,** adjusting levels of government expenditure and taxation, directly affects the government's components of consumption and investment. It also influences private expenditure, especially consumption, which depends on *disposable income,* or income net of taxes. **Monetary policy** also affects private expenditure. If the central bank acts to increase the money supply, as described in Chapter 13, it increases the liquidity of households and firms, lowers interest rates, and stimulates private consumption and investment.

The power of the phase diagram is that it indicates the necessary directions for these policies, depending on the state of the economy. Figure 21–6 provides such a policy map. It shows the same external and internal balance lines, as in the previous diagrams, but adds a new element: four policy quadrants, I to IV, within which the policy prescription always is the same.

Take, for example, point 1, which has been placed on the external balance line but in the inflationary zone. For many years, Brazil has been in this situation, with buoyant exports and balance in foreign payments but chronic inflation running from 40 to well over 100 percent a year. Because the demand for nontradables exceeds supply, we know that one necessary correction is a reduction in real absorption, monetary and fiscal *austerity,* that would reduce demand and move the economy due west from point 1. But, if that is the only policy taken, the economy would not reach internal balance until point 4, in the

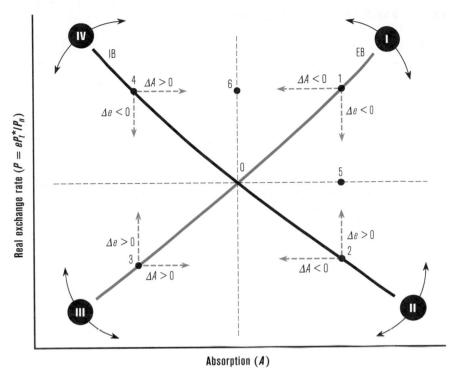

FIGURE 21-6. Policy Zones
From any position of disequilibrium, two policy adjustments generally are
needed to restore internal and external balance. In each of quadrants I to IV, a
particular combination of exchange rate and absorption policy is prescribed.

zone of external surplus. One imbalance is exchanged for another. To avoid generating a surplus, reduced absorption needs to be accompanied by an appreciation of the exchange rate, a move due south from point 1. The result would be a
move approximately toward the equilibrium or bliss point, 0.

Note three things about this result. First, this combination of policies, austerity
and appreciation, would work from any point within Quadrant I to return the
economy to equilibrium. That is, the same combination is needed whether the
economy had inflation with a moderate external surplus or inflation with a moderate deficit, either just above or just below the EB line. If the economy starts just
below external balance, with a moderate deficit, it may seem strange *(counterintuitive)* to recommend an appreciation that, on its own, would worsen the
deficit. But the reduction in absorption, needed to reduce inflation, also reduces
the deficit because it also lowers the demand for tradables. Indeed, it reduces the
demand for tradables too much and throws the economy into surplus; this is the
reason that an appreciation is needed. Of course, the relative intensity of each policy is different, depending where in quadrant I the economy starts. But the basic
principle holds: Anywhere in quadrant I, the right combination of policies is austerity and appreciation, the combination that moves the economy toward point 0.

Second, in general, two policy adjustments are required to move toward
equilibrium. This is a simple example of the general rule enunciated by Dutch

economist Jan Tinbergen: To achieve a number of policy goals, it generally is necessary to employ the same number of policy instruments. Here we have two goals, internal and external balance, and need adjustments in both absorption (austerity) and the real exchange rate (appreciation) to reach them both. It is not always necessary to use two goals, however. If the economy lies just to the east of equilibrium at point 5, then a reduction in absorption achieves internal and external balance simultaneously. And, if the initial situation is point 6, due north of 0, then appreciation alone does the job.

Third, we could view the policy prescription in either of two ways. Austerity is needed to reduce inflation (move west) and appreciation is used to avoid surplus (move south). Or appreciation can be targeted on internal balance (move south toward point 2) but alone would cause a deficit, so that austerity then is required to restore external balance. Therefore, no logic in macroeconomics suggests that one particular policy should be assigned to one particular goal. Economic institutions often do this anyway. In practice, the central bank might use the exchange rate to achieve external balance while the finance ministry uses the budget for internal balance. But, if these two approaches are not coordinated, they may well fail to reach equilibrium.

With these principles established for quadrant I, it is fairly routine to go around the map in Figure 21–6 and see what policy responses are required:

- In quadrant II at a point like 2, with an external deficit but internal balance, exchange-rate devaluation is needed to restore foreign balance but, taken alone, would push the economy into inflation. Fiscal and monetary austerity also are needed to avoid inflation and reach equilibrium. We could reverse this assignment of policies and use austerity to achieve external balance and devaluation to stimulate the economy. Many African countries have been in this situation right up to the present, with low inflation but an insufficiency of export earnings and foreign investment to pay for the imports required for economic development.

- In quadrant III at point 3, an expansionary fiscal-monetary policy eliminates unemployment but at the cost of a foreign deficit, so devaluation is needed to reach equilibrium. Or devaluation stimulates employment and so requires expansion to eliminate the resulting surplus. This is the situation of a mature industrialized economy during a recession, with unemployed labor and capital, but it is not so common in developing countries.

- In quadrant IV at point 4, exchange-rate appreciation can eliminate the external surplus while fiscal expansion prevents unemployment. Or fiscal expansion can end the surplus while appreciation prevents the resulting inflation. A few countries in Asia, such as Taiwan (see Box 21–2) and Malaysia in the 1980s, have been in this situation.

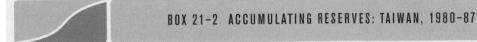

BOX 21-2 ACCUMULATING RESERVES: TAIWAN, 1980–87

By 1980, Taiwan had established an economic growth record that was being cited as a model for other developing countries. The government's macroeconomic policy always had been conservative. When the second oil crisis hit in 1979–80 and as Taiwan began to lose diplomatic standing while China regained its place in the official world order, macroeconomic policy was tightened further.

The central bank began to undervalue its exchange rate and became more restrictive in its monetary policy. The Taiwan dollar was depreciated from 36 per U.S. dollar in 1980 to 40 in 1983, while the real rate depreciated 15 percent against an average of the U.S. dollar, yen, and Hong Kong dollar, representing Taiwan's major trading partners. (Hong Kong trade was destined mainly for China.) From 1980 to 1984, increases in the money supply as a share of GDP were below the long-term trend. Fiscal policy was neutral, however: Both expenditures and revenue fell as shares of GDP and left the deficit roughly constant. The results of exchange rate and monetary policies were dramatic. While exports rose moderately as a share of GDP, imports plunged from about 45 percent of GDP in 1980 to 35 percent in 1986. Reserves rose from under 15 percent of GDP in 1980 to over 60 percent by 1987.

From the national income accounts, a current-account surplus must be matched by a surplus of saving over investment: $S - I = E - M$. The necessary savings surplus was generated by both a rise in saving, from around 30 to almost 40 percent of GDP, and a fall in investment, from over 30 to under 20 percent of GDP. The savings surplus was generated in part by structural factors and in part by the rise in real interest rates caused by monetary stringency. Real interest rates on loans, which had been slightly negative in 1980, rose to a range of 8–10 percent a year from 1982 to 1986. Furthermore, domestic credit was tight. The central bank sterilized the rise in foreign reserves by forcing a sharp drop in the increments to private domestic credit: Net new loans fell to only 5 percent of GDP by 1986.

A price was to be paid for accumulating reserves. The unemployment rate, which had been 1.2 percent in 1980, rose to 2.9 percent in 1985. The growth rate of GDP, which was nearly 10 percent a year from 1970 to 1980, was a little below 7 percent from 1980 to 1985, after which it recovered to about 8 percent a year. Still, measured against most other countries' performances, this was an enviable record. By the mid-1980s, informed opinion in Taiwan turned against mercantilist policies while the U.S. government exerted pressure on Taiwan to reverse its policies. The real exchange rate was appreciated 25 percent, fiscal and monetary policies became more expansionary, and the days of large surpluses and unrestrained reserve accumulation were over.

Source: The data for this case comes from the Republic of China, *Taiwan Statistical Data Book 1993* (Taipei: Republic of China, 1993).

So the principles of macroeconomic stabilization are simple: If policy makers know where to place their economy on this map, they know how to move toward equilibrium. But how do policy makers know where they are? The answer lies partly in measurement, partly in art. Regularly available data on the balance of payments, changes in reserves, and inflation can help locate an economy with respect to the external and internal balance lines. Data on the nominal and real exchange rates, the budget deficit, and the money supply can indicate movements from one policy quadrant to another. Some kinds of data, such as private sector short-term borrowing abroad, however, may not be readily available to policy makers. Such was the case in Korea at the beginning of that country's financial crisis in 1997. In principle, barring such surprises as an unknown large short-term foreign debt that has to be repaid immediately, econometric models can locate the economy and indicate the policies needed to balance it. In practice, especially but not only for developing economies, such models can be too imprecise and too unstable to be wholly dependable. The art of stabilization policy comes in knowing just how hard to push on each component of policy and how long to keep pushing. In this, experience in managing a particular economy is as important a guide as the models estimated by economists.

TALES OF STABILIZATION

Throughout this book we referred to different kinds of economic problems that are associated with developing countries, including the Dutch disease, debt crises, terms-of-trade shocks, foreign-exchange shortages, destructive inflation, and droughts or other natural catastrophes. The Australian model and its phase diagram can be used to show how these and other shocks affect macroeconomic balance and how they should be handled.

The Dutch Disease

Chapter 17 described the strange phenomenon of the Dutch disease, in which a country that receives higher export prices or a larger inflow of foreign capital may end up worse off than without the windfall. The Dutch disease was first analyzed by Australian economists Max Corden and Peter Neary, using a version of the open-economy model.[6] Figure 21–7 traces the impact of a windfall gain using the phase diagram.

---

[6]W. Max Corden and J. Peter Neary, "Booming Sector and Deindustrialisation in a Small Open Economy," *Economic Journal* 92 (1982).

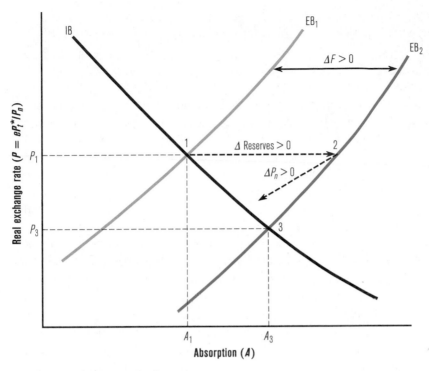

FIGURE 21-7. The Dutch Disease
An export boom or capital inflow shifts the EB curve rightward and leaves the
economy at point 1 in surplus. As reserves accumulate and the money supply
rises (or as the government and consumers spend the windfall), absorption
rises and the economy moves eastward, into inflation. As nontradable prices
rise, the real exchange rate appreciates. At the new equilibrium, point 3,
because P is lower, the supply and demand is balanced with less production
of T goods and more output of N goods than before. The loss of tradable
output is what makes this a "disease."

An economy in equilibrium at point 1 suddenly begins to receive higher
prices for its major export or is favored by foreign aid donors or foreign
investors. All the oil producers, from Saudi Arabia to Indonesia to Mexico, were
in this position in the 1970s, as were coffee (and many other commodity)
exporters during the boom of the mid-1970s. Egypt and Israel were rewarded
with large aid programs by the United States after the Camp David accord of
1978, as was Ghana by the World Bank and others during its stabilization of the
1980s (see Box 21–3). Both Chile in the late 1970s and Mexico after its stabilization in the late 1980s received large inflows of private capital, much of it a return
of previous flight capital. Foreign exchange windfalls are more frequent than
sometimes is supposed.

When the windfall occurs, the supply of tradable goods rises at any given
price. This can be shown as a rightward shift in the supply curve in Figure 21–2A.

BOX 21-3 RECOVERING FROM MISMANAGEMENT: GHANA, 1983–91

In 1983, after a decade of economic mismanagement, Ghana's gross domestic product was 20 percent below its 1974 peak, investment was only 4 percent of GDP, exports had sunk to 6 percent of GDP, and inflation rocketed to 120 percent for the year. After a decade of economic decline, Ghana's military government, headed by Flight Lieutenant Jerry Rawlings, was ready to undertake drastic measures to stabilize the economy and restart economic development.

Working closely with the International Monetary Fund, Ghana focused on three deep-seated problems: exchange-rate reform, fiscal adjustment, and monetary policy. At first, the government maintained its fixed exchange rate but drastically devalued the cedi from 2.75 to the dollar in 1983 to 90 to the dollar by 1986. In 1986, Ghana adopted a restricted floating currency, using periodic auctions to determine the rate. The official exchange market was broadened in 1988, when many foreign exchange bureaus were authorized to trade currencies and virtually absorbed the parallel market in currency; by 1990, the banks were empowered to trade in an interbank currency market. This completed the move to a floating rate regime. By the end of 1992, the cedi traded at 520 per dollar.

In 1983, with fiscal revenues less than 6 percent of GDP, the urgent need was to restore revenues and control expenditures. The deficit was cut from 6.2 to 2.7 percent of GDP in the first year of austerity, and by 1985, the government had begun a major public investment program to stimulate growth. By 1988, the government had restored total expenditures to 15 percent of GDP, 20 percent of which was investment, and was running a surplus of nearly 4 percent of GDP.

Throughout the period, the money supply was constrained but inflation remained stubbornly above 20 percent a year until 1991, when it was reduced to 16 percent and real interest rates finally became positive. Because food prices play a large role in the consumer price index, investment in food production was seen as an important component of any long-run attack on inflation.

The aid donors responded handsomely to Ghana's stabilization and the accompanying economic reforms: The sum of net official transfers and net long-term capital rose from just over $100 million in 1983 to $585 million in 1991.

Stabilization helped restore economic growth. From the depression of 1983–91, GDP grew by 5.1 percent a year and investment rose to 17 percent of GDP. The improvement, although dramatic in relation to the early 1980s, still left Ghana with a lot to be done: In 1991, income per capita remained 25 percent below its 1973 level.

Source: This account is based on Ishan Kapur et al., *Ghana: Adjustment and Growth, 1983–91* (Washington, DC: International Monetary Fund, 1991).

In the phase diagram of Figure 21–7, there is a rightward shift in the EB curve. At point 1, for example, which had been in external equilibrium along EB_1, the economy now is in surplus, so the new EB curve must be to the right; for example, at EB_2. The economy cannot remain at point 1 because the inflow of reserves increases the money supply; this adds to demand and, because the windfall increases private income and government revenue, leads to greater expenditure. So absorption rises, a move from point 1 toward point 2. This moves the economy off its internal balance, into inflation.[7]

The resulting rise in P_n has two effects: a reduction in real absorption that partially corrects the initial rise in A and, assuming the official rate is fixed, a real appreciation of the exchange rate. (The real rate also appreciates if the nominal rate is floating, because the greater supply of foreign currency drives down the price of foreign currency.) Therefore, the economy first moves from point 1 toward 2 in Figure 21–7 then begins to head in the general direction of the new equilibrium, point 3. In this case, market forces are likely to be sufficient to reach the new equilibrium, unless the authorities prevent appreciation and maintain real absorption and so keep the economy in an inflationary posture like point 2.

What, then, is the problem? The economy is at a new equilibrium, its terms of trade improved, its currency appreciated and so citizens have more command over foreign resources, people spending and consuming more without having to work any harder. There are two flaws in this otherwise idyllic picture. First, such windfalls generally are temporary. When export prices fall or the capital inflow dries up, the EB curve shifts back and a costly adjustment is necessary. We analyze that process in the next section.

The second problem is that, in shifting from the old to the new equilibrium, adjustments in the economy must be made. The real exchange rate P is lower, so X_t has fallen, while X_n has risen. Because the booming export sector does not retrench, nonboom tradables bear the brunt of the adjustment. Frictions in the labor market are likely to mean at least temporary unemployment as workers switch from tradable to nontradable production. If the tradable sector includes modern manufacturing, then long-term development may be set back because manufacturing is the sector likely to yield the most rapid productivity growth in the future. And if tradable industries close, it is more difficult to make the inevitable adjustment back toward point 1 when the windfall is over. This decline in nonboom-tradable production turns a foreign exchange windfall into a "disease."

---

[7]If the windfall is an inflow of capital, this treatment is precise. In the case of a rise in export prices, however, the move from point 1 to 2 is an approximation. Strictly speaking, a rise in export prices should raise P_t^*, a depreciation of the real exchange rate that moves the economy upward from point 1, after which the economy moves east toward EB_2.

What can be done to cure the disease? The government could try to move the economy back toward the old (and probably future) equilibrium at point 1. Its tools are the official exchange rate, which would have to be devalued against the tendencies of market forces, and expenditure, which would have to be reduced through restrictive fiscal and monetary policies that also reduce inflation (lower P_n or at least its growth). The resulting buildup of reserves and bank balances have to be sterilized through monetary policy so they are held as assets and not spent. It is a neat political trick to manage an austere macroeconomic policy in the face of a boom, because all the popular pressures are for more spending. Not too many countries have managed it. Indonesia is among the few that have; we discussed Indonesia's therapy for Dutch disease in Box 17–4.

Debt Repayment Crisis

When Mexico announced in 1982 that it no longer could service the debt it acquired during the oil boom of the 1970s, many other developing countries followed Mexico's lead and the financial world entered a decade of debt crisis (Chapter 15). Most Latin American countries largely have overcome their debt problems, but many African countries continue to struggle to repay the money they borrowed, mostly from aid agencies. Although debt service insolvency encroaches gradually on an economy and can be foreseen, it often appears as a national crisis because economic management has been inept.

The formal analysis of a debt crisis is similar to that of another common phenomenon, a **decline in the terms of trade** that leads to a foreign exchange shortage, which in turn is simply the reverse of the Dutch disease. Therefore, the oil exporters, such as Indonesia, Nigeria, and Venezuela, faced a similar kind of crisis once oil prices began falling in the 1980s.

Figure 21–8 captures this process. An economy in balance at point 1 needs to find additional resources to repay its foreign debt or needs to adjust to falling terms of trade. The supply of tradables therefore shifts to the left in Figure 21–2A; in the phase diagram, the EB curve also shifts leftward to EB_2.[8] If the crisis leads to debt relief or additional foreign aid, the curve moves less far and might settle at EB_3.

Now in foreign deficit, the economy begins losing reserves. If the government has to repay some of the debt or falling export prices cut into its revenues, the government needs to reduce its expenditures as well. Both cause a reduction in absorption. These actions move the economy toward external balance but also into unemployment. To gain the new equilibrium at point 3, it also is necessary to devalue the currency. This could be done by the central bank under a

---

[8]Strictly speaking, we cannot analyze the fall in export prices this way, but it is a reasonable approximation for many situations. See note 7.

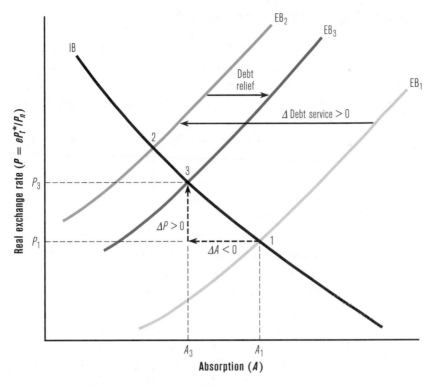

FIGURE 21-8. Debt Crisis or Declining Terms of Trade
An economy in equilibrium at point 1 suddenly needs to repay its debt (or faces falling export prices). External balance shifts from EB_1 to EB_2, although debt relief or increased foreign assistance might reshift the balance line back to EB_3. If policies accommodate the fall in reserves and income, absorption declines. A devaluing exchange rate, via central bank action or market forces, helps the economy move to its new equilibrium at point 3. With more tradables produced and less consumed, the surpluses can be used to repay the debt.

fixed rate or by the foreign exchange market under a floating rate. At the new equilibrium, the country produces more and consumes fewer tradables, because P has risen. This, of course, is a loss of welfare for the populace. The surplus of X_t over D_t is used to repay the debt or simply compensates for reduced export prices.

Debt crises and the hardships they cause are not an inevitable consequence of borrowing to finance development. If the borrowed resources are invested productively, they increase the potential output of both tradables and nontradables. Added production increases income and generates the capacity to repay the debt out of additional income, without a crisis and an austerity program. Countries such as Korea and Indonesia have been large international borrowers, but prior to the financial crisis of 1997–99, they escaped debt crises.

Stabilization Package: Inflation and a Deficit

External shock is not the only way an economy gets into trouble. Reckless or misguided government policies often are to blame. Impatient with sluggish development or intent on benefiting its constituencies, a government expands its spending and incurs a budget deficit. Unable to finance the deficit by borrowing from the public, the ministry of finance sells short-term bills to the central bank; this adds to the money supply. The economy drifts into inflation and a foreign deficit, at a point like point 1 in Figure 21–9, far from equilibrium at point 2 on the economy's original external balance curve EB_1. When economies become unstable in this way, private investors get skittish and try to invest in nonproductive assets like land or, more often, invest abroad; this deepens the external deficit. The government, recognizing the error of its ways or just hoping for some outside help to avoid painful adjustment, calls in the IMF.

The core IMF stabilization program consists of a reduction in the government's budget deficit and programmed targets for domestic credit that, in effect, cap the growth of the money supply. Together, these measures reduce absorption in the economy and move it westward from point 1, closer to external and internal balance. IMF packages frequently include an exchange-rate devaluation as well. Whether this is needed or not depends on the precise location of the economy (point 1) relative to equilibrium (point 2). In some cases, the reduction in absorption is sufficient to reach both internal and external balance. As pictured in Figure 21–9, a small devaluation is needed to reach point 2 and avoid unemployment.

However, IMF programs usually come with substantial aid attached, not only from the fund, but from the World Bank and bilateral donors. The aid package, by adding to the economy's capacity to buy tradables, shifts the EB curve to the right, to EB_2 in the diagram, and moves equilibrium to point 3. Note two things about this aid package. First, it reduces the need for austerity to some extent, as A_3 is greater than A_2. Second, it reduces the need for devaluation of the exchange rate. Indeed, as shown, there is little or no need to devalue to move from 1 to 3. Donors and the IMF nevertheless frequently insist on devaluation. Sometimes, that may be a requirement just to reach a point like 3. In other cases, donors and the IMF may have in mind a self-sustaining stabilization that will be valid even after aid is reduced and the external balance curve moves back toward EB_1. Whatever the motive, it is important to realize that aid itself is a partial substitute for both devaluation and austerity. In essence, the aid does what higher production of tradables otherwise must do and it finances expenditures that otherwise must be cut. Ghana's experience, which fits this description, is discussed in Box 21–3.

Another kind of stabilization also can be illustrated with Figure 21–9, **rapid (or hyper-) inflation.** In Bolivia's hyperinflation of the mid-1980s (see Chapter 5) or the chronic inflations in Brazil and Argentina, external balance is a secondary consideration or not a major problem. Point 4 in the diagram depicts this situation. Austerity still is required to move toward equilibrium at point 2 or 3 (if

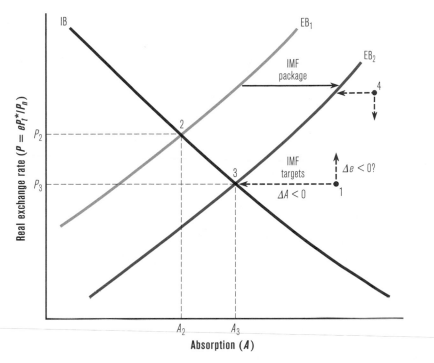

FIGURE 21-9. Stabilization from Inflation and a Deficit
An economy at point 1, far from equilibrium at point 2, above all needs
to reduce absorption through austerity: reduced budgetary deficits and
slower growth of the money supply. An IMF and donor package of aid
might bring equilibrium closer by shifting the external balance to EB_2,
but the aid package is conditional on the austerity program. Whether
any exchange rate action is required depends on the precise initial
position, point 1.

there is an aid package). But devaluation only intensifies inflation. Instead, the
currency must be appreciated, which also dampens inflation. One way to
achieve this would be to fix the nominal rate and let the continuing (if decreasing) inflation in nontradable prices (P_n) appreciate the real rate P. This is the
exchange-rate anchor, a device used often in Latin America, especially in Chile
during the late 1970s, in Bolivia during the mid-1980s, and in Argentina during
the 1990s. It has the disadvantage that a lower real rate discourages export
growth. Yet investment in new exports may be part of a strategy to open the
economy, diversify exports, and move the external balance curve to the right.

Drought

The human tragedy of drought or other natural disasters in places such as
Ethiopia, the West African Sahel, and India before the Green Revolution dwarfs
issues of macroeconomic management. But the adept management of an
economy racked by natural disaster is essential to reduce the misery of starving

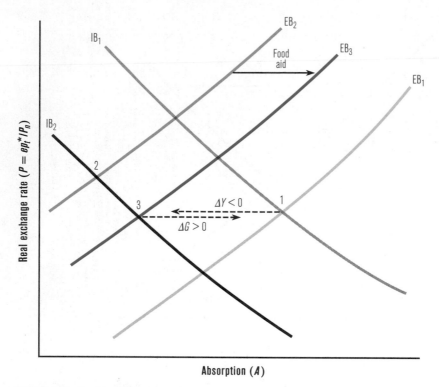

Absorption (A)

FIGURE 21-10. Drought

Drought or another natural disaster reduces the capacity to produce both
nontradables and tradables, so the curves shift to the west. Disaster relief
from abroad augments the external balance curve and shifts it to EB_3, with
equilibrium at point 3. Remaining temporarily at point 1, the economy
becomes inflationary. The reduction in output and therefore in income
reduces absorption, but the government's need to spend more on relief
tends to offset this move toward equilibrium. The outcome could be
continued inflation.

or displaced people. Drought, for example, reduces a country's capacity to produce food, export crops, and in some countries, generate electricity from
hydropower. At the same time, income is lower because farmers and others
have less product to sell. Government then needs to provide social safety nets;
this means spending more on the provision of food, transportation, health
services, and sometimes shelter. Foreign governments often provide financial,
food, and technical aid under these situations.

The macroeconomic reflection of a drought is depicted in Figure 21–10. The
economy begins in equilibrium at point 1. Drought reduces the economy's
capacity to produce both nontradables (some foods, hydroelectricity, water supplies) and tradables (export crops, importable foods, some manufactures). We
show this as a leftward shift in both the IB and EB lines: Reduced output of X_n at
any given price means a larger zone in which D_n exceeds X_n; this is inflationary.

Similarly for X_t; and this enlarges the area of deficit. The new external balance curve, EB_2, may be augmented (shifted back to the right) by foreign aid to EB_3, in which case, the new equilibrium is point 3.

The economy, still at point 1, is inflationary. The fall in incomes creates a tendency for absorption to shrink on its own and move the economy leftward toward the new equilibrium. At the same time, the government tries to spend more to relieve hunger, disease, and other problems. The outcome depends on the relative force of these tendencies. The impact of most natural disasters is temporary, typically lasting a year, although some African droughts have been much longer. It is appropriate to try to ride out such shocks with minimal adjustment, especially if foreign aid can bear much of the burden. Therefore, for example, even if an exchange-rate adjustment is called for to reach equilibrium, it is unlikely to work very well during a drought and probably should be resisted. This could be said for fiscal austerity, too, except that the rise in prices can deepen the suffering of those already hurt by the drought. If the government is able to shift its expenditures so that a greater portion goes into alleviating the impact of the drought, it may be able to relieve the worst suffering while restricting the rise of total expenditures and containing inflation.

Index